THE NEW INTERNATIONAL COMMENTARY
ON THE
NEW TESTAMENT

General Editors

NED B. STONEHOUSE
(1946–1962)

F. F. BRUCE
(1962–1990)

GORDON D. FEE
(1990–2012)

JOEL B. GREEN
(2013–   )

The Gospel of
JOHN

J. RAMSEY MICHAELS

WILLIAM B. EERDMANS PUBLISHING COMPANY
GRAND RAPIDS, MICHIGAN

Wm. B. Eerdmans Publishing Co.
2140 Oak Industrial Drive NE, Grand Rapids, Michigan 49505
www.eerdmans.com

© 2010 J. Ramsey Michaels
All rights reserved
Published 2010 by
Printed in the United States of America

26 25 24   8 9 10 11 12

Library of Congress Cataloging-in-Publication Data

Michaels, J. Ramsey.
The gospel of John / J. Ramsey Michaels.
p.   cm.   — (The new international commentary on the New Testament)
Includes bibliographical references and indexes.
ISBN 978-0-8028-2302-1 (cloth: alk. paper)
1. Bible. N.T. John — Commentaries.   I. Title.

BS2615.53.M53   2010
226.5′077 — dc22
                                            2010013943

CONTENTS

Editor's Preface — viii
Author's Preface — x
Abbreviations — xiv
Bibliography — xvi

INTRODUCTION — 1
  I. THE NATURE OF JOHN'S GOSPEL — 1
  II. THE AUTHORSHIP OF THE GOSPEL — 5
    A. "John" in Ancient Traditions — 6
    B. The Tradition Pro and Con — 12
    C. That Disciple — 17
  III. TRUTH CLAIMS — 24
  IV. JOHN AND THE OTHER GOSPELS — 27
  V. THE STRUCTURE OF JOHN'S GOSPEL — 30
  VI. LOCATION AND DATE — 37
  VII. THEOLOGICAL CONTRIBUTIONS — 39

TEXT, EXPOSITION, AND NOTES — 45
  I. PREAMBLE: THE LIGHT (1:1-5) — 45
  II. THE TESTIMONY OF JOHN (1:6–3:36) — 57
    A. John and the Coming of the Light (1:6-13) — 58

Contents

B. Our Testimony and John's (1:14-18)	74
C. John and Jesus (1:19-34)	93
D. Jesus and John's Disciples (1:35-51)	117
E. Jesus at Cana and Capernaum (2:1-12)	139
F. Jesus in the Temple at Passover (2:13-22)	156
G. Jesus and Nicodemus at Passover (2:23–3:21)	171
H. John's Farewell (3:22-36)	211
III. JESUS' SELF-REVELATION TO THE WORLD (4:1–12:50)	228
A. Jesus and the Samaritans (4:1-42)	229
B. Jesus in Galilee Again (4:43-54)	270
C. Jesus and the Sick Man in Jerusalem (5:1-18)	285
D. Jesus' Answer to the Jews in Jerusalem (5:19-47)	305
E. Across the Lake and Back (6:1-21)	338
F. Jesus and the Crowd at Capernaum (6:22-40)	359
G. Jesus and the Jews at Capernaum (6:41-59)	382
H. Jesus and His Disciples at Capernaum (6:60-71)	404
I. To Jerusalem, or Not? (7:1-13)	419
J. Jesus in the Temple (7:14-36)	431
K. The Last Day of the Festival: Jesus and the Pharisees (7:37–8:29)	459
L. The Last Day of the Festival: Jesus and the Jews Who Believed (8:30-59)	501
M. Jesus and the Man Born Blind (9:1-38)	537
N. Blind Guides and the Good Shepherd (9:39–10:21)	570
O. Titles and Works (10:22-42)	593
P. Going to Bethany (11:1-16)	612
Q. The Raising of Lazarus, and Its Consequences (11:17-54)	625
R. To Jerusalem Again (11:55–12:19)	659
S. The Hour of Glorification (12:20-36)	683
T. The Verdict on the World (12:37-50)	706
IV. JESUS' SELF-REVELATION TO THE DISCIPLES (13:1–17:26)	719

A. Jesus at Supper (13:1-20)	719
B. The Departure of Judas (13:21-35)	745
C. Four Questions (13:36–14:31)	761
D. Indwelling and the Love Command (15:1-17)	799
E. The World and the Advocate (15:18–16:16)	817
F. The Disciples' Response (16:17-33)	840
G. The Prayer for the Disciples (17:1-26)	856
V. VERIFICATION OF JESUS' SELF-REVELATION IN HIS PASSION AND RESURRECTION (18:1–21:25)	883
A. The Arrest and Hearing (18:1-27)	883
B. Jesus, Pilate, and the Jews (18:28–19:15)	912
C. The Crucifixion and Burial (19:16-42)	945
D. The Empty Tomb and the First Appearance: Jesus and Mary (20:1-18)	984
E. The Second Appearance: The Disciples and Thomas (20:19-31)	1004
F. The Third Appearance and Simon Peter's Commission (21:1-25)	1025

INDEXES

Subjects	1059
Authors	1065
Scripture References	1069
Early Extrabiblical Literature	1089

EDITOR'S PREFACE

I take great pleasure in introducing this commentary on John's Gospel to the larger Christian community of scholars and students. In one of my earliest years in the role of editor of this series, I had opportunity to visit Professor Leon Morris at his home in Melbourne, New South Wales, who was at that time in his ninetieth year. He agreed to work on a revision of his commentary that had first appeared in 1971. The revised edition appeared in 1995. But for a number of reasons the "revision" turned out to be much more cosmetic than substantial. So after his passing, I approached my former colleague and long-time friend, J. Ramsey Michaels, as to whether, in keeping with what was happening elsewhere in the series, he would like to offer a replacement volume. The present superb exposition of the Gospel of John is the end product of his agreeing to do so.

It is a special personal pleasure to welcome Ramsey's contribution to this series, since our own relationship dates to 1974 when Andrew Lincoln and I joined him and David Scholer on the New Testament faculty at Gordon-Conwell Seminary in Massachusetts, where the four of us (and our spouses) spent five wonderful years together. I had taught the Gospel of John at Wheaton College before moving to Gordon-Conwell, and it was this move that also shifted my primary New Testament focus from John to Paul, since the Johannine material was in Ramsey's very good hands. So I owe Ramsey a personal debt of gratitude for this move, which turned out to mark most of the rest of my New Testament career (apart from a commentary on the Revelation due out in 2010).

Whereas one might well question whether the scholarly/pastoral world needs yet another commentary on this Gospel, anyone who takes the time to read or use this work will easily recognize that the answer is "yes." Here is a substantial, truly original, work of extraordinary insight and helpfulness to pastor and scholar alike, which should have a considerable life span well after both author and editor have gone to their eternal reward. What

Editor's Preface

the careful reader and user of this commentary will recognize is the large number of insights into this Gospel, which, for want of a better term, must be judged as "new." But that does not mean "eccentric"; rather they are the result of many years of focused labor — and love — for John's Gospel. I am therefore pleased to commend it to one and all.

Gordon D. Fee

AUTHOR'S PREFACE

I am pleased to be a contributor to the New International Commentary on the New Testament. The first general editor of the series, Ned Stonehouse, was my mentor for a year at Westminster Seminary in the 1950s, and the current editor, Gordon Fee, was my colleague at Gordon-Conwell for a decade in the 1970s and 80s. This commentary represents a second effort, building to some extent on the first (1984 and 1989),[1] but attempting a far more detailed exposition of the text. I used to tell my friends that I keep trying until I get it right. The charm of the enterprise, of course, is that one never quite "gets it right." Moreover, as I get older I am increasingly conscious of the mortality rate among some who have written on John's Gospel. Edwyn Hoskyns's commentary had to be finished and edited by F. N. Davey (1947), R. H. Lightfoot's by C. F. Evans (1956), J. N. Sanders' by B. A. Mastin (1968), and Ernst Haenchen's by Robert W. Funk and Ulrich Busse (1980). Yet I am encouraged by the example of C. H. Dodd, who completed his first great work on the Gospel of John, *The Interpretation of the Fourth Gospel,* in 1953 at the age of 69, and his second, *Historical Tradition in the Fourth Gospel,* ten years later.

It may help readers to know from the start what this commentary will provide and what it will not. First, I have not begun to monitor all the publications on the Gospel in the seventeen years that have passed since I first signed the contract with Eerdmans (I may even have missed a few from before that!). Rather, I have tried to immerse myself in the text itelf, while interacting repeatedly with the major commentators, past and present, such as Bultmann, Schnackenburg, Brown, and Barrett (the first tier, more or less), and a number of others whose work I have used a great deal, including Leon

---

1. See my *John: A Good News Commentary* (San Francisco: Harper and Row, 1984) and *John,* NIBC 4 (Peabody, MA: Hendrickson, 1989). The latter differs from the former only in being based on the NIV rather than the TEV, or Good News Bible.

Author's Preface

Morris, my predecessor in the NICNT series, Westcott, Hoskyns, Lindars, Lincoln, Carson, Beasley-Murray, Keener, Moloney, and my own younger self. The list could go on and on. To my surprise I found Rudolf Bultmann's commentary the most useful of all, a work widely admired for all the wrong reasons. Bultmann's theories of source, redaction, and displacement have not survived and should not, yet his eye for detail is unsurpassed, and his close reading of the text as it stands — even when he discards it — perceptive and illuminating. It is only a slight oversimplification to say that Bultmann interprets the Gospel correctly (more or less), finds it unacceptable, and then rewrites it. His greatness lies in the first of those three things, not the second or the third. To a degree, I have also dealt with the relevant periodical literature, but for something close to an exhaustive bibliography the student will have to look elsewhere. Keener's 167 pages (!) is a good, up-to-date place from which to start.[2]

Second, I have not spent a great deal of time on the "background" of the Gospel (whatever that might mean), whether in Judaism, Hellenism, Hellenistic Judaism, Qumran, Gnosticism, or whatever. It is customary to do this in relation to the Gospel of John but not to any great extent in relation to the other three Gospels, because of the assumption that this Gospel somehow has a unique "background" not shared by the others. I am not so sure that this is true. I am more sure that its background, like that of all the Gospels, is mixed, that its main ingredients are the Jewish Bible, Second Temple Judaism (both Palestinian and Hellenistic), and primitive Christianity, and that the interpreter should have an eye open for relevant parallels (be they background or foreground) in Gnosticism as well. "Background," to my mind, is better assessed in relation to particular passages than in generalities.

Third, and consequently, I have kept the Introduction relatively short, at least in relation to the size of the commentary as a whole. Not only the Gospel's historical and cultural background, but its use of sources, its relationship to other Gospels and other New Testament documents, its literary style, its christology and theology, all of those issues are as well, or better, addressed as they come up in connection with the relevant texts than at the outset, before one has even started reading. Leon Morris's introduction ran to almost sixty pages, Raymond E. Brown's to well over a hundred,[3] C. K. Barrett's to almost 150, Schnackenburg's to just over two hundred — and

---

2. See Craig S. Keener, *The Gospel of John: A Commentary* (Peabody, MA: Hendrickson, 2003), 2.1257-1409.

3. This is not quite fair to Brown, inasmuch as his introduction was expanded after his death into a 356-page book (Raymond E. Brown, *An Introduction to the Gospel of John: Edited, Updated, Introduced, and Concluded by Francis J. Moloney,* Anchor Bible Reference Library; New York: Doubleday, 2003).

Author's Preface

Craig Keener's to 330 pages! Yet, by contrast, Bultmann's commentary in German had no introduction at all, and when Walter Schmithals added one for English readers in 1971, it took up a modest twelve pages! So I will not apologize for a comparatively short introduction centered largely on the question of authorship. In any event, I have always suspected that the so-called "Introduction" should come *after* the Commentary proper, not before. I wrote it last, and it would not be a bad idea to read it last.

Finally, I have given the priority to understanding the text in its present form, just as it has come down to us, rather than tracing the history of how it came to be. The sources of John's Gospel, whether one or more of the other Gospels, the oral traditions behind them, or a putative "Signs Source," or "Revelation Discourse," are of secondary interest, often consigned to footnotes. I do not assume that something in the Gospel which is there by default, as it were, having been taken over from an earlier source, is necessarily *less* important to the writer than the editorial work the writer has brought to it. In the current jargon, the approach taken here is synchronic, not diachronic. I have assumed that the Gospel of John as we have it is a coherent literary composition, and I have attempted to read it as such — even while alerting the reader to the supposed difficulty of doing so in certain places.[4] Sometimes I am asked, "Does the Gospel of John put words in Jesus' mouth?" My answer, which will become evident in the Commentary, is "Perhaps so, though not as often as some might think, and when I conclude that it does, my job as a commentator is to leave them there."

Given the choice of using the NIV (or TNIV) translation, or making one of my own, I chose the latter course. I prefer not to use up space either defending or quarreling with the peculiarities of a given English version. My own translation is literal, and deliberately so. Its sole value is to give the reader without knowledge of Greek some idea of the structure and syntax of the original. It is not intended to stand on its own, and it should never ever be made to do so! As for the text, I have generally followed the Nestle-Aland Greek New Testament (26th and 27th editions, depending on what I had available). When I departed from it (for example, at 1:15 and at 12:17), I have indicated why, sometimes at considerable length.

This second effort of mine has been largely carried out during retirement years, yet it is the product of a half-century in the classroom, at Gordon

---

4. That is, certain so-called *aporias,* or awkward transitions, prompting theories of displacement (for example, the proposed reversal of chapters 5 and 6), theories of two farewell discourses separated by "Rise, let's get out of here!" (14:31), and attempts to separate certain passages from the Gospel proper, either as later additions by a different hand (for example, chapter 21, or 6:52-58), or as earlier and more primitive formulations (for example, parts of 1:1-18 and the so-called "Signs Source").

Author's Preface

Divinity School, Gordon-Conwell Theological Seminary, Andover Newton, Missouri State University, and in retirement Fuller Seminary in Pasadena and Seattle, and Bangor Seminary in Portland, Maine. I am grateful to the students in all those places whom I taught and who taught me a thing or two. Three of them — Ben Witherington (1995), Rod Whitacre (1999), and Craig Keener (2003) — have written fine commentaries of their own on the Gospel of John. So has Homer A. Kent Jr., professor and later president of Grace Theological Seminary (*Light in the Darkness: Studies in the Gospel of John*, 1974), who in the Spring of 1953, as I recall, introduced me to John's Gospel in the classroom. To them I dedicate this volume. Homer's lectures were very well organized, but what I remember best were twenty-one assigned "problem texts" he gave us to deal with, one to a chapter. That, with the help of Westcott's commentary on the English text and Merrill Tenney's *John: The Gospel of Belief,* was what got me started.

In more recent years, I benefited from interaction with colleagues, including Gordon Fee at Gordon-Conwell (now my General Editor), Charlie Hedrick at Missouri State, and the late David Scholer at Fuller. Still more recently — down the "home stretch," as it were — I had a lot of encouragement from a clergy support group in New Hampshire consisting of six or seven pastors of small American Baptist churches (my own pastor among them). We worked together mostly on case studies, giving me a sense of what the rural and small city pastor has to deal with, outside the orbit of the megachurch. I am grateful for their prayers, and I hope the commentary meets their expectations, for they are fairly typical of the audience for which I am writing.

And of course there is my wife Betty, who has loved me and whom I have loved ever since that Spring of 1953 when I first got acquainted with the Gospel of John. To her, with my love, I dedicate this volume.

J. Ramsey Michaels

ABBREVIATIONS

ANF	Ante-Nicene Fathers. 10 vols. Grand Rapids: Eerdmans, n.d.
APOT	*Apocrypha and Pseudepigrapha of the Old Testament,* edited by R. H. Charles. 2 vols. Oxford: Oxford University Press, 1913
ASV	American Standard Version (1901)
BDAG	Bauer, Walter. *A Greek-English Lexicon of the New Testament and Other Early Christian Literature.* 3d ed. revised and edited by F. W. Danker. Chicago: The University of Chicago Press, 2000
BDF	Blass, F. and Debrunner, A. *A Greek Grammar of the New Testament and Other Early Christian Literature,* edited by R. W. Funk. Chicago: The University of Chicago Press, 1961
BibSac	*Bibliotheca Sacra*
CBQ	*Catholic Biblical Quarterly*
CEV	Contemporary English Version (1995)
DJG	*Dictionary of Jesus and the Gospels.* Downers Grove, IL: InterVarsity Press, 1992
Douay	Holy Bible: Douay Version (1956)
ERV	English Revised Version (1881)
ESV	English Standard Version (2001)
FC	Fathers of the Church: A New Translation. Washington, DC: Catholic University of America Press, 1947-63
GCS	*Die griechischen christlichen Schriftsteller der ersten Jahrhunderte*
GNB	Good News Bible (1976)
HTR	*Harvard Theological Review*
ISBE	*International Standard Bible Encyclopedia.* Grand Rapids: Eerdmans, 1979-88
JB	Jerusalem Bible (1966)

JBL	*Journal of Biblical Literature*
JSNT	*Journal for the Study of the New Testament*
JSNTSup	Supplements to Journal for the Study of the New Testament
JTS	*Journal of Theological Studies*
KJV	King James Version (1611)
LCL	Loeb Classical Library. Harvard University Press.
LSJ	H. G. Liddell and R. Scott, *A Greek-English Lexicon,* revised by H. S. Jones. Oxford: Oxford University Press, 1996
LXX	The Septuagint, or Greek Version of the Old Testament.
NA^{27}	Nestle-Aland. *Novum Testamentum Graece.* 27th ed. Stuttgart: Deutsche Bibelgesellschaft, 2001
NAB	New American Bible (1970)
NASB	New American Standard Bible (1977)
NEB	New English Bible (1961)
NIBC	New International Biblical Commentary. Peabody, MA: Hendrickson, 1989
NICNT	New International Commentary on the New Testament
NIV	New International Version (1978)
NJB	New Jerusalem Bible (1999)
NLT	New Living Translation (1996)
NPNF	Nicene and Post-Nicene Fathers of the Christian Church. Grand Rapids: Eerdmans, n.d.
NRSV	New Revised Standard Version (1989)
NTS	*New Testament Studies*
OTP	*Old Testament Pseudepigrapha,* edited by J. H. Charlesworth. Garden City, NY: Doubleday, 1983-85
PL	*Patrologia Latina*
RB	*Revue Biblique*
REB	Revised English Bible (1989)
RHPR	*Revue d'Histoire et de Philosophie Religieuse*
RSV	Revised Standard Version (1952)
SBL	Society of Biblical Literature
SNTS	Studiorum Novi Testamenti Societas
Strack-Billerbeck	Strack, H. L., and Billerbeck, P. *Kommentar zum Neuen Testament aus Talmud und Midrasch.* 6 vols. Munich: Beck, 1922-61
TDNT	*Theological Dictionary of the New Testament.* 10 vols. Grand Rapids: Eerdmans, 1964-83
TEV	Today's English Version
TNIV	Today's New International Version (2005)
WUNT	Wissenschaftliche Untersuchungen zum Neuen Testament
ZNW	*Zeitschrift für die neutestamentliche Wissenschaft*

BIBLIOGRAPHY

I. PRIMARY SOURCES

These include texts and translations of the Gospel of John and of ancient sources relevant to its interpretation, other than those listed under the the table of Abbreviations. This involves a judgment call, in that English (and other) translations are viewed as in some sense primary texts rather than as commentaries.

Apocrypha, II: Evangelien (ed. E. Klostermann). 3d ed. Berlin: Walter de Gruyter, 1929.
Authorized Daily Prayer Book (rev. ed.). New York: Bloch, 1960.
The Babylonian Talmud (ed. I. Epstein). 18 vols. London: Soncino, 1935-61.
Bell, H. I., and Skeat, T. C. (eds.). *Fragments of an Unknown Gospel and Other Early Christian Papyri.* London: Published by the Trustees, 1935.
The Catholic Study Bible. NAB. Oxford: Oxford University Press, 1990.
Charles, R. H. *The Book of Enoch.* Oxford: Clarendon, 1912.
Danby, Herbert. *The Mishnah.* Oxford: Oxford University Press, 1933.
Fenton, Ferrar. *The Holy Bible in Modern English.* Merrimac, MA: Destiny, 1966.
Field, F. *Notes on the Translation of the New Testament.* Cambridge: At the Cambridge University Press, 1899.
García Martínez, F. *The Dead Sea Scrolls Translated.* Leiden: Brill, 1994.
Ginzberg, Louis. *Legends of the Jews.* Philadelphia: Jewish Publication Society, 1909ff.
Grant, R. M. *Second-Century Christianity.* London: SPCK, 1957.
———. *Gnosticism.* New York: Harper & Brothers, 1961.
Harvey, W. W. *Sancti Irenaei Episcopi Lugdunensis: Libris quinque adversus Haereses.* 2 vols. Cambridge: Typis Academicis, 1857.
Hawthorne, Gerald F. "A New English Translation of Melito's Paschal Homily,"

in *Current Issues in Biblical and Patristic Interpretation* (ed. G. F. Hawthorne; Grand Rapids, Eerdmans, 1975), 147-75.

Hennecke, Edgar, and Schneemelcher, Wilhelm. *New Testament Apocrypha.* 2 vols. Philadelphia: Westminster, 1964.

James, M. R. *The Apocryphal New Testament.* Oxford: Clarendon, 1924.

Joseph Smith's "New Translation" of the Bible. Independence, MO: Herald, 1970.

Knox, Ronald. *The New Testament of Our Lord and Saviour Jesus Christ: A New Translation.* New York: Sheed & Ward, 1946.

Lattimore, Richmond. *The New Testament.* New York: North Point, 1996.

Layton, Bentley. *The Gnostic Scriptures: A New Translation.* New York: Doubleday Paperback, 1995.

Lewis, Agnes Smith. *A Translation of the Four Gospels from the Syriac of the Sinaitic Palimpsest.* London: Macmillan, 1894.

Mekilta de-Rabbi Ishmael on Exodus (ed. J. Z. Lauterbach). Philadelphia: Jewish Publication Society, 1976.

Midrash Rabbah (ed. H. Freedman and M. Simon). 10 vols. London: Soncino, 1961.

Montgomery, Helen Barrett. *The New Testament in Modern English.* Centenary Translation. Philadelphia: Judson, 1924.

The New Testament and Psalms: An Inclusive Version. New York: Oxford University Press, 1995.

The New Testament in Basic English. New York: E. P. Dutton, 1941.

The New World Translation. Brooklyn: Watchtower and Tract, 1961.

Neusner, Jacob. *Sifre to Deuteronomy: An Analytical Translation.* Atlanta: Scholars Press, 1987.

Nock, A. D., and Festugière, A.-J. *Corpus Hermeticum, Tome I: Traités I-XII.* Paris: Société d'Édition, 1960.

The Odes of Solomon: The Syriac Texts (ed. James Charlesworth). Missoula, MT: Scholars Press, 1977.

Palestine in the Fourth Century A.D.: *The Onomasticon by Eusebius of Caesarea.* Jerusalem: Carta, 2003.

Pesikta de-Rab Kahana (ed. W. G. Braude and I. J. Kapstein). Philadelphia: Jewish Publication Society, 1975.

Phillips, J. B. *The New Testament in Modern English.* London: Geoffrey Bles, 1963.

Roberts, C. H. (ed.). *An Unpublished Fragment of the Fourth Gospel in the John Rylands Library.* Manchester: Manchester University Press, 1935.

Robinson, James M. (ed.). *The Nag Hammadi Library in English.* 3rd ed. San Francisco: Harper & Row, 1988.

Rotherham, J. B. *Emphasized New Testament.* Grand Rapids: Kregel, 1959.

Stern, Menahem (ed.). *Greek and Latin Authors on Judaism.* 3 vols. Jerusalem: Israel Academy of Sciences and Humanities, 1976-84.
Tertullian's Homily on Baptism (ed. E. Evans). London: S.P.C.K., 1964.
The Twentieth-Century New Testament (rev. ed.). New York: Fleming H. Revell, 1904.
Vermes, Geza. *The Complete Dead Sea Scrolls in English.* New York: Allen Lane: Penguin, 1997.
Völker, W. (ed.). *Quellen zur Geschichte der christlichen Gnosis.* Tübingen: Mohr (Siebeck), 1932.
Wade, G. W. *Documents of the New Testament.* London: Thomas Murby, 1934.
Wakefield, Gilbert. *A Translation of the New Testament.* Cambridge, MA: Harvard University Press, 1820.
Westcott, B. F., and Hort, F. J. A. *The New Testament in the Original Greek.* New York: Harper and Brothers, 1882.
Wetstein, J. J. *Novum Testamentum Graece.* Amsterdam, 1751.
Wilkinson, John. *Egeria's Travels to the Holy Land.* Jerusalem: Ariel, 1981.
Williams, Charles B. *The New Testament: A Private Translation in the Language of the People.* Chicago: Moody, 1960.

II. COMMENTARIES ON THE GOSPEL OF JOHN

Modern commentaries will normally be cited merely by the author's last name and the page number. If the author has written secondary commentaries, or other works that are in the Bibliography, these will be cited by a keyword from the title.

Augustine. *Homilies on the Gospel of John.* NPNF. 1st ser., 7.7-452. Grand Rapids: Eerdmans, 1978.
Barrett, C. K. *The Gospel According to John.* 2d ed. Philadelphia: Westminster, 1978.
Beasley-Murray, G. R. *John.* Word Biblical Commentary 36. Waco, TX: Word, 1987.
Bengel, J. A. *Gnomon of the New Testament.* 5 vols. Edinburgh: T&T Clark, n.d.
Bernard, J. H. *A Critical and Exegetical Commentary on the Gospel According to John.* 2 vols. International Critical Commentary. Edinburgh: T&T Clark, 1928.
Brodie, Thomas L. *The Gospel According to John: A Literary and Theological Commentary.* New York: Oxford University Press, 1993.
Brown, Raymond E. *The Gospel According to John.* 2 vols. Anchor Bible 29 and 29A. Garden City, NY: Doubleday, 1966 and 1970.

Bibliography

Bultmann, Rudolf. *The Gospel of John: A Commentary.* Philadelphia: Westminster, 1971.

Calvin, John. *Calvin's Commentaries 7: The Gospels.* Grand Rapids: Associated Publishers, n.d.

Carson, Donald. *The Gospel According to John.* Grand Rapids: Eerdmans, 1991.

Chrysostom. *Homilies on the Gospel of St. John.* NPNF. 1st ser., 14.1-334. Grand Rapids: Eerdmans, 1978.

Godet, F. *Commentary on the Gospel of John.* 2 vols. New York: Funk and Wagnalls, 1886.

Haenchen, Ernst. *John 1: A Commentary on the Gospel of John, Chapters 1–6.* Philadelphia: Fortress, 1984.

———. *John 2: A Commentary on the Gospel of John, Chapters 7–21.* Philadelphia: Fortress, 1984.

Hoskyns, Edwyn C. *The Fourth Gospel* (ed. F. N. Davey). London: Faber and Faber, 1947.

Keener, Craig S. *The Gospel of John: A Commentary.* 2 vols. Peabody, MA: Hendrickson, 2003.

Kent, Homer A., Jr. *Light in the Darkness: Studies in the Gospel of John.* Winona Lake, IN: BMH, 1974.

Lightfoot, R. H. *St. John's Gospel: A Commentary* (ed. C. F. Evans). Oxford: Oxford Paperbacks, 1960.

Lincoln, Andrew T. *The Gospel According to Saint John.* Black's New Testament Commentary 4. Peabody, MA: Hendrickson, 2005.

Lindars, Barnabas. *The Gospel of John.* Greenwood, SC: Attic Press, n.d.

Marsh, John. *Saint John.* Westminster Pelican Commentaries. Philadelphia: Westminster, 1968.

Michaels, J. Ramsey. *John.* NIBC 4. Peabody, MA: Hendrickson, 1989.

Moloney, F. J. *The Gospel of John.* Sacra Pagina 4. Collegeville, MN: Liturgical Press, 1998.

———. *Belief in the Word: Reading John 1–4.* Minneapolis: Fortress, 1993.

———. *Signs and Shadows: Reading John 5–12.* Minneapolis: Fortress, 1996.

———. *Glory, Not Dishonor: Reading John 13–21.* Minneapolis: Fortress, 1998.

Morris, Leon. *The Gospel According to John: Revised Edition.* NICNT. Grand Rapids: Eerdmans, 1995.

Origen. *Commentary on the Gospel of John: Books 1-10* (trans. R. E. Heine). FC 80. Washington, DC: Catholic University of America Press, 1989.

———. *Commentary on the Gospel of John: Books 13-32* (trans. R. E. Heine). FC 89. Washington, DC: Catholic University of America Press, 1993.

Sanders, J. N., and Mastin, J. A. *A Commentary on the Gospel According to St. John.* London: Adam & Charles Black, 1968.

Schlatter, Adolf. *Der Evangelist Johannes.* Stuttgart: Calwer Verlag, 1960.

Schnackenburg, Rudolf. *The Gospel According to St. John.* 3 vols. New York: Crossroads, 1982.
Wesley, John. *Explanatory Notes upon the New Testament.* London: William Bowyer, 1755.
Westcott, B. F. *The Gospel According to St. John: The Greek Text with Introduction and Notes.* Grand Rapids: Eerdmans, 1954.
Whitacre, Rodney A. *John.* IVP New Testament Commentary 4. Downers Grove, IL: InterVarsity Press, 1999.
Witherington, Ben III. *John's Wisdom: A Commentary on the Fourth Gospel.* Louisville: Westminster John Knox, 1995.

III. OTHER SECONDARY WORKS CITED

Abbot, Ezra. "The Distinction between *aiteō* and *erōtaō*," in *The Authority of the Fourth Gospel* (Boston: Ellis, 1888), 113-36.
Abbott, Edwin A. *Johannine Vocabulary.* London: Adam and Charles Black, 1905.
———. *Johannine Grammar.* London: Adam and Charles Black, 1906.
Aland, K. "Eine Untersuchung zu Joh 1:3-4: Über die Bedeutung eines Punktes." *ZNW* 59 (1968), 174-209.
Alter, Robert. *The Art of Biblical Narrative.* New York: Basic Books, 1981.
Anderson, Paul N. *The Christology of the Fourth Gospel: Its Unity and Disunity in the Light of John 6.* WUNT. Tübingen: Mohr, 1996.
Anderson, Paul N., Just, Felix, S. J., and Thatcher, Tom (eds.). *John, Jesus, and History,* Volume 1: *Critical Appraisals of Critical Views.* Atlanta: Society of Biblical Literature, 2007.
Atwood, Craig D. *Community of the Cross: Moravian Piety in Colonial Bethlehem.* University Park, PA: Pennsylvania State University Press, 2004.
Aune, David E. *Prophecy in Early Christianity and the Ancient Mediterranean World.* Grand Rapids: Eerdmans, 1983.
Bammel, Ernst. *"Philos tou Kaisaros."* Theologische Literaturzeitung 77 (1952), 205-10.
———. "John Did No Miracles: John 10:41," in *Miracles* (ed. C. F. D. Moule; London: Mowbrays, 1965), 197-202.
Bauckham, Richard (ed.). *The Gospels for All Christians: Rethinking the Gospel Audiences.* Grand Rapids: Eerdmans, 1998.
———. *Jesus and the Eyewitnesses: The Gospels as Eyewitness Testimony.* Grand Rapids: Eerdmans, 2006.
———. *The Testimony of the Beloved Disciple.* Grand Rapids: Baker Academic, 2007.

Bibliography

Black, Matthew. *An Aramaic Approach to the Gospels and Acts.* 3d ed. Oxford, Clarendon, 1967.

Boismard, M.-É. *Le Prologue de Saint Jean.* Lection Divina 11. Paris: Cerf, 1953.

———. *Du Baptême à Cana.* Paris: Cerf, 1956.

Borgen, Peder. "Observations on the Midrashic Character of John 6." *ZNW* 54 (1963), 232-40.

———. *Bread from Heaven: An Exegetical Study of the Concept of Manna in the Gospel of John and the Writings of Philo.* Supplement to *Novum Testamentum* 11. Leiden: Brill, 1965.

———. "God's Agent in the Fourth Gospel," in *The Interpretation of John* (2d ed.; Edinburgh: T&T Clark, 1997), 83-95.

Bornkamm, Günther. "Die eucharistische Rede im Johannes-Evangelium." *ZNW* 47 (1956), 161-69.

Brown, Raymond E. *The Community of the Beloved Disciple: The Life, Loves, and Hates of an Individual Church in New Testament Times.* New York: Paulist, 1979.

———. *The Death of the Messiah: From Gethsemane to the Grave. A Commentary on the Passion Narratives of the Four Gospels.* 2 vols. New York: Doubleday, 1994.

———. *An Introduction to the Gospel of John: Edited, Updated, Introduced, and Concluded by Francis J. Moloney.* Anchor Bible Reference Library. New York: Doubleday, 2003.

Brownlee, William H. "Whence the Gospel According to John?" in *John and the Dead Sea Scrolls* (ed. J. H. Charlesworth; New York: Crossroad, 1990), 168-70.

Bultmann, Rudolf. *Theology of the New Testament.* 2 vols. New York: Charles Scribner's, 1951.

Bunyan, John. *Grace Abounding to the Chief of Sinners.* London: Penguin, 1987.

———. *The Pilgrim's Progress* (ed. Roger Sharrock). London: Penguin, 1987.

Burney, C. F. *The Aramaic Origin of the Fourth Gospel.* Oxford: Clarendon, 1922.

Burridge, R. A. *What Are the Gospels? A Comparison with Graeco-Roman Biography.* Grand Rapids: Eerdmans, 2004.

Cadbury, H. J. "The Ancient Physiological Notions Underlying Joh. 1:13a and Heb. 11:11." *The Expositor* 9 (1924), 430-39.

Carter, Warren. *Pontius Pilate: Portraits of a Roman Governor.* Collegeville, MN: Liturgical Press, 2003.

Charlesworth, James. *The Beloved Disciple.* Valley Forge, PA: Trinity Press International, 1995.

Cohee, Peter. "John 1.3-4." *NTS* 41 (1995), 470-77.

Colwell, E. C. "A Definite Rule for the Use of the Article in the Greek New Testament." *JBL* 52 (1933), 12-21.
Crossan, J. Dominic. "Mark and the Relatives of Jesus," *Novum Testamentum* 15 (1973), 81-113.
Cullmann, Oscar. "Samaria and the Origins of the Christian Mission," in *The Early Church* (London: SCM, 1956), 185-92.
Culpepper, R. Alan. *Anatomy of the Fourth Gospel*. Philadelphia: Fortress, 1983.
Dalman, G. *Sacred Sites and Ways*. London: SPCK, 1935.
Daniell, David. *The Bible in English*. New Haven: Yale University Press, 2003.
The Complete Poems of Emily Dickinson (ed. T. H. Johnson). Boston: Little, Brown, n.d.
Dodd, C. H. *The Interpretation of the Fourth Gospel*. Cambridge: At the University Press, 1953.
———. "Note on John 21,24." *JTS* n.s. 4 (1953), 212-13.
———. *Historical Tradition in the Fourth Gospel*. Cambridge: At the University Press, 1963.
Duke, Paul. *Irony in the Fourth Gospel*. Atlanta: John Knox, 1985.
Edwards, R. B. "Χάριν ἀντὶ χάριτος [Jn 1:16]: Grace and Law in the Johannine Prologue." *JSNT* 32 (1988), 3-15.
Edwards, M. J. "'Not Yet Fifty Years Old': John 8:57." *NTS* 40.3 (1994), 449-54.
Fee, Gordon D. "Once More — John 7:37-39." *Expository Times* 89 (1977-78), 116-18.
Fish, Stanley. "Progress in *The Pilgrim's Progress*," in *Self-Consuming Artifacts* (Berkeley: University of California Press, 1974), 224-64.
Fitzmyer, J. A. *The Gospel According to Luke*. Anchor Bible 28 and 28A. Garden City, NY: Doubleday, 1981 and 1985.
Fortna, Robert T. *The Gospel of Signs*. SNTS Monograph Series 11. Cambridge: Cambridge University Press, 1970.
———. *The Fourth Gospel and Its Predecessor*. Philadelphia: Fortress, 1988.
France, R. T. "Jesus the Baptist?" in *Jesus of Nazareth: Lord and Christ* (ed. J. B. Green and M. Turner; Grand Rapids: Eerdmans, 1994), 94-111.
Gardner-Smith, P. *Saint John and the Synoptic Gospels*. Cambridge: Cambridge University Press, 1938.
Garvie, A. E. *The Beloved Disciple*. London: Hodder & Stoughton, 1922.
Giblin, C. H. "Suggestion, Negative Response, and Positive Action in St John's Gospel (John 2:1-11; 4:46-53; 7:2-14; 11:1-44)." *NTS* 26 (1979-80), 197-211.
Gourbillon, J.-G. "La parabole du serpent d'airain." *RB* 51 (1942), 213-26.
Grelot, J. "Jean VII, 38: Eau de rocher ou source du Temple?" *RB* 70 (1963), 43-53.
Gundry, Robert H. *Mark: A Commentary on His Apology for the Cross*. Grand Rapids: Eerdmans, 1993.

Bibliography

———. *Jesus the Word According to John the Sectarian.* Grand Rapids: Eerdmans, 2002.

Gunther, J. J. "The Relation of the Beloved Disciple to the Twelve." *Theologische Zeitschrift* 37 (1981), 129-48.

Hägerland, Tobias. "The Power of Prophecy: A Septuagintal Echo in John 20:19-23." *CBQ* 71.1 (2009), 84-103.

Harner, Philip B. *The "I Am" of the Fourth Gospel.* Facet Books 26. Philadelphia: Fortress, 1970.

———. "Qualitative Anarthrous Predicate Nouns: Mark 15:39 and John 1:1." *JBL* 91 (1973), 84-86.

Hedrick, C. W. "Authorial Presence and Narrator in John," in *Gospel Origins and Christian Beginnings* (Sonoma, CA: Polebridge, 1990), 75-93.

———. "Vestigial Scenes in John: Settings without Dramatization." *Novum Testamentum* 47.4 (2005), 354-66.

Hirsch. Emmanuel. *Studien zum vierten Evangelium.* Tübingen: Mohr (Siebeck), 1936.

Horbury, William. "The Benediction of the *Minim* and Early Jewish Christian Controversy." *JTS* 33 (1982), 19-61.

Howard, W. F. *The Fourth Gospel in Recent Criticism.* London: Epworth, 1945.

Hunn, Debbie. "Who Are 'They' in John 8:33?" *CBQ* 66.3 (2004), 387-99.

Jeremias, Joachim, *Jerusalem in the Time of Jesus.* Philadelphia: Fortress, 1975.

Käsemann, Ernst. *The Testament of Jesus.* Philadelphia: Fortress, 1968.

Kimelman, Reuven. "*Birkat Ha-Minim* and the Lack of Evidence for an Anti-Christian Jewish Prayer in Late Antiquity," in *Jewish and Christian Self-Definition* (London: SCM, 1981), 226-44.

Koester, Craig R. "Messianic Exegesis and the Call of Nathanael (John 1.45-51)." *JSNT* 39 (1990), 23-34.

Kopp, C. *Holy Places of the Gospels.* New York: Herder and Herder, 1963.

Lane, William. *The Gospel According to Mark.* NICNT. Grand Rapids: Eerdmans, 1974.

Law, Robert. *The Tests of Life: A Study of the First Epistle of St. John.* 3d ed. Edinburgh: T&T Clark, 1914.

Levenson, Jon. *The Death and Resurrection of the Beloved Son.* New Haven: Yale University Press, 1993.

Lewis, C. S. *Miracles: A Preliminary Study.* New York: Macmillan, 1947.

Lightfoot, J. B. *The Apostolic Fathers.* 5 vols. Peabody, MA: Hendrickson, 1989.

Lincoln, Andrew T. "God's Name, Jesus' Name, and Prayer in the Fourth Gospel," in *Into God's Presence: Prayer in the New Testament* (ed. R. N. Longenecker; Grand Rapids, Eerdmans, 2001), 155-80.

Longenecker, Bruce W. "The Unbroken Messiah: A Johannine Feature and Its Social Function." *NTS* 41.3 (1995), 428-41.

Mackowski, R. M. *Jerusalem, City of Jesus.* Grand Rapids: Eerdmans, 1980.

BIBLIOGRAPHY

Malina, Bruce J., and Rohrbaugh, Richard L. *Social Science Commentary on the Gospel of John.* Minneapolis: Fortress, 1998.
Martyn, J. Louis. *History and Theology in the Fourth Gospel.* New York: Harper & Row, 1968.
Meier, John. *A Marginal Jew.* 3 vols. New York: Doubleday, 1991, 1994, 2001.
Metzger, Bruce M. *A Textual Commentary on the Greek New Testament.* London/ New York: United Bible Societies, 1971.
Michaels, J. Ramsey. "Nathanael Under the Fig Tree." *Expository Times* 78 (1966/67), 182-83.
———. "The Centurion's Confession and the Spear Thrust." *CBQ* 29 (1967), 102-9.
———. "The Temple Discourse in John," in *New Dimensions in New Testament Study* (ed. R. N. Longenecker and M. C. Tenney: Grand Rapids: Zondervan, 1974), 200-213.
———. "The Johannine Words of Jesus and Christian Prophecy," in *SBL 1975 Seminar Papers* (Missoula, MT: Scholars Press, 1975), 233-64.
———. "Origen and the Text of John 1:15," in *New Testament Textual Criticism: Its Significance for Exegesis. Essays in Honour of Bruce M. Metzger* (Oxford: Clarendon, 1981), 87-104.
———. "Evangelism and the Lost," in *Lost and Found: A Biblical/Pastoral Critique* (Valley Forge, PA: American Baptist Churches, 1988), 3-16.
———. "John 12:1-11." *Interpretation* 42.3 (1989), 287-91.
———. "John 18.31 and the 'Trial' of Jesus." *NTS* 36.3 (1990), 474-79.
———. "Everything That Rises Must Converge: Paul's Word from the Lord," in *To Tell the Mystery: Essays on New Testament Eschatology in Honor of Robert H. Gundry* (Sheffield: JSOT Press, 1994), 182-95.
———. "Betrayal and the Betrayer: The Uses of Scripture in John 13.18-19," in *The Gospels and the Scriptures of Israel* (JSNTSup 104; ed. Craig A. Evans and W. Richard Stegner; Sheffield: Sheffield Academic, 1994), 459-74.
———. "Baptism and Conversion in John: A Particular Baptist Reading," in *Baptism, the New Testament and the Church: Historical and Contemporary Studies in Honour of R. E. O. White* (JSNTSup 171; Sheffield: Sheffield Academic, 1999), 136-56.
———. "The Itinerant Jesus and His Home Town," in *Authenticating the Activities of Jesus* (ed. B. D. Chilton and C. A. Evans; Leiden: Brill, 1999), 177-93.
———. "By Water and Blood: Sin and Purification in John and First John," in *Dimensions of Baptism: Biblical and Theological Studies* (JSNTSup 234; ed. Stanley E. Porter and Anthony R. Cross; Sheffield: Sheffield Academic, 2002), 149-62.
———. "Atonement in John's Gospel and Epistles," in *The Glory of the Atone-*

ment: Biblical, Historical and Practical Perspectives. Essays in Honor of Roger R. Nicole (ed. Charles E. Hill and Frank A. James III; Downers Grove, IL: InterVarsity, 2004), 106-18.

Miller, E. L. *Salvation-History in the Prologue of John: The Significance of John 1:3/4.* Leiden: Brill, 1989.

Minear, Paul S. *John: The Martyr's Gospel.* New York: Pilgrim, 1984.

Möller, Mogens. "'Have You Faith in the Son of Man?' (John 9.35)." *NTS* 37.2 (1991), 291-94.

Moloney, F. J. *The Johannine Son of Man.* Rome: LAS, 1976.

Moore, George Foote. *Judaism in the First Centuries of the Common Era.* 2 vols. Cambridge, MA: Harvard University Press, 1927.

Moore, Stephen D. "Are There Impurities in the Living Water That the Johannine Jesus Dispenses? Deconstruction, Feminism and the Samaritan Woman," in *The Interpretation of John* (ed. John Ashton; 2d ed.; Edinburgh: T&T Clark, 1997), 279-99.

Moule, C. F. D. "A Note on 'under the fig tree' in John i 48, 50." *JTS* n.s. 5 (1954), 210-11.

Neyrey, J. H., and Rohrbaugh, R. L. "'He Must Increase, I Must Decrease' (John 3:30): A Cultural and Social Interpretation." *CBQ* 63.3 (2001), 464-83.

Nicol, W. *The Semeia in the Fourth Gospel.* Leiden: Brill, 1972.

Niklas, Tobias. "'Unter dem Feigenbaum': Die Rolle des Lesers im Dialog zwischen Jesus und Natanael (John 1.45-50)." *NTS* 46.2 (2000), 193-203.

O'Connor, Flannery. *The Habit of Being.* New York: Farrar Straus & Giroux, 1979.

Odeberg, Hugo. *The Fourth Gospel Interpreted in Its Relation to Contemporaneous Religious Currents in Palestine and the Hellenistic-Oriental World.* Uppsala: Almqvist & Wiksells, 1929.

Pagels, Elaine. *The Johannine Gospel in Gnostic Exegesis.* SBL Monograph Series 17. Nashville: Abingdon, 1973.

Parker, Pierson. "Bethany Beyond Jordan." *JBL* 75 (1955), 257-61.

Pennells, S. "The Spear Thrust (Mt. 27:49b, v.l./Jn. 19:34)." *JSNT* 19 (1983), 99-115.

Peterson, Erik. "Die Einholung des Kyrios," *Zeitschrift für systematische Theologie* 7 (1929/30), 682-702.

Potterie, I. de la. "Jésus, roi at juge d'après Jn 19, 13: *ekathisen epi bēmatos*." *Biblica* 41 (1960), 217-47.

———. "'C'est lui qui a ouvert la voie': La finale du prologue johannique." *Biblica* 69.3 (1988), 340-70.

Price, Reynolds. *Three Gospels.* New York: Scribner's, 1996.

Rackham, R. B. *The Acts of the Apostles: An Exposition.* London: Methuen, 1951.

Reinhartz, Adele. *Befriending the Beloved Disciple: A Jewish Reading of the Gospel of John.* New York: Continuum, 2001.

Richter, G. "Die Fleischwerdung des Logos im Johannes-Evangelium." *Novum Testamentum* 13 (1971), 81-126; 14 (1972), 257-76.

Riesner, Rainer. "Bethany Beyond the Jordan (John 1:28)." *Tyndale Bulletin* 38 (1987), 29-63.

Robertson, A. T. *A Grammar of the Greek New Testament in the Light of Historical Research.* 4th ed. rev. New York: George H. Doran, 1923.

Robinson, J. A. T. "Elijah, John and Jesus: An Essay in Detection," in *Twelve New Testament Studies* (Naperville, IL: Allenson, 1962), 28-52.

———. "The 'Others' of John 4:38," in *Twelve New Testament Studies* (Naperville, IL: Allenson, 1962), 61-66.

———. "The Parable of the Shepherd (John 10:1-5)," in *Twelve New Testament Studies* (Naperville, IL: Allenson, 1962), 67-75.

———. *The Priority of John.* Oak Park, IL: Meyer-Stone, 1987.

Sayers, Dorothy. "A Vote of Thanks to Cyrus," in *Unpopular Opinions.* London: Gollancz, 1946.

Schneiders, Sandra M. *The Revelatory Text.* San Francisco: HarperSanFrancisco, 1991.

———. "A Case Study: A Feminist Interpretation of John 4:1-42," in *The Interpretation of John* (ed. John Ashton; 2d ed.; Edinburgh: T&T Clark, 1997), 235-59.

Scrivener, F. H. *Bezae Codex Cantabrigiensis.* Cambridge: Deighton, Bell, 1864.

Smith, George Adam. *Jerusalem.* 2 vols. London: Hodder & Stoughton, 1907-8.

Staley, Jeffrey L. *The Print's First Kiss: A Rhetorical Investigation of the Implied Reader in the Fourth Gospel.* SBL Dissertation Series 82. Atlanta: Scholars Press, 1988.

———. "Stumbling in the Dark, Reaching for the Light: Reading Character in John 5 and 9." *Semeia* 53 (1991), 55-80.

Tabor, James D. *The Jesus Dynasty: The Hidden History of Jesus, His Royal Family, and the Birth of Christianity.* New York: Simon and Schuster, 2006.

Tenney, Merrill C. "The Footnotes of John's Gospel." *BibSac* 117 (1960), 350-64.

Thatcher, Tom. *The Riddles of Jesus in John: A Study in Tradition and Folklore.* SBL Monograph Series 52. Atlanta: Society of Biblical Literature, 2000.

Thomas, J. Christopher. *Footwashing in John 13 and the Johannine Community.* JSNTSup 61. Sheffield: Sheffield Academic, 1991.

Thompson, Marianne M. *The God of the Gospel of John.* Grand Rapids: Eerdmans, 2001.

Updike, John. *Self-Consciousness: Memoirs.* New York: Knopf, 1989.

Van Belle, G. *Les parenthèses dans l'Évangile de Jean.* Leuven: Peeters, 1985.

BIBLIOGRAPHY

Wilcox, Max. "The 'Prayer' of Jesus in John xi.41b-42." *NTS* 24 (1977-78), 128-32.
Wilkinson, John. *Jerusalem as Jesus Knew It.* London: Thames & Hudson, 1978.
Wilson, R. McLean. *The Gospel of Philip.* London: A. R. Mowbray, 1962.
Yates, J. E. *The Spirit and the Kingdom.* London: SPCK, 1963.
Zerwick, M. *Biblical Greek.* Rome: Pontifical Biblical Institute, 1963.
Zimmerman, M. and R. "Der Freund des Braütigams (Joh 3, 29): Deflorations — oder Christuszeuge." *ZNW* 90 (1999), 123-30.

INTRODUCTION

I. THE NATURE OF JOHN'S GOSPEL

God, according to Emily Dickinson, is "a distant — stately Lover" who woos us "by His Son." A "Vicarious Courtship," she calls it — like Miles Standish sending John Alden to court "fair Priscilla" on his behalf in Henry Wadsworth Longfellow's famous poem. "But lest the soul — like fair Priscilla," she adds, mischievously, "choose the Envoy — and spurn the groom," He "vouches with hyperbolic archness, 'Miles' and 'John Alden' were Synonym — ."[1] The avid reader of the Gospel of John may detect here an echo of John 13:20 ("the person who receives me receives the One who sent me"). Jesus is indeed God's Envoy in this Gospel, as in the others (see Mt 10:40; Lk 10:16), but in no other Gospel is he so unmistakably "One" with the Father who sent him (10:30), the "I Am" who existed before Abraham (8:59), and the "Word" who was with God in the beginning, and was himself "God the One and Only" (1:1, 18). Jesus in the Gospel of John is an unforgettable figure, so much so that God the Father becomes, in the eyes of some, the "neglected factor" in New Testament theology, particularly in this Gospel.[2] It is in fact tempting to "choose the Envoy and spurn the groom," but it is a temptation to be resisted, and it is resisted, resolutely, on virtually every page of the Gospel. Over and over again, Jesus reminds his hearers that the Son does nothing on his own, that his words are words the Father has given him to speak, and his works only what the Father has given him to do. His authority rests not in himself but in his total obedience to the Father's

---

1. See *The Complete Poems of Emily Dickinson* (ed. T. H. Johnson; Boston: Little, Brown, n.d.), 169-70. Interestingly, Dickinson wrote this poem in 1862, only four years after Longfellow wrote *The Courtship of Miles Standish*.

2. See Marianne M. Thompson, *The God of the Gospel of John* (Grand Rapids: Eerdmans, 2001), who seeks to correct this misunderstanding.

INTRODUCTION

will. Perhaps because of this intriguing mix of self-assertion and humility, equality with God and submission to the Father, Christian readers through the centuries have fallen in love with the Jesus of the Gospel of John, and consequently with the Gospel itself.

Not all readers of the Gospel have felt the same way. It is not everyone's favorite Gospel. As to its style, the translators of the NAB complain that

> The Gospel according to John comprises a special case. Absolute fidelity to his technique of reiterated phrasing would result in an assault on the English ear, yet the softening of the vocal effect by the substitution of other words and phrases would destroy the effectiveness of his poetry. Again, resort is had to compromise. This is not an easy matter when the very repetitiousness which the author deliberately employed is at the same time regarded by those who read and speak English to be a serious stylistic defect. Only those familiar with the Greek originals can know what a relentless tattoo Johannine poetry can produce.[3]

To which David Daniell, no stranger to good English style, replies, "Any stick, it seems, will do to beat the Gospel of Love."[4] No consensus here.

As to content, some hear only Jesus' self-assertion in the Gospel, and none of his humility. In the face of its programmatic assertion that "the Word came in flesh and encamped among us" (1:14), there are those who have asked,

> In what sense is he flesh who walks on the water and through closed doors, who cannot be captured by his enemies, who at the well of Samaria is tired and desires a drink, yet has no need of drink and has food different from that which his disciples seek? He cannot be deceived by men, because he knows their innermost thoughts even before they speak. He debates with them from the vantage point of the infinite difference between heaven and earth. He has need neither of the witness of Moses nor of the Baptist. He dissociates himself from the Jews, as if they were not his own people, and he meets his mother as the one who is her Lord. He permits Lazarus to lie in the grave for four days in order that the miracle of his resurrection may be more impressive. And in the end the Johannine Christ goes victoriously to his death of his own accord. Almost superfluously the Evangelist notes that this Jesus at all times lies on the bosom of the Father and that to him who is one with the Father the angels descend and from

---

3. *The Catholic Study Bible* (Oxford: Oxford University Press, 1990), "Preface to the New American Bible First Edition of the New Testament."

4. *The Bible in English* (New Haven: Yale University Press, 2003), 754.

him they again ascend. He who has eyes to see and ears to hear can see and hear his glory. Not merely from the prologue and from the mouth of Thomas, but from the whole Gospel he perceives the confession, "My Lord and my God." How does all this agree with the understanding of a realistic incarnation?[5]

Likewise, in the face of the Gospel's classic declaration that "God so loved the world that he gave the One and Only Son, so that everyone who believes in him might not be lost but have eternal life" (3:16), Adele Reinhartz, a Jewish New Testament scholar, comments that the gift offered here

> is the promise of eternal life through faith in Jesus as the Christ and Son of God. From the implied author's perspective, this gift is not a casual offering that I as a reader may feel free to take up or not, as I please. Rather, it is for him vitally important — for my own sake — that I accept the gift by believing in Jesus as the Christ and Son of God. Accepting the gift leads to eternal life; rejecting it leads to death. . . . The Beloved Disciple's strong interest in my response is conveyed also in the continuation of the passage in 3:19-21, which reframes the gift in ethical terms. . . . Thus the Beloved Disciple judges me as "evil" if I reject his gift, that is, if I refuse to believe in Jesus as the Christ and Son of God. Conversely, he judges me as "good" if I accept his gift through faith in Jesus as savior. The universalizing language of this passage, which views the coming of the Son of God into the world as a whole, stresses that this gift is offered to me and all readers who have ever lived or ever will live. At the same time, I and all other readers are to be judged according to our response to the gift, and are subject to the consequences of our choice.
>
> The Beloved Disciple, as the implied author of the Gospel of John, therefore takes his offer with utmost gravity and urges his readers to do the same. It is a matter of life and death, good and evil. . . . The Gospel, and therefore also its implied author, recognizes two types of people, those who come to the light and those who do not, those who do evil and those who do not, those who believe and those who do not, those who will have life and those who will not. The Beloved Disciple as implied author exercises ethical judgment with respect to his readers by separating those who do good — who believe — from those who are evil. In doing so, he also aligns one group with himself, as the one whose witness is conveyed through the medium of the Gospel itself, and consigns all others to the role of "Other."[6]

---

5. Ernst Käsemann, *The Testament of Jesus* (Philadelphia: Fortress, 1968), 9.
6. Adele Reinhartz, *Befriending the Beloved Disciple: A Jewish Reading of the Gospel of John* (New York: Continuum, 2001), 24-25.

INTRODUCTION

Coming from one who gladly embraces for herself the role of "Other,"[7] this is a remarkably perceptive account of what the Gospel of John is all about, reminding us that understanding and acceptance are not necessarily the same thing. But sometimes they do go together, as in this comment by Robert Gundry, a Christian New Testament scholar who views John's Gospel as the word of God and yet understands it, in much the same way as Reinhartz, as "countercultural and sectarian":

> John not only leaves the world outside the scope of Jesus' praying and loving and of believers' loving. He also describes the world as full of sin; as ignorant of God, God's Son, and God's children; as opposed to and hateful of God's Son and God's children; as rejoicing over Jesus' death; as dominated by Satan; and as subject to God's wrath, so that God's loving the world does not make for a partly positive view of it. Rather, God loved it and Christ died for it in spite of its evil character. What comes out is the magnitude of God's love, not a partly positive view of the world.[8]

While this Gospel was without question "countercultural," even "sectarian," in its own time, not all would agree that it is any more so than the other three Gospels, or any Christian community in the first century.[9] Yet in our day and age it is, as Gundry recognizes, both countercultural and sectarian.[10] It cuts against the grain of both liberal and conservative versions of Christianity. Against those who value "inclusion" above all else, and watch their churches grow smaller even as they become more "inclusive," it offers a rather "exclusivist" vision of a community of true believers, "born from above" and at odds with the world. And even though one of its legacies is the

---

7. Reinhartz explores four ways to read the Gospel of John: a "compliant" reading, with the beloved disciple as "Mentor"; a "resistant" reading, with the beloved disciple as "Opponent"; a "sympathetic" reading, with the beloved disciple as "Colleague"; and an "engaged" reading, with the beloved disciple as "Other." The last she acknowledges, from her Jewish perspective, as the closest to her own (see *Befriending,* 131-67).

8. Robert H. Gundry, *Jesus the Word According to John the Sectarian* (Grand Rapids: Eerdmans, 2002), 63-64.

9. See, for example, *The Gospels for All Christians: Rethinking the Gospel Audiences* (ed. Richard Bauckham; Grand Rapids: Eerdmans, 1998), in particular the essay by Bauckham, "John for Readers of Mark," 147-71. See also D. A. Carson's brief but conclusive demonstration that the Sermon on the Mount (and Matthew's Gospel generally) is no less "sectarian" than the Gospel of John (*John, Jesus, and History,* Volume 1 [Atlanta: Society of Biblical Literature, 2007], 157).

10. Gundry makes this point at some length in the third chapter of *Jesus the Word According to John the Sectarian,* "A Paleofundamentalist Manifesto for Contemporary Evangelicalism, Especially Its Elites, in North America," 71-94.

expression "born-again Christian" — a phrase that has become in some quarters a code word for a certain kind of political activist — it offers little encouragement to such activism. In sharp contrast to Jesus and his disciples in this Gospel, most "born-again Christians" (though not all) are very much at home in the world. Though aware of some of its shortcomings, they value it enough to want to change it in ways that would never have occurred to the writer of this Gospel. The point is not that they are wrong to do this; the point is that their activism has little to do with being "born from above" in the Johannine sense. Most of them express — quite sincerely — a deep appreciation, even love, for John's Gospel, yet in too many cases it is fair to say that their appreciation exceeds their understanding.

In light of all this, the task of writing a commentary is a very specific one. The commentator's job is not to "sell" or market the Gospel of John — that is, persuade people to like it. Many Christian believers are already quick to identify it as their favorite Gospel, and those who are not committed believers will not necessarily like it better the more they understand it. Quite the contrary in some cases. It is not a matter of liking or disliking. Believers and unbelievers alike need to be confronted with John's Gospel in all its clarity, so that they can make up their minds about the stark alternatives it presents — light or darkness, truth or falsehood, life or death — and its extraordinary claims on behalf of Jesus of Nazareth. Quite simply, Is it true? The short answer, the Gospel of John's own answer, is "Yes, it is true!" At the end of it we read, "This is the disciple who testifies about these things and who wrote these things, and we know that his testimony is true" (21:24). The claim echoes Jesus' own claims within the narrative: "There is another who testifies about me, and I know that the testimony he testifies about me is true" (5:32), "Even if I testify about myself, my testimony is true" (8:14), and "I was born for this, and for this I have come into the world, that I might testify to the truth" (18:37). The Gospel writer — and those who vouch for him — is no less confident than Jesus himself of the "truth" to which he testifies. But who is he, and what reason is there to accept his truth claim?

II. THE AUTHORSHIP OF THE GOSPEL

It is commonly assumed by biblical scholars, though not by most readers of the Bible, that all four Gospels are anonymous — even while continuing to call them "Matthew, Mark, Luke, and John"! "John" in fact is often viewed as somehow *more* anonymous than the other three, by those who prefer to speak of Matthew, Mark, Luke, and "the Fourth Gospel." But are any of them in fact anonymous? Yes and no. Yes, in the sense that none of their authors reveal their names anywhere in the written text, as Paul does so conspicuously at the beginning of each of his letters, or like Peter, James, and Jude in their letters, or John in the book of Revelation. No, in the sense that the author of "Luke" speaks of himself in the first person as if known to his readers, and even names the person to whom he is writing (Lk 1:3), while the author of "John" is identified at the end of the Gospel, not by name but as "the disciple whom Jesus loved" (see 21:20-24). And no, in that every known Gospel manuscript has a heading or superscription: "According to Matthew," "According to Mark," "According to Luke," and "According to John" respectively.[11] While it is generally acknowledged that these headings were not part of the Gospels as they came from the pen of their authors, they are without question part of the Gospels in their "published" form as a fourfold collection, probably as early as the middle of the second century. The presumption was that there was one "gospel," or good news of Jesus Christ, preserved in four versions "according to" *(kata)* the testimonies of four named individuals. For this reason it was assumed (almost unanimously) in the ancient church that "the disciple whom Jesus loved," who was said to have written the Gospel we are discussing, was named "John."

A. "JOHN" IN ANCIENT TRADITIONS

The cumulative testimony of the church fathers to "John" and his Gospel is impressive. **Theophilus of Antioch** in the late second century, in agreement with the superscription to the Gospel, attributes at least its opening lines to "John," whom he names as one of the "spirit-bearing men" whose authority ranks with that of "the holy writings."[12] He does not, however, further identify "John" either as "son of Zebedee," or "apostle," or "disciple of the Lord." His testimony could have been simply taken from the superscription, "According to John."

Irenaeus, near the end of the century, after recounting the traditions about the other three Gospels, concluded, "Afterwards, John, the disciple of the Lord, who also leaned upon His breast, did himself publish a Gospel during his residence at Ephesus in Asia."[13] The mention of "Ephesus in Asia" is consistent with the book of Revelation, where someone named "John" writes

---

11. "According to" is κατά. This is commonly judged to be the earliest form of the heading, as witnessed by the two fourth-century manuscripts, Vaticanus (B) and Sinaiticus (ℵ). Most later witnesses (and even the very early P^{66} and P^{75} in the Gospel of John) have the slightly longer form εὐαγγέλιον κατά . . . ("A Gospel According to" Matthew, Mark, Luke, and John, respectively).

12. *To Autolycos* 2.22 (see ANF, 2.103).

13. *Against Heresies* 3.1.1 (ANF, 1.414).

to seven churches in Asia which he obviously knows well, beginning with an oracle directed to the church at Ephesus (see Rev 1:4; 2:1). Irenaeus's phrase, "the disciple of the Lord," is further explained by the words "who also leaned upon His breast," echoing the account in the Gospel itself in which "the disciple whom Jesus loved" was first introduced (see 13:23). Irenaeus is telling us that this "disciple of the Lord" was in fact named "John." It is natural to assume that he was referring to John the son of Zebedee, the only one of the twelve apostles named John (see Mt 10:2//Mk 3:17//Lk 6:14). This John, with his brother James, was one of the first four disciples to be called, according to Matthew, Mark, and Luke (see Mt 4:21//Mk 1:19//Lk 5:10), along with two other brothers, Peter and Andrew. Almost always, James and John (in contrast to Peter and Andrew) are seen together in the Gospel tradition. In the Gospel of John itself they are mentioned only once, and not by name but simply as "the sons of Zebedee" (21:2). In Mark, Jesus even gives the two of them one name in common, "Boanerges," interpreted as "sons of thunder" (Mk 3:17). They even speak in unison, as when they ask permission to send fire from heaven on a Samaritan village (Lk 9:54), or ask to sit one on Jesus' right and one on his left in his glory (Mk 10:37). They are both present (never only one!) with Peter (and, sometimes, Andrew) at the raising of Jairus's daughter (Mk 5:37//Lk 8:51), at the transfiguration (Mt 17:1//Mk 9:2//Lk 9:28), on the Mount of Olives (Mk 13:3), and in the garden of Gethsemane (Mt 26:37//Mk 14:33). Only once in the entire Gospel tradition does John son of Zebedee speak or act alone — when he tells Jesus, "Master, we saw someone driving out demons in your name, and we prevented him because he was not following with us" (Lk 9:49; see also Mk 9:38), and is told, "Do not prevent [him], for whoever is not against us is for us" (Lk 9:50; see also Mk 9:40). Even here, the verb "we saw" *(eidomen)* seems to include his brother James as well. In the book of Acts we do see him without his brother, but still not by himself but with Peter, who speaks for both of them (see Acts 3:4-6, 12-26; 4:8-12, 19-20; 8:20-23; compare Lk 22:8).

While Irenaeus does not designate "John" either as "son of Zebedee" or "apostle," it seems clear that this is who he means by "John, the disciple of the Lord." Elsewhere he is very explicit about this person. Writing to a Roman presbyter named Florinus to warn him against Valentinian Gnosticism, he recalls how

> while I was still a boy I knew you in lower Asia in Polycarp's house when you were a man of rank in the royal hall and endeavouring to stand well with him. I remember the events of those days more clearly than those which happened recently . . . so that I can speak even of the place in which the blessed Polycarp sat and disputed, how he came and went out, the character of his life, the appearance of his body, the dis-

courses which he made to the people, how he reported his intercourse with John and with the others who had seen the Lord, how he remembered their words, and what were the things concerning the Lord which he had heard from them, and about their miracle, and about their teaching, and how Polycarp had received them from the eyewitnesses of the word of life, and reported all things in agreement with the Scriptures.[14]

Irenaeus also passes on a tradition from this same Polycarp, bishop of Smyrna in the early second century, that "John, the disciple of the Lord, going to bathe at Ephesus, and perceiving Cerinthus within, rushed out of the bath-house without bathing, exclaiming, 'Let us fly, lest even the bath-house fall down, because Cerinthus, the enemy of the truth, is within,'" adding that "the Church in Ephesus, founded by Paul, and having John remaining among them permanently until the time of Trajan, is a true witness of the tradition of the apostles."[15] Here, by implication at least, is a testimony that "John," no less than "Paul," is indeed an apostle. Later, Irenaeus again cites "John, the disciple of the Lord," in refutation of Cerinthus and other heretics by attributing to him the opening words of the Gospel of John as we know it ("In the beginning was the Word, and the Word was with God, and the Word was God").[16]

Surprisingly, Irenaeus also quotes **Ptolemy**, one of the Valentinian Gnostic writers against whom his *Against Heresies* was directed, as attributing to this same "John, the disciple of the Lord," the opening words of the Gospel as we know it (Jn 1:1-5, 10-11, 14).[17] Whatever their differences in interpretation, Irenaeus and his opponents seem to have valued equally the testimony of "John, the disciple of the Lord." Ptolemy is also quoted by a later church father as attributing to "the apostle" the statement, "All things came into being through him, and apart from him not one thing that has come into being was made" (Jn 1:3),[18] suggesting that he uses "apostle" and "disciple of the Lord" interchangeably. Thus "John" is identified as "the disciple of the Lord" both by Ptolemy and his enemy Irenaeus, and as "the apostle," explicitly by Ptolemy and implicitly at least by Irenaeus. If the designation "apostle" is strictly limited to Paul and to the Twelve so identified in the synoptic Gospels, then "John" can only be the son of Zebedee and brother of James.

This conclusion has been challenged occasionally on the basis of the

14. Eusebius, *Ecclesiastical History* 5.20.5-6 (LCL, 2.497-99).
15. Irenaeus, *Against Heresies* 3.3.4 (ANF, 1.416).
16. Irenaeus, *Against Heresies* 3.11.1 (ANF, 1.426).
17. Irenaeus, *Against Heresies* 1.8.5 (ANF, 1.328).
18. Ptolemy, *Letter to Flora,* from Epiphanius, *Panarion* 3.33 (see R. M. Grant, *Gnosticism,* 184).

THE AUTHORSHIP OF THE GOSPEL

testimony of **Polycrates**, bishop of Ephesus at the end of the second century. Writing to Victor, bishop of Rome, in defense of a fixed date for Easter, Polycrates cited the "great luminaries" buried in Ephesus who held this view, among them "John, who lay on the Lord's breast, who was a priest wearing the breastplate, and a martyr, and teacher. He sleeps at Ephesus."[19] The identification of "John" with "the disciple whom Jesus loved" mentioned in the Gospel is unmistakable (see Jn 13:25), yet this "John" is not explicitly called either "apostle" or "disciple of the Lord," only "martyr" and "teacher," and, most remarkably, "a priest wearing the breastplate." Only the Jewish high priest wore "the breastplate," or "mitre,"[20] and it is incredible to think of John the son of Zebedee, or for that matter any disciple of Jesus, as having ever served as the Jewish high priest. Possibly Polycrates jumped to a rash conclusion from a notice in the Gospel that one of Jesus' disciples (according to *some* interpretations "the disciple whom Jesus loved") was "known to the Chief Priest" (Jn 18:15, 17). Or possibly he has confused "John" the Christian "martyr and teacher" with "John" the Jewish priest mentioned alongside "Annas the high priest" and "Caiaphas . . . and Alexander, and all who were of the high-priestly family" (Acts 4:6) as interrogators of Peter and John the son of Zebedee after they had healed a lame beggar at the gate of the temple. According to Richard Bauckham, Polycrates could not have confused those two Johns because they are both part of the same narrative, and Polycrates must have therefore had in mind another "John" who had lived in Ephesus and was buried there.[21] But the argument is tenuous, for once such a capacity for confusion is admitted it is hard to set limits to it. Polycrates in almost the same breath confuses Philip the apostle with Philip, one of the seven appointed to serve tables in the apostles' place (Acts 6:5). His gift for muddying the waters seems to know no bounds.

More often, the notion that "John" must necessarily be the son of Zebedee is challenged on the basis of the even earlier testimony of **Papias**, bishop of Hierapolis in Asia Minor, a contemporary of both Polycarp and Ptolemy. While Papias says nothing about the authorship of the Gospel that we call the Gospel of John,[22] he does (like Ptolemy and Irenaeus) clearly re-

---

19. Quoted in Eusebius, *Ecclesiastical History* 5.24.3 (LCL, 1.507); also 3.31.3 (LCL, 1.271).

20. Gr. τὸ πέταλον. "Mitre" is the translation in 3.31.3 (LCL, 1.271). See the lengthy (and convincing) discussion in R. Bauckham, *The Testimony of the Beloved Disciple,* 41-50.

21. Bauckham, *Testimony of the Beloved Disciple,* 50.

22. Papias's discussion of the authorship of the Gospels is limited to Mark and Matthew in the material available to us from Eusebius (see *Ecclesiastical History* 3.39.15-16; LCL, 1.297).

fer to "John" as a "disciple of the Lord." His testimony (preserved for us by Eusebius in the fourth century) has been the subject of considerable debate:

> And I shall not hesitate to append to the interpretations all that I ever learnt well from the presbyters and remember well, for of their truth I am confident. For unlike most I did not rejoice in them who say much, but in them who teach the truth, nor in them who recount the commandments of others, but in them who repeated those given to the faith by the Lord and derived from the truth itself; but if ever anyone came who had followed the presbyters,[23] I inquired into the words of the presbyters, what Andrew or Peter or Philip or Thomas or James or John or Matthew, or any other of the Lord's disciples,[24] had said, and what Aristion and the presbyter John,[25] the Lord's disciples,[26] were saying. For I did not suppose that information from books would help me so much as the word of a living and surviving voice.[27]

Eusebius himself finds that Papias

> twice counts the name of John, and reckons the first John with Peter and James and Matthew and the other Apostles, clearly meaning the evangelist, but by changing his statement places the second with the others outside the number of the Apostles, putting Aristion before him and clearly calling him a presbyter. This confirms the truth of the story of those who have said that there were two of the same name in Asia, and that there are two tombs at Ephesus both still called John's. This calls for attention: for it is probable that the second (unless anyone prefer the former) saw the revelation which passes under the name of John. The Papias whom we are now treating confesses that he had received the words of the Apostles from their followers, but says that he had actually heard Aristion and the presbyter John. He often quotes them by name and gives their traditions in his writings.[28]

Has Eusebius read Papias correctly? The debate, which continues to the present day, hinges on the identification of Papias's "presbyters," whose "words" he values so highly. Are they simply his way of referring to the twelve apostles, seven of whom (Andrew, Peter, Philip, Thomas, James, John, and Matthew) he promptly names? Or are they the next generation of

---

23. Gr. τοῖς πρεσβυτέροις.
24. Gr. τῶν τοῦ κυρίου μαθητῶν.
25. Gr. ὁ πρεσβύτερος Ἰωάννης.
26. Gr. τοῦ κυρίου μαθηταί.
27. Eusebius, *Ecclesiastical History* 3.3-4 (LCL, 2.291-93).
28. *Ecclesiastical History* 3.39.5-7 (LCL, 2.293-95).

church leaders, particularly in Asia, who had followed the apostles and handed down their teaching? If it is the former, then Papias is twice removed from the seven apostles whom he names, for he looks to those who had "followed"[29] them. If it is the latter, he is three times removed from the apostles, for he looks to those who had "followed" the presbyters, so as to learn secondhand what they were saying about those whom they in turn had followed, the original disciples of Jesus.

Eusebius contradicts himself. On the one hand he presupposes the first alternative, that "the presbyters" are in fact "the apostles." This is clear in his paraphrase of what he has just quoted Papias as saying, for in the quotation Papias says, "If ever anyone came who had followed the presbyters, I inquired into the words of the presbyters," and in Eusebius's paraphrase he claims that Papias "confesses that he had received the words of the Apostles from their followers" (literally "from those who had followed them").[30] Nothing could be clearer than that Eusebius identifies Papias's "presbyters" with the "apostles" Andrew, Peter, Philip, Thomas, James, John, and Matthew. Yet this identification pulls the rug from under his insistence that two Johns are in play. *Both* Johns in the Papias citation are called "presbyters" (that is, apostles, according to Eusebius), and *both* are counted among "the Lord's disciples." All that distinguishes them is the tense of a verb. Papias inquired about what the one had "said"[31] and what the other (along with Aristion, who is not called "presbyter") was "saying."[32] Nothing in the citation requires that two individuals are in view. Rather, Papias seems to be saying that one of the seven "presbyters" who used to speak in the past (John) still speaks, together with Aristion, who was a "disciple of the Lord" but not one of the twelve.[33]

Nor do "two tombs at Ephesus both still called John's," necessarily point to two Johns. There are to this day two tombs in Jerusalem, each revered as the tomb of Jesus, but no one has proposed a second Jesus. Eusebius has a reason of his own (which he does not try to hide) for wanting to distinguish John the Apostle from John the Presbyter — it enables him to attribute "the revelation which passes under the name of John" to someone other than an apostle. He does not try to make the case here (candidly acknowledging that some "prefer the former," that is, the apostle as author of the Revelation), but elsewhere he is quite explicit:

29. Gr. παρηκολουθηκώς.
30. Gr. παρὰ τῶν αὐτοῖς παρηκολουθηκότων.
31. Gr. εἶπεν, aorist.
32. Gr. λέγουσιν, present.
33. So Morris, 21: "The trouble is that, for all the popularity in some circles, there is little evidence for the existence of John the Elder. It boils down to Eusebius' interpretation of one sentence in Papias and a much later traveler's tale of two tombs in Ephesus each said to be John's."

that this book is by one John, I will not gainsay; for I fully allow that it is the work of some holy and inspired person. But I should not readily agree that he was the apostle, the son of Zebedee, the brother of James, whose are the Gospel of John and the Catholic Epistle.[34]

Eusebius makes his case, then, in order to assign a different author to *the book of Revelation,* not the Gospel of John. While he acknowledges that the Revelation is "the work of some holy and inspired person" (evidently the elusive "presbyter John"), it is important to him (because of its differences from the Gospel) that it not be the work of the apostle. It is necessary to cherry-pick his testimony in order to use it in support of a different author for the Gospel. Yet while this "presbyter" distinct from the apostle remains something of a phantom in real history,[35] he has taken on a life of his own in modern "Johannine" scholarship. In D. A. Carson's words, "having an extra 'John' around is far too convenient to pass up."[36] It allows us to take seriously the unanimous tradition of the church that the author of the Gospel was "John," while avoiding the difficulties now frequently associated with the traditional ascription to John the son of Zebedee.

B. THE TRADITION PRO AND CON

What are the difficulties? How well does John the son of Zebedee fit the picture that emerges from the Gospel itself of the person it claims as its author, "the disciple whom Jesus loved"? The case in favor of the identification is simple and appealing: "the disciple whom Jesus loved" must have been one of the Twelve whom Jesus had chosen (6:70) because he was present at the last supper (13:23). Of the Twelve, he was the one sitting closest to Jesus, so close that he "leaned on Jesus' breast" (13:25), making it very likely that he was one of the "inner circle" of three (or sometimes four) apostles whom Jesus takes aside (in the other three Gospels) to share in certain crucial moments in his ministry such as the raising of Jairus's daughter, the transfiguration, the last discourse on the Mount of Olives, and the prayer in Gethsemane. These were Peter, the brothers James and John, and sometimes Peter's brother, Andrew —

---

34. *Ecclesiastical History* 7.25.7 (LCL, 2.199).
35. It is of course true that someone who calls himself "the Presbyter" is the author of 2 John (1) and 3 John (1), and putting that claim together with the traditional ascription to "John," it is natural to speak of "John the Presbyter." Yet if "presbyter" is simply a "Johannine" word for "apostle" (which does not occur in Jn, or 1-3 Jn as a term for Jesus' disciples), the author is simply claiming to be one of Jesus' original followers, possibly one of the Twelve (see 1 Jn 1:1, 3, where the "we" seems to carry the same implication).
36. *John, Jesus, and History,* Volume 1, 139.

the first four disciples called, according to Matthew, Mark, and Luke. Of these four, the beloved disciple cannot be Peter, for the Gospel narrative clearly distinguishes him from Peter (13:23-25; 20:2-10; 21:7, 20-23). He can hardly be Andrew, for Andrew is frequently named in the Gospel, and there is no conceivable reason why the disciple would sometimes be named and sometimes not. That leaves the twosome, James and John, the sons of Zebedee. They are a particularly attractive pair because their bold request to sit immediately on Jesus' right and left in his coming glory (Mk 10:37) could imply that those were *already* their customary seats when Jesus and the disciples ate together.[37] But James is eliminated because of his early martyrdom at the hands of Herod Agrippa I (see Acts 12:2), leaving him scant time to write a Gospel, much less become the subject of a rumor that he would live until Jesus returned (see Jn 21:23)! So we are left with half of the twosome, John the son of Zebedee.[38] It is worth noting as well that John is seen in the book of Acts only in association with Peter (Acts 1:13; 3:1-4:22; 8:14-25), even as four of the five appearances of "the disciple whom Jesus loved" in John's Gospel are with Peter (19:26-27 being the only exception).

So again, what are the difficulties? The flaws in the classic argument center on its assumption that the twelve apostles (that is, the twelve listed in the synoptic Gospels) were present at the last supper, and were the only ones present. But "the Twelve" are never listed in this Gospel, nor are they called "apostles." Only once do they come into the narrative (quite abruptly), when Jesus, after many of his disciples deserted, "said to the Twelve, 'Do you want to go away too?'" (6:67), prompting Peter's confession, and Jesus' reply, "Did I not choose you as the Twelve? And one of you is 'the devil'" (6:70). In contrast to the other three Gospels (Lk 6:13 in particular), the earlier moment of "choosing" is seen only in retrospect. Obviously Peter is one of "the Twelve," for it is to him that Jesus is speaking, but only "the devil" Judas Iscariot (6:71) and Thomas (20:24) are explicitly identified as being "one of the Twelve." Who were the other nine? Disciples named in the Gospel are Andrew, Philip, Nathanael (see 1:40-45), another Judas, "not Iscariot" (14:22), and "the sons of Zebedee" (21:2). The latter are presumably James and John, as in the other Gospels, bringing the total to nine. Of these, all but Nathanael are on at least one of the synoptic lists of twelve apostles — assuming that the other Judas can be identified with Luke's "Judas of James"

---

37. Caution is necessary because the two disciples' request had to do with thrones and judicial authority, not seats at a meal, yet the two ideas seem rather closely linked (see Lk 22:30).

38. The classic statement is that of B. F. Westcott a hundred years ago, who argued that the author was (a) a Jew, (b) a Jew of Palestine, (c) an eyewitness, (d) an apostle, (e) the apostle John (*The Gospel According to John,* ix-lix).

INTRODUCTION

(Lk 6:16; Acts 1:13). Lazarus, Martha, and Mary of Bethany are also named, as well as Mary Magdalene, but they are not called disciples, and they seem not to have traveled with Jesus. Other disciples besides "the disciple whom Jesus loved" are mentioned but not named (see 1:40; 18:15-16; 21:2). Consequently there is no way to determine which disciples (beyond Peter, Thomas, and Judas Iscariot) actually belonged to "the Twelve," nor is it ever explicitly stated that the Twelve, and only the Twelve, were present at the last meal and the farewell discourses. Obviously, some of them were present (Peter, Thomas, and Judas Iscariot all being mentioned by name in chapters 13 and 14), but what of the others who are mentioned, Philip, the other Judas, and "the disciple whom Jesus loved"? Did they belong to "the Twelve" so far as this Gospel is concerned?

Perhaps the strongest argument in favor of the Twelve being present at the last meal is the use of the verb "I chose" in 13:18 ("I know which ones I chose"), 15:16 ("You did not choose me, but I chose you") and 15:19 ("I chose you out of the world"), echoing 6:70, "Did I not choose you as the Twelve?" (italics added). While all of Jesus' disciples are "elect" in the sense of having been given him and drawn to him by the Father (see 6:37, 39, 44), only the Twelve are selected, or "chosen." If this is the case, then even though nothing is made of the designation, they are the disciples primarily in view in the farewell discourses, their calling as "the Twelve" being defined by the words, "I chose you, and appointed you that you might go and bear fruit, and that your fruit might last" (15:16). It is fair to assume that (with the obvious exception of Judas Iscariot), they are also in view in 20:19-31, where the designation of Thomas as "one of the Twelve" (20:24) seems to imply that even though Thomas, as "one of the Twelve," would have been expected to be present when Jesus first appeared (vv. 19-23), he was not. This is consistent with certain correspondences between what was promised to the disciples in chapters 14–16 and what happens in these verses after Jesus' resurrection.

To that extent the traditional argument for John the son of Zebedee is sustainable. But does the Gospel of John's "Twelve" match the twelve listed in the other three Gospels and Acts — lists which do not entirely agree even with one another?[39] We have no guarantee that they do, and in that sense the logic of the traditional argument is less than airtight. As for an "inner circle" consisting of Peter, James, John, and sometimes Andrew, there is no such inner circle in this Gospel. While Peter and "the disciple whom Jesus loved" stand out and are left standing at the end, each of the disciples — Andrew,

---

39. Peter, Andrew, James and John of Zebedee, Philip, Thomas, Matthew, Bartholomew, James of Alphaeus, and Judas Iscariot are listed in all three synoptics and Acts; Thaddeus and "Simon the Cananaean" only in Matthew and Mark; "Judas of James" and "Simon the Zealot" (possibly the same as "Simon the Cananaean") only in Luke and Acts.

Philip, Nathanael, Thomas, and Judas-not-Iscariot — has his moment in the sun, or opportunity to ask a question, with "the sons of Zebedee," two-thirds of the synoptic inner circle, making a belated cameo appearance (21:2). Of all the disciples, they alone say nothing and do nothing. Yet their mere presence at the fishing scene in chapter 21 makes the identification of "the disciple whom Jesus loved" as one of them problematic.[40]

It has become almost axiomatic in attempting to identify the beloved disciple that he is not likely to have been sometimes named and sometimes anonymous. While some have ignored that principle, notably those few who identify him as Lazarus, or Thomas, it has for the most part been assumed that the beloved disciple's anonymity is maintained consistently throughout. Defenders of the traditional view that he is John of Zebedee have been content to make an exception on the ground that "the sons of Zebedee" are not actually named, but this is surely a technicality. In calling them "the sons of Zebedee," the writer has in effect named them, for there is little doubt that their names would have been known to most of the Gospel's readers.[41] And like the synoptic writers, he views them as a pair, not as individuals. This undercuts the notion that he is himself one of them. In fact, as we will see in the commentary, if the whole scene is understood to be viewed solely through the eyes of "the disciple whom Jesus loved," then he is distinguishing himself from *all seven* of the disciples said to be gathered for fishing at the lake of Tiberias, not only from the five who are named (Peter, Thomas, Nathanael, and the sons of Zebedee) but from the two who are unnamed, making eight in all. While this is by no means certain, it is consistent with two other scenes in the Gospel. In one, Jesus says to Judas, "What you are doing, do quickly!" and the disciple (as author) adds that "none of those reclining found out for what reason he said this to him" (13:28), obviously excluding himself, for he did know the reason. In the other, he enumerates four individuals (all women) "standing by the cross of Jesus" (19:25), again excluding himself because he is the one "taking the picture," as it were. Then suddenly he "comes out of hiding" as we see him through Jesus' eyes (vv. 26-27), correcting the reader's impression that only women were present at the crucifixion. In the fishing scene, a case can be made that he similarly excludes himself in listing the (other) disciples who were present, until he again comes out of hiding to exclaim, "It is the Lord!" (21:7). If so, he is clearly *not* one of "the sons of Zebedee."

---

40. Bauckham is even more emphatic: "But in fact 21:2, far from allowing the possibility that the beloved disciple is John the son of Zebedee, actually excludes the possibility" (*Testimony of the Beloved Disciple,* 77).

41. Again, Bauckham comments, "Everyone knew the names of the sons of Zebedee.... If the beloved disciple could be one of them, he could also just as well be Thomas or Nathanael" (*Testimony of the Beloved Disciple,* 77).

INTRODUCTION

Yet if the author is not John the Apostle (and if John the Presbyter remains a ghost), how did the name come to be attached so persistently to the Gospel, beginning with the superscription, "According to John"? It is a fair question. The Gospel as it comes to us sends distinctly mixed messages, with a clear identification by name (as do the other Gospels) at the beginning and at least the pretense of anonymity at the end. Why would this Gospel (alone among the four) identify its author as "the disciple whom Jesus loved," yet without providing an actual name? Does it do this in order deliberately to conceal the name, or because its readers were expected to know the name? The effort to correct a rumor "that that disciple would not die" (v. 23) seems to imply the latter, yet why the secrecy about something already well known? If John of Zebedee is the author, why the concealment? John was an acknowledged apostle, and there would have been every reason to claim his apostolic authority. The book of Revelation shows no such hesitation in claiming "John" (quite possibly the son of Zebedee) as its author, naming him as if he needs no introduction (Rev 1:1, 4). In the so-called "Gospel of John," however, the "John" who needs no introduction is a different John, the one known in the other Gospels as "the Baptist" or "the Baptizer." In this Gospel, he is the first person mentioned by name (1:6), and he is always simply "John" (never "John the Baptist," or "Baptizer") — as if there is no need to distinguish him from anyone else with the same name?[42] This is odd if "John" is the author's name as well.[43] To anyone looking at the Gospel for the first time, the juxtaposition of "According to John" as a heading, and "A man came, sent from God. John was his name" (1:6)[44] is striking. The impression given is that the two Johns are the same, and that he is either the author or the hero of the story, or both.

It is of course a misleading impression, for the "John" of 1:6-8, 15-18,

---

42. Contrast the author's care to distinguish between "Judas of Simon Iscariot" (6:71) and Judas "not the Iscariot" (14:22), and among "Mary, who anointed the Lord" (11:2), "Mary of Clopas," and "Mary Magdalene" (19:25). There is possibly one other "John" in the Gospel, the father of Simon Peter (see 1:42; 21:15-17), yet no care is taken to distinguish him from the Baptizer. In fact, as we will see, he may even *be* the Baptizer, if Jesus is speaking not of Peter's paternity but of the fact that he was at first a disciple of "John."

43. It is even more odd that defenders of the traditional view argue precisely the opposite. For example, Westcott (xlvii), "If, however, the writer of the Gospel were himself the other John of the Gospel history, it is perfectly natural that he should think of the Baptist, apart from himself, as John only"; so too Morris (7): "It is difficult to understand why any informed early Christian (who must have known that there were two Johns) should thus court confusion. But it would have been quite natural for John the Apostle to speak of his namesake simply as 'John.'" Yet Luke does this as well (with only three exceptions, all in dialogue, none in narrative), without "courting confusion."

44. On the importance of the name "John" for the Baptizer, see Luke 1:13, 60, 63.

19-34 and 3:23-36 is neither the author nor the hero. And yet he is a major (if not the major) "voice" (1:23) in the Gospel's first three chapters. If the Gospel is viewed as "testimony," his is the first testimony we hear (see 1:7-8, 15, 19, 34; 3:26), and his pronouncement, "The One coming after me has gotten ahead of me, because he was before me" (1:15), seems to have been what prompted the author to begin as he did, with a reminder of Who it was who came "before" John (1:1-5). While this John is obviously not the author, the actual author is quite willing to blend his own voice with John's in testifying to the "glory" and the "grace and truth" of the Word made flesh (see 1:14, 16-17), and implicitly to make John's words his own (see 3:27-36) in exactly the same way that he makes the words of Jesus his own (see 3:13-21). As we will see, it is John, not Jesus, who speaks with the emphatic "I" in the opening chapter (for example, "I am not the Christ," 1:20; "I am a voice of one crying in the desert," 1:23; "I baptize in water," 1:26; "This is he of whom I said," 1:30; "And I did not know him," 1:31, 33; "And I have seen, and have testified," 1:34), and again when he reappears in chapter 3 ("I said I am not the Christ," 3:28; "So this, my joy, is fulfilled. He must grow, but I must diminish"). By contrast, Jesus in these three chapters (even though he will "grow" as John "diminishes," 3:29-30), says surprisingly little in the first person, and nothing at all with the emphatic "I" until at last he reveals himself to the Samaritan woman at the well (4:26).[45] It is at least possible that this Gospel is "According to John" not because someone named John is the actual author but because of the early mention of "John" in 1:6 and the prominence of John's testimony in the Gospel's first three chapters.

C. THAT DISCIPLE

What then of the Gospel itself, aside from its superscription and the traditions of the fathers? What does it say about "the disciple who testifies about these things and who wrote these things," and whose "testimony is true" (21:24)? In this commentary I have taken a "minimalist" approach, focusing on passages where "the disciple whom Jesus loved" is explicitly called that (13:23-25; 19:26-27; 20:2-10; 21:7, 20-24), and excluding the three passages where some have found him lurking but where he is not so designated (1:40; 18:15-16; 19:35). As a result, certain conclusions that have become almost conventional wisdom to some are not drawn. It would, for example, be convenient to

---

45. Jesus' first words in the Gospel are decidedly not centered on himself: "What are you seeking?" (1:38), and "Come, and you will see" (v. 39). After that, he speaks of himself in the third person as "the Son of man" (1:51; 3:14), or "the Son" (3:16-18), or "the Light" (3:19-21), or even as "we" (3:11), conspicuously avoiding the emphatic "I."

argue that this disciple was first of all a disciple of John (1:40), helping to explain why John's name came to be attached to the Gospel. But there is no evidence for this. His anonymity does not mean that he can be identified with any or all unnamed disciples. It is at least as likely that the unnamed disciple with Andrew who heard John say, "Look, the Lamb of God!" was Philip (see 1:43) as that it was "the disciple whom Jesus loved." Nor can he necessarily be identified with the unnamed disciple accompanying Peter after Jesus' arrest who was "known to the Chief Priest" (18:15), and therefore (so the argument goes) more than likely a Judean, and probably not one of the Twelve. That hypothesis, in fact, stands somewhat in tension with the preceding one, for all the named disciples who heard John east of the Jordan (Andrew, Peter, and Philip, not to mention Nathanael) were Galileans, and if the beloved disciple were one of them, he too would likely have been a Galilean.

The most persistent identification, perhaps, is with the anonymous eyewitness to Jesus' crucifixion who "has seen" and "testified," and whose "testimony is true, and that one knows that he tells the truth, so that you too might believe" (19:35). If "the disciple whom Jesus loved" is the witness who "testifies about these things" (21:24), what could be more appealing than an explicit claim that he was an eyewitness to Jesus' crucifixion, and to the blood and water from Jesus' side? Yet if there is such a claim, it is anything but explicit. While "the disciple whom Jesus loved" was indeed present, along with four women, as witness to the crucifixion (19:26-27), nothing in the text links him to the anonymous figure whose eyewitness testimony is noted and confirmed several verses later. He is in the text for a different reason — to accept Jesus' mother as his mother and care for her; if taken literally, the notice that "from that hour the disciple took her to his own home" (v. 27) removes him from the scene well before the spear is thrust into Jesus' side. While he is obviously an eyewitness to much that transpires in the Gospel, in that certain scenes are viewed through his eyes and narrated from his standpoint, no great emphasis is placed on his role as eyewitness. That is left rather to John (that is, the Baptizer, 1:34) and to the anonymous witness at the cross (19:35). Only once does the disciple call attention to what he "saw" (20:8), and even there it is sandwiched between what Peter had just seen in the tomb of Jesus and what Mary Magdalene would see, to the point that we are left wondering which vision was actually his, the scattered graveclothes (vv. 6-7), or the two angels in white (v. 12).

In short, "the disciple whom Jesus loved" is a very elusive figure in the Gospel, and not just because he is unnamed. He is first introduced — or introduces himself — as "one of his disciples" (13:23), but in the narratives that follow he is characteristically in, but not of, the apostolic company commonly designated the Twelve. Peter asks him to find out from Jesus which of them will hand Jesus over to the authorities, and he does so (13:25-26), only to leave Peter and the others in the dark as to who it is (vv. 28-29). When Jesus is crucified, he is not with the other male disciples (wherever they might be!), but with four female disciples, "standing by the cross of Jesus" (19:25). When Jesus gives his mother and the disciple into each other's care (19:26-27), the disciple holds his peace and obeys. When he looks into the tomb of Jesus and "believes" (20:8), he does not pause to share his insight with Mary Magdalene, who is left crying outside the tomb (v. 11); if he and Peter compare notes on the way home (v. 10), we hear nothing of it. If he is present on either of the two occasions when Jesus appeared to the disciples behind locked doors (20:19-23 and 26-29), we hear nothing of that either. Only at the final fishing scene near the lake of Tiberias does he make an appearance and break his silence, to tell Peter, "It is the Lord!" (21:7). Those are his only words to a fellow disciple anywhere in the Gospel, and his only words to anyone after the question at the table, "Lord, who is it?" (13:25).[46] When at the end Peter earns a rebuke for his curiosity about the disciple's fate (21:21), the disciple is again characteristically silent (vv. 22-23) — even as he is solemnly identified as the one who "testifies" (v. 24)!

Some commentators attach great significance to the disciple's association with Peter in four of his five appearances in the Gospel, usually suggesting a rivalry of some kind between the two, and usually to Peter's disadvantage. He and Peter are thought to represent competing segments of the Christian community (Jew and Gentile, institutional and charismatic, or whatever), or perhaps different spheres of responsibility within the Christian movement (such as pastoral and evangelistic, or administrative and prophetic). There is little evidence of such rivalry in the text, except perhaps at the very end (21:20-23). Long before "the disciple whom Jesus loved" even comes into the story, it is Peter who confesses, "Lord, to whom shall we turn? You have words of life eternal, and we believe and we know that you are the Holy One of God" (6:68-69). And Peter's request to the disciple at the table is a perfectly natural one, given the seating arrangement and the perplexity of all the disciples (see 13:22), not a sign of Peter's ignorance or inferiority. If anyone deserves blame, it is the disciple himself for not fully carrying out Peter's request. Nor does the disciple deserve any particular merit for winning the footrace to the tomb of Jesus (20:4). When we are told that he "saw and believed" (20:8), we are hardly allowed to infer (despite Lk 24:12) that Peter saw and did *not* believe. Later, at the lake of Tiberias when he recognizes that "It is the Lord!" (21:7), his words are probably said to be addressed to Peter simply because Peter is the first to act on this information. Obviously the other disciples hear him as well (see v. 12). Only the gentle re-

---

46. The latter is repeated in slightly longer form in 21:20, "Lord, who is the one handing you over?"

buke to Peter at the end (21:22) puts Peter at any kind of disadvantage, and its purpose is only to remind Peter (and, more importantly, the reader) that different disciples have different callings.

Where, then, are we left? With an unnamed "disciple whom Jesus loved" who may or may not be one of the Twelve, but is *not* (in order of appearance) Andrew, Peter, Philip, Nathanael, Judas Iscariot, Thomas, Lazarus, Mary, Martha, Judas-not-Iscariot, Mary Magdalene, or a son of Zebedee. That he is male is evident from Jesus' words to his mother, "Look, your son!" (19:26), but beyond that his anonymity remains intact. While his identity is clearly known to those who vouch that "his testimony is true" (21:24), and probably to the Gospel's original readers, the modern reader can only guess as to who he was.

Two clues are worth exploring, both centering on what happened *after* the events recorded in the Gospel. The first is the rumor that the disciple would not die before the Lord's return (21:23). This does not help very much because the saying of Jesus that might have given rise to such a rumor mentioned "some" *(tines)* who "would not taste death" before the coming of the kingdom of God, not just one (see Mt 16:28//Mk 9:1//Lk 9:27). Some have proposed that the rumor would have had particular relevance to Lazarus, who had already died once and was expected not to die again, but if we stay with the principle that the disciple would not have been sometimes named and sometimes anonymous, Lazarus is ruled out.[47] The most we can infer is that the disciple lived at least into the last decade or so of the first century, and it is not unlikely that this was true of quite a number of Jesus' followers. Papias, after all, attests the "living and surviving voice" of at least two (Aristion and John) well into the second century.[48] The rumor that he would not die, therefore, only eliminates disciples known to have died earlier, and these — James of Zebedee and probably Peter — are eliminated already on other grounds.

The other possible clue, the one instance in which Peter is not in the picture, is more promising. It is that moment at the cross when Jesus says to his mother, "Look, your son!" and to the disciple, "Look, your mother!" (19:26-27). Taken literally, the pronouncement implies that "the disciple whom Jesus loved" is in fact one of Mary's own sons and brother of Jesus, now appointed to care for his mother after Jesus' death. Certainly the expression, "the disciple whom Jesus loved," is consistent with the disciple's being Jesus' own brother. If he is not, Jesus' living brothers are, at the very least, being conspicuously overlooked. Moreover, among the women present near

---

47. For a list of those identifying the disciple as Lazarus, see Charlesworth, *The Beloved Disciple,* 185-92.

48. See above, n. 27.

the cross in Mark (15:40) and in Matthew (27:61), the woman designated as "Mary the mother of James and Joses [or Joseph]" could, as some have suggested, actually have been the Mary mother of Jesus, given that two of Jesus' brothers (in addition to "Simon" and "Judas") were named "James" and "Joses" (or "Joseph"; see Mk 6:3 and Mt 13:55, respectively). Quite possibly Mark has deliberately avoided referring to Mary as Jesus' mother (in keeping with Mk 3:31-35), and Matthew has followed in his footsteps. In Mark, Jesus is called "the son of Mary" and "brother of James and Joses and Judas and Simon" not by Mark himself, but by the people of Jesus' hometown — unreliable narrative voices at best (see Mk 6:3, and compare Mt 13:55). The reader already knows who Jesus' true "brother" and "sister" and "mother" are — those who "do the will of God" (Mk 3:35). Luke appears to have negotiated this tricky terrain by explicitly characterizing Jesus' mother and brothers themselves as "those who hear and do the word of God" (Lk 8:21) — that is, as "model disciples" and "prime examples of those who listen to the word of God 'with a noble and generous mind'" (see Lk 8:15).[49] In John's Gospel, Jesus himself takes the initiative to assign his mother to someone else — as it happens, to a kind of "model disciple" identified only as "the disciple whom he loved." If the disciple is one of Jesus' own brothers, this initiative can be viewed as yet another way of negotiating the same terrain. What is crucial for Jesus' mother and brothers is not their blood relationship to Jesus, but rather (as with any disciple) being objects of his love (see 13:1) who "hear and do the word of God." As we were told from the start, the birth that matters is "not of blood lines, nor of fleshly desire, nor a husband's desire, but of God" (1:13).

    The obvious barrier to any identification of "the disciple whom Jesus loved" with a brother of Jesus is the flat statement that "his brothers did not believe in him" (7:5). Yet at least two of his brothers, James (Gal 1:19; Jas 1:1) and Jude (Jude 1), are known to have eventually come to faith, and there is no evidence that any of them did not. Within fifty days of Jesus' resurrection his mother is seen in the company of "his brothers," along with the eleven disciples (named one by one) and the women who had traveled with them (see Acts 1:13-14). We are not told anywhere in the New Testament the circumstances by which any of them came to believe in him — except that he "appeared to James" after his resurrection (1 Cor 15:7).[50] There is, moreover,

---

49. The language is J. A. Fitzmyer's (*Luke,* 1.723).

50. The account of the appearance to James in the *Gospel of the Hebrews* implies that James was already a believer before the resurrection, and that he was present at the last supper: "James had sworn that he would not eat bread from that hour in which he had drunk the cup of the Lord until he should see him risen from among them that sleep." According to this tradition (in contrast to 1 Cor 15:7), Jesus appeared to James first, and "shortly thereafter the Lord said, Bring a table and bread! And immediately it is added, He

INTRODUCTION

a certain reticence about identifying Jesus' brothers among those who believed. While Paul refers once to James as "the brother of the Lord" (Gal 1:19),[51] James himself (or someone writing in his name) conspicuously does not, calling himself instead "servant of God and the Lord Jesus Christ" (Jas 1:1). Jude too identifies himself as "servant of Jesus Christ and brother of James" (Jude 1).

Quite possibly a similar reticence underlies the phrase "the disciple whom Jesus loved" in the Gospel of John. If one of Jesus' brothers did in fact become a disciple during the course of his ministry, this phrase might have served to distinguish him from his fellow disciples, all of whom Jesus loved (see 13:1, 34), but not as brothers — at least not to begin with. In the course of the narrative, they too (20:17), and finally all believers (21:23), come to be known as Jesus' "brothers," children of the same Father (see 20:17, "my Father and your Father"). Still, on this theory, only one is a child of the same mother, and he leaves his signature to that effect in recording Jesus' words, "Look, your son!" (19:26), and "Look, your mother!" (19:27). Early on in the Gospel, Jesus is seen briefly in Capernaum after his first miracle with "his mother and brothers and his disciples," as if they are all one family (2:12), and even in chapter 7, where his brothers are said not to have believed in him, they are presumably still in Capernaum (see 6:59), perhaps still in the company of, or at least in touch with, his disciples.[52] This should caution us that the contrast between Jesus' brothers and his disciples is not to be overdrawn, for even the disciples are not always characterized as "believers." Sometimes they are (16:27, 17:8), but just as often they are urged to "believe" (14:1), or told of Jesus' intent that later they "might believe" (13:19; 14:29), or said to believe "now" (16:31), with the implication that it might not last. One of them is even urged to be "no longer faithless but faithful" (20:27). As for "the disciple whom Jesus loved," he is explicitly said to "believe" only once, when he looks into Jesus' tomb after the resurrection (20:8). While this is surely not his first moment of belief, it does signal that what defined him from the start was not that he "believed," but that he was "loved."

The identification of the disciple as a brother of Jesus is, like all other theories of his identity, pure speculation. It is not even a real identification,

---

took the bread, blessed it, and brake it and gave it to James the Just and said to him: My brother, eat thy bread, for the Son of man is risen from among them that sleep" (Hennecke-Schneemelcher, 1.165, from Jerome, *Of Illustrious Men* 2).

51. It is likely that the phrase "James and the brothers" (Acts 12:17) places James among the believers (possibly the elders) in Jerusalem, not among the blood brothers of Jesus.

52. Jesus is said to be "walking in Galilee" (7:1), and it is fair to assume that the twelve disciples are still "walking" with him (in contrast to those who no longer did so, 6:66).

for it stops short of providing an actual name. Which brother of Jesus is meant? James has left too many tracks in early Christian traditions, none of them linked particularly to this Gospel, to be a likely candidate, and the brief letter attributed to Jude is strikingly different from the Gospel of John.[53] Moreover, if "Jude" or "Judas" is the beloved disciple, then who is "Judas, not the Iscariot," mentioned in 14:22? If he is the same person, why is he sometimes named and sometimes not? And if he is a different "Judas" or "Jude," why does he go to such pains to distinguish this disciple from Judas Iscariot, but not from himself? We are left with a brother named either "Joses" (in Mark) or "Joseph" (in Matthew),[54] and another named "Simon" (see Mk 6:3; Mt 13:55). Because nothing is known of either of them except that they were Jesus' brothers, it is possible to lay at their doorstep almost any theory one wishes. "Joses" or "Joseph" is a marginally better candidate, perhaps, because of the purported mention of him (along with James) as Mary's son in connection with her presence at the crucifixion (see Mk 15:40, 47; Mt 27:56). But nothing approaching certainty is possible. The major difficulty is moving from chapter 7, with its explicit statement that Jesus' brothers "did not believe in him" (7:5), to chapter 13, where one of his brothers (according to this theory) is reclining at his side at the last meal.[55] How was this brother transformed from someone whom "the world cannot hate" (7:7) into someone whom "the world hates" (15:18-19)? The "brothers" (7:3) are obviously distinguished from "the Twelve" (6:70), and if those present at the last meal are the Twelve, what is one of the brothers doing there even if he did become a believer? Yet "the disciple whom Jesus loved" has a place at the table, and a place of honor at that.

One solution to which some have resorted in order to make room for someone beyond the Twelve at the table is the notion that "the disciple whom Jesus loved" was the host at the meal (hence the place of honor), the "certain one"[56] in the city to whom Jesus' disciples were instructed to say, "The Teacher says, 'My time is near; I am doing the Passover at your place[57] with

---

53. One interpreter who identifies "the disciple whom Jesus loved" as one of Jesus' brothers is J. J. Gunther, who identifies him as this Judas ("The Relation of the Beloved Disciple to the Twelve," *Theologische Zeitschrift* 37 [1981], 129-48; see Charlesworth, *The Beloved Disciple,* 196-97). Another is James D. Tabor, in *The Jesus Dynasty* (New York: Simon and Schuster, 2006), 206-7, who identifies the disciple as James.

54. Is Matthew's "Joseph" simply an assimilation to the name of Jesus' father in Matthew's birth narrative?

55. The only identifiable convert in these chapters is the man born blind (see 9:38), and there is nothing to link him either with a brother of Jesus or with "the disciple whom Jesus loved."

56. Gr. τὸν δεῖνα.

57. Gr. πρὸς σέ.

my disciples'" (Mt 26:18). "The Teacher" implies that this person too was a disciple, who recognized "the Teacher's" authority;[58] yet like "the disciple whom Jesus loved," he conspicuously goes unnamed.[59] Could he be that disciple? If so, could he also be a brother of Jesus? The possibilities multiply, and with them the uncertainties, confirming that this identification, like all the others, is speculative. At the end of the day "the disciple whom Jesus loved" remains anonymous. After nineteen hundred years all we know of him is that Jesus loved him and confided in him at least once (13:26), that Jesus' mother became — or was — his mother (19:27), that he "believed" (at least once, 20:8), that he recognized Jesus when no one else did (21:7), and that he lived long enough to spawn a rumor that he would go on living until Jesus returned (21:23). The church for nineteen centuries has identified him with the Apostle John, son of Zebedee, and that long tradition deserves the utmost respect. Yet at that point, ecclesiastical tradition and critical traditions have largely parted company, and among the latter there is nothing approaching consensus as to his identity or even his authorship of the Gospel. His claim to authorship is unmistakable, yet his anonymity (whatever the original readers of the Gospel might have known) is both conspicuous and deliberate. In a way it need not surprise us, for several key characters in the story he tells — the Samaritan woman, the royal official at Cana, the sick man at the pool, the man born blind, even Jesus' mother — are just as nameless. Unlike Jesus' mother, who, according to Luke, "treasured these things and pondered them in her heart" (Lk 2:19; also 2:51),[60] he tells his story freely, yet like her (and evidently with her) he retains his privacy, a privacy that even the most inquisitive commentator will do well to respect.

III. TRUTH CLAIMS

The anonymity of this Gospel's author implies that in the eyes of the "we" who published it, its truth did not depend merely on the identity of the person

---

58. See John 13:13; also 11:28, where Martha uses this term of Jesus in speaking to her sister Mary.

59. In Mark (14:14) and in Luke (22:11) he is the anonymous "owner of the house" (ὁ οἰκοδεσπότης). For this identification (though without making this man a brother of Jesus), see Witherington, *John's Wisdom* (14), and Bauckham, *Testimony of the Beloved Disciple* (15), both of whom view him as a "nonitinerant" disciple, a Judean resident of Jerusalem. Yet the beloved disciple shows up in Galilee at the lake of Tiberias (21:7) and — at least according to both Bauckham (84-85) and Witherington (70) — even beyond the Jordan (see 1:40), in the company of three Galileans!

60. The twin notices in Luke may well imply a claim that Luke has somehow managed to access these unspoken memories as part of his "orderly account" (see Lk 1:3).

who "testified" and who "wrote" it (21:24). Name dropping was unnecessary. What mattered was not the author's name or whether he was an "apostle" or one of "the Twelve," only that he was present at certain points in the narrative and was very close to Jesus, so close that he reclined "at Jesus' side" (13:23) at the last supper, and "leaned on his breast" (21:20), even as Jesus was now "right beside the Father" (1:18). As we have seen, his testimony does not stand alone, but belongs to a whole series of testimonies, starting with John's, who "came for a testimony, to testify about the light" (1:7). John's testimony, based on what he has "seen" (1:32-34) and "heard" (3:29), resounds through the first three chapters of the Gospel, and in retrospect Jesus himself acknowledged that John "testified to the truth" (5:33).

Jesus, too, "testifies" to what he has seen and heard (3:11, 32), and from chapter 4 on his testimony takes center stage. The voice testifying as "I" is now consistently his voice, and he calls witnesses to back up his testimony: "If I testify about myself, my testimony is not true," he begins; "There is another who testifies about me, and I know that the testimony he testifies about me is true" (5:31-32). That this "other" is the Father is clear from what follows (see 5:37; also 8:18). This, he claims, is evident in "the works that the Father has given me that I might complete them" (5:36), for "The works that I do in my Father's name, these testify about me" (10:25).[61] Like John, he speaks as an eyewitness, testifying now in the first person to that which he has seen and heard: "The things I have seen in the Father's presence I speak" (8:38), and "the things I heard from him are the things I say to the world" (8:26). Consequently he tells those Jews who professed to believe, "If you dwell on my word, . . . you will know the truth, and the truth will set you free" (8:31-32). He calls himself "a man who has spoken to you the truth which I heard from God" (8:40), but in frustration he concludes, "If I speak truth, why do you not believe me? Whoever is from God hears the words of God. This is why you do not hear, because you are not from God" (8:45-46). And to the Gentiles his message is the same: "I was born for this," he tells Pontius Pilate, "and for this I have come into the world, that I might testify to the truth. Everyone who is from the truth hears my voice" (18:37). Pilate's "What is truth?" (18:38) is a redundant question, one to which the reader is expected to know the answer: "I am the Way, and the Truth and the Life" (14:6), and "Your word is the truth" (17:17).

Such truth claims are absolute, and no less so are those of the Gospel in which they are embedded. Jesus, in fact, seems to anticipate, if not a written Gospel at least a testimony to "the truth," replacing yet continuing his own af-

---

61. The Father's testimony is evident as well, he implies, in the voice of God at Mount Sinai (5:37b), and consequently in "the Scriptures," which, he claims, also "testify about me" (5:39).

ter his departure: "And I will ask the Father, and he will give you another advocate, that he might be with you forever, the Spirit of truth" (14:16-17); "But the Advocate, the Holy Spirit, which the Father will send in my name, he will teach you all things and remind you of all things that I said to you" (14:26); "When the Advocate comes, . . . the Spirit of truth that goes forth from the Father, he will testify about me, and you too must testify because you are with me from the beginning" (15:26-27); "I . . . am telling you the truth: it is to your advantage that I am going away, for unless I go away the Advocate will not come to you" (16:7); "But when that one comes, the Spirit of truth, he will lead you in all the truth" (16:13). Not "the disciple whom Jesus loved," but "the Advocate,"[62] or "the Spirit of truth," is the Guarantor of the truth of the testimony, and consequently of the written Gospel — the Spirit in conjunction not with a single individual but with those whom Jesus acknowledges as being with him "from the beginning"[63] (15:27). The latter notice recalls Luke 1:2, with its reference to "those who from the beginning were eyewitnesses and servants of the word," and even more pointedly 1 John 1:1-2, "That which was from the beginning, which we have heard, which we have seen with our eyes, and our hands have touched, concerning the word of Life — and the Life was revealed, and we have seen, and we testify, and we announce to you the Eternal Life which was with the Father and was revealed to us."

No distinction between theological truth and historical truth is evident. If the Advocate guarantees the former, the testimony of those who were with Jesus "from the beginning" guarantees the latter. And in the end the Advocate guarantees both. If the Advocate will finally "lead you into all the truth" (16:13), he will first of all, Jesus says, "remind you of all things that I said to you" (14:26). The Gospel begins with a series of highly theological, unverifiable assertions (1:1-5) — but moves seamlessly from there into straightforward narrative (vv. 6-8), and back again (vv. 9-18), before taking up the historical narrative in earnest ("And this is the testimony of John when the Jews sent priests and Levites to him from Jerusalem," 1:19). To the author, the one is as "true" as the other, and in much the same sense. The modern notion that his account could be theologically "true" yet historically unreliable is as foreign to him as it is to those who in the end vouch for the truth of his testimony (21:24).

At the same time, he gives no hint that the truth of his account implies the falsity of other accounts known to him. He is quick to acknowledge that Jesus "did many, and other, signs" — whether before or after his resurrection — "in the presence of his disciples which are not written in this book" (20:30), and his Gospel carries with it the added acknowledgment of "many

---

62. Gr. ὁ παράκλητος.
63. Gr. ἀπ' ἀρχῆς.

other things that Jesus did" (21:25). His Gospel is "true," he claims, because the Advocate will lead the disciples into "all the truth" (16:13), yet he does not claim "all" the truth for his Gospel. Its truth claims, while absolute, are not necessarily exclusive. While it knows nothing of a canon, it is, one might say, "ready" to be part of a canon — much like Luke's Gospel, with its acknowledgment of "many" who have preceded it (Lk 1:1). It is also "ready" for the canon in the sense that the revelation the Advocate brings will not go on indefinitely, as the ancient Montanists believed, continuing or even supplanting the revelation that Jesus brought once and for all. Rather, the testimony of Jesus and that of the Advocate are inextricably linked. The Advocate illumines and interprets only what Jesus has already revealed (see 16:14). His role, Jesus says, is to "remind you of all things that I said to you" (14:26) — that is, to "remind" or "cause to remember," not simply in the sense of recalling facts and words, but in the sense of enabling a later generation to understand those words, perhaps for the first time (see, for example, 2:17, 22; 12:16).

IV. JOHN AND THE OTHER GOSPELS

Are the Gospel's truth claims consistent with its genre? Is it a genre that aspires to "truth"? There is no reason to distinguish the genre of John's Gospel from that of its companions, Matthew, Mark, and Luke. Each begins at a "beginning" — all but Matthew explicitly — but each at a different beginning: Matthew with Abraham and a genealogy; Mark with John the Baptizer; Luke with a nod to "those who from the beginning were eyewitnesses and servants of the word," and then the Baptizer; John's Gospel with the Genesis beginning, and then the Baptizer. Each tells the story of Jesus with occasional attention to precise chronology, and each focuses disproportionately on the last week of Jesus' life and the events leading to his crucifixion (hence the designation "Gospel"). There is general agreement that the Gospels are not biographies in the modern sense of the word, yet with it a growing consensus that they are recognizable as ancient biographies or "lives,"[64] a genre encompassing something of a spectrum from pure propaganda to rather serious historiography. Richard Bauckham has made a strong case for placing the Gospel of John close to the historiographical end of that spectrum.[65] Whether or not he is

---

64. Gr. βίοι; Lat. *vitae.* See R. A. Burridge, *What Are the Gospels? A Comparison with Graeco-Roman Biography* (1992; 2d ed., Grand Rapids: Eerdmans, 2004).

65. Bauckham, *Testimony of the Beloved Disciple,* 93-112. He concludes that "to its contemporaries the Gospel of John would have looked considerably more like historiography than the Synoptic Gospels would" (112).

INTRODUCTION

correct in placing it *closer* than the other Gospels to serious history is open to debate, but his appeal to the Gospel's topographical and chronological precision is impressive. Incidents are placed, for example, "not just in Galilee, but in Cana or Capernaum; not just in Jerusalem but at the pool of Bethesda near the Sheep Gate; not just in the temple but in Solomon's Portico."[66] Events and discourses take place at named Jewish festivals such as Passover (chapters 2, 6, 11–20), the Tent festival (chapters 7–8) and Hanukkah (chapter 10).[67] Whatever the interpreter's judgment about the historicity of this or that particular incident or pronouncement, the Gospel's genre is consistent both with its extraordinary truth claims and with the genre of the other three Gospels. There can be little doubt that it wants to be taken seriously as history.

The question of whether or not the "Advocate," or "Spirit of truth," is at work in other testimonies to Jesus and other written Gospels is one that "the disciple whom Jesus loved" and those who vouched for him obviously do not address. Yet it is legitimate to ask how the beloved disciple knows of Jesus' "other" words and deeds? He speaks of them as unwritten in "this book" (20:30), but does he know of other books in which they are "written"? More specifically, does he know any or all of the other three Gospels in their final written form? For centuries the conventional wisdom was that he did know the other three, and consciously wrote to supplement them. Eusebius hands down a tradition to the effect that

> The three gospels which had been written down before were distributed to all including himself [that is, John]; it is said that he welcomed them and testified to their truth but said that there was only lacking to the narrative the account of what was done by Christ at first and at the beginning of the preaching. The story is surely true. It is at least possible to see that the three evangelists related only what the Saviour did during one year after John the Baptist had been put in prison and that they stated this at the beginning of their narrative.[68]

As early as the third century Clement of Alexandria wrote that "John, last of all, conscious that the outward facts had been set forth in the Gospels, was urged on by his disciples, and, divinely moved by the Spirit,[69] composed a spiritual Gospel."[70] While this is consistent with the explicit accent on the

---

66. Bauckham, *Testimony*, 99.
67. See Bauckham, *Testimony*, 101. As we will see, the one festival not named (5:1) may have been left anonymous in order to conceal a rare departure from chronological order.
68. *Ecclesiastical History* 3.24.7-8 (LCL, 1.251-53).
69. Gr. πνεύματι θεοφορηθέντα.
70. *Hypotyposeis*, in Eusebius, *Ecclesiastical History* 6.14.7 (LCL, 2.49).

Advocate, or "Spirit of truth," in John's Gospel, it is an oversimplification. Clearly, the synoptic Gospels are also "spiritual," and just as clearly the Gospel of John is as interested in "outward facts" as they are. The similarity of genre bears this out. Still, Clement's assertion that John was written last, with full knowledge of the other three, seemed to be confirmed by its placement in the canon. After all, anyone reading the Gospels in their canonical order would know by the time he reached the Gospel of John what the other three had said, and it seemed only reasonable that the Gospel writer had this knowledge as well. With the dominance of Markan priority from the mid-nineteenth century on, even those who had their doubts as to whether John's Gospel knew all three synoptics still routinely assumed that he knew at least the Gospel of Mark in its final written form.

This changed in the twentieth century, particularly after the work of Percival Gardner-Smith[71] and C. H. Dodd.[72] While there are exceptions, most interpreters today view the Gospel of John as independent of the other written Gospels (even Mark), yet familiar with many of the unwritten traditions behind them.[73] In the places where John and the synoptic Gospels overlap — the ministry of John the Baptizer (Jn 1:19-34), the cleansing of the temple (2:13-22), the healing of the royal official's son (4:43-54), the feeding of the five thousand and walking on the water (6:1-21), the decision of the Jewish council or Sanhedrin (11:45-53), the anointing at Bethany (12:1-8), the triumphal entry (12:12-29), and the entire passion narrative — the pattern of similarities and dissimilarities remains an enigma. As the commentary will show, parallels can be found between John's Gospel and every stratum of synoptic tradition: Mark, the so-called "Q" source, and material distinctive to Matthew and to Luke.[74] Sometimes the wording and/or placement of the synoptic material appears to be more nearly original, while at others John's wording and/or placement seems more primitive. Often it is difficult or impossible to decide. The respective traditions are perhaps best described as intertwined.

In general it is fair to say that John's Gospel differs from the other

---

71. *Saint John and the Synoptic Gospels* (Cambridge: Cambridge University Press, 1938).

72. *Historical Tradition in the Fourth Gospel* (Cambridge: Cambridge University Press, 1965).

73. Interestingly, Eusebius acknowledges that even after Matthew, Mark, and Luke had written their Gospels, "John, it is said, used all the time a message which was not written down" (*Ecclesiastical History* 3.24.7; LCL, 1.251) — this *before* the other Gospels "were distributed to all including himself" (see above, n. 68).

74. For example, Mark and John (see Mk 14:3 and Jn 12:3); "Q" and John (Mt 11:27//Lk 10:22 and Jn 3:35; 13:3; 17:2; 10:14-15; 17:25); Matthew and John (Mt 26:3 and Jn 11:47-53; Mt 27:49 and Jn 19:34; Mt 28:10 and Jn 20:17); Luke and John (Lk 23:4, 14, 22 and Jn 18:38; 19:4, 6; Lk 24:12; and Jn 20:6-8).

three in style and in structure. As to style — which turns out finally to be inseparable from content — Jesus speaks with a very different voice in this Gospel. In Matthew, Mark, and Luke the theme of his proclamation is the kingdom of God; here it is himself and his mission. As Rudolf Bultmann famously insisted, the revelation turns in upon itself. What Jesus reveals from the Father is simply that he is the Revealer, sent from the Father![75] Yet in this way he reveals the Father, which is not so different from saying that he reveals God, or the kingdom of God. What he says is what God has given him to say, and in his "works" or miracles he reveals the God of Israel at work (see 5:17). One way of summing up the difference is to say that much of what is implicit in the other three Gospels becomes explicit in John. The emphatic "I" of the Sermon on the Mount ("You have heard, . . . but now *I* tell you") and other pronouncements ("If *I* by the Spirit of God drive out demons . . .") becomes the magisterial "I am" of the Gospel of John (see 8:24, 28, 58; 13:19; 18:5-6). In the synoptics, Jesus proclaims "the gospel of God" (Mk 1:15), and in so doing reveals himself as God's messenger. In John's Gospel he reveals himself, and in so doing reveals the Father who sent him (see 12:45, "the person who sees me sees the One who sent me"; 14:9, "The person who has seen me has seen the Father"). Yet it is doubtful that this amounts to a simple reinterpretation of the other three Gospels. More likely the competing traditions took shape independently, with the Gospel of John deriving its own unique character from the interplay of inspiration and tradition (the "vertical" and "horizontal" if you will) — that is, on the one hand the testimony of the Advocate, or "Spirit of truth" ("he will testify about me," 15:26), and on the other the testimony of the eyewitnesses (those "with me from the beginning," 15:27), represented by "the disciple whom Jesus loved."

V. THE STRUCTURE OF JOHN'S GOSPEL

As to structure, if John's Gospel is familiar with the so-called Markan outline, common to Matthew, Mark, and Luke, then it has distanced itself from that outline in conspicuous ways. Eusebius acknowledged already in the fourth century that

---

75. In Bultmann's words, "Thus it turns out in the end that Jesus as the Revealer of God *reveals nothing but that he is the Revealer,*" and "the Revelation consists of nothing more than the bare fact of it (its *Dass*) — i.e., the proposition that the Revealer has come and gone, has descended and been re-exalted" (*Theology of the New Testament*, 2.66). This recurring self-reference is what produces the "relentless tattoo" of Johannine poetry so distasteful to the translators of the NAB (see above, n. 3).

The Structure of John's Gospel

> John in the course of his gospel relates what Christ did before the Baptist had been thrown into prison, but the other three evangelists narrate the events after the imprisonment of the Baptist. If this be understood, the gospels no longer appear to disagree, because that according to John contains the first of the acts of Christ and the others the narrative of what he did at the end of the period.[76]

As we have seen in our discussion of the prominence of "John" (that is, the Baptizer) in the first three chapters,[77] there is something to be said for Eusebius's interest in "what Christ did before the Baptist had been thrown into prison." First, the importance of the Baptizer in the so-called "Prologue" should not be overlooked. Scholarly readings, even among those resolved to look at the finished text as a literary entity (that is, synchronically), sometimes tend to follow the "tracks" left by various source theories.[78] For example, the long-held theory that the first eighteen verses of the Gospel either were or contained a distinct pre-Johannine "hymn" of some kind has tended to lock in the notion that those verses were a unit set apart from the rest of the Gospel, to be given separate and special treatment as "the Prologue." The Gospel as a whole is rightly viewed as narrative, much like the other Gospels, but "the Prologue" is often seen differently — almost as another genre. Consequently, the explicit narrative beginning *within* the Prologue (1:6) has to be viewed as no narrative beginning at all, but simply as an "interpolation" embedded in what some scholars have already decided is a pre-Johannine, possibly pre-Christian, hymn. But if what looks like a narrative beginning *is* in fact just that — a reasonable assumption — then the real "prologue" — or "preamble," or "introduction" — is not John 1:1-18 but John 1:1-5.[79] These five verses, unlike most (but not all) of the Gospel, have no narrative context. Whatever their background — for example, in Jewish Wisdom tradition — their present function is to set the stage for introducing "A man . . . sent from God. John was his name" (1:6), and to explain John's repeated claim that "The One coming after me has gotten ahead of me, because he was before

---

76. *Ecclesiastical History* 3.24.12-13; LCL, 1.253-55.
77. See above, pp. 16-17.
78. Other examples include C. H. Dodd, who did not advocate a pre-Johannine "Signs Source," nevertheless described chapters 2–12, Jesus' public ministry, as "the Book of Signs" (in distinction from chapters 13–21, "the Book of the Passion"; Dodd, *Interpretation,* 297, 390); also, many of those who insist that chapter 21 is an original and integral part of the Gospel nevertheless continue to treat 20:30 and 31 as if they were in fact the ending of the Gospel.
79. This was how Chrysostom read it in commenting on John 1:6: "Having in the introduction [εἰσαγωγή] spoken to us things of urgent importance concerning God the Word (the Evangelist) proceeding on his road, and in order, afterwards comes to the herald of the Word, his namesake John" (*Homilies on St. John* 6.1; NPNF, 1st ser., 14.25).

INTRODUCTION

me" (1:15; also v. 30). Indeed, "the Word" who is Jesus does precede John, and therefore takes precedence over him. This is evident at once in the insistence that John "was not the light, but [he came] to testify about the light" (1:8), and in the accompanying excursus on the coming and presence of Jesus in the world (1:9-18). It is as if the Gospel writer cannot resist pouring out in advance the whole story he has to tell in ten memorable verses. If the narrative of John's testimony has already begun (vv. 6-8), then the real "interpolation" is this magnificent excursus, with the narrative of John and his testimony resuming in 1:19-34.[80]

It is John, accordingly, whose eyewitness first-person testimony dominates the first chapter — and frames the first three chapters. Although he disappears as soon as Jesus takes the initiative to find Philip and Nathanael and to set out for Galilee (1:43-51), John the Baptizer is not gone for good. After the wedding at Cana, which confirms several of John's disciples as disciples of Jesus (even with Jesus still within the family circle, 2:11-12), and after Jesus' eventful ministry at the first Passover in Jerusalem (2:13–3:21), we find him in Judea doing just what John had been doing. He who will "baptize in Holy Spirit" (1:33) is baptizing in water (3:22, 26), the same as John.[81] Even though Jesus has much to say of significance in the first three chapters, it is undeniable that he shares the spotlight with John. They speak, as it were, in stereo. Jesus speaks to Nicodemus, yet his words abruptly spring out of their narrative context (see 3:13-21) to become a kind of sequel to the "introduction" or "preamble" of 1:1-5 and the excursus of 1:9-18. John then comes front and center to give his farewell speech (3:27-36). He speaks to his own disciples (vv. 27-30), yet his words, too, spring from their narrative context to become yet another sequel to the Gospel's opening verses (see 3:31-36). Together, the "preamble" of 1:1-5 and the joint testimonies of John and Jesus frame the Gospel's first three chapters. Within these chapters, as we have seen, the dominant voice in the emphatic first person is John's voice, not (as yet) the voice of Jesus (see 1:20, 23, 26, 31, 33, 34; 3:28-30). It is arguable that not just chapter 1 but the Gospel's first three chapters should be designated "the testimony of John." Yet as soon as John says, "He must grow, but I must diminish" (3:30), Jesus' role in the story grows exponentially. John, with his very last words (3:31-36), announces that "the Word" (1:1) is about to speak: "What he has seen and what he heard, to this he testifies" (3:32), and "the one God sent speaks the words of God" (v. 34). At the same

---

80. As we will attempt to show, the testimony attributed to John in 1:15-18 is different, a testimony not made in history but in the present, as John is made a spokesman for the Gospel writer himself and the Christian community of his day.

81. Or at least his disciples were. It seems to have amounted to the same thing (see 4:2).

THE STRUCTURE OF JOHN'S GOSPEL

time, John reinforces the alternatives of faith and unbelief already set forth in 1:11-12 and 3:13-21: "Whoever believes in the Son has eternal life, but whoever disobeys the Son will never see life, but the wrath of God remains on him" (v. 36).

At this point the narrative resumes, the story line corresponding to that of the synoptics except that instead of John's imprisonment (as in Mk 1:14 and Mt 4:12) it is John's sovereign farewell speech that triggers Jesus' journey to Galilee (see 4:1-3). Whether or not Jesus continued baptizing as John had done, we are not told. As is the case with John, the Gospel is more interested in Jesus' testimony than in any baptizing activity he may have carried on. From here on, as we have seen, the "I" who testifies is Jesus. So far, apart from the "Amen, amen, I say to you" formula (1:51; 3:3, 5, 11), he has had little to say in the first person (*"my* Father's house," 2:16; "I will raise it up," 2:19), and nothing with the emphatic "I," but this changes in chapter 4 when he reveals himself to the Samaritan woman with the words, "It is I — I who am speaking to you" (4:26; see also 6:20; 8:24, 28, 58). Moreover, in contrast to John (see 10:41), his testimony is punctuated by a series of miraculous signs. His self-revelation (whether in the emphatic first person, or as "the Son" or "Son of man") extends through chapter 12, at the end of which comes yet another brief monologue without narrative context (12:44-50), this time introduced with the words, "But Jesus cried out and said" (12:44), punctuated with the emphatic "I" (vv. 46, 47, 49) and, like John's farewell speech at the end of chapter 3, terminating a major section of the Gospel.

To this extent, Eusebius' testimony is helpful in structuring the Gospel of John in comparison to the synoptics. Our reading of the Gospel so far yields an outline consisting of a short preamble (1:1-5), the testimony of John (1:6–3:36), and the public testimony of Jesus (4:1–12:50). But Eusebius does not warn us that when we move beyond the first three chapters, the differences between John and the synoptics do not diminish. After John's imprisonment, Matthew, Mark, and Luke recount Jesus' ministry in Galilee at some length, concluding with one — and only one — extended journey to Jerusalem and an account of Jesus' arrest, trial, death, and resurrection there. Our Gospel, by contrast, places Jesus in Jerusalem already in chapter 2, and even after John's imprisonment Jesus is there again in chapter 5, again in chapters 7, 8, 9, and 10, and again in chapters 12 through 20, always in connection with one or another of the Jewish festivals. He is in Galilee only for one miracle in chapter 2 and another in chapter 4 — both in the same town, a town not even mentioned in the other Gospels — and once more for a miracle and an extended discourse at Capernaum in chapter 6. He returns to Galilee after the resurrection (chapter 21), as he does in Matthew and (implicitly) in Mark, but the Galilean ministry which dominates the other three Gospels virtually disappears. Moreover, in the Synoptics everything is public except for the interpretations of certain parables (see Mk 4:34) and a final discourse on things to come (Mk 13 and parallels),[82] while the Gospel of John seems to divide Jesus' ministry into two parts, a "public ministry" to the crowds and the religious authorities in Jerusalem and Galilee (chapters 2–12) and a "private ministry" to his disciples in the setting of the last supper (chapters 13–17). Most noticeably of all, the two events introducing passion week in Mark — the triumphal entry and the cleansing of the temple — are separated (and reversed) in John's Gospel in such a way as to frame the entire public ministry of Jesus (see 2:13-22; 12:12-19).

In view of all this, it is difficult to tell whether John's Gospel knows the outline common to Matthew, Mark, and Luke (an outline remarkably well summarized by Peter in Acts 10:37-41) and deliberately opts for an alternative, or whether it knows only isolated incidents and pronouncements of Jesus from synoptic tradition, and puts these together with what the Gospel writer knows as an eyewitness, independently of the other Gospels. In any event, its structure deserves close attention in its own right, apart from all theories of literary dependence, and apart from all source theories as well. To begin with, the effect of placing the temple cleansing almost at the beginning of Jesus' ministry rather than near the end is far reaching. Any reader familiar with the other Gospels will assume, on reading that "the Passover of the Jews was near, and Jesus went up to Jerusalem" (2:13), that Jesus' Galilean ministry has been extremely brief (see 2:1-12), and that the passion is about to begin.[83] In one sense the reader has been misled, but in another sense not, because all that happens from here on happens with the passion in view. The Scripture remembered in connection with the cleansing of the temple is "Zeal for your house will consume [that is, destroy] me" (2:17), and the only "sign" Jesus gave was "Destroy this sanctuary [that is, his body], and in three days I will raise it up" (2:19). Conspicuous in the synoptic passion narrative is a trial (of sorts) before the Sanhedrin and the Chief Priest, but in John's Gospel the whole public ministry of Jesus (at least from chapter 5 on) is his trial at the hands of the Jewish religious authorities, one in which he is both accused and accuser, and one peppered with such terms such as "testify" and "testimony" (see 3:11, 32; 5:31-34, 36-37, 39; 7:7; 8:13-14, 17, 18; 10:25), "judge" and "judgment" (see 3:18-19; 5:22, 27, 30; 7:24, 51; 8:15-16, 26, 50; 12:31), "true" and "truth" (see

---

82. In a sense, Jesus' claim to the Chief Priest that "I have spoken publicly to the world," and "I spoke nothing in secret" (18:20) is more applicable to the synoptics than to the Gospel of John.

83. The notice is remarkably similar to another, nine chapters later, when the passion actually does begin: "Now the Passover of the Jews was near, and many went up from the region to Jerusalem before the Passover, that they might purify themselves" (11:55).

The Structure of John's Gospel

5:31-33; 7:18; 8:13-14, 16, 17, 40, 45-46; 10:41). In a general way chapters 2 through 12 can be regarded as a book of judgment. In one sense, Jesus is on trial, but in another "the world," represented by the Jewish religious authorities, is being tried — and condemned. Ever since chapter 5 the religious authorities had been seeking Jesus' life, "because he was not only abolishing the Sabbath but was claiming God as his own Father, making himself equal to God" (5:18; see also 7:1, 19, 25, 30; 8:37, 40), but the verdict comes down only after this extended "trial," as the Jewish ruling council formally "resolved that they would kill him" (11:53). Consequently, there is no real trial after Jesus is actually arrested, only a brief hearing before the Chief Priest in which Jesus simply refers back to what he had "always taught in synagogue and in the temple, where all the Jews come together" (18:20). Throughout the public ministry there looms the prospect of Jesus' "hour," which the reader understands as the hour of his death, a death viewed in this Gospel not as defeat but as victory, not as tragedy but as "glorification" (7:39; 12:23, 28). Suspense builds as the reader is told more than once that Jesus escaped arrest "because his hour had not yet come" (7:30; 8:20; see also 8:59; 10:39). Finally, "The hour has come that the Son of man might be glorified" (12:23), not in an arrest but simply by Jesus' sovereign decree (the arrest will take place six chapters later!).

As passion week begins (see 12:1), the book of judgment gives way to a book of glory. Strictly speaking, perhaps, the book of judgment consists of 2:13–11:54 (with the handing down of the verdict in 11:45-54), and the book of glory begins already with the notice of the last Passover (11:55), yet there is also (as we have seen) a definite break at the end of chapter 12, with the Gospel writer's own verdict on an unbelieving world (12:37-43) and a final soliloquy from the lips of Jesus (12:44-50). There is no urgent need to choose between the two options, for in either case 11:55–12:50 is transitional, marking both the end of the public ministry with its emphasis on judgment (see, for example, 12:31, "Now is the judgment of this world. Now the ruler of this world will be driven out") and the beginning of the passion with its decisive revelation of Jesus' glory (see 12:23, 28). At the end of this longer transition is a shorter one (12:44-50) consisting not so much of Jesus' verdict on the world's unbelief (vv. 47-48) as his promise of light and life to those who do believe (vv. 44-46, 49-50), with just a hint that he will have more to say (v. 50) — which in fact he does. If chapters 2 through 12 lead up to the certainty that Jesus must be glorified in death, chapters 13 through 17 prepare the readers of the Gospel — in the persons of their surrogates, the disciples — for that death and its implications. To them, Jesus' "glorification" is not experienced as glorification but as departure or absence, and the thrust of the farewell discourses in 13:36–14:31 and in chapters 15 and 16 is to overcome the scandal of Jesus' absence with the promise of his return, whether in his resurrection (chapter 20) or in the person of the Advocate, or "Spirit of truth," and with a new command to "love each other, just as I loved you" (13:34; 15:12).

In chapter 17 Jesus turns around, as it were, to the Father in prayer, reporting to the Father what his ministry has accomplished and interceding for his soon-to-be-scattered disciples (see 16:32). Like 1:1-5, 3:13-21, 3:31-36, and 12:44-50, this, too, is a passage without a real narrative context. Jesus is no longer "with" his disciples, but rather looks back to a time when "I was with them" (17:12). His "private" ministry to the disciples has become even more private, as even they are shut out, and like the Jewish High Priest the Good Shepherd moves into the "Holy of Holies" to speak to his Father alone, on behalf of his sheep. Yet as soon as he is finished, he is "with" them again, as they cross the Kidron valley together, to a familiar gathering place where he will be arrested (see 18:1-2). With his arrest, the passion narrative proper begins, and whatever else it may be, in this Gospel it brings the verification of promises made earlier — that the sheep, though scattered, would not be "lost" (18:9), that Jesus would be "lifted up" (18:32) and "glorified" at a definite "hour" (19:13-14, 17-18), that he would go away to the Father (20:6-8) and come again to the disciples (20:19, 26), that he would bring with him the Holy Spirit (20:22), and that they would know joy (20:20) and peace (20:19, 21, 26) when they saw him again. The ending of the Gospel (chapter 21) is curiously like a new beginning, an acknowledgment, perhaps, of how the gospel story began in other traditions, with a fishing scene at the lake of Galilee (see Mk 1:16-20; Lk 5:1-11). Christian discipleship begins where the Gospel ends.

At the end of the day there is no one right way to outline the Gospel of John. The preceding observations yield the following:

PREAMBLE (1:1-5).
THE TESTIMONY OF JOHN (1:6–3:30), with a transition on the lips of John (3:31-36) corresponding to the preamble.
JESUS' SELF-REVELATION TO THE WORLD (4:1–12:43), with a transition this time on the lips of Jesus (12:44-50).
JESUS' SELF-REVELATION TO THE DISCIPLES (13:1–16:33), with a much longer transition in the form of Jesus' prayer to the Father (17:1-26)
VERIFICATION OF JESUS' SELF-REVELATION IN HIS ARREST, CRUCIFIXION, AND RESURRECTION (18:1–21:25).

This outline, like all the others, is far from perfect. It does justice to some but by no means all of the evidence. It does not, for example, do justice to the importance of the seven signs Jesus performs, the first sandwiched between the testimonies of John (2:1-11) and the other six displayed in connection with Jesus' self-revelatory discourses to the world. Its chief distinguishing features are that it does not begin with an eighteen-verse "prologue" but with a five-verse "preamble," and that it takes note of certain passages which, like the preamble, have no proper narrative context and can serve as markers dividing one section from another. Yet there are other such passages (for example, 3:13-21 and 5:19-47) which do not similarly serve as division markers. Structure in John's Gospel, as in most great literature, is largely in the eye of the beholder.

VI. LOCATION AND DATE

Where was the Gospel of John written, and when? Those questions are not easily answered. Traditions connecting it with Ephesus in Asia Minor are mostly linked to the assumption that the author was John the son of Zebedee, or (in the view of some modern scholars) the shadowy John the Presbyter. But once we are left with an author who is either anonymous or someone other than "John," the evidence begins to look rather thin. Ephesus, or at least Asia Minor, is still a reasonable guess, given certain similarities between the Gospel of John and such writings as Paul's letters to Colossians (for example, 1:15-20) and Ephesians, and the book of Revelation, and given the role assigned to "the Advocate" by the Montanists in Asia Minor in the second and third centuries.[84] Yet nothing approaching certainty is possible. The earliest textual witnesses to the Gospel of John are papyri from Egypt, above all the so-called Rylands fragment, or P[52], consisting of John 18:31-33, 37-38 (the earliest known fragment of any New Testament book), from the first half of the second century,[85] and the Bodmer papyri (P[66] and P[75]), from the early third century. This obviously does not mean that the Gospel was written there. Virtually all New Testament papyri come from Egypt, whose climate lends itself to their preservation. Yet Egypt cannot be ruled out, nor can Palestine. Syria is perhaps more likely than either, for Ignatius of Antioch shows signs of familiarity with the theology of the Gospel, even though he never

---

84. According to Eusebius, "Of these some like poisonous reptiles crawled over Asia and Phrygia, and boasted that Montanus was the Paraclete [τὸν μὲν δὴ παράκλητον] and that the women of his sect, Priscilla and Maximilla, were the prophetesses of Montanus" (*Ecclesiastical History* 5.14 (LCL, 1.471); also Montanus is said to have claimed, "I am the Father and the Son and the Paraclete" (Didymus, *De Trinitate* 3.41.1, cited in R. M. Grant, *Second-Century Christianity*, 95).

85. *An Unpublished Fragment of the Fourth Gospel in the John Rylands Library* (ed. C. H. Roberts; Manchester: Manchester University Press, 1935).

quotes it,[86] and so too do the *Odes of Solomon*.[87] Moreover, the Jewishness of this Gospel, and the intertwining of its traditions with those behind each of the synoptic Gospels, is consistent with Syrian origin. But there is no way to be certain. If there is such a thing as a distinctively "Johannine" community, we do not yet know enough about it to be able to locate it geographically. When we speak of the author's "community," all we mean is whatever Christian communities the author may be familiar with, wherever he, or they, may be. It is clear that these communities — like most Christian communities at that time — were "sectarian" with respect to the Graeco-Roman world around them, but by no means clear that they were sectarian with respect to other Christian groups.

As to date, we are similarly at a loss. The Gospel obviously predates the Rylands fragment, and if the author was, as he claims, an eyewitness, it was almost certainly written within the first century. Yet if it is in fact independent of the other three Gospels, drawing on traditions intertwined with theirs, but not on Matthew, Mark, or Luke themselves as literary sources, then there is virtually no limit on how soon after the death and resurrection of Jesus it could have been written. While there is nothing to shatter the conventional wisdom that it is the latest of the four Gospels, there is no way to prove it either. This Gospel could have originated any time within the latter half of the first century, and only the rumor that "the disciple whom Jesus loved" would not die (21:23) places it nearer the end of that period than the beginning. If, as seems likely, it was written after the destruction of Jerusalem and the temple by the Romans in AD 70, this would lend special poignancy and irony to the fear of the Jewish leaders that "If we let him go on like this, . . . the Romans will come and take away both our place and our nation" (11:48). In fact, even though they arrested Jesus and put him to death, the Romans eventually came and did exactly that!

---

86. See, for example, Ignatius, *To the Magnesians* 7.1, "And so, just as the Lord did nothing apart from the Father — being united with him — neither on his own nor through the apostles" (LCL, 1.247; compare Jn 5:29; 8:28); *To the Philadelphians* 7.1, "For it [that is, the Spirit] knows whence it comes and where it is going" (LCL, 1.289; compare Jn 3:8); *Romans* 7.3, "I desire the bread of God, which is the flesh of Jesus Christ, from the seed of David; and for drink I desire his blood, which is imperishable love" (LCL, 1.279; compare Jn 6:53-56).

87. See, for example, *Odes of Solomon* 7.12 ("He has allowed him to appear to them that are his own," *OTP*, 2.740; compare Jn 1:11); 8.20-21 ("Seek and increase, and abide in the love of the Lord; and you who are loved in the Beloved; and you who are kept in him who lives," *OTP*, 2.742; compare Jn 15:9); 10:5 ("And the gentiles who had been scattered were gathered together," *OTP*, 2.744; compare Jn 11:52); 11.23 ("Indeed, there is much room in your paradise," *OTP*, 2.746; compare Jn 14:2); 18.6 ("Let not light be conquered by darkness," *OTP*, 2.751; compare Jn 1:5).

VII. THEOLOGICAL CONTRIBUTIONS

It is difficult to say much about the theology or christology of John's Gospel that has not been said many times before, nor is the introduction to a commentary necessarily the best place to try. Better to let the reader draw his or her own conclusions from discussions of particular texts as the commentary unfolds. But two things stand out for me, the first because it is so pervasive throughout the Gospel, the second because it is rarely noticed or appreciated by interpreters.

The first contribution of John's Gospel to the theology of the New Testament takes us back to where we began. It is the notion of Jesus as God's unique Envoy or messenger, simultaneously claiming for himself both Deity and obedient submission to Deity. The strangeness is evident to anyone who places the two pronouncements, "I and the Father are one" (10:30) and "the Father is greater than I" (14:28), side by side. Jesus can say, "My Father is working even until now, and I am working," provoking the accusation that he is "making himself equal to God" (5:17-18), yet immediately insist that he does nothing "on his own," but only what the Father has sent him and commanded him to do (see 5:19, 30). He can warn that "unless you believe that I am, you will die in your sins" (8:24) and "When you lift up the Son of man, then you will come to know that I am," yet immediately add that "on my own I do nothing, but just as the Father taught me, these things I speak" (8:28). He never acts "on his own" in relation to the Father, but always "on his own" in relation to the world. As far as his death on the cross is concerned, no one takes his life from him, he insists, "but I lay it down on my own. I have authority to lay it down, and I have authority to receive it back," yet he quickly adds, "This command I received from my Father" (10:18). His "authority," whether to exercise judgment (5:27) or to lay down his own life, belongs to him only because it belongs first to the Father. His mission is to reveal the Father, but in so doing he reveals himself — first publicly, as we have seen, to the world at large on the stage of contemporary Judaism, and then privately to his own disciples.[88] The obvious objection to all this is that the Judaism of Jesus' day, in contrast to the Gentile world, did not need Jesus to reveal to it its own God — or so it would seem. What was needed rather was someone to

---

88. Certain parallels between the one and the other are worth noticing. Compare, for example, 8:21 ("Where I am going you cannot come"; see also 7:34) with 13:33 ("just as I said to the Jews that 'Where I am going, you cannot come,' so I say to you now"); 8:14 ("you do not know where I come from or where I am going") with 14:5 ("Lord, we do not know where you are going"); 8:19a ("Where is your father?") with 14:8 ("Lord, show us the Father"); 8:19b ("If you knew me, you would know my Father") with 14:7 ("If you all have known me, you will know my Father too"). The disciples are are at first hardly better off than "the Jews," but in their case the revelation is in the end both given and received.

reveal the God of Israel to the Gentiles, a Messiah who would make Israel a light to the nations. This the coming of Jesus will do as well, but it is largely outside the horizons of the Gospel narrative (see 10:16; 11:52; 12:32). Rather, Jesus in this Gospel "came to what was his own," even though "his own did not receive him" (1:11). He came to reveal the God of Israel to Israel in one very specific way — as Father, and in particular as *his* Father, not simply telling the people of God things about God they did not already know, but *showing* them the face of God in his own face (see 12:45; 14:9) and his own life.

The Gospel of John, then, is not just about Jesus but about God, as is evident not only in its christology but in its message of salvation. This, to my mind, is the Gospel's second major contribution to New Testament theology, and it is rather more controversial than the first. From the start, the Gospel speaks of those who "receive" Jesus as the Light and "believe in his name," those who are given "authority to become children of God" by virtue of having been "born . . . of God" (1:12-13). Two chapters later Jesus tells Nicodemus, "unless someone is born from above [or "of water and Spirit"], he cannot see [or "enter"] the kingdom of God" (3:3, 5). But what exactly is the relationship between being "born of God," or "born from above," and "receiving" or "believing in" Jesus? Which comes first? Is a person reborn because he or she believes, or does a person believe as a *result* of being reborn? Conventional wisdom assumes the former as a matter of course, and the word order of 1:12-13 seems on the face of it to support this. Yet those verses make no explicit causal connection either way between faith and rebirth, and as Jesus' dialogue with Nicodemus runs its course, evidence for the opposite view begins to surface. "Receiving" Jesus' testimony is mentioned in 3:11, and "believing" is repeatedly urged in verses 12, 15, and 16. Finally, the stark alternative of "believing" or "not believing" in him is clearly set forth (v. 18), and then restated (in language reminiscent of 1:9-13) as either loving or hating the Light, either "coming to the Light" or refusing to come (vv. 19-21). The person who "hates the Light" does so because he "practices wicked things," and refuses to come "for fear his works will be exposed" (v. 20). By contrast, the person who "does the truth comes to the Light, so that his works will be revealed as works wrought in God" (v. 21).

On this note the interview with Nicodemus — if Nicodemus is still anywhere in the picture — comes to an end. In sharp distinction from the other three Gospels, in which Jesus says, "I have not come to call the righteous, but sinners" (Mk 2:17//Mt 9:13; also Lk 5:32), he does come to call, if not explicitly "the righteous," at least those who "do the truth" — as against those who "practice wicked things." Those who come to him in faith (that is, "come to the Light") demonstrate by so doing that they are *already* "doers of the truth," not by their own merits to be sure, but because their works have been done "in God" (*en theō*, 3:21). They do not prove their faith by their works — at least not yet — but on the contrary prove their works by their faith. To this extent, John's Gospel turns some versions of Reformation theology on their heads![89] It is not as radical as it sounds, however, for the point is simply that God is at work in a person's life *before* that person "receives" Jesus, or "believes," or "comes to the Light." This is evident in the account of the man born blind — the Gospel's classic case study on what it means to be "born of God" — where the point made is *not* that the man was a sinner who "believed" and was consequently reborn. On the contrary, Jesus insists, "Neither this man sinned nor his parents" — that is, his predicament was not the result of sin. Rather, the purpose of the healing was "that the works of God might be revealed in him" (9:3) — that is, God was *already* at work in his life, and his eventual confession of faith (9:38) would reveal that to be the case. He did not believe *in order* to be "born of God." He believed *because* he was "born of God." This interpretation is confirmed by Jesus' repeated insistence that "All that the Father gives me will come to me" (6:37), "No one can come to me unless the Father who sent me draw him" (6:44), and "no one can come to me unless it is given him from the Father" (6:65). The initiative in human salvation is God the Father's, and his alone.

Of the major interpreters of John's Gospel, only Rudolf Bultmann wrestles significantly with this aspect of the Gospel's view of salvation. He writes of "Johannine Determinism," defining it as a "dualism of decision" in contrast to "the cosmological dualism of Gnosticism."[90] But in the end he seems to accent human "decision," or free will, to the point that it trumps the divine initiative: "Man cannot act otherwise than as what he is, but in the Revealer's call there opens up to him the possibility of being otherwise than he was. He can exchange his Whence, his origin, his essence, for another; he can be 'born again' (3:1ff.) and thus attain to his true being. In his decision between faith and un-faith a man's being definitively constitutes itself, and from then on his Whence becomes clear."[91] While it is true that John's Gospel centers on a call to decision, the hearer's decision cannot change but only reveal what has gone on before — the working of God the Father in those who will eventually become his children. Jesus can speak of "other sheep" whom, he says, "I have," even though they have not yet believed (10:16), and the Gospel writer can envision scattered "children of God" — "born of God," therefore — who have yet to be "gathered into one" (11:52). Perhaps the

---

89. This is also consistent with the notion (often dismissed as out of place in John's Gospel) that "those who have done good things will go out to a resurrection of life, but those who have practiced wicked things to a resurrection of judgment" (5:29).

90. *Theology of the New Testament*, 2.21.

91. *Theology of the New Testament*, 2.25.

words of old Simeon in another Gospel put it best: Jesus in the Gospel of John comes "so that the thoughts of many hearts might be revealed" (Lk 2:35). The accent is not on "conversion" (the words for "repent" and "repentance" never occur), or even the forgiveness of sins, but on revelation. The coming of Jesus into the world simply reveals who belongs — and who does not belong — to his Father, the God of Israel. If the Gospel of John reveals who the Son is and who the Father is, it also tells its readers who they are and where they stand with the Father and the Son.

If God the Father is the initiator of Christian salvation according to this Gospel, he is also its end and goal. The Son is sent from the Father and returns to the Father again. This is what the world does not understand according to chapters 2 through 12, and through much of chapters 13 through 17 the disciples do not understand either. In the end they finally grasp that he has in fact "come forth from God" (16:30), but not that he must return to God again. "If you loved me," he tells them, "you would rejoice that I am going off to the Father, because the Father is greater than I" (14:28). Only by virtue of his prayer on their behalf (chapter 17) and of his resurrection (chapter 20) does his intention that "In that day, you will come to know that I am in my Father, and you in me, and I in you" (14:20) come to realization. He sends them, through Mary, the message that "I am going up to my Father and your Father, and my God and your God" (20:18). If the beginning of the story is the work of God the Father in the hearts of human beings, drawing them to the Son, the end of the story is their union with the Son and consequently with the Father. Just as the Gospel's christology is a kind of parabola, with the Son coming down from the Father into the world and going back up to the Father again, so too is its soteriology, its course of salvation, with God the Father drawing a people to God the Son, who leads them in turn back to the Father. Those who, in Emily Dickinson's words, "choose the Envoy — and spurn the groom" have failed to understand the Gospel of John.

The Gospel of JOHN

Text, Exposition, and Notes

I. PREAMBLE: THE LIGHT (1:1-5)

1 In the beginning was the Word, and the Word was with God, and the Word was God. 2 He was with God in the beginning. 3 All things came into being through him, and apart from him not one thing that has come into being was made. 4 In him was life, and that life was the light of humans, 5 and the light is shining in the darkness, and the darkness did not overtake it.

The story to be told in this Gospel begins with the words, "A man came, sent from God. John was his name" (1:6). This means that the five preceding verses must be taken as a kind of preface or preamble, in keeping with the principle stated by John himself that "The One coming after me . . . was before me" (v. 15; see also v. 30). This will be new to generations of readers who are accustomed to setting the first eighteen verses of the Gospel apart as "The Prologue." In identifying the first five verses of John as "preamble," rather than the first eighteen as "prologue," we are breaking with tradition, and within these five verses we break with tradition again by accenting "the light"[1] rather than "the Word" as their major theme. John's Gospel is classically remembered as a Gospel of the Word *(ho logos),* and its christology as a "Logos" christology to be placed alongside other New Testament christologies. But the significance of "Word," or Logos, as a title for Jesus, real as it

---

1. Capitalization is a problem in translating Greek designations for God or Jesus into English. Capitalizing such metaphors as Good Shepherd, or Vine, or Bread, or Lamb of God, or such terms as the Word, the Light, the Life, the Son, even the Father, is one way of signaling to the reader that these expressions are being used as metaphors or titles of deity. Yet with terms not inherently personal in nature the decision to capitalize or not can be a rather subjective one. I have capitalized only where the term seems to function unmistakably as a personal title.

is, must be kept in perspective. It appears only four times in the Gospel, three times in the very first verse, once in verse 14, and never again in the rest of John.[2] "Light," on the other hand, is a dominant image through at least the first half of the Gospel.[3] The preamble begins with "the Word" (v. 1) and finishes on a triumphant note with "the light" (v. 5), giving away at the outset the ending of the story, and succinctly describing the world as the Gospel writer perceives it: "And the light is shining in the darkness, and the darkness did not overtake it." The Gospel of John is about revelation; the text begins with audible revelation ("Word"), moving on to visible revelation ("light"), and thence back and forth between the two (embodied in Jesus' signs and discourses) as the story unfolds.

1-2 Each of the four Gospels begins, appropriately enough, with a reference to some kind of beginning. Mark's heading is "Beginning of the gospel of Jesus Christ" (Mk 1:1). Matthew opens with "an account of the origin of Jesus Christ" (Mt 1:1). Luke acknowledges the traditions of "those who from the beginning were eyewitnesses and ministers of the word" (Lk 1:2). John's "beginning" *(archē)* is the earliest of all, for the vocabulary of John's preamble is decisively shaped by the opening verses of Genesis. Why this is so has puzzled interpreters for centuries. The Gospel of John is not particularly interested in creation. Like the other Gospels, its focus is on revelation and redemption, the new creation if you will. But at the outset, attention is drawn to the beginning of all beginnings, the story of creation in Genesis. Whether or not the purpose is to counter a group in or on the fringes of the Christian movement that denigrated the old creation (Gnosticism comes immediately to mind), we do not know. As interpreters, our best course is to defer judgment for the moment, and wait to see if subsequent evidence in the Gospel sheds light on why the writer has begun in this way.

In any event, the words "In the beginning"[4] unmistakably echo Genesis 1:1, "In the beginning God made the heaven and the earth." Yet the differences are more striking than the similarities. God is the solitary Creator in the Genesis account, while in John creation is jointly the work of God and the

---

2. The fuller expression "the word of God" (ὁ λόγος τοῦ θεοῦ) occurs in 10:35, but not (on most readings) in reference to Jesus. It also appears in Revelation 19:13 as a name for a rider on a white horse (evidently the triumphant Jesus) coming in judgment, but there the term echoes earlier references in the Revelation where it is not obviously christological (for example, 1:2, 9; 6:9; 20:4; see also 19:9).

3. Jesus identifies himself explicitly as light in 8:12, "I am the Light of the world"; compare 9:5, "As long as I am in the world, I am the world's light"; 12:36, "While you have the Light, believe in the Light"; 12:46, "I have come as light into the world" (see also 3:19-21). It is perhaps worth noting that all the references to light come within the first twelve chapters.

4. Gr. ἐν ἀρχῇ.

Word. Genesis, moreover, is interested in God's *act,* not God's being or existence, which is simply presupposed: "God *made* the heaven and the earth." John's Gospel, by contrast, focuses on *being,* in three clauses: (1) "In the beginning *was* the Word," (2) "the Word *was* with God," and (3) "the Word *was* God."[5] Perhaps this is because God in the book of Genesis needs no introduction. God can be safely presupposed, but the same is not true of the Word in the Gospel of John. The Word must be identified, and can only be identified in relation to God, the God of Israel.

After introducing "the Word" in the first clause, the verse presents an interplay between "the Word" *(ho logos)* and "God" *(ho theos)* in two different ways, and in chiastic fashion: the Word was "with God"[6] and, following the order of the Greek text, God was what the Word was.[7] The solemn repetition — Word, Word, God, God, Word — captures the reader's attention from the outset by giving the language a poetic or hymnic quality that immediately sets John apart from the other three canonical Gospels. Because this quality is not typical of John's Gospel as a whole, the impression is given that John will be more different from the other Gospels than is actually the case.

What then is the relationship between the Word and God? The signals are mixed, in that the two are viewed first as distinct entities ("the Word was with God"), and then in some way identified with each other ("the Word was God"). "God" in the first instance has the definite article in Greek *(ho theos),* which is not used in English when speaking of the Jewish or Christian God, but in the second instance it stands without the article.[8] But the placement of "God," or *theos,* first in its clause,[9] before the verb, gives it a certain definite-

---

5. "Was" in Greek is ἦν, repeated three times, the imperfect of the verb "to be." In the LXX of Genesis 1:2, the verb "was" (ἦν) goes not with God but with the earth as a static and formless void, waiting for the spirit of God to move upon it.

6. Πρός is literally "toward" God (see Moloney, 35; Brown, 1.3-5, suggests "in God's presence"). The translation "with God" seems to presuppose the more common Greek prepositions for "with": σύν or παρά followed by the dative, or μετά with the genitive. There is justification for the traditional rendering, however, if πρός is understood in the sense of "at home with" (like Fr. *chez*) or "close to" (see Abbott, *Johannine Grammar,* 273-76; also BDAG, 711, on πρός, III, 7). The meaning is comparable to that of 1 John 1:2, "We announce to you that eternal life which was with the Father (πρὸς τὸν πατέρα) and was revealed to us."

7. In Greek thus: καὶ ὁ λόγος ἦν πρὸς τὸν θεόν, καὶ θεὸς ἦν ὁ λόγος.

8. Some have seen a parallel in Philo's exposition of Genesis 31:13, where he distinguishes between θεός with and without the article, the former referring to "him who is truly God" and the latter to "his chief Word," or λόγος (*On Dreams,* 1.229-30). Such parallels should be used with caution, given that Philo was exegeting biblical language while John's Gospel is formulating its own. Notice that John uses θεός *without* the article in 1:18 for One who is so "truly God" that no one has ever seen him!

9. That is, θεὸς ἦν ὁ λόγος.

ness, warning us against reducing it to a mere adjective.[10] At the same time, the absence of the article alerts the reader that "the Word" and "God," despite their close and intimate relationship, are not interchangeable. While the Word is God, God is more than just the Word.[11] Even though it stands first in its clause, "God" is the predicate noun and not the subject of the clause, that is, "the Word was God," not "God was the Word" (compare 4:24, "God is Spirit," not "Spirit is God"). Even when the subject stands first, the definite article is often used to distinguish the subject from the predicate, as in 1 John 1:5 ("God is light") and 4:8 and 16 ("God is love").[12] In our passage, "God" is virtually an *attribute* of the Word, just as spirit and light and love are attributes of God in these other texts. To some, this makes *theos* almost adjectival (as in James Moffatt's translation, "the Logos was divine"),[13] but it is no more an adjective than "spirit" or "light" or "love" are adjectives. To say "God is Spirit" is not the same as saying God is spiritual, and "God is love" says more than that God is loving. In the same way, "the Word was God" says more than "the Word was divine." While "the Word was deity" is possible, it sounds too abstract, losing the simplicity and style of "the Word was God" with no corresponding gain in accuracy.[14]

God will emerge in this Gospel as "the Father," with the Word as the Father's "only Son" (see vv. 14, 18) or simply "the Son." To express this rela-

---

10. See the classic rule proposed by E. C. Colwell that "definite predicate nouns which precede the verb usually lack the article" ("A Definite Rule for the Use of the Article in the Greek New Testament," *JBL* 52 [1933], 20). On this passage in John, see P. B. Harner, "Qualitative Anarthrous Predicate Nouns: Mark 15:39 and John 1:1," *JBL* 91 (1973), 84-86.

11. As Barrett puts it, "The absence of the article indicates that the Word is God, but is not the only being of whom this is true; if ὁ θεός had been written it would have been implied that no divine being existed outside the second person of the Trinity" (156).

12. That is, ὁ θεὸς φῶς ἐστιν and ὁ θεὸς ἀγάπη ἐστίν, respectively. A partial analogy exists between God in relation to the Word and God in relation to love. The author of 1 John can say on the one hand that "Love is from God" (ἡ ἀγάπη ἐκ τοῦ θεοῦ ἐστιν, 4:7), and on the other that "God is love" (ὁ θεὸς ἀγάπη ἐστίν, 4:8, 16). But the analogy is far from perfect, because the conclusion to which it leads is not that "Love is God" (as "the Word was God").

13. Brown (1.5) rightly calls this rendering "too weak," adding that "after all, there is in Greek an adjective for 'divine' *(theios)* which the author did not choose to use." He concludes that "for a modern Christian reader whose trinitarian background has accustomed him to thinking of 'God' as a larger concept than 'God the Father,' the translation 'The Word was God' is quite correct."

14. The NEB and REB rendering, "what God was, the Word was," is less effective because it seems to imply a third entity to which both "God" and "the Word" are being compared. It does have the advantage of preserving the Greek word order, but a better option would have been "God was what the Word was."

1:1-5 PREAMBLE: THE LIGHT

tionship, later Christian theology introduced the Hellenistic notions of "nature" and of "person": the Father and the Son are two distinct Persons sharing a common nature as God. A classic "Johannine" opening to the Gospel, and one wholly congenial to later Christian theology, would have been, "In the beginning was the Son, and the Son was with the Father, and the Son was God. He was in the beginning with the Father." Instead, the Gospel writer has opted to postpone speaking of "the Son" and "the Father" until after the narrative proper has begun, with the appearance of the "man sent from God. John was his name" (1:6). This is appropriate because elsewhere in the Gospel tradition the Father is defined as Father and the Son as Son precisely in the setting of Jesus' baptism by John in the Jordan River (Mk 1:9-11 and parallels). The choice of different vocabulary in the preamble has contributed to the widespread (but questionable) view among modern scholars that not only the first five verses but much of what is commonly known as the prologue (vv. 1-18) belongs to a pre-Johannine, possibly pre-Christian, hymn.

The first and second clauses of verse 1 ("In the beginning was the Word, and the Word was with God") are echoed more briefly, like an antiphonal response, in verse 2: "He was in the beginning with God."[15] The point is that the Word was God's companion in the work of creation (see v. 3). The writer will not let us bypass the "beginning" and Genesis 1:1 too quickly. Ptolemy, the earliest known commentator on the Gospel of John, in the mid-second century elevated *archē* to the status of a christological title. "John the Lord's disciple," Ptolemy wrote, "desiring to tell of the origin of the universe by which the Father produced everything, posits a certain Beginning [*archēn*] which was first generated by God, which he called Only-Begotten Son and God, in which the Father emitted all things spermatically. By this the Logos was emitted, and in it was the whole substance of the Aeons, which the Logos itself later shaped.... First he differentiates the three: God, Beginning, and Logos; then he combines them again in order to set forth the emission of each of them, the Son and the Logos, and their unity with each other and with the Father. For in the Father and from the Father is the Beginning, and in the Beginning and from the Beginning is the Logos."[16] Creation, the

---

15. Pliny's letter to Trajan around A.D. 110 is often cited in this connection. According to Pliny, Christians told him that "they were in the habit of meeting on a certain fixed day before it was light, when they sang in alternate verses [*invicem*] a hymn to Christ, as to a god" (*Epistles* 10.96; see Theron, 15). Many scholars have conjectured that this "hymn to Christ, as to a god," sung responsively, was either the so-called "prologue" to John or a source underlying the prologue. Such a theory can be neither proved nor disproved.

16. The translation is that of Robert M. Grant, *Gnosticism* (New York: Harper & Brothers, 1961), 182. Grant proposes "principle" as an alternative translation of ἀρχή. The Greek text is as cited in Irenaeus, *Against Heresies* 1.8.5 (Harvey, 1.75-76; see also

work of one divine entity in Genesis, God (Heb. *'ĕlōhîm*), and the work of two in John (God and the Word), becomes in Ptolemy the work of three (God, the Beginning, and the Word).

In this way Ptolemy, a Valentinian Gnostic, created a kind of "trinity" out of the opening verses of John long before trinitarianism became dominant in the church. Nor is his interpretation quite as far-fetched as it sounds, given that *archē* was already a title for Jesus Christ in Asia Minor before the end of the first century.[17] Yet Ptolemy has moved too far from the world of Genesis to be convincing. The "beginning" in Genesis 1[18] is clearly intended in a temporal sense. The same is true in John 1:1, just as "from the beginning" (or *ap' archēs*) is also consistently temporal in the New Testament.[19] John's Gospel has moved beyond Genesis in its own ways, however, first by its transformation of the refrain, "and God said"[20] (Gen 1:3, 6, 9, 11, 14, 20, 24, 26, 29), into the noun "word" or *logos*,[21] and second by its personification of "word" as "the Word." Personification is evident not so much in the pronoun "he"[22] as in the characterization of the *logos* as "God," understood as a personal Being. But if the Word is personal in John 1, is the reader expected to know that the Word is specifically Jesus Christ? Probably so, in view of the fact that when the name "Jesus Christ" is finally introduced (1.16), it is as a given, without explanation or fanfare. Moreover, when "Jesus" makes his appearance as a living character in the story, he does so very abruptly and through the eyes of the baptizer, John, who "sees Jesus coming toward him"

W. Völker [ed.], *Quellen zur Geschichte der christlichen Gnosis* [Tübingen: J. C. B. Mohr/Paul Siebeck, 1932], 93-94). For fuller discussion, see Elaine Pagels, *The Johannine Gospel in Gnostic Exegesis* (SBL Monograph Series 17; Nashville: Abingdon, 1973), 26-27.

17. See Colossians 1:18 ("And he is the head of the body, the church, he who is the beginning [ἀρχή], firstborn from the dead, so that in all he might come first"), and Revelation 3:14, "Thus says the Amen, the faithful and true witness, the beginning [ἡ ἀρχή] of the creation of God" (compare Rev 21:6; 22:13).

18. That is, Ἐν ἀρχῇ in the LXX of Genesis 1:1 and בראשית in the Hebrew Bible.

19. This is the case whether the "beginning" in view is the creation of all things (Mt 19:4, 8; 24:21; Mk 10:6; 13:19; Jn 8:44; 2 Pet 3:4; 1 Jn 3:8) or the beginning of the Christian movement (Lk 1:2; Jn 6:64; 15:27; 1 Jn 1:1; 2:7, 13, 14, 24; 3:11; 2 Jn 5, 6; compare ἐν ἀρχῇ in Acts 11:15).

20. In Hebrew ויאמר אלהים or in Greek καὶ εἶπεν ὁ θεός.

21. This happens already in the Hebrew Bible. See Psalm 33:6, "By the word of the LORD [Heb. בדבר יהוה; Gr. τῷ λόγῳ τοῦ κυρίου] were the heavens made."

22. "He" is οὗτος, literally "this man," but inevitable in any case because λόγος is a masculine noun. Moloney (35) allows for the possible translation of οὗτος as "this man," anticipating the Gospel narrative about Jesus, but the formal introduction of John as the first "man" (ἄνθρωπος) in the story argues against this. The masculine gender of λόγος is a perfectly adequate explanation for the gender of οὗτος.

1:1-5 PREAMBLE: THE LIGHT

(1:29). Evidently the reader knows who Jesus is, and therefore, in all likelihood, that the story is about him from the start. He is first "the Word" (vv. 1-3, 14), then "the Light" (vv. 4, 5, 7-8, 9-10), then the "One and Only" (vv. 14, 18), and finally, in much of the rest of the Gospel, "the Son."[23]

3-4 As soon as the Word has been introduced, "was" gives way to "came" or "came to be" *(egeneto)*, a verb conspicuous in the LXX of the Genesis account.[24] Divine being gives way to divine action, starting with the creation of the world. This is the verb the Gospel writer will use not only for creation (vv. 3 and 10) but for the coming of John as "a man sent from God" (v. 6), for the coming of the Word himself in the flesh of Jesus Christ (v. 14) and for the "grace and truth" that Jesus Christ brings (v. 17). Regarding creation, the same thing is stated twice for rhetorical effect, first positively and then negatively. "All things" came into being through the Word, and "not one thing" came into being without him.[25] The construction is similar to that of verse 1, where the repetitions, "Word, Word, God, God, Word," carried the thought forward in similar chainlike fashion (sometimes known as "staircase parallelism"), except that here strong contrasts are introduced: "through him" and "apart from him"; "all things" and "not one thing."

The classic problem of the verse is that the symmetry is broken by the seemingly redundant clause, "that which has come to be" *(ho gegonen)*, at the end of the verse. Traditional English versions convey the sense of redundancy quite well; for example, "All things were made through him, and without him was not anything made that was made" (RSV); "Through him all things were made; without him nothing was made that has been made" (NIV). Not all English versions agree, however. Some have followed instead an ancient precedent in reading this clause not as an anticlimax to verse 3 but as the beginning of verse 4: for example, "All things came into being through him, and without him not one thing came into being. What has come into being in him was life, and the life was the light of all people" (NRSV); "Through him all things came to be; no single thing was created without him. All that came to be was alive with his life, and that life was the light of men"

---

23. For a different way of making a transition from the speech of God to that of the Son, see Hebrews 1:1-2, "God, who in many and various ways spoke [λαλήσας] to the fathers in the prophets, has in these last days spoken [ἐλάλησεν] to us in the Son [ἐν υἱῷ]."

24. Note the repetition of καὶ ἐγένετο (Heb. ויהי) in Genesis 1:3, 5, 8, 9, 11, 13, 15, 19, 20, 23, 24, 30.

25. The first two elements of the second clause (χωρὶς αὐτοῦ / ἐγένετο) correspond to the last two elements of the first (δι' αὐτοῦ / ἐγένετο). The chainlike contrasting parallelism is framed by the sharper contrast of πάντα ("all things") and οὐδὲ ἕν ("not one thing"). The Greek word order shows the symmetry of the construction:

πάντα / δι' αὐτοῦ / ἐγένετο,
καὶ χωρὶς αὐτοῦ / ἐγένετο / οὐδὲ ἕν.

(NEB).[26] Such a verse division is supported by Kurt Aland, who demonstrated thirty years ago from ancient versions and citations of the fathers that this way of reading the text enjoyed almost universal support in the second and early third centuries.[27]

Is Aland's reading correct? I once thought so,[28] but now I am not so sure. This was a rare point at which Bruce Metzger disagreed with the committee that edited the United Bible Societies *Greek New Testament*. The UBS Editorial Committee read *ho gegonen* with verse 4 in keeping with Aland's argument, but Metzger filed his own minority report in his *Textual Commentary*, arguing that the relative clause belonged with verse 3.[29] The awkwardness Metzger noticed is evident in the NRSV ("What has come into being in him was life, and the life was the light of all people"), where the perfectly accurate rendering, "what *has* come into being," seems to require "*is* life."[30] The present tense, "is" *(estin),* does in fact appear as a variant reading in verse 4 in several ancient manuscripts and versions.[31] But Metzger, this time in agreement with the UBS Editorial Committee, comments, "In order to re-

---

26. Similar renderings of verse 4 include, "Everything that was created received its life from him, and his life gave light to everyone" (CEV), and "What came to be through him was life, and this life was the light of the human race" (NAB).

27. K. Aland, "Eine Untersuchung zu Joh 1:3-4: Über die Bedeutung eines Punktes," *ZNW* 59 (1968), 174-209. For a more recent defense of a similar view, see E. L. Miller, *Salvation-History in the Prologue of John: The Significance of John 1:3/4* (Leiden: Brill, 1989). This, for example, was the reading of Origen, who seems to have known no other (see, for example, his *Commentary on John* 2.112-32 [FC 80.124-29]).

28. J. R. Michaels, *John,* NIBC 4 (Peabody, MA: Hendrickson, 1989), 25.

29. *A Textual Commentary on the Greek New Testament* (London/New York: United Bible Societies, 1971), 195-96. Metzger appealed to "John's fondness for beginning a sentence with ἐν and a demonstrative pronoun (compare 13:35; 15:8; 16:26; 1 Jn 2:3, 4, 5; 3:10, 16, 19, 24; 4:2, etc.)," and concluded, "It is more consistent with the Johannine repetitive style, as well as with Johannine doctrine (compare 5:26, 39; 6:53), to say nothing concerning the sense of the passage, to punctuate with a full stop after ὃ γέγονεν" (196). His most telling point was that "Despite valiant attempts of commentators to bring sense out of taking ὃ γέγονεν with what follows, the passage remains intolerably clumsy and opaque. One of the difficulties that stands in the way of ranging the clause with ἐν αὐτῷ ζωὴ ἦν is that the perfect tense of γέγονεν would require ἐστιν instead of ἦν" (196, n. 2).

30. The alternative would have been to make the imperfect ἦν ("was") determinative, and read ὃ γέγονεν as a pluperfect: "What *had* come into being in him *was* life." This would be an improvement but still awkward.

31. These include ℵ and D, plus the old Latin, a number of other ancient versions, and patristic quotations. For the evidence, see *The Greek New Testament* (4th rev. ed.; Stuttgart: United Bible Societies, 1993), 312. Origen, for example, knows of this reading and considers it "perhaps not without credibility" (*Commentary on John* 2.132 [FC, 80.129]).

lieve the difficulty . . . the tense of the verb was changed from imperfect to present."³²

Peter Cohee, in an attempt to resolve the problem, argues that the seemingly redundant clause was not original, but rather "introduced into the text as a gloss."³³ But even if it is a gloss, the same question remains. Was it added to the end of verse 3, or to the beginning of verse 4? Whether one agrees with his conclusion or not, Cohee's answer is instructive. If it is a gloss to verse 3, he infers that "Someone wished to point out that the absolute statement in the verse proper applied to the mortal sphere of created things, but that there were things — or at least *one* thing — uncreated."³⁴ In effect, Cohee is attributing the gloss to a scribe whose interpretation of John 1:3-4 precisely matched that of Ptolemy. Irenaeus quotes Ptolemy as claiming that "'all things' came into existence 'through' it [*di' autou*], but Life 'in' it [*en autō*]. This, then, coming into existence *in* it, is closer *in* it than the things which came into existence *through* it."³⁵ There is no textual evidence for excluding the clause "that which has come to be" as a gloss, and to do so is precarious.³⁶

If it is *not* a gloss, but part of the original text, then Cohee's mention of a view "that there were things — or at least *one* thing — uncreated" takes on added significance, for it could as easily be the view of the Gospel writer himself as of a later scribe. As soon as he had written, "All things came into being through him," and "not one thing was made without him," it may have

---

32. He therefore rejects the reading on the ground that "the second ἦν (in the clause ἡ ζωὴ ἦν τὸ φῶς), seems to require the first" (*Textual Commentary,* 196).

33. "John 1.3-4," *NTS* 41 (1995), 470-77. Cohee appeals on the one hand to "John's fondness for ending a clause with οὐδείς, οὐδὲ ἕν, or οὐδέν," and on the other (citing Metzger) to "John's fondness for beginning a sentence or clause with ἐν and a demonstrative pronoun." The former he urges as an argument against construing ὃ γέγονεν with verse 3, and the latter against construing it with verse 4! The only conclusion he can draw is that it was added later.

34. Cohee considers it more likely a gloss to verse 4, "to emphasize the contrast between the prepositions δι' of verse 3a and ἐν of 4a, and to equate the respective verbs of these verses. In other words, the author simply wished to state that Life existed in the Word; someone else added the relative clause to comment that, like all things, Life, too, was created, but unlike all other things, Life had its creation *in* the Word" (Cohee, 476).

35. The translation is from Grant, *Gnosticism,* 182-83. The Greek text is in Irenaeus, *Against Heresies* 1.8.5 (Harvey, 1.75-76). Cohee cites this text (474), but does not mention Ptolemy and seems to imply that it represents Irenaeus's own interpretation.

36. Cohee's appeal to the presence of dots on either side of the clause in question in certain Byzantine manuscripts as an acknowledgment of doubt about its authenticity (476) is unconvincing, particularly in light of his own admission that "there are no variant readings" here, but "only one reading with various punctuation indicating different editorial opinions" (470). At most the dots in later manuscripts would be simply a recognition that earlier interpreters had divided the verses differently.

occurred to the writer that some things did not come into being at all, but had always existed.[37] Among these were the two things of immediate concern in these opening verses, eternal "life" and the "light" of human beings. Other examples would have been divine wisdom, truth, and love. Such things are not creations of God but attributes of God. They exist wherever and whenever God exists. The Gospel writer, therefore, had to add the words "that which has come into being" as a qualification: "All things came into being through him, and apart from him not one thing *that has come into being* was made" (my italics).[38] Not all things were created, but all things created were created through the Word. The contrast is not, as Ptolemy thought, between things created *through* the Word and things created *in* the Word, but between things that *came into being* through the Word and things that did not come into being at all, but always *were*. The latter, being attributes of God, are also attributes of the Word.

The first of these is "life," probably not physical life (which according to Genesis 1 *was* created), but spiritual life, or what the Gospel of John elsewhere calls "eternal life." One definition of "eternal," after all, is having neither end nor beginning. Here the Gospel writer moves past "life" quickly to get to the theme of light, which will be developed at greater length in the verses to follow, but in 1 John "life" takes center stage at the start. There, having mentioned "the word [or message] of Life" (1 Jn 1:1), the writer adds, "and the Life was revealed, and we have seen, and we testify and announce to you that eternal Life which was with the Father [*pros ton patera*] and was revealed to us" (1 Jn 1:2).[39] Clearly, "Life" is not something created, but, like the Word, is with God from the beginning. Near the end of 1 John the writer concludes, "And this is the testimony, that God has given us eternal Life, and this Life is in his Son. Whoever has the Son has Life, and whoever does not have the Son of God does not have Life" (1 Jn 5:11-12). The Gospel of John makes the same point at the end of its first major section: "Whoever believes

---

37. For a somewhat analogous qualification of πάντα, see 1 Corinthians 15:27, where Paul cites Psalm 8:6, "For he subjected all things [πάντα] under his feet," and then immediately added that "all things" do not, of course, include the One who did the subjecting!

38. At least one recent version has returned to this traditional verse division. The Revised English Bible (REB), moving away from the NEB, has "and through him all things came to be; without him no created thing came into being. In him was life, and the life was the light of mankind."

39. It appears that what the Gospel of John says of the Word, 1 John says of Life. The Word was "with God" (πρὸς τὸν θεόν, Jn 1:1), while eternal Life was "with the Father" (πρὸς τὸν πατέρα). Consequently it seems appropriate to capitalize "Word" in John's Gospel while leaving "life" in small letters, and to capitalize "Life" in 1 John while leaving "word" in small letters.

1:1-5 PREAMBLE: THE LIGHT

in the Son has eternal life; whoever disobeys the Son will not see life, but the wrath of God abides on him" (Jn 3:36). Here in verse 4, "life" and "light" are equivalent expressions for salvation, and for the time being the preoccupation is with light. In stating that in the Word "*was* life," and that "that life *was* the light of humans,"[40] the writer is giving us a provisional *definition* of the "life" he has in mind. Salvation in the Gospel of John is defined as revelation or knowledge, something of which "light" is a most appropriate symbol. "This is eternal life," we will read, even within Jesus' last prayer to the Father, "that they may know you, the only true God, and him whom you have sent, Jesus Christ" (17:3). Life in this Gospel *is* light, "the light of humans." Once again, physical light is not meant because in Genesis physical light was created as the first of all created things ("God said, 'Let there be light,' and there was light," Gen 1:3).[41] In our text, by contrast, "the light of humans" is not something created, but is part and parcel of the life that is in the Word, and therefore eternal.[42]

Almost always, "light" in the Gospel of John is a metaphor,[43] but the question here is whether the metaphor is to be understood universally, as the intellectual or emotional light distinguishing humans from the rest of creation, or more specifically as the "the light of the world" revealed in Jesus Christ (see 8:12). This question can perhaps be answered definitively only after taking into consideration verse 9 of this chapter ("The light was the True [Light] that illumines every human being who comes into the world"), and 3:19 ("This then is the judgment, that the Light has come into the world, and human beings loved the dark rather than the Light, for their works were evil"). The former points toward the general or universal understanding of verse 4, the latter toward the more redemptive-historical interpretation. But because there has been no mention of any specific "coming" of the light this early in the story, it is wise to give the phrase "the light of humans" the broadest possible application. It is fair to assume that "the light of humans" refers to a capacity for love and understanding given to every human being at

---

40. "Life" (ζωή) is without the definite article the first time it appears in verse 4, but when it appears a second time, it has the article (ἡ ζωή), suggesting the translation "that life" (that is, the life just mentioned).

41. In the LXX, literally, "and light came to be [καὶ ἐγένετο φῶς]." In Genesis, light is among those things that "came to be," while in John's Gospel it belongs to those things that simply "were" (ἦν).

42. Paul makes a transition from physical light to spiritual light somewhat differently: "For God who said, 'Let light shine out of darkness,' has shined in our hearts, bringing to light the knowledge of the glory of God in the face of Jesus Christ" (2 Cor 4:6).

43. When light is not a metaphor, but refers to physical light, the author supplies a qualification to that effect (that is, "the light *of this world*," 11:9).

birth. Despite the strong Johannine emphasis on another birth, "of God" (1:13) or "of the Spirit" (3:6) or "from above" (3:3), the testimony of verse 4 is that physical birth is also a source of "light" from God. At least the burden of proof is on those who would argue otherwise.

5 The tense of the verb changes from imperfect to present. The light "is shining" *(phainei)* in the darkness. Having looked at beginnings, and how "all things came into being" (v. 3), the Gospel writer returns to his own time and his own world. What is striking is that he passes over the whole "biblical" period (what Christians today call the "Old Testament") in silence. Some modern interpreters have found this odd, and have tried to find allusions to the Old Testament, beyond Genesis 1, either in verses 1-5 [44] or verses 6-13,[45] or both. But these supposed allusions are not convincing. This book is a Gospel, not a survey of redemptive history. Having laid claim, briefly and decisively, to the whole created order on behalf of the Word (and implicitly, though only implicitly, to the entire biblical past), the writer moves on to tell the Gospel story, the good news of Jesus. As readers, we are not kept in suspense. We learn immediately that the story will have a happy ending. The light "is shining in the darkness," we are told, not continually through time but specifically *now,* because something decisive happened. What that something was, we are not told. The Christian reader familiar with the rest of the New Testament already knows, and probably the Gospel's original readers knew. But all we are told explicitly is what did *not* happen: "the darkness" did not "overtake" *(katelaben)* the light.[46]

This is the first we have heard of "darkness" *(skotia),* and the writer does not pause to address the philosophical question of where the darkness came from if "all things" were either created through the Word or existed in the Word. The perspective of John's Gospel as a whole, however, suggests that "the darkness" is equivalent to "the world" *(ho kosmos),*[47] and the writer

---

44. Brown (1.27) links verse 4 to the tree of life in the garden of Eden, and verse 5 to the struggle between light and darkness in connection with the Fall.

45. C. H. Dodd (*Interpretation,* 270-71) finds in vv. 4 and 9-10 the notion that the Torah was present in the world throughout the history of Israel, in v. 11 an assertion that "the word of the Lord through Moses and the prophets came to His own people Israel, and Israel rejected it," and in vv. 12-13 a hint that God nevertheless gave some in Israel the status of "sons" (citing Exod 4:22, Deut 14:1, and Hos 1:10, as well as Ps 82[81]:6, which Jesus himself later quotes in Jn 10:35). This is to read between the lines far more than the text warrants.

46. The point is much the same as in 1 John 2:8, where the old commandment the readers have heard is also called a new commandment "because the darkness is passing away, and the true light is already [ἤδη] shining."

47. This can be seen by comparing John 2:8 ("the darkness is passing away") with 2:17 ("the world is passing away").

will make clear in verse 9 that "the world came into being through him." It is probably fair to assume that if "all things" include "the world," they also include "the darkness." Some translators (perhaps with the analogy between darkness and the world in view) have rendered the verb as "comprehend" or "understand," anticipating verse 10 ("the world did not know him").[48] Others accent the idea of conflict, as I have done, with the verb "overtake" or "overcome."[49] Still others, combining the ideas of comprehension on the one hand and confrontation on the other, have proposed such alternatives as "seize," "grasp," or "master."[50] The verb is probably to be read as part of the imagery of darkness, hence "overtake." The physical darkness of night falls quickly, "overtaking" those who stay too long in places where the night brings danger, and the same is true of the spiritual darkness of ignorance and unbelief.[51] This is *not* what has happened, however, in the story to be told here, which was after all handed down in the Christian church as "gospel," or good news. Right from the start it is clear that a confrontation between light and darkness has taken place once and for all, and that the light has emerged victorious. The light shines on in the darkness, and the writer will now proceed to narrate how this all came about.

II. THE TESTIMONY OF JOHN (1:6–3:36)

After the preamble, the first three chapters of the Gospel are framed by John's varied testimonies to Jesus (1:6-8, 15-16, 19-36 and 3:22-36), and his continuing presence gives these chapters their distinctive character. John's is the dominant voice at first, and then as Jesus begins to find his own voice (3:11-21), John bids the reader good-bye (3:30), confirming Jesus' testimony and yielding center stage to "the One coming from above" (3:31-36).

---

48. As in the NIV, "but the darkness has not understood it"; compare, for example, Schnackenburg, 1.246-47; Bultmann, 47-48; Beasley-Murray, 11.

49. So the RSV, NRSV, and NEB; compare Westcott, 5; Morris, 75-76.

50. As in the REB, "and the darkness has never mastered it." According to Barrett (158), "The darkness neither understood nor quenched the light"; compare Hoskyns, 143.

51. This is illustrated in the reading of certain Greek manuscripts (ℵ and D) of John 6:17: "They got in a boat and were on their way across the lake to Capernaum, but the darkness overtook [κατέλαβεν] them, and Jesus had not yet come to them." For similar imagery, but with spiritual rather than physical darkness in view, see 12:35: "Yet a little while the Light is among you. Walk while you have the Light, so that darkness will not overtake [καταλάβῃ] you."

THE GOSPEL OF JOHN

A. JOHN AND THE COMING OF THE LIGHT (1:6-13)

>   6 *A man came, sent from God. John was his name.* 7 *He came for a testimony, to testify about the light, that they all might believe through him.* 8 *He was not the light, but [he came] to testify about the light.* 9 *The light was the true [Light] that illumines every human being who comes into the world.*[1] 10 *He was in the world, and the world came into being through him, and the world did not know him.* 11 *He came to what was his own, and his own did not receive him.* 12 *But to as many as did receive him he gave authority to become children of God, to those who believe in his name,* 13 *who were born not of blood lines, nor of fleshly desire, nor a husband's desire, but of God.*

The narrative, like that of Mark's Gospel (1:4), begins with John the Baptist, or Baptizer, known here simply as "John" (v. 6).[2] As we have seen, the name "John,"[3] right on the heels of the caption "According to John" in the earliest manuscripts of the Gospel,[4] could mislead some readers into thinking that this John is either the author of the Gospel or its main character, and indeed a case could be made that his is the major voice in at least the Gospel's first three chapters. John's ministry of baptism is not even mentioned at first (not until v. 25), but instead he is identified (v. 7) as one who "came for a testimony, to testify about the light" (that is, the "light" mentioned in vv. 4 and 5), so that "they all might believe through him" (v. 7). But almost immediately, as if to deflect the assumption that the story is going to be about him, the narrative is interrupted, as the narrator stops to explain that John himself was not the light (v. 8), then to reflect on the identity of the light (v. 9) and on the coming of the light into the world as a person ("he" and not "it"). The Christian reader will know that the Light is Jesus, but strictly speaking "he" is still anonymous. All we know for certain is that he is not John. We do learn that the world he created "did not know him," and "his own did not receive him," yet that some did receive him, and that those who did are called "the children of God." As for John, and his explicit testimony to "the light," that will come later (see vv. 15-16, 19-34; 3:27-36). In short, the preamble (vv. 1-5) intrudes

---

 1. Or: *The light was the true [Light] that illumines every human being by coming into the world.*
 2. John is said to be "baptizing" (βαπτίζων) in the Gospel of John (1:28; 3:23), but only Jesus is actually called "the Baptizer" (ὁ βαπτίζων, 1:33), and that in reference to baptism not in water but in the Holy Spirit.
 3. The accent on the name "John" (literally, "a name to him John") is strangely reminiscent of the birth narrative in Luke (see Lk 1:13, "and you shall call his name John"; 1:60, "no, but he shall be called John"; 1:63, "John is his name").
 4. In Greek, Κατὰ Ἰωάννην.

upon the narrative, as the Gospel writer pauses to spell out its implications, and in the process summarizes in very few words the whole of the Gospel story (see vv. 10-13).

6 The coming of "John" into the world represents a continuation of the plan of God that began with creation. Just as all things "came into being" through the Word (v. 3), so John "came" as one "sent from God."[5] The terminology invites misunderstanding, perhaps deliberately on the author's part. If John was "sent from God," was he a divine messenger or angel of some kind? The use of the term "man" or "human being" *(anthrōpos)* rules out this possibility, but readers familiar with the whole story will know that Jesus was a "man" too, and viewed as such both by himself (8:40) and others (see, for example, 1:30; 4:29; 9:11, 16; 19:5). Was John "sent" in the same way Jesus was sent? The author writes as if he knows of persons or groups that may think so, and perhaps wants his readers confronted, if only for a moment, with that possibility.[6] But he quickly adds that John was sent only "for a testimony, to testify about the light" (v. 7), and that John himself "was not the light" (v. 8). Later, when his disciples begin comparing him with Jesus, John will insist that "I am not the Christ," but that "I am sent ahead of him" (3:28). He is "sent from God" as a human delegate on a purely human mission,[7] that of bearing testimony to someone greater than himself.

7-8 Preamble and narrative beginning are linked both in style and content. Stylistically, verses 7-8 exhibit the same chainlike repetition or "staircase parallelism" evident in verses 1-5: the pattern of "testimony, testify, light, light, testify, light," recalls the repetition of "Word, Word, God, God, Word" in verse 1, or of "life, life, light, light, darkness, darkness" in verses 4-5. The similarity is remarkable in view of the fact that advocates of a hymnic source behind the so-called prologue have tended to identify verses 1-5 largely as poetry and verses 6-8 as a prose interpolation. As to content, the new factor introduced is "testimony" (or *martyria*). Nothing is said of John's baptizing activity. John has come solely "to testify" (vv. 7, 8), and his testimony has to do with "the light" mentioned in verses 4-5. Later we will learn that John did in fact baptize (1:25-26, 33; 3:23), as in the other Gospels, but baptism is incidental to his real mission, which is to point all people, especially his disciples, to Jesus Christ.

C. H. Dodd found in verses 7-8 an anticipation of much of what is to

---

5. Both "came into being" and "came" are ἐγένετο in Greek.
6. According to BDAG (756), "John the Baptist was not, like Jesus, sent out from the very presence of God, but one whose coming was brought about by God."
7. Even though John is "sent" (ἀπεσταλμένος), his mission is perhaps more like that of the delegation sent to him by the Jewish authorities in Jerusalem (1:19, 24; note the participle ἀπεσταλμένοι in v. 24) than to Jesus' mission from heaven. The distinction between John's mission and that of Jesus will be explored more fully in 3:31-36.

follow concerning John. The statement that John "came for a testimony, to testify about the light" (v. 7a) anticipates John's recorded testimonies in 1:19-34, while the intent "that they all might believe through him" (v. 7b) comes to realization in 1:35-37. Within John's testimonies, the notion that John himself "was not the light" (v. 8a) provides the theme of 1:19-28, where the accent is mainly on what he himself is *not* (that is, not the Christ, not Elijah, not the Prophet, vv. 20-21); the positive aspect of "testifying about the light" (v. 8b) comes to expression in 1:29-34, where John finally sees Jesus and points him out as "Lamb of God" (v. 29) and "Son of God" (v. 34).[8] Whether Dodd has given us here a glimpse into the author's actual programmatic intent or simply a useful pedagogical device is uncertain. But his insight underscores the centrality of "testimony," or *martyria,* in the presentation of John in the Gospel that (perhaps coincidentally) bears his name.

The goal of John's testimony is "that they all might believe through him" — not "in him" but "through him." This is the first appearance of the verb "believe" *(pisteuein),* and we are not yet told what, or in whom, people were to believe. A reasonable guess is that they were to believe in "the light." This would give a certain symmetry to the first twelve chapters of the Gospel, for Jesus' last words to the crowds at Jerusalem at the end of his public ministry were, "Walk while you have the light, so that the darkness will not overtake you. . . . While you have the light, believe in the light, that you may become sons of light" (12:35-36). In one sense, John and Jesus have a common goal and mission, shared also by the Gospel writer, whose stated intent is "that you might believe" (19:35; 20:31). At the outset, the shared mission is universal in scope. Just as "all things" came into being through the Word (v. 3), John testifies in order that "they all," or "all people," might believe (v. 7).[9] Aside from the passing reference to "darkness" in verse 5, the stubborn reality of unbelief is nowhere to be seen. Consequently, there is no hint as yet of the classic Johannine contrast between those who believe and those who do not.

The disclaimer to the effect that John "was not the light" (v. 8) is important for two reasons. First, it raises the obvious question of why such a disclaimer was necessary. Does the author know of readers or potential readers for whom John and not Jesus was the main character in the story? We know that there were such groups in later times,[10] and this is the first of several hints

---

8. See Dodd, *Historical Tradition,* 248-49, who finds echoes of these two verses also in 3:22-30 and 10:41-42.

9. Compare 12:32, where Jesus promises that "I, if I be lifted up from the earth, will draw them all [πάντας] to myself."

10. According to the third-century Pseudo-Clementine *Recognitions* 1.54, "Some even of the disciples of John, who seemed to be great ones, separated themselves from the people, and proclaimed their own master as the Christ" (ANF, 8.92). John is also a major messianic figure in the later Mandean literature.

in the Gospel that the author may be countering their views by attempting to "put John in his place,"[11] exalting Jesus, and him alone, as the Word (vv. 1-2, 14), the true Light (vv. 4-5, 9), and God's One and Only (vv. 14, 18).

Second, the disclaimer has the effect of sidetracking the narrative, just as it is getting started, by shifting the focus of interest *away* from John and his testimony and back to "the light" to which John testified — back, that is, to the preamble and to the overriding question of how it came about that "the light is shining in the darkness, and the darkness did not overtake it" (v. 5). The narrative that began at verse 6 is aborted in favor of a series of theological reflections, not on John's significance but on the significance of the light. With these reflections the whole story is collapsed into a magnificent summary of the Gospel (vv. 6-13), with a response from the believing community (vv. 14-18). The narrative proper, at its orderly and proper pace, will resume in earnest only at verse 19, with a detailed account of John's testimony to a delegation of priests and Levites from Jerusalem.

9 More about the light. In my translation I have taken "light" as the subject and the adjective "true" substantivally as a predicate: "The light was the true [Light]." It is also possible to take both as predicates ("That — or he — was the true Light"), leaving the subject unexpressed and without a definite antecedent. This is commonly done on the assumption that the unexpressed subject is "the Word,"[12] but the Word has not been mentioned, even implicitly, since verse 4.[13] Even if the subject is left unexpressed (as "that," or "he"), it is defined not by an antecedent but by its predicate, as "the light" to which John testified in verse 8. The point of verse 9 is that the light in question here, "the light of humans" mentioned earlier, was the "true" light (see 1 Jn 2:8), not so much in contrast to some "false" or misleading light as in contrast to *all* other light — the physical "light of this world," for example (11:9), or the spiritual "light" given off by the ministry of John, the "burning and shining lamp" (5:35). The light to which John testified was not his own, but the supreme and universal "Light of the world" (8:12), the light "that illumines every human being who comes into the world." For the first time, "light" can be appropriately capitalized, because it is now apparent that "the true Light" is a personal being.

In our translation, the participle "coming" or "who comes" (*erchomenon*) is taken with the phrase that immediately precedes it, "every human being," yielding a redundant yet quite idiomatic expression, "every human being who comes into the world" (compare KJV). The phrase is idiomatic

---

11. See 1:19-28; 3:27-30; 5:33-36; 10:40-42.
12. For example, Bultmann, 52; Schnackenburg, 1.253.
13. Dodd (*Interpretation*, 268) is correct that "In verse 4 a transition is made to φῶς, and φῶς, not λόγος, is formally the subject of the propositions made in verses 9-12."

because "all who come into the world" was a common expression in rabbinic literature for "everyone,"[14] but more redundant than the rabbinic expression in that the latter did not include the word "man" or "human being."[15] The redundant language seems intended simply to recall "the light of humans" (v. 4), now further defined as the light shining on "every human being."

Modern translators are bothered not only by the apparent redundancy, but perhaps also by the fact that on this interpretation no room is left for any explicit mention of the coming of the light into the world. The alternative adopted by most commentators and modern English versions has been to read the participial expression with "light" rather than with "every human being," as, for example, in the REB: "The true light which gives light to everyone was even then coming into the world" (see RSV, NRSV, NIV, NEB, NEB). But there are difficulties with such a translation. The verb "was," instead of standing on its own like the seven other instances of this verb in the first thirteen verses, is pressed into service as a helping verb with the participle "coming" so as to create a periphrastic construction ("was . . . coming") rather uncharacteristic of Johannine style.[16] Moreover, the periphrastic construction gives the impression that the coming of the light into the world was a state, or at most a process, rather than a simple identifiable event.[17] The words "even then," which are not in the Greek text but supplied in the REB translation, represent an effort to give this process a setting in real history, within the ministry of John as sketched in verses 6-8. But if we think of the light as Jesus, then the coming of the light is not a process going on during

---

14. One frequently cited parallel is in *Leviticus Rabbah* 31.6 ("Thou givest light to the celestial as well as to the terrestrial beings and to all who enter the world" (*Midrash Rabbah: Leviticus* [London: Soncino, 1961], 401). On the expression כל באי העלם generally, see Strack-Billerbeck, 2.358.

15. Yet as Leon Morris notes (83), "No argument should be based on the occurrence of ἄνθρωπον, for John uses the redundant ἄνθρωπος quite often" (he cites 2:10 and 3:1, 27; other examples are 5:5; 7:46; 8:40; 9:16; 11:50). Rudolf Bultmann's excision (52) of ἄνθρωπον from the Johannine text as "an explanatory gloss (of the translator)" is not only "arbitrary" (Schnackenburg, 1.255), but raises the question, an added explanatory gloss by whom? To Bultmann "the translator" (of a pre-Johannine hymnic source) is none other than the author of the Gospel. But if the author wrote it, why should it be excised as a gloss?

16. Although there are periphrastic constructions in John's Gospel (1:28; 2:6; 3:23; 10:40; 11:1; 13:23; 18:18, 25), none have the participle separated from its helping verb by a relative clause, as here (see Schnackenburg, 1.254, who calls the periphrastic construction here "not impossible, though the insertion of a relative clause makes it unique").

17. Although the light "comes into the world" in two other places in the Gospel of John, its coming is an accomplished event, not a process (ἐλήλυθεν, "the light *has come* into the world," in 3:19; ἐλήλυθα, "I *have come* as light into the world," in 12:46).

John's ministry, but a simple event, the birth of Jesus. In replying to Pontius Pilate, Jesus himself says as much: "You say that I am a king; *I was born* for this, and for this *I have come into the world,* that I might testify to the truth" (18:37, my italics). It should come as no surprise that being "born" and "coming into the world" are equivalent expressions. If "the light" is a human being, then the light "comes into the world" like any other human, by natural birth, not by some kind of continuing process, least of all during the ministry of John!

Another alternative views the phrase "coming into the world" either as a kind of afterthought,[18] or as a parenthetical expression modifying "the light." In effect, a comma is placed (as in the Nestle Greek text) between "every human being" and "coming into the world." This too could be read as a process, like the periphrastic construction mentioned above,[19] or it could be read simply as a characterization of the light, as, for example, in the NASB ("There was the true light which, coming into the world, enlightens every man"), or the TEV ("This was the real light — the light that comes into the world and shines on all mankind"). It is a "coming-into-the-world" sort of light, just as "the bread of God," or "bread of life" (another designation for Jesus), is a "coming-down-from-heaven" sort of bread (6:33, 50). Just as Jesus, coming down from heaven, "gives life to the world" (6:33), so this light, coming into the world, "illumines every human being."[20]

This view avoids the difficulties of the first alternative, and must be held open as a possibility. Still, the traditional interpretation that "coming into the world" goes with "every human being" remains the most natural one. On such a reading, the "light" is not *explicitly* said to "come into the world" at all. What we might have expected, and what is missing, is a simple affirmation that the light "came" *(egeneto),* echoing the LXX of Genesis 1:3 and announcing a new creation in contrast to the old. Instead, the author postpones the simple affirmation until verse 14, reverting to "Word" (or *logos*), in place of light: "So the Word came [*egeneto*] in human flesh." There is no way that these verses can be placed in any real chronological order. The time reference of the verb "illumines" (v. 9), like that of the verb "shines" (v. 5), is the present, the time when the author writes the Gospel. Already in verse 5, and again at verse

---

18. Schnackenburg, 1.255.
19. See, for example, Edwin Abbott: "There was [from the beginning] the light, the true [light], which lighteneth every man, coming as it does (ἐρχόμενον) [continually] into the world" (*Johannine Grammar,* 221). Abbott later presses the point in favor of a sharp distinction between ἐρχόμενον here and the aorist ἦλθεν in verse 11: "The passage says, first, that the Light was *'continually coming'* to all mankind (more especially to the prophets and saints) and then that it definitely *'came'* in the Incarnation" (367).
20. It acquires virtually an instrumental sense, as in our marginal rendering, "by coming into the world" (see above, n. 1).

9, the author presupposes, without quite saying it, that "the light has come into the world" (3:19), or that "the Word became flesh" (1:14), in the person of Jesus Christ. The only difference between the two verbs is that "illumines" *(phōtizei)* is transitive, while "shines" *(phainei)* is intransitive: the light "is shining" in the darkness, but "illumines," or shines *on,* every human being born into the world. The point is not that the light illumines every human being at birth (that is, at the *time* of "coming into the world"),[21] but simply that the light illumines everyone in the world. The author seems to have chosen his terminology out of a belief that the "True light," or "the light of humans," in some sense illumined everyone since the creation, but his specific point in verse 9 is that this light illumines every human being *now,* because of the revelatory events to be unfolded in this Gospel.

10 Those who read "coming into the world" with "the light" commonly point to verse 10 in support of their interpretation: the light "was coming into the world" (v. 9), and consequently "was in the world" (v. 10).[22] But the statements are too close together for the link to be convincing. There is a certain awkwardness in claiming that the light "was coming into the world" (v. 9), and then, almost in the same breath, that it "was in the world" (v. 10). No sooner is the process mentioned than it is over. The reader is tempted to ask, "Which is it? Was the light on its way, or had it actually arrived?"

Verse 10 settles the matter. The light "was in the world," and it is probably fair to assume that the time frame is the same as in verses 6-9: that is, during the ministry of John, and on the threshold of Jesus' ministry. The author's fondness for word repetitions surfaces again in verse 10, as the expression "the world" is picked up from the end of verse 9 and repeated three times, in three distinct clauses. As in verse 9, the subject is "the light," but with an increasingly human persona. In the first clause, the notion that the light "was in the world" comes as no surprise in view of such phrases as "the light of humans" (v. 4), or "the light . . . that illumines every human being." But was "the light" an "it" or a "he"? In itself, the second clause could be translated either "the world came into being through it," or "the world came into being through him." But the analogy with "all things came into being through him" (that is, through the Word, v. 3) argues for the latter. The "light" of verses 4-5 and 7-9 is here assimilated to "the Word" mentioned in verses 1-2. Finally, in the third and last clause of verse 10, "the world did not know him," the masculine pronoun "him" (*auton,* in contrast to the neuter *auto,* "it," in v. 5) makes it now unmistakably clear that "the Light" is a Person, interchangeable with "the Word." The parallel between "the world came

---

21. For this reason, Morris's paraphrase, "every man at the time of his birth" (83), is misleading as a summary of the view presented here.

22. For example, Brown, 1.10; Barrett, 160.

1:6-13 JOHN AND THE COMING OF THE LIGHT

into being through him" (v. 10) and "all things came into being through him" (v. 3) is striking.[23]

In verse 10 the Gospel writer wants to remind us of creation, and that the entire created order came into being through "the Word," now further identified as "the Light" (and appropriately capitalized in translation). The effect is to heighten the irony and tragedy of a new assertion: "and [yet] the world did not know him." *Even though* he created the world, *still* "the world did not know him"![24] It is natural to ask if perhaps the reason — or at least one reason — for beginning with creation in the first place was to lay the basis for this supreme irony in the story of Jesus. The statement that "the world did not know him" is the second hint of conflict or rejection in the Gospel story, the first being the note in verse 5 that the darkness "did not overtake" the light. Its purpose, however, is not — at least not yet — to set up a dualism between "the world" and some community of faith that *does* "know" Jesus as the world's Light. John himself, within this chapter, will introduce his questioners to Jesus for the first time as someone "whom you do not know" (1:26), admitting that "even I did not know him" (1:31, 33). As the story unfolds, some will come to "know" Jesus and some will not, but for the time being "the world" is an undifferentiated whole, encompassing within itself the potential both for knowledge and ignorance, belief and unbelief.

11 The word repetitions continue: "his own," "his own," "received," "received."[25] The irony of the Light's rejection comes to expression a second time, and even more explicitly: "He came to what was his own [*eis ta idia*, neuter], and his own [*hoi idioi*, masculine] did not receive him." Just as "the world" in verse 10 was an undifferentiated whole, so there is no distinction here between "what was his own" and what was not, or between "his own people" (Jews, for example)[26] and others who did not belong to the Light. Rather, "what was his own" is simply another way of saying "all things," or "the world," while "his own" (masculine) refers generally to "humans" (v. 4), or "every human being" (v. 9) in the world.[27] The author seems to be reflect-

---

23. That is, πάντα δι' αὐτοῦ ἐγένετο (v. 3) and ὁ κόσμος δι' αὐτοῦ ἐγένετο (v. 10).
24. The verb "know" (ἔγνω) is aorist: the world did not "come to know" or "learn to know" the Light, just as it never learned to know God (compare 17:25).
25. In Greek, τὰ ἴδια . . . οἱ ἴδιοι . . . παρέλαβον . . . ἔλαβον.
26. Brown (1.10) identifies τὰ ἴδια as "what was peculiarly his own in 'the world,' i.e., the heritage of Israel, the Promised Land, Jerusalem," and οἱ ἴδιοι as "the people of Israel," citing Exodus 19:5, "You shall be *my own possession* among all the peoples." According to Beasley-Murray, "the Evangelist almost certainly saw the saying as relating especially to Israel in its resistance to the Word of God" (12-13). So too Morris, 85-86.
27. Bultmann, 56. On the grounds that Bultmann sees here "a cosmological reference, rather than a reference to salvation history," Brown contends that "his interpretation flows from his presupposition that the Prologue was originally a Gnostic hymn"

ing, in the broadest possible terms, on a principle known to him from Gospel tradition, that "A prophet has no honor in his own hometown" (4:44).[28] The RSV translation, "He came to his own home," can appeal to 4:44, and to the two other uses of the same phrase in John's Gospel (16:32 and 19:27), where it refers to the homes of Jesus' disciples.[29] Yet it is hard to see how "the world" (v. 10) can be viewed as "home" to the Word, who was "with God in the beginning" (v. 2).[30] Rather, the expression grows out of the reminder in verse 10 that "the world came into being through him."[31] The world is "his own" in the sense of being his creation, and thus his property or possession, not his "home" in the sense of either place of origin or permanent dwelling.[32]

The notion that the Light, or the Word, found no reception in the world stands in sharp contrast to certain Jewish teachings about Wisdom seeking a home and finding it in Israel or Jerusalem.[33] It is more akin to the apocalyptic

---

(1.10). This is by no means the case, for the Gospel writer was as capable of viewing Jesus' ministry within a cosmological framework as was any supposed hymnic source, Gnostic or otherwise.

28. Other forms of the saying occur in Mark 6:4//Matthew 13:57b, Luke 4:24, and *Gospel of Thomas* 31, but only John 4:44 includes the words "his own" (τῇ ἰδίᾳ, redundant with πατρίς, or "hometown"), echoing the language of 1:11.

29. Morris is quite emphatic: "When the Word came to this world he did not come as an alien. He came home. Moreover, he came to Israel. Had he come to some other nation it would have been bad enough, but Israel was peculiarly God's own people. The Word did not go where he could not have expected to be known. He came home, where the people should have known him" (85).

30. See, for example, 8:23, where Jesus tells the Pharisees, "You are from below, I am from above. You are of this world, I am not of this world"; also, 17:14, where he refers to disciples as "not of the world, even as I am not of the world."

31. Compare *Odes of Solomon* 7.12, "He has allowed him to appear to them that are His own; in order that they may recognize Him that made them, and not suppose that they came of themselves"; *The Odes of Solomon: The Syriac Texts* (ed. J. H. Charlesworth; Missoula, MT: Scholars Press, 1977), 36.

32. Bultmann, 56; Schnackenburg, 1.259.

33. For example, Wisdom speaks in Sirach 24.3-11 (RSV): "I came forth from the mouth of the Most High. . . . I dwelt in high places, and my throne was in a pillar of cloud. Alone I have made the circuit of the vault of heaven and have walked in the depths of the abyss. In the waves of the sea, in the whole earth, and in every people and nation I have gotten a possession. Among all these I sought a resting place; I sought in whose territory I might lodge. Then the Creator of all things gave me a commandment, and the one who created me assigned a place for my tent. And he said, 'Make your dwelling [κατασκήνωσον] in Jacob, and in Israel receive your inheritance. . . . In the holy tabernacle I ministered before him, and so I was established in Zion. In the beloved city likewise he gave me a resting place, and in Jerusalem was my dominion. So I took root in an honored people, in the portion of the Lord, who is their inheritance'" (see also Baruch 3:35–4:2).

1:6-13 JOHN AND THE COMING OF THE LIGHT

tradition in the book of *Enoch* about Wisdom finding no permanent home on earth.³⁴ But the story is not the same. "The Word," or "the Light," in John's Gospel is not the "Wisdom" of either the wisdom or apocalyptic traditions in Judaism. The decisive difference is that "he" — not "she" as in the case of Wisdom — is a specific historical person, Jesus of Nazareth. Grammatically, the subject of verses 10 and 11 is the Light (see v. 9), but the author knows, and readers are expected to know, that the real subject is Jesus — even though he will not be named until verse 17, nor brought into the narrative until verse 29. Because verse 11 (even more than v. 10) has the sound of a concrete reference to Jesus and his ministry on earth, even those who appreciate the universality of the context tend to notice at the same time the appropriateness of verse 11 in relation to Israel and the Jewish people. Barrett is ambivalent on the subject,³⁵ while Hoskyns finds here a "double reference to the whole earth and to Israel as God's possession," with "no final distinction between Israel and the world, between Jew and Greek. As the creation of God, all men are his property . . . and Jesus was in the world, not merely in Israel."³⁶ The point is that while the Jews are not viewed here as Jesus' "own" in a special sense in which the Gentiles are not, they may be in mind as *representatives* of the world to which Jesus came, with Judea or Jerusalem as the *stage* on which the drama of Jesus' confrontation with the world is to take place.

12 If "his own" in verse 11 is meant to be inclusive rather than exclusive, then "as many as received him" (v. 12) are not a different group consisting of others who were *not* Jesus' own (Gentiles, for example, in contrast to Jews), but rather a subset of "his own." This sets up a kind of rhetorical contrast, even contradiction. Jesus' "own did not receive him," *yet* many of them did receive him. The contradiction cannot be avoided by attributing different meanings to the two different words for "receive." Rather, "receive" in verse 11 *(parelabon)* and in verse 12 *(elabon)* are to be taken as synonymous.³⁷ The

---

34. "Wisdom could not find a place in which she could dwell; but a place was found (for her) in the heavens. Then Wisdom went out to dwell with the children of the people, but she found no dwelling place. (So) Wisdom returned to her place and she settled permanently among the angels" (*Enoch* 42.1; Charlesworth, *OTP*, 1.33).

35. Barrett claims that "the 'home' to which Jesus came was Israel," and that "Jesus came to the framework of life to which as Messiah he belonged," yet concludes that "It was the world that rejected Jesus" (163). His ambivalence is as old as Chrysostom, who saw the text "calling the Jews 'His own,' as his peculiar people, or perhaps even all mankind, as created by Him" (*Homily* 9.1; NPNF, 14.32).

36. Hoskyns, 146.

37. See Barrett, 163; Bultmann, 57; Morris, 86. At most, it could be argued that παρέλαβον (used only two other times in John) was appropriate with οἱ ἴδιοι because of its connotation of taking to oneself or one's home (14:3; compare 19:16, where it involves taking into custody).

latter, in fact, echoes the former and reinforces the contrast between the two clauses. The "contradiction" is deliberate, allowing the second clause to qualify and balance the first (as in 3:32-33, "No one receives his testimony," *yet* "the person who did receive his testimony confirmed thereby that God is true").[38] The use of "received" here anticipates verse 16: "Of his fullness we have all received, and grace upon grace." To "receive" the Light is to receive Jesus' "testimony," and to partake "of his fullness" (1:16).[39] Not surprisingly, this "receiving" belongs to "those who believe" *(tois pisteuousin)* in Jesus' name (v. 12b). "Receiving" and "believing" are virtually synonymous in this Gospel, both involving a conscious, active choice, and each interpreting the other. John had come "to testify about the light, that they all might believe through him" (v. 7), but now we learn that matters are not that simple. Even when the Light came, "his own did not receive him," that is, they did *not* believe — and yet some of them did! This is what the story is about.

Grammatically, the author places a middle term between "receiving" and "believing." "Receiving" implies a gift and a giver. "Giving" and "receiving" are natural correlatives in any language, not least in biblical Greek (see, for example, 3:27; 16:23-24; 17:8). Despite the word order, the subject of verse 12 is not the "many" who "received" the Light, but rather (as in vv. 10-11), an unexpressed subject, the Light himself (v. 9). The main verb, accordingly, is not "received," but "gave," with "them" as indirect object. The author, however, has highlighted the recipients instead of the giver by placing them front and center in a relative clause.[40] This is not all. The recipients are given "authority to become children of God" *(tekna theou)* and then, as we

---

38. Abbott (*Johannine Grammar,* 466) cites this and several other passages (4:1-2; 7:8-10, 16; 8:15-16; 16:14-15, 32, as well as the formula "the hour is coming and now is") as examples of what he calls John's "self-corrections," but they are too diverse to justify identifying this as a characteristic Johannine literary device. An example from another Gospel is Matthew 28:17, "When they saw him, they worshipped," *yet* "some doubted."

39. For "receive," the author prefers the more active λαμβάνειν (literally, "take"; forty-six occurrences) over the more passive δέχεσθαι ("accept" or "welcome"; only one occurrence). For other examples of "receiving" or "taking" either Jesus or his testimony or the Holy Spirit, see 3:11, 5:43, 7:39, 12:48, 13:20, 16:24, 17:8, and 20:22. Another compound, καταλαμβάνειν (1:5, 12:35, and the variant reading in 6:17; see above on v. 5), also means "take" in an active sense, but with hostile intent (more like "overtake," as with the woman "taken" in adultery in 8:3, 4).

40. According to Barrett, "The relative clause thrown to the beginning of the sentence as a *nominativus pendens* and resumed by αὐτοῖς is characteristic of John's style" (163). C. F. Burney cited this construction years ago as evidence of a Semitic original (*Aramaic Origin,* 64-65), but Bultmann (57) calls it "a not uncommon rhetorical device which is by no means specifically Semitic" (compare Brown, 1.10; Morris, 86-87). But true parallels to the construction found here are difficult to find in John's Gospel (the closest, perhaps, being 6:39, 10:29, and 17:2, 22, 24).

have seen, further identified as "those who believe." Finally, the author highlights them once more by returning to the nominative with which verse 12 began: "who were . . . born of God" (v. 13). The two nominative constructions frame the main clause so as to shift attention from the Light to the recipients of the light, first by contrasting them with those who did *not* receive the Light (v. 12a) and then by decisively spelling out their identity as "children of God" (v. 13).[41]

The point of verse 12 is that to receive "him" (that is, the Light, or Jesus as the Light) is to receive "authority" *(exousian)* from him to become God's children. "Authority" in the Gospel of John is something Pontius Pilate claims for himself falsely, but which must be given "from above" (19:10-11). It is something the Father gives to the Son, whether authority to exercise divine judgment (5:27), or to lay down his life and take it again (10:18), or "over all flesh, that he might give eternal life to all that you have given him" (17:2). The last of these is the one with the most direct bearing on our passage, for it involves the gift of life to believers.[42] If one were to bring the two passages together, it would be possible to conclude that the recipients of the Light here are given not just life, or the status of God's children, but the divine "authority" of Christ himself. While this is a legitimate Johannine theme (see 17:22), it is a rather heavy one to introduce so early in the Gospel. At this point it is wise not to overinterpret this "authority." It clearly does *not* mean that "those who received him" have a choice of either becoming "children of God" or not! It is nothing like the authority Pilate thought he had, to either crucify Jesus or let him go (19:10). Rather, if the word "authority" were to disappear from the text altogether, the meaning would be about the same! To say "He gave them *authority* to become children of God" is little different from saying, "He gave them to become children of God," in the sense of granting them the status of children.[43]

---

41. No causal sequence is spelled out here, and none should be assumed. The text does *not* say they were given authority to become God's children *because* they received the Light or as a reward for doing so. If the principle later introduced that "A person cannot receive anything unless it is given him from heaven" (3:27) is operative here as well (see also 6:65), it could as easily have been the other way around.

42. An often-cited parallel is found in Poimandres, the first tractate of the *Corpus Hermeticum* (1.28): "Why, O men of earth, have you given yourselves up to death, when you have authority [ἔχοντες ἐξουσίαν] to partake of immortality [τῆς ἀθανασίας]?" (my translation; the text is from A. D. Nock and A.-J. Festugière, *Corpus Hermeticum,* Tome I: *Traités I-XII* [Paris: Société d'Édition, 1960], 16). The parallel is noteworthy because the *Corpus Hermeticum* contains a whole tractate on "Rebirth" (Tractate 13, Περὶ Παλιγγενεσίας). An important difference is that in Hermetic literature the "authority" is something humans (at least some humans) possess naturally by birth, while in John's Gospel it is a gift linked to the coming of the Light.

43. See BDAG, 242, citing Matthew 13:11, "To you it is given to know," and John

"Children of God" is not a distinctively Johannine phrase, nor is it common in the New Testament as a whole. It appears in the Gospel only here and in 11:52, and in 1 John 3:1, 2, 10 and 5:2.[44] Paul uses it four times (Rom 8:16, 21; 9:8; and Phil 2:15),[45] more or less interchangeably with "sons of God" (see Rom 8:14-15, 19, 23; 9:4). Bauer's lexicon understands it "in Paul as those adopted by God," and "in John as those begotten by God,"[46] but the distinction is not clear-cut. "Giving authority to become," or granting status as children of God, is not so different from "adoption" in the Pauline sense (Rom 8:15, 23; 9:4; Gal 4:5). Yet John's Gospel parts company with Paul in two ways. First, the term "sons of God" never occurs,[47] probably because the Gospel writer wants to preserve the uniqueness of Jesus' relationship to God as "the Son." Jesus is introduced, in fact, not simply as "Son" *(huios),* but as "unique Son," or "One and Only" (vv. 14, 18). Second, John's Gospel goes on to unpack the metaphor involved in "children of God" in a way in which Paul never does (v. 13).[48]

Before defining "children of God" (v. 13), the author pauses to identify God's "children" unmistakably as "those who believe in his name" (v. 12b), a phrase equivalent to "those who believe in him" — that is, in the Light.[49] The longer expression, "to believe in the name," occurs only here

---

5:26, "For as the Father has life in himself, he has also given to the Son to have life in himself" (to the latter of which Jesus adds, "and he has given him *authority* [ἐξουσία] to pass judgment, because he is Son of man," 5:27). Compare Bultmann, 57, n. 5.

44. Τέκνα θεοῦ occurs without the article here and in 1 John 3:1 and 2, and with definite articles (τὰ τέκνα τοῦ θεοῦ) in 11:52 and 1 John 3:10 and 5:2. As a rule the phrase lacks the article when it precedes verbs of being or becoming, as it does here (see the discussion above on θεός without the article in 1:1).

45. Paul tends not to use the definite article (see Rom 8:16-17; Phil 2:15), except when the phrase is caught up in his rhetoric with other expressions that include the article (as in Rom 8:21 and 9:8).

46. BDAG, 995.

47. The closest the Gospel of John comes to "sons of God" is "sons of light" (υἱοὶ φωτός, 12:36), a phrase which, taken literally, would be virtually equivalent to "sons of Jesus," but which means simply those who are of the light, or belong to the light (compare 1 Thess 5:5).

48. Paul explores instead the metaphor of adoption (Gal 4:1-7). Aside from the Gospel of John, only 1 John (3:9) and 1 Peter (1:23) among the New Testament books pause to examine the metaphor of being God's children, both by referring in some way to the divine "seed" or "sperm."

49. The equivalence of "believe in him" and "believe in his name" is clearly seen in 3:18: "The one who *believes in him* is not condemned, but the one who does not believe is condemned already because he has not *believed in the name* of the only Son of God." The three other characteristic constructions of πιστεύειν are simply "to believe," with no object expressed (as in v. 7), "to believe that" (with ὅτι), and "to believe someone" (with the dative) in the sense of believing what that person says.

1:6-13 JOHN AND THE COMING OF THE LIGHT

and in 2:23 and 3:18, while the simpler "to believe in" *(pisteuein eis)* dominates the Gospel of John, with thirty occurrences.[50] Two things are noteworthy about the phrase, "those who believe in his name." One is that in 3:18 it is linked explicitly to a title, "the One and Only Son of God" (3:18), and it is possible that here too it anticipates the references to "a father's One and Only" in verse 14 and "God the One and Only" in verse 18. The other is that the present tense of the participle, "those who believe," suggests that the author has in mind Christian believers (or potential believers) *in his own day,* even as he writes his Gospel (compare 20:31: "These things are written *that you might believe* that Jesus is the Messiah, the Son of God, and that believing you might have life *in his name*").[51] The Gospel is written to just such a community of believers, and the author now takes time to remind his readers of their new identity as children of God, and what it means.

13 In simplest terms, "children of God," or "those who believe in the name," are those "born [or begotten] of God" *(ek theou egennēthēsan).* It is important to notice here what is *not* said. The text defines no temporal or causal relationship between "believing" and being "born of God," either to the effect that individuals are born of God *because* they believe,[52] or that they believe because they are *already* born of God. The point is simply that both expressions refer to the same group. "Born of God," or "born of him," occurs six times in 1 John (2:29; 3:9; 4:7; 5:1, 4, and twice in 5:18), but only here in John's Gospel. Three equivalent phrases do occur, however, in Jesus' dialogue with Nicodemus: "born from above" (3:3), "born of water and Spirit" (3:5), and "born of the Spirit" (3:6). There if anywhere Jesus spells out what "born of God" means theologically.[53] Here the Gospel writer spells out instead what it does *not* mean, above all that it is something other than physical birth (see Nicodemus's question in 3:4). He is not of course denying that believers are born physically, but he is saying that this is not what makes them "children of God." Believers are born like anyone else into the world (see v. 9), but their

---

50. The statistics are very different in 1 John, where "believe in" occurs only once (5:10), and "believe in the name" twice (3:23 and 5:13, the latter with εἰς and the former with a dative: "believe the name" or "believe by the name"). Neither expression appears in 2 or 3 John.

51. See also 17:20 and 20:29, where Jesus makes reference to a later generation of believers distinct from those who believed during his ministry (compare also perhaps 10:16, as well as 11:52, the only other occurrence of "children of God" in this Gospel).

52. Bultmann (59) assumes without argument that this is the case. But the accent in verse 13 on divine sovereignty and on the absence of any human involvement in the birth of "the children of God" points, if anything, in the opposite direction.

53. 1 John concentrates rather on what it means ethically: those "born of God" are those who do what is right (2:29), and do not sin (3:9; 5:18). They are those who love (4:7), believe that Jesus is the Messiah (5:1), and so overcome the world (5:4).

physical birth is merely a metaphor for the birth referred to here. Birth "from God" can be understood only as *new* birth, or rebirth, and the emphasis is on the *difference,* not the similarity, between the new and the old.[54]

The author accents the distinction between physical and spiritual birth by means of three negative phrases. "Not of blood lines" is literally "not of bloods." The plural is unexpected because it refers in the Old Testament not to physical birth but to acts of bloodshed.[55] According to Schnackenburg, "It is found only in classical Greek for birth," but even here the evidence is meager.[56] It is remotely possible that the writer avoids the singular, "of blood," simply because Christian believers are in fact born anew through the blood of Christ, but this would have been a reason for avoiding the terminology of blood altogether, not for resorting to an ambiguous plural.[57] More likely, the plural points simply to the participation of two parents in the act of procreation, not to the physiological details of either conception or birth. In the second phrase, the words "of fleshly desire" (literally, "of the will of flesh") are not equivalent to the "lust" *(epithymia)* of the flesh (1 Jn 2:15), even though the subject is sexual intercourse between a man and a woman. Both here and in the next clause, "desire" or "will" *(thelēma)* refers simply to choice or initiative, not to sexual or any other kind of desire, legitimate or illegitimate. "Flesh" *(sarx)* refers to human nature as such (see v. 14), not to an evil principle or impulse in human nature, as is often the case in Paul.[58] The third phrase, "a husband's desire," reiterates the second but makes it more specific, in that "human initiative" in procreation is defined (in John's first-century world!) as "the husband's initiative."[59] The word for "husband" *(anēr),* in

---

54. Compare Paul's emphasis in connection with the image of new creation (καινὴ κτίσις): "the old things have passed away; look, new things have come" (2 Cor 5:17).

55. See 2 Samuel 16:8, etc.

56. Schnackenburg, 1.264; Bultmann (60) cites Euripides, *Ion* 693: ἄλλων τραφεὶς ἐξ αἱμάτων ("a son sprung from strange blood"). See also H. J. Cadbury, "The Ancient Physiological Notions underlying Joh. 1:13a and Heb. 11:11," *The Expositor* 9 (1924), 430-39.

57. Hoskyns, 146-47. This is never explicit in John's Gospel, but according to 1 John 5:6 Jesus came "through water and blood, not by the water alone, but by the water and the blood" (compare Jn 19:34), and according to 1 John 1:7 "the blood of Jesus his Son cleanses us from every sin."

58. Paul writes of "the lust of the flesh" (ἐπιθυμίαν σαρκός, Gal 5:16; compare Rom 13:14), and at least once (Eph 2:3) he uses "lusts of the flesh" (ταῖς ἐπιθυμίαις τῆς σαρκός) interchangeably with "choices" or "initiatives" (τὰ θελήματα) of the flesh. "Flesh" does not have the same negative connotations even in 1 John 2:16, where it is more an occasion for sin (like "eyes" in the next phrase) than the source of sin.

59. This phrase is omitted in the first hand of B, probably by accident (because of the repetition of οὐδὲ ἐκ θελήματος), and in some patristic quotations (perhaps because of seeming redundancy).

1:6-13 JOHN AND THE COMING OF THE LIGHT

distinction from the generic word for human being (vv. 4, 9), normally means "man" in the sense of male, here in a context involving procreation a husband or sexual partner (compare Eph 5:22, 24, 25; Col 3:18-19; 1 Pet 3:1, 7).[60] Together, the three negative expressions make a simple point: to be "born of God" is not a physical or literal birth, but a metaphor for a transformed life.

Some ancient versions and patristic citations presuppose a singular relative pronoun and a singular verb ("who . . . was born") instead of the plural, "were born." The subject then becomes not the recipients of the Light, but the Light himself, the "him" of verse 12 in whose name they believed. In short, verse 13 becomes an explicit statement of the virginal conception and birth of Jesus. It is important to note that this reading is found in no Greek manuscript, and that it has no serious claim to originality.[61] Theologically, however, it was a natural, perhaps inevitable, development because verse 13 would have seemed to later scribes and Christian readers a perfect affirmation of the mystery of the virgin birth as narrated in Matthew and Luke. To some it would have set the stage admirably for the affirmation of verse 14 that "the Word came in human flesh."[62] Another proposal has been that the plural was original, but that the author phrased verse 13 in such a way as to make a subtle allusion to the virgin birth of Jesus.[63] "Taken literally," according to Haenchen, "these words express the virgin birth for

---

60. A further implication is that God in the expression "born of God" is also visualized as male (that is, "born of God," is equivalent to "begotten of God"). This assumption is most clearly evident in 1 John 3:9, with its reference to God's "seed" (σπέρμα, probably referring to the male sperm) remaining in the believer to keep the believer from sin.

61. The variant could easily have arisen from the tendency of a copyist to link the relative pronoun directly to the immediately preceding αὐτοῦ at the end of verse 12 rather than the more remote ὅσοι at the beginning of the verse. The reading occurs in one old Latin version, *b* ("qui . . . natus est"), one Latin lectionary, and partially in the Curetonian Syriac and some manuscripts of the Peshitta. Tertullian (*De Carne Christi* 19), who also supported the singular reading, attributed the plural to Valentinian Gnostics who were trying to support their doctrine that the elect, or gnostic pneumatics, were born of a secret divine seed. But as Schnackenburg (1.264) and Bultmann (59) point out, the plural attributes this divine birth to all believers, not just an elite group, so that the reading would not have established the point the Valentinians were trying to make. Instead, Tertullian provides unwitting testimony to the great antiquity of the commonly accepted plural reading.

62. Thus it is easy to see how an original plural could have been changed by scribes to the singular. If the singular were original, however, it is difficult to imagine why anyone would have blunted such an eloquent testimony to the unique and supernatural birth of God's "One and Only" (μονογένης, vv. 14 and 18).

63. Boismard, *Le Prologue de Saint Jean* (56) appeals to 1 John 5:18: "We know that one who has been born of God [understood as the believer] does not sin, but he who was born of God [understood as Jesus] keeps him, and the evil one does not touch him."

all Christians."⁶⁴ But the virgin birth of Jesus, according to Matthew and Luke, was a real physical birth from a real womb, and this is not the case with Christian believers. There is no actual virgin from whose womb they are born. The whole point of verse 13, as we have seen, is that the imagery of birth is *not* to be taken literally in their case. Its language, as Schnackenburg puts it, "seems to exclude not merely a human father, but any kind of human cooperation."⁶⁵

Efforts to read the virgin birth into verse 13 lose sight of an important feature of the last three verses of this section. After the profound christological reflection on "the Word" (vv. 1-3), and on "the true [Light] that illumines every human being who comes into the world" (v. 9), the writer shifts the center of interest to the recipients of the Light, known as "those who believe in his name," or "children of God" (vv. 12-13).⁶⁶ The Word, or the Light (we are not even sure what to call him at this point) recedes momentarily into the background, as a pronoun ("him" or "his"), or as the unexpressed subject who "came to . . . his own" (v. 11) and "gave authority to become children of God" (v. 12). Christology gives way to ecclesiology, and the Christian community to which the Gospel of John was written takes center stage.

B. OUR TESTIMONY AND JOHN'S (1:14-18)

>14 *So the Word came in human flesh and encamped among us; we looked at his glory — glory as of a father's One and Only,¹ full of grace and truth.* 15 *John testifies about him and has cried out, saying²*

---

64. Haenchen, 1.118.

65. Schnackenburg, 1.265. It is true that the reference to "a husband's desire" does focus on the husband or father, but the other two phrases ("not of blood lines, nor of fleshly desire") are sufficiently sweeping to support Schnackenburg's contention.

66. Rhetorically, the shift corresponds to a subtle change in style. The chainlike word repetitions and alternations that have characterized the author's style from the start (with alternations of "Word" and "God," "life" and "light," "light" and "darkness," "witness" and "light," and repetitions of "world") taper off after the repetition of "his own" and "received" in verses 11 and 12a. The effect is a quickening of the rhetorical pace, building to a kind of crescendo with the phrase "born of God" at the end of verse 13 (the repetition of οὐδὲ ἐκ θελήματος in v. 13 has the quite different effect of preparing for this crescendo by creating suspense and expectation).

1. This translation, which follows the NIV, has three advantages over "only-begotten" or "only Son": (1) it avoids the metaphor of begetting or birth, which is not present in the Greek μονογενής; (2) it preserves the notion of uniqueness, which is conspicuous in that word; (3) it avoids confusing the two different words μονογενής and υἱός.

2. This translation is based on the Westcott and Hort text. If I had followed the Nestle and Bible Society texts, as most English versions have done, the translation would

1:14-18 OUR TESTIMONY AND JOHN'S

— he it was who said, "The One coming after me has gotten ahead of me, because he was before me" — 16 that of his fullness we have all received, and grace upon grace. 17 For the law was given through Moses; grace and truth came into being through Jesus Christ. 18 No one has seen God, ever. It was God the One and Only, the One who is right beside the Father, who told about him.

Stylistically, the next few verses stand apart from what precedes by their conspicuous use of the first-person plural: "So the Word . . . encamped *among us*, and *we looked* at his glory" (v. 14) and "Of his fullness *we have* all received" (v. 16, my italics). The change can be expressed in one of two ways. Either the author is revealing his own identity as one of the "children of God" introduced in verses 12 and 13 who "received" the Light, or else he is invoking this group implicitly in verse 14 to testify to their faith in much the same way in which he invokes John explicitly in verse 15 ("John testifies about him and has cried out, saying . . ."). In the first instance the author is speaking personally, in the second rhetorically.

If personally, a further question arises: Is the "we" exclusive or inclusive? Is the author distinguishing himself from his readers, as if to say, "The Word came in human flesh and encamped among *us* [the original disciples of Jesus], and *we* [the eyewitnesses of what is written in this Gospel] looked at his glory"? The analogy of 1 John 1:1-4 makes it tempting to introduce just such an "apostolic we" into the discussion,[3] but there is no "you" corresponding to the "we" to support such a distinction here.[4] On the contrary, two verses later we read, "Of his fullness we have *all* received" (v. 16), matching the inclusiveness of "as many as did receive him," who "believe in his name" (v. 12). Despite the analogy of 1 John 1:1-4, it is by no means cer-

---

have been: *John testifies about him and has cried out, saying, "This was he of whom I said, 'The One coming after me has come ahead of me, because he was before me.'" For of his fullness we have all received, and grace upon grace.*

3. The "apostolic we" is evident in 1 John 1:1 and 3: "That which was from the beginning, which *we* have heard,, which *we* have seen with *our* eyes, and *our* hands have touched, concerning the word of life . . . what *we* have seen and heard *we* announce *also to you* [καὶ ὑμῖν], so that *you too* [καὶ ὑμεῖς] may have communion *with us* [μεθ' ἡμῶν], and truly our communion is with the Father and with his Son Jesus" (my italics). Quite clearly, the "we" is limited here to the apostles or eyewitnesses, while the "you" refers to the readers.

4. Contrast also 1 John 1:5, "And this is the message *we* have heard from him and announce *to you*." While an audience consisting of "you" is visible twice in John's Gospel (19:35 and 20:31; see Introduction), "we" and "you" are never used together so as to distinguish explicitly between two groups. Even where such a distinction may be implied (20:31), the point is made in the immediate context (20:29) that those who have "seen" have no advantage over those who have not.

tain that the author writes self-consciously as an eyewitness here. Such an expression as "we looked at his glory" can be taken literally, as in Luke 9:32, where at Jesus' transfiguration the disciples "stayed awake and saw his glory," but it can just as easily be figurative, as in 2 Corinthians 3:18, where Paul concludes that "all of us, with unveiled faces, seeing the glory of the Lord as though reflected in a mirror, are being transformed into the same image from one degree of glory to another; for this comes from the Lord, the Spirit" (NRSV). In either case, the readers (and if he is *not* an eyewitness, the author himself) are drawn into the once-for-all experience of Jesus' original disciples, just as they are in Jesus' final benediction to Thomas, "Because you have seen me you have believed; blessed are those who have not seen and have believed" (20:29). The fact that the author never returns to the first-person plural again until the very end of the Gospel ("*we know* that his testimony is true," 21:24) suggests that he is speaking rhetorically here as much as personally. Having provided the "children of God" with an extended introduction in verses 12-13, he now joins his voice with theirs and speaks from their perspective.

14 Depending on context, the conjunction *(kai)* with which verse 14 begins can be translated simply as "and" or with further nuances, either resumptively (as "so," or "and so") or calling attention to a contrast ("and yet").[5] The simple "and" leaves unclear the relationship (temporal or otherwise) between what has been said in verse 11-13 and what is added here. The third option ("and yet") would be attractive if one were to adopt the singular reading, "was born," in verse 13: that is, *even though* Jesus was born "not of blood lines, nor of fleshly desire, nor a husband's desire, but of God," *yet* he did truly come into human flesh, as a true human being. But it does not work nearly as well with the plural reading. The second option ("*So* the Word came") is best because the verse is not asserting anything new. "The Word came in human flesh" simply recalls and reaffirms "He came to what was his own" (v. 11).[6] The author is not announcing a mysterious transformation of the divine Word, as Haenchen proposes,[7] into something other than itself (that is, flesh), but simply confirming verses 1-13 by making it explicit that "the true Light," who "came to what was his own," was none other than "the Word" *(ho logos)* introduced in verse 1, who had been "with God in the beginning" and was himself "God."

---

5. See BDF, 227 (§ 442); also BDAG, 495.
6. This is the case even though "came" is ἐγένετο here and ἦλθεν in verse 11.
7. Haenchen speaks freely and repeatedly of a "transmutation from one form to another (εἰς ἄλλο γένος)" while admitting that "the Prologue does not betray how the Evangelist understood it" (1.130); see also G. Richter, "Die Fleischwerdung des Logos im Johannes-Evangelium," *Novum Testamentum* 13 (1971), 81-126; 14 (1972), 257-76.

"Came" here *(egeneto)* is not to be sharply distinguished from the same verb in verses 2, 6, 10, and 17. When the subject is "all things" (v. 2) or "the world" (v. 10), it means "came into being" (as in the LXX of Genesis 1), but when the subject is "a man" (v. 6), or "grace and truth" (v. 17), it can mean either "came into being" or simply "came." In the case of "the Word" (who always existed, vv. 1-2), "came into being" is hardly an option. Here, however, the verb has a predicate, "flesh" *(sarx)*. The point is not that the Word was *transformed* into flesh, for (as Schnackenburg points out) "the Logos remains the subject in the following affirmation ('and dwelt among us') and made his divine glory visible — in the flesh — to believers."[8] Rather, the meaning is that the Word came into the world *as* flesh, or *in* flesh. The affirmation is much the same as the confession of faith by which the utterances of prophets are to be tested according to 1 and 2 John: "Jesus Christ come in flesh" (1 Jn 4:2), or "coming in flesh" (2 Jn 7).

Ernst Käsemann's rhetorical question is a good one: "Does the statement 'The Word became flesh' really mean more than that he descended into the world of man and there came into contact with earthly existence, so that an encounter with him became possible?" In itself, it does not. If one must choose between Käsemann and Haenchen (see n. 7), Käsemann has the better case. But when he goes on to suggest that the significance of "The Word became flesh" is "totally overshadowed by the confession 'We beheld his glory,'"[9] he is on much weaker ground.[10] On the contrary, "The Word came in human flesh" is a decisive affirmation, repeated in a variety of ways by the Gospel writer and by Jesus himself throughout the Gospel: "He came to his own" (1:12), "The Light has come into the world" (3:19), "The bread of God is that which comes down from heaven" (6:33), "I have come down from heaven" (6:38; compare 3:13), "I am the living Bread that came down from heaven" (6:51), "This is the bread that came down from heaven" (6:58),[11] "I have come as light into the world" (12:46), "I went forth from the Father, and have come into the world" (16:28).[12] Rudolf Bultmann writes eloquently of

---

8. Schnackenburg, 1.266; compare Brown, 1.32, "Thus, in becoming flesh the Word does not cease to be the Word, but exercises its function as Word to the full."

9. See Käsemann, *The Testament of Jesus,* 9.

10. Compare Beasley-Murray, 13.

11. The examples from John 6 are of particular interest because "the Bread that came down from heaven" is finally identified more specifically as Jesus' "flesh" (ἡ σάρξ μου, v. 51).

12. To these could be added Martha's confession that Jesus is "the Messiah, the Son of God who comes into the world" (11:27), and even the belief of the crowd after the feeding of the five thousand that he was "the prophet who comes into the world" (6:14). That Jesus "comes into the world" by birth, like any other human being, is clear from his reply to Pilate, "I was born for this, and for this I came into the world" (18:37).

the "offense" of "the Word became flesh,"[13] but the offense of these other texts scattered throughout the Gospel is just as great (compare 6:61, "Does this offend you?"). John 1:14 is programmatic for them all, whether they speak of "flesh," or of "coming down from heaven," or "coming into the world." Whatever the terminology, God enters the world he has made in a manner for which humans are totally unprepared.

There is a parallelism of sorts between "came in human flesh" and "encamped among *us*" (italics added). Those who speak here as "we" or "us" are unmistakably "flesh," a purely human community, even though "born of God" and not "of fleshly desire" (v. 13). The imagery of the phrase "encamped [*eskēnōsen*] among us" is that of pitching a tent. The point of the metaphor is not that the Word's presence on earth was temporary,[14] for none of the other four New Testament occurrences of the verb "encamped" (*skēnoun*), all from the book of Revelation, have to do with a temporary dwelling. Two of these (Rev 12:12 and 13:6) refer to those who "dwell" in heaven (presumably angels), while the other two (Rev 7:15 and 21:3) promise that God will "dwell" with his people, not for a limited time but forever.[15] More likely, the metaphor's point is that the world is not the proper home of the Word (that would be "with God," v. 1, or "right beside the Father," v. 18), but a kind of second home, or home away from home. It is fully consistent with the notion that he came not "to his own home" but "to what was his

---

13. Bultmann is worth quoting at length on this point: "Thus the *offence* of the gospel is brought out as strongly as possible by ὁ λόγος σὰρξ ἐγένετο. For however much man may await and long for the event of the revelation in the human sphere, he also quite clearly expects . . . that the Revelation will somehow have to give proof of itself, that it will in some way be recognisable. The Revealer — although of course he must appear in human form — must also in some way appear as a shining, mysterious, fascinating figure, as a hero or θεῖος ἄνθρωπος, as a miracle worker or mystagogue. His humanity must be no more than a disguise; it must be transparent. Men want to look away from the humanity, and see or sense the divinity — or they will expect the humanity to be no more than the visualisation or the 'form' of the divine. All such desires are cut short by the statement: the Word became flesh. It is in his sheer humanity that he is the Revealer" (63).

14. Käsemann, for example, translates it as "dwelt for a little while," linking it to "the paradoxical 'a little while' of the farewell discourses in 14.19; 16.16ff.; as already in 7.33; 12.35; 13.33" (*Testament of Jesus,* 10). It is noteworthy that the NIV in 1983 changed its "lived for awhile among us" (in the 1973 and 1978 editions) to "made his dwelling among us" (see the Preface to the tenth anniversary edition, 1988, p. viii).

15. Compare Morris, 91: "The term had come to be used in a conventional fashion of settling down permanently in a place (e.g., Rev. 12:12; there can be no more permanent dwelling than in heaven!)." It is worth noting also that in Revelation 7 and 21, when God "encamps" (σκηνώσει) with his people, "they will not hunger or thirst *any more*" (7:16), and "there will be *no more* death or sorrow or pain" (21:4, my italics). This is no temporary encampment.

own" (v. 12). The question of whether the Word's stay on earth was temporary or permanent, and of what it meant for Jesus to "go away" when his ministry was over (7:33; 8:21; 13:33), is a broader and more profound question, one not to be settled on the basis of this verse alone.

Beyond this, the tent imagery evokes the Exodus, and the tenting of God with the people of Israel in their desert wanderings. This is evident in the close association of the phrase "encamped among us" with the "glory" *(doxa)* of the Word. Near the end of Exodus, the author concludes: "Moses could not enter the Tent of Meeting because the cloud had settled upon it, and the glory of the LORD filled the tabernacle" (Exod 40:35, NIV). The similarity of sound between the Greek *skēnē* ("tabernacle" or "tent") and the Hebrew *shākan,* "to dwell," or "settle," used of the Lord dwelling with Israel or in his temple, seems to have influenced the LXX translators at some points and perhaps the choice of words here as well.[16] But possibly the most relevant parallel is one in which this is *not* the case: "I will put my dwelling place among you, and I will not abhor you. I will walk among you and be your God, and you will be my people" (Lev 26:11-12, NIV).[17]

Similar covenant language is echoed in the prophets and in the New Testament. For example:

> "My dwelling place will be with them; I will be their God, and they will be my people" (Ezek 37:27, NIV).

> "'Shout and be glad, O Daughter of Zion. For I am coming, and I will live among you,' declares the LORD. 'Many nations will be joined with the LORD in that day and will become my people. I will live among you and you will know that the LORD Almighty has sent me to you'" (Zech 2:10-11, NIV).

> "I will dwell and walk among them, and I will be their God, and they will be my people" (2 Cor 6:16).

> "See, the tent of God is with humans, and he will encamp with them, and they will be his people, and God himself will be with them as their God" (Rev 21:3).

In our text there is no *direct* reference to the Exodus nor to God's ancient covenant with Israel. When the author wants us to think of Moses or the

---

16. For a list of examples, see Schnackenburg, 1.269. As is often noted, the Hebrew noun *Shekinah* was later derived from the verb שׁכן, "to dwell," and used (after the biblical period) as a designation for the divine presence (as, for example, in ʾAbot 3.2, "if two sit together and study the words of the Torah, the *Shekinah* is in the midst of them").

17. Here the Hebrew is מִשְׁכָּנִי, but the LXX has no form of σκηνή or σκηνοῦν here, but rather "I will place my covenant [τὴν διαθήκην μου] among you."

desert wanderings explicitly, he will mention Moses by name (v. 17). Yet if those speaking are "children of God" (vv. 12-13), covenant language is appropriate, for in almost the same breath in which the God who encamps on earth says, "I will be their God, and they will be my people," he can also say, "I will be to you a father, and you will be to me sons and daughters" (2 Cor 6:18), or "Whoever overcomes will inherit these things, and I will be to him God and he will be to me a son" (Rev 21:7).

The "glory" *(doxa)* of the Word is seen by the children of God, appropriately enough, as the glory of "a father's One and Only."[18] With this, the Gospel's terminology takes a decisive turn from the expressions "God" and "the Word" (vv. 1-2) toward what is to be the dominant relationship from now on, between "the Father" and "the Son."[19] The classic declaration of that relationship in the Gospel tradition is of course the voice from heaven at Jesus' baptism, "You are my beloved Son; with you I am well pleased" (Mk 1:11; Lk 3:22; compare Mt 3:17).[20] It is widely recognized that the synoptic term "beloved" *(agapētos;* compare Mt 12:18; Mk 12:6; Lk 20:13) and the Johannine "One and Only" *(monogenēs;* compare 1:18; 3:16, 18; 1 Jn 4:9) are almost equivalent terms, both accenting the uniqueness of Jesus' relationship to the Father.[21] The reference to "a father" seems to have been introduced to explain the otherwise abrupt "One and Only." Otherwise, we might have wondered, "*Whose* One and Only?" The answer is "a father's One and Only" (perhaps with the implication: "You know, as in the baptism story"), or literally, "a One and Only from a father" *(para patros).*[22] At the same time,

---

18. Gr. ὡς μονογενοῦς παρὰ πατρός. The term "One and Only" (μονογενής) distinguishes Jesus' sonship from that of Christian believers generally (the "children of God" of v. 13). Jesus' sonship is unique. He alone is "the Son," or "One and Only," and believers are always God's "children" (compare 11:52), never God's "sons" (though compare "sons of light," in 12:37). The ambiguity of our translation (with "One and Only" capitalized, but with "father" in lower case) is an attempt to reflect the ambiguity of the text, in which both words are indefinite yet fraught with meaning in the setting of the Gospel as a whole.

19. Both terms will become definite in verse 18, μονογενής by virtue of being linked to θεός, and πατήρ by acquiring the definite article, "the Father." The point of ὡς ("as") is not that the glory of the Word is simply analogous to the glory of "a father's One and Only," but that it actually is that glory (see BDAG, 1104; also Brown, 1.13).

20. Compare the voice from heaven at Jesus' transfiguration in the three synoptic Gospels (Mk 9:7; Mt 17:5; Lk 9:35).

21. Both are used in the LXX to translate Heb. יחיד, which can mean either "unique" or "beloved" (for examples, see Schnackenburg, 1.271, n. 183).

22. A rather similar use of παρά is found in 5:44, where Jesus tells the Jewish authorities in Jerusalem that "the glory that is from the only God [τὴν δόξαν τὴν παρὰ τοῦ μόνου θεοῦ] you do not seek." The parallel confirms what the reader already knows, that the "father" of the "One and Only" is himself the "only" God, and the object of Jewish worship.

the choice of words could imply that "the One and Only" was also "sent" from his father, just as John was "sent from God" (v. 6). The notion that the Word "came" is, after all, still very much in the author's mind.[23] Yet in the absence of any explicit word for "coming" or being "sent," it is probably safer to view the reference to a father (or the Father) as simply part of the definition of "One and Only."[24]

In this Gospel (unlike the synoptics), the notion of Jesus as God's "One and Only," or more commonly as "the Son," arises out of a certain perception of his ministry as a whole, not out of a specific incident such as the baptism or the transfiguration. The Gospel of John, in fact, makes no direct mention of either of these events. Similarly, "we looked at his glory" is not a claim based on a single experience (contrast Lk 9:32; 2 Pet 1:17-18), but a testimony to Jesus' entire life on earth. His "glory" *(doxa),* closely identified with "the glory of God," is revealed in his miracles (2:11; 11:40), but above all when he is "glorified" *(doxazesthai)* in his death on the cross and the events leading up to it (7:39; 11:4; 12:16, 23, 28; 13:31; 17:1, 5). The verb for "we looked at" *(etheasametha)* is used of John's vision of the Spirit descending on Jesus (1:33), once of observing a miracle (11:45), and three times in 1 John of believers' perceptions of God or Christ (1 Jn 1:1; 4:12, 14). It is also used of Jesus' own perception (1:38; 6:5) or that of his disciples (4:35) in the presence of potential converts or an opportunity for mission. In two of these instances the expression "Lift up your eyes and look" (4:35), or "Lifting up his eyes and looking" (6:5), suggests a deliberate act of the will. For this reason "we looked at" (like the "beheld" of the KJV) is a marginally better translation than "we saw."

"Full of grace and truth"[25] probably modifies "a father's One and Only." Some English translations depart from the Greek word order so as to make it modify "the Word,"[26] but by the time "grace and truth" are mentioned the author has exchanged the terminology of "the Word" for that of Son and father.[27]

---

23. Later, within the Johannine narrative, Jesus will claim to be "the one from God" (ὁ ὢν παρὰ τοῦ θεοῦ, 6:46; compare 7:29; 9:16, 33; 16:27, 28; 17:8).

24. BDAG, 757. See also Bultmann (71), who adds that the simpler "μονογενοῦς του πατρός would be ambiguous" (that is, the double genitives could be read: "of the only Father"; so too Haenchen, 1.120).

25. Gr. πλήρης χάριτος καὶ ἀληθείας.

26. See, for example, the RSV ("And the Word became flesh and dwelt among us, full of grace and truth"), or the GNB ("The Word became a human being and, full of grace and truth, lived among us"). Those who adopt this interpretation can argue that πλήρης is nominative, agreeing with ὁ λόγος, "the Word," not genitive like μονογενοῦς, "One and Only," or accusative like δόξαν, "glory." There is, however, wide agreement that πλήρης here may well be indeclinable; see BDAG, 827; BDF, §137(1).

27. Lightfoot, 86.

The difference is small because in either case the phrase refers to "Jesus Christ" (compare v. 17). Other versions set off the expression translated here as "glory as of a father's One and Only" with commas, in apposition to "his glory," implying that "filled with grace and truth" modifies "glory."[28] This is less satisfactory because attributes such as "grace and truth" are more appropriately applied to persons than to another attribute such as "glory." It is, after all, Jesus the man who is "full of the Holy Spirit" according to Luke 4:1, and Stephen, a man, who is "full of grace and power" according to Acts 6:8.[29] If the Holy Spirit confers "power" *(dynamis)* in Luke-Acts, so that "power" and the Spirit are almost synonymous,[30] the Spirit in John's Gospel is closely associated with "truth" *(alētheia),*[31] to the point of being identified as "the Spirit of truth" (14:17; 15:26; 16:13). "Grace and truth," while coordinate grammatically, seem not to be coordinate in meaning, just as "grace and power" are not coordinate in meaning in the book of Acts. Rather, "truth" specifies what "grace" it is that Jesus possesses.[32] He is full of the grace, or gift, of truth (that is, of the Spirit of truth). This suggests that "full of grace and truth" may be simply another way of affirming that Jesus was "full of the Holy Spirit," as in Luke 4:1.[33]

Another line of interpretation derives "grace and truth" from the Exodus tradition, and two closely associated Hebrew words for "mercy" (or "covenant loyalty") and "truth" *(ḥesed wĕ'ĕmet).*[34] Unlike "grace and truth" in our text, these two words are almost synonymous in meaning, both focusing on faithfulness to God's covenant with Israel. This option is attractive because of the possible echoes of the Exodus and the Sinai covenant in verse

---

28. This is the case (though somewhat ambiguously) in the NASB, NRSV, and NEB, among others (compare G. Delling in *TDNT,* 6.285).

29. The two expressions, "full of grace and truth" (πλήρης χάριτος καὶ ἀληθείας) and "full of grace and power" (πλήρης χάριτος καὶ δυνάμεως), are strikingly similar. The vocabulary is characteristic of Luke. Stephen was part of a group described as "full of Spirit and wisdom" (6:3), and is said to be "a man full of faith and the Holy Spirit" (6:5), and at his martyrdom still "full of the Holy Spirit" (7:55). See also Luke 5:12 ("a man full of leprosy"); Acts 9:36 ("she was full of good works and alms"); 11:24 ("a good man and full of Holy Spirit and faith"); 13:10 ("full of all deceit and all trickery"); and 19:28 ("full of wrath").

30. See, for example, Luke 1:35; 4:14; 24:49; Acts 1:8; 10:38.

31. See 4:23-24, where Jesus speaks of worshipping God "in Spirit and truth" (ἐν πνεύματι καὶ ἀληθείᾳ). This is even more conspicuous in 1 John ("It is the Spirit who testifies, because the Spirit is the truth," 5:6), and in 2 John, where "the truth" is described exactly as if it were the Spirit: "because of the truth that remains in us and will be with us forever" (2 Jn 2; compare Jn 14:16, 17).

32. Compare BDF, §442(16): "The co-ordination of two ideas, one of which is dependent on the other (hendiadys), serves in the NT to avoid a series of dependent genitives."

33. Compare Abbott, *Johannine Vocabulary,* 281.

34. Heb. חסד ואמת.

14.[35] When Moses asked to see the glory of the Lord (Exod 33:18), the Lord warned him that "you cannot look at my face, for no one can look at my face and live" (33:20). Then he placed Moses on a rock and passed by, saying, "The LORD, the LORD, compassionate and gracious God, slow to anger, *great in mercy and truth*" (Exod 34:6, my italics).[36] Moses cannot look at God's face, but he can learn to know God's attributes of "grace and truth."[37] The covenantal background is noteworthy because Moses will be mentioned by name three verses later (v. 17), and we will be reminded explicitly of what God told Moses on the mountain: "No one has seen God, ever" (v. 18; compare 5:37; 6:46; 1 Jn 4:12). Still, the precise terminology, "full of grace and truth," is, as we have seen, closer to what could be called the "empowerment language" of Luke-Acts, centered around the gift of the Holy Spirit (compare Lk 4:1; Acts 6:3, 5, 8; 7:55; 11:24). The two worlds of thought are not mutually exclusive. Jesus is the recipient of "grace" here, empowered as the Father's "One and Only" with the very attributes God revealed to Moses long ago. The role of the Spirit in all this is not yet explicit, but we will hear more of it later (see 1:32-34; 3:34).

15 The author now adds the testimony of "John" (compare v. 6) to his own testimony and that of the "children of God." Testimony was the purpose for which John came (vv. 7-8), and now we are allowed to hear what he said. Origen, who defined this as the first of six such testimonies of John to Jesus (the other five being 1:23, 26-27, 29-31, 32-34, and 36), included all of verses 15-18 as words of John.[38] Few modern commentators have followed him. Most conclude that John's testimony consists only of verse 15. According to the Greek text of Nestle and most English translations, the testimony is, "This was he of whom I said, 'The One coming after me has come ahead

---

35. Compare Dodd, *Interpretation*, 175-76; Barrett, 167; Brown freely renders the phrase "enduring love" (1.14).

36. The Hebrew for "great in mercy and truth" is רב-חסד ואמת (*rab-ḥesed wĕ'ĕmet*), rendered in the LXX as πολυέλεος καὶ ἀληθινός ("very compassionate and true"). This is as close as Exodus comes to the Johannine "full of grace and truth."

37. Dodd comments that חסד ואמת "is variously translated, but most characteristically as ἔλεος καὶ ἀλήθεια. There is, however, evidence that in the later stages of the LXX . . . χάρις came to be preferred to ἔλεος as a rendering of חסד, and the combination of χάρις καὶ ἀλήθεια is so unusual in Greek that we must suppose that the expression was derived from a Hebrew source" (*Interpretation*, 175; compare Schnackenburg, 1.272). For the combination χάρις ἔλεος εἰρήνη in a Johannine context in which ἀλήθεια is also conspicuously present, see 2 John 3.

38. *Commentary on John* 2.212-13 (FC, 80.152-53). "This whole speech, therefore," he claims, "was from the mouth of the Baptist bearing witness to the Christ. This fact escapes the notice of some who think that the speech from the words, 'We all received of his fullness' up to 'he has declared him' was from the mouth of John the apostle" (§213).

of me, because he was before me'" (v. 15). Because the testimony is introduced in the present tense ("John testifies about him and has cried out, saying"),[39] it appears that the author is speaking of John as if he were still alive, a living witness to the author's own generation.[40] The double time perspective is confusing: first, John *said* (past tense) that someone coming after him had gotten ahead of him because he existed before John; now John looks back on that pronouncement and *testifies* (present tense) to the readers of the Gospel that this person was none other than God's "One and Only" (v. 14). Later we will learn that John had already made the same identification *within* his ministry, when he saw Jesus coming toward him and announced (to no one in particular), "This is he about whom I said, 'After me is coming a man who has come ahead of me, because he was before me'" (v. 30). Two things are curious: first, John's pronouncement seems to come abruptly and prematurely, before the narrative proper has even begun; second, John looks *back* (not once but twice) on something he had said earlier without ever being represented as saying it in the first place.[41]

The matter is complicated by a textual variant.[42] Origen followed a different textual tradition, reading "This was he who said" instead of "This was he of whom I said."[43] Our single most important Greek manuscript, Codex Vaticanus (B), the fifth-century Codex Ephraemi Rescriptus (C), and

---

39. "Testifies" is μαρτυρεῖ (present tense), while the verb κέκραγεν ("has cried out") is perfect, but, as Barrett observes, "used with the force of a present" (167; compare BDF, §341). The verbs are almost synonymous in John's Gospel, which uses κράζειν to mean "proclaim" or "announce," while deploying a different verb, κραυγάζειν, for a mere shout or outcry (see W. Grundmann in *TDNT*, 3.901-2; also Dodd, *Interpretation*, 382, n. 1, who finds that "John used κράζειν where most other Christian writers used κηρύσσειν, and in the same sense").

40. According to Schnackenburg, "John's clarion call, which never ceases to ring out, testifies for all time that the incarnate Logos was the greater" (1.274; compare Morris, 95-96). Brown, by contrast (1.15), views μαρτυρεῖ as simply a historical present (compare BDF, §321), referring to John's witness in the past, and κέκραγεν as equivalent to a historical present. Somewhat inconsistently, however, he agrees that "John the Baptist's witness to Jesus and proclamation of him is looked on as still in effect against the claims of the sectarians."

41. The closest he comes to it is the phrase "the One coming after me" (ὁ ὀπίσω μου ἐρχόμενος, v. 27).

42. For fuller discussion, see my article, "Origen and the Text of John 1:15," in *New Testament Textual Criticism: Its Significance for Exegesis. Essays in Honour of Bruce M. Metzger* (Oxford: Clarendon, 1981), 87-104.

43. Thus, οὗτος ἦν ὁ εἴπων instead of οὗτος ἦν ὃν εἶπον. Although Origen's exposition of verse 15 in its normal sequence in the Gospel has not survived, he cites the clause in question twice, both times as οὗτος ἦν ὁ εἴπων (*Commentary on John* 6.3 and 6.6; see E. Preuschen, *GCS*, 4.108, 113; the numeration in the English translation is 6.13 and 34 [FC, 80.171, 178]).

Cyril of Alexandria all agree with the text of Origen,[44] and on this evidence Origen's reading was adopted by Westcott and Hort, with the more familiar reading relegated to the margin.[45] Few English versions, even among the closest followers of the Westcott and Hort text (such as ERV, ASV, NASB, RSV, and NRSV) followed it at this point.[46] B. F. Westcott (without endorsing the reading) commented that it made "intelligible sense by emphasising the reference to the Baptist's testimony: 'this John, and no other, was he who spake the memorable words.'"[47] The Westcott and Hort text made such a reading almost inevitable by setting off "This was he who said" with dashes.[48] But it is not the only way to construe the variant reading. The words of the variant, "This was he who said," or "He it was who said," are, as Westcott recognized, not words attributed to John the Baptist but words of the Gospel writer introducing John. As such they can hardly be separated

---

44. In each of the manuscripts οὗτος ἦν ὁ εἴπων was what the original copyist wrote, but later correctors changed it to what later became the accepted reading, οὗτος ἦν ὃν εἶπον. The same thing happens in later manuscripts of Origen's *Commentary on John* (as is evident in the English translation, ANF, 10.350, 352), and of Cyril of Alexandria. See Michaels, "Origen," 95, n. 21.

45. *The New Testament in the Original Greek* (New York: Harper and Brothers, 1882), 1.187. Unfortunately, the two editors did not discuss the variant in their "Notes on Selected Readings" appended to their second volume, possibly because they were not in agreement. B. F. Westcott did not defend or presuppose the reading in either of his commentaries on the Gospel of John, and it appears likely that its adoption was the decision of F. J. A. Hort.

46. There are, however, a number of exceptions: Rotherham's *Emphasized New Testament* (Grand Rapids: Kregel, 1959); *The Twentieth Century New Testament* (New York: Revell, 1904); G. W. Wade, *Documents of the New Testament* (London: Thomas Murby, 1934); Charles B. Williams, *The New Testament: A Private Translation in the Language of the People* (Chicago: Moody, 1960); the *New World Translation* of the Jehovah's Witnesses (Brooklyn: Watchtower and Tract, 1961); and Richmond Lattimore, *The New Testament* (New York: North Point, 1996). The United Bible Society's *Greek New Testament* in its third edition preferred ὃν εἶπον with an "A" rating (see Metzger, *Textual Commentary*, 197-98), and in its fourth revised edition (1993) eliminated its note on the variant altogether!

47. *The Gospel According to St. John* (London: John Murray, 1908), 1.66.

48. See, for example, *The Twentieth Century New Testament*: "John bears witness to him; he cried aloud — for it was he who spoke — . . ."; G. W. Wade, *Documents*: "the statement was his own, his alone"; Lattimore: "John bears witness concerning him, and he cried out, saying [for it was he who was speaking] . . ."; also the *New World Translation*: "(John bore witness about him, yes, he actually cried out — this was the one who said [it])"; Williams does the same, while avoiding dashes: "John testified to Him, and cried out, for this was the one who said . . ."; Metzger reconstructs it as ". . . and cried, saying — this was he who said [it] — 'He who comes after me ranks before me' . . ." (*Textual Commentary*, 198).

from the testimony to which they are attached. If the connection is maintained, then *the whole sentence* should be set off with dashes, yielding the translation I have adopted in this commentary: "John testifies about him and has cried out, saying — he it was who said, 'The One coming after me has come ahead of me, because he was before me' — that 'Of his fullness,' etc."[49] Instead of John the Baptist looking back on something he had said earlier, this is the Gospel writer himself, interrupting his own discourse to identify John by means of a well-known quotation. The quotation is aptly chosen because it makes three points important to the Gospel writer, especially in the Gospel's first major section (chapters 1–3): that Jesus came "after" John *(opisō mou)*,[50] that he nevertheless had gotten "ahead" of John *(emprosthen mou)*, and that this was because he had existed "before" John *(prōtos mou)*. The first of these assertions is reinforced when John refers to Jesus within the narrative as "the One who comes after me" (1:27a, 30; see also 3:27), the second when John says, "I am not worthy to untie the strap of his sandal" (1:27b), and "He must grow, but I must diminish" (3:30); the third was established at the very outset when the author demonstrated that Jesus existed not only before John but before the world's creation (vv. 1-5).[51] This saying of John, in fact, as we have seen, provides a possible clue to the author's purpose in beginning the Gospel as he has done, with Jesus as the preexistent "Word" or "Light."

Which reading is to be preferred? External evidence favors the Nestle text, but only slightly.[52] Transcriptional probability, on the other hand, argues

---

49. For further discussion, see Michaels, "Origen," 96-99.

50. There is an ambiguity, perhaps intentional, to the preposition "after" (ὀπίσω). It can mean "after" in time (that is, later than, BDAG, 575, on ὀπίσω, 2, b), or it can mean coming "after" in the sense of following as a disciple (BDAG, 575, on ὀπίσω, 2, a, β; compare Mk 1:17; 8:34; Mt 16:24). If it is the first, then ὀπίσω μου is being contrasted with πρῶτός μου ("before me"); if the second, then the contrast is with ἐμπρόσθεν μου ("ahead of me"). Very likely the reader is intended to notice both contrasts.

51. A curious feature of the so-called "Inspired Version" of the Reorganized Church of Jesus Christ of Latter-Day Saints is an insertion between the end of verse 15 and the beginning of verse 16, accenting once again the preexistence of the Word: "For in the beginning was the Word, even the Son, who is made flesh, and sent unto us by the will of the Father. And as many as believe in his name shall receive of his fullness." *Joseph Smith's "New Translation" of the Bible* (Independence, MO: Herald, 1970), 443.

52. The evidence from Origen shows that ὁ εἴπων is a very ancient Alexandrian reading, at least as ancient as any existing Greek manuscript, so that its presence in the first hand of B and C cannot be merely a slip of the pen corrected by later hands. On the other hand, the support for ὃν εἶπον is more widespread and diversified, and includes equally strong Alexandrian support, above all P[66] and P[75]. If either or both of these papyri had agreed with B and Origen, our English versions today might look quite different.

for the Westcott and Hort reading.[53] The best recourse for a commentary is to leave open both possibilities and make the reader aware of their implications. If we follow Nestle and most English versions, John's testimony is "This was he of whom I said, 'The One coming after me has come ahead of me, because he was before me.'" The Gospel writer presents John the Baptist as a present witness quoting something he had said at some point in his ministry and assuring the Gospel's readers that Jesus was the One about whom he had been speaking. If we follow Origen and the Westcott and Hort text ("This was he who said, 'The One coming after me has come ahead of me, because he was before me'"), then this is not John's actual present testimony to the readers of the Gospel, but simply the author's way of reintroducing John by reminding the readers of something they already knew John had said. On this reading, the whole sentence, "He it was who said, 'The One coming after me has come ahead of me, because he was before me,'" is a digression, although an important one in the setting of chapters 1–3. John's *present* testimony to the readers of the Gospel comes rather in the next verse, introduced appropriately with the conjunction "that" *(hoti):* "John testifies about him and has cried out, saying . . . that of his fullness we have all received, and grace upon grace."

16 By contrast, those who follow the Nestle text in verse 15 must translate the conjunction *(hoti)* with which verse 16 begins as "because" or "for," creating only a vague link between verses 15 and 16,[54] and leaving open the question of whether or not John is still the speaker. Those who follow Westcott and Hort may translate it in the same way,[55] but (as we have just

---

53. That is, it is easier to imagine ὁ εἴπων being changed to ὃν εἶπον than the other way around. If the former were original, the tendency of scribes would have been to conform it to John's pronouncement within the Gospel narrative, "This is he about whom I said [οὗτός ἐστιν ὑπὲρ οὗ ἐγὼ εἶπον], 'After me is coming a man who has gotten ahead of me, because he was before me'" (v. 30). The minimum alteration necessary to do this would have been a simple change of ὁ εἴπων to ὃν εἶπον. If ὃν εἶπον were original and John were already the speaker, we would have expected the verb to be ἐστίν rather than ἦν, for John appears at the beginning of the verse as a present, living voice testifying to a present, living Jesus. On the other hand, ἦν was used nine times within the Gospel's first ten verses, and (along with ἐγένετο) characterizes the author's style. For this reason I prefer the Westcott and Hort text; see Michaels, "Origen," 101-2.

54. The vagueness of the connection is even more evident in the variant reading καί ("and"), found in A, the majority of later Greek manuscripts, and most Latin and Syriac versions. But the support for ὅτι is overwhelming, with P⁶⁶ and P⁷⁵ alongside ℵ, B, D, and the earliest Latin versions. Ὅτι is more consistent with the Westcott and Hort reading in verse 15, and M. É. Boismard goes so far as to argue that an original καί was changed to ὅτι "sous l'influence d'une exégèse en faveur à Alexandrie dès le temps d'Origène" (*Prologue de Saint Jean,* 82; compare Bultmann, 76, n. 3; Schnackenburg, 1.275).

55. The *New World Translation* (see n. 46) renders ὅτι as "For," starting a new

seen) have the additional option of translating it as "that," introducing not an old but a new testimony of John, and the one with which the author is primarily concerned (v. 16). That is, John who once *said,* "The One coming after me has now come ahead of me," now *says* that of his fullness we have all received, and so on.[56] If this is the case, Origen's view that the testimony of John extends beyond verse 15 is vindicated. Modern scholars have been reluctant to follow Origen on this point, probably because verses 16-18 do not sound like anything else attributed to John in the Gospel tradition and would be difficult to defend as genuine utterances of his. But it is not a question of a "genuine" utterance of John. The point is rather that the Gospel writer is attributing certain words to John rhetorically in order to make John, like himself, a spokesman for the Christian community, the "children of God" who "believed in the name" of Jesus, "the One and Only from the Father." Without quotation marks in the Greek text, it is impossible to distinguish between direct and indirect discourse, and verse 16 (introduced by *hoti*) should probably be read as indirect discourse: "John testifies about him and has cried out, saying . . . that of his fullness we have all received, and grace upon grace." In this case, the writer is not attributing specific words to John but only summarizing the import of his testimony for Christian believers.

Some have seen in John a representative of the old covenant,[57] but there is little direct evidence of this in the text. Rather, like the Gospel writer and like a number of characters within the Gospel who confess their faith in Jesus Christ, John represents the believing community of the author's day. He is not an Old Testament prophet but a New Testament Christian — perhaps the first Christian, in that he is the first to put his faith in Jesus (see 1:20, 29-34; 3:29-30). "Of his fullness"[58] recalls "full of grace and truth" (v. 14). The implication is that the Christian community has not only looked at One "full of grace and truth," but has "received" from him those very gifts. "We have all received" corresponds, as we have seen, to "as many as received him" back in verse 12. To receive the Giver is to receive and partake of his gifts. "Of" *(ek)* is

---

sentence and giving the impression that what follows are the author's words, not words of John the Baptist. Richmond Lattimore renders it "because," and gives the impression that John is still being quoted. Those who translate ὅτι as "because" or "for" can argue that this is its meaning in both the preceding and following verses ("*because* he was before me," v. 15; "*For* the law was given through Moses," v. 17).

56. Michaels, "Origen," 103.

57. Barrett, for example, claims that "John the Baptist represents the Old Testament, and vv. 15-17 are intended to make clear the Old Testament setting in which the work of Jesus is to be understood" (167). On verse 16 he adds that "If John the Baptist is speaking, 'we' must be the prophets. Otherwise, the reference is to the apostolic church" (168).

58. Gr. ἐκ τοῦ πληρώματος αὐτοῦ.

partitive, with the meaning, "*from* his fullness."⁵⁹ We do not receive all of Christ's "fulness" *(plērōma)*, but draw "grace and truth" from it as from a boundless supply. The accompanying words, "and grace upon grace,"⁶⁰ bear this out.⁶¹ "Grace," like "grace and truth" in verse 14, probably refers to, or at least includes, the gift of the Spirit.⁶² This is all the more appropriate if the testimony is being attributed to John the Baptist, who later sees the Spirit descending and remaining on Jesus, identifying him as the one who baptizes in Holy Spirit (vv. 33-34). Here, with the words, "Of his fullness we have all received," John takes his place among those who have received that baptism,⁶³ while the phrase "grace upon grace" locates the gift of the Spirit within a series of divine "graces" or gifts.⁶⁴ Such language is quite literally "charismatic," but the reality to which it points has more to do with revelation than with empowerment for ministry, as in Luke-Acts or Paul.⁶⁵ The One from whose "fullness we have all received" is, after all, "the Word" (vv. 1, 14) or "the Light" (vv. 4-5, 9-11), and revelation is to be the Gospel's theme.

17 Whatever may be true of the conjunction *hoti* in verse 16, the same connective at the beginning of verse 17 means "because" or "for," introducing an explanation of the cryptic "grace upon grace." If verse 16 were read as direct discourse, this would suggest that the citation of John's testimony has now ended, and that the Gospel writer is now supplying an inter-

---

59. BDF, §169(2).

60. Gr. καὶ χάριν ἀντὶ χάριτος.

61. BDF, §442(9) labels καί here as epexegetical: "that is to say," grace upon grace. Morris puts it more strongly: "and what is more" (98, n. 119).

62. Bultmann comments that "The meaning of χάρις in vv. 14 and 16 corresponds more nearly to the Pauline πνεῦμα" (79, n. 2).

63. Compare, perhaps, 3:27, "A person cannot receive anything unless it is given him from heaven."

64. Compare Philo, *On the Posterity of Cain* 145: "Wherefore God ever causes His earliest gifts [πρώτας . . . χάριτας] to cease before their recipients are glutted and wax insolent; and . . . gives others in their stead [ἀντ' ἐκείνων], and a third supply to replace the second [ἀντὶ τῶν δευτέρων], and ever new in place of earlier boons [ἀντὶ παλαιοτέρων], sometimes different in kind, sometimes the same" (LCL, 2.412-15). In both passages ἀντί, which strictly means "in place of," is used to accent the boundless generosity of the Giver (compare Bultmann, 78, n. 2; also R. B. Edwards, "Χάριν ἀντὶ χάριτος [John 1.16]: Grace and Law in the Johannine Prologue," *JSNT* 32 [1988], 3-15).

65. Compare 16:14, where the Spirit, personified as "Advocate" (παράκλητος, 16:8) or "Spirit of truth" (16:13), becomes the mediator between Jesus and those who "receive" him: "He will take from what is mine [ἐκ τοῦ ἐμοῦ λήμψεται] and announce it to you." The phrase "from what is mine" (ἐκ τοῦ ἐμοῦ) corresponds to "of his fullness" (ἐκ τοῦ πληρώματος αὐτοῦ) in our text, but the purpose of the Spirit's act is revelation (ἀναγγελεῖ ὑμῖν), not empowerment. If there is a point in common with the Spirit in Paul or Luke-Acts, it is prophecy.

pretation.⁶⁶ But if it is read as indirect discourse, the issue does not arise. The author has merged his own persona so thoroughly with that of the Baptist that distinguishing between them is futile. Ironically, yet aptly enough, tradition has given them the same name, John.⁶⁷ The explanation of "grace upon grace" is that the "grace" or gift of the law through Moses has now, through Jesus Christ, given way to "grace and truth." Some commentators find here an almost Pauline contrast between law and grace,⁶⁸ but this is not evident in the text. The accent rather is on continuity. The law is itself grace from God, "given through Moses" as a preparation for more and greater grace to come. The point is not that the law failed because it could not provide "grace and truth," but that it paved the way for the latter to come into being "through Jesus Christ" (compare 1:45; 5:45-47).⁶⁹ "Grace and truth," therefore, are more than simply the "mercy and truth" revealed to Moses (Exod 34:6). Here, as in verse 14, they are closely linked to the person of Jesus, but now with the stipulation that they are something believers have "received" (v. 16) from Jesus. This is consistent with the notion that together they refer to the gift of the Spirit (compare 7:37-39). In contrast to verse 14, both "grace" and "truth" have definite articles here (rendered literally by Lattimore: "the grace and the truth"). Possibly the articles are markers recalling verse 14: "the aforementioned grace and truth," or "that grace and that truth belonging to the Father's One and Only."⁷⁰ Or they may simply have definite articles in order to stand parallel to "the law" *(ho nomos)*.

In the case of the law, the passive "was given" points to God as the Giver,⁷¹ even though it was given "through Moses."⁷² "Grace and truth," by

---

66. While Origen extended John's comment all the way to the end of verse 18, his Gnostic opponent Heracleon ended it with verse 17 and assigned verse 18 to the Gospel writer (*Commentary on John* 6.3; E. Preuschen, *GCS,* 4.108; in the English translation, 6.13 [FC, 80.171]).

67. See Chrysostom, *Homilies on St. John,* 6.1 (NPNF, 1st ser., 14.25).

68. See, for example, Barrett, 169; also Bultmann (79), who nevertheless admits that "the contrast is otherwise foreign to John and comes from the Pauline school." Edwards (see n. 64), without going this far, argues from the preposition ἀντί, "in place of," that the new grace in Christ supersedes the old grace of the law.

69. Brown makes a similar point (1.16), despite his very different translation of "grace and truth" as "enduring love," based on the analogy with חסד ואמת. Similarly Morris (99): "John may well be claiming accordingly that God's revelation of these attributes was wrongly ascribed to Moses. They were not revealed through him, but they came through Jesus."

70. BDF, §252. For possible analogies in Johannine literature, see John 3:5, 6 ("born of water and Spirit," followed by "born of *the* Spirit"), and 1 John 5:6 ("through water and blood," followed by "in *the* water and in *the* blood").

71. BDF, §130(1); also M. Zerwick, *Biblical Greek* (Rome, 1963), 76 (§236).

72. This does not prevent Jesus from asking elsewhere, "Did not Moses give you

contrast, "came into being" *(egeneto),* just as the world "came into being" (vv. 3, 10), just as John "came" as a messenger (v. 6), and just as the Word "came" in human flesh (v. 14). More specifically, "grace and truth" came into being "through Jesus Christ" just as all things came into being "through him" (vv. 3, 10).[73] The coming of "grace and truth" is a kind of new creation,[74] and the Word through whom all things came to be finally has a name — "Jesus Christ."[75] Because of the differing verbs, therefore, the phrases "through Moses" and "through Jesus Christ" are not strictly parallel. Jesus is not a new Moses receiving and delivering a new law, but the Word in human flesh, calling "grace and truth" into being. Although, as we have seen, "grace and truth" points to the gift of the Spirit, the focus of our text is not on the Spirit as such, or on any other particular gift, but on "Jesus Christ," who made both new creation and the new birth (vv. 12-13) possible.

18 The christological interest continues. The confessional "we" and "us" of the believing community testifying to its experience (vv. 14-16) now gives way to a tone of pure christological declaration not unlike that of the Gospel's opening verses, and to a significant limitation on human experience: "No one has seen God, ever"[76] (compare 6:46; 1 Jn 4:12). The principle is classically Jewish, going back to the experience of Moses when God told him, "you cannot see my face; for no one shall see me and live" (Exod 33:20). Instead, it was granted to him to have the Lord pass by; then, the Lord told him, "I will take away my hand, and you shall see my back; but my face shall not be seen" (33:23; compare 34:6). In our text the accent is on "God," which comes first in its clause even though it is the direct object, not the subject (compare, v. 1).[77] This is difficult to show in English without restructuring (for example, "God has never been visible to anyone"). Another clause follows, with a similar accent on "God," now further identified as "One and

---

the law?" (7:19), although the notion of Moses as giver is qualified in the case of circumcision (7:22), and of "bread from heaven" (6:32).

73. Compare 1 Corinthians 8:6: "But for us there is one God, the Father, from whom are all things, and we for him, and one Lord, Jesus Christ, through whom are all things [δι' οὗ τὰ πάντα] and we through him" (ἡμεῖς δι' αὐτοῦ).

74. Christian interpreters have from time to time seen echoes of the creation narrative (Gen 2:7) in the Johannine accounts of Jesus taking dirt from the ground to put on the eyes of the man born blind (9:6; see Irenaeus, *Against Heresies* 5.15.2; ANF, 1.543), and (more commonly) of him breathing on his disciples, saying, "Receive Holy Spirit" (20:22; see, for example, Barrett, 570; Brown, 2.1037).

75. The full name, "Jesus Christ," occurs only here and in 17:3 in the Gospel of John (see, however, 1 Jn 1:3; 2:1; 3:23; 4:2; 5:6, 20; 2 Jn 3, 7).

76. The placement of the adverb "ever" (πώποτε) last in the English sentence reflects the emphasis it has in the Greek (this adverb recurs in 5:37 and in 1 Jn 4:12, though not in the same emphatic position).

77. The same word order was present in verse 1 (καὶ θεὸς ἦν ὁ λόγος).

The Gospel of John

Only" (thus, *monogenēs theos*, "God the One and Only"),[78] recalling "a father's One and Only" (v. 14), and here further described as "the One who is[79] right beside the Father."[80] The terminology makes it clear that "the One and Only" is himself God, as surely as "the Word was God" at the beginning (v. 1). His place "right beside the Father" (literally, "in the Father's bosom")[81] echoes the assertion at the outset that the Word was "with God" (v. 1; compare "with the Father," 1 Jn 1:2), and it would be easy to infer that this is a glimpse of the postresurrection Jesus, corresponding to the preexistent Jesus of the Gospel's opening verses.[82] Yet there is no "now" in the sentence, and the accent is more on the nature and status of "God the One and Only" than on the time reference of the pronouncement.

The two clauses, "No one has seen God, ever," and "It was God the One and Only . . . who told about him," stand quite independent of one another grammatically, requiring us to infer the precise relationship between them. For example, "No one has seen God"; *therefore* "God the One and Only . . . told about him," or "No one has seen God," *but at least* "God the One and Only . . . told about him," or "No one has seen God"; *instead* "God the One and Only . . . told about him."[83] In any event, because "No one has

---

78. This is the reading of the best and most ancient manuscripts (P⁶⁶, ℵ*, B, C*, and others), and of the NIV ("God the One and Only") and NRSV ("God the Only Son"), while A, Θ, and the majority of later manuscripts read ὁ μονογενὴς υἱός, followed by the KJV ("the only-begotten Son") and the RSV ("the only Son"). The latter is by far the easier reading; "Son" and "One and Only" go naturally together, while "God" and "One and Only" do not. Later scribes would have tended to change the less familiar μονογενὴς θεός into the more familiar ὁ μονογενὴς υἱός (compare Jn 3:16, 18; 1 Jn 4:9), not the other way around.

79. On "the One who is [ὁ ὤν] as a designation for God, see Exodus 3:14 LXX, as well as Philo, Josephus, and, in the New Testament, Revelation 1:4, 8; 4:8; 11:17; 16:5. Whether or not ὁ ὤν is intended to reinforce θεός here is difficult to say. Later, when this Gospel has the opportunity to use ὁ ὤν with ἐγώ εἰμι (as in Exod 3:14, LXX), it does not do so (see 8:24, 28, 58; 13:19).

80. The indefinite "a father" of verse 14 now becomes definite. This is the first of many references (most of them on the lips of Jesus) to "the Father" in distinction from "the Son."

81. Gr. εἰς τὸν κόλπον τοῦ πατρός. According to the NRSV, "close to the Father's heart"; compare 13:23, where "the disciple whom Jesus loved" is first introduced reclining at table "at Jesus' side" (ἐν τῷ κόλπῳ τοῦ Ἰησοῦ).

82. Bultmann, for example, asks, "Does it refer to the pre-existent one, who was in the bosom of the Father, or to the post-existent one, who is now with the Father?" (82), and considers it more likely "that ὤν is to be taken as a true present, and that it is therefore said of the Revealer who has returned to the Father" (82, n. 6).

83. Just such a connective (εἰ μή, "except that") is added in one later Greek manuscript (W), in old Latin versions, and in Latin citations in Irenaeus (compare the εἰ μή, "except," in 3:13 and 6:46).

seen God, ever," hearing takes the place of seeing. Faith here, as in Paul, "comes by hearing" (compare Rom 10:17), and this is all the more appropriate in a setting where Jesus Christ has been introduced as "the Word." He is now said to have acted as the Word when he "told about" God. "Told about" *(exēgēsato)* can be a rather straightforward, even colorless, term for reporting something or telling a story,[84] or it can be an almost technical term for delivering revelations from the gods or authoritative interpretations of sacred writings.[85] Here it is almost certainly the former. There is no evidence (unless this is it) for a technical use of this word anywhere in the New Testament or early Christian literature. But it is not for that reason unimportant; the assertion that Jesus "told about" God presupposes that he is the exception to the principle laid down in the first half of the verse.[86] Because he is himself God, and "right beside the Father," he (and he alone) has seen God and can therefore "tell about" God.[87] This he will do in the narrative to follow, though not immediately.[88]

C. JOHN AND JESUS (1:19-34)

> 19 *And this is the testimony of John when the Jews sent priests and Levites to him from Jerusalem to ask him, "Who are you?"* 20 *And he confessed, and did not deny; he confessed that "I am not the Christ."* 21 *And they asked him, "What, then? Are you Elias?" And he said, "I am not." "Are you the Prophet?" And he answered, "No."* 22 *So they*

---

84. See Luke 24:35; Acts 10:8; 15:12, 14; 21:19.
85. See F. Büchsel, in *TDNT,* 2.908; BDAG, 349.
86. Compare 6:46, "Not that anyone has seen the Father except [εἰ μή] he who is from God, he has seen the Father." The Gospel of John repeatedly mentions things Jesus has seen in the presence of the Father which he now communicates to the world (see 3:11, 32; 5:19; 8:38). The link between seeing God and being able to reveal God is evident in Sirach's rhetorical question, "Who has seen him and will describe him?" (τίς ἑόρακεν αὐτὸν καὶ ἐκδιηγήσεται, Sirach 43.31, LXX). As Büchsel notes (*TDNT,* 2.908), "Jn 1:18 is like an intentional answer to this question."
87. Another, more subtle, interpretation is that ἐξηγήσατο should be interpreted according to its etymological meaning, "to lead." See, for example, Boismard (*Le Prologue de Saint Jean,* 91, 95): "Il nous a conduit dans le sein du Père" (that is, "He has led us to the bosom of the Father"). R. Robert (*Revue Thomiste* 87.3 [1987], 435-41, and 89.2 [1989], 279-88) tries to combine the meanings, "to tell, or narrate" and "to lead, or guide." For a refutation, see R. H. Gundry, *Jesus the Word According to John the Sectarian* (Grand Rapids: Eerdmans, 2002), 98-100.
88. Moloney (47) struggles with the fact that ἐξηγήσατο has no direct object, thus inviting the rather forced interpretations described just above. He concludes, wisely, that "The object of the verb (God) must be supplied by the reader: 'He has told God's story.'"

The Gospel of John

said to him, "Who are you? We have to give an answer to those who sent us. What do you say about yourself?" 23 He said, "I am a voice of one crying in the desert, 'Make straight the way of the Lord,' just as Isaiah the prophet said." 24 And they were sent from the Pharisees. 25 And they asked him, and said to him, "Why then do you baptize, if you are not the Christ, nor Elias, nor the Prophet?" 26 John answered them, saying, "I baptize in water; among you stands One whom you do not know, 27 the One who comes after me, the strap of whose sandal I am not worthy to untie." 28 These things came about in Bethany, across the Jordan, where John was baptizing.

29 The next day he sees Jesus coming to him and says, "Look, the Lamb of God, who takes away the sin of the world. 30 This is he of whom I said, 'After me comes a man who has gotten ahead of me, because he was before me.' 31 And I did not know him, but the reason I came baptizing in water was so that he might be revealed to Israel." 32 And so John testified, saying that "I have watched the Spirit coming down as a dove out of the sky, and it remained on him. 33 And I did not know him, but the One who sent me to baptize in water said to me, 'Whoever it is on whom you see the Spirit coming down and remaining on him, this is he who baptizes in Holy Spirit.' 34 And I have seen, and have testified that this is the Son of God."[1]

The account of John's testimony picks up where it left off in verses 6-8 and 15. The whole section from verses 19 to 34 encompasses two testimonies, one negative and one positive, framed by the noun "testimony" in verse 19 and the verb "testify" in verses 32 and 34. The negative testimony in verses 19-28 has a specific setting in an encounter between John and a delegation sent from Jerusalem to question him (v. 19).[2] In verses 29-34 there is no longer any sign of this delegation, and John's positive testimony seems directed to no one audience in particular. Yet his pronouncements about Jesus speak directly to the delegation's concerns. For example, the question, "Why then do you baptize?" (v. 25), is not answered until John says, "the reason I came baptizing in water was so that he might be revealed to Israel" (v. 31). The mysterious phrase, "the One who comes after me" (v. 27), is more fully explained in verse 30, "After me comes a man who has gotten ahead of me, be-

---

1. Some ancient manuscripts and versions (א, afterward corrected, plus the old Latin *b* and *e* and the old Syriac versions) read "the Chosen One of God" (ὁ ἐκλεκτός τοῦ θεοῦ) instead of "the Son of God" (ὁ υἱός τοῦ θεοῦ). Other old Latin witnesses read *electus filius*, "the Chosen Son," a reading reflected also in the Sahidic Coptic. The overwhelming manuscript evidence, however, favors "the Son of God."

2. Some manuscripts (for example, P^{66}, P^{75}, and א) omit the words "to him" (πρὸς αὐτόν), but the variant makes little difference in the meaning.

cause he was before me" (compare v. 15). The claim that "I baptize in water" (v. 26) is left hanging until John completes the contrast with the information that the One coming after him is the One "who baptizes in Holy Spirit" (v. 33).[3] In short, the issues raised by the delegation on one day are resolved on the next, not for the delegation's benefit but for the readers of the Gospel. This is John's two-pronged testimony. Part one is negative and is terminated by a notice of place ("in Bethany," v. 28), while part two is positive and is introduced with a notice of time ("the next day," v. 29). We will look at them separately.

19 Verses 19-28 are linked to the preceding material by "And" (v. 19), once more resisting the notion that verses 1-18 should be set apart from the rest of the Gospel as "Prologue." The clause "And this is [rather than "this was"] the testimony of John" gives to the testimony a certain contemporary quality, like the testimony of verses 15 and 16. At the same time, however, it calls attention to a particular occasion in the past, probably well into John's ministry rather than near its beginning. John had by this time attracted enough attention for the religious establishment in Jerusalem to want to find out who he was and what he was claiming for himself.[4] "You" in the delegation's question is emphatic, as if challenging John: "You — who are you?" or "Who do you think you are?"

"The Jews" as an identifiable group are here introduced for the first time in the Gospel. The context makes clear that they are the religious leaders of Israel, for they have the authority to send out envoys to investigate John's claims and conduct. Because the delegation consists of "priests and Levites" (two terms occurring nowhere else in this Gospel), we are given the impression that "the Jews" too are a priestly group, presumably the "chief priests" mentioned in ten other places in the Gospel.[5] This would be appropriate because the delegation is concerned about John's baptism, a matter of ritual purity (see 3:25). But more likely, "the Jews" *(hoi Ioudaioi)* serves here and throughout the Gospel as an umbrella term for both priestly and scribal lead-

---

3. Compare Mark 1:6: "I baptize you in water, but he will baptize you in Holy Spirit." Dodd traces what he calls a "disjunction" between the two parts of the saying about water and Spirit baptism in Matthew (3:11), Luke (3:16), and especially here in John, where the two parts of the saying stand seven verses (and one whole day) apart (*Historical Tradition,* 253-54).

4. Compare Luke 3:15-16, where, after a considerable summary of John's preaching (3:7-14), the people begin to ask "in their hearts concerning John, whether he might be the Christ," and he answers their unspoken question with the pronouncement, "I indeed baptize in water, but the One mightier than I is coming. . . . He will baptize you in Holy Spirit and fire." In retrospect, Luke places this exchange at a time "when John was finishing his course" (Acts 13:25).

5. See 7:32, 45; 11:47, 49; 12:10; 18:3, 35; 19:6, 15, 21.

ers in Israel,[6] especially in Jerusalem.[7] Because of the close link to Jerusalem, "Judeans" (that is, residents of Judea) is a possible translation in some places,[8] but the accent in the term is on religion rather than geography, specifically on religious authority and the determination of religious practice. Whether rendered as "Jews" or "Judeans," the term reflects the perspective of those outside rather than within Judaism.[9] Its use here suggests that the Gospel was written for a predominantly Gentile-Christian audience.

20 John, probably with good reason, interprets the delegation's question "Who are you?" as "Are you the Christ?" (see Lk 3:15), and answers accordingly. The first clue that the question may have been asked with hostile intent is the language of his reply: "And he confessed, and did not deny; he confessed that 'I am not the Christ'" (v. 20).[10] The repetition of "and he confessed" is striking, and just as striking is its negative reinforcement with the words, "and did not deny" — this in spite of the fact that what he issues is patently a denial![11] "Confessed" does not refer to confession of sins but to maintaining one's allegiance to Jesus Christ in the face of hostile interrogation, and this is what John is doing here implicitly. On a later occa-

---

6. Priests were distinguished from scribes by their involvement in the temple cult. "Scribes," in particular the Pharisees, were lay scholars and teachers of the law.

7. The Greek word order, in fact, allows the reading, "the Jews from Jerusalem." Throughout the Gospel are references to various "festivals of the Jews" in Jerusalem, governing further references to "the Jews" in narratives and discourses to follow; see, for example, 2:13 (governing 2:18, 20 and 3:1); 5:1 (governing 5:10, 15, 16, 18); 7:2 (governing 7:11, 13, 15, 35; 8:22, 31, 48, 52, 57; 9:21-22; 10:19, 24, 31, 33), and 11:55 (governing 12:9, 11, etc.).

8. See, for example, 7:1, "After this Jesus walked in Galilee, for he would not walk in Judea (ἐν τῇ Ἰουδαίᾳ), because the Jews (οἱ Ἰουδαῖοι) were seeking to kill him"; also 11:7-8, "Then after this he said to his disciples, 'Let us go into Judea [εἰς τὴν Ἰουδαίαν] again'; his disciples said to him, 'Rabbi, now the Jews [οἱ Ἰουδαῖοι] are seeking to stone you, and you are going there again?'" (see also 3:25). Only in chapter 6 do we see "the Jews" in Galilee (6:41, 52), possibly because we are told at the outset (as in the Jerusalem discourses) that "the Passover was near, a festival of the Jews" (6:4; compare 2:13, 5:1, 7:2, and 11:13; see n. 6).

9. See M. Stern (ed.), *Greek and Latin Authors on Judaism* (3 vols.; Jerusalem: Israel Academy of Sciences and Humanities, 1976-84), passim.

10. The "I" (ἐγώ) is emphatic, echoing the emphatic "you" (σύ) in the delegation's question (v. 19). A possible implication is that although John is not the Christ, someone else, not too far away (compare μέσος ὑμῶν, v. 26) *is* the Christ.

11. The Mormon "Inspired Version" of the Bible makes dramatic changes at this point: "And he confessed, and denied not that he was Elias; but confessed, saying, I am not the Christ. And they asked him, saying, How then art thou Elias? And he said, I am not that Elias who was to restore all things." *Joseph Smith's "New Translation" of the Bible*, 444. The concern to harmonize John's disclaimer with Matthew 11:14 and 17:12 is evident.

sion, "the Jews" are said to have "already decided" that anyone who "confessed" Jesus as the Christ would be put out of the synagogue (9:22; compare 12:42). Here the readers of the Gospel know, because John "came for a testimony, to testify about the light" (v. 7; compare vv. 15-16), that when he says, "I am not the Christ," he means that "the Christ" is Jesus![12] John's apparent denial is actually a confession of his faith in "the Christ," so that "the Jews" and their delegation are thwarted. He tells them nothing, while at the same time bearing implicit testimony to Jesus. The readers also seem to know that John was eventually imprisoned for his testimony,[13] and his language here allows them to conclude that he was imprisoned as a confessing Christian. His disclaimer, "I am not the Christ," echoes and reinforces the notion that "he was not the light" (v. 8). While both passages may reflect an awareness of some who honored John as "the light" or as "the Christ," the purpose of the disclaimer is not to put John down but to set the stage for his explicit testimony to Jesus in the section to follow.

The full name "Jesus Christ" has been used in verse 17, but this is the first mention of the title "the Christ" (*ho Christos,* literally "the Anointed One"), the Greek equivalent of "the Messiah" (v. 41), who was expected to come (presumably as King) "from the seed of David and from Bethlehem, the village where David was" (7:42). "The Christ" was also expected, by some at least, to perform many "signs" or miracles (7:31) when he came, and to "remain forever" (12:34), and by the Samaritan woman to "tell us all things" (4:25). To the Christian readers of the Gospel, he is also "the Son of God," and above all he is Jesus. The Gospel's whole purpose is that its readers might believe "that Jesus is the Christ, the Son of God, and that believing you might have life in his name" (20:31; compare 11:27). John, in his answer to the Jerusalem delegation, is the first to articulate that belief, however indirect and implicit his "confession" may be.

21 The delegation has not asked, "Are you the Christ?" in so many words, but in light of John's reply they proceed as if they had: "What, then? Are you Elias?"[14] The expectation that Elijah would return to prepare the peo-

---

12. "Confessing" (rather than "denying") Jesus as the Christ or Son of God is supremely important not only in the Johannine writings (compare 1 Jn 2:22-23; 4:2-3, 15), but elsewhere in the New Testament (see, for example, Mt 10:32-33; Lk 12:8-9). For this reason, Bultmann's comment that "Ὁμολογεῖν does not of course refer here to the confession of faith, but is used like ἀρνεῖσθαι as a juridical term" (38, n. 1) rests on a false dichotomy.

13. This is evident in a later parenthetical remark, "for John had not yet been thrown into prison" (3:24). No further explanation is necessary because the writer assumes that the story of John's imprisonment is well known.

14. We have used the Greek-derived spelling "Elias" in our translation, based on the Greek text, but the more familiar "Elijah" in discussion, in keeping with the Hebrew Bible and most modern English translations.

ple for the day of the Lord is as old as the prophecy of Malachi, where the pronouncement, "See, I will send my messenger, who will prepare the way before me" (Mal 3:1, NIV), anticipates the concluding promise, "See, I will send you the prophet Elijah before that great and dreadful day of the LORD comes" (Mal 4:5; compare Sirach 48.10). In the synoptic tradition, John himself becomes an Elijah figure, explicitly in Matthew (11:14; 17:12-13), implicitly in Mark (1:2; 9:13) and Luke (1:17), on the assumption that Elijah prepares the way not for God, or the "great and dreadful day of the LORD," but for Jesus the Messiah.[15] But John's Gospel seems to reflect the older tradition, going back to Malachi and Sirach, in which Elijah is the forerunner not of "the Christ," but of the God of Israel, and therefore a messianic figure in his own right. This is the Elijah figure John has in mind when he says, "I am not." Next the delegation asks, "Are you the Prophet?" and again the answer is no. The Gospel writer does not pause over these second and third denials to insist that they are actually confessions, as in the case of "I am not the Christ." If he had written, "Again John confessed and said, 'I am not,'" we might have inferred that John was implicitly acknowledging *Jesus* as "Elijah" and "the Prophet," as well as "the Christ," but as it is we have no clear signal that this is the case.[16] If John thought of Jesus as Elijah, it would explain why he twice identifies Jesus as someone who "was before me" (vv. 15, 30),[17] and yet the readers of the Gospel are intended to understand Jesus' preexistence in terms of his identity as "the Word" (vv. 1-2), not as an Elijah figure. There is no evidence in the Gospel of John that Jesus fulfills the Elijah role.

As for "the Prophet," the title seems to have been derived from the promise of Moses that "The LORD your God will raise up for you a prophet like me from among your brothers. You must listen to him" (Deut 18:15, NIV). Of such a prophet, God had told Moses, "I will put my words in his mouth, and he will tell them everything I command him. If anyone does not

---

15. Justin Martyr in the second century attributed to his Jewish opponent Trypho the notion that "Christ — if He has indeed been born and exists anywhere — is unknown, and does not even know Himself, and has no power until Elias come to anoint Him, and make Him manifest [φανερόν] to all" (*Dialogue with Trypho* 8.4; ANF, 1.199). The statement appears to rest in part on Jewish tradition and in part on Christian traditions about John and Jesus: on the one hand the synoptic notion that John was Elijah, and on the other the evidence of the fourth Gospel that John (even though *not* Elijah) baptized Jesus so that he might be "revealed [φανερωθῇ] to Israel" (Jn 1:31).

16. The delegation's second and third questions are as emphatic as the first: "Are you [σύ] Elijah?" and "Are you [σύ] the Prophet?" But John's answers become less and less emphatic: "I am not" (οὐκ εἰμί, without the emphatic ἐγώ), and simply "No," suggesting that he is not attributing these titles to Jesus or anyone else in particular (contrast n. 10).

17. See Brown, 1.64; J. A. T. Robinson, "Elijah, John, and Jesus: An Essay in Detection," *Twelve New Testament Studies* (Naperville, IL: Allenson, 1962), 30.

listen to my words that the prophet speaks in my name, I myself will call him to account" (18:18-19). On the other hand, "a prophet who presumes to speak in my name anything I have not commanded him to say . . . must be put to death" (18:20). An expectation of "the Prophet" as a single messianic figure fulfilling Deuteronomy 18:15-18 is not widely attested in Judaism. A number of texts look forward instead to a reinstitution of the prophetic office (for example, 1 Macc 4:46; 14:41; compare 9:27). Yet the desert community at Qumran prescribed that its members follow the rules taught by its founders "until the prophet comes, and the messiahs of Aaron and Israel" (1QS 9.11; compare 4QTestimonia).[18] Luke knows of such an expectation in Judaism, applying the Deuteronomy prophecy to Jesus in one of Peter's speeches (Acts 3:22; compare v. 26), and (less clearly) in Stephen's (7:37). In John's Gospel, Deuteronomy 18 seems to inform Jesus' language when he insists that the words he speaks are not his own, but are words the Father has given him and commanded him to speak (for example, 7:17-18; 8:28; 12:49-50; 14:10). Yet his use of the term "Father" betrays the fact that "the Son," not "the Prophet," is his operative self-designation.[19] He is identified twice as "the Prophet" by others (6:14; 7:40), but not by any who would qualify as reliable examples of the kind of faith the readers of the Gospel ought to have.[20] In itself, John's admission that he is neither "Elijah" nor "the Prophet" tells us nothing about Jesus.

22 The delegation presses its question again, this time dropping the emphatic "you," with its note of challenge. With this, they invite John to state his identity in his own terms. Their use of the phrase "those who sent us" reminds us once again that they are a delegation from "the Jews" in Jerusalem,[21]

---

18. See F. García Martiínez, *The Dead Sea Scrolls Translated* (Leiden: Brill, 1994), 13-14, 137.

19. See Hebrews 1:1-2: "In the past God spoke to our forefathers through the *prophets*, . . . but in these last days he has spoken to us by his *Son*" (my italics). When John's disciples identify Jesus as one of whom "Moses wrote" (1:45), or when Jesus himself claims that Moses "wrote about me" (5:46), Deuteronomy 18 may well be in mind along with other texts, but with the implication that Jesus is "the Christ" or "the Messiah" in a general sense (see 1:41), not specifically "the Prophet" of Deuteronomy 18.

20. In 6:14 it is a conclusion reached about Jesus by those to want to take him by force and make him king (v. 15), while in 7:40 it is simply a spontaneous reaction of some in the crowds around Jesus, a title linked loosely to "the Christ" (vv. 41-42; compare v. 52). "Prophet" (without the article) is used twice (4:19; 9:17) by those who are not yet believers, but on their way to true faith. Only once (4:44) does Jesus, even implicitly, refer to himself as "a prophet."

21. Somewhat ironically, the same phrase anticipates John's (1:33) and Jesus' own repeated references to "the One who sent me" (4:34; 5:24, 30; 6:38, 39; 7:16, 18, 28, 33; 8:26, 29; 9:4; 12:44, 45; 13:20; 15:21; 16:5), or "the Father who sent me" (5:23, 37; 6:44; 8:16, 18; 12:49; 14:24).

the real antagonists of both John and Jesus. Far from challenging John, they are almost pleading with him for an answer so that they will not be in trouble with "the Jews" for coming back empty-handed (compare the plight of those sent to arrest Jesus at the Feast of Tabernacles in 7:32-36, 45-49). Their plea sets the stage for John's self-description in the next verse.

23 All four Gospels describe John the Baptist with a quotation from Isaiah 40:3 (compare Mk 1:3, Mt 3:3, and Lk 3:4), but only here is the quotation attributed to John himself. The Gospel writer even calls attention to John as the speaker by prefacing his pronouncement with the delegation's question, "What do you say about yourself?" (v. 22). "I," he replies, "am a voice of one crying in the desert, 'Make straight the way of the Lord,' just as Isaiah the prophet said." While the last clause, "just as Isaiah the prophet said," could be a parenthetical comment by the Gospel writer, it is more likely part of John's reply.[22] The same text was cited by the Qumran community as a justification for their withdrawal to the Judean desert (1QS 8.14), but our Gospel divides the text differently and puts no particular emphasis on the phrase "in the desert."[23] While the quotation preserves the older tradition that John carried on his ministry in the desert, its purpose is not to locate his activity geographically. In this Gospel, in fact, John is seen preaching and baptizing *not* in the desert but in villages (such as "Aenon, near Salim," 3:23) with ample water supplies.

The purpose of the quotation is rather to present John as a solitary and anonymous "voice" *(phōnē)* for God, the first such voice within the Gospel story.[24] Although a clear distinction is evident between "the Word" (vv. 1-2, 14) and a mere "voice,"[25] yet even a "voice" is no small thing. Jesus' own voice will echo and reecho through the Gospel, and those who belong to him

---

22. John's words, "Isaiah the prophet," echo the delegation's inquiry about "the prophet" (v. 21). Although John is not "the prophet," he fulfills the prophecy of one biblical prophet in particular.

23. John, like the other three Gospels, construes "in the desert" with what precedes ("a voice of one crying in the desert"), while the Qumran community, both in 1QIs[a] and in 1QS 8.14, followed the Masoretic division ("In the desert, prepare the way," García Martínez, 12). Aside from this indirect reference, the fourth Gospel does not even locate John's ministry in the desert (contrast Mk 1:4; Mt 3:1; 11:7; Lk 1:80; 3:2; 7:24).

24. Origen comments, "But he cries and shouts that both those who are afar may hear him speaking and those who are hard of hearing may understand" (*Commentary*, 6.100). "For what other wilderness," he asks, "is harder to deal with than a soul that is bereft of God and of all virtue?" (6.102; FC, 80.196-97).

25. A similar distinction is made in 5:35, where John, who we know "was not the light" (τὸ φῶς, 1:7), is called "the burning and shining lamp" (ὁ λύχνος). Brown (1.43) cites Augustine to the effect that "John the Baptist was a voice for a while (John v. 35), but Christ is the eternal Word in the beginning" (compare also Origen, *Commentary*, 6.94, 98; FC, 80.195-96).

will be those who "hear his voice" (compare 5:25, 28; 10:3-5, 16, 27; 18:37). As for John, he claims no messianic role or dignity for himself. Later, in his only other self-identification in the Gospel, he will call himself "the bridegroom's friend who stands by and hears him, and rejoices with joy at the voice of the bridegroom" (3:29). To him, Jesus is both "the bridegroom" and the coming "Lord" whose way must be made straight.[26] To the delegation, "the Lord" is simply the God of Israel, but John will soon alert them that someone else is in the picture (vv. 26-27). The imperative, "make straight," in the quotation is the only hint in this Gospel that John called the Jewish people to repentance.[27] Everywhere else, his sole mission is to testify about Jesus and make him known to "Israel" (1:31).

24 The Gospel writer now supplies the information parenthetically (and belatedly) that the delegation was "sent from the Pharisees."[28] "Sent" ironically echoes the earlier notice that John himself was "sent" from God (v. 6). Two "missions" confront one another here, John's mission from God and the delegation's mission from "the Jews" (v. 19). "Pharisees" helps define "the Jews." The parenthetical comment seems to contradict what has gone before because the Pharisees were emphatically not a priestly group, and would not have been likely to send out a delegation of "priests and Levites." But the Gospel writer, probably with a Gentile readership in mind, is not interested in fine distinctions between scribal and priestly authority. Later he will describe "the chief priests and Pharisees" as acting together repeatedly to have Jesus arrested (7:32, 45; 11:47, 57; 18:3), and the same alliance is presupposed here.[29]

---

26. That Jesus is "Lord" (κύριος) is the view not only of the Gospel writer at several points in the narrative (4:1; 6:23; 11:2; 20:20; 21:12), but of Jesus' disciples (13:13; compare the repeated address κύριε), above all in the setting of Jesus' resurrection (20:2, 13, 18, 25, 28; 21:7).

27. Εὐθύνατε replaces the ἑτοιμάσατε ("prepare") of the LXX, and of Matthew, Mark, and Luke. John's Gospel appears to have telescoped Isaiah 40:3a with v. 3b, εὐθείας ποιεῖτε, "make straight the paths of our God."

28. Some ancient manuscripts, including the majority of later ones, add a definite article οἱ before ἀπεσταλμένοι, suggesting the translation, "And those who were sent were of the Pharisees" (that is, they themselves belonged to the Pharisees). This would directly contradict the assertion that they were "priests and Levites" (v. 19). The most significant ancient manuscripts, however (including P[66], P[75], ℵ*, B, A*, and C*, and Origen) omit the article, which has the effect of making ἀπεσταλμένοι ἦσαν a periphrastic construction ("they were sent"), as in our translation.

29. Another interpretation, as old as Origen, finds here a second delegation, by reading the text, "And [some] were sent also from the Pharisees." According to Origen, "two embassies come to the Baptist. One consists of 'priests and Levites' sent from Jerusalem by the Jews. . . . The other comes from the Pharisees, who send also because they are in doubt about the answer which had been given to the priests and Levites" (*Commen-*

25 The delegation goes on to ask, "Why then do you baptize, if you are not the Christ, nor Elias, nor the Prophet?" This is the first mention of John's activity as a baptizer, and it comes rather abruptly. Evidently the readers are expected to know already that this "John" is actually "John the Baptist" (see Mt 3:1; Mk 6:25; Lk 7:20, 33) or "John the Baptizer" (Mk 1:4; 6:14, 24). Three verses later the Gospel writer finally makes explicit that "John was baptizing" (v. 28), but even there the interest is not in what he was doing but in where he was doing it. John's baptizing activity, we now learn, is the reason the delegation came to him in the first place. Once-for-all ritual baptism was used in Judaism only for proselytes, and anyone presuming to baptize those who were already Jews by birth was in effect putting them in the position of proselytes. Such a procedure would have signaled that a new age was at hand and that all Israel needed cleansing.

The delegation's assumption seems to have been that certain messianic figures would "baptize" at the beginning of the messianic age, probably in the sense of purifying the world, or Israel in particular, from sin. To them, consequently, anyone who baptized in water was making some kind of messianic claim. Their belief, while not explicitly documented in Judaism, has its roots in biblical prophecy, where God is the One who will purify Israel and no distinction is made between cleansing with water and cleansing by the Spirit. The best example is Ezekiel 36:25-27: "I will sprinkle clean water on you, and you will be clean; I will cleanse you from all your impurities and from all your idols. I will give you a new heart and put a new spirit in you; I will remove from you your heart of stone and give you a heart of flesh. And I will put my Spirit in you and move you to follow my decrees and be careful to keep my laws" (NIV).[30] For those who expected such figures as "the Christ," or "Elijah," or "the Prophet," it was natural to suppose that they would be the instruments through whom God would carry out this great work of purification.

---

tary on John, 6.50; FC, 80.182). Origen, like others since, was misled by the apparent discrepancy between priests and Levites and the Pharisees, for he went on (6.51-52) to contrast the "gentleness and curiosity" of the priests and Levites, as "scrupulous servants of God," with the "arrogant and rather senseless words" of the Pharisees (in v. 25). Some modern commentators, without proposing two embassies, nevertheless find here a new line of questioning introduced by the notice that the delegation included some Pharisees (for example, Brown, 1.43-44; Dodd, *Tradition,* 263-64).

30. Brown (1.51) adds to this Zechariah 13:1 ("On that day a fountain will be opened to the house of David and the inhabitants of Jerusalem, to cleanse them from sin and impurity," NIV), and from the Qumran literature 1QS 4.20-21, where God "will purify for himself the configuration of man, . . . cleansing him with the spirit of holiness from every irreverent deed," and "sprinkle over him the spirit of truth like lustral water (in order to cleanse him) from all the abhorrences of deceit and from the defilement of the unclean spirit" (García Martínez, 7).

26 John replies with an implied distinction between water baptism and the eschatological cleansing his questioners have in mind: "I baptize in water; among you stands One whom you do not know." The implication is that this other figure will carry out a far more significant baptism than John's. He is the One with whom they should be concerned. Those familiar with the synoptic tradition will expect him at this point to say that such a One will baptize "in Holy Spirit" (Mk 1:8), or "in Holy Spirit and fire" (Mt 3:11; Lk 3:16). He finally does (v. 33), but not until the next day, and not (so far as we know) in the presence of the delegation from Jerusalem. Instead, he taunts the delegation with two disturbingly contradictory pieces of information: first, that this greater One already "stands among you";[31] second, that he is someone "*you* do not know" (italics added). The emphatic "you" *(hymeis)* implies that John does know him, and later he will tell the readers of the Gospel (without the delegation present) how he learned of him (see vv. 32-34). Bultmann is quick to comment that John "does not of course mean that Jesus is present in person,"[32] but J. H. Bernard is not so sure: "Apparently Jesus was actually present on this occasion, which was subsequent to His Baptism. . . . there is no record, at any rate, of [John's] being further questioned as to what he meant, or to which person in the company his words were applicable" (compare NLT, "right here in the crowd").[33] Behind John's strange remark lies a traditional Jewish notion of the hidden Messiah who comes into the world but remains incognito until it is time for him to be revealed.[34] The phrase "among you" is probably intended to place him not specifically on the

---

31. Metzger (*Textual Commentary,* 199) comments that the perfect tense of the verb ἕστηκεν (the reading of both the Bible Society and the Nestle text) "conveys a special force here (something like, 'there is One who has taken his stand in your midst')." It is the reading of P[66], A, C, and the majority of later manuscripts. Other witnesses (including B and L) read what Metzger calls "the more syntactically appropriate present tense" (στήκει). But the difference between the two readings need not be reflected in translation. The perfect here (like κέκραγεν, "has cried out," in v. 15) is simply the equivalent of a dramatic present (hence our translation, "among you stands"). The fact that most ancient versions (Latin, Syriac, and Coptic) translated the verb as present tells us little as to which Greek reading they had in front of them.
32. Bultmann, 91, n. 2.
33. Bernard, 1.40.
34. See, for example, *4 Ezra* 12.32: "This is the Messiah whom the Most High has kept until the end of days"; also 13.52: "Just as no one can explore or know what is in the depths of the sea, so no one on earth can see my Son or those who are with him, except in the time of his day" (*OTP,* 1.550, 553). See also Justin Martyr, *Dialogue* 8.4 (see above, n. 15), and especially *Dialogue* 110.1, "Now I am aware that your teachers . . . maintain He has not yet come; or if they say that He has come, they assert that it is not known who He is [οὐ γινώσκεται ὅς ἐστιν]; but when He shall become manifest and glorious [ἐμφανὴς καὶ ἔνδοξος], then it shall be known who He is" (ANF, 1.253).

scene or among the delegation, but more broadly among "the Jews" whom the delegation represents. The "you" has an adversarial sound: the Messiah (if that is the proper term) is among *you,* John says, and yet *you* do not know him![35] John's role is to make him known, not to the delegation or to the religious establishment in Jerusalem, but to "Israel" (see v. 31).

27 John next provides the delegation a tantalizing clue, with the phrase "the One who comes after me" (v. 27). The reader has seen this phrase before (v. 15) and knows to whom it refers, but the delegation from Jerusalem does not. "The Coming One" *(ho erchomenos),* or "the One coming into the world," was a familiar phrase in Jewish expectation, either as a title in itself or in connection with other titles such as "the Prophet" (6:14) or "the Christ" (11:27). Jesus is hailed at his triumphal entry with the words, "Blessed is the Coming One," not only in our Gospel (Jn 12:13) but in all four (compare Mk 11:9//Mt 21:9//Lk 19:38). According to Matthew (11:3) and Luke (7:19), John the Baptist himself sent word to Jesus from prison, asking, "Are you the Coming One, or do we look for another?" The delegation would have recognized "the One who comes" as a messianic title comparable to the three they had mentioned, but what could "the One who comes *after me"* possibly mean on the lips of one who renounced all such titles for himself? That the Coming One would come *after* John had departed the scene? Hardly, for John had just stated that the Coming One was already present. That the Coming One was John's disciple? The expression, "to come after" someone, can mean to follow as a disciple (as in Mt 16:24; Lk 9:23; 14:27), yet how could John disclaim messianic status and in the same breath claim a messianic figure as one of his followers? Surely the phrase "the One who comes after me," a mere fragment of a longer pronouncement (1:15; also v. 30),[36] would have raised more questions than it answered for the delegation of priests and Levites, and those they represented.

Next, John makes explicit what so far he has only hinted at, that the

---

35. To Brown (1.53), John's words are "not meant as a reproach to the audience for its blindness, for John the Baptist freely admits (v. 33) that he himself could not recognize Jesus without help from God." Yet the language echoes 1:10 ("He was in the world . . . and [yet] the world did not know him"), and parallels the words of Jesus at certain points in the Gospel (for example, 7:28b-29; 8:14, 19, 55; 17:25), as well as the adversarial reply of the man born blind that "you do not know where he is from [ὑμεῖς οὐκ οἴδατε πόθεν ἐστίν], and yet he opened my eyes" (9:30). John's implication is that God has withheld the revelation from the Jerusalem establishment and entrusted it to his chosen messengers.

36. Later copyists seem to have sensed the abruptness and incompleteness of the phrase, for in A and in the majority of later Greek manuscripts (as well as most Latin and the later Syriac versions), the words from 1:30, "who has gotten ahead of me" (ὃς ἔμπροσθέν μου γέγονεν; compare v. 15) have been added.

Coming One is indeed greater than he. His metaphor is that this is One "the strap of whose sandal I am not worthy to untie" (compare Mk 1:7; Mt 3:11; Lk 3:16; Acts 13:25). In contrast to the synoptic Gospels but in agreement with Acts, the text here omits mentioning explicitly "One stronger than I." It also agrees with Acts against the Synoptics in its use of "sandal" in the singular rather than the plural, and of "worthy" *(axios)* instead of "sufficient." Yet it agrees with Mark and Luke (against Matthew and Acts) in mentioning the "strap" of the sandal, with Mark and Matthew (against Acts) in using an ambiguous expression *(opisō mou)* for "after me," in preference to a clearly temporal one *(met' eme,* as in Acts 13:25; Lk 3:16, lacks the prepositional phrase altogether). And it agrees with Matthew alone in adopting the full participial expression ("the One who comes after me"). It appears that the Gospel of John is either making use of all three of the other Gospels and Acts, or none of them, and the odds strongly favor none. C. H. Dodd has argued convincingly "that this part of the Baptist's preaching . . . was preserved in several branches of the tradition, and that variations arose in the process of oral transmission. . . . it would be unsafe to assume that the significant features peculiar to the Fourth Gospel in this passage are no more than the author's free embellishments of matter drawn at second hand from the Synoptics."[37] The Gospel writer seems to have chosen carefully from this common tradition to direct some of John's words (vv. 26-27) to the delegation from Jerusalem, and others (vv. 30 and 33) to the Christian readers of the Gospel. The effect is to keep John's questioners in the dark, while making Jesus known to those prepared to follow him (vv. 29-34).

28 The Gospel writer now intervenes to tell us — belatedly again — *where* this all took place ("in Bethany, across the Jordan"), and *why* (because "John was baptizing"). Readers could have inferred the latter from the delegation's last question (v. 25), but the parenthetical notice now makes it explicit. "These things came about" *(egeneto)* once more echoes the *egeneto* of creation (vv. 3, 10), and of the coming of John himself and of the Word (vv. 6, 14, 17). Having announced in general terms that John "came" (v. 6) and that his purpose was to "testify" (vv. 7-8; compare v. 15), the writer supplies two notices, "This is John's testimony" (v. 19) and "These things came about" (v. 28), the first introducing John's encounter with the delegation from Jerusalem, and the second concluding it. This is the first concrete instance of his testimony in a narrative setting. The second notice terminates the encounter in the same way that similar notices elsewhere in the Gospel (introduced similarly with "These things") terminate significant stages of certain discourses or narratives — even when there is more to follow; see, for example, 6:59, "These things he said"; 8:20, "These words he spoke"; 13:21,

---

37. *Tradition,* 256; see also Brown, 1.52.

"Having said these things" (compare 18:1); 20:31, "These things are written." There is more of John's testimony to follow here as well (vv. 29-34), but verse 28 signals the end of its first phase.

The point of the reference is not that John baptized "in the Jordan River" (as in Mk 1:5; Mt 3:6; compare Lk 4:1), but that he baptized at "Bethany, across the Jordan," wherever that may have been, presumably because there was a good water supply there — as there was at "Aenon, near the Salim" (3:23). In contrast to the Synoptics, this passage says nothing of a "desert" (see above, n. 23). The location of "Bethany, across the Jordan," is unknown. As far back as the third century, Origen found the reference puzzling, and for him historical probabilities took precedence over literary probabilities. Even while admitting that Bethany "occurs in nearly all the manuscripts" and "that, in addition, this was the earlier reading," Origen proposed emending the text to "Bethabara," a place which, in his day, was "pointed out on the bank of the Jordan. There they say John baptized."[38] But while "Bethabara" is found in a few later witnesses (including K, 33, the old Syriac versions, and the Sahidic Coptic), the manuscript evidence overwhelmingly favors "Bethany." The latter is also the more difficult reading. If "Bethabara" had been original, there would be no reason to alter it to "Bethany," while a change in the opposite direction would have been quite plausible, for the reasons Origen gave.[39] "Bethany" invites confusion with another Bethany, the home of Mary, Martha, and Lazarus (11:1), not "across" but on the west side of the Jordan, only "fifteen stadia" (about three kilometers) from Jerusalem (11:18).[40]

Some have proposed that the reference is not to a village otherwise unknown, east of Jericho or the Dead Sea, but to the entire district of Batanea, the biblical Bashan, well to the north, in the tetrarchy of Herod Philip.[41] The

---

38. *Commentary on John,* 6.204-5 (FC, 80.224-25). The effect is to put the place not "beyond the Jordan," but precisely at the Jordan, in agreement with the synoptic tradition. It is noteworthy that the sixth-century Madeba map actually locates "Bethabara" on the *west* side of the river. Yet Eusebius in the fourth century located "Bethaabara" [*sic*] "across the Jordan," adding that "The place is shown in which also many of the brethren even now are eager to take a bath" (see *Palestine in the Fourth Century* A.D.: *The Onomasticon by Eusebius of Caesarea* [Jerusalem: Carta, 2003], 38).

39. See Metzger, *Textual Commentary,* 199-200.

40. Pierson Parker identified the two Bethanys by reading the phrase as "across from the point of the Jordan where John had been baptizing" ("Bethany Beyond Jordan," *JBL* 75 [1955], 258). His proposal does not work because elsewhere in the Gospel the phrase clearly refers to the east bank (that is, the present kingdom of Jordan). This is the case both in 3:26, spoken from the standpoint of "Aenon near the Salim" in either Judea or Samaria (compare vv. 22-23), and in 10:40, written from the standpoint of Jerusalem (compare 10:22-23).

41. See W. H. Brownlee, "Whence the Gospel According to John?" in *John and the Dead Sea Scrolls* (ed. J. H. Charlesworth; New York: Crossroad, 1990), 168-70, who

suggestion is intriguing because it would explain why all of John's named disciples were Galileans (1:44; 21:2), and how they could reach Cana of Galilee from "Bethany" by "the third day" (2:1). Yet the spelling cannot be made to correspond. Moreover, place names in the Gospel of John referring to large areas such as Judea, Galilee, or Samaria always have the definite article, while the names of cities or towns, such as Jerusalem, Bethsaida, Nazareth, Cana, Capernaum, Aenon, Bethlehem, the other Bethany, and Ephraim, usually do not.[42] By this standard, "in Bethany" appears to refer to a town or village. If the tradition behind the text is that John baptized throughout the district of Batanea east of the Sea of Galilee, then the Gospel writer has either misunderstood the tradition or consciously transformed it. This does not, of course, rule out the possibility that Bethany may have been further north and closer to Galilee than later tradition has placed it, perhaps even within the borders of Batanea. All we know from the Gospel is that John baptized there, and that Jesus had a temporary home there (1:39). It appears to have had some importance for Jesus, for it is later called a "place" (*topos*, 10:40; 11:6) to which he returned and "remained there" (10:40; compare 1:39; 11:6), and a place where "many believed in him" (10:42).

29 With this, the delegation from Jerusalem is gone. We have no idea how they reacted to John's testimony, or what "answer" they brought back to those who sent them from Jerusalem (v. 22). Center stage is John's, and his alone. All of what follows are his words, except for brief narrative introductions in verse 29 ("The next day he sees Jesus coming to him and says . . ."), and verse 32 ("And so John testified, saying that . . ."). He first presents Jesus as "the Lamb of God, who takes away the sin of the world" (vv. 29-31), and then gives explicit testimony as to how he reached that conclusion (vv. 32-34). The section is unified by John's repeated references to "baptizing in water" (vv. 31, 33; compare v. 26), by twin notices that "I did not know him" (vv. 31, 33), and by three closely related statements of who "This is" (vv. 30, 33, 34), a presentation formula recalling the synoptic accounts of Jesus' baptism (Mt 3:17) and transfiguration (Mk 9:7 par.). There is no voice from heaven here, except for John's private revelation from "the One who sent me to baptize in water" (v. 33). Instead, John's is the authoritative voice, telling us decisively

---

traces the view to C. R. Conder in the quarterly of the *Palestine Exploration Fund* (1875 and 1877); also R. Riesner, "Bethany Beyond the Jordan (John 1:28)," *Tyndale Bulletin* 38 (1987), 29-63.

42. The exceptions are four occurrences of "Jerusalem" (2:23; 5:2; 10:22; 11:18) with the article (out of a total of twelve), one occurrence of "Cana" (4:46) with the article (out of four), and the unidentified "Salim" with the article (3:23). The article with "Bethany" in 11:18 is in dispute textually and (whether original or not) was probably used with the express purpose of distinguishing the Bethany that was near Jerusalem from the one where John baptized.

who Jesus is ("the Lamb of God," and "the Son of God"), and what he does ("takes away the sin of the world," and "baptizes in Holy Spirit").

The notice that it is now "the next day" will be repeated twice (vv. 35, 43), punctuating the narrative from here to the end of the chapter, and the consciousness of a time sequence will continue into chapter 2 ("on the third day," 2:1; "a few days," 2:12). As the scene begins, Jesus is "coming to" John, an expression which in this Gospel normally suggests giving allegiance to someone (see 6:35, 37, 44-45, 65; 7:37). The phrase echoes "the One who comes after me" (v. 27), confirming the impression that Jesus is a disciple of John, or at least a potential disciple. It is even possible to infer that Jesus is "coming" to John for the first time, as if for baptism, but the story as it unfolds makes that unlikely (see vv. 32-34).

The narrative introduction is in the present tense. As soon as John "sees" Jesus approaching, he "says," "Look [ide],[43] the Lamb of God, who takes away the sin of the world." But to whom is he presenting Jesus? Not to the now absent delegation of priests and Levites, and not yet to his disciples (see vv. 35-37). Rather, in principle at least, John is presenting Jesus "to Israel" (v. 31). The "hidden Messiah" is no longer hidden. Yet, for the moment at least, we the readers are John's only audience and therefore in a sense "Israel's" representative. But why "the Lamb of God"? "Lamb" is bound to evoke the image of sacrifice,[44] and yet the expression "who takes away the sin of the world" resists any notion of "the Lamb of God" as a passive victim. Jesus, in speaking of his death on the cross, will later declare, "I lay down my life, that I might take it again. No one takes it away from me, but I lay it down of my own accord" (10:17-18). Similarly, "the Lamb of God" here is victor, not victim. He who "takes away" sin is not himself "taken away" by anyone or anything. According to 1 John 3:5, "You know that he was revealed so that he might take away sins, and in him there is no sin." Three verses later the author explains, "For this the Son of God was revealed, that he might destroy the works of the devil" (3:8b).[45] The form of the expression "the Lamb of

---

43. The Gospel of John prefers ἴδε (15 occurrences) to ἰδού (4 occurrences), sometimes giving it a certain performative quality. This is the case in 1:47 where ἴδε defines Nathanael, unexpectedly, as a "true Israelite," in 19:14 where Pilate uses it — even though ironically — to make Jesus a king, and in 19:27 where it seems to establish a relationship that did not exist before.

44. In some commentators this is linked to the notion of the Passover lamb, on the basis that in John's Gospel Jesus dies on the very day and hour when the paschal lamb was slaughtered (19:14), and that none of his bones were broken (19:33, 36; compare Exod 12:10). But because the Passover lamb was not a sacrifice for sin, the reference is more commonly thought to be to the Jewish sacrificial system generally.

45. Schnackenburg finds "a sure starting-point in 1 Jn 3:5, a verse which echoes this text and provides a sort of commentary on it" (1.298).

God," in fact, parallels "the Son of God," as well as other titles such as "the Chosen One of God" (a variant for "Son of God" in v. 34; see above, n. 1), "the Holy One of God" (6:69), "the gift of God" (4:10), "the bread of God" (6:33), and "the word of God" (10:35). The definite article (*ho amnos,* "the Lamb") suggests a title as well known as any of those, or as "the Christ" or "the Prophet" (v. 25), but no such title is attested in the Hebrew Bible or early Judaism.[46] In the book of Revelation we hear of a well-known messianic figure, "the Lion of the tribe of Judah" (5:5), who appears on the scene as "a lamb" (*arnion,* without the definite article, 5:6), and is then consistently identified throughout the book as "the Lamb" (with the article).[47] Similarly, the Gospel of John seems to presuppose an indefinite "lamb" used as a metaphor (as in Isa 53:7),[48] which it transforms into a definite title, "the Lamb of God."[49] While the book of Revelation has no exact equivalent to the phrase as a whole, it does support the notion that "the Lamb of God" in John's Gospel is an active and not a passive figure. "The Lamb of God" on John's lips is likely a formulation modeled after "the Son of God," which makes its first appearance in the Gospel (also on John's lips) five verses later. In effect, "the Son of God" (v. 34) seems to function as an explanation of what "the Lamb of God" means.[50] If John had said, "Look, the *Son* of God, who takes away the sin of the world," the meaning would have been almost the same.

46. There is general agreement that the statement in the *Testament of Joseph* 19.11 that from the seed of Levi and Judah will come "the Lamb of God, who will take away the sin of the world, and will save all the nations, as well as Israel" (*OTP,* 1.824) is a Christian formulation based on this very verse in the Gospel of John.

47. It is intriguing to notice that the Lamb in Revelation is first introduced "standing" (ἑστηκός) among or "in the midst [ἐν μέσῳ] of the throne of God and the four living creatures and in the midst [ἐν μέσῳ] of the elders," just as John anticipated his presentation of Jesus as "Lamb of God" with the comment that "among you stands [μέσος ὑμῶν ἕστηκεν] One whom you do not know" (v. 26). Yet it is difficult to make much of the similarity because in the Revelation "standing in the midst" signals disclosure (compare Jn 20:19, 26), while here (perhaps ironically) it accents nondisclosure. When John goes on to reveal Jesus as the Lamb in the Gospel, it is not as a standing figure but as one "coming to him" (v. 29), or "walking" (v. 36). The parallels, therefore, are probably coincidental.

48. The "servant of the LORD" described in Isaiah 52:13–53:12 is compared to a sheep or a lamb (ὡς πρόβατον . . . ὡς ἀμνός, 53:7, LXX) in his silence and his willingness to become a sacrifice (this text is quoted and applied to Jesus in Acts 8:32-35; see also 1 Pet 1:19, ὡς ἀμνοῦ . . . Χριστοῦ).

49. Compare Dodd, *Interpretation,* 230-38, followed by Beasley-Murray, 24-25. Brown (1.58-63) accepts this interpretation as the view of John the Baptist, but not as the interpretation intended by the Gospel writer.

50. This may be related to Genesis 22, where Abraham told Isaac, "God himself will provide the lamb [πρόβατον, LXX] for the burnt offering" (22:8). In early Christian interpretations the "lamb" that God provides turns out to be his own Son. For example,

Why then *doesn't* John say, "Look, the Son of God"? What is it that the metaphor of "the Lamb" brings to the title? The answer is neither gentleness nor silence nor a willingness to be sacrificed, but purity. When we are told in 1 John 3:5 that Jesus "was revealed so that he might take away the sins," the author adds, "in him there is no sin" (compare 1 Pet 2:22). Without using the term "Lamb," the passage in 1 John makes the point that Jesus is a Messiah "without defect" (like the Passover lamb of Exod 12:5).[51] When he is revealed, the author promises, "we will be like him, for we will see him as he is; and everyone who has this hope in him purifies himself, even as he is pure" (1 Jn 3:2-3). If "taking away" *(airōn)* the world's sin is equivalent to "cleansing" *(kathairōn)* the world of its sin,[52] then John's pronouncement here corresponds to what he says in Luke of the Mightier One to come: that he will "thoroughly cleanse his threshing floor and gather the wheat into his barn, but he will burn up the chaff with unquenchable fire" (Lk 3:17; see also Mt 3:11). The distinctive feature that the Gospel of John brings to this picture of judgment is that the One who purifies the world is himself pure. The One who takes away sin is himself sinless.

Can we go a step further and say that the sinless Lamb "takes away the sin of the world" by shedding his own blood? Such an idea seems far removed from the thought of John the Baptist as we meet him in the synoptic tradition, even though his baptism was said to be "for the forgiveness of sins" (Mk 1:4; Lk 3:3). It is much more at home in the larger setting of the fourth Gospel as a whole, where Jesus as the good Shepherd "lays down his life for the sheep" (10:11, 15; compare 11:52) and gives his flesh "for the life of the

---

Melito of Sardis: "On behalf of the just Isaac a lamb appeared for the sacrifice, that Isaac might be loosed from his bonds. Being sacrificed it redeemed Isaac; so also the Lord being sacrificed saved us. . . . For the Lord was the lamb as the ram which Abraham saw caught in the bush" (*Eclogues* 5-6, in R. M. Grant, *Second-Century Christianity: A Collection of Fragments* [London: SPCK, 1957], 72). In the New Testament, see Romans 8:32 ("For God did not spare his own Son") in relation to Genesis 22:12 and 16 (compare Jn 3:16; also 8:56, "Abraham rejoiced that he would see my day, and he saw it and was glad"). For Jewish traditions about the "binding of Isaac" ("Aqedath Isaac"), see L. Ginzberg, *Legends of the Jews,* 1.279-86; 5.249-51, and for a full discussion, J. Levenson, *The Death and Resurrection of the Beloved Son* (New Haven: Yale University Press, 1993). Levenson comments that "the dynamics underlying this ritual-mythical pattern come full circle in this New Testament material: the son takes the place of the sheep who took the place of the son" (208).

51. This expression was elaborated in early Christianity in 1 Peter 1:19 ("as of a faultless and flawless lamb") and in Melito, *On the Passover* 12 ("a faultless and perfect lamb").

52. Compare the play on words in John 15:2: "Every branch in me that bears no fruit he takes away (αἴρει), and every branch bearing fruit he trims clean (καθαίρει), so that it will bear more fruit."

world" (6:51), claiming that "unless you eat the flesh of the Son of man and drink his blood, you do not have life in yourselves" (6:53; compare vv. 54-57). It is even more at home in 1 John, where "the blood of Jesus his Son cleanses us from all sin" (1 Jn 1:7; 5:6, 8; compare 2:2, 4:10), and in the Revelation, where Jesus is introduced as the One who "loosed us from our sins in his blood (Rev 1:5). While the Gospel writer never speaks of "the blood of the Lamb" (contrast Rev 5:9; 7:14; 12:11), and stops well short of attributing to John the explicit notion of cleansing from sin through Jesus' blood, he nevertheless allows John's testimony to evoke for his readers just such imagery. Yet if we read the pronouncement with Jesus' redemptive death in mind, we must still be careful to remember that he is not a victim here, but the victor. Just as the author of Hebrews presented Jesus as High Priest, but a high priest like no other in offering up his own blood rather than the blood of animals (Heb 9:25-26), so the Gospel writer presents him here as "the Lamb," but a lamb like no other in that he himself initiates the sacrifice, and by his own will accomplishes purification (compare Heb 1:3). Both in Hebrews and in the Gospel of John, Jesus is priest and sacrifice at the same time. "For their sake," he will say, referring to his disciples, "I consecrate myself, so that they too might be consecrated in truth" (17:19). "The Lamb of God," paradoxically, functions as a kind of priestly title, for it attributes to Jesus the work of purification and cleansing from sin. As to the time frame, it is clearly future from the standpoint of both John and the Gospel writer, even though the verb "takes away," like the verb "baptizes" (v. 33, referring to a future act of baptizing in Holy Spirit), is a present participle. The point of John's testimony is not to fix the time of the world's purification, but to identify it as the work of Jesus, and of him alone.

30 While in narrative time it is still "the next day" after John spoke with the delegation from Jerusalem, we now hear of something John said publicly *before* that encounter (how long before we do not know): "After me comes a man who has gotten ahead of me, because he was before me" (compare v. 15). Having briefly echoed that earlier pronouncement in the encounter itself ("the One who comes after me," v. 27), John now in retrospect cites it in full. It is in fact cited *only* in retrospect in this Gospel (vv. 15, 27, 30), never in its original narrative setting, and we can only conjecture what that setting might have been.[53] Here, as in verse 15, John testifies to the fact that Jesus "was before me," something none of his hearers in "Bethany, beyond the Jordan" would have understood, but something the readers of the Gospel

---

53. One part of the saying "the One coming after me" (compare 1:27) does appear in its own narrative setting in the synoptics, with the affirmation that the Coming One is "mightier" (Mk 1:7; Mt 3:11; compare Lk 3:16), but without any notice of his having existed "before" John or getting "ahead" of him.

understand because of verses 1-5. Having presented Jesus as "the Lamb of God," he now further identifies him as "a man" whom he had announced earlier: "This is he of [54] whom I said, 'After me comes a man,'" and so on. With these words he calls our attention to the fulfillment of his own prophecy, something he never does in the synoptic tradition.[55] Only in the fourth Gospel does John point Jesus out in person as the "Coming One" of his expectations. "After" *(opisō)* carries the same ambiguity here that it had in verse 15: Jesus comes "after" John in time so that John can predict his coming as something future, and yet Jesus also comes "after" John in the sense of coming *to* him as a disciple would do. The Gospel writer is content to let both implications stand, for he regards both as true. From them he has constructed a kind of riddle which he likes well enough to repeat. In this riddle, *opisō* has two opposites, one for each of its alternative meanings. Even though Jesus is "after" John in time, he actually existed long "before" *(prōtos)* John was born. Even though Jesus came "after" John as a disciple and candidate for baptism, he has gotten "ahead" *(emprosthen)* of John as God's chosen messenger. The two are interconnected in that Jesus surpasses John in importance precisely "because" of his priority in time.

31 In claiming that "I did not know him," John further confirms that he is speaking of a time prior to his meeting with the delegation from Jerusalem.[56] At that time he had said. "Among you stands one whom *you* do not know" (v. 26, italics added), implying that he himself *did* know the One of whom he spoke. Now he looks back to a still earlier occasion when, he claims that even "I did not know him" (the "I" here, like the "you" in verse 26, is emphatic). The "hidden Messiah" (see above, n. 34) was at first hidden even from John, whose task it was to make him known! At this point we expect John to explain how he learned to recognize the Coming One, but he makes us wait for that (vv. 32-34). Instead he tells us what he had neglected to tell the delegation from Jerusalem (v. 25), that is, *why* he baptized. The

---

54. The preposition ὑπέρ is a strong one for "of" or "about" (literally, "on whose behalf"), and some ancient witnesses, including the majority of later ones, read περί ("about" or "concerning") instead. But the weaker meaning for ὑπέρ is not uncommon in Paul (see, e.g., 2 Cor 8:23; 12:8; Phil 1:7; 4:10; 2 Thess 2:1), and the two options are probably interchangeable here (Abbott, *Johannine Grammar,* 555-56; BDF, §231).

55. The emphatic "I" ("This is he of whom I [ἐγώ] said" — perhaps in contrast to "just as Isaiah the prophet said," v. 23) suggests that he is doing this quite consciously. For οὗτός . . . ἐστιν as a way of introducing the fulfillment of a prophecy, see Matthew 3:3, "For this is he who was spoken of by Isaiah the prophet" (referring to John himself); compare Acts 2:16, "this is that" (τοῦτό ἐστιν, referring to a prophecy of Joel).

56. The quotation in verse 30 of what John had said earlier ends where the verse ends. Verse 31, therefore, is a pronouncement spoken at the same time John said, "Look, the Lamb of God" (that is, "the next day," v. 29).

reason "I came baptizing in water," John says, was so that the Coming One "might be revealed to Israel" (again, see 1 Jn 3:5, "he was revealed so that he might take away sins").

What is this revelation to "Israel," and how does John's baptism bring it about? "Israel," mentioned here for the first time, stands in contrast to "the Jews" in Jerusalem who sent the priests and Levites to question John (v. 19). To them he revealed nothing, but to "Israel" he will reveal the Messiah. "Israel" remains at this point undefined. John's pronouncement leads us to expect a public disclosure of some kind during his ministry, but none will be forthcoming. We, the readers, are John's only audience, so we alone are in on the secret that the Coming One whom he now sees "coming to him" (v. 29) is in fact Jesus. A few verses later, two of his disciples will learn of it (vv. 35-37), and they will tell others, but that disclosure will fall short of the wholesale "revelation to Israel" that John seems to promise (see, however, 2:11; 21:1, 14). As to what baptism has to do with the revelation, this too is unclear for the moment. John has some further explaining to do.

32 John has been speaking continuously since the beginning of verse 29. Now the narrative voice intervenes, as if to give John a moment to get his breath. Instead of the present tenses of verse 29, where he simply "sees Jesus coming" and "says, 'Look, the Lamb of God,'" we have an aorist main verb, and a more formal beginning: "And so John testified, saying that 'I have watched the Spirit coming down as a dove out of the sky, and it remained on him.'" There is something definitive about the way this testimony is introduced, recalling John's earlier testimony before the Jerusalem delegation: "And he confessed, and did not deny; he confessed, that 'I am not the Christ'" (v. 20). At the same time, it echoes the programmatic heading of verse 19: "And this is the testimony of John." The theme of testimony frames the whole of verses 19-34, but it comes to fullest expression here in John's account of what he saw: "I have watched the Spirit come down as a dove out of the sky, and it remained on him." John is the first eyewitness in a Gospel that values eyewitness testimony (compare 19:35; 20:8, 20, 24-29). He becomes here the spokesman for all who have "looked," whether literally or spiritually, at the Word in human flesh, and seen "glory as of a father's One and Only" (v. 14).[57] John's vision leads him to the same conclusion, that Jesus is indeed "the Son of God" (v. 34).[58]

The scene John describes in his testimony is not explicitly said to be Jesus' baptism, but because we are familiar with the baptism from the synop-

---

57. Τεθέαμαι here ("I have watched") echoes ἐθεασάμεθα ("we looked at") in verse 14.

58. Compare 1 John 4:14, "And we have looked [ἡμεῖς τεθεάμεθα] and we testify [μαρτυροῦμεν] that the Father has sent his Son as Savior of the world."

tic accounts, it is hard to imagine it any other way. John sees "the Spirit coming down as a dove out of the sky" on Jesus, just as Jesus himself saw it according to Mark (1:10) and Matthew (3:16). Because of the metaphor of the dove, "out of the sky" is probably the appropriate translation for the Greek phrase *ex ouranou* rather than "out of heaven." While the Spirit comes from heaven, doves do not, and John is using the language of appearance.[59] Unlike Jesus in the synoptics, he does not see "heaven" (Luke) or "the heavens" (Matthew, Mark) either "opened" (Matthew, Luke) or "torn apart" (Mark), nor is there a voice from "heaven" or "the heavens" to verify his testimony. John offers an account of something seen on earth, not a window to the world beyond (contrast 1:51). But what is unique about his testimony in comparison to the synoptic accounts of Jesus' baptism is that he witnesses not simply a process but its result. Having seen the Spirit "coming down" on Jesus, he makes a point of noticing that "it remained on him." Because there is no voice from heaven, there is no explicit termination to the vision. The relationship it dramatizes between Jesus and the Spirit is a continuing one (compare 3:34). The verb "remained" *(menein)* becomes a significant term in this Gospel (with 40 occurrences, plus 27 more in the Johannine letters) for the mutual relationship between God and believers. How long the Spirit "remained" on Jesus we are not told, but in the case of believers the Spirit comes to stay (compare 14:16-17). It is fair to assume at this point that the Spirit will continue to rest on Jesus until (and unless) we have an explicit notice to the contrary (see 19:30).

33 John's disclaimer, "and I did not know him, but . . . ," repeats word for word the beginning of verse 31, and is followed similarly by a reference to his work of "baptizing in water" (compare also v. 26). What is new is that we now learn whose purpose it was that the Coming One should be "revealed to Israel" (v. 31). It was not John's own plan, but the plan of "the One who sent me." This expression, which Jesus will use frequently in reference to his own mission,[60] reminds us that John, too, was "sent from God" (v. 6;

---

59. As in the synoptics, the question remains of whether John is saying that he saw the Spirit (however visualized) descend *in the manner of* a dove, or whether he saw what actually appeared to be a dove. In the synoptics, the Lukan phrase "in bodily form" (Lk 3:22) seems intended to settle that question in favor of the second alternative, and the uses of the verb "saw" in Matthew and Mark, and the verb "watched" in John, tend to suggest that Luke's interpretation was correct. Why look for other ways for him to have visualized the Spirit when we have a specific one ready at hand?

60. For "the One who sent me," see 4:34; 5:24, 30; 6:38, 39; 7:16, 18, 28, 33; 8:26, 29; 9:4; 12:44, 45; 13:16, 20 (twice); 16:5. But Jesus, unlike John, can also speak of "the Father who sent me" (5:23, 37; 6:44; 8:16, 18; 12:49; 14:24, 26). While the two different words for "send," ἀποστέλλειν and πέμπειν are synonymous in this Gospel, the latter is used only as an aorist active participle ("the One who sent," or "those who sent"), while the former occurs always as either a finite verb or a perfect passive participle.

also 3:28).[61] Like the delegates from Jerusalem who first questioned him (v. 22), John was an agent or emissary — but from an immeasurably higher authority!

Only twice in the entire Gospel are we given the precise words of God, here and in 12:28, where "a voice from heaven" responds to Jesus' prayer, "Father, glorify your name," with the assurance, "I have both glorified and I will glorify again." Here "the One who sent" both John and Jesus tells John, "Whoever it is on whom you see the Spirit coming down and remaining on him, this is he who baptizes in Holy Spirit." The divine vocabulary matches John's own vocabulary (v. 32) almost word for word. In real time, God's promise comes first and John's testimony echoes what God had told him, but in narrative time it is the other way around: John's words come first (v. 32), and the words of God echo and confirm his testimony (v. 33). We are not told the circumstances under which God spoke to John. The retelling of it makes it sound less like a public voice from heaven than like the private assurances to Paul, whether from God or the risen Jesus, that "I have many people in this city" (in a dream at Corinth, Acts 18:10), or that "My grace is enough for you, for power is perfected in weakness" (in answer to Paul's prayer, 2 Cor 12:9). Yet the context, recalling the traditional story of Jesus' baptism, leads us to expect a public disclosure of some kind. The concluding words, "This is he who baptizes in Holy Spirit," while spoken to John privately, are consistent with such a disclosure, for they echo John's presentation formula, "This is he of whom I said, 'After me comes a man who has gotten ahead of me, because he was before me'" (v. 30).

34 The formal introduction to John's eyewitness testimony, "And I have seen, and have testified" (v. 34; compare 19:35), now sets the stage for John's definitive statement of who Jesus is, and a narrative of the call of his first disciples (vv. 35-51). The voice of God, "This is he who baptizes in Holy Spirit" (v. 33), echoing John's words, "This is he of whom I said" (v. 30) is reechoed in turn by John himself: "This is the Son of God." The effect of the repeated presentation formula (vv. 30, 33, 34) is to give John's testimony the same authority and status that the voice from heaven has in the synoptic tradition (at least in its Matthean form, "This is my Beloved Son, in whom I take pleasure," Mt 3:17; compare 17:5; Mk 9:7; Lk 9:35). John's voice dominates the narrative. Nowhere is the title, "Gospel of *John*," more apt than here. John uses the emphatic "I" nine times in verses 19 to 34 (and once more in 3:28), but no one else (including Jesus) ever uses it within the

---

61. "Sent" in both instances is ἀπεσταλμένος. There is no discernible difference in meaning between the two verbs for "send," ἀποστέλλειν and πέμπειν, either in the case of John or of Jesus.

Gospel's first three chapters.⁶² John's testimony here, like the voice at the baptism in the synoptic tradition, is "public" as far as the readers of the Gospel are concerned, even though there is no identifiable audience within the narrative. John, and not a heavenly voice, confirms Jesus' identity to the reader, even though it remains for him to be "revealed to Israel" (compare v. 31). For the first time, the "One and Only" (vv. 14, 18) is explicitly defined as "the Son of God" *(ho huios tou theou)*. The variant reading, "the Chosen of God" *(ho eklektos tou theou)*, has a strong claim to originality because "the Chosen," if it were original, might well have been changed to the more familiar "Son," while a change in the opposite direction seems less likely (see the TNIV, "God's Chosen One"). Still, the manuscript support for "the Chosen" is not strong (see above, n. 1). A plausible solution is that "the Chosen" was indeed changed to "the Son," but that the change was made by the Gospel writer! If the author found "the Chosen of God" in his source, it would have been natural to interpret it as "the Son of God," reflecting his own characteristic vocabulary (compare v. 49; 3:18; 5:25; 10:36; 11:4, 27; 19:7; 20:31), and just as natural for the traditional designation, "the Chosen," to have survived in some later manuscipts. "Chosen," like "One and Only" or "Beloved" (as in Mt 3:17 and parallels), points to Jesus' unique position of favor in his Father's eyes. Like them it is a title that would have been at home in early baptism or transfiguration accounts — just the sort of narratives the Gospel writer would have used in reporting John's testimony.⁶³ It is appropriate that John, the first eyewitness, should also be the first to identify Jesus as "the Son of God," the title by which (along with "the Christ") the author wants his readers to know and believe in him (compare 20:31). Having already acknowledged Jesus implicitly as "the Christ" (by disclaiming the title for himself, v. 20), John now confesses him openly as "the Son of God."⁶⁴

If "Son of God" within the developing Johannine tradition clarifies and interprets "the Chosen of God," in the Gospel's present literary framework it clarifies and interprets (as we have seen) the otherwise difficult "Lamb of God" (v. 29). If this is the case, then the participial expression, "he who baptizes in Holy Spirit" (v. 33), also has a likely equivalent in "the Lamb of God,

---

62. In striking contrast, ἐγώ or κἀγώ occurs 148 times in the rest of the Gospel, all but eight of which are on Jesus' lips.

63. Compare the Lukan transfiguration account: "This is my Chosen Son [ὁ υἱός μου ὁ ἐκλελεγμένος]; listen to him" (Lk 9:35, where both ἀγαπητός and ἐκλέκτος are found as variant readings); see also Luke 23:35, where ὁ ἐκλέκτος is used mockingly of Jesus (with "the Christ of God") as he hangs on the cross.

64. If John is *not* calling Jesus "the Son of God," then it remains for Nathanael to introduce the title in verse 49 ("Rabbi, you are the Son of God; you are the King of Israel"), a place where it has less emphasis because of the accent on something "greater" to follow (vv. 50-51).

who takes away the sin of the world" (v. 29). Both are priestly acts in that they refer to a work of purification from sin which Jesus will accomplish, accenting first its worldwide goal and second the Spirit as the instrument by which he will carry it out. This work of purification — whether as "Lamb of God" or as "the Baptizer" — will begin with Jesus' own baptizing ministry (3:22, 26; 4:1), but will come to full realization only in his sacrificial death and consequent bestowal of the Holy Spirit on his disciples (20:22-23).

D. JESUS AND JOHN'S DISCIPLES (1:35-51)

> 35 *The next day John was there again, and two of his disciples.* 36 *And looking right at Jesus as he walked by, he says, "Look, the Lamb of God!"* 37 *And his two disciples heard him speaking, and they followed Jesus.* 38 *Jesus turned and noticed them following, and he asks them, "What are you seeking?" Then they asked him, "Rabbi" — which means teacher — "where do you stay?"* 39 *He said to them, "Come, and you will see." So they came, and saw where he was staying, and they stayed with him that day. It was about the tenth hour.* 40 *Andrew, the brother of Simon Peter, was one of the two who had heard what John said and followed him.* 41 *First thing, he finds Simon, his own brother, and says to him, "We have found the Messiah" — which means Christ.* 42 *He brought him to Jesus. Looking right at him, Jesus said, "You are Simon, the son of John; you shall be called Cephas" — which means Peter.*
>
> 43 *The next day he decided to set out for Galilee, and he finds Philip, and Jesus says to him, "Follow me."* 44 *Now Philip was from Bethsaida, from the town of Andrew and Peter.* 45 *Philip finds Nathanael and says to him, "We have found someone of whom Moses wrote in the law, and of whom the prophets wrote, Jesus, son of Joseph, from Nazareth."* 46 *And Nathanael said to him, "Can anything good come out of Nazareth?" Philip says to him, "Come and see."* 47 *Jesus saw Nathanael coming to him, and says of him, "Look, a true Israelite, in whom is no deceit!"* 48 *Nathanael says to him, "How do you know me?" Jesus answered and said to him, "Before Philip called to you under the fig tree, I saw you."* 49 *Nathanael answered him, "You, Rabbi, are the Son of God. You are the King of Israel."* 50 *Jesus answered and said to him, "Because I said to you that I saw you underneath the fig tree, you believe. You will see something greater than these things."* 51 *And he says to him, "Amen, amen, I say to you all, You will see the sky opened, and the angels of God going up and coming down over the Son of man."*

The Gospel of John

As the sequence of days continues, Jesus gathers around him four, possibly five, disciples, all Galileans: first, Andrew and an unnamed companion, both disciples of John; then Andrew's brother Simon Peter; then Philip, who may or may not be Andrew's unnamed companion; finally Nathanael, known already to Jesus as a "true Israelite" (v. 47). This is the "call" of the disciples according to this Gospel, not by their fishing nets at the lake of Galilee as in Matthew, Mark, and Luke, but at "Bethany across the Jordan, where John was baptizing" (v. 28) and where Jesus had a temporary residence. Moreover, in contrast to the other Gospels, their reason for following him is given. They follow him because John has proclaimed him in their hearing as "the Lamb of God" (v. 36), and they acknowedge him as "the Messiah" (v. 41), as "someone of whom Moses wrote" (v. 45), and as "the Son of God" and "the King of Israel" (v. 49). Jesus decides to go to Galilee, enlists them all to accompany him, and promises them a vision — as yet unexplained — of "the sky opened, and the angels of God going up and coming down over the Son of man" (v. 51).

35 The adverb "again" calls attention to the repetition of the phrase "the next day" (v. 35), and consequently to the Gospel writer's consciousness of a series of days (see vv. 29, 43; 2:1). Again John "was there,"[1] but the difference between this day and the preceding one is that now he has an audience: two of his disciples. Although John has used the ambiguous terminology of someone coming "after me" (see vv. 15, 27, 30), this is the first we are told explicitly that he even had disciples. Presumably his disciples were drawn from among those he baptized (compare 4:1, where "baptizing" and "making disciples" are coordinate terms), but it is doubtful that all who were baptized became his disciples.

36 In a dramatic reenactment of verse 29, John looks at Jesus, not "coming to him" as before, but "as he walked by."[2] The verb of motion prepares us for the movement of the disciples, who "followed" him (vv. 37-38) — not metaphorically but literally — as he kept on walking. In the presence of the two disciples, John repeats his presentation of Jesus as "the Lamb of God" (compare v. 29), but without the accompanying reference to "taking away the sin of the world." This means that the readers understand more than the disciples do about Jesus, but the omission does not impugn in any way the disciples' faith.[3] Rather, it focuses attention on the single issue of Jesus'

---

1. The verb is εἰστήκει, literally "was standing, " but the emphasis of this verb is "less on 'standing' than on *being, existing*" (BDAG, 483, with this verse as an example).

2. Gr. περιπατοῦντι. This verb is used of Jesus' travels throughout the first half of the Gospel (for example, across the lake, 6:19; in Galilee, 6:66 and 7:1; in Solomon's portico in the temple, 10:23; among the Judeans, 11:54).

3. Contrast Jeffrey Staley, to whom the disciples' confessions in response to John's announcement (vv. 41, 45, 49) are "rash . . . based upon a minimal knowledge," and "border on the ludicrous" (*The Print's First Kiss,* 80).

1:35-51 JESUS AND JOHN'S DISCIPLES

identity rather than on his priestly work of purification and redemption. For the moment, the Gospel writer is interested in simply piling up titles for Jesus, allowing each to interpret and help define the others: "the Lamb of God" (v. 36), "the Messiah" (v. 41; compare v. 45), "the Son of God" (v. 49; compare v. 34), "the King of Israel" (v. 49), and "the Son of man" (v. 51). Jesus is all of these and more, and the Gospel writer wants us to hear it from a chorus of voices, finally including Jesus' own (v. 51). The simple "Lamb of God" is sufficient for that purpose.

37-38 On hearing John's words, his disciples immediately fall in line behind the "peripatetic" Jesus.[4] They "followed" him, and leading the way he had to turn around in order to see them "following." "What are you seeking?" he asks them. These are the first words Jesus speaks in the Gospel, and he will repeat them to different audiences at two other crucial points in the narrative.[5] They answer with a question of their own, "Where do you stay?" (v. 38). They are not avoiding Jesus' question, but in effect telling him precisely what they are looking for. They speak not out of idle curiosity, but precisely as "followers." They want to know where Jesus is "staying" because they assume he is on his way there. He is their leader now, and they want to know where he is leading them.[6]

John's disciples call Jesus "Rabbi," and the Gospel writer intervenes to tell us that this word means "Teacher" (*didaskale*, v. 38). Like the belated notices in verse 24 that the delegation sent to John was sent from the Pharisees, and in verse 28 that the encounter took place in Bethany, this is one of many authorial comments or narrative asides in this Gospel intended to help the reader understand what is going on.[7] In this instance the comment implies

---

4. If this is the beginning of their "walk" with Jesus, the end of it (for some) is in 6:66, where "many of his disciples turned back and no longer walked (περιεπάτουν) with him."

5. "What are you seeking?" is τί ζητεῖτε. Jesus asks essentially the same question of the soldiers sent to arrest him (τίνα ζητεῖτε, 18:4, 7), and of Mary Magdalene (τίνα ζητεῖς, 20:15). Both are in a garden, one in a hostile setting and the other in a setting of joyful reunion, and in both instances the question leads to a self-disclosure of some kind (18:5-6, 8; 20:16). Here too there is self-disclosure, but not immediately (see 1:51; 2:11).

6. Compare the later question, in a very different context, when the disciples want to follow Jesus to heaven: "Where are you going?" (13:36-37; 14:5; compare 16:5).

7. Ferrar Fenton noticed this phenomenon as early as 1903, and placed such narrative asides in brackets in his translation (*The Holy Bible in Modern English* [Merrimac, MA: Destiny, 1966], 1017); see also A. E. Garvie, *The Beloved Disciple* (London: Hodder & Stoughton, 1922), 14-29; M. C. Tenney, "The Footnotes of John's Gospel," *BibSac* 117 (1960), 350-64; R. A. Culpepper, *Anatomy of the Fourth Gospel,* especially 15-49; G. van Belle, *Les Parenthèses dans l'Évangile de Jean* (Leuven: Peeters, 1985), and C. W. Hedrick, "Authorial Presence and Narrator in John," in *Gospel Origins and Christian Beginnings* (Sonoma, CA: Polebridge, 1990), 75-93.

The Gospel of John

that John's disciples are now Jesus' disciples because they consider him their "Teacher."[8] It is the first of three such translations of Hebrew expressions in the immediate context (see vv. 41, 42). We cannot assume that the Greek-speaking readers of the Gospel actually needed the translations. Quite possibly the writer simply wants to accent his own credibility as someone familiar with Jewish terms and customs.[9] Other narrative asides will deal explicitly with such customs, and with matters of time, place, and the motivation of certain characters in the story.

39 Jesus invites the two, "Come, and you will see,"[10] and we are told that "they came, and saw where he was staying, and they stayed with him that day." Two things are noteworthy: first, we are again reminded that these events took place within a single day, or what was left of it; second, the verb "to stay," or "remain" (Gr. *menein*), represents another paradigm for discipleship, alongside "to follow" (Gr. *akolouthein*).[11] To "follow" is to embark with Jesus on a journey, while to "stay" or "remain" is to maintain a lasting personal relationship with him. That the disciples "stayed" with Jesus (presumably in Bethany) for the rest of the day testifies to their commitment as disciples.

At this point, another narrative aside tells us that "It was about the tenth hour." The "tenth hour" would be 4 p.m., if we assume that this Gospel, like the others, is following the Jewish time reckoning in which the daylight hours begin at 6 a.m., not at midnight as in Roman law.[12] This is not a long

---

8. See verse 49; also 3:26, where those who continue to be John's disciples address John as "Rabbi"; also 4:31; 9:2; 11:8, where Jesus' disciples do the same, 13:13, where Jesus says that his disciples know him as "the Teacher" (ὁ διδάσκαλος; compare 11:28), and 20:16, where Mary Magdalene calls him "Rabbouni," also translated as διδάσκαλε. More problematic are 3:2 and 6:25, where those using the term are potential rather than actual disciples.

9. Staley, *The Print's First Kiss*, 82.

10. This translation assumes the reading ἔρχεσθε καὶ ὄψεσθε (with P⁶⁶, P⁷⁵, B, L, and others). The καί is consecutive, introducing a promise resulting from the command (BDF, §442[2]; in effect, "If you come, then you will see"). Other ancient manuscripts (including ℵ, A, Θ, all Latin versions, and the majority of later manuscripts) have the twin imperatives ἔρχεσθε καὶ ἴδετε, "Come and see" (as in v. 46). The difference is small in any case.

11. See, for example, 8:31: "If you dwell [ἐὰν ὑμεῖς μείνητε] on my word, then you are truly my disciples," and 15:7, "If you make your dwelling [ἐὰν μείνητε] in me, and my words come to dwell in you, ask whatever you want and it will be done for you. In this my Father is glorified, that you bear much fruit and become my disciples." See also 21:22, where discipleship for Peter means "following," and for the beloved disciple "staying" or "remaining."

12. See 4:6, where Jesus came to the well in Samaria at "the sixth hour," and 19:14, where Jesus was presented for crucifixion at "the sixth hour," both referring apparently to 12 noon, not 6 a.m. For fuller discussion, see Morris, 138, n. 91, who makes the

1:35-51 JESUS AND JOHN'S DISCIPLES

sojourn with Jesus.[13] The reference to the "tenth" hour, which has no obvious symbolic significance,[14] and which qualifies or even subverts the notice that "they stayed with him that day,"[15] probably reflects historical tradition, not the creativity of the Gospel writer. Yet while "tenth" is not symbolic, "hour" may very well be, for Jesus will soon begin to speak of another decisive "hour" (2:4).[16]

40 At this point the Gospel writer begins to take an interest in these disciples as individuals. First he mentions "Andrew" (v. 40), who is promptly identified in relation to "Simon Peter," a name apparently well known to the readers of the Gospel (compare 6:8). Andrew is Simon's brother (Mk 1:16// Mt 4:18; Mt 10:2//Lk 6:14) and is introduced here in order to bring Simon Peter into the story as quickly as possible, even though Simon is *not* (as in Mark and Matthew) one of the first two to follow Jesus. Consequently, the second of the two disciples goes unmentioned. Because this disciple is unnamed, some have identified him with the anonymous "disciple whom Jesus loved," who will be introduced in the latter half of the Gospel, beginning at 13:23. There is little ground for this conjecture. At most it could be argued that if the "beloved disciple" is (as 21:24 claims) the source or author of the Gospel, he might have deliberately left himself out of the account.[17] But a number of characters in the Gospel are left anonymous, and for a variety of reasons. Here the story is about Andrew and Simon Peter, not about Andrew's unidentified companion.

41 Having identified Andrew as "the brother of Simon Peter," the author now tells us that Andrew "finds Simon, his own brother" and tells him, "We have found the Messiah." The reader is then told that Messiah "means Christ," just as Rabbi (v. 38) meant "teacher." There is repeated play

---

telling point that even in the Roman world the reckoning from midnight was only for legal purposes, and that "for all other purposes they seem to have computed from sunrise. For example, they marked noon on their sundials with VI, not XII."

13. Jesus is often said to have "stayed" (μένειν, 2:12; 4:40; 10:40; 11:6, 54), or "spent time" (διατρίβειν, 3:22), or "sat" (καθῆσθαι, 6:3), or "gathered together" (συνάγειν, 18:2) with disciples or potential disciples for varying lengths of time in the Gospel narrative.

14. Schnackenburg, 1.309, in contrast to Bultmann, 100, n. 9.

15. It is possible to read the subversion as deliberate, as if to say, "Yes, they stayed with him that day, but the day was practically over!" Yet there is no hint that the writer wants to minimize or make light of the disciples' faith (contra Staley, *The Print's First Kiss;* see n. 3). At most it could be argued that he is simply being careful not to overstate his case for the disciples' status as eyewitnesses. Such honesty gains him credibility with his readers.

16. See also 4:21, 23; 5:25, 28; 7:30; 8:20; 12:23, 27; 13:1; 16:2, 4, 25, 32; 17:1; 19:14, 27.

17. He obviously did not do so in four other incidents (13:23-30; 19:25-27; 20:2-10; 21:7, 20-24).

here on the verb "to find," probably linked to Jesus' opening question, "What are you looking for?" (v. 38). The text evokes Jesus' words in the synoptic tradition, "Seek, and you will find" (see Mt 7:7//Lk 11:9),[18] words which seem to be known and echoed, at least negatively, in this Gospel as well. In contrast to those to whom Jesus will later say, "You will seek me, and you will not find me" (7:34, 36; also 8:21; 13:33), John's disciples "find" here all that they are "seeking": Jesus himself and where he was staying, and other disciples with whom to share the story.

Another notable feature here is that Andrew finds his brother Simon "first thing" *(prōton)*. Both the text and the meaning are uncertain. *Prōton,* the reading of the best ancient manuscripts,[19] should be read adverbially (as in our translation) to mean that the "first" thing Andrew did was to locate Simon Peter. Less plausibly, it could be read adjectivally, with the implication that Simon was "first" among the disciples,[20] even though he was not chronologically the first to become a disciple. A variant reading *(prōtos)*[21] makes Andrew the first disciple of Jesus who made a convert, with the thought already in mind that Philip will similarly "find" Nathanael (v. 45).[22] Still another reading, *mane* ("in the morning") in a few old Latin versions, may not be a real variant at all but may simply reflect an attempt by Latin translators to convey the true meaning of *prōton:* if Andrew found Simon "first thing" after spending the remainder of the day with Jesus, then it must have been the next morning. This interpretation seems inescapable in any case.[23] Yet if

---

18. See Origen, *Commentary on John,* 2.221 (FC, 80.154).

19. These include P[66], P[75], B, A, Θ, Ψ, and a later hand of א, plus most Latin, Syriac, and Coptic versions.

20. In the synoptic lists of the Twelve, Simon Peter is consistently listed first (Mk 3:16; Mt 10:2; Lk 6:14; compare Acts 1:13), and in one Gospel he is even designated as "first" (πρῶτος, Mt 10:2). But in the synoptic calling accounts, Simon is also called first, either individually (Lk 5:1-11) or with his brother Andrew (Mk 1:16-18//Mt 4:18-20). See Abbott, *Johannine Grammar,* 14.

21. This is the reading of א, L, and the majority of later Greek manuscripts.

22. See Metzger, *Textual Commentary,* 200. Alternatively, on the supposition that the unnamed disciple is "the disciple whom Jesus loved," πρῶτος has been interpreted to mean that Andrew "first" found his brother Simon before John the son of Zebedee found his brother James! See Barrett, 181-82.

23. Other possible ways of reading πρῶτον are unconvincing: for example, the notion that Andrew found Simon Peter "first" and someone else later (Philip, for example, on the supposition that Andrew is the subject of v. 43a; see below, n. 32), or that Andrew found Simon Peter *before* the events described in verses 35-39, making Simon himself the unnamed disciple of verse 40 (!). This would not only necessitate reading the present tenses εὑρίσκει and λέγει (v. 41) as if they were pluperfects, but would seriously conflict with the main point of the passage as a whole — that John's disciples followed Jesus on the basis of John's testimony.

"first thing" implies "the next day" (as in vv. 29 and 35), why not just say so? The Gospel writer appears to be taking liberties with his own sequence of successive days. A possible reason is that if he had said "the next day" instead of the simple "first thing," there would have been an extra day in the sequence. As it is, he tacitly assumes, without being explicit, that the call and renaming of Simon Peter (vv. 40-42) took place on the same day as the call of Nathanael (vv. 43-51). Strictly speaking, the call of Simon has no day of its own assigned to it in the sequence of days, but functions as a kind of appendix to the day which the disciples of John spent with Jesus. The odd arrangement of days has a two-pronged effect. As far as Nathanael is concerned, the account of his call has the whole "next day" to itself (vv. 43-51), without competition from a traditional account of Simon and the changing of his name. As far as Simon Peter is concerned, he gains a place alongside the first two disciples to be called, even though he was not present with them at the opening scene. If not quite the "first" of the disciples (as in Mt 10:2), he is still among the first, and (unlike Nathanael) will continue to play a significant role from time to time in the Gospel story (see 6:68-69; 13:6-10, 24, 36-38; 18:10-11, 15-18, 25-27; 20:2-6; 21:3-11, 15-22).

Andrew's testimony to Simon, "We have found the Messiah," echoes the proclamation of John, "Look, the Lamb of God!" (v. 36). John's disciples hear "the Lamb of God" as "the Messiah." To the Gospel writer and his intended readers, this is not a misunderstanding. "The Lamb of God" and "the Messiah" *are* synonymous terms to this writer, and yet it must be added that such designations as "Lamb of God" (vv. 29, 36) and "Son of God" (v. 34) further characterize "the Messiah" as one who is pure and who carries out a work of purification, whether described as "taking away the sin of the world" (v. 39) or as "baptizing in Holy Spirit" (v. 33). Andrew's simple pronouncement, "We have found the Messiah," shows no awareness of this dimension of the Messiah's work, yet later, when Simon Peter's turn comes to speak for himself, he confesses Jesus as "the Holy One of God" (6:69). It is unfair to conclude, therefore, that Andrew's testimony here to Simon, and Philip's testimony to Nathanael (v. 45), are somehow inadequate or unworthy of true disciples, or, as Moloney puts it, "a blatant untruth."[24] Obviously the author and the readers of the Gospel hold to a "higher" christology than these first few disciples, but as Moloney himself aptly remarks, "the disciples have not read the prologue."[25]

42 When Andrew brought Simon to Jesus, Jesus "looked right at him" (see also v. 36) and called him by name:[26] "You are Simon, the son of

---

24. Moloney, 60 (compare Staley's comment, n. 3, above).
25. Moloney, *Belief in the Word,* 70 (compare 66).
26. We are not told whether Jesus knew Simon's name supernaturally (Bultmann,

John;[27] you shall be called Cephas." The latter is not a name, but the Greek transliteration of an Aramaic word for "rock."[28] Here it functions as a kind of nickname, which the Gospel writer promptly renders into Greek as "Peter," explaining why Andrew was introduced just above as "the brother of Simon Peter" (v. 40).[29] "Simon, the son of John" is usually read as the equivalent of "Simon Barjona" (or "Simon, son of Jona") in the Matthean account of the changing of Simon's name (Mt 16:17), but "John" and "Jona" are quite different names in Hebrew.[30] The only "John" mentioned so far is the one who has just proclaimed Jesus as "Lamb of God" (v. 36), and it is at least as likely that Jesus is addressing Simon as an adherent or disciple of John as that he is making reference to Simon's actual father.[31] While Simon is not explicitly said to be John's disciple, he is with his brother Andrew and other disciples of John "in Bethany, beyond the Jordan, where John was baptizing" (v. 28),

---

102, n. 1), or whether Andrew had told Jesus about him. If the knowledge is supernatural, nothing is made of it. More to the point is the Johannine notion that Jesus, as Good Shepherd, "calls his own sheep by name" (10:3; compare 20:16).

27. In contrast to Matthew 16:18, the emphatic "You are" (οὐ εἶ) is simply descriptive, not performative. In Matthew, when Jesus says, "You are [σὺ εἶ] Peter," his words transform "Simon Barjona" into "Peter." Here when he says, "You are [σὺ εἶ] Simon, the son of John," he is merely stating what was the case all along. Even the words that follow, "you [σύ] shall be called Cephas," are a promise or prediction, not a transformation. "Simon" will become "Cephas" at a later time, specified in Matthew but not in John's Gospel.

28. The name "Cephas" is used only here in the Gospels, but eight times in Paul's letters (1 Cor 1:12; 3:22; 9:5; 15:5; Gal 1:18; 2:9, 11, 14). Paul uses the name "Peter" only in Galatians 2:7-8, where his language seems to have been dictated by that of a specific agreement drawn up by the Jerusalem church. Otherwise, Paul seems to have regarded Cephas as a real name, not a nickname, and consequently not to be translated, as the Gospel writer has done here.

29. For this reason, πέτρος should be rendered in English as the name "Peter" rather than as "rock," the etymological meaning of the name. "Rock" in koine Greek is consistently πέτρα, not πέτρος (which was used in classical Greek for a loose rock or stone), and this Gospel, unlike Matthew (16:18), shows no interest in the wordplay.

30. Compare Schnackenburg, 1.311, n. 86, who nevertheless understands this "John" as Simon's father. A fragment, probably from the *Gospel of the Hebrews,* has υἱὲ Ἰωάννου in place of Βαριωνᾶ (see *Apocrypha, II: Evangelien* [ed. E. Klostermann; Berlin: Walter de Gruyter, 1929], 8), and it is of course possible that in a similar way our Gospel writer has read the very uncommon proper name "Jonah" (Ἰωνᾶς, or יוֹנָה, otherwise unattested between the time of Jonah the biblical prophet and the third century A.D.), as the more familiar "John" (Ἰωάννης or יוֹחָנָן), inviting confusion with another "John" who up to now has been the principal character in his story.

31. BDAG, 1024. See 1 Peter 5:13, where the implied author, this same Peter, sends greetings from "Mark my son"; also, "your sons" (Mt 12:27; Lk 11:19) as a designation for adherents of the Pharisees (compare Lk 5:33).

not at home in Bethsaida (v. 44). If this is the case, then when Jesus tells "Simon, the son of John," that his new name will be Cephas, it marks a transition for both disciples (or all three) from being John's disciples to becoming disciples of Jesus. The initiative in this transfer of allegiance lies not with them, but with Jesus. Jesus' pronouncement to Simon marks a point in the Gospel at which Jesus takes center stage, and John for the time being disappears. From here on, Jesus will call and direct his own band of disciples, and John will be seen only once more, just long enough to say an eloquent good-bye (3:22-36).

43 If our interpretation of "first" (v. 41) is correct, then "the next day" here means the next day after two of John's disciples followed Jesus, not the next day after Jesus' encounter with Simon. Grammatically, the subject of the verb "he decided" is not immediately specified, but contextually it can only be Jesus.[32] Not only was Jesus speaking at the end of the preceding verse, but in the larger context Jesus was the leader and John's disciples the followers. Having taking the initiative by promising Simon a new name (v. 42), Jesus now continues to direct the action. His decision "to set out for Galilee" anticipates the wedding "in Cana of Galilee" (2:1), and may even presuppose Jesus' invitation to the wedding (2:2). Having "decided" to make the journey, Jesus himself now does some "finding." He "finds" Philip[33] and "says to him" (now for the first time explicitly to anyone): "Follow me." Only when he utters these classic words of invitation (see 21:19, 22 and compare 8:12; 12:26) is it made explicit that Jesus is actually the subject of all three verbs, the one doing the deciding, the finding, and the speaking.

In contrast to verses 38-39, Jesus' invitation to discipleship is now very direct. He does not ask, "What are you looking for?" (as in v. 38), because Philip is not looking for anything. Jesus does the looking — and the finding. Nor does Philip ask, "Where do you stay?" (v. 38), because Jesus is not "staying" anywhere. Instead, we have here an account of a "call" more like those in the synoptic Gospels, where Jesus meets certain individuals, says "Follow me" (as in Mk 2:14, for example), or "Come along after me"

---

32. Moloney, *Belief in the Word* (70, n. 56) agrees, but calls the text "notoriously troublesome." The adverb πρῶτον in verse 41 could mislead the reader into thinking that after Andrew found Simon Peter he did some more "finding," making him the one who "decided to set out for Galilee" and who "finds Philip" in verse 43 (see above, n. 23). Yet it is hardly plausible that, having "followed" Jesus, Andrew would now determine the itinerary for himself!

33. Only in the Gospel of John (compare 6:5-8; 12:21-22; 14:8-10) is Philip anything more than a name on a list of Jesus' apostles (compare Mk 3:18; Mt 10:3; Lk 6:14; Acts 1:13). He is not to be confused with the Philip who was appointed to serve tables and who became an evangelist to Samaria and to the Ethiopian eunuch in the book of Acts (Acts 6:5, chapter 8, and 21:8).

(as in Mk 1:17), and they either follow or do not. Here too Jesus is on a journey, and invites Philip to join him. The initiative is his, and his alone.

44 Despite these differences between the call of Philip and that of the first three disciples, the pattern of narration does follow that of verses 40-42, where Andrew found Simon Peter. In a narrative aside, the author pauses to tell us that "Philip was from Bethsaida, from the town of Andrew and Peter," just as he paused to tell us earlier that "Andrew, the brother of Simon Peter, was one of the two who had heard what John said and followed him" (v. 40). In each instance, the identification of one disciple is preliminary to the "finding" of another, who then becomes the center of attention — Simon Peter in the first instance, Nathanael in the second. The two narrative asides serve to establish a relationship between the two brothers and Philip, who comes from the same town. The relationship between Andrew and Philip surfaces again later in the Gospel, where Andrew never appears without Philip (see 6:5-9; 12:21-23), and Philip only once without Andrew (14:8-10).

In the present context, it also lends credibility to Schnackenburg's suggestion that Philip is the unnamed disciple of verse 40.[34] This proposal, while not provable, explains why Jesus so quickly "finds" Philip (v. 43), and why Philip then proceeds to do just what Andrew had done (v. 45).[35] The notice that Philip was "from Bethsaida" hardly means that the scene of the action has shifted there from "Bethany, beyond the Jordan" (v. 28).[36] Bethsaida was in Galilee (12:21), and at this point Jesus has only "decided to set out for Galilee" (v. 43). He has not arrived there. Quite possibly the Gospel writer expects his readers to know that Bethsaida is in Galilee, for knowing that would help them understand why Philip responded so quickly to Jesus' invitation.[37] For

---

34. Schnackenburg, 1.310. The suggestion is not necessarily dependent on Schnackenburg's conjecture (which he admits is "questionable") that verse 43 was added by a redactor (1.313).

35. Another unprovable, though intriguing, possibility is that Andrew and Philip are the two unnamed disciples in 21:2, where they are otherwise conspicuous by their absence.

36. According to Lindars (116), we now "suddenly discover that the setting is in or near Beth-saida . . . about seventy miles from the scene of the Baptist's ministry." He concludes "that John's topographical care deserts him at this point" (see also Bultmann, 102-3: "it is not possible to know whether this happens before he crosses the Jordan, or when he has already reached Galilee").

37. The notion that Andrew and Peter were from Bethsaida is independent of the synoptic tradition, where their home seems to be in Capernaum, some miles to the south (Mk 1:29 par.). But as Schnackenburg observes, the information here "shows precise knowledge" (1.314), that is, to the effect that the two brothers and Philip had grown up in Bethsaida. The effort of Abbott (*Johannine Grammar,* 228) to suggest (on the basis of a supposed difference between the prepositions ἀπό and ἐκ) that "Philip, though resident in Bethsaida, has sprung 'from' Capernaum, the city of Andrew and Peter," is far from convincing. The two prepositions appear to be used interchangeably.

him, and for Peter and Andrew as well, it was an opportunity to return home, parting company with John and his disciples. While nothing is said explicitly of Andrew and Simon Peter accompanying Jesus and Philip (and presumably Nathanael) to Galilee, the presumption later on is that "his disciples" were present at the wedding in Cana (2:2, 11), and then with Jesus in Capernaum (2:12). The implication of the narrative is that by this time they numbered either four or five, depending on whether Philip and the unnamed disciple are the same.

45 The vocabulary of verse 41 repeats itself. Philip "finds" Nathanael and "says" to him, "We have found" someone. In the first instance it was "the Messiah" (v. 41); here it is "someone of whom Moses wrote in the law, and of whom the prophets wrote." Taken literally, Philip's plural "we" suggests a deliberate repetition of Andrew's language, and consequently an awareness of the encounter between Jesus and the two disciples of John and of Andrew's testimony to Simon Peter. This would also lend plausibility to the conjecture that Philip was the unnamed disciple of verse 40. Moloney claims that Philip here "repeats the lie of Andrew: 'We have found. . . .'" The only person Philip found is Nathanael (v. 45a), but he *was found* and called by Jesus."[38] This presupposes an overly sharp distinction between finding and being found, a distinction appropriate to discussions of divine sovereignty and human free will, but not to the dynamics of storytelling. In Jesus' parables, for example, finding (Mt 13:44-46) and being found (Mt 18:12-14; Lk 15:32) are almost interchangeable metaphors for salvation, and the same is true here.

Nathanael is unknown to the synoptic tradition,[39] and all efforts to identify him with someone named in the synoptic Gospels (Bartholomew, for example, or Matthew) are speculative.[40] Philip's witness to Nathanael advances the narrative in three ways. First, it reminds us of the Gospel writer's interest in "Moses," still accenting (as in v. 17) promise and fulfillment, continuity rather than discontinuity, between Moses and Jesus. Later, Jesus himself will endorse Philip's claim ("If you believed Moses, you would believe me, for he wrote about me," 5:46). Second, it anchors the notion of "the Messiah" in the entire Hebrew Bible, both the law and the prophets.[41] This sug-

---

38. Moloney, 55.

39. The name "Nathanael" means, in Hebrew, "God has given," and the writer could be anticipating already here his characteristic theme that Jesus' disciples are those whom God has "given" him (see 6:37, 39; 10:29; 17:2, 6-7, 24; 18:9). Yet there is no way a first-time reader, even one who knew Hebrew, could have been expected to catch such a reference. Only on encountering the later references to believers as God's gift would it have been possible to think back on Nathanael as the author's prime example. For now at least, Nathanael's name is just a name, not to be scrutinized for deeper meaning.

40. See Schnackenburg, 1.314; Morris, 143.

41. The operative phrase here is "Moses and the prophets," as in Luke 16:31 (also

gests that the whole Bible testifies to a single "Coming One," as John thought (vv. 15, 26-27), in contrast to the delegation from Jerusalem, with their pedantic alternatives of "the Christ," "Elias," and "the Prophet" (v. 25).[42] Third, Philip finally names the One who is both the long-expected Messiah and the main character in the present story: "Jesus, son of Joseph, from Nazareth."

Ironically, the only characters in the Gospel who speak Jesus' name are individuals or groups who do *not* believe in him: "the Jews" in Galilee who asked, "Is this not Jesus, the son of Joseph, whose father and mother we know?" (6:42); the man born blind, who testified that "the man called Jesus" had healed him (9:11); some Greeks at the Passover who would tell this same Philip, "Sir, we want to see Jesus" (12:21); the soldiers sent to arrest "Jesus the Nazarene" (18:5, 7); and, finally, Pilate's mute inscription over the cross, "Jesus the Nazorean, the King of the Jews" (19:19). Philip, like the man born blind, will soon come to believe in Jesus (2:11; compare 9:38), but at the moment he is only a "follower" in the sense of hearer and companion on a journey, not yet a "believer." None of this means that these would-be followers are wrong in their understanding of Jesus. Even though Philip's testimony "falls short of the full truth,"[43] readers of the Gospel would have viewed it as a valid pointer toward that truth. Even without birth narratives, they would have known that "son of Joseph" and "Son of God" are not contradictory terms. "The Word came in human flesh," after all (v. 14), and "son of Joseph" is as legitimate an expression as any for "human flesh." As to the virgin birth, the term "son of Joseph" neither implies nor excludes it, as the birth narratives in Matthew and Luke both recognize. Whether it is a matter of the Gospel writer's conscious irony,[44] or of simply recording faithfully the terms by which Jesus' contemporaries described him, there is no basis here for calling into question the genuineness of Philip's commitment to Jesus.

46 The last phrase, "from Nazareth," catches Nathanael's attention:

24:27), on the assumption that "Moses" refers to the Torah, or first five books of the Hebrew Bible, and "the prophets" to all the rest (even when "the psalms" are mentioned separately, as in Lk 4:44, the effect is the same). To someone reading the Gospels in their canonical order, Philip's words in John 1:45 reinforce the risen Jesus' claims for himself in Luke 24:27, 44.

42. This may help explain the emphasis on "Moses" when in fact most messianic texts in the Hebrew Bible are found not in the Torah, but in the prophets or the psalms. If "the Messiah" (or "Christ") and "the prophet" (vv. 21, 25) are the same, then "Moses" becomes a conspicuous witness to Jesus the Messiah (see Deut 18:15-18; other possible messianic texts within the five books of Moses include Gen 3:15; 49:10; Num 24:17).

43. Moloney, *Belief in the Word,* 70-71.

44. According to Barrett, "It is in accord with his ironical use of traditional material that he should allow Jesus to be ignorantly described as 'son of Joseph' while himself believing that Jesus had no human father" (184; also Morris, 144).

1:35-51 JESUS AND JOHN'S DISCIPLES

"Can anything good come out of Nazareth?"[45] Contrast the first two disciples' encounter with Jesus. They had asked, "Where do you stay?" (v. 38), but this time it is a question not of where he is "staying" temporarily, but of where his home is. Nathanael's question is rhetorical and skeptical, where theirs was serious and searching, yet Philip's answer, "Come and see," echoes Jesus' earlier answer, "Come, and you will see" (v. 39).[46] Nathanael's skepticism about Jesus probably does not arise out of small-town rivalries (Nathanael was from Cana, according to 21:2), but out of a stubborn provincialism in reverse that refuses to see anything great or glorious in that which is familiar or close to home. Nathanael takes offense at "Nazareth" for much the same reason that the human mind in every generation takes offense at the Word coming "in human flesh" (v. 14).[47] Whether or not it also reflects the writer's awareness of later Jewish polemic against "the sect of the Nazoreans" (Acts 24:5) is more difficult to determine. If it does, then Philip's words, "Come and see," stand as an invitation to the Jewish community to put old prejudices aside and test the claims of Jesus and the Christian movement fairly on the basis of personal experience.

47 Verbs of motion are noticeable once again. Just as John had seen Jesus "coming to him" (v. 29) and then again "as he walked by" (v. 36), and had said "Look, the Lamb of God!" so Jesus now sees Nathanael "coming to him" and says, "Look, a true[48] Israelite, in whom is no deceit!" The purity of the true disciple mirrors the purity of the Lamb himself. The expression, "a true Israelite, in whom is no deceit," recalls the story of Jacob, above all the change of name from "Jacob" to "Israel" (Gen 32:28), anticipated by Isaac's statement to Esau that "Your brother came deceitfully and took your blessing," and Esau's reply, "Isn't he rightly named Jacob? He has deceived me these two times: He took my birthright, and now he's taken my blessing!"

---

45. Grammatically, it is Jesus who is from Nazareth. Abbott correctly links the accusative τὸν ἀπὸ Ναζαρέτ with the accusative Ἰησοῦν: "Jesus, son of Joseph, the [Jesus] of Nazareth" (*Johannine Grammar,* 38).

46. The parallel would be even closer if the variant reading ἴδετε were adopted in verse 39 (see above, n. 10). But quite possibly the variant itself originated as a partial assimilation to ἴδε here (see Barrett, 181).

47. Contrast Moloney, who argues that Nathanael is right, in the sense that Jesus is *not* from Nazareth, but from God: "The earliest Church recognized Jesus as being 'of Nazareth,' but the Johannine story insists that the believer look beyond his historical origins. In this Nathanael poses a good question" (55). This interpretation sets Jesus' human and divine origins too sharply against each other.

48. "True" (ἀληθῶς) is an adverb (more literally, "truly an Israelite"); compare 8:31, "If you remain in my word, you are truly (ἀληθῶς) my disciples." The terminology here reinforces the notion that "grace and truth [ἀλήθεια] came through Jesus Christ" (v. 16; compare v. 14). At the same time, it introduces the notion of genuineness, which is in turn reinforced by its negative corollary, "in whom is no deceit."

(Gen 27:35-36, NIV). Nathanael is a true "Israel," forever free of the "deceit" *(dolos)* that marked the life of the old "Jacob" (compare Ps 32:2; 1 Pet 2:1).

As in verse 29, the expression "coming to him" hints at the notion of allegiance. Nathanael is already on his way to becoming a disciple and, despite his initial skepticism,[49] there is no hint that he is coming to Jesus as a "sinner." Even though Jesus is "the Lamb of God, who takes away the sin of the world" (v. 29), he is not said to be calling "sinners" here (contrast Mk 2:17 par.; Lk 5:8). "Sin" in this Gospel belongs to "the world," and to the realm of darkness and death. In contrast to 1 John (1:5–2:2; 5:16-17), this Gospel has little reflection on the "sins of the righteous." Jesus is calling "true Israelites," in fulfillment of John's intention that he "might be revealed to Israel" (v. 31). If not explicitly "righteous," they are at any rate "chosen" by Jesus (compare 6:70; 13:18; 15:16, 19), "given" to him and "drawn" to him by the Father (compare 6:37, 39, 44, 65; 10:29; 17:2, 6, 9, 24). Nathanael as "a true Israelite, in whom is no deceit" is typical of them all,[50] and Jesus' promise to Nathanael turns out finally to include the whole group (v. 51).

48 Nathanael hears Jesus' words as directed to him personally, and asks, "How do you know me?"[51] There is no false modesty here. With a touch of humor, the Gospel writer highlights Nathanael's candor as a way of confirming Jesus' view of him as a man without deceit.[52] Jesus now goes on to explain his knowledge of Nathanael: "Before Philip called to you[53] under the fig tree, I saw you." Grammatically, the words are ambiguous,[54] but the

---

49. There is no indication in the text that Jesus had actually heard Nathanael's skeptical comment about Nazareth in the preceding verse. Yet it quickly becomes clear that he knows Nathanael's heart and his previous activities, and it is fair to assume that he knows what was said about Nazareth as well (compare 20:27, where Jesus immediately invites Thomas to touch his wounds, even though he had not been present at 20:25 when Thomas had expressed his skepticism to the other disciples).

50. It is worth noting that in Isaiah 53:9 and in 1 Peter 2:22, where it is cited, the absence of "deceit," or δόλος, is linked to being without sin.

51. At this point a conscious dialogue begins, continuing back and forth to the decisive pronouncement at the end of the chapter. First, "Nathanael *says* to him," then "Jesus *answered and said* to him," then in turn "Nathanael *answered* him" (v. 49), then again "Jesus *answered and said* to him" (v. 50), and finally, "and *he says* to him, 'Truly, truly *I say to you all*'" (v. 51).

52. Compare Morris, 145-46: "A more guileful man would have 'modestly' asserted his unworthiness."

53. "Called" (φωνῆσαι) is not the word commonly used for calling or recruiting someone as a disciple (that is, καλεῖν), but means simply to call out or speak to someone.

54. The participle ὄντα ("being," or "when you were") could be read either with the first occurrence of σε, or "you" ("Before Philip spoke to you under the fig tree, I saw you"), or with the second ("Before Philip spoke to you, I saw you when you were under the fig tree"). See Abbott, *Johannine Grammar,* 278.

most likely meaning is that "under the fig tree" is where Nathanael was when Philip "found" him and told him about Jesus (v. 45).[55] This would imply as well that Jesus knew of his comment about Nazareth (see n. 49). The point of saying, "*Before* Philip called to you," is not to raise the question "How long before?" or "On what occasion?" but simply to establish priority. What counts is not that *Philip* found Nathanael (v. 45), but that *Jesus* had already found him, just as surely as he found Philip to begin with (v. 43). By now the initiative rests wholly with Jesus, and Philip (consciously or not) has been acting as Jesus' agent.

Why a fig tree? Assuming that it was simply because that was where Philip found Nathanael, the question still remains, Why call attention to such a detail? One proposed answer is that "Under what tree?" was an accepted way of asking for evidence.[56] Another is that a specific biblical text is in view, Zechariah 3:10, against the messianic backdrop of 3:8.[57] But if Nathanael represents "Israel" in a symbolic reenactment of biblical history, then Jesus' role is the role of God, and a different text, Hosea 9:10, comes to mind: "Like grapes in the wilderness, I found Israel. Like the first fruit on the fig tree, in its first season, I saw your ancestors" (NRSV). The point would then be a comparison between Jesus finding the new Israel among the disciples of John, and God finding the old Israel in the days of the patriarchs.[58] Jesus spoke elsewhere of the delight of discovering an unexpected treasure in a field, or of selling everything to acquire one magnificent pearl (Mt 13:44-46); the image in Hosea of finding fruit unexpectedly in a barren land was well suited to make a similar point. As we have seen, Jesus in this Gospel considers his disciples a precious find, a gift from the Father, but it is too early in the Gospel account to make such a thought explicit (see above, n. 39). The reference to finding Nathanael "under the fig tree," therefore, remains at this point something of an enigma.

55. The alternative view, that Jesus saw Nathanael under the fig tree at some unspecified time *prior to* his meeting with Philip, raises all kinds of fruitless questions about what Nathanael had been doing there that made him recall the occasion and conclude that Jesus had read his mind (for example, meditating on the law, recounting to himself the story of Jacob, etc.). Beasley-Murray is surely correct in finding "no hidden subtlety here, just a statement of place where the two met" (27; compare the extended discussion in Chrysostom, *Homily* 20; NPNF, 1st ser., 14.71).

56. C. F. D. Moule ("A Note on 'under the fig tree' in John i 48, 50," *JTS* n.s. 5 [1954], 210-11) cited the story of Susanna in the additions to Daniel (*Susanna* 51–59), together with some talmudic evidence (compare Dodd, *Historical Tradition,* 310). Brown classifies this with a number of other proposals as "pure speculation" (1.83), while Barrett regards it as "anything but conclusive" (185).

57. C. R. Koester, "Messianic Exegesis and the Call of Nathanael (John 1.45-51)," *JSNT* 39 (1990), 23-34.

58. See my article many years ago, "Nathanael Under the Fig Tree," *Expository Times* 78 (1966/67), 182-83.

49 Jesus' supernatural knowledge of Nathanael's character and circumstances (compare 2:24-25; 4:17-18)[59] calls forth a spontaneous confession of faith: "You, Rabbi, are the Son of God. You are the[60] King of Israel." The first of these titles reinforces the testimony of John on the basis of the Spirit's descent on Jesus that "this is the Son of God" (v. 34). It is the only title for Jesus used more than once in the chapter. The second title, "the King of Israel" (see 12:13), is precisely what we would expect from "a true Israelite." Nathanael, as "Israel," acknowledges "Jesus, son of Joseph, from Nazareth" as his King and Lord.[61] The designation of Israel's king as God's son goes all the way back to the biblical Psalms (compare Pss 2:6-7; 89:26-27), and in the present context the two are virtually synonymous ways of affirming Jesus as "the Christ" or "Messiah" (compare vv. 41, 45).

The Gospel writer and his readers know that Jesus is God's Son in a more profound sense than Nathanael could have understood (see 1:14, 18), yet he allows Nathanael (like John in v. 34) to speak for him and for the entire Christian community. Nathanael's confession anticipates the writer's hope that all who read "might believe that Jesus is the Christ, the Son of God, and believing have life in his name" (20:31). To Nathanael, within the story, "King of Israel" defines what "Son of God" means, but for the author and his readers "Son of God" (that is, "God the One and Only, . . . right beside the Father," v. 18) defines what "King of Israel" means. There is ambivalence about Jesus' kingship in this Gospel. He eludes efforts to make him king (6:15), yet the crowds in Jerusalem echo Nathanael's words in welcoming him as "King of Israel," in fulfillment of Zechariah 9:9 (12:13, 15). The inscription over the cross, in common with the other Gospels, reads, "the King of the Jews" (19:19; compare v. 14), but the Gospel writer puts the irony in context with a serious dialogue between Jesus and Pilate over kingship (18:33-38) and a reminder to Pilate that Jesus "made himself the Son of God" (19:7). "My kingship is not from this world," Jesus tells Pilate, "You say that I am a king; for this I was born, and for this I came into the world, that I might testify to the truth. Everyone who is from the truth hears my voice" (18:36, 37). Those who are "from the truth," like Nathanael, are the "Israel"

---

59. See also, for example, 4:50-53; 5:42; 6:6, 64; 7:19-20; 8:37, 40; 11:4, 14; 13:11, 18-19, 36-38; 14:29; 16:1-4, 19; 21:18-19.

60. "King" (βασιλεύς) is definite even without the definite article because it is a predicate nominative that precedes the verb. Thus the variant reading in some ancient manuscripts (σὺ εἶ ὁ βασιλεύς) has exactly the same meaning (see also 12:13).

61. T. Niklas, "'Unter dem Feigenbaum': Die Rolle des Lesers im Dialog zwischen Jesus und Natanael (John 1.45-50)," *NTS* 46.2 (2000), 195, 197, finds rather a sharp and intentional contrast between Philip's "son of Joseph" (v. 46) and Nathanael's "Son of God" (v. 49). Compare Moloney's interpretation of Nathanael's skepticism about Nazareth (n. 47).

of which Jesus is King. Nathanael and his companions will learn shortly that Jesus' identity as Son and Revealer of God defines and takes precedence over his identity as King.

50 Jesus takes Nathanael's confession in stride and promises him even more. His response is wordy,[62] and could be read as a kind of rebuke, but it is doubtful that any rebuke is intended.[63] Jesus accepts Nathanael's words as a genuine expression of belief. While there have been general references to those who "believe" in the Light (v. 7) or in Jesus' name (v. 12), Nathanael is the first *individual* in the Gospel who is explicitly said to "believe." Jesus' reply should probably be punctuated as a statement (NIV: "You believe"),[64] but even if it is punctuated as a question (RSV, NRSV: "Do you believe?"), Jesus is not casting doubt on Nathanael's faith, only on the merit of the evidence on which it is based.[65] Jesus' supernatural knowledge of the past or the present, while impressive, is not the most important reason for believing in him.

Three chapters later many Samaritan villagers "believe" in Jesus on the basis of a woman's testimony that "he told me everything I ever did" (4:39; compare vv. 17-19, 29), but after spending two days with Jesus they say to her, "No longer do we believe because of what you said, for we have heard for ourselves and we know that this is truly the Savior of the world" (4:42). Similarly here, Nathanael's faith based on Jesus' supernatural knowledge of his meeting with Philip[66] will give way not to a deeper faith but to

---

62. The English translation, "and said to him, 'Because I said to you that I saw you [καὶ εἶπεν αὐτῷ ὅτι· εἶπόν σοι ὅτι εἶδόν σε] underneath the fig tree,'" reflects quite well the repetitiveness and wordiness of the Greek sentence. What Abbott (*Johannine Grammar*, 155-56) calls the "suspensive" use of ὅτι (that is, as "because" in a clause prior to the main clause) is characteristic of Johannine style (compare 8:45, 14:19, 15:19, 16:6, 19:42, and especially 20:29, where Jesus tells Thomas, in a manner reminiscent of our passage, "Because [ὅτι] you have seen me, you have believed. Blessed are those who did not see, and believed").

63. Compare Schnackenburg, 319: "How else could Nathanael have come to believe, except through Jesus' first words to him?"

64. Abbott points out that in John's other uses of the "suspensive" ὅτι (see n. 60) "the verb in the apodosis is always affirmative," and that "This turns the scale in favor of an affirmative" here (*Johannine Grammar*, 196).

65. Moloney's comment, even *after* Nathanael's confession, that "Up to this point the narrative has not witnessed an expression of genuine faith" (*Belief in the Word*, 75), is hardly fair to Nathanael.

66. The phrase "underneath the fig tree" (ὑποκάτω τῆς συκῆς) is simply a stylistic variation of "under the fig tree" (ὑπὸ τὴν συκῆν) in verse 48 (compare Mk 4:21 with Lk 8:16). It should be interpreted in light of the latter, not the other way around. Morris, for example (146, n. 111), uses it to rule out the notion that Jesus saw Nathanael at the time Philip called him, and to place the incident instead at some unspecified *earlier* time (see above, n. 54).

more conclusive verification. In the case of the Samaritans the verification came in what they heard for themselves from the lips of Jesus, while for Nathanael the verification consists of things he "will see" (compare Philip's invitation to "come and see," v. 46). Nathanael's experience moves from being seen (vv. 47, 48) to seeing (vv. 50, 51). If Jesus is to be "revealed to Israel" as John promised (v. 31), then "Israel," like John, must "see" Jesus[67] (compare vv. 32-34) and the "greater things than these," of which Jesus now speaks.[68]

51 Jesus now goes on to explain the "greater things," addressing first Nathanael alone, and then immediately a wider audience: "Amen, amen, I say to you all." Commentators often resolve the discrepancy by arguing either that verse 51 is "an addition of the Evangelist's,"[69] or (on the contrary) an originally independent saying imported into the Johannine context.[70] But even if such theories were provable, they would have little relevance to the interpreter's task, which is to make sense of the narrative as it stands. Three considerations must be kept in mind. First, Philip's invitation to Nathanael back in verse 46 to "Come and see" makes it a fair inference that Philip is also assumed to be present. Second, the narrative flow of the chapter allows us — invites us, in fact — to go a step further and assume that *all four* individuals who have met Jesus — Andrew, Simon Peter, Philip, and Nathanael — are with him at this point. These four (or five, if the unnamed disciple is not Philip) seem to constitute the group designated as "his disciples" in the next chapter (2:1, 11, 12, 17, and 22). Third, the plural "you all" *(hymin)* should be understood finally as including the readers of the Gospel. Whatever experiences are in store for Jesus' disciples are in store for us as well — not just vicariously but actually — as we read the Gospel and enter into its world (compare 20:29-31).

The double "Amen" formula occurs 25 times in John's Gospel as a way of solemnly attesting the truth of what is about to be said. It is never doubled

---

67. Compare Brown, 1.87. It is highly unlikely, however, that there is any direct reflection here on the (incorrect) etymology of the name "Israel" as "seeing God" (above all in Philo; for example, *De Somniis* 1.171). For such an interpretation, see M.-É. Boismard, *Du Baptême à Cana* (Paris: Cerf, 1956), 123-27.

68. The notion of "greater things" is conspicuous in this Gospel. The Father is "greater" than Jesus (14:28), and his gift to Jesus is "greater than all" (10:29). As the present is "greater" than the past (for example, Jacob, 4:12; John, 5:36; Abraham, 8:53), so the future is "greater" than the present (in addition to Nathanael's "greater things than these," see 5:20, "works greater than these [μείζονα τούτων] he will show him," and 14:12, "the works I do [the believer] will do also, and greater than these [μείζονα τούτων] he will do, because I am going to the Father").

69. Bultmann, 98, 105.

70. See Moloney, *The Johannine Son of Man,* 24, n. 6.

in the other Gospels, where Jesus uses the single "Amen" 31 times in Matthew, 13 times in Mark, and 6 times in Luke. The formula does not demand the plural "you." Jesus could have used the singular *(soi)* as he does with Nicodemus (3:3, 5, 11) and with Peter (13:38; 21:18).[71] "Amen" (sometimes doubled) was fairly common in Jewish literature as a response to a prayer or vow,[72] but Jesus' use of it to *introduce* certain pronouncements is virtually unique.[73] The 25 instances of "Amen, amen" in John's Gospel are quite varied and resist easy generalization. Sometimes (as here) they attest the truth of a single pronouncement (3:3; 8:51; 13:21); other times they introduce (10:7; 12:24) or punctuate a longer speech of Jesus (for example, 5:19, 24, 25), or highlight Jesus' responses within an ongoing dialogue or controversy (see 6:26, 32, 47, 53).[74] Sometimes they call attention to his identity as "Son" (5:19) or "Son of God" (5:25) or "Son of Man" (here and in 6:62). Sometimes (as here) they predict the future (see 13:21, 38; 14:12; 16:20, 23; 21:18). Sometimes they point the way to salvation or eternal life (3:3, 5; 6:47, 53; 8:51). It is easy to say (as many commentators do) that the formula accents certain sayings of Jesus as especially important, but if Jesus is "the Word" (vv. 1, 14), and if everything he speaks is what he has received from the Father (for example, 3:34; 7:16; 8:26, 28, 38; 12:49), then all of his sayings are true and revelatory in the eyes of the Gospel writer. It is just that Jesus pauses occasionally to vouch more explicitly for their truth. In a sense, the double "Amen" formula here (and even more explicitly in 3:11) solemnly attests the truth of *all* that Jesus will say from here on. So far he has said little: only "What are you looking for?" (v. 38) and "Come, and you will see" (v. 39), two concise pronouncements on Simon's name (v. 42) and Nathanael's character (v. 47), and a brief further exchange with Nathanael (vv. 48, 50). The substance of his revelation is yet to come, and the "Amen, amen" pronouncement marks its be-

---

71. Thus the shift to the plural is deliberate, not something made inevitable by the "Amen" formula. The analogy with Nicodemus is instructive. Jesus addresses Nicodemus in the singular but shifts to the plural as the conversation proceeds (3:11-12) in order to show that Nicodemus is a representative figure. Nathanael is a representative figure as well, and now that the conversation is at an end the plural makes it clear that this is the case.

72. Of the 25 occurrences of "Amen" in the Hebrew Bible, five are doubled, either as "Amen, amen" (Num 5:22; Neh 8:6) or "Amen and amen" (Pss 41:14; 72:19; 89:53). All of these appear in the LXX as γένοιτο γένοιτο except for Nehemiah 8:6 (which appears as a single ἀμήν), but for ἀμὴν ἀμὴν in certain LXX manuscripts see 1 Esdr 9.47 (B); Tob 8.8 (S). For the doubled "Amen" in Hebrew, see also 1QS 1.20; 2.10, 18.

73. See, however, Jeremiah 28:6, where "Amen" is rendered in the LXX as ἀληθῶς.

74. Bernard comments that the expression "always carries a reference to what has gone before — either a reply to an observation . . . or an explanation and expansion of something that has already been said" (1.67).

ginning. The promise that "you will see" echoes (perhaps deliberately) the "Come, and you will see" of verse 39. There the disciples "saw where he was staying," but here Jesus begins to make known the full extent of what they — and we — "will see" in the chapters to come.

The allusion in Jesus' pronouncement to Jacob's dream at Bethel (Gen 28:12) is neither as direct nor as unmistakable as is commonly assumed.[75] There is no stairway or ladder reaching to heaven, no Jacob asleep and dreaming, no vision of the Lord, no covenant promise.[76] John Chrysostom discussed the pronouncement at some length without any reference to the Genesis text: "For on Him as on the King's own Son, the royal ministers ascended and descended, once at the season of the Crucifixion, again at the time of the Resurrection and the Ascension, and before this also, when they 'came and ministered unto Him' (Matt. iv. 11), when they proclaimed the glad tidings of His birth, and cried, 'Glory to God in the highest, and on earth peace' (Luke ii. 14), when they came to Mary and Joseph."[77] The links between Jesus' promise to Nathanael and Jacob's dream are two: first, the angels (using the same phrase, "the angels of God"), and second, the verbs "going up and coming down" in just that order (since angels have their home in heaven, we might have expected the opposite). While these similarities are sufficient to establish a connection, they do not justify reading the pronouncement as in any way a midrash or paraphrase of the Genesis text — as if to equate "the Son of man" either with the stairway or with the sleeping Jacob at the bottom.[78]

---

75. Contrast H. Odeberg: "The allusion in this utterance to Gen 28:12 is immediately apparent and generally recognized" (*The Fourth Gospel,* 33).

76. Jacob's comment after the vision that "the LORD is in this place, and I did not know it" (ἐγὼ δὲ οὐκ ᾔδειν, Gen 28:16) evokes rather John's two disclaimers, "and I did not know him" (κἀγὼ οὐκ ᾔδειν αὐτόν, vv. 31, 33), made just before testifying to Jesus as "Son of God."

77. *Homily* 21 (NPNF, 1st. ser., 14.73). Origen's commentary is unfortunately not extant on this passage. The earliest commentator to mention Jacob at Bethel seems to have been Augustine, whose exegesis is on the whole less plausible than Chrysostom's. Augustine noticed that Jacob "anointed the stone which he had placed at his head" (Gen 28:18), and saw this as "a pointing out of Christ," the anointed Stone of Isaiah 28:16 and 1 Peter 2:6. The angels he interpreted as "good preachers, preaching Christ; this is the meaning of 'they ascend and descend upon the Son of man.'" *On the Gospel of John,* 7 (NPNF, 2d ser., 7.56-57). For a good brief survey of patristic views, see Bernard, 1.70-72.

78. The Hebrew text says that in Jacob's dream the angels were ascending and descending "on it" (בו), meaning on the ladder or stairway (LXX, ἐπ' αὐτῆς, where the genitive refers to place). Some have inferred from this that the Son of man is a sort of "ladder" or mediator between heaven and earth. But in certain early Jewish traditions (e.g., *Genesis Rabbah* 68.12, in *Midrash Rabbah* [London: Soncino, 1961], 626), בו was read as "on him," meaning on (or upon) Jacob. Because this agrees with the grammar of John 1:51 (ἐπὶ τὸν υἱὸν τοῦ ἀνθρώπου, where the accusative implies motion toward or over someone), oth-

1:35-51 JESUS AND JOHN'S DISCIPLES

More to the point is the fact that angels are associated with the Son of man nine other times in the Gospels,[79] and are viewed on at least three different occasions as Jesus' actual or potential protectors during his sojourn on earth (see Mt 2:13-14, 19-21; 4:6, 11; 26:53; Mk 1:13; Lk 22:43).[80] Chronologically, Jesus' promise to Nathanael and the other disciples comes closest to the notice at the temptation in Mark and Matthew that "the angels were ministering to him" (Mk 1:13; compare Mt 4:6, 11). In simplest terms, "the angels of God going up and coming down over the Son of man" represent the "glory" *(doxa)* to be displayed in Jesus' ministry (compare v. 14), from the wedding at Cana (2:11) to the raising of Lazarus from the dead (11:4, 40) — all of it preliminary to the Son of man's final "glorification" in the passion narratives.[81] Probably no significant distinction should be made between the angels "going up" (as if to bring Jesus' prayers up to the Father) and "coming down" (as if to bring to Jesus revelations from God).[82] Rather, the two participles simply reinforce the notion that God is with Jesus from the beginning of his ministry to

---

ers have identified the Son of man with Jacob at the bottom of the stairs, as the recipient of divine revelation (compare Odeberg, 35). But if anyone corresponds to the biblical Jacob, it is Nathanael, the "true Israelite," not Jesus. According to Brown (1.90), "The whole theory is dubious." Barrett (187) and Schnackenburg (1.321-22) are similarly cautious.

79. The terms are "the angels" (Mk 13:27), "the holy angels" (Lk 9:26), "his angels" (Mt 13:41; 16:27; 24:31), "his holy angels" (Mk 8:38), "all the angels" (Mt 25:31), and, most significantly, "the angels of God," as here (Lk 12:8, 9). Compare also Revelation 14:6-20.

80. The "twelve legions of angels" which Jesus could have summoned at his arrest but did not (Mt 26:53) are particularly noteworthy. It is intriguing to ask if they are the same as Jesus' "helpers" or "assistants" (ὑπηρέται) in John's Gospel who might have fought on his behalf but do not because his kingdom is "not of this world" (see 18:36, and compare Bernard, 2.610-11).

81. The notion that "the angels of God" represent "the glory of God" is a natural and appropriate one. Notice the pairing of "angel of the Lord" (ἄγγελος κυρίου) with "glory of the Lord" (δόξα κυρίου) in Luke 2:9; also the association of "Son of man" with both "glory" and "angels" in Mark 13:26-27//Matthew 24:30-31, in Mark 8:38//Matthew 16:27//Luke 9:26, and in Matthew 25:31. In John's Gospel, aside from the present passage, "glory" replaces "angels" as the operative term for the vindication of Jesus. Even the variations in terminology are similar: the Gospel of John can speak of "the glory of God" (11:4, 40; 12:43), or "his [that is, Jesus'] glory" (1:14; 2:11; 12:41; compare 17:24), inviting comparison with such terms as "his angels" and "the angels of God" (see n. 79).

82. For such a distinction, see Schnackenburg (1.321): "From the Son of Man on earth, the angels go up to God with his desires and prayers, and come down to serve him." Still less should the verbs "going up" and "coming down" be used to argue that the Son of man is in some mystical sense *both* at the bottom and the top of the stairway, so that the disciples will see "the connexion of the earthly man with his heavenly counterpart," or "between the celestial appearance, the Glory, δόξα, of Christ, and his appearance in the flesh" (Odeberg, 36).

the end. The reference to "the sky opened" echoes the synoptic accounts of Jesus' baptism,[83] while the angels (as we have seen) would have evoked for some his desert temptation. Just as the writer of this Gospel omits the transfiguration, yet sums up the whole ministry of Jesus with the testimony that "we looked at his glory" (v. 14), so he omits Jesus' baptism and temptation, yet affirms the reality of the Spirit "remaining" on him (vv. 31, 33) and of angels "going up and coming down" over him (v. 51), not in one or two incidents but throughout his ministry, up to and including his resurrection.

As to the term "Son of man" itself, it makes its first appearance here as a title for Jesus comparable to "the Lamb of God" (vv. 29, 36), "the Son of God" (vv. 34, 50), "the Messiah," or "Christ" (v. 41), and "the King of Israel" (v. 50). In its strategic context here, it trumps all the others — even "Son of God" — as the defining title for Jesus in this Gospel. This is appropriate because, unlike the others, "Son of man" is not a title someone else gives to Jesus, but one that he claims for himself, just as in the other Gospels.[84] What is unclear is whether or not Nathanael was familiar with the term, and whether or not Jesus expected him to be. Neither Nathanael's response nor that of the other disciples is given. Unlike the rest of the "Son of man" sayings in the Gospel of John, this one ends the conversation. It invites comparison with Jesus' response to the High Priest before the Sanhedrin: "From now on[85] you will see the Son of man seated on the right hand of power and coming on the clouds of heaven" (Mt 26:64; compare Mk 14:62). There Jesus was responding to an enemy questioning his supposed claim to be "the Christ, the Son of God" (or, in Mark, "the Son of the Blessed"); here he responds to a disciple confessing him as "Son of God" and "King of Israel." But in each instance he resolves the issue with a reference to himself as "Son of man,"[86] and a promise that "you will see" something to vindicate the Son of man. In Matthew and Mark, "Son of man" comes near the beginning of the pronouncement; he

---

83. Compare Matthew 3:16; Luke 3:21. As in the baptismal accounts, οὐρανός is best rendered as "sky" rather than "heaven" because the language is that of a vision (compare Acts 7:56, Rev 4:1), and in a vision the visible "sky" (not heaven) is opened to reveal what lies beyond it.

84. If this were the only occurrence of "Son of man" in John's Gospel, it could be argued that Jesus meant someone other than himself, but such an argument cannot be sustained throughout the rest of the Gospel (see 9:37, where Jesus explicitly claims the title for himself, and 12:32-34, where he speaks of himself being "lifted up" and the crowd responds as if he had said 'Son of man'; also 6:51-58, where to eat Jesus' flesh is to eat the flesh of the Son of man).

85. Even textual copyists seem to have noticed the similarities, for many ancient manuscripts add the words "from now on" (ἀπ' ἄρτι) from Matthew 26:64 between the "Amen, amen" formula and ὄψεσθε in verse 51.

86. Compare Mark 8:31, where he replies to Peter's acknowledgment that "You are the Christ" (v. 29) with a reference to himself as "Son of man."

is enthroned in heaven and coming again, and that is his vindication. Here "Son of man" comes last in the sentence; angels minister to him already on earth, and that is his vindication.[87] Standing where it does, at the very end of Jesus' initial call of his disciples, "Son of man" cries out for definition. Nathanael does not ask, "Who is this Son of man?" (12:34), or "Who is he, Lord, that I might believe in him?" (9:36), yet the unspoken question lingers.

E. JESUS AT CANA AND CAPERNAUM (2:1-12)

1 And the third day a wedding took place in Cana of Galilee, and the mother of Jesus was there, 2 and Jesus with his disciples had also been invited to the wedding. 3 And when the wine gave out, the mother of Jesus says to him, "They have no wine." 4 And Jesus says to her, "What is that to me or to you, woman? My hour has not yet come." 5 His mother says to the servants, "Do whatever he tells you." 6 Now there were six stone water jars, placed there for the purification rituals of the Jews, each holding two or three measures. 7 Jesus tells them, "Fill the water jars with water," and they filled them to the top. 8 And he tells them, "Now draw some out and take it to the banquet master"; so they took it. 9 When the banquet master tasted the water-turned-to-wine and did not know where it came from (though the servants who had drawn the water knew), the banquet master called for the bridegroom 10 and said to him, "People always put out the good wine first, and then the not-so-good when they have had too much to drink. You have kept the good wine until now." 11 This Jesus did in Cana of Galilee as a beginning of the signs, and revealed his glory, and his disciples believed in him. 12 After this he went down to Capernaum, he and his mother and brothers and his disciples, and there they remained for a few days.

A few verses earlier Jesus "decided to set out for Galilee" (1:43), but at the end of the chapter his journey there with his disciples had not yet begun. Now we are "in Cana of Galilee," where, we are told, "the third day a wedding took place" (2:1). Here (as in 1:19) we expect a full stop and a fresh start, and the modern chapter division caters to this expectation. But instead the writer uses the conjunction *kai* ("and") to move us on with scarcely a break. "Ignore the chapter division," he seems to tell us, "and you will see what Jesus said you would see" (that is, in 1:51). Moreover, "the third day"

---

87. Compare Lindars, 122: "The point is that Jesus is *on earth*, and the revelation of his glory as the Son of Man does not have to wait for his exaltation to heaven."

reminds us that we are still in the time-conscious world of 1:19-51, punctuated by the repeated expression, "the next day," in 1:29, 35, and 43. Four successive days have gone by, and "the third day" normally means "two days later," or "the day after tomorrow" from the standpoint of the events just described. This brings the total to six.[1] Nowhere are the six days totaled up, however, and it is probably futile to look for symbolic parallels either in the six days of creation, or the six days prior to Jesus' last Passover (12:1), or the six days preceding the glory of Jesus' transfiguration (compare Mk 9:2; Mt 17:1). Perhaps the most attractive suggestion is that of Moloney, who finds in the Jewish midrash *Mekilta on Exodus* an account of the giving of the law on Mount Sinai in which "the third day" (compare Exod 19:11, 15, 16), being preceded by four days of preparation, is actually the sixth day overall, just as in John 1:19–2:11. The strength of his proposal is that he can appeal to the principle stated already in the Gospel that "the law was given through Moses; grace and truth came into being through Jesus Christ" (1:17).[2] But the midrash is later than John's Gospel, and the parallel is one that would likely have been lost on the Gospel's readers. Rather, the author's interest is in the sequence, not in the total of six. If there had been more days, or fewer, the point would have been much the same. Nor is it helpful to find in "the third day" a subtle allusion to the resurrection of Jesus.[3] Rather, "the third day" here, instead of "the next day," merely signals the fact that additional time was needed to make the journey from the place where John had been baptizing to "Cana of Galilee."[4] Because "the third day" can sometimes be used rather imprecisely (like "a couple of days" in English; see Lk 13:32), and because the location of "Bethany, beyond the Jordan" (1:28) is unknown and Cana's location not absolutely certain,[5] it is useless to speculate how long the actual

---

1. Those who assign 1:40-42 to a separate day (see, for example, Carson, 167-68; compare Bultmann, 98, n. 4; 114, n. 3) end up with a total of seven (but see the discussion above on πρῶτον in 1:41).

2. Moloney, 50-51. His point is that after the sequence of days, "The glory of God is revealed 'on the third day,'" just as in John 2:11 (50); see *Mekilta de-Rabbi Ishmael* (ed. J. Z. Lauterbach; Philadelphia: Jewish Publication Society, 1976, 2.210).

3. Dodd, *Interpretation,* 300 (see 1 Cor 15:4; also Mt 16:21; 17:23; 27:64; Lk 9:22; 13:32; 18:33; 24:7, 21, 46). John's Gospel, in the only place where it echoes this tradition, uses a different phrase, "in three days" (2:19-20; compare Mk 8:38, 9:31, 10:34, and 14:58).

4. Cana, unlike Bethsaida (1:44, but see 12:21), Nazareth (1:45-46), and Capernaum (2:12), is specifically designated "of Galilee" (compare v. 11; 4:46; 21:2; also Josephus, *Life* 86: "a village of Galilee which is called Cana"), not to distinguish it from other villages of the same name elsewhere (see, for example, Josh 19:28; Josephus, *Antiquities* 13.391 and 15.112), but to signal that Jesus' plan "to set out for Galilee" (1:43) is still in effect.

5. The presence of Jesus' mother at the wedding, as well as Nathanael's comment

2:1-12 JESUS AT CANA AND CAPERNAUM

journey would have taken. The narrative shows no interest in the journey as such, nor in Jesus' arrival in Galilee. The scene has changed, and for the moment Jesus and his disciples are not in the picture. But "Galilee" is important, for Galilee, not Judea, will be the scene of the first miracle.

1 The story begins abruptly with the notice that "a wedding took place." The verb for "took place" is the now familiar *egeneto* (literally, "came," or "came about," as in 1:3, 6, 10, 14, 17, and 28). We know nothing of the circumstances of the wedding, or the identity of the bridegroom and the bride, only that the mother of Jesus was "there" (*ekei*, accenting the importance of the place). His mother's presence provides a reason for the presence of Jesus and his disciples (v. 2) and sets the stage for a brief exchange between Jesus and his mother (vv. 3-4) and the ensuing miracle. The fact that "the mother of Jesus" is never named in this Gospel (see vv. 3-5, 12; 6:42; 19:25-27) is less surprising than is often assumed. Jesus' brothers are not named either (v. 12; 7:3-5, 10), and his father Joseph is named only by Philip (1:45) and by "the Jews" in Galilee (6:42), never by the Gospel writer. In this respect, John's Gospel is not so different from Mark's, where Jesus' mother Mary and his brothers Jacob, Joses, and Simon are named only once (Mk 6:3), and that by the citizens of his hometown, not the Gospel writer.[6]

2 Almost as an afterthought, we are told that "Jesus with his disciples had also been invited [literally, "called"] to the wedding." The verb is singular, suggesting that Jesus was invited and brought his disciples along,[7] but it is wrong to infer, as some have done, that their presence was what led to the shortage of wine (v. 3).[8] Nor can it be assumed that Jesus was invited to the wedding while he was still beyond the Jordan, at Bethany. The notice that Jesus "decided" to go to Galilee (1:43) suggests that he acted on his own initiative (compare 5:21; 17:24; 21:22), not in response to an undisclosed wed-

---

about Nazareth (1:48), suggests that Cana was near Nazareth (Nathanael, according to 21:2, was from Cana). The reference to Capernaum in 2:13 and the story of Jesus and the royal official in 4:46-54 suggests that Cana was also within a day's journey of Capernaum (the text consistently speaks of "going down" from Cana to Capernaum: 2:13; 4:47, 49, 51). On the basis of the oldest traditions and the continuity of the name, Cana should probably be identified with Khirbet Qana, in hill country above a broad plain eight miles north of Nazareth, rather than Kefr Kenna, just four miles northeast of Nazareth, which has been shown to pilgrims and tourists since the sixteenth century (for the classic argument, see E. Robinson, *Biblical Researches in Palestine* [London: John Murray, 1841], 3.204-8; G. Dalman, *Sacred Sites and Ways* [London: S.P.C.K., 1935], 101-6).

6. It is possible that Mary the mother of Jesus is named by the Gospel writer in Mark 15:40, 47 and 16:1, but if so, she is named precisely *not* as Jesus' mother, but as the mother of his brothers James and/or Joses.

7. Hence the uncommon translation of καί: not "Jesus *and* his disciples," but "Jesus *with* his disciples."

8. Compare Bultmann, 115, n. 6.

ding invitation! The narrator is simply bringing Jesus and his disciples to the wedding as quickly and simply as possible, to get to the account of the miracle. Here for the first time, the phrase "his disciples" refers to the disciples of Jesus (compare vv. 11, 12, 17, and 22) rather than to John's disciples (as in 1:35, 37).[9] The disciples (evidently Andrew, Peter, Philip, Nathanael, and perhaps one other)[10] are introduced here, but play no part in the actual miracle story (vv. 3-10). The only reason for mentioning them is to prepare for the concluding notice that when Jesus "revealed his glory" in the miracle of the wine, "his disciples believed in him" (v. 11).

Jesus' father Joseph and his brothers and sisters, on the other hand, are not mentioned.[11] In one second-century tradition about the incident, Jesus "was invited with his mother and his brothers"[12] (rather than his disciples),[13] suggesting a time when he was still within the family circle and had no disciples. The notion that at some stage of the tradition the story was told as a remarkable incident from Jesus' childhood (like Lk 2:42-51, or even the stories found in the *Infancy Gospel of Thomas*) is an intriguing one,[14] but in John's Gospel this is obviously not the case because of the presence of disciples and all that has gone before.[15]

9. Brown comments (1.98), "They have abandoned the ascetic ways of John the Baptist for the less abstemious practices of Jesus (Luke vii 33-34)."

10. Many commentators (for example, Bultmann, 115, n. 5; Barrett, 190) assume that "his disciples" are somehow already "the Twelve" (compare 6:67, 70), but the reader would have no way of knowing this.

11. The presence of his brothers in verse 12 may well imply their presence at the wedding as well, but unlike the disciples they did not believe (7:5), and they are therefore not essential to the story. The narrative, like those in the other Gospels, may well presuppose that his father Joseph is deceased.

12. *Epistula Apostolorum* 5 (E. Hennecke, *New Testament Apocrypha* [Philadelphia: Westminster, 1963], 1.193). This work places the incident just between a brief account of Jesus being taught letters as a child (4), and his ministry proper: "And he made water into wine and awakened the dead and made the lame to walk; for him whose hand was withered, he stretched it out again, and the woman who suffered twelve years from a haemorrhage touched the edge of this garment and was immediately whole." At this point the apostles (who claim to be writing the account) abruptly come into the picture: "and . . . we reflected and wondered concerning the miracle he performed" (5).

13. Compare Bultmann, 114, who doubts that the disciples were originally in the story at all.

14. Compare Lindars, 127-28.

15. It is noteworthy that R. T. Fortna, in his reconstruction of a so-called "Signs Gospel" underlying the Gospel of John, considers the disciples part of the original story in the source, not an addition by the Gospel writer (*Gospel of Signs*, 30). Fortna takes issue with Bultmann at this point (see n. 13), yet Bultmann argues that "the correction of 'brothers' by 'disciples' might well have occurred in the σημεῖα-source, if the miracles were linked together to form a continuous narrative" (114, n. 6).

2:1-12 JESUS AT CANA AND CAPERNAUM

3 The story unfolds with a remarkable economy of language. "When the wine gave out" is only two words in Greek.[16] The comment of Jesus' mother, "They have no wine," echoing the narrator, suggests that she speaks merely as a guest, not as someone with direct responsibility for the wedding banquet. Her words, "they do not have," rather than "we do not have," puts her at a certain distance from the situation. As far as we can tell, she is simply pointing out a fact, not asking Jesus to do anything, least of all for herself. Her pronouncement sounds almost like a parody of Jesus' own comment in the synoptic tradition just before the feeding of the four thousand: "They do not have anything to eat" (Mk 8:2; Mt 15:32). There it was a matter of possible starvation; here it is a possible social disaster!

4 Jesus' abrupt reply, "What is that to me or to you?" (literally, "What to me and to you?") is a startling expression here because its five other New Testament occurrences are all in stories of demon possession, addressed to Jesus by people who are possessed.[17] The same idiom in Hebrew occurs in a wider range of settings in the Old Testament.[18] There the meaning can range from conflict between two parties (Jdg 11:12 and 1 Kgs 17:18, "What do you have against me?") or avoidance of conflict (2 Chr 35:21, "What quarrel do I have with you?"), to simple disengagement of one party from another (2 Kgs 3:13, "What have we to do with each other?"; compare Hos 14:8, "What has he [Ephraim] to do with idols?"). It is more ambiguous in 2 Samuel 16:10 and 19:23, where King David seems to demand disengagement between himself and "Abishai son of Zeruiah," and at the same time between *both of them* and "Shimei son of Gera," guaranteeing that Shimei will not be put to death. Disengagement is the point of Jesus' reply to his mother as well, but with the same ambiguity we find in the two texts from 2 Samuel. If Jesus is taking his mother's comment as an implicit request for him to act, it is natural to understand his reply as personal disengagement from her and what she is asking, as if to say (in the impatient tone of the modern idiom), "What do you want from me?" But if he hears her comment simply as a state-

---

16. In Greek, ὑστερήσαντος οἴνου, a genitive absolute. At least one scribe seems to have sensed *too much* economy of language. The first hand of ℵ (in agreement with a number of old Latin witnesses) is more wordy: "They had no wine because the wine of the wedding had been used up. Then [ℵ adds] the mother of Jesus said to him 'There is no wine'" (instead of "They have no wine" — presumably to avoid echoing "They had no wine" in the preceding sentence).

17. Compare Mark 5:7 and Luke 8:28 (τί ἐμοὶ καὶ σοί); with Mark 1:24, Matthew 8:29, and Luke 4:34 (τὶ ἡμῖν καὶ σοί).

18. Yet it is not necessarily a Semitic idiom, or limited to texts based on Hebrew originals. See, for example, Epictetus, *Dissertations,* in relation to wind for sailing (1.1.16), to Zeus or the gods (1.22.15; 1.27.13), and to an annoying person (2.19.16); also *Corpus Hermeticum* 11.21, in relation to God (see Schnackenburg, 1.328).

ment of fact (which it appears to be), his reply could be read as a disengagement of *both of them* from the troubles of the wedding party, as if to say, "What is that to me or to you?"[19]

It is difficult to decide between these alternatives. On the one hand, Jesus' knowledge of the inner thoughts of people he encounters (see 1:48; 2:24-25; 4:17-18) suggests that he might well be looking beneath the surface of his mother's remark and responding to an unspoken request to work a miracle. Moreover, as Brown points out, "the fact that he speaks of '*my* hour' would seem to indicate that he is denying only his own involvement."[20] Commentators have found in this Gospel a recurrent pattern of Jesus at first refusing a request, then establishing his independence of human agendas by referring to a decisive "hour" or "time" of glorification, but then granting the request after all (for example, Jesus and his brothers in 7:2-10; Jesus and the sisters of Lazarus in 11:1-7).[21] On the other hand, each incident is different, and their distinctiveness must be respected. For example, only Jesus' brothers in chapter 7 ask anything of him explicitly, and the Gospel writer is quick to tell us that their request was made in unbelief (7:5). Neither Jesus' mother here nor the sisters of Lazarus in chapter 11 make any actual request, and there is no evidence here (unless this is it) that Jesus and his mother have contrary intentions. Given the portrait of Jesus that emerges in this Gospel, there is little doubt that the narrative comment made in connection with the feeding of the five thousand applies here as well: "For he himself knew what he was going to do" (6:6). His mother's remark that "they have no wine" (v. 3) is not so much a request for Jesus to perform a miracle as a signal to the reader that he is going to do so. Her subsequent word to the servants, "Do whatever he tells you" (v. 5), will signal further that this is her expectation as well. In short, Jesus and his mother are thinking along the same lines, not at cross purposes.

If this is the case, then Jesus' words are meant not as disengagement from his mother or what she has in mind, but as disengagement of *them both* from the wedding banquet and its immediate needs. His mother's matter-of-fact pronouncement, "They have no wine," could evoke an impression of extreme need or deprivation (as in Mk 8:2; Mt 15:32). Yet whatever we may think of the importance of being a good host, or of honor

---

19. Compare Richmond Lattimore, *The New Testament* (New York: North Point, 1996); Reynolds Price, *Three Gospels* (New York: Scribner's, 1996), 184.

20. Brown (1.99) does, however, take account of 2 Samuel 16:10. Schnackenburg is more dismissive: "It never means, 'What concern is that of yours or mine?' The καί must be understood as marking a certain contrast" (1.328).

21. See C. H. Giblin, "Suggestion, Negative Response, and Positive Action in St John's Gospel (John 2:1-11; 4:46-53; 7:2-14; 11:1-44)," *NTS* 26 (1979-80), 197-211. For a similar pattern in another Gospel, see Luke 13:31-33.

and shame in the New Testament world, a shortage of wine at a wedding is not in quite the same category as a life-threatening illness (4:46-54), physical helplessness (5:1-8), being without food (6:5-13), blindness (9:1-7), or death (11:11-16, 38-44). Jesus' words to his mother are not a rebuke, nor an unambiguous refusal to act, but simply a reminder that the need she has pointed out is a relatively minor one. "Don't worry," he seems to say, "Their predicament is nothing to us. They will survive quite nicely even if 'They have no wine'!" He could even be saying, "Don't worry, woman. What is it to us? It is a small thing, and easily fixed." The issue is not compassion, but the revealing of Jesus' glory (compare 1:14), and it is important to make clear at the outset (to his mother, but above all to the reader) that whatever revelation is to take place here is only a beginning, and a modest one at that. This he does with the additional comment, "My hour has not yet come." We are left with a twofold question: First, how would Jesus' mother have understood this pronouncement? Second, how is the reader of the Gospel to understand it?

Both here and in 19:26, Jesus addresses his mother as "woman" *(gynai)*, the same term he uses in addressing the Samaritan woman (4:21) and Mary Magdalene (20:15; compare the angels in v. 13).[22] While the term implies no disrespect,[23] it makes Jesus' mother a stranger, just as the Samaritan woman was a stranger to Jesus, and just as Mary Magdalene was a stranger as long as she thought he was the gardener.[24] Yet the designation is not surprising if we keep in mind that Jesus never calls her "mother" (or "Mary") in *any* of the four Gospels. Only in John's Gospel, in fact, does he ever speak to her directly as an individual.[25] The three other instances in this Gospel are instructive in that each is linked, directly or indirectly, either to a decisive "hour," or to something "not yet." In 4:21 Jesus tells the Samaritan woman that "an *hour* is coming," or "an *hour* is coming and now

---

22. See also the woman taken in adultery (8:10, in material added later to the Gospel), and women in two of the synoptic healing narratives (Mt 15:28; Lk 13:12).

23. There is no evidence that the term is used with disrespect anywhere in the New Testament (compare Lk 22:57; 1 Cor 7:16), or (with rare exceptions) in ancient literature generally (see BDAG, 208-9). Hermas, in his opening vision, uses it interchangeably with "Lady" (κύρια): "Did I not always look at you as a goddess? Did I not always respect you as a sister? Why do you charge me falsely, O woman [γύναι], with these evil and unclean things?" (*Shepherd of Hermas, Vision* 1.1.7).

24. Jesus first called her "Woman" (20:15), but then abruptly, "Mary" (v. 16), bringing a moment of recognition and intimacy. There is no corresponding moment of intimacy in relation to his mother. The closest to it is 19:26, where in the presence of the disciple whom he loved, Jesus calls her "your mother," not his own.

25. In Luke 2:49 the twelve-year-old Jesus responds to his mother's question about his whereabouts by addressing her and his father jointly.

is" (v. 23), when worship will be "in Spirit and truth." In 19:27, as soon as Jesus had given his mother into the beloved disciple's care, we are told that "From that *hour* the disciple took her home." In 20:17 Jesus tells Mary Magdalene not to hold on to him, "for I have not yet ascended to the Father." In yet another instance Jesus tells a parable about "the woman," who "when she gives birth, has pain because her *hour* has come. But when the child is born, she no longer remembers the pain, because of the joy that a human being is born into the world" (16:21). This woman represents Jesus' disciples, who "now have pain, but I will see you again, and your heart will rejoice, and no one will take your joy from you" (v. 22; compare 16:2, 4, 32). The evidence is complex. The "hour" can be a time of suffering that will pass, or a moment of decisive change and vindication, or both at once. As a mother and as a woman, the mother of Jesus knows of such times in life, above all giving birth and coping with death. While she has no way of knowing that Jesus' hour will in some sense be hers as well (19:27), she has good reason to sense in her son's words a momentous destiny of some kind. Beyond that, it is difficult to know how she would have heard his pronouncement. What determines her quick response (v. 5) is not so much the term "hour" as Jesus' assurance to her that it "is not yet here." If she believed that by his "hour" Jesus meant simply the right time to perform a miracle, then his reply would have been a clear refusal to act. But if he meant a decisive future crisis, the "not yet" could signal just the opposite: that there was still time to address such mundane things as a shortage of wine at a wedding![26]

As to the readers of the Gospel, it is necessary to distinguish between first-time readers and those who have read or heard the Gospel before. For the latter, the answer is easy. They will remember that when the religious authorities later tried to arrest Jesus, they could not do so because "his hour had not yet come" (7:30; 8:20). But then at the Passover, when some Greeks asked to see him, Jesus replied, "The hour has come for the Son of man to be glorified" (12:23), and prayed, "Father, save me from this hour — no, this is why I came to this hour! Father, glorify your name" (vv. 27-28; compare 17:1, "Father, the hour has come. Glorify your Son, that your Son may glorify you"). Such readers will know that Jesus' "hour" is the moment of his

---

26. For the notion that "there is still time" (even though it grows shorter), see 9:4-5, "We must work the works of the One who sent me while it is day. Night is coming when no one can work; as long as I am in the world, I am the world's light"; 11:9-10, "Are there not twelve hours of daylight? If anyone walks in the daylight, he does not stumble, for he sees the light of this world. But if anyone walks at night, he stumbles because the light is not with him"; 12:35-36, "For a little while the light is still with you. Walk while you have the light, so that the darkness will not overtake you. . . . While you have the light, believe in the light, that you might become children of light."

death, "his hour to be taken out of this world" (13:1), the "sixth hour" of the Day of Preparation of the Passover (19:14). None of this is apparent to first-time readers. Jesus' ministry is just beginning (compare v. 11), and they have little more to go on than Jesus' mother. Yet from the preceding testimony of John, they can infer that perhaps Jesus' "hour" is the moment when he will carry out his priestly work of purification by "taking away the sin of the world" (1:29) and "baptizing in Holy Spirit" (1:33). Now they learn that the time for the decisive cleansing is "not yet." They will also remember that Jesus promised them a vision of "angels going up and coming down over the Son of man" (1:51) — a process rather than a single moment — and they may well be wondering whether that vision too belongs to the future "hour," or whether it is closer at hand.

5 Jesus' mother does not answer him, but turns instead to "the servants," mentioned here for the first time.[27] Her comment confirms that she has not interpreted Jesus' words in verse 4 as a refusal to act. She assumes that he *will* act, first because he considers the shortage of wine a matter easily remedied ("What is that to me or to you?"), and second because whatever dark crisis may be on the horizon, it is "not yet here." There is still time for small things, and she instructs the servants accordingly: "Do whatever he tells you." Her optimism is not attributable to any supernatural knowledge on her part (only Jesus has that), nor to a motherly intuition that although her child says one thing he really means another. Instead, she is a reliable hearer and interpreter of Jesus' words to her in the preceding verse. Her response is a clue to what the reader's response should be: Let the miracle proceed!

"Do whatever he tells you" sounds like a command that at some point might have been issued to Jesus' disciples (for example, 13:17, "Now that you know these things, blessed are you if you do them"). As we have noted, Jesus' disciples seem to disappear between verse 2 and verse 11, and play no part in the actual account of the miracle. Within the account, it appears that these anonymous servants to whom Jesus' mother said, "Do whatever he tells you," take the disciples' place, for their role here corresponds more or less to the disciples' role in the feeding of the five thousand (see 6:5-13). They function as the disciples' surrogates or stand-ins, for it is their obedience that accomplishes the miracle. Except for Jesus and his mother, only they and the disciples will even know that a miracle has taken place (vv. 9 and 11). They are the ones who actually "do" the miracle. Jesus simply gives the orders. To

---

27. The definite article with "servants" suggests that their presence at the wedding should be self-evident to the reader, just as the presence of "the banquet master" (v. 8) and "the bridegroom" (v. 9), introduced similarly with definite articles, is self-evident. The parallel with Pharaoh's words, "Go to Joseph and do what he tells you" (Gen. 41:55, NIV) is probably coincidental.

a certain extent this is also true of the disciples in the feeding of crowds (in the synoptic Gospels, though not in John), and of the bystanders at the raising of Lazarus, but less so than here, for Jesus has no direct contact here with either the water or the wine. In some sense, like his disciples, he stands apart from the actual miracle, watching it happen. As far as he is concerned, it will be a miracle of speech,[28] orchestrated by his two simple commands: "Fill the water jars with water" (v. 7), and "Now draw some out and take it to the banquet master" (v. 8).

6 Stories involving water in the Gospel of John ordinarily make some reference to natural water sources, such as the springs at "Aenon, near the Salim" (3:23), or Jacob's well (4:6), or the pools of Bethsaida (5:2), or Siloam (9:7), but here the interest centers instead on "six stone water jars." There must have been a well or a spring at Cana from which the jars were routinely filled, but it plays no part in the story. Why are the water jars mentioned instead of the water source? The narrator explains that they were "placed there for the purification rituals of the Jews."[29] But are the jars emphasized because they were a prominent feature of the story as handed down in the tradition, and "the purification rituals" introduced simply to explain why they were so conveniently "there" *(ekei)*, that is, at hand? Or does the story center on the jars instead of the natural water source precisely *because* they had to do with "the purification rituals of the Jews"? If Jesus is indeed the pure "Lamb of God, who takes away the sin of the world" and "baptizes in Holy Spirit," the latter possibility is superficially attractive. Is Jesus' great work of purification being contrasted with another, lesser kind of cleansing? Is there an intentional contrast here between the old Jewish rules about purity and the liberating "new wine" of the new covenant in Jesus Christ?[30] So far in the Gospel the only possible basis we have seen for such a distinction is the principle that "the law was given through Moses; grace and truth came into being through Jesus Christ" (1:16), but the accent there, as we have seen, was on continuity rather than contrast. While there may be a certain irony in the reference to Jewish purification (compare 3:25), in the absence of direct evidence it is better to take the phrase simply as an explanation of why the jars were "there."

---

28. Compare Moloney, *Belief in the Word,* 86.

29. This is probably why they were of stone rather than of clay. Brown (1.100) suggests that stone jars, if contaminated, could be cleaned, while clay jars would have to be broken (compare Lev 11:33).

30. See Dodd, *Interpretation,* 299; Barrett, 192; Brown, 1.104-5; Carson, 173. Schnackenburg is (rightly) much more cautious (1.339): "It is not certain that the evangelist is really so hostile to Jewish purifications . . . since he also mentions Jewish ritual customs without disparagement (compare 7:22; 11:55; 18:28; 19:40)." Others (Bernard, Bultmann, Haenchen, Lindars) do not even raise the possibility of anti-Jewish polemic here.

2:1-12 JESUS AT CANA AND CAPERNAUM

More to the point is the sheer quantity of water required to fill the six[31] jars. If each jar held "two or three measures" (a measure equaling about nine gallons), the total amount of water turned to wine would be enormous — somewhere between 110 and 160 gallons! If the Gospel writer had accented the water source instead of the water jars, there would have been no way to measure this amount. It appears that the sheer magnititude or extravagance of the miracle is one of the writer's interests. We have only to compare the twelve baskets of fragments left over after feeding five thousand people with five loaves and two morsels of fish (6:13),[32] or the "153 large fish" which the disciples caught in their net at Jesus' command (21:11), or (in a different vein) the whole pint of precious perfume which Mary of Bethany poured out on Jesus' feet (12:3), or the seventy-five pounds of spices used to embalm Jesus' body after his death (19:39). If even these seem tame in comparison to certain Jewish and early Christian accounts of the extravagant bounty (of wine specifically, and of oil) in the messianic age,[33] it is because the Gospel writer is claiming a basis for his figures in actual history. Here the magnitude of the impending miracle stands in almost humorous contrast to the smallness or triviality of the need (v. 4, "What is that to me or to you?"). But the humor makes the serious point that when Jesus gives life, he gives it abundantly, far beyond all need or expectation (see 10:10).

7-8 Jesus told the servants to fill the jars, and they filled them "to the top,"[34] complying both with Jesus' mother (v. 5) and with Jesus. In narra-

---

31. Some commentators have seen six as one short of perfection, confirming the imperfection of "purification rituals of the Jews" (see Moloney, *Belief in the Word,* 85). Others mention this suggestion, but with caution (Barrett, 191; Morris, 160-61), or, better, with outright rejection (Schnackenburg, 1.332; Brown, 1.100; Lindars, 130).

32. This accent on abundance (ἐπερίσσευσαν, 6:13) is of course a conspicuous part of the synoptic accounts of the feeding of multitudes as well (compare Mk 6:43; 8:8, 19-21; Mt 14:20; 15:37; 16:9-10; Lk 9:17).

33. See, for example, *1 Enoch* 10.19, *2 Baruch* 29.5, and above all Papias in the mid-second century, who attributes to "John the Lord's disciple" a messianic prophecy about "vines with 10,000 branches, and on every branch 10,000 shoots, and on every shoot 10,000 clusters, and in every cluster 10,000 grapes, and pressed from every grape 25 measures of wine" (Irenaeus, *Against Heresies* 5.33.3; Harvey, 2.417-18).

34. The phrase "to the top" (ἕως ἄνω) is redundant, inviting symbolic interpretations. Those reading the Gospel a second time and searching for such meanings might recall that just before his last miracle Jesus lifted his eyes "up" (ἄνω) in prayer (11:41; compare 17:1), and that when he was crucified his robe was woven as one piece "from the top" (ἐκ τῶν ἄνωθεν, 19:23). Jesus himself is "from above" (ἐκ τῶν ἄνω, 8:23; ἄνωθεν, 3:31) and requires birth "from above" (ἄνωθεν, 3:5). Some might also think of the pool of Siloam, "sent" (like Jesus himself) to be the instrument of healing (9:7). None of this is apparent on first reading, however, and although the phrase may be evocative, it is doubtful that any such interpretation is intended.

tive time it takes only a moment to fill the six huge jars. In real time it could have taken hours, for it was, in Haenchen's words, "by no means a simple undertaking."[35] As we have seen, it is in the activity of the servants under Jesus' orders that the miracle takes place. Ordinarily, the reader's assumption would be that the water is being drawn for "purification," not for drinking, but this assumption is quickly proved wrong. As soon as the jars were filled, Jesus told the servants, "Now draw some out and take it to the banquet master,"[36] and again they obeyed (v. 8). A miracle requires verification, and the banquet master, however unwittingly, will provide it. Because the verb "to draw out" *(antlein)* is used elsewhere in this Gospel for drawing water from a well (see 4:7, 15), B. F. Westcott suggested that the servants simply drew additional water from the well at Cana (so far unmentioned) and that only this small sample, not the contents of the six great jars, was changed into wine.[37] But if this were the case, why would the six water jars be mentioned at all? Why go to the trouble of filling them if they play no part in the miracle? Why would Jesus have had them filled up for some future purification ritual in which he himself would not participate? Moreover, while the banquet master would have been duly impressed, the small sample would not have solved the initial problem that "They have no wine" (v. 3). Westcott's interpretation seems to have been an attempt to avoid the nineteenth-century embarrassment at Jesus' providing an alcoholic beverage for a wedding celebration in such quantity, but in this Gospel the principle is much the same whether it is a matter of wine, or bread, or fish. Jesus is able to provide for us "more than abundantly, beyond all that we ask or think" (Eph 3:20).

35. Haenchen adds that the maximum weight of the water would have been "up to 700 kilograms or more than 1500 lbs." We have no way of knowing how far the jars were from Cana's water source, or the size of the buckets used to draw water from the well, or even whether the jars were totally or only partially empty. Haenchen is probably right that the story "appears to reckon with the maximum case. For only if the jars were entirely empty and then filled to the brim with water is it certain that a prodigious amount of water was actually changed into wine" (1.173).

36. "Banquet master" (ὁ ἀρχιτρίκλινος) is rare in Greek literature (see *Heliodorus* 7.27.7, in the sense of a slave serving as headwaiter or wine steward; more common are συμποσίαρχος and τρικλινιάρχης). Here it is probably not a slave but a family member or friend of the bridegroom (see 3:29) appointed to do the honors at a specific celebration (like the ἡγούμενον, "leader," in Sirach 32.1-2). In our passage, "the servants" (vv. 5, 9), "the banquet master" (vv. 8-9), and "the bridegroom" (v. 9) all have the definite article, suggesting that their presence at the wedding is normal and expected, and their roles well defined.

37. B. F. Westcott (1.84). Westcott's explanation that "That which remained water when kept for a ceremonial use became wine when borne in faith to minister to the needs, even the superfluous requirements, of life" places altogether too much emphasis on the passing reference to Jewish purification rituals.

9-10 At this point the miracle is already accomplished, but no one except Jesus knows it. The reader will find out first, from the expression "the water-turned-to-wine." The servants who drew the water will find out next, presumably from the banquet master's comment (v. 10). Then it will come out that Jesus' disciples also knew what had happened (v. 11),[38] and we can infer from her earlier instructions to the servants that Jesus' mother may have known as well. But as far as we can tell, neither the banquet master nor the bridegroom nor the bride nor the other wedding guests ever found out. On the contrary, the writer tells us that when the banquet master tasted the newly made wine he "did not know where it came from," that is, he did not know that it came from the six stone water jars as the product of a miracle.[39] The miracle itself is not announced but taken for granted, buried within a participle (*gegenēmenon,* within the phrase "water-turned-to-wine") — as if the reader knows it has already happened. There have in fact been clear signals all along the way, from the remark of Jesus' mother that "They have no wine" (v. 3), to her command to the servants, "Do whatever he tells you" (v. 5), to Jesus' step-by-step instructions (vv. 6-8). Obviously something was going to happen, and that something had to do with a shortage of wine and a huge amount of water. This author is not going to feign surprise when there is none. From the reader's standpoint the transformation was virtually inevitable. Consequently the Gospel writer is less concerned with the miracle itself than with its verification.

The verification of the miracle is ironic in that the banquet master does not realize that he is verifying anything. On tasting the wine he "called for the bridegroom" (v. 9), with a humorous remark about the high quality of the wine: "People always put out the good wine first, and then the not-so-good when they have had too much to drink. You have kept the good wine until now" (v. 10). This story has long been identified as a miracle story, the first miracle in the Gospel of John (v. 11), yet its form is closer to what has been identified in the synoptic Gospels as a pronouncement story. A story, sometimes a miracle, sometimes a controversy, is told for the sake of a key pronouncement of Jesus (or even a series of pronouncements) as a kind of punch line to the story (see, for example, Mk 2:1-12, 14-17, 18-22, 23-28; 3:1-5). Here too the account leads up to a pronouncement that gives the story its meaning, but with the striking difference that the crucial words are not Je-

---

38. Whether the disciples knew what had happened from the servants, their surrogates within the narrative, or simply from observation, is never made clear.

39. See 4:11, "From where [πόθεν] do you have the living water?" Again the text teases us toward a symbolic interpretation (compare n. 34). It is said of Jesus himself in this Gospel, no less than of the water he provides or the wine he creates, that no one knows "where he is from" (see 7:28; 8:14; 9:29; 19:9; compare 1:26, 31, 33). The same is true of "everyone born of the Spirit" (3:8).

sus' own, but those of the banquet master, testifying to what Jesus has done. This happens occasionally in the Synoptics as well (see Mk 1:27; 4:41; Lk 5:26), but when it does the ones testifying are fully aware of the miracle, while the banquet master in our story shows no such awareness. The readers of the Gospel, like "the servants who had drawn the water," know what has happened, but he does not. Yet, ironically, his testimony is all the more convincing precisely *because* it is an unwitting testimony. An ignorant and therefore unbiased observer provides the best possible confirmation of what we as readers already know, that Jesus has turned water into wine.

The banquet master's words are spoken to the bridegroom, who now makes his cameo appearance in the story. If the servants who drew the water function in the story as surrogates or stand-ins for Jesus' disciples, the bridegroom functions in a strange way as a stand-in for Jesus. The words of the banquet master, "You [*sy*] have kept the good wine until now" (v. 10), ought to have been directed to Jesus. In some sense, from the reader's standpoint they *are* directed to Jesus, for Jesus is the one who "kept the good wine until now." The bridegroom gets the credit for what Jesus has done! We can only wonder about his reaction because he seems to have known no more than the banquet master about where the wine "came from." By his silence he accepts the compliment and takes credit for the wine's quality.[40] But Jesus' disciples, and the reader, know better. This ending underscores the fact that throughout the narrative, Jesus, like his mother and his disciples, has stood somewhat apart from what was happening at the wedding (v. 4, "What is that to me or to you?") and even somewhat apart from his own miracle. As we have seen, he simply gives directions and the miracle happens. Like his disciples, he has a surrogate or silent partner *within* the wedding festivities, the bridegroom who gets credit for providing the good wine. It is probably no coincidence that Jesus himself is seen as a bridegroom a chapter later in this Gospel (3:29), and elsewhere in the Gospel tradition (Mk 2:19-20 par.).

The theme of Jesus as bridegroom in the synoptic Gospels comes, appropriately enough, in a context dealing with the distinction between "old" and "new" wine (Mk 2:22 par.), and accenting the coming of the new in the person of Jesus. The closest parallel to the banquet master's comment comes in a saying of Jesus added in Luke to this tradition, "No one who has drunk what is old desires new, for he says, 'The old is good'" (Lk 5:39; compare *Gospel of Thomas* 47). Instead of "old" the banquet master speaks of "the good wine" as that which normally comes "first," and instead of "new" he notes with surprise that in this case "the good wine" is that which comes

---

40. Chrysostom also noticed this, but concluded that "what we needed to learn was, that Christ made the water wine, and that good wine; but what the bridegroom said to the governor he did not think it necessary to add" (*Homily* 22.3; NPNF, 1st ser., 14.78).

later, kept "until now."⁴¹ As in the synoptics, the accent of the pronouncement is on "now," and on the newness and superiority of that which Jesus now brings.⁴² Yet the tension between the "already" and the "not yet" should not be overlooked. Jesus has clearly told his mother, "My hour is not yet here" (v. 4), and the Gospel writer will now confirm this with a notice that the miracle of the wine was only a "beginning" (v. 11).⁴³ When put in its literary context, the banquet master's remark becomes simply a compliment on the quality of the wine. The "not yet" is what dominates the story as a whole. Jesus has provided "good wine," but the best is yet to come.

11 The Gospel writer now stands back from the story to provide a summary of its significance. Such editorial summaries in this Gospel frequently begin, as here, with the demonstrative pronoun "this" (4:54; 21:14), or "these" (for example, 1:28; 6:59; 8:20; 12:16; 13:21; 17:1; 18:1; 20:31).⁴⁴ Here the pronoun is feminine, in agreement with the feminine noun *archēn,* "beginning," which should probably be read as a predicate to the pronoun: "This he did *as* a beginning of the signs."⁴⁵ The summary speaks of "the signs" (with the definite article), as if the writer knows of them as a specific set of events from which a selection can be made,⁴⁶ and the word "beginning" obviously implies that we will hear more of them (see 4:54, "And this Jesus did again as a second sign when he came from Judea to Galilee").

In effect, the summary transforms the story that precedes it. In contrast to the story itself, where Jesus merely gives the orders and the servants

---

41. The pronouncement vaguely recalls the riddle of Jesus' relationship to John in the previous chapter (1:15, 30), where Jesus is the latecomer who arrives on the scene "after" John (ὀπίσω μου) and perhaps as John's disciple, yet who has surpassed John because he was actually "first" (πρῶτός μου) in time.

42. See, for example, Dodd, *Historical Tradition,* 227; Lindars, 131; Barrett, 193; Brown, 1.105; Schnackenburg, 1.338.

43. Compare Moloney, *Belief in the Word,* 87.

44. In this respect the Gospel writer's style corresponds closely to that of Jesus himself, whose brief rhetorical summaries *within* his own discourses often begin similarly, with ταῦτα (for example, 14:25; 15:11, 17; 16:1, 4, 25, 33).

45. This is supported by the absence of the article with ἀρχήν (contrast 10:6). On the construction, see BDF, §292; also Bultmann, 118, n. 6, and the text cited there from Isocrates, *Panegyricus* 10.38.

46. Compare "his signs" (2:23), "these signs" (3:2), "the signs" (6:2), "more signs" (7:31), "such signs" (9:16), "many signs" (11:47; 20:30), "so many signs" (12:37), "other signs" (20:30). Many (following Bultmann) have concluded from this that the writer is drawing on a "Signs Source" consisting of a series of narratives of one sign after another (see R. T. Fortna, *The Gospel of Signs* and *The Fourth Gospel and Its Predecessor;* also W. Nicol, *The Semeia in the Fourth Gospel*), but whether this is true or not the commentator's task is to give primary attention to the *present* narrator's references to "signs" as markers in the present narrative.

"do" the miracle (v. 5), the summary states unambiguously that this was something Jesus himself "did." Jesus' words are regarded as equivalent to actions. "Sign" *(sēmeion)* is a distinctively Johannine word for Jesus' deeds, used to accent the revelatory character not only of his miracles, but of everything he "did" (see 20:30, where everything Jesus "did in the presence of this disciples" is summed up under the heading of "signs").[47] In this respect, the word "signs" *(sēmeia)* is similar to "works," the other word used in this Gospel for Jesus' miracles, which also refers more broadly to everything Jesus did in fulfillment of his mission from God. In "doing" this first sign, we are told, Jesus "revealed" or "made known" *(ephanerōsen)* for the first time something about himself, specifically his "glory," glory defined for us earlier "as of a father's One and Only, full of grace and truth" (1:14).

The Gospel writer's straight-faced summary *could* be read ironically. Those who have seen the humor of the banquet master's final remark about good wine have commonly assumed that the humor ended there, but this is not self-evident. The writer's verdict that in performing this particular miracle Jesus "revealed his glory" has, on the face of it, a dry humor of its own. What kind of "revelation" or "manifestation" is it when most of the major characters in the story — banquet master, bridegroom, wedding guests — have no idea of "what just happened here"?[48] Can *this* be the "revelation to Israel" that John promised a chapter earlier (1:31)? The humor, or at least the appearance of it, comes in the pitifully narrow scope of the disclosure: "and his disciples believed in him." The "Israel" of 1:31 turns out to be four, maybe five, people! No one else is said to have seen Jesus' glory and believed — not the banquet master or the bridegroom, not Jesus' mother who seemed to know what was coming, nor even the servants who knew where the wine came from (v. 9) — only a handful of disciples watching from the sidelines.[49] They are outsiders to the miracle, yet the revelation it brings is for them and

---

47. The terminology of Jesus "doing" (ποιεῖν) signs is maintained quite consistently throughout the Gospel (see 2:23; 3:2; 4:54; 6:2, 14, 30; 7:31; 9:16; 10:41; 11:47; 12:18, 37; 20:30)

48. Chrysostom (*Homily* 23.1) addresses this fact and tries to deal with it: "How then did he 'manifest forth his glory'? He manifested it at least for His own part, and if all present hear not of the miracle at the time, they would hear of it afterwards, for unto the present time it is celebrated, and has not been unnoticed" (NPNF, 1st ser., 14.80).

49. This is in keeping with the uses of φανεροῦν elsewhere in the Gospel. Jesus "reveals" God's name to those "whom you gave me out of the world" (17:6), and after the resurrection "reveals" himself three times "to the disciples" (21:1, 14). Even when his brothers urge him to "reveal yourself to the world," it is "so that *your disciples* may see the works you are doing" (7:3-4, my italics). Only in 3:21 and 9:3 is the scope of the "revelation" or "disclosure" left undefined. At one point, one disciple is impelled to ask, "Lord, how is it that you are going to reveal [ἐμφανίζειν] yourself to us and not to the world?" (14:19).

2:1-12 JESUS AT CANA AND CAPERNAUM

them alone, not for those who actually participated in the miracle. Similarly we the readers of the Gospel are outsiders even to the *telling* of the miracle, yet the story invites us to see Jesus' glory through the disciples' eyes (compare 1:14) and with them believe (see 20:30-31).

For this reason, we should probably *not* read verse 11 as humor or irony, tempting as it might be to do so. Rather, the summary transforms the story seriously and legitimately, so that it accomplishes just what the Gospel writer intends. The promised vision of "the sky opened, and the angels of God going up and coming down over the Son of man" (1:51) is starting to come into focus. At least one disciple, Nathanael, was said to "believe" even then (1:50). Now the disciples are beginning to see the "greater things" that will bring them to the next level of faith,[50] and eventually, when Jesus' "hour" has come and he is raised from the dead, to yet another level (see v. 22). The phrase "in Cana of Galilee" (echoing v. 1) frames the whole account with a characteristically Johannine interest in place (compare "there" in vv. 1 and 6). When Jesus comes to Cana again, the writer will remind us that it was "where he made the water wine" (4:46). At the same time, "Cana of Galilee" provides a point of reference for the notice to follow that "he went down to Capernaum" (v. 12).

12 This verse is transitional. The Gospel writer loses interest in exact chronology,[51] and the sojourn at Capernaum "for a few days" (literally, "not many days," as in Acts 1:5) provides a cushion of sorts between the series of six days that began at 1:19 (compare 1:29, 35, 43 and 2:1) and Jesus' first Passover (v. 13).[52] Jesus "went down" from Cana to Capernaum, just as he is urged to do later by a nobleman from Capernaum (4:47, 49), and, with his mother and brothers and his disciples, "remained there" *(ekei)* for an unspecified length of time.[53] Once again place is important, and later we will see Je-

---

50. The notice that the disciples "believed in him" (καὶ ἐπίστευσαν εἰς αὐτόν) is the first use of the characteristic Johannine expression (πιστεύειν εἰς) for "believing in" Jesus. It can be regarded as an abbreviated form, and therefore an equivalent, of "believing in his name" (πιστεύειν εἰς τὸ ὄνομα αὐτοῦ; see 1:12).

51. Μετὰ τοῦτο ("after this," or "next"; see 11:7, 11; 19:28), like the more common μετὰ ταῦτα (see 3:22; 5:1, 14; 6:1; 7:1; 13:7; 19:38; 21:1), is a rather imprecise connective. Here the author may have chosen the singular τοῦτο with the preceding "sign" (σημεῖον) still in mind (compare 4:54, τοῦτο . . . δεύτερον σημεῖον).

52. Chrysostom takes the series of chronological notices between 1:29 and 2:12 quite seriously: "He received baptism then a few days before the passover" (*Homilies* 23.1; NPNF, 14.80).

53. Some manuscripts (including A) have the singular, "he remained" (ἔμεινεν), but the weight of evidence clearly supports the plural, "they remained" (ἔμειναν). The plural could imply that Jesus' mother and brothers and sisters were also at Capernaum only temporarily, but there is obviously no suggestion that they accompanied him on his subsequent journeys, and there is a later hint that Capernaum may have been their home (below, n. 55).

155

sus back in Cana performing a miracle for someone in Capernaum (4:46-50). The presence of Jesus' mother and his disciples is a natural carryover from the preceding account of the wedding, but the presence of his brothers (and sisters?)⁵⁴ is more surprising. As we have seen, Jesus' brothers were present *instead of* the disciples in at least one early account of the wedding (*Epistula Apostolorum* 5; see above, n. 12). Their inclusion here may be a tacit acknowledgment of such a tradition, for their presence at the wedding seems to be assumed, not instead of but with the disciples. Even so, they would have had no knowledge that a miracle took place unless Jesus or the disciples told them. In any event, their inclusion anticipates Jesus' later encounter with them (also in Galilee), where they urge him to "go to Judea" and "reveal" himself on a much wider scale than he had done before (7:3). There we learn that, unlike the disciples, they "did not believe in him" (7:5), at least not yet, but here at the outset of his ministry, Jesus and his mother, brothers, and disciples stay together briefly as a community in the town where the family seems to have been living.⁵⁵ Here a basis is laid, perhaps, for one of the disciples (possibly a brother?) taking Jesus' mother into his care (19:27), and for Jesus finally referring to his disciples as "my brothers," and children of the same Father (20:17-18). Deliberately or not, some such transformation is here anticipated as Jesus' natural brothers and his disciples are seen together as "family."

F. JESUS IN THE TEMPLE AT PASSOVER (2:13-22)

> 13 *And the Passover of the Jews was near, and Jesus went up to Jerusalem.* 14 *And he found in the temple those selling cattle and sheep and doves, and the money changers sitting.* 15 *And he made a kind of whip out of cords and drove them all from the temple, with the sheep and the cattle, and he spilled the coins of the money changers and overturned the tables,* 16 *and to those selling doves he said, "Get these out of here! Stop making my Father's house a house of trade!"* 17 *His*

---

54. It is difficult to say whether or not "brothers" (ἀδελφοί) is generic or specifically masculine. In the other Gospels, Jesus' sisters are sometimes mentioned explicitly with the brothers (Mk 6:3, and in a textual variant in 3:32), and sometimes not (Mk 3:31, 33), in the latter instances leaving us with the same question as here. There is no reason from the text to think that Jesus' "brothers" are anything but the natural children of "Joseph" (1:45) and "the mother of Jesus" (2:1).

55. Although Jesus is "from" Nazareth (1:45-46), the comment of "the Jews" at Capernaum (6:42; compare vv. 24, 59) suggests that this was where he lived as an adult and where his family was well known (see Mt 4:13, where, after leaving Nazareth, Jesus "settled down" [κατῴκησεν] in Capernaum, just as the family had earlier 'settled down' in Nazareth, 2:23).

2:13-22 JESUS IN THE TEMPLE AT PASSOVER

disciples remembered that it is written, "Zeal for your house will consume me." 18 *So the Jews answered and said to him, "What sign do you show us, because you are doing these things?"* 19 *Jesus answered and said to them, "Destroy this sanctuary, and in three days I will raise it up."* 20 *So the Jews said, "Forty-six years it has taken to build this sanctuary, and you are going to raise it up in three days?"* 21 *But he was speaking of the sanctuary that was his body.* 22 *So, when he was raised from the dead, his disciples remembered that this was what he meant, and they believed both the scripture and the word Jesus spoke.*

In contrast to the miracle of the wine, in which Jesus simply spoke and the servants carried out his orders, here Jesus himself acts decisively (2:13-15), and then interprets his action by his speech (vv. 16-22), centering on two key pronouncements (vv. 16 and 19). These sayings, while directed to the religious authorities in Jerusalem as part of a controversy provoked by his actions, are (like the miracle at Cana) intended primarily for his own disciples (vv. 17 and 22).

13 Once again the conjunction "and" *(kai)* links the account very closely to what has preceded. Just as in 1:19 and in 2:1, we expect a break in the action, but the conjunction drives the story forward without hesitation (compare the repeated "and" at the beginning of vv. 14, 15, and 16). A reader coming to the Gospel of John having just finished any of the other Gospels might have the impression here that this is to be a very short Gospel indeed! Jesus has been in Galilee, done a miracle there, and then stayed in Capernaum for an unspecified length of time. Now that the time of Passover is "near" (as later in 6:4; 11:55), Jesus travels to Jerusalem and finds money changers in the temple (as in Mt 21:12; Mk 11:15; Lk 19:45). Anyone familiar with the synoptic chronology might conclude that we are already into the last week of Jesus' life!

This is of course not the case. The preceding notice (v. 11) has made it very clear that what Jesus did in Cana was only a "beginning." Naturally there has always been vigorous discussion over the question of whether Jesus cleansed the temple in Jerusalem near the beginning of his ministry (as here),[1] or near the end (as in the Synoptics),[2] or whether he did so twice.[3]

---

1. See J. A. T. Robinson, *The Priority of John*, 127-31.
2. This is almost a consensus among modern scholars (see, for example, Barrett, 195; Beasley-Murray, 38-39). Lindars (135-36) argues that John originally placed it in chapter 12, but in a second edition moved it to make room for the story of the raising of Lazarus as the immediate cause of Jesus' death. Brown (1.118) proposes that on his first journey to Jerusalem Jesus "uttered a prophetic warning about the destruction of the sanctuary," but that "Jesus' action of cleansing the temple precincts took place in the last days of his life."
3. So Morris, 166-68; Carson, 177-78. Perhaps the best argument for such a har-

Such discussions belong either to canonical criticism or to the study of the historical Jesus. They are outside the scope of a commentary on any one Gospel, for each Gospel knows of just one cleansing and leaves the reader in no doubt as to when it took place. The reader of John's Gospel has every reason to assume that Jesus purified the temple just once, and that he did so very early in his ministry. There is no hint in the text that the Gospel writer is correcting an earlier, different chronology. Rather, he purports to give an independent, first-time account of the event.

The phrase "the Passover of the Jews" (like "the purification rituals of the Jews" in v. 6) presupposes that the readers are not themselves Jews or Jewish Christians, and do not keep the Jewish Passover.[4] At the same time it signals that at this festival Jesus will confront "the Jews," that is, the religious authorities in charge of the festival, and hints that there will be controversy (see vv. 18, 20). Having "gone down" from Cana to Capernaum (v. 12), Jesus now "went up," not to Cana again but to Jerusalem, as he and others are customarily said to do for all the festivals (see 5:1; 7:8, 10, 14; 11:55; 12:20). We are not told that his disciples accompanied him to Jerusalem as they did to Cana (2:2) and Capernaum (2:12), yet as the story unfolds their presence seems to be presupposed (see vv. 17, 22).[5]

14-15 The narrative assumes that Jesus went to Jerusalem specifically in order to visit the temple (compare 5:14, 7:14, 8:59, 10:23, and 11:56), where he "found . . . those selling cattle and sheep and doves, and the money changers sitting." The prepositional phrases "in the temple" (v. 14) and "from the temple" (v. 15) frame the author's concise account of Jesus' drastic action. Definite articles mark the groups against whom Jesus directed his anger: "the sellers," whether of cattle, sheep, or doves (vv. 14, 16), and "the money changers" (vv. 14-15). In contrast to the Synoptics, "buyers" are not mentioned. These groups had apparently set up shop in the outer courtyard of the temple (the so-called "court of the Gentiles") for the convenience of worshipers, so that money could be changed and animals for sacrifice purchased right on the spot.[6] Quickly

---

monization is the possibility that Jesus may have cleansed the temple early in his ministry when he was still part of a movement centering around John the Baptist (compare Mt 21:32, where Jesus says to the temple authorities, "John came to you in the way of righteousness"), but there is no hint in this Gospel that Jesus was acting on anything but his own sovereign initiative. John has been prominent in the narrative both before (1:19-34) and after (3:22-30) the story of the cleansing, but he is completely out of the picture here.

4. Compare "the Passover of the Jews" (11:55); "the Passover, the festival of the Jews" (6:4); "the festival of the Jews [called] Tents" (7:2); "a festival of the Jews" (5:1). Only in 10:21 does the writer introduce a Jewish festival ("the Rededication in Jerusalem") without mentioning "the Jews" explicitly.

5. Compare Origen, *Commentary on John* 10.150-51; FC, 80.290.

6. While Jewish sources hint at such a custom (for example, Zech 14:21; M. She-

2:13-22 JESUS IN THE TEMPLE AT PASSOVER

fashioning a whip out of cords,[7] therefore, Jesus drove "them all" from the temple. "Them all" *(pantas)* is masculine, suggesting that he used the whip (or threatened to do so) on merchants and animals alike.[8] As for the money changers,[9] he overturned their tables and spilled their coins.[10] All this he did without a word of warning.

16 Jesus reserves his speech for the sellers of doves,[11] but his words are just as applicable to the other merchants and the money changers: "Get these out of here! Stop making[12] my Father's house a house of trade!"[13] We are not to suppose that Jesus' comments *followed* his drastic

---

qalim 1.3), the New Testament accounts of the temple cleansing are themselves its best attestation (see J. Jeremias, *Jerusalem in the Time of Jesus,* 48-49). Money changing was necessary somewhere in the city because Roman currency was not allowed in the temple. Jerusalem carried on lively trade with Tyre to the north, and only the Tyrian shekel was acceptable in paying the temple tax (*M. Bekhorot* 8.7), perhaps because the Tyrian coins were pure silver, like the "sanctuary shekel" of Num 18:16; compare Morris, 170).

7. Some important ancient manuscripts (including P^{66}, P^{75}, and the old Latin) add ὡς before φραγέλλιον, "whip," suggesting improvisation: "a kind of whip," which seems to be implied in any case. Φραγέλλιον is a loanword from Lat. *flagellum.*

8. Compare Brown, 1.115; Schnackenburg, 1.346. Haenchen, on the other hand, explains the masculine πάντας from the masculine τοὺς βόας, "the cattle," concluding that Jesus used the whip only on the animals (1.183). While the notion that Jesus would use a whip on humans is troubling to some, the text makes no distinctions. If, however, the sellers saw their property disappearing, they would have been quick to follow, to retrieve their investment.

9. The word for "money changers" here (κολλυβιστής) is the same word found in the synoptic accounts of the temple cleansing (Mt 21:12; Mk 11:15; compare Lk 19:45 D), and different from the word used in verse 14 (κερματιστής). To this writer they are simply stylistic variations, interchangeable in meaning (compare τὸ κέρμα, "coins," in the same clause). Logically, the overturning of the tables should precede the spilling of the coins, but the Greek reverses the order, possibly to link τῶν κολλυβιστῶν as closely as possible to τὸ κέρμα.

10. There are two minor textual variants here. Some manuscripts (including P^{75} and B) have the plural τὰ κέρματα for "coins" instead of the collective singular τὸ κέρμα (P^{66}, ℵ, A, and others), but the difference is of little consequence. For "overturn," some manuscripts have ἀνέστρεψεν (P^{75}, A, and the majority of later manuscripts) or κατέστρεψεν (ℵ and others) instead of the less common ἀνέτρεψεν (P^{66}, B, and others), but these seem to have been influenced by the κατέστρεψεν of Mt 21:12 and Mk 11:15. Again, the difference in meaning is negligible.

11. As Moloney concisely observes, "Cages, unlike oxen and sheep, cannot be sent scurrying away" (77).

12. The force of the present imperative μὴ ποιεῖτε is that the dovesellers must stop something they are already doing (the implication is, "How dare you").

13. Doves were the offerings of the poor (Lev 5:7), but Westcott's caution (1.91) is well taken: "There is no reason to think that those who sold the offerings of the poor were, as such, dealt with more gently than other traffickers."

actions, as if he had driven everyone else from the temple and was now left alone with the dovesellers. Nor is this the missing warning that actually *preceded* his actions, as if he had said, "Get these animals out of here, or I'll drive them out myself!" Rather, his words are to be read as more or less simultaneous with his actions, given in order to interpret his actions, and for the reader. The heart of Jesus' interpretation is his use of the term "house" *(oikos)* rather than "temple" *(hieron,* as in vv. 14-15), and his reference to God as "my Father."

Jesus refers to the temple as God's "house" in the synoptic accounts as well (Mk 11:17; compare Mt 21:13; Lk 19:46), citing God's intention in Isaiah 56:7 that "My house will be called a house of prayer for all the nations" and contrasting it with present circumstances, in which "You have made it a refuge for bandits" (compare Jer 7:11).[14] The temple is a sacred place or place of worship *(hieron)* not in and of itself, but because of its relationship to the God of Israel as God's "house" *(oikos),* the place where God dwells. Here in John's Gospel, without quoting Scripture, Jesus makes the same point, but goes beyond it in two ways. First, he denounces trade in the temple not because it is dishonest or corrupt, but because it exists there at all.[15] Playing on the word *oikos,* he contrasts God's "house" not with "a refuge for bandits," but with a "house of trade" *(oikon emporiou).*[16] Second, and more important, Jesus refers to the temple not simply as "God's house" but as "my Father's house."[17] Here for the first time in John's Gospel he calls

---

14. Isaiah 56:7 and Jeremiah 7:11 go together naturally in the Gospel tradition, having in common the key phrase "my house" (ὁ οἶκός μου), with God understood as the speaker.

15. For Jewish polemic against buying and selling, see Sirach 26.29 ("A merchant can hardly keep from wrongdoing, and a tradesman will not be declared innocent of sin") and 27:2 ("As a stake driven firmly into a fissure between stones, so sin is wedged in between selling and buying"). See also *Gospel of Thomas* 64, where Jesus says (without explicit reference to the temple), "Tradesmen and merchants will not enter the places of my Father."

16. See the the last verse of Zechariah, "And there shall no longer be a trader in the house of the LORD of hosts on that day" (Zech 14:21, RSV), where "trader" (compare 11:7, 11) is כְּנַעֲנִי, translated in the LXX as Χαναναῖος, "Canaanite." Many commentators (for example, Dodd, *Interpretation,* 300; Brown, 1.119) find an allusion here to the Zechariah passage, with the implication that Jesus' purging of "trade" from the temple was a messianic act. It is doubtful, however, that any reader could have been expected to notice this. The Gospel writer ignores it, calling attention instead to a very different biblical text (v. 17; see Bultmann, 124).

17. Compare Luke 2:49, ἐν τοῖς τοῦ πατρός μου (literally, "in my Father's things"). Only here in John's Gospel does Jesus speak of the Jerusalem temple in this way, but he uses a similar expression, "in my Father's household" (ἐν τῇ οἰκίᾳ τοῦ πατρός μου), to refer to heaven, or the heavenly temple (14:2).

2:13-22 JESUS IN THE TEMPLE AT PASSOVER

God "my Father,"[18] a clear signal to the reader that he is now speaking explicitly as the Father's "One and Only" (see 1:14, 18), or "the Son of God" (1:34, 49). With this, he begins a conversation with the Jewish authorities that will extend through the first half of John's Gospel. His implicit claim might have drawn the same reaction here that it does at the next stage of the conversation, when "the Jews" will begin to seek his life because "he said that God was his own Father, making himself equal to God" (5:18). But it draws no such reaction. The merchants and money changers are too busy fleeing the premises and retrieving their property to challenge his claim, and when Jesus is finally challenged (v. 18), the response is to his actions, not his words. It is as if no one heard. To everyone but the reader, Jesus' claim that God is his Father goes unnoticed.[19]

17 The first response to Jesus' action (and the only response to his pronouncement) comes from his own disciples. To this point the reader has had no way of knowing that the disciples are even present with Jesus at the Passover festival in Jerusalem. Now suddenly they are in the picture. The Gospel writer intervenes in one of his narrative asides to tell us that they "remembered" a certain biblical text. This is the first Scripture citation in the Gospel of John,[20] but it comes as no surprise because Jesus' disciples have already identified him as "someone of whom Moses wrote in the law, and of whom the prophets wrote" (1:45). The text chosen is appropriate in this context because it picks up the word "house," which Jesus has just used twice (v. 16). A reader familiar with the other Gospels might have expected the Scripture cited by Jesus himself in the synoptic accounts, in which the God of Israel is the speaker: "My house shall be called a house of prayer" (Isa

---

18. He continues to do so throughout the Gospel; see 5:17, 43; 6:32, 40; 8:19 (twice), 49, 54; 10:18, 25, 29, 37; 14:2, 7, 20, 21, 23; 15:1, 8, 10, 15, 23, 24; 20:17. In even more instances Jesus speaks of "the Father," with exactly the same meaning. As Moloney remarks, "A very Johannine feature has been added to the narrative" (*Belief in the Word*, 96-97).

19. Implicit in this claim is a proprietary interest in the Jerusalem temple as a legitimate place of worship (4:20, 22). The view of Bernard (1.87) that "the action of Jesus was a protest against the whole sacrificial system of the Temple," because "The killing of beasts, which was a continual feature of Jewish worship, was a disgusting and useless practice" (1.87), is unwarranted and gratuitously anti-Jewish. Jesus' acknowledgement of the temple as "my Father's house" and his "zeal" on its behalf (v. 17) point to exactly the opposite conclusion (see Morris, 172).

20. The writer generally prefers the periphrastic expression γεγραμμένον ἐστίν, as here (compare 6:31, 45; 10:34; 12:14), to the shorter γέγραπται (8:17), although they are interchangeable in meaning (see 20:30, 31). Here the expression should be translated "is written" rather than "was written" (despite its dependence on the aorist ἐμνήσθησαν) because the accent is on the present testimony of Scripture to the readers of the Gospel (compare 5:39), not on the writing of Scripture in the far distant past.

56:7). But here the disciples remember a different text, one in which the psalmist speaks and God is being addressed: "Zeal for your house will consume me" (Ps 68[69]:10 LXX). It is as if Jesus himself is speaking in the words of the psalmist.

When did their remembering take place? Did they, as most commentators suppose, remember the psalm right on the spot, just as Jesus in the other Gospels quoted Scripture in the very act of driving the merchants from the temple?[21] Or did they remember it later?[22] It is difficult to be certain because the verb for remembrance *(emnēsthēsan)* is introduced so abruptly.[23] But the nature of the quotation itself provides a clue. The quotation is from a psalm widely known and used in early Christian writings,[24] and agrees closely with the LXX except for the future tense of the verb: "Zeal for your house will consume me," instead of "has consumed me," as in the LXX.[25] The effect of this change is to shift the accent from the "consuming zeal" with which Jesus drove the merchants from the temple at that early stage in his ministry to the long-range results of his action. "Consume" can also mean "devour" or "destroy," and what the disciples "remembered" was that Jesus' zeal for the house of God would eventuate in his own destruction.[26] Even though John's Gospel has placed the cleansing of the temple at the beginning rather than the end of Jesus' ministry, it preserves a causal connection between that action and Jesus'

---

21. See Dodd, *Historical Tradition,* 158; Schnackenburg, 1.347; Barrett, 198; Hoskyns, 194; Bernard, 1.91; Westcott, 92; Moloney, *Belief in the Word,* 97-98.

22. See Bultmann, 124, and especially Abbott, *Johannine Grammar,* 478-79.

23. Later copyists tried to make it less abrupt by adding δέ ("and" or "but") after ἐμνήσθησαν, or καί ("and") or even τότε ("then") before it, suggesting (however subtly) that the disciples remembered the text from the Psalms right then and there. But our earliest manuscripts (including P[66], P[75], ℵ, and B) have allowed the ambiguity to stand.

24. The words that immediately follow in the same verse of Psalm 69 ("the reproaches of those who reproach you have fallen on me") are cited in Romans 15:3, with the added comment that "Whatever was written before was written for our instruction" (15:4). Later in John's Gospel (15:25), Jesus himself takes on the persona of the psalmist, citing the fulfillment in his own life of the words, "They hated me without cause" (Ps. 69:5). Here the quotation illustrates a point similar to the one Paul was making in Romans: "But now they have both seen and hated both me and my Father" (15:24).

25. "Will consume" is καταφάγεται; "has consumed" (LXX) is κατέφαγεν. There seems to have been some mutual cross-fertilization between the New Testament and LXX manuscript traditions, as some LXX manuscripts (for example, B) have the future καταφάγεταί, while some later New Testament manuscripts (including the Textus Receptus, some of the old Latin and Syriac, and the Vulgate) have the aorist, as in the LXX.

26. Compare Bultmann (124), Schnackenburg (1.347), Dodd (*Historical Tradition,* 158), and most others (Barrett, 199, is an exception, finding here a reference only to "consuming zeal").

execution by the Jewish authorities.[27] But how would Jesus' disciples have known this at the time? It is fair to say that they are not distinguished by great prophetic insight in the Gospel of John (or any other Gospel!), and it is doubtful that the Gospel writer would attribute to them such insight here. The future "will consume," or "will destroy," tends to support the view that their "remembrance" of the psalm was after the fact — as in the two other uses of the verb "remember" *(emnēsthēsan)* in John's Gospel (one in the near context, in v. 22, "when he was raised from the dead," and the other in 12:16, "when Jesus was glorified").[28]

18 Jesus finally draws a response, not from the merchants and money changers, but from "the Jews," building on the notice that the festival was "the Passover of the Jews" (v. 13). Even though the Passover was a festival for all the Jewish people, those in charge were the religious authorities in Jerusalem, the same authorities who earlier sent emissaries to question John (1:19). Here they engage Jesus in a brief dialogue extending through the next three verses: "So the Jews answered and said to him" (v. 18); "Jesus answered and said to them" (v. 19); "So the Jews said" (v. 20).

Strangely enough, these religious authorities take no explicit offense at Jesus' reference to "my Father's house" (v. 16).[29] Their "answer" is not to his words but to his actions: "What sign do you show us because[30] you are

---

27. Compare Brown, 1.124. Brown, however, goes a step further to propose that what immediately precedes in the psalm ("I have become a stranger to my brothers, an alien to my mother's sons") is implied here as well, in that after 2:12 "Jesus left his brothers to come to Jerusalem, and they would be separated from him through unbelief during his ministry." Here he is on far shakier ground, for to this point nothing negative has been said about Jesus' brothers, and there is nothing in Jesus' actions in the temple to suggest any alienation from them.

28. The case is not airtight because the future tense could be explained simply by the fact that Jesus' purification of the temple was future from the standpoint of the ancient psalmist. That is, the psalm can be read as an explicit prophecy. But Psalm 69 and others like it are not normally cited that way in the New Testament. Rather, their present and perfect tenses are usually retained (see, for example, Ps 69:5 in Jn 15:25; Ps 41:10 in Jn 13:18; Ps 22:19 in Jn 19:24). The shift to the future here is exceptional, suggesting that the "consuming" or "destroying" is future not only from the psalmist's standpoint but from that of the Johannine narrator as well.

29. Chrysostom notices this: "See, He even calls Him 'Father,' and they are not wroth; but when He went on and spoke more plainly, so as to set before them the idea of His Equality, then they became angry" (the latter referring, apparently, to 5:17-18; *Homilies* 23.2; NPNF, 14.81).

30. According to Abbott, "the meaning of ὅτι seems to be '[We ask thee this question] because'" (*Johannine Grammar,* 157; compare BDF, §456[2]). Bultmann instead tries to read ὅτι as "that" (124), resulting in a far more cumbersome paraphrase: "What kind of sign can you show as a proof that you are doing this *lawfully* (or alternatively that you are *allowed* to do this)?" As is often the case, simpler is better.

doing these things?" (italics added). The irony in their demand for a "sign" *(sēmeion)* is that the Gospel writer considers everything Jesus "did" as "signs" by which he "revealed his glory" to believers (see v. 11), and he expects his readers to see Jesus' actions the same way.[31] Therefore in demanding a sign because Jesus was "doing these things," the religious leaders are simply displaying their ignorance and misunderstanding.[32] The "signs" have been given. "These things" are themselves the signs, but unlike Jesus' disciples (v. 11), "the Jews" in Jerusalem have neither seen nor believed (compare 6:30; 9:39-41; 12:37-41).

19-20 The Gospel writer's presentation of Jesus' response mimics the challenge of the Jewish authorities. Just as they "answered and said to him" (v. 18), so he "answered and said to them" (v. 19). Jesus' answer is a kind of riddle: "Destroy this sanctuary, and in three days I will raise it up." He seems to be introducing yet a third word for the temple in which they were standing. First it was called "the temple" *(to hieron,* vv. 14 and 15); then Jesus called it a "house" *(oikos),* specifically "my Father's house" (v. 16); now it is a "sanctuary" *(naos),* specifically "this sanctuary." A distinction sometimes made is to the "sanctuary" as the central shrine, or holy place within the larger "temple" precincts.[33] But the reaction of his hearers (v. 20) suggests no such differentiation. Their response, moreover, echoes Jesus' pronouncement in three respects, mimicking or mocking his claim. They repeat his expression, "this sanctuary," corresponding to the way in which Jews commonly referred to their own temple in Jerusalem.[34] They repeat his use of the verb "raise," while using it interchangeably with the verb "build" (v. 20), either of which can be used for building a house or a place of worship.[35] Finally, they repeat "in three days,"[36] but in such a way as to characterize it as an absurdly short

---

31. See also 20:30-31; 21:25.

32. Compare the demands in the synoptic tradition by "the Pharisees" (Mk 8:11), or "the Scribes and Pharisees" (Mt 12:38), or "the Pharisees and Sadducees" (Mt 16:1), or simply "others" in the crowds (Lk 11:16), for "a sign" (Mt 12:38) or "a sign from heaven" (Mt 16:1; Mk 8:11; Lk 11:16). There Jesus regarded all such demands as characteristic of an evil generation, and either refused them out of hand (Mk 8:12) or promised just one sign, "the sign of Jonah" (Mt 12:39-40; 16:4; Lk 11:29-30), which referred (as here) to his own resurrection.

33. See LSJ, 1160 and BDAG, 533; compare Brown, 1.115. Most commentators, however, are hesitant to press the distinction (see Barrett, 199; Moloney, *Belief in the Word,* 99).

34. See Mk 14:58, and compare "this mountain" (Mk 11:25) and "this place" (Acts 6:14).

35. For ἐγείρειν in the sense of erecting or restoring a building, see BDAG, 214 (for example, of Jerusalem's walls, Sirach 49.13; of the temple, 1 Esdras 5.44; Josephus, *Antiquities* 15.391; 20.228).

36. The same phrase occurs in Matthew 27:40//Mark 15:29 (compare "through

period of time in comparison to "forty-six years" (v. 20).[37] They do not, however, pay attention to the imperative "destroy" *(lysate)* with which Jesus' riddle began. They seem to have perceived the verb as imperatival in form but not in meaning. Jesus is not commanding them to destroy anything, but rather setting up a condition: "*If* you destroy this sanctuary, in three days I will raise it up."[38] The accent is not on the destruction of the "sanctuary," but on the promise to "raise it up."[39] Consequently, the Jewish authorities take offense not at being told to destroy their own temple, but at Jesus' claim that he himself will build it again, and in such a short time.

A messianic reading of 2 Samuel 7:13-14 could suggest that rebuilding the temple was a work of the Davidic Messiah, even as David's son had built the first temple (compare Zech 6:12-13). Jesus' words might then have been interpreted as a messianic claim, particularly in the wake of his comment about "my Father's house" (v. 16). Caution is necessary because the Messiah

---

three days," Mt 26:61//Mk 14:58). As Delling points out (*TDNT,* 8.218), "three days" in biblical usage can be either a short or a long period depending on the context" (it is a long time, for example, in Mk 8:2, Lk 2:46, and Acts 9:9!), but here the contrast with "forty-six years" makes it unmistakably very short.

37. Normally the aorist οἰκοδομήθη ("was built") would imply that the temple was finished, but according to Josephus it was not. He wrote that the temple was begun in the eighteenth year of Herod's reign (about 20 B.C.; *Antiquities* 15.380; according to *War* 1.401 the fifteenth year, or 23 B.C.), and not completed until about A.D. 63, just seven years before its destruction (*Antiquities* 20.219). But if the temple was in regular use, people would have thought of it as finished, and would have spoken as "the Jews" do here (compare Ezra 5:16, LXX, where the aorist is used of an earlier temple which "from then until now has been under construction, and is not yet finished"). "Forty-six years" should be read as a piece of historical evidence placing the event around A.D. 26 or 27, not a symbolic number as Augustine thought (*Tractates* 10.11-12, NPNF, 1st ser., 7.73-74), nor a veiled reference to Jesus' age (see 8:57; see Brown, 1.116; Schnackenburg, 1.351-52; Bultmann, 127). Not surprisingly, the date is more consistent with the beginning than with the end of Jesus' ministry (see Lk 3:1), and thus with the Johannine placement of the temple cleansing.

38. See BDF, §387(2); Dodd, *Interpretation,* 302, n. 1. Bultmann disagrees (125), placing the emphasis rather on the imperative itself, which he sees as ironic, in the tradition of certain biblical prophecies (citing Amos 4:4, Isa 8:9-10, and Jer 7:21; compare Mt 23:32). This is not consistent with the reply of "the Jews" in verse 20.

39. In this respect the saying is different from the charge against Jesus at his trial in Matthew and Mark, where the accent is as much on destruction as on restoration, and where Jesus himself does the destroying: "I am able to destroy [δύναμαι καταλῦσαι] the temple of God and in three days build it" (Mt 26:61; compare 27:40); "I will destroy [ἐγὼ καταλύσω] this temple made with hands and in three days build another not made with hands" (Mk 14:58; compare 15:29). The accent on destruction is even stronger in *Thomas* 71 ("I will destroy [this] house, and no one will be able to rebuild it") and in the charges against Stephen in Acts 6:14 (that Jesus "will destroy this place and change the customs which Moses delivered to us").

is pictured as the builder of the temple only rarely and only in later rabbinic literature, while in earlier Jewish material God is more often the Builder.[40] But even though the reader knows that Jesus is "God the One and Only, the One who is right beside the Father" (1:18), it is unlikely that he is claiming to be God, even implicitly, at this early point in the narrative. More likely, he is endorsing and claiming for himself Nathanael's confession of him as both "the Son of God" and "the King of Israel" (1:49). The issue is joined, and will continue to be joined, over "christology" in the strict sense of the word, that is, over the question of whether or not Jesus is the Messiah.[41] This is consistent with the emphatic "you" in the mocking reply of the Jewish authorities: "and *you* are going to raise it up in three days?" Even though "the Jews" began by responding to Jesus' actions rather than his words (v. 18), seeming to ignore his provocative reference to "my Father's house" (v. 16), their problem in the end is not with what he has done, but with who he is, or claims to be. Their scornful last words (v. 20) go unanswered, just as the banquet master's comic misunderstanding of the miracle at Cana went unanswered.[42] Jesus' first confrontation with "the Jews" is over almost as soon as it began.

21 While "the Jews" have the last word in the dramatic exchange just described in the text, they do not have the last word in the text itself. That belongs rather to the Gospel writer, just as in did in the story of the wedding (2:11). The writer now intervenes to explain that Jesus "was speaking of the sanctuary that was his body." This belated piece of information forces the reader to go back and look at verse 19 again. So far, most readers have probably been guided in their interpretation of Jesus' riddle by the way in which the Jewish authorities heard it. They would assume that although "the Jews" were wrong to mock Jesus' pronouncement about "this sanctuary," they at least interpreted it correctly. Now they learn that this is not so, and a re-reading of verse 19 is required. What are the implications of rereading "this sanctuary" in Jesus' pronouncement as "this *body*"?[43] Clearly, the demonstrative pronoun

---

40. See, for example, 4QFlorilegium 1.1-13, and for further references and discussion, R. H. Gundry, *Mark*, 899-900.

41. Notice that the issue is still unresolved as late as 10:24: "How long will you keep us in suspense? If you are the Messiah, tell us plainly."

42. Again John Chrysostom noticed, and wondered, "Why did He so keep silence? Because they would not have received His word; for if not even the disciples were able to understand the saying, much less were the multitudes" (*Homily* 23.3; NPNF, 1st ser., 14.82).

43. A line of interpretation as old as Origen (for example, *Commentary on John* 10.228-32, 263; FC, 80.305-6, 313) sees in the reference to Jesus' body a reference to the church as well as to the physical body of Jesus. But the accent on "this" and the reference to "destroying" the body and raising it "in three days" do not lend themselves to such an interpretation. Even though, as Schnackenburg puts it, this writer's "ecclesiology is based

"this" is just as appropriate as before, if not more so. Paul spoke rhetorically of his body, or the human body generally, as "this corruptible," or "this mortal" (1 Cor 15:53-54), or simply as "this" (2 Cor 5:2), or "this tent" (some manuscripts of 2 Cor 5:4), or even "these hands" (Acts 20:34).[44] The verb "destroy," however, takes on new significance. Destroying a body (that is, killing a person) is obviously quite different from destroying a temple! The verb recalls verse 17: "Zeal for your house will consume [or destroy] me." Jesus' death is once again part of the scenario, and the implication is that "the Jews" (that is, the religious authorities in Jerusalem) will bring it about. The imperative, as we have seen, expresses a condition: "*If* you destroy this body, in three days I will raise it up." When Jesus seemed to be referring to the temple in Jerusalem, that was not a realistic possibility. He was not saying that "the Jews" would destroy their own temple, nor did they attribute to him any such notion. But if he means by "this sanctuary" his own body, his pronouncement becomes a kind of accusation as well as a promise. The imperative begins to sound like a challenge: "Go ahead, destroy this body! If you do, I will raise it up in three days!" For the first time he hints at what he will say explicitly later on ("You are seeking to kill me," 8:37, 40; compare 7:19-20), and what in fact they will soon begin to do (5:18; compare 7:1, 25; 8:59; 10:31-33; 11:53). Other features of the pronouncement quickly fall into place. The verb "raise up" *(egeirein)* is more commonly used of raising up persons (whether from sickness, sleep, or death) than buildings.[45] "Three days" is (as Jesus' hearers had noticed) a ridiculously short time in which to build a temple, but (in light of certain synoptic traditions) an appropriate and familiar one in connection with Jesus' resurrection. Just as in the synoptic tradition, the only "sign" given turns out to be his own resurrection.[46]

---

entirely on Christology" (1.352), the Pauline notion of the church as the "body" of Christ never appears in the Gospel of John.

44. The notion that Jesus pointed to himself when he first made the pronouncement (which some commentators mention but none will admit to holding!) is absurd because it would, as Schnackenburg remarks, "make the Jewish misunderstanding incredible" (1.349).

45. While ἐγείρειν is occasionally used of a building in Greek literature (n. 35), all but one of the 144 uses of the verb in the New Testament refer to living entities rather than buildings (the response of "the Jews" in v. 20 being the only exception). It is one of two verbs (along with ἀνίστάναι) used repeatedly in the New Testament for the resurrection of Jesus.

46. See Matthew 12:40: "No sign will be given . . . except the sign of Jonah. For as Jonah was three days and three nights in the belly of the fish, so the Son of man will be three days and three nights in the heart of the earth." The Synoptics use various expressions in speaking of Jesus' resurrection (τρεῖς ἡμέρας, Mt 12:40), "after three days" (μετὰ τρεῖς ἡμέρας, Mk 8:31; 9:31; 10:34); "on the third day" (τῇ τρίτῃ ἡμερᾳ, Mt 16:21; 17:23; 20:19; 27:64; Lk 9:22; 18:33; 24:7, 21; Acts 10:40; 1 Cor 15:4). While the precise expression used here, "in [or within] three days" (ἐν τρισὶν ἡμέραις), occurs only in sayings

We are left, then, with two competing solutions to Jesus' riddle about "this sanctuary" (v. 19): a wrong one (from a Johannine perspective) in verse 20, and the right one (supplied by the Gospel writer) in verse 21.[47] What the two solutions have in common is that the controversy is not over what Jesus has just done in the temple precincts (despite the initial response of "the Jews" in v. 18), but over who Jesus is. The implication of the final words of verse 20 is "Who do *you* think you are?" (compare 8:53b). The reader already knows who Jesus is, the Father's "One and Only" (compare 1:14, 18), and has Jesus' own words about "my Father's house" (v. 16) to prove it. The reader also knows how the controversy will turn out: zeal for his Father's house will "consume" or "destroy" Jesus (v. 17), but when the Jewish authorities "destroy" his body, he himself will raise it up (v. 19). The outcome of the conflict is not in doubt, for Jesus is fully in control.[48]

22 The Gospel writer's narrative aside continues. Here the particle "So" (*oun* in Greek), often used in resuming a narrative after a parenthetical comment by the narrator,[49] instead continues and elaborates the comment itself. Having just stated that Jesus "was speaking of the sanctuary that was his body," the Gospel writer goes on to explain that this was a conclusion to which the disciples came only after he was in fact "raised from the dead." The verb "was raised" corresponds to the the words "I will raise up" in Jesus' own pronouncement, except that the Gospel writer reverts to the more common passive form in which does not explicitly raise himself or his own body.[50] The notice that "his disciples remembered" echoes verse 17, where

---

about destroying the temple (Mt 27:40; Mk 15:29), it is vague enough to be consistent with either form, "after three days" or "on the third day."

47. The "wrong" solution surfaces again at the end of Jesus' ministry in synoptic accounts of his trial, where certain "false witnesses" charge him with threatening to "destroy the temple of God and in three days build it" (Mt 26:61), yet even here a variant form of the charge (Mk 14:58) adds that the temple he would build was "not made with hands" (ἀχειροποίητον). The qualification could represent a move in the direction of the Johannine "right" solution, in which the temple Jesus will raise up is no literal temple, but his own body (compare 2 Cor 5:1), but it could also signal a claim that Jesus builds as God builds, in that ἀχειροποίητον "comes to mean 'made by God'" (Gundry, *Mark*, 900, concludes that Jesus was charged with having "arrogated to himself another divine role").

48. The notion of Jesus "raising up" himself or his own body (ἐγερῶ αὐτόν, v. 19) is not the usual way of referring to Jesus' resurrection (see v. 22), yet is wholly consistent with the perspective of this Gospel (compare 10:17-18, "I lay down my life that I might take it again. . . . I have authority to lay it down, and I have authority to take it again").

49. Compare BDF, §451(1); Abbott, *Johannine Grammar*, 470.

50. The difference is slight because the intransitive passive ἠγέρθη is middle or active in meaning, without particular reflection on God the Father as the One who "raised up" Jesus (see BDAG, 214-15; compare ἐγερθεὶς ἐκ νεκρῶν, 21:14; also 11:29, where Mary "rose quickly" and came to Jesus).

they were said to have remembered a passage of Scripture. There certain clues suggested that the recollection was after the fact; now the Gospel writer makes this explicit. It was indeed not in the temple on that first Passover, but much later, "when he was raised from the dead," that they remembered. The writer bases his comment (v. 21) on their collective authority. He knows what Jesus meant by his pronouncement[51] because the disciples themselves (who were presumably present on the scene) eventually came to that realization. "Meant" is an appropriate translation because it is a matter not simply of recalling certain words that Jesus had spoken, but of coming to understand their significance in light of subsequent events.[52]

When the disciples "remembered" Jesus' pronouncement, we are told, they also "believed both the scripture and the word Jesus spoke." "Believed" recalls verse 11, where these same disciples "believed in him" after the miracle at Cana of Galilee. There it was a matter of putting one's trust in Jesus as a person; here it is a matter of believing something to be true (that is, "the scripture and the word Jesus spoke").[53] The contrast is not between a superficial preresurrection faith in Jesus as a person and a deeper postresurrection faith by which one learns to see him as the fulfillment of Scripture and receive the revelation he brings from God.[54] The point is rather that the crucial act of faith came first, when Jesus "revealed his glory, and his disciples believed in him" (v. 11), and that what happened later, "when he was raised from the dead" (v. 22), simply verified and validated that initial faith. As we will see, the verification of Jesus' words by later (sometimes postresurrection) events so that his disciples might "believe" is a conspicuous theme in this Gospel (see, for example, 13:19; 14:29; 16:4).

---

51. Τοῦτο ἔλεγεν ("this was what he meant," v. 22) echoes ἔλεγεν περί ("he was speaking of," v. 21). As Abbott comments, "in this prediction about the Temple, *'remembered'* is probably a short way of saying 'remembered and recognized'; and ἔλεγεν περί is but a longer form of ἔλεγεν" (*Johannine Grammar*, 341). For ἔλεγεν as "meant," compare the parenthetical comment in 6:71: "But he meant [ἔλεγεν] Judas, son of Simon Iscariot."

52. Compare 12:16, "These things his disciples did not understand at first, but when Jesus was glorified, then they remembered [τότε ἐμνήσθησαν] that these things were written about him and that they had done these things for him"; also 14:26, where remembrance with understanding is probably the point of Jesus' promise that the Holy Spirit "will remind [ὑπομνήσει] you of all that I said to you."

53. The former is πιστεύειν εἰς; the latter πιστεύειν with the dative. For extended discussions, see Abbott, *Johannine Vocabulary*, 32-80, and Dodd, *Interpretation*, 182-84.

54. Compare perhaps 20:8-9, where the beloved disciple "saw and believed" (ἐπίστευσεν) on looking into Jesus' tomb, but where we are then told that he and Peter "did not yet know the scripture, that he must rise from the dead." The parallel is far from perfect, however, because the contrast in chapter 20 is not between pre- and postresurrection faith, but between two stages of postresurrection faith, one immediate and the other the product of subsequent reflection.

The disciples "believed" two things after the resurrection: "the scripture" and "the word" that Jesus had just spoken. By "the scripture" is meant the specific text from Psalm 69, "Zeal for your house will consume me" (v. 17),[55] not the Jewish Scriptures as a whole.[56] This text they treated as a prophecy come true. The words of the psalmist had become in effect words of Jesus. Zeal for his Father's house had indeed destroyed him. As for "the word Jesus spoke," it is clearly his pronouncement, "Destroy this sanctuary, and in three days I will raise it up" (v. 19), in particular the promise of "raising it up," and the disciples "believed" this as well. Jesus had predicted his death (in the words of the scripture) and his resurrection (in his own words), and *both* predictions had now come true.[57] The Gospel writer's notice here is a signal that Scripture and the words of Jesus will be treated in much the same way in this Gospel. Certain things will happen in the story "to fulfill" certain texts of Scripture (12:38; 13:18; 15:25; 17:12; 19:24, 36), and other things will happen "to fulfill" certain sayings of Jesus (18:9, 32). Some biblical texts are cited (as they are here) in the first person, as if Jesus is the speaker (compare 13:18; 15:25; 19:24), and sometimes Jesus' own words are so closely entwined with words of Scripture that it is difficult to tell which is which (7.38, 19:28). To believe Scripture and to believe Jesus amount to much the same thing (compare 5:46-47). The disciples' belief in "the word Jesus spoke" stands in sharp contrast to the unbelief of "the Jews," because the latter had heard that same word and mocked it (v. 20). While there is no similar contrast with respect to "the scripture" because Jesus had quoted no text of Scripture in their presence (as he does in the Synoptic accounts), the implication is that the lines between faith and unbelief are beginning to be drawn. So far in the Gospel, first Nathanael (1:50) and then the disciples as a group (2:11 and here) have explicitly "believed," and no one has explicitly been said to "disbelieve" or "not believe." Yet here at Jesus' first Passover in Jerusalem, without using the actual word, the Gospel writer has given us the first specific example of the unbelief that we know Jesus will face (see 1:10-11).

55. Compare Lindars, 144; Moloney, *Belief in the Word,* 102; Sanders and Mastin, 120; compare Haenchen, *John 1,* 185.

56. The term ἡ γραφή is always used in John's Gospel for specific texts, never for the Jewish Scriptures as a whole; see 7:38, 42; 10:35; 13:18; 17:12; 19:24, 28, 36, 37 (the only possible exception is 20:9, but even here it is likely that a specific text is in mind even though it remains unidentified). When the writer wants to refer to the Jewish Scriptures more generally, he uses the plural (5:39).

57. The failure to see that *both* death and resurrection are in view leads some commentators to ignore the Psalm 69 citation and look for other texts not even mentioned in this passage that specifically point to resurrection (above all, Ps 16:10, cited in Acts 2:31 and 13:35; for example, Westcott, 1.95; Morris, 179-80; Carson, 183).

G. JESUS AND NICODEMUS AT PASSOVER (2:23-3:21)

23 *Now while he was in Jerusalem at the Passover, with the festival going on, many believed in his name, for they could see the signs he was doing.* 24 *But as for Jesus, he would not entrust himself to them, for he knew them all.* 25 *He had no need for anyone to testify about the person, for he himself knew what was in the person.* 3:1 *But there was one person, a man of the Pharisees, Nicodemus by name, a ruler of the Jews.* 2 *He came to him at night and said to him, "Rabbi, we know you have come from God as a teacher, for no one can do these signs you are doing unless God is with him."* 3 *Jesus answered and said to him, "Amen, amen, I say to you, unless someone is born from above, he cannot see the kingdom of God."* 4 *Nicodemus says to him, "How can a person be born when he is old? Can he enter his mother's womb a second time and be born?"* 5 *Jesus answered, "Amen, amen, I say to you, unless someone is born of water and Spirit, he cannot enter the kingdom of God.* 6 *What is born of the flesh is flesh, and what is born of the Spirit is spirit.* 7 *Don't be surprised that I told you, 'You people must be born from above.'* 8 *The wind blows where it will, and you hear the sound of it, but you don't know where it comes from or where it goes. So it is with everyone born of the Spirit."* 9 *Nicodemus answered and said to him, "How can these things be?"* 10 *Jesus answered and said to him, "You are the teacher of Israel, and you don't understand these things!* 11 *Amen, Amen, I say to you that we speak what we know, and we testify to what we have seen, and you people do not receive our testimony.* 12 *If I have told you people earthly things and you do not believe, how will you believe if I tell you heavenly things?* 13 *And no one has gone up to heaven except he who came down from heaven, the Son of man [who is in heaven].*[1] 14 *And just as Moses lifted up the snake in the desert, so the Son of man must be lifted up,* 15 *so that everyone who believes might have eternal life in him.* 16 *For God so loved the world that he gave the One and Only Son, so that everyone who believes in him might not be lost but have eternal life.* 17 *For God sent his Son into the world not to*

---

1. The bracketed words are found in a number of Greek manuscripts, including A, Θ, Ψ, families 1 and 13, the majority of later manuscripts, virtually all Latin versions, and two Syriac versions. One Syriac and one old Latin version have the words, "who *was* in heaven," while a few later Greek manuscripts and a Syriac version have "who is *from* heaven." By far the weight of manuscript evidence (including P^{66}, P^{75}, ℵ, B, and L) favors omission of this clause. Yet it is a difficult reading, because if Jesus is himself the Son of man, the question of how he could be on earth and in heaven at the same time is raised. If it was original, it is easy to see why it might have been dropped. Therefore I have placed it in brackets.

judge the world, but so that the world might be saved through him. ¹⁸ *Whoever believes in him is not judged; whoever does not believe is already judged, because he has not believed in the name of the One and Only Son of God.* ¹⁹ *This then is the judgment, that the Light has come into the world, and human beings loved the dark rather than the Light, for their works were evil.* ²⁰ *Everyone who practices wicked things hates the Light and does not come to the Light, for fear his works will be exposed,* ²¹ *but whoever does the truth comes to the Light, so that his works will be revealed as works wrought in God."*

There is no easy way to divide this long section, which spells out in some detail the contrast between belief and unbelief. The notice about those who "believed in his name, for they could see the signs he was doing" (vv. 23-25) leads smoothly into a dialogue with Nicodemus, the only named representative of this group (3:1-11). The dialogue then fades into a monologue in which Jesus seems to be addressing no one but the reader (3:12-21). The theme of his brief discourse is as broad as the Gospel itself, recalling themes introduced in the so-called "Prologue" (1:1-18) — above all, the coming of the Light into the world, the alternatives of receiving or rejecting the Light, and the necessity of "believing in his name" and being "born of God" (see 1:9-13).

23 Jesus is still "in Jerusalem at the Passover, with the festival going on," though not explicitly in the temple. In contrast to the Jewish leaders in the temple, "many believed in his name, for they could see the signs he was doing." These "many" are unidentified, although there is reason to think that some of them were leaders as well. One at least was "a man of the Pharisees" and "a ruler of the Jews" (3:1), and we will learn later of "many of the rulers" who similarly "believed" in Jesus (12:42). The expression, "believed in his name," recalls 1:12-13, where the "children of God" who "received" the Light and were "born of God" are concretely identified as "those who believe in his name." Here we are told that they did so on the same ground on which his disciples "believed in him" at the Cana wedding, that is, on the basis of "the signs he was doing" (compare 2:11). If "signs" *(sēmeia)* are understood as miracles, no miracles comparable to what Jesus had done at Cana are recorded at this Passover in Jerusalem, and none will be until explicit notice is given that a "second sign" has taken place (4:54). In the present narrative, "the signs" can only be Jesus' actions in driving the merchants and money changers from the temple,[2] "signs" recognized as such by those who "believed in his name" but

---

2. This does not exclude the possibility that at some stage of the tradition, before the account found its way into John's Gospel, the "signs" at Jesus' first Passover in Jerusalem may have consisted of specific miracles, possibly of healing. The healing of the sick man in chapter 5, for example, is placed at an unidentified "festival" (5:1), which in an

2:23–3:21 Jesus and Nicodemus at Passover

not by "the Jews" at the temple who challenged his authority. The latter had seen what Jesus was doing (v. 18), but had still demanded, "What sign do you show us?" Here too the accent is on the verb "was doing" *(epoiei)* more than on "the signs." It now becomes clear (if it was not before) that "the signs" are simply Jesus' "deeds," not necessarily miraculous but full of revelatory significance. First Jesus' disciples, and now these believers at the Passover festival, saw significance in things Jesus had done, while "the Jews" (vv. 18 and 20) saw only a threat to their authority as guardians of the temple.

Nothing in the text suggests that the faith of these Passover "believers" was anything but genuine.[3] Later we will hear that those who have *not* "believed in the name of the One and Only Son of God" prove thereby that they are "already condemned" (3:18). These "believers" are clearly not in that position. But are "those who believe in his name" *necessarily* given "authority to become children of God" simply because of their belief? It would be natural to assume so (on the basis of 1:12), but what immediately follows suggests that their faith, genuine though it may be, is not sufficient to identify them as those "born of God" (see 1:13).

24-25 Even though many "believed" *(episteusan,* v. 23), the Gospel writer is quick to add parenthetically that "as for Jesus, he would not "entrust [*episteuen*] himself[4] to them."[5] In one sense this is not surprising, for Jesus in

---

earlier form of the story could have been this first Passover (see Michaels, *John,* 84-85). But while such a possibility cannot be excluded, it has no bearing on the interpretation of the text of the Gospel as it stands, in which the healing in chapter 5 is obviously later. In the present form of the text, what impressed not only these Passover believers (v. 23) but also Nicodemus (3:2) and the Galileans mentioned later who "saw all that he did in Jerusalem at the festival" (4:45), was the cleansing of the temple, and that alone.

3. Origen (*Commentary on John* 10.310; FC, 80.324-25) distinguished between "believing in Jesus" and "believing in his name" with the comment, "We must cling, therefore, to him rather than to his name, that, when we perform miracles in his name, we may not hear the words which were spoken of those who boasted in his name alone" (an allusion to Mt 7:22-23). Abbott *(Johannine Vocabulary)* tried to make a similar case by linking "belief in the name" to "a lower kind of trust, a profession of belief in baptism" (37), but the text offers no basis for any such distinction.

4. "Himself" is αὐτόν (literally "him," but with a reflexive meaning). Some important manuscripts (including P[66]) have ἑαυτόν here (the more common pronoun for "himself"), but αὐτόν is the more difficult reading. It is easy to see why it would have been changed to ἑαυτόν, but not why the opposite change would have taken place. The entire verse in Greek sounds cumbersome and redundant, with four occurrences of the emphatic or reflexive pronoun αὐτός (αὐτός . . . αὐτόν αὐτοῖς . . . αὐτόν), leading to an elaborate repetition in verse 25 of the thought that Jesus "knew them all." The first αὐτός serves to underscore the contrast between the two uses of πιστεύειν; thus the translation, "But as for Jesus, he. . . ." The effect is to place the emphasis strongly on Jesus "himself" (αὐτός) and on his knowledge.

5. For πιστεύειν as "entrust," compare Luke 16:11, Romans 3:2, 1 Corinthians

this Gospel is not known for greeting the faith even of his own disciples with great enthusiasm. His reaction is usually either silence (2:11; 4:53; 11:27), or a warning of some kind (6:70; 16:31-32), or a reference to something "greater" (1:50) or more "blessed" (20:29). Here he goes further, seeming to reject the faith of these Passover believers altogether. This is very odd in a Gospel where Jesus will hold out all kinds of promises to those who believe: they are "born of God" (1:13); they are not condemned to death, but have "eternal life" (3:16, 18; 5:24; 6:47); if they die, they will rise to life, never to die again (11:25-26); they will "see the glory of God" (11:40); they will receive the Spirit (7:39); and they will do the works Jesus did, and even "greater works" (14:12).

Why do none of these promises apply to the believers here? We are not told why, except that Jesus "knew them all."[6] "He had no need for anyone to testify[7] about the person, for he himself knew what was in the person."[8] It is all very well to "believe," but Jesus, and Jesus alone, determines whether or not a person's faith is accepted. He knows these "believers," just as surely as he knew that Nathanael was "a true Israelite" (1:47). But what is it about them that he knows, and why does this prevent him from accepting their allegiance? It cannot be simply that their faith was based on "signs,"[9] for the same was true of Jesus' disciples (2:11), and he quite clearly "entrusted himself" to them (2:12). Later, he will encourage even those who oppose him to

---

9:17, Galatians 2:7, 1 Thessalonians 2:4, 1 Timothy 1:11, and Titus 1:3. While "entrusting oneself to someone" (πιστεύειν αὐτόν τινι) does not occur elsewhere in the New Testament, it is not uncommon in Greek literature (for example, *Aristeas* 270; Josephus, *Antiquities* 12.396; and a number of texts cited in BDAG, 817).

6. Greek (διὰ τὸ αὐτὸν γινώσκειν πάντας). Because both the subject and the object of the infinitive are in the accusative case, this clause could also be translated, "because they all knew him," but this makes no sense in the context. The effort of one early translator (Gilbert Wakefield, *Translation of the New Testament,* 1820) to render it this way (evidently in light of Mk 1:34, where Jesus forbade the demons to speak "because they knew him") is ingenious but unconvincing.

7. The expression, "no need for anyone to testify" (ἵνα τις μαρτυρήσῃ) is simply another way of saying that Jesus had complete knowledge (compare 16:30, "You have no need for anyone to ask you," where the point is that Jesus not only knows everything, but reveals everything without being asked; see also 1 Jn 2:27 and 1 Thess 4:9, 13).

8. "Person" is a word traditionally translated as "man," though not gender specific. "About the person" is περὶ τοῦ ἀνθρώπου, and "in the person" is ἐν τῷ ἀνθρώπῳ. While not gender specific, ἄνθρωπος in this sense is generic, referring not to an individual but to any person (see BDAG, 82).

9. This is a very widely-held view (see, for example, Bultmann, 131; Schnackenburg, 1.358; Brown, 1.126-27; Morris, 181), based in part on Jesus' rebuke to the nobleman at Cana (4:48), read in light of the preceding notice (4:45) that Galileans had been present at this festival.

"believe the works" he performs in order to understand his relationship to God the Father (10:38). Rather, what Jesus knows about these Passover believers is what he knew about Nathanael. Just as he knew that Nathanael was someone "in whom is no deceit" (1:47), so he knew generally what was "in the person," and therefore what was (or was not) "in" these believers. Later he will say to another group (unbelievers in this case) at another Jewish festival, "No, I know you, that you do not have the love of God in yourselves" (5:42).[10] As his disciples come to recognize, Jesus "knows" everything (see 16:30; 21:17). He shares in the omniscience of God the Judge of all, who can "test the mind and search the heart, to give to all according to their ways" (Jer 17:10, NRSV; compare Ps 7:10; Prov 24:12),[11] and nowhere in the Gospel is his divine knowledge more evident than here.[12]

The phrases "about the person" and what was "in the person" imply a generalization about humanity and the human condition (see n. 8). The assessment is the narrator's assessment, even though attributed to Jesus. It is a conclusion drawn from Jesus' refusal to "entrust himself" to certain people who sought him out, a refusal that can be seen in the synoptic Gospels as well as the Gospel of John.[13] The mention of a "person" *(anthrōpos)* echoes the opening verses of the Gospel, where the writer speaks of "the light of humans" (1:3), and of "the true [Light] that illumines every human being who comes into the world" (1:9), but it also anticipates 3:19, where we are told that "the Light has come into the world, and human beings [*hoi anthrōpoi*] loved the dark rather than the Light, for their works were evil." The latter restates the principle that "the world did not know him" (1:10) and "his own did not receive him" (1:11). "Humans" or "persons" *(hoi anthrōpoi)* are

---

10. See also 5:38, "And you do not have his word remaining in you" (ἐν ὑμῖν μένοντα).

11. Such texts are echoed in the pronouncements of the risen Jesus in the book of Revelation, who repeatedly mentions things that he says "I know" (οἶδα) about each of the seven congregations in Asia (Rev 2:2, 9, 13, 19; 3:1, 8, 15), and who claims that "I am he who searches hearts and minds, and I will repay each of you according to your deeds" (Rev 2:23, NIV).

12. Other examples: he knows the Samaritan woman's past (4:17-18; compare vv. 29, 39), and that the nobleman's son will live (4:50); he knows what he will do to feed a crowd of five thousand (6:6); he knows who will disbelieve and who will betray him (6:64), and why the blind man was born blind (9:3); he knows that Lazarus has died (11:11-14) and will rise again (11:4, 11, 40); he knows his own mission, and the events leading to its completion (13:1, 3; 18:4; 19:28), and he knows that Thomas has asked to verify his identity by touch (20:27).

13. Compare, for example, Jesus' flight from the crowds again and again in Mark's Gospel, and his use of parables to hide the truth from some while revealing it to others. In John, compare his flight from those who acknowledged him as "the Prophet who comes into the world" and tried to make him a king (6:14-15).

equivalent in this Gospel to "the world," or "his own," those who should have received him because he created them and illumined them at birth (1:3, 9), but did not. Now we learn that Jesus knew this from the start because he knew what was "in" them. In this Gospel there is something wrong with what is merely "human." Jesus insists that "I do not receive glory from humans" (5:41; also 5:34), in contrast to unbelievers who receive "glory from one another" (5:44), and in contrast even to those who "believed in him" (12:42, as here), yet "loved the glory of humans instead of the glory of God" (12:43).

In the latter case a reason is given for the negative verdict on their faith: "because of the Pharisees they would not confess him for fear of being put out of the synagogue" (12:42). Perhaps this was also the reason why Jesus would not "entrust himself" to those who believed at this first Passover. We are not told. The only distinction between these Passover believers and the disciples who "believed in him" after the Cana wedding is simply that he "revealed his glory" to the one group (2:11) but not to the other. There is, as we will see, a strong note of divine election throughout this passage, as in the Gospel as a whole. Jesus chooses his own disciples (6:70; 13:18). They do not choose him (15:16).

3:1 Someone once said, "If you want people to read what you've written, don't write about Man, write about a man." The repetition of the noun "person" or "man" *(anthrōpos)* links the story of Nicodemus closely to what precedes. Having hinted at the evil in the heart of the human "person" generally (2:25), the writer now focuses on one "person" in particular. Nicodemus is the first character since chapter 1 to be identified by name,[14] and he is further described both as a man "of the Pharisees" and "a ruler of the Jews." The mild adversative in the expression, "But there was one person," raises the question of how typical Nicodemus is of the "many" who "believed in Jesus' name" and to whom he did not "entrust himself" (2:23-25). Is Nicodemus a typical example of this group or is he an exception? Did Jesus "entrust himself" to Nicodemus or not?

On the face of it, there are signals that raise suspicions. Not only is

---

14. Like John (1:6), Nicodemus is identified both as a "man" or "person" (ἄνθρωπος), and by name, with the same expression used to name John (ὄνομα αὐτῷ, "his name," literally "a name to him"). "Nicodemus" was a Greek name, adapted into Hebrew as Naqdimon. There is no sure way to identify our Nicodemus with anyone else of that name mentioned in Jewish literature. The wealthy Naqdimon ben Gorion at the time of the siege of Jerusalem in 70 (*b. Ta'anit* 19b-20a, *b. Ketubbot* 66b-67a, and *b. Giṭṭin* 56a) would probably have been too young to have been a "ruler" in the time of Jesus. Among five names of Jesus' disciples given in the Talmud (*b. Sanhedrin* 43a) are a Naqai (sometimes thought to be the Aramaic form of Naqdimon) and a Buni (mentioned in *b. Ta'anit* 20a as Naqdimon's other name), but there is no proven connection (compare Schnackenburg, 1.365).

2:23–3:21 JESUS AND NICODEMUS AT PASSOVER

Nicodemus part of a group whose faith Jesus did not find acceptable, but he belongs both to "the Jews" and to "the Pharisees" in particular, that is, to those who had sent a delegation to John (1:19, 24), and been told that John proclaimed One "whom you do not know" (1:26). As one of "the Jews," he seems to belong with those who had challenged Jesus' authority at the temple (2:18, 20). More specifically, he is "a ruler [*archōn*] of the Jews."[15] By "ruler" it is frequently understood that he belonged to the Jewish ruling council, or Sanhedrin,[16] but this is far from certain. More likely, the term is used more generally here to refer to a leader of some kind among the Jewish people (see "Israel's teacher," v. 10). While the "many" who believed at this first Passover are not identified as "rulers," the group mentioned later who "believed in him but because of the Pharisees would not confess him" are introduced specifically as "rulers" (12:42). The Gospel writer, even while suggesting that the faith of such "rulers" was inadequate, seems to take a certain satisfaction in pointing out their attraction to Jesus and his teachings. Later, when the Pharisees ask (rhetorically), "Have any of the rulers believed in him, or any of the Pharisees?" (7:48-49), the writer quickly brings Nicodemus, both ruler and Pharisee, on the scene (7:50-51)[17] as if in refutation of their claim, confirming the impression here that he belongs to those who "believed in his name" at this first Passover.

2 Nicodemus "came to him," just as Jesus had come to John (1:29) and Nathanael had come to Jesus earlier (1:47). Wherever this expression occurs in the Gospel, it raises at least a possibility that the person is "coming" in faith, or giving allegiance in some way (see 3:26; 5:40; 6:35, 37, 44-45, 65; 7:37; 10:41; note especially the parallelism between "coming to me" and "believing in me" in 6:35 and 7:37-38). This appears to be the case here. If he was one of those who "believed in his name" (2:23), it is natural that Nicodemus "came to him."[18] But why "at night"? It is not uncommon for this writer to pay attention to the time of year (10:22) or time of day, whether the

---

15. Compare Luke 18:18, where a wealthy "ruler" (ἄρχων) addresses Jesus as "Good teacher" and asks what he must to "inherit eternal life."

16. Even some English versions assume this (NIV, NEB, REB), but the New Testament evidence is inconclusive (see Delling, *TDNT*, 1.489; BDAG, 113-14). What is clear is that the Jewish ἄρχοντες, or "rulers," are a group of leaders distinguished from the "elders" and the "scribes" (Acts 4:5, 8), from the "chief priests" (Lk 23:13; 24:20), and from "the Pharisees" (Jn 7:48; 12:42; this is the case even though Nicodemus belonged to both groups). It is interesting that Joseph of Arimathea, who is quite clearly identified as a council member (Mk 15:43; Lk 23:50), is never called a "ruler."

17. Instead of repeating all the terminology of 3:1, the writer simply states that Nicodemus was "one of them" (7:50).

18. Later, Nicodemus is twice identified by this act of "coming" to Jesus (ὁ ἐλθὼν πρὸς αὐτόν, 7:50, 19:39).

precise "hour" (1:39; 4:6; 19:14) or more generally, "night" (13:30; 21:3; compare 6:16-17; 20:19) or "morning" (18:28; 20:1; 21:4). Here it is important to distinguish between Nicodemus's possible reason for coming at night and the Gospel writer's reason for calling attention to it. As for the first, he may have come out of fear, or a desire for secrecy. This would align him with those other "rulers" who believed in Jesus, but "because of the Pharisees would not confess him for fear of being put out of the synagogue" (12:42). Later, his companion, Joseph of Arimathea, is said to have been "a disciple of Jesus, but secretly, for fear of the Jews" (19:38). At that point Nicodemus himself is reintroduced, and possibly the accompanying reminder that he had come to Jesus "at night" (19:39) implies that he too was a secret disciple, and for the same reason. But in contrast to the "rulers" of 12:42, who "loved the glory of humans instead of the glory of God" (12:43), the writer puts no blame either on Joseph in chapter 19 or on Nicodemus here.[19]

As for the Gospel writer, why does he call our attention to "night" as the setting of the encounter? Every other use of "night" in this Gospel has negative associations. "Night" was when Judas departed (13:30). "Night" was when the disciples caught no fish (21.3). "Night" is when "no one can work" (9:4), and when someone who tries to walk "stumbles because the light is not in him" (11:10). It is virtually equivalent to "the dark" (3:19) or "the darkness" (1:5; 8:12; 12:35, 46) in this Gospel. But what does this say about Nicodemus? Did he come at night because he "loved the dark" (3:19) and "walked in the darkness" (8:12; 12:35)? Or did he come *out of* the darkness, offering allegiance to One already identified as "the Light" (see 1:4-9)? On this reading, Nicodemus "comes to the Light, so that his works will be revealed as works wrought in God" (v. 21).[20] The reader has little basis on which to decide between the two options, and for the time being must leave Nicodemus's motives and spiritual condition an open question.

Nicodemus says, "Rabbi, we know[21] you have come from God as a teacher." There is no reason to doubt either his sincerity or the aptness of his characterization of Jesus. "Rabbi" is the same designation by which the dis-

---

19. Compare the disciples "behind locked doors for fear of the Jews" when they saw the risen Lord (20:19; compare v. 26).

20. See Barrett, 205; Morris, 187; Schnackenburg, 365-66; Moloney, 91. Yet those who hold this view seldom apply Jesus' positive characterization of those who "come to the Light" (3:21) to Nicodemus without some qualification.

21. "We know" (οἴδαμεν) can refer simply to what is common knowledge (compare 9:31), and does not have to be a signal that Nicodemus is speaking for a larger group. Here, however, he does speak for such a group, and οἴδαμεν probably reflects this (compare 7:27 and 9:29, where it is used again in connection with the issue of where Jesus is from). As we will see, Jesus presupposes just such a wider audience in two of his responses to Nicodemus (vv. 7, 11-12).

ciples addressed Jesus earlier (1:38, 49), and instead of explicitly translating it again as "teacher" (as in 1:38), the Gospel writer allows Nicodemus to do it for him. The use of the title marks Nicodemus as a disciple (see 3:26; 4:31; 9:2; 11:8), or at least a potential disciple (6:25). Jesus is known to his disciples in this Gospel as "Teacher," and he accepts that designation (13:13-14). In recognizing Jesus as one who has "come from God," Nicodemus is saying as much as Jesus' disciples were willing to say later even after lengthy instruction prior to his passion (16:30). Yet the acknowledgment does not in itself imply either Jesus' preexistence, or that he has come down from God in heaven (compare vv. 13; 6:33, 38, 42, 63). The reader knows these things (from 1:1-14), but also knows that even John could be identified as a man "sent from God" (1:6) with no connotations of preexistence or divinity at all. Whatever one may say about Nicodemus's faith, his knowledge is far from complete. The reader is way ahead of him. But when Nicodemus goes on to mention "these signs," the immediate impression is just the opposite: Nicodemus, like the rest of the Passover believers, seems to know of "signs" done in Jerusalem that the reader knows nothing about. This, as we have seen, is unlikely (see 2:23). "Signs" here (as in 2:23) should be understood rather as "deeds" or "works"[22] that the reader *does* know about: that is, Jesus' provocative actions in the temple, and (since Nicodemus calls him "teacher") perhaps his words as well. To Nicodemus they are "signs" because he finds them significant, drawing from them the conclusion that Jesus has "come from God" because "God is with him."[23]

3 A casual reading could suggest that Jesus simply ignores what Nicodemus has just said, but this is not the case. Rather, the form of Nicodemus's comment, "*no one can* do these signs . . . *unless* God is with him" (v. 2), anticipates the form of Jesus' immediate response (v. 3): "Amen, amen, I say to you, *unless* someone is born from above, *he cannot* see the kingdom of God" (italics added). Jesus' words echo, even mimic, Nicodemus's words of praise, reversing the clauses so that together the two pronouncements form a chiasm.[24] Far from ignoring Nicodemus's comment, he matches one impossibility with another. Just as it is *impossible* to do what Jesus has been doing *unless* "God is with him," so it is *impossible* to "see the kingdom of God" *unless* one is "born from above." With this a dialogue begins, clearly marked off like the dialogue between Jesus and "the Jews" at the

22. The verb "to do" is again conspicuous here (ποιεῖν ἃ σὺ ποιεῖς; compare 2:11, 18, 23).

23. Jesus twice makes the same claim for himself: "And the One who sent me is with me [μετ' ἐμοῦ]; he has not left me alone" (8:29; compare 8:16); "And yet I am not alone, because the Father is with me" (μετ' ἐμοῦ, 16:32).

24. In Greek, Nicodemus says οὐδεὶς γὰρ δύναται . . . ἐὰν μή, and Jesus (turning the expression around) replies, ἐὰν μή . . . οὐ δύναται.

temple in 2:18-20. That is, Jesus "answered and said to him" (v. 3); Nicodemus "says to him" (v. 4); Jesus "answered" (v. 5); Nicodemus "answered and said to him" (v. 9); Jesus "answered and said to him" (v. 10). The last answer concludes the dialogue as Nicodemus fades from the scene.

This second "Amen, amen" pronouncement, like the first (1:51), is Jesus' reply to an acknowledgment of who he is by someone addressing him as "Rabbi" (Nathanael in 1:49, and now Nicodemus). This time he speaks to Nicodemus alone rather than to a group, as in the case of Nathanael.[25] Yet the necessity of rebirth is not just for Nicodemus but for "someone" or anyone *(tis)*, and the intended audience will become more inclusive as the dialogue proceeds (see vv. 7, 11, and 12), maintaining the impression that Nicodemus is representative of a larger group. The phrase "born from above" (that is, *anōthen*) recalls for the reader the elaborate characterization of God's "children" as those born "not of blood lines, nor of fleshly desire, nor a husband's desire," but "born of God" (1:13).[26] It is not a matter of physical birth, but of divine rebirth or transformation.[27] The reader can recognize, therefore, that "from above" means simply "of God," or "from God."[28] God must become Father[29] to those who would "see the kingdom of God."

While Jesus has been hailed as "King of Israel" (1:49), the phrase "the kingdom of God" is mentioned only twice in the entire Gospel of John: here and in Jesus' attempted clarification in verse 5 (compare "my kingdom," repeated three times in 18:36). To "see the kingdom of God" could mean either to have a visionary experience like that promised to Nathanael and his companions (1:51),[30] or to experience salvation. Jesus

---

25. Thus, ἀμὴν ἀμὴν λέγω σοι rather than ἀμὴν ἀμὴν λέγω ὑμῖν, as in 1:51.

26. The closest synoptic parallel is Matthew 18:3, "Amen, I say to you, unless [ἐὰν μή] you turn and become as children [ὡς τὰ παιδία], you will by no means [οὐ μή] enter the kingdom of heaven." While the form is similar, there is no spiritual rebirth here, but only the use of children as a metaphor for discipleship (compare Mk 9:33-37; 10:13-16).

27. The compound verb "born again" (ἀναγεννᾶσθαι) does not occur in John's Gospel or 1 John, but in the New Testament only in 1 Peter (1:3, 23; see also Justin, *Apology* 1.61.4). For the noun "rebirth," or "regeneration" (παλιγγενεσία), see Matthew 19:28 (with reference to a reborn world) and Titus 3:5 (with reference to baptism); also Tractate 13 in the *Corpus Hermeticum,* "On Rebirth."

28. See verse 31, where "the One who comes from above" (ὁ ἄνωθεν ἐρχόμενος) is almost immediately interpreted as "the One who comes from heaven" (ὁ ἐκ τοῦ οὐρανοῦ ἐρχόμενος), that is, from God (compare 19:11).

29. "Father," because "born again" means "begotten again," as by a male progenitor. The only mother "from above" in the New Testament is "the Jerusalem above" (ἡ δὲ ἄνω Ἰερουσαλήμ), which Paul refers to as "our mother" (Gal 4:26; also vv. 28-29).

30. Compare Wisdom 10.10, with reference to Jacob's vision at Bethel: "When a righteous man fled from his brother's wrath," wisdom "showed him the kingdom of God [βασιλείαν θεοῦ] and gave him knowledge of angels."

speaks often in the synoptic Gospels of "entering" or "inheriting" the kingdom of God, but only once of "see[ing] the kingdom of God." Some of "those standing here," he said, "will not taste of death until they see the kingdom of God" (Lk 9:27). Luke implies that this was fulfilled eight days later when three of the disciples "saw his glory" (9:32). Here in John's Gospel it is those who were "born of God" who "looked at his glory" when "the Word came in human flesh" (1:13-14), and to whom "he revealed his glory" in Cana of Galilee (2:11). "Seeing glory" (17:24) or "seeing life" (3:36) are also expressions for final salvation, however, and the same is true of "seeing the kingdom of God" (compare v. 5, where Jesus explains "seeing" as "entering"). Nicodemus (unlike the "ruler" who questioned Jesus in Lk 18:18) has not asked about salvation or eternal life, but Jesus responds to him as if he had: salvation is impossible — *unless* a person is "born from above."[31]

4 His reply indicates that Nicodemus hears the pronouncement very differently from the reader: "How *can* a person be born when he is old? *Can* he enter his mother's womb a second time and be born?" (italics added). First, it is often assumed that he hears the adverb *anōthen* not as "from above" (which would make no sense to him), but as "again."[32] In one sense, this is not a misunderstanding because it would seem that a birth "from above" is necessarily a second, or new, birth.[33] But a better way of putting it is that he seems not to have heard the adverb at all. His reply focuses solely on the notion that a person already alive must be "born." Such a birth is by definition a "new" or "second" birth, even without an accompanying adjective or adverb.[34] Second, he hears "born" as a reference to physical birth as from a "mother's womb," not to the act of begetting, as from a father,

---

31. The notion of impossibility comes up in the synoptic Gospels as well, when Jesus sets high standards for "entering the kingdom of God," and his disciples ask, "So who can [τίς δύναται] be saved?" He then replies, "With humans it is impossible [ἀδύνατον], but not with God, for all things are possible [δυνατά] with God" (Mk 10:23-27 par.).

32. For these two alternative meanings, see BDAG, 92. The common assumption that the word has a "double meaning" here (for example, Brown, 1.130; Morris, 188-89; Barrett, 205) is questionable. While ἄνωθεν can mean either "from above," or "again," there is no reason to think it means both at the same time, except in the sense that "from above" necessarily *is* "again."

33. The only way this would not be the case is if the writer were assuming that the first, or physical, birth of the elect was itself somehow a birth "from above," simply because they were God's elect, predestined from birth to be the children of God. This is highly unlikely, however, given the sharp distinction in 1:13 between physical birth and being born "of God."

34. See Schnackenburg, 1.369: "Nicodemus has only taken up and analyzed 'being born'; he seems to have ignored completely the ἄνωθεν of Jesus."

whether human or divine.³⁵ His rhetorical questions assume that Jesus is calling for a second physical birth, and Nicodemus dismisses any such idea as "impossible" and patently absurd.³⁶ With this he becomes a spokesman for precisely the kind of misunderstanding the Gospel writer warned against at the outset ("not of blood lines, nor of fleshly desire, nor a husband's desire," 1:13). As far as the reader is concerned, the sarcasm backfires. What turns out to be ridiculous is not Jesus' pronouncement, but Nicodemus's crudely literal interpretation of it. Entering the womb a second time is as absurd as building a temple in three days (2:20), or having a camel go through the eye of a needle (see Mk 10:25). Yet at the same time the incredulous words, "How can?" and "Can he?" actually reinforce the point that salvation is "impossible" without the rebirth of which Jesus has spoken.

5 Jesus responds by restating what he said before in slightly different words: "Amen, Amen, I say to you, unless someone is born of water and Spirit,³⁷ he cannot enter the kingdom of God." Jesus calls attention to the adverb "from above," which Nicodemus had overlooked, by redefining it as "of water and Spirit,"³⁸ and he redefines "seeing" as "entering" the kingdom of God. "Entering" picks up on Nicodemus's own terminology about "entering" the mother's womb, but brings the discussion back to the matter of salvation, which Nicodemus seems to be avoiding. It is not a question of "entering" the womb again (v. 4), but of "entering" the kingdom of God (see Mt 5:20; 7:21; 18:3; 19:23-24; Mk 9:47; 10:23-25; Lk 18:25; Acts 14:22). Jesus will develop the idea of being "born of the Spirit" in verses 6-8, but "water" is mentioned only here. Nicodemus will respond to neither.

The reference to "water and Spirit" has called a forth a variety of interpretations. The reader will notice, for example, that John earlier contrasted his own role of "baptizing in water" (1:26, 31, 33) with Jesus' role as the One who would "baptize in Holy Spirit" (1:33). This suggests that being "born of water and Spirit" could have something to do with water baptism and baptism in the Spirit, whether viewed together or separately.³⁹ We will learn

---

35. Compare the questions about rebirth in *Corpus Hermeticum* 13.1-2 (Περὶ Παλιγγενεσίας): "From what womb is a man born, and of what seed?"

36. Nicodemus goes so far as to characterize the person who enters the womb a second time as "old," either because he himself (as "a ruler of the Jews") is old, or merely to heighten the absurdity of it all. As Schnackenburg puts it, "the extreme case of the aged makes flagrantly clear what is true of every age, that there is only one birth" (1.368).

37. It is difficult to decide whether or not "spirit" should be capitalized. I have opted for capitalization in verse 5 because when Jesus repeats the word in verses 6 and 8 he does so with the definite article, "the Spirit," suggesting that the Holy Spirit is meant.

38. In Greek, ἐξ ὕδατος καὶ πνεύματος.

39. This is the view of the majority of commentators (for example, Westcott, 108-9; Bernard, 1.104; Hoskyns, 213-14; Brown, 1.141-44; Beasley-Murray, 48; Schnacken-

shortly that Jesus himself, like John, "baptized" (presumably in water) in Judea, to the point that his baptizing ministry was perceived as rivaling John's (3:22, 26; 4:1-3). His comment here might therefore be understood as an endorsement of John's ministry of baptism, and (if it had begun by this time) his own as well. Another proposal (mostly in popular literature) has been that "born of water" refers to physical birth, whether from the standpoint of water in the mother's womb, or of water as a euphemism for the male sperm (compare 1 Jn 3:9).[40] This need not mean simply that a person must first be born physically (which should go without saying) and then born spiritually. The phrase could be read "of water, even Spirit," with "water" expressing the idea of physical birth and "Spirit" making it immediately clear that physical birth is only a metaphor for the birth of which Jesus speaks.[41] Thus "born of water and Spirit" means simply "born of Spirit."[42] Defenders of this view can point out that in verses 6 and 8 Jesus forgets about water and mentions only the Spirit. The difficulty, however, is that while "water" is a possible metaphor for physical birth, it is not an obvious one. The Gospel writer already used a number of expressions for physical birth and "born of water" was not among them (see 1:13).[43] He did this, moreover, in order to draw the sharpest possible contrast between physical and spiritual birth (*"not"* of blood lines, etc., *"but"* of God) rather than to point out analogies between them. In the present context Jesus himself will draw an equally

---

burg, 1.369; Barrett, 209; Moloney, 92-93). There are a number of nuances to this view, depending on one's theological convictions. The point could be either that "water" (that is, water baptism) is necessary, or that it is insufficient without the accompanying work of the Spirit (or even both at the same time!).

40. "Euphemism" is perhaps not the right word, because the terminology of "water" or a "drop" was used contemptuously (like dust or clay) to remind humans of their humble origin (e.g., *m. 'Abot* 3.1, "a putrid drop"; *3 Enoch* 6.2, "a white drop"; 1QH 5.21, "an edifice of dust, kneaded with water"; 9.21, "a vessel of clay, and kneaded with water"; compare 11.24).

41. This is the view of Odeberg, *The Fourth Gospel* (48-71, and the texts cited there), who understands "water" as a term for the male seed, but spiritualized as "celestial σπέρμα . . . an efflux from above, from God," so that "the spiritual man, or . . . member or citizen of the βασιλεία τοῦ θεοῦ owes his existence as such to the procreative power of the efflux from God, the σπέρμα in the spirit" (63-64; compare Morris, 191-93).

42. Others get rid of water in more heavy-handed fashion by simply omitting ὕδατος καί as an interpolation (for example, Bultmann, 138, n. 3). But even if they are an interpolation (which is unlikely, and for which there is no manuscript evidence), why remove them from the text? It is widely acknowledged that the Gospel of John grew in stages in any case, and if someone in the Johannine community cared enough to add them to the tradition, why would this not make them *more* important for understanding the Gospel in its present form, not less? (compare Moloney, 99).

43. See Lindars, 152.

sharp contrast between the two: "What is born of the flesh is flesh, and what is born of the Spirit is spirit" (v. 6). The incongruity of understanding water as physical birth can easily be seen by substituting "flesh" (which clearly *does* mean physical birth) for water, yielding a self-contradictory phrase, "born of flesh and Spirit" or "born of flesh, even Spirit."

On the face of it the baptismal view has more in its favor, yet it sets rather narrow limits to the application of both "water" and "Spirit." While both terms are used in connection with baptism (1:33), they are also used in a variety of other ways in this Gospel that have nothing to do with baptism. "Water," for example, can evoke images either of cleansing (9:7; 13:5), or of sustaining life by the quenching of thirst (4:10-14; 6:35; 7:37-38), and in this respect it is explicitly identified as "the Spirit" (7:39). "Spirit," too, can be either the "life-giving" Spirit (6:63) or the agent of purification (as in 1:33). As has often been observed, "water" and "Spirit" are governed by a single preposition (*ek*, "of," or "from"), suggesting that they are viewed together here, not separately.[44] "Water" by itself, so far at least in the narrative, has no particular significance. The water of John's baptism (1:26, 31) anticipates a greater baptism "in Holy Spirit" (1:33), and ordinary water (for "purification," as it happens, 2:6) waits to be transformed into "the good wine" that reveals the glory of Jesus (2:9-10). Here, too, "water" needs "Spirit" in order to have significance.

Moreover, if "water and Spirit" together were introduced to explain "from above," then the latter should in turn help explain "water and Spirit." The reader's first encounter with the Spirit in this Gospel was "coming down" from the sky (1:32-33), and the present passage confirms that first impression that the Spirit is indeed "from above." Nor is it strange to think of water as coming "from above." We need not imagine anything so esoteric as Odeberg's celestial divine seed, or "efflux from above" (n. 41). We need only think of rain.[45] John's Gospel never uses the imagery of rain, yet when Jesus tells the Samaritan woman of "living water," and she asks him, "From where [*pothen*] do you have the living water?" (4:11), his implied (though unstated) answer is, "from above" *(anōthen)*. The woman looks down into the well for her water, but Jesus has water from the opposite direction. Similarly, Nicodemus may not know from where *(pothen)* the wind comes (v. 8), but the reader knows that the Spirit is "from above." As for the water in the pool

---

44. Odeberg, as we have seen, makes this point, and its validity is not dependent on the peculiarities of his own interpretation.

45. See *b. Ta'anit* 2a, where R. Jochanan said, "Three keys the Holy One, blessed be He, has retained in His own hands and not entrusted to the hand of any messenger, namely, the Key of Rain, the Key of Childbirth, and the Key of the Revival of the Dead" (*Babylonian Talmud: Seder Mo'ed* [London: Soncino, 1938], 4.3). All three focus on life, and God's power to give life.

of Siloam where the man born blind washed and received his sight, the Gospel writer pauses to remind us (9:7) that the very name "Siloam" means "sent," as if from God in heaven.

In short, if both water and Spirit mean "life" in the Gospel of John, then birth from "water and Spirit" means the beginning of new life "from above," or what this Gospel calls "eternal life" *(zōē aiōnion)*. The word "life," used only twice in the Gospel so far (1:4, "In him was *life,* and the *life* was the light of humans"), will recur again and again beginning in this chapter (vv. 15 and 16, twice in v. 36, plus thirty more occurrences in chapters 4–21).[46] "Born of water and Spirit," therefore, becomes simply the writer's way of defining "the kingdom of God" as "life" or "eternal life," with the effect of actually *replacing* "kingdom of God" with "life" (the term "kingdom of God" never occurs again in the Gospel of John). Such an interpretation does not exclude a baptismal reference, but allows the reader to think more broadly about "water and Spirit" than simply the act of water baptism. It is confirmed by the fact that "water and Spirit" also evokes a number of biblical prophecies about spiritual cleansing in connection with the promise of a new covenant with the people of Israel,[47] yet even without knowing these prophecies the reader is well equipped (possibly at once, and certainly on a second reading or hearing) to understand Jesus' words adequately within the framework of the Gospel itself.

6 Jesus continues by reminding Nicodemus of the principle that like produces like. In contrast to other expressions of this principle in the New Testament (for example, Mt 7:16-20; 12:33-35; Gal 6:7-8; Jas 3:12), his point is not that "flesh," or "what is born of the flesh" (compare 1:13), is "at enmity with God" (compare Rom 8:7), or at war with "spirit" (compare Gal 5:17) or with "what is born of the Spirit" (compare Gal 4:29). His point is simply that "flesh" and "spirit" are different spheres of reality, each producing offspring like itself. "What is born," whether of flesh or Spirit, is neuter here (in contrast to "everyone born" in v. 8), perhaps as an equivalent to the Greek neuter nouns "infant" or "child."[48] "Flesh" is human nature, which, because it is mortal, tries to gain a kind of immortality by reproducing itself (see 1:13). Instead it produces only that which is mortal like itself. "Spirit" differs from "flesh" not in being immaterial as opposed to material,

---

46. Even in the synoptic tradition "life" and "kingdom of God" can be used interchangeably (specifically with the verb "enter"; see Mk 9:43, 45, 47; compare also Mt 7:14; 18:8, 9; 19:16, 17, 29).

47. This point is made at some length by Carson (191-96) with particular reference to Ezekiel 36:25-27.

48. "What is born" is τὸ γεγεννημένον in Greek; "infant" is τὸ βρέφος; "child" is τὸ τέκνον or τὸ παιδίον (all with the neuter definite article; see also Lk 1:35, τὸ γεννώμενον, "the child to be born").

but in being immortal as opposed to mortal. "Flesh" is subject to death; "spirit" is not. Even the Word, when he "came in human flesh," became subject to death, while "the Spirit" (and consequently "spirit")[49] means life, and only life. This verse, with what precedes it, affords a basis in the Jesus tradition for Paul's pronouncement that "Flesh and blood cannot inherit the kingdom of God, nor does corruption inherit incorruption" (1 Cor 15:50). The latent implication of Jesus' word is that those "born of the Spirit" are no longer "flesh" but are themselves "spirit" (see v. 8) — not that they are no longer human or no longer in the body, but that they "have eternal life" (compare vv. 15-16) and are consequently no longer mortal (compare 8:51; 11:26).

7 Jesus now repeats for yet a third time the notion that a person must be "born from above" (compare vv. 3, 5). "Don't be surprised" is almost equivalent to "No wonder," linking the pronouncement to what Jesus has just said in verse 6.[50] *If* it is true that "What is born of the flesh is flesh, and what is born of the Spirit is spirit" (v. 6), then, *of course,* "You people have to be born from above."[51] But the expression "you must" is not used here as an imperative, "Be born from above," as if it were something a person could simply choose to do. The impersonal verb *dei,* "it is necessary," points to a divine necessity (in John's Gospel alone, see 3:14, 30; 4:4, 24; 9:4; 10:16; 12:34; 20:9).[52] Yet the necessity is not an inevitability, as if Jesus were promising, "You *will* be born from above, like it or not." Rather, what "is necessary" is what God has decreed *as the means* by which a person sees or enters the kingdom of God. "You must be born from above" is simply a more direct and positive way of saying, "Unless you are born from above, you cannot see the

---

49. The distinction between "Spirit" and "spirit" in an English text is rather arbitrary (among the more difficult calls are 6:63b and 19:30). Normally I have capitalized "Spirit" where it appears to refer to the Spirit of God (as almost everywhere in John's Gospel), and left it uncapitalized where it refers simply to redeemed humanity or the human spirit.

50. The verb "surprised" or "amazed" (θαυμάζειν) can mean either favorably or unfavorably impressed, depending on the context (see BDAG, 444), but in this instance Nicodemus's potential "surprise" sounds fairly neutral, suggesting neither hostility on the one hand nor admiration on the other.

51. See 1 John 3:12-13, where the author first makes the point that Cain killed his brother because his works were evil and his brother's were righteous, and then draws the conclusion, "So don't be surprised [μὴ θαυμάζετε] if the world hates you." The expression functions somewhat differently in John 5:28, where Jesus supports a conclusion already drawn (vv. 25-27) with the comment, "Don't be surprised at this" (μὴ θαυμάζετε τοῦτο) and a summary of traditional Jewish beliefs pointing to this conclusion.

52. This is most often the meaning in the other Gospels as well, although δεῖ can also be used in the somewhat weaker sense of that which is morally appropriate or fitting (for example, Mt 18:33; 23:23; Mk 13:14; Lk 12:12; 13:14, 16; 15:32; 18:1; 19:5).

kingdom of God." This third formulation differs from the first two in speaking not of an indefinite "someone" (as in vv. 3 and 5), but specifically of "you" (*hymas,* plural). The pronoun embraces both Nicodemus and those he represents (compare his own use of the plural "we know" in v. 2), primarily the believers to whom Jesus "would not entrust himself" at this first Passover (2:23-24).[53] They had "believed in his name," but something more was "necessary": they had to be "born from above."

8 Jesus now introduces an odd metaphor — odd because the metaphor and the reality it represents are expressed by the same noun *(to pneuma),* which can be translated as either "the Spirit" or "the wind." The reader, in light of verses 5 and 6, would ordinarily read it as "the Spirit," except that the accompanying verb, "blows" *(pnei),* is a word never used of the Spirit in the New Testament, but used quite naturally of the wind.[54] Moreover, its "sound" *(phōnē)* is far more easily understood as the sound of the wind than as the "voice" of the Holy Spirit.[55] Schnackenburg calls the verse "a short parable," with the interpretation introduced by the words, "So it is with everyone born of the Spirit."[56] The analogy is of course that the wind is invisible; we cannot see or know "where it comes from or where it goes," or why it changes direction, yet we hear the sound of it and see its effects. Jesus could have then concluded simply, "So it is with the Spirit," but this would have made no sense with the same word being used for both wind and Spirit. Consequently, he concludes by mentioning "everyone born of the Spirit" (echoing "what is born of the Spirit" in v. 6). Because "born of the wind" is not a plausible option, the reader knows that Jesus is once more using *pneuma* to mean "Spirit" (as in vv. 5-6),[57] and that "wind" was only a momentary metaphor.

What is less clear is whether or not Jesus' words should be read as a conscious statement about "the children of God," those who "received him" and "believed in his name" (compare 1:12-13), or would later do so — that

---

53. Alternatively, the plural "you" could be understood as referring to the Jewish people as a whole. The same options present themselves in vv. 11 and 12, but at this point it is more likely that the reader will think of the Passover believers of 2:23-24.

54. See 6:18, with ἄνεμος, "wind"; compare also Matthew 7:25, 27; Luke 12:55; Acts 27:40; Revelation 7:1 (for πνεῦμα as wind with the cogate verb πνεῖν, see *Epistle of Jeremiah* 60; Diodorus Siculus 24.1.2).

55. A consistent reading with "Spirit" would yield something like "The Spirit breathes where he will, and you hear his voice, but you don't know where he comes from or where he goes" (compare Barrett, 211). For φωνή as the Spirit's voice in tongues-speaking, see Acts 2:6; 1 Corinthians 14:7, 8, 10, 13, but this is an issue far removed from the world of John's Gospel, particularly in these early chapters.

56. Schnackenburg, 1.373.

57. This is evident in the variant reading ἐκ τοῦ ὕδατος καὶ τοῦ πνεύματος (ℵ; compare the old Latin and Syriac), echoing verse 5.

is, about the author and readers of the Gospel themselves (the "we" of 1:14). Are Christian readers to infer that *they* are those whose origin and destiny, whose comings and goings, are a mystery to the rest of the world? Jesus will later make just such a statement about *himself*: "I know where I came from and where I am going, but you do not know where I come from or where I am going" (8:14), and this will become a recurring theme in his teaching.[58] Unlike Nicodemus, who thought he knew that Jesus had "come from God as a teacher" (v. 2), his opponents later in the story will admit that "We do not know where this man is from" (9:29). Pilate will ask him, "Where do you come from?" and Jesus will not answer. He will tell his questioners and those sent to arrest him, "Where I go you cannot come," and they will not understand what he means (7:34; 8:21). But there is no such mystery about the comings or goings of Jesus' disciples. They, in fact, are as baffled as the Jewish authorities about where Jesus is from or where he is going. "You will seek me," he tells them, "and just as I said to the Jews that where I go you cannot come, so I say to you now" (13:33). Only after many questions and much anxiety does he finally make known to them his origin and destiny: "I came forth from the Father, and I have come into the world; again, I am leaving the world and going off to the Father" (16:28; compare 13:3). Even then, they seem to grasp only the first half of his pronouncement, coming back full circle to what Nicodemus had said at the beginning: "By this we believe that you have come from God" (16:30; compare 3:2).

Yet here, in speaking to Nicodemus, Jesus sees Christian believers, with all their limitations, in the same way he sees himself, as in some sense "from God"[59] and destined to return to God again.[60] While they may not know it,[61] Jesus knows it, and his pronouncement serves to remind the Gospel's readers of their divine heritage and calling.[62] The readers, standing out-

---

58. Compare Ignatius, who makes the same claim for the Spirit: "the Spirit is not deceived, being from God; for he knows where he comes from and where he is going" (*To the Philadelphians* 7.1).

59. To be born "of the Spirit" (ἐκ τοῦ πνεύματος, vv. 6, 8) is to be born "of God" (ἐκ θεοῦ as in 1:13, or ἐκ τοῦ θεοῦ as in 1 John), and to be "born of God" is to be "of God" or "from God" (ἐκ τοῦ θεοῦ εἶναι; see 8:47; 1 Jn 4:4, 6; 5:19). They are also "from God" in the sense that God gave them to Jesus in the first place (6:37, 39, 44; 10:29; 17:2, 6, 24; 18:9).

60. This becomes evident in some of Jesus' promises to his disciples and to the readers, especially in the farewell discourses (see 12:26; 13:36; 14:2-3, 6; 17:24).

61. At best, it is possible to infer (with Bultmann, 143, n. 1) from 12:35 that those who "walk in the light," in contrast to those walking in darkness, "know where they are going" (compare 1 Jn 2:11). But this is a stretch. Bultmann's citation of 14:4 as direct evidence of such knowledge is unconvincing in light of Thomas's puzzled question that immediately follows (14:5).

62. Gnostic parallels come inevitably to mind. According to Bultmann, "It is a fundamental tenet of Gnosticism that the Redeemer is a 'stranger' to the world, which

side the story, are not subject to quite the same limitations as the disciples within the story. The reminder that the world does not understand them, even as it did not understand Jesus, places them in a privileged position, affirming their identity as a sectarian community belonging to God, a counterculture in a hostile society (compare 15:18-19).[63]

9-10 The dialogue now draws to a close as it began: Nicodemus "answered and said to him" (v. 9), and Jesus in turn "answered and said to him" (v. 10). Nicodemus's last question, "How can these things be?" not only echoes his earlier question in verse 4 ("How can a person be born when he is old?"), but recalls the whole series of impossibilities that dominated verses 2-5: "no one can" (v. 2); "he cannot" (v. 3); "How can?" and "Can he?" (v. 4); "he cannot" (v. 5). Nicodemus is still unable to fathom the mystery of which Jesus has spoken. "These things" are not the elusive ways of the wind in Jesus' metaphor, but (as in v. 4) the mystery of being born "of the Spirit" (v. 6) or "from above" (v. 7).[64]

"You are the teacher of Israel," Jesus replies, "and you don't understand these things!" There is strong irony in his words: "these things" *(tauta)* on Jesus' lips echoes what Nicodemus has just said, and "the teacher" (where we might have expected simply "*a* teacher") frames the whole dialogue of verses 2-10 by reminding us of Nicodemus's initial confidence about Jesus that "we know that you have come from God as a teacher" (v. 2). Jesus, in a kind of mock confession,[65] now defers to Nicodemus as "*the* teacher" *(ho didaskalos),* while at the same time reminding him that he does *not* know or understand what Jesus is saying. Jesus' reply can be punctuated as either a question or a statement of fact. Most commentators read it as a rhetorical question, expressing surprise that Nicodemus is not familiar with the new

---

does not know his origin or his destination. . . . By virtue of their secret relationship with the Redeemer, the same is true of the redeemed, the spiritual men; indeed for them the decisive Gnosis is to know whence they themselves have come and whither they are going." While Bultmann was committed to the notion that "John took over the Gnostic view of the Redeemer and applied it to the person of Jesus," he admits that with regard to the believer "he has moved further away from the Gnostic view as a result of rejecting the idea of the pre-existence of souls and of the cosmic relationship between the Redeemer and the redeemed" (Bultmann, 143, n. 1).

63. Compare 1 John, where the similar phrase "everyone born of God (πᾶς ὁ γεγεννημένος ἐκ τοῦ θεοῦ) is used of those who have broken with the world to the extent that they do not or cannot sin (see 1 Jn 3:9; 5:18).

64. Even Nicodemus's choice of the verb for "be" or "come to be" (γενέσθαι) sounds (especially when read aloud) like the verb "to be born" (γεννηθῆναι, repeated in various forms in vv. 3, 4, 5, 6, 7, and 8).

65. In a curious way, the form of Jesus' pronouncement recalls Nathanael's confession, "You, Rabbi, are the Son of God; you are the King of Israel" (1:49; compare also 6:69; 11:27).

birth: "You are the teacher of Israel, and you don't understand these things?" Sometimes the implication is drawn that "these things" are clearly taught in Jewish Scripture, and therefore quite accessible to Nicodemus and to all who faithfully study and teach the Scriptures. This, however, is not the case.[66] While the Hebrew Bible predicts the coming of the Spirit and freely uses the imagery of water, nothing in it prepares Nicodemus (or the Christian reader) for Jesus' solemn declaration that "unless someone is born from above, he cannot see the kingdom of God" (v. 3). There is no interrogative particle here, and Jesus' words can just as easily be read as an exclamation: "You are the teacher of Israel, and you don't understand these things!"[67] The words "you don't understand" simply confirm the repeated notion of impossibility (from the human standpoint) that has marked the dialogue from its beginning. The argument is from the greater to the lesser: if even "the teacher of Israel" does not understand this birth "from above," how can anyone else? If there is surprise here, it is an ironic or feigned surprise, for Jesus has already stated clearly that Nicodemus has no knowledge or understanding (see v. 8) of the new birth or those "born of the Spirit." Still, the question, "How can these things be?" was not an exercise in futility. The answer will come in due course, not by human wisdom or ingenuity but by divine revelation.

11 With this, "the teacher of Israel" disappears from the scene. If verse 10 was a question, it goes unanswered, and if it was an exclamation it puts Nicodemus to silence. He is still being addressed ("Amen, amen, I say to *you*," singular), but he himself does not speak again until 7:50-51, when he offers a timid word in Jesus' defense. For the third time in the chapter (compare vv. 3, 5) and the fourth time in the Gospel Jesus adopts the "Amen, amen" formula to introduce a series of pronouncements of special importance: "we speak what we know, and we testify to what we have seen, and you people do not receive our testimony." The plural verbs "we speak," "we know," "we testify," "we have seen," and the plural pronoun "our" where we might have expected the singular "my," are striking. This is the characteristic revelatory language of John's Gospel, but when we hear it again it from Jesus' lips it will always be in the first-person singular, not the plural: "I speak" (8:26, 38; 12:50), "I know" (8:14, 55), "I testify" (5:31; 8:14, 18), "I have seen" (8:38).

Why is it plural here? One possible answer is that Jesus includes his

---

66. Compare Bultmann, 144: "Jesus' answer is not intended to imply that the scribe ought himself to have been able to give the answer, which would mean that one should look for the scriptural references which, in the Evangelist's view, contain the doctrine of rebirth. Rather, Jesus' answer makes it clear that the teachers of Israel *can* give no answer. They necessarily fail when they are faced with the decisive questions."

67. See Abbott, *Johannine Grammar,* 200, who nevertheless still regards the pronouncement as an expression of surprise: "The teacher of Israel . . . and ignorant of this!"

disciples with himself in the pronouncement. Just as Nicodemus is part of a larger group, so too is Jesus. Yet Jesus' disciples have not been mentioned since 2:17 and 22. They play no explicit part in his encounter with Nicodemus, even though their presence with Jesus in Jerusalem is presupposed (see below, v. 22). Another suggestion is that Jesus aligns himself with the biblical prophets, or perhaps specifically with John, who was earlier said to "have seen" and "testified that this is the Son of God" (1:34). Another is that Jesus and the Father speak with one voice.[68] Still another is that the plurals refer not only to Jesus and his disciples within the narrative, but to his continuing testimony in and through the Johannine community in its mission to, and its conflict with, the Jewish synagogue at the time the Gospel was written.[69] Or perhaps Jesus is simply mocking Nicodemus, as he did with the phrase "the teacher of Israel," by echoing the self-assured "we know" of verse 2.[70] A solemn "Amen, amen" pronouncement, however, is an unlikely vehicle for satire. Jesus is deadly serious in assuring Nicodemus of the validity of the revelation he brings to the world. The fact is that there is no way to tell who, if anyone, is included with Jesus in the "we" and the "our." Plural or not, the accent is on Jesus' activity, and his alone. As the writer will shortly make clear, it is "the One who comes from above" or "from heaven" (v. 31) of whom it is said, "What he has seen and heard, this he testifies, and no one receives his testimony" (v. 32), and this person can only be Jesus. In the present verse Jesus could just as easily have said, "*I* speak what *I* know, and *I* testify to what *I* have seen, and you people do not receive *my* testimony."

The question therefore remains: Why the plurals? The most plausible answer is that *it is still too early in the Gospel* for Jesus to speak authoritatively in the first person as the Revealer of God. Aside from the "Amen, amen" formula itself, Jesus does not begin to speak authoritatively as "I" until he meets the Samaritan woman in chapter 4.[71] All ten of the occurrences of the emphatic

---

68. See Abbott, *Johannine Grammar,* 312 (compare 8:16-18); also Chrysostom, *Homily* 26: "The expression 'we know,' He uses then either concerning Himself and His Father, or concerning Himself alone" (NPNF, 1st ser., 14.92). But the words, "we testify to what we have seen," can hardly be true of Jesus and the Father in quite the same sense.

69. See Barrett, 211; Schackenburg, 1.375-76. Bernard finds here not "the actual words of Jesus so much as the profound conviction of the Apostolic age that the Church's teaching rested on the testimony of eye-witnesses" (1.110, citing 1 Jn 1:1-2 and 4:14). Hoskyns (216) combines several of these interpretations into one with the comment that "Jesus did not confront Judaism alone," citing 5:30-47, and appealing to John, Moses and the prophets, Jesus' disciples, and (implicitly) the author and readers of the Gospel as examples of those included in the "we."

70. According to Brown (1.132), "the use of 'we' is a parody of Nicodemus's hint of arrogance."

71. See, for example, 4:14: "Whoever drinks of the water which *I* will give" (ἐγὼ δώσω); 4:26, "*I* am he [ἐγώ εἰμι], the One speaking to you"; 4:32, "*I* [ἐγώ] have food to eat

"I" *(egō)* in chapters 1–3 are on the lips of John, not of Jesus.[72] Here if anywhere we might have expected it because here Jesus solemnly attests to the validity not of a single pronouncement (as with the "Amen, amen" formula) but of everything he has said or will say. He speaks with unique and sovereign authority, but the plurals serve to deflect the uniqueness somewhat until John has yielded up the spotlight to Jesus (vv. 27-30), and until Jesus has been more formally presented as "the One who comes from above" and who "testifies to what he has seen and heard" (vv. 31-32). Only then will Jesus be ready to use the emphatic "I," and he promptly does so (repeatedly) in the next chapter.[73]

What is surprising about Jesus' testimony, both here and elsewhere in the Gospel, is that it is based, like John's, on what he has "seen" (compare "seen and heard," v. 32). This we might have expected from John (see 1:34; 3:29), but not necessarily from Jesus — *until* we remembered that the Word was "with God in the beginning" (1:1-2) and that although "No one has seen God," it was Jesus, "the One who is right beside the Father, who told about him" (1:18; also 5:37; 6:46; 8:38). Jesus, because of his preexistence, "speaks what he knows" and "testifies to what he has seen" in a way no human witness can do — not John (1:34), not the anonymous witness to the crucifixion (19:35), and not the Christian community (1 Jn 1:1-2). Their testimonies are all derivative, while his is the very fountainhead of Christian revelation. The conclusion, "you people[74] do not receive our testimony," also echoes the opening account of Jesus' reception in the world, "his own did not receive him" (1:11), and at the same time anticipates the notice that "no one receives his testimony" (3:32). If the Gospel writer knows the end from the beginning, so too does Jesus in his final words to Nicodemus. But we have yet to hear from him an echo of the note of hope sounded in 1:12, that "to as many as did receive him he gave authority to become children of God, to

---

that you do not know"; 4:38, "*I* [ἐγώ] have sent you to harvest." Such language continues to characterize Jesus' speech throughout the rest of the Gospel.

72. See 1:20, 23, 26, 27, 30, 31 (twice), 33, 34; 3:28. The closest Jesus comes to such a pronouncement in chapters 1–3 is his promise that "I will raise" (ἐγερῶ) the temple in three days (2:19). While the "I" here is not the emphatic ἐγώ, Jesus' opponents respond with an emphatic "you" (καὶ σύ, v. 20).

73. Bultmann's comments are remarkably similar: "The Evangelist has retained the plural because in a peculiar manner he disguises the person of Jesus and conceals the fact that ultimately Jesus is the only one who speaks from knowledge and who bears witness to what he has seen. He wants the discourse to retain its air of mystery, and he does not yet wish to state clearly that Jesus is the Revealer" (146); compare also Staley, *The Print's First Kiss,* 61: "Jesus never uses the first person pronoun *egô* in these three chapters — only John does; and in Jesus' one extended monologue (3:11-21), he speaks of himself only in the third person or first person plural. This peculiarity also changes after chapter 4."

74. The translation "you people" rests on the plural verb (οὐ λαμβάνετε), in keeping with the plurals in vv. 2 and 7.

2:23–3:21 JESUS AND NICODEMUS AT PASSOVER

those who believe in his name." Ironically, even though Jesus is speaking to one who presumably had "believed in his name on seeing the signs he was doing" (2:23), the promise of that verse is at this point unfulfilled. The reader has learned what is "impossible" (vv. 2, 3, 4, 5, 9), but has not yet heard the positive message of salvation. That will come in verses 14-21.

12 Having made his point about divine revelation, Jesus now reverts to "I" in speaking of himself (not, however, the emphatic "I"). Possibly the "Amen, amen" formula still governs the brief discourse that follows. Nicodemus seems to have disappeared, but Jesus continues to address those whom Nicodemus represents, whether all of Israel (v. 10) or those who believed in Jesus at the Passover (2:23-24). His pessimism about them (as expressed in v. 11) also continues, with a charge that "you do not believe," and the rhetorical question "How will you believe?" These indictments are framed by two conditional clauses: "If I have told you people earthly things," and "if I tell you heavenly things." The first is oriented to the past and to reality, assuming that Jesus has actually told them "earthly things." The second points to the future or "something impending," holding out the possibility that Jesus *will* tell them "heavenly things."[75] The argument is from the past to the future, and from the lesser to the greater: if they have already heard "earthly things" and not believed, how can they believe "heavenly things"?[76]

The reader is left wondering: What are the "earthly things" *(ta epigeia)* of which Jesus has spoken? Are they the experience of the new birth (vv. 3, 5, 7) and the work of the Spirit in the lives of believers (v. 8b)? Or are they the purely physical realities of birth (v. 4) or the wind (v. 8a)? If the former, then why is the new birth said to be "from above" (vv. 3, 7)? But if the latter, how can one *not* believe in such natural occurrences as birth, or the blowing of the wind? A third alternative is to view the "earthly things" as just such natural occurrences or physical realities, yet "not regarded as complete in themselves but as pointing parabolically to Christ and to God's activity in

---

75. "If I have told you" is a first class or real condition with εἰ (εἰ . . . εἶπον ὑμῖν); the second is a future condition with ἐάν (ἐάν εἴπω ὑμῖν); BDF, §372 (1) and §373 (3). For another Johannine example of two different conditional clauses in the same sentence, compare 13:17, "Now that (εἰ) you know these things, blessed are you if (ἐάν) you do them."

76. Compare Wisdom 9.16, "We can hardly guess at what is on earth, and what is at hand we find with labor; but who has traced out what is in the heavens?" (RSV); *4 Ezra* 4.21, "so also those who dwell upon earth can understand only what is on earth, and he who is above the heavens can understand what is above the height of the heavens" (*OTP*, 1.530); also *b. Sanhedrin* 39a, where Rabban Gamaliel says to the Emperor, "You do not know what is on earth, and yet [claim to] know what is in heaven." When the Emperor claims to know the number of the stars, Gamaliel tells him to count his teeth, adding "You know not what is in your mouth, and yet wouldst know what is in Heaven!" (*Babylonian Talmud. Seder Nezikin III: Sanhedrin* [London: Soncino, 1935], 248).

him, and intended to provoke faith" — that is, as parables or metaphors.[77] Much later, Jesus will make a distinction to his disciples between speaking "in parables" and speaking "openly about the Father" (16:25; also v. 29). The specific "parable" in mind there involves physical birth as well (16:21-22), and it is quite possible that Jesus is making a similar distinction already in this early encounter with Nicodemus and his friends.[78] On this interpretation, the phrase "earthly things" is almost synonymous with metaphor or figurative language. The presumption is that when we are dealing with spiritual realities such as birth from above ("heavenly things," if you will), they are more easily understood when couched in metaphorical language. But if the metaphors are not understood and the hearers do not come to faith (as is the case here), there is little hope that a direct and explicit presentation of the "heavenly things" will do any good.[79] Logically, the reader could infer from this that Jesus will not speak of "heavenly things" in this Gospel. In fact the opposite is true, for in due course he will do exactly that.

13 Jesus now explains why he, and he alone, has the right to speak of the "heavenly things" *(ta epourania)*. This second "Son of man" pronouncement, like the first (1:51), uses the imagery of ascent and descent to make a statement about his unique relationship to God. Now it is no longer angels "going up and coming down," but the Son of man himself. Yet here, as in the first pronouncement, the actual title "Son of man" is introduced only at the end. With these words, Jesus reinforces the note of impossibility and human limitation which has dominated his conversation with Nicodemus from the start, while at the same time transcending it with a mighty and decisive exception: "*no one* has gone up to heaven *except* he who came down from heaven, the Son of man" (italics added). Jesus' words now reaffirm what the Gospel writer claimed from the start, that "No one has seen God, ever. It was God the One and Only, the one who is right beside the Father, who told about him" (1:18). Others in Jewish tradition (especially certain apocalyptic traditions) were said to have seen God or ascended into heaven, but Jesus here denies that any of them actually did so.[80]

---

77. See Barrett, 212, who adds, "Jesus has spoken parables which should have evoked in Nicodemus faith (in Jesus himself); they failed in their purpose, and it will therefore be useless to speak directly, without parable, of τὰ ἐπουράνια; compare Mark 4.11f."

78. Compare H. Sasse, in *TDNT,* 1.681.

79. Consequently, while Sasse's reference to John 16:25 (see n. 78) is appropriate, Barrett's reference to Mark 4:11f. (n. 77) is not, because in Mark the purpose of "parables" is not to make Jesus' proclamation easier to understand, but harder. Mark's "parables" (παραβολαί), unlike John's παροιμίαι in chapter 16 (or τὰ ἐπίγεια here), are actually "riddles" designed to hide the truth.

80. Rhetorical denials of this kind were common enough in Jewish literature

Only he has been to heaven. Only he can tell of "heavenly things," and his revelation alone can be trusted (compare v. 11). Through him all the impossibilities become possible, and through him the way to rebirth and eternal life is opened for those who believe.

Taken literally, the pronouncement implies that Jesus has *already* "gone up to heaven,"[81] which is hard to visualize if, as we have been told, he was "with God in the beginning" (1:1-2), or "right beside the Father" (1:18). One suggestion often made is that *ei mē* ('except') functions here as a simple adversative ("but," or "but only") yielding the paraphrase, "No one has ascended, *but* one has descended, the Son of man."[82] Yet none of the New Testament passages commonly cited as parallels (for example, Mt 12:4; Lk 4:27; Rev 21:27) are true parallels. In each instance, the "exception" is not a real exception because it does not belong to the class specified (that is, "the priests" in Mt 12:4 were not included among "David and his companions," "Naaman the Syrian" in Lk 4:27 was not included among "lepers in Israel," and "those written in the book of life" in Rev 21:27 are not included among "things common or unclean"). Here, on the other hand, "the Son of man" obviously *does* belong to the class ostensibly excluded by the sweeping term "no one," and does thereby qualify as a genuine exception. "Except" *(ei mē)* should therefore be translated in the usual way, not as a simple adversative.

Another proposed solution is that the speaker is no longer Jesus but the Gospel writer, looking back on Jesus' ministry from a postresurrection perspective.[83] On such a reading, the pronouncement becomes one of the writer's "narrative asides," interrupting Jesus' speech to remind the Johan-

---

(compare Deut 30:12; Prov 30:4; Bar 3.29), yet they existed alongside traditions about those who had ascended (for example, Enoch, Abraham, Moses, Elijah, Isaiah). For examples, see Odeberg, 72-98, who concludes that no rejection of these traditions is implied (97-98). The point is rather that "the saints and prophets could do nothing without the Son of Man; if they ascended to heaven it was in the Son of Man, in union and communion with him." Odeberg's examples, however, do not distinguish between *visions* of heaven and actual *ascent* into heaven. Possibly Jesus' pronouncement is intended to rule out only the latter (even 1:18 and 6:46, which exclude visions of *God,* do not necessarily exclude the sort of heavenly visions described in, say, Ezekiel, or the book of Revelation). John's Gospel even has a couple of its own (8:56; 12:41).

81. "Gone up" is ἀναβέβηκεν, perfect tense.

82. See Moloney, *Johannine Son of Man,* 55; Westcott, 115-16; Bernard, 1.111; Carson, 200. Their point is that the revelation of heavenly things takes place not by virtue of anyone's ascent into heaven but by virtue of the Son of man's descent from heaven (compare Schnackenburg's more precise paraphrase, "No one has ascended to heaven [and brought tidings]; only one [has brought tidings]: he who descended from heaven, the Son of man," 1.393).

83. See, for example, Barrett (213), Haenchen (*John 1,* 204), and Beasley-Murray (44-45).

nine church that no one has ascended to heaven except Jesus because he came down from heaven in the first place (compare 6:62; 20:17). The impression that Jesus has already ascended is reinforced by a variant reading explicitly identifying the Son of man as "he who is in heaven."[84] The difficulty with this interpretation is that the text gives no signal of a change of speakers. The conjunction "and," both in this verse and the next, links each pronouncement closely to what precedes it, suggesting that Jesus is still the speaker, even though his audience within the narrative now seems to have vanished along with Nicodemus. The term "Son of man" (both here and in the following verse) confirms this, for in John's Gospel (as in the Gospel tradition generally) "Son of man" is Jesus' title for himself, not a title given him by others.

How then do we make sense of the pronouncement with the earthly Jesus as the speaker? The issue, of course, is not whether the historical Jesus would have spoken in this way, but whether the Johannine Jesus might have been represented as doing so.[85] This is the Gospel, after all, in which Jesus says, "I and the Father are one" (10:30), and even within the present chapter we are told that "He who comes from above is above all" (v. 31). To be "above all" is, on the face of it, not so different from being "in heaven."[86] Yet to ask at what point in the narrative between chapters 1 and 3 did Jesus go up to heaven is to ask the wrong question. The "ascension" in view here is not so much an event in time as a way of describing who Jesus is.[87] Like the angels

---

84. Greek ὁ ὢν ἐν τῷ οὐρανῷ. While the variant reading (see above, n. 1) could have arisen from a scribe's marginal note alluding to the risen Jesus, it scarcely matters whether the variant is accepted as original or not. If the perfect ἀναβέβηκεν, "has gone up," is read with "the Son of man" as its subject, it implies *in any case* that as a result of having ascended he is now in heaven.

85. Precritical commentators, reading a text that included the words "who is in heaven," are generally more helpful on this point than modern interpreters. Chrysostom wrote, "For not in heaven only is He, but everywhere, and He fills all things" (*Homilies on John* 27.1; NPNF, 1st ser. 14.94), and Augustine commented, "Behold, He was here, and was also in heaven; was here in His flesh, in heaven by His divinity; yea, everywhere by His divinity. Born of a mother, not quitting the Father" (*Tractates on the Gospel of John* 12.8; NPNF, 1st ser., 7.84).

86. Compare Ephesians 4:9-10, where Christ is identified as the One who both descended and ascended "far above all the heavens [ὑπεράνω πάντων τῶν οὐρανῶν], that he might fill all things."

87. Brown (1.132) notices in John's Gospel a "strange timelessness or indifference to normal time sequence," citing 4:38, where Jesus speaks as if he has already sent out his disciples. In other instances, the perspectives of either the Son's preexistence (5:19-20) or postresurrection existence (17:11-12) are drawn into the present tense of Jesus' discourse. We may also compare the new Jerusalem in the book of Revelation, where the accompanying participle, "coming down from heaven," does not refer to a point in time but simply describes the nature of the Holy City (Rev 3:12; 21:2, 10).

with whom he is associated (1:51), he is both an "ascending" and a "descending" Son of man (see 6:33, 38, 42, 51, 58, 62), for he knows "heavenly things," and makes them known on earth.[88]

14-15 Another "and" *(kai)* introduces yet another "Son of man" pronouncement, the third so far in the Gospel. Once again (as in 1:51 and in v. 13) "Son of man" comes last in its clause, prompting the unspoken question, "Who is this Son of man?" Nine chapters later, when that question is finally asked, it seems to be in response to the pronouncement exactly as given here: "How can you say that the Son of man must be lifted up? Who is this Son of man?" (12:34).[89] There the reader is also told that the word "lifted up" indicated the manner of Jesus' death (12:33). Yet here in chapter 3, when he says, *"just as* Moses lifted up the snake in the desert, *so* the Son of man must be lifted up" (italics added), no such help is given. Nothing in the verb itself suggests death by crucifixion. On the contrary, all the New Testament uses of this verb *(hypsōthēnai)* outside of John's Gospel imply prosperity or gain, and in Jesus' case exaltation to heaven (Acts 2:33; 5:31; compare Phil 2:9). The incident in Numbers 21:8-9 was a popular subject for reflection and edification both in early Judaism and early Christianity,[90] but instead of attempting to expound the passage (as he does, for example, with "bread from heaven" in chapter 6), he relies on a simple analogy *[just as . . . so]* based solely on the one word, "lifted up," a word that does not even occur in the biblical passage!

Why "lifted up?" If the verb does not come from the text of Numbers 21, where does it come from and why does Jesus use it? On the face of it, "to be lifted up" does not sound very different from "going up" (v. 13). The no-

---

88. Compare John Calvin: "For *to ascend to heaven* means here 'to have a pure knowledge of the mysteries of God, and the light of spiritual understanding'" *(Calvin's Commentaries 7: The Gospels* [Grand Rapids: Associated Publishers, n.d.], 640). While Moloney's attempt to eliminate altogether the theme of ascent and descent from John's Gospel is unconvincing, still his assertion that "the Johannine Son of Man is *not* concerned with vertical movement" *(Johannine Son of Man,* 226) is true in the sense that Jesus' ascent is not *literally* up nor his descent *literally* down.

89. The wording is almost identical: ὑψωθῆναι δεῖ τὸν υἱὸν τοῦ ἀνθρώπου in 3:14; δεῖ ὑψωθῆναι τὸν υἱὸν τοῦ ἀνθρώπου in 12:34. Jesus had said nothing in the context of 12:34 about "the Son of man," only that "I, if I be lifted up [ἐὰν ὑψωθῶ] from the earth, will draw them all to myself" (v. 32).

90. Early Judaism remembered that the bronze snake was eventually destroyed as a graven image (2 Kgs 18:4), and emphasized that it did not in itself bring salvation (Wis 16.5-7, 10-11; *m. Rosh ha-Shanah* 3.8; Philo, *Allegory of the Laws* 2.79-81; *Agricultura* 95-96). Early Christianity viewed it as a type of Christ on the cross, but not in any obvious dependence on the Gospel of John (see *Barnabas* 12.5-7; Justin, *1 Apology* 60; *Dialogue* 91, 94, 112; Tertullian, *Against Marcion* 3.18.7). None of these midrashic reflections on the Numbers passage use any form of the verb ὑψοῦν, "to lift up."

tion of ascending to heaven is still at work here, but the analogy with Moses and the snake requires a transitive rather than an intransitive verb. Moses put the snake on the pole; it did not get there by itself. The writer has therefore transformed the colorless "placed" or "set" of the biblical narrative (Num 21:8-9) into "lifted up" *(hypsōsen)*, an action more appropriate to the theme of exaltation. Yet the analogy itself seems very far-fetched. How can Jesus' exaltation or ascension be like that of a snake fastened to a pole? The pronouncement has the look of a riddle (like the riddle about destroying the temple in 2:19), confounding Jesus' hearers and even many readers of the Gospel, at least those reading it for the first time. In chapter 2, the readers were given an explanation (2:21-22), but this time, as we have seen, no explanation is given until nine chapters later (12:33). How is the reader to solve the riddle without looking ahead for the answer? First, it is important to remember that we are reading a "Gospel," which is by definition an account of Jesus' passion and resurrection. All four Gospels have passion predictions, and the combination of the title "Son of man" with the impersonal verb *dei* ("must," or "it is necessary") recalls some of the explicit passion and resurrection predictions in the other Gospels.[91] Second, the precedent of 2:19, with its explanation in 2:21-22, alerts us to the possibility of *implicit* passion and resurrection predictions. If Jesus' body is to be destroyed and raised again in three days (2:19), we may well suspect that the Son of man's strange "exaltation" here like a snake on a pole is not quite the unambiguous triumph that the verb "lifted up" might otherwise suggest. Perhaps here too the solution to the riddle is that Jesus will die and rise again.[92] Finally, the verb "lifted up" recalls the beginning of the third so-called Servant Song in Isaiah: "Look, my servant will understand, and he will be lifted up and glorified exceedingly" (52:13, LXX). There the verbs "lifted up" *(hypsōthēnai)* and "glorified" *(doxasthēnai)*, which become in John's Gospel the two verbs decisively associated with Jesus as "Son of man,"[93] introduce one who is known

---

91. See Mark 8:31: "And he began to teach them that the Son of man must [δεῖ τὸν υἱὸν τοῦ ἀνθρώπου] suffer many things and be rejected by the elders and chief priests and scribes, and rise after three days" (compare Lk 9:22; 17:24-25; 24:7).

92. Is it possible that Jesus' pronouncement here is simply a further answer to the Jewish authorities' demand for a "sign" (σημεῖον) back in 2:18? In the biblical account, Moses was said to have placed the bronze snake "on a sign" (ἐπὶ σημείου, 21:8-9, LXX), and in Luke 11:30 Jesus responds to a request for a sign with an analogy (much like the one here) between "the Son of man" and a well-known biblical figure: "As [καθώς] Jonah became a sign to the Ninevites, so [οὕτως] too will the Son of man be to this generation" (Mt 12:40 is more explicit: "For as Jonah was in the belly of the fish three days and three nights, so will the Son of man be three days and three nights in the heart of the earth").

93. For "exalted" or "lifted up," see 8:28 as well as 12:32-34, and for "glorified" see 12:23; 13:31-32 (compare 7:39; 8:54; 11:4; 12:16; 17:1, 5).

not for glory or exaltation, but for redemptive suffering on behalf of his people (Isa 52:14–53:12). Such clues anticipate (and justify) for the perceptive reader the later explicit notice that Jesus would be "lifted up" by crucifixion and rising again, and in no other way (12:33; see also 18:32).

Even aside from the grotesque analogy between Jesus and a snake, the Numbers 21 passage is only partially suited to the use to which Jesus has put it. Moses lifted up the snake, while God (in one sense) or (in another) the Jewish authorities who had Jesus crucified, "lifted up the Son of man."[94] It is doubtful that Moses represents either.[95] He put the snake on the pole so that anyone bitten by a snake "would look at the bronze snake and live" (Num 21:9, LXX), while in John's Gospel the purpose is "that everyone who believes might have eternal life in him" (v. 15). Numbers 21 does not mention "believing," and the Gospel of John does not mention "looking at" the crucified Son of man.[96] The only real correspondence is between the verb "live" in Numbers and "eternal life" in John, and even this parallel is superficial because "live" refers simply to healing, while "eternal life" means salvation, or "entering the kingdom of God" (see v. 5).[97]

This is the first mention of "eternal life" in the Gospel of John. The point of introducing it here is that "eternal life" is the new life resulting from being "born of water and Spirit" (v. 5), or "born from above" (vv. 3, 7). "Life" was mentioned briefly near the beginning of the Gospel as being "in him," that is, "in" the Word, and here too "eternal life" is "in him," that is, "in" the Son of man.[98] While the word order suggests that it is a matter of "believing in" the Son of man,[99] the verb "to believe" *(pisteuein)* is never

---

94. As we have seen (compare v. 7), δεῖ often refers to a divine necessity, while the use of a passive verb to refer indirectly to acts of God is a common grammatical device in the New Testament (compare Whitacre, 91; on this "theological passive," see also M. Zerwick, *Biblical Greek,* 76). Yet Jesus can also say to his enemies in the heat of debate, "When you lift up [ὑψώσητε] the Son of man, then you will know that I am" (8:28).

95. Compare 6:32, "Amen, amen, I say to you, not that Moses gave you the bread from heaven, but that my Father gives you the true bread from heaven."

96. Not surprisingly, "believing" is mentioned in several early Christian expositions of Numbers 21 (for example, *Barnabas* 12.7; Justin, *1 Apology* 60; also Justin, *Dialogue* 91, though with due warning against believing in the serpent, who was "cursed by God from the beginning"). John's Gospel, for its part, speaks occasionally of "seeing" or "looking at" Jesus in connection with believing in him (for example, 6:40; 12:45; 19:35).

97. John's Gospel is also familiar with the verb "live" as simply an expression for healing (4:50, 53), but with the implication that physical "life" (at least in the context of healing) always points toward "eternal life." The same is true of the verb "to be saved" (11:12).

98. Compare 1 John 5:11, "And this is the testimony, that God has given us eternal life [ζωὴν αἰώνιον], and this life [αὕτη ἡ ζωή] is in [ἐν] his Son."

99. For the expression, "believe in the Son of man," see 9:35. Most English ver-

used with *en* (the preposition for "in") in the Gospel of John, but always with *eis* (literally "into," as in 1:12; 2:11, 23), or with a noun in the dative case (meaning to accept something as true, 2:22). Jesus is not speaking explicitly of "believing in him," therefore, but simply of "believing" (used absolutely, as in 1:6), and as a result "having eternal life in him."¹⁰⁰ "Eternal life" is where the emphasis lies. Ironically, this life is promised to "everyone who believes" precisely in a context in which some have "believed in his name" and yet *not* been given "eternal life" because Jesus "would not entrust himself to them" (2:23-25). The promise of the verse is contingent on the Son of man being "lifted up." Just as the new birth is "necessary" *(dei,* v. 7) in order to enter the kingdom of God, so the crucifixion of the Son of man is "necessary" *(dei)* in order to have that "birth from above" and consequently the kingdom of God, now defined as "eternal life." Here if anywhere is the turning point of the chapter.

16 Here the same question arises as in verse 13. Is Jesus still speaking, or does the Gospel writer now intervene to reflect on what has just been said? This time there is no title "Son of man" to assure us that Jesus is still the speaker, and the conjunction "for" *(gar)* is one of the characteristic ways of introducing authorial comments or narrative asides in this Gospel.¹⁰¹ Some English versions, therefore, place quotation marks after verse 15, signaling that Jesus' speech has ended and that what follows are the Gospel writer's words.¹⁰² The majority, however (including the most recent versions), extend Jesus' speech to the end of verse 21,¹⁰³ and the wisest course is to follow their example. While few interpreters would seriously argue that Jesus actually uttered the words found in verses 16-21 to Nicodemus and his companions at the first Passover in Jerusalem, Jesus has been introduced as "the Word," the only Revealer of God. It is fair to assume that once he is so introduced all au-

---

sions (RSV, NRSV, NIV, NAB, and many others) have "everyone who [or whoever] believes in him." It is difficult to tell whether this is because they followed a different reading, εἰς αὐτόν (as in v. 16), with ℵ, Θ, Ψ, and the majority of later manuscripts, or whether they simply construed the preferred reading ἐν αὐτῷ (P⁷⁵ and B) with the verb "believe" rather than with "having eternal life." Still other variants are ἐπ' αὐτῷ (P⁶⁶ and L) and ἐπ' αὐτόν (A). The reading εἰς αὐτόν is highly suspect because a number of witnesses that have it have also imported the whole phrase, "might not be lost, but," from verse 16.

100. Compare ERV, NASB, NEB, REB, and JB. Whether or not this construction is used because of the analogy with Moses and the snake (with the natural desire to avoid any implication of "believing in" a graven image such as the bronze snake) is difficult to say (compare n. 96).

101. See, for example, 4:44; 6:64; 7:5; 13:11; 20:9.

102. Notably the RSV and NAB (also *Twentieth Century New Testament, New Testament in Basic English,* E. J. Goodspeed, Ferrar Fenton, and Weymouth).

103. These include the NASB, NIV, NRSV, NEB, REB, JB, NLT, and CEV (as well as the *New World Translation,* Phillips, C. B. Williams, and Helen Barrett Montgomery).

thoritative revelation in the Gospel comes from him, whether through his own lips or the pen of the Gospel writer.[104] Without a clear notice in the text that his speech is over, the reader should keep on listening as to the voice of "the One who came down from heaven, the Son of man," for only he can speak of "heavenly things" (vv. 12-13). As we have seen, it is still too early in the Gospel for Jesus to use the pronoun "I" in delivering these oracles of God, as if he is God himself, so the text resorts to first-person plurals (as in v. 11) or to the third person (as here). The conjunction "for" does introduce an explanatory comment, but the comment is Jesus' own. Jesus builds on the language and thought of verses 14 and 15 to explain precisely *why* "the Son of man must be lifted up" (v. 14). He confirms that the necessity is divine, grounded in "God," and God's love for the world. Having looked at the cross from the human side, by a strange analogy with a snake fastened to a pole, he now places it within the eternal purposes of God. The grammar of the verse reflects this, as Jesus echoes the correlative construction of verse 14 ("And *just as . . . so*") with a corresponding one ("God *so* loved . . . *so that* he gave").[105]

This is the first mention of love in the Gospel of John, and it is rather untypical in that the object of God's love is "the world" *(ton kosmon)*. Nowhere else in John's Gospel (or anywhere else in the New Testament!) is God explicitly said to "love" the world, yet it cannot come as a surprise to any reader who remembers that "the world came into being through him" (that is, through the Word, 1:10), and consequently that the world was "his own" (1:11). Jesus has already been identified as "the Lamb of God who takes away the sin of the world" (1:29), and will be identified as "the Savior of the world" (4:42). God's love for the world, though seldom explicit, is a given. At the same time, God has a unique and specific love for "the One and Only Son."[106] We have already learned that a "One and Only" shares in a father's glory (1:14), and that Jesus as God's "One and Only" is himself God, "right beside the Father" (1:18). Now it becomes explicit that "the One and Only" is God's "Son" (see 1:34, 49), and that both terms are interchangeable with "Son of man" (vv. 13, 14).

---

104. This is of course all the more the case if the "Amen, amen" of verse 11 is assumed to be still in effect. As Brown comments (1.149), "Of course the evangelist has been at work in this discourse, but his work is not of the type that begins at a particular verse. All Jesus' words come to us through the channels of the evangelist's understanding and rethinking, but the Gospel presents Jesus as speaking and not the evangelist."

105. In Greek, καθὼς . . . οὕτως in verse 14; οὕτως . . . ὥστε here.

106. The majority of later manuscripts and some earlier ones (P⁶³, A, L, Θ, Ψ, Latin and Syriac versions) add αὐτοῦ, "his," to "One and Only Son," but stronger manuscript evidence (P⁶⁶, P⁷⁵, B, and the first hand of ℵ) favors simply the definite article. The possessive pronoun is implied in any case, but the shorter reading gives the phrase the quality of a title.

The striking, even shocking, thing about God's love for the world in relation to God's love for his "One and Only Son" is that the former takes priority! The verb "to love" *(agapan)* in this Gospel implies not so much a feeling as a conscious choice.[107] Often it implies a preference for one person or thing or way of life over another.[108] The shock of the pronouncement is that here God puts the well-being of "the world" *above* that of "the One and Only Son." The notion that God "gave" or "gave up" his only Son points unmistakably to Jesus' death,[109] confirming the interpretation of "lifted up" (v. 14) as crucifixion. We might have expected "God *sent* the One and Only Son" (as in 1 Jn 4:9), because "sent" is the operative verb for the mission of Jesus throughout the rest of the Gospel, beginning in the very next verse.[110] But it is important that this first reference to Jesus' mission specify its purpose as a redemptive mission. The "giving" includes all that the "sending" does and more, for in sending his "One and Only" into the world, God gave him up to death on a cross.[111] The analogy that comes to mind is Abraham, and his willingness to offer up his "one and only" son Isaac as a sacrifice in obedience to God (Gen 22:1-14).[112] This analogy, unlike that with Moses and the

---

107. This is surely implied by the fact that love is a command in John's Gospel (13:34; 15:12, 17) and in the New Testament generally. It is not a product of one's feelings, but is something that a person can simply decide to do.

108. Compare E. Stauffer, in *TDNT*, 1.36: "Particularly characteristic are the instances in which ἀγαπᾶν takes on the meaning of 'to prefer,' 'to set one good or aim above another,' 'to esteem one person more highly than another'" (in John's Gospel, compare 3:19; 12:43).

109. Compare Levenson, *Death and Resurrection of the Beloved Son:* "The verb takes us back to . . . the gruesome command of Exod 22:28b: 'you shall give Me the first born among your sons,'" adding that "the father's gift that the Fourth Gospel has in mind is one that necessarily entails a bloody slaying of Jesus, very much . . . along the lines of the slaughtering of the paschal lamb that Jesus becomes and also supersedes" (223).

110. For "sent," with forms of ἀποστέλλειν, see 3:17, 34; 5:36, 38; 6:29, 57; 7:29; 8:42; 10:36; 11:42; 17:3, 8, 18, 21, 23, 25; 20:21; a different verb is used when the "sending" of Jesus is expressed with a participle, as in "the One who sent me" (ὁ πεμψάς με, 4:34; 5:24, 30; 6:38, 39; 7:16, 18, 28, 33; 8:26, 29; 9:4; 12:44, 45; 13:20; 15:21; 16:5; compare 1:22, 33; 13:16), or "the Father who sent me" (ὁ πατὴρ ὁ πεμψάς με, 5:23, 37; 6:44; 8:16, 18; 12:49; 14:24).

111. Other New Testament writers tend to use the compound παραδιδόναι in this way (for example, Rom 4:25, 8:32), but in John's Gospel this verb ordinarily refers to Jesus being "delivered up" either by Judas (6:64, 71; 12:4; 13:2, 11, 21; 18:2, 5; 21:20) or by religious or political authorities (18:30, 35, 36; 19:11, 16). The closest parallels to John 3:16 are passages in which Jesus either "gives" or "delivers" *himself* to death for those he loves (see Gal 1:4, 2:20; Eph 5:2, 25).

112. While "one and only" (יחיד in Hebrew) is rendered as ἀγαπητός in the LXX (Gen 22:2, 12, 16), the author of Hebrews refers to Isaac as Abraham's μονογενής (Heb 11:17). Both terms are used in the LXX to translate יחיד.

bronze snake, is never made explicit, but hints elsewhere in the Gospel suggest that what God asked of Abraham was something God himself would do in the course of time.[113] Like the Moses analogy, it has its limits because God is not acting out of obedience to anyone but out of love for the world he has made. But while God's love is universal, it guarantees eternal life not for the whole world indiscriminately but for "everyone who *believes.*" The last clause of verse 16 sounds like a refrain, echoing verse 15 with only two small changes: first, it is a matter not simply of "believing" but of "believing in" Jesus;[114] second, to "have eternal life" is further explained by its natural opposite, to "not be lost" (*mē apolētai;* compare 6:39-40; 10:28; 12:25).[115] This is the first hint of dualism in the discourse. Just as "eternal life" is more than simply the prolongation of physical life, so "being lost" is more than just physical death. It is, as the next verse will show, eternal condemnation and separation from God. There are no "lost sheep" in the Gospel of John (contrast Mt 10:6; 15:24; Lk 15:6), for Jesus' "sheep" will never be lost and those who are "lost" are not his sheep (see 10:26-28).

17 Having made his point that "the One and Only Son" is given up to death (v. 16), Jesus now introduces the more neutral verb "sent" in place of "gave" to describe his mission (see n. 110). Just as verse 16 (introduced by "for") explained the "lifted up" of verse 14, so verse 17 (also introduced by "for") explains the reference to not being "lost" in verse 16. The same contrast expressed by the words, "*not* be lost *but* have eternal life," is repeated in different words: "*not* to condemn the world, *but* so that the world might be saved." The effect is to interpret "lost" as "judged" or condemned,[116] and "having eternal life" as "being saved," thus heightening the note of dualism introduced in the preceding verse. To be sure, the accent is on the positive, as if Jesus is correcting those who mistakenly thought God's purpose in sending the Son was to condemn the world. He will offer the same positive corrective

113. See 1:29 and 8:56.
114. That is, πᾶς ὁ πιστεύων εἰς αὐτόν (rather than ἐν αὐτῷ, as in v. 15). The effect of the rephrasing is to focus on "the One and Only Son" as the sole legitimate object of Christian faith (compare v. 18b).
115. When *not* contrasted with eternal life or salvation, however, the verb "lost" has a wider range of meaning; it can refer to bread that is spoiled or wasted (6:12, 27), or to physical death (10:10), or to the downfall of a nation (11:50). In 17:12 and 18:9 the verb allows for the possibility of either physical or spiritual ruin, or both.
116. Κρίνειν in John's Gospel can mean either "to judge" or, more specifically, "to condemn." Because the more unambiguous κατακρίνειν, "to condemn," never occurs in John's Gospel (except in 8:10-11 in a section added by later scribes), κρίνειν has to do double duty for both. Here the contrast suggests that here it means to condemn (the opposite of "save"). As Schnackenburg puts it, "'Judgment' is here used in the purely negative sense of reprobation, condemnation to punishment or death" (1.402).

(speaking in the first person) nine chapters later: "And if anyone hears my words and does not obey them, I do not judge [that is, "condemn"] him, for I have come not to judge the world but to save the world" (12:47; compare "Savior of the world," 4:42). He wants to make it clear in both instances that God's intent is a saving one, yet there is a negative subtext to his words. The early notices that "the world did not know him" (1:10) and "his own did not receive him" (1:11) still stand.[117] Jesus knows, and the readers know, that not everyone in the world will be saved. Some *will* be condemned, but he will not blame their condemnation on God. He will insist rather (in the next two verses) that they are self-condemned (compare 12:48, "The person who rejects me . . . has that which judges him; the word which I spoke, that will judge him in the last day").

18 The dualism now becomes explicit, with a sharp distinction between "Whoever believes in him" and "whoever does not believe." Jesus has just said that he did not come to condemn. This is obviously true of those who believe, for they are "not judged," but it is also true of unbelievers. Jesus does not condemn them either because they are "already judged" by their own unbelief. These are the only two alternatives, and Jesus speaks as if the issue has been decided. While the carrying out of "judgment" or condemnation may be future (see 12:48), the verdict is handed down in the present, solely on the basis of whether or not a person has "believed in the name of the One and Only Son of God."[118] The criterion for judgment is not righteousness or good works, but faith.

This raises two problems. The first is that some *have* "believed in his name" (2:23), and yet Jesus "would not entrust himself to them." So far as we know, at this point in the discourse he still has not. We can infer here that these Passover believers are "not judged" — certainly not "already judged" — but can we infer to the contrary that they are already "saved" (v. 17), or "have eternal life" (vv. 15-16)?[119] Despite the two clear alternatives presented here, their fate remains a mystery. The second problem is that a judg-

---

117. Even the style of the solemn threefold repetition of "the world" ("into *the world* not to condemn *the world*, but so that *the world* might be saved") recalls the style of the Gospel's introductory section: "He was in *the world,* and *the world* came into being through him, and *the world* did not know him" (1:10).

118. The closest parallel, perhaps, to this judgment based solely on faith is a verse within the longer ending of Mark: "The one who has believed and is baptized will be saved, but the one who has disbelieved will be condemned" (Mk 16:16).

119. Notice that although there is a "realized eschatology" of condemnation here (ἤδη κέκριται), there is no corresponding "realized eschatology" of salvation (as, for example, in 5:24). The idea that a person "might have [ἵνα . . . ἔχῃ] eternal life" (vv. 15-16) or "be saved" (ἵνα σωθῇ, v. 17) is at this point a divine intention for the future, not a reality in the present.

ment solely on the basis of faith, without reference to good deeds of any kind, is virtually unknown either in early Judaism or early Christianity (see, for example, Mt 3:7-11; 13:41-42, 49-50; 25:31-46; 1 Pet 1:17; Rev 20:12-13, 22:12). Even Paul, for all his emphasis on justification by faith alone, envisions a final judgment on the basis of a person's works and the state of the heart that produced them (see Rom 2:6-11; 1 Cor 3:13-15; 4:5; 2 Cor 5:10). Later in John's Gospel itself, Jesus will speak of an hour when "all who are in the tombs will hear his voice, and those who have done good things will go out to a resurrection of life, but those who have practiced wicked things to a resurrection of judgment" (5:29). Because of this, the conventional wisdom that in this Gospel unbelief is the only sin for which anyone is condemned is at best a half truth. The present verse, taken out of context, may seem to support it, but those who read on will quickly discover that the truth is more complicated. Deeds are in the picture as well as faith, and (in contrast to some versions of Reformation theology) actually *precede* faith.

19 By now the emphasis has shifted noticeably from the positive to the negative. Everything in verses 16 and 17 had to do with salvation and eternal life except for the brief disclaimers, "not be lost" (v. 16) and "not to condemn the world" (v. 17). But verse 18 presents a stark alternative between being "not judged" (as a result of believing) and being "judged already" (for unbelief). Now the focus shifts entirely to "judgment" *(krisis),* this time in the sense of "verdict" (a negative verdict as it turns out) and the reason for the verdict, to the point of sounding as if there were no salvation or eternal life for *anyone:* "This then is the judgment, that the Light has come into the world, and human beings loved the dark rather than the Light, for their works were evil" (compare 12:43). With this, Jesus drops the terminology of "the Son of man" (vv. 13-15) or "the One and Only Son" (vv. 16-18). Instead he calls himself "the Light," echoing the dualistic language of the Gospel's opening paragraphs. The reader will recall 1:5, for example ("the light is shining in the darkness, and the darkness did not overtake it"), and 1:10-11 ("He was in the world, . . . and the world did not know him. He came to what was his own, and his own did not receive him"). The theme of Jesus' rejection by the world, stated programmatically in those early verses, now becomes explicit on his own lips. The second alternative in the preceding verse ("whoever does not believe is already judged," v. 18) is now generalized and assumed to be the norm. All "human beings" are exposed (at least for the moment) as unbelievers, in keeping with Jesus' knowledge of what was "in the person" (that is, in every human being, 2:25). The somber pronouncement that they "loved the dark rather than the Light" stands in tragic contrast to the good news that "God so loved the world that he gave the One and Only Son" (v. 16). Here again, and more explicitly than before, "love" *(agapan)* implies choice or preference (see above, n. 108). God put human salvation ahead of even the safety of his own Son, but instead of returning God's love, human beings chose "the dark" instead. Just as "the Light" is a metaphor for God's presence in the world in the person of Jesus, so "the dark," or "the darkness," is a metaphor for whatever opposes God and resists "the Light" — in short, a metaphor for evil.[120] Jesus now makes this explicit by giving the reason *why* humans preferred their own darkness to God's Light — "for their works [*ta erga*] were evil." Despite the strong accent on belief in verses 15 and 16b, and the stark alternatives of faith and unbelief in verse 18, Jesus wants it made very clear that divine judgment, whether present or future, is based on works after all (as in 5:29).

20-21 A noticeable feature of Johannine style in these early chapters is a sweeping negative assertion followed by a conspicuous exception. For example, "his own did not receive him" (1:11) is followed by "to as many as did receive him he gave authority to become children of God" (1:12). "No one receives his testimony" (3:32) is followed by a notice that "the person who did receive his testimony confirmed thereby that God is true" (3:33). Here too the generalized assertion that "human beings loved the dark rather than the Light" is followed by a division of "human beings" into two groups (as in v. 18), depending on whether or not a person "comes to the Light" (vv. 20, 21). The metaphor of "coming to the Light" brings faith back into the picture, and Jesus will now insist that faith and good works go hand in hand. The person who has no faith — that is, who "hates the Light and does not come to the Light" — is the person whose works are "evil," that is, "who practices wicked things" (compare 5:29). "Coming to the Light" is at one level an expression of allegiance no different from "coming to Jesus" as Nathanael (1:47) and Nicodemus (3:2) had done (compare 3:26; 5:40; 6:35, 37, 44-45, 65; 7:37), or coming to John as Jesus himself had done earlier (1:29). If Jesus is the Light who came into the world (v. 19), then to "come to the Light" is simply to come to Jesus in faith. But more than that, the metaphor implies full disclosure, for light by its nature illumines dark places and makes secret things public, in this case a person's "works." The disclosure is expressed by two verbs, similar in meaning but with opposite connotations. One kind of person "does not come to the Light, for fear his works will be *exposed*" (v. 20). The other kind "comes to the Light, so that his works will be *revealed*" (v. 21).[121] The former proves by not coming that his works are "evil" (v. 19)

---

120. For σκοτία, compare John 1:5; 8:12; 12:35, 46; 1 John 1:5; 2:8, 9, 11 (σκότος, while common enough in the synoptic Gospels, occurs only here in John). "Light" and "darkness" are not quite symmetrical opposites because "darkness" is never personified and therefore not to be capitalized.

121. "Exposed" is ἐλέγχειν, while "revealed" is φανεροῦν. The similarity of the two verbs is easily seen in Ephesians 5:13: "But all things exposed [ἐλεγχόμενα] by the light are revealed [φανεροῦται], for light is that which reveals" (τὸ φανερούμενον).

or "wicked" (v. 20 and 5:29). The latter proves by "coming to the Light" that he is a doer of "the truth," and that his works are "in God."

All of this could come as a surprise to those who read the Gospel through the glasses of later Christian (particularly Reformation) theology, where faith precedes works, and where we prove our faith by our works (see Jas 2:18). Here by contrast good works *precede* faith, just as evil works precede unbelief, and we prove our works by our faith![122] This suggests that the purpose of Jesus' coming in the Gospel of John is not so much "conversion" as "revelation" of who belongs to God already and who does not.[123] It is perhaps no accident that the New Testament word for "conversion" or repentance *(metanoia)* never occurs in John's Gospel or letters. As we have seen, Nathanael came to Jesus not as a sinner but as "a true Israelite, in whom is no deceit" (1:47). He came because in some way he *already* belonged to God, and Jesus knew that God was drawing him. The case of Nicodemus (3:2) is more complicated. The notice that Jesus "knew what was in the person" (2:25b) may imply that he was a sinner, but clearly he did not come as a sinner throwing himself on Jesus' mercy. In any event, the fact that Nicodemus came "at night" suggests that he was not unambiguously "coming to the Light" as one who "does the truth" and whose works are "wrought in God."

The expression "whoever does the truth" is surprising because the reader is expecting "whoever does *good things*" in contrast to those who practice "wicked things" (see 5:29). But "doing truth," a Hebrew term for "acting faithfully" (see Gen 32:10; 47:29; Neh 9:33), was used at Qumran in connection with entering into the covenant (see 1QS 1.5; 5.3; 8.2).[124] There,

---

122. Protestant commentators naturally have difficulty with this. Ernst Haenchen, for example, agrees that it is what the text says, but insists that it cannot be what the text means. "As it is put in these verses," he comments, "it appears that the light reveals only what is already good or evil: whoever is good is not afraid of God and therefore comes to Jesus: whoever is bad is afraid and stays away. Yet this moralizing statement, in which everything depends solely on the quality of man already present, cannot be the meaning of the Evangelist." He concludes that a person's true character "is determined only in the encounter with Jesus: whoever opens himself to Jesus in spite of, or with, his sins, is good" (*John 1*, 205). Bultmann takes the text more seriously, but backs away from its full implications: "in man's decision it becomes apparent what he really is. He does indeed reach his decision on the basis of the past, but in such a way that this decision at the same time gives the past its real meaning, that in unbelief man sets the seal on the worldliness and sinfulness of his character, or that in faith he destroys its worldliness and sinfulness" (159).

123. For a fuller discussion, see my article, "Baptism and Conversion in John: A Particular Baptist Reading," in *Baptism, the New Testament and the Church: Historical and Contemporary Studies in Honour of R. E. O. White* (JSNTSup 171; Sheffield: Sheffield Academic Press, 1999), 145-48.

124. The Hebrew for "doing truth" (עשׂה אמת) comes into Greek as ποιεῖν ἀλήθειαν (or τὴν ἀλήθειαν).

The Gospel of John

"truth" is part of a series of virtues, along with righteousness, justice, humility, and loving-kindness.[125] In John's Gospel, "truth" has not been mentioned since the "grace and truth" of 1:14 and 17, and the issue is more or less the same here as it was in those early verses: Is the meaning determined by assuming Hebrew influence on the language of the Gospel,[126] or is it determined by looking at the usage of "truth" *(alētheia)* in John's Gospel (and the three Johannine letters)[127] more generally?

In 1:14 and 17 we concluded that the expression "grace and truth" referred not to the ancient covenant but to the new reality that came into the world with the coming of Jesus Christ and the gift of the Spirit. Here too it is possible that "doing the truth" means living for that new reality in the new community of faith (compare "worshiping in Spirit and truth," 4:23, 24; "walking in truth," 2 Jn 4 and 3 Jn 3, 4). Perhaps the most radical expression of the newness of "truth" is that of Ptolemy, a second-century Valentinian Gnostic, who noted that the "images and allegories" of the Jewish law were "well and good while truth was not present. But now that the truth is present, one must do the works of truth[128] and not those of its imagery."[129] While John's Gospel obviously does not share Ptolemy's presupposition of radical discontinuity between the old law and "the truth," it does share the assumption that "the truth" came decisively into being *(egeneto,* 1:17) in Jesus Christ.[130]

The matter is best resolved by taking into account the whole clause: "whoever does the truth *comes to the Light.*" In itself, "doing the truth" means just what it did in the Hebrew-speaking world: acting faithfully as

---

125. This is the case also in Genesis 32:10 and 47:29, and in two LXX passages where there is no obvious Hebrew equivalent: Isaiah 26:10, where not "doing truth" (ἀλήθειαν οὐ μὴ ποιήσῃ) is linked closely to not learning "righteousness" (δικαιοσύνη), and Tobit 4.6, where "doing truth" (οἱ ποιοῦντες ἀλήθειαν) or "doing the truth" (ποιοῦντος ... τὴν ἀλήθειαν) is linked to "doing righteousness" (4:7). In Tobit 13.6 "doing truth before [God]" (ποιῆσαι ἐνώπιον αὐτοῦ ἀλήθειαν) stands alone, but with much the same meaning as at Qumran.

126. That is, חסד ואמת, "mercy and truth," in 1:14 and 17; and עשה אמת, "to do truth" (in the sense in which it was understood in the Hebrew tradition) here.

127. See, for example, "If we say we have communion with him and walk in the dark we lie, and do not do the truth" (οὐ ποιοῦμεν τὴν ἀλήθειαν, 1 Jn 1:6; compare also the reference to "doing falsehood" [ποιῶν ψεῦδος] in Rev 22:15).

128. Gr. τὰ τῆς ἀληθείας δεῖ ποιεῖν, literally "do the things of truth."

129. *Letter to Flora,* in Epiphanius, *Panarion* 33.6.5. The translation is from B. Layton, *The Gnostic Scriptures* (New York: Doubleday, 1995), 313; the text is from *Quellen zur Geschichte der christlichen Gnosis* (ed. W. Völker; Tübingen: Mohr [Siebeck], 1932), 91.

130. For a closer parallel to Ptolemy's terminology of truth as something "present" (παρούσῃ), see 2 Peter 1:12.

one who gives allegiance to God. But the point of Jesus' pronouncement here is that the person who truly acts in faithfulness toward God *will* eagerly and willingly "come to the Light [that is, to Jesus and the new community], so that his works will be revealed as works done in the power of God." The verse does not so much presuppose the distinctly Christian (or Johannine) understanding of truth as create it, or at least introduce it. The familiar Hebrew notion of "doing the truth" is here redefined in a Christian sense as "coming to the Light," just as in 1 John 1:6-7 it is defined as "walking in the Light" so that consequently "we have communion with one another, and the blood of Jesus his Son purifies us from all sin." The explicitly Christian term here is "the Light," for the Light has already been personalized as Jesus (see 1:10) and is appropriately capitalized. "Truth" has not (yet) been personalized and should not be capitalized, although the careful reader may remember that "the Light" was formally introduced at the beginning as "the *true* Light." "Truth" in the Gospel of John takes on the meaning of "reality," the new reality that comes into the world in the person of Jesus, and to which Jesus testifies.[131] It becomes, in fact, almost synonymous with Light, and consequently with Jesus himself (compare 14:6). To "do the truth" is to do what is right by acknowledging to all the world who we are and to whom we belong.

Whether or not a person "comes to the Light" depends on a person's "works" (*ta erga,* vv. 20-21). The Light will either "expose" them as evil (v. 20),[132] or "reveal" them as "works wrought in God" (v. 21). The cognate expression, "works wrought,"[133] is echoed in two other places where the works in question are works of God: 6:28 ("What shall we do to *work the works* of God?") and 9:4 ("We must *work the works* of the One who sent me").[134] The phrase "in God" does not in any way anticipate the pronounce-

---

131. Compare Dodd, *Interpretation,* 170-78. Dodd argues that "while the mould of the expression is determined by Hebrew usage, the actual sense of the words must be determined by Greek usage. It is 'truth', i.e. knowledge of reality, that comes through Jesus Christ" (176). Later he concludes, "To put the matter even more strongly, He is not only the revealer of ἀλήθεια, He is Himself ἡ ἀλήθεια" (178).

132. Some ancient manuscripts (including P[75] and A) changed the order of τὰ ἔργα αὐτοῦ (v. 20) to agree with the order in verse 21; others (including P[66]) added the phrase "that they are evil" (ὅτι πονηρά ἐστιν), prompted either by the concluding clause in verse 19 ("because their works were evil"; compare also 7:7), or by a desire to end the sentence like verse 21, with a ὅτι-clause.

133. In Greek, τὰ ἔργα . . . εἰργασμένα.

134. The construction has a faintly Hebraic sound to it, but is at home in either Hebrew or Greek (A. T. Robertson, *Grammar,* 477-78). More often in John's Gospel, it is a matter of "doing" (ποιεῖν, 5:36; 7:3, 21; 8:39, 41; 10:25, 38; 14:10, 12; 15:24; 17:4) or "completing" (τελειοῦν, 4:34; 5:36; 17:4) one's works (in most instances the works for which Jesus came into the world).

ments of Jesus' farewell discourses, or of 1 John, about the mutual indwelling of the believer "in" the Father or the Son.[135] Rather, it is instrumental. "Works wrought in God" are works done in the power of God or with God's help, and thus virtually equivalent to "the works of God" (6:28; 9:3). The latter expression is significant because in both instances it refers to the works of God through human beings, whether those who believe in Jesus (6:28-29), or Jesus himself and the man born blind (9:3-4). The case of the blind man is particularly relevant here because of Jesus' reference to the works of God being "revealed" in him. On the face of it, there is little difference between saying "so that his works will be revealed as works wrought in God" (v. 21), and saying "so that the works of God will be revealed in him" (9:3). Can it be that Jesus (as presented by the Gospel writer) already has in mind this individual (the man born blind) as a classic example of the person who "does the truth" and "comes to the Light"? Obviously the first-time reader has no way of knowing whether this is so or not. Nathanael and Nicodemus are, as we have seen, the two examples much closer at hand. Nathanael, "a true Israelite, in whom is no deceit" (1:47), was clearly one who "did the truth" and therefore "came to the Light." His works, we may conclude, were "wrought in God." Nicodemus, on the other hand, is at best a flawed and ambiguous example, placed in the story to tease us into asking whether he belongs in verse 20 or verse 21, and then to ask the same question about ourselves.

Thus the end of Jesus' long exchange with Nicodemus and the Passover believers of 2:23-25 is a restatement of the familiar Jewish notion of a judgment according to works, but with a distinctive twist. It is a matter not of salvation as a reward for good works, but of good works as a motivation for "coming to the Light" in faith. Those who "do the truth" will "come to the Light" not to glorify themselves as righteous, but to show publicly that their works are "wrought in God," that is, that God has been at work in their lives all along. Being "born from above" (vv. 3, 7) is a process just as surely as natural birth is a process, not something that happens in a single moment of "conversion." The end of the process is "coming to the Light," but as we will learn later, no one "comes to the Light," or to Jesus, without being "given" and "drawn" to him by the Father (compare 3:27; 6:37, 39, 44, 65; 10:29; 17:2, 6, 24). Salvation depends on divine election, and divine work in the lives of the elect, not on merit earned by good works. But whether Nicodemus and the Passover believers in Jerusalem belong to the Light or to the darkness is left, quite intentionally, as an open question.

---

135. See, for example, John 14:20; 15:1-4; 17:21, and 1 John 2:24; 3:24; 4:13, 15. More specifically, ἐν θεῷ here is not equivalent to the ἐν τῷ θεῷ of 1 John 4:15.

H. JOHN'S FAREWELL (3:22-36)

> 22 *After these things, Jesus and his disciples came into the Judean land, and he spent time with them there and was baptizing.* 23 *Now John too was baptizing, in Aenon near the Salim, because there were many springs there, and people were coming and being baptized.* 24 *For John was not yet put in prison.* 25 *So an issue came up among John's disciples with a Judean about purification,* 26 *and they came to John and said to him, "Rabbi, he who was with you across the Jordan, to whom you bore testimony, look, he is baptizing, and they are all coming to him!"* 27 *John answered and said, "A person cannot receive anything unless it is given him from heaven.* 28 *You yourselves can testify for me that I said I am not the Christ, but that I am sent ahead of him.* 29 *He who has the bride is the bridegroom, but the friend of the bridegroom who stands by and hears him rejoices with joy at the bridegroom's voice. So this, my joy, is fulfilled.* 30 *He must grow, but I must diminish.* 31 *The One coming from above is above all. He who is from the earth is from the earth and speaks from the earth. The One coming from heaven is above all.*[1] 32 *What he has seen and what he heard, to this he testifies, and no one receives his testimony.* 33 *The person who did receive his testimony confirmed thereby that God is true,* 34 *for the one God sent speaks the words of God, for he gives the Spirit without measure.* 35 *The Father loves the Son and has given all things in his hand.* 36 *Whoever believes in the Son has eternal life, but whoever disobeys the Son will never see life, but the wrath of God remains on him."*

This section can be divided into either three parts or four: first, a narrative introduction briefly situating Jesus and John in "the Judean land" and "Aenon near the Salim," respectively (vv. 22-24); second, a comment by John's disciples about Jesus and his baptizing ministry (vv. 25-26); third, John's reply to their implied question (vv. 27-30), and (perhaps fourth) some further reflections arising out of that reply (vv. 31-36). The question is, To whom do these "further reflections" belong? Are they simply a continuation of John's answer to his disciples, or are they reflections of the Gospel writer? The issue is much the same here as in 2:23–3:21, where we determined that Jesus was in some sense the speaker all the way to the end. Even if, say, 3:16-21 were the composition of the Gospel writer, our conclusion was that the Gospel writer

---

1. Some manuscripts (including P⁷⁵, the first hand of ℵ, and D) omit the words, "is above all" (ἐπάνω πάντων ἐστιν), yielding the translation, "He who comes from heaven testifies to what he has seen and heard, and no one receives his testimony." But the witness of P⁶⁶, B, and the majority of later manuscripts and versions suggests that the longer reading is original.

simply allowed Jesus, "the Word," or "the Light," to be the vehicle of the Gospel's revelation. The question here is whether John, who was "not the Light" (1:8) can similarly be a vehicle of revelation.[2] While some English translators seem to have more difficulty allowing John to speak for the Gospel writer than allowing Jesus to do so,[3] there is no indication of a change of speaker after verse 30. I have therefore included all of verses 31-36 in quotation marks as a continuation of John's words. There is no way to be absolutely certain of this, and at the end of the day it does not matter. In any event, 1:1-5 and 3:31-36 appropriately frame the Gospel's first three chapters, the former introducing Jesus as "the Word" and the latter providing a setting in which "the Word" will soon begin to speak decisively.

22 "After these things" signals the end of Jesus' speech and the resumption of the narrative,[4] with its characteristic geographical focus. Having "set out for Galilee" (1:43) from "Bethany, beyond the Jordan, where John was baptizing" (1:28), and having gone "down to Capernaum" from "Cana in Galilee" (2:11-12), and thence "up to Jerusalem" (2:13), Jesus now comes "into the Judean land" (that is, into Judea) with his disciples. We have heard nothing of Jesus' disciples since 2:17 and 22, where we glimpsed them not within the actual narrative but "remembering" it after the resurrection. The disciples have had no real part in the story since 2:12, when they "remained there" in Capernaum with Jesus and his mother and brothers. At that time they numbered no more than five, and whether or not their number has grown we do not know. Now Jesus is "spending time with them there" again, only this time "there" *(ekei)* is in Judea. Some interpreters have reasoned that since Jerusalem is already in Judea, the narrative presupposes that Jesus is coming from somewhere else, Galilee perhaps. But this would require either a rearrangement of the text (for which there is no evidence), or the assumption that the author is simply taking over the language of an earlier source in which Je-

---

2. See 1:15-18, where the same question — where John's words ended and the words of the Gospel writer began — came up. There the ὅτι of verse 16 suggested that what immediately followed was attributed to John as indirect discourse, while verses 17 and 18 could have represented either a continuation of this speech or a postscript by the Gospel writer.

3. Most English versions settle the issue of 3:16-21 and 3:31-36 the same way, but there are exceptions: the NEB, REB, NRSV, the *New World Translation,* and Charles B. Williams continue Jesus' speech through verse 21, yet end John's at verse 30, attributing verses 31-36 to the Gospel writer. None known to me does the exact opposite (though Weymouth and Ferrar Fenton do so partially). Still, many versions have no hesitancy in extending the quotation to the end in both instances (for example, NIV, NASB, CEV, *Jerusalem Bible, New Living Translation,* J. B. Phillips, Helen B. Montgomery).

4. This common connecting phrase, μετὰ ταῦτα, occurs here for the first time in John's Gospel (though compare μετὰ τοῦτο, "after this," in 2:12).

sus was coming from Galilee to Judea.⁵ More likely, "into the Judean land" means simply into the Judean countryside in distinction from the city of Jerusalem.⁶ A "canonical" reading could tempt us to imagine a parallel here to the later Christian mission from "Jerusalem" to "all Judea and Samaria" to "the end of the earth" (Acts 1:8), for Jesus will shortly move on to "Samaria" (Jn 4:4), announce a great "harvest" there (4:35-38), and be hailed as "Savior of the world" (4:42). But even aside from the lack of evidence that John's Gospel knows the book of Acts, the parallel is doubtful, for when Jesus leaves Judea, his intended destination is not Samaria, and certainly not "the end of the earth," but Galilee, where he had been before (4:3; compare v. 43).

Jesus' sojourn with his disciples is of undetermined length, a kind of interlude between significant ministries in Jerusalem (2:13–3:21) and Samaria (4:1-42). Unlike other such interludes in the Gospel (that is, 2:12, 10:40-42, and 11:54) its location (in contrast with John's specific location, v. 23) is given vaguely as "the Judean land." We know only that Jesus and his disciples were somewhere in Judea, but we do learn for the first time that Jesus "was baptizing" (compare v. 26). This will later be qualified by the notice that "Jesus himself was not baptizing, but his disciples were" (4:2), yet so far as we know at this point in the story, Jesus is indeed "baptizing in water" just as John had done earlier (see 1:26, 31). John had said that Jesus, by contrast, would "baptize in Holy Spirit" (1:33), but the statement here that Jesus "was baptizing" (without further qualification) clearly implies water and not Spirit baptism.⁷ The remarkable feature of the notice is that the reader is allowed no actual glimpse of Jesus (or his disciples) actually baptizing anyone, but is simply told, as if by hearsay and from a distance, that it occurred. The narrative will center instead on John and his disciples.

23 John, whom we have not heard from since 1:37, now makes his reappearance. The notice that John "too" was "baptizing" confirms the assumption that Jesus and John were baptizing in much the same way and for much the same reason.⁸ John's earlier claim that "the reason I came baptizing in water was so that [Jesus] might be revealed to Israel" (1:31) must now be

---

5. See Barrett, 219-20, who proposes several possible rearrangements, but concludes that "the passage makes sense as a whole and [sic] its present position."

6. Compare χώρα in 11:55. Bultmann (170) cites Aeschylus, *Eumenides* 993, "both country and city" (καὶ γῆν καὶ πόλιν); see also Schnackenburg, 1.410 ("γῆ = χώρα, 11:54"), and 2.364, on 11:55 ("Χώρα here . . . means the rest of the country as opposed to the capital, probably with particular reference to Judaea").

7. Obviously if baptism in the Spirit were implied, there would be no need for the disclaimer in 4:2.

8. Compare Moloney, 105: "There is no hint in these introductory remarks that there was any qualitative difference between the two baptisms. The focus is on the baptizers, not the respective merits of their baptismal rites."

qualified, for by now Jesus has been "revealed to Israel" (see 1:29, 36; 2:11) and yet John continues to baptize. What then was the common reason why both John and Jesus were baptizing? It would be easy to supply an answer from the synoptic tradition, where John's was "a baptism of repentance for the forgiveness of sins" (Mk 1:4), but this is never made explicit in our Gospel. All we know is that baptism had to do with "purification" (v. 25) and that it involved people "coming" to the baptizer (compare v. 26), who by baptizing them made them his "disciples" (4:1). As in 1:28 ("Bethany, beyond the Jordan"), John's baptizing ministry is given a quite specific location: "in Aenon near the Salim," and for John as for Jesus place is important: "there were many springs[9] there." While this location may have been known to the readers of the Gospel, it cannot now be identified with absolute certainty. The very name "Aenon" means a spring or well, and Arabic names beginning with '*Ain* are common to this day. Although the site may not have been far from the Jordan River, the notice makes clear that John did not depend solely on the Jordan for his water supply. "Salim" means peace,[10] but because the names of villages do not normally have the definite article, it has been suggested that "the Salim" was the name of a plain south of Beth Shan where Aenon was located (compare "the region near the desert," 11:54).[11] Eusebius's fourth-century gazetteer, the *Onomasticon,* places Aenon about eight miles south of Beth Shan, and just to the northeast of Samaria, where there are in fact a number of springs.[12] Two Aenons are shown on the sixth-century Madeba map. One, east of the Jordan just across from "Bethabara," is labeled "Aenon, where Sapsaphas is now"; the other, west of the Jordan and further north, is labeled "Aenon near the Salim." The second corresponds to the *Onomasticon,* but whether the designation is dependent on John's Gospel itself, or whether the Gospel (or one of its sources) added the words "near the Salim" to specify which Aenon was meant is uncertain. In any event, "Aenon" in John's Gospel

---

9. "Many springs" are literally "many waters" (ὕδατα πολλά), a phrase used several times metaphorically in the book of Revelation (1:15; 17:1, 15; 19:6). The only significance of such parallels is perhaps an impression of great abundance (compare Jn 7:38, "streams of living water").

10. It is doubtful that the Gospel writer found significance in the name, for if he had he would likely have pointed it out (compare 9:7).

11. On these identifications, see G. Dalman, *Sacred Sites and Ways* (London: SPCK, 1935), 89-90, 233-35, and especially C. Kopp, *Holy Places of the Gospels* (New York: Herder and Herder, 1963), 129-37.

12. This was also the testimony of the pilgrim Egeria in the fourth century (compare J. Wilkinson, *Egeria's Travels to the Holy Land* [Jerusalem: Ariel, 1981], 108-110). Another theory places Aenon and Salim well *within* Samaria, where the names survive to this day ("Salem" or "Salim," three and a half miles to the east of Nablus, and "Ainun," seven miles north). But this puts the two villages too far apart, and Ainun has no spring (see Kopp, *Holy Places,* 136-37).

3:22-36 John's Farewell

is obviously west of the Jordan, for the previous site of John's activities is clearly said to be "beyond the Jordan" (v. 26), to the east. Still, it is not exactly "in the Judean land" (v. 22). Jesus and John, though engaged in the same activity, are not together nor even particularly near each other. As we will see, John learns of Jesus' activities only indirectly.

24 As a parenthetical aside, the writer now supplies the information that "John was not yet put in prison."[13] Like the Gospel's first narrative asides (1:24, 28), it comes belatedly, as an afterthought. Logically, it should have preceded verse 23, as an explanation of how John can be in the story at all. While the notice sounds redundant in its present position, it sends a signal to the reader that the author knows the story of John's imprisonment, but that it is not the story he is going to tell.[14] Instead of having John forcibly removed from the scene by Herod's soldiers, he will allow him to make his own exit voluntarily and say his own eloquent farewell (vv. 27-30). Jesus' continuing journey from Judea back to Galilee again (4:3) will be triggered not by John's imprisonment (as in Mk 1:14 and Mt 4:12), but by a perception that Jesus was "making and baptizing more disciples" than the still active John (4:1).[15]

25-26 At this point we learn that John still had disciples of his own (as in Mk 2:18; 6:29; Lk 5:33; 11:1; Mt 11:2), even though at least two of them had gone off to follow Jesus (1:35-40). Here John's disciples, having raised an "issue"[16] with an unidentified "Judean" or "Jew"[17] about "purifica-

---

13. Stylistically the periphrastic construction ἦν βεβλημένος ("was put") echoes the periphrastic ἦν . . . βαπτίζων of verse 23 ("was baptizing"; compare 1:28).

14. In the synoptic Gospels too we learn of John's imprisonment either prematurely (Lk 3:19-20), or only very briefly (Mk 1:14; Mt 4:17; compare Mt 11:2), or in retrospect while recounting his death as well (Mk 6:17-29; Mt 14:3-12).

15. Chrysostom suggested that the point of verse 24 is to show that John continued to baptize right up to the time of his imprisonment. Even though his real work was done when he baptized Jesus, he continued to baptize so as not to arouse his disciples' jealousy by making them think he was immediately yielding center stage to Jesus (*Homilies* 29.1; NPNF, 1st ser., 14.100).

16. This word (ζήτησις) probably retains something of its basic meaning of a search or investigation. Nothing in the context suggests an atmosphere of intense controversy with the anonymous "Jew" (if anything, the controversy implied by their question is with Jesus and his followers). The phrase ἐκ τῶν μαθητῶν is probably not partitive (as in 1:35), as if to involve only "some" of John's disciples. Rather, ἐκ suggests simply that John's disciples initiated the inquiry.

17. Some important witnesses (including P[66], ℵ*, Θ, all Latin and some Syriac and Coptic versions) support the plural Ἰουδαίων over the singular Ἰουδαίου (P[75], B, ℵ[2], A, and many others), but in view of the plural in 2:6, plus the frequent controversies in this Gospel between Jesus and "the Jews," it is more likely that the singular (only here, aside from 4:9 and 18:35) was changed to the plural than the other way around (compare Metzger, *Textual Commentary*, 205).

tion,"[18] come to John with the report, "Rabbi, he who was with you across the Jordan, to whom you bore testimony, look, he is baptizing, and everyone is coming to him!" (v. 26).[19] The term "Jew" (or *Ioudaios*) can, as we have seen, refer either to a "Judean" in particular or a "Jew" more generally. The reference to "purification" recalls "the purification rituals of the Jews" (2:6), yet at the same time *Ioudaios* also reminds us that Jesus' current activities were geographically in "the Judean land" (v. 22). Just how the issue of "purification" brought Jesus and his activities to their attention is uncertain.[20] Quite possibly an anonymous "Jew" or "Judean" had come from Judea with news of Jesus' success there, perhaps even with an account of his own "purification" by Jesus through baptism. While there is no way to be sure of this, it would help explain the conclusion (probably exaggerated) that "they are all coming to him" (v. 26).[21]

The words of John's disciples take us back to the world of chapter 1, when Jesus and John had been together "beyond the Jordan" (1:28), and John repeatedly "bore testimony" to Jesus (1:19, 34; see also 1:7-8, 15). They phrase their comment in such a way as to challenge John and even distance themselves from him. Jesus, they say, was "with *you*," not "with us,"[22] and was someone "to whom *you* [*sy*] bore testimony."[23] When they add, "Look, he[24] is baptizing, and they are all coming to him!" their words seem to carry the implied question: "What are *you* going to do about it?"[25]

18. Gr. περὶ καθαρισμοῦ.

19. The play on the expression to "come to" someone (ἔρχεσθαι πρός) as a disciple is noteworthy. John's disciples "come to him" (as his disciples) only to point out that people are "all coming to him" (that is, to Jesus) as disciples.

20. In view of the accent on purification, the remark of John's disciples is noteworthy for what it does *not* say. As Chrysostom noticed, "they do not say, 'He whom thou didst baptize' baptizeth" (*Homilies* 29.2; NPNF, 1st ser., 14.101). The omission is consistent with this Gospel's practice of never mentioning that John baptized Jesus.

21. Gr. πάντες ἔρχονται πρὸς αὐτόν. Compare the fear of the Jerusalem authorities concerning Jesus that "they will all [πάντες] believe in him" (11:48), and the lament of the Pharisees that "the world [ὁ κόσμος] has gone off to follow him" (12:19).

22. "With you" (μετὰ σοῦ) probably implies discipleship (as in Mk 3:14; 5:18, 40), but John's disciples do not explicitly identify Jesus as having been one of their own number.

23. In this Gospel the verb μαρτυρεῖν, "testify," is normally used with the preposition περί, "about," or "concerning." Aside from the phrase, "to testify to the truth" (5:33; 18:37), it takes the dative only here and in verse 28.

24. Jesus is anonymous throughout the exchange. In the disciples' remark he is οὗτος ("this one," v. 26, probably with a touch of disdain; compare 7:27; 9:16, 29); in John's reply he is ἐκείνου ("that one," v. 28; compare v. 30).

25. Augustine made the implied question explicit: "What sayest thou? Ought they not to be hindered, that they may rather come to thee?" Consequently, Augustine relates

27-28 John's direct reply to his disciples' challenge comes in verse 28, where his own emphatic pronouns, "You yourselves" *(autoi hymeis)* and "for me,"[26] together mimic their emphatic repetition of the singular "you." But first he responds with a more general observation: "A person cannot receive anything unless it is given him from heaven" (v. 27). What "person" is John referring to here, himself or Jesus, or the believer?[27] Probably all of the above, but Jesus first of all because the focus of the disciples' question was on Jesus and his activities. The striking universalism of the news that "they are all coming to him" (v. 26) demands a response, and the form of John's response echoes that of Jesus to Nicodemus.[28] In the earlier instance it was a matter of being born "from above," here of being given something "from heaven." John's point is that even if "they are all coming" to Jesus (which is doubtful; see v. 32), it is because God has given them, and if not so many are coming to John, it is because God has given him less. Jesus himself later makes a similar point in almost the same words: "*No one can* come to me *unless* the Father who sent me draws him" (6:44), and "*No one* can come to me *unless* it is given him by the Father" (6:65, italics added).[29] Chapter 6 will remind us that John's words are applicable in a variety of ways. The one who "receives" can be the believer, receiving salvation (as in 6:44 and 65), or it can be John or Jesus, receiving those who come (see 6:37, 39; see also 10:29; 17:2, 6, 24).[30]

John's answer to himself rather than Jesus: "Of whom, think you, had John said this? Of himself. 'As a man, I received,' saith he, 'from heaven'" (*Tractates on the Gospel of John*, 13.9; NPNF, 1st ser., 7.90).

26. "For me" (μοι) is omitted in some manuscripts (including P[75] and ℵ), possibly because the cluster of three emphatic pronouns in a row (αὐτοὶ ὑμεῖς μοι) seemed redundant to some scribes.

27. Ἄνθρωπος is probably used here in a very generalized sense as "anyone" (equivalent to the indefinite pronoun τις; see BDAG, 81[4]; BDF, §301[2]). Thus "a person cannot" (οὐ δύναται ἄνθρωπος) is simply another way of saying "no one can" (οὐδεὶς δύναται; compare 6:44, 65). If we think of the saying as applicable to John himself, we are reminded of Jesus' question in Mark, "The baptism of John — was it from heaven [ἐξ οὐρανοῦ], or from humans?" (Mk 11:30). If we think of it as applicable to the believer, Paul's words come to mind, "What do you have that you did not receive?" (1 Cor 4:7).

28. That is, "A person cannot [οὐ δύναται] receive anything unless [ἐὰν μή] it is given him from heaven" recalls the οὐ δύναται, "cannot," and the ἐὰν μή, "unless," of 3:3 and 5.

29. Both 6:44 and 6:65 exhibit the same combination of οὐ (or οὐδείς) δύναται and ἐὰν μή.

30. Compare Brown, who shows how chapter 6 expands on 3:27 in two distinct though related ways: first, "No one can come to Jesus unless God directs him. Faith or coming to Jesus is God's gift to the believer. This resembles vi 65"; second, "No one can come to Jesus unless God gives him to Jesus. The believer is God's gift to Jesus. This re-

Having stated a very general principle, John now goes on to answer his disciples directly. Picking up their own verb "bore testimony" (v. 26), he insists that they too were present with Jesus "beyond the Jordan," and that "You yourselves can testify for me," that is, they know very well what John had said there about himself and about Jesus. Again we are in the world of chapter 1, yet not necessarily in scenes where John's disciples were actually said to be present. When he told the delegation from Jerusalem, "I am not the Christ" (1:20), his disciples had not yet made their appearance, and he never said to anyone in so many words, "I am sent ahead of him."[31] The latter is a composite of John's message based partly on the introductory notice that he was "sent from God" (1:6), and partly on his repeated references to Jesus as coming "after me" (*opisō mou,* 1:15, 27, 30). If Jesus was "after" John, then John was "ahead of" *(emprosthen)* Jesus — in historical time, though clearly not in status or rank![32]

John's disciples had been privy to none of these pronouncements, certainly not to the introduction of John as "a man sent from God" (1:6). Therefore, John's words here are directed not so much to them in a concrete historical situation as to us, the readers of the Gospel, in a literary framework. We have read the Gospel's opening verses and know that John was "sent from God." We have heard him speak three times of "the One coming after me" (1:15, 27, 30), and have been told repeatedly that John was *not* "the Light" (1:8), *not* the Christ, *not* Elias, *not* the Prophet (1:20-21), but that Jesus *is* the Light (1:4-5, 9; 3:19-21), the One and Only Son (1:14, 18, 34; 3:16, 18), the Lamb of God (1:29, 36), and the Son of man (1:51; 3:13, 14). While John's disciples remembered in a general way that he had "borne testimony" to Jesus (v. 26), they seem not to have heard his actual testimony, for if they had they would not have been surprised that Jesus' ministry was flourishing. John, therefore, will testify again, to them and to us (vv. 29-30).

29-30 John's final testimony introduces the metaphor of the bridegroom. Jesus in the synoptic tradition uses the bridegroom as a metaphor under similar circumstances when challenged about the behavior of his disciples in comparison to both John's disciples and the Pharisees over the question of fasting: "Can the wedding guests fast while the bridegroom is

---

sembles vi 37" (1.155). Yet Jesus' terminology is different in that he consistently speaks of God as "the Father." John not only avoids "Father," but uses the passive "it is given" and the circumlocution "from heaven" to avoid speaking of God's action directly. Jesus prefers the active voice (6:44; also vv. 37, 39), and even when he repeats word for word John's passive "unless it is given him" (ἐὰν μὴ ᾖ δεδόμενον αὐτῷ, 6:65) clearly identifies "the Father" as the Giver.

31. In Greek, ἀπεσταλμένος εἰμὶ ἔμπροσθεν ἐκείνου.

32. Compare 1:15 and 30, where Jesus gets "ahead of" (ἔμπροσθεν) John in status because (as 1:1-5 had already shown) he *preceded* him in time.

with them? As long as they have the bridegroom with them, they cannot fast. But the day will come when the bridegroom is taken from them, and then they will fast on that day" (Mk 2:19-20; compare Mt 9:15; Lk 5:34-35). Already in the Gospel of John we have met a literal bridegroom who was congratulated for having "kept the good wine until now" (2:10), and who by his silence took credit for having done so. Now John points to another bridegroom, one who the reader knows was the real provider of the "good wine." He expands the metaphor into a brief parable with three characters: the bridegroom, the bride, and "the friend [*philos*] of the bridegroom."[33] The context clearly shows that the bridegroom is "he who was with you beyond the Jordan, to whom you bore testimony" (v. 26), that is, "the Christ" (v. 28). The bride is a shadowy figure, barely in the story at all, mentioned only to help us identify the bridegroom and distinguish him from the bridegroom's friend: "He who has the bride is the bridegroom." This is consistent with wedding parables generally in the New Testament, where the bride is conspicuous by her absence.[34] As for "the friend of the bridegroom who stands by and hears him," and "rejoices with joy at the bridegroom's voice,"[35] John himself takes on that role by adding explicitly, "So this, my joy, is fulfilled."

So much for the cast of characters. What is John's point? There is, as Bultmann noticed, "a certain humour" in the pronouncement, "He who has the bride is the bridegroom,"[36] yet it also comes as a serious illustration of the principle that "A person cannot receive anything unless it is given him from heaven" (v. 27). The bride is God's gift to the bridegroom (compare 6:37, 39; 10:29; 17:2, 6, 24), not to the bridegroom's friend, so that if "they are all coming" to the bridegroom for baptism (v. 26), it is none of the friend's business! Implicit in all this is the notion that "the bride" in some way represents Jesus' disciples. Later we will learn not only that the disciples are those whom the Father has given Jesus, but that they are his "sheep" who "hear his voice" (10:3-5, 16, 27; compare 5:25, 28, 37; 18:37; 20:16), and that their

---

33. The "friend of the bridegroom" in Jewish wedding custom was a שׁוֹשְׁבִין (*shoshebin*, "groomsman," or "best man"; see *m. Sanhedrin* 3.5). Yet there was not necessarily just one such person. In some traditions there were two, one representing each family; in 1 Maccabees 9:39 "the bridegroom [ὁ νυμφίος] came out with his friends [οἱ φίλοι αὐτοῦ] and brothers." For Jewish texts on the *shoshebin,* see Strack-Billerbeck, *Kommentar,* 1.45-46, 500-504, and, in particular, *t. Ketubbot* 1.4.

34. No bride is mentioned in Mark 2:19-20 and parallels, nor in Matthew 22:1-14, where a king gives a wedding banquet for "his son," nor in Matthew 25:1-13, where ten virgins await the bridegroom, but not the bride (except in a few manuscripts of 25:1, including D, Θ, and the Latin and Syriac versions), nor at the wedding in Cana in John 2:1-11.

35. John himself was only a "voice" (φωνή), in contrast to "the Word" (1:23), but here we learn that "the Word" too has a "voice," the decisive voice in this Gospel.

36. Bultmann, 173.

"joy" will one day be "fulfilled" (15:11; 16:24; 17:13; compare 1 Jn 1:4; 2 Jn 12). They too are Jesus' "friends" (*philoi*, 15:13-15; compare 21:15-17; 3 Jn 15). In short, their experience matches that of John, his first "friend." Whatever else he may be in this Gospel, John is, as we have seen, a confessing Christian (compare 1:15-16, 20, 29, 34). The "friend of the bridegroom" becomes almost indistinguishable from the bride, for at any wedding she, just as surely as the bridegroom's friend, "rejoices with joy at the bridegroom's voice." But because neither John nor any individual disciple, male or female, could ever be appropriately identified as Jesus' "bride," all he can be is "friend of the bridegroom."[37] Consequently, the metaphor is stretched to the breaking point.[38] All that differentiates John from other disciples (aside from the fact that he came first) is that he pointed his own disciples to Jesus (1:35-37), yet even in this respect Andrew was like him in that he brought his brother Simon Peter to Jesus (1:41-42), even as Philip brought Nathanael (1:45). They too, in their own way, were "friends of the bridegroom," bringing others to the Messiah they had found.

The description of the bridegroom's friend as one who "stands by" recalls our first glimpse of John with his disciples, when he "was [standing] there" (1:35) with two of them, and, "looking right at Jesus," said, "Look, the Lamb of God" (1:36). Now he can no longer see Jesus, but in his mind he "hears him" and rejoices at the sound of his voice. John's experience anticipates that of the Gospel's readers, who are thereby encouraged to echo his final words and make them their own. This involves again the recognition of a divine necessity: "He must grow, but I must diminish." Just as surely as God requires that a person "must" be reborn (3:7), and that the Son of man "must" be lifted up (3:14), so God requires that Jesus "must" (*dei*) come first and the believing disciple (whether John or anyone else) second. The pronouncement confirms John's earlier acknowledgment that "The One coming after me has gotten ahead of me" (1:15, 30), adding that this is how it "must" continue to be. John draws a sharp contrast between "growing" and "diminishing."[39] Jesus is now moving center stage in the Gospel, while John's role, significant

---

37. There is a possible analogy in the Matthean parable of the ten virgins (Mt 25:1-13). There the virgins are functionally equivalent to the absent bride, and yet they cannot be the bride because they are plural and must be plural in order to make a distinction between those who were wise and those who were foolish.

38. Some, by contrast, would press the metaphor to the limit, placing John in the role of the *shoshebin* who "stands by" outside the bridal chamber until he "hears" from within the bridegroom's voice announcing the joyful news that the marriage has been consummated, and that the bride was a virgin! (compare J. Jeremias, *TDNT,* 4.1101; Schlatter, 108; Whitacre, 97). See, however, M. and R. Zimmerman, "Der Freund des Braütigams (Joh 3, 29): Deflorations- oder Christuszeuge," *ZNW* 90 (1999), 123-30.

39. "Grow" is αὐξάνειν in Greek, and "diminish" is ἐλαττοῦσθαι.

as it has been, is coming to an end. Readers familiar with the rest of the New Testament will notice that in Luke, John and Jesus both "grew" in parallel fashion (Lk 1:80; 2:40), as Augustine recognized,[40] but here the two are moving in opposite directions. Jesus' "growth" is measured in the context by the impression that "they are all coming to him" (v. 25), and that he was "making and baptizing more disciples than John" (4:1), just as in the book of Acts "the word of God grew" when the Christian movement spread and the number of disciples increased (Acts 6:7; 12:24; compare 19:20). In this Gospel, Jesus is "the Word," and he will "grow," at least to begin with, in much the same way.[41] As for John, the verbal acknowledgment that "I must diminish" takes the place of any explicit notice of John's imprisonment. We know that John will soon be "put in prison" (v. 24), but we are spared the details. Instead, he exits the narrative in his own way and on his own terms.[42] To misquote a later pronouncement of Jesus, "No one takes my freedom or my stature from me; I lay it aside for myself" (see 10:18).[43] John, like Jesus, knows that "A person cannot receive anything unless it is given him from heaven" (v. 27), and consequently he does not cling to freedom or to life as if he were entitled to them. He retains control over his destiny precisely by yielding control to Jesus, and to the God who "sent" them both (see 1:6; 3:17, 28, 34).[44]

31 Most recent commentators have noticed the similarity between

---

40. *Tractates on the Gospel of John* 14.4: "As regards the flesh, John and Jesus were of the same age, there being six months between them: they had grown up together; and if our Lord Jesus Christ had willed to be here longer before His death, and that John should be here with Him, then as they had grown up together, so they would have grown old together" (NPNF, 1st ser., 7.95).

41. Efforts to interpret the verbs "grow" and "diminish" astrologically, as part of a metaphor of a rising and falling star (Bultmann, 175: "the old star is sinking; the new star rises") are not quite "absurd" (Barrett, 223), but not quite convincing either. Nor is Matthew Black's theory of a wordplay in a supposed Aramaic original helpful in dealing with the text as it stands (*An Aramaic Approach to the Gospels and Acts* [3d ed., 1967], 147; see Barrett, 224).

42. This is the case in all the earliest and most reliable manuscripts. At the end of verse 36, however, a few later witnesses, including one minuscule (2145), one old Latin version *(e),* and one late Syriac version (the margin of the Harklean Syriac), add the explicit notice, "and after these things John was delivered up," in keeping with similar notices in the synoptic tradition.

43. Jesus too in this Gospel goes to his arrest and death on his own initiative, and with a much longer farewell (not only 10:17-18, but chapters 13–17, and 18:1-11).

44. See J. H. Neyrey and R. L. Rohrbaugh, " 'He Must Increase, I Must Decrease' (John 3:30): A Cultural and Social Interpretation," *CBQ* 63.3 (2001), 464-83, especially their conclusion: "Rarely does one find in Greek or Israelite literature a public figure who willingly and peacefully allows his honor and prestige to diminish without envy and hostile reaction" (482-83).

3:13-21 and 3:31-36, some even to the point of rearranging the text so that the one comes right after the other.[45] There is no textual evidence for such a move, and the present order of the text must be respected. Still, the similarity of the two passages suggests that Jesus and John both speak as reliable narrators in this Gospel, and with much the same voice. While John's acknowledgment that "he must grow, but I must diminish" (v. 30) could signal that John now falls silent and Jesus begins to speak, it is perhaps more likely that John has a few more words to say.

"The Coming One" *(ho erchomenos)* refers consistently to Jesus in this Gospel (compare 6:14; 11:27; 12:13), as in the others. To John he had been "the One coming after me" (1:15, 27), but now he is "the One coming from above" *(anōthen,* as in vv. 3, 7) or "the One coming from heaven." The whole verse forms a chiasm in three parts *(a, b,* and *a'*):

    a. The One coming from above is above all.
    b. He who is from the earth is from the earth, and speaks from the earth.
    a'. The One coming from heaven is above all.

Each of the three clauses is redundant in itself, and the first and last clauses *(a* and *a')* are redundant in relation to each other, for to come "from above" and to come "from heaven" are the same thing. These two clauses refer to Jesus, recalling 3:13: "And no one has gone up to heaven except he who came down from heaven, the Son of man." Their common conclusion that he "is above all" tends to support the appropriateness (if not the originality) of the disputed ending of verse 13, "who is in heaven." "From above" takes us back to Jesus' opening words to Nicodemus: "unless someone is born from above, he cannot see the kingdom of God." Now we learn that such a birth is possible because of Jesus himself, "the One coming from above," or "from heaven," the One who has spoken of "heavenly things" *(ta epourania,* v. 12). The preposition "from" *(ek),* repeated four times in this one verse, speaks both of someone's origin and nature. Jesus is "from" heaven, and therefore a heavenly being. Because he is "above all," it is not surprising that "they are all coming to him" (v. 26).

The second clause *(b)* is also redundant, and the compounded redundancy has a powerful rhetorical effect. "He who is from the earth" can only

---

45. Bultmann, for example, from whom we expect such rearrangements, places 3:31-36 right after 3:21 (160), while Schnackenburg, from whom we do not, places it just before 3:13 (1.380-92). Barrett comments rightly that "Schnackenburg is not wrong . . . that v. 31 continues the thought of 3.12, but it does so with greater force and clarity when vv. 13-17, 27-30, are allowed to intervene" (224).

be John himself, who has insisted all along on his own subordinate status (1:15, 20-22, 26-27, 30; compare 1:8), and continues to do so here.[46] John is "from" this earth, and therefore "of" the earth, a mere human.[47] His testimony is "from the earth," for he speaks from a human perspective and not "from heaven."[48] Yet on the principle that "A person cannot receive anything unless it is given him from heaven" (v. 27), God speaks even through John. His "earthly" testimony is reliable, but the greater testimony "from above" belongs to Jesus.

32 We immediately hear more of Jesus' "testimony," as John echoes what Jesus had said earlier to Nicodemus ("we speak what we know, and we testify to what we have seen," 3:11). Referring to "the One coming from heaven," John claims that "What he has seen and heard, to this he testifies." Later Jesus will use the emphatic "I" to make the same point about himself: "And what I heard from him, these things I speak in the world" (8:26; see also 5:30; 8:40; 15:15), and "The things I have seen in the Father's presence I speak" (8:38). Like John or any other witness (see 1:32-34), Jesus can testify only to what he has seen or heard,[49] but because he was "with God in the beginning" (1:1-2), his testimony is unique and final. All other Christian testimony (for example, 1 Jn 1:1-3) is secondary to his, and depends on his. Yet Jesus' testimony is not accepted by the world — this despite the impression

---

46. See Barrett, 224-25. Many commentators differ, arguing that the phrase "has a more general application" to all who are "unable to transcend the things of this world *(epigeia)* and thus cannot accept the revelation of the heavenly *(epourania)* that takes place in Jesus" (Moloney, 111). This is Schnackenburg's view as well, but his judgment here is linked to his rearrangement of 3:31-36 right after 3:12. Significantly, he admits that whoever shifted 3:31-36 to its present position after 3:30 may well have understood "He who is from the earth" as John (1.383).

47. Here Jesus in the Gospel of John answers the question he raised in Mark, "The baptism of John — was it from heaven, or from humans?" (Mk 11:30). See also Mt 11:11 and Lk 7:28, where John is the greatest among "those born of women"; also the contrast between Jesus and the first Adam (1 Cor 15:47). It is important not to confuse the expression "from the earth" (ἐκ τῆς γῆς) with "from [or of] the world" (ἐκ τοῦ κόσμου), or "of this world" (as in 8:23, "You are from below; I am from above. You are of this world; I am not of this world"). The latter suggests not merely human limitation, but dualism and opposition to God (see 8:24, "you will die in your sins").

48. Compare 5:33-34, "You have sent word to John, and he has testified to the truth. I, however, do not accept the testimony from a human" (παρὰ ἀνθρώπου).

49. It is characteristic of the Gospel's style that "has seen" is perfect tense (ἑώρακεν; compare 1:34; 8:38; 19:35; 20:18, 25, 29), while "heard" is aorist (ἤκουσεν; compare 8:26, 40, 15; this in contrast to 1 Jn 1:1 and 3, where both verbs are perfect). It is doubtful that any difference in emphasis is intended (as proposed in BDF, §342[2]). In John 5:37, "heard" is perfect tense only because it is used with πώποτε, "ever," or "at any time."

that "they are all coming to him" (v. 26). John's disciples could not have been more mistaken, for Jesus himself had told Nicodemus, "You people do not receive our testimony" (3:11), and John now generalizes from this that "no one receives his testimony." Both pronouncements confirm the grim verdict that "his own did not receive him" (1:11), and that "human beings loved the dark and not the Light, because their works were evil" (3:19).

33 None of these generalized declarations of unbelief, however, are absolute. There are always exceptions, and the story line of John's Gospel thrives on the exceptions. As soon as we heard that "his own did not receive him" (1:11), we learned of those "did receive him" (1:12). As soon as we were told that "human beings loved the dark and not the Light" (3:19), we learned that this was true of some but not of others (3:20-21). Here, right on the heels of a notice that "no one receives his testimony" (v. 32), comes a reminder that someone in fact "did receive his testimony" (v. 33). But who was this someone? Most interpreters conclude that it refers to anyone, anywhere, who ever "received" Jesus or "believed in his name" (as in 1:12), and that it functions as a kind of invitation to the reader to do exactly that. Yet the aorist participle with the definite article *(ho labōn)* suggests a more specific reference, possibly to John himself, who has just acknowledged "receiving" only what heaven had to give (v. 27), and who "received" from Jesus "fullness" and "grace upon grace" (1:16).[50] The two options are not mutually exclusive, for John is, as we have seen (1:15-16, 20, 34), the first among many believers in Jesus in a Gospel that has come (whether by chance or design) to bear his name.

Whether the reference is to John or to those who followed his example is in the end irrelevant, for the point of the verse is not the identity of the one who "received," but the assertion that in receiving Jesus' testimony a person has "confirmed thereby that God is true." "Confirmed" *(esphragisen)* is literally "certified," or "marked with a seal," attesting to the validity of a document to which the seal is attached.[51] But the metaphor is weakened here to refer more generally to confirming or attesting the truthfulness of something or someone.[52] The accent is not on the process of "sealing" or "certification," but

---

50. Without going this far, B. F. Westcott commented that "The reference appears to be directly historic, going back to the time when the disciples were first gathered around the Lord" (1.133).

51. In Christian tradition the verb comes to refer to the work of the Holy Spirit in conversion (2 Cor 1:22; Eph 1:13; 4:30), and "the seal" (ἡ σφραγίς), consequently, to baptism (see Hermas, *Similitudes* 9.16.4, "The seal, then, is the water. They go down into the water dead, and come up alive. The seal, then, was preached to them also, and they made use of it to enter the kingdom of God"). No such meaning is applicable here, where the "confirming" or "certification" is done not by God but by the believer.

52. See G. Fitzer, in *TDNT*, 7.949.

on "God." Those who "receive" Jesus' testimony confirm not that Jesus is true *(alēthēs)* but that *God* is true (compare 8:26).[53] The point is much the same as in 1 John 5:10, where we read, "The person who believes in the Son of God has the testimony in himself; the person who does not believe God has made him a liar, for he has not believed in the testimony which God has testified about his Son." After hearing about "the person who believes in the Son of God," we would have expected "the person who does *not* believe in the Son of God," but instead the text speaks of "the person who does not believe *God*."[54] To not "believe in the Son of God" is to deny God himself and make God a liar. In both passages, God entrusts his own credibility to the Son.

34 This interpretation is borne out in the next verse, where "God" is mentioned twice in quick succession: "for the one *God* sent speaks the words of *God*" (italics added).[55] John, himself "sent from God" (1:6; 3:28), nonetheless acknowledges Jesus as God's supreme agent, uniquely qualified to speak for God as John could never do. With this he confirms Jesus' own claim that "God sent his Son into the world not to condemn the world, but so that the world might be saved through him" (3:17). Yet for a moment John withholds the actual title "Son," as he pauses to remind us of how he came to know Jesus as "Son of God" (compare 1:34). The reminder comes as a cryptic comment, "for he gives the Spirit without measure" — cryptic, because it is not at once clear who is giving what to whom. Is it God giving the Spirit to Jesus, or to believers, or both? Or is it Jesus giving the Spirit to believers? Or the Spirit giving spiritual gifts to believers?[56] The preceding clause implies rather clearly "God" as the Giver, and "the one God sent" as the recipient. If so, then "the Spirit" is the gift, and John is simply expanding on his earlier testimony that "I have watched the Spirit coming down as a dove out of the sky, and it remained on him" (1:32). "Without measure" *(ou gar ek metrou)* is simply another way of saying that the Spirit "remained" on Jesus (1:32, 33).

---

53. See 13:20, "the person who receives [ὁ λαμβάνων] me receives [λαμβάνει] the One who sent me," and 12:44, "the person who believes in me does not believe in me, but in the One who sent me."

54. Not surprisingly a number of later manuscripts in 1 John 5:10 substitute "the Son," or "the Son of God," or "Jesus Christ," for "God" as the one who is "made a liar" by those who disbelieve.

55. Barrett rightly observes that the conjunction "for" (γάρ) "is to be noted: to accept the testimony of Christ means to attest the truth of God *because* Jesus as God's accredited envoy speaks the words of God" (226).

56. Two variant readings suggest that some scribes feared that the clause could be (mis)read with "the Spirit" as the subject, and tried to avoid that impression. One group (including A, D, Θ, Ψ, the Syriac and much of the Latin, and the majority of later manuscripts) did it by inserting ὁ θεός before τὸ πνεῦμα, making "God" explicit as the subject. Another reading (including the first hand of B) omitted τὸ πνεῦμα altogether.

The point is not that God "gave" the Spirit to Jesus "once upon a time" at Bethany beyond the Jordan (1:28), but that God "gives" the Spirit to Jesus always and everywhere in the course of his mission to the world.[57] That is why this Gospel never specifies Jesus' baptism as the moment of the Spirit's descent. Just as Jesus' glory is revealed not in a particular incident, such as the transfiguration, but throughout his ministry (see 1:14), so the Spirit comes and remains on Jesus not on one specific occasion, such as the baptism, but all the time, as his constant companion and possession. To say that the Spirit is his "without measure" is to recognize Jesus as a man "full of grace and truth" (1:14), of whose "fullness we have all received" (1:16). The phrase is probably intended to distinguish Jesus from the prophets, who (it is implied) received the Spirit "by measure" *(ek metrou)* in order to prophesy,[58] and so to identify Jesus uniquely as God's Son, or "One and Only."[59] It confirms John's earlier testimony, "This is the Son of God" (1:34), and is itself confirmed in the next verse, where John goes on to speak explicitly of "the Father" and "the Son" in much the same way in which Jesus himself will speak later in the Gospel (see 5:19-23, 26; 14:13).

35 John now draws a further conclusion from the revelatory scene to which he had testified earlier (see 1:32-34): "The Father loves the Son and has given all things in his hand." With these words, he defines the earlier scene very much along the lines of the synoptic accounts of Jesus' baptism ("You are my beloved Son, in whom I take pleasure," Mk 1:11). The measureless gift of the Spirit (v. 34) is proof of the Father's love, and along with the Spirit, the Father "has given" the Son "all things."[60] The Son therefore "speaks the words of God" (v. 34), and to his voice one must listen (compare v. 29).

At first glance, the notion that "The Father loves the Son" stands in a

---

57. Compare perhaps 6:32, "Amen, amen, I say to you, it is not Moses who has given you [οὐ . . . δέδωκεν] that bread from heaven, but it is my Father who gives you [δίδωσιν] the true bread from heaven."

58. See the late midrash, *Leviticus Rabbah* 15.2: "Even the Holy Spirit resting on the prophets does so by weight, one prophet speaking one book of prophecy and another speaking two books" (*Midrash Rabbah* [London: Soncino, 1961], 4.189). John's expression, ἐκ μέτρου (literally, "from a measure"), occurs nowhere else in Greek literature (ἐν μέτρῳ or κατὰ μέτρον would have been expected). Schlatter (111) attempts to take the ἐκ literally as "from," but it seems to function here much as it does in the expression ἐκ μέρους, "in part" (1 Cor 12:27; 13:9, 10, 12).

59. Compare the distinction in Hebrews 1:1-2 between God's speech through the prophets and through the Son.

60. See 13:3, "Knowing that the Father had given him all things [πάντα] into his hands." This thought too is paralleled in certain synoptic passages: "All things [πάντα] have been handed over to me by my Father" (Mt 11:27//Lk 10:22); "All authority has been given me in heaven and on earth" (Mt 28:18).

kind of tension with Jesus' pronouncement that "God so loved the world that he gave the One and Only Son." If "love" has the connotation of choice or preference), it is natural to ask, "Whom does the Father love more, and whose welfare does the Father put first, his Son's or the world's?" But this is the wrong question, for the reader has known from the start that God's gift of his Son in death was not irrevocable. From the beginning a resurrection or vindication of some kind was presupposed (see 1:5, 51; 2:19-22). Despite (or perhaps because of) being "lifted up," the Son is "right beside the Father" (1:18), and "above all" (v. 31). Now it becomes explicit that in his exaltation "all things" *(panta)* are his. The effect of the notice that "The Father loves the Son" is not to subvert the message of John 3:16, but to further define the term "One and Only Son," and thus to heighten the reader's wonder at the breadth and depth of God's love. If the Father gave up even the Son whom he loved above all to death on a cross, how great must be his love for us and for our world! Just as the Spirit was God's immeasurable gift to his Son, so the Son is God's immeasurable gift to the world.

36 The echo of 3:16 continues, as John puts before his disciples the same stark alternatives Jesus had offered Nicodemus and his companions: "Whoever believes in the Son has eternal life, but whoever disobeys the Son will not see life, but the wrath of God remains on him." Jesus' positive intention "that everyone who believes in him might not be lost but have eternal life" (v. 16) comes to realization in the first clause, yet the dualism of Jesus' encounter with Nicodemus is maintained. As the reader has known from the start (see 1:11), not everyone will believe and not everyone will have eternal life. Verse 36 echoes verse 18, except that the common Johannine expression, "whoever does not believe" (v. 18b), gives way to "whoever disobeys the Son" (v. 36b), a phrase found nowhere else in John's Gospel. While the contrast with "whoever believes in the Son" (v. 36a) makes clear that the meaning is the same, the change of verb helps define "believing" as obedience, or "coming to the Light" (compare vv. 20-21), rather than mere intellectual assent.[61]

The contrast between the two clauses also assumes that having "eternal life" *(echei,* "has") and "seeing life" mean the same thing, just as "seeing" and "entering" the kingdom of God meant the same thing in Jesus' dialogue with Nicodemus (vv. 3, 5).[62] But the tenses of the verbs are different. "Has" is present tense: the one who believes "has" eternal life now, as a pres-

---

61. So rightly Lindars (171): "it combines the implications of 'he who does not believe' (verse 18) and 'every one who does evil' (20), whose condition blinds him to the truth of the Gospel." For a similar interplay of the same two verbs, see 1 Peter 2:6-8.

62. "To see life" occurs only here in the New Testament (though compare 1 Pet 3:10), but "to enter into life" occurs several times in the synoptic Gospels, probably as an equivalent expression (Mt 18:8-9; 19:17; Mk 9:43, 45).

ent possession. Jesus' intention that those who believe "might have" (vv. 15, 16) eternal life has become reality.[63] "Will not see," by contrast, is future: the person who "disobeys the Son" not only does not have eternal life now, but will never "see life" in the future. As in verse 18, the point is *not* that the disobedient are now suddenly condemned by a vengeful God, but, on the contrary, that their spiritual condition and their relation to God remains unchanged. In verse 18, the unbeliever was said to be "already condemned," while here "the wrath of God remains on him." This last echo of John's testimony of the Spirit's descent on Jesus (1:32-34) is ironic: just as the Spirit came down and "remained on him" (1:32-33), so God's wrath "remains on" the unbeliever. "The wrath of God," mentioned only here in John's Gospel, recalls one notable saying attributed to John in the synoptic Gospels ("Who warned you to flee from the coming wrath?" Mt 3:7//Lk 3:7). Here, however, the use of *menein*, "to remain," implies that divine wrath is not simply a future threat but a present reality as well. Human beings are *already* under "the wrath of God," just as they are already in "darkness" (compare 1:5; 3:19). Those who remain unchanged by the coming of the Light "remain in darkness" (compare 12:46), and the wrath of God "remains" on them. The grim verdict of this verse is that for some hearers and readers nothing has changed. As Jesus will put it later to some of the Pharisees, "Your sin remains" (9:41). The joint testimony of Jesus and John is that a person gains eternal life only by "coming to the Light" (vv. 20-21), or "believing in the Son" (v. 36). With these words, John's testimony is finished, and he disappears from the story.[64]

III. JESUS' SELF-REVELATION TO THE WORLD (4:1–12:50)

John has said that "the one God sent speaks the words of God, for he gives the Spirit without measure" (3:34). In the next nine chapters Jesus will speak "the words of God" to an ever more hostile world, represented by the Jewish religious establishment in Jerusalem. He begins auspiciously among foreigners, revealing his identity to a woman in Samaria (4:26), and he is hailed as "the

---

63. Barrett (227) calls this "the climax of the chapter, and a final indication that it is right to read it in the order in which it stands in the MSS." John's pronouncement corresponds closely to the conclusion of the main argument in 1 John: "Whoever has [ὁ ἔχων] the Son has [ἔχει] life; whoever does not have [ὁ μὴ ἔχων] the Son of God does not have [οὐκ ἔχει] life" (1 Jn 5:12).

64. As we have seen (n. 42), some later manuscripts add a final notice removing John from the scene, but this is contrary to the Gospel writer's intention, for John is still active in ministry, implicitly at least, in 4:1.

Savior of the world" (4:42); but after this he meets nothing but rejection, whether in Jerusalem (chapters 5, 7-12) or in Galilee (chapter 6). Unlike John, he validates his testimonies with a series of miracles (chapters 5, 6, 9, 11), but in the end the verdict is that "Even after he had done so many signs before them, they would not believe in him" (12:37). The revelation ends with another soliloquy like the last words of John (3:31-36), but this time on the lips of Jesus (12:44-50), and this time not saying farewell but reminding the reader that he has yet more to say because "the Father who sent me, he has given me a command what I should say and what I should speak; . . . so then the things I speak, just as the Father has told me, thus I speak" (12:49-50).

A. JESUS AND THE SAMARITANS (4:1-42)

> 1 *Now when the Lord found out that the Pharisees had heard that Jesus was making and baptizing more disciples than John* 2 *— although Jesus himself was not baptizing, his disciples were —* 3 *he left Judea and went back again into Galilee.* 4 *But he had to go through Samaria.* 5 *So he comes to a town of Samaria called Sychar, next to the field Jacob gave to Joseph his son.* 6 *There too was Jacob's spring. So Jesus, weary from the journey, was sitting like this at the spring. It was about the sixth hour.* 7 *A woman from Samaria comes to draw water. Jesus says to her, "Give me to drink."* 8 *(For his disciples had gone into the town to buy provisions).* 9 *So the Samaritan woman says to him, "How come you, a Jew, are asking drink from me, a Samaritan woman? For Jews will have nothing to do with Samaritans."* 10 *Jesus answered and said to her, "If you knew the gift of God and who it is who says to you, 'Give me to drink,' you would have asked him, and he would have given you living water."* 11 *She says to him, "Sir, you have no bucket and the well is deep. From where, then, do you have this living water?* 12 *Are you greater than our father Jacob, who gave us the well and drank from it himself, with his sons and his livestock?"* 13 *Jesus answered and said to her, "Everyone who drinks of this water will thirst again,* 14 *but whoever drinks of the water that I will give him will never ever thirst. Instead, the water I will give him will become in him a spring of water rushing to eternal life."* 15 *The woman says to him, "Sir, give me this water, so that I will not thirst and have to keep coming back here to draw."* 16 *He says to her, "Go call your husband. Then come back here."* 17 *The woman answered and said to him, "I have no husband." Jesus says to her, "You have said it well, 'I have no husband,'* 18 *for you have had five husbands, and the one you have now is not your husband. What you have just said is true."* 19 *The woman*

says to him, "Sir, I can see that you are a prophet. 20 Our fathers worshiped on this mountain, and yet you people say that the place where one must worship is in Jerusalem." 21 Jesus says to her, "Believe me, woman, that an hour is coming when neither on this mountain nor in Jerusalem will you worship the Father. 22 You people worship what you do not know. We worship what we know, for salvation is from the Jews. 23 And yet an hour is coming and now is when the true worshipers will worship the Father in Spirit and truth, for those are the kind the Father is looking for to worship him. 24 God is Spirit, and those who worship him must worship in Spirit and truth." 25 The woman says to him, "I know that Messiah is coming, who is called Christ. When he comes, he will tell us all things." 26 Jesus says to her, "It is I — I who am speaking to you."

27 And at that his disciples came, and were surprised that he was speaking with a woman, though no one said, "What are you looking for?" or "What are you speaking with her about?" 28 So the woman left her water jar and went into the town and says to the men, 29 "Come, see a man who told me everything I ever did. Could this be the Christ?" 30 They came out of the town, and were coming to him. 31 Meanwhile his disciples were asking him, "Rabbi, eat." 32 But he said to them, "I have food to eat that you do not know about." 33 So his disciples were saying to each other, "Has anyone brought him anything to eat?" 34 Jesus says to them, "My food is that I might do the will of the One who sent me and complete his work. 35 Do you not say that there are still four months and then the harvest comes? Look, I say to you, Lift up your eyes and look at the fields, that they are white for harvest. 36 Already the harvester is receiving payment and gathering a crop for eternal life, so that the sower might rejoice together with the harvester. 37 For in this the saying is true that one is the sower and another the harvester: 38 I have sent you to harvest that on which you have not labored. Others have labored, and you have entered into their labor."

39 Now many of the Samaritans from that town had believed in him because of the woman's word testifying that "He told me everything I ever did." 40 So when the Samaritans came to him, they asked him to stay with them, and he stayed there two days. 41 And many more believed because of his word, 42 and they said to the woman that "We no longer believe because of your speech, for we ourselves have heard, and we know that this is truly the Savior of the world."

The narrative resumes after John's speech to his disciples (3:27-36), as the narrator returns to the subject of Jesus, his travels, and his baptizing ministry (see 3:22, 26). On his way back to Galilee he encounters first an individual

4:1-42 JESUS AND THE SAMARITANS

woman at a well in Samaria (4:1-26), and then a whole village (vv. 27-42). He speaks to the woman first of water and eternal life, and then of true worship, and the woman becomes a messenger to the men of her village, who eventually learn that Jesus is "the Savior of the world" (v. 42). The story as it unfolds picks up certain themes both from John's speech and from his own in the preceding chapter. For example, the imagery of bridegroom and bride (3:29) shows up, implicitly at least, in the dialogue between Jesus and the woman he meets at a well. Moreover, the theme of "believing" with the promise of "eternal life" (see 3:16-21, 36) surfaces again in Jesus' promises to her (4:14), and to his disciples in connection with the prospect of a rich "harvest" among the Samaritans (see vv. 36, 39, 42), while his hope "that the world might be saved" (3:17) is echoed in the Samaritans' confession of him as "Savior of the world" (4:42). That which was announced in discourse comes to expression concretely in this narrative of an otherwise unknown mission of Jesus and his disciples to a foreign and traditionally hostile community.

1 The narrative's opening (vv. 1-3) is very cumbersome because of two things: first, the mention of the Pharisees (v. 1), and second, the abrupt parenthetical notice that Jesus himself was not literally baptizing anyone (v. 2). If the account had begun simply, "Now when the Lord realized that he was making and baptizing more disciples than John, he left Judea and went back into Galilee," it would have gracefully resumed the preceding narrative without seeming awkward or overloaded with subordinate clauses. There we learned that Jesus was indeed baptizing in Judea (3:22), and that John's disciples seemed to perceive his ministry as more successful than John's (v. 26). Now we find that Jesus came to view things in much the same way, and consequently left the area. But the mention of the Pharisees complicates the picture. What seems to have troubled Jesus was not that he was having more success than John, but that the Pharisees had heard that this was the case. We have met the Pharisees once before as those who had sent delegates to question John about his ministry of baptism (1:24), and we can only assume that Jesus wanted to avoid a similar round of questions. The Gospel writer refers to Jesus as "the Lord,"[1] a term characteristic of Luke's narrative

---

1. "The Lord" (ὁ κύριος) is the reading of P66, P75, A, B, C, L, and the majority of later manuscripts, plus two old Latin versions, the Sinaitic Syriac, and the Sahidic Coptic. Other witnesses (ℵ, D, Θ, among others, plus most of the old Latin and Syriac versions, and the Bohairic Coptic) have instead the more common "Jesus" (ὁ Ἰησοῦς). Both the manuscript evidence and the likelihood that a scribal change would have been in the direction of a more familiar and expected reading favor "the Lord" as original. The argument that "Jesus" is original and was changed to "the Lord" to avoid an awkward repetition of the proper name (see Metzger, *Textual Commentary*, 205-6) is less convincing. Such a change would only have raised, needlessly, the question of whether "the Lord" and "Jesus" were the same. The text does not give evidence of aiming for smoothness in any case.

material, but absent in Markan or Matthean narrative and used only sparingly in John's Gospel.[2] Aside from the biblical quotation in 1:23, it is the first use of "Lord" in this Gospel, and may have been introduced here to reinforce John's eloquent testimony (3:27-36) to Jesus' supremacy (compare "above all," v. 31). Yet "the Lord's" knowledge is not supernatural (as in 1:47-48 or 2:24-25), for he is said to have "found out," or "come to know," of the Pharisees' awareness of his and John's ministry, presumably by being informed.[3]

The situation vaguely recalls Matthew's account, where Jesus left for Galilee after his temptation in the desert because he "heard" that John had been imprisoned (Mt 4:12). Here John is not imprisoned, but merely "diminished" (3:30) in the public eye, and those who "hear" are first the Pharisees and only then Jesus. There is a similarity in that news about John triggers a change of scene for Jesus. Yet in contrast to Matthew (and the synoptic tradition generally) Jesus does not emerge from the obscurity of a forty-day retreat in the desert to begin a "public ministry" in Galilee. As far as the reader is concerned, Jesus has already been "revealed to Israel" (1:31), "revealed his glory" at Cana in Galilee (2:11), confronted "the Jews" in Jerusalem (2.13-22), performed "signs" there (2:23; 3:2), and conducted a baptizing ministry in Judea (3:22, 26). Many have "come to him" (3:26) and "believed in his name" (2:23). Even now he is "making and baptizing more disciples than John." The terminology suggests that water baptism was the normal way by which a person became a "disciple," whether of John or Jesus.[4] This is undisputed in the case of John, who is, after all, remembered in Christian tradition as "the Baptist" or "the Baptizer," but not in the case of Jesus. It is commonly assumed that John baptized, and the earliest Christians baptized, but that Jesus did not. At his command after the resurrection, we are told (Mt 28:19), his followers reverted to the practice of John. The notice here (and in 3:22 and 26) seriously qualifies that widely held assumption. The reader already knows that at least two (probably more) of Jesus' first disciples were drawn from among the disciples of John (1:35, 40), and can assume that as John's

---

2. There are six Johannine examples, but three of these (20:20; 21:7, 12) are simply narrative echoes of lines uttered by characters in the story ("I have seen the Lord," 20:18; compare v. 24; and "It is the Lord," 21:7), leaving only 4:1, 6:23, and 11:2. The latter two refer to things that happened to "the Lord" *outside* the immediate narrative, either before or after what is being described (see 6:11 and 12:3 respectively). In this sense, 4:1 is unique.

3. This is in keeping with the Gospel's common use of the aorist (ἔγνω) of the verb "know" (γινώσκειν) to mean "learn," "find out," or "come to know" (see Jn 1:10; 4:53; 5:6; 6:15; 7:51; 10:38; 11:57; 12:9; 13:28; 16:19; 17:25; 19:4).

4. Compare Matthew 28:19-20, where "making disciples" is defined as "baptizing" and "teaching."

4:1-42 JESUS AND THE SAMARITANS

disciples they had been baptized in water. Now for the first time Jesus is said to have added to their number,[5] and to have done so in the same way, by baptizing. The implication is that water baptism was the normative rite of initiation for Jesus no less than for John, for in baptism a person "comes to him" (3:26) and is made a "disciple." But does our text imply that this was the case throughout Jesus' ministry, or only for a brief interlude in Judea, presumably while he was still under John's influence?[6] Arguments from silence cancel each other out. Jesus is never again said to have baptized, yet nowhere are we told that he gave up the practice either. Because he continued to "make disciples," even though the precise phrase is not used again, and invited people to "come to me" (for example, 6:35, 45; 7:37), the distinct possibility remains that he also continued to baptize.[7]

2 In dealing with this issue, the commentator must decide whether to look at it from the standpoint of historicity (Was the historical Jesus *in fact* a baptizer like John?), or from the standpoint of the Gospel writer's literary intention (Does this Gospel *intend to present* Jesus as a baptizer like John?). The two questions are not quite interchangeable. The Gospel writer adds an immediate qualification, signaling that whatever the answer to the first question, the answer to the second is "No. Jesus is *not* simply a baptizer like John." Like certain other narrative asides in the Gospel, the disclaimer comes very belatedly, as if to say, "Oh, I forgot to tell you this before" (compare 1:24, 28; 3:24). Three times he has said Jesus "was baptizing" (3:22, 3:26, and now 4:1). He could have added the disclaimer at 3:22 or 3:26, but now he finally lets the reader in on the secret: "Jesus himself was not baptizing, his disciples were."[8] The qualification could be read as a virtual retraction, and is routinely understood by some to be the work of someone other than the Gospel writer.[9] More likely, it comes from the Gospel writer himself (compare

---

5. Their number must have increased considerably, for two chapters later (6:66-70) it is *reduced* to twelve!

6. The latter is commonly taken for granted, often with the added claim that John is right over against the Synoptics (see, for example, John Meier, *A Marginal Jew*, 2.123).

7. See R. T. France, "Jesus the Baptist?" in *Jesus of Nazareth: Lord and Christ* (ed. J. B. Green and M. Turner; Grand Rapids: Eerdmans, 1994), 94-111.

8. Moloney (116) reads it *not* as a belated comment, but a change from 3:22 and 26: "Once there was one baptizer, John (1:28); then there were two, John and Jesus (3:22-23); now there are many baptizers, all the disciples of Jesus (4:2). There is a proliferation of baptizers, and the purpose of the baptismal activity of the disciples of Jesus is to draw more people to their master." But the point is not so much that Jesus' disciples *are* baptizing as that Jesus himself is not personally doing so. John's testimony in 3:27-36 suggests that "more disciples" are being baptized not simply because there are more baptizers, but because Jesus is greater than John.

9. Meier (*A Marginal Jew*, 2.121-22) attributes the remark to a later redactor who "apparently found the idea of Jesus baptizing objectionable, and in his usual [*sic*] wooden,

Paul's self-correction in 1 Cor 1:16), for it is consistent with his practice of consistently downplaying Jesus' role as a baptizer and accenting the distinctions between him and John. If it is the Gospel writer's work, his belated comment is better read simply as an appeal to a technicality. If Jesus sponsored and supervised a ministry of baptism in Judea, it is fair to say he "was baptizing," whether he personally anointed or dipped candidates in the waters of the region or whether his disciples did it for him. The comment is not a serious denial that Jesus baptized, but merely distinguishes him from John by deemphasizing that aspect of his ministry.[10] This leaves us with the question of whether or not the historical Jesus was in fact a baptizer like John. None of the other Gospels even hint at such a thing, yet the thrice-repeated notice that Jesus "was baptizing" in Judea is difficult to ignore — all the more difficult in light of the apparent effort to minimize its significance.

3 To avoid the Pharisees' questions, Jesus now resumes his journey, leaving Judea (compare 3:22) and heading back to Galilee. "Back again" reminds the reader that he has been in Galilee before (see 1:43; 2:1-12),[11] and later, when he finally arrives (4:43-54), there will be further reminders of his previous visit (vv. 46, 54). The journey will take only two or three days in real time (4:40, 43), but it will seem like more in narrative time as the writer goes into considerable detail about what happened on the way. From the standpoint of Jesus' itinerary verses 4-42 are a long digression, yet they are the heart and core of the unfolding story line, and in them Jesus will undertake his decisive self-revelation to the world.

4 The "digression" begins with a terse notice, "But he had to go through Samaria." The "but" is a very mild adversative, as if to say, "But remember, 'Judea to Galilee' necessarily involves Samaria as well." Much has been written about whether the necessity was geographical or theological. Did Jesus "have to" *(edei)* go through Samaria for the same reason a person "must" *(dei)* be born from above (3:7), or the Son of man "must" be lifted up (3:14), or Jesus "must" grow and John diminish (3:30)? Or did he "have to" go there simply because it was the most direct route? Was it a matter of God's will (compare 4:34), or geographical convenience? Some commentators are

---

mechanical way . . . issues a 'clarification' correcting any false impression the narrative might give." Meier's knowledge of what is "usual" for his supposed redactor on the basis of one brief sample is rather puzzling. Where are all the other "wooden" and "mechanical" comments, and do they all come from the same redactor?

10. It also tends to validate what must have been the churches' practice at the time John's Gospel was written, in which Jesus' disciples baptize "in his name" (see Mt 28:19; Acts 2:38; 8:16; 10:48; 19:5; compare 1 Cor 1:13, 15).

11. While πάλιν is omitted in certain manuscripts (A, B*, and the majority of later manuscripts), it is present in the most reliable witnesses (including P⁶⁶, P⁷⁵, ℵ, D, L, and virtually all the Latin and Syriac versions) and is undoubtedly original.

quick to introduce the theological factor,[12] but the reference should probably be read simply as a geographical observation, carrying forward the story line by explaining how a journey to Galilee brought Jesus to a well in Samaria.[13] While the impersonal verb *dei* ("must" or "it is necessary") often points to a theological necessity, only here in John's Gospel is a form of this verb used by the Gospel writer as part of the narrative. All other instances are within quotations, whether of John (3:30), Jesus (3:7, 14; 4:24; 9:4; 10:16), someone responding to Jesus (4:20; 12:34), or Scripture (20:9). As narrative, it recalls the often-cited notice in Josephus that "Samaria was now under Roman rule, and for rapid travel it was essential [*edei*, as here] to take that route, by which Jerusalem may be reached in three days from Galilee."[14] Moreover the explicit mention of Jesus' starting point (Judea) as well as his destination (Galilee), in contrast to other instances where only the destination is named,[15] suggests that the reader is expected to appreciate the logic of "going through Samaria." Later, after Jesus' ministry in Samaria and Galilee, the writer will frame the whole chapter into a single narrative by telling us again that Jesus had "come from Judea into Galilee" (v. 54), a subtle reminder that his journey had embraced Samaria too.

5 The town of Sychar (unlike such Galilean places as Bethsaida, Cana, and Capernaum) is introduced as if unknown to the readers of the Gospel.[16] All they need to know is that it is "a town of Samaria called Sy-

---

12. For example, Brown, 1.169; Morris, 226; Moloney, 116; Michaels, 69 (I have since changed my mind).

13. Compare Bultmann (176); Schnackenburg (1.422); Carson, 215-16; Barrett, 230. Despite their differences, Jews and Samaritans seem not to have deliberately avoided one another's territory (see Lk 10:30-33; 17:11-19). While Jesus warned his disciples in Matthew not to enter Samaritan towns (Mt 10:5), in Luke he explicitly sent them there to prepare for his own arrival (Lk 9:52; compare 10:1).

14. *Vita* 269 (LCL, 1.101); see also *Antiquities* 20.118. Josephus's "three days" exhibits (coincidentally) the same interest as John's Gospel in how long such journeys take; see John 2:1, "on the third day"; 4:40, "two days"; 4:43, "after the two days."

15. The latter is the common practice in John's Gospel in describing Jesus' itinerary, sometimes because the starting point is clear from the context (as in 1:43; 2:12, 13; 4:43, 46; 5:1; 10:40; 12:1), but also when it is not (3:22; 6:1).

16. Its location is still unknown. Identified on the sixth-century Madeba map as "[Sy]char, now [Sy]chora," it is believed to correspond to the present-day Arab village of Askar, a mile east of Nablus on the slope of Mount Ebal. (The Mishnah refers vaguely to a valley or plain of En Soker, or "spring of Soker," *Menaḥot* 10.2). Because the name Shechem was much better known, two Syriac manuscripts and some interpreters (beginning with Jerome) have read "Shechem" here, but if Shechem were original, there would have been no reason to change it to the unfamiliar Sychar. The biblical Shechem, known as Tell Balatah since the excavations of Sellin and Wright, is less than a mile from Askar, and has by it a very deep spring, shown to visitors as "Jacob's well." While this is likely

char,"[17] close to sites important in Samaritan tradition. The writer places it "next to the field Jacob gave to Joseph his son," a place associated with Shechem, the Samaritan capital. In Genesis, Jacob was said to have given to Joseph "one portion more than to your brothers, the portion that I took from the hand of the Amorites with my sword and with my bow" (Gen 48:22, NRSV).[18] Even though Sychar is not Shechem (see n. 16), it is nearby, and the traditions evoked by the story are associated with Shechem by Samaritans and Jews alike.

6 The naming of the country (twice) and the town, the allusion to Jacob's gift of the field to Joseph, and the notice that "There too [*ekei*] was Jacob's spring," demonstrates once more the narrator's interest in the precise location of Jesus' activities.[19] It also gives credibility to the Samaritan woman's comment later (v. 12):[20] if the field was Jacob's, so too was the "spring" (*pēgē*, a word referring to the water supply, not to the hole in the ground that led to it).[21] The writer now sets the stage for Jesus' encounter with a Samaritan woman. The place is "at the spring." The time is "about the sixth hour," or

---

the spring John's Gospel has in mind, there is no evidence that a town even existed there in Jesus' time. The movements in the story between the spring and the town make better sense if the distance is one kilometer (as from the spring to Askar) than if it is only 250 feet (as from the spring to Tell Balatah). Yet Askar has its own spring, and the question remains why, *if* Sychar is the modern Askar, the woman came the extra distance to draw water. Was it the spring's depth and purity, or its association with Jacob? Or was she unwelcome at her own town's spring? There is no evidence for the latter. As far as the reader knows, Jacob's spring was the natural place for her to come.

17. Compare the otherwise unknown "town called Ephraim," vaguely located "in the region near the desert" (11:54), as well as John's mysterious "Bethany, beyond the Jordan" (1:28) and "Aenon near the Salim" (3:23).

18. "Portion," literally "shoulder," is שכם (in the LXX, Σικιμα), playing on the name Shechem. It is not entirely clear to what event Jacob is referring. Genesis 33:19 (NRSV), where he had bought "from the sons of Hamor, Shechem's father, . . . the plot of land on which he had pitched his tent," implies a peaceful acquisition of the land, while Genesis 34:25-29, where his sons "killed Hamor and his son Shechem with the sword" and "plundered the city" (presumably Shechem), suggests something quite different. Nor do the biblical texts mention a spring or well.

19. Compare the repeated use of "there" (ἐκεῖ) in 2:1, 6, 12; 3:22, 23, and in the present story notice how ἐκεῖ is repeated in verse 40 so as to frame the whole (". . . and he remained *there* two days").

20. Chrysostom asks, "Why is the Evangelist exact about the place? It is, that when thou hearest the woman say, 'Jacob our father gave us this well,' thou mayest not think it strange. For this was the place where Levi and Simeon, being angry because of Dinah, wrought that cruel slaughter" (*Homilies* 31; NPNF, 1st ser., 14.107).

21. The latter is "the well" (τὸ φρέαρ, vv. 11, 12). See verse 14, where πηγή refers to a water supply that has nothing to do with a "well." The distinction affects the meaning of the phrase ἐπὶ τῇ πηγῇ: not "on the well," but "at the spring" (see BDAG, 363).

4:1-42 JESUS AND THE SAMARITANS

noon,[22] the same time of day as Jesus' crucifixion, as the reader will find out in due time (19:14).[23] The setting recalls three classic biblical incidents in which a man met a prospective bride at a well: when Abraham's servant seeking a bride for Isaac met the virgin Rebekah (Gen 24:1-27), when Jacob met Rachel (Gen 29:1-12), and when Moses met Zipporah in Midian (Exod 2:15-21).[24] Each story is different, and the language of the story told here cannot be traced to any one of them. But the introduction to the story here is strikingly similar to Moses' encounter as Josephus transformed it (*Antiquities* 2.257), in which Moses "sat down on the brink of a well and there rested after his toil and hardships, at midday, not far from the town."[25] Jesus too, being "weary from the journey, was sitting like this at the spring." "Like this" *(houtōs)* is a storyteller's flourish,[26] as if to demonstrate by gesture the weariness that forced Jesus to stop and rest.[27] Yet the imperfect "was sitting" suggests not so much the action of sitting down as rather a state of being already seated quietly, waiting for what will happen next (compare "Mary was sitting in the house," 11:20).[28] The stage is set. Let the encounter begin.

7 The narrative use of the present tense signals another exchange comparable to Jesus' encounter with John's disciples (1:35-51) or with Nicodemus (3:1-10): "A woman from Samaria *comes* to draw water," and "Jesus *says* to her, 'Give me to drink'" (italics added). The verb "comes" echoes verse 5: Jesus "comes" to Sychar, the woman now "comes" to the spring, and they meet. For a third time the country is named (compare vv. 4, 5) when the woman is introduced, somewhat redundantly, as "a woman from

---

22. For evidence that "the sixth hour" was noon, see above on 1:39.

23. The expression is exactly the same in both passages, ὥρα ἦν ὡς ἕκτη, not merely "the sixth hour," but "*about* the sixth hour").

24. See, for example, Robert Alter, *The Art of Biblical Narrative* (New York: Basic Books, 1981), 51-62; Paul Duke, *Irony in the Fourth Gospel* (Atlanta: John Knox, 1985), 101-3; Sandra M. Schneiders, *The Revelatory Text* (San Francisco: HarperSanFrancisco, 1991), 187-94.

25. The translation is from LCL, 4.277. In the LXX we are told only that, "having come into the land, he sat down on the well" (Exod 2:15). The other two biblical incidents give the time either as "toward evening, the time when women go out to draw water" (Gen 24:11), or (more vaguely) "still broad daylight" (Gen 29:7).

26. For οὕτως used in this way, see 13:25; also the variant reading added to 8:59 in certain ancient manuscripts.

27. According to Chrysostom, "He sat 'thus.' What meaneth 'thus'? Not upon a throne, not upon a cushion, but simply and as He was [Gr. ὡς ἔτυχεν, "as it happened"], upon the ground" (*Homilies* 31; NPNF, 1st ser., 14.109).

28. See NASB, NRSV, REB (implied also by the KJV and ERV, "sat thus," and the NLT, "sat wearily"). Most modern English translations, however, render it "sat down," as if the verb were aorist (for example, RSV, NEB, NIV, NAB, JB, TEV, CEV, J. B. Phillips, Richmond Lattimore, Reynolds Price).

Samaria."[29] Unlike Nicodemus (3:2), she does not "come to Jesus" as one professing allegiance, nor does she come "at night." Knowing nothing of Jesus, she simply comes to the spring at high noon for water. To modern ears, Jesus' request, "Give me to drink," sounds abrupt, even impolite, but the narrative is bare, stripped of pleasantries and preliminaries.[30] His words are only slightly more abrupt than those of Abraham's servant on meeting Rebekah: "Let me drink a little water from your jar" (Gen 24:17). If there is one biblical point of reference for Jesus' meeting with the Samaritan woman, it is probably that story, echoed here and at the same time transformed. A servant representing a bridegroom meets the virgin bride at a well by asking for a drink of water, and Rebekah quickly responds, "Drink, sir!" (Gen 24:18). In our narrative, Jesus has recently been identified as a bridegroom (3:29), but the Samaritan woman, we will shortly learn, is neither bride nor virgin, and is not so quick to grant Jesus' request (v. 9). In the Genesis story, real thirst is not the issue, for the request is part of a conscious and prayerful plan to find a bride for Isaac (Gen 24:12-14). Here too it is tempting to suspect that Jesus has a plan to evangelize Samaria, that he is not really thirsty, and that his request for water is just a ploy (see 6:6, "He himself knew what he was going to do"). Yet all the clues point in the opposite direction. Jesus' weariness, conveyed both by word and implied gesture, makes his thirst a wholly natural and inevitable part of the story. Those who knew of his passion would also know that his thirst at that time, again "about the sixth hour" (see 19:14, 28), was real and not feigned. Here too, when he says bluntly, "Give me to drink," he does so for only one reason. He is thirsty. Nothing that he says later (vv. 10, 13-14) changes that.

8 As in several other narrative asides in John's Gospel (1:24, 28; 3:24; 4:2), the notice that his disciples "had gone into the town to buy provisions" comes belatedly, as if it were an afterthought. We were not even told that the disciples had accompanied him from Judea to Samaria. Yet the notice serves a definite purpose in its present position, for Jesus has just met the woman, and the writer is taking the opportunity to tell us that the two were

---

29. "From Samaria" (ἐκ τῆς Σαμαρείας) must obviously be read with "woman," not with the verb (see Bultmann, 178, n. 4). She is a woman "from" or "of" Samaria. Yet the expression is not quite equivalent (as Bultmann implies) to Nicodemus as a man "of the Pharisees" (ἐκ τῶν Φαρισαίων, 3:1), for the ἐκ is not partitive here but denotes the woman's ethnic origin. The phrase puts the woman at a certain distance from the presumed readers of the Gospel as a resident of a foreign country.

30. Dorothy Sayers, referring to those who "infer that He never said 'Please' or 'Thank you,'" observed that "perhaps these common courtesies were left unrecorded precisely because they were common" ("A Vote of Thanks to Cyrus," in *Unpopular Opinions* [London: Gollancz, 1946], 28). It is amusing to hear Jesus made to say "Please" to the Samaritan woman in some of the more paraphrastic versions (NLT, CEV, Phillips)!

alone, accenting the drama of what is to follow. Beyond this, it sets the stage for the disciples' later return, and their shock "that he was speaking with a woman" (v. 27). Jewish custom frowned on a man of God carrying on an extended conversation with a woman,[31] and it did not help that Jesus and this woman were alone.[32]

9 Instead of playing out the bride's compliant role in a traditional well story ("Drink, sir!" Gen 24:18), the woman balks at Jesus' request: "How come you, a Jew, are asking drink from me, a Samaritan woman?"[33] While she consciously identifies herself as a woman and as a Samaritan, she does not invoke Samaritan custom so as to refuse Jesus' request outright. Instead, she wonders aloud why Jesus would ask her for water, given the customs of his own people. She[34] then adds an explanation, that "Jews will have nothing to do with Samaritans" (not that "Samaritans will have nothing to do with Jews," which was equally true). To "have nothing to do with" can mean either to have no dealings in a general sense, or specifically to not "use [vessels] together" in situations where ritual purity is at stake.[35] The second option seems plausible

---

31. See Sirach 9.1-9; also *Pirqe 'Abot* 1.5: "Hence the Sages have said: 'He that talks much with womankind brings evil on himself and neglects the study of the Law and at the last will inherit Gehenna'" (translation from Danby, 446). The accent seems to have been on "much," for a story in the Talmud tells of a Galilean rabbi who asked a wise woman, "By what road do we go to Lydda?" "Foolish Galilean," she replied, "did not the Sages say this: Engage not in much talk with women? You should have asked: By which to Lydda" (*'Erubin* 53b; translation from *Babylonian Talmud: Seder Mo'ed* [London: Soncino, 1938], 2.374).

32. Being alone together was not an inevitable feature of the biblical stories of a bridegroom meeting a bride by a well. They are alone in Genesis 24:1-27, but not in Genesis 29:1-12 (where Jacob first met some shepherds), or in Exodus 2:15-21 (where seven daughters came out to draw water). Even in the first story, Josephus's retelling has Abraham's servant meeting "a number of maidens going to fetch water," and choosing from among them the one who grants his request for a drink (*Antiquities* 1.244-48).

33. How did she know he was a Jew? Chrysostom supposes, "From His dress, perhaps, and from His dialect" (*Homilies* 31; NPNF, 1st ser., 14.109), but it is of no interest to the Gospel writer.

34. Her comment is commonly viewed as that of the Gospel writer, explaining to the reader why she said what she did. Yet the writer seems to attribute it to the woman herself (see Hoskyns, 242; Lindars, 181), just as he attributed 3:16-21 to Jesus and 3:31-36 to John, and just as he will attribute to Jesus the comment that "salvation is from the Jews" (v. 22b). In this instance, however, the writer may regard the comment as unreliable, because he has already told us that the disciples are off to town precisely to deal with Samaritans (v. 8).

35. The verb in Greek is συγχρῶνται (see BDAG, 953-54). The second option was the proposal of David Daube, "Jesus and the Samaritan Woman: The Meaning of συγχρῶνται," *JBL* 69 (1950), 137-47, followed by a number of commentators since (for example, Barrett, 232-33; Brown, 1.170; Morris, 229; Moloney, 121; Carson, 218). Jews

because it is a question of drinking from the same cup or jar.³⁶ Yet the reader was probably not expected to understand all the particulars of ritual purity (it is mentioned only generally and vaguely in 2:6 and 3:25).³⁷ Therefore the translation, "have nothing to do with," or "have no dealings with," is preferable. The added comment is fully consistent with the woman's question, and by it the writer assures us that in fact she had a point: Jesus is "a Jew," and if "Jews will have nothing to do with Samaritans," then he is in danger of violating Jewish custom.³⁸ Only here in the whole New Testament, ironically in the very act of doing what Jews do not normally do, is Jesus explicitly called "a Jew."³⁹ The writer implicitly endorses this label, yet a further irony remains. Jesus comes as an outsider and stranger to the whole world: to the Samaritan woman he is "a Jew," yet four chapters later, to "the Jews" in Jerusalem he is "a Samaritan" (8:48). At the end of the present scene, this stranger to the world will be revealed as "Savior of the world" (v. 42).

10 Jesus' answer playfully engages the woman as a debate partner in much the same way he engaged Nicodemus (3:3), by mimicking her own words.⁴⁰ She had said, "How come *you* . . . are *asking*," and he replies with a contrary-to-fact condition, "If you knew, . . . *you* would have *asked*."⁴¹ With

---

viewed Samaritan women in particular as "menstruants from their cradle" (*Niddah* 4.1), so that one could never be sure they were not unclean.

36. Augustine noticed this, even without Daube's help: "You see that they were aliens: indeed the Jews would not use their vessels. And as the woman brought with her a vessel with which to draw the water, it made her wonder that a Jew sought drink of her — a thing to which the Jews were not accustomed. But He who was asking drink was thirsting for the faith of the woman herself." *Tractates* 15.11 (NPNF, 1st ser., 7.102).

37. Compare Lindars, 181: "The difficulty of this view is that it fails as an explanation for Gentiles, being a case of expounding *ignotum per ignotus;* also the verb has no object, so that 'vessels' has to be understood." So too Haenchen, 1.220; Schnackenburg, 1.425; Beasley-Murray, 58.

38. The narrative aside is missing altogether in a number of ancient textual witnesses: ℵ*, D, and several old Latin versions (*a, b, e,* and *j*). It is, however, precisely the sort of comment that characterizes this writer. Possibly some scribes preferred to see Jesus' request as contrary only to Samaritan, not Jewish practice, and the woman's response, consequently, as based on a misunderstanding. While it was a matter of custom and not law, even the appearance of Jesus as a lawbreaker may have been distasteful to some.

39. While Ἰουδαῖος here could be translated either "Jew" or "Judean," it cannot mean "Judean" in contrast to "Galilean." To the woman, Galileans and Judeans were all Ἰουδαῖοι because they worshiped God in Jerusalem (v. 20), in "the land of Judea" (see 3:22).

40. This device is not unknown in other Gospels. See, for example, Matthew 15:2-3, where the Pharisees ask Jesus, "Why [διὰ τί] do your disciples transgress [παραβαίνουσιν] the tradition of the elders?" (v. 2), and Jesus responds with a question of his own, "Why [διὰ τί] do you also [καὶ ὑμεῖς] transgress [παραβαίνετε] the command of God?" (v. 3).

41. The italicized words call attention to the repetition in Greek of the emphatic "you" (σύ), and of the verb "ask" (αἰτεῖν).

this he exposes her ignorance of two things: first, "the gift of God," and second, "who it is who says to you, 'Give me to drink'" — that is, who Jesus is.[42] Both are things the reader of the Gospel should know, even though the woman does not. "The gift [*tēn dōrean*] of God" could be the law, "given through Moses" (1:17), or it could be Jesus himself, God's "One and Only Son" (3:16). But if John's farewell speech, still fresh in the reader's mind, is allowed to provide the framework, God's gift is the Spirit, given "without measure" to the Son, to whom all things are given (3:34-35). "Gift" as a term for the Holy Spirit recalls the book of Acts (2:38; 10:45; 11:17), most notably in Samaria itself (8:20),[43] where Peter speaks of "the gift of God" in connection with Simon Magus's attempt to buy from the apostles the power of conferring the Spirit by the laying on of hands. Here at Jacob's spring, "the gift of God" is uniquely in the hands of Jesus, identified almost from the start as "he who baptizes in Holy Spirit" (1:33). He speaks of himself, oddly, in the third person ("who *it is* who says to you, . . . you would have asked *him*, . . . *he* would have given you"), just as when he refers to himself as "the Son of Man," or "the Son." His answer clothes him in mystery, challenging the woman's assumption that she knows who he is ("you, a Jew," v. 9). At the same time, he gives her a metaphor for "the gift of God" appropriate to the setting: "living water," a term referring to fresh running water, like that from Jacob's spring, in contrast to stagnant water from a cistern.[44]

11 The woman answers with a little more respect, addressing Jesus as "Sir" *(kyrie)*, but adding, "you have no bucket and the well is deep. From where, then, do you have this living water?" She is the first person in the Gospel to address Jesus with this title, but because she is not (yet) a disciple, *kyrie* has to mean "Sir" here and not "Lord."[45] Yet to the reader it echoes the Gospel writer's introduction of Jesus into the present narrative as "the Lord"

---

42. Moloney (117) makes these two things "the basis for the entire discussion between Jesus and the woman. The first part of the discussion will concentrate on the living water, the gift of God (vv. 10-15 . . .), and the second will be concerned with who it is who is speaking (vv. 16-30 . . .)."

43. In each of these instances, the same word for "gift" (ἡ δωρεά) is used.

44. Gr. ὕδωρ ζῶν (BDAG, 426). See the LXX of Genesis 26:19, Leviticus 14:5, Zechariah 14:8, and a variant reading in Jeremiah 2:13 (A and a corrector of א); also *Didache* 7.1-2.

45. English versions tend to translate it "Sir" when the speaker is not a committed disciple (as here; also vv. 15, 19, 49; 5:7; 6:34; 8:11; 9:36; 11:34; compare 12:21; 20:15), and "Lord" when it is one of the Twelve (6:68; 11:3, 12; 13:6, 9, 25, 36, 37; 14:5, 8, 22; 21:15, 16, 17, 20, 21), or Mary or Martha (11:21, 27, 32, 39), or the man born blind on coming to faith (9:38). But the distinction is very arbitrary, as one can easily see by comparing the former blind man's words in 9:36 and 38, or by comparing Mary and Martha's words (11:32, 39) with those of "the Jews" (11:34). It is unlikely that the term is ever addressed to Jesus without at least a hint of allegiance (above all, see 13:13; 20:28).

(*ho kyrios,* v. 1). The woman's remark confirms that she knows nothing of "the gift of God," nor of Jesus's identity. Only his last two words, "living water," register with her, and she has no idea "from where" *(pothen)* such water might come. She, not Jesus, has a bucket to draw water from the well, and if the "living water" he has in mind is not from the well, where does it come from? Does he still want a drink from her, or does he have water of his own? The woman is like the banquet master at Cana, who did not know "where" *(pothen)* the wine at the wedding came from (2:9), or Nicodemus, who did not know "where" *(pothen)* the wind came from or was going (3:8). The implied answer to her question can only be "from above" (as in 3:3, 7 and 31). She thinks first of the depths of the well ("the well is deep"), but Jesus has water from quite another direction.

12 Inevitably, her question about "the living water" leads to a question about Jesus' identity: "Are you greater than our father Jacob, who gave us the well and drank from it himself, with his sons and his livestock?" In mentioning "our" father Jacob who gave "us" the well, she speaks as a Samaritan. The well is a Samaritan artifact and holy place,[46] linking the Samaritans to the patriarchs and the biblical narrative. Later, in Jerusalem, "the Jews" will ask Jesus a similar rhetorical question: "Are you greater than our father Abraham?" (8:53). The reader is expected to understand that he is in fact greater than both. The woman's comment about the well cannot be verified from the biblical text (that is, from Gen 48:22), but expands on the Gospel writer's introductory setting of the scene (v. 5). If "the field Jacob gave to Joseph his son" included the well (vv. 5-6), then Jacob's well, no less than his field, was Jacob's gift to Joseph, and consequently to the Samaritans, who considered themselves Joseph's descendants.[47] If Jacob "drank from it himself, with his sons and his livestock," it must be a water source of great abundance. The merits of the well become for the woman a matter of ethnic pride. What water source could be greater or more satisfying than that which "our father Jacob" left for his Samaritan children? Her remark reminds us, however subtly, that in contrast to Jacob and his sons, Jesus has *not* drunk from the well. His thirst remains unquenched (see 19:28).[48]

---

46. The woman's word for the well is φρέαρ (translated here as "well"), in contrast to the Gospel writer's πηγή (translated as "spring"). The most plausible distinction is that the latter refers to a natural water source and the former to something dug or constructed by human beings (see above, n. 21). Possibly this is why she can say that Jacob (and not God) "gave us the well."

47. So Josephus, *Antiquities* 11.341: "tracing their line back to Ephraim and Manasseh, the descendants of Joseph" (LCL, 6.479).

48. According to Stephen D. Moore (in *The Interpretation of John,* 2d ed., ed. John Ashton; Edinburgh: T&T Clark, 1997), 280: "What Jesus longs for from this woman, even more than delicious spring water, is that *she* long for the living water that *he*

13-14 For the first time Jesus explains that the "living water" he has in mind is not from Jacob's spring. "This water" (v. 13) is not the same as the water that "I will give." "This water," like any other, quenches thirst temporarily; the water Jesus gives quenches thirst forever. He tells her that "whoever drinks of the water that I will give him will never ever thirst. Instead, the water I will give him will become in him a spring of water rushing to eternal life" (v. 14). His extraordinary promise redefines both water and thirst. The point is not that he offers some magic water that quenches *physical* thirst forever (as the woman is quick to assume, v. 15), but that he offers a different kind of water to quench forever a different kind of thirst. His words make clear to the reader, if not to the woman, that the phrase with which he concluded his last speech, "living water" (v. 10b), was a metaphor. It is a very odd metaphor, in that only when it is taken *literally* (that is, as "living" rather than simply "running" water), does it disclose the reality to which it is pointing. If Jesus' last two words before were "living water" (v. 10), his last two words now are "eternal life" (v. 14). "Living" water means "life-giving" water. Just as in the dialogue with Nicodemus, "eternal life" is the burden of Jesus' message (3:15, 16).

The other notable feature of this pronouncement is the emphatic "I" (*egō*, v. 14), which Jesus adopts now for the first time in the Gospel.[49] First he had spoken of "the gift of God," then of himself indirectly in the third person and what "he would have given" (v. 10); then the woman told how Jacob "gave us the well" (v. 12). Now, finally, Jesus begins his formal self-revelation, identifying himself plainly as the sovereign Giver of life: "whoever drinks of the water that *I* will give him will never ever thirst. Instead, the water I will give him will become in him a spring of water, rushing to eternal life." The promise, however, is generalized, and not addressed (like v. 10) to the Samaritan woman in particular.[50] Hence the male-sounding pronoun "him" repeated three times: "give *him* . . . give *him* . . . in *him*."[51] While the

---

longs to give *her*. Jesus thirsts to arouse *her* thirst. His desire is to arouse her desire, to be himself desired. . . . His desire is to fill up *her* lack." This thought, while very appealing (compare Augustine's comment above, n. 36), draws too heavily on the image of Jesus as bridegroom, and goes beyond what the reader is able to conclude at this point from the narrative. The real nature of Jesus' thirst emerges only in the passion, at 19:28.

49. The emphatic ἐγώ occurs with δώσω in all manuscripts in the first clause of verse 14, but only in some manuscripts (ℵ, D, N, and others) in the last clause ("the water I will give him will become in him a spring"). Probably the omission was original, for the emphatic ἐγώ would have been understood in any case.

50. The same was true in the case of Nicodemus, where the necessity of rebirth was held out to "someone" (τις, 3:3 and 5), or to "you people" (ὑμᾶς, 3:7), not just to Nicodemus personally.

51. Gr. αὐτῷ . . . αὐτῷ . . . ἐν αὐτῷ.

pronoun is generic and by no means excludes the woman, it does move the center of attention away from her and the scene at the well, as if to say to the reader, male or female, "This means you. This is *not* a story about a bridegroom meeting his bride at a well. It is a promise of eternal life for you, whoever and wherever you may be."[52] The "spring of water" is no longer Jacob's spring at Sychar. It is a spring within the believer, "rushing to eternal life." The spring is not itself "eternal life," but rather "the gift of God" (v. 10), the Spirit, an identification made explicit later (7:39). Jesus is simply promising to do what John said he would do: baptize in Holy Spirit (1:33). Just as in the encounter with Nicodemus (3:5), "water and Spirit" amount to much the same thing, and together guarantee a person "eternal life" (see 3:15, 16). "Rushing" *(allomenou)* confirms that the "spring" Jesus has in mind is the Spirit. This verb is used twice in the book of Acts (3:8; 14:10) of human beings leaping or jumping to prove that they are healed of their lameness, but only here of water as from a spring. Its closest parallels are in the LXX, where the same verb describes "the Spirit of the Lord" or "the Spirit of God" in action, "rushing" on Samson (Jdg 14:6, 19; 15:14, LXX) or on Samuel (1 Kgs 10:10, LXX; compare 10:6; 11:6; 16:13).[53] "Rushing" also suggests abundance, a continuing, self-replenishing supply of good fresh water that never runs dry (compare 1 Sam 10:10).

"Eternal life" is future here. The phrase "to [or for] eternal life" (as in 4:36; 6:27; 12:25) signals its futurity.[54] But "future" does not mean "after death." Death does not even enter into the equation for those who have "eternal life" (see 5:24; 6:50; 8:51; 11:25-26). Rather, "eternal life" belongs to the immediate future, so immediate that Jesus can speak of it as something the believer already "has" (3:36; 5:24; 6:47, 54). It is tempting to play down, as some have, the futurity of "eternal life," emphasizing that what Jesus promised was not simply never-ending life but new life, a qualitatively different kind of life. Sometimes the question is asked, "Who would even want to go on living forever and ever?" The answer, I suspect, is quite a few of us,[55] but the question misses the point. *Of course* the life Jesus offers the Samaritan woman is a new, qualitatively different kind of life — but *not* because of the adjective "eternal" attached to it. "Life" in the Gospel of John is, by definition, not the

---

52. This is the proper response to Sandra Schneiders, "A Case Study: A Feminist Interpretation of John 4:1-42" (in *The Interpretation of John,* 2d ed., 240), who objects to translating the masculine pronoun into English as "him." Her point is well taken as far as standard English translations are concerned, but in a translation accompanying a commentary it is important to reflect such specific features of text as masculine pronouns.

53. See Abbott, *Johannine Grammar,* 243-44.

54. The same is true of the purpose clauses in 3:15 and 16, 6:40, and 17:2.

55. See John Updike, *Self-Consciousness: Memoirs* (New York: Knopf, 1989), 212-57.

physical life that God created through the Word, but the divine life that was "in him" (1:4) from the beginning, part and parcel of his own being. There is no "life" mentioned anywhere in the Gospel which is *not* by implication "eternal."[56] But when the adjective is explicitly added, it does serve to accent the "endless" or "never-ending" character of divine life. Here it reinforces the point that whoever "drinks of the water that I will give him will *never ever* thirst" (my italics), just as Jesus' sheep "will *never ever* be lost" (10:28), and those who believe in him will "*never ever* die" (11:26; compare 8:51-52). To the Gospel writer, "eternal life" is a redundant expression, but he is willing to risk a little redundancy to make the point that salvation is forever.

While the parallels with Jesus' conversation with Nicodemus are conspicuous, there is one major difference. Instead of telling the Samaritan woman again and again what is "impossible" (as with Nicodemus in 3:3, 5, and 12), he freely offers the Spirit and eternal life to whoever "drinks of the water that *I* will give him." For the first time, he speaks openly as God's messenger, offering salvation to this woman and to all who hear or read his words.

15 The woman is not put off by all the masculine pronouns (see n. 52). "Sir, give me this water," she replies, just as Jesus had told her she should have done already (v. 10). Yet she still does not understand "the gift of God." In asking for "this water," she wants the "living water" Jesus has just promised (v. 14), but her actual words echo instead his reference to drinking "this water" only to get thirsty again (v. 13). Her choice of words betrays the fact that she is still thinking of physical water, not from Jacob's spring perhaps, but physical nonetheless. Drinking water guaranteed every day, "so that I will not thirst and have to keep coming back here to draw" (compare 6:34, "Sir, give us this bread always"). It is difficult to imagine what kind of literal arrangement she might have had in mind. The writer presents her comment as something faintly ridiculous, like the notion of building a temple in three days, or entering one's mother's womb a second time. Like the Jews at Jerusalem (2:20), or like Nicodemus (3:4), or even Jesus' own disciples (see v. 33), she has not learned to recognize his metaphors. She understands now that she, not Jesus, is the one in need, but she does not yet understand the true nature of either her own "thirst," or the "living water" that will quench it.

16 Jesus respects the woman's recognition of her need, and responds to her as to a potential believer: "Go call your husband. Then come back here." Any notion that this is literally a story about a bridegroom and a

---

56. See 1 John 5:11-12, "And this is the testimony, that God has given us eternal life, and this life is in his Son. Whoever has the Son has life, and whoever does not have the Son does not have life." "Eternal life" and "life" are used interchangeably in John 3:36, 5:24, 5:39-40, and 6:53-54.

bride now disappears. In such a story the appropriate line would have been "Go call your father," not your husband (see Gen 24:23; 29:12; Exod 2:21). Instead, Jesus takes on the role of missionary, or messenger of God, "bridegroom" to a whole people (compare 3:29). As the model for all Christian missionaries, he wants salvation for families or households, not just individuals (see 4:53, "he and his whole family").[57] Therefore he says, "Go call your husband."[58] At the same time, he echoes the woman's own expression, "back here," from the preceding verse: "Then come back here" (*enthade* in both instances). But why is the place, or the water source, still important, even though Jesus has just said that the true "spring of water rushing to eternal life" is not in the ground but within the believer (v. 14)? Does he still have water baptism in mind (see 3:22, 26; 4:1-2), as Christian missionaries do in the book of Acts (16:15, 33; 18:8)? It cannot be ruled out, because the notion of "drinking" the Holy Spirit can stand right alongside that of water baptism (see 1 Cor 12:13). Yet nothing is said of baptism, and in any event Jesus' request quickly becomes moot when we learn not only that the woman has no husband but that Jesus knew it all along! The reader is tempted to conclude, with Bultmann, that the request was "only a means of demonstrating his own omniscience,"[59] but that fails to do justice either to Jesus' missionary strategy or the literary strategies of the Gospel writer. "Go call your husband" is Jesus' way of gaining access to the entire Samaritan community. Because she has no husband, the woman will summon the whole town, and they will come (vv. 28-30), not just "back here" to the spring, but specifically to Jesus (see v. 30, "They were coming . . . to him"), and thus to salvation.

17-18 When the woman says, "I have no husband," Jesus repeats her own words, and heartily endorses her answer: "You have said it well, 'I have no husband,' for you have had five husbands,[60] and the one you have now is not your husband. What you have just said is true."[61] Whether she was

---

57. The book of Acts has several examples (11:14; 16:15, 31-33; 18:8; see also 1 Cor 1:16; 16:15).

58. Chrysostom hints at a similar interpretation: "Christ saith, 'Call thy husband,' showing that he also must share in these things" (*Homilies* 32; NPNF, 1st ser., 14.113).

59. Bultmann, 187.

60. The woman says, "I have no husband" (οὐκ ἔχω ἄνδρα), but Jesus changes the word order (ἄνδρα οὐκ ἔχω), putting "husband" front and center. Then he accents "five husbands" by placing it first as well (see Morris, 234, n. 40).

61. "You have said it well" and "What you have just said is true" frame the whole pronouncement and mean exactly the same thing. "Well" (καλῶς) means "rightly" or "truly," as in 8:48, 13:13, and 18:23. "*Just* said" is an effort to render the demonstrative τοῦτο, "this." Origen's reading of Jesus' words as a "a reproof . . . as though her former statements were not true" (*Commentary on John* 13.53; FC, 89.80) led him to conclude that what the woman said in verses 9, 11, and 12 were lies! (compare Abbott, *Johannine Grammar*, 9-10). All this from a simple demonstrative pronoun!

in fact consciously telling the truth, or whether "I have no husband" was, as Lindars puts it, "a white lie,"[62] is another question. If she was lying, her lie adds a definite note of irony to Jesus' commendation of her for telling the truth! The "five husbands" have lent themselves persistently to an allegorical interpretation, as the supposed five false gods of the five foreign tribes that the Assyrians brought into Samaria after destroying Israel's northern kingdom (see 2 Kgs 17:24-32 and Josephus, *Antiquities* 9.288).[63] This interpretation reduces the woman to a mere symbol or representative of "Samaria," whose present illegitimate lover is the God of Israel (see v. 22, "You people worship what you do not know")! For some feminist interpreters, it may help avoid the distasteful notion that Jesus was exposing an immoral woman's past, but it flounders on the stubborn fact that the woman herself heard Jesus' words as a comment on her personal history, not on the history of her people (vv. 29, 39).[64] And her references to "our father Jacob" (v. 12), and later to "our fathers" who "worshiped on this mountain" (v. 20), give clear evidence that she knew the difference.[65]

This does *not* mean that Jesus' words made her feel guilty, or even that he intended them to.[66] She is not so much convicted of sin as merely amazed at his knowledge of her past and present. In this respect, she is like Nathanael, whom Jesus identified as a "true Israelite" and said he had seen

---

62. Lindars, 185: "The reason could be that she wants to get the water without going all the way back to Sychar first."

63. According to 2 Kings 17:24, the tribes were "from Babylon, Cuthah, Avva, Hamath, and Sepharvaim" (NRSV), but according to 17:29-32 there were *seven* gods in all, because two of the tribes, the Avvites and the Sepharvites, had two gods each. According to Josephus, "each of their tribes — there were five — brought along its own god" (LCL, 6.153). The interpretation, therefore, depends on Josephus, and has been traced to a thirteenth-century marginal notation citing John 4:18 in a manuscript of Josephus (see W. F. Howard, *The Fourth Gospel in Recent Criticism,* 183). But as Morris cautions (235), not even Josephus explicitly states that there were just five gods.

64. See Schneiders, "A Case Study," 235-60, a curious combination of a literal and a representative (or symbolic) understanding of the Samaritan woman. The weakness of her approach is evident in her paraphrase of v. 29: "Come and see a man who told me [that is, us] all I [that is, we] have ever done!" (249).

65. A. S. Peake (quoted in Howard, 183) summed up concisely the arguments against the allegorical approach: "It is a pity for this interpretation that these gods were seven and not five; that they were worshipped simultaneously and not successively; and it is hardly likely that idolatry should be represented as marriage, when its usual symbol is adultery, or that the author should have represented Yahweh under so offensive a figure." So too Bultmann, 188; Beasley-Murray, 61.

66. The text neither mentions divorce nor specifies how it came about that she had five husbands. The Gospels tell of at least one case in which a woman had *seven* husbands without ever being divorced or judged immoral (Mk 12:18-23 and par.).

"under the fig tree" before they met (1:48). Yet the reader will also remember that sometimes Jesus' supernatural knowledge does carry intimations of judgment, as in the reminder that "He had no need for anyone to tell him about any person, for he himself knew what was in the person" (2:25). Such intimations can be found here, but they do not add up to a picture of the sovereign Lord either condemning or forgiving a poor, helpless sinner. She is *not* one of the prostitutes or sinful women with whom we see Jesus dealing on some occasions (Lk 7:36-50; Jn 8:1-11). She is made of sterner stuff. While his exposure of her five husbands and her present lover does not reflect well on her character, it is still just part of the repartee, the lively give-and-take that has gone on for nine verses now between "you, a Jew" and "me, a Samaritan woman" (v. 9). Jesus the "Jew" has gained the upper hand, but she is by no means ready to plead, "Lord, be merciful to me, a sinner," nor does Jesus ask her to. She has proved herself a worthy debate partner, and the debate continues.

19-20 Jesus has scored a major point, and the woman acknowledges this by addressing him no longer simply as "a Jew" (v. 9) but as "a prophet" (compare 9:17).[67] Her recognition of him as "prophet" is preliminary, however, to a question she directs to him as a Jew: "Our fathers worshiped on this mountain, and yet you people[68] say that the place where one must worship is in Jerusalem." Prophet he may be, but Jesus is still "a Jew," and she "a Samaritan woman" (v. 9). It is a mistake to read too much into her expression, "I can see." This verb for "see" *(theōrein)* is quite common in John's Gospel (24 occurrences), but it does not necessarily imply deep theological insight. More likely, it is used here as part of the woman's rhetorical strategy to frame a question to a supposed "expert" about the proper place to worship God. Should it be "on this mountain" (which was probably within view), or "in Jerusalem"? Who is right, Jew or Samaritan? As a Samaritan, she waits to hear whether Jesus will speak as just another partisan Jew, or as a true "prophet" whose words she can take seriously. Just as Paul was not fully convinced of the true religiosity of the Athenians when he said, "I can see [*theōrō*] how religious you are in every way" (Acts 17:22),[69] so the woman is not fully con-

---

67. For any readers acquainted with Luke there is irony here, given the Pharisees' claim in Luke about the woman who anointed Jesus: "If this man were a prophet, he would have known what kind of woman this is, that she is a sinner" (Lk 7:39). Here Jesus as prophet knows "what kind of woman" this woman of Samaria is, yet he continues to deal with her as a legitimate dialogue partner.

68. "You people" is simply the plural ὑμεῖς; the NIV makes it explicitly "you Jews."

69. The parallel is not exact because Paul's comment was based on certain "objects of worship" that he had literally seen (ἀναθεωρῶν, v. 23), while the woman's comment is a conclusion drawn from what Jesus has just said.

vinced that Jesus is actually a "prophet" whom the Samaritans can accept. Her question is meant to test him.

"This mountain," to the woman, was Mount Gerizim (Deut 27:4-8), based on the Samaritan version of the Hebrew Bible (known as the Samaritan Pentateuch; the Hebrew text has "Mount Ebal").[70] The woman's expression "our fathers" (in contrast to "you people") suggests that in her eyes this history belonged to the Samaritans and not to the Jews.[71] According to Josephus (*Antiquities* 11.321-24), Alexander the Great gave the Samaritans permission to build a temple there, and the names of the builders (Sanbelletes and Manasses; see *Antiquities* 11.302) correspond rather closely to the names of the defectors from Nehemiah's Jerusalem over a hundred years earlier according to the biblical account (see Neh 13:28). Little is known of that temple except that the Jewish ruler John Hyrcanus destroyed it two hundred years after Alexander, around 128 B.C. (*Antiquities* 13.255-56). It was not standing in Jesus' time, therefore, or at the time John's Gospel was written. As far as we know, there was only a "place" (see v. 20), not an existing temple on Mount Gerizim. Jerusalem was also on a mountain (Heb 12:22; Rev 21:10), with an actual temple (2:20) as its "place" of worship (11:48). Jerusalem was where the Jews, and even "some Greeks," came specifically "to worship" at the major Jewish feasts in Jesus' time (12:20). Jesus has already claimed the Jerusalem temple as "my Father's house" (2:16), and it will be the scene of his ministry through much of the Gospel (see 5:14; 7:14; 8:20, 59; 10:23; 18:20). His answer, therefore, is inevitable. He will speak as "a prophet," but a distinctly Jewish prophet.

21 At first Jesus sounds like a prophet who stands above all partisan bickering. "Believe me, woman, that an hour is coming when neither on this mountain nor in Jerusalem will you worship the Father" (v. 21). "Believe me" is an expression solemnly attesting the truth of what one is about to say, more or less equivalent to "Amen, amen" (1:51; 3:3, 5, 11), but here the reader of the Gospel will see overtones of an outright invitation to "believe" in Jesus, as his disciples had done (1:50; 2:11), and as the Samaritan villagers would shortly do (vv. 39, 41).[72] Never is the woman explicitly said to "believe," but her subsequent actions (vv. 28-29) strongly suggest that she did.

---

70. According to Deuteronomy 11:29, Gerizim had been a place of blessing and Ebal a place of cursing, suggesting to some interpreters that "Mount Gerizim" (with the Samaritan Pentateuch) may have been the correct reading in Deuteronomy 27:4.

71. Tom Thatcher, *The Riddles of Jesus in John*, 220, reads the "our" as including both Samaritans and Jews, but the precedent of verse 12 ("*our* father Jacob, who gave *us* the well") makes this unlikely.

72. The closest parallel within John's Gospel is 14:11, where Jesus tells those who are already his disciples, "Believe me [πιστεύετέ μοι], that I am in the Father and the Father in me, or if not, then believe because of the works themselves."

Here she has already called him "prophet" because he knew her past (v. 19), and as prophets like to do, he now speaks of the future. It is the second time he has told a "woman" *(gynai)* about a coming "hour" (compare 2:4). This time the "hour" is not a decisive moment in his own life that has "not yet" come, but a whole new era in which existing religious divisions will be broken down.[73] Jesus promises the woman a future in which "neither on this mountain nor in Jerusalem will you worship the Father" (v. 21).

Two things are noteworthy about his promise. First, "you will worship" is plural, referring to the Samaritans, and echoing the woman's distinction between "we" and "you" (v. 20). Second, in this promised future the Samaritans will worship "the Father." For Jesus to call God "the Father" in speaking to a non-Jew is startling. To the woman, "father" is a title belonging either to Jacob (v. 12) or other human ancestors (v. 20), not to God. Barnabas Lindars is surely correct that Jesus' words "should not be taken to mean worship of the universal Father in a non-sectarian (Jewish, Samaritan, or even Christian) way, which would be quite foreign to John's theology, but worship in and through the Father-Son relationship which is made possible by incorporation into the Son."[74] This is the first time in the Gospel that Jesus himself has mentioned "the Father" in this way (with the article but with no possessive pronoun, "my").[75] Significantly, it will become his characteristic designation for God in all his discourses throughout the Gospel (75 instances in all). To call God "the Father" is tantamount to calling himself "the Son,"[76] and to say that the Samaritans "will worship the Father" is to imply that they will do so through Jesus the Son.[77] The Christian reader is supposed to understand this even though the Samaritan woman does not. It is no accident that Jesus begins to speak of "the Father" at about the same time he begins to use the emphatic "I" *(egō)* to refer to himself (see vv. 14, 26). Clearly, the

---

73. See Brown's helpful distinction (1.517-18) between the uses of "hour" with the definite article or possessive pronoun ("the hour," "my hour," "his hour"), and those where "hour" is used indefinitely, as here. The latter, he suggests, "apply the effects of Jesus' hour to those who believe in him" (compare 5:25, 28-29; 16:2, 25, 32).

74. Lindars, 188. In settings where Paul (for example) preaches to Gentiles, God is more likely to be called "the living God" (Acts 14:15), or "the living and true God" (1 Thess 1:9), or "the God who made the world" (Acts 17:24), than "Father." The closest Paul comes to "Father" in preaching to Gentiles is "We are his offspring" (Acts 17:28), but this is meant more in the sense of universal fatherhood as Lindars describes it than like fatherhood in the Gospel of John.

75. The Gospel writer has mentioned "the Father" once (1:18), and John did so in his farewell speech (3:35), but Jesus has referred only to "my Father's house," using the possessive pronoun (2:16).

76. John has already used "the Father" and "the Son" together (3:35), and Jesus will do so again and again as well, beginning in 5:19.

77. See 14:6, "No one comes to the Father except through me."

discussion is moving toward the issue of christology, or specifically "who it is who says to you, 'Give me to drink'" (v. 10).

22 Having said that, Jesus nevertheless takes his stand *within* the religious divisions that still exist: "*You* worship what you do not know. *We* worship what we know, for salvation is from the Jews" (v. 22, italics added). His words now echo even more sharply the woman's distinction between "our fathers" and "you people" (v. 20).[78] Like the woman's rhetorical "I can see" (v. 19), his pronouncement evokes Paul among the Athenians: "So what you worship unknowingly I proclaim to you" (Acts 17:23). Even the noticeably neuter expression, "*what* you do not know," corresponds to Paul's "*what* you worship unknowingly" (italics added). The point is not that John's Gospel presupposes either the Lukan account or the incident to which it refers, but that in a general way Jesus is addressing the Samaritan woman in the same manner in which Jews (and later, Christians) customarily addressed *Gentiles*. This is why the indictment of Samaritan worship sounds so harsh.[79] Jesus' mission is not merely to a particular sect on the margins of Judaism, but to the whole Gentile world. Its conclusion will be that he is "Savior of the world" (v. 42), but on the way to this conclusion it must be shown that Gentiles either worship false gods as idols (see Acts 14:15; 1 Thess 1:9; Rom 1:21-23) or worship the true God in ignorance (as in Acts 17:23). In the case of the Samaritans, only the latter course is possible. They worship the God of Israel, but ignorantly. The Samaritan woman did not know "the gift of God" (v. 10), and now we learn that the Samaritans as a people did not know God. Consequently, Jesus insists, "Salvation is from the Jews." This is the only time in any of the Gospels that Jesus explicitly mentions "the Jews," and in doing so he takes his stand with "the Jews," confirming the woman's first characterization of him (v. 9). He sounds as harshly and narrowly Jewish here as in his encounter in Mark and Matthew with another Gentile woman, when he said, "Let the children be fed first, for it is not good to take the children's bread and give it to the dogs" (Mk 7:27; see also Mt 15:26).[80] Yet there

---

78. Efforts to make "you people" refer to *both* Jews and Samaritans, and "we" to the Christian community (Odeberg, *The Fourth Gospel,* 170-71, citing 3:11 as a parallel) not only ignore the dynamics of the conversation, but violate the immediate context, making it necessary to excise the clause, "for salvation is from the Jews," as a gloss (see n. 80).

79. Lindars calls it "not a contemptuous assertion of Jewish superiority" (188), but it certainly could be read that way.

80. Some scholars, unable to fathom such irony, have assigned either the last clause, "for salvation is from the Jews" (Odeberg, *The Fourth Gospel,* 171), or the whole of verse 22, to a later editor, effectively removing it from the Gospel (see Bultmann, 189, n. 6; Haenchen, *John 1,* 222). Another desperate move was that of Abbott, who assigned verse 22 "to the Samaritan woman as her account of what the Rabbis say" (*Johannine Grammar,* 100; also *Johannine Vocabulary,* 140). Such expedients stumble on the ἀλλά

is a certain irony in his pronouncement as well, given his repeated insistence elsewhere in the Gospel that "the Jews" did not know God either (7:28; 8:19, 55; 15:21; 16:3).

How heavy is the irony? Is Jesus mocking the whole "we"-against-"you" distinction by making himself its harshest spokesman? Probably not, because the last clause, "Salvation is from the Jews," is difficult to read as anything but a straightforward, serious assertion. It is the only instance of the word "salvation" *(sōtēria)* in John's Gospel, just as the Samaritans' confession at the end of Jesus' visit (v. 42) is the only instance of the word "Savior" *(sōtēr)*. If salvation is *from* the Jews, it is *for* the whole world, and if Jesus is Savior of the world, then he too (as the woman was quick to recognize, v. 9) is from the Jews. His words to the woman here are not exclusionary, therefore, but quite the contrary. He offers her the messianic salvation that comes "from the Jews," but without asking her to become a Jew.

23 Having stated as bluntly and starkly as possible the present state of affairs between Jews and Samaritans (v. 22), Jesus nevertheless reiterates his promise for the future, and explains it further: "And yet an hour is coming and now is when the true worshipers will worship the Father in Spirit[81] and truth" (v. 23). In one sense, Jesus is adding nothing to what he said in v. 21 about "worshiping the Father." Worship "in Spirit and truth" *is* worship of "the Father," and worship of "the Father" *is* worship "in Spirit and truth." The two expressions are virtually interchangeable, and to that extent redundant when used together. Despite the present division and the inadequacy of the Samaritan religion, the promise of v. 21 still stands! It is here repeated, and at the same time transformed. Jesus transforms the promise by expanding "an hour is coming" (v. 21) with the added words, "and now is."[82] He also defines the proper place of worship positively rather than negatively, answering the natural question: If "neither on this mountain nor in Jerusalem" (v. 21), then where? "In Spirit and truth" is his answer. Finally, instead of "you [Samaritans] will worship" (v. 21), he now says, "the true worshipers will worship," uniting Jew and Samaritan alike in common worship of "the Father" (that is, through 'the Son').

Both expressions, the shorter "an hour is coming" (v. 21), and the lon-

---

("and yet") of verse 23, and leave verses 21 and 23 standing awkwardly side by side. In favor of the text as it stands, see Schnackenburg, 1.436, Barrett, 237, and the bibliography assembled by Moloney (132). Nor is it plausible, given the text as it stands, to attribute the pronouncement to the Gospel writer as an editorial comment or narrative aside. Clearly, it is part and parcel of Jesus' answer to the woman.

81. In keeping with the personal nature of "Spirit" in this Gospel (see v. 24), I have capitalized it here as in most other places (for example, 1:32-33; 3:5, 6, 8, 34).

82. For the longer form, "an hour is coming and now is," compare 5:25; see also 16:32; 1 John 4:3.

ger one, "an hour is coming and now is" (v. 23), refer to the *same* future. The one is not sooner or more imminent than the other.[83] Both refer to a time present to the Gospel writer and his implied readers, but future to Jesus and the Samaritan woman within the narrative. It is an impending, even imminent future, for it is the goal toward which the narrative itself is moving (see vv. 35-36). It is a time in which the holy places now dividing Jew from Samaritan no longer matter. Just as the woman will not keep coming to Jacob's spring for the water Jesus has in mind (v. 15), so her place of worship will be "neither on this mountain nor in Jerusalem," but "in Spirit and truth." "Spirit and truth," like "grace and truth," are a hendiadys, that is, coordinate grammatically but not coordinate in meaning. Just as "truth" specified what "grace" or gift it was that Jesus possessed and brought into the world (1:14, 17), so "truth" here defines "Spirit" as "true" Spirit, or "Spirit of truth" (see 14:17; 15:26; 16:13; 1 Jn 4:6). Jesus told Nicodemus explicitly of being "born of the Spirit" (3:5, 6, 8), and has told the woman too about the Spirit without using the actual word. Instead he has spoken of "the gift of God," or "living water" (v. 10), or "the water I will give" (v. 14). Now, finally using the word, he identifies "Spirit" with "truth," essentially with the "grace and truth" that "came into being through Jesus Christ" (1:17). "The true worshipers" are those whose character reflects and embodies that "truth."

24 Worship "in Spirit and truth" does not necessarily mean nonliturgical or noninstitutional worship, nor does it favor "inward" individual worship over "outward" corporate worship. Rather, it is worship appropriate to the nature and character of God, and if God's nature is revealed only in "God the One and Only, the One who is right beside the Father" (1:18), then such worship is impossible until "the One and Only" has come. Now that the Revealer is present in the person of Jesus, such worship can and will become a reality. The pronouncement "God is Spirit" (v. 24) is a rare instance in which Jesus actually reveals something about God, and not just that he himself is the Revealer.[84] What he reveals is not new (although it is never explicitly stated in the Hebrew Bible or LXX). To say "God is Spirit" is not so different from saying God is invisible (1:18; 6:46), incorruptible, not to be worshiped in the form of idols or images (Rom 1:22; Acts 17:29), and that God does not live in temples made with human hands (Acts 7:48-49; 17:24). Because he has just implied that Jews know this and Samaritans do not

---

83. This is *not* the case in 5:25, 28-29, where the longer form comes first (v. 25) and refers to a nearer future in which the author and his readers live, while the shorter form (vv. 28-29) refers to a more distant time at the end of the age, when "those who are in the tombs will hear his voice and come out," etc.

84. See Bultmann's classic statement in his *Theology of the New Testament* (2.66): "Thus it turns out in the end that Jesus as the Revealer of God reveals nothing but that he is the Revealer."

(v. 22), Jesus' words at one level sound like a continuation of his polemic in favor of Judaism. Yet it is more, for he is summoning Jew and Samaritan alike to a new kind of worship, and this can only mean through a new Mediator. Small wonder that when the woman replies, her first words will be, "I know that Messiah is coming, who is called Christ" (v. 25).

This new kind of worship is not something Jesus is urging on the woman, as if to say, "This is the way I would like you to worship." It is not an option, but something that "must" occur (*dei,* v. 24) in the near future, just as surely as a Jew at present "must" (v. 20) worship in Jerusalem. A Jew whose worship is centered other than in Jerusalem is defining himself as something other than a Jew, and someone who worships other than "in Spirit and truth" is no "true worshiper." The question for the woman is not "How shall we worship?" but "Who are the true worshipers?" Not the Jews and not the Samaritans, but those who "worship the Father in Spirit and truth." They are "the kind the Father is looking for [*zētei*] to worship him," Jesus adds (v. 23). This pronouncement is crucial,[85] for by now it is self-evident to the reader that only those "born of the Spirit" (3:5, 6, 8) worship "in Spirit and truth." It is Jesus' way of repeating to this woman and the Gentiles what he had already said to Nicodemus and the Jews, that they must (3:7) be "born from above." He is not so much giving advice as stating a divine necessity or inevitability. Yet there is an element of appeal here that was not present in the conversation with Nicodemus. Those who worship "in Spirit and truth" are "the kind the Father is looking for" (v. 23). God *wants* those who are "born from above" (3:3, 7). God *wants* to be their "Father," and God *wants* their worship.[86] Jesus may have implied this to Nicodemus, but he never said it explicitly. As we saw, all he gave Nicodemus was a series of impossibilities. Now he is on a mission in a sense in which he was not before. If "the Father" is actively seeking *(zētei)* "true worshipers" to worship "in Spirit and truth," so too is Jesus "the Son." [87] Without using the imagery of shepherd and sheep, he anticipates here his role as Shepherd, bringing in "other sheep, not of this fold" (10:16), gathering into

---

85. C. K. Barrett comments, "This clause has perhaps as much claim as 20.30f. to be regarded as expressing the purpose of the gospel. Such worshippers are what God seeks in sending his Son into the world" (238).

86. There is admittedly a fine line between ζητεῖν as divine longing (see Mt 18:12; Lk 15:8; 19:10) and as divine requirement or demand (see 8:50; Lk 12:48; 13:6-7; 1 Cor 4:2). See H. Greeven, in *TDNT,* who puts 4:23 in the second category, yet concludes that "the seeking of Jesus is accompanied by and grounded in a claim to what belongs to Him, while on the other side ζητεῖν as requirement does not have the ring of pitiless rigour but rather of patient and hopeful expectation" (2.892).

87. This will become explicit in the next chapter: "Amen, amen, I say to you, the Son can do nothing of himself, but only what he sees the Father doing, for whatever things he does, these the Son does as well" (5:19).

4:1-42 JESUS AND THE SAMARITANS

one the scattered "children of God" (11:52). This he will call a "harvest" (vv. 35-38), and he will bring it to completion in two days (vv. 40, 43). The mission is not an end in itself, but part of God's plan for gaining "true worshipers" and true worship (see v. 34).

In just four verses, Jesus has used the verb "worship" seven times and the noun "worshipers" once. He picks up the verb from the woman's two uses of it in her question to him as "prophet" (v. 20) and repeats it again and again. The verb "worship" *(proskynein)* will occur only twice more in the entire Gospel (9:38; 12:20), and seems ill suited to this exchange because it means to fall down or prostrate oneself, as before a *visible* object of worship (see 9:38).[88] Such a meaning makes more sense in the woman's question (v. 20) than in Jesus' answer (vv. 23-24). While by no means an "oxymoron,"[89] his answer reminds the Samaritan woman that "worship" (in the sense of falling down and prostrating oneself) is a metaphor for a state of the heart. In the prophetic tradition of "Rend your hearts and not your garments" (Joel 2:13), he is saying that "the true worshipers" are known not by their bodily posture (any more than by their place of worship), but by the Spirit's presence among them. Readers are expected to recognize themselves in these "true worshipers," and in so doing see themselves no longer as Jews or Gentiles, but as Christians, a "new race," or "third race" who worship "in a new way."[90] This will mean worshiping God as "the Father" (vv. 21, 23) through Jesus the Son.

25-26 The woman grasps his meaning, at least in part, and pursues the discussion as best she can. Jesus had said, "You people worship what you do not know" (v. 22), and she replies by citing one thing at least that she can say, "I know." She knows that "Messiah is coming, who is called Christ," and that "When he comes, he will tell us all things." She has heard Jesus say (twice), "an hour is coming" (vv. 21, 23), and she hears this as a messianic promise in fulfillment of Samaritan expectations. When she says, "he will tell *us* all things," she still means by "us" the Samaritans in distinction from the Jews. Yet "Messiah" does not seem to have been a term used

---

88. The literal sense of "falling down" or "bowing down" is present in a number of New Testament occurrences of προσκυνεῖν, either with the verb πίπτειν, "to fall," as almost a helping verb (see Mt 2:11; 4:9; 18:26; Acts 10:25; 1 Cor 14:25; Heb 11:21; Rev 5:14; 7:11; 11:16; 19:10; 22:8), or in some other way (Mt 28:9; Mk 15:19; Rev 3:9).

89. This is what H. Greeven calls it (*TDNT*, 6.764), adding that "Proskynesis demands visible majesty before which the worshipper bows" (765).

90. For "new race," see *Epistle to Diognetus* 1; for "third race" see *The Preaching of Peter,* cited in Clement of Alexandria, *Stromateis* 6.5: "For what has reference to the Greeks and Jews is old. But we are Christians, who as a third race worship him in a new way" (see Hennecke-Schneemelcher, *New Testament Apocrypha* [Philadelphia: Westminster, 1964], 2.100).

by the Samaritans, who (at least in the later sources that we have) called their coming Prophet or Teacher rather the *Taheb,* "he who returns," or "he who restores." The Samaritan expectation may have been based on the prophet like Moses expected in some Jewish circles as well, in fulfillment of Deuteronomy 18:15-18.[91] John's Gospel gives evidence of being acquainted with such a tradition,[92] and it comes as no surprise to the reader when Jesus at once lays explicit claim to the title of "Messiah" with the decisive words, "It is I — I who am speaking to you" (v. 26). The reader already knows that Jesus is "the Messiah," or "the Christ" (see 1:41), but what is striking is that he first embraces and owns the title for himself on Samaritan soil in front of a Samaritan woman. Six chapters later, by contrast, "the Jews" in Jerusalem are still trying to determine whether he is making such a claim or not (10:24). As for the woman, she speaks of "Messiah" and "Christ" from a certain distance, borrowing Jewish terminology that is not altogether familiar to her. It is fair to say that she speaks as any Gentile might, not like a Samaritan in particular.[93]

The notion that the Messiah "will tell us all things" is fully in keeping with Jesus' role throughout this Gospel.[94] He is "the Word" who reveals God (1:1), or "God the One and Only" who reveals the Father (1:18). He speaks of both "earthly" and "heavenly" things (3:12), telling what he knows (3:11) and testifying to "what he has seen and what he heard" (3:32). As "the one

---

91. This is to be expected in view of the Samaritans' acceptance of only the Torah as Scripture. The so-called *Taheb* is mentioned in at least one later (fourth-century) Samaritan source (*Memar Markah* 4.12), but what connection (if any) can be made between this figure and the woman's "Messiah" or "Christ" (v. 25) is uncertain (see Moloney, 133-34). Josephus tells of one Samaritan in Jesus' time possibly playing the role of *Taheb* with respect to sacred vessels on Mount Gerizim that were supposed to go back to Moses' time (*Antiquities* 18.85; see LCL, 9.61-62, note *c*), but no specific titles are used.

92. Note the references in this Gospel to "the Prophet" (1:21; 6:14; 7:40, 52); also, for the notion that Moses wrote about Jesus, see 1:45; 5:46.

93. Possibly there is a trace of accommodation to a Jewish stranger in her borrowing of two Jewish titles. The words "who is called Christ" (ὁ λεγόμενος χριστός) are the woman's words, not the Gospel writer's narrative aside. She is clearly not translating "Messiah" into Greek for Jesus' benefit (!), or even for the reader's (as in 1:41). Rather, the expression recalls others in which a person has two names, whether one is a translation of the other or not: "Thomas who is called Didymus" (11:16; 20:24; 21:2), "Simon who is called Peter" (Mt 10:2), "Jesus who is called Justus" (Col 4:11), or "Jesus who is called Christ" (Mt 1:16; 27:17, 22). While she knows that "the Christ" is a title (v. 29), she shows her Gentile orientation here by treating "Christ" and "Messiah" as if they were (interchangeable) proper names.

94. The terminology is also quite in keeping with Jesus' later promises of "the Advocate," or "Spirit of truth" (see, for example, 16:13-15).

4:1-42 JESUS AND THE SAMARITANS

God sent" he "speaks the words of God" (3:34). Carefully avoiding the first-person pronoun, he had identified himself to this woman at first simply as "who it is who says to you, 'Give me to drink'" (v. 10), but then he began to promise water that "*I* will give" (v. 14), and now he embraces gladly the role of Messiah and Revealer: "It is I — I who am speaking to you" (v. 26). For the first time in the Gospel he adopts the formula, "I am" *(egō eimi)* or "It is I," to make known his identity, here as "Messiah" or "Christ" (however the woman may have understood these titles), but elsewhere in the Gospel more broadly as God's agent or messenger.[95] At this point the reader knows better than the woman who Jesus is, and that he will "tell us all things," just as she said, if we only read on.

27 Jesus' disciples have gone unmentioned since v. 8, when we learned that they "had gone into the town to buy provisions."[96] Now they are back, interrupting Jesus' conversation with the woman before she can respond to his abrupt claim that he is "the Messiah" she knows is coming. They are "surprised,"[97] not that he is speaking with a Samaritan (they, after all, had just come from shopping in a Samaritan town), but that he is speaking with a woman. Their reference to "speaking" echoes Jesus' own "I who am *speaking* to you" (v. 26, italics added), accenting the irony that the One "speaking with a woman" is none other than "the Messiah, who is called Christ"! The Gospel writer seems to know that they were surprised even though they said nothing, and takes the liberty of supplying two questions which they might have asked but did not: "What are you looking for?" and "What are you speaking with her about?"[98] The implication is that they wanted to ask these questions but did not dare (compare 16:5,

---

95. For ἐγώ εἰμι by itself, as Jesus' self-revelation, see 6:20; 8:24, 28, 58; 13:19; 18:5, 6, 8. It is also used once by the man born blind, identifying himself as the well-known former beggar in Jerusalem (9:9). In other passages, Jesus uses ἐγώ εἰμι with a variety of images to explain his redemptive work (see 6:35, 47; 8:12; 10:7, 9, 11, 14; 11:25; 14:6; 15:1, 5). Ἐγώ εἰμι by itself, as here, occurs in the LXX (especially in Isaiah) as a formula for God's self-revelation; see Isaiah 43:10; 45:18; 51:12, and for an especially close parallel to Jesus' words to the Samaritan woman here (ἐγώ εἰμι, ὁ λαλῶν σοι), see Isaiah 52:6 (ὅτι ἐγώ εἰμι αὐτὸς ὁ λαλῶν). But the question of whether or not Jesus is claiming to be God in saying "I am," or "It is I," does not come up until 8:58.

96. Schnackenburg (1.424-25) comments that their disappearance and reappearance "need not be considered a piece of stage setting manipulated by the evangelist. Things could have happened that way." Of course, but historicity does not preclude artistry in the telling!

97. "Surprised" (ἐθαύμαζον) can have a mildly negative connotation (see 5:20; 7:15), but need not imply that they took offense (as perhaps in 5:28 and 7:21).

98. Schnackenburg (1.443) may well be right that τί means "what" here (not "why"), just as in the first unspoken question. As he says, "John uses λαλεῖν with the accusative object . . . remarkably often, 30 times in all."

19; 21:12).⁹⁹ The Gospel writer could not have known such a thing without being an eyewitness, and even then the disciples would have had to have voiced the questions, at least to one another (as they will in v. 33).¹⁰⁰ But eyewitness or not, this writer is quite capable of functioning as an omniscient narrator who (like Jesus himself) knows what his characters are thinking and what motivates them (see, for example, 2:24-25; 6:6; 11:51-52; 12:6). Here he assigns significance to questions *not* asked. "What are you speaking with her about?" reinforces yet again the notion of a "speaking" Messiah (v. 26), and "What are you looking for?" recalls Jesus' comment to the woman that "the Father is *looking for*" those who will worship "in Spirit and truth" (v. 23, italics added).¹⁰¹ The answer to the unspoken question is that Jesus is doing the Father's work in "looking for" just such "true worshipers" as this woman (see v. 34, "that I might do the will of the One who sent me and complete his work").

28-29 The woman's actions speak louder than words. She "left her water jar and went into the town and says to the men, 'Come, see a man who told me everything I ever did. Could this be the Christ?'" The point is not that "such a jar would be useless for the type of living water Jesus has interested her in,"¹⁰² for she still has no clear idea of what he meant by "living water." Nor is it her way of finally giving Jesus the drink of water he had asked for (v. 7).¹⁰³ At this point the jar is empty, not full, for, as far as we know, she never drew the water for which she came to the well in the first place. Rather, to anyone who has read other Gospels, the woman's action recalls that of Jesus' first disciples in Mark, in "leaving" their nets to follow him (Mk 1:18; also Mt 4:20, 22). The difference is that Jesus has not called her or sent her on a mission. The initiative is hers.¹⁰⁴ She is in a hurry to get back to town

---

99. So Chrysostom, *Homilies on St. John,* 33.3: "Still in their amazement they did not ask Him the reason, so well were they taught to keep the station of disciples, so much did they fear and reverence Him" (NPNF, 1st ser., 14.117).

100. In a number of instances Jesus' opponents in this Gospel direct their questions to each other rather than to Jesus, but then Jesus directs his answers back at them (see, for example, 6:41-43, 52-53, 60-61; 7:15-16; 8:22-23).

101. Commentators have difficulty with the question, "What are you looking for?" Moloney (134) sees "sexual innuendo" in it, while Brown (1.173) suggests that the disciples thought "perhaps he had asked her for food after they had gone to get some." Some have proposed that this first question was for the woman rather than Jesus (Wesley, *Explanatory Notes,* 233; Bernard, 1.152; Morris, 243; Carson, 227), but important manuscripts (including ℵ and D) close off this option by adding "to him" (αὐτῷ) just before the two questions, and this seems presupposed in any case.

102. See Brown, 1.173.

103. Barrett, 240.

104. See Chrysostom, *Homilies on St. John,* 34.1: "They, when they were called, left their nets; she of her own accord leaves her water pot, and winged by joy performs the

with news of her encounter, and the water jar will only slow her down.[105] In a sense, her mission to the town is an extension of Jesus' own mission, for just as he "left" Judea and "went" into Galilee (v. 3), she now "left" her water jar and "went" into town (v. 28).

She speaks "to the men" of Sychar (v. 28) about "a man" (*anthrōpon*, v. 29) who, she claims, "told me everything I ever did." Why not "to the people," about "a person"? A gender-inclusive translation does not work well here. While the crowd of townspeople may have included both men and women, the wordplay of the text on "the men" and "a man" suggests that the accent is on the men of Sychar. The reader is meant to wonder at this point, "How will 'the men' respond to the testimony of a woman?" (see v. 42). The woman herself seems aware of this dynamic, couching her testimony in the form of a hesitant, though calculated, question, "Could this[106] be the Christ?" — in contrast to Andrew's positive declaration earlier, "We have found the Messiah" (1:41). She speaks not as a theologian, but out of a personal encounter with a man who had told her "everything I ever did." While the exaggeration[107] may have been intended to draw the men to Jesus by appealing to their prurient curiosity about her past, it was also true to her image of a Messiah who, she believed, would "tell us all things" (v. 25). She is no more embarrassed or repentant about her past in front of them than she was with Jesus. Neither shame nor humility nor uncertainty about Jesus' identity keeps her from issuing her invitation. "Come, see," she tells the men of Sychar, just as Philip had told Nathanael (1:46).

30 The men's immediate response was to follow the woman back in the direction from which she had come. She "went into the town" (v. 28), and they promptly "came out of the town" (v. 30). The aorist tenses show that these actions are completed, but the added note that they "were coming to" Jesus (imperfect tense) describes an action in progress. As the scene is about to change, they are en route to Jacob's well. Jesus and his disciples — and the reader — can expect them shortly. To "come to him" implies at least poten-

---

office of Evangelists. And she calls not one or two, as did Andrew and Philip, but having aroused a whole city and people, so brought them to Him" (NPNF, 1st ser., 14.118). This analogy is of course weakened by the fact that John's Gospel tells nothing of the first disciples "leaving" their nets, or anything else.

105. "Water jars" (ὑδρίαι) have been mentioned before (2:6-7), but the woman's jar is obviously much smaller than the six jars at the Cana wedding, and has nothing to do with "purification."

106. The question (with μήτι) expects a negative answer, as if to say, "He isn't the Christ, is he?" See BDF, §427(2). But here the remarkable thing is that she is even raising such a question, so that the effect is not to rule anything out, but on the contrary to introduce a possibility not considered before.

107. As in the Roberta Flack ballad: "Telling my whole life with his words. . . ."

tial allegiance (as with Nathanael, perhaps, in 1:47; see also 1:29; 3:2, 26), and the reader is left to wonder whether or not the allegiance will become actual. Are they in fact (whether they know it or not) "coming to him" for baptism, as the Judeans before them did (see 3:26)? We are not told.

31-33 "Meanwhile" signals the change of scene back to the well, and to Jesus with his disciples. The writer links the two scenes with the use of another imperfect verb: even as the Samaritans "were coming," Jesus' disciples "were asking" him to eat some of the food they had bought in town. "Rabbi, eat" sounds just as abrupt as Jesus' first words to the woman, "Give me to drink" (v. 7). Their request reminds us that Jesus never got his drink of water from the woman, and now we will see him abstaining from food as well. Food, like water, becomes a metaphor, but not one that the disciples understand. "I have food to eat," he replies, "that you don't know about." He continues the emphatic *"I" (egō)* that he had begun to use with the woman (vv. 14 and 26), and it distances him even from his loyal followers. They are as puzzled about Jesus' "food" as the Samaritan woman was about "living water." His reference to what "you [*hymeis,* also emphatic] do not know" excludes them, just as his earlier inference that she did not know "the gift of God" (v. 10), and his comment that she and her people worshiped "what you do not know" (v. 22) had excluded her.[108] Jesus erects for the moment a similar barrier between himself and his disciples, but only in order to teach them — and incidentally, the reader — something of his mission to the world (see vv. 34-38). The disciples immediately prove him right by demonstrating that in fact they do *not* know about the "food" of which he speaks (v. 33). Like the Samaritan woman, they take the metaphor literally, asking, "Has anyone brought him anything to eat?"[109] Their question is addressed not to Jesus but "to each other,"[110] and, like the two unspoken questions earlier (v. 27), seems to have the Samaritan woman in mind.

34 Jesus' explanation of the food metaphor can be read either as a

---

108. Compare also John's words to the delegation from Jerusalem about "One whom you do not know" (ὃν ὑμεῖς οὐκ οἴδατε, 1:26).

109. Like the woman's question to the Samaritan townspeople, this question expects a negative answer, as if to say, "Surely no one has brought him anything to eat?"

110. Again they seem to be afraid to ask him (compare 16:5, 19; 21:12). So Chrysostom, *Homilies on St. John* 34.1: "Why now wonderest thou that the woman, when she heard of 'water,' still imagined mere water to be meant, when even the disciples are in the same case, and as yet suppose nothing spiritual, but are perplexed? though they still show their accustomed modesty and reverence toward their Master, conversing one with the other, but not daring to put any question to Him. And this they do in other places, desiring to ask Him, but not asking" (NPNF, 1st ser., 14.119). Yet as we have seen (above, n. 100), in this Gospel even Jesus' opponents often put their questions to each other rather than Jesus.

simple continuation of his original remark (v. 32), or as a response to what the disciples' have just said (v. 33). Even though their question was not directed at him, he is still the One who "knew what was in the person" (2:25), and consequently what people want to ask before they ask it (see, for example, 6:43, 61; 16:5, 19). So he takes the opportunity to explain what he means by "food" (v. 34), and to add yet another, closely related metaphor, that of the "harvest" (vv. 35-38). "My food," he explains, "is that I might do[111] the will of the One who sent me and complete his work." This is Jesus' first use of the phrase, "the One who sent me" (John had used it in 1:33),[112] or, more specifically, "the will of the One who sent me" (see 5:30; 6:38). Later he will explicitly define "the will of the One who sent me," or of "my Father," as gaining "eternal life" and resurrection for "all those he has given me" (6:39-40). For now this remains unspecified, but he will spell it out shortly in a similar way, as a "harvest," or the gathering of "a crop for eternal life" (v. 36). If "living water" was a metaphor for the Spirit, "food" is a metaphor for obedience, or the fulfillment of a mission. In a very different setting in a different Gospel, Jesus is quoted as saying, "A person shall not live by bread alone, but by every word coming from the mouth of God" (Mt 4:4, citing Deut 8:3).[113] The disciples will soon learn that Jesus' "food" — that is, his "work," in obedience to words coming from God[114] — will in certain ways become theirs as well (see 6:27).

35 Food is the product of a "harvest," which "comes" at a certain time of year, any time between April and June depending on the crop and the rainfall.[115] Six months between sowing and harvest were normal, but "four

---

111. Moloney (142) finds a difference here between the present ποιῶ (supported by ℵ, A, and the majority of later witnesses) and what he calls the future (actually aorist subjunctive) ποιήσω (supported by P66, P75, B, C, D, and others), preferring the former because it points "to the present nature of Jesus' acceptance of the Father's will." But it is difficult to see any real distinction. If, as he says (138), the καί ("and") is epexegetic (that is, if "finishing the work" explains "doing the will"), then both should be aorist, in keeping with the better manuscript evidence. Even if the present is preferred as the more difficult reading (Schnackenburg, 1.447), the meaning is virtually the same.

112. In all, Jesus speaks of "the One who sent me" 18 times in this Gospel, and "the Father who sent me" eight times.

113. See also Wisdom 16.26: ". . . so that your sons, whom you loved, O Lord, might learn that it is not the production of crops that feeds a human being, but that your word preserves those who trust in you."

114. See 5:17, "My Father is working even until now, and I am working." Also, 5:36, "the works [τὰ ἔργα] that the Father has given me that I might complete them." Jesus in his last prayer will report to the Father that he has "completed the work" (τὸ ἔργον τελειώσας) which the Father gave him to do (17:4). There too the context implies that this "work" involves the giving of "eternal life" (17:2-3).

115. See Brown, 1.174; Schnackenburg, 1.449.

months" seems to have been a kind of best-case scenario.[116] In a parable in another Gospel, Jesus made the point that patience is required in waiting for "the harvest" (*ho therismos,* understood as "the kingdom of God"),[117] but that nothing can hold it back when it is ready. When its time comes, immediate action is required (Mk 4:26-29). Here he uses the same image to expand on his comment to the Samaritan woman both that "an hour is coming" (vv. 21, 23), and that it "now is" (v. 23). The "hour" he now calls "the harvest," and it is fair to conclude that this harvest corresponds in some way to the salvation promised in his reference to the Father's search for "true worshipers" to worship "in Spirit and truth" (vv. 23-24).[118] Just as in the Markan parable, Jesus weighs the need for patience over against a call for immediate action, and the call for action wins out. Conventional wisdom dictated a four-month wait,[119] but Jesus announces decisively ("Look, I say to you") that the time for waiting is over: "Lift up your eyes and look at the fields, that they are white for harvest." The reader knows what the disciples do not, that the townspeople are on their way back to the well even as Jesus speaks (v. 30), and that if the disciples look they will see them coming into view. "Look, I say to you," no less than the more characteristic "Amen, amen, I say to you" (1:51; 3:3, 5, 11) introduces a decisive revelation.[120] Jesus is telling his disciples that the "harvest" he has in mind is a harvest of souls, not of grain, and that its time has come. Two chapters later, he himself will "lift up his eyes

---

116. See Bultmann, 196, n. 4.

117. For similar imagery, accenting patience yet insisting that "the Parousia of the Lord is near," see James 5:7-8.

118. In Revelation 14:15 a "harvest" is explicitly called an "hour," but in this instance an hour of judgment and not salvation: "Send your sickle and harvest, for the hour has come to harvest [ἦλθεν ἡ ὥρα θερίσαι], for the harvest [ὁ θερισμός] of the earth is ripe."

119. While it is possible that a four-month span between sowing and harvest had become proverbial, no evidence exists of any actual proverb to that effect. Nor can we infer that Jesus' statement supplies real information as to the time of year his visit to Samaria took place (that is, that it was literally four months before harvest, roughly December or January). As Morris comments (246), "Jesus' request for water points to a time of heat," and "four months before harvest there would have been plenty of surface water." Nor can his comment that the fields were now "white for harvest" be taken literally. Schnackenburg is right: "The text cannot be used a firm pointer for the chronology of Jesus' ministry" (1.449).

120. Compare Paul's "Look, I tell you a mystery" (ἰδοὺ μυστήριον ὑμῖν λέγω, 1 Cor 15:51). At the same time, the contrast between what "you say" (ὑμεῖς λέγετε) and what "I say to you" (λέγω ὑμῖν) superficially evokes the so-called antitheses in Matthew between what "you have heard it said" and what "I say to you" (Mt 5:21-48). But the parallel is illusory because Jesus is dealing here not with authoritative teaching, but merely with a common cliché.

and look," just as he tells his disciples to do now, and will see "that a great crowd was coming toward him" (6:5), just as the Samaritans "were coming to him" now (v. 30). Such a harvest recalls an occasion in two other Gospels where he said, "The harvest is great, but the laborers are few. Pray, therefore, the Lord of the harvest, that he send forth laborers to his harvest" (Mt 9:37-38//Lk 10:2). In Matthew the "harvest" (in a grand mixture of metaphor!) consisted of "sheep not having a shepherd" (Mt 9:36), and the same is true here, except that instead of "the lost sheep of the house of Israel" (Mt 10:6), the "harvest" consists of Samaritans, who were specifically excluded according to Matthew (10:5).

"White for harvest" (or "white unto harvest," KJV) seems to have come into our language as an expression for "ripe" or ready for harvest almost solely on the basis of this text.[121] No clear evidence exists that "white" *(leukai)* commonly had this meaning in ancient Greek.[122] Yet "white" is evocative. The analogy between white fields and the white hair of old age suggests ripeness or maturity (see Dan 7:9; Rev 1:14; Hermas, *Vision* 1.2.2; 2.4.1; 3.10.2-5),[123] and it is more than possible that white's usual connotations of purity or redemption are in play as well.[124]

36 "Already" aptly sums up the message of the preceding verse, so aptly that some interpreters want to place it at the end of that verse instead of the beginning of this one (that is, "white for harvest *already*").[125] But this ad-

---

121. Chrysostom commented, "For as the ears of corn, when they have become white, and are ready for reaping, so these, He saith, are prepared and fitted for salvation." *Homilies on St. John* 34.2 (NPNF, 1st ser., 14.119).

122. J. J. Wetstein (*Novum Testamentum Graece* [Amsterdam, 1751], 1.865) listed four parallels, the closest being Ovid, *Fasti* 5.357, "An quia maturis albescit messis aristis."

123. The third-century *Acts of Thomas* 147 adopts the language of this passage to speak of old age: "The field is become white and the harvest is at hand, that I may receive my reward. My garment that grows old . . . I have worn out, and the laborious toil that leads to rest I have accomplished. I have kept the first watch and the second and the third, that I may behold thy face and worship thy holy radiance." Hennecke-Schneemelcher, *New Testament Apocrypha* (Philadelphia: Westminster, 1964), 2.520.

124. In the Revelation, John sees "a great crowd whom no one can number, from every nation and tribe and people and tongue, standing before the throne and before the Lamb, wearing *white robes* and with palm branches in their hands" (Rev 7:9, my italics), and later "a *white cloud* and someone like a son of man" seated on it, initiating "the harvest of the earth" (Rev 14:14-15; see above, n. 118). Each "white" image is a sequel to a vision of 144,000 (7:1-8; 14:1-5), described in 14:4 as "firstfruits to God and the Lamb." No such symbolism is evident here, however.

125. This reading is reflected in the RSV, NEB, and REB, and in the versification of the Nestle-Aland 27th edition. Compare 1 John 4:3, and see Moloney (144) and Bernard (1.157).

verb normally precedes the verb it modifies, both in John's Gospel and in the New Testament generally.[126] Here it effectively links the metaphor of fields now "white for harvest" to two closely related images, "the harvester" and "the sower." "Harvest" requires a "harvester," which in turn implies a "sower." Together they comprise what looks like a brief parable: "Already the harvester is receiving payment and gathering a crop for eternal life, so that the sower might rejoice together with the harvester." The picture of a harvester "receiving payment" and "gathering a crop," and of the sower and harvester "rejoicing together" is the stuff of which parables are made, but one phrase is out of place: "for eternal life" (compare v. 14). Here the symbolism intrudes into the telling of the story, confirming that the "harvest" is to be a harvest of souls. A "crop for eternal life" is no ordinary crop, just as "a spring of water rushing to eternal life" (v. 14) is no ordinary spring. If Jesus is telling a parable here, he is in the same breath supplying it with an interpretation.[127]

Moreover, the order of clauses is odd. "Receiving payment" precedes "gathering a crop," which could imply that the harvester is paid in advance. Alternatively, if "payment" *(misthon)* were understood as "reward" rather than "payment" or wages, the two clauses could be read as synonymous: the crop itself *is* the reward. The "and" then becomes merely explanatory, in that the harvester gains his reward precisely by "gathering a crop for eternal life."[128] But "payment," in the sense of actual wages, is a regular part of New Testament imagery related to planting, watering, and harvest (see Mt 20:1-16; Lk 10:7; 1 Cor 3:8, 14; 1 Tim 5:18; Jas 5:4), and is likely in the picture here as well.[129] Here it probably "has no special meaning of its own,"[130] except to point to the harvest's completion. While "already" is obviously crucial to Jesus' meaning, the accompanying verbs for "receiving" and "gathering" are present tense, not aorist. The point is that the great "harvest" is under way, not that it is "already" complete. The harvester is overtaking the sower, just as in the imagery of Amos "the one who plows shall overtake the one

---

126. This is the case in 14 other instances in John. Only once (9:27) does it follow the verb (see also 1 Jn 4:3). Of its 61 occurrences throughout the New Testament, I found only eight exceptions, five of them in Luke or the book of Acts. This is the view of most commentators, and is reflected in (among others) the NIV, NRSV, and NAB.

127. So too Lindars: "By specifying *eternal life,* John has dropped the metaphor and provided the application" (196).

128. So Schnackenburg: "The reception of the reward hardly refers here to the metaphor of payment of wages (compare Mt 20:8ff.). The reward is probably the gathering of the harvest itself; the καί, therefore, gives the precise explanation of the reward" (1.450). See also Abbott, *Johannine Grammar,* 227.

129. See Barrett, 241.

130. So Bultmann (197), who calls it "a way of referring to the end of the harvest, for the point of the story depends on the temporal relationship of seed-time and harvest."

who reaps, and the treader of grapes the one who sows the seed" (Am 9:13, NRSV). Given the normal sequence of sowing first and then harvesting, this harvest illustrates the principle that "the last will be first and the first last" (see Mt 20:16),[131] in order that "the sower might rejoice together with the harvester."[132] Here, as in 3:29, "joy" or "rejoicing" marks the completion of an assigned task, this time the joint task of sower and harvester.[133]

37-38 At this point the question resurfaces: Are we dealing with a parable here, or something else? If it is a parable, there is no need to ask, "Who is the harvester, and who the sower?" All we need to know is that "The harvest is at hand; the reaper has overtaken the sower. This is the promised age of fulfillment."[134] If it is allegory, those characters cry out for identification. In an actual harvest, the sower and the harvester could be the same person, or different people. Without making an immediate identification, Jesus draws on a traditional proverb or saying to differentiate the two: "For in this the saying is true that one is the sower and another the harvester." The "saying" *(ho logos)* he has in mind is not a specific text, but a principle expressed in a number of ancient texts, both Jewish and Greek, that the world is not always fair. People do not always get to enjoy the fruit of their labor.[135] But Jesus gives the hard saying a positive twist. It is "true" *(alēthinos),* but not in the way it is customarily understood. "In this" points forward rather than back,[136] introducing Jesus' forthcoming explanation of how or in what sense the saying is "true": "I have sent *you* to harvest that on which *you* have not labored. Others have labored, and *you* have entered into their labor" (v. 38).

---

131. See my article, "Everything That Rises Must Converge: Paul's Word from the Lord," in *To Tell the Mystery: Essays on New Testament Eschatology in Honor of Robert H. Gundry* (Sheffield: JSOT Press, 1994), 182-95, arguing that the imagery of "first and last" points not to reversal but to equity or equality. So too with sower and harvester.

132. Compare 1 Corinthians 3:8, "Now the one who plants and the one who waters are one [ἕν εἰσιν], and each will receive his own payment according to his own labor."

133. For "joy" as a characteristic of a successful harvest, see Psalm 126:5-6 (NRSV): "May those who sow in tears reap with shouts of joy. Those who go out weeping, bearing the seed for sowing, shall come home with shouts of joy, carrying their sheaves" (also Isa 9:2, "as with joy at the harvest").

134. See Barrett (242), who adds, "If, however, John is writing allegorically we must seek a precise meaning for the terms ὁ σπείρων, ὁ θερίζων."

135. Sometimes it is a matter of divine punishment (see Deut 20:6; 28:30; Job 31:8; Mic 6:15), sometimes of human injustice (see Mt 25:24, 26; Lk 19:21-22), other times simply of circumstances, or "the wry injustices of fate" (Lindars, 196). For the latter, as implied here, see Ecclesiastes 6:2 and Philo, *Allegory of the Laws* 3.227 (LCL, 1.454-55).

136. As in John 9:30, 13:35, and probably 15:8 (also 1 John 2:3, 5; 3:16, 24; 4:2, 9, 10, 13). In John 16:30 the phrase points back to what has preceded (in 1 Jn 3:10 and 19, 4:17, and 5:2 it could be read either way).

The Gospel of John

The good news is that the disciples themselves are the harvesters, and therefore beneficiaries, not victims, of the traditional saying. They have "entered into" the labors of "others," and therefore into the "joy" of a good harvest.[137]

The pronouncement still bristles with difficulties. Who are the "others" *(alloi)* into whose labor the disciples have entered? Jesus and the Samaritan woman? John and John's disciples? John and Jesus? God and Jesus? Moses and the prophets? All of the above? And when exactly did Jesus "send" his disciples to carry out this spiritual "harvest"? Because this Gospel (unlike the Synoptics) has no record of any missionary tour by Jesus' disciples during his ministry on earth (contrast Mk 6:6-13; Mt 10:5-16; Lk 9:1-6, 10:1-12), most modern commentators assume that (in Schnackenburg's words), "Jesus places himself mentally in the future when he has already sent out his disciples"[138] (see 17:18; 20:21). On this view, "you" no longer refers to the disciples *within* the narrative, but instead to the readers of the Gospel *outside* the narrative, representing the postresurrection "Johannine community."[139] While it is quite appropriate for readers to apply any and all of Jesus' words to themselves, the exclusion of the actual participants in the story from any chance of making sense of what he said is troubling. A better alternative is to look for instances *within* the preceding narrative in which Jesus "sent" his disciples somewhere. When he stopped to rest by the well, they went into the town to buy food (v. 8), but this hardly qualifies as a mission.[140] More to the point, they were baptizing in Judea just before the visit to Samaria. In one breath the Gospel writer tells us that Jesus "was baptizing" (v. 1) and that his disciples were doing so (v. 2). Evidently they were acting as his agents or representatives. While the verb "send" was not used there, the idea was clearly present. This raises the possibility that sending them "to harvest" is a metaphor for sending them "to baptize," as they had done in Judea.[141] Unlike

---

137. "Entered into" is εἰσεληλύθατε. See Matthew 25:21 and 23: "Well done, good and faithful servant! . . . Enter into [εἴσελθε] the joy of your master."

138. Schnackenburg, 1.452; see also Bultmann, 199-200; Haenchen, *John 1*, 225-26. Brown (1.183) is less certain, but his only alternative is to spring verse 38 loose from its narrative context and read it as an independent saying.

139. In a similar vein, Oscar Cullmann revived a view as old as F. C. Baur, that those "sent" were the apostles Peter and John after the resurrection, who conducted a mission to Samaria (Acts 8:14-25), and that the "others" who preceded them were the Hellenists, led by Philip (Acts 8:13). See "Samaria and the Origins of the Christian Mission," in *The Early Church* (London: SCM, 1956), 185-92. For a critique, see J. A. T. Robinson, "The 'Others' of John 4:38," in *Twelve New Testament Studies* (Naperville, IL: Allenson, 1962), 61-66.

140. Nor does the fact that he was "weary" (κεκοπιακώς) from his journey (v. 6) *in itself* identify him as one who "labored" (κεκοπιάκασιν, v. 38) so that the harvest could take place.

141. See Carson (231), but especially Moloney, who implies (without quite say-

Paul, who claimed that "Christ sent me not to baptize but to proclaim the gospel" (1 Cor 1:17), they are perhaps "sent" specifically to baptize, that is, to reap the harvest of the gospel.[142]

Jesus' pronouncement offers the disciples (and us) an important caution about religious conversion, and perhaps about water baptism in particular. "Conversion" (if there is such a thing in the Gospel of John) is a complex process, not a single event in a moment of time. Those who "come to the Light" are those who already "do the truth," and by their coming they reveal that their works have been "wrought in God" (3:21). A variety of factors have brought them to Jesus, and no one person can claim credit for "converting" them or "winning them to Christ." There are no "soul winners" in this Gospel, only "harvesters," and the harvester must not forget the labor of "others." As for these "others," they remain (and should remain) indefinite. To identify them is to limit them. They are "all of the above," and more — Moses and the prophets, John, Jesus, the woman, even the Samaritans themselves! But salvation is the work of God (see v. 34); to borrow Paul's imagery, one person may plant a seed, another may water the crop, yet neither the one nor the other amount to anything, but only "God, who makes it grow" (1 Cor 3:6-7).

At this point, just as he calls them to the great "harvest," Jesus' disciples seem to disappear. His pronouncement goes unanswered. We will not meet them again (at least not explicitly) until a certain Passover in Galilee, when he will sit with them on a mountain and once again "lift up his eyes and see a great crowd coming toward him" (6:3). Yet it is probably fair to assume that they accompanied him to Galilee (v. 43) and Jerusalem (5:1), even though they are not mentioned. Can we also assume that they stayed two days in Sychar (vv. 40-42) and baptized the Samaritans? This can be posed either as a historical question (Did Jesus' disciples *in fact* baptize during his public ministry? If so, did they baptize Samaritans?), or as a literary question (Does the Gospel writer mean to *imply* that they did so? Is baptism in any way part of the Gospel's story line?). Either question is difficult, but the first is outside the scope of a commentary — at least of this commentary! The second is not. Clearly, Jesus' speech to his disciples about doing God's will and reaping a harvest (vv. 34-38) is calling them to do *something* in relation to the Samaritan townspeople — something about

---

ing so) that the disciples went ahead and baptized the Samaritans: "The baptisms of Jesus and John the Baptist have come to an end (compare 3:24; 4:2). The disciples have emerged, sent ones of Jesus (4:38a), as the only baptizers" (141). But if they are truly "sent ones of Jesus," then their baptisms are his as well. For the notion that Jesus and/or his disciples continued to baptize throughout his ministry, see R. T. France, "Jesus the Baptist?"

142. See also 1 Corinthians 3:6, where Paul is the sower or planter, not one who waters or harvests the crop, and 3:10, where he describes himself as one who lays foundations, not one who builds on foundations.

which the ensuing narrative (vv. 39-42) is noticeably silent. The reticence of this Gospel about baptism — even Jesus' own baptism — suggests that what is not told, yet implied, is that Jesus' disciples did baptize the Samaritans, just as earlier they had baptized many Judeans (v. 2; compare 3:22, 26; 4:1). But because the Gospel writer wants to present Jesus as one who will baptize "in Holy Spirit" (1:33), not in water like John, he avoids the language of baptism, adopting instead that of the "harvest" (vv. 35-38), and of "coming to Jesus" and "believing" in him (vv. 30, 39-41).

39 The scene shifts back to the Samaritan townspeople on their way, with the woman, back to Jacob's well. The notice that "many believed in him" (aorist tense) should perhaps be read as a pluperfect: they *had* "believed in him because of the woman's word testifying that 'He told me everything I ever did.'" While this verse is not normally classed as one of the Gospel's so-called "narrative asides," it is somewhat parenthetical, a belated explanation of why the Samaritans had responded so quickly to the woman's invitation when "They came out of the town, and were coming toward him" (v. 30). They came, we are now told, because they "believed" her word, and to that extent "believed in him" as their "Christ," or Messiah. Other than the disciples themselves (1:50; 2:11, 22), they are the second group explicitly said to have "believed" in Jesus, the first being "many" at the Passover in Jerusalem (2:23).[143] In contrast to those Passover "believers," to whom he "would not entrust himself" (2:24), Jesus does entrust himself (temporarily at least!) to these believing Samaritans (vv. 40-42). As for the Samaritan woman, her invitation to them (v. 29) is now called her testimony, identifying her as a woman of faith by placing her alongside John and Jesus, and all who "speak what we know, and . . . testify to what we have seen" (3:11).

40 The Samaritans' faith explains not only why they were "coming to Jesus" (v. 29), but also, now that they had come, why they asked him "to stay [*meinai*] with them." The reader will recall that when Jesus met his first disciples they had asked him, "Where do you stay?" (1:38), and that "they came, and saw where he was staying, and they stayed with him that day" (1:39). This time he "stayed" *(emeinen)* with the Samaritans at Sychar, not one day but two. In both instances a kind of bonding *(menein,* "to remain" or abide) takes place between Jesus and those who view him as "the Christ," and a community of believers comes into being. While the believing Samaritan community is much larger than the little community of four or five disciples formed at Bethany (1:35-51), we will hear nothing of its subsequent history, for Jesus will soon move on (vv. 43-44).

---

143. The key word here is "explicitly." We can assume that others in Judea who "came to him" (3:26), and were "baptized" (3:22, 26) and made "disciples" (4:1), also "believed," even though that verb is not used.

4:1-42 JESUS AND THE SAMARITANS

41-42 What happened during the two days? All we know is that Jesus taught the Samaritans in person, and consequently that "many more believed because of his word" (v. 41). "Because of his word" stands in contrast to "because of the woman's word" (v. 39). The Samaritans say nothing to Jesus, but are quick to remind the woman of the contrast. "We no longer believe," they tell her, "because of your speech, for we ourselves have heard, and we know that this is truly the Savior of the world" (v. 42). Their comment could be read as a disparagement of the woman, suggesting that her "word" is not as good as the "word" of Jesus. Some interpreters point to the Samaritans' use of the term "speech" *(lalia)* as if it meant simply "idle talk" or "chatter," in contrast to a "word" *(logos)* or "logical discourse."[144] But no such distinction can be maintained. Jesus himself has identified himself as "I who am speaking" *(ho lalōn,* v. 26), and he later uses "my speech" and "my word" almost interchangeably for his self-revelation (8:43).[145] He also equates his disciples' "word" (or *logos*) with his own (15:20), and places those who believe in him on the basis of "their word" on the same level with the original disciples themselves (17:20; compare 20:29). Far from disparaging the woman's testimony, the Samaritans[146] are claiming to have verified it. Even though there is great value in taking things on faith (see v. 50), verification has its place as well (see v. 53). "Come, see," she had told them (v. 29), and they did exactly that. "Could this be the Christ?" she had asked, and now they had their answer: "we ourselves have heard, and we know that this is truly the Savior of the world." The contrast is not between the hesitant or unreliable "word" of the woman and the decisive "word" of Jesus, but between good news and its subsequent verification.[147] Like Jesus himself, the Samaritans could now say, "we speak what we know, and we testify to what we have seen" (3:11). But instead, like the woman (v. 29), they emphasize what they

---

144. So John Calvin, who commented that "the Samaritans appear to boast that they have now a stronger foundation than a woman's tongue, which is, for the most part, light and trivial" (*Calvin's Commentaries,* Volume 7: *The Gospels* [Grand Rapids: AP&A, n.d.], 667). While few modern commentators fully agree, Schnackenburg finds "a note of contempt" here (1.457), and Bultmann characterizes λαλιά as "mere words which in themselves do not contain that to which witness is borne" (201).

145. The verb λαλεῖν, "to speak," is used 49 times in this Gospel to refer to Jesus' own revelatory speech.

146. Those speaking to the woman (v. 42) must be understood as speaking for *all* the Samaritan townspeople, not just the "many more" (v. 41) who believed after Jesus stayed with them. This is signaled by the οὐκέτι ("no longer"), implying that some of them at least had believed first on the basis of the woman's testimony.

147. See Origen on this verse (*Commentary on John* 13.353; FC, 89.144): "For it is impossible for one who is taught by someone who has seen him and who describes him, to have the same experience that occurred, in respect of the intellect, to the one who has seen him. It is better indeed to walk by sight than by faith."

have "heard" from Jesus during the two days, for their test of a Messiah (like hers) was that he would "tell us all things" (v. 25).

We do not, of course, know exactly what Jesus said to the Samaritans during the two days, but we can infer something of his message from what he said to the woman, and from his discourses elsewhere in the Gospel. Whatever it was, it led them to conclude that he was "truly the Savior of the world." The phrase recalls on the one hand Jesus' reminder to the woman that "Salvation is from the Jews" (v. 22), and on the other his earlier pronouncements that "God so loved *the world* that he gave the One and Only Son" (3:16, my italics), and that "God sent his Son into *the world* not to condemn *the world,* but so that *the world might be saved* through him" (3:17; compare 12:47).[148] The universality is hard to miss. The Samaritan community speaks for all Gentiles, acknowledging Jesus as "Savior" not simply of Samaritans in addition to Jews, but of the whole world. While "Savior," or being "saved," is not necessarily limited just to eternal or heavenly salvation (see 11:12; 12:27), the accent on "eternal life" in Jesus' earlier pronouncements (3:14-16) suggests that the Samaritans are looking to Jesus for more than temporary help or deliverance. They are embracing nothing less than the hope of "eternal life." On such a basis they are good candidates for baptism, and Jesus' disciples may well have baptized them, but the Gospel maintains its silence on this issue.

B. JESUS IN GALILEE AGAIN (4:43-54)

> 43 *So after the two days he went out from there into Galilee.* 44 *For Jesus himself testified that a prophet has no honor in his own hometown.* 45 *Now when he came to Galilee, the Galileans received him, having seen all that he did in Jerusalem at the festival, for they too had come to the festival.* 46 *So he came back again to Cana of Galilee, where he made the water wine. And in Capernaum there was a certain royal official whose son was sick.* 47 *When he heard that Jesus had come from Judea to Galilee, he went to him and asked that he might come down and heal his son, for he was about to die.* 48 *So Jesus said to him, "Unless you [people] see signs and wonders, you will never believe."* 49 *The royal official said to him, "Lord, come down before my little child dies!"* 50 *Jesus said to him, "Go, your son lives!" The man believed the word Jesus said to him, and he went.* 51 *Already,*

---

148. 1 John combines the terminology of John 3:16-17 with that of the confessing Samaritans: "And we have seen and we testify that the Father has sent his Son to be Savior of the world" (σωτῆρα τοῦ κόσμου, 1 Jn 4:14).

4:43-54 JESUS IN GALILEE AGAIN

while [still] on his way down, his slaves met him, saying that his child lived. 52 *So he inquired of them the hour at which he got better, and they told him that "Yesterday at the seventh hour the fever left him."* 53 *The father knew then that it was that very hour at which Jesus had said to him, "Your son lives," and he believed, he and his whole family.* 54 *And this Jesus did again as a second sign when he came from Judea to Galilee.*

The long digression (vv. 4-42) is over, and Jesus resumes his journey from Judea "back into Galilee" (v. 43; see v. 3). There he receives a warm reception from Galileans who, like others at Jerusalem (2:23-25) had witnessed what he had done at the Passover festival (v. 45). One concrete example is given: when Jesus returns to Cana, the scene of his first miracle, "a certain royal official" comes to him from Capernaum to ask healing for his son (vv. 46-47). Instead of going there, Jesus abruptly points out the characteristic need people have for verification or visible proof (v. 48), yet when the man persists, he sends him back alone with the assurance, "Go, your son lives!" (v. 50). The official takes him at his word and goes home. Having believed without verification, he is given the verification as his slaves come out to meet him with the news that his son got better at the very moment Jesus spoke those words. Consequently, "he believed, he and his whole family" (v. 53). This the Gospel writer calls Jesus' "second sign" (v. 54; see 2:11)

43-44 In keeping with the notice that he stayed "two days" at Sychar in Samaria (v. 41), we are now told that "after the two days" he left (v. 43). What immediately follows (v. 44) is best understood as an explanation (introduced by *gar,* "For") as to why he limited his visit to just two days. In one sense, no explanation is required because Galilee was his destination from the start (v. 3), and even two days could be regarded as overly generous. But much has happened in Samaria — something Jesus could call a "harvest" (vv. 35-38), with a general acclamation of him as "Savior of the world" (v. 42). Therefore an explanation is needed as to why he decided to move on.

The reason given is that "Jesus himself testified that a prophet has no honor in his hometown" (v. 44).[1] The writer presents this in a narrative aside, as something Jesus himself once "testified," not necessarily at this time, but in his teaching as remembered and recorded by his followers.[2] In

---

1. Gr. ἐν τῇ ἰδίᾳ πατρίδι.
2. Bultmann attributes to the aorist ἐμαρτύρησεν "a pluperfect meaning" (204), referring to something Jesus had said *before* he arrived in Galilee. This may be so but does not have to be. The aorist implies only that it was said prior to the time the author writes the account. Therefore "testified" is appropriate.

fact, sayings to that effect are found in each of the other Gospels: "A prophet is not without honor except in his hometown" (Mt 13:57; Mk 6:4),[3] and "Truly, I say to you that no prophet is acceptable in his hometown" (Lk 4:24).[4] In each instance the saying is found in the setting of a visit of Jesus to his actual hometown (or *patris,* Mt 13:54; Mk 6:1), in Luke explicitly Nazareth (Lk 4:16). Here in John, by contrast, the saying has no apparent connection with Nazareth, even though Jesus is just as clearly a native of Nazareth as in the other Gospels (see Jn 1:45-46). Perhaps for this reason, most interpreters (and some modern versions) understand *patris* as Jesus' "hometown" in the synoptic Gospels, but as his "own country" in John.[5] Consequently they try to identify it either with Galilee, his destination (v. 45), or with Judea, the starting point of his journey (vv. 3, 54). But if Galilee is meant,[6] why does Jesus immediately head for a place where he had "no honor"?[7] The saying sounds more like a reason for avoiding a place than seeking it out. Or was he deliberately looking for a place where he had no honor because he wanted to avoid the spotlight (as perhaps in vv. 1-3)? If so, he must have been disappointed because when he arrived in Galilee, "the Galileans received him" (v. 45). Yet if he meant Judea,[8] why is the pronouncement quoted here instead of at v. 3, when he first left Judea? And even if it belongs back there, it does not fit because his reason for leaving Judea was not that he found no honor there, but that he found so much honor that it was an embarrassment to him (see 3:26; 4:1). No, the saying is introduced as a reason for leaving *Samaria*! And yet Samaria cannot possibly be his "own country," nor Sychar his "hometown," even though his enemies will later denounce him as a "Samaritan" (8:48). The presumption throughout Jesus' encounter with the Samaritan woman has consistently been that

---

3. In Matthew, Jesus adds the words, "and in his household"; in Mark, "and among his relatives and in his household."

4. Similar sayings are widely attested in the ancient world, the best known of which is Philostratus, *Epistle* 44: "Other men regard me as the equal of the gods, and some of them even as a god, but until now my own country [ἡ πατρίς] alone ignores me" (LCL, 2.437). See also Epictetus, *Discourses* 3.16.11; Dio Chrysostom, *Discourses* 47.6.

5. See the NIV; the NRSV uses "own country" here and "hometown" in Luke 4:24 and Mark 6:4, but then, rather inconsistently, "own country" in Matthew 13:57. Bultmann is quite emphatic: "Πατρίς v. 44 of course means 'fatherland' and not 'hometown'" (204). This is by no means self-evident.

6. This is the majority view (see Brown, 1.187; Schnackenburg, 1.462; Carson, 235-36; Haenchen, *John 1,* 234). The appeal is simply to the fact that Jesus is a Galilean according to John's Gospel (see 6:42; 7:41, 52). If his "hometown" is Nazareth, as we know from Luke, then his "own country" must be Galilee.

7. Gr. τιμὴν οὐκ ἔχει.

8. See Origen, *Commentary on John* 13.372 (FC, 89.148); among moderns, Westcott, 170-71.

she is a Samaritan and he a Jew (see vv. 9, 20, 22). Moreover, he did find "honor" in Samaria (v. 42).

The difficulties surrounding every proposed identification of Jesus' "own country" or "hometown" suggests that a precise identification is not the point. The saying, after all, is a generalization. Its subject is not Jesus, but "a prophet," any prophet.[9] Instead of explaining why Jesus was rejected in his actual hometown of Nazareth, the saying simply explains why he kept moving instead of settling down in one place. *Patris* refers to a town or village here, just as in Matthew, Mark, and Luke, but it can be any town or village, not a particular one.

The meaning is that no prophet should stay in one place so long that it becomes his "hometown." In the immediate context it is the Samaritan town of Sychar, but under other circumstances it could have been Bethany, Cana, or Capernaum. The point is simply that Jesus' ministry was an itinerant one.[10] He did not stay in any one place long enough to make it his home. To do so would have been to wear out his welcome and have "no honor" there.[11] The same principle comes to expression in the rules laid down in the second-century *Didache* regarding Christian prophets or missionaries: "Let every apostle who comes to you be received as the Lord, but he shall stay only one day, or if necessary a second as well. But if he stays three days, he is a false prophet" (*Didache* 11.4-5). These instructions belong to what the writer calls

---

9. Bultmann (205) cites Emmanuel Hirsch to the effect that "Jesus leaves Samaria so quickly lest it become a πατρίς for him." Hirsch regards the saying not as an original part of the Gospel, but as a later editor's addition. In his own words: "Der Sinn dieses Zusatzes kann dann bloss sein, die Kürze des Verweilens bei den Samaritern zu begründen. Jesus blieb nicht solange, dass die Samariterstadt seine πατρίς wurde, weil ein Prophet nichts gilt da, wo er eine Heimat hat oder zu habe versucht. Das Wort sieht das Wandern und nicht lange bleiben also dem Propheten gemäss an." *Studien zum vierten Evangelium* (Tübingen: Mohr [Siebeck], 1936), 55.

10. This seems to be the case also in Luke 4:24: "Truly, I say to you that no prophet is acceptable [δέκτος] in his hometown" (compare *Gospel of Thomas* 31 = Papyrus Oxyrhynchus 1.6). If "acceptable" means "acceptable to God," as it does elsewhere (for example, in v. 19), then the point is that no prophet *acceptable to God* stays home; that is, the only true prophet is an itinerant prophet. See also Matthew 8:20 and Luke 9:58: "Foxes have holes, and birds of the air have nests; but the Son of man has nowhere to lay his head." Significantly, perhaps, Luke's version of that saying comes right after Jesus has left a village in Samaria (9:51-56). For fuller discussion, see my article, "The Itinerant Jesus and His Home Town," in *Authenticating the Activities of Jesus* (ed. B. D. Chilton and C. A. Evans; Leiden: Brill, 1999), 177-93.

11. Whether "honor" (τιμή) refers simply to honor from the Samaritans, or honor with God as well is more difficult to say. Within the framework of the proverbial saying it is principally the former, but the uses of "honor" elsewhere in the Gospel (5:23; 8:49; 12:26), as well as the analogy with Luke 4:24, suggest honor with God.

"the ways of the Lord" (*Didache* 11.8), suggesting a basis in Jesus' own practice during his ministry.[12]

None of this is explicit in John's Gospel. Despite Jesus' frequent travels — from Bethany (1:28) to Cana (2:1) to Capernaum (2:12) to Jerusalem (2:13) and Judea (3:22), and back again to Galilee (4:3) by way of Samaria (4:4) — the itinerant nature of his ministry has not been a major theme. If we look at "A prophet has no honor in his own hometown" within the Gospel's literary framework, its background is theological. It echoes what we have known all along — that Jesus "came to what was his own, and his own did not receive him" (1:11). What we now learn is that he does not come as a poor beggar looking for "honor" or "acceptance," or a "home" in this world. In coming into the world, he does not give himself unreservedly to any one place. Rather, he sets his own agenda. Like the Spirit, he knows "where he comes from and where he is going" (3:8; compare 8:14). The first hint of this was at the first Passover in Jerusalem, when "many believed in his name" but the writer intervened to tell us that "Jesus himself did not entrust himself to them, for he himself knew them all" (2:24). Specifically, "he himself knew[13] what was in the person" (2:25). The writer's comment here is similar, except that instead of simply telling us what Jesus "knew" within himself, it cites as evidence something he actually said. In contrast to the Passover scene in Jerusalem, he did "entrust himself" to the Samaritans (v. 40), but what "Jesus himself testified"[14] was that he could do so only temporarily, or he would wear out his welcome. He who comes "from above," or "from heaven" (3:31), has only "encamped among us" (1:14). He cannot make a permanent home anywhere on earth. "Honor" requires that "the Savior of the world" (v. 42) move on to fulfill his mission to the world.[15]

45 The echo of Jesus' first Passover, and of those who "believed in his name" there (2:23), quickly becomes explicit. We now learn that "the Galileans" had been there too and had seen "all that he did in Jerusalem at the festival," that is, the driving of the money changers and their animals from the temple precincts (2:13-22).[16] Consequently, on his return to Galilee, they

---

12. Bultmann (200) mentions *Didache* 11.5 in connection with the "two days" that Jesus spent at Sychar (v. 40), but not in connection with the pronouncement quoted in v. 44. Also, he rather cancels out the proposal with a competing suggestion that Jesus may have limited his visit so as "not to appear too contradictory to the Synoptic tradition, which makes no mention of Jesus' ministry among the Samaritans" (200).

13. Gk. αὐτὸς γὰρ ἐγίνωσκεν.

14. Gk. αὐτὸς γὰρ Ἰησοῦς ἐμαρτύρησεν.

15. For a Lukan equivalent of the same principle, see Luke 4:43, "I must proclaim the gospel of the kingdom of God in the other towns as well, for this is why I was sent."

16. Already in the third century, Origen recognized that it was this and not miracles that they had witnessed in Jerusalem, proving that "the Savior's power is seen no less

4:43-54 JESUS IN GALILEE AGAIN

"received him."[17] The notice should be taken at face value. Most modern interpreters fail to do so, partly because of Jesus' rejection of those earlier "believers" in Jerusalem (2:24-25), and partly because of his skeptical reaction three verses later to the royal official's plea for healing for his son (v. 48).[18] But no such negative reaction is recorded here, no reaction at all in fact, and none should be assumed.[19] As far as the reader can tell, to "receive" Jesus is a good thing. If it does not imply saving faith, it implies hospitality at least, comparable to that of the Samaritans (v. 40), and an atmosphere in which faith can (and for the Samaritans did) grow and flourish. But who were these Galileans who "received him"? Are all Galileans meant? Surely not everyone in Galilee had been in Jerusalem for Passover. Or are they the citizens of one unidentified Galilean town that Jesus passed through on his way back to Cana (v. 46)? We are not told. Perhaps the best way of reading verse 45 is as a sort of heading to the whole narrative of Jesus' encounter with the royal official and the healing of his son. That is, the writer makes the general observation that "the Galileans received him" (v. 45), and then provides us with one specific illustration of this (vv. 46-54), possibly with the implication that further examples could have been given if needed (see 20:30-31; 21:25).

46 Jesus' journey "back again into Galilee" (v. 3) is now complete, as he comes "back again to Cana of Galilee, where he made the water wine." Right on the heels of a reference to what "he did [*epoiēsen*] in Jerusalem at the festival" (v. 45) comes the reminder that he also "made [*epoiēsen*] the water wine" (see 2:11). The writer shifts attention from the temple cleansing to a miracle story (the one miracle so far in the Gospel) in order to set the

---

in these acts than in his power to cause the blind to see, the deaf to hear, and the lame to walk" (*Commentary on John* 13.384; FC, 89.150).

17. Gr. ἐδέξαντο αὐτόν. Contrast the Samaritan village in Luke, where the Samaritans "did not receive him" (οὐκ ἐδέξαντο αὐτόν, Lk 9:53). This is the only use of the verb δέχεσθαι for "receive" or "accept" in John's Gospel, which ordinarily uses λαμβάνειν for "receiving" Jesus (1:12; 5:43; 13:20; compare 3:11, 32-33; 12:48; 17:8).

18. Bultmann (204) states confidently that "the acclaim which Jesus finds in Galilee is not true recognition, just as the faith of the people of Jerusalem (2.23) was not true faith." Morris concurs: "Their very acceptance of him thus was in its way a rejection" (254). Schnackenburg (1.464) goes so far as to call this verse a "derogatory judgment" (!) on the Galileans, a judgment "confirmed by Jesus' words in v. 48." This interpretation, conspicuous by its absence in the ancient commentaries of Origen (*Commentary on John* 13.381-90) and Chrysostom (*Homilies on St. John* 35), begins to surface in Augustine (*Tractates on John* 16.1-3).

19. Moloney sees this, but is not deterred: "Jesus' response to this signs-faith is not recorded in 4:45, but it is implicit. The enthusiasm of the Galileans in v. 45 is based on a limited understanding of Jesus" (160). This is a moderate statement compared to those expressed in the preceding note, especially given Moloney's view that most faith in Jesus in this Gospel (including that of the disciples) is based on limited understanding.

stage for a second miracle. The miracle story that follows (vv. 46-54) has some similarities to two synoptic accounts in which Jesus healed someone's child from a distance: in one instance a Roman centurion (Mt 8:5-13; Lk 7:1-10), and in the other a "Canaanite" or "Greek" woman near Tyre (Mt 15:21-28; Mk 7:24-30). The first of these was set in Capernaum (Mt 8:5; Lk 7:1), and here too we are told that "in Capernaum there was a certain royal official whose son was sick."

The "royal official" is literally a "royal," the adjective being used as a noun.[20] "Royals" were not necessarily the royal family, as in British usage today, but could be servants (military or otherwise) of the "king" *(basileus)*, that is, either of the Roman emperor, or (in this setting) of Herod Antipas, the "tetrarch" or administrator of Galilee.[21] John's "royal official," therefore, is less specific than Matthew and Luke's "centurion." He could be military or civilian, Jew or Gentile. All we know is that he and his ailing son are at Capernaum, and Jesus is at Cana. The distance between them is geographical, not ethnic or cultural. In contrast to the Samaritans (as well as the synoptic centurion and Syro-Phoenician woman), his race and religion are not part of the story.

47 If Jesus were to retrace his earlier steps, he would have "come down" in due course to Capernaum (see 2:11-12),[22] but the royal official cannot count on such an itinerary. Instead he takes the initiative to find Jesus at Cana. The news he heard that Jesus had come "from Judea to Galilee" (compare vv. 3, 54) suggests that he knew Jesus had been in Judea, evidently because he, or other Galileans, had seen Jesus there (v. 45). Yet he is not said to

---

20. Some ancient manuscripts (D, one or two old Latin, and some Bohairic Coptic manuscripts) have a variant reading βασιλίσκος, "petty king," here and in verse 49. Without adopting this variant, Heracleon (as Origen represented him) wrote, "because his kingdom is small and temporal, ... he was called a royal official [βασιλικός], as if he were some petty king [μικρός τις βασιλεύς] appointed over a small kingdom by a universal king" (Origen, *Commentary on John* 13.416; FC, 89.157). The variant may have arisen because of scribes' difficulty with the adjective "royal" being used as a noun, and interpretations like Heracleon's may have made βασιλίσκος seem more plausible (Sanders and Mastin, 155, argue for the variant reading on the ground that "royal official" represented a partial harmonization with Matthew and Luke's "centurion").

21. While Herod was not really a king (see Josephus, *Antiquities* 17.188, for the distinction between "king" and "tetrarch"), he is called βασιλεύς in Matthew 14:9, Mark 6:14, and *Gospel of Peter* 1.2. Josephus frequently uses the plural "royals" (οἱ βασιλικοί) in a military sense to refer to "the royal troops" or "the king's men," whether of a Seleucid king (*War* 1.45), or the various Herods (see, for example, *Life* 400; *Antiquities* 15.289; 17.266, 270, 281).

22. The consistent use of the verb καταβαίνειν ("come down"), as in 2:12 (see vv. 47, 49, 51) reflects a knowledge that Cana was in the hill country and Capernaum on the Sea of Galilee.

have remembered the miracle at Cana, nor would we expect him to, given that only Jesus' disciples and a few servants knew what had happened there. That memory is for the reader alone (v. 46). Nevertheless, knowing that Jesus was there, the royal official "went to him[23] and asked that he might come down and heal his son, for he was about to die." Why did he think Jesus had the power to heal? Had Jesus performed healings in Jerusalem? As we have seen, the text gives no evidence of that. A better answer is that he had acted with authority in Jerusalem (see 2:14-20), and the royal official assumed that his authority extended to physical healing as well. But more to the point, *the reader* knows he has the power to heal simply because of who he is, and will regard the royal official's plea for healing as a normal and expected thing — as normal and expected, say, as a centurion pleading for his ailing servant, or a Gentile woman for her possessed daughter. Because the royal official's request is given in indirect rather than direct discourse, it is difficult to tell whether the information that his son "was about to die" is part of what he actually said to Jesus, or whether it is supplied for the reader's benefit to explain the urgency of his request.[24] Probably the latter, for when he then makes it explicit in direct discourse (v. 49), he seems to be heightening the note of urgency as far as Jesus is concerned.

48 Jesus at first seems to balk at the royal official's request, just as in the case of the Canaanite or Syro-Phoenician woman, and (possibly) the centurion in Matthew.[25] The difference is that he does not do so because of the royal official's race, as in the case of the woman. The likelihood, in fact, is that the royal official is a Jew, for the comment that "Unless you [people] see signs and wonders, you will never believe" is at least as applicable to Jews as to Gentiles (see 1 Cor 1:22). Yet the plural is probably not intended to place the royal official in any ethnic group, Jew or Gentile, Judean or Galilean.[26] Rather, Jesus' skepticism is about human nature and human motiva-

23. Gr. ἀπῆλθεν πρὸς αὐτόν. Some manuscripts (ℵ*, C, families 1 and 13, 33, and 565) have instead ἦλθεν πρὸς αὐτον ("came to him"), corresponding to the actions of Nicodemus (3:2), the Judeans (3:25), and the Samaritans (vv. 30, 40) in "coming to Jesus." There is little difference in meaning. Both imply at least potential allegiance. But "went" (ἀπῆλθεν) is preferable, both on the basis of manuscript evidence and because the story is being told at this point from the perspective of the royal official at Capernaum rather than of Jesus at Cana.

24. The latter is the case in Luke 7:2, "The servant of a certain centurion was ill and about to die" (ἤμελλεν τελευτᾶν).

25. Jesus says to the woman, "Let the children be satisfied first; it is not good to take the children's bread and give it to the dogs" (Mk 7:27; compare Mt 15:26). In Matthew 8:7 it is a question of whether Jesus' words are read as a statement ("I will come and heal him"), or as a skeptical question ("Am I to come and heal him?"). In Luke 7:6 Jesus says nothing, but goes willingly to help the centurion.

26. Abbott (*Johannine Vocabulary*, 50) takes it as a matter of class: "I know the

tion in general, just as it was earlier in Jerusalem (2:25) when "he had no need for anyone to tell him about any person." It is a matter of human characteristics generally, not those of any one group.

These characteristics are not all bad. "Unless you . . . see signs and wonders, you will never believe" is not so much a rebuke or an insult as a simple fact. Near the end of the Gospel, one of Jesus' disciples (Thomas in 20:25) will use exactly the same grammatical structure to say it again and embrace it as his own: "*Unless I see* in his hands the print of the nails, and put my finger into the print of the nails, and put my hand into his side, *I will never believe*" (italics added). Humans want evidence; they want verification, which is not in itself a bad thing. Jesus invited his first disciples to "Come and see" (1:39). Philip invited Nathanael to do the same (1:46), and the Samaritan woman told the Samaritans, "Come, see a man who told me everything I ever did" (4:29). Each time, sight and hearing led to faith. "Signs and wonders,"[27] as distinguished from "signs" in a more general sense for things Jesus did, are visible miracles accompanying and accrediting the ministries of either Jesus himself (Acts 2:22) or his apostles (Acts 2:43; 4:30; 5:12; 6:8; 14:3; 15:12; Rom 15:19; 2 Cor 12:12; Heb 2:4), or of false prophets (Mt 24:34; Mk 13:22; 2 Thess 2:9).[28] "Sign" *(sēmeion)* by itself can also have this meaning on the lips of Jesus' opponents when they demand from him a miracle to accredit or validate what he is doing (as in 2:18; see also 6:30; Mt 12:38; 16:1; Mk 8:11; Lk 11:16). The question here is whether Jesus' relationship with the royal official is adversarial, as in those examples, or something more like his relationship with Thomas. Is Jesus treating him as an enemy, or a potential disciple? If the former, then the royal official proves him wrong almost immediately (v. 50), calling into question the principle that Jesus "knew what was in the person" (2:25). The better course is to recognize the similarity with the Thomas episode. Jesus is not rebuking or rejecting the royal official so much as leading him toward faith, just as in the encounter with Thomas (20:27), and in the Synoptics with the centurion and the Syro-Phoenician woman.[29]

49 Unlike the Syro-Phoenician woman (Mk 7:28), the royal official has no clever answer. All he can do is repeat his plea with renewed urgency: "Lord, come down before my little child dies!" The writer signals the ur-

---

ways of your class, the Herodians, the courtiers, the men of the world." This too limits the application more than it should be limited.

27. Gr. σημεῖα καὶ τέρατα.

28. The phrase seems to go back to Exodus 7:3 (LXX), where God tells Moses that "I will harden Pharaoh's heart, and I will multiply my signs and wonders [τὰ σημεῖά μου καὶ τὰ τέρατα] in the land of Egypt."

29. See Abbott *(Johannine Vocabulary,* 50), who paraphrases, "None of you, as a rule, will believe without seeing signs and wonders! Is it to be so with you also?" and concludes that "It is exclamatory as regards the class but interrogative as regards the individual."

4:43-54 JESUS IN GALILEE AGAIN

gency with a shift from indirect to direct discourse, with the royal official now referring to his "son" (v. 47)[30] affectionately as "my little child,"[31] and addressing Jesus as "Lord" *(kyrie)*. Most English versions, with the Samaritan woman still in mind, render *kyrie* as "Sir" (as in vv. 11, 15, 19). But the two encounters are very different. There is none of the teasing give-and-take of that earlier conversation. The royal official speaks out of desperation. "Lord, come down," in contrast to the Samaritan woman's "Sir, give me this water" (v. 15), has the sound of a genuine prayer (see Isa 64:1). It is a prayer of faith, presupposing that if Jesus "comes down" to Capernaum he can prevent the child's death. In a later incident, the sisters Martha and Mary attribute to Jesus a similar power to prevent their brother's death, and when he fails to arrive in time, they each tell him, "Lord, if you had been here, my brother would not have died" (11:21, 32; see also v. 37). In both accounts, Jesus exceeds faith's expectations — there by raising the brother Lazarus from the dead, here by healing the child from a distance. Together, they frame Jesus' ministry of healing in this Gospel.

50 Instead of "coming down" from Cana to Capernaum with the royal official, Jesus simply tells him, "Go, your son lives!"[32] The repetition of "your son lives" two more times, once in indirect discourse (v. 51) and once verbatim (v. 53) gives it the character of a healing formula. The point, of course, is not that the child still clings to life as by a slender thread, but that he will recover. He is healed. Most English versions translate it idiomatically as a future, "Your son will live" (RSV, NRSV, NIV, NEB, REB, NLT), but if it is future, it is an immediate future. There is value in retaining the present tense of the Greek, for it captures this Gospel's accent on "life" as a present possession. Jesus' power to save physical life becomes here a metaphor for his gift of eternal life (see 3:15, 16, 36; 4:14, 36). "Go" *(poreuou)* means that the royal official should go back to Capernaum, without Jesus, to rejoin his son.[33] So "the man believed the word Jesus said to him, and he went." It is as if he had heard Mary's command to the servants at the Cana wedding, "Do whatever he tells you" (2:5). More specifically, the language parallels the story of the centurion in Matthew and Luke, when the centurion told Jesus, "For I too am a man under authority, having soldiers under him, and I say to this one, 'Go,' and he goes,[34] and to another, 'Come,' and he

---

30. Gr. τὸν υἱόν.
31. Gr. τὸ παιδίον μου.
32. Gr. ὁ υἱός σου ζῇ.
33. See Matthew 8:13, where Jesus tells the centurion "Go [ὕπαγε], as you have believed let it be to you," and Mark 7:29, where he tells the Syro-Phoenician woman, "Go [ὕπαγε], the demon has left your daughter!"
34. Gr. πορεύθητι, καὶ πορεύεται, in agreement with πορεύου and καὶ ἐπορεύετο in the present passage.

comes, and to my slave, 'Do this,' and he does it" (Mt 8:9; also Lk 7:8). The centurion's assumption is that this is how Jesus operates as well. In John's Gospel we see him operating in just that way, and with similar results. Another similarity is that the centurion also told Jesus to "say the word," and his servant would be healed (Mt 8:8; compare Lk 7:7), and here the royal official "believed the word Jesus said to him."[35]

With this, the faith of "the man"[36] becomes explicit. He has seen no signs or wonders, yet he believes. His faith is in Jesus' word, and in that alone. Some commentators conclude from this that it is in some way incomplete, or at least preliminary to the full-blown faith expressed when the healing is verified (v. 53).[37] Yet at the corresponding point in the synoptic story of the centurion Jesus says, "I have not found such faith in Israel" (Mt 8:10; Lk 7:9), and in the story of the Gentile woman, "Great is your faith" (Mt 15:28). While there is no such commendation here, the man's action is an eloquent response to Jesus' remark about "signs and wonders" (v. 48). Perhaps the commendation comes indirectly and belatedly near the end of the Gospel when Jesus says to Thomas, "Because you have seen me, you have believed. Blessed are those who did not see, and believed" (20:29).[38] Like these unnamed beneficiaries of Jesus' last beatitude, the royal official believes without having seen. To this extent his faith, like theirs, surpasses that of Thomas.

Clearly, there are stages of faith here, as elsewhere in the Gospel. For example, Jesus' disciples believed in him at first because he "revealed his glory" in a miracle at Cana (2:11), but only later, "when he rose from the dead," did they "remember" and "believe" his word (v. 22). Our closest precedent is the case of the Samaritans, who first "believed in him because of the woman's word" (v. 39), but later heard Jesus for themselves and "believed because of his word" (vv. 41-42). The contrast there was not between faith and sight, but between a secondhand and a firsthand report. The narrative moved from faith (genuine faith, as far as we can tell) to its subsequent verifi-

---

35. Gr. ἐπίστευσεν . . . τῷ λόγῳ ὃν εἶπεν αὐτῷ. Such examples suggest that while John's account is independent of the Synoptics (see Brown, 1.193; Dodd, *Historical Tradition*, 188-95), they share common language at a number of points. Yet no single pattern of priority emerges. Sometimes the one appears more nearly original, sometimes the other.

36. Perhaps significantly, the "royal official" (βασιλικός, vv. 46, 49) is now simply "the man" (ὁ ἄνθρωπος), and when he learns that his child is healed, he is called "the father" (ὁ πατήρ, v. 53). As Jesus meets his need, his worldly status is stripped away.

37. So Barrett, 248; see also Brown, 1.191, 512-13.

38. Bultmann can be seen wavering between two ways of viewing the royal official's faith: "It does not of course refer to faith in its full sense, for this is not reached until v. 53; but inasmuch as the father believes without seeing (20.29), his faith shows one aspect of true faith, which is then followed by the experience of the miracle" (208).

cation, but at both stages it was a matter of hearing the word, not of seeing anything in particular. Here the movement is from faith to sight: when the royal official took Jesus at his word (v. 50), he exercised genuine faith, verified later by what actually happened (v. 53). This is similar to the presumed situation of the Gospel's readers as well. The royal official is someone with whom they can identify, for their faith in Jesus' word, the word written down in this Gospel, will eventuate in "life" in Jesus' name (20:30-31).

51 Yet another similarity between this story and that of the centurion (in Luke) is that a journey is interrupted. They are quite different journeys, however. In Luke it is Jesus' journey from the gates of Capernaum to the centurion's house: "Already, while Jesus was [still] not far[39] from the house, the centurion sent friends, telling him, 'Lord, don't trouble yourself, for I don't deserve for you to come under my roof'" (Lk 7:6). Here it is the royal official's much longer journey from Cana to his home in Capernaum: "Already, while [still] on his way down,[40] his slaves met him, saying that his child lived." In Luke (as in Matthew) the initiative for the healing to take place at a distance comes from the centurion himself. In John's Gospel, as we have just seen, it comes from Jesus (v. 50).[41] The slaves' good news "that his child lived" is reported in indirect discourse, confirming but not repeating word for word Jesus' pronouncement, "Your son lives" (v. 50).[42] A fondness for synonyms is apparent in the use of "child" *(pais)* as yet a third word for the sick boy, alongside "son" (vv. 47, 50, 53) and "little child" *(paidion,* v. 49).[43] The word of the slaves verifies the word of Jesus, even before the father arrives in Capernaum to see for himself. It was just the opposite among the Samaritans, where Jesus' word verified the woman's testimony (v. 42).

52 What remains to be verified is the exact time of the child's recovery. The man seems to have taken Jesus' assurance, "Your son lives" (v. 50), literally (as our translation has done), not as a promise that he would get

---

39. Gr. ἤδη δὲ αὐτοῦ οὐ μακρὰν ἀπέχοντος.
40. Gr. ἤδη δὲ αὐτοῦ καταβαίνοντος.
41. In this respect, John's story is closer to that of the Canaanite or Syro-Phoenician woman (see Mt 15:28; Mk 7:29). For Jesus to take the initiative is surely in keeping with John's theology, but again priority is difficult to assign.
42. This is the case in the earlier and better manuscripts (including P^{66}, P^{75}, ℵ, A, B, C), but not all. Some manuscripts (including D, K, L, N, 33, 579, 892, 1241) make it direct discourse, with ὁ υἱός σου as in verse 50.
43. See also the varied designations for the royal official himself (n. 30), and the well-known synonyms for "love," "sheep," and "feed" in 21:15-17. Παῖς can also mean "servant," as in the story of the centurion (certainly in Lk 7:7, and probably in Mt 8:6, 8, and 13), but the preceding use of "son" and "little child" demands that it be translated "child" here, in distinction from the royal official's "servants" or "slaves" (οἱ δοῦλοι αὐτοῦ) who came out to meet him.

better but as a declaration that he was healed from that very moment. Consequently the man is curious about the timing. The relevant narratives in one Gospel (Matthew) show a similar interest, but to a lesser extent: the centurion's servant was healed "in that hour" (Mt 8:13), and the Canaanite woman's daughter was healed "from that hour" (Mt 15:28; see also Mt 9:22; 17:18). John's account is much more specific: "he inquired of them the hour at which he got better, and they told him that 'Yesterday at the seventh hour the fever left him.'"[44] Here the account switches back to direct discourse, for the slaves' precise testimony is important to the story. Yet the "seventh hour" (that is, one o'clock in the afternoon)[45] means nothing to the reader because the time of the royal official's encounter with Jesus (vv. 47-50) was not given. All it tells us is that the child's recovery can be linked to a specific moment when "the fever left him." The belated mention of "fever" is the closest the writer comes to indicating the nature of the illness.[46]

53 For the first time the "royal official," or "the man," is called "the father," possibly because we will see him shortly as head of "his whole family." Through him the reader learns the significance of the seventh hour, for it was he who "knew then that it was that very hour at which Jesus had said to him, 'Your son lives.'" The verb "knew" in the aorist tense here suggests that he just now realized this or found it out, and the reader learns it with him. Consequently, "he believed, he and his whole family."[47] His initial faith (v. 50) is confirmed in what sounds like a formal act of conversion or religious commitment. The expression "he and his whole family" corresponds to a number of incidents of conversion in the book of Acts where someone with his or her "family" or "household" (*oikos* or *oikia*) is "saved" (Acts 11:14), or "baptized" (16:15), or "believes," and is "saved" and "baptized" (16:31-33; also 18:8). Here the "whole family" must include the son, the slaves who

---

44. In *b. Berakot* 34b, R. Gamaliel, whose son was ill, sent two scholars to ask R. Chanina to pray for him. He did so, and when he had finished he said, "Go, the fever has left him." They made a note of the exact moment, and when they returned to R. Gamaliel, he said, "You have not been a moment too soon or too late, but so it happened: at that very moment the fever left him and he asked for water to drink." *The Babylonian Talmud: Seder Zera'im* (London: Soncino, 1948), 215-16.

45. So most modern English versions (for example, NRSV, NEB, REB, NLT). The RSV and NIV retain the more literal "seventh hour," but there is no obvious symbolism here in connection with the number seven. As in the case of the "tenth hour" (1:39), the number seems to have been simply part of the story as originally told.

46. While nothing so specific as this is found in the synoptic stories of the centurion or the Syro-Phoenician woman, the story of the centurion in Matthew is immediately followed by an incident in which Peter's mother-in-law is suffering from a fever, and Jesus "touched her hand and the fever left her [ἀφῆκεν αὐτὴν ὁ πυρετός], and she got up and waited on them" (Mt 8:15; also Mk 1:31; Lk 4:39).

47. Gr. ἐπίστευσεν αὐτὸς καὶ ἡ οἰκία αὐτοῦ ὅλη.

met the father on the way to Capernaum (v. 51), and possibly a wife and other children. The verb "believed" is singular, accenting the father's faith (as in v. 50), but the presumption is that the rest of the family followed his example.

What is different from the book of Acts is that no missionary is present to recognize or preside over these "conversions." In Acts it was either Peter (11:14) or Paul (16:15, 31-33; 18:8), but here Jesus has not come down to Capernaum. There is no sojourn here to match the two-day stay with the Samaritans at Sychar (v. 40). The whole point of the story was that the healing took place at a distance, evidently in order to place Jesus at Cana to correspond with the earlier miracle at the wedding (vv. 46, 54). But what about Jesus' disciples? If we can infer that they may have reaped a harvest by baptizing the Samaritans, can we also infer that they did so in Capernaum? Probably not. Filling in gaps is well and good, but as we move further and further from what is explicit, such theories become more problematic. But Jesus is no stranger to Capernaum (2:12). He will get there eventually (6:17), and he has sufficient standing there to teach in its synagogue (6:59). The very existence of this story and the story of the centurion in Matthew and Luke is evidence that someone in Capernaum took due note of the fact that a local dignitary "believed, he and his whole family."

54 The Gospel writer's comment on the incident, "And[48] this Jesus did again as a second sign when he came from Judea to Galilee," accomplishes two things for the narrative. First, it marks the completion of the journey that began when Jesus "left Judea and went back again into Galilee" (v. 3). The journey, long delayed in Samaria (vv. 4-42),[49] has brought him "to Galilee" (vv. 43, 45), and in particular "back again to Cana of Galilee, where he made the water wine" (v. 46). Second, it provides a sequel to the notice given just after that miracle: "This Jesus did in Cana of Galilee as a beginning of the signs, and revealed his glory, and his disciples believed in him" (2:11). The repetition of "again" or "back again" (*palin,* vv. 3, 46) has hinted that a sequel may be coming, and the redundant *palin deuteron* ("again . . . second")[50] now introduces the sequel. A second "sign" presupposes a first, which can only be the "beginning of the signs" mentioned earlier. But several questions remain. What do the two signs have in common that warrants bracketing them? Why was there no such notice when Jesus drove the money changers from the tem-

---

48. The "and" (δέ) is bracketed in the NA[27] text because important witnesses omit it (ℵ, A, D, K, L, and the majority of later manuscripts and versions), but P[66], P[75], and B, among others, include it.

49. The delay is only two or three days (vv. 41, 43), but because of all that happens there, it seems longer to the reader, especially to anyone writing a commentary!

50. See 21:16, where Jesus asked Simon Peter "again a second time" (πάλιν δεύτερον) if he loved him (compare πάλιν ἐκ δευτέρου, Mt 26:42; Acts 10:15). See BDAG, 221.

ple in Jerusalem? What about the "signs he was doing" at the Passover in Jerusalem (2:23; 3:2)? Do they not count? What links these two incidents? Is it only the location in "Cana of Galilee" (v. 46; 2:1 and 11), or something more? The answers are not easy. "Cana of Galilee" is not named again in this final notice, and there is room for argument whether the actual healing took place at Cana or at Capernaum. The point is simply that Jesus did it "when he came from Judea to Galilee," that is, when he completed what he set out to do after baptizing and making disciples in Judea (vv. 1-3).

This "second sign" is as important for what it is not as for what it is. It does *not* represent a widening or extension of Jesus' ministry from Jews to Gentiles or to the whole world. That took place already among the Samaritans (v. 42). Rather, it represents a return to familiar places and people, perhaps to his own mother and brothers (see 2:1, 12). It is a tacit acknowledgment of what the synoptic tradition makes very clear, that Jesus was a Galilean, and that Galilee was the primary scene of his ministry. Moreover, this "second sign" should *not* be read as promising a whole series of signs up to seven, or whatever number the interpreter finds in the Gospel. The numbering stops at two.[51] "Second" simply reinforces the adverb "again" *(palin)*, at the same time qualifying it to make the point that Jesus did not do *exactly* the same thing "again," but something comparable.[52] As we have seen, "signs" are not necessarily miracles, but simply things Jesus "did" to which the Gospel writer assigns "significance" or revelatory value. Jesus' deeds collectively can be called "signs" (*sēmeia*, 2:11; 6:2; 7:31; 9:16; 11:47; 12:37; 20:30) just as they can be called "works" *(erga)*,[53] and in two instances besides this one a particular deed is called a "sign" (*sēmeion*, singular, in 6:14; 12:18). But the "signs" are not numbered (only paired, and just this once), not limited to Galilee, and probably not limited to miracles. All the writer is saying with this notice is that Jesus, now back in Galilee, is still

---

51. Robert Fortna has argued (*The Fourth Gospel and Its Predecessor*, 66) that the designation of the miraculous catch of fish after Jesus' resurrection as the "third" time he revealed himself (21:14) goes back to a stage of tradition in which the numbering of the signs continued. While this is (remotely) possible, it has no bearing on the text of the Gospel as it stands, which explicitly states that it was Jesus' "third" appearance *after his resurrection* (see πάλιν, "again," in 21:1). Even Fortna is hesitant about pressing his case (79).

52. To unpack our translation a little, it could be paraphrased, "And this Jesus did *again* — that is, as a *second* sign — when he came from Judea to Galilee." Just as "beginning" in 2:11 should be read as predicate to ταύτην ("This he did . . . *as* a beginning"), so here "second sign" should be read as predicate to τοῦτο.

53. Jesus' deeds are called "works" when they are seen as "works of God" (5:20, 36; 7:3; 9:3, 4; 10:25, 32, 37, 38; 14:10, 11, 12; 15:24). "Work" (ἔργον, singular) can refer either to a specific deed of Jesus (7:21) or to the "works of God" in their entirety (4:34; 17:4).

being Jesus, still "revealing his glory" (as in 2:11), and that whole families are coming to faith (v. 53). Quite possibly, as we have seen, the healing of the royal official's son is only a sample of the kind of thing Jesus was doing among the Galileans when they "received" him (v. 45).

Finally, what of the "significance" or revelatory value of this healing? It lies in the repeated word of healing, "Your son lives" (vv. 50, 53; compare v. 51). The healing highlights Jesus' power to give life, whether physical or eternal life (see 3:15, 16, 36; 4:14, 36), and this will be the overriding theme of the chapters to follow (for starters, see 5:21, 25, 26). If revelation of Jesus' glory was the message of the first sign (2:11), the gift of life is the message of its sequel, and as the Gospel story unfolds the reader will learn that revelation and eternal life amount to much the same thing (see 17:3). Within the story, "Your son lives" is a kind of refrain accomplishing the child's healing, but in the Gospel's larger framework the association of "son" and "lives" evokes the notion that "the Son" and "life" go together (see 3:36; 1 Jn 5:12, 20). Freed from its immediate narrative context, it becomes a word of praise to God ("Your Son lives"), proclaiming nothing less than the resurrection of Jesus himself (see 5:26; 6:57; 14:19). Is it too much to suspect that such a thought might have crossed the minds of some of the story's first readers?

C. JESUS AND THE SICK MAN IN JERUSALEM (5:1-18)

1 *After these things there was a festival of the Jews, and Jesus went up to Jerusalem.* 2 *At the Sheep's [place] in Jerusalem is a pool, called in Hebrew Bethsaida, having five porticoes.* 3 *In these would lie a multitude of the sick, blind, lame, or shriveled up.* 5 *There was a certain man there who was thirty-eight years in his sickness.* 6 *When Jesus saw him lying there, and found out that he had been like that for a long time, he said to him, "Do you want to get well?"* 7 *The sick man answered, "Sir, I have no one to put me into the pool when the water is stirred up, and whenever I get there, someone else goes down ahead of me."* 8 *Jesus said to him, "Get up, pick up your mat and walk."* 9 *And all at once the man got well, and he picked up his mat and walked. But it was the Sabbath that day.* 10 *So the Jews said to him who had been cured, "It is the Sabbath, and it is not lawful for you to pick up your mat."* 11 *But he answered them, "The one who made me well, that man told me, 'Pick up your mat and walk.'"* 12 *They asked him, "Who is the man who told you, 'Pick up and walk'?"* 13 *But he who had been healed did not know who it was, for Jesus had ducked out — there was a crowd in the place.*

14 *After these things Jesus finds him in the temple and said to him,*

> "Look, you have gotten well. Don't sin any more, or something worse may happen to you." 15 The man went away and told the Jews that it was Jesus who made him well. 16 And for this the Jews began pursuing Jesus, because he did such things on the Sabbath. 17 But Jesus had an answer for them: "My Father is working even until now, and I am working." 18 So for this the Jews kept seeking all the more to kill him, because he was not only abolishing the Sabbath but was claiming God as his own Father, making himself equal to God.

"After these things"[1] (v. 1; compare 2:13; 3:22) links the ensuing account only very loosely to what has preceded. The same phrase occurs again at the beginning of chapter 6 and chapter 7, each time signaling a change of scene or a turn in the narrative (see also v. 14). A number of scholars over the years have proposed reversing the order of chapters 5 and 6, so that Jesus' ministry at Cana in Galilee to the royal official (4:43-54) is followed immediately by the feeding of the multitude, still in Galilee near the shore of the lake (6:1-15).[2] This explains why Jesus at the beginning of chapter 6 is assumed to be already in Galilee, simply crossing from one side of the lake to the other (6:1). But there is not a shred of manuscript evidence for such a move. Readers who dutifully follow the course of this rearranged Gospel from chapter 4 to chapter 6 to chapter 5 to chapter 7 will discover at the beginning of chapter 7 that Jesus is suddenly "walking around" in Galilee (7:1) without any notice of how he got there from Jerusalem, and within nine verses is back in Jerusalem again (see 7:10). The rearrangement solves one problem only to create another.[3] While it may tell us something of the original historical sequence of certain events in Jesus' life, it tells us nothing of the literary sequence of John's Gospel. Its mistake lies in trying to "improve" the text by making it more chronologically aware and intentional than it intends to be. "After these things" means little more than "The next thing I would like to tell is this." Better to interpret the text as it stands than rewrite the text. With this in mind, let us move from chapter 4 to chapter 5, *not* to chapter 6. The new chapter finds Jesus in Jerusalem, where he again (as in 4:43-54) performs a miracle that gives "life" to someone who is "sick."

1 Instead of "going down" to Capernaum from Cana in Galilee (*katabēthi*, 4:49), Jesus "went up"[4] to Jerusalem, just as he had done at Passover (see

---

1. Gr. μετὰ ταῦτα, as in 2:13; 3:22.
2. See, for example, the commentaries of Bernard (1.171), Bultmann (209), and Schnackenburg (2.5-9), all of whom not only propose such a transposition, but incorporate it into the arrangement of their commentaries.
3. Schnackenburg (2.5) argues the opposite, but unconvincingly.
4. Gr. ἀνέβη.

5:1-18 Jesus and the Sick Man in Jerusalem

2:13). Having firmly established that Jesus is a Galilean (2:1-12; 4:3, 47, 54), the author makes Galilee his point of reference and brings Jesus to Jerusalem only for "a festival of the Jews."[5] Ordinarily the "festival" is named, as either Passover (2:13; 11:55), Tents, or Tabernacles (7:2), or Dedication (now known as Hanukkah) (10:22). Here alone it is unnamed, either deliberately or because the story was preserved and handed down without a precise temporal setting. In 2:13-22 it may have been important that the festival was "the Passover of the Jews" because of veiled references to Jesus' death and resurrection (2:17, 19-22), anticipating Jesus' last Passover. Here we find nothing linking the events of the chapter to a specific festival. What turns out to be important instead is that "it was the Sabbath that day" (v. 9; see vv. 10, 16).

If the author has purposely left the festival nameless, he could have done so in order to conceal a departure from chronological order. If the healing to be recorded in this chapter was remembered in connection with Jesus' first Passover described in chapter 2, then it could have originally been one of the impressive "signs he was doing" that attracted the attention of "many," including Nicodemus (see 2:23; 3:2). If, as many believe, the story of the temple cleansing was transferred at some point in the tradition from the last week of Jesus' life to that first Passover in Jerusalem, it would have tended to overshadow other stories already associated with that early visit. The healing recorded in chapter 5 could have been one of those accounts "rescued" from its original setting, given a new literary setting of its own, and made the basis of further controversy between Jesus and the Jewish authorities in Jerusalem (vv. 16-18, 19-47; see also 7:21-23). None of this, however, sheds light on the Gospel in its present form, where the events described are clearly subsequent to Jesus' first visit to Jerusalem and Judea (2:13–3:36), and to his ministries in Samaria and Galilee (4:1-54). Whatever the historical facts or traditions, in its *literary* setting this unnamed "festival of the Jews" could be any festival between the first Passover in Jerusalem (2:13) and the second Passover (presumably a year later) at the time Jesus fed the multitude in Galilee (6:4). It is unlikely, therefore, that the author intends us to think of it as Passover. He has left it nameless, and we should do the same. The only reason for mentioning it is to bring Jesus to Jerusalem from Galilee, and for this any "festival" will do. Again (as in 2:13) the mention of "the Jews" in charge of the festival tells us who Jesus' antagonists will be (see vv. 10, 15, 16, 18).

---

5. Gr. ἑορτὴ τῶν Ἰουδίων, without a definite article. Some ancient manuscripts (including ℵ, C, L, 33) have "*the* festival of the Jews" (ἡ ἑορτὴ τῶν Ἰουδίων), as if the author (and perhaps the readers as well) have a specific festival in mind, whether Passover (later called "the festival of the Jews," 6:4), or Tents (sometimes referred to in Jewish literature simply as "the festival"), or Pentecost (which would have come fifty days after the Passover of chapter 2). But the question is moot because the most reliable ancient witnesses (including B, P[66], P[75], A, and D) lack the definite article.

2   The author might have taken Jesus directly to the temple for this "festival of the Jews" (see 2:14), but first he sketches a scene in Jerusalem for the benefit of readers unfamiliar with the city. Jesus will get to the temple soon enough (v. 14), but attention focuses for now on a "pool" at the "Sheep's [place],"[6] leading into the city, probably (as Brown locates it) "northeast of the Temple where the sheep were brought into Jerusalem for sacrifice."[7] The author claims that this pool "is" (*estin,* present tense) in Jerusalem, even after the city's destruction in A.D. 70 (assuming that John's Gospel is written after 70).[8] Quite likely he is right, for archeological evidence from later times suggests that the pool was still used as a healing sanctuary to the god Asclepius long after the city was destroyed and rebuilt by the Romans.[9] While he knows that the readers have little likelihood of ever visiting the spot, the author invites them to visualize the scene as it unfolds.

The Hebrew name of the place, probably unfamiliar to them and quite uncertain in the manuscripts, is less important to the story than the author's description of the pool's "five porticoes" or "colonnades," and the "multitude of the sick, blind, lame, or shriveled up" lying there (v. 3). The most important ancient witnesses (including P[75], B, the Vulgate, and Coptic versions) give the name as "Bethsaida" (P[66] offers a slight variation of this), Others (including ℵ and 33) have "Bethzatha," and still others "Belzetha" (D, and the old Latin), or "Bethesda" (A, C, and the majority of later manuscipts). Conventional wisdom is quick to dismiss "Bethsaida" because it appears to be based on a confusion between this pool in Jerusalem and the town in Galilee that was home to Philip, Andrew, and Simon Peter (see 1:44; 12:21).[10] Yet

---

6. "The Sheep's" (ἡ προβατική) is simply an adjective derived from "sheep" (τὸ πρόβατον; see 10:1-16, 26-27; 21:16-17). Used substantively, as here, it is "the Sheep's place," possibly understood as "the Sheep Gate" (see Neh 3:1, 32; 12:39; in the LXX, ἡ πύλη ἡ προβατική). This would explain why προβατική is feminine. Alternatively, if "pool" (κολυμβήθρα, also feminine) were read as dative (ending with the iota subscript — ᾳ) instead of nominative, then the phrase would be "at the Sheep Pool." As Bultmann notes, however (240), the nominative participle "called" (ἡ ἐπιλεγομένη) implies that what is "called" by a Hebrew name has already been named in some way (see BDF, 212 [§412-13]; BDAG, 374-75). "Pool" should therefore be read as nominative in agreement with the participle, as the subject of the sentence and the focus of attention (see also Metzger, *Textual Commentary,* 207-8).

7. Brown, 1.206.

8. According to J. A. T. Robinson, who dates the Gospel *before* 70, John's language presumes that Jerusalem is still standing, yet Robinson is quick to admit that the use of the present tense does not in itself demand this conclusion (*The Priority of John* [Oak Park, IL: Meyer-Stone, 1987], 70).

9. See, for example, R. M. Mackowski, *Jerusalem, City of Jesus* (Grand Rapids: Eerdmans, 1980), 79-83; Robinson, *Priority of John,* 54-59.

10. See Metzger, *Textual Commentary,* 208.

5:1-18 JESUS AND THE SICK MAN IN JERUSALEM

this author is quite capable of letting a single name do double duty for two different towns or places (see "Bethany" in 1:28, in 11:1, 18, and in 12:1). If he did so here, scribes might well have tried to correct him (just as Origen did at 1:28), by changing "Bethsaida" to "Bethzatha" or "Bethesda" on the basis of what was known about this section of Jerusalem,[11] or this pool in particular.[12] This is at least as likely as a change in the opposite direction, and for this reason we have followed the earliest manuscripts in reading the name as "Bethsaida" (see n. 11). The "five porticoes," or covered colonnades,[13] should not be interpreted allegorically, any more than the "six stone water jars" at Cana (2:6) or the Samaritan woman's "five husbands" (4:18).[14] The five porticoes simply contribute to the impression of a great amount of space,[15] appropriate to the "multitude" (v. 3) of those who gathered there.

3, 5 The scene unfolds, not merely as something that met Jesus'

---

11. Josephus writes of a hill in Jerusalem called "Bezetha," opposite the Antonia fortress, which gave its name to an area known also as Caenopolis, or "New City" (see *War* 5.149-51). But "New City" is not the translation of "Bezetha." George Adam Smith pointed out that this name "cannot mean New-City: probably it stands for Bethzaith, 'house' or 'district' of olives" (*Jerusalem*, 1.244). While "Beth-zaith" is likely a variation of "Bethzatha," it is also close enough to "Bethsaida" to suggest that the earliest manuscripts (P^{66}, P^{75}, and B) represent not just an assimilation to 1:44, but were in touch with the original name of the place (see 1 Macc 7:19 and R. H. Charles, *APOT*, 1.91, n. 19).

12. Probably with this pool in mind, the *Copper Scroll* at Qumran (3Q15, col. 11) refers to "Bet-Eshtadatain" (a dual form in Hebrew, implying twin pools) as "the reservoir where you enter the small pool" (G. Vermes, *The Complete Dead Sea Scrolls in English* [Allen Lane: Penguin, 1997], 588).

13. Among modern interpreters the five colonnades are commonly visualized as framing a square or rectangular pool on four sides, with one additional portico or colonnade in the center dividing the pool into two bathing areas (thus matching the twin pools of the *Copper Scroll*; see n. 12). This is possible but by no means certain (see Robinson, *Priority of John*, 55, who comments that such a description fits "reservoirs for supplying water to the temple area of the city," but "would have been highly unsuitable for a healing sanctuary" because invalids who entered the pool would have been "in imminent danger of drowning"). Robinson points instead to certain small grottoes discovered at a lower level "with steps leading down to them, together with some rectangular stone basins presumably for washing" (56; see also Mackowski, *Jerusalem*, 81; J. Wilkinson, *Jerusalem as Jesus Knew It*, 98).

14. Allegorical interpretations are as old as Augustine: "That water, then — namely that people — was shut in by the five books of Moses, as by five porches. But those books brought forth the sick, not healed them. For the law convicted, not acquitted sinners" (*Tractates on John* 17.2; NPNF, 1st ser., 7.111).

15. "Five porticoes" was one more than the four surrounding the outer court of the Jerusalem temple, according to Josephus (see, for example, Josephus, *Antiquities* 15.395-402; *War* 5.190-92; also Mackowski, *Jerusalem*, 123-28).

eyes when he arrived in Jerusalem, but as what went on at the pool on a regular basis, whether at the Jewish festivals or all the time. It is a customary or repeated scene that the reader is invited to visualize, not a one-time event. Within the five porticoes or covered colonnades "would lie[16] a multitude of the sick, blind, lame, or shriveled up" (v. 3). "The sick" could be read either as a general designation of the whole group (as if it were followed by a colon), or it could be read as referring (rather vaguely) to one group among the four. In any event, the "sickness"[17] (v. 5) of the man who will be at the center of the story (v. 7) is not specified. His inability to get into the pool (v. 7) will suggest that he is either one of the "lame" or the "shriveled up," but we are never told explicitly.

At the end of verse 3, the manuscripts diverge. Codex D and some of the old Latin add "paralytics" to the list, possibly because of a similar-sounding story in the synoptic Gospels in which Jesus says, "Get up, pick up your mat and go home," to a man explicitly called a "paralytic" (Mk 2:10-11; see also Mt 9:6). D had only a few followers in the Latin tradition, but other manuscripts made far more sweeping changes. The first, shorter addition, "waiting for the moving of the water," appeared also in D and its followers, but in a wide range of later manuscripts and versions as well. Its effect is to explain why so many sick people would congregate in these five covered colonnades at the Bethsaida pool. They were waiting for something, and the reader can infer already that "the moving of the water" in some way represented an opportunity for healing (see v. 7). A much longer addition explains why in much greater detail: "For an angel of the Lord would come down from time to time in the pool and stir up the water. The first one in after the stirring of the water would get well from whatever disease he had."[18] Interestingly, all the main verbs in this added material confirm the impression that this was not a single event that happened on one memorable day, but something that happened again and again as a common occurrence.[19]

---

16. The verb κατέκειτο ("would lie," or "used to lie") appears to be an iterative imperfect (see BDF, §325; Robertson, *Grammar,* 884), referring to a usual or customary scene of a crowd of sick persons gathered at the pool.

17. Gr. τῇ ἀσθενείᾳ. The man is then identified as ὁ ἀσθενῶν ("the sick man," v. 7).

18. Some early manuscripts (D and some old Latin) have the first of these but not the second; others (such as A), the second without the first. But the earliest and most reliable witnesses (including P⁶⁶, P⁷⁵, ℵ, B, C*, and 33) have neither. The first variant appears to have been added by scribes to prepare the reader for the sick man's statement in verse 7; the second, to explain further why the water was stirred and why healing properties were attributed to its movement. See Metzger, *Textual Commentary,* 209.

19. The verbs are all imperfects with the same iterative quality as the κατέκειτο of verse 3. This is confirmed by the phrase κατὰ καιρόν ("from time to time"). These verbs

5:1-18 JESUS AND THE SICK MAN IN JERUSALEM

These additions (especially the second one) obviously make the Gospel's readers much more knowledgeable about the situation than they would otherwise be — too knowledgeable, in fact.[20] All we are supposed to know for the moment is that a large crowd of the sick and disabled gathered regularly at a famous pool in Jerusalem. Our attention is meant to focus on "a certain man" (v. 5)[21] and his experience "there" *(ekei)*. We will learn of what went on at the pool not from a narrative aside by the author (which is what v. 4 would be if it were genuine), but from the narrative itself. We will see the man through Jesus' eyes (v. 6), hear the man's own account of his predicament (v. 7), and witness a miracle (vv. 8-9). The only piece of information we are given in advance is how long the man has been sick — "thirty-eight years." Here again commentators have looked for allegorical meanings (see n. 14), but again unconvincingly.[22] More likely, this is a tradition handed down from the time the story was first heard, remembered, and retold, serving here to heighten the impression of a knowledgeable (if not omniscient) author-narrator.[23] The man's "sickness," like that of the royal official's son at Cana (4:46) is not named (see also 6:2; 11:3-4). In the earlier incident we learned that it involved a "fever" (4:52), and in this instance we learn that it makes him unable to walk or get into the water.

---

are κατέβαινεν ("would come down") or (in some manuscripts) ἐλούετο ("would bathe"); also ἐτάρασσε ("would stir up"), ὑγιὴς ἐγίνετο ("would get well"), and κατείχετο ("had").

20. Whether the longer addition is based on a scribe's imagination or on local legend, it has the effect of endorsing the supposed healing qualities of the pool by attributing them to "an angel of the Lord" (ἄγγελος κυρίου). It is doubtful that the author wants to do this, given the fact that Jesus completely bypasses the pool in healing the man with a word. Moreover, despite the promise of angels "going up and coming down over the Son of man" (1:51), angels play only a very minor role in this Gospel (see only 12:29; 20:12).

21. Gr. τις ἄνθρωπος; compare τις βασιλικός ("a certain royal official," 4:46). Just as he was first the "royal official" (4:46, 49), then "the man" (v. 50), then "the father" (v. 53), so the man in this story is called "a certain man" (5:5), then "the sick man" (v. 7), "him who had been cured" (v. 10), "he who had been healed" (v. 13), and finally just "the man" (v. 15).

22. See, for example, Deuteronomy 2:14, "And the length of time we had traveled from Kadesh-barnea until we crossed the Wadi Zered was thirty-eight years, until the entire generation of warriors had perished from the camp, as the LORD had sworn concerning them" (NRSV; see Marsh, 250). Augustine makes a much more elaborate argument: "If, therefore, the number forty possesses the perfecting of the law, and the law is fulfilled only in the twin precepts of love, why dost thou wonder that he was weak and sick, who was short of forty by two?" (*Tractates on John* 17.2; NPNF, 1st ser., 7.113).

23. Similar information is given at times in the synoptic Gospels and Acts; for example, "twelve years" (Mk 5:25); "eighteen years" (Lk 13:11); "eight years" (Acts 9:33). Here (as in Lk 13:11), the time reference may have something to do with the charge of Sabbath breaking (see v. 9b): if the man had waited this long for healing, what would one more day have mattered? (presumably Jesus would have answered as he does in Lk 13:16).

6 Arriving in Jerusalem (v. 1), Jesus surveyed the whole scene just described (or so we can assume), but what we are explicitly told that he "saw" is the one man "lying" there,[24] the man to whom we have just been introduced. When Jesus "found out"[25] that he had been like that[26] for a long time," he asked the man, "Do you want [*theleis*] to get well?" In contrast to his encounter with the royal official at Cana (4:47-48), Jesus now takes the initiative to heal. His question is straightforward. It carries no hidden rebuke or psychological analysis, as if to say, "Do you *really* want to get well, or have you become quite comfortable in your life of dependency all these years?"[27] Instead, Jesus is asking, "What do you want? What can I do for you?" He is saying just what he said to blind Bartimaeus in Mark: "What do you want me to do for you?" (Mk 10:51).[28] Bartimaeus had an answer ready ("that I might see," v. 51b), but here Jesus supplies the obvious answer for the sick man: "to get well."[29] "Well" or "healthy" is used only of this healing in John's Gospel, and it is used repeatedly (see vv. 9, 11, 14, 15, and 7:23, as well as the scribal addition in v. 4). To "get well" is as generalized and unspecific as being "sick." John's Gospel is not interested in the clinical details or symptoms of the illnesses Jesus cured, only in his ability to make things right by giving life to those in need (see 4:50, 53, "your son lives").

24. Gr. τοῦτον . . . κατακείμενον.
25. "Found out" is literally "knew" (γνούς), or "came to know." Jesus' knowledge is not supernatural here (as in 2:25, where the verb γινώσκειν is imperfect), but natural (as in 4:1, aorist, as here). Presumably Jesus learned that the man had been sick a long time by being told. If he had known it by divine omniscience, he would have known precisely how long ("thirty-eight years," v. 5), but the text never claims that he knew that.
26. Literally, "that he already had a long time." The main verb of the clause, "had" (ἔχει, more literally "has," historic present), echoes the notice in the preceding verse that the man "had been" (ἔχων) sick (literally, "in his sickness") for thirty-eight years. "In his sickness" (ἐν τῇ ἀσθενείᾳ αὐτοῦ) is implied here as well. Hence our translation, "he had been like that" (for this use of ἔχειν in reference to the time or circumstances of one's life, see BDAG, 422).
27. Lindars hints at such a reading (215): "It is possible to imagine that Jesus' question has been prompted by the fact that the man has made no attempt to reach the water when it last bubbled up. His reply will then appear to be quite dignified and free from bitterness. The answer is, 'Yes, but experience has taught me that it is hopeless to try.'" But this would have required a different framing of the question: "*Don't you want* [οὐ θέλεις] to get well?" (see J. Staley, "Stumbling in the Dark, Reaching for the Light: Reading Character in John 5 and 9," *Semeia* 53 [1991], 71, n. 8). Moreover, it implies that Jesus is taking account of information which the reader cannot yet know (except from later scribal tradition!). This is possible but not likely.
28. Contrast the leper in Mark, to whom it was a matter of what *Jesus* "wanted": "If you want [ἐὰν θέλῃς], you are able to make me clean" (Mk 1:40), and whom Jesus promptly answered, "I want to [θέλω]. Be clean" (v. 41).
29. Gr. ὑγιὴς γενέσθαι.

5:1-18 JESUS AND THE SICK MAN IN JERUSALEM

7 The sick man hears Jesus' words simply as an offer of help from a kind stranger, so he suggests something Jesus might do for him. "Sir,"[30] he replies, "I have no one [literally, "no man"][31] to put[32] me into the pool when the water is stirred up." He needs "a man" (probably male in this instance), either a slave[33] or a good friend,[34] to assist him, and Jesus is a likely candidate. Without the "helps to the reader" provided by later scribes (see v. 3, and n. 18), we are left to infer that the pool must have had healing qualities (or at least that the sick man thought it did), and that these qualities were in effect only at certain times when the pool was "stirred up,"[35] presumably by an intermittent spring of some sort. "Whenever I get there," the sick man complains, "someone else goes down ahead of me."[36] There is reason to suspect his motives. Unless others in the "multitude" at the pool (v. 4) had a slave or close friend by their side, most of them were in the same situation as he. No such healthy companions are mentioned in the author's opening sketch of the scene (v. 3). The reader is left wondering. In trying to recruit Jesus to help him, is the sick man gaining an unfair advantage?[37]

8 Jesus will have none of it. Instead, ignoring the pool and its supposed healing powers, he tells the man, "Get up, pick up your mat and walk." The setting of the incident, so elaborately introduced (vv. 2-3), is virtually forgotten. Jesus and the sick man are still at the pool, but it no longer matters. They could be anywhere. Readers familiar with other Gospels will remember a story in which Jesus and a paralytic are in Galilee, not Jerusalem, and in a house, not by a pool. Unlike the sick man here, this man had friends to help him

---

30. The designation κύριε is "Sir" here, as in the case of the Samaritan woman (4:11, 15, 19), not "Lord," as on the lips of the royal official (4:49). The sick man attributes no supernatural healing powers to Jesus at this point.

31. Gr. ἄνθρωπον οὐκ ἔχω.

32. "Put" is literally "throw" (βάλῃ), but the verb βάλλειν is common in this weakened sense (BDAG, 163; see, for example, Jn 13:5; 18:11; 20:25).

33. On ἄνθρωπος as a slave or servant, see BDAG, 81.

34. To a modern reader familiar with all the Gospels, the contrast with Mark 2:3-4 is striking. There the paralyzed man had not one but *four* faithful companions to carry him on his mat to the roof and let him down from there to be healed. It is difficult to say whether or not the writer of John's Gospel knows this story and is tacitly acknowledging the contrast.

35. Gr. ταράχθη.

36. The scribe or scribes responsible for the explanation added in later manuscripts (v. 4) seem to have interpreted this to mean that only the "first one" (πρῶτος) into the pool after the stirring of the water would be healed, but the language of v. 7 does not require this. "Someone else" (ἄλλος is indefinite, and need not be limited to just one person.

37. His complaint, with its emphatic "I" and its close juxtaposition of ἐγώ and ἄλλος, sounds whining and self-centered: "whenever *I* get there [ἐν ᾧ δὲ ἔρχομαι ἐγώ], *someone else* [ἄλλος] goes down ahead of me."

(not one but four!) who carried him on a "mat" (Mk 2:4),[38] and dug through a roof to get to Jesus. Jesus' words to this man were the same: "Get up, pick up your mat and walk" (Mk 2:9). In both instances the healing was immediate, and the ensuing action matched the command almost word for word. The paralytic "got up and at once[39] picked up his mat and went out" (Mk 2:12). In our story, "all at once[40] the man was well, and he picked up his mat and walked" (v. 9).

A natural question to ask in both stories is, Why mention the "mat"? Why not just say "Get up and walk?"[41] In Mark the answer is fairly clear. The paralytic was brought in to Jesus on a "mat," but now he no longer needs it. Carrying his mat signals his newfound independence and marks his departure from the scene. He does not walk simply to demonstrate his ability to walk, but he goes home, and because the mat is his property he takes it with him (see Mk 2:11, 12). In John's Gospel, although the mat has not been mentioned before, the reader can infer something similar. In telling the sick man, "Get up, pick up your mat and walk," Jesus is not saying, "Get up and walk around to prove to everyone that you are healed." He is saying, "Get up, leave this place and take your mat with you, because you aren't coming back. You don't need to stay here any longer."[42]

9 The notice that the man "got well" recalls Jesus' initial question whether he wanted to "get well" (v. 6).[43] Whatever doubts there may have been about the man's motives (see v. 7), Jesus knows that he truly wants to "get well," and he grants his wish unreservedly, with no requirement, or even any mention, of "faith" (contrast 4:50, 53; also Mk 2:5). The story now takes a decisive turn, with the abrupt comment that "it was the Sabbath that day" (v. 9b). The notice, like some other narrative asides in John (see 1:24, 28; 3:24), comes belatedly. Both here and later in the case of the blind man at the pool of Siloam (9:14), the author waits until the healing is over to tell us that

---

38. A "mat" (κράβατος, as here) was a poor man's bed that could also serve as a pallet or stretcher (see BDAG, 563). Matthew and Luke prefer other terms, such as κλίνη (Mt 9:2, 6; Lk 5:18), or its diminutive κλινίδιον (Lk 5:19, 24).

39. Gr. καὶ εὐθύς.

40. Gr. καὶ εὐθέως.

41. At one point in the Markan story of the paralytic, Matthew and Luke change Jesus' command to exactly that (Mt 9:5; Lk 5:23). At that moment, Jesus is simply deliberating what he might say. Two verses later, when he actually says it, Matthew and Luke follow Mark's wording more closely: "Get up, pick up your mat and go to your house" (Mt 9:6; Lk 5:24). When he obeys, Mark and Luke have him taking his mat (Mk 2:12; Lk 5:25), while Matthew simply states that he "got up and went to his house" (Mt 9:8).

42. Up to this point the "mat" seems more at home in the Markan story than here, suggesting that details from that story might have influenced the telling of this one. But as soon as the Sabbath is mentioned (v. 9), the place of the mat, and the act of carrying of the mat, in the story becomes unmistakably clear.

43. Gr. ὑγιὴς γενέσθαι in verse 6; ἐγένετο ὑγιής here.

5:1-18 JESUS AND THE SICK MAN IN JERUSALEM

it is the Sabbath, in contrast to several healing stories in other Gospels in which we know from the start that this will be an issue (see Mk 2:23; 3:2; Lk 13:10; 14:3). The effect of the news is to change the story's direction. Its setting is the weekly Sabbath now, not simply an unnamed yearly "festival of the Jews" (v. 1), and the Sabbath will determine the story line from here on.

10 At this point the question of why Jesus mentioned the carrying of the mat resurfaces. A new reason now emerges. "The Jews" make an abrupt appearance,[44] reminding "him who had been cured"[45] of what the reader has just been told (that "It is the Sabbath"), and warning him that "it is not lawful for you to pick up your mat." The reader now learns that whatever else it may have been, the mention of carrying the mat (vv. 8 and 9) was a way of setting the stage for this warning, and for the ensuing charges of "the Jews" against Jesus of breaking the Sabbath (see vv. 15-16). This was a function it did *not* have in the Markan story of the paralytic in Capernaum. But it was part of the oral law that "taking out from one domain into another" was one of thirty-nine activities considered to be work and forbidden on the Sabbath,[46] and it is probably to some version of that law that "the Jews" are referring.

Are we to infer that Jesus knew this when he told the sick man to carry off his mat? From what we know of the Johannine Jesus, we can be sure that nothing he says or does is unintentional. He knew exactly what he was doing, and his command to "Get up, pick up your mat and walk" was a deliberate challenge to the religious authorities in Jerusalem and their Sabbath laws.[47] With their words, "it is not lawful,"[48] the issue is joined (compare Mk 2:24,

---

44. We have met οἱ Ἰουδαῖοι ("the Jews") twice before, as those who sent messengers from Jerusalem to question John (1:19), and as Jesus' antagonists in Jerusalem on his first visit there (2:18, 20), but not since then.

45. The man is identified in a variety of ways, first as "the sick man" (ὁ ἀσθενῶν, v. 7), now after the healing (v. 11) as "him who had been cured" (τῷ τεθεραπευμένῳ, the only instance of this verb for healing in John's Gospel), and finally (for variety's sake) as "he who had been healed" (ὁ ἰαθείς, v. 13).

46. *Mishnah Shabbat* 7.2 (Danby, 106). Ironically, the four who carried the paralytic to see Jesus in Mark may not have been guilty of Sabbath breaking: "[If he took out] a living man on a couch he is not culpable by reason of the couch, since the couch is secondary" (10.5; Danby, 109). In any event, the issue does not come up there.

47. Schnackenburg (2.97) makes precisely this point, even though he considers it a secondary feature of the narrative: "The evangelist makes it look like deliberate provocation.... Originally, Jesus' instruction was simply part of the pattern of the story (compare Mk 2:11), but the evangelist uses it to show how Jesus is bound to carry out only the will of his Father and to 'work' when he sees the Father 'working' (verses 17, 19), even if this means conflict with the Jewish sabbath laws." Provocation may also be implied by the initial reference to the length of the man's infirmity (v. 5): if he had been sick for thirty-eight years, what harm could be done by waiting another day to avoid the Sabbath?

48. Gr. οὐκ ἔξεστίν.

26; 3:4). If not a Sabbath breaker himself, Jesus has at least contributed to the delinquency of one.⁴⁹

11-12 Always quick to make excuses (see v. 7), the Sabbath breaker replies, "The one who made me well, he told me, 'Pick up your mat and walk.'" For their part the Jewish authorities are quite willing to accept his excuse, perhaps in the hope that it will lead them to the real target of their investigation. We seem to be witnessing here a resumption of the aborted confrontation at the Passover festival three chapters earlier. "The Jews" held their peace before (after 2:20), but we have not heard the last of them. "Who is the man who told you, 'Pick up and walk'?" they ask, and we sense that they are on Jesus' trail once again. Already the issue is shifting, as it will explicitly later in the chapter (vv. 16-18) from the Sabbath question to that of Jesus' identity. To the healed man, Jesus is "the one who made me well" (v. 11), but to the Jerusalem authorities he is simply "the man who told you, 'Pick up and walk'" (v. 12). They have no interest in, and no direct knowledge of, the healing. To them Jesus is not a healer or miracle worker, only a Sabbath breaker. All they care about is his identity, whether in order to charge him for breaking the Sabbath, or to connect him to the earlier act of provocation in driving the money changers from the temple (2:14-16). Their question, "Who is the man?" will echo and reecho through this Gospel in various ways, with multilayered answers.⁵⁰

13 For now the question of "who it was" goes unanswered. Jesus' identity remains a mystery to those who do not believe. "He who had been healed" did not know Jesus' name, and could not point him out because "Jesus had ducked out"⁵¹ — there was a crowd in the place." The implication is that he made his escape quite intentionally, knowing what the authorities had in mind.⁵² The "crowd in the place"⁵³ brings the narrative back to the opening description of "the place" (the pool at Bethsaida, v. 2), and the "multitude" of

---

49. In the first Sabbath dispute in the Synoptics (Mk 2:23-28 and par.), the issue is similarly the action of those associated with Jesus, not Jesus himself.

50. Jesus, who called himself "Son of man" (1:51; 3:13, etc.), is repeatedly called "a man" or "this man" by his enemies (7:46; 9:16, 24; 10:33; 11:47; 18:17, 29; 19:5), potential disciples (4:29; 7:51; 9:11), and even himself (8:40). The last answer to the question, "Who is the man?" (τίς ἐστιν ὁ ἄνθρωπος) is Pilate's "Here is the man" (ἰδοὺ ὁ ἄνθρωπος, 19:5).

51. Gr. ἐξένευσεν. Colloquial English ("ducked out") captures quite well the sense of the verb, which suggests a dodge or a turning of the head (compare νεύει, 13:24, and see Barrett, 255; also Field, *Notes,* 88, 100).

52. This is the first of several instances in which an elusive Jesus escapes potential arrest or even stoning, sometimes with the notice that "his hour had not yet come" (7:30; 8:20; also 7:32-34, 45-46; 8:59; 10:39; 12:36; and see Lk 4:30).

53. Gr. ὄχλου ὄντος ἐν τῷ τόπῳ.

5:1-18 JESUS AND THE SICK MAN IN JERUSALEM

the sick lying there (v. 3). Yet this "crowd" cannot simply be identified with that "multitude," for it seems to be made up of onlookers standing and milling around, more like the ubiquitous "crowds" in Mark's Gospel. As we have seen, the healing could have happened anywhere, but the author reminds us again of the pool and the opening scene, just in time to set the stage for an abrupt change of venue to a very different kind of "place."

14 "After these things" again (as in v. 1) marks an undisclosed time lapse and a break in the narrative. At the first Passover (2:14), Jesus had "found in the temple" money changers and sellers of livestock. This time, at another "festival of the Jews" (see v. 1) he "finds" the man he had healed, again "in the temple."[54] Presumably the temple was his destination from the start, when he "went up to Jerusalem" for the festival (v. 1), until he was caught up in the scene at the pool. Having left that "place" abruptly (v. 13), he would inevitably go to the temple, "the place where one must worship" (4:20),[55] above all at Jewish festivals. In short, Jesus had reasons to be in the temple that had nothing to do with the man at the pool. Still, their meeting is not a chance encounter. Jesus "finds" the man quite intentionally, just as he "found" Philip (1:43) when he enlisted him as a disciple, just as Andrew "found" Simon Peter (1:41) and Philip "found" Nathanael (1:45).[56]

Instead of "Follow me" (1:43), Jesus makes a more modest — but at the same time more ominous — demand. First he reminds the man of the miracle at the pool: "Look, you have gotten well."[57] Then he adds the thinly veiled warning, "Don't sin any more,[58] or something worse may happen to you." If the notice that "it was the Sabbath that day" (v. 9) caught the reader up short and changed the course of the story, so too does this belated warning from Jesus. It is the first occurrence of the verb "to sin" in John's Gospel. Neither the first disciples, nor Nathanael, nor Nicodemus, nor even the Samaritan woman (despite 4:18), were said to have "sinned." Nor did the healing of the royal official's son address any "sins" of either the child or the father.[59] The

---

54. Gr. εὑρίσκει . . . ἐν τῷ ἱερῷ.

55. See 11:48, where Caiaphas the Chief Priest fears that the Romans will take away "our place [ἡμῶν τὸν τόπον] and our nation."

56. See also 9:35, where Jesus "found" the man born blind and asked him, "Do you believe in the Son of man?"

57. Gr. ἴδε ὑγιὴς γέγονας (see vv. 6, 9, 11).

58. Gr. μηκέτι ἁμάρτανε.

59. The one place in Johannine tradition where sin does enter the picture is the story inserted in the majority of later manuscripts about a woman caught in adultery (Jn 7:53–8:11). Possibly the language of 5:14 has influenced the ending of that story, where Jesus' last words to the woman are "Nor do I condemn you. Go, and from now on sin no more" (μηκέτι ἁμάρτανε, 8:11). But there Jesus adds no warning about "something worse."

reader may have sensed a certain selfishness and duplicity in the behavior of the sick man at the pool, but there has been no hint up to now that Jesus judged or condemned him, or for that matter forgave him. All he said was "Do you want to get well?" (v. 6), and "Get up, pick up your mat and walk" (v. 8). Yet if we remember Jesus' first visit to Jerusalem, we will also remember that he "knew what was in the person" (2:25). If Jesus knew "what was in" people in general (enough not to "entrust himself" to them), we need not be surprised that he knew what was in this particular man — specifically that he was a sinner. Jesus would hardly have failed to notice what even the attentive reader is able to infer. Yet why does Jesus issue this warning? "Look, you have gotten well" is what we expect (see vv. 6, 9, 11, 15). "Don't sin any more, or something worse will happen to you," is not. It sounds as if it belongs in that other story, the one in which Jesus proposed healing someone with the words, "Your sins are forgiven" (Mk 2:5), and then demonstrated dramatically that "Your sins are forgiven" and "Get up, pick up your mat and walk" amount to the same thing (Mk 2:9-12). No such demonstration has taken place here, yet the man Jesus healed is supposed to understand that "Look, you have gotten well" is equivalent to "Look, your sins are forgiven." Or if he does not understand it, at least the reader is expected to. Either way, the warning follows as a logical corollary.

This story in John's Gospel and the story of the paralytic in Mark appear to be intertwined in the Gospel tradition. At least one detail, as we have seen — the picking up of the mat — turned out to be even more at home in this story than in the other, because of the issue of working on the Sabbath. Now we find that another — the link between healing and the forgiveness of sin — was integral to the Markan story from the start, but comes in here almost as an afterthought. While Mark's account of the paralytic helps us fill in the gaps and make sense of the narrative in John, can we assume that John's readers would have been familiar with Mark? Probably not. Without help from Mark, what do we make of Jesus' warning to the man he had healed? It implies that a connection between sickness and personal sin is at least a distinct possibility. The possibility is later raised explicitly by Jesus' disciples on encountering the beggar who was blind from birth (9:2), and Jesus did not claim that such a connection was unthinkable, only that it did not apply in that instance (9:3). On the other hand, the issue never came up in the case of the royal official's son, nor does it when Jesus learns of the illness of his friend Lazarus (11:3). Jesus in this Gospel views sickness first of all as an opportunity for healing and salvation (see 9:3-4; 11:4), not as a punishment for sin, and the same is true here.

At most there is an *analogy* between sin and sickness in that both can lead to death or not, depending on circumstances and severity. "Lord, come down before my little child dies!" the royal official said (4:49), and Jesus assures his disciples that the illness of Lazarus will *not* "lead to death" (11:4). In heated debate, Jesus warns his hostile questioners, "You will die in your sin" (8:21), or "in your sins" (8:24), and another Johannine writing draws a distinction between sin "leading to death" and sin "not leading to death" (1 Jn 5:16-17).[60] In the present passage, too, death (whether physical or spiritual) is presumably the "something worse"[61] of which Jesus warns the man.[62] His fate remains uncertain. The sick man has "gotten well," and by implication his past sins have been forgiven,[63] yet he is not "born from above," as Jesus told Nicodemus a person must be (see 3:3, 6). His status, like that of Nicodemus himself, is still undecided. We do not know, and will never know for certain, whether this man is one "who practices wicked things" and "does not come to the light" (3:20), or one who "comes to the light, so that his works will be revealed as works wrought in God" (3:21). But we can guess.

15 The immediate outlook is not good. The man said nothing in reply, no word of thanks, no expression of belief, no commitment to stop sinning. Instead, he "went away"[64] and told the Jews that it was Jesus who made him well." Much later, after the raising of Lazarus, we will hear of many who "had come to Mary and seen the things he had done" and "believed in him" (11:45), and of others who instead "went off"[65] to the Pharisees and told them the things Jesus had done" (11:46). Those who were not believers became informants, and their information led to the Sanhedrin's decision that Jesus must die (see 11:47-53). The long process that ended with that decision begins here at this early "festival of the Jews," and here too the informant is not a believer, at least not yet and perhaps never. As soon as Jesus said to him, "Don't sin any more," he "went away" and did exactly that. As for the "something worse" awaiting him, it is left to our imaginations.

16 "The Jews" at Jerusalem did not care that "it was Jesus who made him well" (v. 15), only that Jesus had done so by telling him to pick up his mat (v. 12). "For this"[66] they "pursued" or "persecuted" Jesus. Here, as at the beginning of the chapter, the imperfect tenses are noteworthy. The verb "pursued" (*ediōkon*, imperfect) describes a repeated or constant action, a

---

60. Gr. πρὸς θάνατον and μὴ πρὸς θάνατον respectively.

61. Gr. χεῖρόν τι.

62. The warning is intentionally vague, as in the saying of Jesus, "The last things become worse than the first" (see Mt 12:45//Lk 11:26; also 2 Pet 2:20).

63. We may compare not only Mark 2:5, 9-10, but also James 5:15: "And the prayer of faith will save the ailing one, and the Lord will raise him up, and if he has committed sins, they will be forgiven him." The latter is obviously not a perfect analogy because the sick person is a Christian believer (τις ἐν ὑμῖν, 5:14).

64. Gr. ἀπῆλθεν.

65. Gr. ἀπῆλθον.

66. Gr. διὰ τοῦτο, "on account of this," or "for this reason."

fixed policy of regarding Jesus as a marked man.[67] If we assume that this was already the case in light of his actions in the temple earlier, then it could be translated "kept pursuing." But if it was not (and we have no evidence that it was), then the verb should be rendered "began pursuing," and this is the course we have followed in translation. By the same token, what Jesus "did" on the Sabbath is not viewed here as a single act of healing, but as part of a regular pattern of behavior. Probably we are meant to conclude that Jesus "did such things[68] on the Sabbath" more than once, even though only one instance has been given (see 20:30; 21:25).[69] It is important to note that this was the perception not only of "the Jews" but of the Gospel writer. Like the other Gospel writers, he is convinced that Jesus actually did violate Sabbath law, but equally convinced that he was fully justified in doing so.

17 Jesus immediately gives his justification for breaking the Sabbath. He "had an answer"[70] for the Jewish authorities who claimed that he broke the Sabbath. It was not an answer remembered as having been given at a specific time and place, or in relation to specific words from "the Jews." We have no reason to believe that it is still the Sabbath, or that Jesus is still in the temple.[71] No real dialogue takes place between Jesus and "the Jews." He makes his pronouncement (v. 17), and instead of saying anything to him in reply they simply make plans to kill him (v. 18). Then Jesus "gave answer"

---

67. Much later Jesus will look back on this fixed policy as if it were a single completed act, telling his disciples: "if they persecuted me [ἐδίωξαν, aorist], they will persecute you" (15:20).

68. Edwin Abbott, after commenting that "the evangelist seems to indicate a 'beginning' to persecute, dating from a special act," added that "perhaps 'these things' means 'such things as this' " (*Johannine Grammar,* 337). Translating ταῦτα as "such things" is a way of doing justice to the iterative quality of the imperfect ἐποίει, referring to things Jesus did repeatedly or customarily.

69. Later Jesus will speak of "one work" he has done on the Sabbath (7:21, with v. 23), but we also hear of crowds who followed him "because they had seen the signs he had been doing for those who were sick" (6:2). These signs (whether on the Sabbath or not) are not all recorded, but we know that Jesus will heal on the Sabbath at least one more time (see 9:14).

70. Gr. ἀπεκρίνατο. For this rendering, see Brown, 1.212. The aorist middle ἀπεκρίνατο occurs in John's Gospel only here and in v. 19. Everywhere else in the give-and-take of Johannine dialogue the aorist passive (ἀπεκρίθη) is used. Abbott suggests that the middle implies a formal defense against a charge, yet he admits that this is *not* involved in the uses he surveys of this verb form in the LXX. It is safer to stay with his more generalized conclusion that "there is some notion of publicity, or oracular response, or solemnity, so that the meaning is different from that of ἀποκριθῆναι" (*Johannine Grammar,* 392).

71. Contrast Lindars (218): "It must be assumed that the Jews' 'persecution' of Jesus meant that they searched for him at once, and having found him (still in the Temple, perhaps; compare verse 14) challenged him with the point at issue."

5:1-18 JESUS AND THE SICK MAN IN JERUSALEM

again (v. 19),[72] this time at great length (vv. 19-47), with no interruptions from "the Jews" and still no response. It is not so much an actual debate on an actual occasion as a literary construction based on what "the Jews" in Jerusalem must have thought and what Jesus would have said in reply.[73] It is the writer's first real venture into the mind of Jesus, speaking for himself in the first person.[74] "My Father is working even until now," he says, "and I am working." He had spoken of "my Father" once before, when he said in the temple, "Stop making my Father's house a house of trade!" (2:16), but it did not register. This time it does. "The Jews" at Jerusalem now hear the expression "my Father" and grasp its implications (see v. 18). Jesus is picking up the thread of a rather familiar discussion in Judaism about the Sabbath. The notion that God "rested" after creating the world in six days (Gen 2:2-3) could not be interpreted to mean that God is now inactive in the world. On the contrary, God is at work constantly, giving and sustaining life, rewarding the righteous and punishing the wicked. In short, God, and God alone, lawfully breaks the Sabbath.[75]

---

72. Again, ἀπεκρίνατο.

73. Significantly, the middle ἀπεκρίνατο also occurs in Luke 3:16, where it refers to John the Baptist's answer to an *unspoken* question of "the people" in general (see also Acts 3:12).

74. This in contrast to the Gospel's opening verses (1:1-18), and to Jesus' encounter with Nicodemus (3:11-21) and John's farewell (3:31-36), where Jesus and John respectively are made to speak not so much for themselves as for the Gospel writer and his community.

75. The discussion is evident both in later rabbinic material and closer to Jesus' time in the writings of Philo. According to *Exodus Rabbah* 30.9, a group of Rabbis on a journey to Rome were challenged by a sectarian who asked why God did not observe the Sabbath. "Wretch!" they replied, "Is not a man permitted to carry on the Sabbath in his own courtyard?" adding that "Both the higher and lower regions are courtyards of God, as it says, The whole earth is full of his glory" (*Midrash Rabbah: Exodus* [London: Soncino, 1961], 355-56). According to R. Phinehas in *Genesis Rabbah* 11.10, God "rested from the work of [creating] His world, but not from the work of the wicked and the work of the righteous, for He works with the former and with the latter. He shows the former their essential character, and the latter their essential character." He then showed from Scripture that the punishment of the wicked and the rewarding of the righteous are both called "work" (*Midrash Rabbah: Genesis* [London: Soncino, 1961], 86). Philo, in commenting on Genesis 2:2, said, "First of all, the Creator, having brought an end to the formation of mortal things, begins the shaping of others more divine. For God never leaves off making, but even as it is the property of fire to burn and of snow to chill, so it is the property of God to make: nay more so by far, inasmuch as He is to all besides the source of action" (*Allegory of the Laws* 1.5; LCL, 1.149-51). Elsewhere he added, "Moses does not give the name of rest to mere inactivity. The cause of all things is by its nature active; it never ceases to work all that is best and most beautiful. God's rest is rather a working with absolute ease, without toil and without suffering" (*On the Cherubim* 87; LCL, 2.61).

With the pronouncement, "My Father is working even until now, and I am working," Jesus injects himself into the equation. The result is a kind of riddle,[76] open to several possible interpretations. Does it mean that after creating the world God continued working until now, but that now Jesus takes over in God's place? Or does it mean that God continued working and is still at work, only now *through* Jesus the Son?[77] Or that God has been at work ever since creation, first through the preexistent Son and now through the incarnate Son? Or is it simply that God is still at work, and Jesus is God's imitator, like a son apprenticed to his father? [78] There is no sure way to tell what the relation is between the Father's work and the work of the Son. Interpretations will vary according to the degree of sophistication the reader brings to the text. The implication in any event is that because God breaks the Sabbath Jesus can do so as well, and for that reason alone the "riddle" (if that is the right word) is highly provocative.[79] Beyond this, all the reader has to go on is Jesus' earlier comment to his disciples that "My food is that I might do the will of the One who sent me and complete his work" (*ergon,* 4:34). Not surprisingly, he now identifies "the One who sent me" unmistakably as "my Father" (compare 2:16), implicitly claiming for himself the title of God's "One and Only" (1:14, 18; 3:16), or "Son" sent into the world (see 3:17, 34-35). The stage is set for a confrontation, or more precisely a series of confrontations, not limited to a single occasion, or to one Sabbath or one unnamed festival, but spanning the rest of the first half of John's Gospel (chapters 5–12).

18 The answer to Jesus' "answer" echoes v. 16, where "for this," that is, for healing on the Sabbath, the Jerusalem authorities "began pursuing" Je-

---

76. Curiously, it is not listed among Jesus' riddles in Tom Thatcher's survey, *The Riddles of Jesus in John* (184-87). It is difficult to see why 2:16, for example, is included and 5:17 is not. Thatcher admits, "This list may not be exhaustive. Other large sections of FG in which Jesus speaks of his identity and mission, such as chapters 5 and 15, may include statements which FE understood to be riddles but which cannot be identified by these criteria" (187). Possibly he excludes 5:17 because "the Jews" expressed no confusion (see his four criteria, 183), but essentially they drew a blank (v. 18), just as they did after the pronouncement in 2:16 (see 2:18).

77. "Until now" (ἕως ἄρτι) can refer to conditions prevailing up to, but not including, the present (2:10; 16:24), or to conditions up to *and* including the present, and beyond (1 Jn 2:9, and probably here).

78. As has often been noted, the words in themselves and out of context could simply be read, "My father has always been a working man, and I'm a working man too"! On the apprenticed son, see Dodd, *Historical Tradition,* 386, n. 2, and in *RHPR* 42 (1962), 107-15.

79. In its implication, the pronouncement is comparable to the principle laid down in all three synoptic Gospels that "the Son of man is Lord of the Sabbath" (see Mt 12:8, Mk 2:28; and Lk 6:5).

5:1-18 JESUS AND THE SICK MAN IN JERUSALEM

sus. Here too it is "for this,"[80] for what he has just said, that they "kept seeking all the more to kill him." The reader now learns that when the authorities "began pursuing" Jesus (v. 16), their intent was "to kill."[81] Now they are "all the more"[82] determined to do so, and they will persist in this intent throughout the Gospel (see 7:1, 19, 20, 25; 8:37, 40; 11:53; 18:31).[83] Again the imperfect tenses are conspicuous. They "kept seeking" to kill Jesus, not only because he was breaking the Sabbath on a regular basis — in their eyes "abolishing" it[84] — but for an even deeper reason: he "was claiming God as his own Father."[85] They are referring of course to what he has just said, "My Father is working even until now, and I am working" (v. 17), but they make no explicit attempt to interpret what he means either by his "work" or the Father's "work." All they seem to hear is the expression, "my Father."[86] That, perhaps together with his use of the emphatic *"I" (kagō)* is what provokes them. From it they conclude three things: that Jesus is referring to God, that he is claiming God as "his own Father," and therefore that he is claiming to be "equal to God."[87]

As far as the Gospel writer is concerned, these are perfectly legitimate conclusions: Jesus *did* "break the Sabbath,"[88] he *did* claim God as "his own

---

80. Again, διὰ τοῦτο (see above, n. 66).

81. Gr. ἀποκτεῖναι.

82. Gr. μᾶλλον.

83. Abbott, by contrast (*Johannine Grammar*, 568), suggests that μᾶλλον signals a change of plans: "they *rather* sought to kill him [*than merely to persecute him as before*]." But the verses listed confirm the reader's impression that "pursuing" or "persecuting" Jesus always entailed seeking his death (compare Schnackenburg, 2.462, n. 31). The same will be true of the persecution of Jesus' disciples (see 15:20-21; 16:2).

84. Gr. ἔλυεν. The verb λύειν in relation to the Sabbath (as here), or the law (see 7:23; also Mt 5:19), or the Scripture (see 10:35), appears to mean more than simply transgress or violate or disregard, but rather to annul, destroy, or abolish (see BDAG, 607). It is never used of the Sabbath in any of the other Gospels.

85. "Claiming" is ἔλεγεν. That is, he was "saying that" God was his Father.

86. Gr. ὁ πατήρ μου. Odeberg (*The Fourth Gospel*, 203) disagrees, commenting that Jesus' blasphemy "consisted not in his calling the Holy One his Father, but in his presuming upon a peculiar sonship in virtue of which he had the right of performing the same 'continual work' as his Father." In short, he was a rebellious Son, saying in effect, "'I am equal with, as good as, my Father.'"

87. Gr. ἴσον τῷ θεῷ.

88. The verb "break" (ἔλυεν) could imply that Jesus did away with, or abolished, the Sabbath (see BDAG, 607). Yet the notice simply reinforces what was said in verse 16 (that Jesus "did such things" on the Sabbath). To the Jewish authorities this may have been tantamount to abolishing the Sabbath, yet they would also have assumed that one man cannot "abolish" an ordinance of God, only violate it. Jesus will later be charged not with abolishing the Sabbath, but simply "not keeping" it (οὐ τηρεῖ, 9:16). As for the Gospel writer, what is said here must be read in light of what Jesus says elsewhere, that one legitimately keeps the Sabbath by healing or doing good (see 7:23; also Mk 3:4; Lk 13:16; 14:3).

Father," and he *did* claim to be "equal to God."[89] The text presents these affirmations not simply as what "the Jews" thought Jesus was saying, but as what he was saying, and what was in fact the case.[90] Yet the repeated mention of "the Jews" (vv. 16, 18) also highlights the fact that such claims were highly problematic within Judaism, as much so or more than breaking the Sabbath. Philo, for example, even while acknowledging that "to imitate God's works is a pious act," cautioned that "the mind shows itself to be without God and full of self-love, when it deems itself as on a par with God;[91] and, whereas passivity is its true part, looks on itself as an agent. When God sows and plants noble qualities in the soul, the mind that says, '*I* plant' is guilty of impiety."[92] Philo's warning against the emphatic "I" *(egō)* suggests that in John as well part of the offense may be traceable to Jesus' emphatic conclusion, "and *I* am working."[93] Jesus' claim that God was "his own Father"[94] meant that God was (in C. H. Dodd's words) "his father in a sense other than that in which any Israelite might speak of Him as 'our Father in heaven.'"[95] This could mean that he was speaking as Israel's Messiah,[96] or it could mean (as both "the Jews" and the Gospel writer assume) that he was speaking as a divine being. To the Gospel writer these are not mutually exclusive options, but to Jesus' questioners the latter was the primary concern. In a later confrontation they will say, "It's not about a good work that we stone you, but about blasphemy, and because you,

---

89. The emphasis is somewhat different from Paul's in Philippians 2:6, where Jesus did not consider "being equal to God" (τὸ εἶναι ἴσα θεῷ) something to be "grasped" or "seized" (ἁρπαγμόν). To the author of John, this would have been because equality with God was already his.

90. Contrast Dodd, who argues that "if the evangelist had been asked whether or not he intended to affirm that Christ was ἴσος τῷ θεῷ, he would have replied that ἴσος, whether affirmed or denied, is not the proper term to use in this context" (*Interpretation*, 327-28). On the contrary, it is precisely the term of the Gospel writer's choosing, not as a straw man or a misconception that needs to be corrected, but as a true characterization of Jesus. It only needs to be elaborated and spelled out, and this Jesus will do in the discourse that follows. Still, Dodd's discussion of the matter (320-28) is highly illuminating.

91. Gr. ἴσος εἶναι θεῷ.

92. *Allegory of the Laws* 1.48-49 (LCL, 1.177). The Apostle Paul, significantly, once said the very thing Philo warned against (ἐγὼ ἐφύτευσα, "I planted"), but was quick to add, "but God made it grow" (1 Cor 3:6). Here too we will see Jesus adding crucial qualifications in the discourse that follows.

93. Gr. κἀγὼ ἐργάζομαι.

94. Gr. πατέρα ἴδιον.

95. Dodd, *Interpretation*, 325.

96. See, for example, (NRSV) 2 Samuel 7:14, "I will be a father to him, and he shall be a son to me," and Psalm 89:26-27, "He shall cry to me, 'You are my Father, my God and the Rock of my salvation!' I will make him the firstborn, the highest of the kings of the earth." This is in keeping with what the reader already knows about Jesus: that he is both "Son of God" and "King of Israel" (see 1:49).

being a man, are making yourself God" (10:33).[97] To the Jewish mind, making oneself "equal to God" (5:18) represented at the very least a first step toward the outright blasphemy of making oneself "God" (*theos*, 10:33),[98] and in that sense a denial of Jewish monotheism.[99] Yet the reader of the Gospel has known from the start that "God" (*theos*) is exactly what Jesus is (see 1:1, 18), so that to hear it from Jesus' own lips (implicitly) and from his opponents (explicitly) comes as no surprise, but as confirmation. With the notice that the issue is "not only" (*ou monon*) the Sabbath, but Jesus' claims about himself, we move decisively from the realm of legal observance to the realm of christology. The question "Who is the man?" (v. 12) will more and more take center stage. Jesus' answer (vv. 19-47) will primarily address that question, and only secondarily (and indirectly) the issue of the Sabbath.

D. JESUS' ANSWER TO THE JEWS IN JERUSALEM (5:19-47)

19 *So Jesus gave his answer, saying to them, "Amen, amen, I say to you, the son can do nothing on his own, except what he sees the father doing. For whatever things he does, these in the same way the son does too.* 20 *For the Father loves the Son and shows him everything that he himself is doing, and to your amazement he will show him greater works than these.* 21 *For just as the Father raises the dead and brings them to life, so too the Son brings to life those he wants.* 22 *For the Father judges no one, but has given all the judgment to the Son,* 23 *so that all will honor the Son just as they honor the Father. Whoever*

---

97. The grammar is similar: "making himself [ἑαυτὸν ποιῶν] equal to God" (5:18), and "make yourself [ποιεῖς σεαυτόν] God" (10:33).

98. In the Graeco-Roman world, the often-quoted words of Apollonius of Tyana assume only a difference of degree between the two designations: "Other men regard me as the equal of the gods [ἰσόθεον], and some of them even as a god [θεόν], but until now my own country alone ignores me" (Philostratus, *Epistle* 44).

99. Judaism guarded its monotheism rigorously against any notion of "two Powers" (שְׁתֵּי רְשׁוּיוֹת) or authorities, or a "second God" (see the classic discussions in G. F. Moore, *Judaism*, 1.364-67; Odeberg, *The Fourth Gospel*, 203-4; and Dodd, *Interpretation*, 324-27). See *Sifre Deuteronomy* §329, adducing Deuteronomy 32:39 ("there is no god beside me") as the correct reply both to those who say "there is no authority" and those who say "there are two authorities in heaven" (J. Neusner, *Sifre to Deuteronomy: An Analytical Translation* [Atlanta: Scholars Press, 1987], 2.374). So too *Mekilta to Exodus 20.2:* "Scripture, therefore, would not let the nations of the world have an excuse for saying that there are two Powers, but declares: 'I am the Lord thy God.'" And "Rabbi Nathan says: From this one can cite a refutation of the heretics who say: There are two Powers" (*Mekilta de-Rabbi Ishmael* [trans. J. Z. Lauterbach; Philadelphia: Jewish Publication Society, 1976], 2.231-32).

does not honor the Son does not honor the Father who sent him. 24 Amen, amen, I say to you that the person who hears my word and believes the One who sent me, has eternal life and does not come into judgment, but has passed from death into life. 25 Amen, amen, I say to you that an hour is coming and now is when the dead will hear the voice of the Son of God, and those who hear will live. 26 For just as the Father has life in himself, so too he gave to the Son to have life in himself, 27 and he gave him authority to do judgment, because he is the Son of man. 28 Don't be amazed at this, for an hour is coming in which all who are in the tombs will hear his voice, 29 and those who have done good things will go out to a resurrection of life, but those who have practiced wicked things to a resurrection of judgment.

30 "As for me, I can do nothing on my own. Just as I hear I judge, and my judgment is right, because I am not seeking my will but the will of the One who sent me. 31 If I testify about myself, my testimony is not true. 32 There is another who testifies about me, and I know that the testimony he testifies about me is true. 33 You have sent word to John, and he has testified to the truth. 34 I, however, do not accept the testimony from a human; I only say these things so that you might be saved. 35 He was the burning and shining lamp, and you chose to rejoice for a time in his light. 36 But I have testimony greater than John's. For the works that the Father has given me that I might complete them, the very works that I do testify about me that the Father has sent me. 37 And so the Father who sent me, he has testified about me. You have never heard his voice nor seen his form, 38 and you do not have his word dwelling in you, because he whom that One sent, him you do not believe. 39 You search the Scriptures, because you think that in them you have eternal life. And yet those are the [writings] that testify about me. 40 And you are unwilling to come to me that you might have life.

41 "I do not accept glory from humans. 42 No, I know you, that you do not have the love of God in yourselves. 43 I have come in my Father's name, and you do not accept me. If another comes in his own name, him you will accept. 44 How can you believe, when you receive glory from each other, but do not seek the glory that comes from the Only God? 45 Do not think that I will accuse you to the Father. Your accuser is Moses, in whom you have set your hope. 46 For if you believed Moses, you would believe me, for he wrote about me. 47 But if you do not believe his written words, how will you believe my spoken words?"

This time, instead of being one brief pronouncement (v. 17), Jesus' answer is his longest speech so far, and his longest uninterrupted speech to opponents

5:19-47 JESUS' ANSWER TO THE JEWS IN JERUSALEM

anywhere in the Gospel (vv. 19-47).[1] Its purpose is to explain in detail the brief riddle, "My Father is working even until now, and I am working" (v. 17), so as to refute his opponents and at the same time instruct the Gospel's readers. The answer has two parts: first, an examination of the two kinds of "works" he has in common with his Father, giving life and judging (vv. 19-29); second, an actual exercise of judgment in which he presents testimony from several witnesses on his own behalf and against his accusers, and reaches a verdict (vv. 30-47). In the first part, Jesus speaks of himself mainly as "the Son" in relation to "the Father" (vv. 19-23, 25-27), while in the second part he shifts back to the emphatic "I" (*egō,* vv. 31, 34, 36, 43, 45) with which the confrontation began (see v. 17). All of it goes unanswered, at least for the time being.

19-20 Jesus again gives an "answer"[2] to words not actually spoken. In a strange way, his answer recalls the answer of the sick man at the pool to the Jewish authorities. Just as he claimed that he carried his mat on the Sabbath not on his own initiative but at the command of Jesus (v. 11), so Jesus now says that he does not act "by himself," but only at God's prompting. His repeated use of the verb "to do"[3] (v. 19) speaks directly to the charges that he "did such things on the Sabbath" (v. 16), and his denial that he acted "on his own"[4] addresses the claim that he was "making himself equal to God" (v. 18).[5] He begins his defense with the fifth "Amen, amen" saying in the Gospel (see 1:51; 3:3, 5, 11). Like two of the others (3:3 and 5), it deals with life's impossibilities.[6] "The son," he claims, "cannot"[7] do anything "on his own." As in the earlier examples, the impossibility is qualified by an "except" or "unless" clause. There, we heard that no one can see or enter the kingdom of God "unless" *(ean mē)* they are reborn (3:3, 5). The accent was on the exception. Here too, the son can do nothing on his own "except" *(ean*

---

1. The only longer uninterrupted speech is addressed to his disciples (14:23–16:16).
2. Gr. ἀπεκρίνατο, as in verse 17.
3. Gr. ποιεῖν, ποιοῦντα, ποιῇ, and ποιεῖ.
4. Gr. ἀφ' ἑαυτοῦ.
5. This does not mean that Jesus is in any way denying that charge. Rather, he is explaining what it means for him to be "equal to God." See Chrysostom, *Homilies on John,* 38.3: "He saith this not to take away, but to confirm, His Equality" (NPNF, 1st ser., 14.134); so Augustine, even more eloquently, envisioning what he might say to the heretic: "If there is God the greater and God the less, then we worship two Gods, not one God. . . . This I do not assert: for I understand equality as implying therein also undivided love; and if undivided love, then perfect unity" (*Tractates on John,* 18.4; NPNF, 1st ser., 7.118). Here Augustine anticipates and speaks to the issues raised by Dodd, *Interpretation,* 325-28.
6. In the earlier setting, as we saw, the οὐ δύναται echoed the words of Nicodemus (3:2).
7. Gr. οὐ δύναται.

mē) what he sees his father doing.[8] This time the clause is commonly read as adversative rather than exceptive, yielding the translation, *"but only* what he sees the father doing" (my italics).[9] Jesus will insist repeatedly in this Gospel that he never says or does anything "on his own" (see v. 30; also 7:17, 28; 8:28; 12:49; 14:10; the same is true of "the Spirit of truth," 16:13).[10] On the contrary, a person who speaks "on his own" is a person who "seeks his own glory" (7:18). Jesus is not such a person (see 5:41, 44; 8:50, 54). He does nothing "on his own," but "seeks the glory of the One who sent him" (7:17-18).[11] In this respect he behaves like a prophet,[12] but even more like a son apprenticed to his father, who learns from his father by imitation. Jesus goes so far as to say that the son "sees" what the father does, and does the same things himself. He has said before (3:11), John has repeated (3:32), and Jesus will say again (8:38), that he "has seen" certain things which he now reveals to the world, and more specifically that he "has seen the Father" (so 6:46). The perfect tenses seem to refer to Jesus' preexistence, when he was "with God in the beginning" (1:2). But what of the present tense, "sees," here? Is Jesus claiming that he, as God's Son, literally "sees" the Father on a regular basis during his ministry in Galilee and Jerusalem?

More likely, the terminology comes from the parable-like character of Jesus' words. That is, a son, any son learning his father's trade, does what he "sees" his father doing.[13] Interpreters who notice the parabolic language tend

---

8. Yet another example is John's pronouncement, "A person cannot [οὐ δύναται] receive anything unless [ἐὰν μή] it is given him from heaven" (3:27).

9. So most modern English translations (including RSV, NRSV, NIV, NEB, REB, NLT). See Robertson, *Grammar,* 1025. But New Testament examples of this adversative use of ἐὰν μή are few (Gal 2:16 is a classic, though controversial, instance).

10. Only once does Jesus claim to do something on his own initiative, when he says, "I lay down my life, that I might take it again. . . . I lay it down on my own" (ἀπ' ἐμαυτοῦ), adding that "I have authority [ἐξουσία] to lay it down, and I have authority to take it again" (10:18). Here, however, the contrast is between Jesus' initiative and that of other human beings who wanted to take his life from him, not between Jesus and the Father. He is in fact quick to add, "This command I received from my Father" (v. 18).

11. Again Chrysostom speaks to the issue, defining "nothing of himself" as "nothing in opposition to the Father, nothing alien from, nothing strange to Him, which is especially the assertion of One declaring an Equality and entire agreement" (*Homilies on John,* 38.4; NPNF, 1st ser., 14.134).

12. See 11:51, where Caiaphas the High Priest did not speak "on his own" (ἀφ' ἑαυτοῦ) but rather "prophesied."

13. "The son" (ὁ υἱός) and "the father" (τὸν πατέρα), even with the definite articles, can mean "a son" and "a father" in the sense of any son or father, just as "the heir" (ὁ κληρονόμος) in Galatians 4:1 means "an heir" or "any heir" to his father's estate (see also "the husband" and "the wife" in Eph 5:23). On this generic use of the article, see Robertson, *Grammar,* 757; Abbott, *Johannine Grammar,* 47.

5:19-47 JESUS' ANSWER TO THE JEWS IN JERUSALEM

to use it as evidence of sources behind the Johannine narrative, leading back (possibly) to actual words of the historical Jesus.[14] This is quite plausible, but is not our interest here. A commentary's job is to ask how the use of parabolic language affects the *present* form of the text, that is, the dynamics of Jesus' reply to "the Jews," and the Gospel writer's christological message to his readers. This is not the last time the Johannine Jesus incorporates parables (in the sense of illustrations from daily life) into his discourses. John has done so already (3:29), and three chapters later Jesus will say to another group of questioners under similar circumstances that "the slave" (any slave) does not remain in a household forever, but that "the son" (any son) remains forever (8:35). A slave can be sold, but a son cannot, for he is part of the family. Jesus then applies the designation "son" to himself: "So if the Son makes you free, you will really be free" (8:36). Later still, he will tell his disciples, "I no longer say you are slaves," adding that "the slave" — any slave — does not "know what his master is doing," while they by contrast are like "friends," because "I made known to you everything I heard from my Father" (15:15). He is "the master" or "Lord," and they are his "friends" (15:13-15). Again he moves smoothly from parable to straightforward theological discourse.

The same is true in our passage, where "the son" is any son, yet at the same time specifically Jesus. That a son "sees" what his father does (v. 19), or that a father "shows" his son what to do (v. 20) is a natural part of the story, not necessarily a profound disclosure either about Jesus' preexistence or his visionary experiences. The accent is not on the "seeing" or "showing" per se, but on the theme of imitation, and on the consequent identity of the Son's works with those of the Father. Jesus drives the point home with a series of four clauses, each introduced by *gar* ("for"). The first two of these affirm the identity of the works of the Father and the Son (vv. 19, 20), while the latter two specify just what works are involved and in what way (vv. 21, 22). In the first two, Jesus sets no limit either to the number or extent of these works, or to the degree to which they match: "For whatever things he does, these in the same way the son does too" (v. 19), and "For the Father loves[15] the Son and shows him everything that he himself is doing" (v. 20).[16] In these two pro-

---

14. See Brown, 1.218, and on such parabolic forms in John's Gospel, see Dodd, *Historical Tradition,* 366-87. Dodd concludes from this and several other examples that "in spite of such degree of rewriting as we must always expect from our evangelist, they find their natural place in the family to which the Synoptic parables belong," that John "drew independently upon the common and primitive tradition, and that he has preserved valuable elements in that tradition which the Synoptic evangelists have neglected" (386-87).

15. Gr. φιλεῖ.

16. In the translation I have (perhaps somewhat arbitrarily) left "son" and "father" lower case in verse 19, while capitalizing them in verses 20-23, largely because of the ref-

nouncements the parabolic language continues: an adult son's work resembles his father's when he is apprenticed to a father who loves him. And what is true in everyday life is just as true of Jesus, "the Son," and God, "the Father."[17]

What are "the things he does" (v. 19) that the Father shows to the Son? The next clause identifies them as "works" *(erga),* with the promise of works "greater than these" (v. 20). What are "these," and what are the "greater works"? "These" are apparently the "things" Jesus customarily did on the Sabbath ("such things," v. 16), typified by the healing of the man at the pool. Jesus has already identified them with the works of the Father "until now" (v. 17), that is, the works of God subsequent to creation. The "greater works" are yet to come, but will they come at the last day, or simply later in the Johannine story? Two later miracles explicitly qualify as "greater," the gift of sight to a man born blind (see 9:32), and the raising of a man four days dead (11:39). But at this point in the narrative there is no way to know for certain what the "greater works" will be. All we are told is that Jesus' antagonists will be "amazed"[18] at what the Father will show Jesus (v. 20), and what Jesus consequently will show them. Aside from his introductory formula, "Amen, amen, I say to you" (v. 19), this is the first time Jesus acknowledges the existence of his audience, and he does so in order to promise that God will vindicate him against their charges. While "amazement" is a common reaction to Jesus' words and deeds in the synoptic Gospels,[19] surprises in general can be either pleasant or unpleasant.[20] In this instance, given that those being addressed are bent on killing him (v. 18), "amazement" is more like "dismay" than "delight." Jesus will return repeatedly to the emphatic "you" *(hymeis)* in the second part of his discourse (vv. 30-47), as he resorts more and more to direct polemic against his accusers and would-be assassins (see vv. 33, 34, 35, 38, 39, 42, 44, and 45). Only momentarily does he pause here to anticipate this later polemic, hinting that God will intervene decisively to settle the argument in his favor.

21 With the third (of four) explanatory clauses introduced by *gar*

---

erence to "greater works" and to the distinctly divine works of giving life and exercising judgment.

17. Compare John's testimony: "The Father loves [ἀγαπᾷ] the Son and has given all things [πάντα] in his hand" (3:35). The only appreciable difference between φιλεῖν and ἀγαπᾶν in these two texts is that the former calls attention to friendship and the latter to choice or election.

18. Gr. ἵνα ὑμεῖς θαυμάζητε.

19. In the case of his miracles, see Mt 8:27; 9:33; 15:31; 21:20; Mk 5:20; Lk 8:25; 9:43; 11:14; 24:12, 41, and in relation to his words, see Mt 22:22; Lk 4:22; 20:26.

20. BDAG (444) defines θαυμάζειν as being "extraordinarily impressed or disturbed," adding that "the context determines whether in a good or bad sense." For a mildly negative use of the term, see 4:27, and Luke 11:38 (less mild, as a Pharisee takes offense at Jesus' failure to wash before eating).

5:19-47 JESUS' ANSWER TO THE JEWS IN JERUSALEM

("for"), Jesus now becomes specific about the "works" of God. He assumes (and the Gospel writer assumes) that his opponents will not disagree with his assertion that God "raises the dead,"[21] and "brings them[22] to life."[23] For all practical purposes the assumption is that they are Pharisees, who themselves believed in resurrection.[24] They are troubled only that he continues to call God "Father" (see v. 18). "Just as" introduces the agreed-upon premise that God "raises the dead and brings them to life." The sticking point is the conclusion Jesus draws: "So too[25] the Son brings to life those he wants." All he is doing is repeating in effect that "My Father is working even until now, and I am working" (v. 17), while defining that common "work" as resurrection, or bringing the dead to life. That *Jesus* brings the dead to life is something "the Jews," Pharisees or not, can neither understand nor accept. Not so the Gospel's readers. They — we — are not the audience being addressed (the emphatic "you" of v. 20), and are not "surprised" by what Jesus says. We are mere eavesdroppers to the exchange, yet we know, at least in part, what he means by saying, "the Son brings to life those he wants." We heard him say to the sick man, "Get up" (5:8). We heard him say to the royal official, "Your son lives" (4:50, 53). We heard his testimony that God "gave the One and Only Son" so that those who believe "might have eternal life" (3:16), and John's testimony that "whoever believes in the Son has eternal life" (3:36). And because we know that Jesus is "the Son" (1:14, 18), it comes as no surprise or scandal to us that he gives life.

---

21. Gr. ἐγείρει τοὺς νεκρούς.

22. Because "bring to life" (ζῳοποιεῖν), like ποιεῖν, is normally a transitive verb, "the dead" should probably be understood as the implied object of *both* ἐγείρει and ζῳοποιεῖ even though the latter has no object expressed. Thus the comment that "the Father raises the dead and brings them to life" sounds redundant. It is not redundant, however, for as we will see (v. 29), there is a resurrection that is *not* to life.

23. See *b. Ta'anit* 2a, "Three keys the Holy One blessed be He has retained in His own hands and not entrusted to the hand of any messenger, namely, the Key of Rain, the Key of Childbirth, and the Key of the Revival of the Dead." Also, the second benediction of the standard synagogue prayer, the *Shemoneh Esreh:* "Thou, O Lord, art mighty for ever, thou revivest the dead, thou art mighty to save" (*Authorized Daily Prayer Book* [rev. ed.; New York: Bloch, 1960], 133).

24. That God raises the dead was a commonplace in both Pharisaic Judaism and early Christianity (see v. 28; also Acts 24:15; 26:8). While the Sadducean party disagreed (see Acts 23:8), John's Gospel is not interested in such distinctions within Judaism. "Sadducees" are never mentioned, and when "priests" or "chief priests" come into the story, even they are commonly linked to the Pharisees (see 1:19, 24; also 7:32, 45; 11:47, 57; 18:3). Nothing in this discourse or anywhere in John's Gospel seems intended to speak to one party in Judaism over against another. Jesus wants to divide the opposition only over whether they believe in him or not, not on the basis of any other issue.

25. "Just as" is ὥσπερ γάρ; "so too" is οὕτως καί.

Jesus' real audience, "the Jews," heard none of these things, and if they had, they would not have believed them. So for them it is a very different matter. The notice that the Son gives life stands as a tacit rebuke to them for wanting to take life (v. 18).[26] Jesus' language echoes his response in the synoptic tradition to a charge of Sabbath breaking in Galilee. "Is it lawful on the Sabbath to do good or to do evil," he had asked (Mk 3:4), "to save life[27] or to kill?" His work, he insists — and God's — is to give life,[28] not take it away. He claims, moreover, to give life not just to "the dead" but to "those he wants"[29] suggesting that although he does not act "by himself" or on his own initiative (v. 19); he is no robot. He acts with a certain autonomy, doing what "he wants" *(thelei)* within the limits of his mission as One "sent" from the Father, and in the framework of his responsibility to obey the Father (see 4:34). In short, he does not back away from the implications of the emphatic "I" in his initial pronouncement, "My Father is working even until now, and I am working" (v. 17).[30] At this point, Jesus does not say in so many words that the Son "raises the dead." He evidently wants to define the Son's works more broadly to include healings and a variety of other ways of giving life, from changing water into wine and providing "living water" not from a well (chapters 2 and 4), to multiplying loaves and fish to feed a multitude (chapter 6), or even bringing in an enormous, unexpected catch of fish (chapter 21). Even these are works of the Father, although he does not say so explicitly,[31] and we will soon learn that Jesus, like the Father, "raises the dead," both now and in the future (see vv. 25, 28-29; 6:39-40, 44, 54). In the case of Lazarus, we will see him doing exactly that (11:25, 43-44).

22-23 In one sense, the opposite of "life" is death (v. 24, "from death to life"), but in another, the opposite of "life" is "judgment." Judgment is the theme of the last of the four clauses introduced by *gar:* "For the Father judges no one, but has given all the judgment to the Son" (v. 22).[32] This

---

26. That is, "kill" (ἀποκτεῖναι, v. 18).

27. Admittedly the vocabulary is different: "to save life" is ψυχὴν σῶσαι.

28. Gr. ζῳοποιεῖν.

29. Gr. οὓς θέλει. At the end of the Gospel, the writer calls attention to a saying in which he himself was thought to have been a beneficiary of this very claim. "If I want [θέλω] him to remain until I come," Jesus had said about him, "what is that to you?" (21:22; see also 17:24).

30. Chrysostom puts it bluntly: "Yet 'can do nothing of Himself' is opposed to 'whom He will'; since if He quickeneth 'whom He will,' He can do something 'of Himself,' (for to 'will' implies power,) but if He 'can do nothing of Himself,' then He cannot 'quicken whom He will'" (*Homilies on John,* 38.4; NPNF, 1st ser., 14.135-36).

31. See the classic discussion by C. S. Lewis in *Miracles: A Preliminary Study* (New York: Macmillan, 1947), 163-65.

32. Gr. κρίνει ("judges") and τὴν κρίσιν πᾶσαν ("all the judgment").

seems to contradict what was said earlier, that the Son's mission was "not to judge the world, but so that the world might be saved through him" (3:17; see also 12:47). "Bringing to life" and "judging" are handled quite differently in this Gospel. Both the Father and the Son get credit for raising the dead and giving life, but neither wants to be known as the world's "Judge." Here the Father defers to the Son in that regard, while elsewhere the Son either avoids the role (8:15) or assumes it indirectly or with qualifications.[33] For example, those who reject the Son are "already judged," in that "the Light has come into the world" ("the Light" being the Son), and they "loved the dark and not the Light, because their works were evil" (3:18-19). Or, Jesus says, they "have that which judges them: the word which I spoke, that will judge them in the last day" (12:48). Even when he admits that "For judgment I have come into this world," the judgment he brings involves healing as well as condemnation, for it is as much "that those who do not see might see" as that "those who see might go blind" (9:39). Such disclaimers make the point that while "life" or salvation comes solely on God's initiative, those who are "judged" bring the judgment on themselves.

Nothing is said here of what "all the judgment" entails. "All" implies that the judgment is universal in scope. Its universality is echoed in its purpose that "all" will "honor the Son just as they honor the Father" (v. 23). John said it already, in slightly different words: "The Father loves the Son and has given all things in his hand" (3:35). Here Jesus accents "judgment" in particular as that which the Father has given, but judgment is not so much an end in itself as a means of bringing "honor" to the Son. The verb "to honor"[34] occurs four times in a single verse (v. 23), but behind them all lies the assumption that the Father himself was the first to "honor" the Son, by making the Son his agent or representative on earth. Agency comes to expression in a variety of ways both in this Gospel and in the others. An agent acts on behalf of whoever sends him, and whatever is done to, or for, the agent is done to, or for, the sender.[35] This gives

---

33. In the present context, when he finally does take on the role of judge, he claims it is not "by myself" (ἀπ' ἐμαυτοῦ), but "just as I hear," and not for "my will, but the will of the One who sent me" (see v. 30).

34. Gr. τιμᾶν.

35. In John's Gospel alone, see 12:44-45 ("The person who believes in me does not believe in me but in the One who sent me, and the person who sees me sees the One who sent me"), 13:20 ("The person who receives whomever I send receives me, and the person who receives me receives the One who sent me'), 14:9 ('The person who has seen me has seen the Father"), 15:20 ("If they have pursued me, they will also pursue you; if they kept my word, they will also keep yours"), and 15:23 ("The person who hates me also hates my Father"). In the other Gospels, see Matthew 10:40; Mark 9:37; Luke 9:48; 10:16. On agency, see Peder Borgen, "God's Agent in the Fourth Gospel," in *The Interpretation of John* (2d ed.; Edinburgh: T&T Clark, 1997), 83-95.

the whole pronouncement an ironic twist. At first, Jesus seems to assume that of course those in his audience all "honor the Father," desiring only that they will now "honor the Son" in the same way (v. 23a). But he immediately undercuts his own assumption with the comment that "whoever does not honor the Son does not honor the Father who sent him" (v. 23b). "The Jews" who comprise his audience (vv. 16, 18) obviously think they are honoring God by guarding God's uniqueness and trying to kill Jesus for "making himself equal to God" (v. 18).[36] Yet they are not honoring "the Father," for "the Father" implies a Son, and if they do not recognize "the Son" they cannot recognize or worship God as "Father."[37] Ironically, the very words he speaks (v. 23) carry out the "judgment" that he says God has given him (v. 22). By not honoring Jesus as "the Son," his hearers are dishonoring "the Father who sent him,"[38] that is, dishonoring the God they claim to worship.[39] Jesus' words to the Samaritan woman, "We [Jews] worship what we know" (4:22), are no longer true of those who dishonor Jesus. His rebuke to them remains quite general and impersonal — "whoever does not honor"[40] — but it will grow ever more personal and direct as the discourse moves on (see vv. 37-38, 42, 44).[41]

24 Again (as in v. 19) Jesus uses the "Amen, amen" formula to highlight what he will say next. Here, as in 3:3 and 5, two such pronouncements follow in quick succession and with similar meaning (vv. 24 and 25). The first of these drops "the Son" as a self-designation and shifts back to the "I" of verse 17. Jesus accents the solemn declaration, "I say to you," by referring to "my word," and to the necessity of "hearing." It is as if he repeated the "Amen, amen" formula in bold italics, adding a kind of Johannine equivalent to another common Gospel formula, "Whoever has ears to hear, let him hear."[42] This is what the pronouncement does for "the Jews" to whom Jesus is speaking.

---

36. See 16:2, where Jesus warns his disciples that "an hour is coming for anyone who kills you to think of it as offering worship to God."

37. The reader knows this, for Jesus told the Samaritan woman a chapter earlier of "true worshipers" — in distinction from both Jew and Samaritan — who would "worship the Father in Spirit and truth, for those are the kind the Father is looking for to worship him" (4:23). As we saw, this "true worship" is worship through Jesus the Son.

38. The phrase "the Father who sent him" brings together the two expressions, "my Father" (2:16; 5:17) and "the One who sent me" (4:34). From here, Jesus will use "the One who sent me" (see vv. 24, 30) and "the Father who sent me" (see v. 37) interchangeably, as if the sending of Jesus into the world is what defines who "the Father" is.

39. See especially 8:54-55, "It is my Father who glorifies me, him whom you say that 'He is our God.' And you have not known him, but I know him." Also 7:28, 8:19, and Jesus' warnings to his disciples in 15:21 and 16:3.

40. Gr. ὁ μὴ τιμῶν.

41. The directness is measured by the increasing frequency of the pronoun "you" (ὑμεῖς) in vv. 30-47.

42. See Mark 4:9, 23; Luke 8:8, 14:35. Matthew has it more simply, "Whoever

5:19-47 JESUS' ANSWER TO THE JEWS IN JERUSALEM

For the Gospel's reader it does more, identifying Jesus' "word" *(logos)* as first of all a life-giving word, not a word of judgment. It is familiar ground, for the implied reader knows that Jesus is himself "the Word" (1:1, 14), and that "In him was life" (1:4). While this is the first time Jesus has referred to "my word," the expression echoes earlier references to "the word Jesus spoke" (2:22), and to "his word" (in contrast to the Samaritan woman's, 4:41).[43] "My word" does not of course mean Jesus' word in distinction from the Father's, for John's testimony was that "the one God sent speaks the words of God" (3:34).[44] On the contrary, the appropriate response of "the person who hears my word," Jesus says, is not to believe him, but to "believe the One who sent me."[45] The presumption is that God is speaking through Jesus. To believe Jesus is to believe God, or as he put it a moment before, to honor the Son is to honor "the Father who sent him" (v. 23). The reader now learns that Jesus' "word" is the means by which he "brings to life those he wants" (v. 21). Whoever "hears" the Son's word and "believes" the Father "has eternal life" as a present possession, and consequently "does not come into judgment." Here, as in Jesus' conversation with Nicodemus, "life" and "judgment" are mutually exclusive realities (see 3:16-18). The point is not that those who believe are already judged and acquitted, and thereby granted eternal life.[46] Rather, those who "have life" escape judgment altogether, while those who "come into judgment" do not have life. Moreover, those who "hear" and "believe" do not have to wait for some future "life after death," but have already "passed[47] from death into life" (see also 1 Jn 3:14). There is indeed "life after death," but "life" in this instance is present, while

---

has ears, let him hear" (11:15; 13:9, 43; so too Rev 2:7, 11, 17, 29; 3:6, 13, 22; 13:9), but the formula never appears in John's Gospel.

43. As the Gospel goes on, Jesus refers several more times to "my word," usually as ὁ λόγος ὁ ἐμός when addressing opponents (8:31, 37, 43, 51; but see 8:52), and as ὁ λόγος μου in speaking to his disciples (see 14:23; 15:20; 17:6). The use of the latter expression here is consistent with the notion that Jesus is momentarily talking past "the Jews" here, and inviting the Gospel's readers to "eternal life."

44. See 7:16, "My teaching is not mine, but belongs to the One who sent me."

45. The verb "believe" (πιστεύειν) with the dative case (in this instance with τῷ πέμψαντί με, "the One who sent me") does not mean to believe in God (TEV, CEV) or even trust in God (NEB, REB), but to believe God by accepting what God says (RSV, NRSV, NIV). It is the construction used of the royal official believing what Jesus said (4:50).

46. According to Barrett (261), "The thought is closely akin to the Pauline doctrine of justification, according to which the believer does come into judgement but leaves the court acquitted." On the contrary, the phrase "already judged" (ἤδη κέκριται) is used quite differently in 3:18, where those "already judged" are precisely those who have *not* "believed in the name of the One and Only Son of God."

47. Gr. μεταβέβηκεν.

"death" belongs to the past. This is the first mention of "death"[48] in John's Gospel. "Death" is presumed to be the situation in which people in the world find themselves by default, apart from the "light" that comes in the person of Jesus. Up to now it has been called "darkness" (see 1:5; 3:19), the opposite of "light" — just as "death" is the opposite of "life." The author and his readers both know that "the light is shining in the darkness" already, and that "the darkness did not overtake it" (1:5; see also 1 Jn 2:8). They know that death's power is broken for those who believe, and that they themselves have "passed from death into life." The characteristically Johannine promise of "eternal life" here and now is for them, outside and beyond the story, not for Jesus' accusers within the story, who know none of these things and have no way of comprehending what Jesus is saying. Quite conspicuously, he does not say to them, "If *you* hear my word and believe," but "the person who hears[49] my word and believes," looking beyond them to a more receptive audience typified by the readers of the Gospel.[50]

25 The second "Amen, amen" pronouncement builds on the ending of the first. If some have "passed from death into life" (v. 24), then "the dead" have come alive, and this means resurrection. If the first "Amen, amen" was primarily for the readers of the Gospel, the second is intended both for them and for "the Jews" at the festival in Jerusalem. Jesus makes the double time perspective explicit with the same formula he used in speaking to the Samaritan woman (4:23): "an hour is coming and now is."[51] It is as if he said to his accusers, "an hour is coming," and the Gospel writer chimed in with the postscript, "and now is," signaling to the reader that what Jesus promised back then was now coming to realization. Yet the words are unmistakably Jesus' own. He is simply repeating what he said in the preceding verse. This time it is intelligible to his immediate hearers, for it corresponds to what they themselves expected to happen in the future: "the dead will hear the voice of the Son of God, and those who hear will live." True, they still have the difficulty of acknowledging the "voice" at the resurrection as the voice of "the Son of God,"[52] but the notion of God raising the dead is not for-

---

48. Gr. θάνατος.

49. Gr. ὁ ἀκούων, literally "the one hearing."

50. The noncomprehension becomes explicit in 8:51-53, where Jesus makes a similar kind of promise (v. 51), and "the Jews" (v. 52) neither understand nor give evidence of ever having heard such a thing before (see also 8:43, "Why do you not understand my speech? Because you cannot hear my word," and 6:60, "This word is hard. Who can hear it?").

51. Gr. ἔρχεται ὥρα καὶ νῦν ἐστιν.

52. "The Son" and "the Son of God" are used interchangeably. The former is very common on Jesus' lips in this Gospel, but the longer expression is found only here and in 3:18, 10:36, and 11:4.

5:19-47 JESUS' ANSWER TO THE JEWS IN JERUSALEM

eign to them. Their viewpoint is like Mary of Bethany's in a later conversation with Jesus about her brother Lazarus: "I know he will rise in the resurrection at the last day" (11:24), and Jesus will shortly agree that they are right about that (v. 28). But his extraordinary claim is not only that he is the Son who will awaken the dead, but that the future is now. The time has come and the long-expected resurrection is under way — metaphorically in the experience of the Gospel's readers (see v. 24), but literally as well in the course of the narrative itself (11:43-44, "Lazarus! Out!" . . . and "The one who had died came out"). This "the Jews" are not prepared to accept, yet for the time being they say nothing. Jesus and his "voice" holds center stage. The very words that he speaks convey — not to them but to the Gospel's readers — the "eternal life" about which he speaks.

What does it mean to "hear the voice of the Son of God"? More pointedly, what does it mean for "the dead" to do so? Common sense tells us the dead can hear nothing. Yet Ezekiel prophesied, "O dry bones, hear the word of the LORD" (Ezek 37:4), and Jesus will point to a time when "all who are in the tombs will hear his voice" (v. 28). Sleep was, and is, a common metaphor for death (see 11:11-14; also Mk 5:39; 1 Cor 15:51; 1 Thess 4:13). Daniel was told, "Many of those who sleep in the dust of the earth shall awake" (Dan 12:2), and how better to awaken someone from sleep than by the sound of a voice? Paul quotes such a voice in Ephesians: "Awake, sleeper, and arise from the dead, and the Christ will shine on you" (Eph 3:14). But the voice that awakens the dead in John's Gospel is the Christ's own voice, "the voice of the Son of God," reminding us that just as sleep is a metaphor for physical death, so death itself can be a metaphor for spiritual sleep, "darkness," or alienation from God (again, see 1:5; 3:19; also 8:12; 12:35, 46; 1 Jn 1:5; 2:8). Therefore those who "hear the voice of the Son of God" in this Gospel include not only Lazarus, who was physically dead (11:44), but his sister Mary, still alive (11:29), and Jesus' disciples, whom he called his "sheep" (10:3), plus "other sheep" he promised to bring later (10:16, 27), and finally "everyone who is of the truth" (18:37). All these belong to the ranks of "the dead,"[53] and to all of them the promise goes out that "those who hear will live" (v. 25).[54] The promise goes out as well to Je-

---

53. Gr. οἱ νεκροί.
54. The verb "to hear" is used differently in different pronouncements. In v. 24, one must not only "hear" the word (ἀκούειν with the accusative), but also "believe" what is said (πιστεύειν with the dative). In v. 25, to "hear" the Son of God's voice (ἀκούειν with the genitive) means to take heed, or to hear and obey, implying belief. In vv. 28-29, all who are physically dead will "hear his voice" (again ἀκούειν with the genitive), but this time "hear" does not necessarily imply belief, for not all will attain a "resurrection of life" (v. 29). Thus the claim of Abbott (*Johannine Vocabulary*, 116) that the accusative implies simply hearing while the genitive implies both hearing and obedience works for vv. 24 and 25 but not for vv. 28-29. All that can be said is that sometimes hearing implies faith

sus' accusers on the scene, but with no evidence that they either "heard his word " or "believed the One who sent him" (v. 24; see vv. 37-38).

26 The form of Jesus' next pronouncement echoes that of verse 21: "For *just as* the Father has life in himself, *so too* he gave to the Son to have life in himself" (italics added).[55] What does it mean to "have life," and what does it mean to have it "in himself"? Up to now, those who "have eternal life" are those who believe in Jesus (3:15, 16, 36; 5:24), and it is natural to assume that they have it because Jesus had it first (see 1:4, "In him was life"). "In himself"[56] adds little to this, and should not be overinterpreted. It does not mean, for example, that the Father "made his Son to be the source of life" (GNB), even though that is true, nor does "life" here necessarily refer to "a creative life-giving power exercised toward men."[57] This would make verse 26 simply a doublet of verse 21. The formal parallelism suggests that the two pronouncements are indeed closely related, yet they are not quite synonymous. To have "life in oneself" is not something only the Father and the Son share, but something believers can claim as well. Those who "eat the flesh of the Son of man" can be said either to "have life in themselves" (6:53),[58] or simply to "have eternal life" (v. 54).[59] The two expressions mean the same thing: eternal life is theirs as an assured present possession, and that is all Jesus is saying here about himself and the Father. While his life is dependent on the Father's (vv. 19-20), it is nevertheless his own (see v. 21), implying that no one can take it from him (see 10:17-18). Ironically, the reminder comes just as the Jewish authorities were "trying all the more to kill him" (v. 18), underlining the futility of their efforts.

27 If v. 26 builds on v. 21, v. 27 builds on v. 22. There, Jesus said that the Father had "given all the judgment to the Son." This he offered as an illustration of the principle that "whatever things [the Father] does, these in the same way the Son does too" (v. 19). Here he adds that the Father "gave him authority[60] to do judgment because he is the Son of man." The expres-

---

and sometimes not (see BDF, §173[2]; Robertson, *Grammar,* 506). It depends on the context and the rhetoric, not on whether the verb is used with the accusative or the genitive.

55. "Just as" is ὥσπερ γάρ; "so too" is οὕτως καί (on v. 21, see above, n. 25).

56. Gr. ἐν ἑαυτῷ.

57. Brown, 1.215. So too Bultmann, who comments that God and Jesus "possess the creative power of life; whereas the ζωή which man can enjoy is the kind of life proper to the creature" (260).

58. Gr. ἔχετε ζωὴν ἐν ἑαυτοῖς.

59. See also 5:42, "you do not have the love of God in yourselves" (ἐν ἑαυτοῖς). Bultmann knows that 6:53 is a problem for him, but characteristically dismisses it as a later redaction. Life ἐν ἑαυτοῖς, he claims, "is attributed to the believers (inasmuch as they receive the sacrament) only in the editorial addition, 6:53" (260, n. 3).

60. Gr. ἐξουσίαν.

sion "to do judgment"⁶¹ corresponds to "bring to life" (v. 21), and the two together comprise that which the Son "does" in imitation of the Father (v. 19). As in chapter 3, "the Son of man" and "the Son" or "the Son of God" are pretty much interchangeable (see 3:13-17), but "the Son of man" here, in contrast to all its other occurrences in the Gospels (1:51; 3:13 and 14 so far), lacks definite articles in Greek.⁶² A sufficient reason for this is Colwell's rule that "definite predicate nouns which precede the verb usually lack the article."⁶³ If the rule is in play here, then "Son of man" means "the Son of man," just as in all other Gospel passages, and that is how I have translated it.

Many commentators look for different explanations, either that the title without the article is intended to evoke some specific biblical text (Dan 7:13, perhaps, or Ps 8:4), or that Jesus means simply that God has given him "authority to do judgment" because he is "a son of man" (that is, a human being). The latter is unlikely, even though at least one ancient source may have read it that way.⁶⁴ It fails to take account of this Gospel's pessimism about human beings and the human condition (see 2:24-25; 3:19; 5:41; 12:43; contrast Mt 9:8). Jesus may well be alluding here to texts or traditions, both biblical and extrabiblical, linking "Son of man" in some way with "authority" or "judgment" or both.⁶⁵ The classic example is Daniel 7:13-14, LXX, where the prophet sees "one like a son of man"⁶⁶ coming on the clouds of heaven to the Ancient of Days to be presented in his presence, "and authority was given him." This authority is an "eternal authority, which will not be taken away." In the interpretation a few verses later, the Ancient of Days "gave the judgment" to, or for, "the saints of the Most High" (7:22), who seem to have been represented by the figure of the "Son of man."

Even though the scene in Daniel decisively shaped the New Testament image of Jesus as "the Son of man" (in Mark alone, see, for example, 2:10, 28; 13:26; 14:62), New Testament writers dropped the indefinite expression, "one like a son of man," in favor of an actual title with definite arti-

---

61. Gr. κρίσιν ποιεῖν.
62. Gr. υἱὸς ἀνθρώπου, rather than ὁ υἱὸς τοῦ ἀνθρώπου.
63. See above on 1:1. Also Morris, 284 (n. 82).
64. According to the *Testament of Abraham,* which gives evidence of familiarity with the Gospel of John (see Bultmann, 261, n. 5), Abraham sees "the son of Adam, the first-formed, who is called Abel," who sits "to judge the entire creation, examining both righteous and sinners," and God tells Abraham that "I do not judge you, but every man is judged by a man" (13.2-3; *OTP,* 1.890).
65. While neither of these terms occurs in Psalm 8, both are implicit in the comment that God has "subjected all things" (πάντα ὑπέταξας, 8:7, LXX) under the feet of "man" (ἄνθρωπος) or "the son of man" (υἱὸς ἀνθρώπου, 8:4). Christian reflection on this psalm is evident in Heb 2:5-9.
66. Gr. ὡς υἱὸς ἀνθρώπου.

cles, "the Son of man," formed apparently on the model of "the Son of God."[67] This seems to have been true in *1 Enoch* as well, where "the Son of man, to whom belongs righteousness" is identified as "the One who would remove the kings and the mighty ones from their comfortable seats and the strong ones from their thrones" (*1 Enoch* 46.3-4; *OTP*, 1.34). Just as in the Gospel tradition (Mt 19:28; 25:31), he is seen "sitting on the throne of his glory," delivering oppressors "to the angels for punishments in order that vengeance shall be executed on them — oppressors of his children and his elect ones" (62.5, 11; *OTP*, 1.43).[68] The similarities to Daniel and *1 Enoch* are just as clear in John's Gospel as in any of the others, but are not made closer or more striking by the absence of the article, which is probably attributable to Colwell's rule, and that alone. In our passage, the reader is evidently expected — whether solely on the basis of Daniel, or with the help of traditions found in the other Gospels and *1 Enoch* — to be able to associate "the Son of man" with "judgment" and the "authority" to judge. While nothing is said as to whether the judgment is present or future, the analogy between "doing judgment" and "bringing to life," both "given" to the Son by the Father (vv. 26 and 27), accents its present aspect (see v. 30, where Jesus begins to exercise his role as judge).

28-29 "Don't be amazed at this," Jesus adds, implying that they are, and should not be (see v. 20, "to your amazement").[69] What exactly is "this" which amazes them? Not simply that Jesus is "the Son of man" (v. 27), as Chrysostom thought,[70] but probably all of vv. 24-27, if not all of vv. 19-27. What is so "amazing" (that is, offensive to his hearers) in these verses? Is it the timing ("an hour is coming *and now is*," v. 25), or is it the involvement of "the Son" in all that God does? Probably the latter. Timing is an issue only briefly (vv. 24, 25), but the relation between the Father and the Son has dominated the whole discourse up to this point. So-called "realized eschatology" may be a major concern of the modern reader (at least since C. H. Dodd), but there is no reason to think it made any more of an impression on Jesus' audience here than on the Samaritan woman when he told her "an hour is coming

---

67. The book of Revelation is an exception, but its similarly indefinite expression, "one resembling a son of man" (ὅμοιον υἱὸν ἀνθρώπου, 1:13; 14:14) does not refer unambiguously to Jesus unless and until he so identifies himself (see 1:17-18).

68. The closest parallel in *1 Enoch* to John 5:22 and 27 is in certain manuscripts (B and C) of *1 Enoch* 69.27: "And he sat on the throne of his glory, and the sum of judgement was given unto the Son of Man, and he caused the sinners to pass away and be destroyed from off the face of the earth" (R. H. Charles, *The Book of Enoch* [Oxford: Clarendon, 1912], 140-41; see also *OTP*, 1.49, n. g2)

69. Μὴ θαυμάζετε τοῦτο could also be read as a question ("Does this amaze you?" See BDF, §427[2]), but with little difference in meaning (Barrett, 263).

70. *Homilies on John,* 39.3; NPNF, 1st ser., 14.140.

and now is" (4:23). Their problem with Jesus is not that he said the end had come, but that he claimed God as his Father (v. 18). His main desire for them is that all will "honor the Son just as they honor the Father" (v. 23). Whether present or future, the work of "bringing to life" and "doing judgment" is the Son's work no less than the Father's. Jesus now clinches the point by repeating it in connection with that which is most familiar to his hearers, the resurrection and judgment "at the last day" (for this expression, see below, 6:39, 40, 44, 54; 11:24; 12:48).

But instead of "the last day," he says "an hour is coming," echoing verse 25, except that the transforming postscript, "and now is," is conspicuous by its absence.[71] This final "hour" is a time when "all who are in the tombs" (that is, those who are *literally* dead, not just spiritually dead in their sins) will hear "his voice." In the context, "his voice" can only be "the voice of the Son of God" (v. 25) or "Son of man" (v. 27), not simply the voice of God as in traditional Jewish expectation. Jesus is not just repeating conventional wisdom. The offense in what he is saying is that he puts himself at the center of his accusers' own expectations about "the last day," pressing ever more strongly the claim that God is "his own Father," and that he is "equal to God" (v. 18). Christology, not eschatology, is what unites the entire discourse. Jesus, Son of God and Lord of the present, is Lord of the future as well.

Two problems for modern readers arise from vv. 28 and 29. The first is that a futuristic eschatology is not what we have learned to expect from the Gospel of John. "Eternal life" is supposed to be a present possession, not a future hope, but here Jesus seems to be buying into what some modern interpreters might consider the "misguided" eschatology of his Jewish contemporaries. This is why some commentators have rejected these verses as an interpolation or later redaction.[72] But to the Gospel writer and his readers it is not a problem. Far from asking us to choose between a present and a future resurrection, this author considers the reality of the latter the best argument for the former. If Jesus is going to raise the dead literally at the last day, why should we be surprised that he does so figuratively or spiritually even now?

---

71. The same two expressions occurred in Jesus' dialogue with the Samaritan woman, but with a quite different rhetorical effect. There, Jesus first said, "an hour is coming" (4:21), and then used the longer expression, "an hour is coming and now is," to define what he meant (4:23). Here, by contrast, the two expressions do not refer to the same "hour." The longer one comes first, announcing a future about to begin, or one that has begun for the readers (v. 25). The shorter expression, "an hour is coming" (v. 28), points to a more remote future (equivalent to "the last day") and a literal, not just spiritual, resurrection and judgment.

72. Above all, see Bultmann, 261: "In any case vv. 28f. have been added by an editor, in an attempt to reconcile the dangerous [*sic*] statements in vv. 24f. with traditional eschatology."

The second problem is that good works, not faith, seem to determine salvation. This too is unexpected in John's Gospel. It is not a matter of hearing and believing (as in v. 24), nor of simply hearing (as in v. 25) with the understanding that to hear means to awake and live. Rather, *all* the dead "will hear his voice" (v. 28), all will attain "resurrection"[73] (v. 29), but for some it will be a resurrection of "life" and for others a resurrection of "judgment."[74] Life is reserved for "those who have done good things,"[75] while judgment awaits "those who have practiced wicked things."[76] But again the problem exists only for modern readers, who have learned from centuries of biblical interpretation to set faith against works. It is not noticeably a problem for Jesus' hearers on the scene, nor for the implied readers the author has in mind. The implied reader is expected to remember what Jesus told Nicodemus and his companions two chapters earlier: that human beings "loved the dark and not the Light, because their works were evil" (3:19), that "everyone who practices wicked things hates the Light and does not come to the Light" (3:20), but that "whoever does the truth comes to the Light" (3:21). So here as well, the test of whether one's works are "good" or "wicked" is whether or not one "comes to the Light" (see 3:20, 21), that is, whether one comes to Jesus or not (see v. 40, "you are unwilling to come to me[77] that you might have life"). Coming to the Light, or to Jesus, and "hearing my word" (v. 24) or "voice" (v. 25) amount to the same thing. Either way, believing in Jesus is what counts. Those who "do good things" or "do the truth" are those who believe. Those who "practice wicked things" are those who do not. Whatever may have been the case in Judaism, or in other branches of early Christianity, or other books of the New Testament, faith and works in the Gospel of John come down to the same thing (see, for example, 6:29, "This is the work of God, that you believe in the One he sent").

In one respect, however, Jesus' words differ here from what he said to Nicodemus and his friends at the first Passover (3:20-21). There, the alternatives began with the negative ("practicing wicked things") and ended with the positive ("doing the truth"). Here by contrast Jesus ends on a negative note. The "resurrection of life" for those who have done "good things" comes first,

---

73. Gr. εἰς ἀνάστασιν.

74. For the double resurrection, see Daniel 12:2, where "Many of those who sleep in the dust of the earth shall awake, some to everlasting life, and some to shame and everlasting contempt." Also Acts 24:15, where Paul speaks of the hope he shares with the Jewish people "that there will be a resurrection of both the righteous and the unrighteous," and Revelation 20:4-6 and 11-15, where the two resurrections are separated by a thousand years.

75. Gr. οἱ τὰ ἀγαθὰ ποιήσαντες.

76. Gr. οἱ δὲ τὰ φαῦλα πράξαντες.

77. Gr. ἐλθεῖν πρός με.

5:19-47 JESUS' ANSWER TO THE JEWS IN JERUSALEM

and then the "resurrection of judgment" for those who have "practiced wicked things." Judgment *(krisis)* is where the emphasis lies, and the judgment is aimed squarely at Jesus' hearers and accusers, as the following verses will show.

30 If there is a break anywhere in Jesus' long discourse to "the Jews," it is here. He goes back to where he began, "the Son can do nothing on his own" (v. 19), only now in the emphatic first person: "As for me, *I* can do nothing on my own" (v. 30, italics added). His self-identification as "the Son" is explicit now if it was not before. The first-person singular (often emphatic) will dominate the discourse from here on. In a sense, vv. 19-29, with their simultaneous accent on "bringing to life" (vv. 21, 24, 25, 26, 29) and "judging" (vv. 22-23, 27, 29), were all preliminary to what Jesus will say now — words primarily of judgment. He begins to "judge,"[78] not "by himself," but "just as I hear"; that is, he judges at the Father's prompting and in keeping with the Father's instructions.[79] Previously the metaphor was "seeing," or what the Father "showed" him (vv. 19-20). Now the metaphor is "hearing," but the point is the same. Like a son apprenticed to his father, Jesus acts on God's initiative, not his own. His judgment is "right,"[80] or fair, precisely because it is *not* his own. He has no vested interest in the outcome.[81] "I am not seeking my will," he explains, "but the will of the One who sent me." Consequently his judgment is the very judgment of God (see vv. 22, 27). None of this is new to the Gospel's readers. They already know that Jesus' food is to "do the will of the One who sent me and complete his work" (4:34), and they have seen him at work in the healing of the royal official's son and the sick man at the pool.[82] Now they learn that his "work" involves judgment as well, and they will have a similar opportunity to watch him perform a work of judgment against his accusers (vv. 31-47).

31 While Jesus has repeatedly claimed to "judge" (vv. 22, 30) or "do judgment" (vv. 22, 27), he is never called "Judge" in the sense of one

---

78. Gr. κρίνω.

79. For Jesus to "hear" in this sense is not simply to hear reports of what has happened (as in 9:35; 11:4, 6), but specifically to hear revelation from God (see 3:32; 8:26, 40; 15:15; compare 16:13).

80. Gr. δικαία.

81. Elsewhere (7:24), Jesus contrasts "right" (δικαία) judgment with judgment "by sight" or "by appearance" (κατ' ὄψιν), which seems to correspond to judgment "according to the flesh" (κατὰ τὴν σάρκα). See 8:15-16, where he tells the Pharisees, "You judge according to the flesh; I do not judge anyone, and [yet] if I do judge, my judgment is true [ἀληθινή], for I am not alone, but I and the Father who sent me."

82. See 6:38, where Jesus claims that he has "come down from heaven not to do my will but the will of the One who sent me," defining "the will of the One who sent me" as resurrection and the giving of life (vv. 39-40). Here, by contrast, it is judgment.

presiding over a court of law, either here or anywhere else in John's Gospel.[83] Instead, he merely "testifies" or gives "testimony"[84] against his accusers. He begins by acknowledging his limitations: "If I testify about myself, my testimony is not true."[85] "About myself"[86] (v. 31) echoes "on my own" (v. 30). In both instances the purpose of the disclaimer is to bring God into the picture (v. 32). What Jesus has in mind is the principle of Jewish law that "One witness is not enough to convict a man of any crime or offense he may have committed. A matter must be established by the testimony of two or three witnesses" (Deut 19:15, NIV).[87] This ruling was for the protection of the accused. Here Jesus is the accused (vv. 16, 18), yet he introduces the principle as if he were the prosecutor, admitting that his testimony alone is not sufficient to convict his adversaries of a crime. He needs at least one more witness (see vv. 32-40). This creates an ambiguity for the reader. Who exactly is on trial here, Jesus or "the Jews"? The tables are being turned, right before our eyes. Jesus the prosecutor now calls his Witness.

32 "Another"[88] testifies on his behalf, Jesus claims, fulfilling the ancient requirement of two witnesses (compare 8:18). The reader knows that he can only mean "the One who sent me" (vv. 24, 30), the One he has repeatedly called "Father" (see vv. 17-23). His accusers do not know this, but he will shortly make it explicit (see v. 37). Nothing has been said so far about the Father's "testimony" for Jesus, but now in a single verse we hear, almost redundantly, of "the One testifying about me," and of "the testimony he testifies about me." This testimony, Jesus claims, is "true,"[89] but what is it? When was it given, and how? Someone familiar with the New Testament canon or the fourfold Gospel will think of the Father's voice at Jesus' baptism ("You are

---

83. On the contrary, see Luke 12:14; Jesus becomes "the Judge" (ὁ κριτής) only in 2 Timothy 4:8; James 4:12; 5:9.

84. Gr. μαρτυρῶ ("testify" or "bear witness") and μαρτυρία ("testimony" or "witness"), respectively.

85. This in contrast to earlier references, which presuppose that Jesus' "testimony" is true (see 3:11, 32), as well as an explicit notice later on that "Even if I testify for myself, my testimony is true" (8:14). Joseph Smith's "Inspired Version" (454) boldly conforms the present statement to 8:14: "Therefore if I bear witness of myself, yet my witness is true." Chrysostom, more willing to deal with the text as it stands, comments that Jesus "spake these words in anticipation; as though He had said, 'Ye will surely say to me, we believe thee not; for no one that witnesseth of himself is readily held trustworthy among men'" (*Homilies on St. John*, 40.1; NPNF, 1st ser., 14.144).

86. Gr. περὶ ἐμαυτοῦ.

87. The principle was invoked particularly in capital cases (see Deut 17:6). Jesus introduces the Deuteronomy text only implicitly here, but he will make it explicit later (see 8:17).

88. Gr. ἄλλος.

89. Gr. ἀληθής.

5:19-47 JESUS' ANSWER TO THE JEWS IN JERUSALEM

my beloved Son," Mk 1:11) or the transfiguration ("This is my beloved Son," Mk 9:7), but we have heard nothing of such a voice in John's Gospel.[90] When God identified Jesus by "the Spirit coming down and remaining on him" (1:33), the one "testifying" was John who saw it, not God (1:32, 34). A reference in 1 John to "the testimony of God which he testified about his Son" (1 Jn 5:9, 10) could be read in relation to Jesus' baptism (see 5:6), but nowhere in the Gospel is the testimony linked to any specific incident. Just as Jesus' glory is revealed not at a particular moment but throughout his ministry (see 1:14), and just as the Spirit not only comes but "remains on him," constantly and "without measure" (1:33, 3:34), so the Father testifies for him and about him not just once but again and again, in all that Jesus says and does.

33 All this is known to the reader, but not to Jesus' immediate hearers, "the Jews." Jesus now focuses on them with the emphatic pronoun, "you": "*You* have sent word to John, and he has testified to the truth" (italics added). The remark identifies these "Jews" unmistakably with "the Jews" (1:19) or "Pharisees" (1:24) in Jerusalem who sent a delegation across the Jordan to ask John who he was and why he was baptizing (1:19-28). Jesus here confirms what the Gospel writer kept telling us, that John "testified to the truth," whether to them (1:19-20), or to his own disciples (1:32, 34; 3:26), or to "all" (1:7, 15-16). In "testifying to the truth,"[91] John was simply doing what Jesus would do after him (see 8:14, 40, 45; 18:37), but in the Gospel's first three chapters John was the predominant "witness," and it is natural that his name should come up now. His encounter with the delegation from Jerusalem was inconclusive and ended abruptly. "We have to give an answer to those who sent us," they told John (1:22), but what answer did they bring back, and more important, what was the reaction of "the Jews" in Jerusalem? The text does not say, but Jesus now implies that their questions were satisfactorily answered, and that their view of John is now positive. Significantly, he later moved from "Bethany, beyond the Jordan" (1:28) to "Aenon near the Salim" (3:23), west of the Jordan and closer to Jerusalem. There "the Pharisees" seem to have kept an eye on him, for when Jesus began to baptize more disciples than John, they knew it (4:1). Now Jesus reminds them of John's "testimony to the truth," with the implication that because they themselves cared enough to solicit it,[92] they have every reason to take it seriously.

---

90. God speaks once from heaven later in the Gospel (12:28), but the voice is never explicitly called a "testimony."

91. Quite possibly "the truth" (τῇ ἀληθείᾳ, with the definite article) picks up the preceding reference to the "true" (ἀληθής) testimony of "another" (v. 32), as if to say, "John also testified to this truth."

92. So Chrysostom: "For He said not, 'John testified of Me,' but 'Ye first sent to John, and ye would not have sent had ye not deemed him trustworthy'" (*Homilies on St. John*, 40.2; NPNF, 1st ser., 14.144).

34 Jesus adds a disclaimer. The reason for mentioning John, he tells his accusers, is for their sake, not his. The emphatic "I" brings this out: "*You* sent word to John (v. 33). . . . *I* do not accept the testimony from a human"[93] (v. 34, italics added). John, we remember, was "from the earth," and spoke "from the earth" (3:31), and with "another" to testify on his behalf (5:32), Jesus does not need John's testimony. He introduces John only "so that you might be saved."[94] It is tempting here to downplay the surprising reference to Jesus' accusers being "saved." While it is true that John came so that "they all might believe through him" (1:7), there is little to suggest that these antagonists are potential believers, and much evidence to the contrary (see vv. 38, 40, 42-44, 46-47). Nowhere else in this long discourse does Jesus even come close to inviting them to "believe" or be "saved."[95] Possibly he means no more than "I only say these things for your benefit," referring not to their eternal destiny but to their "comfort level" in this encounter with Jesus and his claims.[96] Still, it is doubtful that the notion of "salvation" can be excluded altogether. Only a chapter before, the Samaritans hailed him as "Savior of the world" (4:42), and there is little doubt that "the Jews" in Jerusalem who are "trying to kill him" (5:18) do in fact belong to "the world." Earlier, Jesus insisted that "God sent his Son into the world not to judge the world, but so that the world might be saved through him" (3:17), yet he added almost in the same breath that "whoever does not believe is already judged" (3:18), and that "This is the judgment, that the Light has come into the world, and human beings loved the dark and not the Light, because their works were evil" (3:19). Such evidence suggests that salvation and judgment can stand side by side — however uneasily — in Jesus' teaching. He desires salvation for his hearers even while pronouncing judgment.[97] Yet the possibility that they might be "saved" is fragile and fleeting, for "judgement" (v. 30) is his major theme. The reader has little reason to expect that these religious authorities will in fact be "saved," whatever their response to John and his testimony may have been.

35 Jesus takes the opportunity to reminisce about John, building on the Gospel writer's words near the beginning, "He was not the light, but [he

---

93. Gr. παρὰ ἀνθρώπου (compare 2:25).
94. Gr. ἵνα ὑμεῖς σωθῆτε (once again, the "you" is emphatic).
95. As we have seen, even verse 24 is not an exception.
96. See BDAG, 982: "thrive, prosper, get on well." The editors do not place v. 34 here, however, but under the heading, "be saved, attain salvation" (983). For the meaning "to benefit" or "do well," see 11:12.
97. See also 12:47-48, where Jesus claims, "I have not come to judge the world but to save the world," yet quickly adds, "The one who rejects me and does not receive my words has that which judges him; the word which I have spoken, will judge him in the last day."

5:19-47 JESUS' ANSWER TO THE JEWS IN JERUSALEM

came] to testify about the light" (1:8). Agreeing that "*He was not* the light," Jesus gives John his proper role: "*He was* the burning and shining lamp" (italics added). Not "the light," but "the lamp,"[98] a bearer of light sent to testify to "the true [Light] that illumines every human being" (1:9). "Burning" evokes an image of judgment associated in the Gospel tradition both with John (Mt 3:10-12) and with Jesus (Mt 7:19; Jn 15:6), while "shining"[99] accents the revelatory character of John's ministry (see 1:31). While John — in this Gospel above all — came to reveal Jesus and not himself, he undeniably had a derivative "light" of his own (like the physical "light of this world," 11:9), and Jesus now reminds his hearers that "you chose to rejoice for a time in his light." Jesus' picture of John's reception by the Jewish authorities is quite different here than in the other Gospels. He does not suggest that they rejected John (Mt 21:25), nor that they thought he was demon-possessed (Mt 11:18), nor that "they did to him whatever they pleased" (Mk 9:13; Mt 17:12). The picture is more like that of Josephus, where John was said to have enjoyed great popularity among "the Jews," and his death was blamed on Herod alone.[100]

Some have found in Jesus' words an allusion to God's promises to Jerusalem in Psalm 131(132):16-17, LXX: "I will clothe her priests with salvation, and her holy ones shall rejoice with great rejoicing. There I will raise up a horn to David; I have prepared a lamp for my anointed.[101] His enemies I will clothe with shame, but on him my holiness will flourish."[102] If the parallel is intended, the pronouncement must be taken ironically. While John is indeed a "lamp" for God's "anointed" (or "Christ"), the religious authorities seeking Jesus' life are hardly Jerusalem's "priests" or "holy ones," and (despite v. 34b) by no means "clothed with salvation." If anything, they are his enemies, "clothed with shame." They evidently "rejoiced" in John's light without embracing the "truth" to which he testified. The questions of the delegation they sent (1:19-24) suggest that they may have entertained the possi-

---

98. Gr. ὁ λύχνος.

99. Gr. φαίνων (compare 1:5, where the light that is the Word is also "shining in the darkness").

100. According to Josephus, *Antiquities* 18, "to some of the Jews [τῶν Ἰουδαίων] the destruction of Herod's army seemed to be divine vengeance . . . for his treatment of John, surnamed the Baptist" (116), so that "the destruction of Herod's army was a vindication of John" (119; see LCL, 9.81-85).

101. Gr. λύχνον τῷ χριστῷ μου, an expression that could also be translated "a lamp for my Christ."

102. See Moloney, 191. Others have found an allusion to Sirach 48.1, where Elijah was compared to a "fire" (πῦρ) and his word to a "torch" (λαμπάς). This is unlikely, not only because of the different vocabulary but because John's role is clearly distinguished from Elijah's in this Gospel (see 1:21).

bility that John was a messianic figure (see Lk 3:15), and "rejoiced" in such hopes "for a time," only to have them dashed by John's disclaimers.[103] Another possible scenario is that they were concerned about what they *feared* were his messianic claims, and relieved to find out that he harbored no such ambitions for himself. In that case their "rejoicing" would have come later, as a result of his having (as Josephus put it) "exhorted the Jews to lead righteous lives, to practise justice toward their fellows and piety towards God, and so doing to join in baptism."[104] "For a time"[105] would then signal what the reader knows to be true in any event: that John's ministry has run its course and is now over. Jesus has "grown," while John has "diminished" (see 3:30).[106] He may be in prison (3:24), or he may be dead, but whatever his status, he is mentioned only in the past tense (compare 10:41). He has spoken his last words even to the Christian community (see 1:15-18; 3:31-36), and as for "the Jews," the fact that they "chose"[107] to bask in his glory for awhile no longer matters. All that matters is what they now "choose" to do with Jesus and his claims (see v. 40).

36 The brief digression about John (vv. 33-35) is over. The emphatic "I" is again conspicuous, as Jesus repeats his claim that "another" witness testifies on his behalf (v. 32). That testimony, he claimed, was "true" (v. 32), and now he adds that "*I* have testimony greater[108] than John's."[109]

---

103. According to Chrysostom, "him they deemed so trustworthy as not to require even concerning himself any other testimony. For they who were sent said not, 'What sayest thou concerning Christ?' but 'Who art thou? What sayest thou of thyself?' So great admiration felt they for the man" (*Homilies on St. John*, 40.2; NPNF, 1st ser., 14.144).

104. *Antiquities* 18.117 (LCL, 9.81-83). According to a variant, reading preserved by Eusebius, people were "overjoyed" or "delighted" (ἤσθησαν) at John's preaching (see LCL, 9.82; see also the Slavonic Josephus: "they were glad"; LCL, 3.644).

105. Gr. πρὸς ὥραν, literally "for an hour." For this expression, see 2 Corinthians 7:8; Galatians 2:5; Philemon 15.

106. Contrast Schnackenburg: "Though the Baptist's death is presupposed (ἦν), the sentence is not focused on the temporal limits of John's activity, but on the attitude of those who approached this shining 'lamp': they wanted to rejoice in him only 'for a while'" (2.122). Schnackenburg adds that "For the evangelist, and for the whole of primitive Christianity, John was not something in the past but a living abiding witness to Christ" (2.122). But this is a false dichotomy, for in this Gospel, John is *both* "something in the past" *and* "a living abiding witness to Christ."

107. Gr. ἠθελήσατε.

108. The translation presupposes the reading μείζω for "greater" (with ℵ, L, Q, and the majority of later manuscripts), which is equivalent to the accusative μειζόνα (D, 1424) and refers to "the testimony." The alternative reading μείζων (P^{66}, A, and B) is nominative, referring to Jesus: "I, being greater than John, have the testimony." The latter makes less sense and is not favored by the word order. Moreover, the notice that Jesus does not accept human testimony (v. 34) leads us to look for a "greater" testimony that he will accept.

109. Literally, "a testimony greater than John" (with τοῦ Ἰωάννου as genitive of

5:19-47 JESUS' ANSWER TO THE JEWS IN JERUSALEM

Ironically, the "lesser" testimony of John has been given explicitly in the Gospel more than once (1:29 and 34, for example), while the "greater" testimony remains implicit. The "greater" testimony is the testimony of Jesus' "works,"[110] more specifically "the works that the Father has given me that I might complete them" (see 4:34, "that I might . . . complete his work"). "The very works that I do," he now reiterates, "testify about me,"[111] and their testimony is "that the Father has sent me." The key word here is not "works," but "the Father."

In effect, Jesus is renewing the claim that started all the trouble in the first place, that "My Father is working even until now, and I am working" (v. 17). The sticking point for his hearers is not the "works" per se, but the claim that they are the Father's works. Jesus is still responding to the charge of "claiming God as his own Father, making himself equal to God" (v. 18). He is not "making himself" anything, he insists, for his works are the Father's testimony on his behalf, adding a decisive second testimony to his own (see vv. 31-32).

37-38 Jesus now makes this explicit. His next lines, "And so the Father who sent me" (v. 37), pick up the last clause of the preceding sentence, "that the Father has sent me" (v. 36), at last identifying "another" witness (v. 32) as "the Father."[112] The conjunction *kai* ("and") is here translated "and so," because it does not introduce a testimony *in addition* to that of Jesus' works, but draws a conclusion from it.[113] The testimony of Jesus' works *is* the testimony of his Father.[114] "He"[115] has been testifying about Jesus all along

---

comparison), but John, while clearly a "witness" (μαρτύς or μαρτυρῶν), is not a "testimony" (μαρτυρία, feminine). The expression used is an abbreviated form of a more precise phrase (such as μείζω τῆς τοῦ Ἰωάννου, "greater than that of John"; see Bultmann, 265, n. 3; Abbott, *Johannine Grammar*, 188).

110. Gr. τὰ ἔργα.

111. Jesus will appeal to his works again and again as a basis on which to "believe" (see 10:25, 37-38; 14:11).

112. Alternately, the "other" could be the "other Advocate" (ἄλλον παράκλητον) of 14:16 ("The Johannine Words of Jesus and Christian Prophecy," 247), but such an interpretation would hardly have been open to even the most perceptive reader at this point.

113. See BDAG, 495: "to introduce a result that comes from what precedes: *and then, and so.*"

114. So Schnackenburg, 2.123-24. Another option is that the Father's testimony is the testimony at Jesus' baptism, but that is unlikely because there is no such voice in John's Gospel. Still another is that the Father testifies about Jesus in the words of Scripture (so Bultmann, 266; Lindars, 229). But he has not yet mentioned the Scriptures (see v. 39; vv. 46-47), and there is no reason to introduce them prematurely.

115. Gr. ἐκεῖνος, a favorite pronoun in this Gospel, referring in v. 35 to John, here and in v. 38 to the Father, and to Moses in vv. 46-47. The pronoun is redundant here, adding emphasis. Some ancient manuscripts (including P66, A, Θ, and a majority of later wit-

(v. 37) in everything Jesus has said or done, but his accusers do not know it. They have "never heard his voice nor seen his form."[116] That they had never seen God was a commonplace, something with which they would have to agree. "No one has seen God, ever," the Gospel writer told us early on (1:18).[117] That they had not even heard God's "voice" was more problematic. Jesus compares the Father's "voice" testifying through his works to the voice of God long ago at Mount Sinai. In contrast to the people of God at Sinai who "heard the voice of words, but saw no likeness, only a voice" (Deut 4:12), Jesus' accusers do not even hear God's voice. The people back there were afraid, and begged not to hear (see Exod 19:16, 19; 20:18-19; Heb 12:19, 26), but these "Jews" at Jerusalem hear nothing.

His point is more than that they were not personally present at Sinai. When he adds, "You do not have his word dwelling in you" (v. 38),[118] he proves again that "he knew what was in the person," just as at the first Passover in Jerusalem (see 2:25). By "his word" he means the message of God delivered at Sinai (see 10:35, "the word of God"), but with the understanding that God whose mighty voice was heard there is still speaking, only now through his Son (see Heb 1:1; 12:25). If they will not hear the Son, they cannot hear the Father (see v. 24, "the person who hears *my* word"; v. 25, "the dead will hear the voice of the *Son of God*").[119] God's word is not "dwelling in" them because Jesus' word is not in them.[120] "He whom that One sent," Jesus tells them, "him you do not believe" (v. 38).[121] Step by step Jesus unmasks his hearers' unbelief, just as he did earlier at Passover (see 3:11-12). It is not a matter of believing *in* Jesus so much as believing him, in the sense of believing his claim that God was his "Father" (vv. 17-18) who "sent" him (vv. 36, 37, 38). The theme of unbelief will continue to the end of the discourse (see vv. 44-47)

---

nesses) add more emphasis with αὐτός ('himself'), or even ἐκεῖνος αὐτός ("he himself," D), but the simple "he," or "that One," is thoroughly characteristic of Johannine style and is supported by strong manuscript evidence (P^{75}, ℵ, B, L, and others).

116. Gr. εἶδος.

117. See 1 John 4:12; also John 6:46, "Not that anyone has seen the Father, except he who is from God, he has seen the Father."

118. Gr. ἐν ὑμῖν μένοντα.

119. So Odeberg, *The Fourth Gospel,* 223-24, who concludes, "the only possibility of hearing the *Father's* voice or seeing his shape is hearing the *Son's* voice and seeing him, in the spiritual sense of the words."

120. See 8:31, "If you dwell [μείνητε] in my word, you are truly my disciples," and 15:7, "If you dwell [μείνητε] in me, and my words dwell in you, ask whatever you will, and it will be done for you."

121. Gr. τούτῳ ὑμεῖς οὐ πιστεύετε. The immediate juxtaposition of "that One" (ἐκεῖνος), referring to God, and "him" or "this one" (τουτῳ), referring to Jesus, is striking in the Greek sentence.

5:19-47 JESUS' ANSWER TO THE JEWS IN JERUSALEM

39-40 The indictment continues. Jesus could be challenging "the Jews" to "Search the Scriptures" (reading "search"[122] as an imperative), but the reason would then have been "because in them you have eternal life." Instead he says, "because *you think* that in them you have eternal life." This implies that searching the Scriptures is their idea, and that the verb should be read as an indicative: "You search the Scriptures."[123] The Scriptures (literally "the writings")[124] are their Scriptures (see 8:17; 10:34; 15:25), something they value, just as they valued (though only "for a time") the ministry of John (vv. 33-35). Judaism consistently taught that the Jewish Scriptures, centered in the Torah, were a source of life, and that studying them was a way to gain life. According to Rabbi Hillel, "the more study of the Law the more life," and "If a man has gained a good name he has gained [somewhat] for himself," but "if he has gained for himself words of the Law he has gained for himself life in the world to come."[125] "Searching" was a technical term for studying the Scriptures,[126] but to the writer of this Gospel such "searching" did not always yield truth. Two chapters later, the Pharisees will tell Nicodemus, "Search and see, that a prophet is not arising out of Galilee" (7:52). The reader will know that they are wrong about that (see 7:40), and here too Jesus shows little confidence in what his accusers "think"[127] either about their own Scriptures or about "eternal life." He has told us already how to "have eternal life" (v. 24), not by "searching the Scriptures" but by believing the Son, and the Father who sent him (see also 3:15-16, 36).[128] Still, Jesus takes what his accusers "think" and turns it to his advantage, just

---

122. Gr. ἐραυνᾶτε, which can be either imperative or indicative.

123. A very early noncanonical text, the *Egerton Papyrus 2* (second century), has slightly different wording, "Search the Scriptures, in which [ἐν αἷς] ye think that ye have life; these are they which bear witness of me" (H. I. Bell and T. C. Skeat, *Fragments of an Unknown Gospel* [London, 1935], 26, 28). To some this may seem easier to read as an imperative (as in Bell and Skeat's translation), yet that is not obviously the case (see Dodd, *Interpretation*, 329-30, n. 1). Significantly, in the *Egerton Papyrus* the words are spoken to "the rulers of the people" (τοὺς ἄρχοντας τοῦ λαοῦ), equivalent to "the Jews" in the Gospel of John, and are followed immediately by words about Moses as their accuser (see v. 45).

124. Gr. τὰς γραφάς.

125. *M. 'Abot* 2.7 (Danby, 448).

126. Gr. ἐραυνᾶν (literally, "to search or inquire") was the equivalent of Heb. דרשׁ, "to study or expound."

127. Gr. δοκεῖτε.

128. The contrast between eternal life "in them" (ἐν αὐταῖς, that is, in the Scriptures, v. 39) and eternal life "in him" (ἐν αὐτῷ, 3:15) is especially telling. Paul too rejected conventional Jewish wisdom, on the basis that even though the purpose of God's commandment was life, its result for him was death (Rom 7:10), and that no law could ever have given life (Gal 3:21; see Barrett, 267).

as he did their fondness for John, and their willingness to rejoice in John's light (v. 35).

In a way they are right about Scripture, just as they were right about John. The Scriptures do give life, not directly but indirectly, by pointing to Jesus: "And yet[129] those are [the writings][130] that testify about me." This has been evident almost from the start, when Philip announced to Nathanael, "We have found someone of whom Moses wrote in the law, and of whom the prophets wrote, Jesus son of Joseph, from Nazareth" (1:45). This Gospel is at one with the rest of the New Testament in acknowledging that the Jewish Scriptures from beginning to end testify to Jesus and support his claims (see, for example, Lk 24:25-27, 44-47). Every citation of things Jesus did or of things done to him that were "written" beforehand in Scripture bears this out. We have had one such citation already (2:17), and many more will follow (see 6:45; 7:38; 12:14; 13:18; 15:25; 19:24, 28, 36, 37; 20:9). The message of Scripture is "Come to Jesus" (see 6:45; 7:37-38), yet those who look to Scripture for their life will not "come to me" (v. 40), Jesus says, in order to gain life.[131] They "chose" to delight in John's ministry (v. 35), yet they are "unwilling"[132] to "come to Jesus" as disciples.[133] By rejecting him, they strangle the life-giving power of their own Scriptures.

41 Jesus will return shortly to the subject of Scripture (vv. 45-47), but he pauses to draw a contrast between his accusers' "thinking" (v. 39) and his own (vv. 41-44). "I do not accept glory from humans," he begins. The noun "glory" echoes the verb "to think," or have an opinion.[134] This verb is used repeatedly in the Gospel of human opinions that turn out to be mistaken or in some way problematic (see v. 45; 11:13, 31, 56; 13:29; 16:2; 20:15).

---

129. "And (καί) has the force of "and yet" (see BDAG, 495: "emphasizing a fact as surprising or unexpected or noteworthy: *and yet, and in spite of that, nevertheless*"). This applies as well to a second καί, introducing verse 40: what is "surprising or unexpected" is not simply that the Scriptures testify to Jesus but that in spite of that his accusers are unwilling to come to him to gain life.

130. The word "writings" or "Scriptures" is not repeated here in the Greek text: literally, "those are the ones testifying about me." The pronoun "those" (ἐκεῖναι) stands for "the Scriptures" here, just as the pronoun "he" or "that one" (ἐκεῖνος) repeatedly stood for John (v. 35) or the Father (vv. 37, 38), and will stand for Moses (vv. 46-47) as witnesses to Jesus.

131. Just as in 3:36, "life" and "eternal life" are used interchangeably.

132. Gr. οὐ θέλετε, literally "you do not choose."

133. To "come to" (ἐλθεῖν πρός) has been used several times for giving allegiance or becoming a disciple (see 1:29; 3:2, 25, 26; also "coming to the Light," 3:20, 21), but now Jesus begins to use it in the first person (πρός με), and will continue to do so (see 6:35, 37, 44, 45, 65; 7:37).

134. See BDAG, 254, on δοκεῖν: "to consider as probable, *think, believe, suppose, consider*."

5:19-47 JESUS' ANSWER TO THE JEWS IN JERUSALEM

The "glory" that Jesus speaks of here is similarly "from humans," that is, honor or recognition[135] based on human opinion or approval.[136] Jesus does "not accept"[137] such "glory" or honor, just as he does "not accept" testimony on his behalf "from a human" (v. 34), not even from John. What counts is not the "glory" of human opinion, but glory or honor from God (see v. 44). The very term "glory" recalls the author's personal confession almost at the outset that "we looked at his glory — glory as of a father's One and Only" (1:14), and the notice after Jesus' first miracle that he "revealed his glory, and his disciples believed in him" (2:11). There, "glory" was understood as God's splendor visible in Jesus the Son — if not literally, at least to the eyes of faith (see 11:40; 12:41; 17:24). Here, it is not something visible, but simply praise or recognition, whether from fellow human beings or from God.

42 In saying, "I do not accept glory from humans" (v. 41), Jesus implies two things: first, that he does not care what his accusers may "think" (v. 39) of him or of his claims; second, that they themselves *do* "accept glory from humans," whether from each other (see v. 44) or from anyone who comes along (v. 43). He confronts them head-on: "No,[138] I know you,[139] that you do not have the love of God in yourselves" (v. 42). Yet again (as in v. 38), Jesus knows what is — or more precisely what is *not* — "in the person" (2:25), in this instance, "the love of God." Does he mean that God does not love them, or that they do not love God?[140] Evidently the latter, because Jesus said, "God so loved the world that he gave the One and Only Son" (3:16), and they clearly belong to "the world." All Jesus is saying is that they (with the rest of "the world") "loved the dark and not the Light, because their works were evil" (3:19). He will say it more explicitly later on, even to those among them who (after a fashion) "believed in him" (12:42): they "loved the glory of humans instead of the glory of God" (12:43). Their credo (in Moses' words) was "Hear, O Israel: The LORD is our God, the LORD alone. You shall

---

135. See BDAG, 257, on δόξα: "honor as enhancement or recognition of status or performance, *fame, recognition, renown, honor, prestige*."

136. See also 12:43, "the glory of humans"; 7:18, "his own glory"; 8:50, "my glory."

137. Gr. οὐ λαμβάνω.

138. "No" is ἀλλά, often a strong adversative, but here reinforcing and adding to what he has just said (see BDAG, 45: "before independent clauses, to indicate that the preceding is to be regarded as a settled matter, thus forming a transition to something new").

139. The perfect ἔγνωκα (literally, "I have known") has the force of a present here, suggesting clear and assured knowledge (see BDF, §341, and compare 6:69, "we know").

140. "The love of God" (ἡ ἀγάπη τοῦ θεοῦ) can refer either to God's love for people (1 Jn 4:9), or their love for God (1 Jn 5:1; compare "the love of the Father," 1 Jn 2:15). This is the only instance of the noun "love" (ἀγάπη) in the first twelve chapters of John's Gospel (see, however, 13:35; 15:9, 10, 13; 17:26).

love the LORD your God with all your heart, and with all your soul, and with all your might" (Deut 6:4-5, NRSV), but Jesus knows that in their hearts[141] they have betrayed their credo, and with it Moses, their lawgiver (see v. 45).

43 How can Jesus claim that his hearers do not love God? He does so on the basis of what he knows to be true and has claimed to be true all along, that "God" and his "Father" are the same (see v. 18). "I have come in my Father's name," he continues, "and you do not accept me" (v. 43). We have heard this before, again and again — from the Gospel writer (1:11), from Jesus (3:11), and from John (3:32) — but now Jesus goes a step further. In rejecting him, he says, his accusers are rejecting "the Father who sent him" (see vv. 24, 37), in whose "name" he comes. As the Son he represents the Father and the Father's authority, so that to reject the one is to reject the other (see, for example, 13:20). Consequently they are rejecting their own "God," whom they profess to love. By contrast, "If another[142] comes in his own name, him you will accept." Here he has no particular person in mind, no "false prophet" or "Antichrist" figure (as, for example, in Mk 13:22 par.). Such a person, presumably, would come (falsely) in Jesus' name (see Mk 13:6 par.; Mt 7:22), or like Jesus, in God's name, not in his own. On the contrary, he has in mind virtually *anyone* who (unlike Jesus) speaks on "his own" authority, and "seeks his own glory" (see 7:18). As he will remind his disciples later, "If you were of the world, the world would love its own" (15:19).[143] "The Jews" who question and accuse him are very receptive to people like themselves, Jesus is saying, even gullible, yet their ears are closed to God's true messenger, the "One and Only Son."

44 Having established that his accusers "do not believe" (v. 38), he now asks rhetorically, "How can *you* believe, when you receive glory from each other, but do not seek the glory that comes from the only God?" (v. 44, italics added). The emphatic "you" is again conspicuous, and the implied answer is, they "cannot" believe, just as "no one can" see the kingdom of God *unless* they are born from above (3:3), or receive anything *unless* it is given from heaven (3:27). The entire discourse is haunted by the same specter of "impossibility" that faced Nicodemus and his friends (see 3:1-21),[144] and this time without an "unless" clause to offer a ray of hope (see 3:2, 3, 5, 27). There is no way Jesus' hearers will come to faith, but this does not mean he has failed. From the

---

141. That is, in themselves (Gr. ἐν ἑαυτοῖς).

142. "Another" (ἄλλος) could be read as a distant, and very ironic, echo of the ἄλλος of verse 32, the Father, who according to Jesus "testifies about me."

143. As Barrett puts it, "One who relies upon his own dignity and power, and seeks glory from men, will belong to the same world as the unbelievers (v. 44) and will therefore prove more attractive to them" (269).

144. See 3:12: "If I have told you people earthly things and you do not believe [οὐ πιστεύετε], how will you believe [πῶς πιστεύσετε] if I tell you heavenly things?"

5:19-47 JESUS' ANSWER TO THE JEWS IN JERUSALEM

start, his purpose was not to bring them to faith but to refute their charges by exposing their unbelief, and in that he has succeeded. The core of their unbelief is that they "receive glory from each other, but do not seek the glory that comes from the Only God." Glory "from each other" is equivalent to glory "from humans" (v. 41; compare 12:43), or even one's "own glory" (see 7:18). Jesus views the members of a person's tight-knit group, whether of Pharisees or priests, or even human beings generally, as simply extensions of one's self. We want their approval because they are like us (or we think they are), and we expect them to judge us in the same way we judge ourselves. To seek, or even accept, such human "glory" is an expression of selfishness, the very opposite of seeking "the glory that comes from the Only God."

The choice of words is telling. The whole confrontation began with the charge that Jesus was "making himself equal to God," threatening Jewish monotheism (v. 18). With the phrase "from the Only God,"[145] Jesus embraces the monotheism of his accusers and throws it back in their faces. As I have tried to show by capitalization, the adjective "Only" dominates the expression "the Only God," to the point that some important manuscripts (including P[66], P[75], B, and W) omit "God" altogether, yielding the phrase, "the glory that comes from the Only One." This reading would imply that "the Only God" and "the Only One" were interchangeable titles, just as "One and Only" (1:14, 18) and "the One and Only Son" (3:16, 18) seem to have been interchangeable. Yet "the Only One" by itself is unattested as a title for God, and the shorter reading is therefore likely a copyist's mistake.[146] Jesus' reference to glory "from the Only God" recalls the Gospel writer's early mention of "his glory — glory as of a father's One and Only" (1:14),[147] in both instances implying that Jesus' "glory" as the Son comes from "the Only God" or from "the Father," and from no one else. Jesus' uniqueness as the "One and Only Son" is rooted in the Father's uniqueness as "the Only God," and consequently in Jewish monotheism. For "the Jews" (vv. 16, 18) to deny the Son is to deny "the Father who sent him" (see v. 23), and conse-

---

145. Gr. παρὰ τοῦ μόνου θεοῦ.

146. See Metzger, *Textual Commentary,* 211, who attributes the omission to a scribe's "transcriptional oversight" in reading the uncial letters TOYMONOYΘYOY as TOYMONOYOY. While the manuscript evidence for the shorter reading is very early, it is not widely distributed. Such expressions as "the only true God" (Jn 17:3), and elsewhere in the New Testament "only God" (1 Tim 1:17; Jude 25) and "only wise God" (Rom 16:27), lead us to expect "the Only God" here as well (for the precise expression ὁ μόνος θεός, see *Aristeas* 139; Philo, *On Flight and Finding* 71; more common in the LXX is ὁ θεὸς μόνος, "God alone," 2 Kgs 19:15, 19; Ps 85:10; Isa 37:20).

147. Even though παρά in 1:14 was simply part of the definition of μονογενής, the preposition still helped convey the impression that both the "One and Only" and his "glory" were "from" (παρά) the Father in that the Son was "sent" as the Father's messenger.

quently to betray the monotheism they profess. This is the logic of Jesus' discourse, and of John's Gospel as a whole, strange as it might seem to Jesus' interlocutors.

45 The next step in Jesus' argument is that denying "the Only God" is a betrayal not only of monotheism, but of Moses, who fostered monotheism by writing such things as "I am the LORD thy God; ... you shall have no other gods before me" (Exod 20:2), "See now that I, even I, am he; there is no other god beside me" (Deut 32:39), and "The LORD is our God, the LORD alone. You shall love the LORD your God" (Deut 6:4-5). Jesus hinted as much when he said, "I know you, that you do not have the love of God in yourselves" (v. 42), and now he makes it explicit: "Moses," and all that Moses represents, belongs to him and not to them. Moses it was who "lifted up the snake in the desert," anticipating the gift of life through the Son of man (3:14-15), and Moses it is who now stands with Jesus in judgment on his own people.

Again (as in v. 39) Jesus anticipates what his hearers may "think": "Do not think,"[148] he cautions them, "that I will accuse you to the Father."[149] The negative present imperative implies that they are thinking exactly that,[150] yet they are obviously not. He is speaking rhetorically "The Father" is his term, not theirs, and if (as they suppose) he is mistaken in "claiming God as his own Father" (v. 18), they have nothing to fear from any accusations he might bring. The reader, however, knows better. The reader is expected to know that Jesus is both "Son" and "Son of man," to whom all judgment belongs (vv. 22, 27, 30). In assuring his hearers that "I" will not "accuse you to the Father," he implies that he could do so if he chose,[151] but the remark is preliminary to his real point, that "Your accuser[152] is Moses, in whom you have set your hope." The latter (if anything) is what gets their attention. Appealing to "Moses" is the same as appealing to "the Scriptures," and "setting their hope" in Moses is equivalent to looking to the Scriptures for "eternal life" (see v. 39). Yet it is shocking to hear of Moses in the role of "accuser," Moses who pleaded to God

---

148. Gr. μὴ δοκεῖτε.
149. Egerton Papyrus 2 has it slightly differently: "Think not that I *came* to accuse you [ἦλθον κατηγορῆσαι] to my Father" (echoing somewhat the Matthean Jesus of Mt 5:17 and 10:34).
150. See BDF, §336(3).
151. The phrase "to the Father" (πρὸς τὸν πατέρα) reminds us that Jesus was "with God" (πρὸς τὸν θεόν) to begin with (1:1; compare πρὸς τὸν πατέρα, 1 Jn 1:2). In later chapters he will speak of returning "to the Father" (πρὸς τὸν πατέρα, 14:12, 28; 16:10, 17, 28), and in 1 John he becomes our Advocate "with the Father" (πρὸς τὸν πατέρα, 1 Jn 2:2). All of this may be in Jesus' mind, but he does not press the point. As far as the reader is concerned his "accusations" could be simply his prayers, and to his hostile hearers they are little more than empty threats.
152. Gr. ὁ κατηγορῶν ὑμῶν.

5:19-47 JESUS' ANSWER TO THE JEWS IN JERUSALEM

for his people, "But now, if you will forgive their sin — but if not, blot me out of the book that you have written" (Exod 32:32, NRSV). All Jesus is doing is repeating more forcefully what he said before, that the Scriptures "testify about me" (v. 39),[153] with the implication that if they testify *for* Jesus, they testify *against* those who now challenge him. The Scriptures — and consequently Moses who wrote them — accuse his accusers.

46-47 While "Jesus" acknowledges that "the Jews" have "set their hope" in Moses (v. 45), he denies that they "believe" him: "For if you believed Moses, you would believe me" (v. 46). The condition is contrary to fact:[154] they did not believe Moses; therefore they do not believe Jesus. But the logic also works in reverse. If they do not believe Jesus — and he has repeatedly demonstrated that they do not[155] — then they do not believe Moses either. The reason, Jesus claims, is that "he[156] wrote about me" (see 1:45, "We have found someone of whom Moses wrote in the law").[157] "If you do not believe his written words,"[158] Jesus concludes, "how will you believe my spoken words?"[159] Contrary to what "the Jews" might think (see 9:28-29),[160] trust in Moses and trust in Jesus stand or fall together. Those who believe that "the law was given through Moses" should be the first to acknowledge that "grace and truth came into being through Jesus Christ" (1:17), but the tragedy, as Jesus sees it, is that they have not done so.

---

153. It is noteworthy that in the *Egerton Papyrus 2*, statements corresponding to vv. 39 and 45 respectively come back to back: "Search the scriptures, in which ye think that ye have life; these are they which bear witness of me. Think not that I have come to accuse you to my Father; there is one that accuseth you, even Moses, on whom you have set your hope" (*Egerton* 2.2-3; Bell and Skeat, *Fragments,* 26, 28).

154. See BDF, §360: "the imperfect is temporally ambiguous." This means that the sentence could be translated either "if you believed Moses, you would believe me," or "if you had believed Moses, you would have believed me." The former fits the context better here, but the difference is small in any case.

155. See v. 38, "him you do not believe"; v. 40, "you are unwilling to come to me"; v. 43, "you do not accept me"; v. 44, "How can you believe?"

156. With this, yet another witness for Jesus is identified with the pronoun ἐκεῖνος (see vv. 35, 37, 39).

157. Moses (both here and in 1:45) is important not for his leadership or anything he did (as in 3:14; 6:31-32; 7:22), but for what he "wrote" (ἔγραψεν). Jesus may have a number of specific written texts in mind, but perhaps especially Deuteronomy 18:15-18.

158. Gr. τοῖς ἐκείνου γράμμασιν.

159. Gr. τοῖς ἐμοῖς ῥήμασιν.

160. In *Egerton Papyrus 2,* the words, "Moses, on whom ye have set your hope" are followed immediately by words reminiscent of John 9:29, "And when they said, We know well that God spake unto Moses, but as for thee, we know not whence thou art, Jesus answered and said unto them, Now is your unbelief accused . . ." (Bell and Skeat, *Fragments,* 28).

The end of the argument demonstrates what has become increasingly evident all along, that salvation or "eternal life" rests on acceptance of Jesus and his word, and on nothing else (see v. 24). Jesus has called his "other" Witness, the Father (vv. 32, 36), and (to satisfy the whims of his accusers) two lesser witnesses, John and Moses, but in the end none of these testimonies matter. His own testimony is self-authenticating. As soon as his accusers reject his word (see vv. 38, 40, 42, 43), in effect they reject these other testimonies as well. When he began by saying, "If I testify about myself, my testimony is not true" (v. 30), Jesus was merely playing his opponents' game. But when they try to play the game again three chapters later (8:13), he will tell them what has really been the case all along: "Even if I testify about myself, my testimony is true, because I know where I came from and where I am going" (8:14). All the other testimonies are wrapped up in his own, and when that is rejected his accusers are judged. His parting question, "How will you believe my spoken words?" (v. 47) goes unanswered, just as the same question, "How will you believe?" went unanswered before, at the first Passover in Jerusalem (3:12). His accusers' silence comes as no surprise because they have been silent throughout. Their last words were a question to the sick man at the pool, "Who is the man who told you, 'Pick up and walk'?" (v. 12). Now that Jesus has told them at great length who he is, they have nothing to say.[161] We can only infer that they have not "heard his word," and do not have "eternal life" (see v. 24).[162]

E. ACROSS THE LAKE AND BACK (6:1-21)

1 After these things, Jesus went across the lake of Galilee, or Tiberias, 2 and a large crowd was following him because they could see the signs he was doing for those who were sick. 3 And Jesus went up on the mountain, and there he sat with his disciples. 4 And the

---

161. Chrysostom, for his own rhetorical purposes, imagines all sorts of replies by "the Jews," turning Jesus' monologue into a free-wheeling dialogue. For example, "'And whence,' saith some one, 'is it clear that Moses will accuse us, and that thou art not a boaster? What hast thou to do with Moses? Thou hast broken the Sabbath which he ordained that we should keep; how then should he accuse us? And how doth it appear that we shall believe on another who cometh in his own name? All these assertions thou makest without evidence'" (*Homilies on John* 41.2; NPNF, 1st ser., 14.149).

162. Critical imagination has supplied the response that the Gospel of John itself lacks. According to the reconstructions of Bernard (1.171), Bultmann (209), and Schnackenburg (2.5-9), 5:47 is followed immediately by the response of "the Jews" recorded in 7:15: "The Jews then were amazed," saying, "How does this man know letters, being uninstructed?"

6:1-21 ACROSS THE LAKE AND BACK

Passover, the festival of the Jews, was near. 5 So when Jesus lifted up his eyes and saw that a large crowd was coming to him, he says to Philip, "Where shall we buy loaves so that these may eat?" 6 This he said testing him, for he himself knew what he was going to do. 7 Philip answered him, "Two hundred denarii's loaves are not enough for each of them to get [even] a little." 8 One of his disciples, Andrew, the brother of Simon Peter, said to him, 9 "A child is here who has five barley loaves and two pieces of fish, but what are these for so many?" 10 Jesus said, "Make the people sit down to eat." Now there was a lot of grass in the place, so the men sat down to eat, about five thousand in number. 11 Then Jesus took the loaves, and when he had given thanks, he gave them out to those who were seated, and of the fish, as much as they wanted. 12 And when they had had their fill, he said to his disciples, "Gather the leftover broken pieces, so that nothing is lost." 13 So they gathered, and filled up twelve baskets with pieces left over by those who had eaten of the five barley loaves. 14 Then the men, seeing what he had done as a sign, said that "This is truly the Prophet who is coming into the world." 15 So Jesus, when he found out they were going to come and seize him to make him king, withdrew again, he alone, to the mountain. 16 But as it grew late, his disciples went down to the lake, 17 and got in a boat and were on their way across the lake to Capernaum. It had already gotten dark, and Jesus had not yet come to them, 18 and the lake was rough, with a strong wind blowing. 19 Then, having advanced about twenty-five or thirty stadia, they could see Jesus walking on the lake and coming near the boat, and they were afraid. 20 But he said to them, "It is I. Don't be afraid!" 21 Then they wanted to take him into the boat, and immediately the boat reached land right where they were going.

Abruptly, we find Jesus no longer in Jerusalem but back in Galilee, crossing from one side of the lake to the other. The scene is familiar to anyone acquainted with the other Gospels: a crowd follows him, apparently because of his ministry of healing the "sick" both in Galilee (4:43-54) and Jerusalem (5:1-9), and he retreats to a mountain with his disciples. But the accent, at least at first, is not on the crowd's "hunger" for miraculous "signs" (v. 2), but on its literal hunger, as he multiplies five barley loaves and two fish into enough food to feed the whole crowd of five thousand — with twelve baskets left over! At this point, the crowd's fascination with "signs" takes over. Jesus is seen as "the Prophet who is coming into the world," and an attempt is made to seize him and make him king by force (vv. 14-15). He withdraws again to the mountain, while his disciples embark across the lake back to Capernaum. The notice that it was dark and that "Jesus had not yet come to them" (v. 17) raises the reader's expectation that he will in fact do so, and he does, walking on the water even though the lake is rough, and calming "their fears" with the announcement, "It is I. Don't be afraid!" (v. 20). He has made good his escape. Even his avoidance of kingship is miraculous!

1 "After these things"[1] (see 5:1, 14) picks up the thread of the narrative, but the connection to what precedes is far from clear. We are told that "Jesus went across the lake of Galilee, or Tiberias," but from where? Conventional wisdom has it that the narrative originally had a quite different setting, in which Jesus was already in Galilee somewhere near the lake, just as in each of the synoptic accounts of the feeding of the five thousand (see Mk 6:32 par.). This may very well be true, yet it does not help us to understand what a reader of John's Gospel who was unacquainted with the Synoptics would have made of it. Jesus was last seen in Jerusalem, in the temple (5:14), even though his long discourse (5:19-47) was linked to no specific location. Now all at once he is in Galilee, crossing from one side of lake of Galilee to the other. That is why, as we have seen, a number of interpreters have proposed reversing the order of chapters 5 and 6. Jesus might then have crossed the lake from Capernaum, and this would have been natural because when he crosses back again his destination is Capernaum (v. 17). Yet in chapter 4 Jesus never reached Capernaum, or the lake, performing the miracle from a distance at Cana, "where he made the water wine" (4:46).

If we keep the chapters in order (as we have done), we have two options. One is that the point of reference is Jerusalem, and the author is simply saying that Jesus traveled from Jerusalem to an undefined location "across"[2] lake Galilee, that is, somewhere along its northern shore. If John's Gospel was written for an audience well outside Palestine,[3] this would not be strange. Such an audience would have viewed Jerusalem as the center of the land, with other areas (even quite distant ones) seen in relation to it.[4] Just as Bethany was "beyond[5] the Jordan" in relation to Jerusalem (1:28; 3:26), so the far north of Palestine could have been viewed as "beyond" or "across" lake Galilee from Jerusalem. But this would place the events of the first part of the chapter somewhere near Capernaum on the northwest side of the lake, raising the question why Jesus would have had to cross the lake again to reach Capernaum (see vv. 17, 24, 59).

The more likely possibility is that the long discourse in 5:19-47 was

---

1. Gr. μετὰ ταῦτα.
2. Gr. πέραν.
3. The careful description of the Bethsaida pool (5:2) suggests an audience remote from the scene.
4. See *Sibylline Oracles* 12.104: "A sword will also come upon the land of Solyma [that is, Jerusalem] as far as the last turning of the sea of Tiberias" (*OTP,* 1.447).
5. Gr. also πέραν.

6:1-21 ACROSS THE LAKE AND BACK

understood to have no geographical setting at all, so that when Jesus shows up at the lake of Galilee (by default, as it were) it comes as no surprise. From the start he was known to be a Galilean (1:45), returning to Galilee for a wedding (2:1-12), and spending time at Capernaum with "his mother and brothers and his disciples" (2:13; see also 6:42, where "the Jews" who are there claim to know his father and mother). The reader is able to negotiate the abrupt transition with an awareness that the unnamed "festival of the Jews" that brought Jesus to Jerusalem (5:1) is over, and that he is now back in "Galilee," the region known to have been his home. A crossing from Capernaum, on the north shore of the lake, to a point near Tiberias in the south would then make sense. This could help explain why the lake is given two names here, "Galilee" as well as "Tiberias."[6] At the same time, the double name also lends a degree of support to the hypothesis that the account to follow may have once had a different literary setting. The lake is consistently called "Galilee" in the synoptic Gospels (once Gennesaret, Lk 5:1), but the only other reference to it in John's Gospel calls it "the lake of Tiberias" (21:1), after the town located on its southern shore (see v. 23).[7] The double name could be a tacit acknowledgment of the use of the name "Galilee" in another (possibly earlier) version of the story.

2-3 The "large crowd" introduced here can only have been "following" Jesus across the lake by boat, just as they will do again (in the opposite direction) later in the chapter (v. 24). The writer never addresses the logistical problem of how many boats such a crowd (at least "five thousand," as it turns out, v. 10) would have needed, or what happened to the boats. "Following" implies at least curiosity and at most a kind of allegiance to Jesus (see 1:37-40, 43), because they could see "the signs[8] he was doing for those who were sick."[9] The reader knows of two such signs, one in Galilee (4:54) and the other (not explicitly called a sign) in Jerusalem (5:1-9), both for someone explicitly described as "sick" (4:46; 5:7). Because the second of these was described as one example of things Jesus commonly did "on the Sabbath" (see 5:16), we may well infer that he had repeatedly healed "the sick" both in Jerusalem and in Galilee. Beyond this, any reader familiar with the synoptic tradition (in any form) would have found the picture of "large crowds" pursu-

---

6. In a few manuscripts (including D, Θ, certain old Latin versions, and the text of Chrysostom), the names "Galilee" and "Tiberias" are distinguished by the phrase, "across Lake Galilee into the region [εἰς τὰ μέρη] of Tiberias." This reading may have arisen because when Jesus crossed the lake again, it was toward Capernaum (vv. 17, 24), and the town of Tiberias would have been a natural starting point for such a journey.

7. See also Josephus, *Wars* 3.57; 4.456 (with a different word, λίμνη, for "lake"), and the citation just above (n. 2) from the *Sibylline Oracles*.

8. Gr. τὰ σημεῖα.

9. Gr. ἐπὶ τῶν ἀσθενούντων.

ing him because of his healings a very familiar one. Equally familiar is the picture of Jesus retreating from the crowds in order to be alone, or at least alone with his disciples. At the same time, Jesus is commonly seen teaching or healing the crowds even under these difficult circumstances.

Here in John's Gospel, "Jesus went up on the mountain, and there he sat with his disciples" (v. 3). Three things are noteworthy about the scene. The first is the accent on place: Jesus is "there"[10] on "the mountain" just as earlier he was "there" at Cana (2:1), Capernaum (2:12), Judea (3:22), Sychar in Samaria (4:6, 40), and the Bethsaida pool (5:5). This time it is a definite (though unnamed) mountain in Galilee, with all that a mountain implies in the Bible as a place of divine revelation.[11] The second is that Jesus is again joined "there" by his disciples. We have heard nothing of them since his encounter with the Samaritan woman at Sychar (4:31-38). We can assume that they accompanied him to Cana of Galilee (4:46) and on to Jerusalem (5:1), but we do not know for certain.[12] The third is a striking resemblance between this mountain scene and two incidents in Matthew, one just before the Sermon on the Mount, where Jesus "On seeing the crowds went up on the mountain; and when he had sat down, his disciples came to him; and he opened his mouth and began teaching them" (Mt 5:1-2), and the other in a setting similar to the present one, in which Jesus "came along the lake of Galilee, and went up on the mountain and sat there" (Mt 15:29).

In Matthew, Jesus "sat" either to "teach" his disciples (5:2) or to "heal" the crowds (15:30). In John's Gospel we are not told why he "sat," but it may have been for similar purposes. Not only was the crowd following him precisely because of his healings (v. 2), but, as we have seen, the account comes right after Jesus' parting question to "the Jews" at Jerusalem, "How will you believe my spoken words?" (5:47). How indeed? The answer will come in this chapter (see below, 6:63), as attention continues to focus on what interpreters have called the "sapiential" theme of Jesus as teacher, and on the necessity of believing the words he speaks.[13]

4 The writer pauses to tell us that "the Passover, the festival of the Jews, was near." Every other time we encounter such a notice in this Gospel,

---

10. Gr. ἐκεῖ.

11. Sinai is of course the classic example, but also the "very high mountain" of the transfiguration (see Mk 9:2), and the mountain in Galilee where the risen Jesus arranged to meet his disciples after the resurrection in Matthew (28:16).

12. While it is remotely possible that they may have returned to Capernaum and performed baptisms (4:53), it is, as we have seen, very unlikely.

13. See, for example, Brown, 1.272-74, who distinguishes between "sapiential" and "sacramental" elements in the chapter. "Sapiential" does not imply (as the name might suggest) explicit references to divine Wisdom, but simply an accent on revelation and on Jesus' mission as teacher or revealer.

whether about Passover (2:13; 11:55) or some other festival (5:1; 7:2), its purpose is either to bring Jesus to Jerusalem or to remind us that he is there (see 10:22). Only this once does Jesus stay away from Jerusalem during a Jewish festival. Possibly the principle introduced a chapter later is already in effect, that is, that Jesus "was walking in Galilee, for he chose not to walk in Judea because the Judeans were trying to kill him" (7:1). But why then mention Passover at all? What does the brief notice accomplish for the reader at this point? The most likely answer is that the mention of Passover evokes Moses, keeping alive in the reader's mind the conclusion of the preceding discourse (5:45-47; also 5:37-40), and anticipating further controversy over Moses and the provision of manna in the desert (see below, vv. 30-32, 49, 58). Yet it is only a momentary notice, and should not be allowed to govern the interpretation of the entire chapter.[14]

5 When we last saw Jesus with his disciples (4:30-38), it was similar to the present situation in that a crowd of Samaritans was "coming to him" (4:30). "Lift up your eyes and look at the fields," he had said, implying that he himself had already done so, and adding that "they are white for harvest" (4:35). This time he himself "lifted up his eyes and saw that a large crowd was coming to him." Now as before, what he sees and what his disciples can see present a challenge: "Where shall we buy loaves so that these may eat?" he asks Philip. Food was part of the earlier scene, and food is crucial to the story here as well. Back then, the disciples had just returned from buying food (4:8, 27), and they urged Jesus, "Rabbi, eat" (4:31). He refused, because "My food," he said, "is that I might do the will of the One who sent me and complete his work" (4:34). Food, we learned, was a metaphor for hearing and doing the will of God. Yet undeniably food was also food. The disciples' little foray into the village was significant enough to keep them off center stage throughout Jesus' encounter with the Samaritan woman, and its purpose was to buy real food for a real journey. Now it is Jesus who thinks of food,[15] and again it is a matter of "buying" it,[16] not just for himself and his

---

14. Contrast Brown, 1.231-304, who makes "Jesus at Passover" a heading to the whole chapter on the basis of one brief notice telling us only that Passover was "near" (ἐγγύς).

15. This in contrast both to the situation at Sychar in chapter 4, and to the synoptic accounts of the feeding, where the disciples are the ones who bring up the shortage of food. In the second feeding in Matthew, the disciples ask virtually the same question that Jesus asks here: "Where [πόθεν] do we get enough bread in the desert to feed such a crowd?" (Mt 15:33; see also Mk 8:4). Both evoke Moses' question to the Lord: "Where [LXX: πόθεν] am I to get meat to give to all this people? For they come weeping to me and say, 'Give us meat to eat!'" (Num 11:13, NRSV), but neither exhibits anything like the anger of Moses' words.

16. Here, too, Jesus' lines (more or less) are in another Gospel attributed to the

disciples this time but for a "large crowd" of potential disciples.[17] His question to Philip is the first time he has spoken to an individual disciple since his parting words to Nathanael at the end of the opening scene (1:50-51). Philip is not reintroduced or further identified. The reader is expected to remember who he is (see 1:43-44). In contrast to all three synoptic Gospels, John contains no hint that they are in a "deserted place" (Mk 6:35 par.), and no proposal that Jesus should "dismiss" the crowd (Mk 6:36 par.) to buy food for themselves in neighboring villages. Instead, Jesus seems to want to incorporate the crowd into the existing group of itinerant disciples, buying food along the way and eating together as a community. Despite the notice that Passover was "near" (v. 4), there is no evidence that a Passover celebration was in view. That will come later.[18] "Loaves" would be insufficient for a Passover meal in any case.

6-7 The Gospel writer steps in, characteristically, with a narrative aside explaining to the reader: "This he said[19] testing him,[20] for he himself knew what he was going to do." "Testing" is commonly used in the Gospel tradition in a negative way, when those who opposed Jesus tried to trap him in his words (see 8:6; also Mt 16:1; 19:3; 22:15, 18, 35; Mk 8:11; 10:2; 12:13, 15; Lk 11:16). Such incidents recall the demand of Jesus' opponents for a "sign" at the first Passover in Jerusalem (2:18), and again later in the present chapter (v. 30). Does Jesus have a similarly hostile intent toward his own disciples? At this point it seems unlikely,[21] yet as the chapter unfolds, unbelievers among Jesus' disciples are weeded out as they take offense at his words (see vv. 60, 64, 66). Possibly the notice about "testing" them is a hint that this process has already begun. Still, this would not mean that Jesus was testing his disciples in quite the way he himself is tested elsewhere in the Gospel tradition. His tone is more playful, as when he told his mother at Cana, "What is that to me or to you?" (2:4). There, his mother pointed out a wine shortage and he brushed it off. Here, he feigns anxiety about a food

---

disciples: "Are we to go and buy [ἀγοράσωμεν] two hundred denarii's loaves, and give them to eat?" (Mk 6:37).

17. "Potential disciples" because, as in the case of the Samaritans (4:30), "coming to" Jesus seems to have implied a desire to join him or give him their allegiance (see 1:29, 47; 3:2, 26).

18. See 13:29, where the issue of buying food comes up yet a third time, finally in direct connection with Passover.

19. The expression, "This he said" (either τοῦτο δὲ ἔλεγεν, as here, or τοῦτο δὲ εἶπεν) is characteristic of Johannine style, especially in narrative asides (see 7:39; 12:33; 21:19; compare 8:6, 11:51).

20. Gr. πειράζων αὐτόν.

21. BDAG lists the present passage (along with Heb 11:17) as one where testing takes place "in a favorable sense . . . so that they may prove themselves true" (793)

shortage in order to elicit a reaction from his disciples. In both instances he "knew what he was going to do," but this time the writer tells us so explicitly. If Jesus was in any way "testing" his mother — and nothing to that effect was said — it was a playful kind of test, and she passed with flying colors (2:5, "Do whatever he tells you").

7 How was it with Philip? Did he pass the test or not? His answer was, "Two hundred denarii's loaves are not enough for each of them to get [even] a little," echoing the disciples' incredulous question in Mark's account: "Are we to go and buy two hundred denarii's loaves, and give them to eat?" (Mk 6:37; see above, n. 16).[22] Did Philip give the right answer, or should he have said, "We don't need to buy food because I know you will work a miracle," or "A person shall not live by bread alone, but by every word coming from the mouth of God" (see Mt 4:4)? Either of these would have been a more high-minded or "theologically correct" answer, but Jesus registers no more displeasure with Philip than he did with the disciples in Mark. This suggests that his "testing" of Philip was more for the reader's benefit than for Philip. The Gospel writer wants to avoid any implication that Jesus was genuinely worried about the food supply, or that he was asking a question to which he did not know the answer.[23] It is important for us, not for Philip, that Jesus "knew what he was going to do" (v. 6), for it confirms what we have already been told about Jesus' knowledge and intentionality (see, for example, 1:48; 2:24-25; 4:17-18). It raises our expectations, and Philip's reply raises them still higher. What *is* Jesus "going to do"? Will it be something on the scale of what he did at Cana, or will it be even greater? Perhaps the reader is expected to know.[24]

8 Philip has had his turn, and now Andrew speaks. Andrew, unlike Philip, is formally introduced (actually reintroduced) as "one of his disciples," and "the brother of Simon Peter." He was first introduced as "the brother of Simon Peter," and "one of the two" who had heard John's testimony and followed Jesus (1:40). The formal introduction here could imply that Philip was *not* one of Jesus' disciples, but that can hardly be the case given the account of Philip's call, and his role in recruiting Nathanael (1:43-51). The discrepancy appears to be random, for in a later incident (12:21-22)

---

22. A Roman denarius being a worker's daily wage (BDAG, 223), two hundred denarii would represent the fruit of at least six months' labor. Both here and in Mark the number accents the magnitude of the miracle to follow.

23. So Brown (1.233): "an editorial attempt to forestall any implication of ignorance on Jesus' part"; also Schnackenburg (2.15): "The question is only a teaching device."

24. The comment that "he himself knew what he was going to do" may contain a hint that the reader (even a first-time reader) is familiar with one or more synoptic (or synoptic-like) accounts of a feeding of a "large crowd" of people. Surely this is true of any canonical reader, including virtually all modern readers, and it may well have been the writer's intention from the start.

Andrew is left unidentified, while Philip is said to be "from Bethsaida of Galilee" (in keeping with 1:44).[25] Here, Andrew is not called "one of the Twelve," as are both Judas Iscariot (6:71) and Thomas (20:24), because "the Twelve" have not yet emerged as a distinct group (see 6:67, 70). Rather, like Judas in one instance (12:4), and the beloved disciple in another (13:23), he is simply "one of his disciples." A further possibility is that by again identifying Andrew in relation to his brother, Simon Peter, the Gospel writer is setting the stage for Simon Peter's decisive confession at the end of the narrative (6:68-69). Andrew is never alone in this Gospel, but always part of a matched pair, whether with his brother Simon Peter or with his compatriot Philip.

9 Andrew volunteers the information that, "A child is here who has five barley loaves and two fish," but adds, "what are these for so many?" The "child," whether a boy or a girl, small child or teenager, or a young slave,[26] is unidentified,[27] a shadowy figure who, like the bridegroom at the wedding (2:9) or the royal official's son (4:52), makes a cameo (non-)appearance and is not heard from again. But the child is "here" *(hōde)*. The writer attributes to Andrew the same sense of place that governs his own description of the scene "there," on "the mountain" in Galilee (see v. 3).[28] We can assume that the child belongs to the "large crowd" that was "coming toward" Jesus and his disciples (v. 5), and that the whole crowd is now "here." "Five barley loaves and two pieces of fish" agree with the synoptic accounts of the feeding of five thousand,[29] but the Synoptics know nothing of any "child." The loaves

---

25. In the farewell discourses, four disciples are identified only by their names: Simon Peter (13:36), Thomas (14:5), Philip (14:8), and (except for the clarification that he is "not Iscariot") Judas (14:22).

26. See BDAG, 748. Παιδάριον, "child," a diminutive of παιδίον, which is in turn a diminutive of παῖς, occurs only here in the New Testament. Παιδίον is far more common (see 4:49; 16:21; 21:5), and might have been expected here. If the meaning is "young slave," as BDAG considers possible, this παιδάριον (presumed male) might correspond to the young female slave (παιδίσκη) who makes a similarly brief appearance in the passion narrative (18:17). In any event, the "child" was old enough to carry the food for at least one family.

27. Some manuscripts (A, K, Γ, Δ, Θ, some Latin and Syriac, and the majority text) add to παιδάριον an indefinite article ἕν, "one," or "a certain" (more or less equivalent to τὶς: see BDAG, 292), but this is almost certainly a scribal change aimed at improving narrative style.

28. In a similar way the Samaritan woman's (and Jesus') use of "back here" (ἐνθάδε, 4:15-16) preserves the sense of place (ἐκεῖ, 4:6) in the encounter at the well in Sychar. See also Jesus' command to his disciples at the feeding of the five thousand in Matthew to bring the five loaves and two fish "here" (ὧδε, Mt 14:18), and Peter's remark after the transfiguration, "It is good for us to be here" (ὧδε, Mk 9:5 par.),

29. The feeding of the four thousand is different: "seven loaves" and (almost as an afterthought) "a few small fish" (ἰχθύδια ὀλίγα, Mk 8:5, 7; Mt 15:34).

and fish are already in the disciples' possession. The five loaves, moreover, are simply "loaves"[30] in the Synoptics, not "barley loaves" as here.[31] The fish are literally "fish," as if right from the lake (see Jn 21:6, 8, 11), while in our Gospel they are "pieces of fish" already prepared as food[32] (see 21:9, 10, 13).[33] Andrew's question, "What are these for so many?" keeps alive the expectations raised by the comment that Jesus "knew what he was going to do" (v. 6), and confirms Philip's estimate of the enormity of the task of feeding such a crowd (v. 7). Again we wonder if perhaps we are expected to know what will happen because we have heard the story before (see n. 24). In any event, the stage is set for a miracle.

10 "Make the people sit down to eat," Jesus told his disciples. "Sit down to eat" is literally "recline"[34] as if at tables, when there were no tables. Instead, the writer explains, there was "a lot of grass,"[35] enough to accommodate the "large crowd" (vv. 2, 5) that had gathered "in the place." Grass need not have been mentioned, yet it seems to have been part of the story from the start, perhaps already in oral tradition (see Mt 14:19; also "green grass," Mk 6:9). In our Gospel, "grass" qualifies to some extent the notice that they were "on the mountain" (v. 3), helping the reader to visualize them on its gentle slopes, not at the very top (see v. 15, where Jesus will retreat again "to the mountain"!). Jesus speaks of the crowd as "the people," but the writer tells us that they were in fact "men"[36] just as in the other Gospels, and that they numbered five thousand.[37] The explicit (and extraordinary) number gives concreteness to Andrew's "so many" (v. 9), and credibility to Philip's judgment that "two hundred denarii" would not be enough to feed them (v. 7). Neither disciple had time to count them, but the all-knowing narrator makes a quick — and we presume accurate — estimate, in agreement with the three synoptic accounts. The reader's natural question whether women and children were

---

30. Gr. ἄρτους.

31. Possibly the "barley loaves" are intended to evoke the story of Elisha and the man from Baal-shalisha who brought "twenty loaves of barley" with which Elisha fed one hundred people, with "some left over" (2 Kgs 4:42-44). If so, there is a definite heightening tendency at work. It is also worth noting that in the immediately preceding narrative in the LXX (2 Kgs 4:38, 41), Gehazi is called Elijah's παιδάριον, in the sense of "servant," precisely in the role of one dispensing food.

32. Gr. ὀψάρια.

33. See BDAG, 746: "As food eaten with bread ὀψάριον can mean 'tidbit' in general . . . or specifically fish." It occurs in the New Testament only in John's Gospel.

34. Gr. ἀναπεσεῖν.

35. Gr. χόρτος πολύς.

36. "The people" (τοὺς ἀνθρώπους) are thus identified as "the men" (οἱ ἄνδρες).

37. Matthew and Mark withhold this information until the end of the story for maximum effect (Mt 14:21; Mk 6:44), but Luke introduces it at roughly the same point as here (Lk 9:14).

on the scene in addition to the five thousand men is left unanswered,[38] but the presence of at least one "child" (v. 9) implies that they were. This would bring the number well above five thousand, making the miracle greater, but it does not interest our writer, nor does he call our attention to the irony that the "child" who had the food may not even have been included among the five thousand. "The men," we are told, "sat down to eat" on the grass, in compliance with Jesus' orders to his disciples. We can infer women and children if we wish, but that is up to us.

11 Jesus performs his first "hands-on" miracle. At the Cana wedding, he merely gave orders and let the servants do the miracle for him (2:7-8). The royal official's son and the man at the pool of Bethsaida he healed with a word: "Go, your son lives" (4:50), and "Get up, pick up your mat and walk" (5:8). This time he "took the loaves" in his own hands, "and when he had given thanks, he gave them out to those who were seated, and of the fish as much as they wanted." "Taking" bread[39] is a natural part of all the feeding stories,[40] and of the synoptic accounts of Jesus' last supper with his disciples.[41] "Giving thanks" belongs to the second feeding story in Matthew and Mark (see Mt 15:36; Mk 8:6), but not the first, where "blessing" is the verb used (see Mt 14:19; Mk 6:41; Lk 9:16). "Giving thanks"[42] is also at home, as we might expect, in the Lukan and Pauline accounts of the last supper, or institution of the "Eucharist" (see Lk 22:19; 1 Cor 11:24).[43] In contrast to all the synoptic accounts both of the feeding of crowds and the institution of the Eucharist, Jesus is not explicitly said to "break" the loaves here, yet we can assume that they were broken, given the reference to "pieces of fish" to begin with (v. 9) and to broken "pieces"[44] left over when the meal was finished (v. 12).[45] The decisive act that accomplishes the miracle is the act of "giving thanks." This is what the writer remembers when he refers back to the miracle from a later vantage point (see v. 23, "after the Lord had given thanks"). Its closest

---

38. Only Matthew addresses the question, giving the number as five thousand men (ἄνδρες), "aside from women and children" (χωρὶς γυναικῶν καὶ παιδίων, Mt 14:21).

39. Gr. λαμβάνειν.

40. See Mt 14:19; 15:36; Mk 6:41; 8:6; Lk 9:16; also in John, at the meal of bread and fish after the resurrection (21:13).

41. See Mt 26:26, 27; Mk 14:22, 23; Lk 22:19

42. Gr. εὐχαριστεῖν.

43. In Matthew and in Mark, "giving thanks" (εὐχαριστεῖν) is used only in connection with the cup (Mt 26:27; Mk 14:23), while "blessing" (εὐλογεῖν) is used of the bread (Mt 26:26; Mk 14:22).

44. Gr. κλάσματα.

45. For this reason, too much should not be made of the bread not being "broken" in John's Gospel (as in B. W. Longenecker's article, "The Unbroken Messiah: A Johannine Feature and Its Social Function," *NTS* 41.3 [1995], 428-41).

analogy in John's Gospel is not at Jesus' last meal, nor at the lake when Jesus gave his disciples bread and fish (21:13), but at the raising of Lazarus, where thanksgiving works like petitionary prayer. Jesus "lifted up his eyes and said, 'Father, I thank you that you have heard me, and I know that you always hear me'" (11:41-42), and the miracle followed (vv. 43-44). Here too "giving thanks" shows Jesus' dependence on the Father, and consequently the five thousand were fed.

As soon as he gave thanks, Jesus "gave out" the loaves to "those who were seated,[46] and of the fish, as much as they wanted." In contrast to every account in the other Gospels, in this one Jesus gives the food directly to the crowd, not to the disciples first to distribute to the crowd. "As much as they wanted" seems to refer grammatically to the "pieces of fish," but its placement at the end of the sentence makes clear that the crowd had all they wanted of fish and bread alike.[47] The phrase anticipates what we learn explicitly in the next verse, that their hunger was more than satisfied, with plenty left over.

12 The actual meal is not described, but buried in a subordinate clause, "when they had had their fill," in much the same way that the transformation of water into wine at Cana was buried within a participle (see 2:9).[48] Attention focuses instead on "the leftover broken pieces," just as in the synoptic Gospels,[49] and in the bibical account of Elisha and the twenty barley loaves ("they ate and had some left, according to the word of the LORD," 2 Kgs 4:44). But John's account differs from the others in that Jesus explicitly gives the reason for gathering up the broken pieces: "so that nothing is lost."[50] All we are told in the other accounts is that the disciples "picked up" (see Mk 6:43; 8:8) twelve baskets of leftovers (in one instance), or seven (in

46. The verb changes here, from ἀναπεσεῖν (aorist, v. 10), "sit down to eat," to τοῖς ἀνακειμένοις (present participle), "those who were [already] seated." The former means to begin to sit, or take a seat, and is used only in the aorist in the New Testament. The latter is a natural alternative for the present tense.

47. This I have indicated in the translation by a comma after "fish." If ἐκ τῶν ὀψαρίων is read as a partitive construction (BDF, §164[2]), the writer could be saying that Jesus gave out "some of the fish" (compare the partitive expression, ἐκ τῶν ἄρτων, "of the loaves," in verse 26, and see also 3:25; 7:40; 9:40; 16:17). Bultmann (213) cites B. Weiss to the effect that the fish "were not distributed to all, but only to those who asked for them!" (the exclamation mark is Bultmann's!), but the implied subject of the last clause is "those who were seated," indicating that however much Jesus distributed, it was sufficient for all.

48. Only in retrospect is "eating" explicitly mentioned: "those who had eaten" (τοῖς βεβρωκόσιν, v. 13); "near the place where they ate [ἔφαγον] the bread" (v. 23); "you ate [ἐφάγετε] of the loaves and were satisfied" (v. 26).

49. See Mt 14:20; 15:37; 16:9-10; Mk 6:43; 8:8, 19-20; Lk 9:17.

50. Gr. ἵνα μή τι ἀπόληται.

another), not that Jesus commanded them to do so for any special reason. The accent is on the sheer quantity of what remained, and the magnitude of the miracle. Here Jesus commands them: "gather"[51] (v. 12), and "they gathered" (v. 13) the leftover pieces. The intention "that nothing is lost" is Jesus' intention, and that is what counts, not how many baskets are filled. Twelve or seven or one — it doesn't matter as long as "nothing is lost."

At one level, this is a perfectly natural aspect of the narrative. Jewish custom dictated that no food be wasted after a meal.[52] But why is it worthy of mention? Is our Gospel merely providing a plausible reason for what the other Gospels describe? Jesus' intention seems to run deeper, reflecting God's intention for human beings, not just their food supply. The only previous use of the verb "to be lost" came in his programmatic statement that God "gave the One and Only Son, so that everyone who believes in him might not be lost but have eternal life" (3:16). Later, returning to the subject of food, Jesus will draw a contrast between food that runs out or is "lost" and that which "remains" (that is, "to eternal life, which the Son of man will give you," 6:27). An implied parallel between food and human beings could help explain Jesus' urgency in insisting that nothing be "lost." Tradition bears this out. A eucharistic prayer in the *Didache,* from the second or perhaps even the first century, gives thanks for the "broken bread": "As this broken bread[53] was scattered on the mountains, but was gathered and became one, so let your Congregation[54] be gathered[55] from the ends of the earth into your kingdom, for yours is the glory and the power through Jesus Christ for ever" (*Didache* 9.4). While this text exhibits no direct dependence on John 6:12, it does show acquaintance more generally with the Gospel stories of the feeding of large crowds and probably with the Gospel of John as a whole.[56]

13 Even though the urgency centered on nothing being lost, it is also true that precisely "twelve baskets" were filled, just as in the other three Gospels. In this respect the story stays the same, and it leaves us with all the same questions. Why twelve? And what happened to the twelve baskets after they were collected? Did the disciples load them in the boat and take them back across the lake (v. 17)? Did they leave them for the crowd? (They would

---

51. Gr. συναγάγετε.
52. See Barrett, 277; Strack-Billerbeck, 4.625-26.
53. Gr. κλάσμα.
54. Gr. ἐκκλησία.
55. Gr. συναχθήτω.
56. Its only real point of contact with the Johannine feeding in particular is the verb "gather" (συνάγειν). There is no mention of bread being "lost," and the crucial number is not "twelve" but "one." The notion of "becoming one" (ἐγένετο ἕν) is no part of the feeding narrative in John's Gospel, but is a characteristic theme of John's Gospel generally, always with reference to the people of God (see 10:16; 11:52; 17:11, 21, 22, 23).

hardly have been enough to feed the crowd a second time.) Did they give them back to the child who supplied the five loaves in the first place? Such questions hold no more interest for our writer than for Matthew, Mark, or Luke — less perhaps, for in the other three we know by this time that there were twelve disciples (see Mt 10:1; Mk 3:14; Lk 6:13), and we can visualize each disciple carrying a basket. We have no such information here. If this is the first hint that there are in fact "twelve" disciples, it is only a hint. "The twelve" do not emerge as an explicit entity until the end of the chapter, where their existence as a group is suddenly recognized (v. 67), and Jesus claims to have chosen them (v. 70). So the question, "Why twelve?" remains (at least temporarily) unanswered, along with the obvious question of what was done with the leftover food. Consequently, the brief notice has the same function as in the synoptic Gospels, simply to underscore the greatness of the miracle by contrasting an enormous yield of "twelve baskets" of leftovers with a modest "five barley loaves." If we remember Elisha (see n. 24), we can do the mathematics: "twenty barley loaves" for a hundred people, over against "five" for five thousand!

14 "The men"[57] whose reaction is now described are not outside observers, but "those who had eaten" (v. 13). On "seeing what he had done as a sign," they acknowledged him as "truly the Prophet who is coming into the world." "Signs" are nothing new in this Gospel, and they are always seen either as things Jesus "did" on a particular occasion, as here (see 2:11; 4:54), or as things he "was doing" on a regular basis (2:23; 6:2; see also 2:18; 3:2). Here the crowd had followed him across the lake because of "signs" done for the sick (v. 2), and now, quite naturally, they interpret his provision of food to satisfy their hunger in exactly the same way.[58] They are not wrong about this, nor they necessarily wrong to conclude that "This is truly the Prophet who is coming into the world." "The Prophet" seems to have been the figure to whom Moses referred when he said, "The LORD God will raise up for you a prophet like me from among your brothers" (Deut 18:15). John had denied being "the Prophet," just as he denied being "the Christ," or "Elijah" (1:20-

---

57. Gr. οἱ οὖν ἄνθρωποι (see above, n. 36).
58. "Sign" (σημεῖον) lacks the definite article, suggesting that the direct object of "seeing" (ἰδόντες) is "what he had done" (ὃ ἐποίησεν), and that σημεῖον should be read as a predicate accusative (see BDF, §157): they saw "what he had done" *as* a sign, or *to be* a sign. Alternatively, it could be translated "seeing what a sign he had done," but the difference is small. In any event, the crowd and the Gospel writer agree in viewing the miraculous feeding as a "sign," or σημεῖον. A few manuscripts (including B and P[75]) have the plural ἃ ἐποίησεν σημεῖα, "what signs he had done," or "the things he had done as signs," factoring into the crowd's reaction the earlier healing signs done on the other side of the lake (v. 2). But the singular has wider manuscript support (ℵ, D, W, Latin and Syriac versions), and is probably to be preferred.

21), but the question whether Jesus was "the Prophet" remained an open one. Philip recognized him as "someone of whom Moses wrote in the law" (1:45). The Samaritan woman called him "a prophet," because he acted like one (4:17-19), and he himself, as we have seen, consciously played a prophet's role in Samaria, leaving after two days because "a prophet has no honor in his own hometown" (4:44). Beyond this, the reader knows Jesus as one who "comes" (1:15, 27; 3:31; 5:43), or is "sent" (3:34; 4:34; 5:23, 24, 30, 36, 37, 38), sometimes specifically "into the world" (3:17, 19, and later in the Gospel 9:39; 10:36; 11:27; 12:46; 16:28; 17:18; 18:37). So the confession, "This is truly the Prophet who is coming into the world," rings just as "true" as that of the Samaritans who said, "This is truly[59] the Savior of the world" (4:42).[60] We know by this time that Jesus is more than "the Prophet like Moses," but he is at least that. His own words, after all, are still ringing in our ears: "If you believed Moses, you would believe me, for he wrote about me. But if you do not believe his written words, how will you believe my spoken words?" (5:46-47).

15 True though it may be, the crowd's confession is not exactly what it seems. We are allowed to see it through Jesus' eyes. He "found out" that their real intention was "to come and seize him to make him king." How do we get from "Prophet like Moses" to "king," and how did Jesus learn of their intention? Moses in Jewish tradition embodied all that they expected or could expect in a messianic figure,[61] but "king," for whatever reason, was what interested them here. The Gospel writer does not pause to examine the logic — in this case the illogic — of the crowd's intention. Obviously, if Jesus were truly what they took him to be, "the Prophet who is coming into the world," they would have every reason to respect — even fear — his power, and no reason at all to think of him as a puppet who could be manipulated to fit their agenda. As for Jesus, how did he "find out" what the crowd had in mind? Was his knowledge supernatural, like his knowledge of Nathanael, or

---

59. Gr. οὗτός ἐστιν ἀληθῶς, in both instances.

60. See also 7:40, "This is truly [οὗτός ἐστιν ἀληθῶς] the Prophet."

61. Philo wrote: "For Moses, through God's providence, became king [βασιλεύς] and lawgiver and high priest and prophet; and in each function he won the highest place. But why it is fitting that they should all be combined in the same person needs explanation. It is a king's duty to command what is right and forbid what is wrong. But to command what should be done and to forbid what should not be done is the peculiar function of law; so that it follows at once that the king is a living law, and the law a just king" (*On the Life of Moses*, 2.3-4; LCL, 6.451-53). Elsewhere Philo adds, "For he did not become king in the ordinary way by the aid of troops and weapons or of the might of ships and infantry and cavalry. It was God who appointed him by the free judgment of his subjects, God who created in them the willingness to choose him as their sovereign" (*On Rewards and Punishments*, 54; LCL, 8.343-45).

of the Samaritan woman, or in general of "what was in the person" (2:25)? Or did he acquire it naturally, as when he "found out" that his baptizing ministry was known to the Pharisees (4:1), or how long the sick man had been lying by the pool (5:6)? The aorist participle, "when he found out,"[62] suggests natural knowledge,[63] but it is hard to be certain. The accent, in any event, is on the information itself, not on how Jesus acquired it, and the purpose of the brief notice to make sure the reader knows it.

The reader, as we have seen, is prepared to accept that Jesus was "truly the Prophet who is coming into the world" (v. 14), and even that he deserved to be called "king." Nathanael hailed him from the start as "King of Israel" (1:49), and he will enter Jerusalem with that title ringing in his ears (12:13). Yet he will make it clear in due course that his kingdom is "not of this world" (18:36). What is jarring here is that "they were going to come and seize[64] him to make him king." Such language recalls, perhaps deliberately, Jesus' own pronouncement in Matthew that "the kingdom of the heavens suffers violence, and violent ones seize[65] it" (Mt 11:12). Jesus wanted no part of their scenario, but instead "withdrew again, he alone, to the mountain." Ironically, a time will come when he will be made "king" against his will (see 19:1-5, 13-16), and when that happens it will be the work not of those who seriously confess him as "the Prophet" but of Pilate and the Roman soldiers, who mock all such claims. It will also signal his imminent death. By "withdrawing," Jesus forestalls that eventuality, just as surely here as when he "ducked out" after healing the man at the pool (5:13), or later when he repeatedly escaped capture (7:30; 8:20, 59; 10:39). The vocabulary is different here, more like Matthew's Gospel than John's,[66] but Jesus' action is thoroughly in character, and consistent with earlier notices that "the Jews began pursuing Jesus" and "kept trying all the more to kill him" (5:16, 18).

The notice that Jesus withdrew "again to the mountain" recalls the beginning of the story, when the "large crowd" first followed him and he "went up on the mountain, and there he sat with his disciples" (vv. 2-3). We were never told explicitly that he came down the mountain, but evidently the

---

62. Gr. γνούς.

63. When supernatural knowledge is involved, the writer often prefers the perfect participle εἰδώς (6:61; 13:1, 3; 18:4; 19:28), or the pluperfect indicative ᾔδει (6:6, 64; 13:11).

64. Gr. ἁρπάζειν.

65. Gr. ἁρπάζουσιν.

66. The verb "withdrew (ἀναχωρεῖν) occurs only here in John's Gospel, but ten times in Matthew, often with the implication of avoiding or escaping danger; see Mt 2:12, 13, 14, 22; 4:12; and especially 12:15 (γνοὺς ἀνεχώρησεν ἐκεῖθεν), 14:13, and 15:21. Possibly the use of the verb here is a carryover from an earlier version of the story which John's Gospel has used as a source.

grassy "place" (v. 10) where he multiplied the loaves is understood to have been at least partway down, so that he must go up "again" to escape the same "large crowd" (presumably) that now wants to make him king.[67] He was "with his disciples" before (v. 3), but now he is "alone."[68]

16-17 The inevitable question, "Where are the disciples?" is answered immediately. They "went down to the lake, and got in a boat and were on their way across the lake to Capernaum" (vv. 16-17). This is the first mention of Capernaum in the chapter (see vv. 24, 59). If Capernaum was Jesus' unnamed starting point (see v. 1), it is natural that the disciples might now return there. Two things are said about the timing of their departure: first, "it grew late" (v. 16), and second, "it had already gotten dark" (v. 17).[69] The first of these explains why the disciples went down to the lake and embarked in a boat; the second implies that after they got into the boat and were out on the lake they were still waiting for Jesus, who had "not yet come to them" (v. 17). But why would they be expecting such a thing? How could he "come to them"?[70] If they were expecting Jesus to join them, the notice should have come earlier, *before* they got into the boat. The text would have had to say, "But as it grew late — and it had already gotten dark and Jesus had not yet come to them — his disciples went down to the lake, and got in a boat, and were on their way across the lake to Capernaum." Such a rearrangement is

---

67. One ancient manuscript (D) adds, "and was praying there" (κακεῖ προσηύχετο), echoing Mk 1:35 more closely than the Matthean and Markan parallels to this passage, where he went up in order "to pray" (προσεύξασθαι, Mt 14:23; Mk 6:46). In John's Gospel there is no need to explain why Jesus withdrew to the mountain. We already know that it was to escape those who wanted to make him king.

68. Literally, "he alone" (αὐτὸς μόνος). Just as in Mk 6:47, αὐτὸς μόνος means simply that Jesus is not with his disciples. They too are "alone" (μόνοι, v. 22) in the sense that Jesus is not with them. Later, Jesus will make the point repeatedly that he is never really "alone," because the Father who sent him is with him (8:16, 29; 16:32).

69. In place of "it had already gotten dark" (καὶ σκοτία ἤδη ἐγεγόνει) two ancient manuscripts (ℵ and D) have a different, more characteristically "Johannine" reading: κατέλαβεν δὲ αὐτοὺς ἡ σκοτία ("but the darkness overtook them"). This reading evokes memories of 1:5 (καὶ ἡ σκοτία αὐτὸ οὐ κατέλαβεν, "and the darkness did not overtake" the light), and at the same time anticipates Jesus' last words to "the crowd" at the end of his public ministry: "Yet a short time the Light is in you. Walk while you have the Light, lest darkness overtake you" (ἵνα μὴ σκοτία ὑμᾶς καταλάβῃ, 12:35). While we may be grateful to later scribes for their appreciation of Johannine thought and vocabulary, the variant reading seems to imply a moral judgment on Jesus' disciples in the boat that seems to go well beyond the Gospel writer's intention.

70. The notion that "Perhaps they were sailing close to land expecting to meet Jesus on the shore" (Brown, 1.251; see also Whitacre, 146) is a counsel of despair. First, they were headed "across the lake" (v. 17), not along the shore. Second, if they were meeting Jesus on land, it would be a case not of his coming to them but of their coming to him.

rather forced. The whole phrase, "and it had already gotten dark, and Jesus had not yet come to them," would have to be read as another of the Gospel's belated narrative asides, explaining why the disciples finally (perhaps reluctantly) decided to get in the boat and go back across the lake without Jesus. More likely, the clause belongs right where the Gospel writer put it. The disciples are in the boat on the lake, it is dark, and "Jesus had not yet come to them." "Not yet" implies that he will come. This has to be *the reader's* expectation, not that of the disciples.[71] The writer assumes that his readers know (more or less) what will happen, just as earlier when he told them that Jesus knew what he was going to do (v. 6). Their impression is that Jesus will come. The only question is when.[72]

In short, we are presumed to be familiar with the basic elements of the story, whether from oral tradition or another Gospel account. Yet John's account is different in some respects from that of the other Gospels. In Mark, for example (6:45-46), and in Matthew (14:22-23), the disciples did not get in the boat on their own initiative. Jesus "compelled" them to do so, while he stayed behind to "dismiss" the crowd,[73] and went up the mountain to pray (see above, n. 67). Nothing is said of any attempt to make him king. Mark sets the stage for the miracle with a notice that "it grew late, and the boat was in the middle of the lake, and he alone on the land" (Mk 6:47; see n. 68). In John's account, as we have seen, the words "Jesus had not yet come to them" raise the level of expectancy. The reader is with the disciples in the boat, seeing the event from their perspective even while knowing and expecting more than the disciples can know. Mark, by contrast, is an omnipresent narrator, allowing us first to see the disciples through Jesus' eyes (Mk 6:48, "seeing them"), and then Jesus through the disciples' eyes (Mk 6:49, "seeing him").[74] Each Gospel in its own way prepares us for something extraordinary.

18 In contrast to the accounts in Matthew (14:24) and Mark (6:48), the notice that "the lake was rough, with a strong wind blowing" is intro-

---

71. Bultmann (215) comments that Jesus' coming was something "which neither the disciples nor the uninstructed reader could have expected. The narrator was obviously thinking ahead to what would follow, and the statement shows clearly that for him the real point of the story is the miracle of Jesus' walking on the lake." The key word in his comment is "uninstructed." The properly "instructed" reader knows what is going to happen.

72. So Lindars: "John's version suggests that the miracle of walking on the sea was bound to happen" (247).

73. "Dismissing" the crowd is a repeated theme in all the synoptic accounts of miraculous feedings (see Mt 14:15, 22, 23; 15:32, 39; Mk 6:36, 45; 8:3, 9), but never occurs in John's Gospel.

74. Matthew is more like John in this respect, lingering briefly with Jesus "alone" (μόνος) on the mountain (14:23; compare Jn 6:15), but telling the story of Jesus walking on the water consistently from the viewpoint of the disciples in the boat (14:24-33).

duced not to prepare us for a final calming of the wind (see Mt 14:32; Mk 6:51), but evidently for some other reason. There is no "stilling of the storm" in John's Gospel, and this is odd because in Matthew and Mark the stilling of this storm (if we may call it that) is redundant in a way it would not have been in John. Jesus had already calmed a storm in both of those Gospels (see Mt 8:23-27; Mk 4:35-41) and would not have had to do so again. That he did reinforces, quietly and without fanfare, the principle that "even the wind and the sea obey him" (Mk 4:41). In John's Gospel, by contrast, this is the logical (really the only) place for such an account to be introduced, yet it is not. And if Jesus is not going to calm the storm, why do we need to know that "the lake was rough, with a strong wind blowing?" The words here have a different function, adding[75] an element of danger to the notice that "it had already gotten dark" (v. 17) and helping to account for the disciples' fear (see vv. 19-20).

19 It is not reassuring that by now the disciples were well out in what Mark calls "the middle of the lake" (Mk 6:47). Our Gospel is slightly more specific: "twenty-five or thirty stadia" amounts to three or three-and-a-half miles.[76] Josephus gives the lake's dimensions as "forty stadia in width, and a hundred more than that in length," thus four-and-a-half by sixteen miles.[77] On any reckoning the disciples were far from land and at least halfway to Capernaum by the time they "could see[78] Jesus walking on the lake." This means that "on the lake"[79] cannot mean "by the lake" (as in 21:1).[80] With the boat three miles out to sea, if Jesus were merely walking along the shore,[81] he

---

75. The particle τε, a "marker of close relationship between sequential states or events" (BDAG, 993), links the notice very closely as a postscript to the immediately preceding description of the disciples' predicament: darkness, Jesus' absence, "and what's more" a storm on the lake.

76. A "stadium" or "stade" was the length of a Roman stadium: one-eighth of a mile, or 192 meters, just over 600 feet (see BDAG, 940). The writer avoids exactitude by the use of ὡς, "about," and by giving two possible estimates.

77. Josephus, *War* 5.306 (see LCL, 2.718, note *a:* "The real measurements on a modern map are about 12/2 miles by 7 miles (at its broadest part). Josephus possibly intends to give the average breadth").

78. This verb for "see" (θεωρεῖν) is common in John's Gospel in the sense of "perceive," "notice," or "observe," thus, "could see" (as in 4:19), an intentional kind of seeing, as if they were looking for something (see BDAG, 454).

79. Gr. ἐπὶ τῆς θαλάσσης.

80. See, for example, Brown, 1.252; Bultmann, 215; Barrett, 280-81; Lindars, 247. Matthew has it unambiguously, "upon the lake" (ἐπὶ τὴν θάλασσαν, Mt 14:25).

81. So Bernard, 1.186, who argues that the phrase "does not necessarily mean more than 'by the sea shore,'" and speaks of "a transformation of the Johannine tradition, which is void of miracle [*sic*] into the supernatural story in Mk., Mt." Elsewhere he claims that "Jn. retells Mk's story of Jesus 'walking on the sea' in such a manner as to correct it, by omitting any suggestion of a miracle" (1.clxxvi).

could hardly be seen "coming near the boat"! As he comes near the disciples are said to be "afraid" *(kai ephobēthēsan)*, probably for more than one reason: because it is dark, because of the wind and the waves, and because they do not recognize the figure approaching their boat.[82]

20 Jesus tells them, "It is I. Don't be afraid!" the very same words he uses in both Matthew (14:27) and Mark (6:50). Jesus has used the expression, "It is I" once before in our Gospel, identifying himself to the Samaritan woman as the Messiah she was expecting (4:26). Here he is not making a christological statement, but simply reassuring his disciples by identifying himself as someone known to them, their Teacher (see 1:38), who had been with them on the mountain (v. 3), and had stayed on there alone (v. 15). To them, "It is I"[83] does not in itself signal either messiahship (which they have already acknowledged)[84] or divinity, but simply Jesus' presence.[85] To the reader it hints at something more, perhaps an angelic or divine epiphany.[86] But this becomes a serious option only later when Jesus adds to the expression a series of designations telling what his presence means (beginning with "I am the Bread of life," vv. 35, 47), and when he uses the expression by itself to evoke the eternal God of Israel (see 8:58). For now he is merely announcing and identifying himself.[87]

21 The disciples do not act as if they have just seen an epiphany or theophany. That "they wanted to take him into the boat" implies that Jesus' words had calmed their fears. They knew he was not a "ghost" (see n. 82),

---

82. John's Gospel leaves unsaid what the other Gospels give as the explanation of their fear. According to Matthew, "they were terrified [ἐταράχθησαν], saying that 'It is a ghost!' [φάντασμά ἐστιν]. And they cried out in fear" (ἀπὸ τοῦ φόβου, Mt 14:26). In Mark, "they thought it was a ghost and cried out, for they all saw him and were terrified" (Mk 6:49).

83. Gr. ἐγώ εἰμι.

84. See 1:41, 45, 48.

85. Contrast this with Paul Anderson's comment (*Christology*, 180) that in contrast to Mark, where Jesus means simply "Don't worry, it's only myself," John's account is "starkly theophanic" (in agreement with Bultmann, 216). If, as Anderson argues, "What Mark describes as being afraid of a phantasm, John interprets as *the fear of God*," then Jesus' use of ἐγώ εἰμι (in the theophanic way that Anderson proposes) would not have had the reassuring effect Jesus intended. If they saw him as the God they feared, it is unlikely that they would have wanted to take him into the boat!

86. See, for example, Revelation 1:17-18, "Don't be afraid [μὴ φοβοῦ]. I am [ἐγώ εἰμι] the First and the Last and the Living One" (compare Isa 48:12).

87. Barrett comments wisely that "the fact that John can use ἐγώ εἰμι as a simple self-identification should be borne in mind before elaborate theories based on occurrences of the words elsewhere are accepted. If in the present passage there is any hint of the epiphany of a divine figure it is not because the words ἐγώ εἰμι are used but because in the gospel as a whole Jesus is a divine figure" (281).

nor an angel, nor a threatening divine figure of any kind, but Jesus, their Teacher and Lord (see 13:13). Their reunion with Jesus is also a moment of recognition, not unlike his encounter with Mary on the day of his resurrection (see 20:14-16). Just as Mary seems to have wanted to touch or hold on to him (20:17), so the disciples wanted Jesus with them in the boat. "They wanted" is imperfect,[88] suggesting an unfulfilled wish (as in 7:44; 16:19). The same verb appears in Mark, but with Jesus as its subject: Jesus "walked on the lake, and wanted to pass them by" (Mk 6:48). Mark tells us what Jesus "wanted," or would have done, while in John it is a matter of what the disciples "wanted."[89]

That their wish went unfulfilled is shown by the notice that "immediately the boat reached land right where they were going" (that is, Capernaum, v. 17). The point of the notice is probably not to signal a second, gratuitous, miracle on the lake. We are not meant to infer that Jesus and the disciples were all supernaturally transported halfway across the lake in an instant. The point is rather that by the time Jesus reached the disciples, their boat had already "advanced" (v. 19) to the other side, implying that Jesus had walked *all the way across the lake*. The miracle was not that he defied gravity by walking on the lake's surface without sinking (though he must have done so), nor that he demonstrated his lordship over the wind and waves like the God of Israel (see Ps 77:16-19; 107:23-30). The miracle lay in the crossing itself. How did Jesus get to where he was going? "The wind blows where it will," he had told Nicodemus, "and you hear the sound of it, but you don't know where it comes from or where it goes. So it is with everyone born of the Spirit" (3:8). Now he has demonstrated to his disciples (and to the reader) that his comings and goings are indeed beyond their comprehension.[90] The chapter began with the simple notice that he "went across the lake of Galilee, or Tiberias" (v. 1). Where he came from then the reader did not know for certain, even though it was clearly not a miraculous crossing. All that was known was that "a large crowd was following him" (v. 2). Now he crosses back again under extraordinary circumstances. After feeding the crowd, he fled to the mountain (v. 15) and now from there back across the lake. The crowd is left to wonder where Jesus has gone. We will hear of their bewilderment shortly (see vv. 22-25).

88. Gr. ἤθελον.

89. The difference between the two accounts should not be exaggerated. Even Mark seems to describe Jesus' intention *as the disciples perceived it,* not by taking the reader inside the mind of Jesus (see W. L. Lane, *The Gospel According to Mark,* 236: "The words record the impression that the disciples had at that time that the spectral figure intended to pass by them"). For a similar example of an unrealized intention, see Lk 24:28.

90. This becomes a significant theme as the story unfolds (see, for example, vv. 24-25; 7:34; 8:14, 21-23; 9:29; 13:33, 36; 16:10, 16-19, 28).

6:22-40 JESUS AND THE CROWD AT CAPERNAUM

As for Jesus' disciples, they are silent, just as his enemies were silent after his long discourse in the preceding chapter. We are not privy to their reaction, and we will not meet them again until verse 60, where we will find them more offended by his words than impressed by his actions.

F. JESUS AND THE CROWD AT CAPERNAUM (6:22-40)

> 22 *The next day, the crowd left standing on the other side of the lake saw that no other boat was there except one, and that Jesus had not gotten into the boat with his disciples, but his disciples had departed alone.* 23 *Other boats came along from Tiberias, which was near the place where they had eaten the bread after the Lord had given thanks.* 24 *So when the crowd saw that Jesus was not there, nor his disciples, they got into the boats and came to Capernaum seeking Jesus.* 25 *And when they found him on the other side of the lake, they said to him, "Rabbi, when did you get here?"*
>
> 26 *Jesus answered them and said, "Amen, amen, I say to you, You are seeking me not because you saw signs, but because you ate of the loaves and were satisfied.* 27 *Work not for the food that is being lost, but for the food that remains to eternal life, which the Son of man will give you. For he it is whom God the Father sealed."* 28 *So they said to him, "What shall we do that we might work the works of God?"*
>
> 29 *Jesus answered and said to them, "This is the work of God, that you believe in him whom that One sent."* 30 *So they said to him, "What then do you do as a sign, that we may see and believe you? What work do you perform?* 31 *Our fathers ate the manna in the desert, as it is written, 'He gave them bread from heaven to eat.'"*
>
> 32 *So Jesus said to them, "Amen, amen, I say to you, it is not Moses who has given you that bread from heaven, but it is my Father who gives you the true bread from heaven.* 33 *For the bread of God is that which comes down from heaven and gives life to the world."* 34 *So they said to him, "Sir, give us this bread always."*
>
> 35 *Jesus said to them, "I am the Bread of life. The person who comes to me will never go hungry, and the person who believes in me will never ever thirst.* 36 *Yet I said to you that you have seen me and you do not believe.* 37 *All that the Father gives me will come to me, and the person who comes to me I will never drive out,* 38 *for I have come down from heaven not to do my will but the will of the One who sent me.* 39 *And this is the will of the One who sent me, that of all he has given me I might not lose anything, but raise it up at the last day.* 40 *For this is the will of my Father, that every person who sees the Son*

and believes in him might have eternal life, and I will raise him up at the last day."

For the first time "the crowd left standing on the other side of the lake" are given a voice. Some, or even all of them, had been involved in a plot to kidnap Jesus and make him their king, and now we hear what they have to say as they become Jesus' dialogue partners. As it turns out, they function in the narrative much like "the Jews" at the first Passover (2:18-20), or at the unnamed "festival of the Jews" in chapter 5 (see 5:1, 15, 16, 18). Unlike the latter, however, they are real participants in a real dialogue, not merely an audience for Jesus' uninterrupted discourse (as in 5:19-47). In any event, it will come as no surprise later when they are abruptly called no longer "the crowd" (as in vv. 22, 24), but "the Jews" (vv. 41, 52). In a very real sense, even though they started out as potential disciples (see v. 2), they turn out to be the same antagonists as before. "The Jews" are "the Jews," whether in Jerusalem or Capernaum, and so the controversy resumes.

22 Earlier notices that "it grew late" (v. 16) and had "gotten dark" (v. 17) prepare us for "the next day" (as in 1:29, 35, 43), and with the new day comes a change of scene. We are now back with "the crowd left standing on the other side of the lake," and for the moment are allowed to see things from their perspective. The account is somewhat confusing, because it seems to be based not on what they literally saw "the next day," but on what they remembered from the day before. What they saw was that there were no boats[1] by the lake. What they remembered was that one (and only one) boat had been there. They knew that Jesus' disciples had left in that boat, and that Jesus had not been with them. So where was Jesus? We know from the preceding section that their plan was "to come and seize him to make him king" (v. 15), and we can assume that this was still their intention. But who were they? How many of the "five thousand men" (v. 10) were involved in that plot? There is no way to know. Nothing prevents us from assuming that all five thousand were involved, and yet the narrative proceeds as if only a small, representative group actually followed Jesus across the lake and engaged him in dialogue.

23-24 At the beginning of the chapter, the writer showed no interest in how the "large crowd" got across the lake (v. 2), but now, having men-

---

1. Literally, "that no other boat was there except one" (that is, the one that had been there, but was now gone). The word for boat, πλοιάριον, again shows the writer's fondness for diminutives (see παιδάριον, v. 9; ὀψάρια, vv. 9, 11), but seems to be used here interchangeably with πλοῖον (see vv. 17, 19, 21, not to mention εἰς τὸ πλοῖον in v. 22 itself, and πλοῖα in the best manuscripts in v. 23, including P[75], ℵ, and B). I have therefore translated both words simply as "boat."

6:22-40 JESUS AND THE CROWD AT CAPERNAUM

tioned a boat (or, rather, the absence of one), he must be more specific. "Other boats[2] came along from Tiberias," he explains. How many other boats? Why did they come? What passengers did they bring? We are told none of those things.[3] The "other boats" are in the story only to provide the necessary transportation back across the lake. The boats came from Tiberias because Tiberias was the nearest town. More specifically, it was "near the place where they had eaten the bread after the Lord had given thanks," for that was where the crowd was "left standing" (see v. 22). The writer takes the opportunity to remind us again of the miracle of the loaves they all had "eaten,"[4] the importance of the "place" where it had happened (see v. 10), and even the act of "giving thanks" by which "the Lord"[5] had performed the miracle (see v. 11). The miracle itself is remembered. Only the extraordinary number, "about five thousand" (v. 10), is forgotten. If we dwelt on that, we would have to ask, "How many boats are needed to transport five thousand men? A thousand? A hundred? Fifty?"

Clearly, the writer's tacit assumption is that "the crowd" has by now dwindled to a small, manageable delegation who "got into the boats and came to Capernaum seeking Jesus" (v. 24). They did this because they "saw that Jesus was not there, nor his disciples." That his disciples were not there was no surprise, for the crowd seems to have known that they had already left, and that Jesus had not been with them (v. 22). But why did they think Jesus would be across the lake, rather than on the mountain, or somewhere beyond it, away from the lake. Possibly because the lake was the quickest way to Capernaum, and they knew that Capernaum was not only Jesus' disciples' destination, but his home (see 2:12), and his family's home (see v. 42). In any event, they looked in the direction of the lake, and as it turned out they were right (v. 25). While "seeking" him can reflect potential or actual discipleship (1:38; 13:33; 20:15), more often it signals a desire to cap-

---

2. Depending on how it is accented, αλλα can be either ἀλλά, "but" or "however" (linking the notice to the preceding verse) or ἄλλα, "other," modifying πλοῖα (or πλοιάρια), "boats." I have followed the Nestle-Aland text in opting for the latter (see the variant reading, ἄλλων πλοιαρίων ἐλθόντων, D). For the phrase, ἄλλα πλοῖα, compare Mk 4:36, where "other boats" are abruptly introduced in similar fashion to get all Jesus' disciples with him across the lake after teaching in parables. Possibly John's Gospel is drawing on an account similar to this.

3. Lindars aptly calls it "a happy coincidence, which John does not try to explain" (249).

4. Except for Jesus' initial question (v. 5), the common verb φαγεῖν, "eat" (see 4:31-33), was not used in the account of the feeding of the crowd (see vv. 10-13), yet it occurs repeatedly from here on in reflections on the feeding (v. 26), on eating the manna in the desert (twice in v. 31 and once in v. 49) and the Bread of life (vv. 50, 51, 52, 53, 58).

5. Gr. εὐχαριστήσαντος τοῦ κυρίου. For "the Lord" as a designation for Jesus by the narrator, see 4:1; 11:2.

ture or kill him (see 5:18; 7:1, 11, 19, 20, 25, 30, 34, 36; 8:21, 37, 40; 10:39; 11:8, 56; 18:4, 7, 8). Which is it here? Neither one exactly, but probably more like the second, a continuation of their earlier plan to "come and seize him to make him king" (v. 15).[6] The first thing Jesus will do when they find him is question their motives (v. 26), and the reader has reason to do the same.

25 "Seek, and you will find," Jesus said in two other Gospels (Mt 7:7; Lk 11:9), and the crowd "seeking" Jesus now "found" him, just as his first disciples had done (1:41, 45). He had crossed the lake, just as they thought, but how he had done so remained a mystery. "Rabbi, when did you get here?" they asked him. The title "Rabbi," echoing Jesus' first disciples (1:38, 49; 4:31), exhibits their persistent desire to "follow" him (see v. 2), but like Nicodemus (3:2) they will turn out to be only potential, not actual disciples. "When [πότε] did you get here?"[7] was their spoken question, but the unspoken one, perhaps one they dared not ask (see 4:27; 16:5; 21:12), was "How?"[8]

26 Neither question is answered. Instead, Jesus unmasks their intentions with a pronouncement introduced, like several others before, with "Amen, amen, I say to you." It is the eighth such pronouncement in John's Gospel (see 1:51; 3:3, 5, 11; 5:19, 24, 25), and the first of four in the discourse now beginning. The ensuing discourse, like the dialogue with Nicodemus and like Jesus' speech to "the Jews" at Jerusalem in the preceding chapter, will be punctuated with this "Amen, amen" refrain (see vv. 32, 47, 53), lending solemnity and seriousness to all that he says. Whether in Jerusalem or Capernaum the audience is much the same, and the reader senses already that the outcome too will be similar. The distinction between actual or potential disciples on the one hand, and opponents or persecutors on the other is rapidly breaking down, and we will witness this blurring process as

---

6. "Seizing" him (ἁρπάζειν, v. 15) is not so different, after all, from "arresting" him (πιάσαι; see 7:30, 32, 44; 8:20; 10:39; 11:57). Whether they intend it or not, "making him king" will eventuate in his death (see 19:13-16).

7. "When" (πότε) seems to require an aorist verb. The perfect γέγονας implies something more like, "How long have you been here?" (see Abbott, *Johannine Grammar*, 347). Later textual variants moved in the direction of the aorist (ἦλθες, ℵ; *venisti* in the Latin tradition), or at least of a specific "coming" (ἐλήλυθας, D) rather than simply "getting here" or "being here" (see Barrett, 286). The more difficult γέγονας is clearly to be preferred, and our translation, "When did you get here?" captures quite well the note of duration signaled by the perfect tense.

8. See Chrysostom, *Homilies* 43.2: "Still when they came to Him after so great a wonder, they asked Him not how He crossed over, how He arrived there, nor sought to understand so great a sign. But what say they? 'Master, when camest Thou hither?' Unless any one affirm that the 'when' is here used by them in the sense of 'how'" (NPNF, 1st ser., 14.156).

the narrative moves along. Instead of welcoming them, Jesus immediately calls into question the "discipleship" to which they aspire. The writer could have repeated here what was said of those who had "believed" at the first Passover, that Jesus "would not entrust himself to them, for he himself knew them all" (2:24). Jesus, echoing the notice that they were "seeking" him (v. 24), uncovers their true motivation: "You are seeking me not because you saw signs, but because *you ate of the loaves and were satisfied.*"[9] The italicized words evoke the biblical complaint of the Israelites against Moses in the desert: "If only we had died by the hand of the Lord in the land of Egypt, when we sat by the fleshpots and *ate our fill of bread*" (Exod 16:3, NRSV). The circumstances, to be sure, are quite different. The crowd is not complaining — not yet, at least (though see vv. 41, 43, 61) — and Jesus is not attributing to them any complaint. But they are, he claims, thinking only of themselves and their appetite for food, not for what he now offers. The stage is being set already for an explicit demand for "bread from heaven," comparable to Moses' "manna in the desert," to satisfy their hunger (see vv. 30-31).

More surprising is Jesus' claim that their reason for following him was "not because you saw signs." Clearly, they had seen signs (v. 2), and one sign in particular (v. 14). The writer has told us that on that basis they identified Jesus as "truly the Prophet who is coming into the world" (v. 14), and it would have been natural to infer that this was why they crossed the lake looking for him. But Jesus' comment trumps that of the narrator. Jesus does not deny that they "saw signs," but he insists that signs were not their true motivation. Unlike his first disciples (2:11), they did not see his glory revealed in the signs. Unlike those at the first Passover (2:23), they did not "believe," or even pretend to believe, because of his signs. Rather, they "followed" (v. 2) or "looked for" him (v. 24) because of his impressive healings and (especially) because he fed them. As "the Prophet who is coming into the world" (v. 14), he would teach them the truth (see Deut 18:15-18; Jn 4:25), but a king would ensure their material well-being. In wanting to make him king, Jesus is saying, they were thinking only of themselves. They "ate of the loaves and were satisfied," and like the Samaritan woman (4:15) they wanted the abundance to continue.

27 Because the food that had "satisfied" the crowd was not food they had to work for, the subject of "work" does not come up until Jesus (rather abruptly) brings it up: "Work not for the food[10] that is being lost, but

---

9. The verb "were satisfied" (ἐχορτάσθητε), which corresponds to "had their fill" (ἐνεπλήσθησαν) in the actual narrative of the feeding (v. 12), may have come from an earlier account similar to those preserved in the synoptic Gospels (see ἐχορτάσθησαν in Mt 14:20//Mk 6:42, Mt 15:37//Mk 8:8; Lk 9:17).

10. Gr. τὴν βρῶσιν.

for the food that remains to eternal life, which the Son of man will give you." Jesus assumes here what they all know to be true, that normally one must work for one's food.[11] Food and work belong together for all who are able to work, but for no one more conspicuously than for Jesus himself, who told his disciples, "I have food to eat that you do not know about" (4:32), and "My food is that I might do the will of the One who sent me and complete his work" (4:34). "Work," for Jesus, was not a way of earning food. Rather, his "food" *was* his work, the work his Father had given him to do (see 5:17, 36). Food to him is more than a physical necessity of life. It is a metaphor, and he invites the crowd to think of it in a similar way. He asks them to consider what kind of "food" they are working for, the kind "being lost,"[12] or the kind that "remains to eternal life," and to choose the latter.

The strong contrast between physical and spiritual food recalls an earlier contrast between "this water" and "the water that I will give" (4:13-14). Just as those who drink from the well at Sychar will "thirst again," so those who "ate of the loaves and were satisfied" will not stay satisfied forever. They proved that by following Jesus, looking for something more. Physical food is subject to "being lost" or "perishing," not in the sense of being spoiled or going rotten, but in that it satisfies human needs only temporarily. Jesus implied as much in other Gospels, making the point that "whatever goes into the mouth enters the stomach, and goes out into the sewer" (Mt 15:17, NRSV; see also Mk 7:19). His conclusion there was that food cannot defile a person, but it is just as clear that food cannot nourish a person indefinitely either, for he also said, according to Matthew, "A person shall not live by bread alone, but by every word coming from the mouth of God" (Mt 4:4). What Jesus says now to the crowd lends unexpected irony to his earlier command to his disciples, "Gather the leftover broken pieces, so that nothing is lost."[13] Gathering the leftovers into twelve baskets (v. 13) could keep them from being wasted, but hardly from being "lost" in the sense in which Jesus now uses the term. Literal food, however miraculously produced, is just food. When it is eaten, it is gone.

The "food that remains to eternal life" is quite another matter. "Food" abruptly becomes a metaphor again, just as it was for Jesus when he said, "My food is that I might do the will of the One who sent me and complete his work" (4:34). For the crowd, too, working for "the food that remains to eternal life" will mean doing the will of God, because doing the will of God is

---

11. This principle seems to have been important in early Christianity. Paul reminds the Thessalonians, for example, that "even when we were with you, we gave you this rule: 'If a man will not work, he shall not eat'" (2 Thess 3:8, 10, NIV; see also v. 12).

12. Gr. τὴν ἀπολλυμένην.

13. Gr. ἵνα μή τι ἀπόληται (v. 12).

the way to eternal life (see 1 Jn 2:17, "And the world is passing away, and its desire, but whoever does the will of God remains forever"). The metaphor of food "that remains to eternal life"[14] recalls the spring rushing "to eternal life" that Jesus promised the Samaritan woman (4:14), or the crop "for eternal life" that he promised his disciples (4:36). "Eternal life" is future in all three instances.[15] Here it is that which "the Son of man will give you,"[16] just as he told the Samaritan woman of spring water that "I will give" (4:14).

Even though he speaks in the third person here, the title "Son of man" turns the discussion unmistakably to Jesus himself and his claims. It is his fifth use of "Son of man" in the Gospel (see 1:51; 3:13, 14; 5:27). The reader knows by this time that the term is interchangeable with "the Son" (see 3:14-16; 5:26-27), and that by it Jesus means himself. What follows sounds less like Jesus than like a comment by the Gospel writer, accenting and enhancing Jesus' own "Son of man" christology: "For he it is whom God the Father sealed."[17] Yet it is not a narrative aside. Jesus is still unmistakably being represented as the speaker. We seem to be back in the world of 3:16-21, where the Gospel writer speaks, but does so unashamedly through the lips of Jesus, or of 3:31-36, where the revelatory words are assigned to John. The expression, "God the Father,"[18] occurs only here in John's Gospel, and has a curiously Trinitarian sound to the modern Christian ear (as in "God the Father, God the Son, and God the Holy Spirit"!). "God" and "the Father" are synonymous, just as in Jesus' conversation with the Samaritan woman (see 4:23-24). The reader understands this by now (see 5:18), and even the crowd takes it in stride, ignoring the designation "the Father," and answering Jesus as if he had only said "God" (v. 28). But "Father" is important to the Gospel writer because it signals again that "the Son of man" is in fact the Father's "Son," or "the Son of God," or God's "One and Only" (see 1:18, 34; 3:16), and the reader is expected to pick this up.[19]

---

14. Gr. τὴν μένουσαν εἰς ζωὴν αἰώνιον.

15. So too in 3:15 and 16, in contrast to 3:36 and 5:24, where it is present.

16. "Will give" is δώσει. Some manuscripts (ℵ, D, and certain old Latin versions) have the present δίδωσιν, "gives you," but this appears to be unduly influenced by v. 32, "my Father gives you [δίδωσιν] the true bread from heaven." The future has greater manuscript support (including B, A, L, W, Θ, and P75), and should be retained (see Metzger, *Textual Commentary,* 212-13).

17. See J. R. Michaels, "The Johannine Words of Jesus and Christian Prophecy," *SBL 1975 Seminar Papers,* 257.

18. Or, more literally, "the Father ... God" (ὁ πατήρ ... ὁ θεός). The word order in Greek is τοῦτον γὰρ ὁ πατὴρ ἐσφράγισεν ὁ θεός.

19. Something similar happens in the synoptic Gospels as well, where Jesus promises that "the Son of man is going to come *in the glory of his Father* with his angels" (Mt 16:27, my italics; see also Mk 8:38; Lk 9:26). Here it is simply "the Father," not "my

The Gospel of John

That God the Father "sealed" Jesus could refer to his baptism by John,[20] except that Jesus is never explicitly baptized in this Gospel. Earlier, the person who received Jesus' testimony (possibly John himself) was said to have "confirmed[21] thereby that God is true" (3:33). The notion that Jesus is God's Son, attributed in the other Gospels to a voice from heaven at Jesus' baptism (see Mt 3:17 par.), is attributed in this Gospel to John at an unspecified time when Jesus received the Spirit (see 1:34). Was that gift of the Spirit "without measure" (3:34), wherever and whenever it might have been, the "sealing" to which Jesus now refers? Or was the Son (or "Son of man") "sealed" already in heaven, before the Gospel story even began? Is it simply an aspect of the "sending" of which Jesus has spoken before[22] and will speak repeatedly again?[23] Four chapters later he will refer to himself as the one "whom the Father consecrated and sent into the world" (10:36), and "sealing" could easily be read as a metaphor for this act of consecration. It is difficult to decide between the two alternatives. The reader's best strategy is to be patient, withhold judgment, and read on.

28 This is the first chance the reader has had to hear someone's reaction to Jesus' use of the title "Son of man." Nathanael heard it (1:51), and said nothing. Nicodemus and his friends at the first Passover heard it (3:13, 14), and said nothing (chapter 3). "The Jews" at the unnamed festival heard it (5:17), and said nothing. Here the crowd finally does respond. They might have asked, "Who is this Son of man?" (see 12:34), but they do not. Bypassing christology altogether, they ignore both "Son of man" and Jesus' accompanying reference to "the Father." They seem to have heard only his command to "work," and the mention of "God" at the very end of his pronouncement (v. 27). They keep the discussion going by asking, "What shall we do that we might work the works of God?"[24] They want to know what

---

Father" (as in 2:16 and 5:17), in keeping with the use of the third person "Son of man" instead of "I."

20. See Schnackenburg: "The Evangelist may also have imagined the sealing, which was carried out by God at a specific point, as having occurred specifically at the baptism of Jesus, since this combines most closely God's testimony and Jesus' endowment with the Spirit" (2.38; so too Bernard, 1.191).

21. Gr. ἐσφράγισεν.

22. See 3:17, 34; 5:36, 38 (with the verb ἀποστέλλειν), or (with the synonym πέμπειν) in the expression, "the One who sent me" (4:34; 5:23, 24, 30), or "the Father who sent me" (5:37).

23. Anderson (*Christology*, 200) offers yet another possibility, that "the 'sealing' work of God the Father seems to refer to the semeiological function of the *feeding*. The purpose of the feeding is to be a seal of attestation, a *sign* that the Son is sent from the Father and that the Bread he has to offer is therefore *eternally* nourishing." There is no direct evidence for this.

24. Gr. ἵνα ἐργαζώμεθα τὰ ἔργα τοῦ θεοῦ.

6:22-40 JESUS AND THE CROWD AT CAPERNAUM

works Jesus has in mind that they must do to gain "eternal life" (v. 27). Their question could just as easily have come from Nicodemus and his friends in response to Jesus brief discourse at that first Passover (3:11-21). It can be read, in fact, as a belated reply to that discourse,[25] but if it is, it betrays a subtle misunderstanding of what Jesus said. They seem to be using "the works of God" to mean works that God requires of them for salvation, but to Jesus "the works of God" are works "wrought in God"[26] (3:21), that is, God's own work in their lives or through them, revealed only when a person "comes to the Light" (see 9:3).

29 Jesus will not let them dodge the issue of christology. Still speaking of himself in the third person, he continues, "This is the work of God, that you believe in him whom that One sent." With this, he identifies "the Son of man" as the one "sent," confirming the notion that the "sealing" of the Son of man (v. 27) was indeed an act of consecration at the time of that "sending" (see 10:36). Jesus' words here speak directly to the crowd's question, except that he substitutes "the work of God" for their plural expression, "the works of God." The only "work of God" that counts is God's work in them so that they might "believe" in Jesus, whom God has sent.[27] Just as he said that a person's "works" are revealed in the single act of "coming to the Light" (3:21), so a person does the "work of God" by "coming" to Jesus (see vv. 35, 37) in the sense of believing in him. Faith, as we have seen, is the touchstone by which works are judged, not the other way around. For the first time, Jesus explicitly invites the crowd to "believe"[28] — specifically "in him whom that One sent," or the "Son of man . . . whom God the Father sealed" (v. 27).

30 What Jesus means is simply "believe in *me*" (see v. 35), and his hearers know it.[29] "What then do *you* do as a sign," they ask, "that we may

---

25. In a similar way, as we have seen, 12:34 can be read as a belated reply to 3:14.
26. Gr. ἐν θεῷ . . . εἰργασμένα.
27. Jesus' language vaguely recalls his comment to "the Jews" in Jerusalem that "you do not have his word dwelling in you, because he whom that One sent, him you do not believe" (5:38). The differences are (a) that the earlier instance was a declaration of judgment, while this is an appeal, and (b) that there it was a matter of believing Jesus and here of believing *in* him (compare also 5:24, where it was a matter of "hearing my word" and "believing the One who sent me").
28. The best ancient manuscripts have the present subjunctive πιστεύητε, "trust" or "continue to believe," while the majority of later manuscripts (as well as the earlier D, K, W, and some others) have the aorist πιστεύσητε, "come to believe," or "be converted." The present, which is more likely original, presupposes that the crowd consists of (at least) potential disciples (see verse 2, which tells us that they were already "following" Jesus).
29. On the basis that "the people are able to identify the Son of man as Jesus without any trouble," Bultmann (225) argues that the use of that title in verse 27 was a later interpolation. But the crowd makes the identification only after Jesus has further clarified "Son of man" as "him whom [God] sent" (v. 29).

see and believe *you?*" (v. 30, my italics), and "What work do you perform?"[30] The emphatic "you" signals that Jesus' christological claims have finally begun to get through to them. Their demand for a "sign" confirms the first thing Jesus had said to them, that they were looking for him "not because you saw signs, but because you ate of the loaves and were satisfied" (v. 26). If they had truly "seen signs," they would not now be asking for another sign. At the same time, it picks up the last thing Jesus had said, his invitation to "believe" (v. 29). In effect, they are admitting that the "signs" Jesus has done up to now (vv. 2, 14) have *not* led them to faith, and they want to see something that will. Their request inevitably recalls that of "the Jews" at the first Passover in Jerusalem: "What sign do you show us, because you are doing these things?" (2:18). The situation is becoming confrontational. They are no longer just seekers asking how they might "work the works of God" (v. 28), but antagonists like "the Jews," issuing a challenge. Their words, "that we may see and believe you," recall what the chief priests and Pharisees once said in another Gospel as Jesus hung on the cross: "Let the Christ, the king of Israel, come down now from the cross, that we may see and believe" (Mk 15:32). That demand at least was clear: Jesus would either "come down now from the cross," or he would not. He did not, and they did not believe. This time it is not so clear what they are asking. What sort of "sign" do they require? "The Jews" in chapter 2 did not say, and the crowd here offers only a hint.

31 The hint comes, at least partly, in the form of a quotation from Scripture ("as it is written").[31] Nowhere else in the Gospel of John do we find anyone but Jesus or the Gospel writer quoting Scripture in this manner.[32] The crowd's chosen text, "He gave[33] them bread from heaven to eat," echoing both Exodus 16 and Psalm 78, seems to have been quoted from memory.[34]

---

30. Gr. τί ἐργάζῃ.

31. Gr. καθώς ἐστιν γεγραμμένον.

32. It is true that Jesus' disciples "remember" a specific passage from Scripture (2:17), and that those who crucified Jesus are said to have cast lots for his cloak so that a certain text "might be fulfilled" (19:24). But the former takes place after the resurrection, outside the narrative proper, while the latter represents the perspective of the Gospel writer, not the stated intention of the Roman soldiers. In neither case is the quotation part of a dialogue with Jesus as here, or as (for example) in the Matthean and Lukan accounts of Satan testing Jesus in the desert.

33. "Gave" is ἔδωκεν, in keeping with the biblical texts being cited in Exodus 16 and Psalm 78. Some manuscripts (including ℵ, W, Θ, and others) have δέδωκεν, but this appears to be an assimilation to verse 32.

34. Whether the Gospel writer is quoting from memory, or just trying to give the impression that the crowd is doing so (carelessly perhaps?), is difficult to say. The key phrase, "from heaven" (ἐκ τοῦ οὐρανοῦ) recalls Exodus 16:4, LXX, but the singular "bread" (ἄρτον, instead of the plural "loaves"), and the verbs "he gave" (ἔδωκεν) and "to eat" (φαγεῖν) echo Exodus 16:15 and Psalm 78(77):24. Moreover, the third person, "to

6:22-40 JESUS AND THE CROWD AT CAPERNAUM

The crowd's assumption is that those who ate the manna in the time of Moses were "our fathers." They speak of their Jewish ancestors in the same way the Samaritan woman spoke of her Samaritan ancestors (4:20), but without the exclusivity of her pronouncement ("*Our* fathers worshiped . . . and yet *you* say," 4:20). She had assumed that her "fathers" were not Jesus' "fathers" because he was a Jew, but this Jewish crowd leaves the question open.

Why do they bring up "the manna in the desert"? "Loaves" (vv. 5, 7, 9, 11, 13, 26), or "bread" (v. 23), or "food" (v. 27) have obviously been the main topic under discussion, and they are simply continuing that theme. What is noteworthy is not their mention of "manna," nor the term "bread" in the biblical quotation, but rather the accompanying phrase, "from heaven."[35] Their challenge recalls that of Jesus' antagonists in the synoptic Gospels who asked for "a sign from heaven" (Mt 16:1; also Mk 8:11; Lk 11:16). "Bread from heaven" sounds like simply a particular instance of "a sign from heaven." What exactly do they have in mind? A repeat of the manna miracle in the desert? Does "from heaven" simply mean "from God," or does it mean a visible sign in the sky (see Mt 24:30; *Didache* 16.6)? Are they referring to real bread, or are they using "bread" merely as a metaphor for wisdom from on high, or even for the law?[36] There is no way to tell, and no evidence that even the questioners themselves know what they want. The reader may remember two examples in the narrative so far that might qualify as "signs from heaven" — one realized when John "watched the Spirit coming down as a dove out of the sky" and remaining on Jesus (1:32), and the other held out as a promise when Jesus told Nathanael and the other disciples, "You will see the sky opened, and the angels of God going up and coming down over the Son of man" (1:51). Beyond this, the reader knows that Jesus himself is "from heaven" (3:13, 31), and that he is quite able to grant, if he chooses, whatever "sign" the crowd might be asking of him. When asked for a sign before, he answered with a riddle pointing to his death, and his resurrection "in three days" (2:19). When similarly challenged in the synoptic Gospels, he referred to "the sign of Jonah" (see Mt 12:39-40; 16:4; Lk 11:29-30), more

---

them" (αὐτοῖς), rather than "to you" (ὑμῖν) corresponds not to the Exodus account, but to Psalm 78(77):24 (see also Ps 105[104]:40). In any event, the crowd would not likely have quoted the text in the second person (ὑμῖν), but would naturally have substituted either "us" (ἡμῖν) or "them" (αὐτοῖς) as the psalmist did, and they (or the Gospel writer) chose the latter.

35. Gr. ἐκ τοῦ οὐρανοῦ.

36. According to Moloney (212), "This never-failing nourishment from God was identified, in both the wisdom and Jewish midrashic traditions, with the gift of the Law." Yet in John's Gospel, despite the recognition from the start that "the law was given through Moses" (1:17; see also 5:45-47; 7:19), the law plays no explicit role in the discussion of "bread from heaven."

specifically in Matthew to Jonah's "three days and three nights in the belly of the fish," anticipating his own three-day sojourn "in the heart of the earth" (Mt 12:40). What will his answer be this time?

32 Jesus continues the discussion with another solemn pronouncement introduced by "Amen, amen, I say to you" (compare vv. 26-27). This time he builds explicitly on the crowd's biblical citation, "He gave them bread from heaven to eat." Superficially his words sound like a correction: "It is not Moses who has given you[37] that bread[38] from heaven, but my Father gives you[39] the true bread from heaven." It is not a correction, however, because the unexpressed subject of the verb in the biblical quotation (whether in Exodus 16 or Psalm 78; see above, n. 34) was God, not Moses. The crowd knows that God gave the manna. Jesus is only stating the obvious, reminding them of what they already know.

Why then mention Moses at all? Possibly because the crowd understood "the Prophet who is coming into the world" (v. 14) as a prophet like Moses, so that a comparison with Moses was inevitable. Jesus seems to welcome such a comparison, and is quite willing to build upon it (see 5:45-47). At the same time, by substituting "you" for "them" in the quotation, he recognizes and accepts the continuity (even identity) between those now questioning him and the ancient Israelites whom they call "our fathers" (v. 31). What God gave their ancestors long ago still belongs to them in their historical memory and traditions — hence the perfect, "has given," instead of the aorist, "gave," in the quotation (see n. 37). Jesus acknowledges and respects this continuity they enjoy with their past, but he is not quite finished. He could have contented himself with the obvious, concluding simply that "it is God who has given you that bread from heaven." Instead, he has a triple surprise for them: "it is *my Father* who *gives* you the *true* bread from heaven" (my italics). First, the tense of the verb changes again: not "gave" or "has given," but "gives" here and now (see n. 39). Second, not "that bread from heaven" but "the true bread from heaven," not an ancient gift with results lasting through the centuries but a new gift altogether: Third, instead of "God," he introduces once again the dangerously provocative phrase, "my Father."

"My Father" is a phrase Jesus has used three times before, always in a

---

37. Gr. δέδωκεν (perfect tense). This is the reading of P[75], ℵ, A, T, Θ, Ψ, and the majority of later manuscripts. Other manuscripts (including B, D, L, W, and others) have ἔδωκεν (aorist tense), but the latter appears to be an assimilation to the most likely reading in the biblical quotation (v. 31; see n. 33).

38. That is, the bread just mentioned in the quotation. "The bread," or "that bread" (τὸν ἄρτον, with the definite article), picks up the reference within the quotation to "bread" (ἄρτον) without the definite article (see BDF, §252[1]).

39. Gr. δίδωσιν (present tense).

polemical context. When he drove the money changers from the sanctuary, he said, "Stop making *my Father's* house a house of trade!" (2:16). After healing the sick man at the pool, he said: "*My Father* is working even until now, and I am working" (5:17); this provoked a lengthy controversy (see 5:18), near the end of which he issued the verdict, "I have come in *my Father's* name, and you do not accept me" (5:43, my italics). This time the polemic shows through in the pointed contrast between the crowd's use of "our fathers" (v. 31), and "my Father" on the lips of Jesus. Instead of acknowledging the common ancestry he shares with the crowd, he claims a different origin for himself, "from above," or "from heaven" (see 3:31). Even though they are Jews and he is a Jew (see 4:9, 22), they stand in much the same relationship to him as the Samaritan woman, who spoke similarly of "our fathers" (4:20) only to have Jesus call her repeatedly to the worship of "the Father" (4:21, 23). Here the term "*my* Father" subtly excludes Jesus' questioners while at the same time holding out to them a gracious and immediate gift: "the true bread from heaven." "True"[40] differentiates the bread Jesus is offering from "the manna in the desert" in Moses' day. If Jesus is the "true" Light (1:9), and if the "true" worshipers are those who worship "the Father" (4:23), it comes as no surprise that Jesus now offers "the true bread from heaven." This, he implies, is what the crowd was asking (vv. 30-31), whether they knew it or not, and he is prepared to grant their request.

33 The phrase, "the true bread from heaven," requires some further explanation, and Jesus supplies it: "For the bread of God is that which comes down from heaven and gives life to the world." By "the bread of God" Jesus means "the true bread" that "my Father" gives (v. 32), for to him "God" and "my Father" are synonymous (see v. 27b). The added comment (introduced by *gar*, "for") again has the look of one of the Gospel writer's narrative asides, like the earlier comment (introduced in the same way), "For he it is whom God the Father sealed" (v. 27). If it is read in this way, it is intended for the reader, not for the crowd to whom Jesus is speaking, and should therefore be translated differently: "For the Bread of God is *he who* [instead of "that which"] comes down from heaven and gives life to the world." This is a legitimate translation because the masculine participle, "who comes down from heaven,"[41] can be read as implying a (male) person as the subject, and that person can only be Jesus (see 3:13, "he who came down from heaven, the Son of man"). On this reading, Jesus is already saying implicitly what he makes explicit two verses later: "I am the Bread of life" (v. 35).[42] The alter-

---

40. Gr. τὸν ἀληθινόν.

41. Gr. ὁ καταβαίνων.

42. As I put it in an article many years ago, "Clearly, 6:33 contemplates the whole scope of the incarnation and the redemptive work of the Son in much the same way as the

native translation shows this by capitalizing "Bread," and by using the pronoun "He" (whether capitalized or not).

The problem with this translation is that the noun "bread,"[43] being masculine, requires the masculine participle anyway. The pronouncement is therefore ambiguous: either translation is possible. But if it is read *not* as a narrative aside, but as part of what Jesus was actually saying to the crowd, then our preferred translation — "For the bread of God is *that which* comes down from heaven and gives life to the world" (my italics) — is by far the more likely. On this reading, Jesus is simply explaining to the crowd what he meant by "the true bread from heaven" (v. 32). "Bread" has not yet been personalized, but refers simply to God's (as yet) unspecified gift of life to the world. Jesus is not yet making an overt christological claim, at least nothing beyond referring to God as "my Father" (v. 32), which, as we have seen, he has done three times before. He is simply promising "life," just as he promised "eternal life" to the Samaritan woman (4:14), and to the Samaritans through the "harvest" carried out by his disciples (4:36). The end of that story was that the Samaritans confessed him as "truly the Savior of the world" (4:42), so that it comes as no surprise here that Jesus promises bread from God that "gives life to the world."[44]

34 The crowd responds: "Sir, give us this bread always." If verse 33 were read as the Gospel writer's narrative aside, then they would be ignoring it (as we would expect them to if it were directed solely to the reader!) and responding simply to what Jesus said in verse 32, as if to say, "Sir, give us this 'true bread from heaven.'" But if verse 33 is read as a word of Jesus, the crowd is responding directly to it, as if to say, "Sir, give us this 'bread of God which comes down from heaven and gives life to the world.'" To them, the "bread," of which Jesus speaks is not a person, but a metaphor for a divine gift of some kind. Their request sounds like that of the Samaritan woman: "Sir, give me this water, so that I will not thirst and have to keep coming back here to draw" (4:15). Their use of "Sir" echoes hers, their phrase, "this bread," echoes the woman's reference to "this water," and their imperative, "give us," echoes her imperative, "give me." But there is one important dif-

---

prolog and chapter 3." This was, and still is, subject to the qualification I made then, that "Quite possibly the ambiguity in *ho katabainōn* is intentional. There is no evidence that John intends the reader to distinguish in any way between the voice of Jesus and the voice of a prophetic-apocalyptic community. There was no such evidence in chapter 3 and there is none here." See J. R. Michaels, "The Johannine Words of Jesus and Christian Prophecy," *SBL 1975 Seminar Papers,* 258.

43. Gr. ὁ ἄρτος.

44. Gr. ζωὴν διδοὺς τῷ κόσμῳ. As Chrysostom put it, "Not, saith He, to Jews alone, but to all the 'world,' not mere food, but 'life,' another and an altered 'life.' *Homilies* 45.1 (NPNF, 1st ser., 14.160).

ference. The Samaritan woman was still thinking of literal water (so that she would not "have to keep coming back here"), but the crowd here is no longer asking for literal food such as loaves and fish, or even manna from the sky. They have now begun to grasp that Jesus is in some way offering them "life," or "eternal life," whatever that might mean, and they want this gift of life "always." The "bread" they want is what Jesus called "the food that remains to eternal life" (see v. 27), to them "a gift that keeps on giving," if you will. They want it, yet they do not understand what it is or how to receive it. They stand on the threshold of belief, without quite believing.

35 Jesus answers at some length (vv. 35-40), and when we hear from his interlocutors again, they are no longer "the crowd" (see vv. 22, 24), but "the Jews" (vv. 41, 52). What he says in the intervening verses is decisive in bringing about this apparent transformation. Most conspicuous is his abrupt use of the emphatic "I" (vv. 35, 40), and first person verbs He begins with the "I am"[45] formula, which he has used only twice before, once to the Samaritan woman identifying himself as the Messiah she expected (4:26) and once to his disciples in the boat, simply announcing his presence (6:20). In those cases there was no predicate because the point of reference was obvious from the context. Here there is a predicate: "the Bread of life,"[46] the first of seven such predicates with "I am" in this Gospel.[47] "The Bread of life" is synonymous with "the bread of God" (v. 33), except that the genitive relationships are different. "The bread of God" identifies God as the source of the bread; "the Bread of life" identifies "bread" (or "the Bread") as the source of life (in this case, "eternal life"; see vv. 27, 40). As we have seen, "the bread of God" was what the crowd meant when they asked Jesus to "give us this bread always" (v. 34), and Jesus is now responding to their request. His response is that it is not a question of *giving* them "the bread of God." Rather, he *is* "the Bread" (hence our capitalization), which he now calls "the Bread of life" because it — or rather he — "gives life to the world" (v. 33). From here on it is not so much a question of what Jesus will give as of who Jesus is,[48] and that is where controversies in John's Gospel most often begin (see for example 5:17-18).

As "the Bread of life," Jesus does not immediately promise "life,"

---

45. Gr. ἐγώ εἰμι.
46. Gr. ὁ ἄρτος τῆς ζωῆς.
47. The other six are "the Light of the world" (8:12), "the Door of the sheep" or "the Door" (10:7, 9), "the Good Shepherd" (10:11, 14), "the Resurrection and the Life" (11:25), "the Way, the Truth, and the Life" (14:60), and "the True Vine" or "the Vine" (15:1, 5).
48. Similarly, in his encounter with the Samaritan woman, he uses the emphatic "I" first to tell her what he will give (ἐγὼ δώσω, 4:14), and then to announce who he is (ἐγώ εἰμι, 4:26).

much less spell out explicitly what "life" might mean. He does not press the metaphor so as to speak explicitly of "eating" or "drinking" (as in 4:13-14 and 4:32-34, and even more pointedly later, in vv. 52-58). Instead, he simply promises that "The person who comes to me will never go hungry, and the person who believes in me will never ever thirst."[49] Although stated negatively, the promises are quite emphatic. "Never go hungry" and "never ever thirst" are solemn assurances, putting the matter beyond all doubt.[50] The redundant-sounding[51] "ever" answers the crowd's plea for bread "always" (v. 34).[52]

But for whom are the promises intended? For the crowd to whom Jesus is speaking, or for others? They are for "the person who comes to me," Jesus says, and "who believes in me." We have met such people before in the narrative: the disciples at the Cana wedding (2:11), all who came to Jesus for discipleship and baptism in Judea (3:26), the Samaritan villagers at Sychar (4:30, 39), the royal official at Cana and then at Capernaum (4:50, 53), and in general all who "do the truth" and "come to the Light" because their works are "wrought in God" (3:21). The crowd here "followed" Jesus (v. 2) and "was coming to him" (v. 5; see also v. 24), but Jesus questioned their motives (v. 26) and "did not entrust himself to them" any more than he did to the so-called "believers" at the first Passover in Jerusalem (2:24). Unlike the latter, they have not even claimed to "believe" (see v. 30). The assurances of this verse, therefore, are not for them but for others, a generalized invitation to all who read it to "come" and "believe." The notice that those who come "will never go hungry" continues the metaphor of "bread" from the preceding discussion. The added notice that "the person who believes in me will never ever thirst" reverts to Jesus' encounter with the Samaritan woman two chapters earlier (4:14). The danger for anyone reading the Gospel for a second or third time is the assumption that Jesus is promising life through the drinking of his blood (see vv. 53-56). This is obviously not the case here, for "blood" has not been mentioned. Water is what quenches thirst, and Jesus is again

---

49. It is characteristic of Jesus' "I am" pronouncements in this Gospel to be followed by promises to those who respond and obey (see 8:12; 10:9; 11:25-26; 14:6; 15:2, 5).

50. Constructions with οὐ μή expressing emphatic negation are normally used with the aorist subjunctive, but in this instance the first verb (πεινάσῃ) is aorist subjunctive while the second (διψήσει) is future indicative. The subjunctive is more common, but the indicative is used with the second verb because of the accompanying accent on duration (πώποτε; compare εἰς τὸν αἰῶνα in 4:14). See Abbott, *Johannine Grammar*, 205.

51. For the same redundancy, only with "forever" (εἰς τὸν αἰῶνα) instead of "ever" (πώποτε), see 4:14; 8:51-52; 10:28; 11:26. "Never" in these οὐ μή constructions is already emphatic (as in "No way!" or "By no means!"), but the added expression accents the eternal nature of the promise.

52. Gr. πώποτε (v. 35) in response to πάντοτε (v. 34).

promising "living water" (as in 4:10). With these words he gathers into one a promise of "bread" with the earlier promise of "water" to the woman at the well, both embodied in his own person.

36 Jesus now confirms that these twin promises are *not* for those to whom he is speaking: "Yet I said to you that you have seen me and you do not believe."[53] "Me" is omitted in certain manuscripts, but the evidence favors retaining it.[54] The omission could imply that it was a matter of seeing the signs (vv. 2, 26) rather than seeing Jesus, but the two amount to much the same thing.[55] Both things are true: they have seen his signs, and they have obviously seen him. It is also true that they do not believe (see vv. 29-30, where he invited them to do so and they asked for yet another "sign"). What he says here is therefore not surprising.

What is surprising is his claim that he had said it before: "Yet I said to you."[56] When would that have been? Commentators point to verse 26, where Jesus admits that they "saw signs," but insists they had come looking for him only because they "ate of the loaves and were satisfied."[57] This could imply unbelief, especially when he follows it up by urging them to "believe" (v. 29).[58] But more likely, Jesus is looking back to an earlier discussion with "the Jews" in Jerusalem, when he told of "the Father who sent me," claiming that "You have never heard his voice nor seen his form, and you do not have his word dwelling in you, because he whom that One sent, him you do not believe" (5:37-38). Like Israel at Mount Sinai, they could not see God and re-

---

53. The Greek sentence has a "both . . . and" (καί . . . καί), even though only one "and" appears in the translation (literally, "you have both seen me, and [yet] you do not believe"). See Abbott, *Johannine Grammar,* 146-47, who renders it, *"though* ye have seen me, *yet* ye do not believe" (for a similar use of the καὶ . . . καί construction, see 15:24).

54. It is omitted by ℵ, A, the old Syriac, and certain old Latin versions, but retained by virtually all other manuscripts and versions (including B, P[66], and probably P[75]). See Metzger, *Textual Commentary,* 213.

55. Compare 20:29, where "seeing Jesus" (ἑώρακάς με) and simply "seeing" (ἰδόντες) amount to exactly the same thing; also 15:24, where "seeing" (ἑωράκασιν) Jesus' works is equivalent to seeing him.

56. Gr. Ἀλλ' εἶπον ὑμῖν.

57. So Schnackenburg, 2.46; Moloney, 215; Bultmann, 232 (even after rearranging the text!); Barrett, 293 (who omits με "because it makes the reference to v. 26 much plainer"!).

58. Another suggestion is that of Peder Borgen, "Observations on the Midrashic Character of John 6," *ZNW* 54 (1963), 239, who proposed the translation, "But I have said, *'You'* [that is, in v. 32] because, though you have seen, still you do not believe." This does not work because in identifying the crowd (ὑμῖν, v. 32) with their ancestors who received the manna long ago (οἱ πατέρες ἡμῶν, v. 31), Jesus is not attributing unbelief to them. On the contrary, he is acknowledging — in his own way even honoring — their Jewish heritage.

fused to hear God's voice, a voice still speaking to them through Jesus, whom "that One sent," whom they could see but whom "you do not believe" (5:38). Now, a chapter later at Capernaum, Jesus has told the crowd to "believe in him whom that One sent" (v. 29), but has concluded that, just as he had said before, "you do not believe" (v. 36).[59] The similarity of vocabulary is striking. Admittedly, there is no explicit reference to "seeing" Jesus in chapter 5.[60] The association of seeing with believing arises rather out of the *present* context. They have asked to see a sign, and Jesus has told them that *he* is the sign. The present verse could be paraphrased, "Yet I said to you [back in 5:38] that you do not believe — and you don't, even though you have now seen me." The reader naturally hesitates to reach back to chapter 5 in this way because the audience has changed.[61] There it was "the Jews" (5:10, 15, 16, 18); here it is a (supposedly) more congenial audience, "the crowd" (6:2, 22, 24). They are "seekers" (vv. 24, 26), and we expect Jesus to be "seeker sensitive." He is, up to a point (see vv. 27, 29, 35), but he has now reached his limit. He is the same Jesus who "knew them all," and "knew what was in the person" (2:24-25), and here we see him doing what he has done before (5:37-44) and will do again — unmasking unbelief. The secret that he knows but the reader does not is that actually the audience has *not* changed. "The crowd" turns out to be "the Jews" after all, something soon to be made explicit (see vv. 41, 52).

37 If those who "come" to Jesus and "believe" in him (v. 35) are *not* the crowd to whom he is speaking, who are they? Instead of specifying his disciples, or those who came for baptism in Judea, or the Samaritans at Sychar, or the royal official at Cana, Jesus speaks in more general terms: "All that the Father gives me will come to me, and the person who comes to me I will never drive out." "All"[62] is neuter and singular (literally, "everything"), referring to all believers corporately,[63] while the participle ("the person who

---

59. The parallel is close, even though in chapter 5 it was a matter of believing Jesus (πιστεύειν with the dative), while here it is a matter of believing in him (πιστεύειν εἰς with the accusative).

60. Jesus does say, however, that they have *not* seen the "form" (εἶδος) of Jesus' Father, and it could be inferred by contrast that they do see Jesus, who stands before them (see 1:18; 6:46; 14:9).

61. Bultmann refers to the view of Wendt "that v. 36 refers back to the discourse in 5.17ff." (232, n. 6), and even "that 6.27ff. really belonged to ch. 5." He finds such a rearrangement implausible because in his own rearrangement "ch. 5 must follow ch. 6" (218, n. 4). No rearrangements are necessary, however. The point is simply that in John's Gospel there is a continuity to the discourses so that Jesus' interlocutors (at least in the first half of the Gospel) are always in some sense the same.

62. Gr. πᾶν.

63. See BDF, §138(1).

comes") is masculine singular,[64] focusing on any individuals who might "come to Jesus" in the sense of believing in him or giving him their allegiance.[65] God decides who they are, for they are God the Father's gift to Jesus, and by coming to him they prove that they belong to God (or, as he put it earlier, that their works are "wrought in God," 3:21). Jesus will make a similar point negatively a few verses later: "*No one* can come to me *unless* the Father who sent me draw him" (v. 44, my italics; see also v. 65). Both here and elsewhere in the Gospel tradition,[66] Jesus responds to unbelief with an appeal to divine sovereignty and divine election.

It is in this framework of sovereignty and election that Jesus holds out the universal-sounding declaration that "the person who comes to me I will never drive out." The words "never drive out"[67] are just as emphatic and final as "never go hungry" or "never ever thirst" (v. 35). Yet they do not add up to universalism. There is no indiscriminate "Whosoever Will," as in the old Gospel song.[68] Those who "come to Jesus" are those whom the Father gave him, and no one else. In promising never to "drive out" those who come, Jesus is simply obeying the Father by accepting the Father's gift. He confirms a principle first laid down by John, that "A person cannot receive anything unless it is given him from heaven" (3:27). The corollary is that a person *must* receive that which *is* given from heaven, and this Jesus promises, emphati-

---

64. Gr. ὁ ἐρχόμενος.

65. In similar passages in this Gospel about "those whom God has given" (for example, v. 39; 10:29; 17:2, 6, 24), there is a similar interplay between neuter and masculine pronouns (see Abbott, *Johannine Grammar,* 309).

66. In the synoptic tradition, see, for example, Mk 4:10-12 (note the verb δέδοται, "is given"), and in John's Gospel, 12:37-41. But here the accent is less on judgment of unbelievers than on God's election of believers to eternal life.

67. Gr. οὐ μὴ ἐκβάλω ἔξω. The adverb ἔξω, "outside," sounds redundant after ἐκβάλω, "cast out," just as πώποτε, "ever," did in v. 35 (see above), and is omitted by some manuscripts (including D, the first hand of ℵ, and the old Syriac), perhaps for that reason. But John's Gospel consistently uses the adverb in contexts with a strong meaning such as expulsion from the synagogue (9:34-35; see also 15:6), or casting out the devil (12:31). It is omitted in 2:15, probably because the phrase ἐκ τοῦ ἱεροῦ ("out of the temple") takes its place, and in 10:4, where the verb has lost some of its literal force.

68. In all fairness, the Gospel song is based not on this verse, but on Revelation 22:18. Yet even John Bunyan, Particular Baptist and staunch Calvinist though he was, found comfort in the broadest possible application of these words, thus resolving his agonized soul searching in *Grace Abounding:* "But Satan would greatly labour to pull this promise from me, telling of me, that Christ did not mean me, and such as I, but sinners of a lower rank, that had not done as I had done. But I should answer him, Satan, there is in this word no such exception, but *him that comes,* any *him, him that cometh to me, I will in no wise cast out*" (*Grace Abounding to the Chief of Sinners* [London: Penguin, 1987], 55 [par. 215]).

cally and without qualification, to do. Even more to the point, as John also acknowledged, Jesus himself is "from heaven" (see 3:31), and the Giver is his own Father (1:34; 3:35). This is clearly the case if Jesus, as "the Bread of life" (v. 35), is indeed (as he has implied) "the bread of God . . . which comes down from heaven and gives life to the world."

38 Jesus now makes explicit that he himself has "come down from heaven" by putting it in the first person: "for I have come down from heaven[69] not to do my will but the will of the One who sent me." The perfect "I have come down" accents not so much Jesus' heavenly origin as his "present location on earth,"[70] and his agenda in this world. He is not laboring the point *that* he came down from heaven — the readers already know that (v. 33), and his hearers will not accept it in any case (see v. 42). Rather, he is explaining *why* he came down: "not to do my will but the will of the One who sent me." Anyone familiar with the rest of the Gospel tradition will recall Jesus' words in Gethsemane, "Nevertheless, not my will, but yours, be done" (Lk 22:42; see also Mt 26:39; Mk 14:36). While John's Gospel shows some acquaintance with this tradition (see 12:27; 18:11), nothing suggests that Jesus is seriously torn between these two alternatives in the present context. Rather, the negative expression, "not to do my will," is simply rhetorical, accenting Jesus' positive determination to do "the will of the One who sent me."[71] The point of reference is not something outside the Gospel of John, such as the prayer in Gethsemane, but two things Jesus said earlier *within* the Gospel narrative, first to his disciples in Samaria ("My food is that I might do the will of the One who sent me and complete his work," 4:34), and then to "the Jews" in Jerusalem (". . . because I am not seeking my will but the will of the One who sent me," 5:30). Both previous passages leave "the will of the One who sent me" undefined, and the phrase cries out for definition, which Jesus now finally supplies.

69. Gr. καταβέβηκα ἀπὸ τοῦ οὐρανοῦ. Notice that "from" is ἀπό here, where we might have expected ἐκ (as in vv. 31, 32, 33). Ἀπὸ τοῦ οὐρανοῦ, in fact, occurs *only* here in John's Gospel. Possibly for this reason, some manuscripts (including ℵ, D, Ψ, and the majority of late manuscripts) have the more familiar ἐκ. There is no discernible difference in meaning, and when "the Jews" later quote Jesus' words (v. 42), the phrase they use is ἐκ τοῦ οὐρανοῦ. There was every reason, therefore, to change ἀπό, if original, to ἐκ, and none to change ἐκ to ἀπό. The latter, with its better manuscript support, should be accepted as original, but the two are virtually interchangeable (see Barrett, 394; Bultmann, 233, n. 3).

70. The phrase is Schnackenburg's (2.47), who appeals not only to the tense of the verb but also (less convincingly; see the preceding note) to the use of ἀπό instead of ἐκ. Two other instances in which Jesus points (even more explicitly) to his "present location on earth" are 8:42 and 16:28.

71. The form is much the same as in a number of other sayings of Jesus, in which it is not a question of Jesus' (or the Father's) "will," but of his "word" (14:24) or what he "speaks" (8:28; 12:49; 14:10), or of his "glory" (8:54).

39 Repeating the whole phrase, "the will of the One who sent me," Jesus defines it as God's intention "that of all he has given me I might not lose anything, but raise it up[72] at the last day."[73] "All," or "everything," is again neuter singular, referring (just as in v. 37) to believers in Jesus corporately rather than individually. If anything, the impersonal or corporate quality of God's gift to Jesus becomes even more conspicuous, with references to either losing "it" or raising "it at the last day."[74] The divine intention that Jesus "not lose" that which God has given him echoes and reinforces his promise that he will "never cast out" (those who come to him) (v. 37). Earlier, he had announced God's intent "that everyone who believes in him might not be lost but have eternal life" (3:16). If he were now to reject those who came to him in genuine faith, he would not only be denying them salvation, but he would "lose" that which his Father wanted him to have. Their loss would be his as well. This, he insists, will not happen, and the preceding narrative has given him a certain credibility: "Gather the leftover broken pieces," he had told his disciples, "so that nothing is lost" (6:12). If he showed such care for twelve baskets of lifeless crumbs, how much more for twelve human beings (see v. 70), plus all those for whom he would finally give his life?[75]

It is important to appreciate the stark finality of "losing" or "being lost" in the Gospel of John. To be "lost" is not preliminary to being "found" or being "saved," as in Matthew and Luke.[76] Jesus comes to Israel, but not to

---

72. "Raise up" (ἀναστήσω) could be either aorist subjunctive or future indicative, but in either case it is still part of the purpose clause with ἵνα. Jesus is not saying in so many words that he will "raise it up on the last day" (that comes in v. 40), only that it is God's intention that he do so.

73. More literally, "that everything he has given me, I might not lose [any] of it, but raise it up on the last day." Πᾶν is the subject of its clause, as in v. 37. Abbott (*Johannine Grammar*, 32-33) cites this verse as an example of one kind of anacoluthon, "the Hebrew custom of putting the subject at the beginning of a sentence, and then repeating it as a pronoun, e.g., '*The Lord, he* is God.'" In this instance the pronoun comes in the phrase ἐξ αὐτοῦ, "of it," a partitive expression requiring that "some," or in this case "any," be supplied (see Abbott, 178; also BDF, §164[2]). Our translation avoids the anacoluthon in order to achieve better English.

74. "It" in the first instance (ἐξ αὐτοῦ) could be either neuter or masculine, but the second instance (αὐτό) makes it clear that both are to be read as neuter.

75. That the "twelve" of 6:70 would turn out to be representative of all who would eventually believe is made explicit in Jesus' final prayer (17:20), and again after his resurrection (20:29).

76. As I put it more fully some years ago, "In the first three Gospels, being lost is often *preliminary* to being found or saved, while in John and the rest of the New Testament being lost is consistently the *alternative* to being saved. The former can be characterized as an *optimistic* way of using the language of lostness and the latter a more *pessi*-

"the lost sheep" of Israel (Mt 10:5; 15:24). "Lost" sheep are not "found" in John's Gospel (as, for example, in Lk 15:6). Rather, Jesus' mission is to make sure that his sheep "will never ever be lost, and no one will seize them out of my hand" (Jn 10:29). He does not come "to seek and to save that which is lost" (Lk 19:10), but to keep people from ever being "lost." In this Gospel a person is not *first* lost and *then* saved (as in Lk 15:24), but *either* lost *or* saved. Both are final, not temporary, conditions. Salvation is "eternal life," and "lostness" is just as eternal.[77]

Later in the story we will learn that the intention expressed here that Jesus "not lose anything" did indeed come to realization. At his arrest, he tells the arresting officers of the priests and Pharisees, "I am he. So if you are looking for me, let these go" (18:8), and Gospel writer reminds us that with this he fulfilled the words spoken in chapter 6, that "of those whom you have given me I have lost none" (18:9). There, to be sure, it is a matter of the disciples' immediate physical safety. The Gospel writer knows that eventually they — most of them at least (see 21:22-23) — will die physically, but their safety at the time of Jesus' arrest stands as a sign that "none of them is lost" (see 17:12)[78] or ever will be, in the sense of forfeiting salvation. For those who die physically, the alternative to being lost is resurrection (see 5:24-25, 28-29). God's will is not only that Jesus "might not lose anything" of what God has given him, but that he might "raise it up at the last day." This promise, repeated three more times in the chapter (vv. 40, 44, 54),[79] represents the heart of God's intention for God's people, both in John's Gospel and in Pharisaic Judaism (see, for example, Acts 23:6; 24:15;

---

mistic use of it. Still another distinction is that in a number of Gospel passages, lost is a metaphorical term closely related to the metaphor of God as Shepherd and the people of God as God's sheep, while in other places it is no longer a metaphor but a straightforward description of final ruin or destruction" ("Evangelism and the Lost," in *Lost and Found: A Biblical/Pastoral Critique* [Valley Forge, PA: American Baptist Churches, 1988], 4).

77. Because Paul shares with John this sense of finality, he never refers to anyone as already "lost" as if it were an accomplished fact. Instead he uses present participles to contrast those who are "being saved" and those who are "being lost" (1 Cor 1:18; 2 Cor 2:15-16; see also 2 Cor 4:3-4; 2 Thess 2:9-10). See Michaels, "Evangelism and the Lost," 11.

78. Judas Iscariot, "the one destined to be lost," is the single exception, an exception allowed only "in order that the Scripture be fulfilled" (17:12). Judas is also an obvious exception in 18:9 (see 18:2, 3, and 5), but at 6:39 Judas has not even been introduced (see 6:64, 70-71).

79. Each time this phrase occurs (vv. 39, 40, 44, 54), the manuscripts are divided as to whether it should be "on the last day" (ἐν τῇ ἐσχατῇ ἡμέρᾳ), or "at the last day" (τῇ ἐσχατῇ ἡμέρᾳ). The tendency of the early papyri (P^{66} and P^{75}) and B is toward omission of ἐν, and the evidence strongly favors omission in v. 54. But there is little difference in meaning in any case.

26:6-8). The "last day" is that future "day" (or "hour") when "all who are in the tombs will hear his voice, and those who have done good things will go out to a resurrection of life, but those who have practiced wicked things to a resurrection of judgment" (5:28-29). Jesus' promise differs from conventional Jewish expectation only in his claim that he himself, as God's Son, will be the one raising the dead. Just as the "voice" awaking the dead in his earlier discourse in Jerusalem was said to be that of "the Son of God" (5:25) or "Son of man" (5:27), so here it is "I" who will "raise it up[80] at the last day." This, not the promise of resurrection as such, is what is bound to give offense to his hearers.

40 Jesus' next pronouncement is almost a doublet of the preceding one, but with several telling exceptions. First, instead of "this is the will of the One who sent me" (v. 39), he substitutes "this is the will of my Father," pressing once again his identity as God's Son (see vv. 27, 32, 37). He reinforces this by explicitly identifying those "whom the Father has given him" (vv. 37, 39) as everyone who "sees the Son" and believes. Second, he shifts from the neuter to the masculine, just as he did in verse 37, from the people of God as a corporate entity to the individual — any individual who believes. It is no longer a matter of "all" or "everything" (vv. 37, 39), but of "every person"[81] who sees and believes, and of raising "him,"[82] not "it," in the resurrection "at the last day." Third, instead of stating the Father's intention for believers both negatively (not being lost) and positively (being raised up on the last day) as in v. 39, he states it only positively (as, for example, in 5:24-25): first for the present (having "eternal life") and then for the future (being raised on the last day). This time the "I" is emphatic: "And *I* will raise him up at the last day." It is an unqualified promise from Jesus himself, not simply part of a statement of God's intention, as in v. 39 (see above, n. 72). The reward Jesus holds out is eschatological, but the issue is christological, just as in the preceding chapter. The "I am" of verse 35 and the "I" of verse 40 frame this last speech of Jesus to the crowd,[83] so as to raise pointedly the question, "Is he in fact the Son of God? Is God his Father, or not?" It is now in the crowd's hands. They must decide.

---

80. Gr. ἀναστήσω.
81. Gr. πᾶς (masculine).
82. Gr. αὐτόν (masculine).
83. The placement of the emphatic ἐγώ almost at the end of its clause, rather than at the beginning (as in κἀγὼ ἀναστήσω, vv. 44, 54), contributes to the impression that Jesus is framing the whole speech with his christological claims. It should be noted that in v. 40 ἐγώ is omitted in certain manuscripts (including P[66], A, and D), but the weight of evidence favors retaining it. The omission may have been influenced by its absence in v. 39.

The Gospel of John

G. JESUS AND THE JEWS AT CAPERNAUM (6:41-59)

41 *So the Jews murmured about him because he said, "I am the bread that came down from heaven."* 42 *And they said, "Is this not Jesus, the son of Joseph, whose father and mother we know? How does he say now that 'I came down from heaven?'"*

43 *Jesus answered and said to them, "Stop murmuring with each other.* 44 *No one can come to me unless the Father who sent me draw him, and I will raise him up at the last day.* 45 *It is written in the prophets, 'And they all will be taught by God.' Every person who has heard from the Father and learned comes to me.* 46 *Not that anyone has seen the Father except he who is from God, he has seen the Father.* 47 *Amen, amen, I say to you, whoever believes has eternal life.* 48 *I am the Bread of life.* 49 *Your fathers ate the manna in the desert, and they died.* 50 *This is the bread that comes down from heaven, so that anyone might eat of it and not die.* 51 *I am the living Bread that came down from heaven. If anyone eat of this bread, he will live forever, and the bread I will give him is my flesh for the life of the world."*

52 *So the Jews quarreled with each other, saying, "How can this man give us his flesh to eat?"*

53 *So Jesus said to them, "Amen, amen, I say to you, unless you eat the flesh of the Son of man and drink his blood, you do not have life in yourselves.* 54 *The person who eats my flesh and drinks my blood has eternal life, and I will raise him up at the last day.* 55 *For my flesh is real food, and my blood is real drink.* 56 *The person who eats my flesh and drinks my blood dwells in me, and I in him.* 57 *Just as the living Father sent me and I live because of the Father, so the person who eats me, even that person will live because of me.* 58 *This is the bread that came down from heaven, not as the fathers ate and died, the person who eats this bread will live forever."*

59 *These things he said teaching in synagogue in Capernaum.*

"The crowd" has no answer to Jesus' speech claiming to be "the Bread of life" (vv. 35-40). In fact, they have not been explicitly called "the crowd" since v. 24.[1] We have been calling them "the crowd" for the sake of a coherent story line, but to the Gospel writer they are simply "they" (vv. 25, 26, 28, 29, 30, 32, 34, 35), Jesus' anonymous partners in dialogue. Now they acquire a new, but not unfamiliar, identity as "the Jews."[2] We have met "the Jews"

---

1. First they were "a large crowd" (ὄχλος πολύς, vv. 2, 5), then "the people" (οἱ ἄνθρωποι, vv. 10, 14), finally again "the crowd" (ὁ ὄχλος, vv. 22, 24).
2. Gr. οἱ Ἰουδαῖοι.

6:41-59 JESUS AND THE JEWS AT CAPERNAUM

three times before, first as those who sent a delegation to John from Jerusalem (1:19), then as Jesus' hostile questioners at the first Passover in Jerusalem (2:18, 20), finally at a later festival in Jerusalem after Jesus healed a man on the Sabbath (5:10, 16, 18). So far they have been associated with Jerusalem in Judea, and some have proposed "the Judeans" as the correct translation, possibly with the motive of making John's Gospel sound less "anti-Jewish." Yet here they are in Galilee, and their apparent prior knowledge about Jesus (v. 42) betrays the fact that they are not Judeans but Galileans! The point is not that the Galilean "crowd" has disappeared, to be replaced by a different set of interlocutors, "the Jews," but that "the crowd" *is* "the Jews." They have shown their true colors, at least in part, by trying to "seize him to make him king" (6:15). Jesus has unmasked their unbelief (v. 36), and now they give voice to their unbelief. The scene has changed since chapter 5, but the audience is the same — not the same individuals, of course, but the same people at heart. They are the same "Jews," for they still "do not believe" (5:38; 6:36).

41-42 Just as in chapter 5, "the Jews" never speak to Jesus. There, as we saw, they "began pursuing him" (5:16), and "kept seeking all the more to kill him" (5:18) because of his actions and words, but said nothing. Here, speaking only to each other, they "murmured about him" because he had said, "I am the bread that came down from heaven" (drawing together vv. 33, 35, and 38). "Murmuring" (see also vv. 43, 61) recalls the people of Israel murmuring against Moses in the desert,[3] taking us back to when the crowd asked Jesus for a sign comparable to "the manna in the desert" (vv. 30-31). Yet it signals not so much unrelieved hostility against Jesus as rather confusion or conflict among themselves.[4] The confusion is linked to their identity as specifically Galilean "Jews." They cannot reconcile the notion that Jesus "came down from heaven" with their own knowledge of where he came from. "Is this not Jesus, the son of Joseph," they ask, "whose[5] father and

---

3. See Exodus 16:1-12, where the Lord gave the manna in response to the "murmuring" of the people (in the LXX, γογγύζειν, as here, or διαγογγύζειν), and Exodus 17:3, where the people "murmured" again and the Lord gave them water from the rock (see also Num 11:1; 14:27, 29; 16:41; 17:5; Ps 106[105]:25, and in the New Testament, 1 Cor 10:10).

4. See, for example, v. 52, where they "quarreled [ἐμάχοντο] with each other"; also 7:12 and 32, where γογγυσμός and γογγύζειν are used in contexts of sharply divided opinion about Jesus.

5. On strictly grammatical grounds, the antecedent of "whose" (οὗ) could be either Jesus or Joseph. But the speakers are clearly not claiming knowledge of *Joseph's* "father and mother" (that is, of Jesus' genealogy). The antecedent has to be Jesus. This makes their words sound redundant, in that they first identify Jesus as "the son of Joseph," and then add that they know Jesus' father. Yet Jesus could have been known by reputation as "son of Joseph," even by those not personally acquainted with his father or mother (see 1:45).

mother we know?" (v. 42).⁶ The comment suggests that they are not only Galileans but residents of Capernaum, and consequently on their home turf. As we have seen, the "large crowd" following Jesus at the beginning of the narrative (v. 2) may well have originated in Capernaum, to which they have now returned. Alternatively, some of them could have been from Nazareth, clearly identified earlier as Jesus' place of origin (see 1:45-46), yet Capernaum in this Gospel is as much Jesus' home as Nazareth,⁷ and the confrontation here at Capernaum plays a role similar to that of his rejection at Nazareth in Luke, or at his unidentified "hometown" in Matthew and Mark.⁸

Here, as in the other Gospels, nothing suggests that the conventional wisdom about Jesus' origins was incorrect. Even the two Gospels with virgin birth stories have genealogies in which Jesus' ancestry is traced through his father Joseph, and they do not see this as in any way incompatible with a virginal conception and birth (see Mt 1:16; Lk 3:23). In John's Gospel, as we have seen, even one of his first disciples called him "Jesus son of Joseph, from Nazareth" (1:45), and he himself will later acknowledge that "Yes, you know me and you know where I am from" (7:28), adding that "I have not come on my own, but the One who sent me is true. Him you do not know." The reader can draw no conclusions from the remark of these "Jews" in Capernaum (v. 42) as to whether or not John's Gospel presupposes the virgin birth. The writer is neither acknowledging that Joseph was literally Jesus' father nor winking at the readers as if to say, "You and I both know he was not." His point is rather that Jesus is fully human, that he "came down from heaven" (vv. 38, 41), and that these two things are not incompatible. As Jesus himself will put it later, "the bread that came down from heaven" is his "flesh" (vv. 51, 58). The reader has known from the start that "the Word came in human flesh" (1:14), but "the Jews" cannot comprehend it. "How," they ask, "does he say now⁹ that 'I came down from

---

6. The absence of Jesus' father, Joseph, at the Cana wedding (2:1) and at Capernaum afterward (2:12) suggests that he was probably dead by this time, and yet "the Jews" claim to "know" (ἡμεῖς οἴδαμεν) both the father and the mother, as if both are still alive. This could account for the omission of the words "and mother" (καὶ τὴν μητέρα) by certain ancient witnesses (including the first hand of א, W, and the old Syriac). The omission accents the redundancy, yet avoids implying that Jesus' mother and father are "known" in the same sense, that is, as living acquaintances of those speaking. The weight of evidence favors retaining the mention of Jesus' mother (with Mark and Matthew, and against Luke; see below, n. 7). See Metzger, *Textual Commentary,* 213.

7. As we have seen, the only reference to Jesus' "hometown," or πατρίς in John's Gospel (4:44), gives the term no precise identification, and Jesus never comes to Nazareth.

8. The question, "Is this not Jesus, the son of Joseph," parallels almost exactly the question asked at Nazareth in Luke, "Is this not Joseph's son?" (Lk 4:22), while the inclusion of Jesus' mother agrees with Matthew (13:55) and Mark (6:3).

9. The manuscript tradition is almost evenly divided between "How does he say *now?* (with νῦν, as in P⁷⁵, B, C, T, W, Θ, and others) and "*So* how does he say?" (with οὖν,

heaven?'" "How" probably expresses not only confusion but skepticism, like Nicodemus's repeated "How can it be?" (3:4, 9), a skepticism that will become explicit in their later question, "How can this man give us his flesh to eat?" (v. 52), and in the question of his so-called "disciples" (v. 61), "This word is hard; who can listen to it?" (see also 7:15; 8:33).

43 Jesus "answered" these "Jews" even though they had spoken only to each other, not to him. The writer could have used the rare aorist middle ("gave answer" or "had an answer"),[10] just as in 5:17 and 19, but does not do so this time because Jesus is engaged in a real debate identified as having taken place at a specific location (see v. 59, "while teaching in synagogue at Capernaum"). Because he "knew what was in the person" (2:25), Jesus knew all the thoughts and "murmurings" of enemies and disciples alike (see v. 61), and was quite capable of responding even to unspoken questions (see above, on 4:27). "Stop murmuring" is a warning to his hearers to turn their attention away from "each other"[11] and toward him, and to move beyond their confusion and listen to what God is telling them. His words recall an earlier warning, "Don't be surprised at this" (5:28), signaling more to come, to murmur and be surprised about. And in fact Jesus will now resume at some length (vv. 44-51) his controversial claim to be "the Bread of life" (v. 35) who "came down from heaven" (v. 38).

44 "No one can come to me," he continues, "unless the Father who sent me draw him" (v. 44). The words are a negative corollary to verses 37 ("All that the Father gives me will come to me") and 39 ("that of all he has given me I might not lose anything"), and an echo of John's caution to his disciples three chapters earlier, "A person cannot receive anything unless it is given him from heaven" (3:27). In verses 37 and 39, the "person" who receives something "from heaven" (that is, from "the Father") was Jesus, while here it is anyone who comes to Jesus for salvation. Those who "come to me," Jesus says, do so because his Father "draws" them, and for no other reason. They are God's gift to Jesus, and Jesus is God's gift to them.[12] Jesus is not so much inviting these Galilean "Jews" to "come to him" as providing the *reader of the Gospel* with an explanation why they would not and could not come.

---

as in P⁶⁶, ℵ, A, D, L, Ψ, much of the Latin, and the majority of later manuscripts). Οὖν is so frequent in Johannine discourse that scribes may well have misread it by default in place of νῦν, which is used not temporally here (as it is more commonly is in John's Gospel) but rhetorically (see Metzger, *Textual Commentary,* 213).

10. Gr. ἀπεκρίνατο. Instead we find here the more common aorist passive used as a middle, ἀπεκρίθη.

11. Gr. μετ' ἀλλήλων.

12. Later, recalling this pronouncement, Jesus will tell his disciples, "That is why I have told you that no one can come to me *unless it is given him* from the Father" (6:65; for the italicized words, compare 3:27).

They do not come to Jesus because they are not "drawn" or "dragged" to him.[13] The verb is used literally of drawing a sword (18:10), or dragging a net full of fish into a boat (21:6) or onto shore (21:11). The image is reminiscent of Jesus' promise in the other Gospels that his disciples will "fish for people" (Mk 1:20) or "catch people" like fish (Lk 5:10). Here the Father "draws" people to Jesus, but once a person is "drawn," Jesus claims, "I will raise him up at the last day." He is saying this now for the third time (see vv. 39, 40). The "I" is emphatic, as in verse 40, but this time, one suspects, the emphasis serves to distinguish Jesus from the Father. The Father "draws" people to Jesus now, and Jesus' role "at the last day" will be to "raise them up."[14]

45 For the first time in the Gospel, Jesus cites a biblical text. Earlier, John had quoted what Isaiah "said" (1:23); the Gospel writer called attention to a "written" text that Jesus might have quoted but did not (2:17), and Jesus' questioners here at Capernaum asked him for a sign like manna because, "as it is written, 'He gave them bread from heaven to eat'" (v. 31). Now it is Jesus' turn to quote Scripture: "It is written[15] in the prophets, 'And they all will be taught by God.' Every person who has heard from the Father and learned comes to me."[16] The purpose of the quotation is to interpret the harsh metaphor of "drawing" people to Jesus (v. 44). The quotation assures us that it is indeed a metaphor. No one is "drawn" or "dragged" to Jesus forcibly or against one's will.[17] Rather, a person is "drawn" by being "taught by God."[18] Jesus locates the pronouncement vaguely "in the prophets," but its precise home is Isaiah 54:13, addressed to Israel as a barren and forsaken wife, with a redeeming promise of compassion, and "all your sons taught by God."[19] Jesus does not mention "sons" because in John's Gospel he is the only "Son,"

---

13. Gr. ἑλκύσῃ.

14. Later, when Jesus claims that he himself (κἀγώ) will "draw them all [πάντας ἑλκύσω] to myself" (12:32), the reader will have to decide whether he refers to the work of "drawing" assigned here to the Father, or to the work of "raising up at the last day" which he has repeatedly claimed for himself (6:39, 40, 44, 54), or to something else entirely.

15. Gr. ἐστιν γεγραμμένον.

16. Jesus will quote what is "written" (γεγραμμένον) two more times in the Gospel (10:34; 15:25), and twice more "the Scripture" (ἡ γραφή, 7:38 and 13:18).

17. For the metaphorical use of this verb, see Jeremiah 38(31):3, LXX, "I have loved you with an eternal love, and I have drawn you [εἵλκυσά σε] into compassion." Also, perhaps 2 Sam 22:17, LXX, "He sent from on high; he took me. He drew me [εἵλκυσεν] from many waters." A fragmentary Greek papyrus from Oxyrhynchus speaks of "those who draw us" (οἱ ἕλκοντες ἡμᾶς) and "those who draw you" (οἱ ἕλκοντες ὑμᾶς), but in the *Gospel of Thomas* 3 (which appears to be a Coptic equivalent), the expression is simply "your leaders." See *Apocrypha, II: Evangelien* (ed. E. Klostermann; 3d ed.; Berlin: Walter de Gruyter, 1929), 20-21.

18. Gr. διδακτοὶ θεοῦ.

19. In the LXX, καὶ πάντας τοὺς υἱούς σου διδακτοὺς θεοῦ.

and he limits "all" to "every person who has heard from the Father and learned." Such a person "comes to Jesus" (compare v. 44), something these Galilean "Jews" have not done. He does not invite them explicitly to "come," but leaves the invitation implicit, and open to "all" or "every person" in general, not them in particular. They stand at no special advantage just because Jesus happens to be addressing them. His words are as much for his so-called "disciples" waiting just offstage (see vv. 60, 66), or (even more) for the readers of the Gospel as for his immediate hearers.

The question remains: How does a person "hear from the Father and learn,"[20] so as to be "taught by God"? Is it a voice within, like the voice at the baptism, saying "This is my beloved Son"? Is it a growing and deepening conviction planted in a person's life by what would be called centuries later "Christian nurture"? Probably not. Rather, the point is what it was a chapter earlier when Jesus told "the Jews" in Jerusalem, "the Father who sent me . . . has testified about me. You have never heard his voice nor seen his form, and you do not have his word dwelling in you, because he whom that One sent, him you do not believe" (5:37-38). To "hear from the Father" is to hear *Jesus,* for the One who spoke long ago at Sinai now speaks through the Son, and only through the Son.[21] If they do not hear the Son, they will not hear the Father, and if they do not hear and learn from the Father, they will not come to the Son.

46 As in the earlier passage (5:37), "hearing" calls to mind "seeing." Anticipating just such a connection, Jesus cautions, "Not that anyone has seen the Father except he who is from God, he has seen the Father." His claim for himself goes beyond *hearing* "from the Father," or "from God." Using the third person (as in "the Son of man," or "the Son"), he identifies himself as "he who *is* from God,"[22] that is, as "the One whom God sent" (see 3:34). The abrupt shift to the third person hints at a different voice here, possibly another of the Gospel writer's narrative asides to the reader, but this is unlikely, for no change of speaker is signaled. Rather, the Gospel writer wants to attribute these words to Jesus, just as he attributed 3:16-21 to Jesus,

---

20. The verb ἀκούειν with the preposition παρά, literally "to hear from," means to learn something by hearing (see 1:40, where John's disciples "heard from" John — that is, learned from him — about Jesus; also 7:51; 8:26, 38, 40; 15:15). This means that καὶ μαθών, "and learned," is almost redundant, merely making explicit what is already implicit in having "heard" (see BDAG, 38 [3d]).

21. See Odeberg, *The Fourth Gospel,* 257-58: "The paradox is this: no one can come to the Son without having received the teaching from the Father; no one can hear and learn from the Father except through the Son." Schnackenburg (2.51) tries (not altogether successfully) to combine "the inward voice of God" or "inward 'attraction' of the Father" with "the external hearing of his Son, in whom he reveals himself."

22. Gr. ὁ ὢν παρὰ τοῦ θεοῦ.

and 3:31-36 to John. So Jesus himself now articulates what the reader has known almost from the start, that "No one has seen God, ever. It was God the One and Only, the One who is right beside the Father, who told about him" (1:18). He now makes clear that he "told about" the Father because he "has seen the Father." He hinted as much before (3:11, 32; 5:19), and he will say again, "I speak the things I have seen in the Father's presence" (8:38). Jesus, the Word and God's "One and Only," now remembers his preexistence. His access to the Father was and is direct, and everyone else's is indirect, for he is the sole mediator between God and humanity. Whether or not the Gospel (either here or at 1:18) has in mind those who claim direct visions of God is unclear.[23] Nothing of the kind is suggested by the context. But if it does, the point is surely that those who make such claims are deceiving themselves and others.

47-48 Jesus continues with another "Amen, amen" pronouncement, the tenth in the Gospel and the third in the present chapter. Unlike the previous two in the chapter (vv. 26, 32), it does not introduce Jesus' answer to a question or challenge from "the crowd" (or in this case "the Jews"), but instead continues a speech already begun (as, for example, in 3:11, and in 5:24 and 25). As in several such cases, it is difficult to tell exactly what constitutes the "Amen, amen" pronouncement proper. Jesus is taking a kind of solemn vow that what he is about to say is true, but how far does the vow extend? It is tempting to limit it to the single sentence, "Amen, amen, I say to you, whoever believes has eternal life" (v. 47), but that will not do because, as we have seen, Jesus is "the Word" who was "with God in the beginning," and everything he says is true because he has heard it "from the Father." The "Amen, amen" formula is simply his way of punctuating the revealed truth he brings to the world in these Johannine discourses. In some instances an "Amen, amen" pronouncement can be limited to a single verse or sentence because Jesus' speech ends and either someone else speaks or the narrative resumes (for example, 1:51; 3:3; 8:51, 58; 13:20, 21; 21:18).[24] But more often, "Amen, amen" should be read as introducing a series of pronouncements, not just one (see 3:5, 11; 5:19, 24, 25; 6:26, 32, and v. 53 below).

That is the case here. In itself, "Amen, amen, I say to you, whoever believes has eternal life" (v. 47) echoes 5:24, "Amen, amen, I say to you that the person who hears my word and *believes* the One who sent me, *has eternal life*" (my italics). Here it sounds like a simplified version of the earlier saying. Yet in the present context it cannot be isolated from what immediately follows: "I am

---

23. "Seeing the Father" will later be redefined, when Philip asks Jesus, "Lord, show us the Father," and Jesus replies, "Whoever has seen me has seen the Father" (14:8-9).

24. This is true also of 13:38, where even though Jesus continues to speak, he changes the subject so completely that v. 38 stands alone.

the Bread of life" (v. 48). The operative metaphor for "life" in the present context has been "bread" ever since verses 31-35, leading up to the same pronouncement, "I am the Bread of life" (v. 35), with its corollary, "The person who comes to me will never go hungry, and the person who believes in me will never ever thirst." This time there is no explicit corollary. Rather, "I am the Bread of life" is closely linked to what precedes, as if to say, "Whoever believes has eternal life, [for] I am the Bread of life." This takes us momentarily back to the setting of verses 31-35, and the issue of "manna in the desert." The "crowd" (vv. 22, 24) who had followed Jesus across the lake to Capernaum first raised that issue (vv. 30-31), and now that their true identity as "the Jews" is known (v. 41), Jesus resumes the discussion.

49 The starting point had been the biblical text they themselves cited, "He gave them bread from heaven to eat" (v. 31). Having identified himself as "the bread that came down from heaven" (vv. 35, 38, 41, 48), Jesus now focuses on the verb "to eat."[25] "Your fathers ate the manna in the desert," he begins, echoing and acknowledging the truth of their own words, "Our fathers ate the manna in the desert" (v. 31).[26] Yet he adds the troubling reminder, "and they died." At one level, this is simply a way of saying, "That was then, this is now," just as he said previously that it was not Moses long ago but his Father right now who "gives you the true bread from heaven" (v. 32). But the stark notice that "they died" gives the pronouncement a somber twist.

What is Jesus' point? Is he merely reminding his hearers that their "fathers" were mortal, like the prophets or even Abraham (see 8:52-53)? Or is it that they died without reaching the promised land *because of their disobedience?* Other New Testament writers tell us that "God was not pleased" with "the fathers," even though they "ate the same spiritual food and drank the same spiritual drink," and that they were "struck down in the desert" (1 Cor 10:1-5), or that God was angry at "those who sinned, whose bodies fell in the desert," so that "they were unable to enter because of unbelief" (Heb 3:17-

---

25. Gr. φαγεῖν. This observation has since become a commonplace, often in connection with viewing Jesus' discourse as a type of synagogue homily, focusing first on one and then another word or phrase in the biblical text. See, for example, P. Borgen, *Bread from Heaven* (Supplement to *Novum Testamentum* 11; Leiden: Brill, 1965), 87 (this is in keeping with v. 59, where the discourse is explicitly located at the synagogue in Capernaum).

26. It is possible to argue that Jesus, by saying "your fathers," is distancing himself from Jewish traditions, as he does in speaking of "your law" (8:17; 10:34), or "their law" (15:25), or "your father Abraham" (8:56): that is, "yours, not mine." Brown, for example (1.273), sees "a deep cleavage between Church and Synagogue at the time when the evangelist is writing." But more likely, "your" (ὑμῶν) is neutral here, for when he repeats himself later he mentions merely "the fathers" (v. 58).

19). Is it legitimate to read such thoughts into the simple comment that those who ate the manna "died"? It is tempting to do so because of the references to Jesus' audience "murmuring" (vv. 41, 43, 61), as Israel in the desert had done. But no such connection is made. All Jesus is claiming explicitly is that manna could not sustain the people indefinitely. They died, as everyone must, even Abraham and the prophets. The implication is that his hearers, "the Jews" now questioning him, will die as well. Only later will he call it "dying in their sins" (see 8:21, 24). He mentions death here only to sharpen the contrast with "life," underscoring the claim just made that "whoever believes has eternal life" (v. 47), and "I am the Bread of life" (v. 48). The Christian reader senses that the contrast is imperfect because the death of which Jesus speaks is physical death, while the life he promises is spiritual, a new and qualitatively different kind of life. In the final analysis this is true, yet Jesus' hearers seem unaware of any such distinction. As far as they are concerned, he could as well be promising endless physical life, and his next words will seem to them to bear this out.

50 "This is the bread that comes down from heaven," he continues, "so that anyone might eat of it and not die." The abrupt shift to the third person recalls verse 33, and raises a similar question. Is this still a word of Jesus or an insertion by the Gospel writer? If the latter, then the translation should be, "*This man* is the bread who comes down from heaven, so that anyone might eat of *him* and not die" (my italics). But (just as in v. 33) there is no evidence of a change of speaker. We have to assume that Jesus is still speaking, and that the above translation is correct. Having just claimed to be "the Bread of life" (v. 48), he can nevertheless still speak of "the bread that comes down from heaven" as "it," and not "I," something distinct from himself, momentarily distancing himself from it. Like the manna of old, it is "bread from heaven" (vv. 31, 32), but in contrast to the manna, those who "eat" of it do *not* die. This explains what Jesus meant earlier by calling it "the true" *(ton alēthinon)* bread from heaven (v. 32). It is "true" or "real" in that it sustains life forever, not just for a day. It is no ordinary food, Jesus claims, and if it is no ordinary food the next question he must answer is, How then is it "eaten"? At one level, the reader knows the answer, for Jesus has said, "Amen, amen, I say to you, whoever *believes* has eternal life" (v. 47, my italics). But is the metaphor of "eating" simply dissolved in the reality of "believing," or does the metaphor itself contribute to our understanding of what "believing" is, and what it entails? Surely the latter. And has Jesus introduced the metaphor of eating just to throw a stumbling block in the path of his hostile questioners (see v. 52), or does it have something to teach the Christian reader as well? Again, the latter is clearly the case.

51 The alternation between the first person and the third person continues, as Jesus announces, "I am the living Bread that came down from heaven." In the context, the phrase "the living Bread"[27] echoes both "the Bread of life" (vv. 35, 47) and the notion that "the bread of God . . . gives life to the world" (v. 33). In the larger perspective of John's Gospel it answers to "the living water" that Jesus promised the Samaritan woman (4:10, 11).[28] It may in fact be modeled after the latter, because the participle "living" is appropriate to fresh water from a spring in a way in which it is not appropriate to bread.

Having shifted back to the first person, "I am the living Bread," Jesus might have been expected to give the accompanying invitation in the first person as well: "If anyone eat of me, he will live forever," just as he said earlier, "I am the Bread of life. The person who comes to *me* will never go hungry, and the person who believes in *me* will never ever thirst" (v. 35, my italics; see also 8:12; 11:25-26). Instead, he shifts again to the third person: "If anyone eat of *this bread,* he will live forever" (my italics). But the alternation between "I" and "this bread" is then resolved when he adds, "and the bread I will give him is my flesh[29] for the life of the world." Conventional wisdom has it that this last clause marks a major transition in the chapter from a "sapiential" or wisdom-oriented perspective, accenting belief in Jesus' word and being "taught by God," to a distinctly "sacramental" emphasis on the bread and wine of the Eucharist.[30] Some have gone so far as to claim that while the former is authentically Johannine, the latter is not, so that vv. 51-58 must be understood as coming not from the Gospel writer but from a later hand.[31] Yet not only is there no textual evidence of such a break, but it is widely acknowledged that the literary style of what follows is indistinguishable from that of what precedes.[32]

More specifically, the comment that "the bread I will give him is my flesh" explains finally why Jesus has alternated between the first and the

27. Gr. ὁ ἄρτος ὁ ζῶν.
28. This is not surprising in light of v. 35, where Jesus as "the Bread of life" promises to satisfy not only hunger but thirst. But Jesus never claims to *be* "the living Water" (7:37 is where he might have done so, and he does not). Nor does the phrase "water of life" even occur in John's Gospel (though see Rev 21:6; 22:1, 17).
29. Gr. ἡ σάρξ μου.
30. See Brown, 1.272-74, who also comments that "if 51-58 are a later addition, they were added not to introduce a eucharistic theme but to bring out more clearly the eucharistic elements that were already there" (1.286).
31. For a classic statement of this position, see Bultmann, 218-19. For a survey of arguments both pro and con, see Schnackenburg, 2.56-59, and for a measured response to Bultmann's hypothesis, P. N. Anderson, *Christology of the Fourth Gospel,* 110-36.
32. Even Bultmann agrees: "At this point the editor, *employing the style and language of the foregoing discussion,* has added or inserted a secondary interpretation of the bread of life in terms of the Lord's Supper" (234, my italics), and "From a stylistic point of view the sentence could have been written by the Evangelist" (234, n. 4).

third person, speaking of himself and of "this bread" interchangeably. It forces the reader to go back and look at verse 50 again, where Jesus seemed to distance himself from "this bread." On the contrary, we now realize, he was speaking of it as if it were his own body, in much the same way that Paul, for example, could refer to his own body as "this mortal," or "this corruptible" (1 Cor 15:53, 54), or as "this" (2 Cor 5:2), or "this tent" (2 Cor 5:4), or even "these hands" (Acts 20:32). The presumption all along has been that "the bread of God" (v. 33), or "this bread" (vv. 50, 51), is Jesus himself, or more specifically his "flesh." The notice that "the bread I will give him is my flesh" only makes it explicit. Again Paul's language (in a very different context) is illuminating: "For I know that *in me, that is in my flesh,* nothing good dwells" (Rom 7:18, my italics). Jesus, no less than Paul, *is* his "flesh" (see 1:14), so that saying "the bread . . . is my flesh" is no different in principle from saying "I am the Bread of life" (vv. 35, 47). But one thing is different: for the first time Jesus promises that he will "give" this bread, that is, give himself. "I will give" recalls yet again Jesus' encounter with the Samaritan woman, and the "living water" he promised that "I will give" (4:14). There it was not immediately clear that to give her "living water" was to give himself, but here it is evident that the gift of "living bread" is at the same time a gift of himself.[33] He is giving his own body, his very flesh, "for the life of the world."[34]

At last he is responding explicitly to the crowd's earlier request to "give us this bread always" (v. 34), but in an unexpected and shocking way. He will give "this bread" indeed (v. 34), but "this bread" turns out to be his own body, given up to death! "My flesh" comes to mean virtually "my death," especially with "flesh" so closely linked to the verb "I will give" and the preposition "for."[35] Jesus' language evokes both the notion (evident in Paul) that Jesus gave himself "for" his people,[36] and the language of the words of institution of the Lord's Supper according to Luke and Paul, "This is my body that is given for you" (Lk 22:19), or simply "that is for you" (1 Cor 11:24). It is customary in Christian tradition to speak of Christ's "blood" as a metaphor for his death on the cross, but on occasion the words

33. Another difference is that in the encounter in Samaria "this water" (τοῦτο τὸ ὕδωρ) was the water from the well which quenched only physical thirst and that only temporarily (4:13, 15), whereas "this bread" in the present passage is "the living bread that came down from heaven."

34. Gr. ὑπὲρ τῆς τοῦ κόσμου ζωῆς.

35. Gr. ὑπέρ, literally "on behalf of."

36. "Give" in such texts is either δίδοναι, as here (Gal 1:4; 1 Tim 2:6; Tit 2:14), or παραδίδοναι (Gal 2:20; Eph 5:2, 25), and it can be "for our sins" (Gal 1:4), "for me" (Gal 2:20), "for us" (Eph 5:2; Tit 2:14) "for her" (that is, the church, Eph 5:25), or "for all" (1 Tim 2:6).

"body" and "flesh" (even *without* the verb "to give" or the preposition "for") are used in a similar way in the New Testament.[37] Here too the reader knows — even though "the Jews" do not — that Jesus' "flesh for the life of the world" is his redemptive death. There have been intimations of this already (1:29, 36; 2:17, 19; 3:14, 16), and they will become more and more explicit, often with the same preposition "for," or "on behalf of" (see 10:11, 15; 11:52; 15:13; 17:19). Within the present discourse, the phrase "for the life of the world" explains and personalizes the earlier promise of bread that "gives life to the world" (v. 33). Jesus will personally give "life" to "the world" by giving his own "flesh" over to death, so that (as he said earlier), "everyone who believes in him might not be lost but have eternal life" (3:16), or "so that the world might be saved through him" (3:17).[38]

52 "The Jews," silent since verses 41-42, finally speak again, and again their speech is directed not to Jesus but to "each other."[39] This time they did not simply "murmur" (v. 41), but "quarreled" with each other, asking, "How can this man give us his[40] flesh to eat?" Yet despite the stronger verb, the accent is still on confusion, not hostility, whether toward Jesus or toward each other. There are no factions or stated differences of opinion among them, as there are later in the story when "the crowds" (or "the Pharisees," or "the Jews") are repeatedly divided by Jesus' words or actions (see 7:12, 40-43; 9:16; 10:19-21; 11:45-46). As before (vv. 41-42), they are confused, and their confusion has deepened. Their question, "How can this man give us his flesh to eat?" recalls Nicodemus: "How can a person be born when he is old?" (3:4), or "How can these things be?" (3:9). Unlike Nicodemus, however, they see Jesus not as "Rabbi," or a teacher "come from God" (3:2), but simply as "this man" (as in v. 42), perhaps with a subtle "con-

---

37. See Romans 7:4, "You have been put to death to the law through the *body* of Christ" (that is, through Christ's death); Ephesians 2:13-14, "But now in Christ Jesus you who were once far away have been brought near in the blood of Christ. For he is our peace, who has made both one and destroyed the middle wall of partition, the enmity, in his *flesh*" (here "in the blood of Christ" and "in his flesh" mean virtually the same thing, his death); see also Colossians 1:22, "in the *body of his flesh* through death"; Hebrews 10:5, "a *body* you have prepared for me"; 10:10, "through the offering of the *body* of Jesus Christ once," and 10:19, "through the veil, that is, *his flesh*" (italics added).

38. BDAG, 1030 (b) identifies ὑπὲρ τῆς ζωῆς as a construction expressing purpose, in this case "to bring life to the world" (compare 11:4: "for the glory of God," meaning "to reveal the glory of God").

39. Gr. πρὸς ἀλλήλους (compare μετ' ἀλλήλων, v. 43).

40. "His" (αὐτοῦ) is omitted in some manuscripts, including ℵ, C, D, L, W, Θ, Ψ, and the majority of later Greek manuscripts, but P66, B, and the Latin and Syriac versions retain it (Metzger, *Textual Commentary*, 214). Internal evidence favors retention because the offense seems to be directed at Jesus personally (as in v. 42) rather than at the abstract idea of eating "flesh" (which would not even have to be human flesh).

notation of contempt."⁴¹ What is it that confuses them? Earlier, it was his claim, "I am the bread that came down from heaven" (v. 41). This time it could have been his promise that those who eat of "this bread" will "not die," but "live forever" (vv. 50-51). That issue will come up later (see 8:51-53), but does not engage them here. What does trouble them is Jesus' comment that the "bread" he will give is his "flesh." He has not yet spoken explicitly of "eating" his flesh, but they have no difficulty making the connection. If he is inviting them to "eat of this bread" (vv. 50, 51), and if he calls the bread "my flesh" (v. 51), what else are they to think?

53 Again (as in v. 43) Jesus answers "the Jews," even though they have said nothing to him. The form of his answer matches almost exactly the form of his answer to Nicodemus three chapters earlier (see 3:3, 5): "Amen, amen, I say to you," followed by a negative conditional sentence introduced by "unless":⁴² "*Unless* you eat the flesh of the Son of man and drink [πίητε] his blood, *you do not have* life in yourselves" (v. 53, italics added). It is the eleventh "Amen, amen" pronouncement in the Gospel, and the fourth in the present chapter. Several things stand out in this pronouncement. First, Jesus accepts the inference that in speaking of "this bread" he was inviting his hearers to "eat his flesh" (v. 52), and he now makes it explicit. More than that, he insists that they *must* do so in order to "have eternal life." Second, he reintroduces the term "Son of man," last used it in verse 27, where he promised "the crowd" that "the Son of man" would give them "the food that remains to eternal life," and identified the Son of man as him "whom God the Father sealed." Here "the food that remains to eternal life" turns out to be the very flesh of the Son of man himself. By now his hearers know that Jesus means himself, for he has repeatedly used the first person and third person interchangeably (see vv. 45-46, 48-50, 51), and he now uses "my flesh" and "the flesh of the Son of man" interchangeably. Nor can these "Jews" fail to see the appropriateness of "the *flesh* of the Son of *man*" (my italics). The title here retains its implication of humanity. Jesus is not speaking of animal flesh, nor (in some paradoxical way) of the flesh of God, or of "the Son," but specifically and emphatically of *human* flesh — his own. Third, and far more striking, he adds that they must "drink his blood." Neither those who heard it nor the reader who reads it is quite prepared for those added words. Jesus has promised that "whoever drinks of the *water* that I will give him will never ever thirst" (4:14, my italics), and that "the person who believes in me will

---

41. Gr. οὗτος. See BDAG, 740 (1a). For more examples, see 7:15, 27, 35; 9:29; 18:40; 19:12 (also οὗτος ὁ ἄνθρωπος, 9:16, 24; 11:47). In the present context, some readers may sense in this disdainful use of οὗτος a jarring contrast to the accent on "this" bread in Jesus' speech (vv. 50, 51).

42. Gr. ἐὰν μή.

6:41-59 JESUS AND THE JEWS AT CAPERNAUM

never ever thirst" (6:35), but the drinking of blood is quite another matter. If his hearers wondered, "How can this man give us his flesh to eat?" what must they think now? Jesus' words compound the offense many times over, for nothing was more abhorrent to the Jewish mind that the drinking of animal blood, much less human blood (see Lev 17:10-16; Acts 15:20, 29; 21:25).

Whatever else it may mean, the mention of "blood" confirms the notion that by his "flesh" (v. 51) Jesus meant his death, and a violent death at that. While "flesh and blood" can simply refer to humanity, the "eating" of flesh presupposes killing, and "drinking" blood presupposes the shedding of blood. The notion of eating and drinking the flesh and blood of Jesus inevitably calls to mind the Christian Eucharist, and the various forms of the words of institution found in the synoptic Gospels and Paul. It has become almost commonplace to describe John's language as "eucharistic," but this judgment must be qualified at least to some degree. In Matthew, for example, Jesus says, "Take, eat. This is my body" (Mt 26:26), and "drink of it, for this is my blood of the covenant poured out for the forgiveness of sins" (vv. 27-28). That is about as close as the words of institution come to Jesus' words in the Gospel of John. The other Gospels (and Paul) lack the specific blunt commands to "eat" and to "drink," preferring the more general "take" (Mk 14:22), or "do this" (Lk 22:19; 1 Cor 11:24, 25). In all of the accounts, moreover, the bread is Jesus' "body," never his "flesh," as in this chapter. John's language is actually more "eucharistic" earlier in describing how Jesus "*took* the loaves, and when he had given thanks, he *gave them out*" (v. 11), and much later, by the same lake with his disciples, when the risen Jesus "*takes* the bread and *gives* to them, and the fish as well" (21:13, my italics).[43] Still, it is difficult to read the pronouncement about "eating the flesh" and "drinking the blood" of the Son of man without the Eucharist coming to mind, and through the centuries the passage has been read and reread in that light. The tendency begins even within the manuscript tradition.[44]

---

43. Strictly speaking, even the language of verse 51, "the bread *I will give*," is more explicitly "eucharistic" than that of verses 53-58.

44. See, for example, the English translation of verses 53-59 in the bilingual Codex Bezae (D) from the sixth century (with variants shown in italics): "So Jesus said to them, 'Amen, amen, I say to you, Unless you *receive* [λαβητε] the flesh of the Son of man and drink his blood, you do not have life in yourselves. The person who eats his flesh and drinks his blood has eternal life, and I will raise him up at the last day. For my flesh is real food [*omitting "and my blood is real drink"*]. The person who eats my flesh and drinks my blood dwells in me and I in him, *just as the Father is in me and I in the Father. Amen, amen, I say to you, unless you receive* [λαβητε] *the body* [το σωμα] *of the Son of man as the bread of life, you do not have life in him.* Just as the living Father sent me and I live because of the Father, so the person who *receives* me [ὁ λαμβανων με], even that person lives because of me. This is the bread that came down from heaven, not as your fathers ate and died, the per-

While the eucharistic interpretation makes some sense for even the earliest readers of the Gospel (who may have known and practiced the Lord's Supper), it makes no sense at all in the literary setting of the discourse at Capernaum. "The Jews" are confused by Jesus' reference to "eating" him, and their confusion is hardly to be allayed by referring to a Christian ritual that did not yet exist. More likely, the sacramental or eucharistic interpretation of the text belongs to the "reception history" of the text rather than to the Gospel writer's intention (much less the intention of Jesus within the story!). The text should be read if possible from within the horizons of the dramatic confrontation being described at Capernaum, so as to speak *both* to "the Jews" on the scene (even if it gives offense) and to Christian readers after the fact. The theme of the discourse so far has been Jesus' claim to give "life" or "eternal life" (see vv. 27, 33, 35, 40, 47, 51), and that to receive that life a person must "come to him" (vv. 35, 37, 44, 45) and "believe" (vv. 29, 30, 35, 36, 40, 47). Now the shocking truth emerges that the "life" he promises comes through death, and only through death. To "believe" means to accept fully the reality of death, a violent death at that, as the only way to "eternal life." In short, the "Amen, amen" saying in verse 53, "Unless you eat the flesh of the Son of man and drink his blood, you do not have life in yourselves," defines the "Amen, amen" saying in verse 47, "whoever believes has eternal life." As we have seen, "to have life in yourselves" or "in oneself" is simply to have eternal life as an assured present possession.[45] That is what Jesus promises, but only the prospect of death makes life possible.

Whose death? His own surely, but is that the full extent of it? Quite possibly Jesus is hinting that "coming to him" and "believing" may cost the believer something as well. In biblical language, "eating flesh" and "drinking blood" evoked images of slaughter and utter desolation,[46] and it may be that to eat Jesus' flesh and to drink his blood implies not only benefiting from his

---

son who eats this bread will live forever.' These things he said in the synagogue, teaching in Capernaum *on a Sabbath*" (for the Greek and Latin, see F. H. Scrivener, *Bezae Codex Cantabrigiensis* [Cambridge: Deighton, Bell, 1864], 112-13). The repeated substitution of "receive" (or "take") for "eat," the omission of "and my blood is real drink," and the addition of a new "Amen, amen" pronouncement about receiving "the *body* of the Son of man as the bread of life," all point to a softening, or domestication, of John's harsh language in the interest of adapting it to the language of the Eucharist.

45. See 5:26, where, in the case of both the Father and the Son, to have "life in oneself" is simply to have life.

46. See Ezekiel 39:17-18, where birds and wild animals are summoned to a "sacrificial feast" and told, "you shall eat flesh and drink blood. You shall eat the flesh of the mighty, and drink the blood of the princes of the earth" (NRSV; compare Rev 19:17-18); also Isaiah 49:26 (NRSV): "I will make your oppressors eat their own flesh, and they shall be drunk with their own blood as with wine" (compare Rev 16:6).

death but to some degree sharing or participating in that death. He says as much in the other three Gospels (see Mt 10:38-39; 16:24-25; Mk 8:34-35; Lk 9:23-24; 14:27; 17:33), and later in this Gospel he will make a similar point in illustrating the principle that "unless the grain of wheat falls to the ground and dies, it remains alone, but if it dies it bears much fruit" (see 12:24-25). Ignatius of Antioch, on the way to Rome and longing for martyrdom, seems to have read it that way, for he wrote, "Alive, I write to you desiring death. . . . I want the 'bread of God,' which is the flesh of Jesus Christ . . . and for drink I want his blood, which is incorruptible love" (*To the Romans* 7.2-3).[47] Yet at this point in the narrative it is impossible to be certain. Jesus' words remain a mystery. All we know is that he is calling for a radical acceptance of his death as the only way to eternal life.[48] How radical that acceptance must be has yet to be determined.

54 Having spoke of "my flesh" (v. 51) and "the flesh of the Son of man" (v. 53), Jesus now switches back to "my flesh" and "my blood," reinforcing his identity as "Son of man." In contrast to his exchange with Nicodemus, he adds a positive corollary to the negative conditional sentence introduced by "unless."[49] Balanced against the warning of the preceding verse is a promise: "The person who eats my flesh and drinks my blood has eternal life, and I will raise him up at the last day." This too, we can assume, is governed by the "Amen, amen" formula (v. 53), and the phrase "has eternal life" echoes verbatim the language of the previous "Amen, amen" pronouncement in verse 47.

Much has been written about Jesus' abrupt use of a different verb for "eat" here,[50] and again in verses 56, 57, and 58. This verb is said to mean "to bite or chew food, eat (audibly)," and to be used "to offset any tendencies to 'spiritualize' the concept so that nothing physical remains in it, in what many hold to be the language of the Lord's Supper."[51] Consequently, Raymond

---

47. For modern interpretations along this line, see P. Minear, *John: The Martyr's Gospel*, 77 ("To drink his blood, therefore, is to receive life from him and to share in his vicarious dying"), and P. Anderson, *Christology of the Fourth Gospel*, 213 ("Jesus was sent to give his 'flesh for the life of the world' . . . and *solidarity with him implies the same for his followers*"); also Michaels, *John*, 115-17.

48. Paul seems to express a similar notion in connection with Christian baptism: "For if we have been planted together in the likeness of his death, so we shall be in that of his resurrection" (Rom 6:5).

49. In the case of Nicodemus, Jesus did not set forth the way to "eternal life" positively until he began to speak of "heavenly things" (3:12-21, especially vv. 14-16).

50. Gr. ὁ τρώγων.

51. BDAG, 1019. So too Bultmann, 236: "It is a matter of real eating and not simply of some sort of spiritual participation"; also Moloney, 224. Morris, however, comments, "Some suggest that it points to a literal feeding and therefore to the sacrament. But this does not follow. There is no logic in saying: 'The verb is used of literal eating. Therefore eating the flesh of Jesus must mean eating the communion bread'" (336). As we have

Brown translates the verb used in verse 53 as "eats," and the verb here as "feeds on."[52] But more likely, the verbs are interchangeable in meaning.[53] Therefore we have translated the two verbs identically. Verse 54 simply repeats verse 53 positively, as a promise instead of a warning. The promise is "eternal life," not as a future reward but as a present possession, something a person "has" here and now. Yet the promise has a future dimension as well, for Jesus quickly adds, "and I will raise him up at the last day" (as in vv. 39, 40, and 44).[54] The emphatic "I" echoes here the emphatic "*my* flesh" and "*my* blood."[55] This accomplishes three things: first, it identifies Jesus unmistakably as "the Son of man" (v. 53); second, it presses the extraordinary claim that "at the last day" this man who died a violent death will be very much alive and quite capable of raising others from the dead; finally, it also presupposes that those others are (or may be) physically dead, implying that such phrases as "not die" (v. 50) and "live forever" (v. 51) are not to be taken literally.[56] Eternal life, as we have seen, is not an indefinite extension of one's present physical life, but a new kind of life altogether, resulting from a new birth. More than a future hope, it is a present possession, yet with a future dimension as well.[57] Because it does not exclude physical death, it is meaning-

---

seen (n. 44), eucharistic language is apt to be *less* literal or physical than that of John's Gospel, not more.

52. Brown, 1.281-82; so too Anderson, *Christology of the Fourth Gospel,* 208: "'to feed upon,' or 'to draw nourishment from'"; others, in a different vein, read it as the "eating of delicacies, or eating with enjoyment" (Bernard, 1.210; see Abbott, *Johannine Vocabulary,* 200).

53. That is, in the aorist indicative or subjunctive the Gospel writer prefers φαγεῖν, and in the present tense the verb τρώγειν (in addition to 6:54, 56-58, see 13:18; the "normal" present tense ἐσθίειν never occurs in this Gospel). To the Gospel writer, φαγεῖν and τρώγειν are the same verb, just as to most ancient writers φαγεῖν and ἐσθίειν are the same verb. BDF, §101 identifies τρώγειν as simply "a popular substitution for ἐσθίειν" (so Barrett, 299; Lindars, 269; Beasley-Murray, 95; Morris, 336). Schnackenburg (2.62) straddles the fence.

54. Bultmann (219) attributes this promise to his so-called "ecclesiastical editor," although he admits that it "has its proper place in v. 54; in the other places, particularly in v. 44, it disturbs the line of thought." As we have seen, this is by no means evident.

55. The possessive pronouns are emphasized by placing them before the nouns "flesh" (μου τὴν σάρκα) and "blood" (μου τὸ αἷμα) respectively, both here and in verse 56 (compare αὐτοῦ τὸ αἷμα, with reference to "the Son of man" in v. 53). The emphasis on "I" and "my" in the present verse is weakened slightly in Codex D, where αὐτοῦ (still referring to "the Son of man") replaces μου (see n. 44).

56. See 11:25-26, "even if he die, he will live," so that "everyone who lives and believes . . . will never ever die."

57. See Westcott, 232: "So far from the Resurrection being, as has been asserted, inconsistent with St. John's teaching on the present reality of eternal life, it would be rather true to say that this doctrine makes the necessity of the Resurrection obvious."

less without the explicit promise of resurrection "at the last day" (see 5:28-29), and this Jesus has supplied, not once but four times.

55 Jesus now gives a reason for his two startling pronouncements. "For my flesh is real food," he claims, "and my blood is real drink." He repeats the phrases "my flesh" and "my blood" from the preceding verse, but in a different word order, accenting not the pronoun "my" but the two nouns "flesh" and "blood" (see n. 55). Codex D omits altogether the second clause, "and my blood is real drink" (see n. 44), perhaps to avoid overemphasizing and so legitimizing the offense of drinking blood. But no other manuscripts follow suit. "Food" and "drink" rhyme,[58] forming a natural pair as in Romans 14:17 and Colossians 2:16.

"Real," or "true,"[59] does not mean "literal," as if Jesus were proposing cannibalism. He has already told his disciples of "food to eat that you do not know about" (4:32), defined as doing "the will of the One who sent me" (4:34). In the present discourse he has distinguished "the food that remains to eternal life" from the literal "food that is being lost" (v. 27), and promised "the true bread from heaven" in contrast to literal manna in the desert (v. 32). Yet neither does "real" quite mean "metaphorical" or "spiritual" *as opposed to* literal — as if literal food and drink were somehow unreal.[60] Rather, Jesus' flesh qualifies as "real" food and his blood as "real" drink because they do what food and drink are supposed to do, and do it better.[61] They nourish and give life, not for a day or even a lifetime, but forever (see vv. 50-51, 54). In declaring them "real," Jesus is bearing testimony (although the word is not used), just as he "testified" earlier that God was "real" or "true" (3:33), and claimed that his own "testimony" about himself and John's testimony about him were also "true" (5:31, 32; see also 7:18; 8:14, 17, 26; 10:41; 19:35; 21:24). Similarly, the solemn assurance here that his flesh and blood are "real" food and drink serves to reinforce the "Amen, amen" with which the present speech began (v. 52).[62]

---

58. That is, βρῶσις, "food," and πόσις, "drink."

59. Gr. ἀληθής.

60. The cognate word for "real" or "true" (ἀληθινός) can have such an implication, as in 4:23, where the reference to "true worshippers" implies that worship *not* "in Spirit and in truth" is unreal or false worship, and in 17:3, where the phrase "the only true God" implies that other gods are false or unreal (see also 1 Jn 5:20-21).

61. In much the same way, Jesus can call himself "the good" (ὁ καλός) Shepherd (10:11, 14) without implying that human shepherds who care for their sheep are necessarily false or evil, and "the true" (ἡ ἀληθινή) Vine (15:1) without denying the reality or value of literal vines or vineyards.

62. This would be even more evident if the adverb ἀληθῶς ("truly" or "really") were accepted in one or both instances as the correct reading in place of ἀληθής (with the first hand of P⁶⁶ and of ℵ, and with D, Θ, the majority of later Greek manuscripts, and the

56 Having given this assurance, Jesus repeats word for word what he said a moment before (v. 54), "The person who eats my flesh and drinks my blood," but with a different ending. Instead of "has eternal life," he now claims that such a person "dwells in me, and I in him" — a decisive pronouncement, defining "eternal life" on the one hand, and "eating Jesus' flesh and drinking his blood" on the other. Both involve being united to Jesus.[63] "Eternal life" is life united to him and dependent on him, while to "eat his flesh and drink his blood" is to be united to him in his death. Neither is possible without the other. But how is either one possible? What does it mean to "dwell"[64] in Jesus and have Jesus "dwelling" in oneself? Nothing in the Gospel so far has quite prepared the reader (much less "the Jews" at Capernaum!) for such language. It is as much an enigma at this point in the story as "eating my flesh and drinking my blood." Jesus' first disciples "stayed with him" for part of a day (1:39), but staying or dwelling "with" Jesus and dwelling "in" him are by no means the same thing. He told "the Jews" in Jerusalem, "you do not have [God's] word dwelling in you" (5:38), implying that God's word ought to be "in" them. But the mutual indwelling of which he speaks here is something altogether new. Jesus will not even try to spell it out until much later in the Gospel when he is alone with his disciples.[65] It is in fact a characteristic — the defining characteristic — of true discipleship, or of what it means to "believe" (v. 47).

Mutual indwelling expresses an intimate relationship between Jesus and his disciples, mirroring the relationship between God and Jesus. The reader knows by now something of the relationship between the Father and the Son (see 3:35; 5:17, 19-23), but not in the language of mutual indwelling. Only later will Jesus explain to "the Jews" that "the Father is in me, and I in

---

Latin and Syriac versions). See, for example, the expression ἀληθῶς λέγω ὑμῖν, used in Luke's Gospel as a virtual equivalent to "Amen, I say to you" (Lk 12:44; 21:3; also 9:27). A slight preponderance of manuscript evidence (including P[75], B, the corrector of P[66], C, K, L, T, W, Ψ, and a number of important minuscules) favors the adjective ἀληθής (see Metzger, *Textual Commentary*, 214), yet the persistent occurrence of the adverb in the manuscript tradition may preserve a sense of testimony or solemn declaration in keeping with the writer's intent.

63. Bengel puts it concisely, his only comment on verse 56 being, "He who eateth, and that which is eaten, in very deed are intimately joined together" (*Gnomon*, 2.323).

64. Gr. μένει.

65. See 14:20, 17:21 and 23, and especially the repeated uses of "dwell" or "remain" (μένειν) in 15:4-10. Only once in the first half of the Gospel does Jesus even begin to invite "the Jews" into such a relationship. Significantly the invitation is directed to "Jews" who have believed in him (8:30-31): "If you remain [μείνητε] in my word, you are truly [ἀληθῶς] my disciples, and you will know the truth, and the truth will set you free" (8:31-32; compare 15:7-8). Just as significantly, the invitation is refused (8:33).

the Father" (10:38), and they will not understand. Still later he will invite his disciples to believe the same thing (see 14:11), and will promise them that "In that day you will know that I am in my Father, and you in me, and I in you" (14:20). Codex D, as we have seen (above, n. 44), spells out the relationship already here by adding the words, "just as the Father is in me, and I in the Father," but the added clause has no other support in the manuscript tradition and is clearly not original.[66]

57 Jesus accomplishes much the same result by introducing "the living Father" in the next verse, thereby appealing to his own dependence on the Father as the model for a disciple's dependence on him.[67] The question is whether verses 56 and 57 should be separated by a comma or a period. Does verse 57 simply complete the thought of the preceding verse, or is it a new and distinct pronouncement? Virtually all translations and commentators opt for the latter, placing a period at the end of verse 56 and beginning a new sentence with "Just as" (v. 57).[68] Our translation has followed that precedent, and yet verse 57 does at the same time complete the thought of verse 56 by grounding the mutual indwelling of Jesus and the believer in Jesus' mission from and dependence on the Father. "Just as the living Father sent me, and I live because of the Father," he explains, "so the person who eats me, even that person will live because of me."

Except for the jarring reference to "the person who eats me," these words begin to strike a more familiar chord. The reader knows that Jesus is "sent" from the Father (3:17, 34; 5:36, 38; 6:29), and even though the phrase "the living Father"[69] has not been used, the reader also knows that "the Father

---

66. Possibly verse 56 appeared unfinished, leading a scribe to insert an additional καθώς-clause to complete the analogy between the mutual indwelling of the Father and Jesus, and that of Jesus with his disciples.

67. This strategy is not as evident in Codex D, because D has inserted another lengthy "Amen, amen" pronouncement (possibly reflecting a distinctly eucharistic interpretation of Jesus' words) between verses 56 and 57: "Amen, amen, I say to you, unless you receive the body of the Son of man as the bread of life, you do not have life in him" (again, see n. 44).

68. See Abbott's discussion (*Johannine Grammar*, 128-29) of the "suspensive" use of καθώς (so called because it "keeps the reader's attention in suspense till he reaches the principal verb later on"). Abbott finds this more characteristic of John's Gospel than the "explanatory" or "supplementary" usage in which καθώς follows the verb, and notes several instances (including this one) where καθώς is "followed by καί or κἀγώ in apodosis." In a footnote he considers briefly the notion that verse 57 is simply a continuation of verse 56, the two being separated only by a comma, but concludes that this "would be against the suspensive use of καθώς, and is in other respects improbable" (129).

69. Gr. ὁ ζῶν πατήρ. This term is not paralleled elsewhere, but is hardly surprising, given the wide currency of the term "the living God" (if "the living God" has a "Son," as in

has life in himself" and "gave to the Son to have life in himself" (5:26). Finally, Jesus has said that the "food" by which he appropriates that "life" from God is "that I might do the will of the One who sent me and complete his work" (4:34). Therefore he can say, "I live because of the Father," but what is crucial here is the conclusion he draws from it: "so[70] the person who eats me, even that person will live because of me."[71] While Jesus never speaks of "eating" the Father, he depends on the Father for his "food," that is, his very life, and by the same token those who "eat" Jesus are those depend on him for their life.[72] At this point he does not specify whether the words "I live because of the Father" and "that person will live because of me" are referring only to life in this world or to resurrection life,[73] nor does he repeat the promise, "I will raise him up at the last day" (v. 54). But the effect of the analogy is to define "eating" Jesus as "doing his will and completing his work," in the same way that he does the Father's will and completes the Father's work — even to the point of death, and the prospect of death cries out for the hope of resurrection. To Jesus in this Gospel, life is life, whether in this world or the world to come. "Believing" in Jesus (v. 47) has now been defined as "eating" his flesh and "drinking" his blood (vv. 53-55), "eating" him as union with him (v. 56), and union with him as doing his will and completing his work (v. 57), in short, as discipleship with all that that entails, up to and including the prospect of martyrdom and the hope of resurrection.

58 Jesus concludes his response to "the Jews" (v. 52) by gathering into a few well-chosen words the whole exchange with them, and before them with "the crowd," all the way back to the crowd's demand for "bread from heaven" (v. 31). First he repeats verse 33 almost verbatim: "This is the bread that came down from heaven," changing only the present participle "comes down" (v. 33) to the aorist "came down," to accent his personal claim

---

Mt 16:16 and 1 Thess 1:9-10, does it make him a "living Father"?), and given the mention of "living water" and "living bread" as gifts of God in this Gospel (see 4:10; 6:32, 51).

70. Καί is ambiguous in conditional sentences, as here with καθώς, for it can mean either "and" or "so." Thus, verse 57 could be translated either "Just as the living Father sent me, *so* [κἀγώ] I live because of the Father, *and* [καί] the person who eats me, even that person will live because of me," or "Just as the living Father sent me, *and* [κἀγώ] I live because of the Father, *so* [καί] the person who eats me, even that person will live because of me" (again, see Abbott, 129). We have opted for the latter because of the additional emphasis supplied by "even that person" (κἀκεῖνος) in the last clause.

71. Gr. ζήσει δι' ἐμέ, corresponding to "I live because of the Father" (κἀγὼ ζῶ διὰ τὸν πατέρα).

72. In John Wesley's words, "*I live by the Father* — being one with him — *He shall live by me* — being one with me. Amazing Union!" *Explanatory Notes on the New Testament* (London: Bowyer, 1755), 241.

73. See, for example, 14:19, 'because I live, you too will live' (ὅτι ἐγὼ ζῶ καὶ ὑμεῖς ζήσετε), referring to the hope of resurrection.

that "I came down from heaven" (v. 38). Next, with the words, "not as the fathers ate and died, the person who eats this bread will live forever," he revisits verse 49, "Your[74] fathers ate the manna in the desert, and they died," and verse 51, "If anyone eat of this bread he will live forever." By now it is clear that "this bread" is the flesh of Jesus "for the life of the world" (v. 51), and that eternal life is possible only through his death. The two questions, "How does he say now that 'I came down from heaven'?" (v. 42), and "How can this man give us his flesh to eat?" (v. 52), have now been answered, but as we will see (v. 60), not to everyone's satisfaction.

59 Jesus' speech is over, and the Gospel writer adds a belated "narrative aside": "These things he said teaching in synagogue in Capernaum."[75] The reader knows already that the setting is Capernaum (vv. 17, 24), but this is the first and only mention of the synagogue. There has been no explicit change of venue from the place where the crowd first "found" Jesus after crossing the lake (v. 25), and we are left ot wonder: Did they find him in the synagogue, or did they find him at the lakeshore and then adjourn to the synagogue? Did he first debate "the crowd" by the lake (vv. 26-40) and then "the Jews" in the synagogue (vv. 41-58)? None of these questions is answered explicitly, but the very broad summary in verse 58 suggests that the entire discourse at least as far back as the introduction of the biblical text about "bread from heaven" (v. 31) took place in the Capernaum synagogue.[76] John's Gospel has implied that Capernaum is Jesus' home (see 2:12; 6:42), and other Gospel traditions present him teaching and performing an exorcism in the synagogue there (Mk 1:21-28; Lk 4:31-37).[77] Later, when the High Priest in Jerusalem asks him "about his disciples and his teaching" (18:19), he will reply, "I have spoken openly to the world. I always taught *in synagogue and in the temple,* where all the Jews come together, and I spoke nothing in secret"

---

74. "Your fathers" (v. 49) and "the fathers" (v. 58) seem to be used interchangeably (see above, n. 26).

75. Codex D adds "on the Sabbath" (see n. 44), in keeping with other passages where Jesus taught in synagogue "on the Sabbath" at Capernaum (Mk 1:21; Lk 4:31), or Nazareth (Lk 4:16, "as was his custom"). In the better manuscripts this is not stated but perhaps assumed.

76. This is in keeping with the thesis of Peder Borgen (see n. 25) and others, that the entire discourse be viewed as a kind of synagogue homily developing the theme of manna in the desert from Exodus 16.

77. See also Luke 4:16-30, at the synagogue in Nazareth. Barrett (300) comments that the discourse in John, "with its interruptions suggests a less formal occasion than a synagogue sermon," yet the "interruptions" (vv. 41-42, 52) are, as we have seen, disputes "with each other" rather than with Jesus, and in any case far less dramatic than the interruptions by the demoniac in Mark 1:23-26, and by the hostile crowd at the synagogue in Nazareth in Luke 4:22-23, 28-29. As we have seen (n. 7), even the question, "Is this not Joseph's son?" is common to Luke (4:22) and to John (6:42).

(18:20, italics added). Jesus has been in the temple twice (2:14-22; 5:14), and will teach there at length in later chapters (see 7:14, 28; 8:20; see also 8:59; 10:23), but only this once at Capernaum is he said to have taught "in synagogue."[78] From the standpoint of Jesus' statement to the high priest, the present notice, "These things he said teaching in synagogue in Capernaum," forms a matched pair with the notice a chapter and a half later, "These words he spoke in the treasury, teaching in the temple" (8:20).[79] Perhaps the Gospel writer included the two notices to accent the point Jesus will eventually make to the high priest — that his teaching was for "all the Jews" (18:20) — not secret or esoteric instruction to a small, subversive group of disciples, but a matter of public record. "Ask those who heard what I told them," he will say; "Look, they know what I said" (18:21). Here in chapter 6, "the Jews" in Galilee have indeed heard what he said. Their final response, like that of "the Jews" in Jerusalem at the end of chapter 5, is undisclosed, but there is little reason or precedent for thinking it favorable (see vv. 41, 52). Instead, certain of his "disciples" react (see v. 60).

H. JESUS AND HIS DISCIPLES AT CAPERNAUM (6:60-71)

> 60 *Then many of his disciples, when they heard, said, "This word is hard. Who can hear it?"* 61 *And Jesus, knowing within himself that his disciples were murmuring about this, said to them, "Does this make you stumble?* 62 *So then, [what] if you see the Son of man going up where he was at first?* 63 *The Spirit is that which makes alive; the flesh accomplishes nothing. The words I have spoken to you are spirit, and they are life.* 64 *But there are some of you who do not believe."* *For Jesus knew from the beginning who they are who do not believe, and who it is who will hand him over.* 65 *And he went on to say, "This is why I have told you that no one can come to me unless it is given him from the Father."* 66 *From this, many of his disciples turned back and would no longer walk with him.* 67 *So Jesus said to the Twelve, "Do*

---

78. The absence of the definite article with "synagogue," both here and in 18:20, does not mean that the word should be translated simply as an indefinite "assembly" or "gathering," for the Capernaum synagogue was well known. It simply corresponds to the expression "in church" (rather than "in the church") when referring to Christian public worship and preaching (see Brown, 1.284; Schnackenburg, 2.455).

79. The two notices belong to a larger category of narrative asides in John's Gospel introduced by "these" (ταῦτα) or "this" (τοῦτο), either setting a scene (as here), or terminating an incident (2:11; 4:54; 21:14), or commenting on something said or done (7:39; 11:51; 12:16, 33, 41), or providing a transition from discourse either to narrative (13:21; 18:1), or further discourse (11:11; 17:1), or the Gospel writer's reflections (12:36b).

6:60-71 JESUS AND HIS DISCIPLES AT CAPERNAUM

you want to go away too?" 68 *Simon Peter answered him, "Lord, to whom shall we turn? You have words of life eternal,* 69 *and we believe and we know that you are the Holy One of God."* 70 *Jesus answered them, "Did I not choose you as the Twelve? And one of you is 'the devil.'"* 71 *He meant Judas of Simon Iscariot. For this man, one of the Twelve, was going to hand him over.*

Once again, the audience seems to change abruptly. First they were "the crowd" (vv. 22, 24), then "the Jews" (vv. 41, 52), now Jesus' "disciples" (v. 60). These "disciples" react in much the same way as "the Jews" had done, "murmuring" at what Jesus has said (v. 61), and sounding more like enemies than like disciples, more like the so-called "believers" at the first Passover in Jerusalem, to whom Jesus "would not entrust himself" (2:24) than like "his disciples" who first "believed in him" at the Cana wedding (2:12). The latter seem to have become a fixed group within the narrative, accompanying Jesus to Samaria (4:8, 27, 31, 33), assisting at the feeding of the crowd (6:3, 8, 12), and meeting Jesus on the lake (vv. 16, 22, 24). Since then, they seem to have been silent observers of Jesus' discourse to "the crowd" and to "the Jews." It is unclear whether these "disciples" who are now complaining are part of that group, or whether they are merely those who "heard"[1] (v. 60), potential rather than actual disciples?[2] If Jesus was dealing first with an undifferentiated "crowd" (vv. 22-40), then with the crowd as "Jews," or unbelievers (vv. 41-59), perhaps he is now finally dealing with the same crowd as potential disciples. From the start, "following him because they could see the signs he was doing" (v. 2),[3] they were clearly differentiated from the actual disciples, who sat with him on the mountain (v. 3) and watched them "coming to him," and gave them food. And yet both expressions, "following him" and "coming to him," imply, as we have seen, at least a first step toward discipleship. The term "disciples" (v. 60) implies that they have heard and want to believe, yet they find Jesus' hard words unacceptable. As a result, we are told, they "turned back and would no longer walk with him" (v. 66). Twelve remain, evidently those who have been known as "the disciples" all along. With Simon Peter as their spokesman they declare their allegiance to Jesus

---

1. Gr. ἀκούσαντες.
2. This would be in keeping with 18:21, where Jesus, on being asked about his "disciples" (v. 19, as if looking for a list of names), replies, "Ask those who have heard [τοὺς ἀκηκοότας] what I said to them," implying that they were not a fixed group, but that anyone who "heard" Jesus was at least potentially a "disciple."
3. As in the case of those who "believed" and to whom Jesus did not "entrust himself" at the first Passover (2:23), it was the "signs" Jesus performed that attracted their attention.

(vv. 68-69), and he tells them that he has chosen them as "the Twelve," but that one of them — he does not say which one — is "the devil."

60-61 Like "the Jews," many so-called "disciples" are troubled by Jesus' words about eating his flesh and drinking his blood. "This word is hard,"[4] they complain; "Who can hear it?" (v. 60). Like "the Jews" too, they speak to each other, not to Jesus, for he does not actually hear their words but knows "within himself" what they are saying[5] and calls it by its right name, "murmuring" (v. 61), just as "the Jews" had "murmured" earlier about his claims (vv. 41, 43). What is it that "makes them stumble" (v. 61)?[6] Is it Jesus' claim to have "come down from heaven" (v. 38), or is it the notion of "eating" his flesh (vv. 51-58), or is it both? Such things were incomprehensible to "the Jews" (see vv. 41-42, 52), but in the case of these would-be "disciples" the difficulty may not have been that his words were obscure or difficult to understand, but that they were all too clear. If, as we have seen, he has been saying that life for the world comes about only through violent death, his own and by extension theirs, it is not surprising that they would find such a prospect "hard" to listen to, much less accept and embrace. Their reaction is like Peter's in Mark, when Jesus predicted his own death, Peter "rebuked" him, and Jesus in turn "rebuked" Peter, calling him "Satan" (Mk 8:32-33), and in Matthew, where Peter added, "God forbid it, Lord! This must never happen to you" (Mt 16:22, NRSV), and Jesus called Peter both "Satan" and a "stumbling block" (16:23).[7] Ironically, as we will see, Peter's reaction in John's Gospel is exactly the opposite (vv. 68-69). The onus that falls on Peter in Matthew and Mark falls here on the undefined "many" who stumbled at Jesus' words.

62 "So then," Jesus continues, "if you see the Son of man going up[8] where he was at first. . . ." The implication of the unfinished question is "What then?"[9] But does he mean to say that if they saw "the Son of man go-

---

4. Gr. σκληρός.

5. The language recalls that of Mark's Gospel, when Jesus came to know "in his spirit" (τῷ πνεύματι αὐτοῦ) that certain scribes were questioning "in themselves" or "in their hearts" his authority to forgive sins (Mk 2:8), and when he knew "within himself" (ἐν ἑαυτῷ) that power had gone out from his body to heal the woman with the issue of blood (Mk 5:30).

6. The point of this verb "stumble" (σκανδαλίζει) is not so much that they were angry (BDAG, 926 [2]), as that out of fear they were tempted to turn away from any commitment to him (as in 16:1; see BDAG, 926 [1]), which in fact they did (see v. 66).

7. The meaning of "stumbling block" (σκάνδαλον) is the same as here (see n. 6): Peter was attempting to turn Jesus away from that to which God had called him.

8. Gr. ἀναβαίνοντα.

9. The construction is one kind of ellipsis, "the omission of the apodosis to a conditional subordinate clause" (BDF, §482); also Abbott, *Johannine Grammar*, 175).

ing up," they would *no longer* be troubled?[10] Or that they would be *even more* troubled than they are?[11] Or is he being intentionally ambiguous?[12] There is no ambiguity here. The pronouncement is linked to Jesus' claim that he has "come down from heaven" (vv. 38, 41, 42; also implicitly, vv. 33, 58). If they were to see Jesus "going up where he was at first," it would demonstrate that his claim was true. The reader knows what they do not: that Jesus (and he alone) has "gone up to heaven" (3:13), that only he "has seen the Father" (6:46), and consequently that his claim is indeed true (see also 20:17). The phrase "where he was at first" reaches all the way back to the Gospel's opening glimpse of "the Word" who was "with God in the beginning" (1:2). A glimpse of him "with God" again at the end would reassure these "disciples" at Capernaum that death, whether his or theirs, was not something to fear. No such visible demonstration is promised, however. All they have to go on is Jesus' spoken "word" (v. 60), "hard" though it may be, and what he requires of them is faith in him, and in that "word."[13]

63 "The Spirit is that which makes alive;[14] the flesh accomplishes nothing," Jesus continues. "The words I have spoken to you are spirit, and they are life." He has already assigned the work of "bringing to life" or "making alive" to the Father, and consequently to the Son, associating it closely with "raising the dead" (5:21). Here too it suggests resurrection, echoing Jesus' repeated promise, "I will raise it [or him] up at the last day" (vv. 39, 40, 44, 54). But what is different is the role of "the Spirit" in "making alive," or raising the dead. Nowhere else in John's Gospel is this connection explicitly made,[15] yet

---

10. For example, Odeberg, *The Fourth Gospel,* 267-68; Hoskyns, 300-301; Lindars, 273; also Moloney, but with the proviso that he has no need to prove himself by ascending visibly to heaven because he came from there in the first place (228, 231; also *The Johannine Son of Man,* 122-23).

11. So Bultmann (445), who interprets "going up" not as resurrection or ascension but as crucifixion, confusing ἀναβαίνειν ("going up," see 3:13) with ὑψωθῆναι (being "lifted up," 3:14). As Bernard points out, the former "never refers to the Crucifixion, but to the Ascension" (1.217).

12. So Westcott, 1.247; Schnackenburg, 2.71; Barrett, 303; and with some hesitation Morris, 339.

13. The expression "where he was at first" (ὅπου ἦν τὸ πρότερον, v. 62) need not prompt an explicit connection between "this word" (ὁ λόγος οὗτος, v. 60) and the opening verses of the Gospel is uncertain. The one *explicitly* in view here is the preexistent "Son of man" (3:13), not the preexistent "Word," or λόγος, even though the reader knows they are the same person.

14. Gr. τὸ πνεῦμα ἐστιν τὸ ζωοποιοῦν. For a similar construction, see 1 John 5:6: "The Spirit is that which testifies" (τὸ πνεῦμα ἐστιν τὸ μαρτυροῦν). In keeping with Johannine usage generally, we have capitalized "Spirit."

15. See 20:22, however, where "Holy Spirit" coming as breath from Jesus' mouth (like the breath of God in Gen 2:7) becomes the *evidence* that Jesus is alive, risen from the

anyone familiar with the Old Testament (for example, Gen 2:7; Ezek 37:5) or with Paul's letters[16] will find it unsurprising.

Here "the Spirit" is contrasted to "the flesh" (a term carried over from vv. 51-56), recalling Jesus' comment to Nicodemus that "What is born of the flesh is flesh, and what is born of the Spirit is spirit" (3:6). In much the same vein, Jesus now insists that "the flesh accomplishes nothing."[17] This poses a serious problem for many interpreters because it seems to undercut Jesus' insistence just expressed that "Unless you eat the flesh of the Son of man and drink his blood, you do not have life in yourselves" (v. 53), and that "The person who eats my flesh and drinks my blood dwells in me, and I in him" (v. 56).[18] Especially those committed to a sacramental interpretation of verses 53-58 complain that Jesus seems to be giving them something with one hand only to take it back with the other. Raymond Brown, for example, unable to explain "how the absolute statement, 'The flesh is useless,' could ever have been said of the eucharistic flesh of Jesus," admits to having "interpreted 60-71 as if these verses had no reference to 51-58."[19] But a solution presents itself if we go back to Jesus' first use of the word "flesh" (v. 51):

---

dead, and able to give life to his disciples. Moreover, a comparison of 4:14 with 7:37-39 suggests that "life eternal" and "Spirit" are (or can be) equivalent terms in this Gospel.

16. See 2 Cor 3:6, "For the letter kills, but the Spirit gives life" (τὸ δὲ πνεῦμα ζῳοποιεῖ); 1 Cor 15:45, where Christ himself ("the last Adam") is identified as "life-giving Spirit" (εἰς πνεῦμα ζῳοποιοῦν); Rom 8:10-11, "If Christ is in you, the body is dead because of sin, but the Spirit is life [τὸ δὲ πνεῦμα ζωή] because of righteousness. And if the Spirit of him who raised Jesus from the dead dwells in you, he who raised Christ from the dead will also bring to life [ζῳοποιήσει] your mortal bodies through the Spirit that dwells in you" (also 1 Pet 3:18, "put to death in the flesh, made alive [ζῳοποιηθείς] in the Spirit").

17. Gr. ἡ σάρξ οὐκ ὠφελεῖ οὐδέν. The form of the pronouncement recalls Mk 14:38, "The spirit is willing, but the flesh is weak" (τὸ μὲν πνεῦμα πρόθυμον, ἡ δὲ σάρξ ἀσθενής), and it may well be traditional. Yet the meaning here is quite different.

18. See, for example, Schnackenburg (2.72), who explains that "the statement about the πνεῦμα receives all the emphasis, and the remark about the σάρξ is added to highlight the statement about the πνεῦμα." See also Barrett, 284, 304; Moloney, 231; Beasley-Murray, 96.

19. On this point Brown, following G. Bornkamm, "Die eucharistische Rede im Johannes-Evangelium," ZNW 47 (1956), 161-69, comments further that "51-58 is a later editorial insertion of Johannine material breaking up the unity that once existed between 35-50 and 60-71," without "any real attempt to give a new orientation to 60-71 in light of this addition" (1.302-3). Bultmann, even though he shares much the same assessment of verses 51-58, also entertains the possibility that verse 63a was something *Jesus' disciples* were saying. Thus, "*You say,* 'The Spirit is that which makes alive; the flesh accomplishes nothing,' but *I say,* 'The words I have spoken to you are spirit, and they are life'" (446). At the same time he weakens the case by citing 4:35, where Jesus, quoting something said by others, makes it very explicit: "Do you not say? . . . Look, I say to you."

"and the bread I will give him is my flesh for the life of the world." There, as we saw, "my flesh" was a metaphor for Jesus' *death* "for the life of the world." Here, the point is that "flesh" is no good without "Spirit," that is, death even for a noble cause "accomplishes nothing" — *unless* it is followed by resurrection. Martyrdom for martyrdom's sake, without hope of vindication, is sheer futility, but Jesus has promised vindication, not once but over and over again: "never go hungry," and "never ever thirst" (v. 35), "never cast out" (v. 37), "raise it up at the last day" (v. 39), "have life eternal," and "raise him up at the last day" (v. 40), "raise him up at the last day" (v. 44), "has life eternal" (v. 47), "will live forever" (v. 51), "has life eternal," and "raise him up at the last day" (v. 54), "dwells in me, and I in him" (v. 56), "will live because of me" (v. 57), and "will live forever" (v. 58).

Jesus' "word" (v. 60) sounded "hard" to these would-be disciples because it seemed to be all about "flesh," and consequently all about death. On the contrary, he now claims, "The words[20] I have spoken to you are spirit, and they are life." Not "flesh," but "spirit"[21] — not "death," but "life." It is true that life comes only through death, whether his or theirs (see 12:24), and this they find disturbing, but the other side of the truth is that death is not the last word. In resurrection, "life" trumps "death," and "the Spirit that makes alive" trumps "the flesh." Jesus invites these "disciples" to hear his words in faith as "spirit" and as "life," but he knows already that some of them will not.

64 Jesus now unmasks the unbelief of these so-called "disciples," just as he unmasked the unbelief of "the crowd" here at Capernaum (v. 36) of "the Jews" earlier at Jerusalem (5:38), and of Nicodemus and his friends even before that (3:11-12). His words are gentler this time, and less sweeping, for there are only "some of you," he says, "who do not believe," fewer perhaps than the "many" who "stumbled" at his message (v. 60). The Gospel writer takes the opportunity to add a narrative aside, calling attention once again (as, for example, in v. 6) to Jesus' foreknowledge: "For Jesus knew from the beginning who they are who do not believe, and who it is who will hand him over."[22] Possibly the writer has in mind already the charge that Jesus was unable to retain the loyalty of his own disciples because they all deserted him at his arrest and one of them handed him over to his enemies.[23] The narrative aside makes it clear that none of this took Jesus

---

20. Gr. τὰ ῥήματα.
21. Here we have not capitalized "spirit" (πνεῦμα, without the article), because it appears not to refer to the Holy Spirit per se, as at the beginning of the verse (τὸ πνεῦμα), but to Jesus' words as the Spirit's instrument.
22. That Jesus "knew" (ᾔδει γάρ) who would hand him over to death is echoed in 13:11 (ᾔδει γὰρ τὸν παραδιδόντα αὐτόν; see also the repeated use of the participle "knowing" (εἰδώς) in relation to the events of Jesus' passion (13:1, 3; 18:4; 19:28).
23. Origen cites a Jewish objection (introduced by the pagan Celsus) that must

by surprise, but that all of it was within his knowledge and part of God the Father's plan. The definite "who they are" echoes the indefinite "some of you" from the preceding clause, implying that Jesus knew more specifically than he was telling just who the unbelievers were. The phrase "from the beginning" looks back from the standpoint of the Gospel writer and his readers at Jesus' ministry in its entirety, not at some specific starting point within his ministry.[24] Consequently, it includes even those who "do not believe" in the writer's own time (that is, who they *are*[25] who do not believe). It is virtually equivalent to "beforehand" or "ahead of time," and makes no claim about what Jesus might have known from his baptism or his birth, much less from all eternity.[26]

If Jesus' knowledge of who did not or does not believe looks very generally at the past and the present (see 3:11-12; 5:38; 6:36), his knowledge of "who it is who will hand him over"[27] looks at a specific event in Jesus' future. It has become customary to translate this verb as "betray," but in itself the verb does not connote treachery. Jesus will be "handed over" more than once in this Gospel, and in different ways (see, for example, 18:30, 35, 36; 19:16).[28] Here it is a matter of one person handing Jesus over, and readers familiar with the story from this Gospel or any other will know that he is referring to Judas Iscariot. It is the first hint of Jesus being "handed over" by Judas, but many others will follow (see v. 71; also 12:4; 13:2, 11, 21; 18:2, 5; 21:20). Readers unfamiliar with that story might recall an earlier notice that the Jerusalem authorities were "pursuing Jesus" and "trying to kill him" (5:16, 18), and perhaps conjecture that someone among his disciples was planning to "hand him over," but who, and how, and to what end would still remain a mystery to them.

65 The writer returns to Jesus' direct speech, which builds of course on what he has just said (v. 64a, "But there are some of you who do not be-

---

have been current already in the first century, to the effect that "he who was a God could neither flee nor be led away a prisoner; and least of all could he be deserted and delivered up by those who had been his associates, and had shared all things in common, and had had him for their teacher" (*Against Celsus* 2.9; ANF, 4.433).

24. See 16:4, where Jesus himself introduces the same term, ἐξ ἀρχῆς, to refer to the whole time during which "I was with you" (also, perhaps, ἀπ' ἀρχῆς, "from the beginning," in 15:27; 1 Jn 1:1; 2:7; 3:11; Lk 1:2).

25. Gr. εἰσίν (present tense).

26. Consequently, it has no relation to the Gospel's opening phrase, "in the beginning" (ἐν ἀρχῇ, 1:1-2).

27. Gr. ὁ παραδώσων, a rare future participle.

28. According to BDAG (762), borrowing the language of Raymond Brown (*Death of the Messiah*, 1.211-13), the translation "betray" tends to "blur the parallelism of Judas' action to the agency of others in the passion narrative."

lieve"), not on the writer's narrative aside. Jesus "went on to say,²⁹ 'This is why I have told you that no one can come to me unless it is given him from the Father.'" When had he told them that? Never in exactly those words, but the quotation is indirect, not direct, and verse 44 is close enough: "No one can come to me unless the Father who sent me draw him." Only the "unless" clause is different in the two pronouncements. Instead of "unless the Father who sent me draw him," Jesus now says, "unless it is given him from the Father," recalling the principle first laid down by John to his disciples three chapters earlier, "A person cannot receive anything unless it is given him from heaven" (3:27). The two pronouncements (all three, in fact) can fairly be regarded as amounting to the same thing. Having interpreted the harsh metaphor of people being "drawn" or "dragged" to God as being "taught by God" or "learning from the Father" (v. 45), Jesus now dissolves the metaphor altogether in favor of John's broader appeal to that which is "given" from heaven (3:27), or, in Jesus' own words, "from the Father."

More striking is the pronoun "you." "I have told *you*," Jesus says (my italics), even though in verse 44 he was addressing "the Jews" (see v. 41), not "his disciples" as here. This confirms what the reader has long suspected: that Jesus' audience throughout the chapter (and through much of the public ministry) is always the same, whether they are called "the crowd" (vv. 22, 24), or "the Jews" (vv. 41, 42), or "the disciples" (vv. 60, 66). What he says to one group he says to all. They are all potential disciples or believers, yet they do not believe, at least not as a group, and sooner or later their unbelief is unmasked (see 12:37).

66 Like "the crowd" and like "the Jews," these "disciples" do not reply when their unbelief is exposed. Instead, the narrative resumes. "From this"³⁰ could mean "from then on," but it more likely echoes Jesus' phrase "this is why" or "for this reason" (v. 65), and carries much the same meaning: "as a result of this," or "consequently."³¹ What results is that instead of an-

---

29. Gr. καὶ ἔλεγεν. For this translation of the imperfect, see Abbott, *Johannine Grammar*, who cites this as one of two instances (the other being 8:31) in which "ἔλεγε appears to be used by John as in Mark to mean 'began to say,' or 'went on to say,' or 'used to say'" (341). Abbott renders it here as "began to say" (342), but "went on to say" is more appropriate because Jesus is resuming (and in fact concluding) a speech already begun (at v. 61) and momentarily interrupted by the Gospel writer's narrative aside (v. 64b).

30. Gr. ἐκ τούτου.

31. See BDAG, 297; also 19:12, the only other occurrence of this phrase in John's Gospel: "From this [ἐκ τούτου], Pilate kept seeking to release him." The language of the context is curiously similar to that of the present passage. Jesus had just told Pilate, "You would not have any authority against me unless it were given you from above [εἰ μὴ ἦν δεδομένον σοι ἄνωθεν]. That is why [διὰ τοῦτο] the one who handed me over to you [ὁ παραδούς μέ σοι] has greater sin" (19:11; compare v. 65).

swering Jesus, "many of his disciples turned back and would no longer walk with him." We are not told explicitly whether this was an immediate or a long-range result, but Jesus' words to "the Twelve" in the next verse, "Do you also want to go away?" argue strongly that it happened immediately, right at the scene.[32] Without claiming that the "many" coincide exactly with the "many" who first "murmured" and "stumbled" at what they had heard (vv. 60-61), the writer leaves the impression, first, that Jesus has failed to calm their fears, but, second, that he has been proven right on two counts. One is that there are indeed "some . . . who do not believe" (v. 64), and the other is that "no one can come . . . unless it is given him from the Father" (v. 65). They are themselves living proof of it, as they turn and walk away. They have "followed" Jesus (v. 2), "come to him" (v. 5), hailed him as "the prophet" (v. 14), tried to make him king (v. 15), "looked for" him and "found" him (vv. 24-25), but now they "turned back,"[33] an expression with an almost military sound (see 18:6!). The verb is aorist, marking in this instance not a momentary setback but a decisive turning away. The accompanying verb is imperfect: they "would no longer walk with him,"[34] making their defection permanent.

While this is the first (and only) explicit reference in the Gospel to "walking with Jesus" as a metaphor for discipleship, the metaphor itself is natural and inevitable. When the first disciples first laid eyes on Jesus, he was "walking" (1:36), and they immediately "followed" him (1:37). They then accompanied him to Cana and Capernaum (2:1-12), to Jerusalem, Judea, and Samaria (2:13–4:42), possibly[35] back to Cana (4:43-54) and Jerusalem again (5:1-47), and now to the lake of Galilee and to Capernaum. All this can fairly be described as "walking with Jesus," even though the only time he was said to be literally "walking" was on the lake (6:19), where they either met him in a boat (v. 21) or followed later in other boats (vv. 22-24). Later, Jesus will be seen "walking" in Galilee (7:1), in the temple at Jerusalem (10:23), and generally "among the Jews" (see 11:54), inviting all who hear him not to "walk in the darkness" (8:12) but to "walk while you have the light, so darkness will not overtake you" (12:35; see also 11:9-10; 1 Jn 1:6-7; 2:6, 11; 2 Jn 3-4).

---

32. So Bultmann (448, n. 1): "It comes to the same thing whether it is interpreted as 'consequently' (so 19.12) or as 'from now on.' At all events it is not a gradual development that is in mind, but an apostasy that is now taking place."

33. Gr. ἀπῆλθον εἰς τὰ ὀπίσω.

34. "Walk" is περιεπάτουν. The imperfect here has a futuristic cast to it (see BDF, §323[4]), describing what would be the practice of these failed disciples from this point on. The translation "would no longer walk with him" brings out this future aspect, while at the same time hinting that it was a matter of their conscious choice.

35. Only "possibly" because Jesus' disciples were not explicitly mentioned between 4:38 and 6:3.

"Walking" becomes a metaphor for living one's life,[36] "walking with Jesus" or "walking in the light" a metaphor for being his disciple,[37] and "walking in darkness" a metaphor for unbelief. When these disciples "turned back and would no longer walk with him," the writer implies, they stopped "walking in the light," and began to "walk in darkness."[38]

67 Jesus now addresses a group he calls "the Twelve," introducing the term as if he expects the reader to understand who "the Twelve" are. Any reader familiar with even one of the other Gospels will understand, but no other Gospel introduces them so abruptly as this. Matthew mentions them first as "his twelve disciples" (10:1), after having spoken more generally of "his disciples" (5:1; 8:21, 23; 9:10, 11, 14, 19, 37), and then names each of "the twelve apostles" one by one (10:2-4). Mark records that Jesus "appointed twelve" (3:14),[39] and like Matthew he lists their names (3:16-19). Luke has Jesus summoning "his disciples," and then choosing "twelve of them, whom he also named as apostles" (6:13), again listing their names (6:14-16). John's Gospel has no list, and no explanation of who "the Twelve" might be. John's Gospel knows nothing, for example, of any analogy between "the Twelve" and the twelve tribes of Israel (as in Mt 19:28; Lk 22:30). The only disciples named so far have been Andrew (1:40), Simon Peter (1:40, 42), Philip (1:44), and Nathanael (1:45). Judas Iscariot (v. 71), Thomas Didymus (11:16), and another Judas (14:22) will be named later. All these are names familiar from the lists in Matthew, Mark, and Luke, but only Simon Peter (v. 68), Judas (v. 71), and Thomas (20:24) are *explicitly* said to belong to the Twelve. "The sons of Zebedee" (21:2) and one or two others will be singled out but not named. Consequently the reader cannot with any confidence construct a list from John's Gospel alone.[40] Those who are unfamiliar with other Gospels have nothing to go on except the fact that "his disciples" had gathered up "twelve baskets" after Jesus fed the crowd (vv. 12-13), so that possibly "the Twelve" could be the same disciples who had assisted at the feeding, each now carrying a basket of leftover crumbs.[41] In any

---

36. See BDAG, 803.

37. In much the same way, as we have seen (pp. 150-51), "coming to Jesus" and "coming to the Light" (see 3:20-21) are equivalent expressions in this Gospel.

38. What was not true of Jesus' disciples in the boat (v. 17) was true of them: "the darkness overtook them."

39. Some manuscripts of Mark 3:14 add the same words found in Luke, "whom he also named as apostles."

40. If one took the bold step of including such "friends" as Lazarus, Mary, and Martha, as well as Mary Magdalene and "secret" disciples such as Joseph of Arimathea, one would have too many names instead of too few. Still, because there is no list, this Gospel does not exclude women from "the Twelve" quite so explicitly as the others do.

41. This is the case in the other Gospels as well (see Mt 14:20; Mk 6:43; Lk

The Gospel of John

event, Jesus asks the Twelve as a group, "Do you want to go away too?" giving them the freedom to leave with the unbelieving disciples if they so choose.[42]

68-69 They do not so choose. "The Twelve" now come to represent an inner circle of Jesus' disciples who remained faithful (without necessarily implying that they were the *only* faithful disciples).[43] Simon Peter, speaking for the Twelve, replies, "Lord, to whom shall we turn? You have words of life eternal, and we have believed and we know that you are the Holy One of God." Here for the first time in the Gospel a named disciple addresses Jesus as "Lord,"[44] a term just as easily translated "Sir," and used so far only by strangers or those seeking Jesus' help.[45] But from here on only disciples or believers will address him in this way, and (all but twice) with the more confessional meaning, "Lord."[46] Simon Peter asks rhetorically, "To whom shall we turn?" picking up the verb from the preceding reference to those who "turned back" from following Jesus (v. 66). "To whom" leads us to expect an emphatic "you" in the next sentence, but instead the pronouncement puts the phrase "words of life eternal"[47] front and center, echoing Jesus' own claim that "The words I have spoken to you are spirit, and they are life" (v. 63).[48]

The Twelve recognize the life-giving quality of Jesus' words, even if the other disciples do not. Unlike the others, they do not "stumble" at his

---

9:17), but in every case the notice comes well after the twelve apostles have been clearly identified.

42. The deliberative question with μή expects a negative answer (see Abbott, *Johannine Grammar*, 193; also BDF, §427[2]), yet a translation such as "You do not want to go away too, do you?" goes too far toward making the reply a foregone conclusion.

43. Besides new converts such as the man born blind (see 9:38), and devoted friends such as Lazarus, Mary, Martha, and Mary Magalene, Jesus speaks of "other sheep" (10:16) and "the scattered children of God" (11:52).

44. Gr. κύριε.

45. See 4:11, 15, 19; 5:7; 6:34, where we have translated it as "Sir," and 4:49, where because of its prayer-like quality we have rendered it as "Lord." Jesus' disciples have more characteristically addressed him as "Rabbi" (see 1:38, 49; 4:31; also 9:2 and 11:8).

46. See 9:38; 11:3, 12, 21, 27, 32, 34, 39; 13:6, 9, 25, 36, 37; 14:5, 8, 22; 21:15, 16, 17, 20, 21; the two exceptions where "Sir" is appropriate are 9:36 (because the former blind man does not know to whom he is speaking) and 20:15 (because Mary Magdalene mistakes the risen Jesus for the gardener). Jesus explicitly recognizes and accepts his disciples' confessional use of "Lord" in 13:13, "You call me 'Teacher,' and 'Lord,' and you say well, for I am."

47. Gr. ῥήματα ζωῆς αἰωνίου.

48. "Words" (ῥήματα, without the article) is indefinite because the comment is not limited to "the words" (τὰ ῥήματα) Jesus has spoken here at Capernaum promising resurrection and life (see v. 63), but includes as well all that he will say from now on.

6:60-71 JESUS AND HIS DISCIPLES AT CAPERNAUM

words (v. 61), but recognize that "life eternal" comes through death and in no other way. Simon Peter articulates for them their faith in Jesus, and this is where we finally encounter the emphatic pronouns that we expect: "and *we* believe and we know that *you* are the Holy One of God" (v. 69, italics added). Not "I" but "we."[49] Not "Peter's confession" but that of the Twelve.[50] In contrast to those who did "not believe" (v. 64) but "turned back" (v. 66), they "believe" and consequently "know" who Jesus is.[51] The emphatic "*You* are the Holy One of God"[52] recalls Nathanael's confession in the opening chapter ("*You* are the Son of God. *You* are the King of Israel," 1:49), and anticipates Martha's five chapters later ("*You* are the Christ, the Son of God," 11:27, my italics throughout). These passages, plus the parallel synoptic accounts, led some later scribes to modify or elaborate "the Holy One of God" in the direction of more familiar titles such as "the Christ, the Holy One of God," or "the Christ, the Son of God" (as in 11:27 and 20:31), or "the Christ, the Son of the living God" (as in Mt 16:16), but the manuscript evidence for the simpler expression, "the Holy One of God," is overwhelming.[53]

If we can assume that Jesus and the Twelve are still at the synagogue in Capernaum (v. 59), we have an additional irony: "the Holy One of God" is the same title given him by a demoniac, "a man with an unclean spirit," in that same Capernaum synagogue according to Mark (1:24) and Luke (4:34). If so, the confession by the Twelve confirms that "the Holy One of God" exactly describes who Jesus is. In the synoptics, "Holy One" implied ritual and moral purity, making Jesus a terror and a threat to the world of the demonic,

---

49. Compare and contrast Martha's confession, speaking for herself: "Yes, Lord, *I* believe [ἐγὼ πεπίστευκα] that you are the Christ, the Son of God, who is coming into the world" (11:27, my italics).

50. This is the case in the other Gospels as well, where Jesus asks "them" (αὐτούς or αὐτοῖς), "Who do you [ὑμεῖς] say that I am?" (Mt 16:15; Mk 8:29; Lk 9:20), and then charges "them" (αὐτοῖς, Mk 8:30; Lk 9:21) or "the disciples" (Mt 16:20) not to tell anyone. Only Matthew (16:17-19) singles Peter out for special notice or commendation.

51. The perfect tenses of the verbs "believe" (πεπιστεύκαμεν) and "know" (ἐγνώκαμεν) are translated as presents, suggesting a settled conviction and an assured knowledge respectively (see BDF, §341; also Abbott, *Johannine Vocabulary*, 125; *Johannine Grammar*, 345, although his renderings "perfect belief" and "perfect knowledge" are somewhat overstated).

52. Gr. σὺ εἶ ὁ ἅγιος τοῦ θεοῦ.

53. Textual witnesses for the reading "the Holy One of God" include P[75], B, ℵ, C*, D, L, W, Ψ, and others. Of the other alternatives, only "the Christ, the Holy One of God" (with P[66] and certain Coptic versions) has any claim at all to consideration, but looks very much like a partial assimilation to one of the less likely options, such as "the Christ, the Son of God" (with most old Latin and Syriac versions), and "the Christ, the Son of the living God" (with the majority of later manuscripts). See Metzger, *Textual Commentary*, 215.

and all that was impure or unclean. Here the accent is on his having been set apart by God to complete a task. Later, he will identify himself as one "whom the Father consecrated[54] and sent into the world" as "Son of God" (10:36; see also 17:17-19).[55] "The Holy One of God" is virtually synonymous with "the Son of God,"[56] acknowledging and confirming what Jesus himself had said again and again, that the Father "sent" him (vv. 29, 57; also 3:17; 4:34; 5:23, 24, 30, 36, 37, 38; 6:38, 39, 44) to bring "words of life eternal" to those who would listen. Here, at last, are the listeners.

70 Recognizing that Simon Peter was speaking for the Twelve and not just himself, Jesus answered "them" (not just Peter) with a rhetorical question of his own, "Did I not choose you as the Twelve?"[57] and a startling revelation: "And one of you is 'the devil.'" When and where did Jesus "choose"[58] these disciples and designate them as "the Twelve"? Nowhere in this Gospel. Just as the text requires some familiarity with who the Twelve are, so it seems to require familiarity with a story in which Jesus chose or appointed twelve disciples to travel with him and share in his ministry (that is, a story resembling Mk 3:13-19, Mt 10:1-4, and Lk 6:12-16). Only Luke's account uses the verb "choose"; "And when day came, he called his disciples, and having *chosen* twelve of them, he named them also as apostles" (Lk 6:13, my italics). John's Gospel repeats three more times the notion that Jesus "chose" his disciples, each time presumably referring to the same group (13:18; 15:16, 19), yet in contrast to Matthew, Mark, and Luke it never refers to them (even in 13:16) as "apostles," or as "the twelve apostles," and never records an incident in which Jesus "chose" them.

The reader is free either to fill in the gap from prior knowledge of a synoptic-like account, or simply to take the writer's word for it that Jesus "chose" the Twelve, without wondering why or how or under what circumstances. The latter option is not so strange, given that the reader was also left to wonder when and how Jesus had previously "sent" his disciples "to harvest that on which you have not labored" (4:38), and by what process the Fa-

---

54. Gr. ἡγίασεν.

55. See Bultmann, 450: "It must be said that the title ὁ ἅγιος τοῦ θεοῦ also denotes Jesus as the one who has consecrated himself as a sacrifice for the world; vv. 70f. especially have reference to the story of the Passion."

56. In Mark as well the "unclean spirits" further identify Jesus as "the Son of God" (3:11) or "Son of the Most High God" (5:7; see also Lk 4:41; Mt 8:29, Lk 8:28). In John's Gospel, the title is similar to "the Chosen One of God" (ὁ ἐκλέκτος τοῦ θεοῦ), found in some ancient manuscripts of 1:34.

57. The double accusatives ὑμᾶς and τοὺς δώδεκα represent "the *predicate accusative*, really a sort of apposition" (A. T. Robertson, *Grammar,* 480; also BDF, §157): "I have chosen you *as* the Twelve," or "*to be* the Twelve."

58. Gr. ἐξελεξάμην.

6:60-71 JESUS AND HIS DISCIPLES AT CAPERNAUM

ther "gives" or "draws" disciples to Jesus (vv. 37, 39, 44). It appears, in fact, that when Jesus claims that "I have chosen" the Twelve, he is merely claiming to have "received" what the Father has "given" him (see 3:27), for, as he has insisted repeatedly, "the Son can do nothing by himself, except what he sees the Father doing" (5:19), and "I can do nothing by myself" (5:30). Those whom he has "chosen out of the world" (see 15:19) are none other than those whom, he says, the Father "gave me out of the world," adding, "Yours they were, and you gave them to me, and they have kept your word" (17:6). This applies both to his choice of individuals (of which we have seen glimpses, 1:35-51), and to his designation of them as a special group known as "the Twelve" (of which we knew nothing until now). They are Jesus' sovereign choice *because* — not although — they were first of all chosen by the Father.

Why are "the Twelve" mentioned in these few verses but virtually nowhere else in the Gospel?[59] Apparently to heighten the irony and shock of what comes next: "And one of you is the 'devil.'"[60] Not "a devil," as in virtually all English translations, but "the devil," because of the same grammatical rule that dictated "the Word was God" (rather than "a god," 1:1), and "the King [rather than "a king"] of Israel" (1:49), the rule that "definite predicate nouns which precede the verb usually lack the article."[61] Moreover, "a devil" would imply a plurality of devils, something of which the New Testament knows nothing. Demons or unclean spirits are not quite the same thing, and there is no evidence in the Gospels (unless this is it) that any of the Twelve were ever demon possessed. If "devil" (or *diabolos*) is indefinite, the meaning would have to be "One of you is slanderous" or "an accuser,"[62] not "One of you is a devil." Even when it is read as definite, the etymological meaning, "the accuser," lies very close to the surface, for Judas indeed became Jesus' "accuser" to the religious authorities. For this reason I have put "the devil" in quotation marks in the translation. Judas is "the devil" because he does the devil's work.[63] For Jesus to

---

59. The only other instance is the passing notice that Thomas, "one of the Twelve," was not "with them" (μετ' αὐτῶν) when the risen Jesus appeared to the disciples behind locked doors (20:24), with its possible implication that "them" (even without Judas present) may refer to "the Twelve."

60. Gr. καὶ ἐξ ὑμῶν εἷς διάβολός ἐστιν. "And" (καί) is really "and yet," heightening the irony (see BDF, §442[1]).

61. See above, on 1:1. Here the predicate noun διάβολος precedes the verb ἐστιν, and may therefore be read as definite.

62. See BDAG, 226, who lists first the adjectival meaning, "slanderous" (see 1 Tim 3:11; 2 Tim 3:3; Tit 2:3).

63. Flannery O'Connor refers to a character in one of her novels and another in one of her short stories as being "of the Devil because nothing in him resists the Devil. There's not much use to distinguish between them" (*The Habit of Being* [New York: Farrar, Straus & Giroux, 1979], 367).

call him "the devil" here is not so different from calling Simon Peter "Satan" in Matthew (16:23) and in Mark (8:33). There too the etymology of "Satan" as "the Adversary"[64] is clearly at work. On the traditional Jewish principle that "an agent is like the one who sent him," or "the agent of the ruler is like the ruler himself,"[65] someone who does the devil's work is in that sense himself "the devil" or "Satan."[66] The supreme irony of the pronouncement, of course, is that one of "the Twelve," one of those "chosen" — not just by Jesus but by the Father — turns out to be "the devil"! Has Jesus made a mistake? Or has God? For the moment, the issue is left unresolved, but in time Jesus will return to it, with the firm assurance to his disciples that it was no mistake, or as he will put it, "I know whom I have chosen" (13:18).

71 Jesus' pronouncement leads us to expect some reaction from the Twelve, but instead the Gospel writer inserts another of his "narrative asides" (as, for example, in v. 64), explaining that Jesus "meant[67] Judas of Simon Iscariot. For this man, one of the Twelve, was going to hand him over." Here for the first time Judas[68] is named, as "Judas of Simon Iscariot," revealing both his father's name[69] and his place of origin,[70] and at the same time explic-

---

64. See BDAG, 916.

65. See, for example, *m. Berakot* 5.5; and in the Babylonian Talmud, *Baba Meṣi'a* 96a; *Ḥagigah* 10b; *Qiddušin* 42b, 43a; *Baba Qamma* 113b; etc. This principle has been studied mainly for its bearing on the relation between God and Jesus (see K. Rengstorf, *TDNT*, 1.414-20; also P. Borgen, "God's Agent in the Fourth Gospel," 83-95), and it is important in John's Gospel for this reason, yet it is no less applicable to the devil and those who do the devil's work on earth

66. In John's Gospel, see also 8:44 (in relation to "Jews" who had "believed in him," vv. 30-31) and 13:2 (in relation to Judas); also 1 Jn 3:8, 10, and Acts 13:10, where Paul addresses Elymas as "son of the devil" (υἱὲ διαβόλου).

67. Gr. ἔλεγεν. More literally, Jesus "was saying" or "was talking about" Judas (for ἔλεγεν as "meant," see 2:22).

68. It is difficult to say whether or not the name "Judas" (Ἰούδαν, v. 71) is intended to suggest a spiritual kinship with Jesus' interlocutors "the Jews" (οἱ Ἰουδαῖοι, vv. 41, 52), who will themselves eventually be called children of "the devil" (8:44). Clearly, Judas was a Jew, but so were Jesus' other disciples, and one even shared the name "Judas" (see 14:22).

69. "Judas of Simon Iscariot" means "Judas, son of Simon Iscariot," just as in the case of Simon Peter, "Simon the son of John" (1:42) is equivalent to "Simon of John" (21:15, 16, 17). In the case of Peter it was an open question whether "John" was the name of Peter's actual father or whether Jesus was identifying him as a disciple or "son" of John the baptizer. Here, in the absence of evidence to the contrary, it is likely that this otherwise unknown "Simon" was Judas's literal father. Judas is identified in this way again in 13:2 and 26.

70. In the best ancient manuscripts (P[66], P[75], B, C, L, W, etc.), "Iscariot" is in the genitive case (Ἰσκαριώτου), agreeing with "Simon" (Σίμωνος); that is, strictly speaking, Simon (Judas's father) is the one called "Iscariot." This tends to rule out various theories

7:1-13 TO JERUSALEM, OR NOT?

itly identified as "one of the Twelve," and yet as the one who, Jesus knew, would "hand him over" (v. 64), presumably to those who were seeking his life (see 5:18; 7:1). The writer's interest in Judas, particularly in these narrative asides, continues through subsequent chapters as a kind of private conversation with the reader, accenting Jesus' foreknowledge, Judas's motives and his possession by the devil, and the other disciples' ignorance of what he was up to (see 12:4, 6; 13:2, 11, 28-29; 18:5).

Here, of course, the Twelve are not privy to the writer's parenthetical aside, nor can Judas know that he has been singled out. Yet the pronouncement, "And one of you is 'the devil'" (v. 70) should have caused an uproar, and does not. This is where the Twelve should have "kept looking at each other, perplexed as to which one he meant" (13:22), or asked him each in turn, "Is it I, Lord?" (Mt 26:22; also Mk 14:19). Instead, the Gospel writer postpones that moment until much later, when Jesus puts it another way: "Amen, amen, I say to you that one of you will hand me over" (13:21). What triggers the confusion finally is not Jesus' mention of "the devil" (which seems to have gone right over their heads), but the prospect of Jesus being "handed over," something the reader knows about already because of the two narrative asides (vv. 64, 71), but something about which the Twelve are still totally in the dark. Evidently the pronouncement, "And one of you is 'the devil,'" is more for the readers' benefit than theirs, underscoring (as we have seen) the irony that even being "chosen" does not guarantee either faithfulness or salvation.[71] The reader can grasp the irony, but cannot tell whether or not the Twelve did so, for they held their peace.

I. TO JERUSALEM, OR NOT? (7:1-13)

> 1 *And after these things Jesus was walking in Galilee, for he chose not to walk in Judea because the Jews there were seeking to kill*

---

that "Iscariot" was a term of reproach applied to Judas after the fact, in light of his betrayal of Jesus (for example, in relation to assassins known as the *sicarii,* who carried daggers, or to a Hebrew root verb meaning "falsehood" or "deceit"). Judas himself, however, was also called "Iscariot" (ὁ Ἰσκαριώτης, 12:4; see also Mk 14:10; Mt 26:14; Lk 22:3), because his father's home was obviously thought to identify his place of orgin as well. There is fairly wide agreement that "Iscariot" means in Hebrew "a man [אִישׁ] of Kerioth," probably a place in Moab, across the Dead Sea, mentioned in Jeremiah 48:24, 41 and Amos 2:2. This is reflected in the variant reading, απο Καρυωτου, in certain manuscripts here (including ℵ* and Θ), and in Codex D at 12:4; 13:2, 26; 14:22 (here, in place of Ἰσκαριώτου, D has Σκαριωθ, making it simply a rather obscure proper name).

71. See 17:12, "and not one of them is lost except the son of destruction, that the Scripture might be fulfilled."

him. 2 But the Tent festival of the Jews was near. 3 So his brothers said to him, "Leave here, and go to Judea, so that your disciples may see the works you are doing. 4 For no one does anything in secret when he himself seeks to be in the public eye. As long as you are doing these things, reveal yourself to the world." 5 For his brothers did not believe in him. 6 So Jesus said to them, "My time is not yet here, but your time is always ready. 7 The world cannot hate you, but it hates me because I testify about it that its works are evil. 8 You go ahead to the festival. I am not going up to this festival, because my time is not yet fulfilled." 9 And having said these things, he remained in Galilee. 10 But as his brothers went up to the festival, then he too went up, not openly but as it were in secret. 11 So the Jews were seeking him at the festival, and said, "Where is that man?" 12 And there was great murmuring about him among the crowds. Some said that "He is good," but others said, "No, but he deceives the crowd." 13 No one would speak about him publicly, though, for fear of the Jews.

Jesus continues "walking in Galilee," and we may assume that "the Twelve" (6:70) are still with him, in contrast to those who "turned back and would no longer walk with him" (6:66). Yet they are nowhere to be seen. Instead, his interaction is with his brothers, of whom we have heard nothing since 2:12, when we glimpsed his disciples, his brothers, and his mother all together with him for a time in Capernaum. We may assume that he is still in Capernaum, where he has just spoken at some length in the synagogue (see 6:59). There too he confronted "the Jews," who "murmured about him" (6:41) and "quarreled with each other" (6:52), but threatened him with no bodily harm. Now we are reminded that earlier "the Jews" in Jerusalem "began pursuing" him and were "seeking all the more to kill him" (5:16, 18). A note of danger is now sounded, as the whole section (7:1-13) is framed by notices that in Judea "the Jews there were seeking to kill him" (v. 1), and that when Jesus arrived in Judea for the Tent festival "No one would speak about him publicly . . . for fear of the Jews" (v. 13). The question is whether or not he will attend the festival and so put his life in danger. His brothers, apparently ignorant of the danger, urge him to go, and "reveal yourself to the world" (vv. 3-4). He refuses, urging them to go on ahead, but when they had gone "he too went up, not openly but as it were in secret" (v. 10).

Superficially, this scene involving family members recalls Jesus' interaction with his mother at the Cana wedding, where he first seemed to refuse her implied request (2:4), but then went ahead and did what she wanted him to do (2:7-8). Yet the differences far outweigh the parallels. First, the brothers' request is not implicit but very explicit; second, Jesus' refusal is equally explicit — nothing so mysterious as "What is that to me or to you?"

7:1-13 TO JERUSALEM, OR NOT?

(2:4); third, the author tells us in no uncertain terms that his brothers did not believe in him, while his mother's confidence in what he would do (2:5) suggests that she did in fact believe. Even the superficial parallel between "My hour has not yet come" (2:4) and "My time is not yet here" (7:6) breaks down, as we will see, for Jesus immediately adds, "your time is always ready." All the two stories have in common is that Jesus acts on his own initiative, yet in obedience to the Father's will. No one, friend or enemy, believer or unbeliever, stranger or family member can force his hand. And when he arrives in Jerusalem, those who are seeking his life are waiting for him, and the crowds, like those in Galilee, are divided (7:11-13).

1 The new chapter begins, like the two preceding ones (see 5:1 and 6:1), with the phrase "after these things."[1] This time, in contrast to the two preceding occurrences, the phrase marks a turn in the narrative, but not a change of scene, at least not immediately.[2] The notice that Jesus "chose not to walk in Judea"[3] makes it clear that Jesus' itinerary, and indeed his life, is in his own hands (see 1:43, 5:21, 17:24, and 21:22, where the same verb is used).[4] The variant reading, "had no authority" (see n. 3) seems to imply that Jesus was not in control of his own destiny, either because the Jews or the Romans had forbidden him to go there or because that was not his Father's plan. If it is original, it is the only instance in John's Gospel where Jesus is said *not* to have "authority" to do something (contrast 5:27; 10:18; 17:2). Throughout the Gospel he seems thoroughly in control of what happens to him.[5] Also, it makes the question of why Jesus ended up going to Jerusalem

---

1. Gr. μετὰ ταῦτα.

2. Those who want to reverse the order of chapters 5 and 6 can appeal to the fact that if chapter 5 immediately preceded chapter 7, the thought that "the Judeans were seeking to kill him" would have been relatively fresh in the writer's mind (see 5:18). Yet if chapters 5 and 6 were reversed, then there would have to be a change of scene. Instead of "Jesus was walking in Galilee," we would expect "Jesus withdrew into Galilee" (from Jerusalem, the scene of the events in chapter 5). In short, the same problem that now exists in the transition from chapters 5 to 6 would appear in the supposed transition from chapter 5 to chapter 7. Nothing is gained by rearrangement (*contra* Schnackenburg, 2.138).

3. Instead of "chose not to" (οὐ γὰρ ἤθελεν), some ancient witnesses (including W, some of the old Latin, the Curetonian Syriac, and Chrysostom) have it that Jesus "had no authority" (οὐ γὰρ εἶχεν ἐξουσίαν) to "walk in Judea." But the most important ancient manuscripts (including א, B, P66, and P75) have the more familiar ἤθελεν ("chose"), which is probably to be preferred (see Metzger, *Textual Commentary,* 215-16).

4. The verb "chose" (ἤθελεν) is imperfect, pointing not to a momentary decision but to a fixed policy (see Morris, 348-49, who paraphrases it, "purposely stayed away").

5. This posed a problem for John Chrysostom, whose text had this reading: "What sayest thou, O blessed John? Had not He 'power,' who was able to do all that He would?" Chrysostom concluded, "For when he saith that 'He had not power,' he speaketh of Him as a man, doing many things after the manner of men; but when he saith, that He stood in the

after all (v. 10) even more difficult than it would otherwise be. How could he go if he did not have "authority" to do so? For this very reason it is the more difficult reading, and a plausible case can be made for its originality.[6] Scribes could have changed it either to protect Jesus' free will or to avoid the false impression that he was forbidden by either Roman or Jewish decree from returning to Judea. The commonly accepted reading that Jesus "chose" not to go there[7] has the look of a correction. Yet caution is necessary, because in this Gospel the notion that Jesus "chooses" to act, or acts "on his own," is not incompatible with the thought that his "authority" to do so comes from God. The two stand side by side, for example, in 5:21-27, where the Son "brings to life those he wants" (that is, those he so "chooses," v. 21) because the Father "gave to the Son to have life in himself" (v. 26) and "gave him authority to do judgment" (v. 27); also in 10:18, where Jesus declared, "No one takes [my life] from me, but I lay it down on my own; I have authority to lay it down, and I have authority to receive it back. This command I received from my Father." Both readings are thoroughly in keeping with Johannine style, and the overwhelming manuscript evidence in favor of "chose not to" is telling.

If "chose not to" was what the author of John's Gospel wrote, we are left with two possibilities. The first is that the variant reading, "had no authority," was introduced later as a theological refinement, making the point that all Jesus' "choices" were in the Father's hand. The second, and more likely, explanation is that the variant reading was actually *earlier* than the "original" reading: that is, that the author of the Gospel himself found the words "had no authority" in a source he was using (whether written or oral), and because they raised more questions than they answered changed them editorially to "chose not to." This he might well have done in light of his consistent assumption that all of Jesus' "choices" were in keeping with the Father's will, and based on the "authority" the Father had given him.[8]

Those who were "seeking to kill" Jesus are called "the Jews" (as in 5:18), which could also be translated "Judeans" because of the preceding phrase "in Judea," so we have rendered it as "the Jews there" (that is, in Judea). That there were "Jews" in Galilee as well is evident from chapter 6. Here as in chapter 5, however, "the Jews" in view are the religious authorities in Jerusalem (the author could have written "Jerusalem" instead of Judea, but

---

midst of them, and they seized Him not, he showeth to us the power of the Godhead" (*Homilies on St. John* 48; NPNF, 1st ser., 14.173).

6. See, for example, Barrett, 309-10; Lindars, 281; and Schnackenburg, 2.138.

7. Gr. οὐ γὰρ ἤθελεν.

8. For a similar instance in which a rejected variant reading appears to belong to John's source, and therefore to be earlier than John's "original" text, see 1:34, where the reading "Son of God" is to be preferred over "Chosen One of God."

7:1-13 To Jerusalem, or Not?

he prefers the play on words). Despite mounting hostility, and despite the imagery of violent death (see 6:52-58), Jesus' life seems not to have been in danger in Galilee. Now, however, to return to Judea, where he was wanted for "abolishing the Sabbath" and "making himself equal to God" (5:18), is to risk arrest and execution at the hands of the authorities.

2 A notice that "the Tent festival of the Jews was near" (v. 2) signals that Jesus' resolve not to go to Jerusalem is about to be tested,[9] for the Jewish festivals were times when devout Jews were expected to be in Jerusalem if possible.[10] It was tested once before, when we were similarly told, "the Passover, the festival of the Jews, was near" (6:4). Evidently Jesus' determination to avoid Jerusalem was already in effect then, for he did not go to Jerusalem for the festival even though his practice elsewhere in the Gospel is to do so (see 2:13, 5:1, 10:22, and 11:55). The festivals are said to be "of the Jews," probably because the readers are presumed to be largely Gentile Christians unfamiliar with Jewish customs (see also 2:6, "the purification rituals of the Jews"). "Of the Jews" (rather than "of the Judeans") is appropriate here because the festivals were intended for all Jews everywhere, not just those who lived in Judea.

"The Tent festival" (literally, "the tent-pitching festival"),[11] or "Feast of Tabernacles" (NIV), or "festival of Booths" (NRSV), was an autumn festival six months after the Passover,[12] celebrating the harvest (see Lev 23:33-36, 39-43; Deut 16:13-17). It was a time when the people of Israel were told, "Live in booths for seven days: All native-born Israelites are to live in booths, so your descendants will know that I had the Israelites live in booths when I brought them out of Egypt. I am the LORD your God" (Lev 23:42-43, NIV). The first and last days of the festival were especially significant: "The first day is a sacred assembly; do no regular work. For seven days present offerings made to the LORD by fire, and on the eighth day hold a sacred assembly

---

9. The notice is linked to what precedes by a mild adversative (δέ, "but"): Jesus did not want to go to Jerusalem, *but* a reason for going now presented itself.

10. See Deuteronomy 16:16, NRSV: "Three times a year all your males shall appear before the LORD your God at the place that he will choose: at the festival of unleavened bread, at the festival of weeks, and at the festival of booths." Or as Josephus explained it centuries later: "Moreover, when they should have won their fatherland, they were to repair to that city which they would in honour of the temple regard as their metropolis, and there for eight days keep festival" (*Antiquities* 3.245; LCL, 4.435).

11. Gr. ἡ ἑορτὴ ... ἡ σκηνοπηγία. This festival was known in Hebrew simply as סֻכּוֹת ("tents" or "booths").

12. The Passover was to take place "on the fourteenth day of the first month" (Lev 23:4), and the Tent festival on "the fifteenth day of the seventh month" (Lev 23:34). It appears, therefore, that Jesus has by this time been "walking in Galilee" for at least six months (see 6:4, "the Passover . . . was near").

and present an offering made to the LORD by fire. It is the closing assembly; do no regular work" (Lev 23:35-36, NIV).[13] Many interpreters of John's Gospel find considerable significance in the fact that this "Tent festival" is the setting for chapters 7 and 8 (for some interpreters chapters 9 and 10 as well!).[14] But caution is necessary: if the Gospel's readers had to be told that the Tent festival was "the festival of the Jews" (v. 2), any subtle allusions the author might have made to its rituals — for example, the seven-day "Water Libation Ceremony" (see *m. Sukkah* 4.9-10) in 7:37-39, or the "Ceremony of Light" (*Sukkah* 5.3-4) in 8:12 and 9:4[15] — would have been lost on them. So far as we can tell at this point, the only purpose of the reference to the Tent festival is to confront Jesus with a decision. Will he attend the festival or not? For that purpose it could have just as easily have been Passover, or the festival of Weeks as the Tent festival.

3 Jesus' brothers, last seen with him at Capernaum with his mother and his disciples (2:12), now abruptly make an appearance — probably still at Capernaum.[16] "Leave here, and go to Judea," they urge Jesus, "so that your disciples may see the works you are doing" (v. 3). The reference to "your disciples" is odd because, as far as we know, Jesus' "disciples" were with him in Galilee (see 6:3, 5-13, 16-21), and twelve at least are still "walking" with him there (6:60-71). While Jesus was said to have "made disciples" in Judea (see 3:22; 4:1), if they were meant the reader would have expected the brothers to say "your disciples there," or something to that effect.[17] Perhaps a better explanation is that "your disciples" does not refer to a fixed group but simply means "those who hear you" (as perhaps in 6:60), that is, potential rather than actual disciples. The mention of being "in the public eye" and of showing oneself to "the world" (v. 4) suggests that what Jesus' brothers have in mind is not a disclosure to a small group of dedicated followers, but a pub-

---

13. For a detailed glimpse how these instructions were to be carried out in practice in New Testament times and (especially) later, see the tractate *Sukkah* in the Mishnah (Danby, 172-81).

14. See, for example, Moloney, 232-36. He writes, "The celebration of Tabernacles forms the background for 7:1–10:21. However, Jesus' departure from the Temple in 8:59 divides the account of the events that took place during the feast into two parts, 7:1–8:59 and 9:1–10:21" (233).

15. See Moloney, 234-35.

16. As in 2:12, the question of whether "brothers" (ἀδελφοί) included sisters as well remains an open one.

17. That Jesus did in fact have disciples in or around Jerusalem is of course a distinct possibility even apart from the present reference. Mary, Martha, and Lazarus are, of course, primary examples (see 11:5). But also (in addition to 3:22 and 4:1, and leaving aside 2:23-25 and 8:30-31), there is mention of a garden across the Kedron where Jesus had "often gathered . . . with his disciples" (18:2), and one of his unnamed disciples is said to have been "known to the High Priest" (18:15).

lic appearance at a very public religious festival.[18] When they speak of "the works that you do," it cannot be assumed that they are asking Jesus to perform miracles — or at least that they are asking *only* for miracles. Just as Jesus' "signs" are not limited to miracles but attribute revelatory significance to everything he did (see 12:37; 20:30), so his "works" are not limited to miracles but identify everything he did as that which the Father sent him to do (see 4:34; 5:17, 20, 36).[19]

4 Jesus' brothers now go on to make their case: "For no one does anything in secret[20] when he himself seeks to be in the public eye.[21] As long as you are doing these things, reveal yourself[22] to the world" (v. 4). The accent on "he himself" is odd, and seemed odd to later scribes,[23] but the point is probably the contrast between things done and the person doing them: that is, a person who wants to *be* "in the public eye" should *do* things that bring this about.[24]

This appears to be simply his brothers' version of something Jesus himself said four chapters earlier: "Whoever does the truth comes to the Light, so that his works will be revealed as works wrought in God" (3:21). It also echoes certain pronouncements of Jesus in the other Gospels, above all "Let your light so shine before the people that they might see your good works and glorify your Father in the heavens" (Mt 5:16; also 5:14-15; Mk 4:21-22; Lk 8:16-17; 11:33). There is nothing wrong with asking him to "reveal yourself to the world," for this was clearly his purpose from the start (see, for example, 1:9-10; 3:16-17), and it is exactly what he will do as the chapter moves along.[25]

---

18. Chrysostom's comment points in the same direction: "But who are those that they call disciples here? The crowd that followed Him, not the twelve" (*Homilies on St. John* 48; NPNF, 1st ser., 14.174).

19. Because "signs" (σημεῖα) and "works" (ἔργα) are less important to the Gospel writer than the verb "to do" (ποιεῖν), the request of Jesus' brothers could almost be paraphrased, "Go to Judea, so that your disciples may see *what you do*" (my italics; see v. 4, "As long as you are *doing* these things . . .").

20. Gr. ἐν κρυπτῷ.

21. Gr. ἐν παρρησίᾳ, literally "in the open," or "boldly."

22. Gr. φανέρωσον σεαυτὸν.

23. Instead of "he himself" (αὐτός), some ancient manuscripts (including B and P[66]) have "it" (αὐτό), yielding the translation, "For no one does anything in secret and seeks for *it* to be in the public eye" (my italics). But αὐτός has wider support, including P[66c], P[75], ℵ, and the majority of ancient witnesses, and should probably be retained (see Metzger, *Textual Commentary*, 216; Abbott, *Johannine Grammar*, 564).

24. Abbott (*Johannine Grammar*, 564) comments that "there is probably a contrast between the *'works'* mentioned in vii.3 . . . and the *worker* ('himself') — as in x. 38 ('Even if ye believe not *me*, believe the *works*,' and comp. xiv. 11)."

25. See, for example, v. 26, "And look, he is speaking publicly [παρρησίᾳ], and they are saying nothing to him"; also 18:20, "I have spoken publicly [παρρησίᾳ] to the

5 If this is the case, why does the Gospel writer intervene in such a way as to imply that the brothers' request was somehow misguided or wrongheaded, with the comment, "For his brothers did not believe in him" (v. 5)?[26] The purpose of the narrative aside is not so much to call into question the validity of their request as to explain and justify Jesus' answer (vv. 6-8). There is no reason to doubt their good brotherly intentions — no implication, for example, that they wanted him to go to Judea so that he would be arrested and killed.[27] Still, this is the only explicit statement in any of the Gospels that Jesus' brothers or sisters did not believe in him during his ministry. It is hard to tell whether the Gospel writer has independent knowledge that this was the case, or whether it is simply an inference from such stories in the Gospel tradition as Mark 3:31-35, or such sayings as Mark 6:4 ("A prophet is not without honor except in his hometown and among his kindred, and in his family"). If the author was indeed "the disciple whom Jesus loved" who took Jesus' mother to his own home (see 19:25-27; 21:24), and obviously if he was *himself* one of Jesus' brothers (see Introduction), he would have had independent knowledge. Even if not, he would not have to have known other Gospel traditions, but might simply have inferred it from Jesus' words that immediately follow (vv. 6-7). Why would Jesus say such things to his own brothers unless he knew for certain that they "did not believe in him"?

6-7 What he said was "My time is not yet here, but your time is always ready" (v. 6), and then "The world cannot hate you, but it hates me because I testify about it that its works are evil" (v. 7). The second pronouncements does seem to imply that Jesus' brothers are in fact unbelievers. Here for the first time in the Gospel, Jesus speaks of "the world"[28] not as the object of God's love and salvation (as in 3:16, 17; 4:42; 6:33, 51), but as God's enemy. Finally, the principle articulated at the outset that "the world did not know him" (1:10) comes to expression on Jesus' own lips. Later, he will tell his disciples, "If the world hates you, you know that it hated me first. If you were from the world, the world would love its own. But because you are not from the world, but I have chosen you out of the world, for this reason the world hates you" (15:18-19; see also 17:14, "I have given them your word, and the world hated them, because they are not of the world even as I am not

---

world [τῷ κόσμῳ]; I always taught in synagogue and in the temple, where all the Jews come together, and I spoke nothing in secret" (ἐν κρυπτῷ).

26. Not surprisingly, one ancient manuscript (D), and several old Latin and Syriac versions, add "then" (τότε), on the grounds that at least two of Jesus' brothers, James (see Gal 1:19) and Jude (Jude 1), were known to have been believers after Jesus' resurrection (see 1 Cor 15:7, "then he appeared to James").

27. One could infer this from the contrast to chapter 11, where his disciples did *not* want him to go to Judea because "the Judeans are now seeking to stone you" (11:8).

28. Gr. ὁ κόσμος.

of the world"). If Jesus' brothers were also believers or disciples, the world would hate them too, but it does not. In contrast to the Twelve he has "chosen" (see 6:70), they belong to "the world" and not to God.

The first pronouncement, "My time is not yet here, but your time is always ready" (v. 6), does not have quite the same impact. For some interpreters, it recalls an earlier scene in which Jesus told his mother, "My hour has not yet come" (2:4). The two situations have often been compared. In both instances there is a request, explicit or implicit, from one or more relatives of Jesus. Both times he at first seems to refuse because his time has not come, but then accedes to the request. Yet Jesus' mother did not explicitly ask for anything, but only pointed out, "They have no wine" (2:3). Nor did Jesus unambiguously refuse to act, saying only "What is that to me or to you, woman?" (2:4). Nor is his mother said to be an unbeliever. Her actions indicate the contrary as she instructs the servants, "Do whatever he tells you" (2:5). Even the parallel between "My hour has not yet come" (2:4) and "My time is not yet here" (7:6) is not quite what it seems. Jesus' "hour," as we have seen, at least hinted at his death on the cross, while "time," or "the right time,"[29] does not. What it does imply is that *all* Jesus' movements, all his comings and goings, are in the hands of the Father, because the Father has sent him into the world (see 3:17, 34; 5:36, 38; 6:57). This is not true of his brothers, because they are not similarly "sent." Instead, they are part of "the world" to which Jesus was sent. In the language of today, they are part of the problem, not part of the solution. While the only uses of *kairos* in John's Gospel are here and in verse 8, Jesus makes clear in other situations that his itinerary is in God's hands, not his own. This was evident in his abrupt decision to abandon a fruitful baptizing ministry in Judea and return to Galilee (4:1-3), and will be evident again in his haste to heal at once a man blind since birth, even though it was the Sabbath (see 9:4, 14), and his decision to wait two days until his friend Lazarus died, and then to go quickly despite the danger of arrest and stoning (11:6-10).[30] Such choices are not "logical" in any human terms, but to Jesus they are necessary and inevitable. The timing of his actions matters because he belongs to God. The timing of his brothers' actions does not matter; their "right time" is any time because they have no mission from God but still belong to "the world."

29. Gr. καιρός.
30. In each of the latter two instances, Jesus is very conscious of time (without using the word καιρός). In the first he justifies his urgency with the comment, "We must work the works of him who sent me while it is day. Night is coming when no one can work" (9:4). In the second he tells his disciples, "Are there not twelve hours in a day? If anyone walks during the day, he does not stumble, because he sees the light of this world. But if anyone walks at night, he stumbles because the light is not in him" (11:9-10; see also 12:35-36).

The Gospel of John

Jesus goes on to explain why the world hates him: "because I testify about it that its works are evil" (v. 7). His response echoes the vocabulary of his brothers' request. They had asked him to let those in Judea "see your works" (v. 3), and to reveal himself "to the world" (v. 4), using "world" in a morally neutral sense. Jesus picks up both words, characterizing both "the world" and *its* "works" (in contrast to his own) as evil. Only against the background of that negative testimony can he grant their request to "reveal yourself to the world" (v. 4). He will reveal himself in due course, but in his own way and his own time.

8-9 "*You* go ahead to the festival," Jesus continues. "*I* am not going up to this festival, because my time is not yet fulfilled" (italics added).[31] He understands "go to Judea" (v. 3) to mean "go up to Jerusalem" (as in 2:13; 5:1; 11:55), that is, as a worshiper at the festival (see also 12:20). This he declines to do, and the Gospel writer is quick to tell us that he kept his word and "remained in Galilee" (v. 9), continuing his fixed policy of avoiding Judea and Jerusalem (see v. 1). If the categorical statement, "I am not going up to this festival," is original, it creates an odd situation in which Jesus says one thing (v. 8) and does another (v. 10).

It is difficult to say just how long Jesus "remained in Galilee" (v. 9). That obviously depends on how "near" the Tent festival was (v. 2). To the Gospel writer it is an interval at least worth mentioning, possibly corresponding to other such intervals when Jesus "remained" somewhere outside Jerusalem for a short time, usually with his disciples.[32] In any event, it stands as a buffer between "I am not going up to this festival" (v. 8), and "then he too went up" (v. 10). The writer wants us to understand that Jesus stood by his promise, at least for a brief time! One way of clearing Jesus of the charge of duplicity has been the suggestion that when he says, "I am not going up to this festival," he is

---

31. The pronouns "you" (ὑμεῖς) and "I" (ἐγώ) are emphatic. Instead of "not" (οὐκ), a number of significant ancient manuscripts (including P66, P75, B, L, W, and the majority of later manuscripts) have "not yet" (οὔπω), yielding the translation, "I am not *yet* going up to this festival." This is obviously an "easier" reading than the text our translation has followed, in view of Jesus' abrupt change of plan two verses later, but for that very reason it is suspect. While the textual support for the reading, "I am not going up to this festival," is slightly less strong (with ℵ, D, K, most of the Latin versions, and the earliest Syriac versions), it is more likely original because it is easy to see why scribes might have changed it to "not yet" (in light of v. 10). On the other hand, if "not yet" (οὔπω) were original, it is difficult to see why scribes would have changed it. Even if it was not inserted to alleviate a difficulty, οὔπω could have been inserted simply to correspond to οὔπω in the latter half of the verse ("because my time is not yet fulfilled") (see P66, which calls attention to the parallel by using οὔπω in the first instance and οὐδέπω in the second). See Metzger, *Textual Commentary*, 216; Abbott, *Johannine Grammar*, 210.

32. For example, 1:39 ("that day"), 2:12 ("a few days"), 4:40 ("two days"), 10:40 (unspecified), 11:6 ("two days"), and 11:54 (unspecified).

7:1-13 TO JERUSALEM, OR NOT?

using the verb "go up"[33] in the same loaded sense as in 3:13 and 6:62: that is, "I am not ascending [to heaven] at this festival."[34] But this does not work, for Jesus would still be misleading his brothers into thinking that he was not "going up" to Jerusalem in the idiomatic sense of making a trip there to participate in the Tent festival.[35] One customarily "went up" to Jerusalem, not only because it was situated at a higher elevation than most (though not all) places in Judea and Galilee, but because it was the seat of the temple, where the people drew near to heaven and to God. Jesus gives no hint that his "ascent" to the holy place would be any different from that of his brothers. Instead, he states clearly his reason for not going: "because my time is not yet fulfilled" (v. 9).[36] Here it is even more tempting than in verse 6 to interpret his "time" as the "hour" of his death, but the temptation should be resisted. He is not saying to his brothers (or even to the reader) that if he goes to the festival he will die. The reader will soon learn that he did go to the festival and yet did *not* die (see 7:30; 8:20, 59). His point is the same as before (v. 6), that his "times" are in the Father's hands, not his own, and certainly not in the hands of his Galilean brothers. He will "go up to Jerusalem" only if, and only when, the Father dictates.

10 After an unspecified interval during which he "remained in Galilee" (v. 9), we are told that "he too went up, not openly but as it were in secret" (v. 10). What triggers his change of plan is that "his brothers went up to the festival," just as he had urged them to (see v. 8). He and they, and possibly his disciples, had been together in Galilee, just as they were earlier, after the miracle at Cana (see 2:12), but now he intentionally distances himself from them, evidently because they belong to "the world" (v. 7). He was not so much refusing to go up to the Tent festival as refusing to go up *with them*.

---

33. Gr. ἀναβαίνειν.

34. See, for example, Brown, 1.308; Hoskyns, 313. They might plausibly have appealed to Luke 9:51 ("when the days had been fulfilled for him to be taken up, he himself set his face to go to Jerusalem"), but they do not.

35. So Schnackenburg (2.143), who recognizes that ἀναβαίνω "must mean the same as Jesus' brothers going up to the feast (vv. 8a, 10). There is no room for a double meaning in this instance." It can be added that ἀναβαίνειν ("to go up") is no more evocative of Jesus' death and resurrection than is the simple verb "to go" that his brothers used previously (ὑπάγε, v. 3; see, for example, v. 33; also 8:21, 22; 13:33; 14:4, 28; 16:10, 17). It is less so, in fact, for, as Lindars notices, "John's usual language for the Passion is that of 'going,'" not of "going up" (285). Even when Jesus' death is viewed as an ascent, the classic Johannine term is not "going up" (ἀναβαίνειν) but being "lifted up" (ὑψωθῆναι; see 3:14, 8:28; 12:23, 32).

36. That is, there is no real difference between "My time is not yet here" (οὔπω πάρεστιν, v. 6) and "my time is not yet fulfilled" (οὔπω πεπλήρωται, v. 8); see Mark 1:15, "the time is fulfilled [πεπλήρωται ὁ καιρός], and the kingdom of God has come near." The passive πεπλήρωται points to God as the One who brings to completion or "fulfills" the time (see G. Delling in *TDNT*, 6.294-95).

Whether he goes alone or with his disciples is uncertain. If his disciples accompany him, it is as silent partners, not as participants in what transpires. But what does it mean to go to the festival "not openly,"[37] but "as it were in secret"?[38] "As it were" offers a subtle qualification of the secrecy of Jesus' visit, inviting the question: In what sense was it "in secret"?[39] Would Jesus go to Jerusalem but not attend the festival? Would he attend the festival but make no public appearance? Would he make an appearance but not be recognized? Such questions go unanswered for now, but will be answered later on. All the reader knows at this point is that in going up to the festival Jesus is still not acceding to his brothers' request (vv. 3-4). They wanted him to "reveal" himself to the world (v. 4), but he goes to the festival "not openly." They did *not* want him to act "in secret" (v. 4), but he goes "as it were in secret." The reader wonders, Did he conceal his very presence at Jerusalem, or did he simply conceal his identity? We are not yet told.

11 There is more to Jesus' secrecy than defiance of his brothers. It is still true that Judea is dangerous territory because "the Jews there were seeking to kill him" (v. 1), and secrecy (however understood) will help Jesus avoid arrest and execution. Lest we forget, the Gospel writer reminds us that "the Jews were seeking him at the festival, and said, 'Where is that man?'"[40] The pursuit of Jesus that began at his last visit to Jerusalem (5:18) continues. The danger mounts and the drama builds as we are given almost simultaneous glimpses of Jesus going up to the festival "in secret," and the Jewish authorities in Jerusalem looking for him there with evil intent.

---

37. Gr. οὐ φανερῶς.

38. Gr. ὡς ἐν κρυπτῷ.

39. "As it were" (ὡς) is omitted in certain ancient manuscripts (including ℵ, D, and some of the old Latin and Syriac versions), but its presence in P⁶⁶, P⁷⁵, B, L, and other Latin and Syriac versions, plus the majority of later manuscripts, argues strongly for its retention. "As it were" tacitly acknowledges that the reader is not expected to know exactly what Jesus' "secrecy" may have entailed. Regarding ὡς, Abbott comments, "The particle may be a short way of saying 'people might call it so,' and it is perhaps inserted with a view to the vindication of the Johannine view of the publicity of Christ's life, as in xviii.20, 'In secret spake I nothing'; and in this very feast Christ is described as (vii.26) 'speaking openly (παρρησίᾳ),' and (vii.28) 'he cried aloud in the temple teaching'" (*Johannine Grammar*, 171).

40. The designation "that man" (ἐκεῖνος) recalls the situation in chapter 5 when the man Jesus had healed at the pool first identified Jesus as "that man" (ἐκεῖνος) who had told him to "Pick up your mat and walk" (5:11), leading the authorities to begin pursuing Jesus. While Jesus and the Gospel writer consistently use the pronoun ἐκεῖνος in a neutral or even favorable sense, on the lips of Jesus' enemies it becomes (along with οὗτος) almost a term of derision (see 9:12, 28; 19:21). Chrysostom went so far as to say, "Through their excessive hatred and enmity they would not even call Him by name" (*Homilies on St. John* 49; NPNF, 1st ser., 14.176).

12-13 In the preceding chapter, we saw that "the Jews" (6:41, 52) replaced "the crowd" (6:22, 24) as Jesus' interlocutors. Here by contrast, in Jesus' absence, *both* are in the picture at the same time. "The Jews" are united in their desire to arrest Jesus and take his life, while "the crowds,"[41] like "the Jews" in the preceding chapter, are divided. Their "great murmuring" recalls the murmuring among "the Jews" in the preceding chapter (6:41, 43). Some were on Jesus' side, saying, "He is good,"[42] while others disagreed, saying, "No, but he deceives the crowd."[43] This difference of opinion about Jesus anticipates three sharper divisions later, whether among "the crowd," as here (vv. 40-44), or among "the Pharisees" (9:16), or among "the Jews" (10:19-21). The clear implication is that the crowds knew that Jesus was a marked man as far as the ruling authorities were concerned.[44] Even those who saw him as a deceiver seem to have been reluctant to get involved. The notice that they would not speak of him "publicly"[45] suggests that they were speaking to each other "in secret," just as Jesus was on his way to Jerusalem "in secret" (v. 10).[46] The double dose, as it were, of "secrecy" sets the stage for Jesus' "public" appearance at the Tent festival in the section to follow (see v. 26, "And look, he is speaking publicly"). The question of what is "public" and what is "in secret" will be an ongoing one, as we will see.

J. JESUS IN THE TEMPLE (7:14-36)

> 14 *Already at the middle of the festival, Jesus went up to the temple and began teaching.* 15 *The Jews then were amazed, saying, "How does this man know letters, being uninstructed?"*

41. Gr. οἱ ὄχλοι.
42. The notion that Jesus is "good" (ἀγαθός) does not of course necessarily mean that they gave him their allegiance (see Mk 10:17-18 and Lk 18:18-19, where calling Jesus "good" falls short of genuine discipleship). Possibly those who regarded Jesus as "good" were using the term in the sense of "kind" or "benevolent" (see BDAG, 4, and Mt 20:15), remembering what he had done for the sick man by the Bethsaida pool.
43. The expression is odd, because some in "the crowds" are talking about "the crowd" as if they did not belong to it. The notion of Jesus as "deceiver" (see v. 47; Mt 27:63) seems to anticipate charges later brought against him at his trial (see Lk 23:5, 14).
44. The phrase, "for fear of the Jews" (διὰ τὸν φόβον τῶν Ἰουδαίων), is used elsewhere of Jesus' disciples and their fear of the religious authorities in Jerusalem (see 19:38; 20:19), while a similar expression, "because they feared the Jews," is used of the parents of the man born blind (9:22). In each instance fear leads to either secrecy, privacy behind locked doors, or reticence to speak.
45. Gr. παρρησίᾳ (compare v. 4).
46. For the contrast between "publicly" and "in secret," see verse 4 and 18:20.

16 So Jesus answered them and said, "My teaching is not mine, but belongs to the One who sent me. 17 If anyone chooses to do his will, he will know about the teaching, whether it is from God, or whether I speak on my own. 18 He who speaks on his own seeks his own glory, but he who seeks the glory of the One who sent him is true, and nothing false is in him. 19 Has Moses not given you the law? And none of you does the law? Why are you seeking to kill me?"

20 The crowd answered, "You have a demon. Who is seeking to kill you?"

21 Jesus answered and said to them. "One work I did, and you all were amazed. 22 That is why Moses gave you circumcision — not that it is from Moses; no, it is from the fathers — and on the Sabbath you circumcise a man. 23 If a man receives circumcision on the Sabbath so that the law of Moses not be abolished, you are angry at me because I made a whole man well on the Sabbath? 24 Don't judge by appearance, but judge the right judgment!"

25 So some of the Jerusalemites said, "Is not this the one they are seeking to kill? 26 And look, he is speaking publicly, and they are saying nothing to him. Do the rulers truly know that he is the Christ? 27 No, we know where this man is from, but the Christ, when he comes, no one knows where he is from."

28 So Jesus cried out teaching in the temple, and said, "You know me, and you know where I am from, and I have not come on my own, but the One who sent me is True, whom you do not know. 29 I know him, because I am from him, and he sent me."

30 So they sought to arrest him, and no one laid a hand on him, because his hour had not yet come. 31 And many from the crowd believed in him, and were saying, "The Christ, when he comes, will he do more signs than this man did?" 32 The Pharisees heard the crowd murmuring these things about him, and the chief priests and the Pharisees sent officers to arrest him. 33 So Jesus said, "Yet a short time I am with you, and I am going to the One who sent me. 34 You will seek me and you will not find, and where I am you cannot come." 35 So the Jews said to themselves, "Where will this man go, that we will not find him? Will he go to the dispersion of the Greeks and teach the Greeks? 36 What is this word that he said, 'You will seek me and you will not find, and where I am you cannot come'?"

When Jesus reaches Jerusalem and the temple, a temple ministry begins, extending all the way from 7:14 to 8:59. While the temporal setting of this extended discourse is the "Tent festival" (see above, on 7:2, 8, 10-11), it is also

7:14-36 JESUS IN THE TEMPLE

the Gospel of John's "temple discourse"[1] *par excellence,* defined as much (or more) by its location as by its timing in the Jewish calendar. The discourse takes place either in two days or three, depending on whether 7:53–8:11 is read as part of John's Gospel. The first day (7:14-36) is "at the middle of the festival," when "Jesus *went up to the temple* and began teaching" (v. 14, my italics), and the narrative then jumps from there to "the last great day of the festival" (7:37). If 7:53–8:11 is viewed as part of John's Gospel, that "last" day comes to an end at 8:1, and another day of teaching follows (8:2-59), *after* the Tent festival is over. But if, as most textual scholars believe, 7:53–8:11 does *not* belong to this Gospel, then the discourse on "the last great day of the festival" extends all the way from 7:37 to 8:59, when Jesus "was hidden and *went out of the temple*" (my italics). Within this final day of teaching, there are two other noticeable breaks, one when the Gospel writer pauses to remind us again of the location: "These words he spoke in the treasury, teaching in the temple" (8:20), and the other when we are told that "many believed in him" (8:30) and Jesus goes on to deal at some length with these "Jews who believed him" (8:31-59).

While the two-day scenario is almost certainly the intention of the author, this commentary will attempt to trace the narrative flow of chapters 7 and 8 *both with and without* the intriguing story of the woman caught in adultery that for centuries has separated the two chapters. Either way, the account is punctuated by explicit references to Jesus' presence in the temple at Jerusalem (see also 8:2, "In the morning *he went again to the temple*"; my italics). If the synoptic Gospels have placed Jesus' "temple discourse" at the season of Passover within the last week of his ministry (see, for example, Mt 21:23–24:1; Mk 11:27–13:1; Lk 20:1–21:4, 21:37-38), the Gospel of John seems to have placed it at a different festival, and close to the very center of the story. Jesus has been in the temple before (2:14-20; 5:14), and will be there again (10:23-39), but nowhere else in the Gospel do we find anything like the sustained ministry there that dominates this chapter and the next.

14-15 The notice that Jesus arrived in Jerusalem late ("Already at the middle of the festival") comes as no surprise, in view of his late, and "secret," departure from Galilee (see vv. 9-10).[2] He went immediately to the temple and "began teaching."[3] This begins yet another chapter in Jesus' ongoing debate with "the Jews," that is, the Jewish ruling authorities (see 2:18-21; 5:19-47;

---

1. Whether I coined the term or not, I made it the title of my article, "The Temple Discourse in John," in *New Dimensions in New Testament Study,* 200-213. It becomes the title of Keener's whole chapter on 7:1–8:59 (Keener, 1.703-74).

2. The verb "went up" (ἀνέβη) is the same here as in v. 10, and is used in the same idiomatic sense for a pilgrimage to the Holy City and its temple.

3. The imperfect ἐδίδασκεν here signals the beginning of an action (see Abbott, *Johannine Grammar,* 336-37).

6:41-58). Surprisingly, it is only the second reference to Jesus "teaching" in John's Gospel, the first being 6:59, "These things he said teaching in synagogue in Capernaum." What exactly did he teach? "These things" according to 6:59, that is, the preceding discourse on the Bread of life, but what is he teaching *now,* in the temple? We are not told,[4] for no words of his have been quoted, and two verses later, when he is quoted, he is not so much "teaching" as talking *about* his teaching: "My teaching is not mine, but belongs to him who sent me. If anyone chooses to do his will, he will know about the teaching, whether it is from God, or whether I speak on my own" (vv. 16-17).

The pronouncement calls to mind Rudolf Bultmann's classic dictum that in John's Gospel "Jesus as the Revealer of God *reveals nothing but that he is the Revealer*."[5] Jesus' "teaching" seems to have no content other than the claim that it comes from God. But is this in fact the case? The immediate response of "the Jews" (v. 15) suggests that it is not the case, and that there is more here than mere self-reference. Amazed,[6] they ask, "How does this man know letters, being uninstructed?" The term "letters"[7] (without the definite article) refers to written words in general,[8] not necessarily the Jewish Scriptures in particular, yet it is difficult to imagine what "written words" Jesus would have been reading or quoting other than the Scriptures (see 5:46-47, "For if you believed Moses, you would believe me, for he wrote about me. But if you do not believe his written words, how will you believe my spoken words?").[9] The response of "the Jews" suggests that Jesus' "teaching" included, even if it was not limited to, exposition of the Jewish Scriptures. This

---

4. Contrast Mark 4:2, where we are told explicitly: "And he began teaching them in parables, *and he said to them in his teaching,* 'Listen. See, a sower went out to sow,'" etc. (my italics; see also Mk 12:38).

5. See Bultmann, *Theology of the New Testament* (New York: Scribner's, 1955), 2.66.

6. The reader is by now familiar with the notion of "the Jews," or religious leaders, being "amazed" (ἐθαύμαζον); see 3:7; 5:20, 28. The expression may, but does not have to, imply that they took offense (BDAG, 444). Here it probably does not, particularly if, as we will argue, they do not at this point know Jesus' identity. The "offense" comes later (see v. 21).

7. Gr. γράμματα.

8. See BDAG, 206: "γράμματα without the article used with a verb like ἐπίστασθαι, εἰδέναι means *elementary knowledge,* especially reading and writing." In the added story of the woman caught in adultery Jesus (whatever his intention may have been) demonstrates his ability to write by writing with his finger on the ground (see 8:6, 8).

9. According to a rearrangement of the text proposed by Bernard (1.71), Bultmann (209), and Schnackenburg (2.5-9), the comment of "the Jews" in 7:15 follows right on the heels of Jesus' words in 5:46-47. This "new and improved" version of the Gospel, however, destroys the author's intended connection between Jesus' "teaching" (v. 14), and "the Jews'" reaction to that teaching (v. 15).

was the case in the synagogue at Capernaum (see 6:59), where he expounded the text, "He gave them bread from heaven to eat" (6:31), and there is every reason to believe that it is also the case here at the temple, even though no text has been announced.

Why do the religious authorities consider Jesus "uninstructed"?[10] Their reaction evokes for a modern reader the notice in the book of Acts that the Jewish "chief priests and elders and scribes" in Jerusalem (Acts 4:5) were similarly "amazed" when they saw that Peter and John, who preached to them so eloquently, were "unlettered and ordinary men" (4:13). Is the Gospel writer telling us this in order to highlight a parallel between the ways Jesus and his postresurrection followers were perceived by the religious establishment? Probably not, for John's Gospel shows little evidence elsewhere of acquaintance with the narratives in Acts. The notion that Jesus was "uninstructed" either in reading and writing, or more specifically in the Jewish Scriptures, is very odd, considering the title "Rabbi" given him repeatedly throughout the Gospel. It is true that the title is used only by his disciples (1:38, 49; 4:31; 9:2; 11:8) or by potential disciples (see 3:2; 6:25), yet one of those "potential disciples" (if the phrase is applicable) was Nicodemus, introduced explicitly as "a ruler of the Jews" (3:1). Why then do these Jewish leaders not recognize Jesus as a "Rabbi" of some sort?

Two possible answers present themselves. The first is that their apparent lack of respect is a deliberate slight, fully consistent with their behavior toward Jesus all throughout the narrative to this point. Only once, briefly, have "the Jews" even deigned to face him head-on and address him personally as "you" (see 2:18, 20). Ever since that early confrontation in the temple, they have either tried to arrest him without speaking to him (5:16, 18), or have murmured *to each other* about him (sometimes even in his presence!), referring to him as "this man" (6:41-42, 52) or "that man" (7:11). Here again they avoid direct contact, but merely comment about "this man" and his lack of education. The problem is that their puzzled words, "How does this man know letters, being uninstructed?" (v. 15), carry with them a note of grudging admiration not altogether consistent with their determination to arrest and kill him (see 5:18; 7:1).[11] Moreover, the question persists, How do they know

10. Gr. μὴ μεμαθηκώς. In a curious way, the scene recalls another, presumably unrelated, incident in another Gospel, when Jesus, twelve years old and literally "uninstructed," sat among the Jewish teachers in this same temple, "listening to them and asking them questions," and "all who heard him marveled [ἐξίσταντο] at his understanding and his answers" (Lk 2:46-47).

11. Their comment recalls Jesus' reception at his hometown in the synoptic Gospels (see especially Mk 6:2; Lk 4:22), but with the conspicuous difference that they neither speak his name nor mention his family background. (as they did in Jn 6:42, the closer parallel to the synoptic passages).

he is "uninstructed"? Do they have a personal knowledge of his background, like "the Jews" in Galilee who knew him as "Jesus, the son of Joseph, whose father and mother we know" (6:42)? Or are they concluding on the basis of appearances, whether a Galilean accent (see Mk 14:70; Lk 22:59; Acts 2:7; 4:13), or perhaps his manner of dress, that he is not one of them, but rather one belonging to what they will later characterize as "this crowd that does not know the Law; they are accursed" (v. 49)?

If the latter is the case, a second possibility presents itself, that is, that these "Jews" in Jerusalem simply do not know who Jesus is. Not that they do not know he is "the Son of God," or "the Word," or "the Messiah." That goes without saying. The point is rather that they do not recognize the man who abruptly "began teaching" in the temple midway through the Tent festival as "Jesus, the son of Joseph" (6:42). More important, they do not recognize him as the fugitive they are looking for, who healed the sick man at the pool of Bethesda, told him to break the Sabbath, and then claimed to be God's own Son (see 5:1-18). In short, Jesus' identity is concealed in some way, a notion fully consistent with the author's comment that when he went up to the festival, he did so "not openly but as it were in secret" (v. 10). Yet the Gospel writer shows no interest in how Jesus might have concealed his identity, whether supernaturally (as in the postresurrection encounters in 20:14 and 21:4) or by a disguise of some kind. The whole notion, in fact, would seem rather farfetched, except for the natural question, If they knew that this man now teaching in the temple was Jesus, why did they not arrest him on the spot? (see v. 1, where they "were seeking to kill him," and v. 11, where they "were seeking him at the festival and said, 'Where is that man?'").[12]

In short, the reader cannot be sure at this point whether or not the Jewish authorities knew with whom they were dealing. But the reader does know: they are dealing with Jesus, and the notion that Jesus was "uninstructed," or somehow unqualified to teach, seems intended to strike the reader as highly ironic, if not laughable. The very first word addressed to Jesus in this Gospel was "Rabbi," interpreted immediately as "teacher" (1:38). Jesus himself had even shared with "the Jews" — the Galilean ones at least — his vision from the Jewish Scriptures (Isa 54:13) that no one would be left

---

12. Most commentators fail to notice the incongruity. R. A. Whitacre (183n.) does notice it, but explains it differently, theorizing that "the Jews" in v. 15 are not the same as "the Jews" in v. 13: "Two verses earlier the term clearly referred to Jesus' opponents among the leaders of Israel, but this meaning does not fit verse 15 since they would have already known what Jesus' teaching was like. Here *the Jews* either must refer to Judeans or Jerusalemites or must be a very general term for those who had come to Jerusalem for the feast from throughout the diaspora." As we have seen, however, when "the Jews" are Jesus' interlocutors in this Gospel, they are portrayed rather consistently as the Jewish religious authorities and as Jesus' enemies.

7:14-36 JESUS IN THE TEMPLE

"uninstructed," but that "they all will be taught of God." Those who have "learned" from God, he added (God being understood as "the Father"), would come to Jesus in faith (6:45). Therefore the comment that he himself was "uninstructed" only betrays the ignorance of the Jerusalem authorities.

16-17 Even though "the Jews" had not spoken to him directly, Jesus "answered" them at some length (vv. 16-19).[13] His answer takes up several themes first introduced in his long discourse to them in 5:19-47: that "the Son can do nothing on his own, except what he sees the Father doing" (5:19), that "I can do nothing on my own" (5:30), that "If I testify about myself, my testimony is not true" (5:31), that "I do not accept glory from humans" (5:41) while "you receive glory from each other, but do not seek the glory that comes from the Only God" (5:44), and that "Your accuser is Moses, in whom you have set your hope" (5:45).[14] Echoing the first three of these earlier pronouncements, Jesus tells them (paradoxically) that "My teaching[15] is not mine, but belongs to the One who sent me" (v. 16).[16] But he then adds something he had *not* said in chapter 5: "If anyone chooses to do his will,[17] he will know about the teaching, whether it is from God, or whether I speak on my own" (v. 17).

What does Jesus mean by "to do his will" (that is, the will of "the One who sent me")? We know what it means for *Jesus* to do "the will of the One who sent me" (see 4:34; 5:30; 6:38-39), but what does it mean for "anyone" to do so? Only twice in John's Gospel do we read of those other than Jesus who "do the will of God": here and in 9:31, where the man born blind will remind "the Jews" that "We know that God does not listen to sinners, but if anyone is god-fearing and does his will, this one he hears" (see also 1 Jn 2:17; 5:14). To "do the will of God" is simply to be "god-fearing"[18] and not a "sinner." While the former blind man has Jesus in mind as the prime example of such godliness, he is making a generalization, not a pronouncement about Jesus in particular. Similarly here, "doing the will of God" is to be defined

---

13. Here again (as in 5:17 and 19), Jesus is not answering a direct question but making a more general statement, and because of this the aorist middle ἀπεκρίνατο might have been expected. But this time the author uses the more common aorist passive ἀπεκρίθη, possibly because what follows is not a monologue but a real dialogue of sorts (see v. 21, where ἀπεκρίθη is repeated; also 8:14, 19, 34, 49, 54).

14. These links obviously contribute to the rearrangements proposed by Bernard, Bultmann, and Schnackenburg (see above, n. 9)

15. Gr. ἡ ἐμὴ διδαχή.

16. Jesus seems to enjoy accenting the paradox. As Augustine noticed (see *Tractates on John* 29.3; NPNF, 1st ser., 7.183), he does not say, "*This* teaching is not mine," but "*My* teaching is not mine."

17. Gr. ἐάν τις θέλῃ τὸ θέλημα αὐτοῦ ποιεῖν.

18. Gr. θεοσεβής.

first of all within the framework of Jewish piety, not in the distinctly Johannine sense of believing in Jesus.[19] To "do the will of God" is to live within God's covenant and according to God's law as a devout Jew.[20] It is virtually indistinguishable from "doing the truth" (3:21) or "doing good things" (5:29). The Gospel writer is not here presupposing a distinctly Johannine understanding of "doing the will of God," but is rather starting with the common Jewish understanding of "the will of God" as something revealed and embodied in the Jewish Scriptures, and then equating that with the new imperative he brings of accepting him as God's unique messenger and agent.[21] He is not so much assuming as deliberately introducing a new understanding of what "the will of God" means for his hearers.

In short, Jesus is repeating with different words what he said to them two chapters earlier, that "if you believed Moses, you would believe me" (5:46), reinforcing the notion that his unspecified "teaching" that first led the Jewish authorities to question his qualifications (v. 14) may in fact have been an exposition of Jewish Scriptures. At the same time, his reference to "doing the will of God" (v. 17) suggests that this may also have been a central theme in his unrecorded discourse.[22] Having spoken generally of "the will of God"

19. That is, not like "the work of God" in 6:29, defined as "believing in him whom that One sent." For the opposite view, see Augustine: "It is the same thing as to believe" (*Tractates on John* 29.6; NPNF, 1st ser., 7.185); so also Bultmann, for whom doing the will of God means "no more and no less than believing," rejecting what he calls "the popular but crude misunderstanding of v. 17 which suggests that it wants to make the way of faith easier by advising that a man should first take seriously the ethical demands, which are universally evident, and that this will lead him to an understanding of the dogmatic teaching" (274; so too Barrett, 318; all three cite Jn 6:29).

20. D. A. Carson offers a valuable clarification, which (intentionally or not) speaks to Bultmann's objection: "The point is not that the seeker must attain a certain God-approved level of ethical achievement before venturing an assessment as to whether or not Jesus' teaching comes from God, but that a seeker must be fundamentally committed to doing God's will. This is a faith commitment" (312).

21. So Chrysostom: "What meaneth, 'If any man do His will'? If any man be a lover of the life which is according to virtue, he shall know the power of the sayings." He then adds, "If any man will give heed to the prophecies, to see whether I speak according to them or not" (*Homilies* 49.1; NPNF, 1st ser., 14.177).

22. It is tempting to conjecture that this "teaching" may have been more akin to what we know of Jesus from the synoptic Gospels — Matthew in particular — than from the Gospel of John. It is Matthew, after all, who records a long discourse involving Jesus' interpretation of "the law and the prophets" (Mt 5:17), and the necessity of "doing" and "teaching" the commandments of God (5:19) so as to attain a righteousness exceeding that of the scribes and Pharisees (5:20), ending with stern admonitions to "do the will of my Father who is in the heavens" (Mt 7:21; also 12:50), or to "hear my words and do them" (7:24). It is Matthew too who concludes that Jesus "was teaching them as having authority and not as their scribes" (7:29), a notice fully in keeping with the present context in John. Interestingly,

7:14-36 JESUS IN THE TEMPLE

as the standard of righteousness, Jesus now adds that *doing* God's will is the key to *knowing* "about the teaching, whether it is from God, or whether I speak on my own" (v. 17). Although John's Gospel is customarily remembered as the one stressing faith or knowledge over action, Jesus' words here demonstrate that the two must never be set over against each other. As we have seen, those who "*do* the truth" are those who "come to the light" (3:21), and those who have "*done* good things" are those who "go out to a resurrection of life" (5:29). Later, Jesus will tell his disciples that "I have given you an example, that you might *do* just as I have *done* for you" (13:15), and "Now that you *know* these things, blessed are you if you *do* them" (13:17, my italics throughout). There is a circularity in this Gospel than cannot be overlooked: if it is true that a person must "know" in order to "do," it is just as true that one must "do" in order to "know." The latter is the point made here. If Jesus' hearers had faithfully done as their own lawgiver and their own prophets commanded, they would know the truth about Jesus and believe in him. As it is, they do not; consequently they are unable to understand or accept what Jesus is saying (see v. 19). At the same time, his pronouncement holds the door open for the readers of the Gospel. If *they* do the will of God, *they* will know whether Jesus' teaching comes from God or whether he speaks on his own authority. These are obviously not two equally plausible alternatives that must be carefully weighed in the balance. What they are expected to know (in light of v. 16, and of 5:19-47) is that Jesus' teaching *does* in fact come from God and God alone, and that he is *not* speaking on his own authority.

18 Jesus' next words have the sound of a narrative aside from the pen of the Gospel writer, explaining Jesus' reference to speaking "on my own"[23] (v. 17; see also 5:30). Yet just as in a number of similar cases where the Gospel writer's thoughts are placed in the mouth of the speaker, whoever it might be,[24] the words must be read as Jesus' words, offering his own explanation of what he has just said. "He who speaks on his own" (v. 18), he continues, "seeks his own glory, but he who seeks the glory of the One who sent him is true, and nothing false is in him." The first of these participial expressions is a generalization (that is, "*Whoever* speaks on his own"), while the second looks like a more specific reference to Jesus himself and his message from God. That was the case in 5:43, for example, where Jesus said, "I have come in my Father's name," in contrast to an indefinite "another" who

---

Bultmann (274, n. 4) cites Martin Dibelius to the effect that "Jesus' διδαχή contains an allusion to the Sermon on the Mount," a notion Bultmann himself rejects.

23. Gr. ἀπ' ἐμαυτοῦ.

24. For example, 3:13, 16-21; 4:22; 6:27, 33, 46, 50, and 58, where the speaker is Jesus; 3:31-36, where the speaker is John; and 4:9, where the speaker is the Samaritan woman. See the comments on those passages; also Michaels, "The Johannine Words of Jesus and Christian Prophecy," *SBL 1975 Seminar Papers,* 251-60.

"comes in his own name." But does the expression "he who seeks the glory of the One who sent him" have to refer *exclusively* to Jesus? Probably not.[25] The whole verse draws a stark contrast in an almost chiastic fashion:

    a. He who speaks on his own
    b. seeks his own glory
    b'. but he who seeks the glory of the One who sent him
    a'. is true, and nothing false is in him.

The middle terms *(b* and *b')* contrast a messenger's own "glory" with that of the Sender,[26] while the first and last terms *(a* and *a')* characterize a messenger (any messenger) who "speaks by himself" as the very opposite of "true."[27] By this standard, Jesus is a "true" messenger of God, and "nothing false is in him,"[28] but so is John, who "testified to the truth" (5:33),[29] and so, we will learn later, is "the Advocate," the very "Spirit of truth," who will not speak "on his own" (16:13). So too are Jesus' disciples, who are "sent" as he is sent (17:18; 20:21) and whom he prays might be "consecrated in the truth" (17:17, 19). Still, the primary focus in the present context is on Jesus, on his self-revelation and his truth claims here in the temple at Jerusalem "at the middle of the festival" (v. 14). But the question persists: Do his hearers recognize him as the same man who came to Jerusalem twice before — first driving money changers from the temple area (2:13-22), and then healing a

---

25. So Bultmann, 275, n. 3: "The article in v. 18 is in both cases generic. The way it is phrased leaves open the question whether the principle could, in fact, be applied to others apart from Jesus."

26. "Glory" (δόξα), means praise, honor, or prestige here, just as in 5:41 and 44 (BDAG, 257). Yet here it is less a matter of seeking God's approval (as in 5:44, "the glory that comes from [παρά] the Only God") than of seeing to it that all the honor goes to God and not the messenger.

27. "True" (ἀληθής) includes both the idea of "truthful" (in the sense of speaking the truth) and "honest" or "reliable" (in the sense of being worth of trust; see BDAG, 43). In this instance, the messenger is "true" because God is "true" (see 3:33; 8:26; and compare 7:28).

28. Ἀδικία ("wrong" or "falsehood") occurs only here in John's Gospel (although see 1 Jn 1:9; 5:17), and the phrase "nothing false is in him" should not be overinterpreted. It is simply a corollary of "true" (ἀληθής), implying honesty, and faithfulness to the Sender. "True" messengers" (aside from Jesus, see 8:46, 1 Jn 3:5) are not necessarily sinless but simply honest or reliable. For a similar use of a negative to reinforce a positive, see 1:47, "a true Israelite, in whom is no deceit"; also 1 John 2:27, where God's "anointing 'is true and is no lie'" (see Bultmann, 276: "when contrasted with ἀληθής, ἀδικία has the specific meaning of 'lie, deceit'").

29. See also 3:33, where it was John first of all who confirmed "that God is true" (ἀληθής).

sick man by a pool on the Sabbath (5:1-9)? Or do they see him simply as an eloquent but anonymous and "uninstructed" stranger?

19 Jesus now introduces Moses into the discussion, which is not surprising if his teaching so far has consisted at least in part of biblical exposition. "Has Moses not given you the law?" he asks, "And none of you does the law? Why are you seeking to kill me?" (v. 19). The first of the three questions — if it is a question — is rhetorical. It was a commonplace among Jews that Moses was the lawgiver.[30] Yet the form of the question matches exactly an indicative statement found in the preceding chapter, that "it is not Moses who has given you that bread from heaven" (6:32). In English, the two sentences do not appear to be parallel:

> "It is not Moses who has given you that bread from heaven" (6:32).
> "Has Moses not given you the law?" (7:19).

In Greek, however, the parallel is striking.[31] It seems odd to translate the first as a statement and the second as a question. The reader is tempted to read the second as a statement more or less parallel to the first: "It is not Moses who has given you the law."[32] While this flies in the face of the common Jewish belief (or at least terminology), it is consistent with the notion that the messenger (whether Jesus or Moses) does not speak "on his own" (*aph' heautou*, v. 18). The point would then be, "It is not Moses [but God] who has given you the law." This would also be consistent with 1:17, "For the law was given through Moses" (with the passive voice acknowledging God as the actual Giver). The difficulty is that the reader is expected to fill in too large a gap. In 6:32, Jesus was quite explicit that "it is not Moses who has given you that bread from heaven, *but it is my Father* who gives you the true bread from heaven" (my italics). Nothing like that is made explicit here. Moreover, three verses later Jesus speaks without hesitation of Moses as the one who "gave you circumcision," adding as a qualification not that circumcision is actually from God but rather that "it is from the fathers" — that is, that it goes back to Abraham (v. 22).

---

30. See, for example, 8:5 ("in the law, Moses commanded us . . .").

31. That is, οὐ Μωϋσῆς δέδωκεν ὑμῖν τὸν ἄρτον ἐκ τοῦ οὐρανοῦ (6:32), and οὐ Μωϋσῆς δέδωκεν ὑμῖν τὸν νόμον (7:19).

32. Such a reading would be strangely reminiscent of the second-century Gnostic treatise, Ptolemy's *Letter to Flora* (preserved by Epiphanius, *Panarion* 33.4.1-2: "The words of the Saviour teach us this triple division. The first part must be attributed to God himself and his legislating; the second to Moses (not in the sense that God legislates through him, but in the sense that Moses gave some legislation under the influence of his own ideas); and the third to the elders of the people" (R. M. Grant, *Gnosticism,* 185; see also B. Layton, *The Gnostic Scriptures,* 309).

In short, Jesus is not at the moment thinking theologically of God as the ultimate Source of the law, but historically of Moses as the Jewish lawgiver. With Jewish tradition generally, he has no interest in pitting the one against the other.[33] For all these reasons, it is best to stay with the common punctuation, "Has Moses not given you the law?" The reader must next decide whether the following clause, "And none of you does the law," should also be punctuated as a question (with the KJV, ASV, NASV, Douay, and Confraternity) or as a statement (with the Nestle text and most English translations, including RSV, NRSV, NIV, and NAB). This time the difference is small, but the traditional punctuation as a question is slightly to be preferred.[34] The three closely linked rhetorical questions convey admirably Jesus' mounting exasperation; the first heightens the irony of the second, reinforcing the earlier charge that "Your accuser is Moses, in whom you have set your hope" (5:45), while the third explains how Jesus knows that "none of you does the law." He claims they have broken the law at one specific point, in "seeking to kill me" (see Exod 20:13, "You shall not murder").[35] He is still talking to "the Jews" (see v. 15), and his accusation comes as no surprise to the reader, for they were indeed seeking his life (see 5:18; 7:1 and 11).[36]

20 While the reader is not surprised, Jesus' hearers are both surprised and angered, yet the indignant reply to the accusation comes not from the accused (that is, "the Jews"), but from "the crowd" (v. 20). The abrupt change of interlocutors is not as odd as it appears, for it has happened twice before in the preceding chapter. There, as we have seen, "the crowd" in Galilee (6:22, 24) gave way to "the Jews" (6:41, 52), who were then abruptly replaced by "many of his disciples" (6:60, 66). Although not quite interchangeable, the three groups respond to Jesus in similar ways. "The crowd" challenges him to perform a sign, just as "the Jews" had done earlier (6:30-31; compare 2:18), while both "the Jews" and the so-called "disciples" refuse

---

33. This is also in keeping with the synoptic Gospels, where both Jesus and the Gospel writers customarily refer to the law as "the law of Moses," or as that which "Moses" said or commanded (see, for example, Mk 1:44; 7:10; 10:3-4 and par.; also Lk 2:22; 24:44).

34. See Abbott, *Johannine Grammar*, 200.

35. Ironically, in 18:31 "the Jews" themselves confirm what Jesus says here: "It is not lawful [οὐκ ἔξεστιν] for us to kill anyone"; see J. R. Michaels, "John 18.31 and the 'Trial' of Jesus," *NTS* 36.3 (1990), 474-79.

36. The rhetorical force of the words, "Why are you seeking to kill me?" is not to ask them seriously to give a reason for wanting to kill him (as, for example, in 10:32), but simply to level the charge that this is in fact their intention. The attempt of Lindars to spiritualize the charge on the grounds that "to refuse to accept Jesus is to seek to kill him" (289), and that "the real charge is that of spiritual murder incurred by the rejection of divine truth embodied in Jesus" (290) is not at all convincing.

genuine discipleship as they "murmur" against him (6:41, 43, 61). In the present chapter, "the Jews" in Jerusalem are (still) seeking to kill Jesus (7:1, 11), and the Jerusalem "crowds" take up the "murmuring" (7:12), some defending Jesus and some accusing him. Unlike "the Jews," they are divided in their opinions, yet "the Jews" too "quarreled with each other" earlier (6:52), and will themselves later be torn by "division" over who Jesus is (10:19-21; see also 11:45-46). Now, abruptly, "the crowd" speaks again, this time with one voice: "You have a demon. Who is seeking to kill you?" (v. 20).

The question for the reader is, How significant is the change of interlocutors? How sharply is "the crowd" to be distinguished from "the Jews"? Very sharply, according to many interpreters. Rudolf Bultmann, for example, comments that the crowd is to be distinguished from the Jews "and is ignorant of the latter's intention."[37] This view is difficult to sustain in view of the vehemence with which the crowd speaks. While "You have a demon" is probably not so much a serious charge of demon possession (as, for example, in Mk 3:22, 30), as simply a way of saying "You're crazy,"[38] the hostility in the words is quite characteristic of "the Jews" in two other passages (see 8:48; 10:20).[39] More important, the notion that "the crowd" was ignorant of "the Jews'" intention to kill Jesus is implausible in light of verses 11-13, where "the Jews were seeking him at the festival, and said, 'Where is that man?'" (v. 11), while those in "the crowd," no matter what their opinion of Jesus, would not "speak about him publicly . . . *for fear of the Jews*" (v. 13, my italics). Why the fear, unless they knew that Jesus was a wanted man? Another possibility is that "the crowd" is simply "playing dumb," pretending to be ignorant of the plan, precisely "for fear of the Jews."[40] But that is not

---

37. Bultmann, 277; see also Westcott, 1.268: "*The multitude*, made up chiefly of pilgrims, not the people of Jerusalem (v. 25) and therefore unacquainted with the full designs of the hierarchy"; Bernard, 1.262: "This is a lifelike touch. It was not the 'people,' but the 'Jews', who had begun the plot; the people knew nothing of it"; Moloney, 245: "The people know nothing of this, and thus act as a foil both to Jesus' knowledge of the decision to kill him and to the duplicity of 'the Jews,' who are attempting to debate with Jesus." Morris (361) is more guarded: "This multitude *professes* to know nothing of the plot" (my italics).

38. There is wide agreement on this point, perhaps in part on the basis of 10:20 ("He has a demon, and is mad!"). See, for example, Lindars, 290; Bultmann, 277, n. 11; Brown, 1.312; Barrett, 319; Carson, 314. In the Synoptics, compare Matthew 11:18 and Luke 7:33, where the charge is leveled against John the Baptist simply because of his ascetic lifestyle.

39. This would be even more clearly the case if 8:48 ("Do we not say well that you are a Samaritan, and have a demon") were read as referring back to something "the Jews" had said a chapter earlier (see Lindars, 290). This is unlikely, however.

40. It is difficult to say whether or not Morris (361; above, n. 37) is hinting as some such scenario.

probable either, for it makes the vehemence of the crowd's reply even harder to understand.

The most satisfactory explanation is the one hinted at before: that is, that the crowd is honestly puzzled and offended by Jesus' accusation because they do not realize that the one speaking is Jesus, the healer and accused Sabbath breaker of chapter 5![41] They truly have no idea why the authorities would be seeking to kill this anonymous stranger who had come late to the festival. The disclaimer, "Who is seeking to kill you?" comes from the crowd, but the reader has reason to suspect that it could just as easily have come from "the Jews."[42] They are indeed seeking to kill *Jesus,* but they have no clue that this "uninstructed" pilgrim at the festival is in fact Jesus. If, as we have been told (v. 10), Jesus is present at the festival "not openly, but as it were in secret," their ignorance is not surprising.

21-23 Jesus now risks major trouble by dropping a very broad hint: "One work I did, and you all were amazed" (v. 21), explaining shortly that the single "work" he has in mind was that "I made a whole man well on the Sabbath" (v. 23). This gives away his identity as nothing else could have done. He is indeed Jesus, the wanted man who had healed on the Sabbath (see 5:1-9).[43] In almost the same breath, without waiting for the crowd's reaction, he defends his behavior in having done so. Having offered a purely christological defense before (5:17, "My Father is working even until now, and I am working"), one that only aggravated the situation (see 5:18), he now argues from traditional Jewish practice: "That is why[44] Moses gave you circumcision — not that it is from Moses; no, it is from the fathers — and on the Sabbath you

---

41. See Michaels, "Temple Discourse," 204-6.

42. Hoskyns (315) points out that that the distinction between "the Jews" and "the crowd" is "not maintained (v. 25), and the phrase *the Jews* seems often to be simply equivalent to the *crowd* (viii.31 sqq., xii.9, &c.)." But it does not necessarily follow, as Hoskyns claims, that if this is the case, "their ignorance is simply a lie."

43. To be sure, the author has implied that this "one work" was typical of Jesus' behavior in a number of instances (see above, on 5:16), yet this was the one instance which in the narrative is said to have triggered the resolve of the Jewish authorities to "pursue" Jesus (5:16), and finally to seek his life (5:18). Moreover, the contrast between "*one* work" (emphasized by being placed first) and "you are *all* amazed" is rhetorically effective.

44. "That is why" (διὰ τοῦτο, literally "because of this") is taken by some with the preceding verse: "One work I did, and you all were amazed because of this." This makes good sense, but is unlikely here because John's Gospel rarely if ever places διὰ τοῦτο anywhere but at the beginning of a clause or sentence (see Abbott, *Johannine Grammar,* 288-89). As translated here the connection is vaguer. Jesus is saying that God instituted the priority of circumcision over the Sabbath in order to convince the Jewish authorities that the welfare of "a whole man" takes precedence over the Sabbath all the more.

circumcise a man. If a man receives circumcision on the Sabbath so that the law of Moses not be abolished,[45] you are angry at me because I made a whole man well on the Sabbath?" (vv. 22-23). The parenthetical correction ("not that it is from Moses; no, it is from the fathers") recalls a similar correction earlier by the Gospel writer (4:2, "although Jesus himself was not baptizing, his disciples were"), but here it comes within words attributed to Jesus. The reader can only conclude that it is to be read as Jesus correcting himself. While circumcision is indeed part of the legal system that "Moses gave you" (see Lev 12:3), it goes back finally to Abraham (Gen 17:10-13, 23), Ishmael (17:23-27), and Isaac (Gen 21:4). Just as in the earlier instance the narrative aside did not change the fact that in effect Jesus *was* baptizing (see 3:22, 26), so here the notice obviously does not prevent the writer from immediately referring to circumcision as "the law of Moses" (v. 23). What looks on the surface like a contradiction is in fact only a technicality.[46]

Jesus is here using the common Jewish argument that some things take precedence over the Sabbath, in this case circumcision. The circumcision of a male child took place on the eighth day after birth (see Lk 2:21), and if the eighth day fell on the Sabbath, the child was circumcised anyway.[47] This sounds more like Jesus in the synoptic Gospels than in the Gospel of John. In Matthew, for example, he makes a similar point regarding the Sabbath in relation to temple worship: "Or have you not read in the law that on the Sabbath the priests in the temple defile the Sabbath and are blameless?" (Mt 12:5).[48] When Sabbath law clashed with other laws, sometimes the other laws took precedence. At the same time, Jesus' argument also involves the principle known in Judaism as "light to heavy" *(qal waḥomer),* that is, an argument from lesser to greater. If circumcision, which involved only one part of a man's body, overruled the Sabbath, how much more would the healing of a "whole man"[49] do

45. "Abolish" is λύειν, in the sense of "annul" or "destroy" (see 2:19). As with the Sabbath in 5:18, it is not simply a matter of failing to keep the law, but of ignoring its validity, and in effect annulling it.

46. Still, Bultmann overstates the case when he says, "The note is clearly of only academic interest, for it is of no importance in this context and only disturbs the line of argument" (278, n. 3). At the other extreme, Chrysostom argued that circumcision was "not of the Law, but of 'the fathers,'" proving that "there are many things more authoritative than the Law" (*Homilies* 49.1; NPNF, 1st ser., 14.179). Rather, the Gospel writer wants to emphasize that whoever the human mediators may have been, the law (including *both* circumcision and the Sabbath) is from God, and God alone (see 1:17; 6:32).

47. See *m. Shabbat* 18.3 and 19.2: "They may perform on the Sabbath all things that are needful for circumcision" (Danby, *The Mishnah,* 116); also *m. Nedarim* 3.11: "R. Jose says, 'Great is circumcision, which overrides even the rigour of the Sabbath'" (Danby, 268; for additional evidence, see Keener, 1.716, n. 128).

48. See Keener, 1.716, n. 126.

49. Gr. ὅλον ἄθρωπον. In this case the translation "man" is obviously justified.

so!⁵⁰ Again he echoes the synoptic tradition, as in Matthew, where he once asked, "What man among you who has one sheep and it falls into a ditch on the Sabbath will not take hold of it and lift it out? And how much more a man is worth than a sheep! So then, it is lawful on the Sabbath to do good" (Mt 12:11-12), or in Luke, where he denounced synagogue leaders as "Hypocrites, does not each of you on the Sabbath free his ox or donkey from the manger and lead it to drink? And this daughter of Abraham, whom Satan has bound now for eighteen years, should she not be freed from this chain on the Sabbath day?" (Lk 13:15-16). Neither of these examples involves circumcision (which Jesus never even mentions in the synoptic Gospels), but similar logic is applied to circumcision and the Sabbath in rabbinic traditions.⁵¹ Even in passages which have nothing to do with the Sabbath, Jesus in the synoptic Gospels makes similar use of a contrast between one bodily part, whether "the right eye" (Mt 5:29) or "the right hand" (Mt 5:30), and a person's "whole body" (5:29, 30).⁵²

Here the familiar synoptic-like contrast leads Jesus to ask his hearers to explain why "you are angry at me⁵³ because I made a whole man well on the Sabbath" (v. 23). The implication is that they have no reason to be angry because Jesus has done a good thing on the Sabbath, something at least as good as circumcision which "the law of Moses" commanded, and not something to be criticized, much less punished.⁵⁴ But to whom is he speaking, and

---

50. The analogy between circumcision and healing seems to imply not a polemic against circumcision in the Johannine community, but on the contrary a respect for the practice as a form of healing (see, for example, Haenchen, 2.15, citing *Numbers Rabbah* 12, "the foreskin is a bodily blemish"). This is in keeping with Chrysostom's remark (in *Homilies* 49.1; NPNF, 1st ser., 14.179) that "circumcision was 'partial' health. And what was the health procured by circumcision? 'Every soul,' it saith, 'that is not circumcised, shall be utterly destroyed' (Gen. xvii.14)." In any event, the issue of imposing circumcision on Gentile Christians was not on John's radar screen, and apparently not on Chrysostom's.

51. See, for example, *b. Shabbat* 132a: "If circumcision, which is [performed on but] one of the limbs of a man, supersedes the Sabbath, the saving of life, *a minori*, must supersede the Sabbath"; also *b. Yoma* 85b: "If circumcision, which attaches to one only of the two hundred and forty-eight members of the human body, suspends the Sabbath, how much more shall [the saving of] the whole body suspend the Sabbath!" (*Babylonian Talmud, Seder Mo'ed* [London: Soncino, 1938], 1.660, 3.421). See also Keener, 717, n. 139.

52. Paul too makes the point that "the whole body" is greater than any one of its parts (see 1 Cor 12:17). At least one instance, the synoptic Jesus makes use of a different formula in which a single member becomes the indicator or index to the state of one's "whole body" (Mt 6:22-23; Lk 11:34; see also Jas 3:3, 6).

53. This verb for being angry (χολᾶν), which occurs only here in the New Testament, is related to a word for bitter "gall" (χολή) which appears in Matthew's account of the crucifixion (Mt 27:34), but the connection should not be pressed.

54. For similar words of self-defense from Jesus, see 8:40 ("But now you seek to

7:14-36 JESUS IN THE TEMPLE

to what "anger" is he referring? Is he addressing "the crowd" who had just said, "You have a demon. Who is seeking to kill you?" (v. 20), or is he addressing "the Jews" (vv. 1, 11, 15), who, as the reader well knows, have been all along seeking to kill him? He had hinted at anger just before when he said, "One work I did, and you all were amazed" (v. 21), and as we have seen, "amazement" was both the implied reaction of "the Jews" in Jerusalem two chapters earlier (see 5:20, 28) and their explicit reaction here (v. 15). This suggests that he may still have them in mind, for "amazement" easily turns into "stumbling" or taking offense (see 6:61), and finally into anger. Beyond this, the stubborn fact that "the Jews" were seeking to kill Jesus (5:18; 7:1) speaks for itself. As for "the crowd," they were annoyed at what they saw as his paranoia (v. 20), and from a rhetorical standpoint the "all" (v. 21) seems to include them. Still, they have given no evidence of any awareness — much less anger — that he has healed on the Sabbath. Therefore, even if Jesus is in some sense answering the crowd, it must be added that at the same time he is talking right past them and continuing to address "the Jews" (as in vv. 16-19), once more unmasking their intentions. It is his indirect way of announcing to them, "I am the One you are looking for," just as he will later announce himself to the band of soldiers gathered to arrest him in the garden across the Kidron valley (18:5).

24 "Don't judge by appearance," Jesus concludes, "but judge the right judgment!"[55] The cognate accusative, "judge the right judgment," echoes Hebrew style, and on the surface the pronouncement sounds like a Hebrew prophet's plea for simple justice.[56] But the phrase "by appearance"[57] is striking. A reader familiar with the Old Testament will recall Isaiah 11:3, where it is said of the "stump of Jesse" (apparently a messianic figure) that "He shall not judge *by what his eyes see,* or decide by what his ears hear; but with righteousness he shall judge the poor, and decide with equity for the

---

kill me, a man who has spoken to you the truth which I heard from God"), and 10:32 ("I showed you many good works from the Father; for which of these works do you stone me?").

55. Gr. τὴν δικαίαν κρίσιν κρίνετε. The negative present imperative (μὴ κρίνετε) could be rendered, "Stop judging," implying that they were already "judging by appearance." But the translation, "Don't judge," carries this nuance just as well. Some ancient manuscripts (including ℵ, Θ, and the majority of later manuscripts) have the second imperative as aorist (κρίνατε), implying something like "hand down the right verdict." But the present κρίνετε (supported by P66, P75, B, D, L, W, Ψ, and others) is probably to be preferred. The two verbs appear to be the same.

56. See, for example, Zechariah 7:9, LXX (Κρίμα δίκαιον κρίνατε); also Deuteronomy 16:18, LXX, where the judges in Israel are to "judge the people a right judgment" (κρινοῦσιν τὸν λαὸν κρίσιν δικαίαν).

57. Gr. κατ' ὄψιν.

meek of the earth" (NRSV, my italics).[58] Jesus asks nothing more or less than that they judge with simple fairness, without partiality or favoritism, as he himself judges (see 5:30, "Just as I hear I judge, and my judgment is right, because I am not seeking my will but the will of the One who sent me"). This they have not done and will not do.[59] In one sense, "by appearance" is simply equivalent to "according to the flesh" (see 8:15).

Yet at this crucial point in the narrative, it is hard to avoid the conclusion that the pronouncement also has something to do with Jesus' own "appearance," or "face," as he confronts these "Jews" in Jerusalem. "Don't judge by appearance, but judge the right judgment!" sounds like a plea to recognize Jesus for who he is, not an anonymous uneducated stranger, but a marked man, wanted by the authorities because he "made a whole man well on the Sabbath" (v. 23). In a very different situation near the end of the Gospel, Mary Magdalene judged "by appearance" and concluded that Jesus was the gardener (20:15). Only when he spoke her name did she know who he was (20:16). Elsewhere he is known to his disciples after the crucifixion by the wounds in his hands and side (see 20:20, 27-28). In another Gospel, he is known to them "in the breaking of bread" (Lk 24:31, 35; see also Jn 21:4-7, 12-13). In the present narrative, the issue of recognizing Jesus as the Sabbath healer who has returned to Jerusalem "as it were in secret" (v. 10) sets the stage for the deeper question, "Who is he *really?*"[60]

The odd thing about this encounter at the temple, and especially about Jesus' brief speech defending himself against the charge of Sabbath breaking (vv. 21-23), is that even though the plan to kill Jesus has been front and center (see vv. 1, 11-13, 19-20), nothing has been said about the real reason the authorities were seeking his life. The reason was not merely that he broke the Sabbath, but that he "was claiming God as his own Father, making himself equal to God" (5:18). Here at the Tent festival two chapters later, Jesus has said nothing about his "Father" (and will not do so until 8:16). Instead, he has spoken only (and rather mysteriously) of "the One who sent me." Christol-

---

58. The phrase, "by what his eyes see," in this passage is rendered in the LXX not by κατ' ὄψιν, but by κατὰ τὴν δόξαν (probably not "according to glory" in this instance, but "according to [his] opinion," or according to what *seems* right). See also 1 Samuel 16:7 (NRSV), "for the LORD does not see as mortals see; they look on the outward appearance, but the LORD looks on the heart." Perhaps significantly, the leader chosen on this principle was David (16:11-13), the original "stump of Jesse" and prototype of the Jewish Messiah (see Lindars, 292, who finds messianic significance in the possible allusion to Isa 11:3). Yet a similar principle is attested in the Hellenistic world (see, for example, Lysias, *Orations* 16.19: "It is appropriate neither to love or hate anyone because of appearance [ἀπ' ὄψεως], but to take account of deeds"; see Bultmann, 278, n. 4; Barrett, 321).

59. If 7:53–8:11 is read as part of John's Gospel, it illustrates the point perfectly.

60. See Michaels, "Temple Discourse," 206.

7:14-36 JESUS IN THE TEMPLE

ogy is not yet an issue in this confrontation, even though the reader knows that it has been before (see 5:19-47), and that it will inevitably come up again.

By this time the writer has made it clear that the key to understanding Jesus' identity is "doing the will of God." In this verse, to "judge the right judgment" is the exact opposite of judging "by appearance," and Jesus has already defined "right judgment" as "not seeking my will but the will of the One who sent me" (5:30). He has also claimed that the way to "know about the teaching, whether it is from God or whether I speak by myself," is to "choose to do his will" (7:17). The invitation to "judge the right judgment" (v. 24) now simply reiterates that invitation to "do the will" of God (v. 17). It involves not only recognizing who Jesus is, but acknowledging that his teaching is not his own, but belongs to "the One who sent him" (see vv. 16, 18). The latter is, if anything, even more crucial than the former. Whether he is "Jesus of Nazareth" who healed on the Sabbath, or an anonymous and uneducated stranger at the Tent festival, what matters above all is where his teaching comes from. Is it from God, or is he simply imparting his own wisdom? Only those who "do the will of God" will know.

25-27 The reply to Jesus' short speech (vv. 21-24) comes not from "the Jews" (see v. 15), and not (at least not explicitly) from "the crowd" (v. 20), but from "some of the Jerusalemites," probably in the sense of "some" *within* the crowd. This group functions as a kind of chorus, summarizing the situation for the reader. "Is not this the one they are seeking to kill?" they ask (v. 25), in glaring contradiction to what the crowd has just said to Jesus, "You have a demon. Who is seeking to kill you?" (v. 20). Their words should be read not as a statement of what had been obvious all along (for it clearly has not been), but as a sudden realization, a moment of truth. Finally, they have picked up on Jesus' repeated hints (vv. 20, 21, 23), and have understood that he is indeed the fugitive "the Jews" are looking for. Yet they are puzzled. Why has he not been arrested? "And look," they continue, "he is speaking publicly, and they are saying nothing to him! Do the rulers truly know that he is the Christ?" (v. 26). The notice that Jesus is now speaking "publicly"[61] signals exactly what his brothers asked of him at the beginning of the chapter: now at last he is no longer "in secret" (vv. 4, 10), but "in the public eye"[62] (v. 4), just as they had urged.

These "Jerusalemites" are torn between two alternatives. Could it be that this Jesus, this fugitive, is actually "the Christ" and that "the rulers"[63]

---

61. Gr. παρρησίᾳ.
62. Gr. ἐν παρρησίᾳ.
63. Gr. οἱ ἄρχοντες (evidently the same group as "the Jews" who were seeking his life).

know it? (v. 26). That is, have they changed their minds because they know that he actually *is* "the Christ"? Answering their own question,[64] they conclude, "No, we know where this man comes from, but the Christ, when he comes, no one know where he is from" (v. 27). We have heard nothing of Jesus as "the Christ" for several chapters. Yet when the Gospel writer first named Jesus, it was as "Jesus Christ" (1:17), as if "Christ" were part of his very name. John's acknowledgment that he himself was *not* "the Christ" (1:20; 3:28) carried with it the implication that "the One coming after" (1:15, 27, 30) perhaps was. This impression was confirmed when Jesus' first disciples hailed him as "the Messiah — which means Christ" (1:41), and thus as "someone of whom Moses wrote in the law, and of whom the prophets wrote" (1:45; see also 5:46). Later, in a non-Jewish setting, a Samaritan woman had said, "I know that Messiah is coming, who is called Christ" (4:25), and Jesus had quickly and explicitly responded, "It is I — I who am speaking to you" (4:26). "Could this be the Christ?" the woman had asked the men of her town (4:29), and in due course they had acknowledged Jesus as "truly the Savior of the world" (4:42).

What does all this tell us about Jewish expectations of "the Christ," or "the Messiah"? Not very much. Only that his coming was prophesied both in the law and the prophets, and that he was expected to "baptize" or purify the world in some way (see 1:25).[65] Now the reader learns one thing more: Jesus is supposed to be disqualified as "the Christ" because "we know where this man is from, but the Christ, when he comes, no one knows where he is from" (v. 27). In saying "we know," these "Jerusalemites" refer to what they consider to be common knowledge,[66] whether among them personally, or "the crowd," or "the rulers." He is evidently now recognized in Jerusalem as "Jesus son of Joseph, from Nazareth" (see 1:45; also 6:42), and it is assumed that if his geographical origin and lineage are known he cannot be the Messiah.[67] Such a be-

---

64. The apparent question-and-answer format suggests this reading. Another possibility is that "some" (τίνες) in the group proposed that Jesus was "the Christ," while "others" (ἄλλοι, unexpressed but implied) raised an objection (compare the various "schisms" in this Gospel, and the uses of ἄλλοι in vv. 12, 41; 9:16, and 10:21).

65. The Samaritans (though not necessarily the Jews) seem to have expected as well that when the Messiah came, he would "tell us all things" (4:25).

66. See, for example, 3:2; 9:31; also Mark 12:14; Romans 2:2; 3:19; 7:14; 8:22, 28; 2 Corinthians 5:1; 1 Timothy 1:8.

67. It remains unclear how either these "Jerusalemites" or "the rulers" in Jerusalem would have known Jesus' origins. His first disciples (1:45, 46) and "the Jews" in Capernaum 6:42) knew where he was from, presumably, because they themselves were Galileans, but he has not so identified himself in Jerusalem either here or in chapters 2 or 5 (see, however 18:5, 8 and 19:19). The writer's assumption in telling the story is that Jesus' hostile interlocutors are in some sense everywhere the same, so that what is known of him in one place (6:42) can apply elsewhere as well.

7:14-36 JESUS IN THE TEMPLE

lief is rarely if ever attested in Jewish sources. It is not the same, for example, as the notion of a hidden Messiah who comes into the world but remains incognito until it is time for him to be revealed.[68] Concealment is, after all, implicit in the very idea of being "revealed."[69] Here it is not a matter of recognizing *who* the Messiah is, but of knowing "where he is from."[70] As it stands, the pronouncement flatly contradicts the thought, soon to be expressed, that "the Christ comes from the seed of David, and from Bethlehem, the village where David was" (v. 42), serving to underline the confusion of these "Jerusalemites." It also flatly contradicts what "the Jews" will say two chapters later about Jesus to the man born blind: "We know that God has spoken to Moses, but as for this man, we do not know where he is from" (9:29). The irony of the former blind man's answer is telling: "What is amazing in this is that you do not know where he is from, and he opened my eyes" (9:30).

The irony is already present here. Even though Jesus' hearers *think* they know where Jesus is from (v. 27), they really do not, any more than they could have known where the good wine at Cana was from (2:9), or the "living water" Jesus offered to the Samaritan woman (4:11). His comings and goings are as mysterious to them as the wind (3:8).[71] He is from Nazareth in Galilee, but ultimately he is "from above" (3:31), or "from heaven" (3:13, 31; 6:32, 33, 38, 42, 50, 51). Ironically, what they say about the Messiah *is* true of Jesus: "when he comes, no one knows where he is from." His origins are beyond human comprehension.

28-29 In light of the foregoing, Jesus might easily have said, "No, you don't know where I am from. You only think you do. I am from above. Consequently, I am the Messiah." But that is precisely what he does not say. Instead he continues "teaching in the temple" (v. 28, as in v. 14), with a solemn pronouncement which he "cried out"[72] (v. 28). This verb implies not so much a loud shout or outcry[73] as a solemn proclamation. It was used once of John early on (1:15), and will appear twice more with Jesus as the subject (v. 37; 12:44). Along with "testify" (see 1:15), it seems to take the place of

---

68. As, for example, in *1 Enoch* 48.6; *4 Ezra* 12.32 and 13.52; and Justin Martyr, *Dialogue with Trypho* 8.4 and 110.1.

69. As Barrett puts it (322), "This however does not amount to much more than saying: 'The Messiah will not be known until he is known,' and is not a full parallel to the words in John, which imply that when the Messiah is known to be Messiah it will still not be known whence he has come."

70. Gr. πόθεν ἐστίν.

71. If this is true of "everyone born of the Spirit," readers can surely infer that it is true of Jesus, as he will soon make explicit (see 8:14).

72. Gr. ἔκραξεν.

73. In John's Gospel, this idea is conveyed by κραυγάζειν (see 11:43; 12:13; 18:40; 19:6, 12, 15) rather than κράζειν.

the more common early Christian term for preaching or proclaiming the gospel message.[74] Like "Amen, amen," it calls attention to the importance and the solemnity of what follows. "You know me, and you know where I am from," Jesus admits. Like his first disciples, Jesus knows that being "from Nazareth" (1:45) is quite compatible with being "the Messiah" (1:41), the One "of whom Moses wrote in the law, and of whom the prophets wrote" (1:45). When asked in so many words, he will not hesitate to acknowledge that he is indeed "Jesus the Nazorean" (see 18:5, 8). But what he adds here is crucial: "I have not come on my own,[75] but the One who sent me is True, whom you do not know" (v. 28). He avoids confronting head-on the issue of whether or not he himself is the Messiah, calling attention again (as in v. 16) to "the One who sent me." What his hearers do not understand is that where Jesus "comes from" — his origin — is not a place but a Person. To be "from above," or "from heaven," is to be sent "from God" (see 3:2, 17, 34; 6:46) or from "the Father" (see 5:36, 37; 6:44, 57).

Quite simply, Jesus is telling his hearers that they do not know God — a startling assertion in view of his words to the Samaritan woman three chapters earlier, "You people worship what you do not know. We worship what we know, for salvation is from the Jews" (4:22). There he stood resolutely alongside "the Jews" as those who know and worship God, while here he abruptly charges that they do not (see also 8:19, 55; 15:21; 16:3). The reason they do not, he says, is that "the One who sent me is True" (that is, truly God),[76] so that if they reject the messenger they are rejecting God, who sent him (see above, 5:23; also Lk 10:16b). What has happened between chapter 4 and the present is that God's messenger has been rejected once in Jerusalem (chapter 5), and is now being rejected again. These "Jerusalemites" can no longer claim that they, in contrast to Samaritans or other Gentiles, know the "true" God, for God has revealed himself in this messenger, and only in him.[77] "I," by contrast, "know him," Jesus claims, "because

---

74. That is, κηρύσσειν, "to proclaim" or preach.
75. Gr. ἀπ' ἐμαυτοῦ, as in v. 17.
76. For "True," a very few ancient manuscripts (including P⁶⁶ and ℵ) have ἀληθής (probably under the influence of 3:33 and 8:26), while the great majority of manuscripts, both early and late, have ἀληθινός, almost certainly the original reading. There is little if any difference in meaning. I have capitalized "True" in translation because ἀληθινός here becomes something close to a title for God (as in 1 Jn 5:20; see also Jn 17:3). This was not the case in 3:33, not because ἀληθής was used there instead of ἀληθινός, but because "God" was already explicitly the subject of the clause, whereas here "True" actually defines who "the One who sent me" is.
77. Possibly Jesus' use of ἀληθινός intentionally echoes the adverb ἀληθῶς, "truly," in the Jerusalemites' question, "Do the rulers truly know that he is the Christ?" (v. 26; see Keener, 1.719, n. 153).

7:14-36 JESUS IN THE TEMPLE

I am from him,[78] and he sent me" (v. 29).[79] In this sense Jesus' hearers do *not* know "where he is from," even though he has just acknowledged (with a touch of irony) that they do (v. 28). He is indeed from a certain place, "Nazareth" as it happens (see 1:45-46), but beyond that he is "from" a Person, "the One who sent me," and if they will not receive the messenger they cannot know the Sender.

30 It is unclear whether or not Jesus' hearers understand that he is claiming they do not know God. What is clear is that the solemn words that he "cried out teaching in the temple" (v. 28) made them angry enough that "they sought to arrest him" (v. 30). Whether "they" are the "Jerusalemites" who first realized that he was a wanted man (v. 25), or "the crowd" (v. 20), or "the Jews" (v. 15) is also unclear, at least for the moment. Presumably only "the Jews" would have had the necessary authority.[80] Perhaps the best way to read verse 30 is as a caption or heading for the next seven verses in their entirety. That is, the writer first states that "they sought to arrest him" (v. 30), and then explains at greater length how the attempted arrest was carried out, and why it failed (vv. 31-36).[81] In this case, "they" are promptly identified as "the chief priests and the Pharisees" (v. 32), a mixed group more or less synonymous with "the Jews." Why did the attempt fail? The theological reason comes first. It failed because God determined that it would fail: that is, because Jesus' "hour had not yet come" (v. 30). The Gospel writer takes Jesus' words spoken long before to his mother ("My hour has not yet come," 2:4), and makes them his own.[82] Jesus' "hour" had not come back then at the Cana wedding, and we are reminded here that it *still* has not come. But the present context makes clearer precisely what the decisive "hour" would entail. If an attempt to take him by force fails "because his hour had not yet come," then

---

78. Gr. παρ' αὐτοῦ.

79. In almost the same breath, Jesus is deferential toward "the One who sent me," acknowledging that "I have not come on my own" (v. 28), yet strongly assertive toward those challenging him (ἐγώ . . . εἰμι, v. 29).

80. Moreover, the verb "sought" (ἐζήτουν) is by this time familiar as an almost technical term for the efforts of "the Jews" to arrest or kill Jesus (see 5:18; 7:1, 11, 19, 20).

81. The few commentators who address the issue tend toward the contrary view, that "this attempt seems to be distinct from that of the authorities in vs. 32" (Brown, 1.313; also Barrett, 323: "a popular movement to seize Jesus, to be distinguished from the formal attempt at an arrest"). To be sure, the expression, "no one laid a hand on him," could suggest a merely physical act of trying to lay hold of Jesus, but the the repetition of the same verb, which can mean either "to seize" or "to arrest," in vv. 30 (πιάσαι) and 32 (ἵνα πιάσωσιν αὐτόν) suggests that the two initiatives are the same. Even Barrett admits (somewhat paradoxically) that "it would be unwise to suppose that John meant the distinction seriously" (323).

82. As we have seen, the pronouncement, "My time [καιρός] is not yet here" (7:6), has a different meaning.

his "hour" must be the time of his arrest,[83] and by extension his trial and execution, the fulfillment of the authorities' plan to "pursue" Jesus and finally "kill" him (see 5:16, 18). The notice that "his hour had not yet come" explains why Jesus was not captured or killed in the course of debates with his opponents (see 8:20; also 7:43; 8:59; 10:39), yet also points toward the moment when he will finally say that "the hour has come" (12:23; see also 12:27; 13:1; 17:1), and face that which awaits him.

31 The writer now gives a more detailed account of why and how "they sought to arrest him" (v. 30). The reason, it turns out, was not simply that the authorities did not like the speech he had given in verses 28 and 29, but that "many from the crowd believed in him" (v. 31a). Those who believed said, "The Christ, when he comes, will he do more signs than this man did?" (v. 31b). As we will learn later, the fear of the Pharisees and the chief priests was that "everyone will believe in him, and the Romans will come, and take away both our place and our nation" (11:48). Those who believed seem to have understood that it was not a matter of just "one work" (v. 21), but that what Jesus had done in Jerusalem on that Sabbath day was typical of what he had been doing on a rather wide front (see above, 3:2, "no one can do *these signs* you are doing unless God is with him"; also 2:23; 4:45, 48; 5:16; 6:2). Commentators are generally agreed that Jewish expectations of the Messiah did *not* emphasize that the Messiah would necessarily perform signs or miracles, much less be known by his miracles.[84] As Schnackenburg points out, "What we have here is not Jewish but Christian messianic dogma"[85] — driven presumably by the conviction of early Christians that Jesus had actually performed many miraculous signs during his ministry, more in fact than they could count (see 20:30), and that these signs pointed to his identity as "the Christ" (20:31).[86] On the basis of these signs, we are told, "many of the

---

83. See Luke 22:53, where Jesus tells "the chief priests and the temple guards and the elders" who had come to arrest him, "this is *your* hour, and the authority of the darkness" (my italics).

84. See (among many others) Keener, 1.719; Barrett, 323; Brown, 1.313; Bultmann, 306, n. 3. It is commonly suggested that miracles were more closely linked to certain messianic figures other than the anointed king from the line of David, above all "the Prophet" like Moses (see v. 40; also 1:21), or the Elijah figure thought to precede the day of the Lord. Possibly the notion that "John did no sign" (10:41) was intended to reinforce John's own insistence that he himself was *not* "the Christ," or "the Prophet," or "Elijah" (see 1:21).

85. Schnackenburg, 2.149.

86. See especially Matthew 11:2-5, where the "works of the Christ" of which John heard in prison turn out to be such miracles of Jesus as healing the blind, the deaf, and the lame, cleansing lepers, and raising the dead (see also Lk 7:18-22); also Mark 13:22, where "false Christs" and "false prophets" try to gain acceptance by performing "signs and wonders," and a number of passages both in John (2:18; 6:30) and in the Synoptics (Mt 12:38; Mk 8:11) where Jesus is challenged to perform signs in order to validate his authority.

crowd believed in him." While the Gospel writer (in contrast to 2:23-25) does not evaluate the genuineness of their faith explicitly, his use of the term "murmuring" in the following verse is hardly encouraging.

32 To the Pharisees, and apparently to the Gospel writer as well,[87] this belief on the part of "many" was nothing more than "murmuring" (v. 32), arising as it did out of conflicting perceptions of Jesus (vv. 25-27). To them it was much like the crowd's "murmuring" earlier (v. 12), when they learned that Jesus was wanted by the authorities. Possibly one reason for this was that while "many" believed in Jesus, others did not (see v. 27), so that "the crowd" was divided (as in v. 12, and explicitly in vv. 40-43). The text does not say. But because *any* belief in Jesus as the Messiah was dangerous, given the authorities' fear of the Romans (again, see 11:48), "the chief priests and the Pharisees sent officers to arrest him" (v. 32). This was the attempt which according to the Gospel writer was doomed in advance to failure "because his hour had not yet come" (v. 30). But these "officers"[88] know nothing of the plan of God, and we will hear a very different explanation shortly from their own lips (v. 46, "no man ever spoke like this").

33-34 In response to this move by the religious authorities, Jesus now speaks, but we are not told to whom. "Yet a short time I am with you, and I am going to the One who sent me," he announces (v. 33), adding "You will seek me and you will not find, and where I am you cannot come" (v. 34). While his words are consistent with the preceding notice that "his hour had not yet come" (v. 30), they strongly suggest that the decisive "hour" is near. At the same time, they further define this "hour" as his departure from the world, back to "the One who sent me." Because Jesus has already established that "the One who sent me" is One "whom you do not know" (v. 28), it follows that they do not and cannot know where he is going.

To drive home the point, he uses language which some readers — though not his immediate hearers — might recognize as contrary to what he was supposed to have said elsewhere: "You will seek me and you will not find, and where I am[89] you cannot come" (v. 34). In two other Gospels he

---

87. The notice is phrased in such a way as to leave this impression. "The Pharisees heard the crowd murmuring" implies more than that they (mistakenly) interpreted their words as "murmuring." The Gospel writer's own use of "murmur" and "murmuring" (see v. 12; 6:41, 43, 61), suggests that he views matters in much the same way

88. Gr. ὑπηρέτας. While the word can be used very generally of any kind of helper or messenger, it is used here and elsewhere (see 18:3, 12, 18, 22; 19:6; also Mt 5:25; Mk 14:54, 65; Acts 5:22, 26) of "officers of the court" (perhaps in this case the Sanhedrin, or Jewish ruling council; see BDAG, 1035).

89. "I am" (εἰμί), both here and in verse 36, can also be read as εἶμι, an Attic future of ἔρχεσθαι (hence as "I shall go"; see v. 35, "Where will this man go?"). As Danker points out (BDAG, 286), this is a possible reading in 12:26, 14:3, and 17:24 as well (see

said, "Ask, and it will be given you; seek, and you will find; knock, and it will be opened to you. For everyone who asks receives, and the one who seeks finds, and to whoever knocks it will be opened" (Mt 7:7-8//Lk 11:9-10). Here it is just the opposite: there are those who seek Jesus who will *not* find him. To be sure, Jesus' first disciples "sought" him and "found" him (1:38, 41), and so did Mary Magdalene (20:15, 16), and even the crowds who followed him in the preceding chapter (see 6:24-25), but the Gospel writer knows that this is not true for everyone, and not even true for his disciples all the time (see 13:33). It cannot be, given the dualism of this Gospel, and least of all in this instance, where those who "will seek" Jesus are agents of those who were "seeking" him only to arrest and kill him (v. 30; also vv. 1 and 11, and 5:18).

An intriguing possibility is that Jesus' language here is influenced by the biblical account of Elijah's ascension to heaven, when the prophets of Jericho sent "fifty men who *searched* for three days but did not *find* him" (2 Kgs 2:17, NRSV; my italics).[90] But while that story shaped at least one later account of Jesus' departure from the earth,[91] the writer could hardly have expected readers to pick up such a subtle allusion here. More likely, this is simply the dualism of John's Gospel at work, as Jesus makes explicit in the words that follow: "and where I am, you cannot come."[92]

---

also BDF, §99[1]). I have left it "I am" in order to acknowledge that a different verb is used here than the ὑπάγω of v. 33, of 8:21, 22, and of 13:33.

90. The verbs, according to 2 Kgs 2:17, LXX, are ζητεῖν and εὑρίσκειν respectively, as here. The "three days" is of interest to readers of John's Gospel in light of 2:19, "Destroy this sanctuary, and in three days I will raise it up." Also intriguing is Elijah's repeated statement (familiar to Paul; see Rom 11:3) that "the Israelites have forsaken your covenant, thrown down your altars, and killed your prophets with the sword. I alone am left, and they are *seeking my life*" (1 Kgs 19:10, 14, NRSV, my italics; in the LXX, ζητοῦσι τὴν ψυχήν μου λαβεῖν αὐτήν (literally, "seeking my life to take it").

91. See *Acts of Pilate* 15.1, where Nicodemus tells the Jewish council, "Just as the holy scriptures tell us that Elijah was also taken up into heaven. . . . *And they searched* for him *for three days and did not find him,* and they knew that he had been taken up (2 Kgs 2). And now listen to me, and let us send to every mountain in Israel and see whether the Christ was taken up by a spirit and cast upon a mountain." This proposal "pleased them all," we are told, "and they sent to every mountain of Israel, and searched [ἐζήτησαν] for Jesus and did not find him [οὐχ εὗρον]" (Hennecke-Schneemelcher, *New Testament Apocrypha,* 1.464).

92. "I" (ἐγώ) and "you" (ὑμεῖς) ae both emphatic. Compare 8:23: "You [ὑμεῖς] are from below; I [ἐγώ] am from above. You [ὑμεῖς] are of this world; I [ἐγώ] am not of this world." Moreover, the expression "you cannot come" (οὐ δύνασθε ἐλθεῖν) recalls the accent on "impossibility" (often wrapped up in the phrase οὐ δύναται) in Jesus' conversation with Nicodemus (see 3:1-6) and elsewhere (see, for example, 3:27; 6:44). Here the dualism is not tempered with an "unless" (ἐὰν μή) clause, as it is in most other examples.

7:14-36 JESUS IN THE TEMPLE

35-36 The preceding qualifies as a kind of a riddle, for Jesus' hearers do not know what to make of it.[93] While it is momentarily unclear to whom Jesus was speaking, the response (not surprisingly) comes from "the Jews" (v. 35). Probably these "Jews" are the delegation of "officers" sent by "the chief priests and the Pharisees" to arrest Jesus (v. 32). Because they represent the religious authorities in Jerusalem, the Gospel writer does not hesitate to identify them as "the Jews" (see 13:33, "and just as I said to the Jews that where I am you cannot come, so I say to you now"). What Jesus says to the "officers" he says in effect to those who sent them.[94] In keeping with their consistent practice up to this point (see, for example, 6:41-43, 52), these "Jews" do not speak to Jesus in reply but "to themselves," that is, to one another. Characteristically as well, their response is one of bewilderment: "Where will this man go, that we will not find him?" they ask. "Will he go to the dispersion of the Greeks and teach the Greeks?"

The reader has to smile at this, because Jesus had told them very clearly where he was going (v. 33, "I go to the One who sent me"). If he has come from God (vv. 28-29), he can only be going back to God again.[95] But if they do not know who "the One who sent him" is, they cannot know where he is going. Any thought of a plan to "go to the dispersion of the Greeks and teach the Greeks" is, at one level, absurd. And yet the Christian reader also knows that by virtue of Jesus' death and resurrection, the Christian message *has* gone precisely to "the dispersion of the Greeks," and "the Greeks" (no less than "the Jews") *are* in fact being taught. They may even be numbered among the Gospel's first readers. And so, ironically, these confused messengers from "the Jews" have spoken the truth — without actually knowing the truth. The "dispersion," or "Diaspora," was (and still is) a technical term for the Jewish community scattered throughout the world (in the New Testament see Jas 1:1; also 1 Pet 1:1, where the terminology is applied to Christians scattered in the world). The phrase "the dispersion of the Greeks"[96] should therefore probably be read as "the dispersion (or Jewish Diaspora) *among* the Greeks."[97] Otherwise, the text could give the impression that "the Greeks" and not "the Jews"

---

93. On v. 34 (along with 8:21 and 13:33) as a riddle, see T. Thatcher, *The Riddles of Jesus in John: A Study in Tradition and Folklore* (Atlanta: Society for Biblical Literature, 2000), 257-60.

94. See 18:12, "the officers of the Jews" (οἱ ὑπηρέται τῶν Ἰουδαίων). Jesus applies the same principle (that is, that messengers are equivalent to those who send them) to himself in relation to the Father, and to his disciples in relation to himself (see 13:16, 20; 15:20).

95. See also 6:62: where Jesus spoke of seeing "the Son of man going up where he was at first."

96. Gr. τὴν διασπορὰν τῶν Ἑλλήνων.

97. See BDF, §166, "Genitive of direction and purpose." See Barrett, 325; Brown,

are the ones dispersed. Some have taken this course, on the ground that in John's Gospel "the Jews" refers to Jews living in Palestine, and "the Greeks" to Greek-speaking Jews living in the Diaspora.[98] Remarkably, John's Gospel never uses the common New Testament term for "the Gentiles,"[99] but "the Greeks" seems to be one of his substitute terms (along with "other sheep" in 10:16, "the scattered children of God" in 11:52, and even "the Samaritans" in 4:39 and 40). The contrast between "Jew" and "Greek," familiar enough from the book of Acts (14:1; 16:1; 18:4; 19:10, 17; 20:21) and the letters of Paul (see Rom 1:16; 2:9, 10; 3:9; 10:12; 1 Cor 1:22, 24; 10:32; 12:13; Gal 3:28; Col 3:11), seems to be in play here as well. "The Jews" (or more precisely, their "officers") who hear Jesus' words can only conclude that he plans to leave Judea to undertake a teaching mission to the Gentile world — a mission that the reader knows has already begun (see 17:18; 20:21).

Finally, in their bewilderment, the officers sent to arrest Jesus ask themselves yet again, "What is this word that he said, 'You will seek me and you will not find, and where I am you cannot come'?" (v. 36). The repetition does more than underscore their confusion. It also highlights for the reader the significance of Jesus' pronouncement. It is a pronouncement that he will repeat twice more as the Gospel story unfolds (see 8:21; 13:33), and clearly one of decisive importance.[100] Jesus will not be present indefinitely, but only for "a short time" (v. 33). Then he must go away to "the One who sent him." This further defines what he meant by his "hour" (v. 30). Whatever else it may be, it is a time of departure from the world. The reader is expected to understand that he is going back to God his Father (see v. 33; 6:62), yet six chapters later not even his closest disciples have grasped where he is going, or why (see 13:36; 14:5). As for the officers now sent to arrest him, they have shown that they do not understand, nor are they able to accomplish their mis-

---

1.314; also Schnackenburg, who comments, "The expression ἡ διασπορά had already become a technical term, followed by a genitive to indicate the region concerned" (2.150; see also 2.476, n. 51, and the evidence given there).

98. This view is associated especially with J. A. T. Robinson in his article, "The Destination and Purpose of St. John's Gospel," in *Twelve New Testament Studies* (Naperville, IL: Allenson, 1962), 107-25. Yet in dealing with this particular text, even Robinson is quite cautious, admitting that the words "are unfortunately ambiguous." After setting forth the two alternatives, he states that "The decision between them can in fact only be made in the light of the Johannine context as a whole." He then defends his view on the basis of his assumption (which few others will grant) that "there is no other reference in the Gospel or Epistles to a Gentile mission" (112, n. 7).

99. Gr. τὰ ἔθνη. It uses only the singular (τὸ ἔθνος), and that in relation to "the nation" of Israel (see 11:48, 50, 51, 52).

100. In similar fashion, bewilderment and repetition work together to highlight a later pronouncement of Jesus, this time to his own disciples: "A short time, and you no longer see me, and again a short time, and you shall see me" (16:16; see vv. 17-19).

sion (see vv. 45-47). They cannot arrest him, for "his hour had not yet come" (v. 30). In "a short time," when it does come, he will depart, but on his own terms, and to a place of his choosing, not theirs.

K. THE LAST DAY OF THE FESTIVAL: JESUS AND THE PHARISEES (7:37–8:29)

37 *Now on the last day, the great day of the festival, Jesus was there and cried out, saying, "If anyone thirst, let him come to me and drink.* 38 *Whoever believes in me, just as the Scripture said, 'From his insides will flow streams of living water.'"* 39 *But this he said about the Spirit, which those who had believed in him were later to receive. For the Spirit was not yet, because Jesus was not yet glorified.*

40 *Some from the crowd, then, when they heard these words, were saying, "This is truly the Prophet."* 41 *Others were saying, "This is the Christ." But they were saying, "Does the Christ come from Galilee?* 42 *Did not the Scripture say that the Christ comes from the seed of David and from Bethlehem, the village where David was?"* 43 *So a split took place in the crowd on account of him,* 44 *and some of them wanted to arrest him, but no one laid hands on him.*

45 *Then the officers came to the chief priests and the Pharisees, and those said to them, "Why didn't you bring him in?"* 46 *The officers answered, "No man ever spoke like that."* 47 *Then the Pharisees answered them, "Are you also deceived?* 48 *Has any of the rulers believed in him, or any of the Pharisees?* 49 *But this crowd that does not know the law, they are accursed."* 50 *Nicodemus said to them — he who came to him previously, and was one of them —* 51 *"Does our law judge the man unless it hear from him first and learn what he is doing?"* 52 *They answered and said to him, "Are you also from Galilee? Search and see that a prophet is not arising out of Galilee."*

*[[*53 *And they went off, each to his house,* 8:1 *while Jesus went off to the Mount of Olives.* 2 *In the morning he again showed up at the temple, and all the people were coming to him, and he sat and began teaching them.* 3 *And the scribes and Pharisees brought a woman who had been caught in adultery, and stood her in the center* 4 *and said to him, "Teacher, this woman was caught in the act of committing adultery,* 5 *and in the law Moses commanded us to stone such women. So what do you say?"* 6 *This they said testing him, so that they might have [reason] to accuse him. But Jesus stooped down and wrote with his finger on the ground.* 7 *Then as they kept on questioning him, he straightened up and said to them, "The one without fault among you,*

let him first throw a stone on her." 8 And again he stooped down and wrote on the ground. 9 Then those who had heard went out one by one, beginning from the elders, and he was left alone, and the woman still in the center. 10 So Jesus straightened up and said to her, "Woman, where are they? Has no one condemned you?" 11 And she said, "No one, sir." And Jesus said, "Nor do I condemn you. Go, and from now on sin no more."]]

12 So again Jesus spoke to them, saying, "I am the Light of the world. Whoever follows me will not walk in the darkness, but will have the light of life." 13 Then the Pharisees said to him, "You are testifying about yourself. Your testimony is not true." 14 Jesus answered and said to them, "Even if I testify about myself, my testimony is true, because I know where I came from and where I am going. But you do not know where I come from or where I am going. 15 You judge according to the flesh, 'I' judge no one. 16 And yet if I judge, my judgment is true, because I am not alone, but I and the Father who sent me. 17 And in your law it is written that the testimony of two men is true. 18 I am the one who testifies about myself, and the Father who sent me testifies about me." 19 Then they said to him, "Where is your father?" Jesus answered, "You know neither me nor my Father; if you knew me, you would know my Father." 20 These words he spoke in the treasury, teaching in the temple, and no one arrested him because his hour had not yet come.

21 So again he said to them, "I am going, and you will seek me, and you will die in your sin. Where I am going you cannot come." 22 Then the Jews said, "Will he kill himself, because he said, 'Where I am going you cannot come'"? 23 And he said to them, "You are from below, I am from above. You are from this world, I am not from this world. 24 I just told you that you will die in your sins. For unless you believe that I am, you will die in your sins." 25 So they said to him, "Who are you?" Jesus said to them, "What can I even begin to say to you? 26 I have many things to say about you and to judge, but the One who sent me is True, and the things I heard from him are the things I say to the world." 27 They did not know that he was telling them of the Father. 28 So Jesus said to them, "When you lift up the Son of man, then you will come to know that I am, and [that] on my own I do nothing, but just as the Father taught me, these things I speak. 29 And the One who sent me is with me. He has not left me alone, for I always do the things that please him."

This long section is interrupted by a passage widely regarded as a later addition to John's Gospel, and therefore set off by double brackets in our transla-

7:37–8:29 THE LAST DAY OF THE FESTIVAL

tion (7:53–8:11). The passage is omitted by the earliest papyri (P⁶⁶ and P⁷⁵), by the earliest of the parchment manuscripts (א, B, L, W, Θ, and most others), and by the old Syriac and some of the old Latin and Coptic versions. It appears first in so-called "Western" manuscripts (the fifth-century Codex Beza [D] and most of the Latin versions), and then comes to be rather consistently present in the majority of later manuscripts and versions. Yet because it has been considered an integral part of John's Gospel for so many centuries, and has been routinely included in English versions (often in brackets, which I have used as well), it has become very familiar to modern readers. Certain isolated manuscripts include it as part of sacred Scripture, but place it elsewhere, for example, after John 7:36, after 7:44, at the end of John's Gospel, after 21:25, or after Luke 21:38. While it is almost certainly a later addition to John's text, and there is some evidence that it "interrupts the sequence of 7.52 and 8.12ff.,"[1] it is nonetheless likely that the manuscripts that placed it here did so for a reason. Consequently, I will look at the larger section, 7:37–8:30, first without the intervening story and then with it (in an Excursus), in order to assess the flow of thought and make a judgement as to authenticity on the basis of narrative (as well as purely textual) criticism.

37-38 The phrase, "Now on the last day, the great day of the festival" (v. 37), serves as a marker, setting off what follows from what had transpired "already at the middle of the festival" (v. 14).[2] The Tent festival lasted seven days (see Deut 16:13, 15; Lev 23:33; Ezek 45:25), but Leviticus adds that it was followed by a "closing assembly" on the eighth day, set apart (like the first day) as a "day of rest" (see Lev 23:36, 39; see also Num 29:12-35; 2 Maccabees 10.6). It is unclear, therefore, whether "the last day, the great day of the festival," is the seventh or the eighth day. It is unlikely that the Gospel's readers would even have been aware of the distinction, and the Gospel writer (if he is aware) does not pause to explain it to them. The Mishnah refers to the eighth day, not the seventh, as "the last Festival-day of the Feast."[3] If "the last day" is the seventh day here, it is the exception and not

---

1. See Metzger, *Textual Commentary,* 220-21; also the extended discussion in Barrett, 589-92.
2. By itself the phrase, "Now on the last day," could evoke for the reader the expression, "at [or on] the last day," used repeatedly in the preceding chapter in connection with the hope of future resurrection (see 6:39, 40, 44, 54). While this is obviously not the reference here, the effect is to give Jesus' words from here to the end of chapter 8 a certain urgency (even though tempered somewhat by the notice shortly to follow, that "the Spirit was not yet, because Jesus was not yet glorified," v. 39).
3. *Sukkah* 4.8 (see Danby, 179). The ritual of this eighth day (at least as it took place at a later time) is discussed at length in the fifth-century midrash, *Pesikta de-Rab Kahana* 28 (ed. W. G. Braude and I. J. Kapstein [Philadelphia: Jewish Publication Society, 1975], 424-44).

the rule, and I know of no other exceptions in Jewish literature. Josephus, while recognizing a sequence from the first day to the seventh, also states without qualification that the Jewish people at this time "for eight days keep festival."[4] Many interpreters have argued that John's Gospel must refer to the seventh day because Jesus speaks of "living water" (v. 38), and the ritual of drawing water from the pool of Siloam to the temple went on for only the seven days.[5] On the eighth day the water libation would have stopped.[6] But the argument rests too much on the supposed parallel between the water poured out at the Tent festival and the saying of Jesus, a parallel which the Gospel writer does not even bother to make explicit.[7] Even if the parallel is presupposed, Jesus might plausibly have waited for the customary water libation to come to an end before offering "living water" of his own.[8]

Whether the "last day" was the eighth day or the seventh, Jesus "was there."[9] He has not gone "to the dispersion of the Greeks" (v. 35), nor has he been arrested. Again he "cried out,"[10] just as he had done once before (v. 28). This time he said, "If anyone thirst, let him come to me and drink. Whoever believes in me, just as the Scripture said, 'From his insides will flow streams

---

4. See *Antiquities* 3.245-47 (LCL, 4.435).

5. See *Sukkah* 4.1: "[The rites of] the *Lulab* and the Willow-branch [continue] six and sometimes seven days; the Hallel and the Rejoicing eight days; the *Sukkah* and the Water-libation, seven days; the Flute-playing, sometimes five and sometimes six days" (Danby, 178). Water libation is described in more detail in *Sukkah* 4.9.

6. Here, however, the tradition is not unanimous, for according to R. Judah the water libation went on for all eight days (see the Babylonian Talmud, *b. Sukkah* 48b).

7. See Hoskyns, 320: "The argument presupposes that the words of Jesus were occasioned by the ceremony. But it should be noted, first, that the evidence for the ceremony is wholly Rabbinic, there being no allusion to it in the Old Testament; secondly that, if there was such a ceremony, it was concerned with the drawing of water, not with the drinking of it; and thirdly that the theme reappears constantly in the gospel in passages where there is no connection with the feast of Tabernacles (iv.14sqq., vi.35, xix.34; I John vv. 6-8)." While few interpreters have followed Hoskyns at this point, his arguments have never been fully answered. His third point is particularly telling (even though "constantly" is a bit of an exaggeration!).

8. See Morris, 374; Carson, 321.

9. Gr. εἰστήκει. As in 1:35 ("John *was there* again") and 3:29 ("the friend of the bridegroom who *stands by*"), this verb (literally, "stood" or "was standing") emphasizes not so much a standing position as simply Jesus' continuing presence at the festival. His mere presence was noteworthy in view of the attempt of the priests and Pharisees to arrest him (vv. 32-36).

10. Gr. ἔκραξεν. Here too the verb signals a solemn proclamation, not a mere shout. But Bultmann's repeated characterization of it as "inspired speech" (75, n. 1; 297, 302) is overdrawn if taken to mean that these pronouncements are more "inspired" than other words of Jesus. The verb calls attention to the pronouncement to about the same extent as the "Amen, amen" formula does.

7:37–8:29 THE LAST DAY OF THE FESTIVAL

of living water.'" The invitation to "come and drink" looks as if it should have been preceded by an "I am" pronouncement, for several of Jesus' "I am's" in this Gospel are followed by just such invitations (see 6:35, 51; 8:12; 10:9; 11:25-26; 15:5). He could have said, "I am the Water of Life" (see Rev 21:6; 22:17), or "I am the Spring" (4:14), or even "I am the Rock" (see Ps 78:16; 1 Cor 10:4),[11] but he claims none of these titles. His hearers have grasped that he is the healer wanted by the authorities, but his true identity is still a mystery to them, and for the time being he lets it remain so.

The punctuation problem here is well known. According to the traditional punctuation (which our translation has followed), a full stop has been placed after the Greek imperative "let him drink"[12] (v. 37). A new sentence (and in most translations a new verse) begins with the phrase, "he who believes in me,"[13] identifying the person who "comes" to Jesus and "drinks" from what he has to offer as a person who "believes" in him. Regarding such a person, Jesus immediately cites a text of "Scripture" to the effect that "From his insides[14] will flow streams of living water" (v. 38).[15] The text makes it explicit that what Jesus offers is indeed "living water" — exactly what he offered to the woman at the well of Sychar three chapters earlier (4:10-11). Surprisingly, however, on this reading the source of the "living water" is the "believer," not Jesus. This has seemed odd to many interpreters in light of a later scene at Jesus' crucifixion where a Roman soldier pierced "his side" with a spear, "and immediately blood and water came out" (19:34). The truth of that account is then attested by an eyewitness (19:35), suggesting that the Gospel writer found it notably significant. Moreover, Jesus and not the believer is the one issuing the invitation to "come to me and drink" (7:37), and Jesus' words are promptly interpreted

---

11. That at some point in the tradition the title "Rock" may have been linked to a saying similar to this can be seen from Justin Martyr's *Dialogue with Trypho* 114.4, where Justin speaks of Christian believers being "willing to die for the name of the good Rock [τῆς καλῆς πέτρας], which causes living water [ζῶν ὕδωρ] to burst forth for the hearts of those who by Him have loved the Father of all, and which gives those who are willing to drink of the water of life" (ANF, 1.256).

12. Gr. πινέτω.

13. Gr. ὁ πιστεύων εἰς ἐμέ. The "suspended nominative" (that is, a noun or pronoun standing alone in the nominative case, followed by an explanatory clause; see BDF, §466[4]; Abbott, *Johannine Grammar*, 308-9) is a common stylistic feature of John's Gospel (see, for example, 1:12; 6:39; 8:45; 10:29; 15:2; 17:2, 24).

14. Gr. ἐκ τῆς κοιλίας αὐτοῦ, literally "from his stomach."

15. This is the punctuation adopted by some of our earliest manuscripts (for example, P66), and many of the church fathers, especially in the Eastern Mediterranean area (see also most editions of the Greek text, and many English translations, for example, the KJV, Douay, RSV, NIV, NAB, and REB). Among commentators, see Barrett, 327; Morris, 395; Carson, 322-25; Lindars, 298-301; Hoskyns, 321-23; Bernard, 1.282; Lightfoot, 183.

as referring to "the Spirit, which those who believed in him were later to receive"[16] (v. 39), not dispense.[17]

Consequently many commentators and some translations have punctuated the sentence differently, with a comma after "let him come to me"[18] and a period after "whoever believes in me"; thus, "If anyone thirst, let him come to me, and let him drink who believes in me. Just as the Scripture said, 'From his insides will flow streams of living water.'"[19] On this reading, it is unclear whether the Scripture quotation is being attributed to Jesus or the Gospel writer. Most of those who translate it this way attribute the quotation to Jesus without discussing the issue, but there are exceptions.[20] Either way, the text cited is identifying Jesus as the source of the living water. It is from Jesus' "insides," not the believer's, that the water flows. This seems to many interpreters more in keeping with the other relevant passages in John's Gospel, as well as with most of the biblical texts to which John's Gospel might conceivably be alluding.

Yet it should not be forgotten that Jesus told the Samaritan woman, "Everyone who drinks of this water will thirst again, but whoever drinks of the water that I will give him will never ever thirst. Instead, the water I will give him will become *in him*[21] a spring of water rushing to eternal life" (4:14, my italics). The point there was that the "living water" Jesus offered was self-replenishing. To say that it would become in the believer "a spring of water rushing to eternal life" was simply a more dramatic and more eloquent way of promising that those who drink of it would *"never ever thirst"* (my italics). The Samaritan woman, even in her misunderstanding, promptly drove the point home with her plea, "Sir, give me this water, so that I will not thirst and have to keep coming back here to draw" (4:15). Again, two chapters later, Jesus as "the Bread of life" promises that "The person who comes

16. Gr. λαμβάνειν (compare 1:16).

17. Schnackenburg (2.154) attempts to resolve the problem with this punctuation by translating, "If anyone believes in me, for him — as the Scripture says — rivers of living water will flow from his [Jesus'] heart." This is a strained translation, first because of the need to supply "for him," and second because when Jesus applies Scripture to himself in John's Gospel, it is always with "me" or "my" (2:17; 13:18; 15:25), never with "him" or "his."

18. Gr. ἐρχέσθω πρός με.

19. For this punctuation, see, for example, the NRSV, NEB, JB, GNB, NLT, and, among the commentators, Brown, 1.319; Dodd, *Interpretation,* 349; Bultmann, 303; Keener, 1.728-29; Whitacre, 195.

20. The NEB, for example, places quotation marks after "let him drink," implying that Jesus' pronouncement is over, and that the Scripture citation that follows is supplied by the Gospel writer. Bultmann (303, n. 5) attributes the quotation to a later "ecclesiastical editor."

21. Gr. ἐν αὐτῷ.

to me will never go hungry, and the person who believes in me will *never ever thirst*" (6:35, my italics).[22] Here in the temple his meaning is probably the same. To say of the believer that "From his insides will flow streams of living water" is yet another way of promising that he will "never ever thirst." As he told the Samaritan woman, the "living water" he offers is a never-failing, self-replenishing stream. The point is not, as is often thought, that the believer will necessarily become a channel of "living water" to others,[23] but that the believer's own well will never run dry.[24] As Jesus will later announce, "I have come that they might have life, and have it in abundance" (10:10).[25] These considerations also reinforce the punctuation used in our translation (that is, with a period after "If anyone thirst, let him come to me and drink"). The other punctuation ("If anyone thirst, let him come to me, and let him drink who believes") contradicts the notion that those who believe will "never ever thirst." If they never thirst, they have *no need* to drink. The participle "Whoever believes in me" is best understood as referring not to someone *being invited* to "come and drink," but to a person who has *already* done so, never to thirst again.[26]

The issue is complicated by the uncertainty as to what text of "Scripture" Jesus (or the Gospel writer) has in mind. Among those commonly suggested,[27] the most plausible is Zechariah 14:8 (NIV), "On that day living wa-

22. In 4:14, the translation "never ever thirst" is based on the addition of εἰς τὸν αἰῶνα ("to the age," or "forever") to the already emphatic οὐ μή ("by no means") construction, while in 6:35 it is based on the addition of πώποτε ("at any time"). There is no discernible difference in meaning between the two expressions.

23. See Westcott, 1.178: "He who drinks of the Spiritual Rock becomes in turn himself a rock from within which the waters flow to slake the thirst of others. He is not only satisfied himself: he overflows. The Christian, in some sense, becomes a Christ (1 John ii.)" — yet an accompanying note tells us that "Bishop Westcott . . . 'now inclines' to interpret αὐτοῦ of Christ" (!). For the view that the believer becomes a channel to others, see also Morris, 375; Hoskyns, 322; Barrett, 328; Bernard, 1.282.

24. See Michaels, 139: "That the believer in Jesus will become a channel of God's life to others is implicit in the total message of John's Gospel, but is not the point of either 4:14 or 7:37-38 in particular." See also Carson, 323-24. The point is made already in Isa 58:11, "You will be like a well-watered garden, like a spring whose waters never fail" (NIV; see also *Sirach* 24.31).

25. The reader of John's Gospel may also remember at this point the extravagant quantity of water changed to wine at Cana (2:6), not to mention the abundance of expensive perfume when Mary of Bethany anointed Jesus (12:3), the enormous weight of spices brought to embalm Jesus after his crucifixion (19:39), and the catch of 153 fish after the resurrection (21:11).

26. See, for example, R. H. Lightfoot, who comments that "whereas to come to the Lord and to drink of Him are synonymous, the believer on Him is by no means in the same case as he who thirsts" (183); also Barrett, 327; Carson, 324.

27. These include Psalm 78:16; 114:8; Isaiah 43:20; 44:3; 55:1; Ezekiel 47:1-12;

ter will flow out from Jerusalem," for it is the only text that uses the actual phrase "living water."[28] Moreover, "that day" spoken of in Zechariah was to be a day when all the nations of the world would come to Jerusalem to worship the God of Israel and "keep the Tent festival"[29] (see Zech 14:16 and 19).[30] Yet neither this nor any other biblical text uses the expression "from his insides" in connection with streams of water. Perhaps the closest parallel to that is Justin Martyr's comment that "As, therefore, Christ is the Israel and the Jacob, even so we, who have been quarried out from the bowels of Christ,[31] are the true Israelite race" (*Dialogue with Trypho* 135.3).[32] The verb "quarried"[33] evokes another of Justin's images, that of Christ as "the good Rock" from which "living water" flows (*Dialogue* 114.4; see above, n. 11). It is unclear whether Justin drew his imagery from John's Gospel or from the Apostle Paul (see 1 Cor 10:4) or both, or whether he and John and Paul all drew on a common source. If the latter is the case, then "the Scripture"[34] cited here could have been just such a source — a midrash or paraphrase based on Israel's desert experience of water from the rock (see Ps 78:16). Possibly this was linked to some reference to Israel's disobedience — as in Psalm 78:17-20 and 1 Corinthians 10:5, as well as the two other New Testament instances where Christ is called a "rock."[35] No such explicit link is made here, yet the Gospel writer goes out of his way to comment that Jesus' promise of "living water" was *not* for his immediate hearers at the Tent festival (see v. 39), adding that the pronouncement was received not with unambiguous faith, but with "a division . . . in the crowd on account of him" (v. 43).

As Schnackenburg points out, the two traditions (represented by Zech 14:8 and Ps 78:16 respectively) are "not mutually exclusive."[36] The place was right (the temple) and the time was right (the Tent festival) for the Zech-

---

Joel 3:18. In such texts God is the giver of water, whether from a rock (as in Exod 17:6; Num 20:7-11) or from the city of Jerusalem.

28. Gr. (LXX): ὕδωρ ζῶν.

29. Gr. (LXX): σκηνοπηγία, just as in John 7:2.

30. The phrase "on that day" is repeated over and over again in the chapter (Zech 14:1, "a day is coming," and 14:4, 6, 8, 9, 13, 20, 21). "That day" was to Zechariah what the day of Jesus' utterance is to the Gospel of John: "the last day, the great day of the festival."

31. Gr. ἐκ τῆς κοιλίας τοῦ Χριστοῦ.

32. See ANF, 1.267.

33. Gr. λατομηθέντες.

34. Gr. ἡ γραφή.

35. See Romans 9:33 and 1 Peter 2:8, "rock of offense" (πέτρα σκανδάλου), based on Isa 8:14). Notice also that in Justin's *Dialogue* (135.3), the point being made is that Christians are "the true Israelite race."

36. Schnackenburg, 2.155-56. Also J. Grelot, "Jean VII, 38: Eau de Rocher Ou Source du Temple?" *RB* 70 (1963), 43-53, which he cites.

ariah text to be in play, and the imagery of water from the rock was implicit already when Jesus spoke earlier of "thirst" as well as "hunger" in connection with "bread from heaven" and his own identity as "the Bread of life" (6:35). Whatever "Scripture" Jesus may have had in mind, he has so incorporated it into his own pronouncement that the words have become his own. With it he issues the same invitation as before (6:35), but the question lingers, Who was present to receive it?

39 The traditional punctuation attributes all of verse 38 to Jesus, but what follows can only be read as a characteristic narrative aside by the Gospel writer: "But he said[37] this about the Spirit, which those who believed in him were later to receive. For the Spirit was not yet, because Jesus was not yet glorified" (v. 39). "This he said" could also be translated "this it said," referring to "the Scripture," for "said" echoes "the Scripture said" in verse 38. But the expression "this he said" and others like it are normally used in John's Gospel as explanations of verbal utterances, not written Scripture (see 2:21; 6:6; 8:6; 11:51; 12:6, 33; 21:19).[38] More important, if Jesus has indeed made the words of "the Scripture" his own words, it is unlikely that the Gospel writer intends to separate out what Jesus has linked together. The comment should therefore be read as referring to verses 37-38 in their entirety, including but not limited to the "Scripture" citation.

The translation "*But* this he said" (my italics) attaches to the particle[39] at least a mildly adversative quality. To a degree, the Gospel writer is adding a small caution or qualification to what he has just represented Jesus as saying. He is telling the reader two things: first, that the "living water" Jesus promises is the Spirit; but, second, that his promise of the Spirit was *not* for his immediate hearers at the Tent festival but for Christian believers at a later time — above all, for the readers of the Gospel themselves. The first is no surprise, given Jesus' words to Nicodemus about a new birth "of water and Spirit" (3:5), and his pronouncement at Capernaum that "the Spirit is that which makes alive" (6:63). Clearly, "living water" is nothing other than "eternal life" (see also 4:14), and just as clearly "the Spirit" is the source of eternal life. More surprising is the notice that the gift of the Spirit was something that believers were "later to receive."[40] Like certain other narrative

---

37. Gr. τοῦτο δὲ εἶπεν.
38. See G. D. Fee, "Once More — John 7:37-39," *Expository Times* 89 (1977-78), 116-18. This point is not altogether conclusive because here (in contrast to other Scripture citations in John's Gospel) "the Scripture" has just been represented as having "spoken" almost as a person would speak (for even clearer examples of this tendency to personify "the Scripture," see Gal 3:8 and 22).
39. That is, the δέ in τοῦτο δὲ εἶπεν, which can be rendered either as "and" or "but."
40. Gr. ἔμελλον λαμβάνειν.

asides in this Gospel, its perspective is postresurrection (for example, 2:21-22 and 12:16). That "later" implies "*only* later," and not then and there at the Tent festival, can be seen from the Gospel writer's further comment, "For the Spirit was not yet,[41] because Jesus was not yet glorified" (v. 39b).[42]

What does it mean for Jesus to be "glorified"?[43] The word has not been used before, although the writer has claimed to have seen Jesus' "glory" (1:14), and has described how Jesus "revealed his glory" at the Cana wedding (2:11). What future "glory" or "glorification" remains? Is it a matter of "the sky opened, and the angels of God going up and coming down over the Son of man" (1:51), or of "the Son of man going up where he was at first" (6:62)? Either of these might be a reasonable guess for any reader who does not know the end of the story, but a complicating factor is the notice a few verses earlier that Jesus' "hour," presumably the time for him to be arrested and perhaps put to death, was also "not yet" (v. 30). What could such a grim fate have to do with "glorification" and the gift of "the Spirit"? How do the two contrasting "not yets" relate to each other? Do they cancel each other out? Which comes first? The issue will be resolved later, when the two terms come together, as Jesus' "hour" turns out to be precisely the hour of his "glorification" (see 12:23; 17:1). Yet for the present the reader confronts the same ambiguity here as in chapter 3, when Jesus spoke of being "lifted up" in the same way that Moses "lifted up the snake in the desert" (3:14). Like that image, the reference to Jesus' "hour" (v. 30) suggests suffering and death, yet the mention of Jesus being "glorified" looks past death to final vindication. The vindication has already been promised in a variety of ways (not only in 1:51 and 6:62, but in 2:19, "Destroy this sanctuary, and in three days I will raise it up"), and is implicit in the immediate context in Jesus' invitation to "come to me and drink" (v. 37).

The negative side of the comment is that the gift of the Spirit is *not* for either "the crowds" or "the Jews" at the temple in Jerusalem during the Tent festival, but for the readers of the Gospel *after* Jesus was "glorified," and af-

---

41. Gr. οὔπω.

42. As commentators have been careful to point out, "the Spirit was not yet" does not mean that the Holy Spirit did not yet *exist*. Jesus had obviously stated that "God *is* Spirit" (4:24), and "the Spirit *is* that which makes alive" (6:63, my italics). The point is rather that the Holy Spirit had not yet come, or been given. This is properly clarified in certain textual witnesses (including B) that define "the Spirit" as "the Holy Spirit" and add the participle "given" (δεδόμενον), and in others (including D) that expand the text to read, "the Holy Spirit was not yet *upon them*" (ἐπ' αὐτούς). But the overwhelming textual evidence omits both the participle and the prepositional phrase, allowing readers to fill in the gaps and supply the right meaning for themselves (see Metzger, *Textual Commentary*, 218).

43. Gr. ἐδοξάσθη.

ter he breathed on his disciples, saying, "Receive Holy Spirit" (20:22). Neither of Jesus' two earlier invitations to "drink" drew a positive response, and the same is true here. First, the Samaritan woman failed to grasp his meaning (4:15), and Jesus changed the subject. In the second instance, he followed his invitation (6:35) by clearly excluding his immediate hearers: "Yet I said to you that you have seen me and you *do not believe*" (6:36, my italics). This time the Gospel writer's disclaimer is borne out by what follows. While the immediate reaction to Jesus' utterance is not uniformly negative (see vv. 40-44), neither will we see among his hearers anything remotely resembling "streams of living water."

40-42 "The crowd" is explicitly said to have "heard these words," and various reactions are given. "Some"[44] said of Jesus, "This is truly the Prophet" (v. 40), while "others" said, "This is the Christ" (v. 41). The two titles side by side recall John's reply to questioners denying that he was either one (see 1:20, 21), while the phrase "This is truly the Prophet" echoes almost verbatim what some Galileans said earlier about Jesus when they planned "to come and seize him to make him king" (6:14-15).[45] While there is no reason to assign similar motives to those speaking here, neither is there sufficient reason to attribute to them genuine faith.[46] In the case of those who said, "This is the Christ" (v. 41), there is more reason to do so, in light of the "many" a few verses earlier who were said to have "believed in him," asking if "the Christ" would do "more signs than this man did" (v. 31). Yet there is no further mention of explicit "belief," much less any evaluation of such belief. Readers are left to make of it what they will.

Another voice is quickly heard: "But they were saying, 'Does the Christ come from Galilee? Did not the Scripture say that the Christ comes from the seed of David and from Bethlehem, the village where David was?'" (vv. 41-42). Whether this is a third voice, or a rejoinder from those who had said, "This is truly the Prophet" (v. 40), is unclear.[47] "They" is probably to be

---

44. "Some" (which would have been τινές) is not in the Greek text, but is implied by the partitive genitive with the preposition ἐκ: literally, "from the crowd, when they heard" (see BDF, §164[2]).

45. The agreement extends even to the repetition of the adverb "truly" (ἀληθῶς). All that is missing is the participial phrase, "who is coming into the world."

46. The comparable confession by the Samaritans at Sychar, "This is truly [ἀληθῶς] the Savior of the world" (4:42) is different, in that it is preceded by an explicit claim that they "believed" (4:39, 41-42).

47. The definite article (οἱ) functions here as a demonstrative pronoun, "these" or "they" (see BDAG, 686; BDF, §249). Some important manuscripts (including the first hand of P[66], ℵ, D, Ψ, and the majority of later manuscripts) settle the matter in favor of a third voice by substituting ἄλλοι ("others") for οἱ. But the latter (supported by P[75], B, L, N, T, W, Θ, and the Latin tradition) is the more difficult reading, and probably original.

understood impersonally, implying that (as Raymond Brown puts it, without comment), "An objection was raised."[48] If it were a rejoinder, the issue would be between those who regarded Jesus as "the Prophet" and those who viewed him as "the Christ," but such a debate is unlikely. More plausibly, the issue was between *both* groups and those (perhaps the majority) who denied that he was in any way a messenger of God.[49] Their argument was simple: Jesus was from Galilee. They had already claimed to know where he was from (v. 27), and he had agreed that they did know (v. 28). Consequently, they now argued, he could not be "the Christ" or "Messiah" (see 1:41) as commonly understood, because according to "the Scripture" the Messiah was to come "from the seed of David,"[50] and therefore "from Bethlehem, the village where David was" (v. 42).[51] The issue here was not so much Jesus' ancestry as his birthplace, and "the Scripture" in mind appears to have been Micah 5:2, the same text cited by Herod's chief priests and scribes according to the birth narrative in Matthew (see Mt 2:4-6).[52]

The question raised by this appeal to "the Scripture" centers on how the readers of the Gospel are meant to view it. Are they expected to agree with it or not? In light of the certainty that such a text actually existed, and in light of the principle Jesus himself articulates three chapters later, that "the Scripture cannot be abolished" (10:35), they are hardly free to disagree.[53]

48. See Brown, 1.319.

49. See verse 52, where much the same objection seems to be raised against Jesus as "prophet" that is raised here against his being "the Christ."

50. That David's line would continue forever, and consequently that the Messiah would be David's descendant, was a notion widely attested in the Hebrew Bible (for example, 2 Sam 7:12; Ps 89:4, 29, 36; Isa 11:1-2; Jer 23:5; see also *Psalms of Solomon* 17.21); that he would come from Bethlehem, the city of David, much less so.

51. Curiously but perhaps coincidentally, the rhetorical question, "Did not the Scripture say?" (οὐχ ἡ γραφὴ εἶπεν) echoes Jesus' own words, "just as the Scripture said" (καθὼς εἶπεν ἡ γραφή) in verse 38. In the first instance, as we saw, "the Scripture" was virtually unidentifiable, while here it is unmistakably clear. What they appear to have in common is that both are paraphrases rather than word-for-word quotations. Their similarity may also suggest that to the Gospel writer the second is just as true and just as important as the first.

52. Surprisingly, this text is not attested in Jewish sources in connection with messianic expectations before the fourth century, and some have suggested that it may have been introduced first by Christians in light of the fact that Bethlehem was in fact Jesus' birthplace (see, for example, Dodd, *Interpretation,* 90-91). But this is unlikely because both in Matthew and in John it is attributed to Jesus' opponents, not to Jesus or the Gospel writer. Even Dodd (91) allows for "the possibility that interpretations of the Old Testament which seemed to favour Christian claims may have been deliberately abandoned in the rabbinic schools" (see Schnackenburg, 2.158).

53. As Schnackenburg puts it, "one might ask whether the evangelist would have dismissed so easily an objection formulated on the basis of Scripture" (2.159). The mat-

"The Christ" must indeed come "from the seed of David, and from Bethlehem, the village where David was." If so, and if the readers of the Gospel are truly meant to "believe that Jesus is the Christ, the Son of God, and in believing have life in his name" (20:31), then they must also believe and know that he was in fact "from Bethlehem," just as two other Gospels (Matthew and Luke) claim that he was.[54] In short, they are expected to understand that his opponents, in attempting to disqualify Jesus as "the Christ," are, ironically and in their ignorance, clearly stating his qualifications. Still, when all is said and done, his "qualifications" (on the basis of Jewish messianic expectations) are of secondary importance to the reader. They are trumped, just as his public identity as "Jesus of Nazareth" is trumped, by his origin "from above" or "from heaven," and by his unique relationship to "the One who sent him" (see 7:18, 28-29).

43-44 The result of the dispute was that "a split[55] took place in the crowd on account of him" (v. 43), a heightened version of the "murmuring" among the crowds earlier (vv. 12, 32), and of the "murmuring" and "quarreling" in Galilee over Jesus' words (see 6:41, 52). The "split" is the first of three explicitly noted in this Gospel: this one "in the crowd," the second among "the Pharisees" (9:16), and the third among "the Jews" (10:19-21). Nothing good comes of such "splits," for although in each instance some speak in favor of Jesus and some against him, no one is said to "believe" in him or to "drink" of the "living water" he has offered. In this sense, the Gospel writer's comment that "The Spirit was not yet, because Jesus was not yet glorified" (v. 39) is confirmed. Even though some have said, "This is truly the Prophet," and others, "This is the Christ" (vv. 40-41), all that comes of such acknowledgments is a standoff. "Some of them wanted to arrest him," we are told, "but no one laid hands on him" (v. 44). The writer could have added, "because his hour had not yet come" (see v. 30), but he does not. That

---

ter can be put even more strongly. "The Scripture" (ἡ γραφή) is always authoritative in John's Gospel (see 2:11; 5:39; 7:38; 20:9), and destined to be "fulfilled" (see 13:18; 17:12; 19:24, 28, 36, 37). In only one other instance do Jesus' opponents appeal to Scripture (6:31), and there Jesus is careful not to question what "is written," but simply to clarify its meaning (6:32-33). Nor is it likely that either Jesus or the Gospel writer took issue with the assertion of the crowd that "We have heard out of the law that the Christ remains forever" (12:34; compare 8:35). Even the claim that "the Christ, when he comes, no one knows where he is from," which is *not* backed up by Scripture, is allowed to go unchallenged.

54. In addition to Schnackenburg (see n. 41), see, for example, Bernard, 1.286; Barrett, 330; Brown, 1.330; Keener, 1.730. According to Bultmann, by contrast (306, n. 6), "The Jews, of course, are as little mistaken in this as they were in 6.42; 7.27. That is to say, the Evangelist knows nothing, or wants to know nothing of the birth in Bethlehem."

55. Gr. σχίσμα.

is of course still the overriding reason, but the more immediate reason Jesus is not arrested is that "the crowd," unlike the Pharisees (v. 32), does not act as one or speak with one voice.

45-46 This second attempt to "arrest"[56] Jesus (v. 44) prompts a change of scene, allowing us a glimpse of how the first attempt turned out.[57] Now we are told explicitly what we already assumed must have been the case, that the officers sent to arrest Jesus (vv. 32-36) returned empty-handed to "the chief priests and the Pharisees" who had sent them. In a kind of parody of Jesus' own intent to "go to the One who sent me" (v. 33), they have now returned to those who "sent" them (v. 32) — but with nothing to show for it! The scene is almost comic, as the Pharisees ask, "Why didn't you bring him in?" (v. 45), and the officers reply, "No man ever spoke like that" (v. 46). They are referring to what he had told them when they came to arrest him (vv. 33-34), part of which they had repeated in confusion and disbelief (vv. 35-36). Now their incomprehension surfaces again as a testimony to the overwhelming power of Jesus' words, recalling other Gospel testimonies to the power of his deeds.[58]

47-49 The Pharisees' reply, "Are you also deceived?" (v. 47), reflects the belief already expressed that Jesus "deceives the crowd" (v. 12). Their accompanying question, "Has any of the rulers believed in him, or any of the Pharisees?" (vv. 47-48), is a setup for the appearance of Nicodemus, who will almost immediately prove them wrong (vv. 50-51). Their harsh verdict on "this crowd that does not know the law" is that "they are accursed" (v. 49). As is frequently pointed out, this judgment was characteristic of certain later rabbinic judgments about nonobservant Jews, known as *'am ha'aretz*.[59] In the present situation, it reflects the mistaken assumption that "the crowd," in contrast to the

---

56. Gr. πᾶσαι, as in verse 30.

57. Predictably, Rudolf Bultmann (see 302-9) rearranged the text so that the attempt to arrest Jesus here and the attempt in vv. 32-36 coincide (thus, v. 30 is followed by vv. 37-44, then by v. 31 and vv. 32-36, finally by vv. 45-52). There are still two attempts. The better procedure is to link the attempt in verse 30 to verses 31-36, as we have done and as the Johannine order seems to require.

58. The simple words, "No man *ever* spoke *like that*" (οὐδέποτε ... οὕτως), recall the reaction in Mark to the healing of the paralytic, "We have *never* seen *such a thing*" (οὕτως οὐδέποτε, Mk 2:12), and in Matthew to the healing of a deaf mute, "*Never* has *such a thing* been seen in Israel" (οὐδέποτε ... οὕτως, Mt 9:33; italics added). The vocabulary is different in John 9:32, but the point is much the same: "Not since time began was it ever heard that anyone opened the eyes of someone born blind."

59. Heb. עם הארץ. The text most often cited is the statement of Hillel, "A brutish man dreads not sin, and an ignorant man [or *'am ha'aretz*] cannot be saintly" (*m. Abot* 2.6; see Danby, 448). A similar outlook probably underlies the amazement of "the Jews," who mistook Jesus for such a person when they asked, "How does this man know letters, being uninstructed?" (v. 15). On such attitudes among the Jewish elite generally, see Keener, 1.731-33.

"the rulers" and "the Pharisees," have believed in Jesus, and that this proves their ignorance of the law.[60] That, as we have seen, was not the case. While at one point "many from the crowd" were said to "believe" (v. 31), their belief seems to have amounted to little more than "murmuring" (v. 32), and even when some proclaimed him "the Prophet" or "the Christ" (vv. 40-41), all that came of it was a "split" in the crowd (v. 43), and another failed attempt at an arrest (v. 44). The Pharisees' effort to create a breach between themselves, the elite who do *not* believe in Jesus, and the ignorant rabble who do is doomed to failure. Not all in "the crowd" believe, and not all among "the Pharisees" or "the Jews" disbelieve. The breach, or "split," as we will see (9:16; 10:19-21), cuts right down the middle of both groups. This becomes evident at once.

50 Nicodemus now speaks. He does not come on the scene, but is assumed to be already present because he "was one of them" (see 3:1, "a man of the Pharisees . . . a ruler of the Jews"). For the reader's benefit, he is also explicitly identified as "he who came to him previously" (see 3:2). The only reason to introduce Nicodemus here is as living proof that the Pharisees are wrong in implying that none of "the rulers" or "the Pharisees" have believed in Jesus.[61] If Jesus' encounter with Nicodemus left some doubt as whether Nicodemus in fact "believed," the doubt is now removed. Whatever his faith may have been, the Gospel writer judges it sufficient to disprove the Pharisees' rash claim. This remains true even if his faith proves in the end to be flawed, like that of other Jewish "rulers" (see 12:42-43; but as for Nicodemus, see 19:39).

51 Nicodemus does not directly challenge his colleagues, but merely asks a question: "Does our law judge the man[62] unless it hear from him first and learn what he is doing?" This was a perfectly reasonable point, given the nature of biblical law (see, for example, Deut 1:16-17; 19:16-17). By referring to "our" law (in contrast to Jesus' own terminology!),[63] Nicodemus distances

---

60. Bultmann (310, n. 4) comments that this verse's "conjunction with the previous clause (ἀλλά) implies the idea, 'What if the ὄχλος does believe in him!'"

61. Barrett suggests the opposite, that "Possibly John means that for all his good will and fair-mindedness, Nicodemus remains one of the Jews, not one of the disciples" (332). On the contrary, the notice that he was "one of them" lends weight to his words (mild as they are) on Jesus' behalf, and gives the lie to the implication that none of the rulers or Pharisees have believed in Jesus.

62. The law is personified here, much as "the Scripture" was personified (v. 38), as the subject of the verb "to judge" (κρίνει). Whether "the man" (τὸν ἄνθρωπον) is any accused person or Jesus in particular is difficult to say. The definite article is surprising, and it is worth noting that Jesus will be designated as "the man" (ὁ ἄνθρωπος) precisely at the moment of his condemnation (19:5).

63. Jesus himself, by contrast, consistently speaks of "your" law (8:17; 10:34), or "their" law (15:25). See also 7:19, "Has Moses not given *you* the law?" (my italics).

himself from the "accursed" crowd that "does not know the law" (v. 49), and confirms to the Pharisees that he is indeed "one of them" (v. 50). His deliberative question[64] matches (and possibly mocks) the two deliberative questions of the Pharisees themselves, "Are you also deceived?" (v. 47), and "Has any of the rulers believed in him?" (v. 48).[65] Nicodemus pleads that the Pharisees should "hear" from Jesus first, and "learn what he is doing." On the face of it, "what he is doing" implies "what he intends" or "what he is up to,"[66] but Nicodemus's choice of words reflects his own long-standing interest in what Jesus was "doing," going back to that earlier encounter when he said to Jesus, "no one can *do* these signs you are *doing* unless God is with him" (3:2).[67] For the reader, it also recalls the original charges against Jesus, that he was "*doing* such things on the Sabbath" (5:16), and his reply that "the Son can *do* nothing on his own, except what he sees the Father *doing*. For whatever things he *does*, these in the same way the Son does too" (5:19, italics added throughout). Nicodemus knew (or thought he knew) what Jesus was "doing," and wanted his fellow "rulers" and "Pharisees" to "hear" of it from Jesus' own lips. But their messengers had already heard, and concluded that "No man ever spoke like that" (v. 46), as if his very words were mighty deeds,[68] and the Pharisees had rejected their report. As far as they were concerned, they had heard enough.[69] Ironically, the reader has already heard Jesus' full defense, delivered as if addressed to "the Jews" directly (5:19-47), and yet without comment or response of any kind from them. As we have seen, that lengthy encounter seems to have been a literary creation, not a literal confrontation, for although Jesus "gave his answer" to them (5:19), they never accused him in person, but only "began pursuing him" for breaking the Sabbath (5:16) and "kept seeking all the more to kill him" for claiming God as his Father (5:18). Consequently, Nicodemus's point is well taken. Neither "the Pharisees" nor "the Jews" (if the two can be distinguished) have yet "heard" directly from Jesus to "learn what he is doing."

52 The Pharisees answer Nicodemus with yet another deliberative

---

64. That is, with μή, expecting a negative answer. See Abbott, *Johannine Grammar*, 193, who comments that μή is "used interrogatively in the Fourth Gospel more frequently than in all the Three Gospels taken together."

65. For yet another deliberative question with μή, see v. 35, "Will he go to the dispersion of the Greeks?"

66. Gr. γνῷ τὶ ποιεῖ. See Chrysostom, *Homily* 52, "For the meaning of, 'know what he doeth,' is, 'what he intendeth,' 'on what account,' 'for what purpose,' 'whether for the subversion of the order of things and as an enemy'" (NPNF, n.s., 14.187).

67. See also 2:23, "many believed in his name, for they could see the signs he was doing" (ἃ ἐποίει).

68. See above, n. 58.

69. So Bultmann: "for them the matter was already closed!" (311).

question, "Are you also from Galilee?" Like their two previous ones (vv. 48, 50), it expects a negative answer, "Of course not!" Yet like the question of the officers sent by the Pharisees (v. 35) and the Pharisees' question to them on their return (v. 47, "Are you also deceived?"), it also injects a measure of doubt, as if to say, "Surely you are not a Galilean, but just as surely you're beginning to sound like one!" Their point was that in appearing to defend Jesus, a Galilean, Nicodemus might well be revealing his own Galilean sympathies. This comes as a surprise, because (aside from the one brief remark in vv. 41-42), geographical origin has not been a conspicuous issue between Jesus and the Jewish authorities. Yet the Pharisees' pronouncement enables certain details in the narrative to fall into place. Before he came to the festival, we were told, "Jesus was walking in Galilee, for he chose not to walk in Judea because the Jews there were seeking to kill him" (v. 1), and when he finally "went up" to the festival (v. 10), he naturally came from Galilee. At the festival, he was at first mistaken for someone "uninstructed," who would not normally have been expected to "know letters" (v. 15). Later, those who were thought (in part mistakenly) to have "believed in him" (v. 48) were denounced as "this crowd that does not know the law," and therefore as "accursed" (v. 49). Such details point to certain strongly held stereotypes about Galilee and Galileans among the Pharisees and the ruling authorities in Jerusalem.[70]

Here it merely becomes explicit. "Search and see," they tell Nicodemus, "that a prophet is not arising out of Galilee." "Search and see" is just what Jesus said they customarily did in relation to Scripture.[71] In this instance they send Nicodemus to Scripture to find out not so much what it says as what (they think) it does *not* say. Their contention that "a prophet is not arising out of Galilee" is puzzling. If they mean that no prophet has *ever* arisen out of Galilee, they are mistaken, for Scripture teaches no such thing (see 2 Kgs 14:25, where Nicodemus would have "seen" that Jonah was from Gath Hepher, and known that Gath Hepher was in Galilee).[72] If they are saying that a prophet is not arising out of Galilee *now*, in the person of Jesus, it is

---

70. This is, of course, even more conspicuous if "the Jews" (vv. 11, 15, 35) are understood as "the Judeans," but that is doubtful, as we have seen, given the presence of "the Jews" in Galilee as well (see 6:41, 52).

71. See 5:39, "You search the Scriptures." In Jesus' pronouncement, "search" (ἐραυνᾶτε) could have been read as either imperative or indicative, but was more likely indicative. Here, "search" (ἐραύνησον) is unmistakably imperative. A few ancient manuscripts (D and others) actually add "the Scriptures" (τὰς γραφάς) here, but this is unlikely. For a similar expression using different vocabulary, see Matthew 9:13, where Jesus tells the Pharisees, "Go, learn what it is, 'I desire mercy and not sacrifice.'"

72. Also, the often-quoted *b. Sukkah* 27b, "There was not a tribe in Israel from which there did not come prophets," and one or two late rabbinic references specifying every town or city in Israel (see Keener, 1.734, n. 298).

hard to see how searching the Scriptures would shed explicit light on that question. Therefore it was conjectured that what they were actually saying was, "The Prophet[73] does not arise out of Galilee,"[74] a conjecture that became an actual variant reading when the Bodmer Papyrus (P[66]) was discovered, and published in 1956.[75] If this reading is original (or if "prophet" without the article is interpreted as nevertheless referring to "the Prophet"), then the Pharisees are probably just repeating the argument of verses 41-42 (based on Mic 5:2) that "the Christ" would not come from Galilee. Because there was no particular discussion in Judaism as to where "the Prophet" like Moses (see Deut 18:15-18) would come from, their assumption would have to be that "the Christ" and "the Prophet" could be regarded as more or less interchangeable figures in messianic expectation. This is plausible in light of the fact that when some Galileans decided a chapter earlier that Jesus was "truly the Prophet who is coming into the world," their first thought was to "seize him to make him king" (6:14-15).[76] Elsewhere in the Gospel, Jesus as "the Christ" and Jesus as "King" appear to be closely related notions (see especially 1:41, 45, 49; also 12:13, 15; 18:33; 19:3, 14, 15, 19). Whatever Scripture they may have had in mind, the Pharisees' response to Nicodemus seems to dismiss his question out of hand. As for Jesus, therefore, the reader does not at all anticipate that they will "hear from him first and learn what he is doing" (v. 51).

8:12 Surprisingly, the Pharisees will now proceed to do almost what Nicodemus recommended! Whether they choose to or not, they will now "hear" from Jesus and to some degree "learn what he is doing." As the narrative continues,[77] we are told, "So again Jesus spoke to them" (8:12). "To them" can only mean "to the Pharisees," for the Pharisees are identified as those who answered (v. 13). "Again" implies that he had spoken to them before — probably not directly but by what he said to the officers representing

73. That is, ὁ προφήτης, as in v. 40.

74. See Bultmann, 312, n. 1, a suggestion that he made even in the first German edition, before the publication of P[66]. The conjecture goes back to a Dr. Owen in the eighteenth century (see Metzger, *Textual Commentary*, 219).

75. Since then, "the Prophet" seems also to be supported by a second Bodmer manuscript, P[75]. At the same time, it must be admitted that the weight of textual evidence supports the anarthrous προφήτης.

76. This raises the question of whether "the Prophet" may have been a more characteristically Galilean expectation, but there is no way to be certain of that. The parallelism between "the Prophet who is coming into the world" (6:14) and "the Christ, the Son of God, who is coming into the world" (11:27) further supports the interchangeability of the two titles, at least in the eyes of some Jews at the time.

77. Here, with the earliest and most important manuscripts, we move directly from 7:52 to 8:12, on the assumption that 7:53–8:11 is a later addition to the text. After dealing with 8:12-20, we will go back and look at the narrative with 7:53–8:11 included.

7:37–8:29 THE LAST DAY OF THE FESTIVAL

them, when they came to arrest him (7:32-34). "No man ever spoke like that" was the reaction then (7:46), and the reader will echo those sentiments about what he adds now: "I am the Light of the world. Whoever follows me will not walk in darkness, but will have the light of life."[78]

The pronouncement evokes for the reader the description of Jesus as "the Word" in the Gospel's preamble, "In him was life, and that life was the light of humans" (1:4), with the further explanation that "The light was the true [Light] that illumines every human being who comes into the world" (1:9). Now "the Word" speaks with his own voice, telling "the world" (represented by the Pharisees) what the readers of the Gospel already know, that he is the world's "Light" whether so recognized or not. Earlier, he had pronounced a negative verdict on "the world" and on "human beings" in general, who "loved the dark and not the Light, because their works were evil" (3:19), but now he offers hope.[79] The form of the pronouncement — with "I am" and a predicate, followed by an invitation and/or promise — recalls 6:35 ("I am the Bread of life. The person who comes to me will never go hungry, and the person who believes in me will never ever thirst"), and 6:51 ("I am the living Bread that came down from heaven. If anyone eat of this bread, he will live forever").[80] As we have seen, Jesus' invitation and prom-

---

78. It has often been suggested (see Keener, 1.739) that this pronouncement was especially appropriate in the setting of the Tent festival (see *m. Sukkah* 5.2-3, describing the lighting of four giant candlesticks "at the close of the first Festival-day" in the "Court of the Women" in the Jerusalem temple, so that "there was not a courtyard in Jerusalem that did not reflect the light of the Beth ha-She'ubah" — that is, "The place of the Water-drawing"). The place is right, for "the treasury" where this discourse was said to take place (see v. 20) was in fact near or within "the Court of the Women," but the time ("at the close of the first Festival-day") is obviously wrong (see 7:37). There is no more reason (less in fact) to believe that this tradition is determinative for understanding Jesus' pronouncement here than there was in 7:37-38. As Keener admits, "John does not restrict his light imagery to this feast" (also C. H. Dodd, who mentions the Tent festival's light celebration but cautions that "no stress is laid upon it" (*Interpretation*, 349).

79. For an anticipation of this note of hope, see 3:21, "but whoever does the truth comes to the Light, so that his works will be revealed as works wrought in God." Here too, as we have seen, Jesus was speaking, but not yet in the magisterial first person (ἐγώ εἰμι) as the Revealer of God.

80. See also 10:9 ("I am the Door. Through me if anyone enter he will be saved, and will go in and go out and will find pasture"), 11:25-26 ("I am the Resurrection and the Life. The person who believes in me, even though he die, will live, and everyone who lives and believes in me will never die forever"), and 15:5 ("I am the Vine, you are the branches; the person who dwells in me and I in him, this person bears much fruit"). In such instances, the invitation is expressed either by an "if" clause (as in 6:51 and 10:9) or by a participle ("whoever," or "the person who," as in 6:35, 8:12, 11:25-26, and 15:5), but with little difference in meaning.

ise in 7:37 ("If anyone thirst," and "Whoever believes in me") looked as if it should have been preceded, or was once preceded, by just such an "I am" declaration.

What does it mean for Jesus to be "the Light of the world"? The world has no light of its own, but rather "the Light has come into the world" from without (3:19), from God, who is Light and the Giver of light (see 1 Jn 1:5). The natural point of comparison is the sun, yet Jesus never explicitly mentions the sun in connection with the metaphor of light.[81] In another Gospel, when he told his disciples, "You are the light of the world," he compared them to stationary light sources other than the sun: "a city set on a hill" (Mt 5:14), or a lamp "on the lampstand" (5:15). Here, by contrast, he himself is "the Light of the world" (in keeping with 1:4, 5, 7, 9, 10; 3:19-21), but not a fixed or stationary light source like a lampstand or a city, or even like the sun. Rather, he is on the move, for his implied invitation is to *"follow,"* and his promise is to "not *walk* in darkness" (my italics).[82] He had told the Pharisees before (through their messengers) that they could *not* follow him ("where I am you cannot come," 7:34), but now he promises that those who do "follow" him will "not walk in the darkness, but will have the light of life." The promise goes right over the heads of the Pharisees, for just like the earlier promise of "living water" (7:38), it is not for them but for those who believe (see 7:39), and specifically for the readers of the Gospel. "The Light of the world" is a moving light,[83] for as Jesus has said, "Yet a short time I am with you, and I go to the One who sent me" (7:33). He returns to this thought each time he returns to the subject of light: *"when I am in the world,* I am the Light of the world" (9:5); *"Yet a short time* the Light is among you; walk *while you have the Light,* so that the darkness will not overtake you.... *While you have the Light,* believe in the Light, that you might become sons of light" (12:35, 36, my italics; see also 11:9-10). Jesus is "the Light of the world" in that he offers salvation to those who believe and are ready to join him on his journey back to "the One who sent him." The metaphorical expression, "the Light of the world," is functionally equivalent to what the Samaritans acknowledged him to be three chapters

---

81. He does so only implicitly: "If anyone walk in the day, he does not stumble, because he sees the light of this world" (that is, the sun, 11:9).

82. For the imagery of Jesus' life as "walking," see 1:36; 6:60; 7:1; 10:23; 11:54; and for discipleship as "following" him, see 1:37-38, 40, 43; 6:2; 10:4, 5, 27; 12:26; 13:36-37; 21:19, 22.

83. An analogy comes to mind with the "pillar of fire" that led the Israelites in the desert "to give them light, so that they could travel by day or night" (Exod 13:21, NIV). Yet even though some have linked the lighting celebration at the Tent festival to those Exodus events (see Keener, 1.739), the parallel is probably unintended. The imagery is more appropriately interpreted from within John's Gospel itself.

earlier ("the Savior of the world," 4:42), or to what John called him even before that ("the Lamb of God who takes away the sin of the world," 1:29). The metaphor of light contributes to the imagery the notion of a journey soon to begin, and the assurance of knowing where the journey leads (see 12:35, where anyone who "walks in that darkness does not know where he is going"; also 1 Jn 2:11). The "light of life" (v. 12b) is light for that journey, light that gives eternal life and salvation to those who follow "the Light of the world."

13 The Pharisees' response to Jesus' words signals a notable turning point in the Gospel (a turning point easily overlooked), not because of what they say, but because they answer him at all. Not once have "the Pharisees" (except for Nicodemus) or "the chief priests" spoken even one word to Jesus in this Gospel, and not since chapter 2, when he drove the money changers from the temple, have "the Jews" done so (see 2:18 and 2:20). Everywhere else in the Gospel up to this point, they have either plotted against him silently (5:16, 18; 7:30, 32), or spoken *about* him to each other (7:11, 45-49), even in his very presence (see 6:41-42, 52; 7:15, 35-36).[84]

Now for the first time "the Pharisees" confront him directly and speak to him face to face: "You are testifying about yourself. Your testimony is not true" (v. 13). On the face of it, their objection is unremarkable. It is quite explicit in the Mishnah,[85] and Jesus himself said virtually the same thing in the course of a long monologue that "the Jews" seem not to have heard: "If I testify about myself, my testimony is not true" (5:31). On Jesus' lips the pronouncement was purely rhetorical, for he went on to adduce a whole series of witnesses on his behalf (5:32-40). Here the objection is quite serious. Like Jesus' earlier pronouncement, it has in mind a biblical principle, which Jesus himself will shortly make explicit (v. 17), that "One witness is not enough to convict a man accused of any crime or offense he may have committed. A matter must be established by the testimony of two or three witnesses" (Deut 19:15, NIV; see also Deut 17:6, where it is more specifically a question of a capital offense). The flaw in the Pharisees' argument is that at least two witnesses were required for the *conviction* of an offender, not for his acquittal. Because it has long been established that they are seeking Jesus' life, and that he is a wanted man (see 5:18; 7:1, 25, 32), they are putting the burden of

---

84. Note such expressions as "with each other" (πρὸς ἀλλήλους, 6:52) and "to themselves" (πρὸς ἑαυτούς, 7:35), and "this man" (οὗτος, 6:41, 52; 7:15, 35) or "that man" (ἐκεῖνος, 7:11) with reference to Jesus. This phenomenon occurs in the other Gospels as well (see, for example, Mt 21:38; Mk 2:6-8; 11:31; 14:4; Lk 4:36; 7:39, 49), and in John's Gospel even among Jesus' disciples (6:60; 16:17-18; see also Mk 4:41; 8:16-17; 10:26).

85. See, for example, *m. Ketubbot* 2.9, "But none may be believed when he testifies of himself" (Danby, 247).

proof precisely where it does not belong.[86] They are at least now willing to speak to him directly, but they are still not quite ready to do what Nicodemus urged, that is, "hear from him first and learn what he is doing" (7:51). They want a corroborating witness. The reader knows that he has not one but several such witnesses (see 5:32-40). This time he will present only One (vv. 16-18), and will do so in his own time and on his own terms. Quite predictably, they will *not* be satisfied.

14 Jesus could have answered (in keeping with 5:31), "If in fact I am testifying about myself, you are right. My testimony is not true." Instead, he says just the opposite: "Even if I testify about myself, my testimony is true" (v. 14a). He does not leave it at that, however, but adds significantly, "because I know where I came from and where I am going. But you do not know where I come from or where I am going" (v. 14b). *Without* the added words, he would have flatly contradicted what he said in 5:31. They supply the needed qualification and clarification, reminding the reader that although Jesus is testifying *about* himself, he is not testifying *by* himself, on "on his own."[87] Those who hear him, he says, must take account of "where I came from and where I am going." This is consistent with the notion that as "the Light of the world" (v. 12), he is on his way somewhere, inviting those who will to "follow" in his steps. For the moment, he leaves unanswered the questions, "Where has he come from?" and "Where is he going?" There are not two answers but one. Jesus' origin and his destination are the same, whether viewed as a Place or as a Person. He has come "from above" (3:31) or "from heaven" (3:13, 31; 6:33, 38, 51, 58), and he will return there (3:13, 6:62), or, to put it another way, God the Father is both "the One who sent him" (see 4:34; 5:24, 30, 37; 6:38, 39-40, 57; 7:16, 28-29), and the One to whom he will return (7:33). The heart of the pronouncement is Jesus' claim that "I know" this, and that "you do not know."[88] It is virtually the same claim he made to the crowd earlier, that "the One who sent me is True, whom you do not know. I know him, because I am from him, and he sent me" (7:28b-29). The only difference is that there he also said "You know me, and you know where I am from" (7:28a), admitting that they knew he was a Galilean (see also 7:41). Here it is a matter of his divine origin, and this they do not know, any more than they know his destination (see 7:33-36).

15-16 Jesus' next comment, "*You* judge according to the flesh; '*I*'

---

86. In invoking this principle in 5:31, as we have seen, Jesus put himself in the position of prosecutor and "the Jews" as defendants. Here his interlocutors, by parroting his words, turn the tables, but in doing so fail to take the responsibility of calling witnesses, insisting instead that he do so.

87. Gr. ἀφ' ἑαυτοῦ (see 5:19; 7:17-18).

88. Gr. ὑμεῖς δὲ οὐκ οἴδατε.

judge no one" (v. 15, italics added), is puzzling, in that he abruptly speaks of "judging" instead of "testifying" (as in vv. 13-14).[89] At first glance, the pronouncement seems to follow more appropriately the story of the woman caught in adultery (7:53–8:11) than the preceding dialogues in chapters 7 and 8.[90] Yet it does reinforce Nicodemus's rhetorical question to his fellow Pharisees, "Does our law judge the man unless it hear from him first and learn what he is doing?" (7:51). In failing to do that, and requiring of Jesus a corroborating witness, they are judging "according to the flesh," and therefore unjustly (compare 7:24, "Don't judge by appearance, but judge the right judgment!").

By contrast, Jesus claims not that he judges wisely or fairly, but that "'I' judge no one." While this claim was borne out in the story of the woman caught in adultery (vv. 10-11), it comes as a surprise to the reader in view of earlier pronouncements that "the Father . . . has given all the judgment to the Son" (5:22; also 5:26), and "Just as I hear I judge, and my judgment is right" (5:30; see also 8:26). On the other hand, Jesus also stated that "God sent his Son into the world not to judge the world, but so that the world might be saved through him" (3:17; also 12:47). The matter is further complicated when Jesus adds, "And yet *if I judge,* my judgment is true, because I am not alone, but I and the Father who sent me" (v. 16, my italics). Jesus "judges no one," yet in the same breath looks at the possibility that he might in fact do so! This is not as strange as it appears because in this Gospel sweeping generalizations are from time to time immediately followed by significant exceptions.[91] The likely point here is that "I" means "I *by myself"* (as in 5:30; 7:17). That is why "I" is placed in quotation marks in our translation. When the "I" is not "alone,"[92] so that it is no longer just "I" but "I and the Father[93] who sent me" (v. 16), then Jesus as "the Son" does not hesitate to judge, nor does he hesitate to claim that "my judgment is true" (again, see 5:30).[94] While Jesus has spo-

89. For a similar shift, but in the reverse direction, see 5:30-31.

90. While the verb κρίνειν ("to judge") does not occur in that story, the compound κατακρίνειν ("to condemn") does occur twice (8:10 and 11).

91. See, for example, 1:11-12 ("his own did not receive him, . . . to as many as did receive him"); 3:19-21 ("human beings loved the dark and not the Light, . . . but whoever does the Truth comes to the Light"), and 3:32-33 ("no one receives his testimony. The person who did receive his testimony confirmed thereby that God is true"). And for a different kind of apparent contradiction, see 12:44, "The person who believes in me does not believe in me, but in the One who sent me."

92. Gr. μόνος.

93. Some ancient manuscripts (including ℵ*, D, and the old Syriac versions) omit "Father" so as to read simply "the One who sent me" (as more commonly in John's Gospel), but virtually all other important witnesses (including P[66] and P[75]) include "Father," making its appearance in v. 18 less abrupt (see Metzger, *Textual Commentary,* 223).

94. For a partial analogy, see Hebrews 2:13, where the author (speaking as if it

ken freely of "the One who sent me" (see 7:16, 28, 33), and has even implied that "the One who sent him" was God (7:17), he has only once used the more concrete expression, "the Father who sent me" (see 5:37), and that in a discourse which the religious leaders in Jerusalem seemed not to hear. The expression will puzzle his hearers (see v. 19, and later v. 27), and their confusion will only be heightened by what he will say next.

17-18 Jesus now repeats what he has said about "judging" (vv. 15-16) with regard to "testimony" and "testifying." This time he states explicitly the biblical principle the Pharisees had in mind when they said, "You are testifying about yourself. Your testimony is not true" (v. 13). Drawing on Deuteronomy 17:6 and 19:15, he acknowledges that "in your law it is written that the testimony of two men is true" (v. 17).[95] The phrase "in your law" stands in noticeable contrast to Nicodemus's expression, "our law" (7:51). The implication is that while Nicodemus was still "one of them" (7:50), Jesus was not (see above, n. 63). Still, the phrase "it is written"[96] signals that Jesus too recognizes the law's authority. His use of the phrase "your law" is not, as some have suggested,[97] a sign of the Gospel's hostility toward Judaism.[98] Instead, two other factors are at work. First, it strengthens Jesus' argument by appealing to that which the Pharisees themselves acknowledged to be true. The fact that Jesus too accepts the law's authority is assumed, but is not crucial to his argument. Second, the terminology places Jesus in the tradition of the biblical prophets who spoke in God's name and from God's perspective *against* Israel's most cherished institutions because they had been corrupted in practice (see, for example, Isa 1:13-14, "*your* incense . . . *your* evil assemblies . . . *your* New Moon festivals . . . *your* appointed feasts"). Here they have corrupted their own law, and Jesus offers a corrective.

The principle in view here is one to which Jesus assents, and on which he is quite willing to build his argument (see also Mt 18:16). The testimonies "of two men" are needed to establish truth, and Jesus flatly claims,

---

were Jesus speaking) quotes Isaiah 8:17, "I [ἐγώ] will be confident in him" (that is, in God), and then in words drawn from the very next verse, Isaiah 8:18, immediately defines "I" as "I and the children which God gave me."

95. Both here and in v. 16 ("And yet if I judge . . ."), the combination of καί and δέ, and the placement of δέ rather late in its clause, gives emphasis to the pronouncement, as if to say, "and what's more," or "and especially" (see Abbott, *Johannine Grammar,* 106-7; Barrett, 339)

96. Gr. γέγραπται. More common in John's Gospel is the form ἐστὶν γεγραμμένον, but the meaning is the same (see 2:17; 6:31, 45; 10:34; 12:14; and compare 12:16, 15:25). In 10:34, Jesus goes on to say explicitly, "The Scripture cannot be broken" (v. 35).

97. See, for example, Dodd, *Interpretation,* 82; Brown, 1.341; Schnackenburg, 2.487.

98. See Keener's discussion (1.741).

"I am the one who testifies[99] about myself, and the Father who sent me testifies about me" (v. 18). To the reader this is nothing new (see 5:37), but the Pharisees seem not to have heard anything like it before (see v. 19). What does surprise the reader is the wording of the citation, to the effect that it is a matter of "two men,"[100] for "the Father who sent me" is obviously not a man but "God" (see 7:16-17). Unless Jesus is being deliberately ironic and therefore misleading,[101] he is using an argument from the lesser to the greater: if the testimony of "two men" is valid in a court of law, *how much more* the testimony of one man, plus God his Father in heaven — particularly if God the Father has sent him to act on God's behalf?

19 The Pharisees respond by asking, "Where is your father?" (v. 19a). The translator must decide whether to capitalize "father" or leave it lowercase.[102] The custom of capitalizing it on Jesus' lips (in v. 18, as elsewhere) argues for the former, yet the dynamics of the conversation (particularly Jesus' expression, "two men," in v. 17) are decisive in favor of the latter. The Pharisees can only assume that Jesus is speaking of human witnesses, and therefore of his human father. In asking "Where is your father?" they are not questioning the legitimacy of his birth,[103] but simply demanding to hear from his second witness. Their distant cousins in Galilee claimed to know both his father and mother (6:42), and he was known publicly as "Jesus, son of Joseph, from Nazareth" (see 1:45).[104] Even the people of Jerusalem

---

99. The form of this pronouncement (ἐγώ εἰμι ὁ μαρτυρῶν) resembles (probably intentionally) the form of Jesus' classic "I am" sayings (as in v. 12, and earlier in 6:35, 47). Yet as Bultmann noted (282, n. 5), it is not the same because "I" is actually the predicate and not the subject of the sentence (as if to say, "It is I who testify").

100. Gr. δύο ἀνθρώπων. The biblical texts say merely "witnesses." Whether or not "two men" is intended to exclude women is uncertain. According to Josephus, Moses said, "Put not trust in a single witness, but let there be three or at the least two, whose evidence shall be accredited by their past lives. From women let no evidence be accepted, because of the levity and temerity of their sex" (*Antiquities* 4.219; LCL, 4.581). Yet on women's testimony in the Gospel of John, see 4:39 and 42.

101. Bultmann (282) calls it a "satirical reply," and "not an argument at all but an expression of scorn." But while scorn is surely present (see v. 19b), from the Gospel writer's perspective the argument is very real and quite compelling.

102. "Father" is capitalized in the Douay, KJV, ERV, ASV, NASV, RSV, NRSV, Moffatt, and Knox (among others), but is left lower case in most modern English versions, including Confraternity, NIV, NEB, REB, NAB, TEV, and NLT (Richmond Lattimore's translation leaves *all* references to "the father" in lower case).

103. Something like this could be inferred from 8:41, "We [ἡμεῖς] are not born of immorality," or from 8:48, "You are a Samaritan, and you have a demon" (see Hoskyns, 332-33).

104. As Westcott remarks (2.7), their question was not "Who is your father?" but "Where is your father?"

claimed to know where he was from (7:27, 41), and Jesus agreed that they did (7:28). The Pharisees' intention here is simply to remind him that his "father" is far away, possibly deceased, and certainly not available to testify on his behalf. Even if he were available, it would not be enough, for to them Jesus is the accused, and therefore according to Jewish law two *additional* witnesses are required to prove his innocence.[105]

To Jesus himself, of course, it is a matter of establishing not his own innocence, but the guilt of his accusers, and for this purpose two witnesses are quite sufficient. He sees himself not as defendant but (alongside the Father) as Judge (see v. 16), and he hands down an immediate verdict: "You know neither me nor my Father; if you knew me, you would know my Father" (v. 19b). He is telling the Pharisees just what he told the Jerusalemites a chapter earlier: that they do not know God (see 7:28-29).[106] Beyond that, he is telling them that the two testimonies of which he has just spoken, his own and his Father's, are *both* wrapped up in his own testimony — in short, that his testimony is self-authenticating. He is simply repeating what he said a few verses earlier, that "Even if I testify about myself, my testimony is true, because I know where I came from and where I am going" (v. 14), and before that when he told "the Jews" in Jerusalem who first accused him that "you do not have [the Father's] word dwelling in you, because he whom that One sent, him you do not believe" (5:38). Not Jesus, but his accusers, stand condemned.

20 Belatedly, the Gospel writer reveals just where this spirited exchange took place: "These words he spoke in the treasury, teaching in the temple, and no one arrested him because his hour had not yet come" (v. 20). The notice recalls 6:59, where, in similarly belated fashion, he told the readers, "These things he said teaching in synagogue in Capernaum" (6:59). There, it was already clear that Jesus was in Capernaum (see 6:17, 24), and it was left unclear at precisely what point his synagogue discourse began. Here too, Jesus has been "teaching in the temple" all along (see 7:14, 28), but this time the specific exchange with the Pharisees in the temple "treasury"[107] seems to have had a definite beginning at verse 12, with the solemn pronouncement, "I am the Light of the world." The "treasury" was simply a stor-

---

105. See Whitacre, 213: "Since the two witnesses required by the law do not include the accused, this would not be a valid legal argument. So Jesus seems to use the law in a nonlegal way to bear witness to his relationship with the Father" (also Brown, 1.341).

106. For both an echo and a striking contrast to this sharp exchange, see 14:7, where Jesus first tells his disciples, "If you have known me, you will know my Father too," to which Philip replies, "Lord, show us the Father" (v. 8), and Jesus tells Philip, "Such a long time I have been with you, and you have not known me, Philip? The person who has seen me has seen the Father" (v. 9).

107. Gr. ἐν τῷ γαζοφυλακείῳ.

age place for contributions and other valuables,[108] on the face of it an odd setting for either a debate or any kind of formal teaching. The "treasuries" (plural) were probably the thirteen trumpet-shaped receptacles adjoining the so-called Court of the Women, between the inner sanctuary and the outer Court of the Gentiles (see *m. Sheqalim* 6.5; Josephus, *War* 5.200; 6.282). It was probably into one of these that the widow placed her two small coins in the story recorded in Mark (12:41-44) and Luke (21:1-4). The Court of the Women, as we have seen (n. 78), was a place for celebration during the Tent festival (*m. Sukkah* 5.2-3), but the celebration would have been over by the time of this encounter between Jesus and the Pharisees. There are in any case no more references to the festival here or anywhere else in the chapter. Here, by contrast, "treasury" is singular, and the phrase "in the treasury" may in fact refer to the Court of the Women as a whole.[109] In two other Gospels, Jesus comments to his disciples about the offerings being placed there (see Mk 12:41, 43; Lk 21:1), but here the location seems to have little to do with the nature of the controversy between Jesus and the Pharisees.[110]

Quite possibly the point of the reference is that the temple treasury was a very public place, making it all the more remarkable that "no one arrested him." The situation recalls the surprised question of "some of the Jerusalemites" midway through the festival, "Is not this the one they are seeking to kill? And look, he is speaking publicly, and they are saying nothing to him" (7:25). Superficially, the closer parallel is the notice five verses later, "So they sought to arrest him, and no one laid a hand on him, because his hour had not yet come" (7:30). Yet despite the repetition of both the verb, "arrest," and the key phrase, "his hour had not yet come," the difference here is that they did not try and fail, but that no one even *tried* to arrest Jesus. The Pharisees are now as baffled and helpless on meeting Jesus in person as the officers they sent to arrest him were a chapter earlier (see 7:32-34, 45-46). "Why didn't you bring him in?" they had asked those officers (7:45), and "Are you also deceived?" (7:47), but they themselves have done no better. Once again, the Gospel writer's explanation is that Jesus' "hour had not yet come."

---

108. See BDAG, 186.

109. See George Adam Smith, *Jerusalem* (London: Hodder and Stoughton, 1907-8), 2.510. Smith implies that this may have been the case in 2 Maccabees 3.24 and 28 as well, in connection with Heliodorus's ill-fated attempt to "enter" and pillage "the treasury" (also singular).

110. Origen commented that the notice "is to show that if all contribute the things to support the needy into the treasury of the temple on behalf of the common good, Jesus, more than all others, should have brought things that were beneficial. These were the words of eternal life and his teaching about God and himself" (*Commentary on John* 19.53; FC, 89.180).

21 In contrast to the notice locating the synagogue discourse at Capernaum (6:59), the notice locating this part of the temple discourse in the treasury (v. 20) does not end the discourse, nor does it signal a change of audience (as in 6:60). Rather, Jesus continues to speak "to them," that is, to the Pharisees, just as in verses 12-20. But instead of "So again Jesus spoke to them, saying . . ." (as in v. 12), the Gospel writer now tells us, "So again he said to them"[111] (v. 21). The difference is subtle but important. This time the point is not simply that Jesus "again said to them," but that he said "again" something he had said to the same audience before — that is, *"I am going* and *you will seek me,* and you will die in your sin. Where I am going *you cannot come"* (v. 21b, italics added). The reader may remember that Jesus did in fact say something like this in the preceding chapter: "Yet a short time I am with you, and *I go* to the One who sent me. *You will seek me* and you will not find, and where I am *you cannot come"* (7:33-34; the italics indicate the extent of the parallelism). But was the audience the same? In a sense, Yes, as we have seen. In 7:33-34 Jesus was speaking to the officers that "the chief priests and the Pharisees" had sent to arrest him (7:32), and thus in effect to "the Jews" themselves (7:35, seen as interchangeable with "the chief priests and the Pharisees"). These were the words they had in mind when they came back with the report, "No man ever spoke like that" (7:46). Here too "the Pharisees" and "the Jews" are interchangeable, for the Pharisees are Jesus' audience in verses 12-20 (see v. 13) and by default also in verse 21, yet the response to Jesus' words comes from "the Jews" (v. 22), just as in 7:35. The main difference between the two pronouncements (or two versions of the pronouncement) lies in the grim prediction added here, "you will die in your sin." Oddly, however, it is not what captures the attention of Jesus' hearers. He will in fact have to repeat it two more times (see v. 24). What does capture their attention are the same words that did so before, "Where I am going, you cannot come" (compare 7:34).

22 The Pharisees, now designated simply as "the Jews," are as baffled by the pronouncement as the officers they sent earlier (see 7:35-36), and their theory about its meaning is just as absurd. Instead of asking, "Will he go to the dispersion of the Greeks and teach the Greeks?" (7:35), they now ask, "Will he kill himself, because he said, 'Where I am going you cannot come?'" (v. 22). Again they speak to each other instead of to Jesus (reverting to their old ways), again they totally misunderstand what Jesus has said, and again their absurd conclusion has an ironic element of truth. Jesus will not, of course, "kill himself" (killing him is rather *their* plan; see 7:19, 25), but he will say two chapters later, "I lay down my soul that I might receive it back. No one takes it from me, but I lay it down on my own. I have authority to lay it down, and I have author-

---

111. Gr. εἶπεν οὖν πάλιν αὐτοῖς.

7:37–8:29 THE LAST DAY OF THE FESTIVAL

ity to receive it back" (10:17-18). His life is in his own hands, regardless of their intent.[112] What they have *not* grasped is that the death of which Jesus has spoken is *their* death: "you will die in your sin" (v. 21).

23 "You are from below,"[113] Jesus replies, "I am from above.[114] You are from this world, I am not from this world." With this, he echoes John's testimony, "The One coming from above is above all. He who is from the earth is from the earth and speaks from the earth" (3:31), except that it is now not a matter of their being "from the earth" as John was, but of being "from this world."[115] This is Johannine dualism in its starkest form. The difference is that "the world" or "this world" in John's Gospel is defined by its rejection of "the Light" that comes from God (see 1:10; 3:19). Jesus has come to "testify about it that its works are evil" (7:7). "The earth," by contrast, has no such connotation, for it is merely the place where human beings live, as distinct from heaven, the dwelling place of God. Yet the juxtaposition in this verse of "from below" and "from this world" indicates that "below" does not refer to an underworld or nether region below the earth. Rather, it refers *to the earth itself and its inhabitants,* viewed as "the world" and therefore as resistant to God and to God's revelation in Jesus Christ.[116] It is "from below" in relation to the region above, that is, "from heaven" (see 3:13, 31; 6:41, 42, 50).

24 The implication of all this is to reinforce the warning that "you will die in your sin" (v. 21), a warning the Pharisees seem not to have heard. Jesus therefore now repeats it almost verbatim,[117] not once but twice: "I just told you that you will die in your sins. For unless you believe that I am, you will die in your sins" (v. 24). At one level, this is simply the negative corollary of his claim to be "the Light of the world" (v. 12). If those who follow him "will not walk in darkness, but will have the light of life" (v. 12), the implication is that those who do *not* follow will not have life, but will instead "die in their sins." For the time being, their sins are not specified, but appear to be simply a corollary of belonging to "the world" (v. 23). Jesus makes the grim prediction three times in all, but the third time he adds a qualification: "For unless[118] you believe that I

---

112. Origen bluntly writes, "perhaps, if I may put it this way, Jesus killed himself in a more divine manner" (*Commentary on John* 19.98; FC, 89.190).
113. Gr. ἐκ τῶν κάτω.
114. Gr. ἐκ τῶν ἄνω.
115. Gr. ἐκ τούτου τοῦ κόσμου.
116. See also 18:36, "My kingdom is not from this world." For the kindred phrase "from the world" (ἐκ τοῦ κόσμου), see 15:19; 17:14, 16. In the book of Revelation, the phrase "the inhabitants of the earth" carries much the same negative connotation that "the world" carries in the Gospel of John (see Rev 3:10; 6:10; 8:13; 11:10; 13:6, 12, 14; 17:2, 8).
117. There is probably no significant difference between "die in your sin" (ἐν τῇ ἁμαρτίᾳ ὑμῶν, v. 21) and "die in your sins" (ἐν ταῖς ἁμαρτίαις ὑμῶν, v. 24).
118. Gr. ἐὰν μή.

am, you will die in your sins." The conditional clause offers a glimmer of hope, as the form of the pronouncement recalls such other sayings in John's Gospel as "unless someone is born from above, he cannot see the kingdom of God" (3:3) or "unless you eat the flesh of the Son of man and drink his blood, you do not have life in yourselves" (6:53). While Jesus is not exactly issuing an invitation (he has done that already in v. 12), he is saying that there is one thing "the Jews" can do so as *not* to "die in their sins," and that is to "believe that I am."

The expression "I am," standing by itself as it does here without a predicate, is ambiguous. They must believe that "I am," he says, but what, or who, is he? Must they believe that he is "the Light of the world" (v. 12), or that he is "from above" (v. 23), or both? Jesus has used the expression "I am" by itself twice before, once to the Samaritan woman (4:26), and once to the disciples in a boat on the Sea of Galilee (6:20).[119] In both instances "I" was the predicate, not the subject, yielding the translation, "It is I," and in both instances Jesus was identifying himself with someone known to the hearer. First it was the Messiah as visualized by the Samaritan woman (see 4:25), and later Jesus was simply announcing his presence to his fearful disciples that it was he and not someone else. There is less certainty here. A prevailing modern interpretation, going back at least to C. H. Dodd,[120] sees the expression as one derived from the God of Israel's self-predication "I am" or "I am He,"[121] especially according to Isaiah, as if to say, "I am the LORD," or "I am God."[122] But Jesus' hearers seem not to understand Jesus' words in that way, and it is doubtful that even the Gospel's readers can be expected to grasp such a subtle allusion at this point.[123]

25-26 Given this ambiguity, the question, "Who are you?" (v. 25), is a natural one. If they must "believe that I am" in order not to "die in their sins," it is important to know just who, or what, Jesus is claiming to be.[124] He

119. Nor have we heard the last of it (see vv. 28, 58; 13:19; 18:5-6, 8).

120. *Interpretation,* 93-96; also Brown, 1.533-38; Harner, *The "I Am" of the Fourth Gospel.*

121. In the Greek LXX, ἐγώ εἰμι, and in the Hebrew, אני הוא; literally ("I — He").

122. See, for example, Isaiah 41:4; 43:10, 25; 45:18, 19; 48:12; 51:12; 52:6; also Deuteronomy 32:39.

123. As we will see, 8:58 is quite another matter. According to Keener (1.770), "Given the absolute use in 8:58 and John's propensity for double entendres, however, the implications of deity may carry over to the other uses as well. The implied deity of such 'I am' statements would recall the implied reader to the introduction (1:1-18)." Yet while the reader does know in a general way that "the Word was God" (1:1), it is by no means evident as yet that this is what Jesus is telling the Jews they must believe. Rather, his focus continues to be on the Father (see vv. 26-29).

124. This is not the last time the question will be asked. See 10:24, where "the Jews encircled Jesus and said to him, 'How long will you take away our soul? If you are the Christ, tell us plainly.'"

replies with a fairly lengthy speech (vv. 25-29), interrupted only by a brief narrative aside (v. 27). For the reader, this speech is the perfect opportunity for Jesus to say, "I am the Word" (see 1:1, 14), or "I am the Son of God" (see 1:24, 49; 5:25), or "I am God" (see 1:1, 18), but he does not. His opening words,[125] in fact, are virtually untranslatable.[126] They are usually rendered either quite literally as "What I am telling you from the beginning,"[127] or else as a question: "[How is it] that I even speak to you at all [or "to begin with"]?"[128] This seems unlikely if it is taken to imply that Jesus finds it useless to talk to these people,[129] but if it is read as a serious question answered immediately by what follows, it makes better sense.[130] That is, "What can I even begin to say to you?[131] I have many things to say about you and to judge, but the One who sent me is True, and the things I heard from him are the things I say to the world."

If this, or something like it, is the correct translation, then Jesus is not directly answering the question, "Who are you?" — at least not immediately. On the contrary, he turns attention *away from* himself to the Father. There is much that he could say, and would say if he were speaking on his own initiative,[132] but in fact he is not.[133] Rather, he claims, "the One who sent me is

---

125. Gr. τὴν ἀρχὴν ὅ τι [or ὅτι] καὶ λαλῶ ὑμῖν.

126. See BDAG, 138; BDF, §300; also Abbott, *Johannine Grammar*, 142-44; Bultmann, 352-53.

127. The sense requires rather "What I told you — or have been telling you — from the beginning." A variant reading in the margin of one ancient witness (P[66]) tries to help by adding the words εἶπον ὑμῖν before τὴν ἀρχήν, yielding the translation, "I told you in the beginning what I am telling you [now]." But the manuscript evidence is too weak, and the added words are clearly a scribal attempt to clarify a difficult text.

128. With τὴν ἀρχήν understood adverbially, equivalent to the adverb ὅλως, "entirely" or "at all." For examples of this usage (which requires reading ὅτι as "that"), see Bultmann, 352, n. 1.

129. As, for example, in the third-century Pseudo-Clementine *Homilies* 6.11 (*GCS*, 110): "If you do not follow the things I am saying, why do I speak at all?" (τί καὶ τὴν ἀρχὴν διαλέγομαι). Or, according to Chrysostom, "What He saith, is of this kind; 'Ye are not worthy to hear My words at all, much less to learn who I am'" (*Homilies on John* 53; NPNF, 1st ser., 14.191);

130. The close connection between the two verses is supported by the threefold repetition of the verb λαλεῖν, "to speak" or "to say": λαλῶ ("I say," v. 25), λαλεῖν ("to say," v. 26), and λαλῶ ("I say," v. 26).

131. Or more literally, "To begin with [τὴν ἀρχήν], what do I even say to you?" (reading ὅ τι as "what" or "something which").

132. That is, "on my own" (ἀπ' ἐμαυτοῦ, as in v. 28; also 5:30; 7:17, 28; and see 5:19; 7:18).

133. The strong adversative ἀλλά is crucial to the meaning of the sentence. The Father's directive sets limits to what Jesus is free to say or not say to the world.

True,"[134] and consequently he says only what he has been told to say. The focus of his reply, then, is not the solitary expression "I am" which caught his hearers' attention, but rather the whole pronouncement (v. 24), of which it is only a part. Having already stated clearly that "*'I'* judge no one" (v. 15, my italics), he now wants it just as clearly understood that in saying "unless you believe that I am, you will die in your sins" (v. 24), he is not speaking on his own authority but is issuing a warning from the Father. He has repeated it three times by now (vv. 21, 24), but "the Jews" have persistently refused to hear it. It is something that he says, "I heard from him" v. 26), whether before coming into the world, or in his present personal relationship with God the Father (see v. 40; also 3:32; 5:30; 15:15), and consequently it is the Father's judgment, not his own. The Father has decreed that those who do not believe in Jesus his Son will "die in their sins."

As for the unanswered question, "Who are you?" the reader knows the answer even if Jesus' audience does not. The reader knows that he is indeed "from above" (v. 23), and "the Light of the world" (v. 12), and (looking further afield) "the Bread of life" (6:35, 48), and the "Messiah" (4:25-26). It is clear by this time that he is all that and more (see 1:1-18; 5:19-30), and it will become clear to "the Jews" as well if they listen to what the Father is telling them. Until they do, the grim prediction, "You will die in your sins," still hangs over their heads. Yet, as Jesus will tell them momentarily, a day will come when their question, "Who are you?" will be answered once and for all (see v. 28, "When you lift up the Son of man, then you will know that I am").

27 Jesus has not used the expression "the Father," or "my Father," in any of this, yet the Gospel writer and the readers of the Gospel all know that "the One who sent me" (v. 26) is in fact God the Father (see 5:37; 6:39, 40, 57; 8:16, 18). "The Jews" to whom Jesus is speaking say nothing, and the writer pauses to explain in a narrative aside that they do not share this knowledge: "They did not know that he was telling them of the Father" (v. 27).[135] As we have noted, Jesus has mentioned "the Father" only sparingly in this discourse, and when he did (vv. 16 and 18), his use of the term invited only confusion (see v. 19a, "Where is your father?"). The comment here confirms the earlier charge against them that "You know neither me nor my Father; if you knew me, you would know my Father" (v. 19b). They seem to have forgotten that the reason they were seeking his life in the first place was not simply that he broke the Sabbath (see 7:21-23), but that he was "claiming God as

---

134. See 7:28, "I have not come on my own, but the One who sent me is True, whom you do not know" ("True" deserves capitalization here as well).

135. In two other narrative asides (10:6; 12:16), the Gospel writer similarly explains that certain characters in the story "did not know" (οὐκ ἔγνωσαν) what was being said or done.

his own Father, making himself equal to God" (5:18), and that his relationship to "the Father" was the major theme of a lengthy earlier discourse (see 5:19-47). With this brief notice, the Gospel writer signals that the question of who Jesus' "Father" is will soon move front and center once again, so as to press home the two related questions of who Jesus is, and whether or not his Father is also Father to "the Jews" themselves (see vv. 37-59).

28 After the interruption Jesus continues his speech seamlessly: "When you lift up the Son of man, then you will come to know that I am, and [that][136] on my own I do nothing, but just as the Father taught me, these things I speak" (v. 28). The clause, "When you lift up[137] the Son of man," is startling, given the implication five chapters earlier that to be "lifted up" (3:14) meant to be put to death by crucifixion (see 12:33 and 18:32, where this becomes explicit). Given the conventional wisdom that crucifixion was a Roman, not a Jewish, method of execution,[138] and given the fact that when Jesus' life is threatened by Jews it is always by stoning, not crucifixion (see v. 59; also 10:31), it is all the more startling that those who will "lift him up" in this way are those specifically identified as "the Jews" (see v. 22).[139] Even so, the tone of Jesus' pronouncement is not accusatory. It is as if he had said, "When the Son of man is lifted up," rather than "When *you* lift up the Son of man." The accent is not on the guilt of "the Jews," but on the promise that "then you will come to know[140] that I am" — in sharp contrast to their present situation, in which "They did not know that he was telling them of the Father" (v. 27).[141] Each time the "lifting up" of Jesus on the cross is mentioned

---

136. A second "that" is supplied because the conjunction "that" (ὅτι) should be understood as governing not just the expression "I am," but the entire clause that follows (so Schnackenburg, 2.203, and most English versions). Carson, however, argues for a full stop after "I am," commenting that "nothing in the Greek text corresponds to NIV's 'that.' Rather, Jesus goes on to say, 'And I do nothing on my own . . .', recapitulating the argument" (345; see also Westcott, 2.11). Yet "I do" (ποιῶ) in the second clause is probably to be understood as having the ἐγώ of the preceding ἐγώ εἰμι clause as its subject as well (compare ἐγὼ . . . ποιῶ, v. 29). The full stop and the new beginning come rather with the change of subject in verse 29, "And the One who sent me is with me."

137. Gr. ὅταν ὑψώσητε.

138. There were exceptions. According to Josephus, the Hasmonean Jewish king Alexander Jannaeus "ordered some eight hundred of the Jews to be crucified, and slaughtered their children and wives before the eyes of the still living wretches" (*Antiquities* 13.380; LCL, 7.417).

139. It is, however, consistent with the Johannine passion narrative, in which Pilate handed Jesus over "to them [that is, to 'the Jews'] to be crucified" (ἵνα σταυρωθῇ, 19:16; see vv. 12, 15).

140. Gr. τότε γνώσεσθε.

141. See Schnackenburg, 2.202, who asks, "How should this announcement by Jesus be understood? From the point of view of damnation ('Then it will be too late'), or

in this Gospel, something good comes of it, whether the prospect "that everyone who believes might have eternal life in him" (see 3:14-15) or that, as Jesus says, "I will draw them all to myself" (12:32). Here it is the knowledge of who Jesus is, and what his relationship is to the Father. He has told these same people earlier, "You know neither me nor my Father; if you knew me, you would know my Father" (v. 19). Now he promises that this will change, but only when they "lift him up." Still, despite their present ignorance, he does not hesitate to speak of "the Father" explicitly: "just as the Father taught me, these things I speak." The lofty announcement, "I am," cannot mean "I am the Son of man" (as if that title finishes an otherwise unfinished sentence).[142] Nor does it mean that Jesus acts on his own authority. On the contrary, to know Jesus as the one who says "I am" is to know him as the One sent from the Father, and thus finally to know his Father as well.

The accent here on a future time when Jesus will be "lifted up" recalls his promise of the Spirit earlier in the day[143] at the Tent festival (7:37-38), with its accompanying caution that "the Spirit was not yet, because Jesus was not yet glorified" (7:39). In this Gospel, certain events cannot happen, and certain things cannot be known, until Jesus is "lifted up" or "glorified" on the cross. The promise given here adds a new dimension to what he said when he first came to the temple and began to teach: "If anyone chooses to do his will, he will know about the teaching, whether it is from God, or whether I speak on my own" (7:17). There, as we saw, he implied that those who faithfully did the will of God as prescribed by their Jewish faith would thereby come to "know" that his teaching was from God. By now it is apparent that these "Jews" have not done so, yet they can still come to "know" (v. 28) these things by virtue of his death and resurrection — this even though they are themselves instrumental in his death! The promise is of course conditional, just as it was from the start. When Jesus has been "lifted up" and "glorified," they must still "choose to do the will of God" (see 7:17), by faith in the Crucified One whom they have pierced.[144]

---

from the point of view of salvation ('Then they will be given the knowledge')?" After a nuanced discussion, he concludes that "it is left open where this recognition will lead, to faith and salvation or to total obduracy and final destruction. But: 'they shall look upon him whom they have pierced.' The exalted one, the pierced one, is a sign from God which no-one can ignore" (2.203).

142. It would be a mere tautology to say they would know that "I am the Son of man." It would mean only that they realized that the "Son of man" whom they had just crucified was Jesus — hardly a new revelation.

143. Or on the previous day, if 7:53–8:11 is read into the Gospel.

144. See (perhaps) 19:37; Revelation 1:7; also Schnackenburg's comment above, n. 141. For a possible example of such knowledge coming too late, see *2 Clement* 17.5, where "the unbelievers" (οἱ ἄπιστοι, though *not* identified as "Jews") exclaim at the last

EXCURSUS ON 7:53–8:11

29 Having introduced (or rather reintroduced) the explicit term "the Father" (v. 28), Jesus now reverts to the phrase that has mostly characterized the discourse up to now, "the One who sent me" (see 7:16, 28, 33; 8:26; also 4:34; 5:24, 30; 6:38, 39), on the assumption that "the One who sent me" is in fact "the Father" (see 5:37; 6:40, 44; 8:16, 18). "He has not left me alone," Jesus adds, echoing his earlier claim that "I am not alone, but I and the Father who sent me" (v. 16; see also 16:32).[145] Now he supplies the reason why he is not alone: "for I always do the things that please him."[146] "Always" signals that his relationship to the Father is unbroken (see 11:42, "I know that you *always* hear me"), and the pronouncement is another way of saying, "My food is that I might do the will of the One who sent me, and finish his work" (4:34; also 5:30; 6:38).[147] Its main thrust is that Jesus is a man not only of speech (vv. 25-28) but of *actions* pleasing to God, not least that he has pleased the Father with regard to the Sabbath (see 5:17).[148] In due course he will challenge his hearers to prove him wrong (see vv. 46, 49; 10:25, 37-38; 18:23).

Excursus on 7:53–8:11

If 7:53–8:11 is read as an authentic part of John's Gospel, the larger unit (7:37–8:29), introduced by the phrase, "Now on the last day, the great day of the festival" (7:37), turns out not to be a unit at all. Rather, the unit introduced there ends with the notice, "And they went off, each to his house, while

---

day, "Woe to us, for it was you [ὅτι σὺ ἦς], and we did not know" (see J. B. Lightfoot, *The Apostolic Fathers* [Peabody, MA: Hendrickson, 1989], 2.255: "The preacher seems to be alluding to this language of our Lord, as recorded by St. John").

145. It is doubtful that any of these pronouncements has anything at all to do with Jesus' cry of dereliction according to Mark (15:34) and Matthew (27:46), "My God, my God, why have you forsaken me."

146. Gr. τὰ ἀρεστὰ αὐτῷ. In this respect Jesus becomes an example to believers (see 1 Jn 3:22, "And whatever we ask from him we receive, because we keep his commands, and we do the things that are pleasing [τὰ ἀρεστά] before him"). The passage may also have influenced Ignatius in the early second century, who wrote "that there is one God, who made himself known through Jesus Christ his Son, who is his Word proceeding from silence, who in all things [κατὰ πάντα] was well pleasing [εὐηρέστησεν] to the One who sent him" (*To the Magnesians* 8.2).

147. It also bears comparison also with certain traditions about Jesus as God's "beloved" or "only" Son in whom the Father is "well pleased" (εὐδόκησα, Mk 1:11; Mt 3:17; 17:5).

148. To Chrysostom, the Sabbath was still the issue, for Jesus was here "continually setting Himself against that which they asserted, that He was not of God, and that He kept not the Sabbath. To this He replieth, 'I do always those things that are pleasing to Him'; showing that it was pleasing unto Him even that the Sabbath should be broken" (*Homilies on John* 53; NPNF, 1st ser., 14.191).

Jesus went off to the Mount of Olives" (7:53–8:1). The "last day, the great day of the festival," is over, and with it the festival itself; a new day begins with the words, "In the morning he again showed up at the temple, and all the people were coming to him, and he sat and began teaching them" (v. 2). Still, the reference to "teaching" (as in 7:14 and 28) and the adverb "again" (as in 8:12) signal a certain continuity with the preceding.

7:53–8:2 "They" who "went off, each to his house" (7:53) are evidently "the chief priests and Pharisees" (including Nicodemus), and perhaps their officers who had just returned from their unsuccessful attempt to arrest Jesus (see 7:45-52). In a curious way (and probably coincidentally) their exit for the night in different directions seems to anticipate the notice near the end of the story of the woman caught in adultery, that "those who had heard went out one by one, beginning with the elders" (8:9). Jesus' antagonists scatter (v. 53), only to come together again (8:3) and again scatter, so that Jesus "was left alone, and the woman still in front of him" (v. 9). The awkwardness will come in 8:12, when Jesus "again . . . spoke to them," as if they had never left.

Whatever one may think of the appropriateness of the story of the woman caught in adultery at this point in John's Gospel, its opening verses make it difficult to view the story as anything but a part of some Gospel somewhere — whether John or Luke or an apocryphal Gospel. Efforts to understand it as a unit complete in itself or as a free-floating piece of tradition are unconvincing because of this clear link to a preceding narrative of some kind. If the disputed passage were 8:3-11, such a theory would make sense, for those verses could conceivably stand alone. But 7:53–8:11 do not stand alone, and it is not hard to understand why most scribes felt compelled to place them somewhere within the text, whether here, or after 7:36 or 7:44, or after Luke 21:38.[149] The pattern of days teaching in the temple and nights spent on the Mount of Olives is thoroughly in keeping with passion week, according to Luke (see 19:47; 21:37-38; 22:39). Yet despite striking similarities in vocabulary between these verses and Luke 21:37-38, the link is tenuous because placing these verses after Luke 21:38 would be highly redundant.[150] Possibly they come from a lost passion account resembling

---

149. The placement of the passage at the very end of John's Gospel, after 21:25 (in a number of later manuscripts known as Family 1), seems to have been a counsel of despair, without attention to context, motivated simply by a concern that the story not be lost.

150. One has only to put them side by side (with the verbal similarities in italics) to sense the redundancy: "Days he was *teaching* in the *temple,* and nights he would go out and lodge on the *Mount that was called Olives,* and *all the people* would come to him *in the morning* in the temple to hear him (Luke). And they went off, each to his house, while Jesus went off to the *Mount of Olives. In the morning* he again showed up at the *temple,*

Excursus on 7:53–8:11

Luke in certain respects, yet clearly the scribes who placed the passage here in John's Gospel did so for a reason. Even though the phrase "all the people"[151] — instead of "the crowd," or "the crowds" — is far more familiar to Luke's readers than to John's (see Lk 1:10; 2:10, 31; 3:21; 6:17; 7:29; 8:47; 9:13; 18:43; 19:48; 20:6, 45; 21:38; 24:19), what is important to John's readers is that the next day Jesus "began teaching," just as he had done at the Tent festival (see 7:14), and that the incident in question happens as part of his teaching ministry.

3 The incident begins when "the scribes and Pharisees brought a woman who had been caught in adultery, and stood her in the center" (v. 3). While the mention of the Pharisees seems appropriate after the Pharisees' attempt to arrest Jesus in the preceding chapter (see 7:32, 45-52), "the scribes" appear nowhere else in John's Gospel. The operative phrase is either just "the Pharisees" (7:32, 47, 48 and frequently), or else "the chief priests and the Pharisees" (7:32, 45; see also 11:47, 57; 18:3).[152] More to the point, the reader would have expected the Pharisees to try again to arrest Jesus (see 7:30, 32, 44) instead of merely inviting his judgment as to the fate of another fugitive. The notice that they did this "so that they might have [reason] to accuse him" (v. 6) seems to forget that they *already* had ample reason to accuse him (see 5:16, 18), and that they were in fact already seeking his life (see 7:1, 11, 19, 21-23, 25). Instead the woman takes "center" stage (*en mesō*, v. 3b) as the accused — a kind of surrogate for Jesus himself. Her case calls into question the judgment of her accusers, as Jesus will show, illustrating his warning, "Don't judge by appearance, but judge the right judgment!" (7:24), and more explicitly his later comment, "You judge according to the flesh, 'I' judge no one" (8:15).

4-5 The woman has been "caught in the act of committing adultery" (v. 4), presumably by at least two witnesses who are present and ready to testify against her (see Deut 17:6; 19:15). "Teacher," her accusers ask Jesus, "this woman was caught in the act of committing adultery, and in the law

---

and *all the people* were coming to him, and he sat and began *teaching* them" (Woman caught in adultery). While Luke describes Jesus' customary or repeated practice during his last week on earth, the story preserved here describes one *particular* night and morning. The redundancy is alleviated somewhat if it is assumed that Luke 21:37-38 was "composed to fill the gap caused by the removal of this paragraph" (Barrett, 589), that is, that it originally followed 21:36, so that those who "went off, each to his house" are those to whom he was speaking in 21:5-36, presumably his own disciples.

151. Gr. πᾶς ὁ λαός.
152. As for Luke's Gospel, while Luke knows and uses the expression "the scribes and the Pharisees" (see Lk 5:21, 30; 6:7; 11:53; 15:2), the Lukan passion narrative consistently prefers "the scribes and the chief priests" (Lk 19:47; 20:1, 19; 22:2, 66; 23:10; see also 9:22).

Moses commanded us to stone such women. So what do you say?" Their use of the title "Teacher"[153] is more characteristic of synoptic controversy narratives[154] than of John's Gospel, where everywhere else (except for Nicodemus in 3:2), "Teacher" occurs only on the lips of Jesus' disciples (see 1:38; 11:28; 13:13, 14; 20:16). Their question, "So what do you say?" is intended to test whether or not Jesus is willing to affirm the law of Moses. Despite being charged with breaking the Sabbath (5:16, 18), he has already appealed to the law in his own defense (7:19, 21-23), and will do so again (8:17-18), and they would like very much to trap him into contradicting or disregarding the law on a specific point other than the Sabbath.

Some have argued that affirming the law would also have been a trap for him because the Romans at the time did not allow the Jewish people to carry out the death sentence.[155] This is unlikely in view of Pilate's two explicit statements to the Jewish leaders regarding Jesus himself after his arrest, "Take him yourselves and judge him according to your law" (18:31), and "Take him yourselves and crucify" (19:6). If the Gospel writer represents Pilate as commanding them to carry out the death penalty, he must have believed they had the right to do so.[156] Thus the intent of the scribes and Pharisees could not have been to put Jesus in a dilemma between the conflicting demands of Jewish and Roman law, but rather to trap him purely on the basis of Jewish law. As far as they were concerned, there could be only one "right" answer to their question: that the stoning should proceed as the law required. Clearly, their intention was flawed because according to biblical law in such cases *both* the man and the woman who had committed adultery should have been stoned, and if the woman was indeed "caught in the act," her partner must have been present and should have been arrested as well.[157] Yet Jesus ignores their error.

---

153. Gr. διδάσκαλε.

154. Among many instances in all three synoptic Gospels, see Matthew 8:19 ("a scribe"); 12:38 ("scribes and Pharisees"); 22:16 ("the Pharisees"), 24 ("Sadducees"), 36 ("one of the Pharisees"); Lk 10:25 ("a legal scholar"), 18:18 ("a certain ruler").

155. Among others, see Keener, 1.737; Barrett, 591-92; Morris, 782; Whitacre, 206; also Brown, 1.337 (though with some caution as to whether the Jewish Sanhedrin in fact had this power).

156. See my article, "John 18.31 and the 'Trial' of Jesus," *NTS* 36.3 (1990), 475-76.

157. See Leviticus 20:10, "If a man commits adultery with another man's wife — with the wife of his neighbor — both the adulterer and the adulteress must be put to death" (NIV); Deuteronomy 22:22-24, "If a man is found sleeping with another man's wife, both the man who slept with her and the woman must die. You must purge the evil from Israel. If a man happens to meet in a town a virgin pledged to be married and he sleeps with her, you shall take both of them to the gate of that town and stone them to death — the girl because she was in the town and did not scream for help, and the man because he violated another man's wife. You must purge the evil from among you" (NIV).

It only confirms, after all, his judgment that they "judge according to the flesh" (see v. 15). Instead, he adopts a very different strategy.

6 At this point, a narrative aside informs the reader, "This they said testing him, so that they might have [reason] to accuse him." Such narrative asides are, as we have seen, very characteristic of this Gospel writer,[158] and are frequently introduced with the expression, "This he said," or something similar (see 6:6; 7:39; 11:51; 12:33; 21:19; also 2:21; 12:6). The parallel to Jesus' own words to Philip in 6:6 is particularly striking: "This he said testing him, for he himself knew what he was going to do." But here (uniquely in John's Gospel) Jesus is the one being tested: "This they said, testing him." They too knew (or thought they knew) what they were going to do, and were "testing" Jesus to see if he was on board with their plans. The closer kinship of the reference is to a number of incidents in the other Gospels in which Jesus' opponents "tested" him either by asking for a sign (Mt 16:1; Mk 8:11; Lk 11:16; compare Jn 2:18; 6:30), or questioning him (as here) about his interpretation of the law (see Mt 19:3; 22:35-36; Mk 10:2; Lk 10:25, 29), or in one instance about the payment of taxes to Caesar (see Mt 22:18, "Why are you testing me?"). In contrast to 6:6, where the notice is intended only to underscore Jesus' total control of the situation, the purpose here (as in the synoptic Gospels) is to alert the reader that "the scribes and Pharisees" asked the question not to learn wisdom from their respected "Teacher," but solely "that they might have [reason] to accuse him."

Jesus' response is surprising. Nothing in any of the stories in Matthew, Mark, or Luke quite prepares us for it. He "stooped down and wrote with his finger on the ground." Much has been written about what words Jesus may or may not have written, but it is all speculative.[159] Essentially his response is a non-answer, equivalent to silence, as is clear from the comment to follow that "they kept on questioning him" (v. 7). His body language is, if anything, even more striking than the reference to writing on the ground. The account is punctuated by notices that he "stooped down" and wrote (v. 6),

---

158. See above, on 1:38.

159. See, for example, Keener, 1.737; Schnackenburg, 2.165-66; Brown, 1.333-34. A common view is that the action has something to do with Jeremiah 17:13, "those who turn away from thee shall be written in the earth, for they have forsaken the LORD, the fountain of living water" (RSV), the point being not that those were the actual words written, but that Jesus was acting out that prophecy. It is remotely possible that Jesus wrote down what he would shortly say to the woman's accusers (v. 7), with the implication that what is "written" is of greater authority than what is merely spoken (see Jesus' citations of Scripture as "written"; also Pilate's comment in 19:22). But this is very doubtful in light of Jesus' repeated emphasis on the authority of the spoken words his Father has given him (as, for example, in 8:26, 28, and 38), and in any case does not adequately explain why he wrote on the ground a second time (v. 8).

"straightened up" and spoke to the gathered crowd (v. 7),[160] again "stooped down" and wrote (v. 8), and finally "straightened up" and spoke again, this time to the woman (v. 10).[161] While it cannot be proven that the story rests on the testimony of an eyewitness (Who would it be? The woman?), details of this kind, even if they had no apparent meaning, would not have been easily forgotten by anyone on the scene. If not attributable to an eyewitness, they point to a storyteller eminently skilled at creating a dramatic effect.[162]

7 In the face of Jesus' silence and apparent disregard for their question, the scribes and Pharisees "kept on questioning him," presumably asking the same question again. Finally "he straightened up and said to them, 'The one without fault among you, let him first throw a stone on her'" (v. 7). His words seem to presuppose that the woman has already been tried and convicted, for according to Scripture, when a person has been convicted on the testimony of at least two witnesses, "The hands of the witnesses must be the first[163] in putting him to death, and then the hands of all the people" (Deut 17:7, NIV). If the woman has indeed been "caught in the act of committing adultery" by the requisite two witnesses (see v. 3), and if the witnesses are indeed present (as would seem to be the case), then Jesus is inviting one of them to do what the law requires. If for any reason the actual witnesses were not present, then anyone who picked up a stone in response to Jesus' words would in effect be taking on himself the role of witness against the woman. The law required that such witnesses not be "malicious" or "lying" witnesses (see Deut 19:16-18). Jesus' version of that requirement is that this person be "without fault,"[164] a term denoting not so much abstract "sinlessness" (in the sense in which later Christian theology has believed Jesus himself to be sinless), as simply personal integrity before God in the matter at hand.[165] That is, whoever takes on himself the role of

---

160. The Greek expressions are κάτω κύψας and ἀνέκυψεν respectively.

161. The Greek expressions are κατακύψας and ἀνακύψας respectively.

162. The reader is almost led to expect the storyteller's adverb οὕτως, "like this," as in 4:6, but it does not occur, and the story achieves the desired effect quite nicely without it.

163. Gr. ἐν πρώτοις (LXX).

164. Gr. ἀναμάρτητος.

165. See K. H. Rengstorf, ἀναμάρτητος, *TDNT,* 1.333-35. See, for example, *Epistle of Aristeas* 252, where the Egyptian king asks one of the translators of the Hebrew Bible into Greek, "How can one be without fault [ἀναμάρτητος]?" The reply was, "By doing everything with considered judgment, not influenced by misrepresentations, but being your own judge of what was said, and in your judgment directing aright matters concerned with petitions made to you, and through your judgment bringing them to pass — that is how you would be without fault [ἀναμάρτητος], O King" (*OTP,* 2.29). Philo uses the word in a context in which he has just written, "Should we then seek to find in the medley of life one who is perfectly just or wise or temperate or good in general? Be satisfied, if you do

witness-executioner must be confident before God that he is doing the right thing — hardly an unreasonable demand.¹⁶⁶

8 This time Jesus' body language, as "again he stooped down and wrote on the ground" (v. 8), signals that he has said all he is going to say. The next move is up to the woman's (and his) accusers. Either they will question him further or they will not. Either they will take up stones to stone the woman or they will not. In contrast to the first time he stooped down (vv. 6-7), they are silent. There are no more questions. A reader familiar with the other Gospels might have expected a notice that "No one could answer him a word, nor did anyone dare question him any more from that day on" (Mt 22:46; see also Mk 12:34; Lk 20:40). In John's Gospel, there are of course many more questions to come (see vv. 12-59), but within the present story the "testing" is over, almost as soon as it began (see v. 6).

9 The actions of "the scribes and Pharisees" speak more loudly than anything they could have said, as "those who had heard went out one by one, beginning from the elders" (v. 9). Again, the scene is one that would have caught the attention of an eyewitness.¹⁶⁷ "One by one, beginning from the elders" is both dramatic and ceremonious, not soon forgotten. At the same time, the phrase "beginning from the elders"¹⁶⁸ evokes Ezekiel's image of judgment on Israel to "begin from my sanctuary" (that is, from the Jerusalem temple, the scene of the present story), so that the agents of judgment "began from the men who were elders, who were inside in the house" (Ezek 9:6, LXX).¹⁶⁹ Instead of condemning the woman, Jesus' words have in effect condemned the temple and the Jewish religious establishment, scribes, Pharisees, chief priests, and elders alike. In this sense the story of the woman caught in adultery mirrors the longer account in which it is embedded, Jesus'

---

but find one who is not unjust, is not foolish, is not licentious, is not cowardly, is not altogether evil. We may be content with the overthrow of vices, [but] the complete acquisition of virtues is impossible for man, as we know him." Only then does he add that "freedom from sin [τὸ ἀναμάρτητον] and guilt is a great furtherance towards a happy life" (*On the Change of Names* 50-51; LCL, 5.167-69).

166. As Schnackenburg admits, "The word need not mean total sinlessness, merely not guilty" (2.481, n. 120). So too Brown, who comments that Jesus "is dealing here with zealots who have taken on themselves the indignant enforcement of the Law, and he has every right to demand that their case be thoroughly lawful and their motives be honest" (1.338).

167. Some later scribes, unsatisfied with such an unvarnished description, felt compelled to add details no eyewitness could have seen: "Those who heard *and were convicted by the conscience* went out one by one" (my italics; see, for example, E, G, and H, from the eighth and ninth centuries).

168. Gr. ἀρξάμενοι ἀπὸ τῶν πρεσβυτέρων.

169. See also 1 Peter 4:17; 5:1.

temple discourse at the Tent festival, in which similarly the accused becomes the agent of God's judgment on the accusers. For the moment, Jesus is "left alone," still bent over, preoccupied with what he is writing, with the woman still standing "in the center" (as in v. 3).[170]

10-11 As before, "Jesus straightened up," and only then spoke. His words are gentler than those to her accusers (v. 7). He asks her two simple questions, as if he did not already know the answers: "Woman, where are they? Has no one condemned you?" "Woman" is his characteristic way of addressing women in this Gospel (4:21; 20:15; see also Mt 15:28; Lk 13:12), even his own mother (2:4; 19:26). While the address implies no disrespect, it does put her at a certain distance, just as in Jesus' encounter with the Samaritan woman, and she replies in the same vein, "No one, sir,"[171] There is no hint that the woman caught in adultery has by this time come to believe in Jesus, or indeed that she ever did. It may be so, but it is not the point of the story. When she acknowledges that no one has condemned her, and Jesus replies, "Nor do I condemn you," he is not so much pronouncing on her eternal salvation as simply confirming that she does not deserve to die. He does not say, as he says in certain other Gospel stories, "O woman, great is your faith" (Mt 15:28), or "Daughter, your faith has saved you. Go in peace" (Lk 8:48). He says only, "Go, and from now on sin no more" (v. 11), recalling his words to the sick man he had healed at the Bethsaida pool, "Don't sin any more, or something worse may happen to you" (5:14). The implication there was that the sick man did *not* believe in Jesus, and that he *did* sin again, almost immediately in fact (see 5:15-16). No such implication is left in the case of the woman, as the story is left open-ended.

When the story is read as part of the Gospel of John, regardless of when it may have been added to the Gospel, it becomes a kind of subtext to Jesus' temple discourse at the Tent festival (that is, to 7:14–8:59). Instead of Jesus being judged and vindicated, the woman is judged and vindicated, and her accusers are judged, just as Jesus' accusers are judged and found wanting in the temple discourse as a whole. And just as her story ends with a stoning that never materialized, so too does the temple discourse itself (see 8:59). Hers is a story within a story, accenting the same truth within a more concise and limited sphere.

---

170. Gr. ἐν μέσῳ. Even though there is no longer a group of accusers to be "in the center" of, she is still the center of the reader's attention in a touching final scene.

171. The address κύριε must almost certainly be translated here as "sir" (as in NIV, NRSV, NAB, NEB, and REB), not "Lord" (as in KJV, ASV, NASB, and RSV).

L. THE LAST DAY OF THE FESTIVAL: JESUS AND THE JEWS WHO BELIEVED (8:30-59)

30 As he was speaking these things, many believed in him. 31 So Jesus said to the Jews who had believed him, "If you dwell on my word, you are truly my disciples, 32 and you will know the truth, and the truth will set you free." 33 They answered him, "We are Abraham's seed, and have never been in slavery to anyone. How do you say that 'You will become free'?" 34 Jesus answered them, "Amen, amen, I say to you, that everyone who commits sin is a slave of sin. 35 But the slave does not remain in the household forever; the son remains forever. 36 So if the Son sets you free, you will really be free. 37 I know that you are Abraham's seed, but you are seeking to kill me, because my word is not getting through to you. 38 The things I have seen in the Father's presence I speak, and you therefore must do what you have heard from the Father."

39 They answered and said to him, "Our father is Abraham." Jesus said to them, "If you are Abraham's children, you would be doing the works of Abraham. 40 But now you are seeking to kill me, a man who has spoken to you the truth which I heard from God. This Abraham did not do. 41 You are doing the works of your father." So they said to him, "We are not born of unlawful intercourse. We have one Father, God." 42 Jesus said to them, "If God were your Father, you would love me, for I came forth from God, and here I am. For I have not come on my own, but that One sent me. 43 Why do you not know my speech? Because you cannot hear my word. 44 You are from the father [who is] the devil, and you choose to do the desires of your father. That one was homicidal from the beginning, and was not standing in the truth, because truth is not in him. When he speaks the lie, he speaks from his own, because he is the liar and the father of it. 45 But I, because I speak the truth, you do not believe me. 46 Who among you convicts me of sin? If I speak truth, why do you not believe me? 47 Whoever is from God hears the words of God. This is why you do not hear, because you are not from God."

48 The Jews answered and said to him, "Do we not say well that you are a Samaritan and have a demon?" 49 Jesus answered, "I do not have a demon, but I honor my Father, and you dishonor me. 50 And I am not seeking my glory. There is One who seeks and judges. 51 Amen, amen, I say to you, if anyone keeps my word, he will never ever see death." 52 So the Jews said to him, "Now we know that you have a demon. Abraham died, and the prophets, and you say, 'If anyone keeps my word, he will never ever taste of death.' 53 Are you

greater than our father Abraham, who died, and the prophets died? Who do you make yourself to be?" 54 *Jesus answered, "If I glorify myself, my glory is nothing. It is my Father who glorifies me, him whom you say that 'He is our God.'* 55 *And you have not known him, but I know him. And if I say that I do not know him, I will be a liar like you. But I know him, and I keep his word.* 56 *Abraham, your father, rejoiced that he would see my day, and he saw and was glad."* 57 *So the Jews said to him, "You are not yet fifty years old, and you have seen Abraham?"* 58 *Jesus said to them, "Amen, amen, I say to you, before Abraham came to be, I am."* 59 *So they took up stones that they might throw on him. But Jesus was hidden, and went out of the temple.*

Even though some (most notably Rudolf Bultmann) have viewed Jesus' "temple discourse" at the Tent festival (that is, 7:14–8:59) as a compilation (and not without reason), it is *in its present form* more like a seamless robe, especially "the last day of the festival," from 7:37 on. In the preceding section, despite notices such as "So again Jesus spoke to them" (8:12), and "These words he spoke in the treasury" (8:20), and "So again he said to them" (8:21), it was difficult to find an excuse to begin a new section. I have begun one here only because of a partial but significant change of audience — like the shifts in chapter 6 from "the crowd" to "the Jews" (6:41), and from "the Jews" to "many of his disciples" (6:60). As we have seen, Jesus' audience (at least in the first half of the Gospel) is in one sense always the same, and almost always hostile (in varying degrees) to his claims. Yet the changes in how the audience is named are worth noticing, and are as useful as anything else in dividing up the discourses. In the present discourse, there were terminological changes back and forth between "the Jews" (7:11, 13, 15, 35; 8:22) and either "the Pharisees" (7:32; 8:13) or "the chief priests and the Pharisees" (7:32, 45), but these were insignificant because the parties were pretty much interchangeable.[1] Now the shift is from "the Jews" (v. 22) to "the Jews who had believed him"[2] (v. 31), a shift that is, on the face of it, far more noteworthy. "The Jews who had believed him" signals quite clearly to the readers of the Gospels that Jesus is now addressing *believers,* not unbelievers, and more specifically Jewish believers in Christ.[3] While many inter-

---

1. "The crowd," or "the crowds," have also been present, but have functioned more as a kind of chorus rather than as Jesus' real dialogue partners (see 7:12, 31-32, 40, 43; also "some of the Jerusalemites," 7:25).

2. Gr. τοὺς πεπιστευκότας αὐτῷ Ἰουδαίους.

3. The terminology in the book of Acts is comparable. See, for example, Acts 21:20, where Paul is told, "You can see, brother, how many thousands there are among the Jews of 'those who have believed [ἐν τοῖς Ἰουδαίοις τῶν πεπιστευκότων], and they are all zealous for the law"; also 15:5, "Then some of those from the sect of the Pharisees who

8:30-59 THE LAST DAY OF THE FESTIVAL

preters have tried to avoid this conclusion because of the harsh words Jesus later speaks to this audience (see, for example, vv. 37-46),[4] the Gospel writer's words ("the Jews who had believed him") are open to no other interpretation. The section to follow details a progressive unraveling of the "faith" of these "believing Jews," first over the issue of slavery and freedom (see vv. 32-33), but eventually over the issue of eternal life (see vv. 51-52) and Jesus' power to confer life. At the end of the day, the question on which these "believers" stumble is christological: "Who do you make yourself to be?" (v. 53), ending in Jesus' magisterial self-revelation, "I am" (v. 58).

30 There could have been a number of possible reactions to Jesus' speech that began, "When you lift up the Son of man" (v. 28) and ended with the claim that "I always do the things that please him" (v. 29). If his hearers had focused on the implication that they would "lift him up" by crucifixion, they might have repeated the words of the crowd, "You have a demon. Who is seeking to kill you?" (7:20). Or, they might have challenged his assertion that "I always do the things that please him" by pressing the charge that he had in fact broken the Sabbath. Their response instead is quite unexpected: "As he was speaking these things, many believed in him"[5] (v. 30). We have heard this expression before, when Jesus first came to Jerusalem and "many believed in his name," and Jesus "would not entrust himself to them" (2:23-24), and again at this same Tent festival, when "many from the crowd believed in him" (7:31), yet nothing much came of it, as their faith was dismissed as mere "murmuring" (7:32).[6]

Here, too, the faith of the "many" who "believed in him" will quickly

---

had believed [πεπιστευκότες] stood up, saying that they must be commanded to be circumcised and to keep the law of Moses." The only difference is that in these passages in Acts, "believe" is used absolutely ("to be a believer") rather than with an object (see, however, the phrase πεπιστευκὼς τῷ θεῷ, used of the Philippian jailer in 16:34).

4. The most common strategies are either to excise the words "who had believed him" as a scribal gloss (see, for example, Brown, 1.354; Lindars, 323-24) or to distinguish sharply between "believing in Jesus" (v. 30) and merely "believing him" (for example, Barrett, 344; Moloney, 275), or to assume that the audience changes back again as soon as real dialogue begins. As long ago as the fourth century, Augustine claimed that those who answered Jesus in verse 33 were "not those who already believed, but those in the crowd who were not yet believers" (*Tractates on John* 41.2, NPNF, 1st ser., 7.230; see also Debbie Hunn, "Who Are 'They' in John 8:33," *CBQ* 66.3 [2004], 387-99). None of these options are at all convincing.

5. Gr. πολλοὶ ἐπίστευσαν εἰς αὐτόν.

6. For other examples of the problematic faith of "many," see 11:45-46 and 12:42-43. One is tempted to invoke the synoptic saying of Jesus, "Many [πολλοί] are called, but few are chosen" (Mt 22:14). The major exception was the case of "many" (πολλοί) of the Samaritans who, having "believed in him" (4:39), came to "know that this is truly the Savior of the world" (v. 42).

The Gospel of John

turn out to be inadequate. This is not apparent at once, but the reader has reason to suspect right from the start that this "belief" is premature. Jesus has just said, "*When you lift up the Son of man,* then you will know that I am" (v. 28, my italics), and this of course has not yet happened. Just as the Spirit will not come until Jesus has been "glorified" (7:39), so perhaps true belief in him is not possible (at least for these "Jews") until he has been "lifted up." Even his first disciples, after all, who genuinely "believed in him," did so only because he "revealed his glory" to them (2:11), and even their faith did not come to full maturity until he "rose from the dead" (see 2:22). Another subtle hint, perhaps, that the belief is premature is the genitive absolute with a present participle, "As he was speaking these things."[7] This is a common way in John's Gospel of marking divisions and endings in Jesus' discourses,[8] but more often the Gospel writer uses "these things" with the *aorist* tense for this purpose, indicating that the discourse, or a significant portion of it, is over.[9] The use of the present tense here could suggest, by contrast, that in this instance Jesus had not finished what he had to say, but that his hearers "believed in him" *before* he had even finished speaking.[10] This would suggest, at the very least, that they needed further instruction, and further instruction is precisely what he tries to provide.

31-32 Jesus now explicitly addresses "the Jews who had believed him," that is, the "many" who were said to have "believed in him" in the preceding verse.[11] "If you dwell on my word," he begins, "you are truly my disciples, and you will know the truth, and the truth will set you free." This often-quoted promise, "you will know the truth, and the truth will set you free" (v. 32), repeats and builds on what he said in verse 28, "When you lift up the Son of man, then you will know[12] that I am," only now with a condition attached.[13] "The truth" that these believing Jews "will know" consists of all that he has just promised them they would know: "that I am, and [that] on

---

7. Gr. ταῦτα αὐτοῦ λαλοῦντος.

8. See Brown, 1.348.

9. For example, "These words he spoke" (ταῦτα τὰ ῥήματα ἐλάλησεν, v. 20; see also ταῦτα εἶπεν, 6:59; ταῦτα εἰπών, 12:21; 18:1).

10. This would be more clearly the case if the text had read ἔτι αὐτοῦ λαλοῦντος ("As he was *still* speaking"), implying an interruption (as in Acts 10:44 or Mt 17:5; yet see also Lk 9:34, ταῦτα δὲ αὐτοῦ λαλοῦντος).

11. Despite the different grammatical constructions (to "believe in" Jesus, using πιστεύειν εἰς, and to 'believe him,' using πιστεύειν with the dative αὐτῷ), there can be no doubt that the same group is in view (for the latter construction used to mean essentially the same as the former; see 5:24, 38, 46; 6:30; 8:45, 46; 10:37, 38; 14:11).

12. Thus, "you will know" (γνώσεσθε, v. 32) echoes "then you will know" (τότε γνώσεσθε, v. 28).

13. So rightly Barrett (344): "This expression is in close parallel with γνώσεσθε ὅτι ἐγώ εἰμι (v. 28)."

504

my own I do nothing, but just as the Father taught me, these things I speak" (v. 28), perhaps with its corollary, "And the One who sent me is with me. He has not left me alone, for I always do the things that please him" (v. 29).[14] The condition he now attaches is that they must "dwell on my word." To "dwell on" Jesus' word presupposes that they have in fact "believed him" (that is, believed in him on the basis of his spoken words, v. 31).[15] Jesus is asking them, now that they have believed, to "follow" him (see v. 12) or "walk with him" (see 6:60) in the sense of giving him their allegiance, finally even to "dwell in him" (6:56) or become united to him in their very being. To be "truly my disciples," he insists, requires nothing less.[16]

The result of such ongoing faith is that "the truth" they have come to know "will set you free" (v. 32).[17] Ironically, it is this additional promise beyond what he said earlier that offends Jesus' hearers and causes them to stumble (see v. 33). "Set free from what?" is the question in their minds, and to that question there can be only one answer. They need to be "set free" from the threat still hanging over their heads that "You will die in your sin" (v. 21), or "your sins" (v. 24). As we saw, "the Jews" never acknowledged that death threat, and these "Jews who had believed him" are still not ready to acknowledge it. Consequently, the question, "Set free from what?" baffles them, and more than that, offends them. Like the false "disciples" of 6:60, they will slip away, and their apostasy begins almost immediately.

33 "We are Abraham's seed,"[18] they reply, "and have never been in

---

14. Contrary to the way in which this text has often functioned in contemporary discourse, therefore, Jesus is not speaking of abstract or academic "truth," but solely of the concrete and very explicit truth about himself and his mission to the world (see below, vv. 40, 44-46; also 3:21; 5:33; 16:13; 17:17, 19; 18:37).

15. The verb "dwell on" (μείνητε) is odd because μένειν, to "dwell," or "remain," implies continuing action (leading us to expect the present tense), even though the tense here is aorist (as in 15:4, 7, 9). The translation "to dwell on" (rather than "to dwell in," as μείνητε ἐν might have led us to expect) is an effort to do justice to the tense of the verb as well as the verb itself, and to the fact that the object is Jesus' "word," not Jesus himself as a person.

16. Much later, Jesus will say something similar even to those who are without question *already* his disciples: "If you make your dwelling [ἐὰν μείνητε] in me, and my words dwell in you, ask whatever you want and it will be done for you. In this my Father is glorified, that you might bear much fruit and become my disciples" (ἵνα . . . γενήσεσθε ἐμοὶ μαθηταί, 15:7-8).

17. Here too a parallel exists with something Jesus will say later to his disciples: "I no longer say you are slaves, because the slave [ὁ δοῦλος] does not know what his master is doing, but I say you are friends, because all that I heard from the Father I made known [ἐγνώρισα] to you" (15:15). As in the present passage, it is knowledge that frees the slave.

18. The phrase "Abraham's seed," or descendants (σπέρμα Ἀβραάμ), recalls such

slavery to anyone. How do you say that 'You will become free'?" Their answer conspicuously ignores Moses' repeated commands in Deuteronomy to "Remember that you were slaves in Egypt" (Deut 5:15, NIV; also 15:15; 16:12; 24:18, 22), and therefore in the present context calls into question their faithfulness to their own covenant. Any reader familiar with the synoptic Gospels will notice that they are also ignoring John the Baptist's warning, "And do not begin to say among yourselves, 'We have Abraham for our father,' for I tell you that God is able of these stones to raise up children to Abraham" (Lk 3:8; see also Mt 3:9).

Yet obviously, these "believing Jews" knew that what they were saying was not literally true. They did remember that their ancestors had been slaves in Egypt, despite being descended from Abraham, and effectively so in Babylon as well, and in their own country at the hands of the Persians, the Greeks, and now the Romans. They are simply expressing a kind of national pride as those who (in Schnackenburg's words) are "free sons of Abraham, who have never inwardly bowed to foreign rule."[19] Even so, their disclaimer misses the point. Foreign rule is not the issue, and Jesus promptly says as much.[20]

34 For the twelfth time in the Gospel, Jesus introduces an answer with his characteristic "Amen, amen" formula, the first time since 6:53 and the first of three within the temple discourse (see vv. 51 and 58): "Amen, amen, I say to you, that everyone who commits sin is a slave of sin" (v. 34). While the "Amen, amen" formula is Johannine, the pronouncement itself evokes a world of thought more often associated with the Apostle Paul, who wrote, "Don't you know that when you offer yourselves to someone to obey him as slaves, you are slaves to the one whom you obey — whether you are slaves to sin, which leads to death, or to obedience, which leads to righteousness? But thanks to God that, though you used to be slaves to sin, you wholeheartedly obeyed the form of teaching to which you were entrusted. You have been set free from sin and have become slaves to righteousness" (Rom 6:16-18, NIV).[21] John's Gospel differs

---

passages as Genesis 13:15 and 17:8, where God promised Abraham the land of Israel, "to you and to your seed forever."

19. Schnackenburg, 2.207. He (and others) cite R. Aqiba's comment that "Even the poorest in Israel are looked upon as freemen who have lost their possessions, for they are the sons of Abraham, Isaac, and Jacob" (*m. Baba Qamma* 8.6; Danby, 343).

20. As he said in three other Gospels, "Give Caesar's things to Caesar, and God's things to God" (Mk 12:17//Mt 22:21//Lk 20:25).

21. Precisely because of the Pauline-sounding language, some interpreters have favored the variant reading in some manuscripts (including D, the old Latin *b,* and the Sinaitic Syriac version), omitting the words "of sin" (τῆς ἁμαρτίας): thus, "everyone who commits sin is a slave" (see, for example, Dodd, *Interpretation,* 177; Brown, 1.355). But the textual evidence is weak, and the Pauline perspective is evident even without the words "of sin."

from Paul only in that the law is not implicated in the Jews' slavery to sin and death, as it is in Paul (see Rom 5:13; 6:14; 7:7-11; Gal 4:21-26).

Jesus' main point here is simply that the actual enslavement of these "believing Jews" was not to Rome, but (in common with the whole world) to sin, and therefore finally to death.[22] Yet this viewpoint (that Israel's problem was not foreign rule but her own sin) was not distinctive to Paul and the Gospel of John alone, or even to early Christianity. It was an authentic strain within Judaism itself from the biblical prophets (notably Jeremiah), through *Second Maccabees,* to the Jewish apocalypse of *4 Ezra* even after the Gospel of John.[23] Here in the temple discourse, Jesus first introduced it with the warning, "You will die in your sin" (v. 21); the theme of sin and death, in particular the overcoming of death, will be his theme from here on to the end of the chapter. His reference to "committing sin," and especially the phrase "a slave of sin," now makes it clear that he was using the noun "slave"[24] (v. 34), and consequently the verb "set free"[25] (v. 32), metaphorically and not literally.

35 The "Amen, amen" pronouncement is not limited to verse 34, but encompasses the next two verses as well. The single metaphor of the "slave" leads into a more complex metaphor or mini-parable about a household, comparable to one he introduced earlier about a son apprenticed to his father (5:19).[26] "But the slave," he continues, "does not remain in the household forever; the son remains forever" (v. 35).[27] That was self-evident. Slaves had no permanent place in the households to which they belonged,[28] unlike family members, and above all in contrast to a firstborn son and heir. Slaves did

---

22. See Romans 5:12; 6:16, and especially 6:23, "For the wages of sin is death, but the gift of God is eternal life in Christ Jesus our Lord" (NIV). Yet the connection between sin and death goes well beyond Paul (see, for example, Jas 1:15, NIV: "sin, when it is full-grown, gives birth to death"). On death itself as slavery, see Romans 8:21 ("slavery to corruption") and Hebrews 2:15, where Christ is said to "free those who all their lives were held in slavery by their fear of death" (NIV).

23. See, for example, *2 Maccabees* 5.17-18; 7.32-33; *4 Ezra* 3.20-27; 6.56-59; 7.10-11.

24. Gr. δοῦλος.

25. Gr. ἐλευθερώσει.

26. The illustration is also reminiscent of Paul's in Galatians 4:1-7, the main difference being that for Paul those who were no better off than "slaves" finally become "sons" (4:5-7), while in John's Gospel they do not, at least not explicitly. The title "Son" is reserved for Jesus alone.

27. As is probably the case in 5:19, the definite articles are generic: "the slave" (ὁ δοῦλος) means any slave in any Roman or Jewish household, and "the son" (ὁ υἱός) any son. The same is true in 15:15, "the slave [ὁ δοῦλος] does not know what his master is doing."

28. As the NIV translates verse 35, "Now a slave has no permanent place in the family, but a son belongs to it forever."

not stand to inherit wealth, and, having been bought, could just as easily be sold. But the metaphor has a theological edge to it, in the stark contrast between "remains forever" and "does not remain . . . forever." The former suggests that some will "live forever" (6:51, 58) or have "eternal life" (see 3:15, 16, 36; 4:14, 36; 5:24, 39; 6:27, 40, 47, 54, 68), while the latter implies just the opposite — that others will die, or, more specifically, "die in their sins" (v. 24). It is a matter of life or death, not just slavery or freedom.

36 Jesus now draws his conclusion from brief parable, a conclusion still governed by the introductory words, "Amen, amen, I say to you." "So," he concludes, "if the Son sets you free, you will really be free" (v. 36). In effect, he renews the invitation and promise that "If you dwell on my word, . . . you will know the truth, and the truth will set you free" (v. 32). It now becomes clear, if it was not before, that "The truth will set you free" actually means "The Son will set you free." Jesus has not called himself "the Son" in their presence,[29] and when he has spoken of his "Father" they have not understood (see vv. 19 and 27), yet the reader knows exactly what he means: *Jesus himself* is "the truth."[30] The door to knowledge, and therefore to freedom and salvation from sin and death, is still open to these Jewish "believers" if only they will, as he said, "dwell on my word" (v. 32). What their new status as "freed slaves" would be he does not define — evidently not "sons," as in Paul (see Gal 4:7 and n. 26), but perhaps "friends" of Jesus (15:15), or "children of God" (1:12; 11:52), or even "children — as opposed to mere 'seed' — of Abraham" (v. 39). Whatever the title, they would be "free" of their present slavery to sin and death, so to "walk in darkness" no longer, but "have the light of life" (see v. 12). In short, "eternal life" would be theirs.

37-38 The note of invitation continues, right alongside a darker note of accusation.[31] Jesus cannot and does not deny the claim of these "believing Jews" that they are "Abraham's seed," or descendants[32] (just as they claimed in v. 33), but he does implicitly deny that they are Abraham's "children,"[33] that is, that their character is anything like Abraham's (he will make this ex-

---

29. He has in fact not even used the term since 6:40 in Galilee, and then only to the crowds (see, however, 5:19, 20, 21, 22, 23, and 26, in words spoken to "the Jews," who seem not to have heard).

30. See 14:6, "I am the Way and the Truth and the Life."

31. This is not so strange if we remember that the same two elements mingled in Peter's sermon to his Jewish audience at Pentecost (for example, "Let the whole house of Israel know for certain that God has made this Jesus *whom you crucified* both Lord and Christ," Acts 2:36, and "Repent, and let each of you be baptized in the name of Jesus Christ *for forgiveness of your sins,* and you will receive the gift of the Holy Spirit," 2:38, italics added; see also Acts 3:13-15 and vv. 17-26).

32. Gr. σπέρμα.

33. Gr. τέκνα.

plicit in v. 39). He does this by bluntly repeating the accusation he made earlier to the crowd, that "you are seeking to kill me" (see 7:19). Back then the charge was denied because Jesus' identity was not even known, but this time it is known, and he adds a reason why they are seeking his life: "because my word is not getting through[34] to you" (v. 37). Having warned them that they must "dwell on my word" (v. 31), he now signals that they are not doing so. His accusation echoes what he said in Jerusalem three chapters earlier, that "the Jews" did not have the Father's word "dwelling in you, because he whom that One sent, him you do not believe" (5:38).

The damning charge is not leveled here for its own sake, however, but in order to lay the basis for one last invitation: "The things I have seen in the Father's presence I speak, and you therefore must do what you have heard from the Father" (v. 38).[35] The pronouncement is difficult, both textually and grammatically, and is not always read in this way. Another possible reading is, "The things I have seen in my Father's presence I speak, and you then are doing the things you have heard from your father," with the implication that theirs is a different "father," presumably the devil (anticipating vv. 41 and 44).[36] A number of textual variants contribute to this very different reading of the text. Some manuscripts add "my" after "Father" in the first clause, and a number of manuscripts correspondingly add "your" after "father" in the second clause, introducing a sharp distinction between two opposed "fathers."[37] But the reading adopted here is supported by the most important ancient witnesses to the text of John's Gospel.[38] It appears that the variations were introduced by scribes who were in a hurry to get to the con-

34. Gr. οὐ χωρεῖ. The verb χωρεῖν implies motion or progress. Bauer suggests "my word makes no headway among you" (BDAG, 1094).

35. This reading, or something close to it, can be found in the NRSV, the NAB, the NIV margin, and the translations of Richmond Lattimore and of Reynolds Price.

36. This reading, or something close to it, predominates among English translations, including the KJV, the Douay, ASV, RSV, NASB, NIV, NEB, REB, GNB, and NLT.

37. The former variant is found in the fourth-century Sinaiticus (א) and several other important uncial manuscripts, such as Θ, Ψ, and D, as well as a considerable number of later minuscule manuscripts from the early Middle Ages. The latter is present in the scribal corrector of א, as well as D, C and Θ, a number of later manuscripts, and Chrysostom.

38. These include above all Vaticanus, or B, L, Origen, and Cyril. With regard to the first variant, the earliest papyri, P[66] and P[75], support the omission of "my" (μου) with "Father" in the first clause and of "your" (ὑμῶν) with "father" in the second clause. Yet their support is compromised to some extent by two other variations in the second clause, where P[75] substitutes λαλεῖτε, "speak," for ποιεῖτε, "do," while P[66] substitutes ἑωράκατε, "you have seen," for ἠκούσατε, "you have heard"). These variants suggest that despite their omission of the possessive pronouns, these ancient scribes may in fact have shared the widely held assumption that Jesus was speaking of two contrasting "fathers" (God and the devil) in this text.

troversy that surfaces in verses 41-44 between having God and having the devil as "father."[39]

Adoption of this shorter reading opens the door to translating the last verb in the sentence[40] as a present imperative, "do" or "you must do," rather than as a present indicative, "you are doing." But this too is disputed, for most commentators who accept this reading still manage to find two "fathers" implied in the text.[41] They still want to read the verb as indicative, pointing to verse 41, where Jesus will say, "You are doing[42] the works of your father," with the clear implication there that they have a different "father" (who turns out to be the devil, v. 44). But two arguments are decisive in favor of reading the verb as imperative. First, the particle "therefore"[43] implies that Jesus is drawing a conclusion from what he has just said.[44] That is, *because* his words represent what he has seen in the Father's presence, his hearers had better listen and "do" what they now hear the Father telling them,[45] that is, through Jesus the Son.[46] Second, the closest parallel in John's Gospel to the language used here is 6:45-46, where Jesus (explaining the biblical text, "And they all will be taught by God") told a group of "Jews" in Galilee that "Every person who has heard from the Father and learned comes to me. Not that anyone has seen the Father except he who is from God, he has seen the Father."[47] That passage, as we saw, was an implied, if somewhat backhanded, invitation to believe (that is, to "learn" and "come to me," 6:45).

---

39. In support of the reading adopted here, see Metzger, *Textual Commentary*, 224-25.

40. That is, ποιεῖτε.

41. Schnackenburg's remark is typical (2.210), "Jesus obviously intends this contrast, but he is still speaking in veiled terms and will not make his idea explicit until later" (see also, among others, Hoskyns, 341; Barrett, 347; Lindars, 327; Carson, 351; Morris, 408; Beasley-Murray, 126; Moloney, 278; Keener, 1.754).

42. Gr. ποιεῖτε.

43. Gr. οὖν.

44. The effort of Abbott (*Johannine Grammar*, 166) to read οὖν as "also" or "accordingly" (indicating correspondence as in 16:22, which he cites), rather than "therefore" (drawing a conclusion as to what Jesus' hearers must "do"), is ingenious but less than convincing.

45. More literally, "what you have heard from the Father" (ἃ ἠκούσατε παρὰ τοῦ πατρὸς).

46. See Brown, 1.356, who rightly argues that "it seems too early in this section of the discourse for the introduction of the theme of the devil as the father of the Jews; it makes the development in 41-44 senseless" (contrast this with Lindars, 327, for whom *Brown's* interpretation "makes nonsense of the argument" [!]).

47. Again it is Abbott who notices the relevant evidence, but his commitment to the notion that Jesus is speaking of two different "fathers" here blinds him to its implication (*Johannine Grammar*, 271-72).

8:30-59 THE LAST DAY OF THE FESTIVAL

Here the invitation becomes explicit (with an imperative), even though there is by this time little expectation of a positive response.[48] Jesus' authority to issue such invitations (in both instances) rests on his preexistence as the Word who was "with God in the beginning" (1:2), or as "God the One and Only . . . right beside the Father," who now reveals the God "no one has ever seen" (1:18; see also 3:11, 32).[49] Because "No one has seen God, ever" (1:18), human salvation depends on hearing and obeying "the One and Only," who is able to tell what he has "seen in the Father's presence" (v. 38).

39 If "do" is read as an imperative, what exactly did Jesus expect his hearers to "do"? He had already urged them to "dwell on my word" (v. 31). The analogy with his earlier pronouncement now suggests that he expected them to "learn" from the Father through him, and thereby "come to me" (6:45), that is, give Jesus their full allegiance. This they will not do, nor will they even acknowledge that the One whom he calls "the Father" is father to them. His use of the term "Father" is still problematic as far as they are concerned (see above, vv. 19 and 27). They still seem not to have grasped that when he speaks of "the Father" he is referring to God. This is all the more remarkable in light of 5:18, where they — or their cohorts — first began to seek his life because he was "claiming God as his own Father, making himself equal to God." Later, when challenged, they will say without hesitation, "We have one Father, God" (v. 41), but here instead they say only, "Our father is Abraham" (v. 39a), doggedly repeating their claim to be "Abraham's seed" (see v. 33). Jesus has already acknowledged that claim and agreed with it (v. 37), but now he makes a crucial distinction: "If you are Abraham's children, you would be doing the works of Abraham" (v. 39b). They may be Abraham's "seed" or "descendants," but "children" implies more.[50] They are

---

48. This interpretation is as old as Origen, who wrote: "The Savior speaks, therefore, after he has seen [the things] with the Father. The Jews, however, who have believed in him have not seen [the things] with the Father, but have heard from the Father, so that they might do what they have heard." He also adduces the passage in 6:45-46, and differs from the view taken here only in suggesting that "they heard from the Father when the Father uttered, *through Moses and the prophets,* the things . . . that must be done" (italics added; see Origen, *Commentary on John* 20.49-50; FC, 89.216).

49. This also helps explain the strong contrast between the emphatic pronouns ἐγώ ("I") in the first clause and ὑμεῖς ("you") in the second (which Moloney, 278, explains as part of the contrast between God and the devil as competing "fathers"). The actual contrast is between Jesus, whose access to "the Father" is direct (based on what he has "seen"), and his hearers, whose access to that same "Father" is indirect (based on what they are now hearing from Jesus' lips).

50. It is not always so clear which of the two is the more spiritually significant term. The classic example is Romans 9:7, which the NIV (in keeping with our text in John) translates "Nor because they are his descendants [σπέρμα] are they all Abraham's children" (τέκνα), while the NRSV (in contrast to John's Gospel) has it, "and not all of

not Abraham's "children" unless their character and behavior show at least a family resemblance to his, and Jesus claims that it does not.

The conditional sentence, "If you are Abraham's children, you would be doing[51] the works of Abraham," must be read as a contrary-to-fact condition. Again (as in v. 38), the manuscript tradition is murky, this time because the sentence is less than perfect grammatically. Strictly speaking, a contrary-to-fact conditional sentence should read, "If you *were* Abraham's children, you would be doing[52] the works of Abraham," and a number of ancient manuscripts have tried to improve the text in just that way.[53] On the other hand, "If you are" leads one to expect a simple conditional sentence, contemplating a reality: "If you really *are* Abraham's children, then *do*[54] the works of Abraham." Not surprisingly, there are manuscripts that move in that direction as well.[55] But the reading, "If you [really] are Abraham's children, you would be doing the works of Abraham," is supported by the overwhelming weight of textual evidence,[56] and is to be followed.[57] Jesus' point is that even though these "believing Jews" are (as they claim) "Abraham's seed," they are not "Abraham's children" because they do not behave as Abraham behaved. Their actions deny the paternity they claim for themselves, for they are not doing "the works of Abraham." Jewish and Christian tradition had much to

---

Abraham's children [τέκνα] are his true descendants" (σπέρμα). The latter is marginally more likely because the context in Romans emphasizes the Abrahamic "seed" with its accompanying "promise" (see 9:8).

51. Gr. εἰ . . . ἐστε ("If you are") and ἐποιεῖτε ("you would be doing").

52. Gr. εἰ . . . ἦτε and ἐποιεῖτε ἄν.

53. Among these are the uncials C, N, W, Θ, families 1 and 13, some of the old Latin versions, and the majority of later manuscripts, which have ἦτε, "were," in place of ἐστε, "are." The imperfect ἐποιεῖτε, even without the particle ἄν, can signal a contrary-to-fact condition (see BDF, §360[1]), but a number of manuscripts make this even clearer with the addition of ἄν (among these are the corrector of ℵ, C, N, L, Δ, Ψ, families 1 and 13, and a number of church fathers).

54. Gr. ποιεῖτε.

55. Ποιεῖτε, which can be translated as indicative ("you are doing") or imperative ("do," as in v. 38), is supported by P[66], B, the Vulgate, and several church fathers, including Origen, Jerome, and Augustine. If this reading were to be adopted, the imperative would be by far the more likely interpretation. A conditional sentence beginning "If you are" is more appropriately followed either by an imperative ("do") or a future indicative ("you will do") than by the present indicative, "you are doing."

56. See P[66], P[75], ℵ, B, D, L, T, the Vulgate, and the Sinaitic Syriac).

57. See Metzger, *Textual Commentary,* 225, and most commentaries. The use of the present tense, "If you are" (εἰ . . . ἐστε), in a contrary-to-fact conditional sentence is not unparalleled. See, for example, Luke 17:6, "If *you have* [εἰ ἔχετε] faith as a grain of mustard seed, *you would say* [ἐλέγετε ἄν] to this fig tree, 'Be uprooted and planted in the sea,' and it would obey [ὑπήκουσεν ἄν] you." There, however, the ἄν sends a clearer signal than here that the condition is contrary-to-fact.

8:30-59 THE LAST DAY OF THE FESTIVAL

say about Abraham's virtues and good works,[58] but Jesus does not go into detail, focusing instead on what Abraham did *not* do, and never would have done (v. 40).

40 "But now," Jesus continues, bringing things back to reality and putting it beyond doubt that what preceded was indeed a condition contrary to fact. The reality, he says again (as in v. 37), is that "you are seeking to kill me, a man who has spoken to you the truth which I heard from God. This Abraham did not do" (v. 40). Jesus seems to have in mind Genesis 18:1-15, where Abraham showed gracious hospitality to "the LORD" in the persons of "three men," understood consistently in later tradition, both Jewish and Christian, as angelic messengers.[59] Jesus too, although "a man" and not an angel,[60] is a divine messenger "from above" (v. 23; see also v. 42) bringing "the truth which I heard from God," but his reception at their hands has been nothing like that of Abraham's illustrious visitors. If anything, it has been more like their reception at the hands of the people of Sodom (Gen 19:1-5), worse in fact, for Jesus accuses these "Jews" of "seeking to kill me." When he made this charge before (v. 37), they did not deny it, but instead repeated their claim that Abraham was their father (v. 39). Now he presses the charge again, reminding them that it grossly contradicts the claim they have just made. Still they will not deny it. With this, they reject his final invitation to

---

58. Within the New Testament, see James 2:21, "Was not Abraham our father justified by works [ἐξ ἔργων] when he offered up Isaac his son on the altar?" Also Hebrews 11:8-19, accenting both his migration to an unknown country and his willingness to sacrifice Isaac. At much greater length, see the (roughly contemporary) *Testament of Abraham*, accenting his hospitality to angelic visitors (*OTP*, 1.871-902), and Philo's *On Abraham*, centering on all three: his migration, his hospitality, and his obedience to God in the case of Isaac (see LCL, 6.2-135).

59. See Josephus, *Antiquities* 1.196; Philo, *On the Migration of Abraham* 107, 113; Justin, *Dialogue* 56. For a blended account of later Jewish traditions, see L. Ginzberg, *Legends of the Jews*, 1.240-45; more specifically, see *Testament of Abraham*, where the divine visitor is the archangel Michael sent to warn Abraham of his impending death (for example, "When Abraham saw the Commander-in-chief Michael coming from afar, in the manner of a handsome soldier, then Abraham arose and met him, just as was his custom to greet and welcome all strangers," *Testament of Abraham* 2.2; *OTP*, 1.882). In other traditions, all three angels were identified (see *b. Baba Meṣi'a* 86b: "Who were the three men? — Michael, Gabriel, and Raphael. Michael came to bring the tidings to Sarah [of Isaac's birth]; Raphael to heal Abraham; and Gabriel to overturn Sodom"; *Babylonian Talmud: Nezikin* [London: Soncino, 1935], 1.500).

60. For what it is worth, this is the only place in John's Gospel where Jesus refers to himself as "a man" (ἄνθρωπος), or human being (except implicitly in v. 17, and except for the title "the Son of man," which occurs twelve times on his lips). Possibly "Son of man" is implied here as well (see 9:36, where the man born blind seems to understand "Son of man" as "that man," referring to Jesus as "the man" who healed him).

"do what you have heard from the Father" (v. 38). The Gospel writer's memorable words, "He came to what was his own, and his own did not receive him" (1:11), are beginning to come true before the reader's very eyes.

41 Jesus can add only one thing at this point, a kind of parody of that last invitation. Instead of pleading with them any longer to "*do* what you have heard from the Father" (v. 38), he now sadly acknowledges that "*You are doing* the works of *your* father" (v. 41a, italics added). The emphatic pronouns "You" and "your"[61] mutually reinforce each other, giving the impression that their "father" is not Jesus' "Father." Nor is Abraham their true father, even though they are Abraham's descendants (see vv. 39-40). The reader senses that Jesus is implying something quite unpleasant, and so do his hearers. Without telling them in so many words who he thinks their spiritual father is, he has succeeded in putting them on the defensive. "We are not born of unlawful intercourse," they quickly reply. "We have one Father, God" (v. 41b). The emphatic "we"[62] in the first clause has led interpreters as far back as Origen to conclude that they are "hinting in a veiled manner that the Savior was born of fornication. They assume this as probable because they do not accept his famous and widely discussed birth from the Virgin."[63] That is, "*We* are not born of unlawful intercourse, but *you* are!" But this is unlikely because they are basically defending themselves at this point, not attacking Jesus. Their emphatic "we" merely echoes and responds to his own emphatic "you" and "your" in questioning their paternity.[64] And just as Jesus was questioning their spiritual paternity, not the legitimacy of anyone's physical birth, so their reply, "We are not born of unlawful intercourse," must be understood metaphorically and not literally.[65] Their added words, "We have one Father, God," seem to make it clear that they are claiming to be legitimate, that is, faithful, children of God, not an unfaithful or adulterous people like Israel of old.[66]

In one sense, this represents progress. These "Jews" have now moved beyond merely claiming to be "Abraham's seed" (v. 33), or to have Abraham

---

61. Gr. ὑμεῖς and ὑμῶν.
62. Gr. ἡμεῖς.
63. Origen, *Commentary on John* 20.128 (FC, 89.233). Also *Acts of Pilate* 2.3 (Hennecke-Schneemelcher, 1.453), where "the elders of the Jews" charge Jesus "Firstly, that you were born of fornication" (ὅτι ἐκ πορνείας γεγέννησαι). In modern times, see Barrett, 348; Hoskyns, 342; and (as a possibility) Brown, 1.357.
64. For these and other arguments, see Schnackenburg, 2.212; also Keener, 1.759-60.
65. For comparable language used literally, see Genesis 38:24, where Tamar was said to be "pregnant from unlawful intercourse" (ἐν γαστρὶ ἔχει ἐκ πορνείας).
66. In Hosea's prophecy, the phrase "children of unlawful intercourse" (τέκνα πορνείας) is used first literally, of Hosea's illegitimate offspring (Hos 1:2) and then metaphorically, of unfaithful Israel (2:6, LXX).

8:30-59 THE LAST DAY OF THE FESTIVAL

as "father" (v. 39), to the point of being able to examine (however uncritically or smugly) their relationship to God. But it is possible to go a step further and ask whether these interlocutors are speaking to Jesus simply as "the Jews" (v. 22), or more specifically as "the Jews who had believed him" (v. 31). The phrase, "not born of unlawful intercourse," evokes other expressions in this Gospel, such as "born not of blood lines, nor of fleshly desire, nor a husband's desire, but of God" (1:13), "born from above" (3:3), "born of water and Spirit" (3:5), "born of the flesh" and "born of the Spirit" (3:6, 8), all with the construction "to be 'born'" or "begotten" *of,* or *from* someone or something.[67] The use of such distinctly Johannine language here suggests that what these "believing Jews" are asserting is that because they have "believed" (vv. 30-31), they are "born of God," just as Jesus said a person must be, and consequently have a right to claim God as their "one Father,"[68] transcending even their cherished descent from Abraham.

If this is the case, it heightens the probability that the Gospel writer, in recounting this harsh debate between Jesus and "the Jews who had believed him" (v. 31), has in mind not so much unbelieving Israel as rather certain factions within Jewish Christianity. In short, the issue is not Christian "anti-Semitism" or "anti-Judaism," as is often assumed, but a clash between certain factions (possibly Jewish and Gentile factions) *within* the Christian community.[69] The author's primary polemic is not against unbelieving Jews but against certain *Jewish Christians* whom he regards as heretics. His claim is that not everyone who claims to be "born of God" or "born from above" actually is. Just as in 1 John so here in the Gospel, certain tests can and must be applied to determine whether or not faith (or regeneration) is genuine,[70] and Jesus will now proceed to apply these tests.

---

67. Gr. γεννηθῆναι ἐκ. See BDAG, 193; compare the repeated expression, "born of God," or "born of him," in 1 John (2:29; 3:9; 4:7; 5:1, 4, 18). Paul, by contrast, seems to prefer such terms as "born *according to* the flesh" (κατὰ σάρκα), or "the Spirit" (κατὰ πνεῦμα, Gal 4:29).

68. Even as they reaffirm Jewish monotheism (see Mal 2:10, NIV: "Have we not all one Father [LXX, πατὴρ εἷς]? Did not one God [θεὸς εἷς] create us?"), their pronouncement is at the same time consistent with early Gentile Christianity (see 1 Cor 8:6; Eph 4:6).

69. At the same time it must be admitted that there are also similarities here to early Christian polemic against unbelieving Israel (above all the charge of "killing both the prophets and Jesus himself"; see Mt 23:31, 34, 37; 27:25; Acts 2:23; Rom 11:3; 1 Thess 2:15). Basically the author is implying that these "believing Jews" are not truly reborn, and are therefore no different from their "unbelieving" cohorts.

70. Among the tests of the new birth in 1 John are "doing righteousness" (2:29), not sinning (3:9; 5:18), loving one another (4:7), believing that Jesus is the Christ (5:1), and overcoming the world (5:4). See Robert Law, *The Tests of Life: A Study of the First Epistle of St. John* (3d ed.; Edinburgh: T&T Clark, 1914). This is not to say that the heresy

42 The first such test is a test of love. We have not heard much of love in this first half of John's Gospel. The only explicit examples of love have been God's love for the world (3:16) and the Father's love for the Son (3:35; see also 10:17). Elsewhere, love is mentioned only to notice its absence (see 3:19; 5:42; also 12:43), and that is the case here as well. Love in this setting means something very close to gracious acceptance of, or hospitality toward, a messenger, here specifically a messenger from God. At the very least, it is the polar opposite of seeking to kill someone (see vv. 37, 40). "If God were your Father," Jesus continues, "you would love me." Again (as in v. 39), he uses a contrary-to-fact conditional sentence: "If God were your Father" — which he is not — "you would love me" — which you do not.[71] With this, Jesus flatly denies their claim to be "born of God" (that is, "not born of unlawful intercourse," v. 41). If God were truly their Father, they would love God's messenger and welcome him into their world, but they have not done so. And Jesus is resolute in his claim to be God's messenger: "I came forth from God, and here I am. For I have not come on my own, but that One sent me." That he has not come "on his own" (see 5:30; 7:17, 28; 8:28), but as one "sent" (see 5:23, 24, 30, 36-38; 6:29, 38, 39, 44, 57; 7:16, 18, 28, 29, 33; 8:16, 18, 26, 29) is by now a familiar theme in his discourses, but one they have still not grasped. At the same time, the expression "here I am"[72] calls attention to his visible presence before them, as a god might appear,[73] but in this instance as a "man" (v. 40) asking to be received and welcomed as God's messenger and therefore as God himself.[74] This they have not done.

43 If love is the first test of true faith, or being "born of God," the second is knowledge or understanding. "Why do you not know my speech?" Jesus asks, and answering his own question concludes, "Because you cannot hear my word" (v. 43). "If anyone chooses to do his will," he had promised

---

in view is the same in 1 John as in the Gospel. In 1 John it seems to be a denial of Jesus' humanity (see 1 Jn 4:2-3), while here the issue appears rather to be his divine origin (see vv. 58-59).

71. A degree of caution is necessary because Jesus can use a similar contrary-to-fact condition even in speaking to those who are without question his true disciples: "If you loved me [εἰ ἠγαπᾶτέ με], you would rejoice [ἐχάρητε ἄν] that I am going to the Father, because the Father is greater than I" (14:28). See also Jesus' repeated question to Simon Peter, "Do you love me?" (21:15-17). But the context in our passage is far different.

72. Gr. ἥκω.

73. See BDAG, 435; also J. Schneider, in *TDNT*, 2.927-28.

74. Certain verses from 1 John are apropos here, even though that letter applies them to loving one another rather than to loving Jesus: negatively, for example, "Whoever does not love his brother whom he has seen cannot love God whom he has not seen" (1 Jn 4:20), and positively, "Everyone who loves the One who procreates [τὸν γεννήσαντα] loves the one who is born of him" (τὸν γεγεννημένον ἐξ αὐτοῦ, 1 Jn 5:1).

8:30-59 THE LAST DAY OF THE FESTIVAL

earlier, "he will know about the teaching, whether it is from God, or whether I speak on my own" (7:17), and later, "When you lift up the Son of man, then you will know that I am" (8:28), and "you will know the truth, and the truth will set you free" (v. 32). Yet they "know" none of these things, whether because they have not chosen to do his will or dwell on his word, or simply because he has not yet been "lifted up" on the cross. They still do not understand his "speech" when he speaks of "the Father" or "the One who sent me," and the reason, he claims, is that "you cannot hear my word."

The point is not that they are *literally* deaf. To "hear" Jesus' word is to hear and obey (just as in v. 37, "you therefore must *do* what you have *heard* from the Father"). Nor is Jesus stating a mere tautology (as if to say they don't understand because they don't understand). The accent falls rather on "cannot." True knowledge or understanding is *impossible* for them, just as surely as it is impossible for anyone not "born from above" to see or enter the kingdom of God (3:3, 5), or for anyone to "come to Jesus" without being drawn by the Father (6:44; see also 3:27; 6:65), or to go with Jesus where he is going (7:34; 8:21). "How can you believe," he asked three chapters earlier, "when you receive glory from each other, but do not seek the glory that comes from the Only God?" (5:44), and the question lingers. Jesus has invited them to "do what you have heard from the Father" (v. 38), and they have not done it, he says, because "you cannot hear my word." In short, they have failed the two tests of life, love and knowledge. Their "belief" (vv. 30-31) has left them unchanged, and is now unmasked as unbelief. They cannot call God their Father because they are not "born from above." Jesus could have said to them again what he said before, "You are from below, I am from above," and "You are from this world, I am not from this world" (v. 23), and "You will die in your sins" (v. 24). But instead he turns their attention to their real "father" (see v. 41), as yet unnamed.

44 Finally, Jesus identifies this different "father": "You are from the father [who is] the devil, and you choose to do the desires of your father" (v. 44a). The emphatic "you" and "your" accents once again the contrast between these "Jews" and Jesus, and between their "father" and his. The expression "from the father the devil"[75] is ambiguous, for "the devil" (genitive case) could be either possessive ("from the father of the devil"),[76] or apposi-

---

75. Gr. ἐκ τοῦ πατρὸς τοῦ διαβόλου.

76. See BDF, §268[2], and Bultmann, 318, both of whom argue that this is, grammatically, the more plausible translation of the text as it stands, yet impossible in the context. It is consequently proposed either "to assume that τοῦ διαβόλου at the beginning is an explanatory gloss which gives the correct sense, or else with K and Orig. to omit τοῦ πατρός" (Bultmann, 319). Bultmann (n. 2) mentions certain later parallels to the notion of the devil's father, but these parallels (not necessarily gnostic, as he claims) are obscure references either to the serpent in Eden as having a father (*Acts of Thomas* 32; *Acts of*

tional ("from the father, the devil"). The former makes no sense, and is quickly set aside (rightly) by most commentators, beginning with Origen.[77] Another option (probably the best from a purely grammatical standpoint) is to take it as an adjective (thus "from the slanderous father"),[78] but as the following two clauses make clear, this "slanderous father" can hardly be other than the devil. This I have tried to capture in the translation, with the phrase, "from the father [who is] the devil" (that is, "the devil" characterizes or defines "the father" as diabolical or slanderous). The meaning is indistinguishable from that of the appositional genitive. It is wise not to lose sight of the etymology of "the devil" (as "the Slanderer" or "the Accuser," for these "Jews" will almost immediately prove Jesus right about them by slandering him as "a Samaritan," and demon-possessed (v. 48).[79]

In adding that "you choose to do[80] the desires of your father" (v. 44a), Jesus echoes, perhaps deliberately, his own opening words at the Tent festival, "If anyone chooses to do his will, he will know about the teaching, whether it is from God, or whether I speak on my own" (7:17). The stark choice is between the "will"[81] of "the One who sent me" (see 7:16), and the "desires"[82] of a far different "father," the devil. The one is life; the other, death. Jesus drives home the point by expanding on who "the devil" was, and is. First, and more briefly, "homicidal" (v. 44b);[83] second, "the liar," and the father of lies (vv. 44b-c). The reader will soon discover that these are not two indictments, but one. That the devil was "homicidal," or murderous, "from the beginning" sig-

---

Philip 110; also Irenaeus, *Against Heresies* 1.30.5-6, 8), or to a demon's repeated mention of its "father" (*Acts of Thomas* 76). Either of these "fathers" could just as easily be the devil himself.

77. Origen is worth quoting: "The text is ambiguous. One meaning suggested by it is that the devil has a father, and so far as the literal meaning is concerned, those addressed by this word appear to be derived from this father. There is another [possible meaning], however, which is preferable, namely, 'You are of this father, concerning whom the title "devil" is predicated'" (*Commentary on John* 20.171; FC, 89.242).

78. Compare 6:70. For διάβολος as "slanderous," see 1 Timothy 3:11, 2 Timothy 3:3, and Titus 2:3 (BDAG, 226).

79. The etymology of διάβολος is still visible in Revelation 12:9-10, where "the one called Devil, and Satan" is further identified as "the accuser of our brothers, who accuses them before our God day and night" (see also Rev 2:9-10).

80. Gr. θέλετε ποιεῖν.

81. Gr. τὸ θέλημα.

82. Gr. τὰς ἐπιθυμίας.

83. Gr. ἀνθρωποκτόνος. This is not the usual word for "murderer" (φονεύς), but more literally "man-killer" or "homicide" (in the Vulgate *homicida*), used here (like διαβόλου) adjectivally (as in *Acts of Philip* 119, where Nicanora tells her jealous husband, "Flee the bitter dragon and his desires [τὰς ἐπιθυμίας αὐτοῦ]; throw from you the works and the arrow of the homicidal serpent" [τοῦ ἀνθρωποκτόνου ὄφεως]; Lipsius-Bonnet, 2.48).

nals that Jesus is referring to the Genesis narrative of the serpent in the garden of Eden.[84] It was the serpent's lie, "You will not surely die" (Gen 3:4, NIV), that first brought death into the world.[85] Consequently, the emphasis here is on the lie rather than on the "homicide" or murder it brought about. That same lie is still at work in the minds of Jesus' hearers, ignoring or denying what he has now said three times, "You will die in your sins" (see vv. 21, 24). Jesus moves quickly from the devil's "homicidal" character to the notion that he "was not standing in the truth, because truth is not in him" (v. 44b).

So far in the present discourse, "the truth"[86] has been understood as the message Jesus brings from God (v. 40), the message that sets people free from sin and death (v. 32). This "truth" is self-referencing, for its content is (in Jesus' words), "that I am, and [that] on my own I do nothing, but just as the Father taught me, these things I speak" (v. 28). In short, "the truth" is that Jesus is the Truth.[87] Yet this same "truth" is very ancient in that it can also be defined as the plan of God in placing Adam and Eve in the garden in Genesis.[88] The present and the remote past come together in Jesus' (and the Gospel writer's) vision. That the devil (in the form of the serpent) "was not standing"[89] in the truth back then is evident "because truth is not in him"

---

84. See 1 John 3:8, "Whoever commits sin is from the devil [ἐκ τοῦ διαβόλου], because the devil sins from the beginning" (ἀπ' ἀρχῆς).

85. This is more likely than the alternative view that the devil's "homicide" was the murder of Abel by his brother Cain (see, for example, Brown, 1.358). That story is obviously in view in 1 John, where the homicide is attributed not to the devil personally, but to Cain (1 Jn 3:12), and so derivatively to "everyone who hates his brother" (3:15). While Cain was "from the Evil One" (v. 12) and therefore the devil's child, he was not himself the devil. Moreover, the accompanying notice in our text that the murderer in question "was not standing in the truth, because truth is not in him" fits the Eden story much better than the narrative of Cain and Abel.

86. Gr. ἡ ἀλήθεια.

87. This is another way of putting Rudolf Bultmann's famous dictum that in John's Gospel, "Jesus as the Revealer of God *reveals nothing but that he is the Revealer*" (*Theology of the New Testament,* 2.66).

88. See Romans 1:25, where idolatry is said to have begun with the changing of "the truth of God" (τὴν ἀλήθειαν τοῦ θεοῦ) by means of "the lie" (ἐν τῷ ψεύδει).

89. There is a textual variation between οὐκ ἔστηκεν (imperfect of στήκειν, "to stand," as in P66, ℵ, and B), and οὐχ ἕστηκεν (perfect of ἵστημι, "to stand" or "be present," as in P75 and the majority of later manuscripts). The only difference this could make is that the perfect could be read with a present meaning ("is standing"), but this is uncertain, and, in any event, the imperfect is better attested (see Metzger, *Textual Commentary,* 226; BDAG, 944). Whether there is a kind of pun on the serpent crawling on the ground and being unable to "stand" (see Irenaeus, *Against Heresies* 1.30.6) is an intriguing question, yet at the end of the day absurd because in spite of the use of the Genesis narrative, "the devil" here is simply the devil. He is not interchangeable, as in some later texts (see n. 83 and n. 85), with the serpent in the garden.

even now. And in the same way, Jesus' hearers are not "dwelling" on his word (see v. 31), because their "father, the devil," is still directing them. Jesus has told them, "You will die in your sins," and the devil is telling them, "You will not surely die." This is the lie[90] spoken of old, and when the devil "speaks the lie" again today, Jesus insists, "he speaks from his own,"[91] because he is the liar[92] and the father of it" (v. 44c).[93] Just as "the truth" that sets people free and gives life is specifically the truth spoken about (and by) Jesus and his Father (see vv. 28, 32, 40), so "the lie" that the devil speaks today is the denial of that same truth. In the words of the author of 1 John, "Who is the liar but the one who denies that Jesus is the Christ; this is the antichrist, the one who denies the Father and the Son" (1 Jn 2:22). Whoever the "liars" may have been in 1 John, in John's Gospel they are these "Jews" who now confront Jesus — even though they were said to have "believed in him" (v. 30). Finally, Jesus will lay that illusion to rest.

45 Jesus has accused these Jewish "believers" of not being God's children, of not loving God's messenger (v. 42) or understanding him, and of being unable even to hear his word (v. 43). But now for the first time he explicitly denies that they "believe," which had been the opening premise of the whole discourse (see vv. 30, 31): "But I, because I speak the truth, you do not believe me" (v. 45; this in explicit contrast to v. 31).[94] The emphatic "I"

---

90. Gr. τὸ ψεῦδος.

91. "From his own" (ἐκ τῶν ἰδίων) is problematic (see Abbott, *Johannine Grammar*, 564-65). To the reader it sounds more or less equivalent to "on his own" or "by himself" (ἀφ' ἑαυτοῦ), as in 7:18, "He who speaks on his own [ἀφ' ἑαυτοῦ] seeks his own [τὴν ἰδίαν] glory." According to Chrysostom, "For men use a lie not as a thing proper [ἰδίῳ], but alien [ἀλλοτρίῳ] to their nature, but he as proper" (*Homilies on John* 54.3; NPNF, 1st ser., 14.195). Another more specific possibility is that the antecedent of ἐκ τῶν ἰδίων is τὰς ἐπιθυμίας (v. 44a). That is, while humans may "choose to do the desires" of the devil, the devil himself speaks out of "his own desires," or lusts, because that is his nature.

92. Gr. ψεύστης ἐστίν. Probably "the liar" rather than simply "a liar," again because of Colwell's rule that "definite predicate nouns which precede the verb usually lack the article" (see above, on 1:1).

93. Once again, as in the expression, "You are from the father [who is] the devil," the wording of the text (καὶ ὁ πατὴρ αὐτοῦ) lends itself to the possibility of finding a reference to the devil's father (thus, "because even his father is a liar"). But this would suggest, if not require, reading ψεύστης as indefinite, which is unlikely. More likely, the antecedent of αὐτοῦ is τὸ ψεῦδος, "the lie." That is, the devil is the liar, and the father of the lie.

94. He has said as much before, whether to "the Jews" in Jerusalem (5:38) or to the crowd that pursued him to Capernaum (6:36), but not to professed believers, at least not explicitly (though see 2:24-25). According to Brown (1.358), "This verse makes it unbelievable that these words have been addressed to 'those Jews who had believed him,' as vs. 31 indicates." This is in keeping with Brown's stated reluctance (1.354) to read the text of verse 31 as it stands (see above, n. 4).

places Jesus as truth-teller over against the devil (v. 44b) as "the liar and the father of it" (v. 44c). The wording of his charge is noteworthy. He does not say, "*Even though* I speak the truth, you do not believe me," but "*Because* I speak the truth, you do not believe me" (italics added). As the devil's children (v. 44), they are predisposed to believe the devil's lie and not the truth of God. Jesus said earlier to others like them, "I have come in my Father's name, and you do not accept me. If another comes in his own name, him you will accept" (5:43), and to his own brothers, "The world cannot hate you, but it hates me *because* I testify about it that its works are evil" (7:7). Later he will tell his disciples, "If you were from the world, the world would love its own, but *because* you are not from the world but I have chosen you out of the world, *therefore* the world hates you" (15:19; italics added). The "truth" that liberates (v. 32) is also the truth that hurts ("For unless you believe that I am, you will die in your sins," v. 24), and consequently they choose not to believe it. They prefer to believe the ancient lie, "You will not surely die."

46-47 Jesus is not finished with his indictment. He concludes with two rhetorical questions, "Who among you convicts me of sin?" and "If I speak truth, why do you not believe me?" (v. 46). As to the first, anyone reading a "longer" version of the Gospel (that is, with 7:53–8:11 included) will see and appreciate in it an implied argument from the lesser to the greater. If none of them could convict or condemn even a poor sinful woman caught in adultery, how could they ever hope to convict or condemn God's One and Only Son? But even without that precedent, the question is no less telling. Its immediate setting is the stark contrast Jesus has just drawn between "the truth" and "the lie" (v. 44), and in asking "Who among you convicts me of sin?" Jesus is referring not so much to sin in the abstract as to the devil's sin, the sin of lying.[95] He has already claimed to "speak the truth," and in not believing him (v. 45), they are in effect calling him a liar. He challenges them to prove it, knowing that they cannot. The second question, "If I speak truth, why do you not believe me?" is not so obviously rhetorical, but Jesus demonstrates that it is by quickly supplying an answer: "Whoever is from God hears the words of God. This is why you do not hear, because you are not from God" (v. 47). He answers his own rhetorical question, "Why?"[96] with the explanation, "This is why."[97]

Here as elsewhere in John's Gospel the dualism is strongly evident.[98]

---

95. Without reference to this passage in particular, BDAG (51) gives a definition of "sin" (ἁμαρτία) as "a prominent feature in Johannine thought, and opposed to ἀλήθεια."

96. Gr. διὰ τί (v. 46).

97. Gr. διὰ τοῦτο (v. 47).

98. See 10:26, where Jesus, again speaking to "the Jews" (οἱ Ἰουδαῖοι, v. 24), says, "But you do not believe, because you are not among my sheep."

The reason they do not believe is that they are not "from God." In the larger Johannine context, this is simply another way of saying that they are not "born from above" (3:3), or "born of God," or "children of God" (1:13) entitled to call God "Father" (8:42), but are, by contrast, "from below," or "from this world" (8:23).[99] Because they are not "from God" they cannot hear "the words of God," that is, they cannot recognize Jesus' words as words from God. Jesus told his disciples earlier that "The words I have spoken to you are spirit, and they are life" (6:63), and Simon Peter, speaking for the Twelve, had agreed: "Lord, to whom shall we turn? You have words of eternal life" (6:68). But this, as we have seen, is a very different audience.

48 Jesus' hearers now prove their descent from the "slanderous" devil by resorting to name-calling: "Do we not say well that you are a Samaritan and have a demon?" (v. 48). The expression, "Do we not say well?"[100] hints that "the Jews" are not saying this for the first time. In the two instances in which Jesus uses such an expression, it is in relation either to something someone has just said, or something said repeatedly or customarily.[101] Here the reader knows that "You have a demon" has in fact been said before (see 7:20), but that was in a setting in which it was by no means clear that those who said it even knew that they were speaking to Jesus. This time it is different. Not only are their words intentionally directed to Jesus, but the charge being leveled is more serious. They are claiming not merely that he is wildly mistaken or insane, but that he is genuinely demon-possessed. Yet their words "Do we not say well?" give the impression that this may have been a rather common opinion about Jesus among some (though not all) the religious authorities in Jerusalem (see 10:20-21); the other Gospels certainly do not contradict that impression (see Mk 3:22).

"Samaritan" is more surprising. Despite the long-standing hostility between Jew and Samaritan, there is no evidence that the mere ethnic epithet "Samaritan" (or "Jew" for that matter) was ever in itself a term of reproach. When the Samaritan woman asked Jesus, "How come you, a Jew, are asking drink from me, a Samaritan woman?" (4:9), she was not calling names, but merely keeping her distance by pointing out facts. It is true that the legal

---

99. For the thought, see 1 John 4:1-6 (in particular vv. 5-6: "They [αὐτοί] are from the world [ἐκ τοῦ κόσμου], therefore they speak from the world and the world hears them. We [ἡμεῖς] are from God [ἐκ τοῦ θεου]; whoever knows God hears us, whoever is not from God does not hear us. From this we know the spirit of truth and the spirit of error").

100. Gr. καλῶς.

101. For example, καλῶς εἶπας (to the Samaritan woman, 4:17); καὶ καλῶς λέγετε (to his disciples, 13:13). See also Mark 7:6, where Jesus cites with approval a biblical prophecy, with the words, "Isaiah well prophesied [καλῶς ἐπροφήτευσεν] about you hypocrites" (setting the stage for a very ironic equivalent three verses later: "How well [καλῶς] you set aside the command of God," v. 9).

8:30-59 THE LAST DAY OF THE FESTIVAL

scholar in Luke, when asked which character in a story was neighbor to the fallen man in the ditch, could not bring himself to say "the Samaritan," but instead replied, "The one who showed mercy" (Lk 10:37). That too was a fact, but that Jesus was a Samaritan was not a fact, but a lie. As the Samaritan woman noticed at once, he was "a Jew" (4:9). Unlike Paul, who became "to the Jews as a Jew that I might gain the Jews" (see 1 Cor 9:20-22), Jesus in this Gospel comes as "a Jew" to the Samaritans and as "a Samaritan" to the Jews — a stranger to everyone, yet offering life and salvation to all.

Even though it is a lie, from the reader's standpoint it is no insult for Jesus to be called "a Samaritan" — not after the story of the Samaritan woman and her village's faithful response to Jesus' mission. Yet the lie's *intent* is slanderous, and therefore the work of the devil, not only because of the Jews' hatred of the Samaritans but because of the explicit link between being "a Samaritan" and "having a demon."[102] These are actually not two distinct charges but one, and Jesus will answer them as one (v. 49). Behind them is the supposition that Samaritans are, if not literally at least figuratively, demon-possessed, by virtue of their centuries-old reputation of worshiping many Gods (see 2 Kgs 17:24-41). Jesus himself, speaking as a Jew, had said of them, "You people worship what you do not know. We worship what we know, for salvation is from the Jews" (4:22). Even down to John's day and later, among Christians as well as Jews, Samaria was associated with heresies labeled as demonic.[103] At the very least, the epithets "Samaritan" and "having a demon" mutually reinforce each other in the minds of Jesus' accusers.

49 Jesus responds quickly and directly to the charge of demon possession, just as he does in the other Gospels (see Mk 3:23-30). The emphatic pronouns are noteworthy in gauging the tone of his response. His accusers had said, "Do *we* not say well that *you* are a Samaritan and have a demon?" (v. 48), and Jesus now answers, "*I* do not have a demon, but I honor my Father, and *you* dishonor me" (v. 49, italics added). His emphatic pronouns

---

102. Another factor sometimes suggested is a possible implication that Jesus is illegitimate (like the Samaritans, as the Jews viewed them), or even that his biological father was literally a Samaritan (see, for example, Hoskyns, 345). This is often urged in connection with the statement, "We [ἡμεῖς] are not born of unlawful intercourse" (v. 41). Yet it would have been easy for them to make such a charge explicitly (as they do in the *Acts of Pilate;* see above, n. 63), and they do not do so.

103. Justin Martyr speaks of "a Samaritan, Simon . . . who in the reign of Claudius Caesar, and in your royal city of Rome, did mighty acts of magic by virtue of the art of the devils operating [τῶν ἐνεργούντων δαιμόνων] in him," and of Menander, "also a Samaritan . . . a disciple of Simon, and inspired by devils" (ἐνεργηθέντα καὶ αὐτὸν ὑπὸ τῶν δαιμόνιων), who "deceived many while he was in Antioch by his magical art" (*Apology* 1.26; ANF, 1.171).

mimic and mock theirs, putting them back on the defensive.[104] Not content with simply denying the charge of demon possession, Jesus adds by way of contrast, "but I honor my Father, and you dishonor me." His pronouncement revisits 5:23, when he was first accused of breaking the Sabbath and "claiming God as his own Father" (5:18). There he stated his Father's intention "that all will honor the Son just as they honor the Father," and that "Whoever does not honor the Son does not honor the Father who sent him" (5:23). Now, in charging that "you dishonor me," he is implicitly accusing them of dishonoring God as well, the God they claim as their "one Father" (see v. 41).[105]

50 Lest he seem to be making grandiose claims for himself, Jesus is quick to add, "And *I* am not seeking my glory. There is one who seeks and judges" (v. 50). Again the "I" is emphatic, suggesting that his accusers are, by contrast, seeking their own glory.[106] The pronouncement itself is consistent with what he has said all along. When he was charged with "making himself equal to God" (5:18), he insisted he could do nothing "on his own" (5:19, 30), and later he explained that "He who speaks on his own seeks his own glory, but he who seeks the glory of the One who sent him is true" (7:18). Jesus seeks the Father's glory, but as far as Jesus' glory is concerned, it is the Father[107] who does the "seeking,"[108] and it is the Father who finally "judges" between Jesus and his accusers.[109] Jesus' "glory," therefore, is his eventual vindication against those who accuse and slander him.

---

104. The four "dueling pronouns" form a kind of chiasm: "we" (plural), "you" (singular), "I" (singular), "you" (plural). Two other instances of Jesus' feisty responses are those to Nicodemus (3:3, also chiastic in structure), and to the Samaritan woman (4:10). These, however, are more playful than antagonistic; a better example (though non-Johannine) is Matthew 15:3.

105. Very broadly speaking, their attitude is also consistent with the principle Jesus articulated "that a prophet has no honor [τιμὴν οὐκ ἔχει] in his hometown" (4:44). For a positive application of a similar principle, see 12:26, "If anyone serves me, the Father will honor [τιμήσει] that person."

106. See also 5:44, addressed to a similar audience: "How can you believe, when you receive glory from each other [δόξαν παρ ἀλλήλων], but do not seek [οὐ ζητεῖτε] the glory that comes from the Only God?"

107. While not explicit, this is pretty much self-evident. Origen, however, cited the gnostic Heracleon as identifying the one seeking and judging as Moses, "the lawgiver himself," citing John 5:45 (*Commentary on John* 20.358-59; FC, 89.279).

108. The same mutuality is evident when the verb "glorify" (δοξάζειν; see v. 54) is used (see, for example, 13:31-32; 17:4-5). The Father and the Son, in contrast to human beings, "glorify" each other, but do not seek to "receive glory from each other."

109. As we have seen, there is a certain ambiguity in this Gospel as to whether judgment is the work of the Father or the Son, but the point is consistently made that the Son never passes judgment on his own initiative, or apart from the Father's will or authority (see vv. 15-16; also 3:17-19; 12:47-48). By the same token, the Father never judges ex-

51 Having stood his ground effectively against those who called him "a Samaritan" and demon-possessed (v. 48), Jesus is ready to make another promise. Oddly, in this discourse his promises of salvation are what provoke the bitterest controversy. It all started with the promise, "If you dwell on my word, you are truly my disciples, and you will know the truth, and the truth will set you free" (vv. 31b-32), reinforced with an "Amen, amen" pronouncement (vv. 34-36), to the effect that "if the Son sets you free, you will really be free" (v. 36). This time the promise is introduced right from the start with the "Amen, amen" formula, the thirteenth occurrence of that formula in the Gospel: "Amen, amen, I say to you, if anyone keeps my word, he will never ever see death" (v. 51). Both promises are conditional on a person's response to Jesus' "word," or message. In one instance it was a matter of "dwelling" on Jesus' word (v. 32); in the other, of "keeping" it (v. 51). At the same time, having revisited 5:23 two verses earlier (with the saying about "honor" in v. 49), Jesus now revisits 5:24, where he had said, "Amen, amen, I say to you that the person who hears my word and believes the One who sent me, has eternal life and does not come into judgment, but *has passed from death into life*" (italics added). The promise of "eternal life" has been common enough in the Gospel up to this point (see 3:15, 16, 36; 4:14, 36; 5:39; 6:27, 40, 47, 54, 68), but only rarely in its negative form of passing "from death into life" (as in 5:24).[110] Another rare exception was 6:50, where Jesus was identified as "the bread that comes down from heaven, so that anyone might eat of it and not die."[111] This was followed shortly by the promise that "If anyone eat of this bread, he will live forever" (6:51).

When stated this way, such pronouncements lend themselves to the notion that Jesus is promising exemption from physical death, and therefore quite literally an endless life here on earth. In 6:52, "the Jews" who heard him did not pick up on this because they were offended above all by something else he said in the same breath: "and the bread I will give him is my flesh for the life of the world" (v. 51). "How can this man give us his flesh to eat?" they demanded, ignoring the promise of "living forever." This time Jesus repeats

---

cept through the Son (see 5:22, 26). Even where the right to judge is said to be delegated to the Son, the reader is not allowed to forget that it is the Father who does the delegating.

110. Surprisingly, it has not been explicitly present in this temple discourse at the Tent festival. It is surely implicit in the promise to "Whoever believes" that "From his insides will flow streams of living water" (7:38) — this, however, with the disclaimer that it was for "later," when Jesus had been glorified and the Spirit had come (7:39).

111. A related expression is to "not be lost" (μὴ ἀπόληται, 3:16, 11:50; also οὐ μὴ ἀπόλωνται, 10:28; and compare 6:39; 17:12), yet it is different in that it refers primarily to a person or group's eternal destiny, and only secondarily (as in 18:9) to their temporal destiny. It is just the opposite with the verb "to die" (in almost any language), which brings to mind first physical death and only secondarily (if at all!) the notion of a fate beyond that.

the same promise even more provocatively (if that is possible), calling attention to it with the "Amen, amen" formula. "If anyone keeps my word," he announces, "he will never ever see death." The translation "never ever" is deliberately redundant, for the expression "not see death" is already emphatic, as if to say "By no means!" or "Never!" and the added phrase ("forever") simply adds to it the prospect of eternal duration (see 4:14; 6:35; 10:28; 11:26). Normally, to "not see death" means to be spared physical death, either forever (as Enoch was; see Heb 11:5), or for a certain period of time (as with Simeon, who was told he would "not see death before he had seen the Lord's Christ," Lk 2:26). Here, although the verb for "see" is different, there is no discernible difference in meaning. Both verbs refer to "seeing" in the sense of experiencing, that is, to "see" death is to die, no matter which verb is used.[112]

Despite all this, the reader of the Gospel knows by this time that Jesus is not using this kind of language in the "normal," that is, literal, way. He is not promising exemption from physical death but from spiritual death, or eternal condemnation. This was evident already in chapter 3, where "eternal life in him" (3:15) was first mentioned in connection with being "born from above" (3:3, 5, 7) and was contrasted not with physical death but with judgement or condemnation (3:17-18), and in chapter 5, where to "have eternal life" or to "pass from death into life" meant to "not come into judgment," that is, to be vindicated and free of condemnation. It was evident also in chapter 6, where Jesus twice stated explicitly that "eternal life" meant, "I will raise him up at the last day" (6:40, 54) — a promise that not only allowed for but actually assumed physical death (see also 5:25, 28-29). If there is any doubt in the reader's mind, Jesus will clear it up in chapter 11, when he tells Martha, "Whoever believes in me, *even if he dies,* he will live, and everyone who lives and believes in me will never ever die" (11:25-26, italics added). But Jesus' audience here in chapter 8 does not have the benefit of such clarifications, and again (as in v. 33) finds his "words of eternal life" (see 6:68) not comforting but offensive.

52-53 Taking Jesus' pronouncement literally, "the Jews" exclaim, "Now we know that you have a demon. Abraham died, and the prophets, and you say, 'If anyone keeps my word, he will never ever taste of death'" (v. 52). Too much should not be made of the slight discrepancy between Jesus' wording, "never ever see death," and their citation of it as "never ever taste of death."[113] It is no more significant than the discrepancy in Jesus' own speech

---

112. On θεωρεῖν, see BDAG, 454, and on ἰδεῖν, see BDAG, 280. It is also worth noticing that in *TDNT* both words for seeing (and others as well) are treated in a single article (5.315-82).

113. Abbott (*Johannine Grammar,* 430-31) makes much of the distinction, but without convincing evidence.

8:30-59 THE LAST DAY OF THE FESTIVAL

between "seeing" and "entering" the kingdom of God (see 3:3, 5). "Seeing" and "tasting" are used almost interchangeably in the New Testament for undergoing the experience of physical death, and carry that implication to about the same degree. The pronouncement as they paraphrase it calls to mind a saying of Jesus in all three synoptic Gospels (in two of them introduced by "Amen, I say to you") that "There are some of those standing here who will never taste of death until they see the kingdom of God come with power" (Mk 9:1), or "until they see the Son of man coming in his kingdom" (Mt 16:28), or "until they see the kingdom of God" (Lk 9:27). This well-known saying is comparable to the promise to Simeon that he would "not see death before he had seen the Lord's Christ" (Lk 2:26), in that "seeing" or "tasting" death is simply a way of measuring the time remaining before some momentous event occurs. It is a way of saying, "It will happen in your lifetime," or "You will live to see it." Jesus' pronouncement in John's Gospel, by contrast, has "forever" attached: "You will not see, or taste, of death — ever!"[114] There is no "before" or "until" clause to tone it down. Consequently, it sounds to "the Jews" as if Jesus is promising endless life here on earth. Their misunderstanding arises not from confusing two Greek verbs, but from a failure all along to grasp what Jesus meant by "eternal life" — just as they have failed all along to grasp who he meant by "the One who sent me," or "the Father" (vv. 19, 27), or what it meant to be "set free" (v. 33).

Offended by what they think Jesus means, they take it as confirmation of what they said before (in v. 48), "Now we know that you have a demon" (v. 52).[115] How can Jesus promise that those who obey his word will never "taste of death," when not even Abraham, whom they call "father" (v. 39), or any of the prophets of Israel, were spared that common fate of all humanity?[116] The point is important enough to them that they repeat it: "Are you greater than our father Abraham, who died, and the prophets died? Who do you make yourself to be?" (v. 53). That it was difficult for some Jews to come to terms with Abraham's mortality is evident from the *Testament of Abraham,* where Abraham negotiates at great length with the archangel Mi-

---

114. See *Gospel of Thomas* 1, where Jesus says, "Whoever discovers the interpretation of these sayings will not taste death" (Miller, *Complete Gospels,* 305; for "taste death," see also *Thomas* 18.3; 19.4, and for "see death," 111.2).

115. The Samaritan Menander, who was (according to Justin Martyr) demon possessed ([ἐνεργηθέντα . . . ὑπὸ τῶν δαιμόνιων]; see above, n. 103), was said to have "persuaded those who adhered to him that they should never die [ὡς μηδὲ ἀποθνήσκοιεν], and even now there are some living who hold this opinion of him" (Justin, *Apology* 1.26; ANF, 1.171). It is difficult to know what relation there is (if any) between such heresies and the Jewish suspicions about Jesus in the Gospel of John.

116. See Psalm 88[89]:49, LXX: "Who is the man who will live [ζήσεται], and not see death [οὐκ ὄψεται θάνατον], or rescue his soul from the hand of Hades?"

chael, functioning as the angel of death, and at the end graciously accepts his inevitable fate.[117] As far as Jesus' questioners are concerned, Abraham and the prophets are dead. The thrice-repeated "died"[118] says so with finality. The reader will recall Jesus' own words to other "Jews" in Galilee, "Your fathers ate the manna in the desert, and they died" (6:49; also v. 58), but the circumstances here are somewhat different. Jesus' point earlier was simply that the manna in the desert sustained that generation only for a time, not forever, like "the Bread of life." This time it is not Jesus saying "Abraham died, and the prophets," but his antagonists. But regardless of who said it, is it true? In one sense, obviously yes. Abraham did die, and so did all the prophets, just as surely as the desert generation died in the time of Moses.[119] Yet Jesus' hearers, if they belonged to the Pharisees (see 7:32, 45; 8:13), would also have believed that Abraham and the prophets would rise from the dead, and Jesus himself in the other Gospels goes further, citing God's self-revelation to Moses at the burning bush, "I am the God of Abraham and the God of Isaac and the God of Jacob" (Exod 3:6), and concluding, "He is not the God of the dead but of the living" (Mt 22:32 and Mk 12:27; see also Lk 20:38, with the added words, "For they are all alive to him").[120] To that extent, Jesus' questioners are mistaken.[121] Jesus, as we will see, is not claiming any special advantage for those who "keep his word" over Abraham or the prophets of old (Isaiah, for example; see 12:41). Still, he is making extraordinary claims for himself, as his hearers understand. Their concluding question, "Who do you *make yourself* to be?"[122] (v. 53), recalls the original suspicion among the Jewish authorities that Jesus "was claiming God as his own Father, *making himself* equal to God" (5:18, my italics). Their question

---

117. See *OTP*, 1.871-904. If E. P. Sanders is correct, the work is roughly contemporary with the Gospel of John ("A.D. 100, plus or minus twenty-five years," *OTP*, 1.875).

118. Gr. ἀπέθανεν (vv. 52, 53); ἀπέθανον (v. 53).

119. See Zechariah 1:5 (NIV), "Where are your forefathers now? And the prophets, do they live forever? But did not my words and my decrees, which I commanded my servants the prophets, overtake your forefathers?"

120. See also Luke 16:22, where Lazarus, the poor man who dies, is taken to "Abraham's bosom," and Abraham tells the rich man, "If they do not hear Moses and the prophets, neither will they be convinced if someone rises from the dead." Also *4 Maccabees* 7.19, where the Maccabean martyrs, "like our patriarchs Abraham and Isaac and Jacob, do not die to God, but live in God," and *4 Maccabees* 16.25, where "those who die for the sake of God live in God, as do Abraham and Isaac and Jacob and all the patriarchs" (RSV).

121. Origen took notice of this as early as the third century when he wrote that, "just as the Jews' statement, 'Now we know that you have a demon,' is false, so also is their statement, 'Abraham is dead, and the prophets'" (*Commentary on John* 20.400; FC, 89.287).

122. Gr. τίνα σεαυτὸν ποιεῖς.

8:30-59 THE LAST DAY OF THE FESTIVAL

reveals that the issue is christological, as it has been all along. It cries out for an answer, and they will not have long to wait (see v. 58).

54-55 Ignoring for a moment the reference to Abraham's death, Jesus speaks directly to the christological question, yet without adding anything new to what he has said before. His answer, in short, is that he is not "making himself" to be anything. "If *I* glorify myself," he insists, "my glory is nothing. It is my Father who glorifies me, him whom you say that 'He is our God'" (v. 54, italics added). He is here basically repeating what he said in verse 50, using the verb "glorify" in place of the expression "to seek glory." At the same time, he reminds his questioners that his "Father" is God, whom they themselves claimed to be their Father as well when they said, "We have one Father, God" (v. 41). Jesus paraphrases what they said as "He is our God,"[123] implying that if their God "glorifies" Jesus (or seeks his glory), they should as well. Because they have not done so, he draws the conclusion that "you have not known him, but I know him." This is the third time he has told them that they do not know God (compare 7:28; 8:19), and he insists repeatedly that he, by contrast, does know God: "And if I say I do not know him, I will be a liar like you.[124] But I know him [compare 7:29], and I keep his word" (v. 55).

The most important claim here — more important than the striking repetition of "I know him," more important than calling them liars — is the claim that "I keep his word," echoing and qualifying his disputed claim that "if anyone keeps *my* word, he will never ever see death" (v. 51, italics added). It is necessary to "keep Jesus' word," not because he is "greater than Abraham" in and of himself, but because he keeps the Father's word. Consequently, his word that gives eternal life *is* the Father's word. This is no surprise to the reader, who has known from the start that "the Word was with God, and the Word was God" (1:1). "I" on Jesus' lips, therefore, is not just "I," but "I and the Father who sent me" (see 8:16).

56 To this point, Jesus himself has not weighed in explicitly on the question of Abraham's mortality. He now does so, with the pronouncement,

---

123. The manuscript tradition is almost equally divided between "our God" (θεὸς ἡμῶν, with P[66], P[75], a corrector of B, A, C, W, Θ, Syriac versions, and the majority of later manuscripts), and "your God" (θεὸς ὑμῶν, with ℵ, B, D, Ψ, and Latin versions). The difference is slight: the former makes Jesus' pronouncement a direct quote of what the Jews had said, while the latter makes it indirect discourse ("him whom who say that he is your God"). Because Jesus does not seem to be quoting verse 41 word for word, it is more likely that scribes would have changed an original use of direct discourse to indirect than the other way around.

124. The name calling is not as abrupt as it sounds, in light of verse 44. If their "father" the devil is "the liar and the father of it," they too are liars, for they are denying God's revelation through Jesus (see 1 Jn 2:22).

"Abraham, your father, rejoiced[125] that he would see my day,[126] and he saw and was glad." The identification of Abraham as "your father," is ironic, like the irony of referring to "him whom who say that 'He is our God'" (v. 54). That Abraham is their father is their claim, not what Jesus thinks (v. 39), but if Abraham "rejoiced that he would see my day," Jesus is saying, and if Abraham is their father as they say, then they should rejoice as well, just as they "chose to rejoice for a time" in John's light (see 5:35). Beyond the irony, the pronouncement raises some difficult questions. First, what precisely does Jesus mean by "my day"?[127] Second, when did Abraham "rejoice" at the prospect of seeing Jesus' "day"? Third, when and how did it finally come about that "he saw and was glad"? These questions need to be confronted one at a time, preferably in just that order (although the first two overlap to some degree).

On the face of it, Jesus' "day" could simply refer to the present — his time on earth even as he speaks here at the Tent festival in Jerusalem. The notion that Abraham foresaw Christ's coming seems to have been a familiar one to Christians well before the Gospel of John was written. Paul, for example, speaks of the "promises" that God made to Abraham, noticing that God did not say (in Gen 13:15), "'and to the seeds,' as to many, but as to one, 'and to your seed,' who is Christ" (Gal 3:16). But something more specific may be in view. "Day of the Lord" in the Hebrew Bible is characteristically a day of judgment or vindication, and the same is true in the New Testament, where "the Lord" is specifically Jesus (see, for example, 1 Thess 5:2; Mt 24:42; also Lk 17:30, "The day when the Son of man is revealed").[128]

In John's Gospel, the only "day" mentioned so far that might qualify as "my day" from Jesus' standpoint is "the last day," a time when, as he has said not once but four times, "I will raise him up" (referring to those whom the Father has given him and drawn to him, and who believe in him, or who

---

125. Gr. ἠγαλλιάσατο.

126. "That he would see [ἵνα ἴδῃ] my day" is not, strictly speaking, a purpose clause (Abraham did not rejoice "in order to see" Jesus' day). Thinking that it might be, some commentators have tried to read "rejoice" as "desired" (by proposing a mistranslation of an Aramaic original; see Brown, 1.359). Rather, the ἵνα-clause is simply explanatory, almost equivalent to a ὅτι-clause, but pointed toward the future (see BDF, §392[1a]; Robertson, *Grammar*, 993). Abraham rejoiced *at the prospect of* seeing Jesus' day.

127. Gr. τὴν ἡμέραν τὴν ἐμήν.

128. See also Luke 17:24, where the phrase "in his day" is linked to "the Son of man" in some, but by no means all of the earliest and best manuscripts (it is missing, for example, in P[75], D, and B, and is consequently bracketed in modern editions of the Greek text). But see 17:22, "Days will come when you will desire to see one of the days of the Son of man, and you will not see it." By contrast, "that day" can also on occasion be the time of Jesus' *absence* (see Mk 2:20). So the evidence is inconclusive.

"eat my flesh and drink my blood"; see 6:38, 39, 44, 54). Later we will learn that "the last day" is also a day of judgment (see 12:48).[129] This interpretation of the "day" that Jesus claimed Abraham saw is appealing, not only because it draws on sayings within John's Gospel itself, but because of traces elsewhere in the New Testament of a belief that Abraham foresaw or somehow anticipated a future resurrection. Paul wrote of God's promise to Abraham, and of Abraham's calling "in the sight of God whom he believed, *who gives life to the dead* and calls things that are not as though they were" (Rom 4:17),[130] and the author of Hebrews claimed that Abraham was willing to sacrifice his son Isaac because "he reasoned *that God was able to raise from the dead* — from which, in a manner of speaking,[131] he did receive him back" (Heb 11:19; my italics).

The striking feature of Abraham's "joy" as Jesus describes it in John's Gospel is that it comes in two stages, the joy of anticipation[132] and the joy of fulfillment.[133] This coincides with Abraham's story in Genesis, where the promise that Abraham would have a son, and become the father of many nations (see Gen 17:15-17) was fulfilled (or at least began to be fulfilled) with the birth of Isaac (Gen 21:1-7).[134] It is natural to infer that it was at the prom-

---

129. Still later, the notion of resurrection "at the last day" is spiritualized to refer to an ongoing relationship between the risen Jesus and his disciples prior to the final resurrection: "Because I live, you also will live. In that day [ἐν ἐκείνῃ τῇ ἡμέρᾳ] you will know that I am in the Father, and you in me, and I in you" (14:19-20; see also 16:23, 26).

130. Paul then compares Abraham's faith to ours, who "believe in him who raised Jesus our Lord from the dead, who was handed over for our trespasses and raised for our justification" (4:24-25).

131. Literally, "in a parable" (ἐν παραβολῇ), that is, figuratively, or "so to speak" (see BDAG, 759).

132. While it was not uncommon for Jewish and Christian writers to speak of Abraham's "joy" (see below, n. 134), the only other instance of this particular verb is *Testament of Levi* 18.14, referring to a future time when "the Lord will raise up a new priest to whom all the words of the Lord will be revealed" (18.1): "Then Abraham, Isaac, and Jacob will rejoice [ἀγαλλιάσεται], and I [that is, Levi] shall be glad [χαρήσομαι], and all the saints shall be clothed in righteousness" (*OTP*, 1.795). While the Johannine Christ fits this author's characterization of the "new priest," the "rejoicing" in John's Gospel appears to be within Abraham's lifetime, not at some future time, and has to do with the promise, not with the fulfillment or realization.

133. The first is ἠγαλλιάσατο, "rejoiced," the second ἐχάρη, "was glad." Brown comments, "It is strange that the first verb is stronger than the second, for we would expect the fulfillment to be stronger than the prospect" (1.359). Possibly this is because Abraham's "laughter" was traditionally associated more with the promise than with the fulfillment (see below, n. 135).

134. On the two stages of joy in Abraham's life, see Philo, *On the Change of Names* 161, "When good is hoped for, it rejoices in anticipation, and thus may be said to feel joy before joy, gladness before gladness" (LCL, 5.225).

ise that Abraham "rejoiced,"[135] and that he "saw and was glad" when the promise was fulfilled, whether at Isaac's birth or at the child's deliverance when Abraham was about to offer him up as a sacrifice (Gen 22:1-14). Those are the moments highlighted in Romans (4:17) and in Hebrews (11:19) respectively, where they are viewed as signs of the resurrection, and they are most likely the moments in view here as well.

Perhaps significantly, the resurrection of the dead in John's Gospel can also be described as a two-stage affair, for Jesus had said, "an hour is coming *and now is* when the dead will hear the voice of the Son of God, and those who hear will live" (5:25, italics added).[136] There too, as in the four instances in which he promised to raise the dead "at the last day" (6:39, 40, 44, and 54), the resurrection is Jesus' work no less than the Father's (see 5:21, "For just as the Father raises the dead and brings them to life, so too the Son brings to life those he wants"). Abraham, consequently, in anticipating and then experiencing (in his own fashion) the resurrection, "saw Jesus' day" and became the beneficiary of the gift of eternal life. As Origen put it, "when Abraham saw the day of Jesus, at the same time that he saw it he also heard his word and kept it, and he no longer sees death.[137] The Jews were also incorrect when they said, 'Abraham died,' as if he were still among the dead."[138] Far from promising anyone who "keeps my word" (v. 51) an advantage over Abraham, as "the Jews" charged, Jesus is classifying Abraham as just such a person, that is, as one who lives, and "will never ever see death." Even though the audience is different (Pharisees, presumably, not Sadducees), this exchange stands as the Gospel of John's nearest equivalent to the synoptic debate over future resurrection (see Mk 12:18-27 and par.).

57 To "the Jews," Jesus' pronouncement implies a claim to preexistence, which they are quick to question: "You are not yet fifty years old,[139]

---

135. Early Jewish versions of the story interpreted Abraham's "laughter" on first hearing the prophecy of Isaac's birth (Gen 17:17) as signifying not incredulity but joy. See, for example, *Jubilees* 15.17, "And Abraham fell on his face, and he rejoiced" (*OTP,* 2.86), and 16.19, where, after Isaac was born, both he and Sarah "rejoiced very greatly" (*OTP,* 2.88). According to Philo, Abraham "falls down and straightway laughs (Gen. xvii.17) with the laughter of the soul, mournfulness on his face, but smiles in his mind, where joy vast and unalloyed has made its lodging" (*On the Change of Names* 154; LCL, 5.221).

136. See also 11:24-26, where Martha speaks of "the resurrection at the last day," and Jesus replies, "I am the Resurrection and the Life. Whoever believes in me, though he die, will live, and everyone who lives and believes in me will never ever die."

137. Gr. καὶ οὐκέτι θάνατον θεωρεῖ.

138. *Commentary on John* 20.397 (FC, 89.287).

139. John's Gospel, unlike Luke (see Lk 3:23, "about thirty years"), says nothing about Jesus' actual age (neither here nor in 2:20!), but an interpretation as old as Irenaeus in the late second century argues that by this time he was closer to fifty than thirty. Irenaeus wrote: "Now, such language is fittingly applied to one who has already passed

8:30-59 THE LAST DAY OF THE FESTIVAL

and you have seen Abraham?"[140] But Jesus has made no such claim. He has said that Abraham saw the future (that is, Jesus' own "day"), and implied that Abraham still lives, but has said nothing to put himself back in Abraham's time. Ironically, their misunderstanding anticipates what he will say next. They, not he, are bringing up the matter of his preexistence, but he, not they, will promptly turn it into an explicit claim (v. 58).

58 Jesus replies with yet another "Amen, amen" saying, the fourteenth in the Gospel and the third in the present discourse (see vv. 34-36, 51): "Amen, amen, I say to you, before Abraham came to be, I am" (v. 58). It is also the third time in the temple discourse that Jesus has used the "I am"[141] formula without a predicate (see vv. 24, 28). Each time before, a predicate could be inferred from the context, whether "I am the Light of the world" (v. 12), or "I am from above" (v. 23), or even (mistakenly), "I am the Son of man" (v. 28), yet enough ambiguity remained to arouse the reader's curiosity and hold "the Jews" at bay. This time the ambiguity dominates: "Before Abraham came to be, I am." I am.... What, or Who? To the modern reader, the sentence appears unfinished. Who is Jesus claiming to be? The striking contrast between coming to be[142] and being recalls the Gospel's opening verses, with their contrast between what "came to be" (1:3, 6, 10, 14, 17) and the "Word" or the "Light" that always "was" (1:1, 2, 4, 9, 10). Here too the imperfect "I was"[143] might have been expected, and would have been sufficient to establish preexistence, but instead Jesus uses the present:[144] not "Before Abraham came to be, I was," but "Before Abraham came to be, I am."

---

the age of forty.... But to one who is only thirty years old it would unquestionably be said, 'Thou art not yet forty years old'" (*Against Heresies* 2.22.6; ANF, 1.392; a few ancient manuscripts, in fact, substitute "forty" for "fifty" in this verse). Irenaeus's argument is not compelling, especially given his strong theological interest in proving that Jesus went through all the stages of human life, including old age (*Against Heresies* 2.22.4). While the figure of "fifty" may have been prompted in some way by the Jewish tradition of the "jubilee year" (see Lev 25:8-12), there is no evidence at all that the writer is looking back at the centuries since Abraham as a series of jubilee years (as proposed by M. J. Edwards, "'Not Yet Fifty Years Old': John 8:57," *NTS* 40.3 [1994], 449-54).

140. Some important manuscripts (including P75, ℵ, and Sy^s) have "Abraham has seen you" (ἑώρακέν σε), but this reading appears to have been an attempt to conform the response more closely to Jesus' pronouncement (v. 56), which had to do not with seeing Abraham, but with what Abraham "saw" (see Metzger, *Textual Commentary*, 226).

141. Gr. ἐγώ εἰμι.

142. Gr. ἐγένετο.

143. Gr. ἤμην.

144. While the imperfect dominates in the Gospel's preamble and what immediately follows, the present tense does appear in 1:5, where the Light "shines" (φαίνει), in 1:9, where it "illumines" (φωτίζει), and above all in 1:18: "the One who is [ὁ ὤν] right beside the Father."

As has often been noticed, this saying of Jesus echoes a number of pronouncements by the God of Israel in the Old Testament (particularly in Isaiah), reminding Israel of who he is, what he has done, and what he will do. Such pronouncements are introduced by "I [am] He" in the Hebrew Bible,[145] and by "I am" in the Greek Old Testament.[146] Their purpose, most often, is to affirm continuity between God's revelations and actions in the past and what he is doing, or will do, in the present and near future. For example, "See now that I myself am He! There is no god besides me. I put to death and I bring to life, I have wounded and I will heal, and no one can deliver out of my hand" (Deut 32:39); "Who has done this and carried it through, calling forth the generations from the beginning? I, the LORD — with the first of them and with the last — I am he" (Isa 41:4); "'You are my witnesses,' declares the LORD, 'and my servant whom I have chosen, so that you may know and believe me and understand that I am he. Before me no god was formed, nor will there be any after me. I, even I, am the LORD,[147] and apart from me there is no savior'" (Isa 43:10-11); "I, even I, am he[148] who blots out your transgressions, for my own sake, and remembers your sins no more" (Isa 43:25); "For this is what the LORD says — he who created the heavens, he is God; he who fashioned and made the earth, he founded it; he did not create it to be empty, but formed it to be inhabited — he says, 'I am the LORD, and there is no other'" (Isa 45:18); "I, the LORD,[149] speak the truth; I declare what is right" (Isa 45:19); "Turn to me and be saved, all you ends of the earth; for I am God, and there is no other" (Isa 45:22); "Listen to me, O Jacob, Israel, whom I have called: I am he; I am the first, and I am the last" (Isa 48:12); "I, even I, am he who comforts you" (Isa 51:12); "Therefore my people will know my name; therefore in that day they will know that it is I who foretold it. Yes, it is I" (Isa 52:6).[150]

From this brief summary, it is clear that the formula in the Greek Bible as in the Hebrew is interchangeable with "I am the LORD," or "I am God." Occasionally, when the Hebrew repeats the first-person pronoun "I"[151] for emphasis (as in Isa 43:25 and 45:19), the Greek treats "I am" as the divine

---

145. Heb. אני הוא (*'Anî Hû*, literally "I He").
146. Gr. ἐγώ εἰμι. The languages differ in that the Hebrew simply conjoins subject and predicate (that is, "I He"), the verb "to be" being understood, while the Greek (usually) employs the verb "to be" (thus simply "I am"), with the predicate being understood.
147. Gr. ἐγὼ ὁ θεός.
148. Gr. ἐγώ εἰμι ἐγώ εἰμι.
149. Gr. ἐγώ εἰμι ἐγώ εἰμι κύριος.
150. All these translations are from the NIV (for simplicity's sake, I have shown only the Greek, not the Hebrew, because in each instance the English translation reflects fairly well the structure of the Hebrew).
151. Heb. אני or אנכי.

8:30-59 THE LAST DAY OF THE FESTIVAL

name, yielding the construction "I am 'I AM'" (as in Isa 43:25 and 51:12), or "I am 'I AM,' the LORD" (in Isa 45:19; see n. 149).¹⁵² The use of "I AM" as a name is reminiscent of Exodus 3:14 (even though the Hebrew is rather different),¹⁵³ where "God said to Moses, 'I AM WHO I AM'" (NIV).¹⁵⁴ It is noteworthy that this encounter began with God telling Moses, "I am the God of your father, the God of Abraham, the God of Isaac and the God of Jacob" (Exod 3:6, NIV), the very passage Jesus cited in the synoptic Gospels as proof that Abraham was still alive (see Mk 12:27 and par.). In the synoptic tradition, with the Sadducees as his questioners, Jesus' task was to show that God was "not the God of the dead, but of the living" (Mk 12:27). Here in John's Gospel, among Pharisees, the issue is not the resurrection per se, but the role of *Jesus* in resurrection, or the granting of "eternal life." How can Jesus say, "If anyone keeps *my* word, he will never ever see death" (vv. 51-52)? How can he promise that "the dead will hear the voice *of the Son of God,* and those who hear will live" (5:25), and that "*I will raise* [them] up at the last day" (6:39, 40, 44, 54; italics added)? The real question is not "Is there a resurrection?" but "Who do you make yourself to be?" (v. 53).

Jesus' answer is unequivocal, and to his hearers deeply offensive. Instead of citing Exodus 3:6 as a word of Scripture, he boldly makes God's pronouncement to Moses his own: "Amen, amen, I say to you, before Abraham came to be, I am." To the reader it sounds unfinished, but Jesus has no need to finish it. His hearers can finish it for themselves: "I am the God of Abraham, the God of Isaac and the God of Jacob," with the implication that "I am not the God of the dead but of the living" (see Mk 12:27), and consequently that "If anyone keeps *my* word, he will never ever see death." Because Jesus is Abraham's God, and "before Abraham," Abraham himself is numbered among those who "will never ever see death." This is as close as the Gospel's opening words, "and the Word was God," come to being made explicit on Jesus' own lips.¹⁵⁵

---

152. This is not invariably the case, for in Deuteronomy 32:39 the emphatic expression, "I myself am he" (in Hebrew, אני הוא), is rendered by a simple ἐγώ εἰμι in Greek.

153. That is, instead of אני הוא ("I [am] he"), or something similar, the Hebrew for "I AM WHO I AM" in Exodus 3:14 uses a form of the verb "to be," אהיה אשר אהיה ("I will be what I will be"), and for the second "I AM" also אהיה ("I will be").

154. Gr. Ἐγώ εἰμι ὁ ὤν.

155. Modern scholars will of course never agree as to whether or not the historical Jesus actually spoke these words. The stakes are simply too high, both in the churches and in the halls of academia. Yet Jesus' use of the emphatic "I" (ἐγώ) throughout the Gospel tradition, both Johannine and synoptic (see, for example, Mk 14:62; Mt 5:21-48; 12:28), as well as his almost oracular references to himself in the third person as "Son of man," stands as a caution against dismissing their historicity out of hand. Jesus was, after

59 At this the temple discourse at the Tent festival comes abruptly to an end. Without a word, Jesus' hearers "took up stones that they might throw on him" (v. 59a). The reader who has the longer version of the Gospel (with 7:53–8:11) senses the irony of a narrative in which the religious authorities first ask Jesus' sober judgment about an adulteress condemned to stoning (8:4-5), then are thwarted by his invitation to "The one without fault among you" to be the first to drop a stone (8:7), but now are finally emboldened to stone even Jesus himself. More than that, the reader senses a discrepancy between their carefully planned scenario in 8:3-5 ("This they said testing him, so that they might have [reason] to accuse him," v. 6), and their spontaneity, even to the point of mob action, here at the end of the discourse. Will they stone Jesus right on the spot, one wonders, without arresting him or holding a trial? Would their leadership (to say nothing of the Roman authorities) permit such a thing?

Even to the reader who does not have the "benefit" of the story about the woman, the mention of stoning comes abruptly, yet not unexpectedly, given the plan of "the Jews" for three chapters now (see 5:18) to kill Jesus. No reason is given as to why they "took up stones" now and not before, or precisely what it was in Jesus' final "Amen, amen" pronouncement (v. 58) that elicited such a reaction. But this is not the last we will hear of stoning (see 10:31, 39; 11:8), and when it is threatened again, the reason is given: "For a good work we do not stone you, but for blasphemy, and because you, being a man, are making yourself God" (10:33). Here too, as we have seen, it is a matter of what Jesus is "making himself" to be (v. 53; see also 5:18). While he is not "making himself" God, he is acknowledging that he is God. His enemies understand his claim long before his own disciples do (see 20:28), and to them it is blasphemy indeed. The question of whether they are acting within or outside the parameters of what the law of Moses commanded, or what the Roman government might allow, is left unresolved, and the question becomes moot as "Jesus was hidden, and went out of the temple" (v. 59b).

The notice that Jesus "was hidden"[156] terminates his self-revelation. He began by going up to the festival "not openly but as it were in secret"[157] (7:10), and now he returns to secrecy again. How he did so, whether by natural or supernatural means, we are not told. The Gospel writer could have added, "because his hour had not yet come" (as in 7:30 and 8:20), but does not need to because by now the reader knows that this was the case. Having eluded those who would have stoned him to death, he then "went out of the

---

all, crucified. Whatever modern scholarship may think, Jesus' opponents seem to have attributed to him extraordinary claims (see v. 59; also Jn 5:18 and Mk 14:62).
156. Gr. ἐκρύβη.
157. Gr. ἐν κρυπτῷ.

9:1-38 JESUS AND THE MAN BORN BLIND

temple." The temple ministry that began when Jesus "went up to the temple and began teaching" (7:14; see also 7:28, 8:20) is now at an end. Where he went from there we are not told.[158]

M. JESUS AND THE MAN BORN BLIND (9:1-38)

1 *And as he was passing by, he saw a man blind from birth,* 2 *and his disciples asked him, saying, "Rabbi, who sinned, this man or his parents, that he should be born blind?"* 3 *Jesus answered, "Neither this man sinned nor his parents, but that the works of God might be revealed in him.* 4 *We must work the works of the One who sent me as long as it is day. Night is coming when no one can work.* 5 *When I am in the world, I am the Light of the world."* 6 *Having said these things, he spat on the ground and made mud from the spittle and smeared the mud on the eyes.* 7 *And he said to him, "Go wash in the pool of Siloam"* — *which means "sent." So he went away and washed and came seeing.*

8 *Then the neighbors and those seeing him formerly, that he was a beggar, said, "Isn't this the one who sits and begs?"* 9 *Some said, "It is he"; others said, "No, but it is like him." The man said, "It is I."* 10 *So they said to him, "How were your eyes opened?"* 11 *That one answered, "The man called Jesus made mud and smeared my eyes and said to me, 'Go to Siloam and wash.' So when I went away and washed, I could see."* 12 *And they said to him, "Where is that man?" He said, "I don't know."*

13 *They brought him to the Pharisees, the man who was once blind.* 14 *Now it was Sabbath on the day Jesus made the mud and opened his eyes.* 15 *So again the Pharisees also asked him how he could see. And he said to them, "He put mud on my eyes, and I washed and I see."* 16 *So some of the Pharisees were saying, "This man is not from God because he does not keep the Sabbath." Others were saying, "How can a sinful man do such signs?" And there was a split among them.* 17 *So*

---

158. A number of ancient manuscripts try to remedy the abruptness of the ending by adding a brief explanation of how Jesus escaped: "and having come through the midst of them, he was going on, and passing by like this" (καὶ διελθὼν διὰ μέσου αὐτῶν ἐπορεύετο καὶ παρῆγεν οὕτως). This addition, found in C, L, N, Ψ, and (with the omission of ἐπορεύετο) in A and the majority of later witnesses, is suspect because it appears (in part) to have been imported from a rather similar scene in Luke 4:30. The most important ancient witnesses (including P⁶⁶, P⁷⁵, ℵ, B, D, W, Θ, the old Latin, and Syriac) do not have it. The final οὕτως ("like this") is another example (as in 4:6) of a storyteller's attempt to lend realism to a scene, and may come from oral tradition. The added words also provide a transition to the next chapter (see 9:1).

The Gospel of John

they say to the blind man again, "What do you say about him, because he opened your eyes?" And he said that "He is a prophet." 18 *So the Jews did not believe about him that he was blind and could see, until they summoned the parents of the one himself who could see.* 19 *And they asked them, saying, "This is your son, whom you say that he was born blind? How then does he see now?"* 20 *So his parents answered and said, "We know that this is our son, and that he was born blind.* 21 *But how he now sees we don't know, or who opened his eyes we don't know. Ask him, he is of age, he will speak for himself."* 22 *These things his parents said because they feared the Jews, for the Jews had already reached an agreement that anyone who confessed that he was Christ would be put out of synagogue.* 23 *This was why his parents said that "He is of age, ask him."*

24 *So for a second time they summoned the man who was blind and said to him, "Give glory to God. We know that this man is a sinner."* 25 *That one answered, "If he is a sinner, I don't know. One thing I know, that I was blind and now I see."* 26 *So they said to him, "What did he do for you? How did he open your eyes?"* 27 *He answered them, "I told you already, and you did not hear. Why do you want to hear it again? Do you want to become his disciples too?"* 28 *And they insulted him, and said, "You are that man's disciple. We are Moses' disciples.* 29 *We know that God has spoken to Moses, but as for this man, we don't know where he is from."* 30 *The man answered and said to them, "For what is amazing in this is that you don't know where he is from, and he opened my eyes.* 31 *We know that God does not hear sinners, but if anyone is god-fearing and does his will, this one he hears.* 32 *It is unheard of that anyone ever opened the eyes of one born blind.* 33 *If this man were not from God, he could do nothing."* 34 *They answered and said to him, "You were born altogether in sins, and you are teaching us?" And they drove him out.*

35 *Jesus heard that they had driven him out, and when he found him he said, "Do you believe in the Son of man?"* 36 *And that one answered and said, "And who is he, sir, that I might believe in him?"* 37 *Jesus said to him, "You have not only seen him, but it is that one who is speaking with you."* 38 *And he said, "I believe, Lord," and he worshiped him.*

Despite the efforts of copyists to link what happens next to what preceded at the Tent festival,[1] it is best to view this chapter as a new story. The narrative

---

1. The scribal addition at 8:59 ends with a notice that Jesus, having left the temple, "was passing by like this" (καὶ παρῆγεν οὕτως), anticipating the words, "And as he was

9:1-38 JESUS AND THE MAN BORN BLIND

is linked only very loosely to the preceding discourse by the conjunction "And" (*kai*, v. 1). There is no way to know how long it was after the autumn Tent festival and Jesus' departure from the temple (8:59) that the events described here are supposed to have taken place. All we are told is that by 10:22 "it was winter," and that the time of the Dedication festival (now known as Hanukkah) had come. Presumably the events of 9:1–10:21 come somewhere between the two festivals, but except for the notice that the healing of the blind man took place on a Sabbath (see 9:14), no time frame is given.[2]

Having provided a grim example of aborted faith and illegitimate birth (8:30-59), the Gospel writer now adds a case study in genuine faith, and birth from above (see 3:3, 5). That a new story is beginning is signaled by the presence of Jesus' disciples with him as he "was passing by" and "saw a man blind from birth" (v. 1). The disciples have been absent throughout the Tent festival (ever since 6:70, in fact), and they make only a cameo appearance here, just long enough to ask one question (v. 2), after which they disappear again, not to reappear until 11:7. The narrative itself consists of the healing of the blind man (vv. 1-7), followed by a succession of scenes between the man and his neighbors (vv. 8-12), the man and the Pharisees (vv. 13-17), his parents and the Pharisees (vv. 18-23), and again the man and the Pharisees, ending with his expulsion from the synagogue (vv. 24-34), after which Jesus finds him and brings him to faith (vv. 35-38).

1 The opening words, "And as he was passing by," are fully consistent with the notion that the temple discourse of the two previous chapters is over, and that a new sequence of events (at an undetermined time, but still in Jerusalem)[3] is under way. The same phrase[4] occurs in the synoptic Gospels at the call of Jesus' disciples by the sea of Galilee (Mk 1:16), and again at the call of Levi (or Matthew) the tax collector (Mk 2:14; Mt 9:9).[5] This too is a

---

passing by" (καὶ παράγων), with which the new chapter begins. Moloney, without accepting (or even mentioning) the textual variant, argues that "The passage is marked by a unity of time, space, and theme. It is taken for granted that the celebration of Tabernacles continues" (290). Consequently, he entitles the entire section from 9:1 to 10:21, "Jesus and Tabernacles II" (see also Hoskyns, 352; Keener, 1.777; Sanders, 254). But to think that (even aside from 7:53–8:11) it is still "the last day, the great day of the festival" (7:37), and at the same time the "Sabbath" (9:14) strains credulity (see Barrett, 356; Brown, 1.371). Would "the Jews" have "taken up stones" to stone Jesus (8:59) on the Sabbath?

2. So Bultmann (330), "There is no attempt in the setting of the scene in v. 1 to link up the narrative with the preceding events" (see also Brown, 1.376; Morris, 424).

3. That Jesus is still in Jerusalem is of course evident from the mention of "the pool of Siloam" (v. 7; see also 10:22).

4. Gr. καὶ παράγων.

5. It is also worth mentioning that each time the phrase occurs in the Synoptics it is followed by the same verb, "saw" (εἶδεν), as it is here. The only difference is that in

"call" narrative of sorts, even though Jesus does not command the blind man to "Come after me," or "Follow me" (as in the synoptic accounts), and the blind man is never explicitly enlisted into Jesus' company of disciples.[6] Rather, the presence of the blind man, aided and abetted by the disciples' question (v. 2), brings Jesus to a stop, and the story begins.

It is clearly important to the narrative that the man had been blind "from birth." Judging from the disciples' question (v. 2), this detail is not just something the Gospel writer is telling the reader, but is obvious to them and to Jesus, either somehow from the man's appearance or because he was a well-known figure in the city.[7] Jesus talked about "birth" in the preceding chapter: birth from Abraham (8:33, 37, 39), legitimate versus illegitimate birth (8:41-42), and birth from God versus birth from the devil (8:44-47). Much earlier, speaking to Nicodemus, he drew a sharp contrast between physical birth and a new birth "from above," or from "water and the Spirit" (3:3, 5; see also 1:13).[8] Now Jesus and his disciples encounter a case in which physical birth has left a person blind.[9] As the story goes on, the man's "birth" defect will continue to be a major issue (see vv. 2-3, 19-20, 32, 34).

2 If readers fail to notice the phrase "from birth," Jesus' disciples[10] are quick to call attention to it. "Rabbi, who sinned," they ask Jesus, "this man or his parents, that he should be born blind?" (v. 2). The notion of "punishing the children for the sins of the fathers" (Exod 20:5; Deut 5:9, NIV; also Tobit 3.3-5) was common enough in the Hebrew Bible and early Juda-

---

Mark and Matthew παράγων has a point of reference: Jesus was "passing by" either "alongside the sea" (παρὰ τὴν θάλασσαν, Mk 1:16; 2:13), or simply "from there" (ἐκεῖθεν, Mt 9:9), that is, from "his own city" (Mt 9:1).

6. In two other stories in Matthew, each involving two blind men, Jesus is said to "pass by" (παράγοντι, Mt 9:27; παράγει, 20:30), and in the second the blind men actually do "follow" him (20:34).

7. More likely the latter, because when the Pharisees question the man's parents, they ask them if "This is your son, whom you say [ὑμεῖς λέγετε] that he was born blind?" (as if it is not self-evident, v. 19). One ancient manuscript (D) adds that he was "sitting" (καθήμενον), perhaps in a familiar location. Even though this reading is not original, it does state what is later explicitly said to have been the case (see v. 8, "the one who sat [ὁ καθήμενος] and begged"; see also Mt 20:30; Mk 10:46).

8. The terminology, "from birth" (ἐκ γενετῆς), instead of the more common "from his mother's womb" (as in the case of those born lame in Acts 3:2 and 14:8, where the notice plays no further part in the story) evokes both 1:13 and the dialogue with Nicodemus.

9. The narrative does not pause to reflect on the broader theological point that mere physical birth leaves us all *spiritually* blind, and therefore in need of rebirth (see, however, vv. 39-41, which stand outside the narrative proper).

10. These "disciples" (οἱ μαθηταὶ αὐτοῦ) are evidently the "Twelve" whom he had chosen (6:70), not an unidentified group of Jerusalem "disciples" (see 7:3), of which little is known.

ism (though not without vigorous dissent; see Ezekiel 18). The notion that a person could be held accountable for his own sins prior to birth is less widely attested and therefore more problematic.[11] Possibly it arises not so much from a particular theological belief as simply an intuitive feeling that because God is just, human sinfulness must somehow lie at the root of all human misfortune.[12] The default assumption was that the victim was to blame, but in the case of someone born blind, the added possibility existed that it might be the parents.

3 While Jesus nowhere rules out such theorizing in principle (see above, 5:14; also Mk 2:5, 9),[13] in this instance he is quick to reject both alternatives: "Neither this man sinned nor his parents, but that the works of God might be revealed in him" (v. 3). What he is saying, of course, is not that the man and his parents are entirely without sin, but that sin is not the reason for the man's predicament.[14] He views the man's blindness from birth not as tragedy but as opportunity. This is commonly understood to mean that the man's blindness affords Jesus an opportunity to work a miracle. The "works of God" are understood to be the works of Jesus.[15] But this interpretation overlooks the striking similarity between Jesus' pronouncement here and at 3:21, at the end of his brief discourse to Nicodemus at the first Passover.[16] The parallel becomes clear when the two sayings are put side by side:

---

11. A rather far-fetched instance commonly cited is *Genesis Rabbah* 63.6 (*Midrash Rabbah* [London: Soncino, 1961], 2.559), on the text, "And the children struggled together within her" (Gen 25:22): "Each ran to slay the other.... Each annulled the laws of the other.... Do not think that only after issuing into the world was he [Esau] antagonistic to him, but even while still in his mother's womb his fist was stretched out against him; thus it is written, *The wicked stretch out their fists from the womb*," citing Psalm 58:3. Nor is the notion of the preexistence of the soul very helpful, for it is only rarely attested in early Judaism (see Wisdom 8.19-20).

12. This is seen most clearly in certain biblical pronouncements by those in despair, such as Psalm 51:5, "Surely I was sinful at birth, sinful from the time my mother conceived me" (see also Job's extended soliloquy in Job 3:1-19).

13. He does, however, insist that those who suffer are not more sinful than those who do not (Lk 13:1-5).

14. See Augustine, *Tractates on John* 44.3: "If no man is sinless, were the parents of this blind man without sin? Was he himself either born without original sin, or had he committed none in the course of his lifetime? . . . For his parents had sin; but not by reason of the sin itself did it come about that he was born blind" (NPNF, 1st ser., 7.246).

15. See Bultmann, 331: "This points forward to the healing miracle; for the one who performs 'God's works' is Jesus, whom the Father has entrusted with the doing of them." He adds that "the purpose of the blind man's suffering is the same as that of Lazarus' illness" (citing 11:4).

16. See my article, "Baptism and Conversion in John: A Particular Baptist Reading," in *The Gospels and the Scriptures of Israel*, 147-50.

"Whoever does the truth comes to the Light, so that his works will be revealed[17] as works wrought in God"[18] (3:21).

"Neither this man sinned nor his parents, but that the works of God might be revealed in him" (9:3).[19]

The parallel suggests that the man born blind is the Gospel writer's prime example and embodiment of the person who "does the truth" and therefore "comes to the Light." Consequently, a different interpretation of "the works of God" presents itself: that is, that they are not so much the miracles of Jesus as the working of God in the man's life, even *before* he met Jesus, setting him apart as the Father's gift to the Son (see, for example, 6:37, 39). As such, they are not fully "revealed" or disclosed in the miracle of restored sight, but only later, when the former blind man finally "comes to the Light" (3:21) by believing in Jesus (see 9:38).[20] For him the act of believing is not so much a "conversion experience" as a revelation of that which he is already, a person who by the power of God "does the truth" (3:21), in sharp contrast to the person "who practices wicked things" and who therefore "does not come to the Light, for fear his works will be exposed" (3:20). On this interpretation, verse 3 seems to have more to do with the blind man's spiritual history than with the mission or miracles of Jesus.

4 So which interpretation is correct? Do "the works of God" have to do with the spiritual life of the man born blind, or with the mission and miracles of Jesus? Verses 1-3, as we have just seen, point to the former, while verses 4-5 accent the latter. "We must work the works of the One who sent me as long as it is day," Jesus continues, "Night is coming when no one can work" (v. 4). Having spoken generally of "the works of God" (v. 3), Jesus now seems to call attention to *his own* mission, and especially the healing he is about to perform. "The One who sent me" is by now a familiar phrase with reference to Jesus' mission (see, for example, 4:34; 5:24, 30; 6:38; 7:16, 28, 33; 8:26, 29), but what is surprising is the plural "we must" (ἡμᾶς δεῖ) with which verse 4 begins: that is, "*We* must work the works of the One who sent *me*."[21] It is commonly argued that Jesus is here enlisting or inviting his disci-

---

17. Gr. ἵνα φανερωθῇ τὰ ἔργα.

18. Gr. ἐν θεῷ.

19. Gr. ἵνα φανερωθῇ τὰ ἔργα τοῦ θεοῦ ἐν αὐτῷ. It is impossible to tell for certain whether the phrase "in him" goes with "might be revealed" (as above, with almost all English translations), or with "the works of God." That is, either "that the works of God might be revealed in him," or "that the works of God in him might be revealed." The difference is minor.

20. This depends, of course, on the authenticity of verses 38-39a (for the textual issue, see below).

21. Later scribes seem to have been confused by the apparent inconsistency. In

9:1-38 JESUS AND THE MAN BORN BLIND

ples (and by extension the readers of the Gospel) to join him in working the works of God,[22] but the difficulty is that the disciples play no part whatever in the blind man's healing or in his coming to faith. In fact, from this point on they disappear from the story. More likely, by "we"[23] Jesus means himself and the blind man, as if to say, "*He and I* must work the works of the One who sent me as long as it is day."[24] In this case a distinction must be made between the way in which Jesus "works the works of the One who sent me," and the way in which the blind man does so. Jesus clearly does so by carrying out his mission, that is, by healing the blind man. But how does the blind man "work the works" of God? Jesus was asked just that question three chapters earlier in Capernaum: "What shall we do that we might work the works of God?" (6:28), and he said, "This is the work of God, that you believe in him whom that One sent" (6:29). There is no reason to suppose that Jesus would have answered the blind man any differently, and in fact the question of belief will emerge explicitly in the last encounter between the two (9:35-38).

The other striking feature of the pronouncement (in addition to the plural "we") is its urgency: "We must,"[25] Jesus insists, "work the works of the

---

place of ἡμᾶς, some ancient manuscripts (including A, C, Θ, Ψ, old Latin versions, and the majority of later manuscripts) have ἐμέ, yielding the translation, "I must work the works of the One who sent me," which is just what would have been expected. This is transparently an attempt to conform the text to normal Johannine usage (for a dissenting opinion, see Bultmann, 331, n. 7). Others (including P66, P75, ℵ, L, and W) change με in the phrase "the One who sent me" to ἡμᾶς, yielding the translation, "We must work the works of the One who sent us" (see Tischendorf; also the NLT). This reading has to be taken more seriously, for like the reading adopted above, it too is an unexpected and therefore quite difficult one. The phrase "the One who sent us" occurs nowhere else in the Gospel, and while Jesus "sends" his disciples (see 4:38), they are not "sent" in quite the same sense in which he is sent. Still, it is more likely that scribes would have tried to conform the pronouns "we" and "I" to one another than create a discrepancy between them. It is best, therefore, to follow codices B and D, with "we" in the first instance and "me" in the second (see Metzger, *Textual Commentary,* 227; also NIV, NRSV, NAB, REB, and most English versions and commentators).

22. See, for example, Brown, 1.372; Barrett, 357; Schnackenburg, 2.241; Hoskyns, 353; Carson, 362; Morris, 426; Keener, 1.779. Alternatively, C. H. Dodd (*Tradition,* 186) sees the verse as a piece of "proverbial wisdom," in which "we" refers to humankind generally. On this view, the original saying was something like "We must work while it is day," and John's Gospel has adapted it to Jesus' use by adding the characteristically Johannine "the works of the One who sent me" (see also Lindars, 342).

23. Gr. ἡμᾶς.

24. For a partial analogy, see Jesus' word to John the Baptist in Matthew: "So it is fitting for us [that is, Jesus and John] to fulfill all righteousness" (Mt 3:15).

25. Gr. ἡμᾶς δεῖ. More literally, "it is necessary for us." On δεῖ as a characteristic expression of necessity in John's Gospel (as in the New Testament generally), see 3:7, 14, 30; 4:24; also 10:16, 12:34, and 20:9.

One who sent me as long as it is day," adding the cautionary note that "Night is coming when no one can work." Even those who understand "we" to refer to Jesus' disciples or to the readership of the Gospel know that they are on shaky ground applying this pronouncement to the church's mission in the present age. On such a view, "day" would be the time allotted for the proclamation of the Gospel, and "night" the time of judgment when it is too late for sinners to repent (as perhaps implied in the gospel song, "Work, for the Night Is Coming"). Most of the New Testament, by contrast, sees the present as "night" and the "day of the Lord" as just that, "day" (see Rom 13:12; 1 Thess 5:1-11; 2 Pet 1:19). The only way to give the pronouncement an application to the present is to view it in generalized human terms, with "day" as a person's lifetime on earth, and "night" as senility or death.[26]

More to the point, as most interpreters recognize, is Jesus' sense of his own time limitations in the Gospel of John. He has already told his mother, "My hour has not yet come," with the implication that there was still time to act. Later he told his brothers, "My time is not yet here" (7:6), implying that his decisions and his itinerary were in God's hand. Still later, the Gospel writer commented, not once but twice, that "his hour had not yet come," implying that it was drawing near (7:30; 8:20). Jesus himself reinforced the first of these notices with the comment, "Yet a short time I am with you, and I go to the One who sent me" (7:33), and the second similarly with the words, "I go and you will seek me," and "Where I go you cannot come" (8:21). Now he is saying it again, in different words. Time is running out, but there is still a window of opportunity,[27] not just for Jesus but for his disciples (see 11:9-10; 13:33; 16:16), and for all who hear his word (see 12:35-36), in this instance the blind man. Jesus will not be "passing by" again (see v. 1). When "day" turns into "night" (see 13:30), with the arrest and execution of Jesus, it will be too late for him. Therefore, "We," says Jesus, " — he and I together — must work the works of the One who sent me as long as it is day. Night is coming when no one can work."[28]

---

26. So, for example, Schnackenburg, with the qualification, "The night, which sets a limit to every person's work, can come in different forms, through death, through external obstacles, through the course of history" (2.242).

27. For a similar thought expressed quite differently, see Luke 13:32-33: "I will drive out demons and heal people today and tomorrow, and on the third day I will reach my goal. In any case, I must [δεῖ με] keep going today and tomorrow and the next day — for surely no prophet can die outside Jerusalem" (NIV).

28. This does not, of course, mean that John's Gospel views the time *after* Jesus' departure and resurrection as a time of unrelieved darkness. On the contrary, the Gospel writer has told us from the beginning that "the light is shining in the darkness, and the darkness did not overtake it" (1:5; see also 1 Jn 2:8). On the whole issue, see Augustine, *Tractates on John* 44.5-6, who concludes, "What shall we say of that night? When will it

5 Because "day" calls to mind the imagery of "light" (see also 11:9), Jesus adds, "When I am in the world, I am the Light of the world" (v. 5). Here he reiterates the claim he made to the Pharisees at the Tent festival in the preceding chapter (8:12),[29] though without the characteristic *egō eimi* formula,[30] and without the accompanying invitation to "follow" and therefore "not walk in darkness," but "have the light of life." Instead of the latter, a story will be told in which those promises literally come true.[31] What better vindication of Jesus as "the Light of the world" than giving sight to a man born blind? At the same time, the pronouncement revisits the Gospel's opening claim that "In him was life, and that life was the light of humans" (1:4), illuminating "every human being who comes into the world" (1:9) — even, as Jesus will now demonstrate, one who "came into the world" unable to see.

6 "Having said these things"[32] marks a transition (as later in 13:21 and 18:1) from speech (vv. 3-5) to action. The healing miracle is narrated quickly and concisely (vv. 6-7), with no wasted words. The blind man will repeat it himself four times, each time more concisely than before (vv. 11, 15, 25, and 30). All we are told is that Jesus "spat on the ground and made mud from the spittle and smeared the mud on the eyes" (v. 6). He neither introduces himself to the blind man, nor verifies that he was in fact born blind, nor does he ask him, "Do you want to get well?" (see 5:6). He simply acts. His use of spittle recalls two healing stories in Mark, one in which he put his fingers in the ears of a deaf mute and then "spit and touched the man's tongue" (Mk 7:33, NIV), and another (specifically involving a blind man) in which he "spit on the man's eyes and put his hands on him" (Mk 8:23, NIV), healing him in two stages (see vv. 24-25).[33] An interpretation as old as Irenaeus identifies Jesus' action here as a mirror image of the work of God in creation.[34] In contrast to the healing of the sick man at the pool, Jesus healed "not by

---

be, when no one shall be able to work? It will be that night of the wicked, that night of those to whom it shall be said in the end, 'Depart into everlasting fire. . . .' But it is here called night, not flame, nor fire" (NPNF, 1st ser., 7.247).

29. The parallel is clearly a factor in the argument of those who see the present narrative as simply a continuation of that temple ministry (see above, n. 1). To Keener, for example, Jesus is "alluding to his announcement *earlier that day*" (1.779; italics added).

30. Here the emphatic ἐγώ is missing, and "Light" (φῶς) lacks the definite article. Yet "Light" is still definite ("the Light") according to Colwell's rule because it precedes the verb "to be" (εἰμι); see Morris, 426, n. 15, and above, on 1:1.

31. See Schnackenburg, 2.242: "The appeal and the promise are also absent. Here, though, this function is performed by the sign itself, towards which this programmatic explanation points."

32. Gr. ταῦτα εἰπών.

33. For extrabiblical instances of the use of spittle in healing, see Keener, 1.779-80.

34. In sharp contrast to Irenaeus, Augustine merely wrote, "As these words are clear, we may pass them over" (*Tractates on John* 44.7; NPNF, 1st ser., 7.247).

means of a word, but by outward action; doing this not without a purpose, . . . but that He might show forth the hand of God, that which at the beginning had moulded man."[35] More specifically, he adds, "that which the artificer, the Word, had omitted to form in the womb [namely, the blind man's eyes], He then supplied in public, that the works of God might be manifested in him, in order that we might not be seeking out another hand by which man was fashioned, nor another Father; knowing that this hand of God which formed us at the beginning, and which does form us in the womb, has in the last times sought us out who were lost, winning back His own, and taking up the lost sheep upon his shoulders, and with joy restoring it to the fold of life."[36]

Many centuries have passed, yet no better interpretation of the verse has been offered.[37] As Irenaeus rightly saw, the accent is on the "mud," not the spittle.[38] The latter is simply a means of making a ball of mud, lending realism to the narrative. A literal reenactment of Genesis would obviously have required Jesus' "breath" rather than "spittle," just as God "breathed" into Adam the breath of life (see Gen 2:7), but it would have destroyed the story's credibility. For that "breath of life" the reader must wait until 20:22, where Jesus "breathed" *(enephysēsen)* on his disciples to give them the Spirit after his resurrection. The Spirit goes unmentioned in this account of Jesus and the blind man, but (in characteristically Johannine fashion) water takes the Spirit's place.

7 To finish the healing, Jesus tells the blind man, "Go, wash in the pool of Siloam." The Gospel writer inserts a comment that "Siloam" means "sent,"[39] and then adds that the blind man "went away and came seeing" (v. 7).

---

35. Yet in connection with the healing at the pool, Jesus could say, "My Father is working even until now, and I am working" (5:17), making much the same point that Irenaeus makes (at much greater length) in his exposition of chapter 9. In the Gospel of John, as has often been noted, Jesus' words and works are almost interchangeable (see, for example, Bultmann, *New Testament Theology* 2.60: "That is the fact — the *works of Jesus* (or, seen collectively as a whole: his work) *are his words*").

36. *Against Heresies* 5.15.2 (ANF, 1.543). Admittedly his interpretation was motivated in part by his anti-gnostic polemic (specifically the references to "another hand by which man was fashioned," and "another Father"), yet it is convincing enough to stand on its own and be taken seriously even today. Obviously, even the anti-gnostic polemic cannot be assumed to be foreign to the Gospel writer's purpose. Also very perceptive is the link Irenaeus establishes between the healing of the blind man (Jn 9) and Jesus as Shepherd (Jn 10, even though Irenaeus's language is drawn more directly from Lk 15!).

37. See Lindars, 343, who adopts it without so much as a nod to Irenaeus: "Jesus does exactly what was done in the creation of man in Gen. 2.6f."

38. While the Genesis account uses the expression "dust from the earth" (χοῦν ἀπὸ τῆς γῆς) rather than "mud" or "clay" (πήλον), see Job 10:9 (LXX): "Remember that you formed me as mud [πήλον], and you are returning me to the earth."

39. Gr. ἀπεσταλμένος. The interpretation (actually a translation from Hebrew to

9:1-38 JESUS AND THE MAN BORN BLIND

The etymology of the name (whatever its origin and whatever its merits)[40] is not strictly necessary to the story, but for that very reason is important to the author — and consequently to the reader. The one preeminently "sent" in this Gospel is Jesus himself (one need look no further than v. 4, "the One who sent me"), but John too was twice said to be "sent" (1:6; 3:28), as Jesus' disciples will also be (4:38; 17:18; 20:21), and as the Spirit will be sent, whether by the Father (14:26) or by Jesus (15:26; 16:7). The perfect participle "sent" is used of John, but not of Jesus,[41] or the disciples, or the Spirit.[42] Still, in light of this Gospel's use of water as an image for eternal life (4:14), or for the Spirit (see 3:5-6; 7:39), the notice that Siloam's waters are "sent" points to their origin "from above," whether immediately from the Gihon Spring up the hill, or ultimately (in the form of rain) "from heaven," or "from God."[43] Beyond that, the notice hints (without quite saying so) that Siloam's waters, like the "water and Spirit" of which Nicodemus was told (3:5), will give the man born blind another birth, and therefore new eyes.[44] While Jesus promises nothing,[45] the

---

Greek) recalls 1:42 (see also 1:38, 41). For the same etymology of the name Siloam, see *Lives of the Prophets* 1.2, in connection with the death of Isaiah. While this document may have undergone some Christian revision, the application is so different here that it is unlikely to have been derived from John's Gospel (see *OTP*, 2.385).

40. "Siloam" evokes Isaiah 8:6-7, "Because this people has rejected the gently flowing waters of Shiloah [LXX, Σιλωαμ], . . . therefore the LORD is about to bring against them the mighty floodwaters of the River — the king of Assyria with all his pomp" (NIV; see also Neh 3:15). The form of the Hebrew (from שלח, "to send") suggests an active "sending" or channel for the water, but the passive participle ἀπεσταλμένος is appropriate because the water itself is "sent," that is, channeled down from the Gihon Spring through Hezekiah's tunnel (see Schnackenburg, 2.243; Bultmann, 333, n. 3). Less convincing is a proposed link to Genesis 49:10, "until Shiloh [שילה] comes," with its long history of messianic application, for (as Schnackenburg admits) this would require misreading a Hebrew ה as ח. Moreover, what does a pool of water have to do with a promised Messiah?

41. See, however, the perfect indicative ἀπέσταλκέν με, "he has sent me," in 5:36 and 20:21.

42. The notice that John was "sent" (1:6) does, however, find an echo in the comment that those who questioned John were also "sent" (ἀπεσταλμένοι) from the Pharisees (1:24).

43. Possibly a link of some kind is intended between "on the ground" (χαμαί, v. 6) and "sent" (ἀπεσταλμένος, as from above, v. 7), pointing to the necessity of both "flesh" and "spirit" in creation, whether the old creation or the new.

44. Caution is necessary in light of the principle that "the Spirit was not yet, because Jesus was not yet glorified" (7:39). Nowhere is it said either that the Spirit came or that the blind man was reborn. Yet the participle "sent" does hint at the Spirit's work (see 1 Pet 1:12, "the Spirit sent [ἀποσταλέντι] from heaven").

45. This in contrast to Elisha when he healed Naaman, the Syrian leper: "Go, wash yourself seven times in the Jordan, and your flesh will be restored and you will be cleansed" (2 Kgs 5:10, NIV). There the Greek for "Go, wash yourself" (πορευθεὶς λοῦσαι,

blind man, without a word, "went away and washed and came seeing."[46]

8-9 The preceding verse left it unclear precisely where the man "came" on returning from the pool of Siloam, and who was there to witness that he could now see. If he returned to the place where Jesus met him, Jesus was evidently no longer present, because later in the chapter he shows no sign of recognizing Jesus (see vv. 36-38). Whether in the same place or elsewhere, the first to notice him were "the neighbors and those seeing him formerly, that he was a beggar,"[47] and they are confused (v. 8). Although the term is not used, there is a division among them over his identity, recalling earlier "splits" in the crowd at the temple over the identity and behavior of Jesus (see 7:12, 25-27, 40-43). "Isn't this the one who sits and begs?" they ask (v. 8), and they cannot agree among themselves, as "Some said, 'It is he,'" and "others said, 'No, but it is like him'" (v. 9).[48] Their confusion stems not just from possible changes in the man's appearance and demeanor, but from their natural difficulty in believing that such a miracle could ever occur (see v. 32). Finally, the man speaks up and identifies himself in a manner recalling Jesus' own repeated self-identification: "It is I"[49] (v. 9; see 4:26; 6:20; 8:24, 28, 58). While this is, strictly speaking, "an instance of a purely secular use of the phrase,"[50] it creates an effect strangely similar to what it would have had on Jesus' lips, for it confirms the reality of the miracle, and consequently the presence in Jerusalem of a miracle worker.

---

with the participle followed by an imperative) is more idiomatic than the Gospel of John's double imperative (ὕπαγε νίψαι), which sounds more Semitic, and is perhaps based on oral storytelling.

46. Bultmann comments, rather mischievously, "One may not ask how the blind man found his way" (333, n. 1). But in fact, a beggar blind from birth would likely have known the city like the back of his hand, and in particular where to find water.

47. This is the first we learn that the blind man was a beggar (προσαίτης), like Bartimaeus, the "blind beggar" (τυφλὸς προσαίτης) of Mark 10:46. Some ancient witnesses (including Γ, Δ, and the majority of later manuscripts) have "blind" (τυφλός) in place of "beggar" (προσαίτης), and others (including 69 and some of the old Latin) combine the two (as in Mark), but the overwhelming textual evidence favors προσαίτης (anticipating προσαιτῶν at the end of the verse).

48. These "others" and still "others" (ἄλλοι ... ἄλλοι) should be understood not as "other" than the group just designated as "the neighbors and those seeing him formerly," but as factions of that larger group. The text is merely saying that the group as a whole raised a question which individual members answered differently (see BDAG, 46; Schnackenburg, 2.497, n. 23).

49. Gr. ἐγώ εἰμι.

50. Brown, 1.373; also Barrett, 359: "This simple use of the words warns the reader against assuming that ἐγώ εἰμι was necessarily to John a religious formula. At this point he is writing simple narrative."

10-12 "The neighbors and those seeing him formerly," momentarily divided (v. 9), now speak with one voice. "How were your eyes opened?" (v. 10) they ask the former blind man.[51] This gives him his first opportunity to tell the story for himself, and he does so: "The man called Jesus made mud and smeared my eyes and said to me, 'Go to Siloam and wash.' So when I went away and washed, I could see" (v. 11). From this we learn that Jesus must have introduced himself by name, even though the author has not told us so, but we learn little else. There is no mention of the spittle (which he probably knows nothing about), but only of the mud (which he would have felt), and the command Jesus gave him to "Go to Siloam and wash."[52] Clearly, the accent is on Jesus. This is only the third time in the Gospel that anyone has spoken Jesus' name, and this time the speaker is someone who knows nothing else about him (for example, that he was "son of Joseph," or "from Nazareth").[53] For now, he knows the healer simply as a man,[54] "the man called Jesus." Later on, in defiance of the Pharisees, he will call him "the prophet" (v. 17) and a man "from God" (v. 32), but still later he will admit that he does not know who this "Jesus" is ("And who is he, sir, that I might believe in him?" v. 36).

The man's neighbors, accordingly, having learned of the "how" (v. 11), now pursue the question of who this "man called Jesus" is and "where" he can be found. "Where is that man?" they ask, and the former blind man replies, "I don't know" (v. 12). The question "Where is that man?"[55] echoes word for word the question of "the Jews" at the start of the Tent festival (7:11), reminding the reader that Jesus is still wanted by the religious authorities, and that his life is still in danger (see 5:18; 7:1, 19, 25; 8:37, 40, 59). That his whereabouts are unknown also hints that he is perhaps still, or again, "hidden" (see 8:59).

---

51. It is uncertain whether or not there is a "then" or "so" (οὖν) in their question; that is, whether they ask "How — or How then — were your eyes opened?" The manuscript evidence is quite evenly divided, with P[75], A, B, the Latin versions, and the majority of later manuscripts omitting οὖν, and P[66], ℵ, C, D, and others retaining it. I have omitted it on the likelihood that the preceding οὖν (in the expression, "*So* they said to him") misled scribes into adding it here. Its presence would suggest that they were responding to something he had said, but in actuality they are addressing him for the first time. Οὖν belongs more appropriately to the narrator than within the quotation.

52. Because of the paraphrase, "Go to Siloam and wash" (instead of "Go wash in the pool of Siloam," v. 7), the preposition εἰς retains its normal meaning of "to" instead of the less common "in" (see BDAG, 289). The interpretation of "Siloam" as "sent" obviously disappears, having been intended only for the reader.

53. See Philip's remark to Nathanael (1:45), and that of "the Jews" in Capernaum (6:42); also the request of certain Greeks, who seem to have at least heard rumors of "Jesus" (12:23).

54. Gr. ὁ ἄνθρωπος.

55. Gr. ποῦ ἐστιν ἐκεῖνος.

After his brief encounter with the blind man, he seems to have "ducked out," much as he did on an earlier occasion (5:13) after healing the sick man at Bethsaida. He will not be seen again until verse 35, where he is said to have "found" the former blind man again and questioned him about his belief.[56] For now, the neighbors and the Pharisees must content themselves with interrogating the former blind man, who functions in the narrative as Jesus' surrogate, and for the Gospel writer as a kind of spokesman for the truth.

13-14 That the man's "neighbors and those seeing him formerly, that he was a beggar" (v. 8) are not just curiosity seekers but are in some way in league with the religious authorities is clear from what they do next: "They brought him to the Pharisees, the man who was once blind" (v. 13). If not quite a citizens' arrest, their action raises the seriousness of the interrogation, and consequently the sense of impending danger, to a higher level, signaled by the Gospel writer's factual notice, "Now it was Sabbath on the day Jesus made the mud and opened his eyes" (v. 14; compare 5:9). Why does it matter that it was the Sabbath? Once again (as in 5:9), the issue will be Sabbath breaking, this time not by the one healed (in picking up his mat, 5:10), but by Jesus himself, who "made the mud and opened his eyes."[57] The notice comes very late in the story, and changes the whole character of the story. From now on, Sabbath observance will be the overriding issue between the man born blind (who in a way becomes a stand-in for Jesus himself) and the Jewish authorities.[58]

15 The former blind man's interrogation moves into a second stage, as "again the Pharisees also asked him how he could see" (v. 15a, as in v. 10, "How were your eyes opened?"). His answer is also the same, but more concise than before: "He put mud on my eyes, and I washed and I see" (v. 15b; compare v. 11). The repetition drives home the point that the man sticks to his story because it is true, yet at the same time the story grows shorter and simpler because readers of the Gospel can fill in the gaps for themselves. For example, the pool is not named this time, and (perhaps more significantly) the man does not say that Jesus "made mud" (as in vv. 6, 11, and 14), only

---

56. Thus Brown's comment (1.371) that Jesus in this chapter "is certainly not in hiding (viii.59)" is not as self-evident as he makes it sound.

57. While there is a prohibition in the Babylonian Talmud specifically against putting saliva on a person's eyes on the Sabbath (*Shabbat* 108b), in this instance that part of the procedure is not mentioned. More likely, the problem was that Jesus had kneaded the mud into a ball in performing the miracle, for the Mishnah lists "kneading" among 39 activities forbidden on the Sabbath (see *m. Shabbat* 7.2; also 24.3, "They may put water into the bran but not knead it"; Danby, 121).

58. Again (as in chapter 5), a deliberate provocation may be implied. If the man was blind from birth and Jesus had the power to heal him, he might easily have kept the Sabbath by simply waiting a day.

9:1-38 JESUS AND THE MAN BORN BLIND

that he "put mud on my eyes" — omitting the detail that may have provoked the charge of Sabbath breaking.

16 The simple answer provokes a "split"[59] among the Pharisees, not over what happened, but (like the 'split' in the crowd in 7:40-43) over the identity and character of Jesus, who made it happen (v. 16). "Some" of them concluded, "This man is not from God because he does not keep the Sabbath," while "others" asked, "How can a sinful man do such signs?" At this point no one, not even he who was born blind, is suggesting that Jesus is more than "a man," whether "the man called Jesus" (v. 11), or a "man from God,"[60] or "a sinful man" (v. 24).[61] A "man from God" would presumably be a prophet like John, "a man sent from God" (1:6). "Some" appealed to Sabbath law, arguing that no true prophet would break the Sabbath, while "others" appealed to the stubborn fact of the healing to reply that no "sinful man" could have performed "such signs."[62]

The comment of this second group recalls those at the early Passover in Jerusalem who were said to have "believed" in Jesus on the basis of "the signs he was doing" (2:23), and Nicodemus, who told Jesus that "no one can do these signs you are doing unless God is with him" (3:2). They also sound like the "large crowd" that followed Jesus in Galilee "because they could see the signs he was doing for those who were sick" (6:2), and those in the crowd at the Tent festival who "believed in him," saying "The Christ, when he comes, will he do more signs than this man did?" (7:31). "Signs" have not been mentioned since then, and Jesus has performed only one more. In none of the other instances was there conclusive evidence of genuine faith, and the same is true here. All that is evident that the Pharisees do not present a united front. There is indeed "a split" among them, but it is also true that the second group, even though not believers, function in the narrative as a voice of reason, speaking for the Gospel writer: "How can a sinful man do such signs?" How indeed?

---

59. Gr. σχίσμα.

60. Gr. παρὰ θεοῦ ὁ ἄνθρωπος. The Pharisees' comment might conceivably also be translated, "This is not the man from God" (as if pointing to a definite messianic figure, such as "the Christ," or "the prophet"), but the word order is against it (to say that unambiguously, the text would have to refer to ὁ παρὰ θεοῦ ἄνθρωπος, or ὁ ἄνθρωπος ὁ παρὰ θεοῦ)

61. The noticeable repetition of "man" (ἄνθρωπος) could evokes for readers familiar with the synoptic tradition the dispute over the Sabbath in Mark, when Jesus said, "The Sabbath was made for man [διὰ τὸν ἄνθρωπον], and not man [ὁ ἄνθρωπος] for the Sabbath. So then the Son of man [ὁ υἱὸς τοῦ ἀνθρώπου] is Lord of the Sabbath" (Mk 2:28). But if this is in the Gospel writer's mind, no allusion to it is necessary because Jesus has already given two perfectly adequate reasons for working on the Sabbath (see 5:17; 7:22-23).

62. Gr. τοιαῦτα σημεῖα.

17 The former blind man is drawn into the "split," much as he was drawn into the previous dispute over his own identity (v. 9). This time the issue is not his identity but that of Jesus, as "they say to the blind man again, 'What do you say about him, because he opened your eyes?'"[63] His answer is characteristically simple: "He is a prophet" (v. 17). It is unclear whether he is simply siding with those Pharisees who had asked, "How can a sinful man do such signs?" (v. 16), implying that he was in some sense a man "from God," or whether he is saying something more. His reply could be also translated, "He is the Prophet,"[64] but this is as unlikely here as it would have been in the case of the Samaritan woman (see 4:19). Rather, he is doing little more than sticking to his story by suggesting that Jesus is "a prophet," or "man from God," perhaps in much the same sense that the Pharisees had determined that John was (see 5:33-35).[65] In identifying Jesus as "a prophet," he is merely making explicit what one faction of the Pharisees (the "others" of v. 16) already implied.

18-19 The Pharisees, who are now called "the Jews" (the terms being still used interchangeably) seem to pay no attention to the man's pronouncement that Jesus is "a prophet" (v. 17). Instead, we are told, "they did not believe[66] about him that he was blind and could see" without questioning his parents for verification. They seem to suspect either that he had his sight all along while pretending to be blind, or that he is a stranger now falsely claiming to be a beggar who was known to be blind. Instead of going to them, they "summoned the parents of the one himself who could see" (v. 18),[67] sug-

---

63. We are not told which faction asked him this question. The adverb "again" (πάλιν) suggests that it comes from all the Pharisees (as in v. 15), not from one faction or the other.

64. This because of Colwell's rule (see above, on 1:1). "The Prophet," as we have seen, was a messianic figure comparable to "the Christ" (see 1:21; 6:14; 7:40). In 1:21, Colwell's rule would have dictated that the definite article was not strictly necessary, but it is nevertheless present, and it is likely here too that, if that was meant, the article would have been present. If the former blind man had been understood as giving Jesus a messianic title, the Pharisees would undoubtedly have expelled him from the synagogue right away (see v. 22) without waiting to hear from his parents, and from him a second time (see v. 34, where after all this they finally "drove him out").

65. It is not a confession of faith, but is comparable instead to the Samaritan woman's comment about Jesus as prophet (4:19), or (at most) her hesitant question to the men of Sychar, "Could this be the Christ?" (4:29).

66. The terminology of unbelief is in keeping with the Gospel writer's frequent characterization of "the Jews" in relation to Jesus himself (see 5:43-44, 46-47; 6:36; 10:25-26; 12:37), even among those who are said to have "believed" (see 8:45-46).

67. The expression is as awkward and redundant in Greek as it sounds in English, mainly because of the participle τοῦ ἀναβλέψαντος ("of the one who could see") after τοὺς γονεῖς αὐτοῦ ("his parents"). For this reason some ancient manuscripts (including P[66]

9:1-38 JESUS AND THE MAN BORN BLIND

gesting a formal interrogation (or inquisition) and raising the threat level still higher, primarily to their son, but also to them and in the long run also to Jesus. Presumably the former blind man is still present when they ask the parents, "This is your son, who you say that he was born blind?" (v. 19).[68] The emphatic "*you* say"[69] suggests that the authorities already have reason to believe that the parents will testify to exactly that, even if it means that some will blame them for their son's condition (see v. 2). "How then does he see now?" they continue, repeating what they previously asked the man himself (v. 15), and what his neighbors asked him before that (v. 10). There is no reason the parents should have known that, not having been present at the healing, unless their son had told them. "The Jews" obviously do not like the answer they have been given, and are questioning the parents in the hope that their son may have told them a different story.

20-21 The parents provide little help. To the authorities' first question, they reply, "We know that this is our son, and that he was born blind" (v. 20), telling them what they already seem to have known. To the second question, "How does he then see now?" they reply, "how he now sees we don't know." Then, surprisingly, they volunteer an answer to a third question that has not been asked: "or who opened his eyes we don't know." They understand that behind the question "How" is the more loaded question "Who" — that is, that the issue in the minds of the religious authorities is christological. Jesus, while not on the scene, is at the very center of the story. The neighbors recognized this when they asked, "Where is that man?" (v. 12), and the authorities' real question now, as yet unspoken, is "*Who* is that man?" The parents, anticipating that question, are quick to insist, "We don't know." Finally, they end the conversation by urging the questioners to ask their son, because "he is of age, he will speak for himself" (v. 21). It is unclear whether or not the parents know that the authorities have already done that (see vv. 13-17), but if their son is in fact present (see n. 68), the opportunity exists for further interrogation right then and there.

22-23 At this point the Gospel writer breaks in with a narrative aside,

---

and some of the old Latin) drop the participle, but the longer reading has much better support and should be retained. The redundancy arises from the Gospel writer's tendency to state the details of the case repeatedly for emphasis. The same scribal discomfort with this redundancy is evident in the few manuscripts (including one old Latin version and one old Syriac) that omit καὶ ἀνέβλεψεν ("and could see") in the preceding clause.

68. The Nestle text and virtually all English translations read this sentence as a question, but it could also be punctuated as a statement of fact, with little or no difference in meaning. Either way, the wording, "This is [οὗτός ἐστιν] your son," suggests that they are presenting him to his parents, and their reply, "We know that this is [οὗτός ἐστιν] our son," confirms that he is indeed present.

69. Gr. ὑμεῖς λέγετε.

explaining what motivated the parents to say what they did.[70] They said it, we are told, "because they feared the Jews, for the Jews had already reached an agreement that anyone who confessed that he was Christ[71] would be put out of synagogue" (v. 22). Then, somewhat redundantly, he adds, "This was why his parents said that 'He is of age, ask him'" (v. 23).[72] The point at issue — though never acknowledged as such — is whether or not Jesus is "Christ," or "the Messiah" (see 1:41; 4:25). This is surprising, because that title has not come up in the present chapter. The question has been whether or not Jesus is "from God" (v. 16) or "a prophet" (v. 17), not specifically "the Christ." Some in the crowd at the Tent festival had called him that, and others had denied it (see 7:41-43), but now it suddenly becomes clear that no one is allowed to confess him as "Christ" with impunity. The "fear of the Jews" that intimidated the crowds even then (7:13) seems to have grown, and the same fear silences the parents of the man born blind. They were afraid of being put "out of synagogue."[73] The point is not that they themselves have necessarily believed in Jesus, but that, like the Jerusalem crowds earlier, they are reluctant even to "speak about him publicly" (again, see 7:13).

The term "out of synagogue" occurs here and in two other places in John's Gospel (12:42 and 16:2), but (aside from patristic references to those three texts) nowhere else in ancient Greek literature. It may have been the Gospel writer's own coinage,[74] and as such its meaning would have been readily understood. Synagogue discipline, involving temporary excommunication (for varying lengths of time and for a variety of reasons), was common enough in early Judaism.[75] Yet the notion of being "put out of synagogue"

---

70. On narrative asides, see above on 1:38.

71. Despite the absence of the definite article, "Christ" (Χριστόν) here is a title (equivalent to "the Christ," or "the Messiah"), not a name, just as it is in Acts 2:36, "God has made him both Lord and Christ" (καὶ Χριστόν). "Christ," in contrast to "prophet," refers not to a class of persons but to a unique messianic figure (thus, although one might speak of "false christs," as in Mk 13:22, no one would speak of "a Christ" as one would of "a prophet").

72. The pronouns are rather confusing. In the last sentence the pronouns αὐτοῦ ("*his* parents") and αὐτόν ("ask *him*") obviously refer to the man born blind. But in the preceding comment, the pronoun αὐτόν (in the reference to "anyone who confessed that *he* was Christ") just as obviously refers not to him but to Jesus, confirming the reader's suspicion that Jesus (absent since v. 7) is nevertheless an unseen presence throughout the chapter.

73. Gr. ἀποσυνάγωγος.

74. Perhaps on the analogy of ἀπόδημος, "away from home."

75. The practice of excommunication is rooted in the Hebrew Bible, first of all in Exodus 31:14, regarding the Sabbath: "whoever does any work on that day must be cut off from his people" (NIV; see also Ezra 10:8). It is spelled out most clearly and in most detail in the sectarian literature from Qumran (see 1QS 6.24–7.25), but various "bans," whether

does raise questions. There is no independent evidence that allegiance to a false Messiah was ever explicitly made grounds for excommunication (though it may have been so obvious as to go without saying). Moreover, it is widely assumed by modern interpreters that the reference goes way beyond temporary excommunication, and has to do rather with a final break between the Jewish synagogue and the Christian movement that is supposed to have occurred near the end of the first century. This is said to have been precipitated by the so-called *Birkath ha-Minim,* or "Heretic Benediction," actually a malediction or curse inserted into the synagogue prayer known as the *Shemoneh Esreh,* or "Eighteen Benedictions."[76] This added twelfth "benediction" said, "For the renegades let there be no hope, and may the arrogant kingdom soon be rooted out in our days, and the Nazarenes[77] and the *minim*[78] perish as in a moment, be blotted out from the book of life, and with the righteous may they not be inscribed. Blessed art thou, O Lord, who humblest the arrogant."[79] Its effect is said to have been to make it impossible for Jewish Christians to worship any longer in the synagogue with fellow Jews. Possibly something of the kind is reflected in Justin Martyr's repeated references in his *Dialogue with Trypho* to the Jews' practice of "cursing in your synagogues those who believe in the Christ" (*Dialogue* 16.4; also 96.2), or to "those in the synagogues who have anathematized and do anathematize those who believe in this very Christ" (*Dialogue* 47.4), or to "insulting the Son of God" and "scoffing at the King of Israel, as your synagogue rulers teach you, after the prayer" (*Dialogue* 137.2).[80]

---

for thirty days or longer, are mentioned in the Mishnah as well (see, for example, *Middot* 2.2; *Ta'anit* 3.8; *Mo'ed Qaṭan* 3.1-2). W. Schrage (*TDNT,* 7.848-49) comments that the purpose of such excommunication was "to amend, convert, or win back the person concerned, not to ban him permanently from the synagogue" (849; see also Morris, 434, n. 36), and the same appears to be true of the few New Testament examples we have of excommunication from early Christian congregations (see Mt 18:15-17; 1 Cor 5:3-5; 1 Tim 1:20).

76. This curse is mentioned in the Talmud (*Berakot* 28b, "These eighteen are really nineteen? — R. Levi said: The benediction relating to the Minim was instituted in Jabneh," *The Babylonian Talmud: Seder Zera'im* [London: Soncino, 1961], 175), but its full text became known only from the discovery of the Cairo Geniza in 1896. For extended discussion, see L. Martyn, *History and Theology,* 34-37.

77. Heb. הנצרים, that is, Christians.

78. Heb. המינים, "heretics."

79. See Barrett, 362 (for a slightly different translation, see Schrage, in *TDNT,* 7.850).

80. The phrase "after the prayer" (μετὰ τὴν προσευχήν) is perhaps significant in light of the *Birkath ha-Minim* as itself part of a Jewish prayer. Also, the twin titles, "Son of God" and "King of Israel," may echo John 1:49, with its confession of faith in Jesus by a "true Israelite."

If this is what is meant by "out of synagogue," the Gospel writer's narrative aside is an anachronism, reading back into Jesus' ministry the situation Jewish Christians faced in his own day, presumed to be around A.D. 90 or later.[81] Yet the Gospel writer is quite explicit and intentional about what he wants to say: that is, that the policy of excommunication did not begin only after the Christian movement was under way (see 16:2), but was "already"[82] in place during Jesus' earthly ministry. If it is an anachronism, it is a very bold and deliberate one.[83] Moreover, it is not limited to a brief narrative aside by the Gospel writer, but becomes part and parcel of the narrative itself, as "the Jews" continue to question the man born blind, and finally, we are told, "drove him out" (v. 34). The difficulty with the widely held theory that the *Birkath ha-Minim* is in play here is that the Gospel of John says nothing about any "curse" or "anathema" on those who are expelled, nor does the later policy amount to formal excommunication. It appears to have been rather a not-so-subtle strategy to persuade "heretics" (including Jewish Christians) to leave on their own.[84]

More likely, "put out of synagogue" refers to some form of temporary exclusion in effect already in Jesus' day (see above, n. 75), enforced only as local synagogues saw fit. Jesus himself, after all, was allowed to speak freely in the synagogue at Capernaum (see 6:59),[85] and when questioned after his arrest, he will claim that "I have spoken publicly to the world; I always taught in synagogue and in the temple, where all the Jews come together, and I spoke nothing in secret" (18:20). The surprised comment of the "Jerusalemites" at the Tent festival, "And look, he is speaking publicly, and they are saying nothing to him," and the question, "Do the rulers truly know that he is the Christ?" (see 7:26) could just as easily have been uttered "in synagogue" as "in the temple." In short, the decree "that anyone who confessed that he was Christ would be put out of synagogue" seems to have been enforced only sporadically, if at all. Its only victim, so far as we know, was the former blind man himself (v. 34).[86] During Jesus' ministry on earth (both here and in

81. See especially Martyn, *History and Theology*, 31-41.
82. Gr. ἤδη.
83. See Carson, 371.
84. Its purposes are in fact quite murky. See, for example, the discussions of Carson, 369-72; J. A. T. Robinson, *The Priority of John*, 72-80; Beasley-Murray, 153-54; Morris, 433-35; also, the more specialized studies of W. Horbury ("The Benediction of the Minim and Early Jewish Christian Controversy," *JTS* 33 [1982], 19-61) and R. Kimelman ("Birkat Ha-Minim and the Lack of Evidence for an Anti-Christian Jewish Prayer in Late Antiquity," in *Jewish and Christian Self-Definition* [London: SCM, 1981], 226-44).
85. Whether Peter was still in the synagogue when he confessed Jesus as "the Holy One of God" (6:69) is uncertain.
86. Martha of Bethany will confess Jesus as "the Christ, the Son of God," two

12:42), the Gospel writer seems more concerned with the *threat* (and consequently the fear) of excommunication than with the carrying out of the threat — this in contrast to Jesus' flat prediction later, "They will put you out of synagogue" (16:2), pointing in all likelihood to the actual experience of some in the writer's own community, doubtless leading up to the *Birkath ha-Minim,* or "Heretic Benediction," but probably not equivalent to it.

Even with the *Birkath ha-Minim* out of the picture, it may still be the case that John's Gospel (like the other three) does blur to some extent the distinction between what Jesus' followers faced during his ministry, and what the Christian community faced at the time the Gospel was written. In the other Gospels, it was not so much a matter of being "put out of synagogue" as of being interrogated and beaten "in the synagogues" (Mk 13:9; also Mt 10:17; 23:34), or "brought before synagogues, rulers and authorities" (Lk 12:11), or delivered "to synagogues and prisons" (Lk 21:12), with the time frame left somewhat ambiguous.[87] Perhaps the closest synoptic parallel is Jesus' warning to his disciples in the Lukan beatitudes, "Blessed are you when people hate you, and when they separate you and insult you and drive out your name as evil, for the sake of the Son of man" (Lk 6:22). Yet no mention is made there of the "synagogue," the perpetrators are not called "the Jews" or "the Pharisees" but simply "people," and in none of the synoptic texts is the issue said to be whether or not Jesus is "Christ," or Messiah. The issue is over "the Son of man,"[88] that is, over the "man" Jesus himself, his identity and his origin, regardless of what title he is given. The same is true in John's Gospel,[89] where (perhaps significantly) the title "Christ" does not occur again until "the Jews" themselves bring it up (10:24). Its role in the present narrative, therefore, should not be exaggerated.

24 Even though they have interviewed the former blind man before (vv. 13-17), "the Jews" take the advice of his parents (v. 21) and question him "for a second time" (v. 24). They could have done so right on the spot (as-

---

chapters later (11:27), but we never learn whether or not she was "put out of synagogue" for it. Possibly so, given the fact that "the rulers wanted to kill Lazarus, because on account of him many of the Jews were turning away and believing in Jesus" (12:10-11), yet it is nowhere made explicit.

87. The ambiguity is noticeable especially in Matthew 10:17 and in Luke 12:11, which do *not* come in a context of prophecies about great future events such as the destruction of the temple or the end of the age.

88. This is clear not only from the phrase "for the sake of the Son of man" (ἕνεκα τοῦ υἱοῦ τοῦ ἀνθρώπου, Lk 6:22), but also from Luke 12:8, where whoever who "confesses" Jesus (presumably in "the synagogues," v. 11) is assured that "the Son of man will confess him before the angels of God" (see also Mk 8:38).

89. This is clear from the phrases "the man called Jesus" (v. 11), "the man [not] from God," and "a sinful man" (v. 16).

suming he was present when they questioned his parents),[90] but instead they "summoned" him,[91] just as they had "summoned" the parents (v. 18), to yet another formal interrogation. The notice that this was the "second" such interrogation heightens the impression of a quasi-judicial proceeding. The former blind man is being given an opportunity to save himself from excommunication. Picking up where their previous conversation left off (see vv. 16-17), they press him to change his story: "Give glory to God.[92] We know that this man is a sinner" (v. 24; compare v. 16). "Give glory to God" was simply their way of saying "Come clean," or "Tell the truth,"[93] swearing him in as a witness on his own behalf — against Jesus. Ironically, he will "give glory to God" precisely by sticking to his story and in the end falling down to worship Jesus (v. 38). In adding, "We know that this man is a sinner," they are trying to put words in his mouth. Their interest is no longer in the factual details of the case, but solely in trying to elicit agreement with their own verdict, handed down in advance, that "This man is not from God because he does not keep the Sabbath" (v. 16). The expression "We know," in contrast to the former blind man's "I don't know" (v. 12), and the "We don't know" of his parents (v. 21), imply that what they were saying about Jesus was a certainty, something with which all right-thinking persons must agree. Yet this was obviously not the case, for some even in their own number had questioned it (see v. 16b, "How can a sinful man do such signs?").

25 The man born blind changes the subject from the character of Jesus back to the basic facts of the case. Echoing the claims he has just heard about what "we know" (v. 24), he replies, "If he is a sinner, I don't know. One thing I know, that I was blind and now I see" (v. 25). With this he retells his story a third time (as in vv. 11 and 15), more briefly than before, yet unchanged. Try as they will, his interrogators cannot make the miracle go away.

26-27 Forced to deal with the facts, they press him for more details, looking in vain for discrepancies: "What did he do for you? How [as in vv. 10 and 15] did he open your eyes?" (v. 26). He has told them all that before — at least all they needed to know (see v. 15, "He put mud on my eyes, and I washed and I see"), and he now says as much: "I told you already, and you did not hear.[94] Why do you want to hear it again?" He might have stopped

---

90. See above, verse 19, "This is your son."
91. Gr. ἐφώνησαν.
92. Gr. δὸς δόξαν τῷ θεῷ.
93. The classic example is Joshua 7:19, where Joshua says to Achan, "My son, give glory [LXX, δὸς δόξαν] to the LORD, the God of Israel, and give him the praise. Tell me what you have done; do not hide it from me" (NIV).
94. One very ancient Greek manuscript (P[66]), the Sinaitic Syriac, and old Latin versions omit "not" (οὐκ), yielding a plausible reading, "I told you already, and you heard." This obviously agrees with the next question ("Why do you want to hear it

9:1-38 JESUS AND THE MAN BORN BLIND

there, but he cannot resist asking one more mischievous question: "Do you want to become his disciples too?" (v. 27). "His" obviously refers to Jesus, changing the subject again from the healing to the healer — that is, back to christology. Moreover, his emphatic "you . . . too"[95] is a striking giveaway that he now thinks of *himself* as a "disciple"[96] of Jesus, whom he has already judged to be "a prophet" (v. 17). While the form of his question expects a negative answer, the very raising of the question stands as an affront to those now investigating him, and they are quick to respond.

28-29 "The Jews" see no humor in the former blind man's remark. Stung by his audacity, "they insulted him," saying, "*You* are that man's disciple. *We* are Moses' disciples. *We* know [as in v. 24] that God has spoken to Moses, but as for this man, we don't know where he is from" (vv. 28-29, italics added). The notice that they "insulted" him[97] is as close as the narrative comes to the "cursing" in the synagogues mentioned in later sources.[98] The emphatic pronouns ("you" and "we") put distance between themselves and the man born blind, in effect putting him "out of synagogue," rhetorically if not yet literally. Their disdain for Jesus shows through not so much in the conspicuous pronouns "that man" (v. 28) and "this man" (v. 29)[99] as in their implication that Jesus stands over against Moses the lawgiver, and therefore over against their law, as a "sinner" and Sabbath breaker (see vv. 16, 24).

As far as the reader is concerned, this merely displays their ignorance, for it has been clear from the outset that "the law was given through Moses; grace and truth came into being through Jesus Christ" (1:17), and Jesus has already told "the Jews" that "if you believed Moses, you would believe me, for he wrote about me" (5:46). They have "not heard" Moses' words any more than they have heard the testimony of the man born blind (v. 27). The notion of setting Jesus and his disciples over against Moses and Judaism is their idea, not the former blind man's and certainly not Jesus' own. Neither Jesus nor the Gospel writer has any quarrel with the claim that "God has spo-

---

again?"), but for that very reason is suspect. The better-attested reading ("I told you already, and you did not hear") is consistent with the Gospel writer's tendency to make the former blind man sound like Jesus himself in his discourses with "the Jews" (see, for example, 10:26, "I told you, and you do not believe"; also 8:43, "you cannot hear my word"; 8:47, "you do not hear").

95. Gr. μὴ καὶ ὑμεῖς.
96. Gr. μαθητής.
97. Gr. ἐλοιδόρησαν.
98. See Justin Martyr's *Dialogue* 137.4, charging the Jews with "insulting [λοιδορῆτε] the Son of God . . . as your synagogue rulers teach you."
99. While these terms are frequently used of Jesus by his enemies (for ἐκεῖνος, see, for example, 7:11; 9:12; 19:21, and for οὗτος, 6:42, 52; 7:27, 35; 9:16), in themselves they are neutral.

ken to Moses" (see 1:17; 7:19), nor in fact with the accompanying assertion that they "don't know where [Jesus] is from" (v. 29). But the latter is a damaging admission, as the former blind man will point out (v. 30), validating Jesus' repeated charge that they do not know God (see 7:28; 8:19, 55; also 15:21; 16:3).[100] Moreover, the alert reader will notice the contradiction between what was said at the Tent festival ("No, *we know where this man is from,* but the Christ, when he comes, no one knows where he is from," 7:27; italics added) and what is being said here. Even though the contradiction is easily resolved (Jesus himself resolved it in 7:28), it underscores the point that Jesus' enemies are grasping at straws, looking for any excuse not to listen to his message.

30 The man born blind responds with his longest speech in the chapter (vv. 30-33). It is important to recognize that he is a reliable witness (in the sense in which literary critics sometimes use the term "reliable narrator"), that is, he speaks for the Gospel writer in much the same way that John did in chapter 1 and in 3:27-36, or that Peter did when he said, "Lord, to whom shall we turn? You have words of eternal life, and we believe and we know that you are the Holy One of God" (6:68-69), or that Martha will do when she tells Jesus, "Yes, Lord, I believe that you are the Christ who is coming into the world" (11:27; compare 20:31). In short, he represents the "Johannine" point of view. Readers of the Gospel are intended to regard his testimony as "the truth," just as if the Gospel writer or Jesus himself had said it.

At the same time, what he says is also fully "in character" with what little we know of him from the preceding narrative. The style and vocabulary of his speech are not necessarily those of Jesus or the Gospel writer, but are distinctly his own. For example, he cannot resist calling attention to the irony of the fact that "the Jews" do not know where Jesus is from (v. 29). "For what is amazing in this," he replies, "is that *you* don't know where he is from, and he opened my eyes" (v. 30, my italics). The pronoun "you" is emphatic, echoing the emphatic "we" of his interrogators (v. 29), while the claim that "you don't know" echoes their own disclaimer, "we don't know," with reference to Jesus in the same verse. At the same time, the conjunction "and" quite clearly has the adversative force of "and yet,"[101] introducing yet a fourth repetition of his story (after vv. 11, 15, and 25), now reduced to its bare essential ("he opened my eyes"). Also worthy of notice is the expression

---

100. The expression "where he is from (πόθεν ἐστίν) calls attention to the world's ignorance of Jesus' mission as one sent from God (see 8:14, "I know where [πόθεν] I came from and where I am going. But you do not know where [πόθεν] I come from or where I am going"; also 2:9, 3:8, 4:11, and 19:9). The reality is that Jesus is "from above" (ἄνωθεν), and thus "from heaven" (see 3:31) or "from God."

101. See BDAG, 495.

9:1-38 JESUS AND THE MAN BORN BLIND

"what is amazing," or "the amazing thing."[102] While this noun occurs nowhere else in John's Gospel, Jesus has used the verb "to be amazed" at least three times in the negative sense of being offended or scandalized, particularly in relation to the healing of the sick man at Bethesda (see 5:20, 28; 7:21). But to the man born blind, "what is amazing" is not so much the miracle itself as the delicious irony of the religious authorities' reaction to it, in particular their ignorance of who Jesus is and where he is from. The man's "amazement," unlike theirs, is closer to amusement than offense, as when one savors a good joke and says, "Oh, that's marvelous!" While he speaks for the Gospel writer, he also speaks in his own style and out of his own personality. Either this unnamed "man born blind" is the creation of a skilled literary artist, or else the Gospel narrative preserves here the memory of a real historical person with very definite character traits. In view of the rather uneven characterizations in the Gospel as a whole, the latter is the more likely alternative.

31 "We know that God does not hear sinners," the man continues, "but if anyone is god-fearing[103] and does his will, this one he hears" (v. 31). "We know"[104] mimics and gently mocks the arrogant and twice-repeated "we know" of his interrogators (see vv. 24, 29), but how far does the irony extend? Is the man born blind fully serious in claiming that "God does not hear sinners," or is he still mimicking the rhetoric of his questioners (see v. 24)? The notion that "God does not hear sinners," while generally in keeping with Jewish and early Christian belief,[105] may come as a surprise to modern read-

---

102. Gr. τὸ θαυμαστόν.

103. "God-fearing" (θεοσεβής) occurs only here in the New Testament, and no similar terms, such as εὐσεβής ("godly") and its cognates, are found in John's Gospel. Possibly the word is chosen here with the implication that those who are "god-fearing" are not only Jews but include as well the Gentile Christian readers of the Gospel of John (compare the expressions σεβόμενοι τὸν θεόν, "fearing God," or simply σεβόμενοι, "fearing" in the sense of "worshiping," used in the book of Acts for Gentiles who worshiped the God of the Jews (see Acts 13:43, 50; 16:14; 17:4, 17; 18:7). The words "if anyone" (ἐάν τις) also support a universalizing conclusion of this kind.

104. Gr. οἴδαμεν.

105. See, for example, Psalms 34:15-16; 66:18-19, and in rabbinic Judaism the saying of R. Huna, "If one is filled with the fear of God his words are listened to" (*b Berakot* 6b; *Babylonian Talmud: Seder Zera'im* [London: Soncino, 1961], 29). As Dodd points out (*Interpretation,* 81), "fear of God" in this text is equivalent to Gr. θεοσεβής or θεοσέβεια. See also *Genesis Rabbah* 60.13, "Why was Rebekah not remembered [with children] until Isaac prayed for her? So that the heathens might not say, 'Our prayer bore fruit'" (*Midrash Rabbah: Genesis* [London: Soncino, 1961], 536); *Exodus Rabbah* 22.3, "Is there then, an impure prayer? No; but he who prays unto God with hands soiled from violence is not answered" (*Midrash Rabbah: Exodus,* 277-78). In the New Testament, see 1 Peter 3:12 (based on Ps 34), and Hebrews 5:7. Cornelius, whose prayer

ers familiar with Jesus' story in Luke of the tax collector who prayed, "God, be merciful to me, the sinner" (Lk 18:13), or even the Johannine principle that "If we confess our sins, he is faithful and righteous so as to forgive us the sins and purify us from all unrighteousness" (1 Jn 1:9). Obviously, under some circumstances God *does* "hear sinners."[106]

Yet the former blind man is being quite serious here, not ironic. His comment reveals something the reader would otherwise not have known, that Jesus accomplished this miracle (and by extension all of his miracles) by prayer.[107] This was evident only once up to now, at the feeding of the five thousand ("and when he had given thanks," 6:11; also v. 23), but Jesus himself will confirm it two chapters later at the raising of Lazarus ("Father, I thank you that you heard me; and I know that you always hear me," 11:41-42). In saying, "God does not hear sinners, but if anyone is god-fearing and does his will, this one he hears," the man born blind is not so much excluding sinners from praying and being heard as simply insisting that *the prayer itself must be an act of* "doing the will of God" (see Mt 6:10; 1 Jn 5:14). Jesus said earlier, "If anyone chooses to do his will, he will know about the teaching, whether it is from God, or whether I speak on my own" (7:17), and the man born blind is now applying that principle to the matter of prayer. The conditional expression, "If anyone,"[108] in both passages marks each as a kind of invitation. Jesus was inviting "the Jews" to do God's will (7:17), so as to learn that his teaching was from God, while the man born blind is inviting them here to do much the same thing[109] (v. 31). In one breath he is attempting to

---

was heard even though he was not a believer in Christ (Acts 10:4, 31), is not really an exception, for he is characterized from the start as "godly" (εὐσεβής) and "God-fearing" (φοβούμενοι τὸν θεόν, Acts 10:2).

106. Augustine noticed this, but viewed it as a sign of the former blind man's limited knowledge: "He speaks still as one only anointed. For God heareth even sinners. For if God heard not sinners, in vain would the publican, casting his eyes on the ground, and smiting on his breast, have said, 'Lord, be merciful to me a sinner'" (*Tractates on John* 44.13; NPNF, 1st ser., 7.248). More likely, the man born blind is speaking here as a reliable witness on behalf of the Gospel writer, who nowhere uses the term "sinner" to refer to a repentant sinner.

107. How did the blind man know this? We are not told. Possibly we might imagine something akin to what is described in Mark 7:34, where Jesus, in healing a deaf mute, "Looked up into heaven, groaned, and said to him, 'Ephphatha,' which is 'Be opened.'" Or in Mark 9:29, where, after driving out a "mute spirit," he told his disciples, "This kind can come out only by prayer." In any event, the former blind man gives no evidence of having actually *heard* Jesus praying (he said nothing of it, for example, in vv. 11, 15, or 25). Rather, he seems to share the assumption of the Markan Jesus that events "forever unheard of" can happen "only by prayer."

108. Gr. ἐάν τις.

109. That is, "does his will" (τὸ θέλημα αὐτοῦ ποιῇ).

vindicate Jesus and at the same time invite "the Jews" as "disciples of Moses" (v. 28) to do what Moses would have done (see 5:45-47), so that their prayers might be heard.

32-33 Playing on the verb "hears," the man continues: "It is unheard of[110] that anyone ever[111] opened the eyes of one born blind.[112] If this man were not from God,[113] he could do nothing" (vv. 32-33). Here more than ever, his voice merges with Jesus' own voice, claiming to be "from God" (see 6:46, 7:29), and the voice of the Gospel writer, pressing the evidence of Jesus' "signs" not only on the Jewish community but on all who read his book (see 20:30-31). He also flatly contradicts what "the Jews" have been saying all along, that "This man is not from God because he does not keep the Sabbath" (v. 16; see also 5:18). In claiming that if he were not from God Jesus "could do nothing" (v. 33), the man obviously means not that Jesus could do nothing at all, but that he could not have done what he has in fact done — that is, "work the works of the One who sent me" (v. 4). In the larger context of the Gospel, the man's remark anticipates Jesus' own later reminder to his disciples that without him they too "can do nothing" (15:5). In short, the man born blind becomes the spokesman and surrogate for the Johannine Jesus, once again confronting "the Jews" with the same claims they have refused to accept all along.

34 The outcome is all too predictable. All that the man's speech accomplishes is to turn the charge of being a "sinner" (see v. 24) against himself. In their anger, his examiners reply, "*You* were born altogether in sins, and *you* are teaching us?" (v. 34, my italics). They are half right. He *is* "teaching" them, just as Jesus tried to teach them in the preceding two chapters (7:14; 8:20), but they are no more receptive to him than they were to Jesus.[114] Where

---

110. Gr. οὐκ ἠκούσθη.

111. "Ever" (ἐκ τοῦ αἰῶνος), with the negative οὐκ ἠκούσθη ('unheard of'), is a redundant (and consequently very strong) expression, looking at eternity past in much the same way as the phrase "never ever" (οὐ μή . . . εἰς τὸν αἰῶνα, 4:14, 8:51-42, 10:28, and 11:26) looks at eternity future. This is probably why the phrase is ἐκ τοῦ αἰῶνος instead of the more common ἐξ αἰῶνος.

112. The key word here is "born" (γεγεννημένου). Opening the eyes of the blind, while uncommon, was not "unheard of" (see, for example, Mk 8:22-26; 10:46-52; Tobit 11.12-13), but the narrative has accented from the start that in this case the man was blind "from birth" (v. 1). While healings even of this kind are not unknown in Graeco-Roman literature (see Keener, 1.792), they do not occur in any biblical or early Jewish traditions. Consequently the man's point would not be lost on his interrogators. Keener adds that if the Gospel writer's audience had heard stories to the contrary, they would "undoubtedly excuse the hyperbole" (1.793).

113. Gr. παρὰ θεοῦ.

114. "Teach" (διδάσκεις) as they understand it implies "lecturing" them authoritatively (see NIV), or telling them what to do (see BDAG, 241; also 1 Tim 2:11, where Paul warns wives against "lecturing" or bossing their husbands).

they are wrong is in singling him out (with the emphatic "you") as one "born altogether[115] in sins."[116] The comment revisits the question with which the chapter began, but in a very heavy-handed way. Nothing so subtle as, "Rabbi, who sinned, this man or his parents, that he should be born blind?" (v. 2). Instead, only the blanket assertion that the man is, and was, a "sinner" from birth, and consequently a "disciple" (v. 28) of the "sinner" Jesus (see vv. 16, 24). Reasoning backward from his allegiance to Jesus, whom they consider a sinner and Sabbath breaker, they conclude that he himself must have been "born altogether in sins." The reader knows they are wrong, first because Jesus has already laid such a notion to rest (see v. 3, "Neither this man sinned nor his parents"), and second because his physical birth is in any case irrelevant. The "man born blind" is no longer blind, for he has been reborn at the hands of Jesus and in the waters of Siloam (vv. 6-7).

Nevertheless, "the Jews" act swiftly on the conclusion to which they have come: "And they drove him out"[117] (v. 34b). "Drove him out" — of where? Out of the room where the interrogation took place? Out of the synagogue? Out of the temple? No specific setting has been given (see v. 24). The reader may notice a striking contrast to Jesus' own promise that "the person who comes to me I will never drive out" (6:37),[118] but the only plausible reference point within the chapter is the Gospel writer's earlier notice that "the Jews had already reached an agreement that anyone who confessed that [Jesus] was Christ would be put out of synagogue" (v. 22). It appears that the threatened excommunication has now gone into effect. Even though the title "Christ" has never come up, the Jewish authorities have interpreted the former blind man's speech as a confession that Jesus is indeed "the Christ," or Messiah, and are acting accordingly.

35-36 Jesus, absent ever since he told the man to "Go wash in the pool of Siloam" (v. 7), seems to have been waiting for just such a develop-

---

115. Gr. ἐν ἁμαρτίαις σὺ ἐγεννήθης ὅλος. "Altogether" (ὅλος) is an adjective in the predicate position modifying "you" (σύ), but its force in the sentence is adverbial (as in 13:10); that is, not "in sins you were born whole," but "you were born wholly in sins" (see BDAG, 704).

116. The emphatic "you" makes it clear that they are not referring simply to "original sin," or to the human condition generally (as, for example, in Gen 8:21) but rather to biblical denunciations of the ungodly ("Even from birth the wicked go astray; from the womb they are wayward and speak lies," Ps 58:4, NIV), or to the self-recrimination of the guilty ("Surely I was sinful at birth, sinful from the time my mother conceived me," Ps 51:5, NIV).

117. Gr. καὶ ἐξέβαλον αὐτὸν ἔξω.

118. The verb "drive out" (ἐκβάλλειν) also evokes the "driving out" of demons in the synoptic Gospels, and in John the promise of Jesus that "the ruler of this world" (presumably the devil) will be "driven out" (ἐκβληθήσεται ἔξω, 12:31).

ment. As soon as he "heard that they had driven him out," we are told, Jesus "found him," just as he "finds" in the temple the sick man he had healed at Bethsaida (5:14; see also 1:43). While he has not yet introduced himself as "the Good Shepherd" (see 10:11, 14), Jesus is already acting like the shepherd in one of his well-known synoptic parables (see Mt 18:13; Lk 15:4-6). This would have been an appropriate time for Jesus to reveal himself to the former blind man with a characteristic "I am" formula, and claim credit for the miracle. He could have said again, "I am the Light of the world. Whoever follows me will not walk in darkness, but will have the light of life" (8:12; see also 9:4), but he does not. Instead, he distances himself from the man born blind and his healing, asking about "the Son of man" who healed him as if he himself were a stranger to the whole incident.[119] "You," he asks him, "do you believe in the Son of man?" (v. 35). The emphatic "you" is all too familiar to the man (see above, vv. 28, 34), but now he is hearing it not from an accuser but from someone who cares about him.[120]

The question, "Do you believe in the Son of *man?*" comes as a surprise, for we would have expected "the Son of God" (as, for example, in 1:34, 11:27, and 20:31). Nowhere else in the Gospels is "the Son of man"[121] ever used as a title by those confessing their faith in Jesus. No one but Jesus even uses the term, except when echoing Jesus' own words (as in 12:34).[122] Even the manuscript tradition had trouble with "the Son of man" in this verse, persistently replacing it with "the Son of God."[123] The reader, of course, knows what Jesus means, for it is evident by this time that Jesus himself *is* "the Son of man." In asking, "Do you believe in the Son of man?" he is simply asking "Do you be-

---

119. One might perhaps compare Luke 24:15-29, where Jesus met two of his disciples after his resurrection in the guise of an anonymous stranger, or John 20:14-15, where his identity was momentarily hidden from Mary Magdalene, or (closer to home), John 7:14-24, where (as we have seen) he appeared at the Tent festival in Jerusalem as an unknown and unlettered stranger.

120. As Barrett phrases it, "Do *you,* over against those who have expelled you, believe?" (364).

121. Gr. ὁ υἱὸς τοῦ ἀνθρώπου.

122. The single exception (and that outside the Gospels) is the martyr Stephen, who says, "Look. . . . I see heaven open and the Son of man standing at the right hand of God" (Acts 7:56). But this too is an echo of the narrator's words in the preceding verse (7:55), couched in words of Jesus drawn loosely from the Gospel tradition (see Lk 22:69; Jn 1:51).

123. Gr. ὁ υἱὸς τοῦ θεοῦ. This is the case in several early uncial manuscripts (including A, L, Θ, Ψ, in the majority of all later Greek manuscripts, and in the Latin and later Syriac versions). But "the Son of man" is the reading of all the earliest and most important textual witnesses (such as P[66], P[75], ℵ, B, D, W, and the Sinaitic Syriac). See Metzger, *Textual Commentary,* who regards the reading "Son of man" as "virtually certain" because of "the improbability of θεοῦ being altered to ἀνθρώπου" (228-29).

lieve in me?" But this is by no means evident to the man born blind. Nowhere up to this point has any of Jesus' listeners commented directly on Jesus' use of this self-designation — neither Nathanael (1:51), nor Nicodemus (3:13, 14), nor "the Jews" in Jerusalem (5:27, 8:28), nor "the crowd" in Galilee (6:27), nor Jesus' unfaithful "disciples" in Galilee (6:53, 62). It is unclear, therefore, just what Jesus is expecting from the man born blind. Does he expect him to understand that the real question is, "Do you believe in me?" More specifically, does he expect him to equate "the Son of man" with "the Christ,"[124] so as to reaffirm his purported confession of Jesus as "the Christ" — the very reason for his expulsion from the synagogue (v. 22)?

It is doubtful that the man would have been able to come to such conclusions unaided, and in fact he is quick to admit that he cannot: "And who is he, sir,[125] that I might believe in him?" (v. 36). Not having read the earlier chapters of the Gospel, the former blind man has no way of knowing who Jesus means by "the Son of man." To him, the term can only refer to the man who healed him,[126] "The man[127] called Jesus" (v. 11) whom he has never seen,[128] but whom he considers "a prophet" (v. 17) or a man "from God" (v. 33). Ironically, he knows that "the Son of man" is "Jesus," yet he does *not* know that this same Jesus is speaking to him, referring to himself as "the Son of man"![129] He also has no idea of what it can mean to "believe in" such a

---

124. Again, see 12:34, where the "crowd" in Jerusalem is confused over the relationship between "the Christ" and "the Son of man."

125. Κύριε, which can also mean "Lord," should be translated "sir" here, because he thinks he is speaking to a stranger.

126. See M. Möller, "'Have You Faith in the Son of Man?' (John 9.35)," *NTS* 37.2 (1991), 292: "From the context it is clear that both Jesus and the man born blind are speaking about the person who cured his blindness. . . . The whole scene demands that Jesus should not reveal himself until after the confession of the faith which is now being sought." This supposition becomes more plausible when "the Son of man" (ὁ υἱὸς τοῦ ἀνθρώπου) is translated back into Aramaic as בר נשׁא, "a man," or "someone," yet even without resorting to this expedient the reader can see how the term echoes the word "man" (ἄνθρωπος), or "this man" or "that man," in the preceding discussions and interrogations (see vv. 11, 16, 24, and implicitly in vv. 12, 28, 29, and 33). See also 8:40, and in the passion narrative Pilate's climactic "Look, the man!" (ἰδοὺ ὁ ἄνθρωπος, 19:5).

127. Gr. ὁ ἄνθρωπος.

128. That the former blind man had never seen Jesus can be inferred from the fact that he was still blind when Jesus met him and told him to wash in Siloam (v. 7), and from the fact that when he returned he did not know Jesus' whereabouts (v. 12).

129. It could of course be conjectured that the man recognized Jesus by his voice (as sheep recognize their shepherd; see 10:3-5, 16, 27), but nothing is said to that effect. If it were the case, it is difficult to know what he would have made of the term "Son of man," and why he would have expressed a willingness to put his faith in someone who was apparently a third party.

9:1-38 JESUS AND THE MAN BORN BLIND

man. He can be grateful to him, but how can he "believe" in someone he has never seen? His reaction, therefore, is a natural one. In asking "Who is he, sir?" he is not so much asking the healer's name (which he already knows, v. 11), or whether he is "the Christ," or "the Prophet," or some other messianic figure (as in 1:19-22), as simply asking to see him. It is as if he had said, "*Where* is he, sir, that I might believe in him?" He seems to regard "belief" not as a mere inward conviction but as a face-to-face encounter with a visible, tangible person, and that is exactly what his belief will turn out to be (see v. 38, "he worshiped him").

37 Here again (as in v. 35) an opportunity presents itself for Jesus to reveal himself in the classical Johannine way, with an "I am" pronouncement, whether understood as "I am [God]," as in 8:58, or simply "It is I" (that is, identifying himself as the man's healer). That is exactly what he did in his encounter with the Samaritan woman when she spoke of "the Christ," and he said, "It is I — I who am speaking to you" (4:26). But again Jesus passes up the opportunity, continuing to speak from a distance, as it were, in the third person: "You have not only seen him,[130] but it is that one who is speaking with you"[131] (v. 37). Why he continues to speak of himself in the third person is not altogether clear. Possibly it is just a corollary of speaking of himself as "Son of man" in the third person. Jesus in this Gospel (as in all the Gospels) speaks of himself as "I" and as "the Son of man" almost interchangeably (see, for example, 6:53-56), yet he never says explicitly, "I am the Son of man" (not even in 8:28, as we have seen).[132] He is quite consistent, therefore, in not doing so here, yet the effect is the same as if he had said "It is I — I who am speaking to you," just as he did to the Samaritan woman.

38 At this point a textual problem presents itself because our manuscripts diverge. A few important early manuscripts omit verse 38 entirely, as well as the opening words of verse 39 ("And Jesus said"), so as to move directly from Jesus' speech identifying himself to the former blind man (v. 37) to the more general pronouncement, "For judgment I came into this world, so that those who do not see might see, and that those who see might go blind" (v. 39). The man born blind disappears from the narrative without a trace, and

---

130. Gr. καὶ ἑώρακας αὐτόν.

131. Gr. καὶ ὁ λαλῶν μετὰ σοῦ ἐκεῖνός ἐστιν. For the καί . . . καί construction with the meaning, "both . . . and," or "not only . . . but also," see 6:36; 7:28; also 11:48; 12:28; 15:24 (see BDF, §444[3]; also Schnackenburg, 2.499, n. 48).

132. The closest he comes to doing so anywhere in the Gospels is in the reading of certain manuscripts in Matthew 16:13, where D, L, Θ, the old Latin versions, and the majority of later Greek manuscripts have Jesus saying, "Who do men say that I, the Son of man, am?" This is almost certainly a conflation of Mark's "I" or "me" (με) with Matthew's "the Son of man," and therefore secondary. The more reliable witnesses (including ℵ, B, and the Vulgate) omit the με.

is never heard from again.¹³³ On this reading, Jesus shifts abruptly from a conspicuous use of the third person to an equally conspicuous first person, and from addressing the man born blind to addressing a very indefinite audience and being heard not by him but by "some Pharisees" (v. 40).

Some have suggested that this reading might be original, the confession of the man born blind having been added from an early baptismal liturgy.¹³⁴ But the transition is too abrupt. Some kind of reply is needed from the man born blind, and it comes appropriately in his confession, "I believe, Lord," followed by the notice that "he worshiped him" (v. 38). This in fact is what we find in most of our earlier and more significant textual witnesses,¹³⁵ and it brings closure to the former blind man's story. "I believe, Lord"¹³⁶ (v. 38a) signals his awareness that his question, "And who is he, sir, that I might believe in him?" (v. 36), has now been answered. The vocabulary is the same, but because he now knows to whom he is speaking, the address *kyrie* no longer means "sir," but "Lord." In keeping with that designation, "he worshiped him"¹³⁷ (v. 38b). The verb "worshiped" implies a visible act of obeisance, signaling his allegiance to Jesus as "Lord" by falling prostrate at his feet.¹³⁸ In this sense, he could not "worship" Jesus until he had seen him face

---

133. This is the reading of P⁷⁵, the first hand of ℵ, W, and the old Latin *b*. Still, the overwhelming weight of manuscript evidence (see n. 135 below) favors the retention of verse 38, and with it the former blind man's confession and act of worship. If the shorter reading were to be adopted, the interpretation of "the works of God in him" in verse 3 as a reference to the blind man's conversion would obviously have to be rethought.

134. See Brown, 1.375. This seems to have been the case in Acts 8:37, where, after the Ethiopian eunuch's words to Philip ("Look, water. What hinders me from being baptized?"), some manuscripts add Philip's words, "If you believe with all your heart, you may," and the eunuch's reply, "I believe that Jesus Christ is the Son of God." There, however, the manuscript support for the added words is very weak, while in our text it is far stronger than the evidence for omission. See Metzger, *Textual Commentary*, who points out that here, "in view of the overwhelming preponderance of external attestation in favor of the longer text, it appears that the omission, if not accidental, is to be regarded as editorial, made in the interest of unifying Jesus' teaching in verses 37 and 39" (229). In fact, as we will see, in verse 39 Jesus is no longer speaking to the former blind man at all, but far more generally to the reader of the Gospel, and, as it turns out, to some Pharisees who overhear his words and challenge him (vv. 40-41).

135. These include P⁶⁶, B, the corrector of ℵ, A, D, L, Δ, Θ, Ψ, most of the old Latin, the Vulgate, the Syriac versions, most of the church fathers, and the majority of later Greek manuscripts.

136. Gr. πιστεύω, κύριε.

137. Gr. καὶ προσεκύνησεν αὐτῷ.

138. See BDAG, 882. Sometimes the verb is used simply in connection with making a fervent request or plea (as in Mt 8:2; 9:18; 15:25; 18:26; 20:20), but no such request is forthcoming here. The point is rather actual worship in the sense of acknowledging Jesus as a king or a deity (as in Mt 2:2, 8, 11; 14:33; 28:9, 17; Acts 10:25; Rev 19:10; 22:8). The

9:1-38 JESUS AND THE MAN BORN BLIND

to face. Jesus' silence[139] signals his acceptance of the man's worship, in contrast to the angel in the book of Revelation in the presence of the prophet John (Rev 19:10; 22:9), or Peter in the presence of Cornelius. Even though he is "Son of man" (v. 37), Jesus does *not*, like Peter, tell his prostrate worshiper, "Get up. I myself am a man too!" (Acts 10:26; see also Acts 19:15). By giving no answer, he acknowledges his deity.

The blind man's story has now been told. He and Jesus together have "worked the works of the One who sent me" (v. 4), just as Jesus said they would. Nothing is said of the forgiveness of his sins, for Jesus has long before made it clear (v. 3) that his sins (whatever they may have been) are not the issue here. Rather, he has simply "come to the Light" (see 3:21), and "the works of God" in his life have been revealed (v. 3). Blind "from birth" (v. 1), he has had his sight restored, signaling nothing less than a new birth. Like the rebirth of which Jesus told Nicodemus (3:5), it is a birth "from water," water from the pool of Siloam "sent" (v. 7) from above. In that sense he was "baptized," so to speak, and as a result "put out of synagogue" (vv. 22, 34). Now he has confessed Jesus as "Lord" and "worshiped him" (v. 38). His is a classic case study in Christian conversion, or so it appears.[140] The only difficulty is the order of events. Confession is supposed to go with Christian baptism, but the blind man made no confession of faith in Jesus when he washed in the pool of Siloam. Jews who confessed Jesus as the Christ were to be put out of the synagogue (v. 22), but the former blind man did not make his confession of faith until *after* he had been put out of synagogue. When he finally did so, his confession was *not* accompanied by water baptism, so far as we are told, even though the Gospel of John makes no secret of the fact that Jesus — or at least his disciples — did in fact perform baptisms (see 3:22, 26; 4:1). The Gospel writer knows what baptism is, and knows what it is to wash clay off one's eyes in a pool, and there is no reason why he would confuse one with the other. The man *could* have said, with Philip's Ethiopian eunuch, "What hinders me from being baptized?" (see Acts 8:37), and Jesus *could* have said,

---

only other uses of προσκυνεῖν in John's Gospel (4:20-24; 12:20) clearly involve the worship of God (the comment in Metzger, *Textual Commentary,* 229, that "προσκυνέω occurs nowhere else in the Fourth Gospel" is obviously incorrect).

139. "Silence" because, as we will see, Jesus' next words (v. 39) are not directed to the man born blind, but to an unidentified audience including "some Pharisees who were with him" (v. 40). He says nothing more to the former blind man.

140. This is in keeping with the influential and now classic argument of Louis Martyn that this chapter tells a story on two historical levels, superficially on the level of Jesus and an actual blind man, but more profoundly on the level of a conflict between church and synagogue somewhere in the Mediterranean world at the time the Gospel of John was written (see *History and Theology in the Fourth Gospel* [New York: Harper & Row, 1968], 3-41).

as he said later to his disciples, "He who has bathed does not have need to wash" (see 13:10), but nothing of the kind is reported. If a baptism took place, the Gospel writer is silent about it, just as he is about any baptismal activity after 4:1-2. Water baptism at this point in the narrative would have been anticlimactic in any case.

While in a general sense the man born blind does provide a kind of case study in the new birth, and perhaps also expulsion from the synagogue (bringing to realization something that seems not to have happened in the life of Nicodemus), the fact remains that the Gospel writer is attempting to write a historical account of something that happened in Jesus' ministry, not in his own time and place. It is not a parable or allegory, but at most a cautionary tale. The author's historical intent places certain constraints on him to narrate what happened "back then," not to bend the facts to conform to whatever may have been the pattern of Christian conversion and separation from the synagogue in his own community. Despite all that has been written in the last forty years or so, we know almost nothing of the author's community, not even whether it was predominantly Jewish Christian or Gentile Christian. Conversions there surely were, and baptisms, and confessions of faith, and perhaps in some instances expulsions from synagogues, and in others voluntary departures. Almost anything can be imagined,[141] but it is doubtful that any one pattern can be imposed on this theoretical "Johannine community."[142] All we know is that in the narrative the man born blind "worshiped" Jesus — worshiped him, we may safely conclude, "in Spirit and truth" (see 4:23, 24).

N. BLIND GUIDES AND THE GOOD SHEPHERD (JOHN 9:39–10:21)

> 39 *And Jesus said, "For judgment I came into this world, so that those who do not see might see, and so that those who see might go blind."* 40 *Some of the Pharisees, those who were with him, heard these things and said to him, "Are we blind too?"* 41 *Jesus said to them, "If you were blind, you would not have sin. But now you say that 'we see.' Your sin remains.* 10:1 *Amen, amen, I say to you, the one*

---

141. For an especially imaginative *tour de force,* see Raymond E. Brown's title, *The Community of the Beloved Disciple: The Life, Loves, and Hates of an Individual Church in New Testament Times* (New York: Paulist, 1979). One suspects (and hopes) that the subtitle on the cover, which does not reappear on the title page, is the work of a market-conscious publisher, not the author.

142. See the essays in the work edited by Richard Bauckham, *The Gospels for All Christians* (Grand Rapids: Eerdmans, 1998), calling into question the very notion of a "Johannine community."

who does not enter through the door into the courtyard of the sheep, but goes up from elsewhere, that one is the thief and robber. 2 *But the one who enters through the door is the shepherd of the sheep.* 3 *To this one the doorkeeper opens, and the sheep hear his voice, and he summons his own sheep by name and leads them out.* 4 *When he has brought out all his own, he goes ahead of them and the sheep follow him because they know his voice.* 5 *But a stranger they will never follow, but will flee from him, for they do not know the voice of strangers."* 6 *This parable Jesus told them, but they did not understand what things they were that he was saying to them.*

7 *So Jesus said again, "Amen, amen, I say to you that I am the Door of the sheep.* 8 *All who came before me are thieves and robbers, but the sheep did not hear them.* 9 *I am the Door. Through me, if anyone goes in he will be saved, and will go in and go out and find pasture.* 10 *The thief does not come except that he might steal and slaughter and destroy. I came that they might have life, and have [it] in abundance.* 11 *I am the good Shepherd. The good shepherd lays down his life for the sheep.* 12 *The one who is a hireling and not a shepherd, whose own the sheep are not, sees the wolf coming and leaves the sheep and flees — and the wolf seizes and scatters them —* 13 *because he is a hireling and it does not matter to him about the sheep.* 14 *I am the good Shepherd, and I know mine and mine know me,* 15 *just as the Father knows me and I know the Father. And I lay down my life for the sheep.* 16 *And other sheep I have, which are not from this courtyard. Those too I must bring, and they will hear my voice, and they will become one flock, one Shepherd.* 17 *That is why the Father loves me, because I lay down my life, that I might receive it back again.* 18 *No one took it away from me, but I lay it down on my own. I have authority to lay it down, and I have authority to receive it back. This command I received from my Father."*

19 *Again a split came about among the Jews on account of these words,* 20 *and many of them were saying, "He has a demon and is mad! Why do you listen to him?"* 21 *Others were saying, "These are not the words of one demon-possessed. Can a demon open the eyes of the blind?"*

Jesus' next words (v. 39) are a generalization, directed not to the man born blind but to the readers of the Gospel. Within the narrative, a new audience overhears him, "some of the Pharisees, those who were with him" (v. 40), and he speaks to them at some length (9:41–10:5), introducing a new set of metaphors involving a shepherd and his sheep. The author pauses to tell us that these Pharisees "did not understand what he was saying to them" (10:6), but Jesus goes on anyway (vv. 7-18), using the same metaphors and presumably addressing the same audience. As the discourse progresses, the metaphors subside as Jesus speaks more directly of himself and the Father (vv. 14-18). By the time he has finished, his audience, now renamed "the Jews" (v. 19), is divided in a "split" or "schism" over his words (vv. 19-21), confirming the notion that they "did not understand."

39 In contrast to verse 37, where we learn what Jesus "said to him," that is, to the former blind man, here we are told only what Jesus "said." No hearers are specified until the following verse, and they are not said to be the intended audience. The man born blind has disappeared from the scene, and will not be heard from again.[1] Jesus' words seem to be addressed to a more general audience, as general as the Gospel's entire readership: "For judgment I came into this world, so that those who do not see might see, and so that those who see might go blind."

The pronouncement is a riddle[2] or paradoxical saying, the kind that "historical Jesus" research might be quite willing to accept as authentic if it were in the Synoptics instead of John. The riddle offers two contrasting reasons why Jesus "came into this world," the first positive and the second negative:

(a) "so that those who do not see might see,"
(b) "so that those who see might go blind."

Such "reversal" sayings are common enough in the synoptic Gospels (see, for example, Mk 8:35; 10:43-44; Mt 23:12),[3] and here too the pronouncement stands on its own (like those in the Synoptics), not as part of an extended discourse. This particular saying is deeply rooted in the Old Testament, particularly Isaiah,[4] yet is introduced in a characteristically Johannine way, with Jesus claiming that "I came into the world" (see 12:46; 16:28; 18:37).[5] In John's Gospel, Jesus comes into the world as "light" (see 1:9; 3:19; 12:46), and the first part of the pronouncement *(a)* revisits rather straightforwardly his claim to be "the Light of the world" (8:12; 9:4), with the implication that as "the Light" he came so that (quite literally) "those

---

1. If verses 38-39a are omitted, his departure is, as we have seen, even more abrupt and unexplained.
2. See Thatcher, *The Riddles of Jesus in John,* 247-52.
3. The same principle of reversal of present circumstances characterizes the beatitudes in Matthew (5:3-12), and the four beatitudes and four woes in Luke (6:20-26).
4. For the giving of sight to the blind, see Isaiah 29:18; 35:5; 42:7, 18, and for the blindness of those who disbelieve, see Isaiah 6:10 (quoted in John 12:40), 29:9, 42:19, and 56:10.
5. Yet this too is paralleled in the synoptic tradition; for example, "I have not come [οὐκ ἦλθον] to call righteous but sinners" (Mk 2:17; see also Mt 5:17; 10:34-35; Lk 12:49).

who do not see might see" — that is, that the blind man might receive his sight. The difficulty comes in the second part of the pronouncement *(b)*, for nothing has prepared us for any intention on Jesus' part "that those who see might go blind" — least of all *literally* blind! This sends a signal that the first part *(a)* does not refer *primarily* to literal blindness either, but to spiritual blindness, the inability to recognize Jesus as God's "Son of man" and worship him as "Lord" (see v. 38).[6]

More important, the opening words, "For judgment I came into the world," make it clear from the start that the accent is on the negative assertion *(b)*, not the positive one *(a)*. That is, the emphasis is on the intent that "those who see might go blind," rather than that "those who do not see might see." The latter is of course also true. We have just seen it happen, at considerable length and in marvelous detail. But it is not what Jesus wants to talk about just now. Instead, he echoes what he said six chapters earlier: "This then is the judgment, that the Light has come into the world, and human beings loved the dark and not the Light, because their works were evil" (3:19).[7] At the same time, he anticipates the verdict on his entire public ministry given three chapters later in Isaiah's words: "He has blinded their eyes and hardened their heart, lest they see with the eyes and understand with the heart and turn, and I heal them" (12:40; see also Mt 13:14-15; Mk 4:12; 8:18). In short, there is both good and bad news in Jesus' pronouncement, but for the moment at least the bad news predominates.

40 No audience for these words has been identified, but an audience (whether the intended one or not) now makes its appearance: "Some of the Pharisees, those who were with him, heard these things and said to him, 'Are we blind too?'" (v. 40). They are not necessarily to be identified with the religious authorities who had repeatedly questioned the former blind man, designated in the narrative either as "the Pharisees" (vv. 13, 15) or "the Jews" (vv. 18, 22). Rather, they are "some of the Pharisees,"[8] possibly a random group or possibly one faction in the dispute mentioned earlier over whether or not Jesus was "from God." Back in 9:16, "some of the Pharisees"[9] were identi-

---

6. See Thatcher, *Riddles,* who comments that "the correct answer to the riddle is that those who 'see' will worship Jesus as the Son of Man (John 9:35-38), while those who do not worship him are 'blind' to his true identity" (248).

7. There too the positive and the negative sides are interwoven, as we have seen: "Everyone who practices wicked things hates the Light and does not come to the Light, for fear his works will be exposed, but whoever does the truth comes to the Light, so that his works will be revealed as works wrought in God" (3:20-21).

8. Gr. ἐκ τῶν Φαρισαίων.

9. Gr. ἐκ τῶν Φαρισαίων τινές. The phrase ἐκ τῶν Φαρισαίων, with or without τινές, is a partitive genitive (BDF, §164[2]); Abbott, *Johannine Grammar,* 89-90), with the meaning "some of the Pharisees."

fied as those who said, "This man is not from God because he does not keep the Sabbath," but it cannot be assumed here that the expression necessarily refers to the same faction, only that it refers to one faction out of two (or perhaps more). They could just as easily be identified with those who asked, "How can a sinful man do such signs?" (v. 16). This would be quite consistent with the notice given here that these Pharisees were "with" Jesus.[10] This could just mean that they were nearby, within earshot (see RSV, NRSV, REB), but it could also imply that they were at worst neutral or at best even sympathetic to his cause.[11] In any event, there is no overt hostility in their question, "Are we blind too?"

Still, the form of the question[12] does expect a negative answer, as if to say, "Surely we are not blind too?" It is not altogether clear whether they have in mind literal or figurative blindness. If the former, they are merely presupposing the obvious: unlike the beggar in the preceding narrative, they can see. If the latter, they are already defending themselves against any implication that they are spiritually blind in refusing to fall down and worship Jesus. The wording of their question argues for the former, as if to ask, "Are *we too* literally blind, like that beggar?" Obviously not.[13] Such a misunderstanding sounds almost too crude to be true, yet it is fairly typical of the ways in which Jesus' words are often misunderstood or taken literally in this Gospel (see, for example, 2:20, 3:4, 4:11, 6:52, 7:35, 8:22, 11:12, and 13:9). If they are not actually blind, they argue, how can Jesus claim to give them sight?[14] They sound a little like "the Jews" at the Tent festival a chapter earlier who said, "We are Abraham's seed, and have never been in slavery to anyone. How do you say that 'You will become free'?" (8:33). That was of course the beginning of a very hostile confrontation, but only the beginning.

10. Gr. οἱ μετ' αὐτοῦ ὄντες.

11. So Thatcher, *Riddles,* 248. The closest parallels are 11:31, where certain "Jews" (οἱ οὖν Ἰουδαῖοι) were said to be "with" Mary (οἱ ὄντες μετ' αὐτῆς) in her house, and 12:17, where a certain crowd (ὁ ὄχλος) had been "with" Jesus (ὁ ὢν μετ' αὐτοῦ) when he raised Lazarus from the dead. While the preposition does not imply discipleship (as perhaps in 3:26), neither does it suggest active opposition.

12. Gr. μὴ καὶ ἡμεῖς τυφλοί ἐσμεν (BDAG, 646; BDF, §427).

13. Admittedly, καί could also be understood as "so" or "then" (see BDAG, 495), yielding the translation, "So are we blind?" or "Are we then blind?" But the word order (καὶ ἡμεῖς) argues for the translation given above.

14. This assumes that they are responding to the first part of Jesus' pronouncement, *(a)* "so that those who do not see might see." Alternatively, if they are responding to the second part, *(b)* "so that those who see might go blind" (as their repetition of his word τυφλοί could imply), their point would be that if they are not in fact blind, then Jesus has obviously not succeeded in blinding them. This is less likely, because the thought of Jesus "blinding" them (whether literally or figuratively!) would have led us to expect a more vehement response.

Here too a confrontation ensues, albeit a milder one (see vv. 6, 19-21), and it is Jesus who provokes it.

41 The confrontation begins with Jesus' explanation of his riddle. Now that he again has a specific audience, he speaks "to them" (v. 41). "If you were blind," he says, "you would not have sin. But now you say that 'we see.' Your sin remains" (v. 41). The "explanation" is as much a riddle as the riddle itself. Like the riddle it purports to explain (see v. 39), it divides naturally into two parts, the first positive and the second negative:

(a) "If you were blind, you would not have sin."
(b) "But now you say that 'we see.' Your sin remains."

The first part *(a)* is a contrary-to-fact conditional sentence. In the second part *(b)*, "But now"[15] brings us back to reality. As in the preceding riddle, the first part revisits in straightforward fashion the story of the man born blind, where he who was literally blind did not "have sin" (see v. 3, "Neither this man sinned nor his parents"). The second part drives home Jesus' indictment of the Pharisees, even these relatively friendly Pharisees. In asking, "Are we blind too?" (v. 40), they had implied that of course they were not, and Jesus calls them on it, rephrasing their puzzled question as an explicit claim that "We see" (v. 41).[16] In doing so, he abruptly changes the subject from literal blindness and sight respectively to what has been his preoccupation all along: their response, or lack of it, to himself and to his word. To "see" is to recognize who Jesus is and worship him, as the blind man finally did. In saying, "We see," therefore, they are lying, for they have not believed in Jesus. The likely point is that everyone is "born blind" in the sense of being unable to "see the kingdom of God" or enter it without a second birth (see 3:3, 5). This in itself is not sin. Nicodemus, for example, was never accused of sin. The sin comes in the lie that "We see," and that consequently no new birth is needed or wanted (see 8:44-45, "When he speaks the lie, he speaks from his own, because he is the liar and the father of it. But I, because I speak the truth, you do not believe me").

"Sin"[17] in John's Gospel is consistently understood as unbelief (see, for example, 8:24; 16:9), and this passage is no exception. Jesus can tell these Pharisees, "Your sin remains" simply on the basis of what he views as their pretension to "see," and their consequent unwillingness to do what the man

---

15. Gr. νῦν δέ.
16. See Abbott, *Johannine Grammar* (164), who notices that "they had not said "'We see,' but 'Are we blind also?'" and argues that "the writer may sometimes use ὅτι to mean "[*to this effect*] *that*" — when he does not propose to give the exact words in a quotation." He cites 10:36 and 18:9 as further examples.
17. Gr. ἁμαρτία.

born blind has just done.[18] He does not explain himself any further to them, yet six chapters later he tells his disciples about them (and others like them) in greater detail and in a grammatically similar way, with two contrary-to-fact conditional sentences about sin followed by a statement of what is "now" in fact the case (see 15:22, 24). Such is Jesus' verdict on these "Pharisees who were with him" (v. 40), and they offer no reply (not even in 10:6, where we are told only that "they did not understand"). The expressions "to have sin" and "your sin remains" seem to refer to being guilty of sin.[19] Ironically, Jesus never explicitly forgives anyone's sin in this Gospel, but in these two instances (plus 8:21-24) he explicitly withholds forgiveness (see 20:23, where the power to forgive or withhold forgiveness is passed on to his disciples). We are left wondering why Jesus is so hard on these supposedly neutral (or even friendly) questioners.

The synoptic Gospels offer a clue. There too (on the basis of Scripture), Jesus points out that in his ministry "the blind see" (Mt 11:5; Lk 7:22; compare Lk 4:18), yet he repeatedly denounces the Pharisees as "blind" (Mt 23:17, 19; also 23:26), or more specifically as "blind guides" (Mt 15:14a; 23:16, 24). "Can a blind person guide the blind?" he asks. "Won't they both fall in a ditch?" (Lk 6:39; compare Mt 15:14b).[20] John's Gospel retains some of the vehemence of such texts, though without speaking of "guides." Instead, as we will see, Jesus drops the metaphor of blindness as he begins to speak of "shepherds," and consequently of "sheep."[21]

---

18. The closest parallel in this Gospel to the expression "your sin remains" (ἡ ἁμαρτία ὑμῶν μένει) is perhaps the parting word of John that "whoever disobeys the Son will never see life, but the wrath of God remains on him" (ἡ ὀργὴ τοῦ θεοῦ μένει ἐπ' αὐτόν, 3:36).

19. This is the case also in 15:22 and 24, and is reflected here in a number of English versions: for example, the RSV ("you would have no guilt," and "your guilt remains"), NIV and TNIV ("you would not be guilty of sin," and "your guilt remains"), NEB and REB ("you would not be guilty," and "your guilt remains"). The NRSV, however, retains the more literal "you would not have sin" and "your sin remains" (see also KJV, NASB, and NAB). The difference is smaller than it appears because even in the latter instances the implication is that sin has consequences, so that the accent is still on a person's guilt or accountability for sin (for the expression "to have sin," see also 1 Jn 1:8).

20. Paul implies that the devout Jew did in fact consider himself "a guide to the blind [ὁδηγὸν εἶναι τυφλῶν], a light to those in darkness, instructor of the foolish, teacher of the young, having the form of knowledge and truth in the law" (Rom 2:19-20). W. Michaelis theorizes that Paul's language here "surely owes its origin to the judgment of Jesus, which Paul must have known" (*TDNT*, 5.99). This is possible, but far from certain.

21. John's Gospel largely avoids the terminology of "guides" (ὁδηγοί), except in 16:13, where "the Spirit of truth" is to "guide" (ὁδηγήσει) the disciples into "all the truth." Jesus is "the Way" (ὁδός) in this Gospel (14:6), but not "the Guide" (ὁδηγός). Instead, he is "the Shepherd" (ποιμήν, 10:11, 14).

10:1-2 Jesus introduces the subject of sheep and shepherds with the fifteenth of his "Amen, amen" pronouncements. Here (as in 8:34-36, and possibly 3:11-21) the "Amen, amen" formula seems to govern not just a verse, but an entire paragraph (10:1-5), which the Gospel writer finally characterizes as "this parable" (v. 6). "Amen, amen, I say to you," Jesus begins, "the one who does not enter through the door into the courtyard of the sheep, but goes up from elsewhere, that one is a thief and robber" (10:1). That the "parable" begins negatively is not as surprising as it might otherwise be, given the negative tone of what has just preceded it (9:41). Moreover, the negative pronouncement has a positive sequel: "But the one who enters through the door is the shepherd of the sheep" (v. 2).[22]

Whether or not this "parable"[23] is comparable to Jesus' use of parables[24] in the other three Gospels could be debated at length. Its closest kinship is with certain parables of "normalcy," describing what is natural or appropriate in everyday life. Doctors, for example, are normally for sick people, not those who are well (see Mk 2:17). Fasting is normal when someone has died, but not at a wedding celebration (Mk 2:18-20). New wine normally goes in new bottles (Mk 2:22). If a sheep falls into a pit, its owner will normally pull it out, even on the Sabbath (Mt 12:11). If a shepherd loses track of even one sheep out of a hundred, he will normally leave the rest to fend for themselves while he goes out to look for it (Lk 15:4). If not common occurrences, these are at least common responses to everyday life situations, or even to emergencies. Similarly here, the first thing that gives legitimacy to the shepherd of the sheep is that he enters the courtyard in the normal fashion, "through the door" (v. 1). If we see someone climbing over the wall instead of entering in the normal way, it is fair to assume he is not the shepherd or owner of the sheep, but most likely a "thief and robber"[25] (v. 1). Even today, someone seen climbing into a house through a window is more likely than not up to no good.

The "courtyard" is a walled enclosure usually attached to a building,[26] serving a variety of purposes[27] but here envisioned as a pen or corral for sheep. It is not altogether clear whether all the sheep in the courtyard belong

---

22. Compare 15:2, where Jesus, after claiming that "I am the true Vine, and my Father is the Vinekeeper" (v. 1), first explains, "Every branch in me that does not bear fruit he takes it away," and then adds, "and every one that bears fruit he trims clean, so that it might bear more fruit."

23. Gr. παροιμία (see v. 6).

24. Gr. παραβολή.

25. Gr. κλέπτης ἐστὶν καὶ λῃστής.

26. See BDAG, 150; also Schnackenburg, 2.279.

27. See, for example, "the courtyard [τὴν αὐλὴν] of the High Priest" (18:15), complete with "the door" (ἡ θύρα, v. 16) and "the doorkeeper" (ἡ θυρωρός, vv. 16-17).

to the one shepherd, or whether several shepherds' flocks are kept together in a common courtyard.[28] The phrase, "the shepherd of the sheep" (v. 2),[29] suggests that the shepherd who "enters through the door" is shepherd to all the sheep in the courtyard, or at least all that figure in the story.[30] If there are other sheep and other legitimate shepherds who also enter "through the door," they go unmentioned. The contrast is between the one shepherd who enters legitimately, and the "thief and robber" who "goes up from elsewhere"[31] to gain access to the sheep.

3 Two more details (in addition to entrance "through the door") signal the shepherd's legitimacy. One is that "the doorkeeper[32] opens" to him, and the other is that "the sheep hear his voice, and he summons his own sheep by name and leads them out" (v. 3).[33] The presence of a "doorkeeper" is the only hint in the text that other shepherds may have their sheep within the courtyard, but this detail is more likely just part of what a reader might have visualized as a normal courtyard setting (see 18:15-17). It is worth no-

---

28. For the latter assumption, see Schnackenburg, 2.279-80, who nevertheless admits that "No mention occurs of other shepherds or their flocks" (2.279) because "The other shepherds and flocks hold no interest for the narrator" (2.280).

29. While ποιμήν lacks the definite article, Colwell's rule allows for the translation, "the shepherd of the sheep." In later manuscript tradition, Codex D and a few other witnesses make this explicit, with the reading αὐτός ἐστιν ὁ ποιμήν τῶν προβάτων (compare Heb 13:20). The same argument, of course, applies to "thief and robber." Although the "thief and robber" could be anyone, in the parable a definite interloper (ἐκεῖνος) is in view.

30. This is still the case even if an article is *not* supplied in translation (as, for example, in a translation such as "he is shepherd to the sheep"). Nothing in the text hints of other shepherds.

31. "Goes up from elsewhere" (ἀναβαίνων ἀλλαχόθεν) is an awkward expression for this illegitimate access to the sheep. While ἀναβαίνων simply implies climbing over the courtyard wall instead of entering through the door, the verb may have been chosen because of its significance in connection with Jesus himself, particularly in light of his pronouncement that "no one has gone up [οὐδεὶς ἀναβέβηκεν] to heaven except he who came down from heaven" (3:13). Jesus is "from above" (ἄνωθεν, 3:31), but the "thief and robber" has a very different place of origin (ἀλλαχόθεν; see also 8:23, "You are from below, I am from above").

32. This generic doorkeeper is masculine (ὁ θυρωρός), as in Mark 13:34, but in contrast to 18:16-17 (see above, n. 27; also BDAG, 462), where a specific feminine doorkeeper was remembered.

33. The effort of Brown (1.392-93, in agreement with J. A. T. Robinson in *Twelve New Testament Studies,* 67-75) to distinguish two parables, vv. 1-3a and vv. 3b-5 respectively, is obviously unconvincing, given the singular expression, "This parable," in v. 6. His argument that vv. 1-3a characterize the Pharisees as "thieves and robbers," in contrast to "strangers" in v. 5, can only be described as premature allegorization, inasmuch as no such identifications have been made in the text. Rather, vv. 1-5 tell a single coherent story.

ticing that "the sheep," not "*his* sheep" — thus presumably *all* the sheep in the courtyard — "hear his voice." Everywhere else in the chapter, to "hear" is to heed and follow (see vv. 8, 16, 27).[34] There is no suggestion that all the sheep in the courtyard "hear" the shepherd's voice but that only "his own sheep" are summoned "by name" and led out of the courtyard. More likely, "the sheep" (that is, all the sheep in the courtyard) are in fact the shepherd's "own sheep," so that the courtyard is in fact emptied out. The phrase "his own sheep"[35] is not introduced in order to distinguish his sheep from someone else's, but simply to accent that they belong to him as objects of his love and care.[36]

The verbs in the present tense ("opens," "hear," "summons," "leads out") refer not to a particular occasion, but to what is normally or customarily true in any courtyard where a shepherd takes care of his sheep and leads them to pasture each day. While it is also customary in any sheepherding culture for shepherds to give nicknames to certain sheep with identifiable features or characteristics, the notion that a shepherd calls *every* sheep "by name"[37] is an exaggeration prompted by the reality to which the imagery points, that is, Jesus' intimate knowledge of, and love for, "his own" disciples (see 13:1).[38] The shepherd "summons" his sheep, much as Jesus will summon Mary to meet him outside Bethany (11:28), or summon Lazarus from the tomb (12:17),[39] and then "leads them out" to freedom and food and water (see v. 9).

4-5 The parable continues with a notice of what happens next, after the shepherd "has brought out all his own" (v. 4). The phrase "all his own"[40] echoes "his own sheep" in the preceding verse.[41] The strong verb "brought

---

34. This is largely the case throughout the Gospel (see 1:37, 40; 3:29, 32; 4:42; 5:24, 25, 28, 30, 37; 6:45, 60; 8:26, 38, 40, 43, 47; 9:27, 31; 11:41, 42; 14:24; 15:15; 16:13; 18:37; a conspicuous exception is 12:47).

35. Gr. τὰ ἴδια πρόβατα.

36. Again, contrast Schnackenburg (2.382; see above, n. 28), who nevertheless admits that "ἴδια could, it is true, simply be a possessive pronoun" (see 1:41, 4:44, and 5:18; also BDF, §286[1])

37. Gr. κατ' ὄνομα.

38. Compare Schnackenburg, 2.281, who regards the naming of every sheep as "scarcely conceivable" in real life. See especially 20:16, where Mary Magdalene recognizes Jesus immediately upon hearing her name from his lips (see also 11:43; 14:9; 21:15, 16, 17).

39. The subsitution of καλεῖ, "calls," for φωνεῖ, "summons" (with the majority of later manuscripts), is more in keeping with Pauline than Johannine vocabulary.

40. Gr. τὰ ἴδια πάντα.

41. Some manuscripts, in fact, including most Latin versions and the majority of later manuscripts, read τὰ ἴδια πρόβατα here as well, or simply drop the πάντα (as in the first hand and the second corrector of ℵ), but πάντα ("all," with P[66], P[75], B, D, L, W, and

out" (literally, "driven out")[42] reminds us that in spite of the implied application to himself and his disciples, Jesus is still speaking in a parable, and therefore about sheep, not persons. Earlier he had said (using the same verb), "the person who comes to me I will never drive out" (6:37), and in the present setting it was the Pharisees, not Jesus, who "drove out" the man born blind (9:34, 35). Here the verb, in the weakened sense of "brought out,"[43] merely resumes the verb "leads them out" in the preceding verse, avoiding a repetition of the same verb. It is not where the emphasis lies.

The verse's main point is rather that the shepherd "goes ahead of them"[44] and the sheep "follow him," just as Jesus' disciples "followed" him from the beginning (1:37-38, 40, 43; see also 8:12). They do so "because they know his voice," reinforcing the point that "the sheep hear his voice" (v. 3). "Knowing" is the result of "hearing," but it is also the result of being known. That the shepherd knows his sheep is evident from the fact that he calls them "by name" (v. 3), and we now learn that this knowledge is in some way mutual, as Jesus will later make explicit (see v. 14). By contrast, the sheep "do not know the voice of strangers" (v. 5), and consequently will follow no one but their proper shepherd.[45] The "stranger"[46] (v. 5) is for the moment undefined, but the contrast with which the parable began suggests that "the thief and robber" mentioned there is still in view (v. 1). This is confirmed by the notion that the sheep "will flee from him" (v. 5), and then by the further mention of "thieves and robbers" in verse 8, and "the thief" in verse 10. The parable ends on the same negative note with which it began (see v. 1).

6 The story might have continued, but it does not. Nothing is said of where the shepherd leads the sheep, or what happens next. Instead, the Gospel writer pauses to identify the preceding five verses as "this parable"[47] (v. 6), and to make it clear that Jesus aimed it at those Pharisees who were

---

the preponderance of the better witnesses) signals the completion of the process described in verse 3 and the beginning of the shepherd's ministry to the sheep in places of pasture *outside* the courtyard.

42. Gr. ἐκβάλῃ.
43. See BDAG, 299 (see, for example, Mt 9:38; Mk 1:12).
44. Gr. ἔμπροσθεν αὐτῶν πορεύεται. Although the setting is very different, the imagery is not unlike that of Mark 14:27-28, where Jesus, after quoting the text, "I will strike the shepherd and the sheep will be scattered" (from Zech 13:7), adds, "but after I am raised up I will go before you [προάξω ὑμᾶς] into Galilee" (compare προάγει ὑμᾶς, Mk 16:7).
45. The expression "they will never follow" (οὐ μὴ ἀκολουθήσουσιν) is an emphatic negation, setting the stage for the sharp contrast, "but will flee" (ἀλλὰ φεύξονται).
46. Gr. ἀλλοτρίῳ.
47. Gr. ταύτην τὴν παροιμίαν.

"with him" and had asked him, "Are we blind too?" (9:40). The notice that Jesus "told *them*" and the reference to "things . . . he was saying *to them*" echo 9:41, where "Jesus said *to them,* "If you were blind, you would not have sin. But now you say that 'we see.' Your sin remains" (my italics). The reader is supposed to understand that the audience is the same. Jesus' verdict against them is now confirmed by the notice that "they did not understand[48] what things they were that he was saying to them" (v. 6). Unlike the sheep who "know" the shepherd's voice (v. 4), they do *not* know what Jesus is telling them. Their inability to see (9:41) is compounded by an inability to hear or understand.

If the Gospel writer goes out of his way to tell the reader that the Pharisees "did not understand," does this mean he expects the reader to understand the parable, or is an explanation needed? If so, is the explanation to be found in verses 7-10, or in verses 11-18, or both? If not, what is the reader to make of the parable as it stands? At the very least, verse 6 seems to invite the reader to make a provisional assessment of the parable's meaning. The efforts of commentators to find in verses 7-18 any kind of coherent or consistent interpretation of the parable invariably end, if not in frustration at least with an acknowledgment of severe limitations.[49] It appears that the model derived from Mark and Matthew, in which Jesus tells a "parable" and then supplies a detailed "interpretation" for the initiated (see Mk 4:1-9, 13-20; 7:14-15, 17-23; Mt 13:24-30, 36-43), is not a useful model here. Instead, verses 1-5 should be allowed to speak for themselves before moving on, and the notice that the Pharisees "did not understand" is as good a place as any for the reader to reflect on the parable's intrinsic meaning and purpose. If verses 1-5 are in fact a single parable, as the phrase "this parable" implies (see above, n. 33), its accent is not on the "door" (vv. 1-2) or the "doorkeeper" (v. 3), but overwhelmingly on the response of the sheep to the shepherd and the relationship between shepherd and sheep (vv. 3-5). The shepherd's legitimacy rests finally not with the doorkeeper or the door, but with the fact that the sheep "hear his voice" (v. 3), and "know" it so well that they can distinguish it from "the voice of strangers" (vv. 4-5). At the same time, the "sheep" are those whose names the shepherd knows, and in being able to recognize the shepherd's voice speaking their names, they also legitimize themselves as "his own" sheep (vv. 3-4). Not sight but hearing makes all the difference.

48. Gr. οὐκ ἔγνωσαν.
49. See, for example, Barrett: "not simply an interpretation but a development of the parable in characteristic Johannine style" (371); also Carson, 383-84. Lindars, by contrast, points to "the repetition of the opening of the parable" (that is, "Amen, amen," v. 7) as "a sign that it is now to be expounded in detail. It seems less likely to be a pointer to fresh traditional material" (358), yet he has to acknowledge not one but several "lines of exposition" (at least three) in the verses that follow (358-60).

7-8 Even though the Pharisees "did not understand" (v. 6), Jesus speaks "again," presumably addressing the same audience:[50] "Amen, amen, I say to you that I am the Door of the sheep" (v. 7). This comes as a surprise to the reader, who might have expected Jesus to identify himself first of all with "the shepherd of the sheep" (v. 2), or if not that at least to "the doorkeeper" (v. 3). Instead, by repeating the "Amen, amen" formula (now for the sixteenth time in the Gospel), Jesus calls attention to the parable's opening line, with its own "Amen, amen," and its key phrase, "through the door"[51] (v. 1).

As "the Door" Jesus claims to be the protector of the sheep from "the thief and robber" (v. 1b). "All who came before me are thieves and robbers," he continues, "but the sheep did not hear them" (v. 8). "Before me"[52] could be either temporal ("all who came before I came"),[53] or spatial ("all who came and stood before me to gain entrance").[54] The temporal understanding can appeal to 9:39, where Jesus said, "For judgment I came into this world," and to verse 10, where he will say, "I came that they might have life," yet the language of "coming" is not easily compatible with the metaphor of Jesus as "the Door." Moreover, the temporal understanding raises the difficult question of what is then implied about Abraham, Moses, the prophets, and John, who came "before" Jesus in time. Are they "thieves and robbers"?[55] "All" sounds very inclusive, yet Jesus has explicitly endorsed Abraham (8:39-40, 56), Moses (5:46-47), and John (5:33-35) as his legitimate predecessors.[56]

---

50. "Again" (πάλιν, as in P[75] and B) suggests that the audience is probably the same, and the variant reading αὐτοῖς (as in P[45] and P[66]) would make it virtually certain. Most later witnesses simply conflate the two (πάλιν αὐτοῖς, "So Jesus said to them again"). And even though "Amen, amen, I say to you" is a stereotyped formula, Jesus would not have had to use it here, and its presence (ending with ὑμῖν) is a further argument against a change of audience.

51. Gr. διὰ τῆς θύρας.

52. Gr. πρὸ ἐμοῦ.

53. This is the dominant view among modern commentators. Schnackenburg, for example, states categorically that πρὸ ἐμοῦ "cannot be meant in anything but a temporal sense" (2.291).

54. See Morris: "We should almost certainly take 'before me' as part of the imagery rather than indicating Jesus' predecessors the religious leaders.... The meaning appears to be that if people are to bring other people into God's fold they must first enter it themselves.... And the only way to enter is through the one door" (451).

55. Most commentators reject this alternative, even while interpreting the phrase "before me" temporally. But there is little evidence for the common supposition that Jesus is referring to "false messianic claimants" (for example, Barrett, 371; Schnackenburg, 2.291). The only possible reference (and a remote one at that!) to false messiahs in John's Gospel places them *after*, not before, the coming of Jesus (5:43).

56. See also 1:17, 45; 12:38-41.

Possibly for this reason, a few ancient manuscripts omit the "all," and many more omit the phrase "before me."[57]

More likely, therefore, the phrase "before me" has a spatial reference. "Thieves and robbers" have come "before" Jesus as before a door.[58] As "the Door," he is a *closed* door to all who confront him and threaten the sheep. These "thieves and robbers" are presumably "the Jews" or "the Pharisees" who have challenged him repeatedly, and have now driven out the man born blind.[59] Throughout the preceding chapters, Jesus confronted these enemies alone, but we now learn that in doing so he was also protecting those whom he said the Father had given him (see 6:37, 44). In this way, his intention "that of all he has given me I might not lose anything" (6:39) is certain to come to pass (see vv. 27-29). "Thieves and robbers" are denied access to the sheep, both because "the Door" stands closed before them and because "the sheep did not hear them" (v. 8b). The latter assertion is true by definition, for throughout the chapter Jesus' "sheep" are identified as those who hear the voice of the Shepherd and of no one else (see vv. 3, 4, 5, 14, 16, 27; also 18:37). Those who listen to other voices are *ipso facto not* his sheep (see v. 26).

9 Jesus repeats the "I am" pronouncement, just as he repeated, "I am the Bread of life" (6:35, 47), and "I am the Light of the world" (8:12; 9:5), and just as he will shortly repeat "I am the good Shepherd" (vv. 11, 14). "I am the Door," he continues, "Through me, if anyone goes in he will be saved, and will go in and go out and find pasture" (v. 9). The difference is that now he presents himself as an *open* door, open not to "thieves and robbers" but to the sheep. It is no longer a matter of coming "before" the door (v. 8) and being denied entrance, but of going "through" the door[60] to a place of safety. As in 6:35, 47 and 8:12, the "I am" pronouncement is followed by an invitation and promise, introduced by "if anyone,"[61] recalling

---

57. "All" (πάντες) is missing in D and two old Latin versions, and "before me" (πρὸ ἐμοῦ) is absent in a number of witnesses (including P75, ℵ*, Γ, Δ, many of the later minuscules, the Sinaitic Syriac, and old Latin versions). See Metzger, *Textual Commentary*, 230.

58. See Acts 12:6 (πρὸ τῆς θύρας); 12:14 (πρὸ τοῦ πυλῶνος); 14:13 (πρὸ τῆς πόλεως); James 5:9 (πρὸ τῶν θυρῶν). See BDAG, 864: "perh. J 10:8 belongs here (Jesus is the door, vs. 7)."

59. Brown (1.393) holds that "the Pharisees and Sadducees remain the most probable targets of Jesus' remarks," but still within a temporal reading of the phrase "before me." He adds, "The unhappy line of priestly rulers and politicians from Maccabean times until Jesus' own day could certainly be characterized as false shepherds, thieves, and robbers who came before Jesus."

60. Compare 14:6: "I am the Way, and the Truth, and the Life. No one comes to the Father except through me" (δι' ἐμοῦ).

61. Gr. ἐάν τις.

such classic promises as 6:51 ("*If anyone* eat of this bread, he will live forever") or 7:17 ("*If anyone* chooses to do his will, he will know about the teaching"), or 8:51 ("*If anyone* keeps my word, he will never ever see death").[62] Like these others, it is an invitation to "anyone" to believe in Jesus and thereby gain eternal life. But because it stands within the metaphorical world of sheep and shepherds, its vocabulary is distinctive. To "go in" and "go out" implies an enclosure, in this instance the "courtyard" (v. 1) housing the sheep. The promise of being "saved,"[63] uncommon in John's Gospel,[64] is probably chosen here to highlight the thought of sheep being "rescued" or "kept safe" from harm, whether from "thieves and robbers" or natural predators (see v. 12).[65] Those addressed, therefore (and "anyone" implies a very general invitation), are promised entry to Jesus' "courtyard," with all the benefits of a shepherd's care. The "courtyard," however, is neither a prison nor a fortress, for the sheep, Jesus promises, "will go in and go out and find pasture" — another way of saying, "if the Son sets you free, you will really be free" (8:36). The metaphors of shepherds and sheep and the courtyard are still at work — not least in the term "pasture,"[66] which sustains animal, not human, life — but the reality to which the metaphors point is also clearly visible, and becoming more so. As the discourse continues, the metaphors will begin to fade, having served their purpose, and Jesus will speak more and more straightforwardly of his mission and his relationship to the Father.

10 Jesus now returns briefly to the subject of the "thieves and robbers," before stating in classic Johannine terms why he came into the world. "The thief does not come except that he might steal and slaughter and destroy," he continues, adding that "I came that they might have life, and have [it] in abundance" (v. 10). The stark contrast between "the thief" and Jesus is striking, as if to guard against any misunderstanding of certain traditional sayings attributed to Jesus in which his "coming" is actually compared to the coming of a thief (see Mt 24:43-44; Lk 12:39-40; Rev 3:3; 16:15; also 1 Thess 5:2, 4). That a thief "steals" is a truism, but "slaughter" and "destroy" are more surprising. These words are part of the metaphor, because

---

62. Italics mine. As we have seen, even the man born blind echoed this terminology (9:31). The pronouncement in 7:37 is a little different, in that the invitation comes not in the "If anyone" clause, but in third-person imperatives, and the promise comes only in the following verse.

63. Gr. σωθήσεται.

64. Only 3:17 and 12:47 use the verb to refer to eternal salvation, and in each instance not of individuals but of the "world" (ὁ κόσμος; see also 4:42, "Savior of the world").

65. This is the case in 11:12 and 12:27 (see BDAG, 982, on 5:34).

66. Gr. νομήν.

"slaughter"[67] has to do with the killing of animals (in this instance, sheep).[68] The supposition is that sheep are stolen not in order to be added to someone else's flock, but to be slaughtered for food, and thus "destroyed." The accent is on "destroy,"[69] for being "destroyed" or "lost" is in this Gospel the very opposite of gaining "eternal life" (see 3:16; 6:39-40). Here the thief comes to "destroy," while Jesus comes "that they might have life." "Life" corresponds to "pasture" within the metaphor, except that the "life" Jesus gives is "in abundance," that is, more than mere survival or safety (v. 9), more than "pasture" (v. 9) in the sense of basic sustenance for a sheep or a human.[70] "Life" is nothing less than "eternal life" with God (just as in 3:16 and 6:40, and frequently throughout the Gospel).[71]

11 Abruptly changing the metaphor, Jesus continues, "I am the good Shepherd."[72] Why "the good Shepherd"? Why not simply "the Shepherd of the sheep" (as in v. 2), corresponding to "the Door of the sheep" (v. 7)? Jesus seems to use the adjective "good" in much the same way that the adjective "true" is used in other instances (see, for example, 1:9, "the true Light"; 6:32, "the true bread"; 15:1, "the true Vine"), to refer to what is "real" or "genuine" in God's sight, the very model or prototype of what a shepherd should be.[73] What makes a shepherd "good" is that he "lays down his life for the sheep," that is, he puts his very life on the line to protect his flock. With this, Jesus leaves behind the imagery of the opening parable (vv. 1-5), with its picture of the shepherd entering through the door and leading the sheep out to pasture. Instead, we see the shepherd and the sheep in the fields *outside* the courtyard, facing the possible attacks of predators.

In the translation, I capitalized "Shepherd" in "I am the good Shep-

---

67. Gr. θύσῃ.
68. See BDAG, 423, and Matthew 22:4; Luke 15:23, 27, 30.
69. Gr. ἀπολέσῃ.
70. The reader will remember the accent on superabundance in two earlier narratives in the Gospel (for example, the six huge jars of water turned to wine [2:6], the twelve baskets of leftover fragments of bread [ἐπερίσσευσαν, 6:13]), and will encounter three more later on: the full pint of perfume Mary poured on Jesus' feet (12:3), the 75 pounds of spices used to embalm his body (19:39), and the enormous catch of 153 large fish (21:11).
71. This "abundant life" should therefore not be viewed (as it has been in some Christian circles) as a "deeper" or "victorious" life gained by a second work of grace subsequent to conversion. It is simply a way of speaking of "eternal life" in the classic Johannine sense of a life that is not merely endless in duration, but new life, a qualitatively different relationship to God.
72. Gr. ὁ ποιμὴν ὁ καλός.
73. As Walter Grundmann puts it, "ὁ ποιμὴν ὁ καλός is the true shepherd who really has a right to the title" (*TDNT*, 3.548). See 1 Thessalonians 5:21, where Paul writes, "Put everything to the test; hold on to what is good" (τὸ καλόν, in the sense of "what is genuine").

herd," but not in the next sentence, "The good shepherd lays down his life for the sheep." The reason is that in the second instance the definite article appears to be generic (like "the doorkeeper" in v. 3, "the thief" in v. 10, or "the hireling" in v. 12).[74] Jesus is speaking of what *any* "good shepherd" (as opposed to a "hireling") would do for his sheep. "Life" (literally, "soul")[75] refers here not to the "spiritual" or immaterial side of a person's being, but, quite the contrary, to a person's physical life in this world (see 12:25),[76] in contrast to the eternal and abundant "life"[77] that Jesus gives (v. 10).[78] The point initially is not that a good shepherd dies for his sheep (that would hardly benefit them),[79] but that he puts himself in danger in order to ensure their safety. Yet the metaphor is moving toward a reality a few verses later in which Jesus as "the good Shepherd" actually "lays down his life" in death to gain for his sheep eternal life (see vv. 15, 17-18; 15:13).

12-13 For the moment, still working with the image of what is expected from any "good shepherd," Jesus drives the imagery home by invoking a contrast. The opposite of "the good shepherd" is "the hireling,"[80] who is no shepherd at all, and has nothing to lose if the sheep are slaughtered because they do not belong to him in the first place. He envisions a scene in which the hireling "sees the wolf coming and leaves the sheep and flees" (v. 12), precisely because he is only a hireling, "and it does not matter to him about the sheep" (v. 13). The outcome is inevitable: "the wolf seizes and scatters them." Whether the predators are humans (as in v. 10), or wild animals as here, the sheep are at their mercy without a "good shepherd" to protect them. Jesus intends no specific identification of "the hireling" any more than for "the doorkeeper" or even "the thief" (while Jesus may have thought of "the Jews" or "the Pharisees" as "thieves and robbers," the singular "thief" remains a generic figure within an imaginative story).[81] He is not even attach-

---

74. For the generic use of the article, see Abbott, *Johannine Grammar*, 47. As Bultmann puts it (370), "The article in front of ποιμήν and μισθωτός corresponds to the style of parables (Mk. 4.3, ὁ σπείρων; Lk. 12.29, ὁ οἰκοδεσπότης, etc.), and figurative sayings (Jn. 4.36; Mk. 2.19; Mt. 24.28, etc.)."

75. Gr. ψυχή.

76. Also Matthew 10:39; 16:25; Mark 8:35; Luke 9:24; 17:33.

77. Gr. ζωή.

78. See BDAG, 1098: "the condition of being alive, earthly life, life itself."

79. So too Bultmann, 370, n. 5: "whereas it is characteristic of a shepherd to risk his life for his sheep, it is not characteristic for him to sacrifice it for them." Dying for the sheep would be implied by the variant reading δίδωσιν ("gives" his soul or life) in a number of textual witnesses both here and in verse 15 (P[45], ℵ*, D, and others). But this reading appears to have been shaped by the reality to which the metaphor is pointing, Jesus' death on the cross (see Mk 10:45).

80. Gr. ὁ μισθωτός.

81. Again, see Bultmann, 370, n. 4.

ing any particular blame to "the hireling," who is simply acting out his role as one who has no investment in the sheep. All that Jesus is saying is that "the hireling" is not a "good" (that is, proper) shepherd, in that he is by definition not a shepherd at all (v. 12).[82] Jesus adds, almost redundantly, that this is "because he is a hireling and it does not matter to him about the sheep" (v. 13), but not before offering a glimpse of the grim but inevitable outcome of the story, in which "the wolf seizes and scatters" the sheep, so that the flock is destroyed (v. 12b). For the reader of the other Gospels, his language evokes a scene just after the Last Supper, on the Mount of Olives, in which Jesus quoted the text, "I will strike the shepherd, and the sheep will be scattered" (Mk 14:27/Mt 26:31, from Zech 13:7).

14-15 Again (as in v. 9) Jesus repeats the "I am" expression: "I am the good Shepherd, and I know mine and mine know me, just as the Father knows me and I know the Father" (vv. 14-15a). Here the metaphor of shepherd and sheep begins to give way to the characteristic pairing of Jesus with "the Father." We have heard nothing of "the Father" since 8:54, but from here to the end of the chapter he will be very much a part of the discussion (see vv. 17, 18, 25, 29, 30, 32, 36, 37, 38). That "I know mine and mine know me" builds (albeit vaguely) on the notion in the introductory parable that "the sheep hear his voice," and that the shepherd summons them "by name" (v. 3). The neuter pronoun for "mine"[83] probably has as its antecedent "the sheep" or "his own sheep" from that scene (vv. 3, 4) and from the later contrast between the shepherd and the hireling (v. 12; see also v. 27).[84] Yet "the Father" is no necessary part of the imagery of shepherd and sheep, and the analogy between the mutual knowledge of Father and Son and of the Son and his disciples is by no means dependent on the Son being visualized as Shepherd and the disciples as sheep (see, for example, Mt 11:27 and Lk 10:22).[85] It is the

82. Gr. καὶ οὐκ ὢν ποιμήν. The expression is odd, in that participles are normally negated with μή (see BDF, §426). Possibly the article governs only the participle (ὁ . . . ὤν), so that both μισθωτός and οὐκ . . . ποιμήν are to be understood as predicate nominatives. That is at any rate what almost inevitably happens in English translation: "The one who is a hireling and not a shepherd" (on the construction, see BDF, §430[1]; Abbott, *Johannine Grammar,* 545-46).

83. Gr. τὰ ἐμά.

84. Brown (1.384) presupposes this in translating the clause, "I know my sheep and mine know me" (so too NIV, TNIV). Yet as we will see, the neuter plural for Jesus' disciples can surface even where the sheep metaphor is not explicit (see 17:10, "and all mine [τὰ ἐμά] are yours, and yours [τὰ σά] mine").

85. Clearly, the mutual knowledge between Father and Son does not make the Father a Shepherd and the Son his sheep! For Jesus' knowledge of the Father, see 8:55, "And you have not known him, but I know him. And if I say that I do not know him, I will be a liar like you. But I know him, and I keep his word" (also 7:29, "I know him, because I am from him, and he sent me"; 8:19, "if you knew me, you would know my Father").

Father, in fact, who makes it possible for Jesus to make the role of a "good shepherd" (v. 11) his own: "And I lay down my life for the sheep" (v. 15). But this time Jesus is not simply telling what any "good shepherd" customarily does for his sheep (as in v. 11), but is instead revealing what he himself does as "good Shepherd." The verb "I lay down"[86] is present (as in v. 11), but points toward the future, when Jesus will give himself over to arresting authorities in order to spare his disciples (18:8), and eventually give himself up to death on the cross (19:30).[87] Still, it is not exactly a futuristic present, for Jesus' life is already at risk, and has been ever since "the Jews began pursuing" him (5:16), and "kept seeking all the more to kill him" (5:18; see also 7:1, 19, 25; 8:37, 40).[88]

16 It would be easy and natural to move directly from verse 15 to verse 17, where Jesus continues, "That is why the Father loves me, because I lay down my life that I might take it back again." But in between comes a different pronouncement: "And other sheep I have, which are not from this courtyard. Those too I must bring, and they will hear my voice, and they will become one flock, one Shepherd" (v. 16). This parenthetical comment[89] looks beyond the "courtyard" of Palestinian Judaism, and probably beyond Judaism itself to the Gentile world. In that world, Jesus is saying, there are those who are already his "sheep," and they will prove it by "hearing his voice," as his own sheep always do (see vv. 3, 4, 14, 27). Later, the Gospel writer will confirm Jesus' pronouncement (and dissolve the metaphor) with the striking comment that even the Jewish High Priest had "prophesied that Jesus was going to die for the nation, and not for the nation alone but in order that the children of God who are scattered might also be gathered together into one" (11:52).[90] Here too the assumption is that Jesus will die (by "laying

---

86. Gr. τίθημι.

87. Bultmann too (383) argues for a change in meaning from verse 11, where the expression means to risk one's life and verses 15 and 17, where it means to lay down one's life in death. While the variant reading δίδωμι ("I give") is more plausible here than the δίδωσιν of verse 11 (see above, n. 79), τίθημι is probably still to be preferred (see Metzger, *Textual Commentary*, 230).

88. Abbott comments, "The present in x.15 'I *lay down* my life for the sheep' is certainly intended to include a reference to the Crucifixion," while adding that "it might refer also to the whole of Christ's work as being a 'laying down of life'" (*Johannine Grammar*, 352).

89. To Bultmann, predictably, the verse "can only be explained as a secondary gloss inserted by the editor." Yet in the same breath he admits that "the same idea is expressed in 11.52 and 17.20 by the Evangelist" (383).

90. That both the "other sheep" here and "the children of God" in 11:52 are Gentiles, and not Jews in the diaspora, is made likely by the deliberate contrast in 11:50-52 between "the people" (v. 50) or "nation" (vv. 50, 52) and "the scattered children of God" (v. 52). In similar fashion, Jesus will speak of being "lifted up from the earth" and

down his life"), but — oddly — that he will survive death, so as to "bring"[91] these "other sheep" under the Shepherd's care. His survival of death, moreover, is not a mere possibility, but a certainty, something that "must"[92] happen, just as surely as "the Son of man must be lifted up" (3:14; also 12:34). The whole scenario recalls Mark 14:27-28, where Jesus quotes a Scripture hinting at his death ("I will strike the shepherd, and the sheep will be scattered," v. 27), yet quickly adds, "but after I am raised up, I will lead you into Galilee" (v. 28; also 16:7).

The outcome is that *all* the sheep (both those "from this courtyard" and the "other sheep") "will become"[93] one flock," with "one Shepherd." Not one "courtyard" or "fold," as in the Vulgate,[94] but "one flock,"[95] a metaphor for the church used only here in John's Gospel.[96] "One flock" is a corollary of "one Shepherd." Jesus' vision is not that Gentiles will be brought into "this courtyard," understood as Judaism, for it is the Shepherd's care, not a particular "courtyard," that defines the "flock." At this point, "one Shepherd" appears to be a self-reference, for Jesus has been the "Shepherd" all along (explicitly so in vv. 11 and 14). Yet in light of what follows later in the chapter the "one Shepherd" could just as easily be God (as consistently in the Old Testament),[97] for Jesus and the Father share in the common work of protecting the sheep and keeping them safe (see vv. 28-30). It is precarious to read into the text any definitive assumption as to what the precise relationship between Jewish and Gentile Christian congregations, or between Jews and Gentiles in any single congregation, should be. With or without the metaphor

---

drawing "them all [πάντας] to myself" (12:32). Clearly, his vision is not limited to Judaism, for he has already drawn to himself Samaritans (see 4:42, "Savior of the world").

91. Gr. ἀγαγεῖν.

92. Gr. δεῖ.

93. Instead of "they will become" (γενήσονται), many ancient witnesses have the singular, "there will be" or "will come to be" (γενήσεται, with P⁶⁶, ℵ*, A, the old Latin and Syriac versions, and a majority of later Greek manuscripts). The effect is to make the "one flock" and "one Shepherd" (jointly) the subject of the clause rather than predicate nominative. But the plural has wider manuscript support (with P⁴⁵, ℵ², B, D, L, W, Θ, Ψ, and important minuscules including 1, 33, and 565), and is the more difficult reading (see Metzger, *Textual Commentary,* 230).

94. The word in the Vulgate is *ovile,* the same word used to translate αὐλή both in this verse and in verse 1 (the KJV, and all other early English versions except for Tyndale, followed the Vulgate, translating ποίμνη as "fold" or "sheepfold"). This is clearly a mistranslation, not a witness to a Greek variant reading (see Metzger, *Textual Commentary,* 231).

95. Gr. μία ποίμνη.

96. The church as a "flock" is more commonly ποίμνιον (as in Lk 12:32; Acts 20:28-29; 1 Pet 5:2-3; also *1 Clement* 16.1, 44.3, 54.2, and 57.2).

97. See, for example, Psalm 23, and, above all, Ezekiel 34.

of shepherd and sheep, Jesus' intent is simply that all his disciples, Jew or Gentile, present and future alike (see 17:20), will become "one" in their relationship to God, their love for each other, and their mission to the world (see 11:52; 17:11, 21, 23).

17 Picking up the thread of verse 15, Jesus continues, "That is why the Father loves me, because I lay down my life, that I might receive it back again" (v. 17). His point is not that the Father's love for him is conditional on "laying down his life" for his sheep (see 3:35, 5:20, and 15:9, where the Father's love for the Son is a given, and 17:24, where Jesus says, "you loved me before the foundation of the world"). Rather, Jesus' love for his sheep and his willingness to die for them is part and parcel of his very nature as God's Son, and therefore as the object of the Father's love.[98] As Shepherd he risks his life for his sheep (v. 11), but as the Father's Son he does more (vv. 15, 17), giving himself up to death on their behalf (see 3:16). That Jesus has now begun to speak explicitly of his death is confirmed by the next clause, "that I might receive it back again."[99] This clause would have no meaning in relation to a shepherd putting his life in danger for his sheep, but in the present context it points to Jesus' resurrection — his clearest pronouncement so far on the subject (see 2:19; 6:62).

18 "No one took it away from me," Jesus continues, "but I lay it down on my own." The aorist "took away"[100] could be a gnomic or timeless aorist,[101] but more likely Jesus is looking back at those earlier instances in which his enemies tried to arrest or stone him and failed to do so (see 7:30, 32, 44; 8:20, 59). His words, "I lay it down on my own," come as a surprise in light of his insistence all along that "I can do nothing on my own" (5:30; see also 7:17, 28; 8:28, 42). The distinction is that Jesus acts "on his own"

---

98. As Barrett puts it, "The relation between the Father and the Son is essential and eternal. John does not mean that the Father loved Christ because the crucifixion took place. But the love of the Father for the Son is a love that is eternally linked with and mutually dependent upon the Son's complete alignment with the Father's will and his obedience even unto death" (377; see also Bultmann, 384).

99. The ἵνα clause, "that I might receive it back," expresses purpose in the sense of *Jesus'* final purpose or intention — not, however, the specific purpose of his act of dying. The latter is said to be rather to benefit the sheep (ὑπὲρ τῶν προβάτων, v. 15), that is, "so that [ἵνα] the scattered children of God might also be gathered together into one" (11:52). The distinction is subtle but necessary.

100. Gr. ἦρεν. The aorist (with P^{45}, ℵ*, and B) is probably to be preferred to the present (αἴρει) as the more difficult reading with very early manuscript support (see, for example, Brown, 1.387; Schnackenburg, 2.509). The tendency of scribes would have been to conform the tense to τίθημι, now about to be repeated for a third time.

101. See BDF, §333(1), and Bultmann, 385, n. 1. There is no need to assume a postresurrection perspective in which "the crucifixion [is] viewed as an event in the past — viewed, that is, from John's own standpoint" (Barrett, 377).

initiative in contrast to the initiative of others who tried unsuccessfully to take his life.[102] He never acts "on his own" in relation to the Father (see 5:19; 7:18).

Jesus will shortly make the distinction explicit, but first he states even more strongly that he acts on his own initiative: "I have authority[103] to lay it down, and I have authority to receive it back." He has mentioned "authority" only once before, in claiming that the Father "gave him authority to do judgment, because he is Son of man" (5:27), in just the same way that "he gave to the Son to have life in himself" (5:26). In both places, Jesus' "authority," including his ability to act "in himself" (5:26), or, as he says here, "on my own," is not something intrinsically his by nature, but something conferred on him by the Father.[104] His pronouncement here about "authority" provides a point of reference for Pilate's unintentionally ironic claim nine chapters later, that "I have authority to release you, and I have authority to crucify you" (19:10). There Jesus is quick to remind him that "You would have no authority against me at all if it were not given you from above" (19:11). Part of the irony is that by then the reader knows that the same is true of Jesus himself, and his own authority, except that his authority is from God and not from Rome. For him, the principle articulated by John still stands: "A person cannot receive anything unless it is given him from heaven" (3:27). Here, therefore, he is quick to add, "This command I received from my Father."

"Received"[105] is the same verb used twice before, in the clauses, "that I might receive it back again" (v. 17) and "I have authority to receive it back" (v. 18a). It is not a case of an active "taking" in the first two instances (as in the NIV and NRSV, "to take it up again") and a more passive "receiving" in the third. Rather, the verb should be translated the same way all three times. Jesus has the authority to "receive" back his life from the Father, because he has first "received" a "command" from the Father, and obeyed it by laying down his life. There is a kind of analogy between the "authority" granted to Jesus from the Father and the "authority" Jesus grants to those who "receive"

---

102. Even under less drastic circumstances, as we have seen, Jesus refused to act on the initiative of his brothers, who wanted him to "go to Judea, so that your disciples may see your works that you do" (7:3), and he will refuse to act immediately on the initiative of Mary and Martha in response to the illness of Lazarus (see 11:6). His response to his mother at the Cana wedding (2:4) was, as we have seen, a bit more complex.

103. Gr. ἐξουσίαν ἔχω.

104. See also 17:2, "just as you have given him authority [ἐξουσίαν] over all flesh, so that all you have given him, he may give to them eternal life," and the discussion above (see 7:1) of the relationship between that which Jesus "chose" not to do, and that which he had no "authority" to do.

105. Gr. ἔλαβον.

him (see 1:12, "But to as many as did receive him he gave authority to become children of God"). "Command,"[106] mentioned here for the first time,[107] encapsulates in a single noun all that is involved in the notion that God "sent" his Son (see 3:17, 34; 5:36, 38; 6:29, 57; 7:29; 8:42), accenting the Father's intention that the Son "lay down his life" and "receive it back again." Implicit in the "command" is the "authority" to do just that. With this, Jesus ends his speech (vv. 7-18) on a rather defiant note.

19-21 If the first part of Jesus' speech to "the Pharisees . . . who were with him" (9:40) resulted in incomprehension (10:6), the second part (vv. 7-18) divides them. "Again a split[108] came about among the Jews," we are told, "on account of these words" (v. 19). "Again" reminds us that there have been other such "splits," whether "in the crowd" (7:43) or among "the Pharisees" (9:16). Probably only the second of these is in view here, for "the Pharisees" and "the Jews" are, as we have seen, largely interchangeable terms. "Many," perhaps the majority, say to their companions, "He has a demon and is mad! Why do you listen to him?" (v. 20), and the "others" reply, "These are not the words[109] of one demon-possessed. Can a demon open the eyes of the blind?" (v. 21). The charge of demon possession has been leveled before, whether simply as another way of saying he was mad (7:20), or in a more serious vein, linking him to the hated Samaritans (see 8:48, 52). Here the charge of madness is explicit. While demon possession and madness were not necessarily identical in the ancient world, they were closely associated.[110] Here the answer of the "others" (v. 21) suggests that they took the rhetoric of demon possession seriously, even if not quite literally. "Can a demon open the eyes of the blind?" they ask, on the assumption that the actions of a demoniac are essentially the actions of the "demon"[111] possessing him. Again (as in 9:16) this second group (even though they do not necessarily believe in Jesus) speak for the Gospel writer, echoing the words of the man born blind, "It is unheard of that anyone ever opened the eyes of one born blind" (9:32). Just as the question "How can a sinful man do such signs?" (9:16) went unanswered because the answer was obvious to the reader, so too those who asked, "Can a demon open the eyes of the blind?"

---

106. Gr. ἐντολή.
107. See also 12:49-50 and the cognate verb ἐνετείλατο in 14:31.
108. Gr. σχίσμα.
109. "These . . . words" (ταῦτα . . . τὰ ῥήματα) effectively echo the Gospel writer's phrase, "on account of these words" (διὰ τοὺς λόγους τούτους, v. 19), even though the words for "words" are not the same, for the terms are used synonymously here, as they are throughout the Gospel.
110. See, for example, Mark 3:21, "they were saying that he was out of his mind," and 3:22, "they were saying that 'he has Beelzebul'" (or "he has an unclean spirit," v. 30).
111. Gr. δαιμόνιον.

are given the last word here.[112] Their question in a way echoes Jesus' own question in the synoptic tradition, "How can Satan cast out Satan?" (Mk 3:23). It also brings the whole section (9:39–10:21) back to the point at which it began, the healing of the man born blind. The dispute over Jesus' "words" (vv. 19, 21) comes down finally to his "works."

O. TITLES AND WORKS (10:22-42)

22 Then came the Rededication in Jerusalem. It was winter, 23 and Jesus was walking in the temple, in the portico of Solomon. 24 So the Jews surrounded him, and were saying to him, "How long will you take away our life? If you are the Christ, tell us plainly." 25 Jesus answered them, "I told you, and you do not believe. The works that I do in my Father's name, these testify about me. 26 But as for you, you do not believe, because you do not belong to my sheep. 27 My sheep hear my voice, and I know them, and they follow me. 28 And I give them eternal life, and they will never ever be lost, and no one will seize them out of my hand. 29 That which my Father has given me is greater than all things, and no one can seize [it] out of my Father's hand. 30 I and the Father are one."

31 Again the Jews lifted stones that they might stone him. 32 Jesus answered them, "I showed you many good works from the Father. For which work among them are you stoning me?" 33 The Jews answered him, "It's not about a good work that we are stoning you, but about blasphemy, and because you, being a man, are making yourself God." 34 Jesus answered them, "Is it not written in your law that 'I said you are gods'? 35 If he said that those to whom the word of God came were 'gods,' and the Scripture cannot be abolished, 36 then you're telling him whom the Father consecrated and sent into the world that 'You blaspheme,' because I said 'I am the Son of God'? 37 If I do not do the works of my Father, don't believe me. 38 But if I do them, even if you don't believe me, believe the works, so that you might learn and know that the Father is in me and I in the Father."

39 So they sought to arrest him again, and he went out from their hand. 40 And he went back again across the Jordan, to the place where John was at first baptizing, and remained there. 41 And many came to him, and they were saying that "Though John did no sign, still everything John said about this man was true." 42 And many believed in him there.

---

112. For similar examples of reliable comments from unexpected sources, see (in addition to 9:16) 3:2; 7:31, 40-41.

The writer pauses to sketch a new scene at the Jewish festival of Rededication (known today as Hanukkah), and a new stage in Jesus' debate with "the Jews." The scene accomplishes two things: first, it attempts to resolve the "split" (v. 19) over Jesus' claim to be "the good Shepherd," drawing on the "sheep" imagery of verses 1-18 (see vv. 26-27); second, it recalls the earlier confrontation at the Tent festival (chapters 7–8), in that "the Jews" continue to challenge Jesus about his claims more generally, focusing now on such titles as "the Christ" (v. 24), "God" (v. 33), and "the Son of God" (v. 34). He answers by repeatedly downplaying the importance of titles, and calling attention instead to "the works I do in my Father's name" (see vv. 25, 32, and 37-38). The outcome is the same as before. "The Jews" try to stone him (v. 31; see 8:59), or, failing that, arrest him (v. 39a), but again without success (v. 39b; see 7:30; 8:20, 59). It remains true that no one has taken Jesus' life from him. Only he has "authority to lay it down" and "authority to receive it back" (see vv. 17-18). His "words" (v. 19) to that effect are thereby vindicated. Once he has made his escape, Jesus leaves the scene of his lengthy debates with "the Jews" for good, returning for a time to revisit the place "across the Jordan" where John testified about him long before (see 1:19-34) and where he had found his first disciples (vv. 40-42). History repeats itself, as "many believed in him there" (v. 42).

22-23 The new scene begins with the notice, "Then came the Rededication in Jerusalem" (v. 22). "Then" is used to set the time frame not for what precedes (9:1–10:21), but for what follows.[1] This is evident from the verb "came" or "came about." When the writer wants to set the time for what has preceded, he uses such expressions as "These things he said teaching in synagogue in Capernaum" (6:59), or "These words he spoke in the treasury, teaching in the temple" (8:20). Here by contrast he is not summarizing, but moving on.[2]

The "Rededication"[3] was an eight-day festival, beginning on the 25th of Kislev (or December), commemorating Jewish independence under Judas Maccabaeus and the consecration of the temple in Jerusalem in 164 B.C., three years to the day after its desecration by the Syrian king Antiochus Epiphanes (see 1 Maccabees 4:59). The author of *2 Maccabees* compared it

---

1. See BDAG, 1012: "to introduce what follows in time (not in accordance w. earlier Gr.) then, thereupon" (see also BDF, §459[2]).

2. This is even more clearly the case if τότε (P^{75}, B, L, W, 33) is replaced by δέ (with P^{66}, א, A, D, and the majority of later witnesses), or omitted altogether (with family 1, 565, and one or two ancient versions; see Lindars, 366, and Sanders, 254). But Lindars' argument (366), that τότε is a later addition because it "properly refers back to a time already mentioned," is both incorrect (relying too exclusively on classical Greek) and unnecessary.

3. Gr. ἐγκαίνια.

to the Tent festival (*2 Maccabees* 1.9; 10.6), and Josephus (*Antiquities* 12.325) called it "the festival of Lights."⁴ The writer does not explicitly identify it as a festival "of the Jews" (see 2:13, 5:1, 6:4, and 7:2), possibly assuming that even his Gentile readers are by now reasonably familiar with such observances. Instead, he simply locates it on the Jewish calendar of festivals by adding, "It was winter" (v. 22b). Three months have elapsed since the Tent festival (7:2). Jesus has presumably been in Jerusalem the whole time, but the events of 9:1–10:21 have had no definite time frame, and no particular relationship either to the Jewish festivals or to the temple. "Rededication" brings Jesus to the temple again, this time not to "the treasury" (see 8:20), but to "the portico of Solomon," a traditional place for teaching and disputation (see Acts 3:11; 5:12).⁵ Clearly, Jesus was "walking" there to teach and invite discussion (as in Mk 11:27), not simply to escape the cold weather, as some have supposed.⁶ "Walking" implies that he simply carried on his ministry as before, on the other side of Jordan (1:36) and in Galilee (6:19, 66; 7:1). This time, in contrast to the Tent festival, he does not publicly or formally "begin teaching" in the temple (7:14), much less "cry out" to all who would listen (7:28, 37), but instead waits for the challenge to his authority that will surely come (see Mk 11:27-28).

24 Accordingly, we are told, "the Jews surrounded him,"⁷ possibly with hostile intent,⁸ as if with stoning already in mind (see vv. 31-33). "How long will you take away our life?" they ask. "If you are the Christ, tell us

---

4. But if indeed the time reference points forward to 10:22-39 and not backward to 9:1–10:21, then there is no attempt here to take advantage of the symbolism of light (as, for example, in 9:5, or in the narrative of giving sight to a blind man).

5. Josephus believed that this eastern portico of the temple was actually built by King Solomon (see *War* 5.184-85; *Antiquities* 15.398-401; 20.221). Whether this is true or not, the demand of the people that Herod "raise the height of the east portico" (*Antiquities* 20.220; LCL, 9.507) suggests that a structure of some kind was already in place in Herod's time.

6. See, for example, Brown, 1.405, who comments that this eastern portico was "the only one of the porticoes whose closed side would protect it from the east wind" (compare Barrett, 379). Even less likely is the suggestion that "winter" is intended to evoke "the spiritual climate" (like "night" in 13:30); see Beasley-Murray, 173, who adds that "the frosty temperature without corresponded to the frozen spirits of 'the Jews'" (!). Rather, the reference to winter is merely a signal that three months have elapsed since the Tent festival, so that Jesus' "hour" (7:30; 8:20) is closer than before. As Bultmann notices, "the seasons of the year reflect the progress of the revelation," but this does not quite justify his conclusion that "the end is near" (361). The "end" awaits the approach of the last Passover, still several months away (see 11:55; 12:1; 13:1).

7. Gr. ἐκύκλωσαν.

8. See BDAG, 574 (in the LXX, see, for example, Pss 21[22]:16; 31[32]:7; 48[49]:5; 87[88]:17; 108[109]:3; 117[118]:10, 11, 12).

The Gospel of John

plainly" (v. 24). The question, "How long will you take away our life?"[9] (v. 24a), virtually defies translation. Most noticeably, it echoes Jesus' own words a few verses earlier, "No one took it away from me," referring to his own "life" or soul, "but I lay it down on my own" (v. 18). If the meaning is the same, they are turning his pronouncement upside down by asking, "How long will you take our life away?" or "kill us."[10] But they can hardly have meant such a thing literally. They have been trying to kill Jesus, not the other way around.[11] Therefore most English versions render it, "How long will you keep us in suspense?" (RSV, NRSV, NIV, REB, NAB, etc.). While this translation makes excellent sense in the context, no such meaning is attested in biblical, classical, or Hellenistic Greek.[12]

It appears that the language of "killing" or "taking away life" is used here metaphorically, as in our colloquial English expression, "the suspense is killing me." While examples from the Greek Old Testament are markedly different, they do exhibit a kindred note of "breathless" expectancy: "To you, LORD, I lifted up my soul" (see Pss 25[24]:1; 86[85]:4; 143[142]:8).[13] Here, however, the expectancy is not a good thing, for *someone else* is "lifting up" or "taking away" their "soul," or life, and *not* toward God. In the wake of the "split" dividing them (v. 19), they are uncertain what to expect, for they are no longer in control. The notion of "killing" or a prolonged death, therefore, is by no means inappropriate as a metaphor for their frustration.

The overriding question is what it has been all along, the subject of all the "splits" among "the crowd" (7:40-44), "the Pharisees" (9:16), and "the Jews" (vv. 19-21): Who is Jesus? Behind the disputes over whether he is "from God" or "a sinner" (9:16), "demon-possessed" or not (vv. 19-21) is the persistent issue of whether or not he is, or is claiming to be, "the Christ" (see 7:26-27, 31, 41-42). This is what frames the anguished demand, "If you are the Christ, tell us plainly" (v. 24b). By "plainly"[14] they seem to mean not just "publicly" (as in 7:4, 26; 18:20), but "in so many words," rather than in meta-

---

9. Gr. ἕως πότε τὴν ψυχὴν ἡμῶν αἴρεις.

10. An echo of Jesus' own words would have been even more evident if the "you" were emphatic: "How long will *you* [σύ] take *our* life away?" This, however, is not the case, possibly because of the emphatic "you" in the next clause, "If you [σύ] are the Christ."

11. Hoskyns's suggestion (386-87) that "Jesus is taking away their life" because his ministry threatens their very existence as a nation (see 11:50) is unconvincing.

12. As commentators have noticed, BDAG (29) offers only one exact parallel, and that from the twelfth century.

13. For a similarly positive use of the metaphor, see also Josephus, *Antiquities* 3.48, where the Israelites under Moses went out against their enemies "with hearts elated [τὰς ψυχὰς ἡρμένοι, literally "having lifted the souls"] at the peril . . . ready to face the horror of it, hoping ere long to be quit of their miseries" (LCL, 4.341).

14. Gr. παρρησίᾳ.

phors such as Bread, Light, Shepherd, or Door (see 11:14; 16:25, 29). Any reader familiar with other Gospels will recall the High Priest's words at Jesus' trial before the Sanhedrin: "Are you the Christ, the Son of the Blessed?" (Mk 14:62), or "Tell us if you are the Christ, the Son of God" (Mt 26:63). There, "the Christ" called forth as its companion title, "the Son of God" (or something equivalent), and in much the same way the subsequent debate here will center less on the issue of whether Jesus is "the Christ" than on whether he is "God" (v. 33) or "the Son of God" (v. 36). Even though the title "Christ" or "Messiah" in early Judaism (see 1:41) did not necessarily imply divinity, in the world of John's Gospel it does, not only to the author (see 20:31) and those who believe in Jesus (see 11:27),[15] but even at some level to Jesus' opponents.[16] Their intense interest in whether or not he is "the Christ" seems to grow, directly or indirectly, out of their initial impression that he "was claiming God as his own Father, making himself equal to God" (5:18). Here as in chapters 7–8, it will turn out that the issue of Jesus as "the Christ" is only preliminary to the issue of Jesus as "Son of God" or "God." Moreover, in asking him now to speak "plainly," "the Jews" show themselves ignorant of the fact that he has already done so (see 7:26). In retrospect, he will insist that "I have spoken plainly to the world; I always taught in synagogue and in the temple, where all the Jews come together, and I said nothing in secret" (18:20).

25 Jesus answers them with a fairly lengthy speech (vv. 25-30). His opening words, "I told you,[17] and you do not believe" (v. 25a), are not literally true. Even though he has spoken "plainly" (7:26), he has never told them in so many words that he was "the Christ." He has claimed this only once, in a very different setting, when the Samaritan woman said, "I know that Messiah is coming, who is called Christ," and Jesus told her, "It is I — I who am speaking to you" (4:25-26). But he immediately explains himself: "The works[18] that I do in my Father's name, these testify about me" (v. 25b). With this, he explains not only the sense in which he can say "I told you," but also the sense in which he can claim that they "do not believe." What they have failed to believe is the testimony of his "works." These works, he reminds them, are in his Father's "name," that is, they are the Father's own works.

---

15. This is evident from the juxtaposition of the two titles, "the Christ, the Son of God" in both passages, and in 20:31 from the placement of the normative Johannine confession right on the heels of Thomas's exclamation, "My Lord and my God!" (v. 28).

16. This may be implied in Haenchen's comment (2.49) that "The Evangelist knows well that Christ means 'the anointed,' as does the term messiah. But he does not use the messianic concept; for him the question is only whether Jesus is the Christ. It is the Christian designation alone that comes into consideration for him."

17. As Haenchen (2.50) notices, even the sound of "I told you" (εἶπον ὑμῖν) echoes the demand, "tell us" (εἰπὲ ἡμῖν, v. 24).

18. Gr. τὰ ἔργα.

With this, he takes them back to where their unbelief began, when he said, "My Father is working even until now, and I am working" (5:17), and they "kept seeking all the more to kill him, because he . . . was claiming God as his own Father, making himself equal to God" (5:18). This, and not the title "Christ," he reminds them, is the real issue. Nor is it purely a question of who Jesus is, for, as he says, "The works that I do" are done in "my Father's name." Despite the emphatic "I," they are the Father's works and not his own.

26 For emphasis, Jesus repeats himself: "But as for you, you do not believe," adding the reason for their unbelief, "because you do not belong to my sheep" (v. 26).[19] Reintroducing the sheep metaphor, he revisits the parable of verses 1-5 and the discourse of verses 7-18. One might have expected rather, "You do not belong to my sheep because you do not believe," but the wording here is in keeping with the theology of the Gospel. The fact that sheep hear their shepherd and recognize his voice does more than simply legitimate the true Shepherd in contrast to "strangers" (see vv. 3-5, 8, 14, 16); it also legitimates them as his sheep. "Hearing" and "knowing" the Shepherd's voice is what *identifies* the sheep.[20] Here for the first time, Jesus defines "hearing" or "knowing" the shepherd's voice more specifically as "believing." Those who do not "believe" prove thereby that they are not Jesus' sheep. Behind it all is a strong accent on election: those who "believe" do so because they are *already* Jesus' sheep (see v. 16, "other sheep I have"), his gift from the Father.

27-28 Jesus now goes on to speak positively about his sheep (vv. 27-28), not so much for the benefit of his immediate hearers as for the readers of the Gospel, those whom he wants to assure that he is "the Christ, the Son of God," so that they might "in believing have life in his name" (20:31). "My sheep hear my voice," he begins, "and I know them, and they follow me" (v. 27), largely repeating what he said before (vv. 3-4, 14). To this he adds the strong assurance that "I give them eternal life, and they will never ever be lost, and no one will seize them[21] out of my hand" (v. 28). Here too he builds on what has preceded, but with particular emphasis on his sheep never being "lost" or "destroyed." The corollary of "eternal life," he claims, is eternal safety from predators (see vv. 10, 12) under his protective "hand." Jesus' goal for his disciples is what it was four chapters earlier, "that of all he has

---

19. More literally, "you are not of my sheep" (ἐκ τῶν προβάτων τῶν ἐμῶν; for the partitive genitive with ἐκ, see BDF, §164[1]).

20. Jesus will later make much the same point to Pilate, without the sheep metaphor: "I was born for this, and for this I came into the world, that I might testify to the truth. Everyone who is of the truth [ἐκ τῆς ἀληθείας] hears my voice" (18:37). Pilate, like "the Jews," was not (v. 38).

21. "Them" is αὐτά (neuter plural) because the antecedent is "my sheep" (τὰ πρόβατα τὰ ἐμά), indicating that the preceding αὐτοῖς (v. 27) is also to be read as neuter, referring to the disciples as "sheep."

given me I might not lose anything" (6:39). This goal will come to realization within the narrative, and when it does, first Jesus (17:12) and then the Gospel writer (18:9) will call it to our attention.

29-30 So far, aside from the phrase "in my Father's name" (v. 25), Jesus' claims about his disciples have been largely centered on himself and his own initiative: "the works that *I* do . . . testify *about me*" (v. 25); "you do not belong to *my* sheep" (v. 26); "*My* sheep hear *my* voice, and *I* know them, and they follow *me*" (v. 27); "And *I* give them eternal life, . . . and no one can seize them out of *my* hand" (v. 28, italics added). Now, however, he acknowledges (as in 6:39) that his "sheep" are in fact a gift from his Father: "That which[22] my Father has given me is greater than all things, and no one can seize [it] out of the Father's hand" (v. 29).[23] "Father" is where the emphasis lies, for it is where the Greek sentence both begins and ends: literally (following the Greek word order), "My Father, that which he has given me is greater than all things, and no one can seize [it] out of the hand of the Father."[24] Perhaps for this reason, the majority of manuscripts, including some early ones, have the relative pronoun and the adjective as masculine, yielding the translation, "My Father, *who* has given to me, is greater than all things" (italics added). This more familiar reading is an easy, almost too easy reading (see n. 22), for the notion that God the Father is "greater than all things" is something that should go without saying. Moreover, it places all the emphasis on the Giver without mentioning the gift at all.[25]

---

22. The reading I have adopted (compare the NRSV), with the neuter relative pronoun (ὅ) and a neuter adjective for "greater" (μεῖζον), is that of B, old Latin and the Vulgate, one Coptic version, and church fathers, including Tertullian, Jerome, and Augustine. A similar reading, with the neuter pronoun (ὅ), but with a masculine adjective for "greater" (μείζων), is found in ℵ and other early witnesses including L, W, and Ψ). The reading "My Father, who has given to me, is greater than all things" (see NIV, and most English versions), with both the masculine pronoun (ὅς) and the masculine adjective (μείζων), is found in P[66], the majority of later Greek manuscripts, and (with slight variations) some early witnesses (including A, Θ, and a later scribal corrector of B). It is easy to see why scribes would have changed the reading adopted here to "My Father . . . is greater than all things," but harder to imagine a change in the opposite direction (see Metzger, *Textual Commentary*, 232, with an acknowledgment that it is not an easy decision).

23. In much the same way, he strongly accented his own initiative in verses 17-18 ("*I* lay down my life. . . . No one took it away from me, but *I* lay it down *on my own*. *I* have *authority* to lay it down, and *I have authority* to receive it back"), yet was careful to preface it with "That is why *the Father* loves me" (v. 17), and to follow it with "This command I received from *my Father*" (v. 18, italics added).

24. For a similar construction, see above, 6:39.

25. If the pronoun (ὅς) refers to the Father, there is no pronoun referring to that which the Father has given. English versions that adopt this reading normally supply "them" as the object, referring to Jesus' "sheep."

By contrast, the point of the reading adopted here is that because the Father is who he is, his gift ("that which he has given me") is "greater than all things." The conclusion that "no one can seize [it] out of the Father's hand" closely parallels what Jesus has just said about himself, that "no one will seize them out of my hand" (v. 28). This can only mean that the gift "greater than all" is Jesus' "flock" (v. 16), that is, his sheep viewed collectively as "That which he has given me."[26] That believers in Jesus are God's gift to him, a gift of inestimable value, comes as a strong word of comfort and assurance to the Gospel's readers. It may come as a surprise to later Christians grounded in the Reformation who have been taught that in ourselves we are corrupt and worthless sinners. "In ourselves" this may be true, but, as we have seen, the Gospel of John views us through a different lens.[27] Value, like beauty, is in the eye of the beholder, and in this case the Beholder is God.[28] This immeasurable value of Jesus' sheep, moreover, is their intrinsic value, for what could be more "intrinsic" than the value assigned to a person or community by God the Creator and Redeemer?

With this Jesus creates a syllogism, not just for the readers' benefit, but as a direct challenge to "the Jews": if (a) no one can seize Jesus' sheep out of his hand, and (b) no one can seize them out of his Father's hand (v. 29), then (c) "his hand" and "his Father's hand" are doing *the same work,* in this instance providing security and protection to the flock. To "the Jews" the syllogism reopens an old wound, recalling the day Jesus began (as they saw it) "claiming God as his own Father, making himself equal to God" (5:18). Without hesitation, he draws the explicit and inevitable conclusion: "I and the Father are one" (v. 30), an assertion every bit as provocative as "My Father is working even until now, and I am working" (5:17), if not more so. As commentators are fond of pointing out,[29] "one" is neuter,[30] not masculine,[31] which would have meant "one person," and might have been viewed as in-

---

26. Gr. ὃ δέδωκέν μοι; see BDF, §138(1).

27. See, for example, Jesus' assessment of Nathanael not as a sinner but as "a true Israelite in whom is no deceit" (1:47), and the discussions above, on 3:21, 5:29, 6:37, 6:44, and 9:3.

28. Even the gnostic *Gospel of Philip* from the second or third century, heretical by many standards, makes a similar point: "When the pearl is cast down in the mud it does not become dishonoured the more, nor if it is anointed with balsam oil will it become more precious. But it has its worth in the eyes of its owner at all times. So with the sons of God, wherever they may be. For they have the value in the eyes of the Father" (*Gospel of Philip* 48; see R. McL. Wilson, *The Gospel of Philip* [London: A. R. Mowbray, 1962], 109).

29. See, for example, Morris, 464 ("one thing" and not "one person"); also Lindars, 370; Beasley-Murray, 174;

30. Gr. ἕν.

31. Gr. εἷς.

consistent with the later doctrine of the Trinity.³² Still, it may not be wise to draw the distinction too sharply, in view of the phrase "one Shepherd"³³ back in verse 16, which, as we have seen, could refer to the Father as easily as to the Son, or to the Father working through the Son. As for the neuter, it would not have to mean more than the two working together in harmony (see 1 Cor 3:8), but the force of the syllogism and the precedent of 5:17 will make it unmistakably clear to "the Jews" that Jesus is in fact "making himself God" (see v. 33). The readers of the Gospel have even more to go on, for they cannot have forgotten the programmatic claims of 1:1 ("and the Word was God") and 1:18 ("God the One and Only . . . right beside the Father").³⁴ At the same time, "one" also makes it clear that Jesus is not claiming to be a "second God" in defiance of Jewish monotheism, but is in some way claiming identity with "the Only God" (see 5:44), the God of Israel.

31 The immediate response of "the Jews" is predictable, as "again"³⁵ they "lifted stones that they might stone him." "Again" looks back at 8:59, when they did exactly the same thing in response to Jesus' pronouncement, "before Abraham came to be, I am" (8:58). At that time, their action terminated the long debate, as Jesus "was hidden, and went out of the temple" (8:59b). Not so here. The debate is just getting started.

32 Instead of pressing the explicit claim that "I and the Father are one" (v. 30), Jesus resumes speaking of his "works" (see v. 25). "I showed you many good works from the Father," he replies, with more than a touch of irony, "For which work among them are you stoning me?" (v. 32). Evidently the works of "the good Shepherd" (vv. 11, 14) are by definition "good,"³⁶ most recently the healing of the man born blind. Jesus' "good" works, he reminds them, are "many," bringing to mind as well the healing at the pool of Bethsaida, which aroused their hostility in the first place (see 5:16; 7:21-23), and perhaps others of which they had only heard reports.³⁷ Possibly his use of

---

32. Schnackenburg comments that "The verse has played a not insignificant part in relation to the doctrine of the Trinity," citing as an example Ammonius of Alexandria "to the effect that the unity relates not to personhood (ὑπόστασις) but to nature (οὐσία)." But while he calls the verse a "vista of the metaphysical depths contained in the relationship between Jesus and the Father" (2.308), he also acknowledges that "These speculations exceed the scope of what the evangelist had in mind" (2.511, n. 121; see also Brown, 2.403).

33. Gr. εἷς ποιμήν, masculine.

34. See also Carson, 394-95.

35. Instead of "again," some ancient manuscripts have οὖν ("therefore," including D and the old Latin) and others have οὖν πάλιν (including P⁶⁶ and A), but the earliest and most reliable manuscripts (including ℵ and B, L, and W) have simply πάλιν ("again").

36. Gr. καλά.

37. See 7:31, "The Christ, when he comes, will he do more signs than this man did?"

the adjective "good" also revisits the Sabbath question (see 5:16; 9:16), about which (in other traditions) he said, "It is lawful to do good[38] on the Sabbath" (Mt 12:12; see also Mk 3:4; Lk 6:9; 13:15-16; 14:5). His point is one he has made before, in very different words: "The thief does not come except that he might steal and slaughter and destroy. I came that they might have life, and have [it] in abundance" (v. 10). His works are "good" in that they involve the giving, not the taking, of life.

33 Ignoring the irony, "the Jews" respond in all seriousness, "It's not about a good work that we are stoning[39] you, but about blasphemy, and because you, being a man, are making yourself God."[40] The charge is prompted by the pronouncement, "I and the Father are one" (v. 30). Here for a third time (just as in 5:18 and 8:53), "the Jews" take offense at what Jesus is supposedly "making himself" to be. Twice before (see 5:19-23 and 8:54-55) he explained that he was not "making himself" anything, but simply acting on behalf of his Father and allowing the Father's works to speak for him.

34-36 Jesus makes the same point again by appealing to "the works of my Father" (v. 37), but not before engaging "the Jews" on the basis of their own Scriptures: "Is it not written in your law,"[41] he asks, "that 'I said you are gods'?[42] (v. 34). The citation is word for word from Psalm 81(82):6, LXX, addressed originally to gods of other nations, rebuking them for their favoritism toward sinners and indifference to the poor (see vv. 2-4). In some traditions, both Jewish and Christian, the passage has been taken to refer to judges in Israel (perhaps on the basis of such biblical texts as Exod 21:6 and 22:7-9, 28, where the term "God" seemed to refer to the courts).[43] Jesus, for his part, goes on to identify these "gods" as those "to whom the word of God came"[44] (v. 35a), an expression more appropriate to biblical prophets than to either

38. Gr. καλῶς ποιεῖν.

39. Both references to "stoning" (λιθάζομεν here and λιθάζετε in the preceding verse) are present tense, as if the stoning were already going on. Obviously it is not (see BDF, §319, "an attempted but incomplete action"), as the purpose clause, "that they might stone" him (ἵνα λιθάσωσιν, v. 31), makes clear. At the end of the encounter (v. 39), they will settle for a less drastic measure, and even that will be unsuccessful.

40. Gr. ποιεῖς σεαυτὸν θεόν.

41. On "your law," see the discussion above on 8:17. Some early manuscripts (including P⁴⁵, ℵ, D, and the old Latin) omit "your" (ὑμῶν), possibly because of Jesus' subsequent endorsement of it as "Scripture" (v. 35), but the analogy with 8:17 ("your law") and 15:25 ("their law") supports its retention (see Metzger, *Textual Commentary,* 232-33).

42. Gr. (LXX): ἐγὼ εἶπα θεοί ἐστε.

43. "God" in these passages, as in Psalm 82:6, is אלהים, a plural form that can mean "God," "gods," or "angels" (see Ps 8:5), or human authority figures such as judges (even Moses in Exod 7:1), all depending on the context.

44. Gr. πρὸς οὓς ὁ λόγος τοῦ θεοῦ ἐγένετο.

gods or judges.[45] He quickly adds, "and the Scripture cannot be abolished" (v. 35b),[46] in effect claiming eternal validity not only for the cited text but for his interpretation of it.[47] By "the Scripture"[48] Jesus means nothing other than what he has just said to be "written in your law" (v. 34), and his acknowledgment that it "cannot be abolished" signals his acceptance of "your" law (that is, the whole of Jewish Scripture) as his own. The accent is not so much on the inerrancy of Scripture (which is, however, taken for granted by both parties) as on its everlasting authority and applicability, right down to Jesus' time.

In later Jewish traditions, the text was frequently applied to Israel as a whole, by virtue of Israel's election and reception of the law at Mount Sinai, sometimes accompanied by the warning, "But you will die like mere men; you will fall like every other ruler" (Ps 82:7, NIV).[49] It is tempting to assign such an interpretation to Jesus here as well, in view of his likely reference to the Sinai revelation in 5:37-38 ("You have never heard his voice nor seen his form, and you do not have his word dwelling in you, because he whom that One sent, him you do not believe"). While that passage has in common with the present one the mention of "the word" of God, or of the Father, and of Jesus as him "whom that One sent" (see 10:36), the reference here is more general. The expression, "those to whom the word of God came," lacks any explicit reference to the Sinai theophany, nor is there any explicit rebuke (as in 5:38), much less a warning about "dying like mere men." Whatever the precise scope and limits of Jesus' interpretation, he seems to assume that his hearers share it, at least broadly speaking, just as they share his conviction that "the Scripture cannot be abolished." On

---

45. For the construction ἐγένετο πρός, with "the word of the LORD" or "the word of God," see Jeremiah 1:2, 4, 11; Ezekiel 6:1; Hosea 1:1.

46. The comment, "and the Scripture cannot be abolished," is not simply parenthetical, but stands within the "if" clause: *If* (a) "he said that those to whom the word of God came were gods," and (b) "the Scripture cannot be abolished," *then* how can they call him a blasphemer for merely claiming, "I am the Son of God"?

47. For λυθῆναι as "abolished," compare 5:18 (regarding the Sabbath) and 7:23 (regarding the law), and see also καταλῦσαι in Matthew 5:17 (regarding "the law and the prophets").

48. Gr. ἡ γραφή, as elsewhere, literally, "the writing."

49. See, for example, *Mekilta on Exodus* (ed. J. Z. Lauterbach, 2.272): "R. Jose says: It was upon this condition that the Israelites stood up before mount Sinai, on condition that the Angel of Death should have no power over them. For it is said: 'I said: Ye are godlike beings,' etc. (Ps. 82.6). But you corrupted your conduct. 'Surely you shall die like men' (ibid., v. 7). In the Babylonian Talmud, see 'Abodah Zarah 5a, and in the Midrash Rabbah, *Exodus* 32.1, 7; *Leviticus* 4.1; 11.3; *Numbers* 7.4; 16.24; *Deuteronomy* 7.12; *Song of Songs* 1.2.5; *Ruth* 1; *Ecclesiastes* 3.16.1. Some of these references incorporate the accompanying warning about "dying like men" (Ps 82:7) and some do not.

that basis he creates his argument from the greater to the lesser. If[50] God called human beings "gods" because "the word of God" came to them, then how could his accusers say, "You blaspheme," just because he had said, "I am the Son of God"?[51] Actually, he had said no such thing explicitly, any more than he had ever told them, "I am the Christ" (see v. 25), yet in speaking again and again of God as his "Father," he had essentially made that claim.

The reader of the Gospel sees more. The mention of those to whom "the word of God came"[52] evokes for the reader the programmatic announcement, "the Word came in human flesh"[53] (1:14) — something "the Jews" at the Rededication festival know nothing about. This is in fact Jesus' only use of the phrase "the word of God" in the entire Gospel,[54] and the reader wonders: What is the relationship between this coming of "the word of God" to those whom the psalm called "gods," and the coming of Jesus the Word "in human flesh"? Robert Gundry has argued that the two "comings" are the same, so that the "gods" to whom "the word of God came" are none other than — or, at least, include — "the Jews" to whom Jesus is now speaking at the Rededication festival.[55] This interpretation is intriguing, because it could provide an appropriate postscript to Jesus' repeated warnings to "the Jews" two chapters earlier that "you will die in your sins" (8:21, 24; see Ps 82:7, "you will die like mere men"). Still, it will not do simply to identify the respective "comings," for the "coming of the word of God" to Israel corporately or to its prophets individually appears to have taken place repeatedly over centuries, while "the coming of the Word in human flesh" is by contrast an unprecedented, once-for-all redemptive event in the person of Jesus. "Those to whom the word of God came" are all Jews up to the time of Jesus, some of whom, like Moses and the prophets, received and became vehicles

---

50. For an argument from Scripture similar in form (with an "if" clause followed by a rhetorical question), but moving from lesser to greater, see 7:23, "If a man receives circumcision on the Sabbath so that the law of Moses not be abolished, you are angry at me because I made a whole man well on the Sabbath?"

51. Gr. υἱὸς τοῦ θεοῦ εἰμι. Colwell's rule applies, justifying the translation, "I am the Son of God" (rather than "a son of God").

52. Gr. ὁ λόγος τοῦ θεοῦ ἐγένετο.

53. Gr. ὁ λόγος σὰρξ ἐγένετο.

54. The only other passages in which Jesus speaks of the Father's "word" (λόγος) are 5:38, 8:55, and 17:6, 14, and 17.

55. *Jesus the Word According to John the Sectarian,* 34-35. Against the objection that Jesus would then have said, "If he called *you* gods" (italics added), Gundry is careful to admit that "the expression 'those ones' includes more people than Jesus' immediate audience, who have just taken up stones with which to stone him (10:31-33); for, again in reference to 1:11, 'he came to his own, and his own did not receive him.' His immediate audience falls short of making up the entirety of 'his own'" (36-37).

of the word, while others proved disobedient.[56] To that extent, Gundry is correct: Jesus' immediate hearers cannot be excluded. They are "gods" only implicitly, however, not explicitly. Yet even an implicit application to them serves to underscore how meaningless the designation really is. Titles do not matter, even when they are grounded in sacred Scripture that "cannot be abolished."

What matters, as Jesus will shortly reiterate (vv. 37-38), are the "works" of God that he has done. The emphasis falls, accordingly, not on such titles as "the Christ" (v. 24), or "God" (v. 33), or "the Son of God" (v. 36), which lend themselves to easy categorization, or even "the Word of God" (see 1:14). Jesus could have phrased it, "If God said that those to whom the word of God came were 'gods,' then how can you accuse the Word of God himself of blasphemy?" Instead he adopts a rather nuanced and cumbersome self-designation centering not on himself as "the Word" but on the Father. He is simply the one "whom the Father consecrated[57] and sent into the world" (v. 36). He himself is only a pronoun ("whom" in the preceding sentence). All the initiative belongs to the Father, who did the "consecrating" and the "sending." Jesus is the Father's agent, acting on the Father's behalf.

That the Father "sent" Jesus into the world is what he has been saying all along (for example, in 3:17; 5:38; 6:29, 57; 7:29; 8:42), but he adds here that the Father "consecrated" him to this mission. Thus, while avoiding the actual title, he confirms publicly what Peter and the Twelve had acknowledged to him in private, that he was "the Holy One of God"[58] (6:69). But what does "holiness" or "consecration" contribute to Jesus' mission to the world? The terminology is used in a variety of ways, but conspicuous among them is the application to priesthood and sacrifice.[59] It is worth remembering that Jesus spoke first of God having "given" his Son (3:16) by being "lifted up" on the cross (3:14), and only after that of having "sent" his Son into the world (3:17). In 6:69, Peter's recognition of Jesus as God's "Holy One" comes in the wake of his rejection by other "disciples" for having spoken so explicitly of his violent death (see 6:51-58, 60, 66).[60] And here the reference to the Father having "consecrated" him in connection with his "sending" re-

---

56. This is borne out by the correspondence between the aorist εἶπεν ("he said," echoing ἐγὼ εἶπα, "I said," in the quotation) and the aorist ἐγένετο ("If he *said* that those to whom the word of God *came* were 'gods'"). Jesus therefore does not view the quotation as a prophecy of the future (that is, of his own coming in the flesh), but as God's comment about what was already the case in the psalmist's day.

57. Gr. ἡγίασεν.

58. Gr. ὁ ἅγιος τοῦ θεοῦ, by implication the "consecrated" One.

59. See BDAG, 9-10.

60. So Bultmann (450), who cites as well Jesus' reference to his impending betrayal by Judas Iscariot (6:70).

calls the Father's "command" (v. 18) empowering him to both "lay down his life" and "receive it back again" (vv. 17-18). All of this lends a certain priestly quality to Jesus' mission, suggesting that he is "sent" specifically to offer himself as a sacrifice. This priestly aspect to his ministry will become explicit in his final report back to "the Father who sent him" (see 17:17-19).

37-38 Having demonstrated from Scripture that titles mean little or nothing, Jesus returns to his main point, his "works,"[61] which he had tried (unsuccessfully) to talk about twice before (vv. 25, 32). At the same time, he revisits previous debates, for in his first confrontation at Jerusalem he had claimed (as his "testimony greater than John's") that "the works that the Father has given me that I might complete them, the very works that I do testify about me that the Father has sent me" (5:36). And later, at the Tent festival, he had told "the Jews" that one's "works" make known one's paternity: "If you are Abraham's children, you would be doing the works of Abraham" (8:39), and "You are doing the works of your father" (that is, the devil; see 8:41-44). Applying the same principle to himself, he now invites "the Jews" to take account of his "works" and assess his parentage: "If I do not do the works of my Father, don't believe me. But if I do them, even if you don't believe me, believe the works" (vv. 37-38a). All he asks for is simple fairness, just as earlier, after an argument based on Scripture (7:22-23), he had invited the crowd in Jerusalem to "judge the right judgment" (7:24). Instead of reminding "the Jews" that they "do not believe" (v. 25), he renews his long-standing invitation to "believe," if not to believe him at least to believe his "works"[62] (v. 38a), which he has repeatedly identified as "the works of my Father" (v. 37).

These are Jesus' last words in the Gospel to "the Jews," and it is striking that after all the recrimination that has gone on through five chapters, he can still end with an open invitation to believe — plus the hope "that you might learn and know that the Father is in me and I in the Father" (v. 38b). Not since 8:32 ("and you will know the truth and the truth will set you free") has he sounded such a positive note toward "the Jews," and there it was to "the Jews who had believed him," inviting them to become "truly my disciples" (8:31). But it ended badly, with an attempted stoning (8:58), and this time will be no better. "That you might learn and know" is, literally, "that you might come to know[63] and continue to know"[64] — another way of urging them (as in

---

61. Gr. ἔργα.
62. Gr. τοῖς ἔργοις πιστεύετε.
63. Gr. ἵνα γνῶτε, aorist subjunctive.
64. Gr. καὶ γινώσκητε, present subjunctive. Some ancient witnesses have "come to believe" (καὶ πιστεύσητε, with A, Ψ, and the majority of later manuscripts) or "continue to believe" (καὶ πιστεύητε, with ℵ), probably because of the apparent redundancy of the repetition of the verb "know," but the earliest evidence (including B, P[45], P[66], and P[75]) favors the retention of γινώσκητε.

8:32) to "know the truth" by becoming his disciples. Realistically, this is not going to happen. The notion "that you might learn and know that the Father is in me and I in the Father" is not so much an actual expectation for these "Jews" at the Rededication as it is an explanation to the reader of what those who "believe" in Jesus (or in his works) can expect to know and understand by virtue of their faith. It is something of which they have not yet been told, but of which they will hear more, the mutual indwelling of the Father and the Son. "The Father is in me,"[65] Jesus claims, "and I in the Father."[66]

Mutual indwelling goes a step beyond mutual knowledge: "I know mine and mine know me," Jesus had said earlier, "just as the Father knows me and I know the Father" (vv. 14-15). But only once before (in 6:56) has he used the language of mutual indwelling, and that in relation to himself and his disciples (those who "eat his flesh" and "drink his blood"), not himself and the Father.[67] In each instance, the reference was "wasted" on its immediate audience, "the Jews," being intended instead for the reader of the Gospel. Jesus will spell it out (without quite explaining it) for the Gospel's readers four chapters later, in his farewell discourse. After expressing surprise that Philip does not yet believe that "I am in the Father and the Father is in me" (14:10), he will tell them all explicitly, "Believe me, that I am in the Father and the Father in me," adding (just as he said to "the Jews") "or if not, believe on account of the works themselves" (14:11). Finally — mystery of mysteries — he will draw even the disciples themselves into the intimate mutual relationship between himself and the Father (see 14:20; 17:21, 23).

The mystery remains, because in such expressions as "the Father is in me and I in the Father," or "You are in me and I in you," the pronoun "in" is being used in two contrasting senses. The Father is not "in" the Son in quite the same sense that the Son is "in" the Father. Nor are the disciples "in" Jesus in quite the same sense that he is "in" them. In both instances the mutuality is limited, in that the Father and the Son (much less the Son and his disciples!) do not have interchangeable roles. As we have just seen (v. 36), the Father "consecrated" and "sent" the Son into the world, not the other way around! All that can be said of the expression of mutual indwelling here is that it restates and reinforces what Jesus said earlier, "I and the Father are one" (v. 30).[68] That much even "the Jews" can grasp, and inevitably their reaction will be much the same as before.

---

65. Gr. ἐν ἐμοί.
66. Gr. ἐν τῷ πατρί.
67. Codex D, however, adds a reference to Jesus and the Father in 6:56 as well: "just as the Father is in me and I in the Father," but as we have seen, this reading is not original.
68. That mutual indwelling is essentially the same as being "one" is confirmed

39 Without hesitation "they sought to arrest him again, and he went out from their hand" (v. 39). "Again" is striking, for we must look all the way back to the Tent festival for a previous attempt to arrest Jesus (see 7:30).[69] The writer in fact repeats almost word for word the language of 7:30: "So they sought to arrest him, and no one laid a hand on him, because his hour had not yet come." Yet the circumstances of the two abortive "arrests" are quite different. The first was an official act of "the Pharisees" involving a delegation of officers (see 7:32-36, 45-47), while the present one appears to have been as impulsive and spontaneous as "lifting stones that they might stone him" a few moments before (v. 31). The reader can visualize "the Jews" still with stones in their hands at least through verse 33, and quite plausibly throughout Jesus' entire speech in verses 34-38. Now in saying "they sought to arrest him again," the writer seems to be making the point that they were simply trying to seize[70] him in order to carry out their stated intention of stoning (see v. 33). In contrast to the confrontation at the Tent festival, which began with a failed arrest (7:30) and ended with a failed stoning (8:59), stoning and "arrest" here are seen as pretty much interchangeable. This is confirmed in the next chapter, when Jesus' disciples will remind him, "Just now the Jews were seeking to stone you, and you are going there again?" (11:8). Yet the outcome is much the same as before: Jesus "went out from their hand" (v. 39),[71] just as two chapters earlier he "was hidden and went out of the temple" (8:59). Here too an exit from the temple is presupposed, though not stated (see v. 23, "in the temple, in the portico of Solomon").

40 It is tempting to view verses 40-42 as an introduction to chapter 11 rather than as a conclusion to chapter 10, because they identify where Jesus was when he first heard of the illness of his friend Lazarus in Bethany of Judea (11:1, 3), and where he waited two days before making a journey there (see 11:5). Yet the natural sequence from "he went out" (v. 39) to "he went" (v. 40) ties these next three verses more closely to what has preceded than to

---

much later in Jesus' final prayer for those who will later believe (17:21-23, italics added): "that they all might be one [ἕν], *just as you, Father, are in me and I in you,* that they too might be in us" (ἐν ἡμῖν), and "that they might be one [ἕν] just as we are one [ἕν], *I in them and you in me,* that they might be perfected into one" (εἰς ἕν).

69. The only previous attempt was the one mentioned in 7:30, and described in more detail in 7:32-36. As we have seen, in 7:44 and 8:20 the point was that no one even *tried* to arrest Jesus.

70. The verb πιάσαι can mean either "arrest" (in an official sense) or "seize" (see BDAG, 812).

71. At the same time, the phrase "from their hand" (ἐκ τῆς χειρὸς αὐτῶν) also evokes the earlier aborted arrests, in which "no one laid a hand [or "hands"] on him" (7:30, 44).

what follows.[72] The reader who wants to know where Jesus "went" when he "went out" learns the answer immediately: he "went back again across the Jordan, to the place where John was at first baptizing, and remained there"[73] (v. 40). It was also called "Bethany" (see 1:28), but the name is omitted here, concealing the odd coincidence of a journey from one Bethany to another (see 11:3, 18). It was the place where Jesus had been "with" John (3:26), where John had hailed him as "the Lamb of God" (1:29, 36) and "the Son of God" (1:34), and where he had taken up at least temporary residence (1:39) and gained his first disciples (see 1:35-51). That he "went back again"[74] and again took up residence for a time (as in 1:38-39) is therefore not surprising. But why just now?

The two sojourns at "Bethany across the Jordan" stand like bookends to Jesus' public ministry. After the rejections and attempted stonings at the Tent festival and the Rededication in Jerusalem, Jesus returns to where faith and discipleship began. Unbelief is not the end of the story. The principle that "He came to what was his own, and his own did not receive him" (1:11) still has as its sequel, "But to as many as did receive him he gave authority to become children of God" (1:12). Before the public ministry of Jesus ends, therefore, we see a kind of reenactment, brief and anonymous though it may be, of the call of his first disciples.[75] We are not told that those first disciples (now twelve in number, see 6:70) accompanied him across the Jordan. Even though he has spoken of them fondly as his "sheep" and a gift from the Father, they have not been participants in the story since the healing of the man born blind (9:2). Yet by the time Jesus learns of Lazarus's illness, their presence with him is presupposed, and the reader learns (belatedly) that they were also with him in Jerusalem (see 11:8, where they remind him of the recent attempted stoning). For the moment, attention will focus instead on a new group of believers (vv. 41-42), who will replicate the disciples' initial encounter with Jesus and (possibly) join their number.

41 To the Gospel writer, the memory of John still haunts the place

---

72. This in contrast to 9:1, where the phrase, "And as he was passing by" (καὶ παράγων), marks the beginning of a new story after Jesus "went out" from the temple (καὶ ἐξῆλθεν, 8:59). The difference is that 10:40-42 is not the new story (which begins at 11:1), but simply a transitional notice.

73. Gr. καὶ ἔμεινεν ἐκεῖ.

74. Gr. ἀπῆλθεν πάλιν. Because of his previous residence and activities there, the translation "back again" for πάλιν is appropriate (see BDAG, 752). Strictly speaking, we were not told that he "went" there before. Rather, he was there *already* when he made his first appearance in the narrative (1:29).

75. Brown puts it more eloquently (1.415): "But for the moment in a place still echoing with the cry of John the Baptist's witness and still bright with the light of his lamp (v. 35), Jesus pauses and is greeted by faith. The darkness has not yet come."

where he first baptized and bore testimony to Jesus, and where Jesus' first disciples acknowledged him as "Messiah" (1:41), "Son of God," and "King of Israel" (1:48). Even though Jesus claimed a "testimony greater than John's," the testimony of his works (see 5:33-36), and even though he has just said that titles mean little in comparison to his works (see vv. 34-38), the Gospel writer reminds us that John's testimony and the titles of Jesus to which he testified are valid as well, now confirmed in retrospect by those who heard him. When Jesus arrived, "many came to him, and they were saying that 'Though John did no sign, still everything John said about his man was true'" (v. 41).[76] They were saying this repeatedly, almost axiomatically,[77] not to Jesus but to one another, or to no one in particular. Such down-to-earth wisdom, while quite different from the divine revelation that Jesus brings, still represents the Gospel writer's viewpoint, and like other such comments in the Gospel is characteristic of those who believe in Jesus — or at least give him a fair hearing. Its closest parallel is perhaps the rhetorical question of some in the crowd at the Tent festival, "The Christ, when he comes, will he do more signs than this man did?" (7:31).[78]

The notice bristles with unanswered questions. Who were the "many" who came to Jesus? Had they been disciples of John, or were they simply residents of the place? If we assume that they were John's former disciples, their comment represents a very different perspective from those at Aenon (3:23) who had complained to John that Jesus was "baptizing, and they are all coming to him!" (3:26). Now they themselves have "come to him,"[79] and the questions multiply. Are *they* now "coming to Jesus" for baptism? Or are they simply coming to welcome him back? None of these questions are answered for us. The comment that "John did no sign" could imply an ongoing difficulty that his disciples — and others — had had with him during the course of his ministry. If some thought he was "the Christ," or "Elijah," or "the Prophet" (see 1:19-21), miraculous signs may well have been expected of him. But if this were the case, his immediate disclaimers should have lowered such expectations. Per-

---

76. See E. Bammel, "John Did No Miracles: John 10:41," in *Miracles* (ed. C. F. D. Moule; London: Mowbrays, 1965), 197-202.

77. Gr. ἔλεγον, imperfect.

78. That comment too was introduced by the imperfect ἔλεγον ("were saying"), suggesting a repeated or characteristic pronouncement. The same is true of the comment of the Samaritans to the woman who met Jesus at the well ("We no longer believe because of your speech, for we ourselves have heard and we know that this is truly the Savior of the world," 4:42), and various comments made by factions in the crowds (see 7:40-41, 9:16, and 10:21). The speeches of the man born blind (9:27, 30-33), while embodying a similar kind of wisdom and common sense, are obviously made just once, as part of a specific cross-examination, and are consequently introduced with aorist verbs.

79. Gr. ἦλθον πρὸς αὐτόν.

haps more likely, the notion that he "did no sign" arose simply out of the inevitable comparison with Jesus, who was known to have done many signs (see 2:23, 3:2, 6:2, and 7:31).[80] This does not mean that Jesus performed signs right here on the spot (as, for example, in Lk 7:21) for the benefit of those who remembered John. Nothing is said to that effect. Rather, just as he had been seen as "making and baptizing more disciples than John" (4:1), so it was by now common knowledge that Jesus performed miracles and John did not.

In any event, the point of the notice is not that "John did no sign," as if to accent the contrast between John and Jesus (that has already been amply demonstrated), but rather the affirmation that "everything John said about this man was true." "Everything"[81] embraces all that John said about Jesus at "Bethany, across the Jordan" (see 1:19-34), and probably all that he said at "Aenon near the Salim" (3:23) as well (see 3:27-36) — that is, that Jesus was "the Lamb of God" (1:29) and "the Son of God" (1:34), "the bridegroom" to whom "the bride" belonged (3:29), that he was "from above," or "from heaven" (3:31), that the Spirit was his "without measure" (3:34), that the Father loved him and gave him all things (3:35), and that only those who believe in him have eternal life (3:36). "Everything" embraces even what has not yet happened — that Jesus will "take away the sin of the world" (1:29), and "baptize in Holy Spirit" (1:33) — assuring us that these things will in fact happen.[82] In short, virtually all that we learn about Jesus in the first three chapters of the Gospel finds confirmation here, in the endorsement of John's testimony — without even using the words "testify" or "testimony."

42 The conclusion is natural, almost anticlimactic. "And many believed in him there" (v. 42) is little more than an echo of the preceding verse, "And many came to him," for in this Gospel "coming to Jesus" and "believing" in him are closely linked, in some cases almost synonymous (see, for example, 3:26; 6:35, 37; 7:37-38). "There" *(ekei)* accents once again that this was the very "place" (v. 40) where John had first baptized, and where Jesus now "remained" (v. 40) for a second time (as in 1:39).[83] The reader has never

---

80. It is possible that the mention of "signs" (σημεῖα) picks up the strong accent on Jesus' "works" (ἔργα) in the preceding debate with "the Jews" at the Rededication (see vv. 25, 32, 37-38). Jesus himself characteristically spoke of his miracles (and his deeds generally) as "works," while those who saw them (as well as the Gospel writer) tended to perceive them as "signs."

81. Gr. πάντα δὲ ὅσα, literally, "all things whatsoever."

82. This is duly noted by Lindars (378) and Brown (1.413), among others.

83. For a similar interest in particular places, using the adverb "there" (ἐκεῖ), see the author's notices at Cana (2:1, 6), Capernaum (2:12), Judea (3:22), Aenon (3:23), Sychar in Samaria (4:6), the pool of Bethsaida (5:5), certain locations in Galilee (6:3, 24), "a town called Ephraim" (11:54), Bethany near Jerusalem (12:2, 9), a garden outside Jerusalem where Jesus was arrested (18:2), and one where he was buried (19:42).

been told explicitly whether John is alive or dead, but the notice that "many believed" signals that the purpose of his mission, "that they all might believe through him" (1:7), has now been fulfilled. His work is done, and his name will not be mentioned again. Nor will we learn anything more about these new believers. Did they remain "there" *(ekei),* "across the Jordan," possibly forming the nucleus of a community known decades later to the author of the Gospel? Or did they accompany Jesus back to the other Bethany, the home of Lazarus and Mary and Martha (see 11:7-16)? Those questions too will remain unanswered.

P. GOING TO BETHANY (11:1-16)

1 *Now there was a certain man who was sick, Lazarus from Bethany, from the village of Mary, and Martha her sister.* 2 *And it was Mary, who anointed the Lord with perfume and wiped his feet with her hair, whose brother Lazarus was sick.* 3 *So the sisters sent to him, saying "Lord, look, one whom you love is sick."* 4 *And when he heard it, Jesus said, "This sickness is not toward death, but for the glory of God, so that through it the Son of God might be glorified."* 5 *Now Jesus loved Martha and her sister and Lazarus.* 6 *Then, as soon as he heard that he was sick, he remained in the place where he was two days.* 7 *Next after this he says to the disciples, "Let us go back to Judea."* 8 *The disciples say to him, "Rabbi, just now the Jews were seeking to stone you, and you are going back there?"* 9 *Jesus answered, "Are there not twelve hours of the day?* 10 *If someone walks in the day, he does not stumble, because he sees the light of this world. But if someone walks in the night, he stumbles, because the light is not in him."*

11 *These things he said, and after this he says to them, "Lazarus, our friend, has fallen asleep, but I am going that I might wake him up."* 12 *So his disciples said to him, "Lord, if he has fallen asleep, he will get better."* 13 *Now Jesus had been speaking about his death, but they thought he was speaking of natural sleep.* 14 *So then Jesus told them plainly, "Lazarus died,* 15 *and I am glad for your sake, so that you might believe, that I was not there. But now, let us go to him."* 16 *So Thomas, the one called Didymos, said to the fellow disciples, "Let us go too, that we might die with him."*

Jesus is still "across the Jordan" (10:40), where "many believed in him" (10:42). There he receives news of the sickness of his friend Lazarus, in Bethany near Jerusalem (11:3). From the start, Jesus promises that the story will not end in death, but will turn out to "the glory of God" (v. 4). The question is whether or not he will put his own life in danger by returning to Judea. The passage invites comparison with 7:1-13, where his brothers urged him to go to Judea and he finally went, but on his own initiative and only after a delay. Here, after a two-day delay, he announces his intention to go back there, and his disciples urge him not to, because of the danger (vv. 7-8). He insists that they are in no immediate danger (vv. 9-10), reasserts his intention to go (v. 11), and again invites them to join him (v. 15). Still unconvinced, they join him nonetheless (v. 16), and with that, disappear from the story.

1 The introduction of Lazarus with the words, "Now there was a certain man[1] who was sick, Lazarus from Bethany," recalls two similar introductions earlier in the Gospel. In Capernaum "there was a certain royal official whose son was sick" (4:46), and at the pool of Bethsaida "a certain man there who was thirty-eight years into his sickness" (5:5). Here as before, the Gospel writer is less than specific about the nature of the "sickness," but in contrast to the two preceding instances the "sick man" is named.[2] More than that, he is identified in relation to someone with whom the readers of the Gospel are expected to be familiar, someone named "Mary," who had a sister, "Martha." Given those names, anyone familiar with Luke's Gospel will remember Luke 10:38-39 as well, where Jesus entered "a certain village, and a certain woman by the name of Martha received him, and her sister was called Mary." John's Gospel presupposes here an acquaintance, if not with Luke's Gospel *per se,* at least with Luke's story (or some story) about these two sisters and their "village." The village is now identified as "Bethany," and Lazarus too is identified, not immediately as their brother, but first simply as someone from their village.[3]

2 "Mary," in turn, is identified as the one "who anointed the Lord with perfume and wiped his feet with her hair," and almost in the same breath

---

1. Gr. ἦν δὲ τις.
2. The coincidence of the name "Lazarus" with Jesus' story about "a certain poor man by the name of Lazarus" (πτωχὸς δέ τις ὀνόματι Λάζαρος, Lk 16:20) continues to fascinate commentators, particularly in view of that story's ending, "If they do not hear Moses and the prophets, they will not be convinced even if someone rises from the dead" (Lk 16:31). But, in contrast to the identification of Mary here (v. 2), John's Gospel shows no awareness of any such connection. For this reason, some have suggested that Luke is building on an early version of the Johannine Lazarus story rather than the other way around (see, for example, Brown, 1.429; Schnackenburg, 2.342).
3. In a somewhat similar way, the writer introduced Philip as being "from Bethsaida [ἀπὸ Βηθσαιδά], from the town [ἐκ τῆς πόλεως] of Andrew and Peter" (1:44). Notice here the same juxtaposition of ἀπό and ἐκ: "from Bethany [ἀπὸ Βηθανίας], from the village [ἐκ τῆς κώμης] of Mary, and Martha her sister." The effort of Abbott (*Johannine Grammar,* 227-29) to distinguish between ἀπό as referring to "domicile" (or residence) and ἐκ to "extraction" (or birthplace) is unconvincing.

we learn that "it was Mary . . . whose *brother* Lazarus was sick" (v. 2, italics added). Mary is mentioned not just because she and Lazarus lived in the same village, but because Lazarus was her own brother (and therefore Martha's as well). Anyone reading the Gospel for the second or third time will notice that the reference to Mary "anointing the Lord with perfume" anticipates a story to be told in the next chapter (see 12:3), but what is the first-time reader to make of it? It makes no sense at all to such a reader, *unless* the Gospel writer is assuming some familiarity with a narrative other than his own, just as in the preceding verse he seems to assume familiarity with some kind of story about "Mary and Martha."

There are two such stories in the canonical Gospel tradition, one in Luke 7:36-50 and one in Mark 14:3-9 (paralleled in Mt 26:6-13). In each of these, the woman who anoints Jesus is anonymous, but the second is located specifically in Bethany, and, perhaps more significantly, is said to be a story destined to be told and retold (see Mk 14:9 and Mt 26:13). Readers acquainted with the telling of that story in *some* form — not necessarily Mark's version, or Matthew's — would be able to appreciate the Gospel writer's comment that the woman who anointed Jesus at Bethany was in fact none other than Mary, sister to Martha, probably familiar as well from another story now found in Luke, and that the "sick man" here at Bethany was in fact their brother. A small world indeed! Still, there are discrepancies. The anonymous woman in Mark and Matthew anoints Jesus' head, not his feet, with perfume (see Mk 14:3 and Mt 26:7), and consequently nothing is said about her "wiping his feet with her hair." Those very details, however, are present in Luke's story (set not in Bethany of Judea, but in Galilee, in the house of a Pharisee named Simon) about a prostitute who abruptly brought in "an alabaster jar of perfume," stood behind Jesus weeping and "began to wet his feet with her tears, . . . wiped them with her hair, kissed them and poured perfume on them" (see Lk 7:37-38, NIV). The story to which John's Gospel refers (for the full story, see 12:1-8) preserves the setting of Mark's account, yet with a number of details preserved not in Mark or Matthew, but in Luke's story about the prostitute.[4] This suggests that John's Gospel is drawing not on any one Gospel's account, but on one of the many retellings to which Jesus refers in Mark 14:9 and Matthew 26:13. He offers no hint that the woman who anointed Jesus was "a woman who had lived a sinful life" (Lk 7:37, NIV), and he differs from both other accounts in giving her a name and placing her in a family that Jesus knew well (Lk 10:38-42) and "loved" (see vv. 3, 5). The

---

4. These include the verbs "anointed" (ἡ ἀλείψασα) and "wiped" (ἐκμάξασα), and the nouns "feet" (τοὺς πόδας) and "hair" (ταῖς θριξίν). Only the noun "perfume" (μύρῳ) is common to all three (see Barrett, 390, who also notes the perfect correspondence between the Gospel writer's vocabulary here and in 12:3).

point of the notice is simply to inform the reader who Lazarus was and why his sickness matters.

3 The story of Lazarus, the "certain man who was sick" (v. 1), is linked to Jesus at his retreat across the Jordan by a notice that "the sisters sent to him, saying, "Lord, look, one whom you love is sick" (v. 3). We are not told how they knew where Jesus was, nor are we introduced to the messengers. Nor do the sisters ask Jesus in so many words to come. Instead they content themselves with a simple statement of fact, not unlike his mother's remark at the Cana wedding that "They have no wine" (2:3). Their comments to Jesus later on (see vv. 21 and 32) reveal that their message was indeed (like his mother's) an implied request. They did expect him to come, and sooner than he did, but the wording of their message reflects a certain almost familial intimacy, and a confidence that he would know what to do. It stands in striking contrast to the very explicit plea of the royal official at Capernaum, a stranger to Jesus, who said, "Lord, come down before my little child dies!" (4:49). Lazarus is not named, but identified simply as "one whom you love."[5] The masculine pronoun is expected to make clear to Jesus that Lazarus is meant. He is the first individual Jesus is explicitly said to have "loved" in this Gospel, although "Martha and her sister" are added almost immediately (v. 5), and one of his disciples is singled out in later chapters as one "whom he loved" (13:23; see also 19:26; 20:2; 21:7, 20).[6]

4 On hearing the message, "Jesus said, 'This sickness is not toward death, but for the glory of God, so that through it the Son of God might be glorified.'" To whom was he speaking? Above all, to the reader of the Gospel, but to whom within the actual narrative? Possibly to his disciples, although at this point there is no evidence that his disciples are even present. They have not been mentioned since 9:2, and do not make an appearance here until verse 7. He could have been speaking to the "many" new disciples who had "believed in him" here across the Jordan (10:42), but there is no way to verify this, for nothing more is said about them. More likely, his words represent an answer to the message he has just received, an answer sent back by messenger to the two sisters in Bethany. This too is unverified for the moment, but appears to be verified later on, when Jesus reminds Martha, "Did I not tell you that if you believe you will see the glory of God?" (v. 40). The only place he could have "told" her such a thing was here, with the assurance

---

5. Gr. ὃν φιλεῖς.
6. In v. 5 and in 13:23 the verb is ἠγάπα. The two verbs for "love," φιλεῖν and ἀγαπᾶν, appear to be used interchangeably (see, for example, 3:35 with 5:20, and 13:23 with 20:2). Some have speculated that the unnamed disciple was none other than Lazarus himself, after he had been raised from the dead. This could explain 21:23, yet no satisfactory reason has ever been given as to why he would have been named here and later left anonymous.

that her brother's sickness was not "toward death,[7] but for the glory of God." Then, explaining what "the glory of God" means, he continues, "so that through it [that is, the sickness] the Son of God might be glorified."

There is more here than the sisters can hope to understand, and much to misunderstand. On the face of it, the promise that Lazarus's sickness was not "toward death" seemed to imply that he would not die, when in fact he would die, and may have been already dead (see vv. 11-14).[8] Jesus will resolve this issue with Martha later (see vv. 25-26), but for the moment at least his words are misleading. The sisters, as practicing Jews, would presumably have understood "the glory of God," and Martha at least will shortly demonstrate a knowledge that "the Son of God" is Jesus (see v. 27). But what would they have made of the prospect that he would be "glorified"[9] (v. 4), much less that it would happen because of their brother's sickness? Jesus has promised nothing of the kind before. Only the Gospel writer, in one narrative aside, has mentioned his "glorification" (see 7:39, "because Jesus was not yet glorified"), and only a few remarks in passing at the Tent festival (7:18; 8:50, 54) have even hinted at a mutual "glorification" of the Father and the Son. Jesus will make it all clearer later on (see 12:23, 28; 13:31-32; 17:1, 4-5), but for the time being it is a riddle even to the first-time reader of the Gospel, and much more so to Martha and Mary. The missing link is the thought that Jesus' "glorification," like his "exaltation" or "lifting up" (3:14; 8:28; 12:32-33), comes to realization paradoxically in his death on the cross (see 12:23-24).[10] Ironically, the sickness that Jesus says is not "toward death" as far as Lazarus is concerned will in the end result in *his own* death, and consequently in his "glorification" — for "the glory of God."

5 Like his reply to his mother at the Cana wedding (2:4), Jesus' reply here (v. 4) could suggest that he was content to let matters take their course. But this is no more the case now than it was then. He does plan to take action, but in his own time and his own way. He will do so, the Gospel writer assures us, because he "loved Martha and her sister and Lazarus" (v. 5). The comment reinforces and validates the message of the sisters that

---

7. Gr. πρὸς θάνατον.

8. For the expression, "toward death" (πρὸς θάνατον), see 1 John 5:16, with its distinction between sins "toward death" (πρὸς θάνατον) and "not toward death" (μὴ πρὸς θάνατον). There, however, spiritual, not physical, death seems to be in view.

9. Gr. ἵνα δοξασθῇ.

10. In all the other instances which speak of the Jesus' "glorification" or "exaltation," the operative title is "Son of man" (3:14; 8:28; 12:23; 13:31), not "Son of God." Jesus in fact rarely uses the full term, "Son of God," for himself, preferring "the Son" or "the Son of man" (see only 3:18, 5:25, and 10:36). A likely reason for "Son of God" here is the wordplay between "the glory *of God*" (τοῦ θεοῦ) and "the Son *of God*" (τοῦ θεοῦ) being "glorified" (italics added).

"one whom you love is sick" (v. 3),[11] making it clear that Jesus loved not only Lazarus but the two sisters as well. Initially, Mary was introduced first and then Martha in relation to her, because Mary was presumed to be known to the readers on other grounds (see vv. 1-2). But now that this has been established, Martha is mentioned first and Mary only as "her sister," without repeating the name. Lazarus is named last because Jesus' love for him is already a given (v. 3), and the accent is now on Jesus' response to the communication just received from the sisters. Of the two, possibly Martha was presumed to have been primarily responsible for the message to Jesus because he says to her later, "Did I not tell you that if you believe you will see the glory of God?" (v. 40).

6 The comment that "Jesus loved" the sisters and Lazarus (v. 5) was necessary in part because what comes next could suggest the opposite. On hearing that Lazarus was sick, Jesus "remained in the place where he was two days" (v. 6). Why the delay, if Jesus "loved" them? Part of the answer, as we have just seen, is surely his determination not to have his hand forced by the wishes of others (besides 2:4, see also 7:6-9). Moreover, anyone who knows the end of the story might well suspect that he waited until Lazarus had died so as finally to raise him from the dead instead of merely healing him, thus adding to "the glory of God." This appears to be confirmed on his arrival when first Martha (v. 21) and then Mary (v. 32) say to him, "Lord, if you had been here, my brother would not have died," and some of "the Jews" who came to comfort them complain that Jesus, having opened a blind man's eyes, could have "made it so that this man would not die" (v. 37). Yet when Jesus arrives at Bethany, Lazarus is already "four days in the tomb" (v. 17). Even if he had left immediately, and therefore arrived two days sooner, Lazarus would have been at least two days dead.[12] Still more to the point, the healing of Lazarus seems not to have depended on the actual presence of Jesus, given the precedent of the healing of the royal official's son (see 4:50). If Jesus could heal a total stranger from a distance, why not a dear friend?

The point of the delay, therefore, must lie elsewhere. The notice is very precise, both as to time and place: "Then . . . he remained in the place where he was[13] two days." "The place where he was" is clearly "across the

---

11. As we have seen (above, n. 6), the two different words for "love" are synonymous (D and two old Latin witnesses have ἐφίλει for ἠγάπα here, conforming the text to verse 3, but this is clearly secondary).

12. This is clear from verse 14, where Jesus, after just two days, "told them plainly, 'Lazarus died.'" The calculation does not depend on the distance between the two Bethanys, which is uncertain because of the uncertainty of the location of "Bethany across the Jordan."

13. Instead of "in the place where he was (ἐν ᾧ ἦν τόπῳ), some ancient manuscripts (including P⁴⁵, D, and the Sinaitic Syriac version) have a simpler reading, ἐπὶ τῷ

Jordan, . . . the place where John was first baptizing," where Jesus had "remained" already for an indefinite length of time (10:40; that is, Bethany: see 1:28), and where "many came to him" and "there" believed (10:41-42). The interval of "two days" recalls Jesus' visit to Sychar in Samaria, where the Samaritans who had just "believed in him" (4:39) then "asked him to stay with them, and he stayed there two days."[14] The question there was why Jesus left after the "two days." The question here is why he waited "two days" before leaving. What the two passages have in common is a possible obligation on Jesus' part to stay on for a measurable length of time (however brief) to nurture the faith of "many" (4:39; 10:41) who "believed in him." That is, Jesus seems to have "entrusted himself" to the Samaritans at Sychar and to these believers "across the Jordan" here in a way he did not to those whose faith he did not accept as genuine (see 2:24-25). These ties cannot be broken instantly, even though both the itinerant character of Jesus' ministry,[15] and here more specifically Jesus' love for "Martha and her sister and Lazarus" (v. 5), dictate that they must in fact be broken. Consequently, Jesus "remained in the place where he was," but for only "two days."

7-8 After the two days, we read, "Next after this he says to the disciples, 'Let us go back to Judea'" (v. 7). This is the only place in the Gospel where the question of going to Judea or Jerusalem comes up in connection with something other than one of the Jewish festivals. The command, "Let us go,"[16] is one that Jesus will repeat more than once as his ministry draws to a close (see v. 15; also 14:31), each time summoning his disciples to a decisive crisis or confrontation (see also Mk 14:42).[17] Perhaps sensing this, they say to him, "Rabbi, just now the Jews were seeking to stone you, and you are going back there?" (v. 8). This is the first we hear of "the disciples" being present with Jesus "across the Jordan." Clearly, "the Twelve" who have been his disciples all along are meant (see 6:70), not the "many" who have just now be-

---

τόπῳ ("at the place"). Its attestation is meager but diverse. If it is original, its connection to "the place" mentioned in 10:40 is viewed as self-evident, but the better-attested reading suggests that the Gospel writer went out of his way to make the link to 10:40-42 explicit.

14. More distantly, the reader will remember Jesus' sojourn with his first disciples at that very place across the Jordan on "that day" (or, rather, part of a day, 1:39), and more generally the series of days marking the call of those first disciples at "Bethany across the Jordan" (see 1:29, 35, 43; 2:1).

15. On the latter, see my article, "The Itinerant Jesus and His Home Town," in *Authenticating the Activities of Jesus* (ed. B. D. Chilton and C. A. Evans; Leiden: Brill, 1999), 177-93.

16. Gr. ἄγωμεν.

17. Only Mark 1:38 comes early in Jesus' ministry, and even there the same urgency and sense of mission are evident in Jesus' conclusion, "for that is what I came out to do" (NRSV).

lieved (10:42).[18] This is evident both from Jesus' language, "Let us go back[19] to Judea," implying that they had been there before, and from their awareness that "just now the Jews were seeking to stone you" (see 10:31). The reader learns (belatedly) that "the Twelve" had been with Jesus all along, even though not mentioned.[20] As for the "many" who believed in Jesus "across the Jordan," like the Samaritans at Sychar they will not be heard from again.

Here as elsewhere "the Jews" are the Jewish religious authorities, but with a geographical reference as well: Jesus should hesitate to go back to "Judea," his disciples are saying, because "the Jews"[21] are seeking to take his life. Even though "the Jews" challenged him in Galilee as well (6:41, 52), only in Judea (more specifically, Jerusalem) have they tried to kill him (see 5:18; 7:1; 8:37, 40, 59; 10:31). To go back there is to put his life in danger. Unlike his brothers in Galilee, who urged him to "Leave here, and go to Judea" so as to "reveal yourself to the world" (7:3-4), his disciples fear for his safety — and possibly their own. Ironically, if Lazarus's illness is indeed "for the glory of God, so that through it the Son of God might be glorified" (v. 4), the advice of Jesus' unbelieving brothers would have been more appropriate!

9-10 In his longest speech so far here on the other side of the Jordan, Jesus replies, "Are there not twelve hours of the day?[22] If someone walks in the day, he does not stumble, because he sees the light of this world. But if someone walks in the night, he stumbles, because the light is not in him." On the face of it, this is simply a long and elaborate way of saying, "My hour has not yet come" (2:4; see also 7:30 and 8:20). At the same time it echoes what he said to these same disciples earlier in the presence of the man born blind, about the need to "work the works of the One who sent me as long as it is day. Night is coming when no one can work" (9:4). The point is the same here. The "hour" of Jesus' death is drawing ever nearer. When it is finally announced (12:23, 27; 13:1), it will come as no surprise but as some-

---

18. This is in keeping with the address, "Rabbi," or "Teacher," which the disciples have used from the start, with the single exception of 6:68, where Simon Peter on their behalf addressed Jesus as "Lord." Interestingly, it was at that point that Jesus first called them "the Twelve" (6:70). In this chapter, the terminology changes to "Lord," on the lips of the disciples (v. 12), Mary and Martha (see vv. 3, 21, 27, 32, 34, 39), and the disciples consistently thereafter (see 13:6, 9, 25; 14:5, 8, 22; 21:15, 16, 17, 20, and above all 20:28). Jesus, however, endorses both titles (13:13), and the distinction should not be exaggerated (see v. 28, where Martha refers to him as "the teacher," and 20:16).

19. Gr. πάλιν.

20. This is further verified by the mention of "Thomas" (v. 16), identified still later as "one of the Twelve" (20:24).

21. Gr. οἱ Ἰουδαῖοι.

22. "Twelve hours" because "the day" does not mean a twenty-four-hour period, but rather daylight or daytime, "the period between sunrise and sunset" (BDAG, 436).

thing signaled well in advance. But until then, Jesus is perfectly safe. Just as at the Cana wedding, there is still time to act (see 2:4), and just as in the case of the man born blind, there is still "work" to be done (see 9:4-5). Only when "night" comes (see 13:30) is Jesus in danger.

But is this the full extent of what he is saying? The reader will notice that he drives the point home not with the customary "I" pronouncement (such as "*My* hour has not yet come"), but with a kind of parable, centering not on himself but on "someone" or "anyone" (v. 10).[23] What is true of his mission, he implies, is true of everyone. A person who walks in daylight can see where he is going and will not stumble, but a person who walks at night is at risk because "the light is not in him."[24] Once the pronouncement is set free from its present context, it is no longer about Jesus (or at least not *just* about him), but about the disciples themselves, or about anyone who hears his message. As he told them earlier, "Night is coming when *no one* can work" (9:4b, italics added). Later, in a very different setting, and with "light" and "darkness" rather than "day" and "night" as the operative metaphors, this interpretation will assert itself: "Yet a short time the light is in you. Walk while you have the light, lest darkness overtake you, and the person who walks in the darkness does not know where he is going" (12:35). The notion of "walking in darkness" or "in the light" (see 8:12; also 1 Jn 1:6-7; 2:11) introduces ethical connotations which are not present here in connection with "walking in the day" or "in the night." Here, Jesus is speaking of ordinary sunlight, "the light of this world," not "the Light of the world" as he claimed to be in his own person (see 8:12; 9:5). His disciples could infer from his language that they too were safe for the time being, until their own appointed "hour" of danger and possible death (see 16:2, 4, 21).

11 Jesus' speech continues, but the Gospel writer is careful to create an interval separating the metaphor he has just used (vv. 9-10) from the one he will now introduce: "These things he said,[25] and after this he says to them, 'Lazarus, our friend, has fallen asleep,[26] but I am going that I might wake him up'" (v. 11). The designation of Lazarus as "our friend"[27] echoes the message

---

23. Gr. ἐάν τις (v. 9); ἐὰν δέ τις (v. 10).

24. Gr. τὸ φῶς οὐκ ἔστιν ἐν αὐτῷ. A similar expression, "the light that is in you" (τὸ φῶς τὸ ἐν σοί) is characteristic of the synoptic Jesus as well; see Matthew 6:23 and Luke 11:35, where, however, in contrast to John's Gospel, it refers to the eye.

25. This and similar expressions are used to summarize significant speeches of Jesus (or others) in this Gospel, or to negotiate transitions from speech back to narrative or to more speech; see, for example, ταῦτα εἶπεν (6:59), ταῦτα εἶπαν (9:22), ταῦτα εἰπών (7:9; 9:6; 11:43; 13:21; 18:1), ταῦτα ἐλάλησεν (12:36; 17:1), ταῦτα εἰποῦσα (20:14), or (on Jesus' own lips) ταῦτα λελάληκα (14:25; 15:11; 16:1, 4, 6, 25, 33).

26. Gr. κεκοίμηται.

27. Gr. ὁ φίλος ἡμῶν.

from the sisters that "one whom you love is sick" (v. 3), but the pronouncement makes no sense when taken literally. If Lazarus were merely sleeping, he would be awake by the time Jesus arrived at Bethany, and would not need Jesus to wake him! Jesus' language is no more realistic here than in the house of Jairus in Mark when he said of Jairus's daughter, "The child is not dead, but sleeps" (Mk 5:39). As in that case, the reader is expected to understand that "sleep" is a metaphor for death. Jesus is announcing his plan to raise Lazarus from the dead. Sleep was a familiar metaphor for death in the ancient world even when no resurrection was expected, and it becomes all the more so in Judaism and early Christianity in light of a firm resurrection faith.[28] The principle that "he himself knew what he was going to do" (6:6) is presumed to be still in effect.

12-13 Like those who were present at the raising of Jairus's daughter (see Mk 5:40), Jesus' disciples take the reference to "sleep" literally: "Lord,[29] if he has fallen asleep, he will get better" (literally, "he will be saved").[30] That is, sleep will be good for him, and he will recover. Jesus will not have to risk his life by going to Judea (see v. 8). The Gospel writer intervenes in his customary way to explain what may have been obvious to most readers: "Now Jesus had been speaking about his death, but they thought he was speaking of natural sleep."[31] For the moment, readers of the Gospel — even the less perceptive ones who needed the narrative aside — are one step ahead of the disciples within the story.

14-15 The disciples are quickly brought up to speed, as "Jesus told them plainly, 'Lazarus died'"[32] (v. 14). "Plainly" or "openly,"[33] translated elsewhere as "publicly" (see 7:4, 26), refers here to literal as opposed to metaphorical speech (see 10:24; also 16:25, 29, where it is explicitly contrasted with speech "in parables" or metaphors).

What he says next is not so clear, either to the disciples or to the reader: "and I am glad for your sake, so that you might believe, that I was

---

28. See BDAG, 551; Keener, 2.840-41 (New Testament examples using the same verb include Mt 27:52; Acts 7:60; 13:36; 1 Cor 7:39; 11:30; 15:6, 18, 20, 51; 1 Thess 4:13-15; 2 Pet 3:4).

29. In addressing him as "Lord" (κύριε), they depart from their customary use of "Rabbi" (v. 8), anticipating the title that Mary and Martha have used (v. 3) and will use later in the chapter (see vv. 21, 27, 32, 34, 39). "Lord" then becomes the dominant title by which Jesus' disciples address him in the remainder of the Gospel (13:6, 9, 25; 14:5, 8, 22; 21:15, 16, 17, 20; see above, n. 13).

30. On this meaning for σωθήσεται, see 5:34, and BDAG, 982.

31. Literally, "of the sleep of slumber" (περὶ τῆς κοιμήσεως τοῦ ὕπνου, see BDAG, 551).

32. Gr. ἀπέθανεν.

33. Gr. παρρησίᾳ.

not there" (v. 15).[34] He seems to be assuming what Lazarus's sisters will tell him when he arrives (vv. 21, 32), that if he had been with Lazarus in Bethany, Lazarus would *not* have died, and he is "glad" that this was not the case — that is, that Lazarus did in fact die. Jesus is "glad," he tells the disciples, not for Lazarus's sake nor for his own, but "for your sake," and he explains immediately what he means by this: "so that you might believe." The disciples have "believed" before (2:11; 6:69), but he addresses them as if he wants them to "believe" now for the first time.[35] In the subsequent narrative, the disciples are never explicitly said to "believe" (in fact, they are not even said to be present), but others do believe: first Martha (v. 27), and then "many of the Jews" who had come to comfort her and her sister (vv. 42, 45; see also v. 48).[36] Jesus' rather obscure pronouncement (v. 15) must be read in light of the equally mysterious message he sent back to the sisters earlier: "This sickness is not toward death, but for the glory of God, so that through it the Son of God might be glorified" (v. 4). Jesus is "glad" he was not "there"[37] because he knows that if he had been present he would not have been willing to allow his friend to die. From a distance he had a choice. He could either have healed Lazarus as he healed the royal official's son (4:50), or he could have allowed nature to take its course. He chose the latter, knowing that the death of Lazarus had a dual purpose: first, "so that . . . Son of God might be glorified" (v. 4), and then, as far as the disciples are concerned, "so that you might believe" (v. 15). These purposes can only come to realization if death is not the end of the story — that is, if Lazarus rises from the dead, as Jesus implied when he said, "Lazarus . . . has fallen asleep, but I am going that I might wake him up" (v. 11). In such a case, Lazarus's illness is *not* after all "toward death," but "for the glory of God," just as Jesus promised (see v. 4).

Without pausing to find out whether or not the disciples have grasped

---

34. The commas in the translation are to be taken seriously. The clause set off by commas, "so that you might believe," is parenthetical. The clause, "that I was not there," goes with "I am glad," not with "believe," which is used absolutely here without an object.

35. The aorist subjunctive (ἵνα πιστεύσητε) could suggest this. See Augustine, *Homilies on the Gospel of John* 49.11, who, while admitting that "He made use of such an expression as if only then they would begin to believe," interpreted it "as meaning, that your faith might be fuller and more vigorous" (NPNF, 1st ser., 7.274). Bultmann agrees that the comment is made "as if 2.11 had not preceded it," but insists that "There is no interest in the development of the disciples" (400, n. 4), and that "Understanding comes to them only after he has left them" (195, n. 2).

36. See Barrett (393), who mentions verses 42, 45, and 48, but not the "belief" of Martha in Jesus as "the Son of God" (v. 27).

37. For ἐκεῖ ("there") with reference to Judea (or Bethany), see verse 8 ("and you are going back *there?*"), in contrast to 10:40 and 42, where ἐκεῖ refers to "the place where he was," across the Jordan (see v. 5).

all this, Jesus concludes with something they will have no difficulty understanding: "But now,[38] let us go to him"[39] (v. 15), echoing verse 8, "Let us go back to Judea." The choice of words is striking. He does not call his disciples to go to Mary and Martha to comfort them, but "to him," that is, to Lazarus himself, as if he were not dead.[40] Again, Jesus' language is consistent with — if it does not actually require — a clear intention to raise Lazarus from the dead.

16 As in 6:68, the disciples respond through a spokesman, not Simon Peter this time but someone not named before, "Thomas, the one called Didymos" (v. 16).[41] "Didymos" meant "twin," but nothing is made of the name.[42] Only later is Thomas further identified as "one of the Twelve" (20:24). Here he speaks not to Jesus but "to the fellow disciples."[43] "Let us go too, that we might die with him." Thomas proposes, echoing Jesus' words, "Let us go to him" (v. 15). The command, "Let us go too," sounds strangely redundant, as if Thomas were somehow speaking to a different group, that is, "we too"[44] in addition to Jesus and those he has just addressed.[45] But no other group is present. Thomas and his "fellow disciples" can hardly be distinguished from "the disci-

---

38. Gr. ἀλλά, here with the force not so much of a strong adversative as simply the strengthening of an accompanying command: "now then," or "so then" (see BDAG, 45).

39. Gr. ἄγωμεν πρὸς αὐτόν.

40. According to Barrett (393), "as if Lazarus were still a living person" (see also Hoskyns, 401).

41. "The one called" (ὁ λεγόμενος) can be used in a variety of ways, either to introduce the translation of a proper name or title, or to join two equivalent names or titles (for example, 4:25).

42. Both "Thomas" (Θωμᾶς) and "Didymos" (Δίδυμος) were Greek proper names. It was unusual to have two Greek names, but the Hebrew word for "twin" (as is often noted) was $t^e\bar{o}m$ (תאום), Aramaic $t^e\bar{o}m\bar{a}$ (תאומא). This was not a proper name in Hebrew, but possibly a Jew who was known to be a twin would have been given the name "Thomas" (Θωμᾶς) because of the similarity of sound. "Didymos" might then have been added to his name, either as the Greek translation of a supposedly "Hebrew" name, or simply as a kind of nickname identifying him as a twin. In certain later traditions, Thomas was identified with Jude or Judas, the brother of Jesus (see Mk 6:3), and was thought to be Jesus' own twin (see *Acts of Thomas* 31, where the serpent says, "For I know that thou art the twin brother of Christ, and dost ever abolish our nature"; Hennecke-Schneemelcher, 2.459; also *Gospel of Thomas* 1, 'These are the secret sayings which the living Jesus spoke and which Didymos Judas Thomas wrote down'; *The Nag Hammadi Library in English*, 126). But there is nothing of this in John's Gospel.

43. Gr. τοῖς συμμαθηταῖς.

44. Gr. καὶ ἡμεῖς.

45. It is as if he were responding not to verse 15 but to what Jesus said in verse 11: "I am going [πορεύομαι] that I might wake him up." The scene would then be comparable to 21:3, where Simon Peter says, "I am going fishing," and the other disciples say, "We too [καὶ ἡμεῖς] are coming with you."

ples" mentioned in verses 7, 8, and 12.[46] Therefore Thomas is addressing the same group, seconding what Jesus has just said — yet with a shocking difference. Instead of simply "going to" Lazarus for an undisclosed purpose (as in v. 15), Thomas urges them to go "that we might die with him."[47]

Die with whom? With Lazarus, or with Jesus? Commentators almost unanimously agree that Thomas is urging his fellow disciples to die with Jesus.[48] A few admit that a reference to Lazarus is "grammatically possible" even though "highly improbable."[49] In fact, however, the reference to Lazarus is more than "grammatically possible." It is, if not grammatically certain, at least the more natural way of reading of the text. The reasons are, first, Thomas's stated intent "that we might die with him" (v. 16) echoes Jesus' announcement, "Lazarus died"[50] (v. 14). Despite the presumed danger (v. 8), nothing has been said explicitly about Jesus "dying." Second, the pronouns in Jesus' pronouncement and that of Thomas are the same, and the reader has a right to expect the same antecedent. Jesus urged that the disciples go "to him" (v. 15), that is, to Lazarus, and Thomas wanted them all to die "with him" (v. 16). Moreover, in the next verse we will learn that when Jesus arrived in Bethany he found "him"[51] already four days in the tomb" (v. 17). If the first and third of these pronouns refer clearly to Lazarus, it is unnatural to assume that the middle one abruptly refers to Jesus! Consequently the conventional wisdom of commentators should be reversed. It is "grammatically possible" that Thomas speaks of dying with Jesus, but more likely that "with him"[52] means with Lazarus.

---

46. As we have seen, Jesus' language in verse 7 and the language of "the disciples" in verse 8 rules out the possibility that Jesus was addressing the "many" who had "believed in him" across the Jordan.

47. Gr. ἵνα ἀποθάνωμεν μετ' αὐτοῦ.

48. See, for example, Barrett (394), Brown (1.432), Bernard (2.381), Sanders and Mastin (267), Beasley-Murray (189), Hoskyns (401), Schnackenburg (2.328), Keener (2.842), Carson (410), Whitacre (283), and Bultmann (400, n. 4), who regards the view that "with him" refers to Lazarus as "bizarre." Only Lindars (392) hints at a possible reference to Lazarus, and that inconclusively: "To go back into Judea is to court danger of death (verse 8), and so to share in the fate of Lazarus. He expresses the loyalty of a true disciple, but he does not know that the disciple must share the death and Resurrection of his Master." Estimates of Thomas's motivation and insight range from "resignation" and "blind devotion" (Bultmann) to "an incredible picture of faith" (Whitacre). The ambivalence of commentators is best illustrated by Barrett, who comments, "His proposal, though it shows courage and devotion to the person of Jesus, shows also a complete failure to grasp the significance of Jesus' death as it is presented in John" (394).

49. See Morris, 484; also Moloney, 337.

50. Gr. Λάζαρος ἀπέθανεν.

51. Gr. αὐτόν.

52. Gr. μετ' αὐτοῦ.

If Thomas is referring to Lazarus, what does it tell us about Thomas and his faith? Obviously it puts him at odds with Jesus' opening statement that "This sickness is not toward death, but for the glory of God, so that through it the Son of God might be glorified" (v. 4). As far as Thomas is concerned, the sickness of Lazarus *is* "toward death," both for Lazarus himself and for Jesus and the disciples — consequently *not* "for the glory of God." His is a counsel not of faith but of unbelief and despair, for he has failed to grasp either the prospect that "the Son of God might be glorified" (v. 4), or the meaning of Jesus' promise that "I am going that I might wake him up" (v. 11).[53] So despite his words, "Let us go too," which imply that they did accompany Jesus to Bethany, he and his fellow disciples disappear at this point and are not seen again until Jesus withdraws to a town called Ephraim near the desert, where he remained "with the disciples" (v. 54). Jesus had expressed to them the hope "that you might believe" (v. 15), but nothing is said of their faith (or even their presence) at the raising of Lazarus. Jesus' hope is fulfilled instead by Martha (vv. 27, 40), and by "many of the Jews" who had come to comfort her and her sister Mary on their brother's death (see v. 45). They, not the disciples, "believed."

Q. THE RAISING OF LAZARUS, AND ITS CONSEQUENCES (11:17-54)

> 17 *So, when Jesus had come, he found him already four days in the tomb.* 18 *Now Bethany was near Jerusalem, some fifteen stadia away.* 19 *And many of the Jews had come to Martha and Mary, that they might comfort them about the brother.* 20 *So Martha, as soon as she heard that Jesus was coming, met him, while Mary was sitting in the house.* 21 *Then Martha said to Jesus, "Lord, if you had been here, my brother would not have died.* 22 *Even now, I know that whatever you ask God, God will give you."* 23 *Jesus said to her, "Your brother will rise."* 24 *Martha said to him, "I know that he will rise in the resurrection at the last day."* 25 *Jesus said to her, "I am the Resurrection and*

---

53. Although the reader is not yet aware of it, Thomas's pronouncement (v. 16) is consistent with his character as revealed in later passages. His acknowledgment that "Lord, we don't know where you are going. How can we know the way?" (14:5) renders suspect the notion that his willingness to travel with Jesus implied any real understanding of Jesus' mission. And his determination not to believe the testimony of his fellow disciples to Jesus' resurrection (20:24) confirms his failure to understand the necessity "that the Son of God might be glorified." This rather consistent development of Thomas's character makes his final confession, "My Lord and my God!" (20:28) all the more striking as a turning point.

the Life. The one who believes in me, even if he dies, will live, 26 and everyone who lives and believes in me will never ever die. Do you believe this?" 27 She said to him, "Yes, Lord, I believe that you are the Christ, the Son of God, who is coming into the world."

28 And having said this, she went and summoned Mary her sister, and told her privately, "The Teacher is here, and is summoning you." 29 And she, as soon as she heard, got up quickly and was coming to him. 30 Now Jesus had not yet come into the village, but was still in the place where Martha met him. 31 So the Jews who were with her in the house and were comforting her, when they saw that she had risen quickly and gone out, followed her, thinking that she was going to the tomb to cry there. 32 Then Mary, as soon as she came to where Jesus was and saw him, fell at his feet saying to him, "Lord, if you had been here, my brother would not have died." 33 So Jesus, as soon as he saw her crying, and the Jews who had come with her crying, got angry in the spirit and shook himself. 34 And he said, "Where have you laid him?" They said to him, "Lord, come and see." 35 Jesus wept. 36 Then the Jews were saying, "See how he loved him." 37 But some of them said, "Could not this man who opened the eyes of the blind man have made it so that this man would not die?" 38 So Jesus, again angry within himself, comes to the tomb. It was a cave, and a stone was lying against it. 39 Jesus says, "Lift the stone." The sister of the deceased, Martha, says to him, "Lord, already it stinks, for it has been four days!" 40 Jesus said to her, "Did I not tell you that if you believe you will see the glory of God?" 41 So they lifted the stone, but Jesus lifted his eyes upward and said, "Father, I thank you that you heard me. 42 And I knew that you always hear me, but I said [it] for the sake of the crowd standing around, so that they might believe that you sent me." 43 And when he had said these things, he shouted in a great voice, "Lazarus! Out!" 44 The one who had died came out, bound with bandages on his feet and hands, and his face wrapped in a cloth. Jesus said to them, "Loosen him, and let him go."

45 So then, many of the Jews, those who had come to Mary and seen the things he had done, believed in him. 46 But some of them went off to the Pharisees and told them the things Jesus had done. 47 So the chief priests and the Pharisees gathered council and were saying, "What do we do because this man is doing many signs? 48 If we let him go on like this, they will all believe in him, and the Romans will come and take away both our place and our nation." 49 But a certain one among them, Caiaphas, being Chief Priest of that year, said to them, "You don't know anything! 50 Don't you realize that it is to your advantage that one man die for the people, and the whole nation not

11:17-54 THE RAISING OF LAZARUS, AND ITS CONSEQUENCES

be lost?" 51 *And this he did not say on his own, but being the Chief Priest of that year he prophesied that Jesus was going to die for the nation,* 52 *and not for the nation alone, but in order that the children of God who are scattered might also be gathered into one.* 53 *So from that day they resolved that they would kill him.* 54 *Then Jesus would no longer walk openly among the Jews, but he went from there to the region near the desert, to a town called Ephraim, and there he remained with the disciples.*

On his arrival in Bethany, Jesus is greeted three times with the comment that he could have kept Lazarus from dying — by Lazarus's sisters, Martha (v. 21), and Mary (v. 32), and by a group of Jews who had come to comfort the sisters (v. 37). Martha comes out to meet Jesus and confesses her faith in him (vv. 20-27). Mary comes later (v. 29), and "the Jews" follow her. Jesus is angry and troubled by the situation (vv. 33, 35, 38), but in the end he prays a prayer of thanksgiving (vv. 41-42) and calls Lazarus from the tomb (vv. 43-44). At this, "the Jews" are divided: some "believe," while others report what has happened to the Pharisees (vv. 45-46). A council is called, and at the urging of Caiaphas, the High Priest, a decision is reached. If Jesus' ministry in Jerusalem up to this point is viewed as a trial (see, for example, 5:31-47; 8:12-20, 21-59), this scene can be understood as the handing down of the verdict: Jesus must die. There is no formal trial of Jesus before the Sanhedrin in this Gospel, and no other declaration of a verdict. In the wake of this decision, Jesus flees for an undetermined length of time to a town "near the desert" called Ephraim (v. 54), but his sojourn there is temporary. The stage is set for the last Passover (v. 55), and for Jesus' passion. No further trial is needed, and none will be forthcoming.

17 Nothing is said of the actual journey to Bethany. Only a participle[1] signals that "Jesus had come" there, and no mention is made of Thomas and the other disciples. On his arrival, Jesus "found him [that is, Lazarus] already four days in the tomb."[2] This can only be read as a kind of heading for the whole section to follow, at least up to verse 39.[3] Jesus cannot have come immediately to the tomb, for as late as verse 34 he is still asking, "Where have you laid him?"[4] The point is simply to set the stage for the

---

1. Gr. ἐλθών.
2. Literally, "having [been] in the tomb already four days" (compare 5:5, "a certain man there who was thirty-eight years in his sickness" (literally, "having [been] thirty-eight years in his sickness"; for the construction, see BDAG, 422).
3. For a similar heading to something spelled out later, see 7:30 ("So they sought to arrest him, and no one laid a hand on him") in relation to 7:32-36, 45-46.
4. Bultmann also notices this (401, n. 1): "V. 17 sounds as though Jesus has come directly to the grave, which would be in contradiction to vv. 34, 38."

627

eventual raising of Lazarus. In case we forget we will be reminded of it just before the miracle, when Martha says to Jesus at the tomb, "Lord, already it stinks, for it has been four days!" (v. 39).

Why the mention of "four days," not once but twice? Commentators often cite a Jewish tradition that "For three days [after death] the soul hovers over the body, intending to reenter it, but as soon as it sees its appearance change, it departs."[5] The tradition is late, and not widely attested, but in the earlier oral law, if a body was to be identified, it had to be done within three days of death, on the theory that otherwise the changes produced by decay would preclude certainty.[6] It is doubtful that such traditions shed much light on the present passage, or would even have been familiar to readers of John's Gospel. If the intent of the reference was to certify that Lazarus was truly dead, the detail of "four days" seems both confusing and unnecessary. Confusing because a Christian reader might be prompted to ask, "Was Jesus *not* truly dead because he was raised within three days?" And unnecessary because the reality of Lazarus's death is nowhere an issue within the story. Not only has Jesus pronounced him dead, and that "plainly" (v. 14), but he is, after all, "already in the tomb," a detail well beyond what is told either in Mark's story of Jairus's daughter (Mk 5:21-43) or Luke's account of the raising of the widow's son at Nain (Lk 7:11-17). One may assume that he would have been just as dead after two days, or one, as after four. The best explanation for the accent on "four days," therefore, is that this is simply the way the story was remembered and handed down. But from a literary standpoint, the notice also serves to prepare the reader for Jesus' stark confrontation with death as decay and uncleanness when he finally stands before the tomb (see v. 39).

18-19 At this point the Gospel writer inserts a narrative aside: "Now Bethany was near Jerusalem, some fifteen stadia away" (v. 18).[7] The reader might have expected to be told the distance from where Jesus had been, across the Jordan, to Bethany, but instead learns the much shorter distance between Bethany and Jerusalem.[8] The likely reason is that the Gospel writer

---

5. *Leviticus Rabbah* 18.1 (*Midrash Rabbah* [London: Soncino, 1961], 4.226); see also *Genesis Rabbah* 100.7 (2.995): "Until three days [after death] the soul keeps on returning to the grave, thinking that it will go back [into the body]; but when it sees that the facial features have become disfigured, it departs and abandons it [the body]."

6. See the Mishnah, *Yebamot* 16.3; "Evidence [of the identity of a corpse] may be given only during the first three days [after death]," even while adding, "but R. Judah b. Baba says: [Decay in corpses is] not alike in all men, in all places, and at at all times" (Danby 244).

7. "Fifteen stadia" would have been just under two miles (see BDAG, 940).

8. Oddly, Chrysostom seems to have assumed that the distance given was the distance Jesus had to travel to reach Bethany, rather than the distance between Bethany and

knows this distance but not the other, because he is unsure of the precise location of the other Bethany "across the Jordan" (see 1:28; 10:42). The reason for the notice is probably to explain the presence in Bethany of "many of the Jews" who "had come to Martha and Mary that they might comfort them about the brother" (v. 19).[9] The fact that their presence in Bethany needs to be explained (most of the residents of Bethany were presumably "Jews" in any case) suggests that they were no ordinary "Jews," but more specifically Jews from Jerusalem,[10] possibly religious leaders linked in some way to the temple. Because Bethany was as close as it was to Jerusalem, it was feasible for people from Jerusalem to come and join in the mourning over Lazarus.[11] The notice is surprising because the last we heard of "the Jews" or "Judeans" was that they were seeking to stone Jesus (v. 8). This group of "Jews" will be heard from again (see vv. 31, 33, 35, 45-46), and the Gospel writer wants to explain from the start why they were so conveniently present.

20 Jesus' entry into Bethany to raise Lazarus from the dead anticipates, first, his triumphal entry into Jerusalem a chapter later (see 12:12-19), and, second, his future coming to earth to raise the dead (see 1 Thess 4:15-17; 1 Cor 15:23, 51-52). He "comes"[12] like a conquering hero, yet to a "village" (v. 1) rather than a great city, and not publicly to the whole village but privately to a family he knows and loves (v. 5). Martha's response evokes the picture of early Christians anxiously awaiting the "coming" of Jesus, for "as soon as she heard that Jesus was coming," she "met him"[13] outside the village (see v. 30), as if to escort him the rest of the way in.[14] Mary, by contrast, re-

---

Jerusalem: "But if Bethany was 'fifteen furlongs off,' which is two miles, how was Lazarus 'dead four days'?" (*Homilies on John* 62.2; ANF, 1st. ser., 14.228).

9. Some ancient manuscripts (including A, Ψ, K, Δ, Θ, possibly P[45], and the majority of later manuscripts) read instead, "who had come to *those [women] who were around* [αὐτὰς περί] Martha and Mary" (italics added): that is, presumably household servants or women friends (for the construction, see Mk 3:34; 4:10; Acts 13:13). This appears to be either a correction prompted by the oddity of one article (τήν) governing both "Martha" and "Mary," or (alternatively) a mistake caused by the combination αὐτὰς περί further on in the sentence (see Metzger, *Textual Commentary*, 233-34).

10. This was at any rate the presumption of one ancient manuscript (D), which read ἐκ τῶν Ἰεροσολύμων ("from Jerusalem") instead of ἐκ τῶν Ἰουδαίων ("of the Jews").

11. Here they are said to have come to "comfort" the sisters (παραμυθήσονται), and in v. 31 specifically Mary (παραμυθούμενοι), while in v. 33 they join Mary in "crying" (κλαίοντας). On consolation and mourning as a ritual custom in early Judaism, see Keener, 2.842-43; G. Stählin, *TDNT*, 5.821.

12. Gr. ἔρχεται.

13. Gr. ὑπήντησεν αὐτῷ.

14. In a well-known article, Erik Peterson, citing 1 Thessalonians 4:17, argued that the language of "meeting" (εἰς ὑπάντησιν or εἰς ἀπάντησιν) was a technical term for "a civic custom of antiquity whereby a public welcome was accorded by a city to impor-

mained "sitting in the house," presumably the house shared by the sisters and possibly Lazarus as well. Too much should not be made of the contrast between the sisters, which is surely derived in part from Luke 10:38-42. Mary seems to have remained at home not because she was less eager to welcome Jesus, but because she had not yet learned of his arrival (see v. 29, where she too, "as soon as she heard, got up quickly and was coming to him").[15]

21-22 Martha greets Jesus with the words, "Lord, if you had been here, my brother would not have died" (v. 21; compare v. 32). Her remark could be read either as a mild rebuke or as a tribute to Jesus' love and power to heal. Her added comment, "Even now,[16] I know that whatever you ask God, God will give you" (v. 22), suggests that it is the latter. As we have seen, even if Jesus had left immediately on receiving her message, Lazarus would still have died, and he could have kept Lazarus from dying without actually coming to Bethany (see, for example, 4:50). It is unclear precisely what Martha expects to happen "even now," but like Jesus' mother at the Cana wedding she trusts him to act (see 2:5), and she "knows," like the man born blind (see 9:31), that whatever Jesus accomplishes he will accomplish through prayer. His method of raising Lazarus from the dead (11.41-42) will bear her out. Her certainty that "whatever you ask God, God will give you" lays a basis for Jesus' own promises to his disciples later in the Gospel that "whatever you ask the Father in my name he will give you" (16:23; see also 14:13-14; 15:7, 16; 16:26-27).[17]

---

tant visitors. Similarly, when Christians leave the gates of the world, they will welcome Christ in the ἀήρ, acclaiming Him as κύριος" (*TDNT*, 1.380-81; also "Die Einholung des Kyrios," *Zeitschrift für systematische Theologie* 7 [1929/30], 682ff.). But caution is needed because a verbal expression (ὑπήντησεν αὐτῷ) is used here, not the more ceremonious εἰς ὑπάντησιν. Even though Martha's intent is to escort Jesus into the village, probably no more is meant by the actual words used than that she "met him." Still, the language does anticipate that of the triumphal entry, when the crowd welcomed Jesus and escorted him into Jerusalem (εἰς ὑπάντησιν αὐτῷ, 12:13; ὑπήντησεν αὐτῷ, 12:18).

15. See Chrysostom, *Homilies on St. John* 52.3: "[Martha] was not more zealous, but it was because the other had not yet been informed, since Martha was the weaker" (ANF, 1st ser., 14.229, citing Lk 10:42 and Jn 11:39).

16. Gr. καὶ νῦν. Some textual witnesses (including P[45], P[66], the corrector of ℵ, A, D, and the majority of later manuscripts) add ἀλλά before καὶ νῦν: "*But* even now." Without the addition, her words could be translated simply "and now," losing the adversative force of verse 22. While ἀλλά is probably not original (the best manuscripts, including P[75], ℵ, and B, do not have it), it likely supplies the correct interpretation of καὶ νῦν (that is, as "Even now," rather than "And now").

17. It is worth noting that Martha, in speaking of Jesus' prayers, uses the same verb for "ask" (αἰτεῖν) that the Gospel writer commonly uses for the prayers of Jesus' disciples. But when Jesus himself prays, his prayer either takes the form of a thanksgiving (as in 11:41), or else a different verb for "ask" (ἐρωτᾶν) is used (as in 14:16; 16:26; 17:9, 15, 20).

23-24 Jesus' reply gives concreteness to Martha's "whatever you ask God" (v. 22). "Your brother will rise,"[18] he promises (v. 23). The reader will recall Jesus' stated intention to go to Lazarus "that I might wake him up" (v. 11), but Martha had not heard those words. At most, she may have heard back from Jesus that "This sickness is not toward death, but for the glory of God, so that through it the Son of God might be glorified" (v. 4). This would have been enough to explain her confidence (v. 22), that somehow everything would turn out for the best. But all she can muster by way of particulars is "I know that he will rise in the resurrection at the last day" (v. 24). Once more, Martha is distinguished by what she "knows," and what she knows is again (as in v. 22) presumed to be true. Lazarus *will* "rise in the resurrection at the last day" (see 5:28-29), and Jesus' words, "Your brother will rise" (v. 23), *could* mean just that, and nothing more. But if that is the case, the reader still remembers that Jesus promised earlier (not once but four times) concerning those who believed that he himself would "raise him [or it] at the last day" (see 6:39, 40, 44, 54). But Martha's comment that Lazarus will "rise in the resurrection at the last day" exhibits no awareness of Jesus' unique role in that great future event. As a Jew (evidently influenced by a Pharisaic belief in the resurrection), the two things she "knows"[19] amount finally to the same thing. That is, all she can imagine for her brother is that Jesus' prayers for him will assure him a place among the righteous "at the last day," when the dead are raised.

25-26 Jesus next enlarges Martha's horizons with yet another of his characteristic "I am" pronouncements. "I am the Resurrection and the Life," he tells her. "The one who believes in me, even if he dies, will live, and everyone who lives and believes in me will never ever die" (vv. 25-26). In contrast to his previous "I am" sayings, which were uttered twice ("the Bread of life," 6:35, 47; "the Light of the world," 8:12; 9:5; "the Door," 10:7, 9; "the good Shepherd," 10:11, 14), this one occurs only once, but with two predicates, "the Resurrection"[20] and "the Life."[21] The first echoes Martha's own reference to "the resurrection at the last day" (v. 24); the second predicate ("the Life") defines what "resurrection" actually means for the believer, whether now or in the future.[22] The other "I am" sayings with their predicates were generally followed by an invitation or promise introduced by a relative

---

18. Gr. ἀναστήσεται.
19. Gr. οἶδα, vv. 22 and 24.
20. Gr. ἡ ἀνάστασις.
21. Gr. ἡ ζωή. This is not the case in all ancient witnesses, for the words "and the life" (καὶ ἡ ζωή) are omitted in P[45], the Sinaitic Syriac, and certain church fathers, possibly because Martha in verse 24 mentions only the resurrection of the dead. But the longer reading is to be preferred (see Metzger, *Textual Commentary*, 234).
22. Although John's Gospel knows of resurrection both "of life" (ζωῆς) and "of judgment" (κρίσεως; see 5:29), only the former is in view here (see 5:24-25).

or conditional clause, or a participle (see, for example, 6:35; 8:12; 10:9). This time, with two predicates, there are also two promises: first, "The one who believes in me, even if he dies, will live" (v. 25); second, "everyone who lives and believes in me will never ever die" (v. 26).[23] It is natural to view the first as the corollary of "I am the Resurrection," and the second as the corollary of "I am the Life." Thus,

(a) *I am the Resurrection* — *that is, the one who believes in me, even if he dies, will live.*
(b) *I am the Life* — *that is, everyone who lives and believes in me will never ever die.*

No such schematization is explicit, however. Both of the promises, each with its implied invitation to "believe," arise out of the two-pronged predicate: "I am the Resurrection and the Life." More to the point, the second promise follows logically from the first. If it is true that the person who believes in Jesus and died (in this case Lazarus) will live again — whether immediately or "in the resurrection at the last day" (v. 24), then it follows that no living believer will ever die — ultimately. They may die physically, like Lazarus, but death's dominion is only temporary, for Jesus himself ("the Resurrection and the Life") will "raise them at the last day" (see 6:39, 40, 44, 54). With this, Jesus explains (in retrospect) his claim to "the Jews" at the Tent festival, "Amen, amen, I say to you, if anyone keeps my word, he will never ever see death" (8:51). It is worth noting that Jesus is not promising Martha in so many words that he will raise Lazarus from the dead that very day. Nothing that he says necessarily goes beyond what she already believed — that Lazarus would rise in the final resurrection — *except* the claim that in order to rise from the dead a person must "believe in me."[24] The issue was not the nature of resurrection, or whether it would take place now or later, but simply the role of Jesus in the gift of resurrection and eternal life. When Jesus concludes by asking, "Do you believe this?" (v. 26), he is asking simply, "Do you believe in me?"[25]

---

23. For the redundant (and therefore emphatic) expression, "never ever die" (οὐ μὴ ἀποθάνῃ εἰς τὸν αἰῶνα), compare, for example, 8:51 ("never ever see death"), and 4:14 ("never ever thirst").

24. See 8:51 and 52, 'If anyone keeps *my* word'; also 5:24, "the person who hears *my* word"; 5:25, "the dead will hear the voice *of the Son of God*"; 5:28, "all who are in the tombs will hear *his* voice" (italics added).

25. Schnackenburg (2.332) reminds us that this is "the only time in the fourth gospel that πιστεύειν governs an accusative," but is careful to add that faith's content is "what Jesus means for believers, and therefore faith is fundamentally an attachment to this messenger of God (εἰς αὐτόν)." This is borne out by 1 John 4:16, the one other Johannine instance (which Schnackenburg also mentions in passing) of πιστεύειν with the accusative.

11:17-54 THE RAISING OF LAZARUS, AND ITS CONSEQUENCES

27 Martha understands this, and answers accordingly: "Yes, Lord, *I* believe[26] that *you* are the Christ, the Son of God, who is coming into the world" (v. 27, italics added). Both the emphatic pronouns and the perfect tense of the verb "believe" recall the confession of Peter on behalf of the Twelve (6:69), implying a settled conviction. Moreover, the content of the two confessions ("the Holy One of God" in the first instance, and "the Christ, the Son of God" here) can probably be assumed to be more or less equivalent. The parallel hints that, at least within the present narrative, Martha (and perhaps her sister Mary as well) have displaced the absent Thomas and his fellow disciples as "believers" or "disciples," and as witnesses to the miracle that Jesus will perform. The two titles Martha has chosen, "the Christ" and "the Son of God," have been fairly conspicuous in Jesus' debates with "the Jews" all along,[27] but are now drawn together here for the first time. Even though Jesus has insisted that titles do not matter as far as his claims are concerned (see 10:34-36), it appears that they do matter as far as believers and readers of the Gospel are concerned. Martha's confession matches almost word for word the very confession the Gospel writer wants to elicit from all his readers (see 20:31, "that you might believe that Jesus is the Christ, the Son of God, and that believing you might have life in his name"). All Martha adds is the further characterization of Jesus as the one "coming into the world."[28] In the immediate context, her comment picks up the preceding notice that "as soon as she heard that Jesus was coming" (v. 20), she went out to meet him. Within the narrative, his "coming" to Bethany to raise the dead stands for his "coming into the world" for the same purpose, whether now or in the future.[29] The intent is not to fix the time of his "coming," present or future, but to define him as "the Coming One,"[30] who does not belong to the world but invades it from the outside (specifically "from above"),[31] to transform or overcome it. Jesus does not respond to her confession of faith, but simply allows it to stand, as he did the confession of the Samaritan villagers (4:42), and the faith of the man born blind (9:38).[32]

28 Perhaps surprisingly, Martha does not escort Jesus into the vil-

---

26. Gr. ἐγὼ πεπίστευκα (perfect, translated as present).

27. For "the Christ," see 7:26, 27, 31, 41, 42; 9:22; and 10:24, and for "the Son of God," see 5:18-25 and 10:36.

28. Gr. ὁ εἰς τὸν κόσμον ἐρχόμενος.

29. In a similar way, his "coming" on a donkey into Jerusalem at the triumphal entry (12:12) identifies him as "the one coming in the name of the Lord" as Israel's king (12:13, 15).

30. See, for example, 1:9, 15, 27, 30; 3:31; 4:25; 6:14; 7:31, 41, 42; 12:13, 15, 46; 14:3, 28; 16:28; 21:22-23.

31. See 3:31, ὁ ἄνωθεν ἐρχόμενος, and ὁ ἐκ τοῦ οὐρανοῦ ἐρχόμενος.

32. Contrast his explicit responses to the confessions of Nathanael (1:50-51), and of Simon Peter and the Twelve (6:70).

lage (see above, n. 14), but returns to her sister Mary in the house (see v. 20), leaving Jesus "still in the place where Martha met him" (v. 30). It is important to her that her sister have a part in welcoming Jesus. So, having made her confession, "she went and summoned Mary, and told her privately, 'The Teacher is here, and is summoning you'" (v. 28). The very language of "summoning"[33] suggests resurrection (see 12:17, where Jesus is said to have "summoned Lazarus from the tomb and raised him from the dead").[34] As far as we know, Jesus had not "summoned" Mary or told Martha to do so (as he told the Samaritan woman, 4:16), yet Martha takes it on herself to "summon" her sister on Jesus' behalf, possibly because she and Mary had acted together from the start in informing Jesus of Lazarus' illness (v. 3), and she wanted the two of them to see things through together. Her language reminds us that the living, no less than the dead, are "summoned" to life by the voice of Jesus (see 5:24, 25; 10:3-4, 27). Martha is careful to speak "privately"[35] to her sister in view of the presence of certain "Jews" who "had come to Martha and Mary, that they might comfort them about the brother" (v. 19). This is confirmed by the fact that when Mary leaves, these "Jews" do not understand at first that she is going out to meet Jesus (see v. 31). Martha's identification of him as "the Teacher" further confirms the sisters' common identity as disciples (see 1:38; 13:13), and the notice that he "is here"[36] may evoke for some readers the common Christian expectation of Jesus' "coming" or *parousia*."[37]

29 Mary, "as soon as she heard,"[38] acted just as Martha had done (v. 20). She "got up quickly[39] and was coming to him" (v. 29). Again, the choice of words hints at resurrection ("got up"),[40] while at the same time con-

---

33. Gr. φωνεῖν.

34. See also the use of the word "voice" (φωνή) in connection with resurrection (v. 43; also 5:25, 28; 1 Thess 4:16; Rev 11:12).

35. Gr. λάθρᾳ.

36. Gr. πάρεστιν.

37. For παρουσία, a word that never occurs in John's Gospel, see Mt 24:3, 27, 37; 1 Cor 15:23; 1 Thess 2:19; 3:13; 4:15; 5:23; 2 Thess 2:1, 8; Jas 5:7, 8; 2 Pet 1:16; 3:4; 1 Jn 2:28). In Barrett's words (397), "It seems not impossible, but more cannot be said."

38. The same phrase, ὡς ἤκουσεν, occurs here and in v. 20.

39. Instead of the aorist ἠγέρθη, some textual witnesses (including P[45], P[66], A, Θ, the majority of later Greek manuscripts, and the Vulgate) have the present ἐγείρεται, but the aorist (with P[75], ℵ, and B, C, D, L, W, and others) is probably to be preferred as the more difficult reading. Most of the manuscripts with the present have also changed the imperfect ἤρχετο, "was coming," in the next clause to a present (ἔρχεται), suggesting a certain discomfort with the abrupt change in tense from aorist to imperfect.

40. "Got up" is ἠγέρθη (or ἐγείρεται; see n. 39 above), literally "woke up," or "was raised." For this verb as a verb of resurrection, see 2:19, 22; 5:21; 12:1, 9, 17; 21:14. Here it is interchangeable with the verb ἀνέστη (v. 31), also conspicuously a verb of resurrection in this Gospel (see vv. 23 and 24; also 6:39, 40, 44, 54; and 20:9).

11:17-54 THE RAISING OF LAZARUS, AND ITS CONSEQUENCES

firming the impression that Mary, like her sister and Lazarus, was a believer ("coming to him").[41] She acts "quickly" to make up for lost time, matching her sister's prompt response to the "coming" of the "Coming One." The imperfect, "was coming to him," sustains the note of haste, raising the reader's level of expectation. What will Mary say to Jesus? What happens next?

30-31 The writer keeps us in suspense with two narrative asides, one about Jesus and one about "the Jews" who were earlier said to have "come to Martha and Mary" to comfort them (see v. 19). Jesus, we are reminded, "had not yet come into the village, but was still in the place where Martha met him" (v. 30). Thus Mary, in "coming to him" (v. 29), was returning to the place from which Martha had come to fetch her. Whether or not Martha accompanied her we are not told. Presumably she did, because she is present later at the tomb of Lazarus (vv. 39-40), but for the moment the narrative focuses not on her but on Mary, and on "the Jews who were with her in the house and were comforting her" (v. 31a). This group of "Jews," we are told next, "when they saw that [Mary] had risen quickly[42] and gone out, followed her, thinking[43] she was going to[44] the tomb to cry there" (v. 31b). They had evidently remained with Mary in the house when Martha went out to meet Jesus (v. 20), and they obviously have not overheard the "private" (v. 28) exchange between the two sisters. Consequently, they are mistaken about Mary's immediate destination, but in "following her," they will stumble into what would otherwise have been a private exchange between Jesus and Mary (or between Jesus and both sisters).

32 Finally, after the two narrative asides (vv. 30-31), we learn that Mary, "as soon as she came to where Jesus was and saw him, fell at his feet saying to him, 'Lord, if you had been here, my brother would not have died'" (v. 32), repeating almost word for word what Martha had said earlier (v. 21).

---

41. On "coming to" (or "toward") Jesus (ἔρχεσθαι πρός) as an act of belief, or allegiance to him, see, for example, 3:21, 26; 6:35, 37; 7:37.

42. "Had risen quickly" (τάχεως ἀνέστη) echoes "got up quickly" (ἠγέρθη ταχύ, v. 29). No different nuance of meaning is intended.

43. "Thinking" (δόξαντες) is almost certainly the original reading (see ℵ, B, C, D, L, W, and in effect P⁷⁵, with its obvious accidental error, δοξάζοντες). The variant, "saying" (λέγοντες, with P⁶⁶, A, Θ, Ψ, and a majority of later manuscripts) could, as Metzger suggests, "have arisen when it was asked how the evangelist could have known the thoughts of the Jews" (*Textual Commentary*, 234), but it may also have come about as a result of the common use of "saying" in the Gospel, and the (mistaken) impression that the following clause was direct rather than indirect discourse. Thus, "saying that 'She is going to the tomb to cry there.'" The Gospel writer (like Jesus himself!) does not hesitate at times to tell what his characters are "thinking" (see v. 13; also 13:29).

44. Εἰς τὸ μνημεῖον would normally be translated "into the tomb," but (as Barrett notes) "In Hellenistic Greek εἰς encroaches upon the use of ἐπί and πρός (398; also BDF, §207[1], Abbott, *Johannine Grammar*, 241-42).

She stops there, however, without the words Martha had added, "Even now, I know that whatever you ask God, God will give you" (v. 22). Consequently, there is no exchange of words between Jesus and Mary, and no explicit confession of faith (as in v. 27). Instead, at the very outset we are told that when she first saw Jesus and spoke to him, she "fell at his feet." This is an act thoroughly characteristic of Mary of Bethany, for wherever she meets Jesus in the Gospel tradition she is at his feet (see v. 2; 12:3; Lk 10:39). Here it is her wordless confession of faith,[45] one that she will later repeat (see 12:3-8).

33 Jesus' reaction is surprising, for "as soon as he saw[46] her crying, and the Jews who had come with her crying," he "got angry[47] in the spirit and shook himself"[48] (v. 33). The language of the verse raises all kinds of questions. We have just learned that Mary fell at Jesus' feet, but we have not been told up to now that she was "crying" (Martha had not cried as far as we know), nor is it at all clear why her crying and that of "the Jews" would have made Jesus "angry" — to the point that he "shook" with anger.[49] Two verses later we will learn that Jesus himself "wept," and that this was viewed as a sign of his great love for Lazarus (vv. 35-36). Why then should the "crying" over Lazarus have made him angry?

Most English translations simply dodge the problem by concealing the reference to anger.[50] Jesus was not angry, they imply, just "deeply moved in spirit and troubled" (RSV, NIV, TNIV), or "deeply disturbed in spirit and deeply moved" (NRSV).[51] But most commentators acknowledge that Jesus is

---

45. We may compare, perhaps, the man born blind when he said, "I believe, Lord," and prostrated himself before Jesus (9:38).

46. Gr. ὡς εἶδεν. By this time the reader will have noticed the repeated expressions with ὡς in this narrative: ὡς ἤκουσεν ("as soon as he heard," v. 6, and "as soon as she heard," vv. 21, 29), ὡς ἦλθεν ("as soon as she came," v. 32), and ὡς εἶδεν ("as soon as he saw," v. 33). All these lend pace and expectancy to the story.

47. Gr. ἐνεβριμήσατο.

48. Gr. ἐτάραξεν ἑαυτόν.

49. It is uncertain whether the "shaking" is physical or simply emotional, but inasmuch as Jesus' anger is "in the spirit" (ἐνεβριμήσατο τῷ πνεύματι), it appears likely that "shook himself," by contrast, refers to his outward physical expression of that inward anger.

50. Even some very early manuscripts (including D, possibly P⁴⁵, and a corrector of P⁶⁶) attempted to soften the reference with the reading ἐταράχθη τῷ πνεύματι ὡς ἐμβριμούμενος ("he was troubled in the spirit *as if* angry"), tacitly acknowledging that the verb did imply anger.

51. See also the KJV, ASV ("he groaned in the spirit and was troubled"), NEB ("he sighed heavily and was deeply moved"). Only a few translations do justice (in varying degrees) to Jesus' anger: for example, NAB ("perturbed and deeply troubled") and REB ("moved with indignation and deeply distressed"), but especially the NLT ("a deep anger welled up within him, and he was deeply troubled").

indeed said to have been "angry," both here and in verse 38.[52] The meaning of the verb is scarcely open to question.[53] The mistake of many translators is to ask prematurely the question, "Why would Jesus be angry?" instead of, "What does the verb actually mean?" Still, once the meaning is established, the question, "Why *was* Jesus angry?" will not go away, and the answers are varied. To some, he was angry at the hypocrisy of "the Jews," or their unbelief — and possibly Mary's unbelief as well.[54] Why were they "crying"? Did they not understand what he was about to do? To still others, he was angry in the face of death, viewed as evidence of the presence of Satan and Satan's dominion, perhaps in anticipation of his own impending encounter with death in the garden of Gethsemane.[55]

None of these answers is entirely satisfactory. Nothing in the text suggests that the crying of "the Jews" (much less of Mary) was in any way hypocritical. Nor are "the Jews" as a group guilty of unbelief, for after the miracle we learn that "many" of them "believed" in Jesus (even though some did not, vv. 45-46). As for the personification of death or the presence of Satan, it is not yet an issue in the Gospel — if it ever is. No sooner do we hear of "the ruler of this world" than we learn that he has been "thrown out" (12:31; see also 14:30; 16:11). Satan will carry out his futile work through Judas Iscariot (13:2), but he has not yet entered Judas (see 13:27), and in any case we have no evidence that Judas is even present until his cameo appearance in the next chapter (12:4). Yet without question Jesus' anger *is* provoked by the sight of Mary "crying, and the Jews who had come with her crying" (v. 33a).[56] Mary, as we have seen, "fell at his feet" (v. 32), and the picture of her "crying" there vaguely recalls a scene in Luke in which a woman "stood behind him at his feet crying, and began to wipe his feet with the tears" (Lk 7:38). Within John's Gospel, it anticipates — for a second time (see 11:2) — the scene a chapter later in which Mary "anointed the feet of Jesus, and wiped his feet

---

52. See, for example, Brown (1.425-26), who nevertheless shies away from it in his translation ("he shuddered, moved with the deepest emotions"); also Schnackenburg, 2.335-36; Barrett, 399; Bultmann, 406; Carson, 415; Hoskyns, 404. Others straddle the fence, and some follow the English translations in downplaying the anger in favor of extreme sorrow or distress (see, for example, Bernard, 2.393; Sanders and Mastin, 271-72; also Lindars, 398-99, who attributes the anger to John's source).

53. See BDAG, 322, who is able to offer many parallels for the meaning "to be angry," but none for the meaning "to be deeply moved."

54. For unbelief or lack of faith as the explanation, see Schnackenburg, 2.336; Bultmann, 406; Hoskyns, 405; Beasley-Murray, 193; Keener, 846. Among modern commentators, the hypocrisy of "the Jews" is mentioned only as an option to be rejected (see, for example, Barrett, 398).

55. See, for example, Brown, 1.435; Westcott, 2.96; Whitacre, 389.

56. The verbs are κλαίουσαν and κλαίοντας, respectively.

with her hair" (12:3). It is a tender and emotional moment, even though Mary merely repeats what Martha had said earlier. Her comment, "Lord, if you had been here, my brother would not have died" (v. 32b), should have introduced an exchange between her and Jesus, as it had done earlier between Jesus and Martha, but it does not. The presence of these "Jews" (see vv. 19, 31) comes as an intrusion, an invasion of privacy ending the encounter, and this could be the reason for Jesus' anger.[57] The Gospel writer may have provided a clue earlier, in the notice that when Martha first summoned Mary, she spoke to her "privately"[58] (v. 28), out of earshot of these "Jews." Jesus' opportunity to do the same is now spoiled by their presence. We can only guess what he might have said to her. Would it have been simply a replay of verses 23-27, or something quite different? Instead, the miracle story runs its course, and Mary disappears (for the time being) from the narrative.

The notion that privacy was the issue has not been explored in the commentaries, but there are hints outside of John's Gospel that this might be the case. For example, the only two occurrences in the synoptic Gospels of the verb "to be angry"[59] occur in connection with the so-called "secrecy phenomena": after Jesus cleansed the leper in Mark, he "*sternly warned* him" and sent him away, saying, 'See that you say nothing to anyone'" (Mk 1:43-44), and when he opened the eyes of two blind men in Matthew, he "*sternly warned* them, 'See that you let know no one know'" (Mt 9:30, italics added).[60] Both of these orders were disobeyed (Mk 1:45; Mt 9:31), but along with other data (particularly in Mark) they testify to Jesus' characteristic desire for privacy in his so-called "public" ministry. This desire is not confined to texts involving the so-called "messianic secret."[61] Jesus seems to have valued his privacy in a variety of situations and probably for a variety of rea-

---

57. Moloney makes gestures in this direction, but in the end reads the story quite differently: "To this point in the narrative nothing has been said of the tears or the mourning of Mary. Only 'the Jews' are reported as mourning (vv. 19, 31). Now, after a demonstration of authentic belief in Jesus, she turns away from him in tears to join 'the Jews.' Will no one come to belief?" (330). At the end of the day he stands with those who see "unbelief" or lack of faith as the central issue.

58. Gr. λάθρᾳ.

59. Gr. ἐμβριμᾶσθαι.

60. This text in Matthew has no parallel in Mark, suggesting that Jesus' concern for privacy or secrecy (whatever its motivation) is not simply a Markan creation.

61. Barrett (399) finds in Jesus' anger an expression of something akin to the Markan "messianic secret": "Jesus perceives that the presence and grief of the sisters and of the Jews are almost forcing a miracle upon him, and as in 2.4 the request for miraculous activity evokes a firm, almost rough, answer; here, in circumstances of increased tension, it arouses his wrath. This miracle it will be impossible to hide (cf. vv. 28, 30); and this miracle, Jesus perceives, will be the immediate occasion of his death (vv. 49-53)."

11:17-54 THE RAISING OF LAZARUS, AND ITS CONSEQUENCES

sons.[62] In the one Markan narrative in which Jesus raises someone from the dead (the raising of Jairus's daughter, Mk 5:35-43), Jesus first separated himself from the "large crowd" hemming him in (see 5:24, 31), and "allowed no one to follow along with him except Peter and James and John" (5:37). Then, outside Jairus's house, "he saw a commotion, and much crying and wailing" (v. 38). "Why the commotion and crying?" he asked, "The child is not dead, but sleeps" (v. 39). Finally, when "they laughed at him" for this, Jesus "put them all outside," taking with him only "the child's father and mother, and those who were with him [that is, Peter, James and John], and went in where the child was" (v. 40). Then the miracle followed, in relative privacy (vv. 41-43). Jesus seems to have wished for just such intimacy here — with a family he knew far better — and because it was not to be, he "got angry in the spirit and shook himself."[63]

34 Nevertheless, whether in private or not, Jesus must do what he came to do. Suppressing his anger,[64] he asks, "Where have you laid him?" (v. 34). The question confirms that he did not know the tomb's location, and therefore had not visited it on his arrival in Bethany (v. 17). He can only be speaking to the two sisters (although Martha is not mentioned as being present until v. 39), for "the Jews" had come only to console the sisters and to mourn (vv. 19, 31). They would have had no responsibility for the burial. Consequently, it is the sisters who reply, "Lord, come and see" (v. 34b). Their request curiously recalls Jesus' first words to his would-be disciples (1:39), and especially Philip's invitation to Nathanael (1:46), but in the present narrative it simply serves to heighten the reader's expectation: What will Jesus find at the tomb, and what will he do? At one level, the reader already knows what he will find (see v. 17), and what he will do there (vv. 11 and 23), but the excitement builds as matters move toward their inevitable conclusion. And suspense builds as well, as the reader is given one more brief vignette (vv. 35-37) before Jesus finally proceeds to the tomb (v. 38).

35-37 That the presence of the Jewish mourners is the reason for Jesus' anger is evident from what happens next. Instead of going immedi-

---

62. See, for example, Mark 1:35; 3:9, 20; 4:1, 34, 35-36; 7:17, 24, 33; 8:23, 26. In John's Gospel, see 2:24-25; 5:13; 6:15; 7:10; 8:59, and the whole of chapters 13–17.

63. The debate among commentators as to whether "in the spirit" (τῷ πνεύματι) refers to Jesus' own spirit or the Holy Spirit is largely beside the point, in view of 1:33 and 3:34 (see also 19:30 and 20:22). During his ministry on earth, Jesus is the bearer of the Spirit to the point that "the Spirit" is indistinguishable from his own "spirit" (hence no capitalization).

64. This is of course not explicit, but something the reader infers. But Chrysostom made it explicit with his comment, "Then rebuking those feelings, (for He 'groaned in spirit' meaneth 'restrained His trouble,') He asked, 'Where have ye laid him?'" (*Homilies on John* 63.1; NPNF, 1st ser., 14.232).

ately to the tomb, "Jesus wept" (v. 35). The word "wept,"⁶⁵ found only here in the New Testament, is distinct from the "crying" of Mary and "the Jews" (v. 33), and is aorist rather than present. Jesus did not join in their continual "crying" but simply "shed tears" of his own.⁶⁶ The response to Jesus' tears comes not from Mary or Martha, but from "the Jews," underscoring the intrusive nature of their presence and again spoiling the intimacy of the moment. Worse, they are divided among themselves, anticipating a more serious split after the miracle is over (see vv. 45-46). Their first reaction was "See how he loved him" (v. 36), confirming what the sisters had said (v. 3) and what the narrator has already told the readers (v. 5). But then "some of them" added a sour note: "Could not this man who opened the eyes of the blind man have made it so that this man would not die?" (v. 37).⁶⁷ The comment recalls that of Martha (v. 21), and Mary (v. 32), but with a note of skepticism not present before, as if calling into question the thought that Jesus loved Lazarus. If he had the power to prevent his friend's death, what he must have lacked was the willingness to do so. At the same time, the comment links these "Jews" from Jerusalem to those in the preceding chapter who knew about the healing of the man born blind, and were finally driven to acknowledge that Jesus had performed that miracle (see 10:21). Despite the acknowledgment, and despite their sympathy for Mary and Martha, they are now reverting to character.

38 Consequently, the second mention of Jesus' anger comes as no surprise: "So Jesus, again angry within himself,⁶⁸ comes to⁶⁹ the tomb" (v. 38a). "Within himself" corresponds to "in the spirit" in the previous instance (v. 33). "Again" is more like "still,"⁷⁰ for Jesus' anger (v. 33) is not likely to have subsided even in his grief. The cause of his anger is much the same as before — probably the intrusive responses of third parties (vv. 36-37), preempting any reaction from his loved ones. On Jesus' arrival at the tomb, the Gospel writer pauses to describe the tomb, so that the reader can

---

65. Gr. ἐδάκρυσεν.

66. "Burst into tears" (BDAG, 211) may be a bit strong, yet given the preceding aorists "got angry" (ἐνεβριμήσατο) and "shook himself" (ἐτάραξεν ἑαυτόν, v. 33), it could well be implied.

67. The repetition of "this man" (οὗτος), with two different antecedents, is as awkward in Greek as in English.

68. Gr. πάλιν ἐμβριμώμενος ἐν ἑαυτῷ.

69. Εἰς is surely "to," not "into," the tomb (see above, n. 44), for the stone is blocking the door. When someone goes "into" a tomb, the expression in this Gospel is "*entered* into the tomb" (εἰσῆλθεν εἰς τὸ μνημεῖον; see 20:6, 8).

70. Gr. πάλιν. See BDAG, 752: "also, again, furthermore, thereupon." This is in keeping with the present tense of ἐμβριμώμενος (that is, "being angry" rather than "got angry").

11:17-54 THE RAISING OF LAZARUS, AND ITS CONSEQUENCES

imagine the procedure Jesus will follow: "It was a cave,[71] and a stone was lying against it" (v. 38b).[72] The stage is set for Jesus to act.

39 "Lift the stone,"[73] Jesus commands the bystanders, but Martha (who has not been heard from since v. 28) interrupts. Martha is abruptly reintroduced here as "the sister of the deceased,"[74] as if we had not met her before, possibly preserving the language of an earlier source in which she was in fact being introduced for the first time.[75] In the present narrative, by contrast, Jesus' reply to her (v. 40) will underscore the major role she has already played. Yet for the moment she has nothing profound to say, only the earthy observation, "Lord, already it stinks,[76] for it has been four days!" With this the introductory notice, "when Jesus had come, he found [Lazarus] already four days in the tomb" (v. 17), is finally confirmed. Even the "already" recalls the earlier reference. "It stinks" implies that there had been no embalming of the body, and although there are hints of embalming (v. 44), there is no mention of spices, or anything remotely comparable to the enormous quantity of myrrh and aloes used to embalm the body of Jesus (see 19:39-40).[77]

---

71. For the use of a cave [σπήλαιον] as a tomb, see, for example, Genesis 25:9-10; also *Testament of Reuben* 7.2 (*OTP,* 1.785) and *Testament of Issachar* 7.8 (*OTP,* 1.804).

72. As Barrett notes (401), "It is not stated whether the shaft of the cave is vertical or horizontal. . . . If the shaft was vertical, ἐπί will mean 'upon'; if horizontal, 'against.'" He favors the latter, on the basis of rabbinic specifications (for example, the Mishnah, *Baba Batra* 6.8; Danby, 375). The account of Jesus' resurrection also seems to presuppose a horizontal shaft, except that the stone in front of the tomb had been taken away (see 20:1). Schnackenburg argues rather for a vertical shaft, "an ante-chamber with an opening in the ground leading to the actual burial chamber," thus matching the traditional tomb shown to tourists today in Bethany as the tomb of Lazarus, but different from Jesus' tomb (2.337-38 and 2.517, n. 63).

73. Gr. ἄρατε τὸν λίθον. This command, so concise and easily remembered, seems to have lived on as an isolated utterance (with slightly different vocabulary and totally different meaning) in later apocryphal traditions of Jesus' words. See *Gospel of Thomas* 77; *Oxyrhynchus Papyri* 1.5: "Raise the stone, and you will find me there" (ἔγει[ρ]ον τὸν λίθο, κακεῖ εὑρήσεις με; see *Apocrypha, II: Evangelien* [3d ed.; Berlin: de Gruyter, 1929], 19).

74. Lazarus is called "the deceased" (τοῦ τετελευτηκότος), rather than "the dead man" (ὁ νέκρος), possibly out of respect (see also v. 44, where he is not "the dead man" but "the one who had died").

75. Possibly for this reason the words "the sister of the deceased" are omitted in a few ancient witnesses (including Θ, some of the old Latin, and the Sinaitic Syriac). The Sinaitic Syriac also has Martha first asking, "Why are they lifting away the stone?" (see A. S. Lewis, *A Translation of the Four Gospels from the Syriac of the Sinaitic Palimpsest,* 187), as if they had already begun to do so (see v. 41).

76. Gr. ὄζει.

77. Brown's comment that "The oils and spices employed in Jewish burial practice prevented unpleasant odor for a while, but there was no real embalming, such as that

The purpose of Martha's blunt objection is to not to single her out for lack of faith, but to allow her to give voice to what everyone on the scene except Jesus must have been thinking, and to elicit from Jesus for the reader's benefit his starkly contrasting response (v. 40).

40 "Did I not tell you," Jesus replies, "that if you believe you will see the glory of God?" His words are spoken to Martha and to her alone,[78] raising acutely the question, When had he told her this? His comment here draws together two previous pronouncements: the first when he sent word back to the two sisters that the sickness of their brother was "not toward death, but for the glory of God, so that through it the Son of God might be glorified" (v. 4), and the second when he said to Martha alone, and in person, "I am the Resurrection and the Life. The one who believes in me, even if he dies, will live, and everyone who lives and believes in me will never ever die. Do you believe this?" (vv. 25-26). Martha then confessed that she did believe (v. 27), and now he tells her that because of her faith, what matters for her is not what she can smell — the foul odor of death — but what she is about to "see" — "the glory of God," understood as the realization of the promise that "the one who believes in me, even if he dies, will live" (v. 25). In the larger setting of the Gospel, the promise to Martha that "you will see the glory of God" reiterates and reinforces Jesus' promise to his first disciples that "You will see the sky opened, and the angels of God going up and coming down over the Son of man" (1:51). If that promise anticipated all of Jesus' signs, particularly the first one, in which he began to display his "glory" (2:11), the promise to Martha anticipates the last of his signs, the raising of her brother, and beyond that Jesus' final "glorification" (11:4). In effect, Jesus has now announced what he will do, and in the same breath interpreted its meaning. All that remains is for the bystanders (that is, "the Jews") to "Lift the stone" and, with Martha, "see the glory of God."

41 The story continues after the brief interruption, with an evident play on words (v. 41, with italics added): "So they *lifted* the stone, but Jesus *lifted* his eyes upward"[79] — in prayer, as he will do again (see 17:1). Even

---

practiced in Egypt, which prevented decomposition" (1.426; see also Keener, 2.848) may be open to question, given the account of Jesus' burial, but in any event no spices are mentioned here.

78. This is signaled by the singular pronoun "you" (σοι), and the second-person singular verbs, "if you believe" (ἐὰν πιστεύσῃς) and "you will see" (ὄψῃ).

79. "Lifted" is ἦραν in the first instance, ἦρεν in the second. That the play on words is deliberate is evident from the other instances in which Jesus either "lifted up his eyes" (ἐπάρας, in 6:5 as well as 17:1) or commanded his disciples to do so (ἐπάρατε, 4:35). In each instance, "lifted up" is the compound verb ἐπαίρειν (either as a participle or an imperative), while here the uncompounded ἦρεν conforms to the preceding ἦραν for the sake of the wordplay. Only two of the four instances of this expression have to do ex-

though the man born blind (9:31), and just recently Martha herself (v. 22), seem to have known that Jesus performed his miracles and healings by the power of prayer, what follows is his first prayer actually recorded in the Gospel. He has consistently referred to God as his "Father," but now for the first time he addresses God as "Father" in prayer.[80] "Father," he says, "I thank you[81] that you heard me. I knew that you always hear me, but I said [it] for the sake of the crowd standing by, so that they might believe that you sent me" (vv. 41-42). He has "given thanks" once before (see 6:11, 23), even though the actual content of his prayer over the loaves was not given. Here his words are given, yet oddly enough this prayer has no content either. Jesus merely gives thanks that the Father has heard his prayer (v. 41). What prayer, and when? Some have argued that Jesus is referring to a prayer at an earlier time, either when he first received news of Lazarus's illness (v. 3), or when he was speaking with Martha (see v. 22).[82] This is possible, but no previous prayer is recorded, and it is safer not to assume one.[83] More likely, Jesus' thanksgiving at just this moment *is* in effect his petition to the Father, just as his thanksgiving over the loaves served as a petition consecrating them and multiplying them for the multitude (6:11, 23). That prayer of thanksgiving was public, but this time it is not immediately clear whether he is praying publicly or privately. His opening words, "I thank you that you heard me" (v. 41) appear to be public, for he adds in the next verse, "I said [it] for the sake of the crowd standing around" (v. 42), implying that they heard.[84] What

---

plicitly with prayer. The other two signal rather an impending spiritual "harvest" (4:35) and the approach of a "large crowd" (6:5).

80. For the simple address "Father" in the synoptic tradition, see Matthew 11:25; Luke 22:42; 23:34, 46; also Mark 14:36 (ἀββὰ ὁ πατήρ), and in John's Gospel see 12:27, 28; 17:1, 5, 21, 24.

81. Gr. εὐχαριστῶ σοι.

82. On this issue see Abbott, *Johannine Grammar,* 331-32, and Morris, 497. Those who hold this view could argue that certain other things Jesus said or did went unmentioned until later (for example, summoning Mary, v. 28, or telling Martha she would see God's glory, v. 40); also that the past tense "I knew" (ἐγὼ δὲ ᾔδειν) in the following clause could refer to what Jesus knew *already* at that earlier time.

83. Origen cited Isaiah 58:9, "And while you are still speaking, I will say, 'Behold, I am here,'" commenting that what God "said to the Savior would surely be something more than that which was written in the promise to just men": thus *"Before* you have spoken, I will say, 'Behold, I am here'"* (italics added). Consequently, "in place of the prayer he intended to offer," Jesus "addresses thanksgiving to the one who anticipated his prayer" (*Commentary on John* 28.40-41; FC 89.300).

84. "I said" (εἶπον) echoes the "he said" (εἶπεν) with which the prayer was introduced. Bultmann, by contrast (408), finds it "obvious that Jesus' words in vv. 41f. are not heard by the bystanders; they only see his attitude of prayer, and in this situation they must understand his prayer as one of request."

follows, however, sounds more like a private exchange between Jesus and the Father, for he speaks to the Father *about* the crowd as if they are out of earshot and cannot hear what he is saying.

42 Jesus' apparently private conversation with the Father begins with the claim, "I knew that you always hear me" (v. 42a), bringing to mind the former blind man's pronouncement that "if anyone is god-fearing and does his will, this one he hears" (9:31), and at the same time Jesus' own claim that "the One who sent me is with me, . . . for I always do the things that please him" (8:29).[85] It is a unique prayer, the prayer of One who has said, "I and the Father are one" (10:30), and "the Father is in me and I in the Father" (10:38).[86] Jesus in this Gospel rarely prays in the conventional sense of the word because his whole life on earth is a prayer, by virtue of his union with the Father.[87] This is what Nathanael was told he would see ("the angels of God going up and coming down over the Son of man," 1:51), and what Jesus has just promised to Martha ("you will see the glory of God," v. 40). But now in "lifting his eyes upward" and giving thanks audibly (v. 41), he has reached out beyond Martha and Mary, praying aloud not because he has to (for God has already heard him), but, as he tells the Father, "for the sake of the crowd standing around, so that they might believe that you sent me" (v. 42b).

This "crowd" of bystanders can only be "the Jews" who had come to mourn with the sisters, interrupting their privacy (vv. 31, 33) and arousing Jesus' anger (vv. 33, 38).[88] It was evidently to them that he said, "Lift the stone" (v. 39), for the writer would have assumed that the women were unable to do so (see Mk 16:3). It is to this "crowd standing around" that Jesus, overcoming his anger, now turns his attention. In some way his prayer is for their benefit. A distinction should be drawn between the *content* of the prayer, which is never stated but which we can assume to be for the raising of Lazarus from the dead, and its *purpose,* which is explicitly said

---

85. Similarly in 1 John, doing "the things that please" God (τὰ ἀρεστὰ ἐνώπιον αὐτοῦ) becomes a condition for having one's prayers answered (1 Jn 3:22).

86. At the same time, Jesus' terminology is not altogether out of place within the traditions of Jewish piety. See, for example, Psalm 118:21: "I thank you that you have answered me and have become my salvation" (NRSV; the LXX is ἐξομολογήσομαί σοι ὅτι ἐπήκουσάς μου). See M. Wilcox, "The 'Prayer' of Jesus in John xi.41b-42," *NTS* 24 (1977-78), 128-32.

87. See A. T. Lincoln's comment that Jesus' relationship with the Father "makes it a matter of course that any prayer of his will be heard — so much so, that he does not need to articulate any individual request" ("God's Name, Jesus' Name, and Prayer in the Fourth Gospel," in *Into God's Presence: Prayer in the New Testament* [ed. R. N. Longenecker; Grand Rapids: Eerdmans, 2001], 157). Jesus does, however, offer specific (though private) petitions to the Father in 12:27-28 and in chapter 17.

88. "The crowd" and "the Jews" have appeared as overlapping, almost interchangeable groups before (see 6:24 and 41; also 7:15 and 20).

11:17-54 THE RAISING OF LAZARUS, AND ITS CONSEQUENCES

to be "so that they might believe that you sent me." That Jesus has "the crowd" (or 'the Jews') in view is apparent from the moment he "lifted his eyes upward" (v. 41), for such body language signals not only prayer (as in 17:1) but mission, an awareness of people in need of what he has come to bring. "Lift up your eyes and look at the fields, that they are white for harvest," he once told his disciples as the Samaritan villagers approached (4:35), and in Galilee when he "lifted up his eyes and saw that a large crowd was coming to him," he asked, "Where shall we buy loaves so that these may eat?" even as "he himself knew what he was going to do" (6:5-6). Later, when he "lifts up his eyes to heaven" for the last time (17:1), the ultimate goal of his prayer will be "that the world might believe that you have sent me" (17:21; see also vv. 8, 23, 25). Here too, even at the tomb of his dear friend, his mind is on his mission to the world, most immediately to "the crowd standing around."

The purpose of his spoken prayer (v. 41) is to make to clear to the bystanders that what he is about to do is not something done "on his own," but something the Father is accomplishing through him. His goal is that they might "believe" as Martha has done (vv. 27, 40), not simply in him as a miracle worker, but as the Father's agent and representative. What he wants them to believe, he tells the Father, is "that *you* sent me" (italics added). As he has said again and again in different ways, "I have not come on my own, but that One sent me" (8:42). Because Jesus first introduced the notion of the Son's dependence on the Father in connection with the giving of life and the raising of the dead (5:19-21), it is all the more important for him to keep that thought in the forefront at this visible sign of resurrection, for the benefit of the bystanders — and perhaps even more the readers of the Gospel, that we too "might believe" these things (see 20:31).

43 Only when he has made it very clear that he is not acting "on his own" does Jesus turn his attention to the tomb, and the dead man within: "And when he had said these things,[89] he shouted in a great voice, "Lazarus! Out!"[90] Here for the first time the principle that a true shepherd "summons his own sheep by name and leads them out" (10:3) comes to graphic expression, side by side with Jesus' promise that "an hour is coming, and now is, when the

---

89. While ταῦτα εἰπών is characteristic Johannine style, it also builds on the εἶπεν of verse 41 and the εἶπον of verse 42. There is therefore an ambiguity as to what "these things" (ταῦτα) refers to. As far as the reader is concerned, "these things" are presumably the whole of verses 41-42, but to "the crowd standing around" they are perhaps only the words they have actually heard, "Father, I thank you that you heard me" (v. 41).

90. Literally, "Here! Outside!" (δεῦρο ἔξω). Δεῦρο is an adverb used as a verb in the imperative, "come" (see BDAG, 220; compare the Samaritan woman's δεῦτε ἴδετε, "Come see," in 4:29). With ἔξω it can be translated with a single adverb used imperatively in English: "Out!"

dead will hear the voice of the Son of God, and those who hear will live" (5:25; also v. 28). It is as if the great day of resurrection is about to begin!

44 In keeping with that future scenario, Lazarus "came out."[91] Yet the facetious comment often made that if Jesus had not called out the name "Lazarus" *all* the dead would have risen is not quite pertinent, because there are substantial differences between this miracle and the general resurrection expected at the end of the age. No one will have to "lift the stone" on that day (v. 39), and (most conspicuously) Lazarus comes out still "bound with bandages on his feet and hands, and his face wrapped in a cloth," so that Jesus has to give "the crowd standing around" yet another command, "Loosen him, and let him go" (v. 44). Despite the rich symbolism, this is a resuscitation, not a resurrection. Later, when Jesus himself is raised, the contrast will be self-evident, for the stone will be already "taken away from the tomb" (20:1), Jesus' body nowhere to be seen, and only "the linen cloths lying, and the cloth which had been over his face not with the linen cloths, but rolled up by itself in one place" (20:7). The so-called "resurrection" of Lazarus is but a *sign* of future resurrection (see 12:18), not the event itself. The promise to Martha that her brother "will rise" still awaits "the resurrection at the last day" (vv. 23-24). For the moment, Lazarus is not being ushered into the age to come, but simply received back into everyday life. This is evident in other Gospel resuscitations: the daughter of Jairus "got up and began walking," and Jesus asked that she be "given something to eat" (Mk 5:42-43), and when the widow's son at Nain "sat up and began speaking," Jesus "gave him back to his mother" (Lk 7:15; see also 1 Kgs 17:23; 2 Kgs 4:36). Here, because Lazarus was already in a tomb, wrapped in ill-smelling bandages and a facecloth, Jesus instead says, "Loosen him, and let him go."

This practical command[92] brings to mind Jesus' promise to "the Jews who had believed him" at the Tent festival that "you will know the truth, and the truth will set you free" (8:32), free from the prospect of dying in their sins (see 8:21, 24).[93] "So if the Son sets you free," he had added, "you will really

---

91. He is still not called "the dead man" (ὁ νεκρός), for he is no longer dead, but simply "the one who had died" (ὁ τεθνηκώς), just as earlier he was called "the deceased" (τοῦ τετελευτηκότος, v. 39; see above, n. 74).

92. Much of what happens in this last of Jesus' signs is carried out by a series of commands in which Jesus speaks and others act so as to accomplish the miracle (as in the first sign at Cana). First he said to the bystanders, "Where have you laid him?" (v. 34), then "Lift the stone" (v. 39), finally "Loosen him" (v. 44). Yet here, in contrast to the Cana wedding, the prayer of Jesus (vv. 41-42) and his explicit command to Lazarus (v. 43) stand at the center of the action.

93. Other parallels, outside of John's Gospel, are more problematic; for example, the words about "binding" and "loosing" in a context dealing with victory over death (see Mt 16:18-19), and Peter's announcement at Pentecost that in raising Jesus from the dead,

11:17-54 THE RAISING OF LAZARUS, AND ITS CONSEQUENCES

be free" (8:36). Freedom and eternal life were synonymous in that setting. Now Lazarus is literally "loosened" or set free, restored to physical life for a few more years, but assured of eternal life forever. In him the promise has come true that "The one who believes in me, even if he dies, will live, and everyone who lives and believes in me will never ever die" (vv. 25-26). Except for a cameo appearance in the next chapter (12:2), nothing more is known of his future, yet his story will have far-reaching consequences. As Jesus knew from the start, God's intent was "that through it the Son of God might be glorified" (v. 4). Events will now move quickly toward that end.

45-46 The raising of Lazarus, like the healing of the man born blind (9:16; 10:19-21), brings about a "split" among "the Jews," although the characteristic word is not used here. "Many" of them, we are told, "believed" in Jesus on the basis of "the things he had done" (v. 45). They are identified as those Jews "who had come to Mary" (vv. 19, 31), followed her to the feet of Jesus, and joined her in crying over Lazarus, arousing Jesus' anger (vv. 33, 38). Their faith now fulfills Jesus' stated intention "that they might believe" (v. 42). It is immediately qualified, however, by the notice that "some of them went off to the Pharisees and told them the things Jesus had done" (v. 46).[94] Either way, the issue was what Jesus had "done"[95] (vv. 45, 46), but the implication is that some of those said to "believe" did not actually believe,[96] and consequently that their motives in informing the Pharisees in Jerusalem were not pure as far as Jesus was concerned.[97] As for those who genuinely believed, they do not simply fade from the scene like the "many" at the first

---

God had "loosed [λύσας] the pains of death, because it was not possible for him to be held by it" (Acts 2:24; see BDAG, 443 on the issue of whether "pains" is a mistranslation of a Hebrew word meaning "bonds" or "chains").

94. Compare the scene earlier at the tomb of Lazarus, where "the Jews" said, "See how he loved him" (v. 37), yet "some of them" (τινὲς δὲ ἐξ αὐτῶν) immediately added, "Could not this man who opened the eyes of the blind man have made it so that this man would not die?" (v. 37).

95. Gr. ἃ ἐποίησεν.

96. See 2:23-25; 8:30-31. Barrett (404) also notes this Gospel's practice of making a sweeping generalization and then immediately qualifying it (for example, 1:11-12, "his own did not receive him. But to as many as did receive him . . ."; 3:32, "no one receives his testimony. The person who did receive his testimony . . ."). A variant reading (τῶν ἐλθόντων instead of οἱ ἐλθόντες, v. 45) avoids the difficulty by making the phrase "some of them" refer to a different group from those who "believed." That is, "many" believed, but "some" (that is, others) went to the Pharisees instead. For this very reason, the reading is suspect, and in any case is supported in only one ancient manuscript (D).

97. Alternatively, it is possible that they went to the Pharisees simply out of excitement and joy over the good news. But this is less likely, for their behavior recalls that of the man Jesus healed at the pool of Bethsaida, who "went away and told the Jews that it was Jesus who made him well."

Passover (2:23), or at Sychar in Samaria (4:39), or at the Tent festival (7:31; 8:30), or on the other side of the Jordan (10:42).[98] Rather, their continuing presence will put both Jesus and Lazarus in danger (see 12:10-11), as they go on to bear testimony that Jesus "had done this sign" (12:17-18).

47-48 When the Pharisees heard what Jesus had done, "the chief priests and the Pharisees," acting jointly (as in 7:32, 45),[99] "gathered council and were saying, 'What do we do[100] because this man[101] is doing many signs? If we let him go on like this, they will all believe in him, and the Romans will come and take away both our place and our nation'" (vv. 47-48). "Gathered council"[102] implies a meeting of the Sanhedrin, the highest ruling authority in Jerusalem other than the Romans,[103] but the absence of the definite article suggests that it may not have been a formal meeting of the whole body.[104] It is in no sense a "trial" of Jesus before the Sanhedrin (even in absentia), but simply a private deliberation authorizing his arrest (see vv. 53, 57). How then does it go beyond that early confrontation after the healing at the pool of Bethsaida, when "the Jews began pursuing Jesus, because he did such things on the Sabbath" (5:16) and "kept seeking all the more to kill him, because he was . . . making himself equal to God" (5:18)? Jesus has been a wanted man ever since (see, for example, 7:1, 30, 32; 8:20, 59; 10:31, 39; 11:8), and it is legitimate to ask what this scene adds to the situation.

Nothing is said here of the specific charges of Sabbath breaking and claiming to be the Son of God. The accent is rather on strategy. Getting rid of Jesus has become more urgent because of fear of what "the Romans" might do. The reference to "many signs" recalls at least two previous miracles of

---

98. While two of these instances (2:23 and 8:30) involved false or inadequate belief, and one other (7:31) carried with it some ambiguity, nothing suggests that the other two instances (4:39 and 10:42) involved anything other than genuine faith.

99. See also 1:24, where a delegation of "priests and Levites" sent to John was said to be "from the Pharisees."

100. Even though the verb is indicative, the question is deliberative (as in the NRSV, "What are we to do?"), not rhetorical (as in the NIV, "What are we accomplishing?" with the implication, "Nothing"). That "you are gaining nothing" is a conclusion reached only later, on Jesus' triumphant return to the city (12:19).

101. On "this man" (οὗτος ὁ ἄνθρωπος) or simply "this one" (οὗτος) as an expression of contempt, see, for example, 6:52; 7:15; 9:16, 28.

102. Gr. συνήγαγον . . . συνέδριον.

103. See *TDNT*, 7.862-66; Keener, 2.1074-76.

104. So Keener (2.1074): "an ad hoc council." Elsewhere in the Gospels and Acts (unless it is plural, referring to "councils" more generally, as in Mt 10:17; Mk 13:9) it is always "the Sanhedrin" (τὸ συνέδριον, Mt 26:59; Lk 22:66, plus thirteen occurrences in Acts), or even "the whole Sanhedrin" (ὅλον τὸ συνέδριον, Mk 14:55; 15:1; also πᾶν τὸ συνέδριον, Acts 22:30).

11:17-54 THE RAISING OF LAZARUS, AND ITS CONSEQUENCES

Jesus that were remembered and commented on after the fact, the healing of the sick man at the pool (5:1-9; see 7:21-23), and the granting of sight to the man born blind (9:1-7; see 10:21; 11:37), plus other signs that may or may not have been known to the authorities in Jerusalem (see 4:46-54; 6:5-15). The raising of Lazarus from the dead seems to have been the last straw. "Many" had believed because of these "many" signs (see v. 45; also 2:23; 7:30; 8:30; 10:42), and the council's exaggerated fear was that more and more — "all," in fact — would do the same,[105] precipitating rebellion against Rome and bringing down the wrath of the Romans on Israel. Ungrounded as they are, such fears still have a certain plausibility within the narrative if we remember those who, after one of Jesus' signs in Galilee, hailed him as "truly the Prophet who is coming into the world," and tried to "seize him to make him king" (see 6:14-15).

Yet if John's Gospel is dated later than A.D. 70, they are also heavy with irony, for the reader would have known that the Romans had in fact done exactly what "the chief priests and the Pharisees" feared. They had taken away "both our place [probably the temple][106] and our nation." Some readers would have viewed this as God's punishment on the Jews for rejecting and crucifying their Messiah. Others would have recognized that these events had come about not because of Jesus and those who believed in him, but because of a series of unrelated circumstances long after Jesus' death and resurrection. Either way, the deliberations and actions of this council would prove futile (see 12:19, "You can see that you are gaining nothing").

49-50 Finally, after the voicing of these concerns, a concrete proposal emerges.[107] The "Chief Priest" speaks, and the matter is settled. Caiaphas is introduced rather oddly, as if readers are unfamiliar with the office of High Priest, as "a certain one among them, Caiaphas, being Chief Priest[108] of that year" (v. 49). The phrase "of that year," repeated twice more in identifying Caiaphas (see v. 51; 18:13), could imply that the Chief Priest

---

105. We may compare the exaggerated comment of John's disciples about Jesus, "Look, he is baptizing, and they are all coming to him!" (πάντες ἔρχονται πρὸς αὐτόν, 3:26).

106. On "the place" (ὁ τόπος) as the temple, see 4:20; also Mt 24:15 ("a holy place"), Acts 6:13 ("the holy place"), 6:14 ("this place"), and 21:28 ("this place," and "this holy place"); see *TDNT*, 8.204; BDAG, 1011.

107. Notice the shift from the imperfect ἔλεγον (they "were saying," v. 47) to the aorist εἶπεν αὐτοῖς (he "said to them"), signaling a very specific proposal from a specific individual.

108. "Chief Priest" (ἀρχιερεύς) is merely the singular of οἱ ἀρχιερεῖς ("the chief priests," v. 47), but the context makes clear that he is not *merely* "one among them" (that is, "*a* chief priest"), but in fact the High Priest, the president of the Sanhedrin and the first among equals (see BDAG, 139).

served for only one year, but this was not the case.[109] If the expression were simply an error,[110] it is odd that it would have been repeated three times. More likely, it is used deliberately and rhetorically to accent the historic nature of the council's decision, and the events that followed. It all happened in "that [fateful] year" when, as we will shortly learn, Jesus would "die for the nation" (v. 51).[111] To the reader living decades later, "that year" marks a milestone in the past, just as surely as "from that day" when Jesus' fate was sealed (v. 53), or "from that hour" when he died (19:27), and in much the same way that phrases such as "in that day" (14:20; 16:23, 26) or "hour" (see 2:4; 4:21, 23; 5:25, 28; 16:4) point to milestones in the future, whether from Jesus' perspective or the reader's.

Caiaphas speaks sharply to his colleagues. "*You* don't know anything!"[112] he charges (v. 49b, italics added), implying by the emphatic pronoun that he understands what they do not. "Don't you realize," he continues, "that it is to your advantage[113] that one man die for the people, and the whole nation not be lost?" (v. 50). In keeping with his tendency to depict "the Jews" as divided among themselves about Jesus (most recently in vv. 45-46),[114] the Gospel writer accents the tension between the Chief Priest and the rest of the council, despite their eventual agreement (v. 53).[115] Appealing to their reason and self-interest, Caiaphas proposes that Jesus be

109. While his two predecessors served for only a year or less (Josephus, *Antiquities* 18.34), Caiaphas's tenure from its beginning (*Antiquities* 18.35) to its end (18.95) spanned eighteen years (see also Lk 3:2 for evidence that he was Chief Priest, along with Annas, at the beginning of John the Baptist's ministry in the desert).

110. Bultmann, for example (410, n. 10), argues that the genitive construction "of that year" (τοῦ ἐνιαυτοῦ ἐκείνου) is not simply equivalent to "in that year," but implies rather that the High Priest's term was precisely one year. But see BDF, §186[2]: "the classical genitive of time within which something takes place."

111. Or as Origen put it, "Caiaphas, who was high priest the year when our Savior brought the dispensation to its completion, when he suffered for man" (*Commentary on John* 28.107; FC, 89.315). So too Schnackenburg, 2.348-49; Barrett, 406; with some hesitation Brown, 1.440).

112. Gr. ὑμεῖς οὐκ οἴδατε οὐδέν, literally, "You don't know nothing."

113. Gr. συμφέρει ὑμῖν.

114. See also the earlier instances in 7:43, 9:16, and 10:19-21.

115. The phrase "to your [ὑμῖν] advantage" maintains the distance between Caiaphas and his colleagues. Some witnesses (including A, W, Θ, Ψ, the majority of later manuscripts, plus the Vulgate and Syriac versions) minimize the distance with the reading "to our [ἡμῖν] advantage," and one important manuscript (ℵ) omits the pronoun altogether. But the stronger evidence (including P⁴⁵, P⁶⁶, B, D, and L) favors the second person. As Metzger notes (*Textual Commentary*, 235), ὑμῖν "is in accord with the tone of contempt represented by the closing words of ver. 49)." The omission could be attributed either to a scribe's uncertainty over which reading was correct, or to the influence of 18:14, or possibly both.

11:17-54 THE RAISING OF LAZARUS, AND ITS CONSEQUENCES

made a scapegoat. Better "one man[116] die for the people, and the whole nation not be lost."[117]

In a curious way, the form of this "prophecy" (see v. 51) recalls a pair of sayings of Jesus himself in a very different tradition about a very different subject: "And if your right eye [or your right hand] offend you, pluck it out [or cut it off] and throw it from you, for it is *to your advantage*[118] that *one* of your members be *lost,* and your *whole body not*[119] thrown into Gehenna" (Mt 5:29, 30; italics added). Yet no one familiar with that passage could view Caiaphas's proposal as anything but a crude parody of it, whether deliberate or not. Caiaphas has taken the principle of sacrificing one bodily member for the sake of the whole and applied it ruthlessly to the body politic.[120] The two sayings are of course not found in John's Gospel, yet Jesus has repeatedly stated his intention that those who believe in him "might not be lost"[121] (3:16), and, more than that, his certainty that his sheep "will never ever be lost" (10:28; see also 6:39).[122] Caiaphas's concern, by contrast, is not with those who believe in Jesus — they are in fact part of the danger (v. 48) — but rather with "the whole nation" and its welfare. His proposal could be interpreted in one of two ways: either to do away with Jesus before he brings down on Israel the wrath of Rome, or to see to it that Rome itself does the job. The latter is what actually happens (see 18:31-32), and it is quite plausible that this was the Chief Priest's intention from the start. Better that Rome put one troublemaker to death than that it destroy the whole nation. The notion of "one man" dying "for the people"[123] may strike the reader (even *before* the Gospel writer spells it out, vv. 51-52) as an odd echo of Jesus' own stated intention to lay down his life "for the sheep"

---

116. Gr. εἷς ἄνθρωπος.
117. Gr. μὴ ὅλον τὸ ἔθνος ἀπόληται.
118. Gr. συμφέρει γάρ σοι.
119. Gr. μὴ ὅλον τὸ σῶμά σου.
120. Still, the application may not be so far-fetched as it seems, given that Jesus is also represented in the synoptic Gospels the same principle corporately (that is, to what is good for the believing community) as well as to the life of the individual (see Mk 9:42-48, Mt 18:6-9).
121. Gr. ἀπόληται.
122. These passages in John's Gospel are not so different from Matthew 18:14, in the very context of Jesus' sayings about the hand and the eye (see the preceding note): "So it is not the will of your Father in heaven that one of these little ones be lost" (ἀπόληται). Despite significant differences between John's Gospel and Matthew and Luke on the subject of being lost (see above on 6:39), this verse in Matthew at least is distinctly "Johannine" in its perspective.
123. Gr. ὑπὲρ τοῦ λαοῦ. That "the people" (τοῦ λαοῦ), and "the nation" (τὸ ἔθνος) are used interchangeably, for merely stylistic reasons, is plausible in light of the Gospel writer's restatement of the proposal in the next verse (ὑπὲρ τοῦ ἔθνους, v. 51).

(10:11, 15).[124] But Caiaphas's intention is very different. To him the "one man" is by no means "shepherd" to the people (as in "one Shepherd," 10:16),[125] and his proposal is sheer political expediency, the creation of a scapegoat.

51 The Gospel writer intervenes to claim the truth of what Caiaphas has just said, regardless of his motivation: "And this he did not say on his own,[126] but being the Chief Priest of that year he prophesied that Jesus was going to die for the nation" (v. 51). Elsewhere in the Gospel, only Jesus (7:17-18; 12:49; 14:10) and the so-called "Paraclete," or "Spirit of truth" (16:13), are said to speak "not on his own," but here the claim is made for Caiaphas, not with respect to his speech or behavior generally,[127] but of his one specific proposal that Jesus "die for the nation." This means not that he is actually a "prophet,"[128] but that on one memorable occasion he "prophesied," that is, he spoke for God. Although the comment links Caiaphas's ability to prophesy to his being "Chief Priest of that year," there is no hard evidence that Jewish priests or high priests necessarily had the gift of prophecy.[129] The Gospel writer is merely seizing the opportunity to attach an ironic double meaning to the Chief Priest's words. He does this by simply repeating the core of Caiaphas's pronouncement, "that one man die for the nation," substituting

---

124. The effect of the pronouncement is to define the preposition ὑπέρ ("for" or "on behalf of") as implying a kind of appeasement or "propitiation," averting the wrath of Rome. In 1 John (contrary to C. H. Dodd, who sees it differently), Jesus' death is viewed in similar fashion in relation to the wrath of God (see ἱλασμός, "propitiation," 1 Jn 2:2; 4:10).

125. In the other Gospels, in fact, Jesus sees the "crowds" (and implicitly the whole "house of Israel") as "sheep not having a shepherd" (Mk 6:34; Mt 9:36), and consequently as "lost" (see Mt 10:5; 15:24).

126. For similar comments explaining the motivation or implication of things just spoken, introduced by "this" (τοῦτο), see 6:6; 8:6; 7:39; 12:6, 33; 21:19.

127. Jesus, by contrast, claims also to *act* "not on his own" but at the Father's direction (5:19, 30; 7:28; 8:28), and implies throughout that this is true of *everything* he says and does.

128. So Origen: "The fact that someone prophesies does not make that person a prophet. Caiaphas indeed . . . was by no means also a prophet" (*Commentary on John* 28.98; FC, 89.314).

129. On the contrary, Josephus claimed that John Hyrcanus I was "the only man to unite in his person three of the highest privileges: the supreme command of the nation, the high priesthood, and the gift of prophecy. For so closely was he in touch with the Deity, that he was never ignorant of the future" (*Jewish War* 1.68-69; LCL, 2.35; see also *Antiquities* 13.282, 299-300). Since certain other high priests also held "the supreme command of the nation," Hyrcanus's prophetic gift seems to have been what made him unique. Even though there were examples of "clerical prophecy," associating prophecy and priesthood (see D. E. Aune, *Prophecy in Early Christianity*, 138-44), the link here is particularly with the office of Chief Priest or High Priest.

11:17-54 THE RAISING OF LAZARUS, AND ITS CONSEQUENCES

"nation" for "people," while omitting the introductory words, "it is to your advantage," and the concluding words, "and the whole nation not be lost." Ironically, the structural elements in the pronouncement that parallel the structure of Jesus' own words (in Mt 5:29-30) are precisely the ones omitted.

The narrative aside transforms the Chief Priest's strategic plan into a plain statement of fact: Jesus was indeed "going to die for the nation." But in what sense "for the nation"?[130] Surely for the nation's benefit, but not in the sense of protecting her from the Roman legions. As we have seen, the Gospel writer must have known that such a hope was futile. Rather, what the reader may have already suspected (from v. 50) now becomes explicit. Jesus would "die for the nation" *redemptively*, just as he would "lay down his life" for his sheep (10:11, 15). Only here in John's Gospel is anything said about Jesus dying redemptively "for," or "on behalf of," the nation of Israel. The Christian reader is tempted to hurry past this assertion so as to concentrate on the writer's more universal interest in "the children of God who [were] scattered" (v. 52), but this temptation should be resisted.[131] Far from merely repeating what Caiaphas has just said, the Gospel writer shifts the subject matter from political expediency to salvation, and the initiative from the Chief Priest and council (v. 50) back to where it belongs, as far as the reader is concerned, with Jesus the Shepherd. There is a hint here (though hardly more than that) of a hope for Israel's restoration comparable to what is found in certain passages in Matthew, Luke, and Acts, and in Paul.[132] That said, the hint is not followed up. Instead, the Gospel writer quickly moves on to something Caiaphas did not actually say, a kind of afterthought that nevertheless finally dwarfs the "prophecy" itself.

52 The Gospel writer now volunteers the information that Jesus would die "not for the nation alone, but in order that the children of God who are scattered might also be gathered into one" (v. 52). The phrase "for the nation" is picked up a second time, in order to set the stage for something new. The form of the pronouncement ("not for this alone,[133] but for that") occurs once more in John's Gospel, when Jesus prays "not for these alone, but also for those who believe in me through their word" (17:20). There, too, the intent is "that they all might be one" (17:21). The distinction is between Jesus' immediate disciples and those who would come to believe in him later, while

---

130. Gr. ὑπὲρ τοῦ ἔθνους.

131. So Lincoln: "That Jesus can be truly said to die for the nation should not be overlooked in favour of the universalizing of the benefits of his death that follows. Unlike the notion of 'the children of God,' the term for 'nation', ἔθνος, is not spiritualized here or in 18.35. It is the Jewish nation that is in view" (330).

132. See, for example, Matthew 1:21; 19:28; 23:39; Luke 22:30; Acts 1:6-7; 3:19-21; also Paul in Romans 11:11-32.

133. Gr. μόνον.

653

here it is between the nation of Israel and "the children of God who are scattered."[134] Who are these "the children of God"? The definite articles[135] suggest that they are a group known to the reader, a group elaborately introduced (without definite articles) near the very beginning of the Gospel: "But to as many as did receive him he gave authority to become children of God, to those who believe in his name, who were born not of blood lines, nor of fleshly desire, nor a husband's desire, but of God" (1:12-13). They are in fact the whole Christian community, consisting of all those who are or will be "born of God" or "born from above" (3:3).[136]

In moving beyond the actual words of the Chief Priest, the writer changes the grammatical construction as well. Instead of "not for the nation alone, but for the children of God," he explains what the phrase "*for* the children of God" would have meant. That is, how exactly is Jesus' death "for" them, or "on their behalf"? In what way does it benefit them? He answers by shifting to a purpose clause: Jesus would die "in order that the children of God who are scattered might also be gathered into one."[137] The "also" *(kai)* is noteworthy, suggesting that "the nation" too will be "gathered" (in some unspecified way) by virtue of Jesus' death on the cross, but the accent is rather on the "gathering into one" of those whom Jesus previously called his "sheep" (see 10:16, "Those too I must bring, . . . and they will become one flock, one Shepherd").[138] The sheep metaphor is now dropped, and Jesus' "sheep" are plainly identified as "the children of God." The striking aspect of the two passages, yet one which is entirely consistent with the theology of John's Gospel, is that Jesus' "sheep" are *already* his sheep before he "brings" them into "one flock," and "the children of God" are his children even *before* they are "gathered into one." Behind both passages is a strong sense of divine election. Those "gathered into one" are those who have "done the truth" and are ready to "come to the Light, so that their works will be revealed as works wrought in God" (see 3:21). They are those whom "the Father has given" Jesus (see 6:37, 39, 44, 65), and in that sense "the children of God."

---

134. A third example can be found in 1 John 2:2, "And he is the atoning sacrifice for our sins, and not for ours alone [μόνον], but for the whole world."

135. Gr. τὰ τέκνα τοῦ θεοῦ.

136. In 1 John, where the term reappears twice more without the article (τέκνα θεοῦ, 1 Jn 3:1, 2), and twice with the article (τὰ τέκνα τοῦ θεοῦ, 3:10; 5:2), the writer clearly claims the designation "children of God" for himself and his readers (καὶ ἐσμέν, "and we are," 3:1).

137. Gr. ἵνα . . . συναγάγῃ εἰς ἕν. The construction is slightly different in 17:20, where the intent is expressed *both* with a prepositional phrase ("for those who believe in me") and with an explanatory purpose clause ("that they all might be one").

138. One very early manuscript (P[66]) heightened the parallel by substituting συναγαγεῖν ("gather") for ἀγαγεῖν ("bring") in 10:16.

53 The meeting of the Sanhedrin is framed by the vocabulary of "gathering." The chief priests and Pharisees "gathered" the council to begin with[139] (v. 47) in order to decide Jesus' fate, but in the end "the children of God" would be the ones "gathered into one" (v. 52). Ironically, the council now starts things in motion toward that end by quickly agreeing to the Chief Priest's proposal: "So from that day they resolved that they would kill him" (v. 53). Over against the divine purpose "that the children of God . . . be gathered into one" (v. 52) now stands the council's firm purpose toward Jesus "that they would kill him" (v. 53). What neither the council nor Caiaphas understands is that the latter would, in the plan of God, inevitably bring about the former.

"From that day" seems to mark a decisive event or turning point,[140] and yet the reader still has to wonder in what way that decision goes beyond the notices six chapters earlier, after Jesus healed the sick man at the pool, that "the Jews began pursuing Jesus" (5:16) and "kept seeking all the more to kill him" (5:18). From that point on we were told repeatedly that they were intent on killing him (see 7:1, 19, 20, 25; 8:37, 40, 58; 10:31). What then is new or different about the notice here that the council finally "resolved[141] that they would kill him"? Only that it is now a quasi-official act of the Sanhedrin at the behest of the Chief Priest. No such resolution is mentioned in Mark or Luke, only a brief notice that "the chief priests and the scribes were seeking how they might seize him by stealth and kill him" (Mk 14:1; also Lk 22:2). But Matthew's Gospel offers a closer parallel: "Then the chief priests and the elders of the people were gathered in the courtyard of the Chief Priest, who was called Caiaphas, and they plotted together[142] that they would seize and kill Jesus by stealth" (Mt 26:3-4).[143] This would not have to imply more than what was stated in Mark and Luke,[144] but the vocabulary at least is similar to John's. Matthew and John agree that at some point prior to Jesus'

---

139. Gr. συνήγαγον.

140. The nearest parallel in John's Gospel is "from that hour" (19:27), marking the "hour" of Jesus' death in relation to Jesus' mother and the disciple whom he loved.

141. Gr. ἐβουλεύσαντο.

142. Gr. συνεβουλεύσαντο.

143. The parallel is even closer if the reading συνεβουλεύσαντο ("plotted together") is adopted in John 11:53 as well (with A, L, Ψ, and the majority of later manuscripts), but this reading is obviously suspect as a harmonization with Matthew. No rationale for the plot is given in Matthew, only for the "stealth" with which it was to be carried out. Matthew adds that "they were saying, 'Not in the festival, so that there will not be an uproar [θόρυβος] among the people'" (Mt 26:5; see also Mk 14:2). Nothing is said as to whether such an "uproar" might attract the attention of the Romans (as in Jn 11:48).

144. The compound verb implies not so much a firm decision or "resolve" (BDAG, 181) as simply a deliberation or "plot" (see BDAG, 957).

arrest the Jewish authorities met together to take action against him. They do not agree on the timing. The notice in Matthew is two days before the Passover (Mt 26:2; Mk 14:1), while in John's Gospel the council meets much earlier. We are not even told that "the Passover of the Jews was near" (v. 55) until *after* Jesus' sojourn in "the region near the desert" for an unspecified length of time (v. 54). And when he finally returns to Bethany, it is still "six days before the Passover" (12:1), not two.

The council's resolution is bluntly stated: "they resolved that they would kill him." The reader knows by now that this has been their intention all along (beginning at 5:18). Jesus accused them three times of seeking his life (7:19; 8:37, 40), and they would neither deny it nor admit it.[145] Now they are admitting it, if not to Jesus at least to themselves. The Gospel writer could have chosen the more judicial term, "put to death," but seems to prefer the verb "kill" in order to confirm very explicitly Jesus' accusations against them (see also 12:10; 16:2; 18:31).

54 We are not told how Jesus learned of the council's decision, only that he "would no longer walk openly among the Jews, but he went from there to the region[146] near the desert, to a town called Ephraim, and there he remained with the disciples" (v. 54). "Ephraim" is believed to have been located to the northeast of Jerusalem, on the northern border of Judea.[147] This

---

145. As we have seen, the seeming denial in 7:20 appears to stem from the fact that Jesus' identity was at that point still unknown.

146. Gr. εἰς τὴν χώραν. One ancient Greek manuscript (D) names "the region" as Σαμφουριν, a name otherwise unknown. G. Dalman (*Sacred Sites and Ways,* 219) considered it a (mistaken) identification of the place with Sepphoris in Galilee, but even aside from the geographical discrepancy Sepphoris was a city, not a "region." Brown (1.441) sees it as a corruption of a Hebrew expression meaning "whose name is Ephraim," making Ephraim the name of the "region" rather than a particular town (see BDAG, 912).

147. Its exact location is unknown (see Brown, 1.441). Eusebius in his fourth-century *Onomasticon* mentions both an Aphra "of the lot of Benjamin . . . a village of Aiphraim near Bethel, about five milestones to the east" (*Onomasticon* 28; see "Ophrah" in Josh 18:23) and "the very large village of Ephraim about 20 milestones from Ailia, on the northern border," identifying the latter with the "Ephron" of Joshua 15:9 (*Onomasticon* 86; "Ailia," to Eusebius, was *Aelia Capitolina,* the name given to Jerusalem by the Romans when they rebuilt it in the second century). See *Palestine in the Fourth Century* A.D.: *The Onomasticon by Eusebius of Caesarea* (Jerusalem: Carta, 2003), 23, 51. Similarly, the sixth-century Madeba map places "Ephron or Ephraea: the Lord was there" in the hill country to the northeast, adjoining the Jordan valley. G. Dalman (*Sacred Sites and Ways,* 217-20) and others have identified Ephraim with present-day *et-Taiyibeh* (whose ancient name is said to have been *Afra*), about 20 kilometers (not 20 miles) from Jerusalem. Dalman attributes the discrepancy to the fact that it "does not lie on any north road from Jerusalem, where the distance could be measured, but 4 kilometres aside to the east . . . so that the notion of such a considerable distance is explainable" (217). In any event,

11:17-54 THE RAISING OF LAZARUS, AND ITS CONSEQUENCES

sojourn is but for a moment in narrative time, marking a break between the council's decision and the events at Passover leading to Jesus' arrest and crucifixion. But in real time (as the reader imagines it), Jesus could have spent weeks, even months, in this "town called Ephraim," for the length of his sojourn there is not given. In that respect it is comparable to his sojourn "across the Jordan" just before the raising of Lazarus (10:40-42). The last firm notice of time was the Rededication festival in the winter (10:22), and the next will be the Passover in the spring (which is "near" in v. 55, and just "six days" away in 12:1). Unless a whole year has passed of which we are told nothing, all the events from 10:22 on must fit into three months or so.

The notice that Jesus "would no longer walk openly among the Jews" (that is, in the vicinity of Jerusalem) recalls the notice earlier that he "chose not to walk in Judea because the Jews there were seeking to kill him" (7:1), and for a time resisted his brothers' advice to "be in the public eye" (7:4). But here, instead of staying where he was, he makes his escape,[148] just as he did before when "the Jews" tried to stone him (8:59) or arrest him (10:39).[149] Nothing is said of what Jesus did or what happened in this "town called Ephraim," except that he "remained with the disciples."[150] The absence of information about his sojourn is puzzling,[151] but suggests that the accent is simply on Jesus "being there," and being "with the disciples." This is borne out by certain other instances in which Jesus "remains" or "spends time" somewhere for an indefinite period (see 2:12; 3:22; 10:40).[152] As for being

---

"It is misleading to read Eusebius's 'milestones' as miles" (see Excursus II to *Palestine in the Fourth Century* A.D., 176-78).

148. That is, he "went from there" (Gr. ἀπῆλθεν ἐκεῖθεν).

149. In 8:59 he "went out of the temple" (ἐξῆλθεν), and in 10:39 he "went out from their hand" (ἐξῆλθεν), and "went back [ἀπῆλθεν πάλιν] across the Jordan" (10:40).

150. The manuscript tradition is divided between "remained" (ἔμεινεν, with P^{66}, P^{75}, ℵ, and B) and "spent time with" (διέτριβεν, with P^{45}, a corrector of P^{66}, A, D, Θ, most of the Latin tradition, and the majority of later manuscripts). The former is probably to be preferred not only because of stronger manuscript evidence, but because the latter shows signs of harmonization with 3:22 (this is evident in some of the same manuscripts which read "his disciples," as in 3:22, and in one which even adds "and was baptizing").

151. C. W. Hedrick identifies this as one of a number of "Vestigial Scenes in John: Settings without Dramatization" (*Novum Testamentum* 47.4 [2005], 354-66). He distinguishes (357) between v. 54a ("a summary statement describing the cessation of Jesus' typical or usual behavior") and v. 54b ("not a summary, like John 11:54a, but rather a description of a particular event, undeveloped and under-dramatized, that goes nowhere so far as the plot is concerned"). Yet because Jesus is already in Judea, the acknowledged "summary" (v. 54a) requires a withdrawal or escape of some kind "from there" (ἐκεῖθεν) to another place (as was the case in 10:39-40).

152. All three of these examples mark the place in question as "there" (ἐκεῖ). But in 3:22, Jesus not only "spends time" but baptizes, leading to a significant exchange be-

657

"there" *(ekei)*, why did Jesus choose this place? It is difficult to say. Ephraim would have been well south of "Aenon near the Salim," where John had baptized (3:23), but an intriguing question is where it was in relation to the unidentified scene of Jesus' baptizing ministry (see 3:22, 26; 4:1). Was there a connection? If the writer knows of one, he makes nothing of it. To him, the notable thing about "Ephraim" is not that anything else important happened there (as was the case in 10:40), but simply that it is *not* Jerusalem, but a place of refuge, however temporary.[153]

As for being "with the disciples," we have heard nothing of them since Thomas "said to the fellow disciples, 'Let us go too that we might die with him'" (v. 16). All through the account of the raising of Lazarus, Jesus' disciples (aside from Mary and Martha) have been conspicuous by their absence. Now they resurface, and from here on, well into the Passion narrative, they will continue to be in the picture (see 12:4-6, 16, 21-26; 13:1–17:26; 18:1, etc.). The implication of the brief notice is that Jesus spent time privately with his disciples, perhaps preparing them for what was to come, yet what evidence we have about Ephraim suggests that it was by no means a remote or uninhabited place, but a populated "town,"[154] perhaps of some size, not a mere "village"[155] like Bethany.[156] At the same time, the detail that it was in "the region near the desert" evokes at least the possibility of refuge and solitude. While a sojourn in "the desert" (comparable to the synoptic temptation stories) would have made a good story, the Gospel writer is probably dealing with a firm historical tradition that Jesus and his disciples, for whatever reason, spent some time before his Passion in a real "town" with plenty of real inhabitants.[157]

---

tween John and his disciples. In 10:40, Jesus' disciples are not explicitly but only implicitly present, and the notice also leads somewhere in that "many believed in him there" (10:42). The only instance other than here in which nothing actually happens is 2:12 (see Hedrick, "Vestigial Scenes," 354-57), but in that instance, as we have seen, Jesus was accompanied by his mother and brothers as well as his disciples, and the point seems to have been precisely the momentary vignette of "family."

153. This is reflected in the terminology: Jesus goes "from there" (ἐκεῖθεν), that is, from Jerusalem, to Ephraim (κἀκεῖ), where he "remained."

154. Gr. πόλιν.

155. Gr. κώμη (see v. 1).

156. This is more or less consistent with the testimony of Eusebius ("the very large village of Ephraim," above, n. 147).

157. See, for example, Brown, 1.444 ("The very obscurity of the reference makes it likely that we are dealing with a historical reminiscence"), and Barrett, 408 ("The name Ephraim serves no allegorical or other purpose, and is probably traditional").

R. TO JERUSALEM AGAIN (11:55–12:19)

55 *Now the Passover of the Jews was near, and many went up from the region to Jerusalem before the Passover, that they might purify themselves.* 56 *So they were seeking Jesus, and saying to one another as they stood in the temple, "What do you think? That he surely won't come to the festival?"* 57 *Now the chief priests and the Pharisees had given commands that if anyone found out where he was, they should make it known, so that they might arrest him.*

12:1 *Then Jesus, six days before the Passover, came into Bethany, where Lazarus was, whom Jesus raised from the dead.* 2 *Then they made a dinner for him there, and Martha was serving, while Lazarus was one of those reclining with him.* 3 *Then Mary took a pound of expensive perfume of genuine nard, anointed the feet of Jesus, and dried his feet with her hair. The house was filled from the fragrance of the perfume.* 4 *But Judas the Iscariot, one of his disciples, the one who was going to hand him over, says,* 5 *"Why was this perfume not sold for three hundred denarii and given to the poor?"* 6 *Now he said this not because it mattered to him about the poor, but because he was a thief, and, having the money box, was stealing from what was being put in.* 7 *So Jesus said, "Let her be, so as to keep it for the day of my burial.* 8 *For the poor you always have with you, but me you do not always have."*

9 *Then a great crowd from the Jews found out that he was there and came, not because of Jesus alone, but that they might also see Lazarus, whom he raised from the dead.* 10 *And the chief priests resolved that they would also kill Lazarus,* 11 *because on account of him many of the Jews were going off and believing in Jesus.* 12 *The next day the great crowd that had come to the festival, when they heard that Jesus was coming into Jerusalem,* 13 *took the branches of the palms and went out to meet him, and they were shouting, "Hosanna! Blessed is the One coming in the name of the Lord, even the King of Israel!"* 14 *And Jesus, having found a young donkey, sat on it, just as it is written,* 15 *"Fear not, daughter Zion. Look, your king is coming, sitting on a donkey's colt!"* 16 *These things his disciples did not understand at first, but when Jesus was glorified, then they remembered that these things were written about him and these things they did for him.* 17 *So the crowd that was with him kept testifying that he called Lazarus from the tomb and raised him from the dead.* 18 *That was also why the crowd met him, because they heard that he had done this sign.* 19 *Then the Pharisees said to each other, "You can see that you're accomplishing nothing. Look, the world has gone after him!"*

This bittersweet narrative brings together several brief independent scenes, skillfully blending the shadow of Jesus' impending death with the prospect of final glory.[1] Its account of Jesus' last journey to Jerusalem is introduced by the notice that "the Passover of the Jews was near" (v. 55), raising expectations that he will return to Jerusalem as he customarily did for the Jewish festivals (see 2:13, 5:1, and 7:10, 6:4 being the sole exception). The note of expectancy is maintained by those already at the festival (vv. 55-57), yet Jesus is never explicitly said to "go up to Jerusalem" for this Passover. Instead, he simply makes an appearance back in Bethany "six days before the Passover" at a dinner where Mary anoints his feet with perfume (12:1-11). But then it is on to Jerusalem and a tumultuous welcome by the crowds there, frustrating the authorities who were seeking his life (vv. 12-19). Despite the welcome and despite the Pharisees' lament, "Look, the world has gone after him!" (v. 19), his anointing by Mary (see vv. 7-8) has already signaled to the reader that his death is inevitable. It is now clear that life for Lazarus will mean death for Jesus — and possibly for Lazarus as well (see 12:10). Yet so far, instead of dying he has been welcomed triumphantly into Jerusalem as "the king of Israel" (v. 13). He has gained the world (v. 19) — but at what price?

55 The reader is fast-forwarded through Jesus' sojourn, and in due course "the Passover of the Jews was near" (v. 55a). An argument could be made that this (and not the end of chapter 12) is the major dividing point of the Gospel, for all that happens from here on happens in connection with this final Passover. The notice echoes almost word for word the notice of Jesus' first Passover: "And the Passover of the Jews was near, and Jesus went up to Jerusalem" (2:13). The difference is that here nothing is said immediately — or ever, for that matter — of Jesus "going up to Jerusalem" for the festival (see 5:1; 7:10). Instead, we learn that "many went up from the region to Jerusalem, before the Passover, that they might purify themselves" (v. 55b). But what is meant by "the region"? Is it a general term for the Judean countryside outside Jerusalem,[2] or does the notice refer to the specific "region near the desert" (v. 54) where Jesus has been staying? Most commentators do not even raise the issue, but its importance should not be overlooked.[3] The correspondence

---

1. See Bultmann (412), who views 11.55–12.19 as "a connected composition, consisting of various fragments."

2. So BDAG, 1093-94; Schnackenburg, 2.364. The closest parallel, however, would be 3:22 (εἰς τὴν Ἰουδαίαν γῆν), where the vocabulary is not the same.

3. Barrett notices it, but does little more than state the alternatives: "Either the district referred to in v. 54, or, more probably, 'the country', 'the provinces', generally" (409). As for English translations, older versions tend to translate the same word (χώρα) in the same way both times (vv. 54 and 55): for example, "a country . . . the country" (KJV, Douay), "the country . . . the country" (ASV, NASB, RSV, Moffatt, NEB, REB). But the more recent tendency is to translate the two instances differently: for example, "a

between "to the region"[4] (v. 54) and "from the region"[5] argues strongly for a reference to the same "region near the desert" where Jesus and his disciples had taken refuge. Thus, "many went up from the [aforementioned] region to Jerusalem," before the Passover, that they might purify themselves" This is consistent with the notion of that region (and the town of Ephraim in particular) as a populated area relatively close to Jerusalem.[6] Self-purification in order to celebrate the Passover was mandated in Scripture (see Num 9:6-12; 2 Chr 30:17-18), and it was probably thought advantageous to do so as close as possible to the actual festival so as not to risk additional defilement.[7] But the Gospel writer is not primarily interested in the details of self-purification.[8] He merely uses it to explain why "many," possibly from the very region where Jesus had been staying, were at the festival ahead of time. More important to him is what they were saying about Jesus once they were there.

56-57 The conversation of these pilgrims centers on whether or not Jesus would make an appearance at the festival, given the decision of the Chief Priest and the council: "So they were seeking Jesus," we are told, "and saying to one another as they stood in the temple, 'What do you think? That he surely won't come to the festival?'" (v. 56). The writer pauses to explain why: "Now the chief priests and the Pharisees had given commands that if anyone found out where Jesus was, they should make it known, so that they might arrest him" (v. 57). The scene is markedly similar to an earlier one at the Tent festival where "the Jews were seeking him at the festival, and said, 'Where is that man?'" There, after considerable murmuring in the crowd, we

---

region . . . the country" (NIV, TNIV), "the region . . . the country" (NRSV, NAB); "a place . . . the country" (TEV, Richmond Lattimore), and (at the extreme) "a place . . . all over the country" (NLT).

4. Gr. εἰς τὴν χώραν.

5. Gr. ἐκ τῆς χώρας.

6. Obviously, if this is the case, Jesus has still been technically "among the Jews" (see v. 54) even in this place of refuge. The inhabitants of the place were loyal enough Jews to come to the Passover festival. The point is not that Jesus wanted to escape to Gentile territory, but that he wanted to avoid "the Jews" in Jerusalem (that is, primarily "the chief priests and the Pharisees").

7. Josephus speaks of the "country-folk [τοὺς ἐπιχωρίους] during their period of purification" in connection with an unnamed Jewish festival (*Jewish War* 1.229; LCL, 2.107), and again of people "assembling for the feast of unleavened bread" (that is, the Passover) at least as early as "the eighth of the month" (about a week early), possibly for this reason (*Jewish War* 6.290; LCL, 3.461).

8. Although the Gospel writer is aware in general of Jewish "purification" (καθαρισμός, 2:6; 3:25), the clause "that they might purify themselves" (ἵνα ἁγνίσωσιν ἑαυτούς) introduces vocabulary that does not occur elsewhere in the Gospel. The closest parallel is perhaps 18:28, with its reference to those who "did not enter the Roman praetorium, so that they might not be defiled [ἵνα μὴ μιανθῶσιν], but might eat the Passover."

were told that "No one would speak about him publicly . . . for fear of the Jews" (see 7:11-13).

Yet there are important differences as well. For one thing, "the Jews" in the earlier situation "were seeking" Jesus (7:11) with hostile intent, "seeking" to kill him as they had intended all along (see 7:1). Here, by contrast, those "seeking" him (v. 56) are not "the Jews" but the "many" who had come early to the Passover festival "from the region" (v. 55). They are "seeking" him in all likelihood *not* with hostile intent, but out of simple curiosity. Their speculation as to whether or not he would come to the festival is more natural and understandable if they know who he is and are acquainted with his previous whereabouts than if they do not. It is not likely that his name would have been such a household word that people from all over Israel would be asking such questions. The curiosity of these pilgrims is consistent with the thought that they are from not just any "region" or "country," but specifically from "the region near the desert" (v. 54) where Jesus had been staying. That they were wondering about these things "as they stood in the temple" (v. 56) heightens the impression that we are dealing here not with a "great murmuring among the crowds" (as in 7:12), but with a particular delegation from a particular place.

Another difference is that the issue of whether Jesus will or will not come to Jerusalem is raised in Jerusalem itself at the festival, not in the place where Jesus is staying (as in 7:1-10, in Galilee). Just as he did not accompany his brothers when they went up to Jerusalem from Galilee (7:8-10), so he did not accompany the "many" other pilgrims from "the region" to this his last Passover. His current whereabouts are unknown to them, and just as unknown to the reader. Their question, "What do you think? That he surely won't come to the festival?" expects a negative answer, yet in a subtle way hints at a positive one, implying that if Jesus does come it will be a bold move indeed.[9] The effect is to invite the reader to ask the same question, raising the level of suspense. Will Jesus show up at the festival or not?

57 As if a reason for the suspense were needed, the writer supplies one: "Now the chief priests and the Pharisees had given commands[10] that if

---

9. "What do you think?" is literally, "What does it seem to you?" (τὶ δοκεῖ ὑμῖν). The follow-up question introduced with ὅτι anticipates the expected answer. E. A. Abbott paraphrases it, "What do *you* (emph.) think? [Do you think, as we do,] that he will never dream of venturing to come to the feast?" He adds the comment that "The intention certainly is to give prominence to Christ's courage in the face of dangers recognized by everybody" (*Johannine Grammar*, 160).

10. "Commands" (ἐντολάς) is the reading of the more important witnesses (including ℵ, B, and W), but the singular "command" (ἐντολήν) has equally strong and wider support (including P⁶⁶, A, D, L, the Latin tradition, and the majority of later witnesses). But because what follows is in fact one "command," it is somewhat more likely that an original plural would have been changed to a singular than the other way around.

anyone found out where he was, they should make it known, so that they might arrest him" (v. 57). This is scarcely a surprise, given the preceding notice that "from that day they [that is, "the chief priests and Pharisees," v. 47] resolved that they would kill him" (v. 53). It is merely a reminder that the council's resolution was now being implemented. What is unclear is the intention of these delegates "from the region." Is it to turn him over to the authorities, or merely to take note of his presence should he make an appearance at the festival? It is a moot question because in any event we are not told whether or not they "found out where he was." Only after Jesus is back in the vicinity of Jerusalem are we told that "the great crowd from the Jews found out that he was there" (12:9, echoing the language of v. 57), and even then they are not said to have made him known to the authorities. So here, as we have seen, the worshipers raising the question of whether or not Jesus will come to the festival do not appear hostile to him (like "the Jews" in 7:11), but neutral (more like "the crowds" in 7:12). Yet regardless of their intent, the decree of "the chief priests and the Pharisees" makes it clear that Jesus is in danger, so that for the reader the suspense mounts.

12:1-2 Jesus abruptly puts in an appearance, not in Jerusalem for the Passover, but less than two miles away (see 11:18) in Bethany, "six days before the Passover," back "where Lazarus was, whom Jesus raised from the dead" (12:1).[11] There is a certain redundancy to the clause "whom he had raised from the dead," for the reader already knows this. The final two references to Lazarus in the Gospel will identify him in the same way (vv. 9, 17). Clearly, the memory of the raising of Lazarus will dominate the scene at Bethany. Symbolic explanations of the "six days" have been proposed, but not very convincingly.[12] The point is rather that the Passover is drawing ever closer, from the generalization that it was "near" (11:55), to the more specific "six days before" (12:1), to "the next day" (12:12), to the very threshold of the festival (13:1). The time reference conflicts with the accounts of Jesus' anointing at Bethany in Mark and Matthew just "two days" (at most) before the Passover (see Mk 14:1; Mt 26:2), and (in contrast to John's Gospel) well *after* his triumphal entry into the city.

The notice that "Then they made a dinner for him there, and Martha was serving, while Lazarus was one of those reclining with him" (v. 2) sets

---

11. The redundancy is even greater if, with many ancient manuscripts (including P[66], A, D, Θ, Ψ, the old Latin, and the majority of later witnesses), the words "the one who had died" (ὁ τεθνηκώς; see 11:44) are inserted between "Lazarus" and "whom he had raised from the dead."

12. For example, that these "six days" somehow correspond to the days of creation, or to the presumed six days at the beginning of Jesus' ministry (see 1:29, 35, 43; 2:1), or Mark's six days prior to the transfiguration (Mk 9:2; Mt 17:1), in each instance the point being that glory is revealed after six days.

the scene for what follows (vv. 3-11). "They made" is indefinite, implicitly referring to Lazarus and his two sisters.[13] The "dinner"[14] may have been arranged to welcome Jesus back from his sojourn and celebrate with him the raising of Lazarus.[15] If so, the likelihood is that his sojourn away from Bethany and Jerusalem has been relatively brief. All three major characters from the preceding chapter are now quickly reintroduced: Martha, who "was serving"[16] (in keeping with her role in another story, which the Gospel writer may have known),[17] Lazarus himself, who is mentioned simply as being present (v. 2), and finally Mary, whose abrupt act becomes the very center of the story (see v. 3). That there were other guests is evident from the reference to "those reclining with him," and these others seem to have included at least some of Jesus' disciples who had been with him at Ephraim and have now returned to Bethany (see v. 4, "Judas the Iscariot, one of his disciples").

3 Mary is the only family member not yet named, and without bothering to mention that she too was present at the dinner, the writer tells us, all in one breath, what she did: "Then Mary took a pound of expensive perfume of genuine nard, anointed the feet of Jesus, and dried his feet with her hair" (v. 3a). This differs from the anointing stories in Mark and Matthew, where the woman who anoints Jesus was not a guest — much less a hostess — at the meal, but "came" to Jesus (Mk 14:3) or "approached" him (Mt 26:7), apparently from outside the house. This is even more evident in Luke, where the woman was "in the town" and "found out that he was eating in the Pharisee's house" (Lk 7:37). In each of the other accounts the woman brings with her an alabaster jar filled with perfume,[18] but here no such jar is mentioned, only the contents, "a pound of expensive perfume of genuine nard."[19] The

---

13. The anointing story in Mark and Matthew, by contrast, is set in the house of a certain "Simon the Leper" in Bethany (Mk 14:3; Mt 26:6; in Lk 7:36-50 the host is a Pharisee who is also named Simon). John's indefinite "they made" (ἐποίησαν) allows for the possibility of harmonization, but no one reading John's Gospel by itself would suspect that the dinner was hosted by anyone other than Martha and Mary.

14. Gr. δεῖπνον.

15. That the dinner was "for him" (αὐτῷ) and that the guests were reclining "with him" (σὺν αὐτῷ) signals that Jesus was indeed the guest of honor.

16. Gr. διηκόνει.

17. See Luke 10:40, where Martha was said to be distracted "over much serving" (περὶ πολλὴν διακονίαν). Nothing has been said up to now in John's Gospel of Martha's role as servant.

18. Mark calls particular attention to the alabaster jar by noting that the woman "broke the jar" when she poured the perfume on Jesus' head (Mk 14:3).

19. The "pound" (λίτραν) was the Roman pound, about 12 ounces rather than 16 (see 19:39), but still an enormous amount of perfume. The other Gospels do not mention the amount of perfume, and only Mark (14:5) mentions its estimated value.

phrase "perfume of genuine nard"[20] is the closest verbal parallel to Mark in all of the Gospel of John, given the rarity both of the noun "nard"[21] and the adjective translated here as "genuine."[22] But here the similarities end. Mary "took" the pound of perfume (which seems to have been ready at hand); she did not already "have" it with her (as in Mk 14:3; Mt 26:7). With it she "anointed" Jesus' feet instead of "pouring" it on his head (as in Mark and Matthew).[23] Consequently, she "dried his feet with her hair," not at all like the woman at Bethany in Matthew and Mark, but more like the anonymous woman in Luke who "placed herself behind him *at his feet* weeping and with her tears began to bathe *his feet,* and she was drying them with the hairs of her head, and kept kissing *his feet* and anointing them with the perfume" (Lk 7:38, italics added).[24] But here too are differences. Luke uses imperfect verbs to describe more of a process than a single act, and his placement of the woman both "behind" Jesus and "at his feet" is difficult to visualize. John, by contrast, uses the aorist tense to describe a single simple act: Mary "anointed the feet of Jesus and dried his feet with her hair."[25] Another difference is that the act of "drying" Jesus' feet with her hair is appropriate in Luke, for she is merely wiping away tears before anointing Jesus with perfume, but less appropriate in John (see also 11:2), where Mary seems to be immediately wiping away the precious ointment she has just administered.[26]

20. Gr. μύρου νάρδου πιστικῆς.

21. See BDAG, 666: "an aromatic oil of the (spike) nard plant." The word occurs only in these two places in the New Testament.

22. See BDAG, 818: "In later writers πιστικῆς means that which belongs to πίστις, 'faithful, trustworthy'" (compare perhaps the adjective ἄδολον in 1 Pet 2:2, "unadulterated milk"). This is the likely meaning here, though it is uncertain whether it is an adjective supplied by one of the Gospel writers (or someone telling the story), or whether it was a kind of brand name under which the perfume was marketed. The parallel would extend even further if the word for "expensive" in Mark were πολυτίμου (with A, G, W, Θ and certain other witnesses) rather than πολυτελοῦς. But this reading (even aside from its weak attestation) is suspect as a scribal harmonization to John.

23. For a convenient chart of the agreements and disagreements among Mark 14:3-9 (leaving Matthew out of consideration), John 12:1-8, and Luke 7:36-38, see Brown, 1.450.

24. The italics help show that Jesus' "feet" are made conspicuous in both passages by repetition (τοὺς πόδας τοῦ Ἰησοῦ and τοὺς πόδας αὐτοῦ in John, and τοὺς πόδας αὐτοῦ three times in Luke).

25. The contrast is most easily seen between the aorist ἤλειψεν ("anointed") in John and the imperfect ἤλειφεν ("kept . . . anointing") in Luke.

26. This is noticed by some commentators (see Barrett, 412, who calls the act "unintelligible"; also Brown, 1.451; Schnackenburg, 2.367). Bultmann (415, n. 1) hints that the reference to drying might be a secondary addition. The further point (made by many of the same commentators) that the letting down of the hair is natural for a "sinful woman" or prostitute (as in Lk 7), but inappropriate for the devout Mary of Bethany, has

While it is possible that the account here has been influenced by some version of Luke's story, John's Gospel has its own reasons for calling attention to the feet rather than the head. For one thing, it could be simply a corollary of identifying the woman who anointed Jesus as Mary of Bethany (see 11:2), for wherever we meet Mary, in John or in Luke, she is always at Jesus' feet (see 11:32; Lk 10:39). But perhaps more important, Mary's act anticipates the action of Jesus at a similar "dinner" a chapter later (13:2), when he himself will "wash the feet of the disciples and dry with the towel with which he was girded" (13:5). Mary's otherwise "unintelligible" act (see n. 26) of wiping away the perfume she has just administered could then be explained not as a detail imported from Luke 7:38, but simply as part of the correlation between her anointing of Jesus and his own subsequent washing of the disciples' feet.[27] In another Gospel, Jesus claims that "the Son of man came not to be served but to serve" (Mk 10:45). In John's account we see Jesus first being served (by *both* Martha and Mary; see v. 2), and then serving. First we are shown the "normal" scene of a disciple at the feet of her teacher (although the extravagance of a whole pound of costly perfume was hardly "normal"!), and later we will witness the striking reversal of that procedure in Jesus' unforgettable act of washing his disciples' feet. Mary's act is as remarkable for its reckless extravagance as the footwashing is for its reversal of expected roles. Whatever the facts of the case historically, pouring the perfume on Jesus' head (as in Mark and Matthew) would not have had the same effect within the dramatic structure of the Gospel.

The concise description of Mary's act concludes with a comment unparalleled in any other Gospel: "The house was filled from the fragrance of the perfume" (v. 3b).[28] The comment calls attention to the reckless extravagance of the act and its consequent effect on the onlookers, eliciting an immediate objection from Judas (vv. 4-5). In more subtle fashion, the comment recalls for the reader Martha's remark at the tomb of Lazarus, "Lord, already it stinks, for it has been four days!" (11:39). The stench of death has now given way to the "fragrance" of eternal life — a note of triumph soon to be qualified by intimations of another death (see vv. 7-8). Beyond this, interpreters as far

---

much less in its favor, for the point of the passage is the sheer recklessness of Mary's love and devotion to Jesus.

27. As Lincoln points out (338), "the particular term for wiping occurs in this Gospel's narrative only in connection with Mary's action (compare 11.2, 12.3) and Jesus' action (compare 13.5)." So too Lindars (416-17): "John seems to have imagined the anointing as washing of the feet, for which drying with the hair would not be inappropriate."

28. On the unusual construction, "filled from" (ἐπληρώθη ἐκ), instead of the simple genitive, "full of," see Abbott, *Johannine Grammar,* 253 (while resisting the symbolic application to the church he attempts to read into it). The closest parallels are 6:13, and Rev 8:5 and Mt 23:25 (albeit with a different verb for "full" or "filled").

back as Origen have gone further, viewing this final comment as John's symbolic equivalent to Jesus' concluding statement in Mark about the woman who anointed him at Bethany: "Amen, I say to you, wherever the gospel is proclaimed in the whole world, what she did will be spoken of in memory of her" (Mk 14:9; see also Mt 26:13). The fragrance of the perfume filling the house is supposed to evoke the thought of the good news about Jesus filling the whole world.[29] This is all very unlikely.[30] John's Gospel is quite familiar with the notion of the universal spread of the message of Jesus to the whole world, but has its own way of expressing it, and when it appears in the Gospel it is easily recognizable (see 10:16; 11:52; 12:24, 32). If John knew of the saying of Jesus in Mark 14:9, introduced by "Amen, I say to you," it is difficult to see why he would not simply have retained it instead of replacing it with a comment of his own cloaked in deep symbolism. The normal route is from symbol to interpretation, not the other way around. Therefore, the simpler explanations of "the fragrance of the perfume" are preferable.[31]

4-5 In other versions of the story an angry objection is raised, either by "some" who were present (Mk 14:4) or by "the disciples" (Mt 26:8).[32] "Why has there been this waste of the perfume?" they ask (Mk 14:4). "For this perfume could have been sold for over three hundred denarii and given to the poor." Then, Mark adds, "they rebuked her" (v. 5).[33] Here, by contrast, the

---

29. Origen is worth quoting in full, even though he seems to be drawing on all three anointing stories at once, as if from a Gospel harmony: "We also ought to know that every good deed done to Jesus is also included in so great a gospel. For example, there was the woman who had performed wicked deeds and repented. She was able to anoint Jesus with a fragrant substance because of her genuine repentance of evil deeds, and she produced the scent of ointment in the whole house, perceptible to everyone there. For this reason it is also written, 'Wherever this gospel is preached among all the nations, that also which she has done shall be told for a memory of her'" (*Commentary on John* 1.67-68; FC, 89.47-48). See also Clement of Alexandria, *Paedagogus* 2.8, "For the feet anointed with fragrant ointment mean divine instruction traveling with renown to the ends of the earth" (ANF, 2.253). Bultmann (405) takes this interpretation seriously, as do Hoskyns (413), Morris (513), Carson (428), and others.

30. Schnackenburg calls it "far from the intention of our passage" (2.367). To Barrett it is "questionable," even though it supports his contention that John knows Mark (413); so too Lindars (417),

31. The notice might even be "a reminiscence of someone who was there" (Morris, 513, who still manages to leave room for a symbolic interpretation).

32. In Luke's story (7:36-50), an entirely different kind of objection is raised (v. 39), to which Jesus responds at great length (vv. 40-48).

33. Mark's version is rather more detailed than Matthew's, in that the objectors speak first "to each other" (πρὸς ἑαυτούς, 14:4), and then "rebuke" the woman herself (καὶ ἐμβριμῶντο αὐτῇ, v. 5). Matthew's version is shorter and simpler: "'Why this waste?' they said. 'For this perfume could have been sold for plenty [πολλοῦ] and given to the poor'" (26:8).

objection is attributed to someone who is actually named (just as Mary was named), "Judas the Iscariot" (v. 4).[34] Judas has been mentioned only once before, as "one of the Twelve" and yet as "the devil," who was going to "hand over" Jesus — how or to whom, we were not told (see 6:70-71; also 6:64). He is now introduced again, and identified in much the same way as "one of [Jesus'] disciples, the one who was going to hand him over" (v. 4), though not as "the devil." Judas does not speak in anger, like those who objected in Mark and Matthew, and these, his only lines in the entire Gospel, sound less like the devil than like a hard-headed, though compassionate, businessman: "Why was this perfume not sold for three hundred denarii and given to the poor?" (v. 5). It was a legitimate question. A denarius was a day's wage, and three hundred denarii might have done a great deal of good (see 6:7). Judas comes off no worse, and perhaps slightly better than the unnamed questioners in the two other Gospel accounts. It is quite conceivable that in the original form of the story it was indeed Judas who raised the objection, and that Mark and Matthew (or their sources) concealed it because it painted Judas in a more favorable light than seemed appropriate, given his immediate act of betrayal (see n. 34). If this is the case, John's Gospel handles the matter differently. An explanation is needed, and quickly supplied.

6 The narrative aside provides information about Judas that the reader would otherwise not have known: "Now he said this not because it mattered to him about the poor, but because he was a thief, and, having the money box, was stealing from what was being put in" (v. 6). This is not the first time the Gospel writer has demonstrated such knowledge. When Jesus told his disciples that "one of you is 'the devil'" (6:70), he knew somehow that Jesus meant "Judas of Simon Iscariot," and that "this man, one of the Twelve, was going to hand him over" (6:71). And here, just a moment before, he has identified Judas again as "the one who was going to hand him over" (v. 4). The reason for this interest in Judas will become clearer (if not entirely clear) a chapter later, when "the disciple whom Jesus loved" (identified finally as the Gospel writer, 21:24) is said to be the first (perhaps the only one) of Jesus' disciples to understand that Judas would "hand over" Jesus to the authorities (see 13:23-27). While he is not quick to share this information with his fellow disciples (see 13:28-29), he shares it repeatedly with the readers of his Gospel (see also 13:2, 11; 18:5). Here he wants them to know that Judas is not speaking out of genuine concern for the poor, but out of greed, knowing that the more that was in "the money box," the easier it would be to skim off something for himself. In this way, the reader learns that Jesus and

---

34. It may be more than coincidental that immediately after the anointing in both Mark (14:10-11) and Matthew (26:14-16), Judas departs to the chief priests and betrays Jesus (see Keener, 2.864).

his disciples carried around a "money box,"[35] and that the funds in it (however collected)[36] were used, among other things, to help the poor (in 13:29 the reason for Judas's departure is seen either as purchasing what was needed for Passover, or giving to the poor).[37] The blunt characterization of Judas as one who said what he said "not because it mattered[38] to him about the poor, but because he was a thief," evokes both "the thief" in Jesus' earlier discourse about shepherds and sheep (10:2, 8, 10), and at the same time the "hireling" to whom "it does not matter[39] ... about the sheep" (10:13).[40] In short, Judas is not the typical well-meaning (if sometimes uninformed) disciple or potential disciple questioning the teacher (as, for example, in 4:9, 11, 15, 19-20; 6:68; 9:36; 11:8, 12, 21-22, 24; 13:6, 8, 9, 36, 37; 14:5, 8, 22). His motives are far more sinister, and his abrupt question is conspicuously *not* introduced by "Lord" or "Rabbi."

7 Jesus himself is kinder to Judas than the Gospel writer's narrative aside. "Let her be," he said, "so as to keep it for the day of my burial" (v. 7). "Let her be"[41] matches exactly his response to those who objected in Mark (Mk 14:6) except that the verb is singular, as the context requires, not plural. But John's account lacks the accompanying words of praise for the woman that are found in Mark, "she has performed a good work for me" (Mk 14:6), and "she has done what she could" (14:8), focusing instead on the main point: "so as to keep it for the day of my burial." The purpose clause, "so as to keep it,"[42] is confusing because it seems to point toward the future, and the phrase "for the day of my burial" seems to bear this out (see 19:40-42). A variant reading, "she has kept it for the day of my burial," alleviates the problem somewhat, but is suspect for that very reason.[43] Mark's wording is even

---

35. Gr. τὸ γλωσσόκομον (see 13:29, and BDAG, 202: "orig. a case for the mouthpiece or reed of a flute, then gener. 'case, container' for anything at all").

36. For a glimpse of the financing of Jesus' ministry, see Luke 8:2-3, where we learn of "certain women who were healed of evil spirits and sicknesses," who "served" or "provided for" (διηκόνουν) Jesus and his disciples "out of their resources" (ἐκ τῶν ὑπαρχόντων αὐταῖς). In her own reckless way, this is exactly what Mary of Bethany has just done.

37. This suggests that Jesus' question to Philip, "Where shall we buy loaves so that these may eat?" (6:5), may not have been merely rhetorical, even though he said it "testing him" (6:6). If so, the "two hundred denarii" mentioned in Philip's answer (6:7) may not have been simply a random number, but something rather close to what Philip knew was in the "money box" (see also Mk 6:37).

38. Gr. ἔμελεν αὐτῷ.
39. Gr. οὐ μέλει αὐτῷ.
40. See Keener, 2.864.
41. Gr. ἄφες αὐτήν.
42. Gr. ἵνα ... τηρήσῃ αὐτό.
43. "She has kept it" (τετήρηκεν αὐτό) is the reading of A, families 1 and 13, and

more comprehensible, "She has undertaken beforehand[44] to anoint my body for the burial" (Mk 14:8).[45] If there is any kind of literary relationship between the story as told in John and in Mark, John's version appears to be the earlier. Both the Markan version and the variant reading in John itself appear to be efforts to clarify what Jesus is saying, namely, that Mary's impulsive act represented a kind of anointing of his body in advance for burial, thereby anticipating his death as no other disciple had done.[46]

The question is whether or not these efforts to interpret the pronouncement in John have done so correctly. Taken literally, Jesus could be saying, "Let her be, so as to keep the perfume [rather than *wasting* it by pouring it out now] until the day of my burial" (that is, seven chapters later, in 19:39-42). This obviously makes no sense, for the perfume is gone, and its fragrance now fills the house (v. 3). The (equally literal) alternative is to read it as "Let her be, so as to keep the perfume" (rather than *selling* it, as Judas had proposed), not "*until* the day of my burial," but as we have translated it, "*for* the day of my burial" (that is, with a view to, or in anticipation of, the burial day).[47] This is precisely how the variant reading (see n. 43) and both Mark and Matthew seem to have understood it. It also fits the context better, in that Jesus is responding to Judas's objection that the perfume should have been "sold" (v. 5), not "kept." The one difficulty — one that would not occur to readers at this point — is how this anointing relates to the actual elaborate preparation of Jesus' body for burial by Joseph and Nicodemus *after* the crucifixion (see 19:39-42).[48] Is the latter simply redundant, or do the two somehow confirm and supplement each other? Both narratives involve an extraordinary quantity of something — "a pound"[49] in one instance ("of expensive perfume of genuine nard," v. 3), and "about one hundred pounds" in the other ("a mixture of myrrh and aloes," 19:39). Quite possibly the apparent repeti-

---

the majority of later manuscripts, as well as two later Syriac versions. By far the more important early witnesses favor the purpose clause (ἵνα . . . τηρήσῃ αὐτό, "so as to keep it"). The perfect τετήρηκεν implies that she has "kept" it up to now, but not that she is still "keeping" it for some future occasion.

44. Gr. προέλαβεν.

45. Matthew's version accomplishes much the same thing: "By putting this perfume on my body, she has done it to prepare me for burial" (Mt 26:13).

46. This presupposes my interpretation that Thomas's remark, "Let us go too that we might die with him" (11:16), is referring not to Jesus but to Lazarus.

47. See BDAG, 291, on εἰς as "for, to, with respect to, with reference to."

48. A similar question arises in Mark's Gospel. What has Mk 14:8 ("She has undertaken beforehand to anoint my body for the burial") to do with Mk 16:1, where three women "bought spices, that they might come and anoint him"? The question does not arise in Matthew, where the women came just "to see the tomb" (28:1).

49. Gr. λίτραν.

tion is not a difficulty but the whole point, in that Joseph of Arimathea and Nicodemus carry out literally (and just as extravagantly!) what Mary has acted out symbolically and in advance. But that story must be told in its own context.

8 According to our best early manuscripts, Jesus continues, "For the poor you always have with you, but me you do not always have" (v. 8). Two important early witnesses, however, omit the entire verse,[50] and the omission must be looked at carefully because the words might easily have been added by a later scribe, assimilating the pronouncement to Matthew 26:11 and/or Mark 14:7.[51] An additional factor is that the text shifts here from singular to plural: "Let her be" (v. 7) is addressed to Judas alone, while "the poor you always have with you" is plural, addressing the whole company. There is no such shift in Mark or Matthew, where those who first raise the objection are plural as well (see Mk 14:6; Mt 26:10), so that the words, "for you always have the poor with you," merely continue the pronouncement in the same vein. An argument could be made that the added words are natural in Mark and Matthew, but unnatural in John. This argument does not work, however, not only because of the weak textual evidence for omitting the verse, but because, as we have seen, John's account of the anointing shows signs of actually being prior to Mark's, at least in certain details (notably v. 7). Nor should it be forgotten that Jesus in the Gospel of John has a way of answering the questions or comments of an individual either with pronouncements directed to a larger group (as with Thomas in 14:6-7, and "Judas, not the Iscariot" in 14:23-24), or else first to the individual who asked and then to the larger group (as with Nathanael in 1:50-51, Peter in 13:36–14:4, and Philip in 14:9-11). It is therefore neither odd nor unnatural for Jesus to respond to Judas in a similar way. The implication is that Judas, despite his unique position as "the devil" (6:71) and "the one who was going to hand over" Jesus (v. 4), is nevertheless at some level expressing thoughts common to others — perhaps all — of the disciples. Judas has not, after all, been revealed as one set apart in any way from the others. Jesus says, "For the poor you always have with you, but me you

---

50. These are D and the Sinaitic Syriac version. In addition, one early papyrus, P[75], omits the words, "with you, but me you do not always have," leaving the sentence, "For the poor you always have." Metzger (*Textual Commentary*, 236) identifies the latter variation as an accidental error, or "parablepsis, the eye of the scribe passing from ἔχετε to ἔχετε" (that is, from "you always have" to "you do not always have," overlooking a whole clause). Virtually all other ancient witnesses (including P[66], ℵ, A, B, W, Δ, Ψ, and the majority of later witnesss) support the text as we have it.

51. See Metzger (236), who nevertheless concluded that "the overwhelming manuscript evidence for the verse seemed to a majority of the Committee to justify retaining it in the text."

do not always have" (v. 8) because it needs to be said, not just to Judas, but to all who were present.

In Mark the statement, "you always have the poor with you," is tempered by the reminder that "whenever you want you can do good to them" (Mk 14:7; for the principle involved, see Deut 15:11). In Matthew (26:11), there is no such addition, possibly because the point has just been made so eloquently that good works done for those in need are done for Jesus himself (see Mt 25:31-46). John's Gospel also lacks the additional words about helping the poor. While the writer's comment that Judas did not truly care about the poor (v. 6) could be read as implying that the readers of the Gospel *should* care, the accent in John is not on "the poor," but on Jesus himself, and his concluding words, "but me you do not always have." What Mary's act of devotion has done is to dramatize a simple fact that both Jesus' enemies and his friends throughout the Gospel have trouble grasping — that he is going away where they cannot follow (see 7:33-34; 8:21; 13:33; 16:16). She has accomplished this without saying a word, but Jesus now says it for her. In effect, whether she knows it or not, she has given him permission to depart by demonstrating her love while he is still present.[52]

9 At this point we are abruptly introduced to "a great crowd from the Jews"[53] who "found out that he was there and came, not because of Jesus alone, but that they might also see Lazarus, whom he raised from the dead" (v. 9). No such "great crowd from the Jews" has been mentioned before, *unless* we are meant to identify them with the "many" Jews who believed in Jesus after the raising of Lazarus, or the "many" who "went up from the region to Jerusalem before the Passover, that they might purify themselves." But the latter (11:55) are never referred to as a "crowd." The former (11:45) can be identified with "the crowd standing around" (11:42) for whose sake Jesus prayed just before calling Lazarus from the tomb. Yet it is unlikely that the same group is in view here, because this "great crowd from the

---

52. For further homiletical development, see my expository article, "John 12:1-11," *Interpretation* 42.3 (1989), 287-91.

53. Instead of ὄχλος πολύς for "a great crowd," some important manuscripts (including ℵ, B, and L) have ὁ ὄχλος πολύς, a difficult reading because πολύς is in the predicate position, making the phrase ill-suited to being the subject of the sentence (see Metzger, *Textual Commentary,* 237). Because it is a difficult reading, some argued for its originality, and the editors have retained the article, while placing it in brackets. Yet support for the anarthrous "a great crowd" (ὄχλος πολύς) is also substantial (with P[66], P[75], A, a later hand of B, as well as Θ, Ψ, 33, and a majority of later witnesses). Moreover, it is unlikely that the writer would have used the article in referring to a group not mentioned before, but introduced here as if for the first time (as in 6:2, ὄχλος πολύς). Possibly the article was added by scribes influenced by the rather consistent presence of the article with ὄχλος elsewhere in the narrative (see vv. 12, 17, 18, 29, 34).

Jews" are not said to have already believed in Jesus.[54] They seem to have come out of curiosity, having heard the story of Lazarus (possibly from the very bystanders who believed according to 11:45). If they believe, it is as a result of what they see or hear now at Bethany, not weeks earlier before Jesus' sojourn near the desert. They have come to Bethany, probably from Jerusalem, on learning that Jesus is there,[55] seeking a glimpse of the miracle worker and verification that Lazarus was indeed alive. If so, we are meeting them for the first time. Nothing is said of what they did when they arrived, or whether they interrupted the dinner. All that counts in the narrative is that they "came" and, presumably, saw what they came to see. The scene remains undeveloped for the time being,[56] but its purpose will become clear later on (see vv. 17-18).

10-11 Instead of commenting further on the arrival of "a great crowd from the Jews" in Bethany, the writer issues a postscript to the decision of the Jewish ruling council (see 11:53, "So from that day they resolved that they would kill him"). He supplies the additional information that "the chief priests resolved that they would also kill Lazarus, because on account of him many of the Jews were going off and believing in Jesus" (v. 10). This is clearly not a second decree, triggered by the fact that Lazarus was present at the dinner at Bethany (vv. 1-2), and that a crowd had come "not because of Jesus alone, but that they might also see Lazarus, whom he raised from the dead" (v. 9). It is rather a more detailed description of what had already been decided, and in almost identical words. The chief priests had not only "resolved that they would kill" Jesus (11:53); they had on that same day, we now learn, "resolved[57] that they would also kill Lazarus." Moreover, the reason was the same. The concern voiced earlier was that "If we let him [that is, Jesus] go on like this, they will all believe in him" (11:48); the concern here is that "on account of him [that is, Lazarus] many of the Jews were going off and believing in Jesus." Lazarus, no less than Jesus, is in danger.

That said, it must be added that the threat to Lazarus never materializes. Nor does the threat against Jesus — in the short run. Instead, something quite different will happen (vv. 12-19). Why? The writer hints at an answer by the way in which he joins the notice about the visit of "a great crowd from the Jews" (v. 9) to the reminder about the council's decree (vv. 10-11). An

---

54. Bultmann, however (416), and Brown (1.456) both identify the crowd here with the crowd in 11:42 that were said to have "believed" in Jesus (11:45).

55. "There" (ἐκεῖ) echoes the same word in verse 2 ("they made a dinner for him *there*"). Whether the crowd came to the village or more specifically to the very "house" (v. 3) where the dinner was held is unclear.

56. It is quite possibly yet another example of a "vestigial scene" which, while undeveloped, is in the narrative for a definite reason.

57. Gr. ἐβουλεύσαντο.

earlier postscript to the decree had been that "the chief priests and the Pharisees had given commands that if anyone found out where [Jesus] was, they should make it known, so that they might arrest him" (11:57). Now we have been told that "a great crowd from the Jews found out that he was there" (v. 9). Evidently when this "great crowd... found out" where Jesus was, they did *not* "make it known" to the chief priests and Pharisees as commanded, but went instead to see for themselves. The reminder that the council's decree was still in effect and that it included Lazarus (vv. 10-11) serves to inform the reader at the same time that the people in general are not cooperating.[58] So far, the formal resolution of the Chief Priest and the council to arrest and kill Jesus is no more successful than the random efforts of "the Jews" have been all along (see, for example, 5:18; 7:1, 32, 45-46; 8:59; 10:31, 39). The concluding words of the notice, that "many of the Jews were going off and believing in Jesus" (v. 11), tell the story. While the "great crowd of the Jews" who came to Bethany to see Lazarus are not necessarily believers (at least not yet), their arrival sends a signal to the reader (if not to the authorities) that arresting Jesus will not be easy.

12-13 "The next day," now *five* days before the Passover (see v. 1), we are introduced to "the great crowd that had come to the festival." The question is whether they are the same "great crowd from the Jews" who came to Bethany to see Jesus and Lazarus (v. 9), or a different crowd. The odd word order[59] could suggest that they are the same,[60] yet their further identification as those who "had come to the festival" hints at a larger group, embracing all or most of the pilgrims who had arrived in Jerusalem by that time. A related question is how they "heard that Jesus was coming into Jerusalem." Even the reader has not been told this explicitly. If they are the same "great crowd" that came to Bethany, they would have heard it directly from Jesus, or the family of Lazarus. If they are a different, larger crowd that we have not met before, then it was either a rumor going around, or else something they heard from the first crowd, those who had come to Bethany to verify the miracle. At this point we are not told, but the truth will come out eventually (see vv. 17-18).

In any event, the crowd acted immediately. As soon as they heard that Jesus was coming, they "took the branches of the palms and went out to meet him, and they were shouting, "Hosanna! Blessed is the One coming in the

---

58. This is consistent with the synoptic tradition (see Mk 14:1-2; Mt 26:5; Lk 22:2).

59. Gr. ὁ ὄχλος πολύς.

60. The definite article could mark a previous reference: "the aforementioned 'great crowd'" (for a similarly resumptive reference to a crowd on "the next day," see 6:22). It is as if the phrase "great crowd" (ὄχλος πολύς) were being treated as one word.

name of the Lord, even the King of Israel!" (v. 13). This is recognizably the "triumphal entry" described in the other three Gospels (see Mk 11:1-10; Mt 21:1-9; Lk 19:28-40), but reduced here to its simplest terms. In contrast to all three Synoptics, John's Gospel describes first what the crowd did (vv. 12-13), and only then (very briefly) what Jesus did (v. 14). None of Jesus' elaborate plans for the occasion (see Mk 11:1-6) come into play. Moreover, the vocabulary is somewhat different. Only John's Gospel gives the name "Palm Sunday" to the event by having the crowd welcome Jesus with "the branches of the palms" (v. 13),[61] accenting even more than the other Gospels the "triumphal" nature of the scene.[62] And only John states explicitly that the crowd went out from the city "to meet him"[63] on his way in (v. 13; compare v. 18), just as Martha had done at Bethany a chapter earlier (11:20, 30). The other Gospels show us the crowd after they had met Jesus, giving us the impression that everyone formed a procession moving in the same direction into Jerusalem — "those who went ahead and those who followed" (Mk 11:9; Mt 21:9).[64] Here, even though the purpose of "meeting" Jesus is to escort him into the city, the "meeting" has an importance of its own, and the cry of "Hosanna" comes *before* the moment of meeting, not after.

"Hosanna!" the crowd exclaims, "Blessed is the One coming in the name of the Lord, even the King of Israel!" (v. 13b). This they say in anticipation, before they have so much as seen Jesus. They have "heard" that he

---

61. Gr. τὰ βαΐα τῶν φοινίκων. The expression is as redundant as it sounds in English, for the first word refers to palm fronds or branches and the second to either palm branches or palm trees (see BDAG, 162-63). The other Gospels have "leafy stalks from the fields" (Mk 11:8) or "branches from the trees" (Mt 21:8), or no mention of branches at all, only clothing (Lk 19:36).

62. See 1 Maccabees 13.51 (βαΐων), on the occasion of the cleansing of the citadel in Jerusalem under Simon Maccabaeus (see also 2 Maccabees 10:7, φοίνικας). Within the New Testament, see Revelation 7:9 ("palm branches [φοίνικες] in their hands"), an especially notable reference because those holding the palms are called "a great crowd [ὄχλος πολύς] that no one could number, out of every nation, and tribes and peoples and tongues, standing before the throne and before the Lamb." If John's language here were intended to evoke some such eschatological scene, it could well anticipate the comment of the Pharisees that "the world has gone after him!" (v. 19) and the visit of the Greeks desiring to see Jesus (v. 20). This is possible, but would be difficult to prove.

63. Gr. εἰς ὑπάντησιν αὐτῷ.

64. Schnackenburg puts it well: "According to the source it was not the crowds accompanying Jesus who now did him homage, as the synoptics describe the scene . . . but visitors to the feast who had already arrived in Jerusalem and now came out to meet him" (2.374; what Schackenburg attributes to a "source" represents as well the Gospel writer's perspective). In Mark those accompanying Jesus are simply "many" (11:8); in Matthew, "the very large crowd" (21:8); in Luke, Jesus' own disciples ("the whole multitude of the disciples," 19:37).

was coming (v. 12), but only in the following verse does he make an appearance (v. 14). The exclamation "Blessed is the One coming in the name of the Lord!"[65] comes directly from Psalm 118:26 (LXX), preceded by the words "O Lord, save now! O Lord, prosper now!" (Ps 118:25). The Hebrew expression "Hosanna," or "Save now,"[66] used there as a petition,[67] has become here (as in Mark and Matthew) an expression of praise to God.[68] In Psalm 118, the last of the *Hallel* Psalms (Pss 113–18) sung at both Passover and the Tent festival, the phrase "coming in the name of the Lord" was customarily understood to refer to each pilgrim in festal procession entering the temple. Here the expression takes on messianic overtones, made unmistakable by the added phrase, "even the King of Israel."[69]

The words of the crowd evoke for the reader a number of associations from within the Gospel itself. "King of Israel" recalls Nathanael's confession of Jesus as both "Son of God" and "King of Israel" (1:49), the former designation interpreting and defining the latter. "Blessed is the One coming in the name of the Lord" recalls John's announcement of Jesus as "the One coming after me" (1:15, 27), or "the One coming from above," or "from heaven" (3:31), again determining in advance what it means to speak of Jesus as "the One coming," or "the Coming One." Even those who tried to make Jesus king after he fed the five thousand hailed him as "the Prophet who is coming into the world" (6:14), and Martha, just before the raising of Lazarus, acknowledged him as "the Christ, the Son of God, who is coming into the world" (11:27). By this time, whether the crowd realizes it or not, the phrase "the One coming in the name of the Lord" has acquired considerable christological weight in the mind of the reader. Jesus himself once told "the Jews" that "I have come in my Father's name, and you do not accept me" (5:43; see also 10:25, "The works that I do in my Father's name, these testify about me"). What "the Jews" could not accept, this crowd, five days before

---

65. Gr. εὐλογημένος ὁ ἐρχόμενος ἐν ὀνόματι κυρίου.

66. Heb. הוֹשִׁיעָה נא; Aram. הוֹשַׁעְנָא.

67. It is so understood in the LXX as well (σῶσον δή).

68. Mark has the simple "Hosanna," as here (11:9), while Matthew has "Hosanna to the son of David" (21:9; compare *Didache* 10.6, "Hosanna to the God of David"). Both conclude by repeating, "Hosanna in the highest." Luke avoids the expression altogether by paraphrasing it as "praising God joyfully with a loud voice" (19:37), and concluding with "peace in heaven and glory in the highest." (For a more literal translation of "Hosanna" as praise, see Rev 7:10, "Salvation belongs to our God who sits on the throne, and to the Lamb.") Modern examples of how a petition can easily become a blessing or an ascription of praise include "God bless you!" and "God save the queen!"

69. Each of the other Gospels adds the messianic tone in its own way: Mark with the added phrase, "Blessed is the kingdom of our father David that is coming" (11:10), Matthew with his "Hosanna to the son of David" (21:9), Luke by inserting "the King" between "Blessed is the One coming" and "in the name of the Lord" (19:38).

Passover, does accept, albeit on its own terms and in the traditional vocabulary of its own liturgy.[70]

14-15 Jesus' own part in the drama is stated in the simplest possible terms, almost as an afterthought: "And Jesus, having found a young donkey,[71] sat on it" (vv. 14-15). For once, the initiative lies not with him but with the crowd. He merely reacts to what the crowd is doing. The economy of language is striking. If the Gospel writer knows the story of how Jesus "found" the donkey, he resists (as the other Gospels do not)[72] the temptation to tell it. He tells only enough to give meaning to the Scripture citation, which he introduces immediately: "just as it is written, 'Fear not, daughter Zion. Look, your king is coming, sitting on a donkey's colt!'" (vv. 14b-15). The citation is linked immediately to Jesus' action (v. 14) by the phrase "sitting on a donkey's colt," but even more significantly to the preceding cry of the crowd by the phrase "your king is coming," echoing "the One coming in the name of the Lord, even the King of Israel" (v. 13). The citation is taken, very loosely, from Zechariah 9:9 (LXX), "Rejoice greatly, daughter Zion! Shout, daughter Jerusalem! Look, your king is coming to you. Righteous and bringing salvation is he, humble and mounted on a pack animal and a young colt." The text as cited is much simpler, preserving only the phrase "daughter Zion" (for Jerusalem), and the key words, "Look, your king is coming!" The "king" in Zechariah is "mounted" rather than "sitting," and the vocabulary for "donkey" is different. John's free citation omits all mention of Jesus' righteousness and humility, and leaves us no room to imagine (as Matthew has done) two animals in the procession.[73] By paring the quotation down to its bare essentials ("Look, your king is coming!"), the Gospel writer actually turns attention *away* from Jesus' action of finding a donkey and sitting on it, and back to the crowd's proclamation, "Blessed is the One coming . . . the King of Israel!" (v. 13). The crucial issue is not what Jesus

---

70. "Blessed is the One coming in the name of the Lord" obviously does not do justice to Jesus' claim that "the Lord" is his Father, nor would we at this point expect it to. If the "One coming" is anyone's son, he is, as Matthew tells us (21:9), "the son of David." As most commentators acknowledge, John's Gospel is drawing here on a source, written or oral, retaining the language of the source and most likely of the event itself.

71. Gr. ὀνάριον.

72. See the lengthy account common to all three Synoptics (Mk 11:1-6; Mt 21:1-7; Lk 19:29-35).

73. Matthew is the only other Gospel to cite the Zechariah passage, and its wording is closer to Zechariah's: "Say to the daughter Zion, 'Look, your king is coming to you, humble and mounted on a donkey, and on a colt, the son of a pack animal'" (Mt 21:5). Matthew places the quotation just after his account of Jesus' elaborate plan to obtain the donkey and the colt, with the comment, "This happened so that what was spoken through the prophet might be fulfilled, saying . . ." (21:4).

did at this particular moment, but who he is, and most notably the crowd's recognition of who he is: "the One coming" and "the King of Israel."

At the same time, it must be noted that Jesus does not reject the crowd's acclamation, as he rejected another crowd's earlier attempt to "seize him to make him king" on the basis of their confession of him as "truly the Prophet who is coming into the world" (see 6:14-15). This confirms the thought that Jesus' flight from kingship back then had to do not with a rejection of kingship per se, but with that earlier crowd's intention to "seize" him by force (6:15), and (even aside from that) with the simple fact that "his hour had not yet come" (see 7:30; 8:20). Here he accepts kingship, but on his own terms, "sitting on a donkey's colt."[74]

16 The account of Jesus' "triumphal entry" into Jerusalem ended with the notice that "Jesus, having found a young donkey, sat on it," followed by the citation from Zechariah (vv. 14-15). But before moving on to speak of the reaction of the Pharisees to what had happened (v. 19), the Gospel writer inserts two narrative asides, the first looking back at the event from the standpoint of Jesus' disciples (v. 16), and the second making very explicit its relationship to the raising of Lazarus (vv. 17-18). The disciples have kept a very low profile ever since Jesus first came to Bethany (11:17), being mentioned only in connection with Jesus' sojourn at Ephraim (11:54), and implicitly (as represented by Judas) at the dinner when Jesus returned to Bethany (see v. 4, where Judas was identified as "one of his disciples"). Nothing has been said of their presence with Jesus on entering Jerusalem, yet their presence is now assumed in the writer's comment that "These things his disciples did not understand at first, but when Jesus was glorified, then they remembered that these things were written about him, and these things they did for him" (v. 16).[75] The threefold repetition of "these things"[76] is striking, referring first to the whole scene (vv. 12-15), then to the Scripture citation in particular

---

74. So Lincoln, 347: "Here the Jerusalem crowd's acclamation is put in the appropriate perspective by the portrayal of Jesus seated on the donkey's colt rather than leading armed resistance on a warhorse." It must be added, however, that John does not labor the point of Jesus' humility, either in the Scripture citation (contrast Mt 21:5, "humble and mounted on a donkey") or in his narrative.

75. The unexpressed subject of the clause "these things they did for him" (ταῦτα ἐποίησαν αὐτῷ) must be understood as "the great crowd that had come to the festival" (v. 12), not the disciples themselves. Strictly speaking, the third-person plural is impersonal, as if to say, "these things were done for him" (see Brown, 1.458; Bultmann, 418, n. 3). It is unnecessary to suppose (with Barrett, 419) that "John's words show awareness of the older tradition, probably Mark," in which the disciples played a significant role by finding the donkey (not to mention Luke, in which "the whole multitude of the disciples" are those who actually welcomed Jesus into the city as king! See Lk 19:37, 39).

76. Gr. ταῦτα.

(v. 15), and finally to the action of the crowd meeting Jesus (vv. 12-14).[77] The point is not that the disciples did not see what was going on, but that they did not recall at the time the text from Zechariah, and consequently did not see the action of the crowd as its fulfillment. They "remembered"[78] only later, when Jesus was "glorified."

This notice, just before Jesus' last Passover, recalls two similar notices at the first Passover, when Jesus came to the festival and drove the money changers from the temple (2:13-22). There too, we were given no hint of the disciples' presence until we were abruptly told that "His disciples remembered that it is written, 'Zeal for your house will consume me'" (2:17). Later, "when he rose from the dead," they also "remembered" what he said, and "believed both the scripture and the word Jesus spoke" (2:22). In that early passage, the reader was expected to know the story of how Jesus "rose from the dead." Here the reader is expected to know, if not precisely when and how Jesus would be "glorified," at least *that* he would be glorified, or vindicated in some way (see 11:4), and that his glorification would have something to do with a dreaded "hour" that had not yet come (see 7:30, 39; 8:20). Both the prophecy of Zechariah on the one hand (v. 15), and the action of the crowd in welcoming Jesus into the city on the other (vv. 12-13), point forward to Jesus' impending glorification, and become intelligible (even to his own disciples) only in light of that glorification. The theme common to both was kingship, and the point of the notice is that Jesus' kingship will come to expression solely in his "glorification" — whatever that might involve.

It is important to pay attention to what the notice does and does not say. In contrast to all three Synoptics, the accent is not on what Jesus himself did — that is, "found a young donkey and sat on it" (v. 14) — but on what was "written about him," what the crowd "did for him," and the correspondence between the two. Just as at the dinner in Bethany when Mary anointed his feet, Jesus is the recipient, not the initiator of the action. The message of the former was that Jesus would soon die and be buried (see vv. 7-9); the message of the latter was that he would be "glorified" as King. The reader is left to wonder how these twin destinies relate to one another — by Jesus being "raised from the dead" (see 2:22), or in some other way?

17-18 An even more obvious question remains. Why exactly did "the great crowd that had come to the festival" go out from the city to meet Jesus, welcoming him as "the One coming in the name of the Lord," and "the King of Israel" (v. 13)? What could have prompted such a provocative public display, given the death sentences against Jesus and Lazarus (11:53; 12:11),

---

77. As we have seen repeatedly, the use of pronouns such as ταῦτα to introduce summary statements is characteristic of this Gospel.

78. Gr. ἐμνήσθησαν.

and especially the warning that "if anyone found out where he was, they should make it known, so that they might arrest him" (11:57)? To answer the question, the Gospel writer adds (belatedly) some necessary information: "So the crowd that was with him kept testifying that he called Lazarus from the tomb and raised him from the dead" (v. 17). "That also," he goes on to explain, "was why the crowd met him, because they heard that he had done this sign" (v. 18). For the modern reader, the "explanation" may raise more questions than it answers. For one thing, it could imply something we would not have suspected up to this point — that *two* "crowds" are on the scene, not just one. The second crowd mentioned (v. 18) is clearly "the great crowd that had come to the festival" (v. 12), but the identity of the first crowd, "the crowd that was with him," is less certain. The matter is complicated by a textual variation. The difference is only one letter, but its implications are considerable. Two readings compete:

(a) According to the text adopted here, "So the crowd that was with him kept testifying that[79] he called Lazarus from the tomb and raised him from the dead."[80]
(b) According to some of the most important ancient manuscripts: "So the crowd that was with him when[81] he called Lazarus from the tomb and raised him from the dead kept testifying."

The latter has impressive manuscript support,[82] and is presupposed by virtually all English translations and most commentators, in part because it is customarily viewed as the more difficult reading.[83] But this is not necessarily the case. According to Text (a), the crowd that "kept testifying" was a crowd that was "with" Jesus (v. 17) at the very time he entered the city, while according to Text (b) they were with him weeks, possibly months earlier, "when he called Lazarus from the tomb and raised him from the

---

79. Gr. ὅτι.
80. This reading is found in P66, D, L, 579, several of the old Latin versions, the Sinaitic Syriac version, and the Coptic versions.
81. Gr. ὅτε.
82. Its support includes ℵ, B, A, W, Δ, Θ, Ψ, most of the important minuscules, both early and late, and the majority of later witnesses.
83. See, for example, Brown (1.458), who admits that ὅτι "makes good sense and removes any obstacle to identifying the crowd in vs. 17 with that in vs. 9," but then adds that "it is probably wiser to opt for the more difficult reading" (that is, ὅτε, "when"). Similarly, Metzger (*Textual Commentary,* 237) prefers ὅτε "because ὅτι appears to be an attempt to clarify the account, which otherwise could be taken to refer to two crowds (compare ver. 18)." So too Bultmann (419, n. 1). As I will try to show, just the opposite is true.

dead" (see 11:42, "for the sake of the crowd standing around, so that they might believe that you sent me").[84] Nothing suggests that they were necessarily present as well at the time Jesus entered Jerusalem on a donkey. In short, Text (a) implies *two* crowds at this "triumphal entry," one accompanying Jesus *into* the city and repeatedly "testifying"[85] to the miracle at Bethany (v. 17), and the other coming out *from* the city to meet him (v. 18). On this reading, the crowd accompanying Jesus and testifying to the raising of Lazarus are probably not the eyewitnesses of the preceding chapter (11:42, 45), but rather the "great crowd from the Jews" (v. 9) who had come to Bethany to see Lazarus and verify the miracle. It is, after all, "the next day" (see v. 12). If they are *not* the same crowd now accompanying Jesus and testifying as he enters the city, it is difficult to explain why they were in the story at all. The very purpose of their abrupt appearance at Bethany (v. 9) seems to have been to prepare the reader for their role here.[86] Text (b), on the other hand, avoids the implication that there were two distinct crowds, and is suspect (despite its strong attestation) for that very reason. On this reading, as we have seen, the crowd "testifying" is "the crowd that was with him *when* he called Lazarus from the tomb" (italics added), that is, "the Jews" who came to mourn with Mary and Martha, witnessed the miracle, and believed (see 11:42, 45). While it is possible that the same crowd was also on the scene when Jesus entered Jerusalem, nothing is said to that effect, and it is far more likely that they had continued "testifying" to their fellow Jerusalemites over a period of time. This understanding is evident in a number of English translations that seem to have been as uncomfortable as some of the early scribes with the notion of two crowds at the triumphal entry. The presumption is that they are eyewitnesses to the miracle who are not literally on the scene, but have "continued to testify" (NRSV), or "continued to spread the word" (NIV, TNIV), ever since they came to believe (see 11:45; 12:11).[87] The imperfect verb "kept testifying" or "was testifying" is read almost as if it were a pluperfect, "had been testifying."

What all this suggests is that the textual question is extraordinarily difficult to decide. The manuscript evidence favors Text (b), yet Text (a)

---

84. "Weeks, possibly months earlier," because of the uncertain length of Jesus' sojourn at Ephraim, in "the region near the desert" (11:54).

85. Gr. ἐμαρτύρει, imperfect.

86. This is the case even if their appearance is classified as another "vestigial scene."

87. Another strategy is to visualize those testifying as being on the scene, but all part of the same "crowd" (see the NLT, "Many in the crowd had seen Jesus call Lazarus from the tomb, raising him from the dead, and they were telling others about it. That was the reason so many went out to meet him").

seems more consistent with internal evidence, especially the narrative flow of the Gospel. However the matter is decided, one thing is clear. The Gospel writer wants to explain why Jesus received such a royal welcome into Jerusalem, and he does so by linking the event to the raising of Lazarus. Whether the report of the miracle came from those present at the scene (11:42, 45), or those who came later to Bethany to verify what happened (12:9), or both, and whether it came over a period of time or on a specific occasion are of secondary importance. What matters is that the raising of Lazarus gained for Jesus the allegiance (at least temporarily) of "the great crowd that had come to the festival" (v. 12), and thus thwarted (again, temporarily) the designs of the chief priests and Pharisees. The account is framed by the twin notices that "the great crowd . . . heard that Jesus was coming into Jerusalem" (v. 12), and that they "heard that he had done this sign" (v. 18). What they "heard" — regardless of which "crowd" they heard it from — was what triggered what they "did for him" (v. 16). The raising of Lazarus from the grave is the last "sign"[88] mentioned in the Gospel, and one of only four explicitly labeled as such (for the others, see 2:11, 4:54, and 6:14). It may be more than coincidental that the only other such "sign" performed publicly (6:14) also resulted in an attempt to make Jesus king. As we have seen, Jesus' response here is quite different from what it was then (see 6:15), in part because his decisive "glorification" is closer at hand (see vv. 16, 23).

19 Finally the Pharisees respond,[89] and even though they are speaking "to each other,"[90] their comment punctuates the narrative for the reader's benefit, much as a Greek chorus might do: "You can see[91] that you're accomplishing nothing," they exclaim. "Look, the world has gone after him!"[92] In one sense, their words simply confirm what we were told earlier, that "many of the Jews were going off and believing in Jesus" (v. 11). But their way of saying it is both exaggerated and laced with irony. Within the Gospel of John it recalls the remark of John's disciples to John (just as exaggerated) that Jesus was "baptizing, and they are all coming to him!" (3:26). Looking beyond

---

88. Gr. τοῦτο . . . τὸ σημεῖον (v. 18).

89. Probably no real distinction is intended between "the chief priests and the Pharisees" (mentioned together in 11:47 and 57), even though only "the chief priests" were explicitly mentioned in verse 10 and only "the Pharisees" here.

90. Gr. πρὸς ἑαυτούς.

91. "You can see" (θεωρεῖτε) is used rhetorically here to introduce a conclusion based on common observation (compare the Samaritan woman's remark, 'I can see that you are a prophet,' 4;19).

92. Gr. ὀπίσω αὐτοῦ ἀπῆλθεν. The expression, "has gone after him" (ὀπίσω αὐτοῦ), implies giving him their allegiance or following him as disciples (see BDAG, 716; this is a possible meaning in 1:15, 27, and 30, and clearly the meaning in Mk 8:34, Mt 16:24, and Lk 9:23).

12:20-36 THE HOUR OF GLORIFICATION

our Gospel, the Pharisees' frustration at "accomplishing nothing"[93] recalls Pilate's frustration in Matthew in just the opposite circumstances, when he wanted to release Jesus but "saw that he was accomplishing nothing, but that instead a riot was starting" (Mt 27:24).

Perhaps more to the point, their words recall a saying of Jesus in other Gospel traditions, asking "What will a man accomplish[94] if he gain the whole world, but lose his life?" (Mt 16:26; see also Mk 8:36; Lk 9:25).[95] In a strange way, the utterance of the Pharisees turns Jesus' pronouncement on its head. The irony is that Jesus himself, who seemed to his enemies to have gained "the world,"[96] would do so only at the cost of his own life. The reader will remember that he has said as much: "And I lay down my life for the sheep. And other sheep I have, which are not from this courtyard. Those too I must bring, and they will hear my voice, and they will become one flock, one Shepherd. That is why the Father loves me, because I lay down my life, that I might receive it back again" (10:15b-17). Like Caiaphas (11:51), the Pharisees speak more wisely than they know. By his death Jesus will gain, if not "the world," at least "the nation" and "the children of God who are scattered" (11:52) — and even "the world" lies at least within the horizons of his saving death (see 1:29, "who takes away the sin of the world"; 6:51, "my flesh for the life of the world"; 17:21, "so that the world might believe"; 17:23, "so that the world might know"). The mixed message that has emerged in this extended narrative (11:55–12:19), of Jesus' impending death on the one hand and his universal kingship on the other, will continue to come to expression in much of what follows.

S. THE HOUR OF GLORIFICATION (12:20-36)

> 20 *Now some of those who were going up that they might worship in the festival were Greeks.* 21 *So these came to Philip, who was from Bethsaida of Galilee, and asked him, saying, "Sir, we want to see Jesus."* 22 *Philip comes and tells Andrew, Andrew comes with Philip, and they tell Jesus.* 23 *But Jesus answers them, saying, "The hour has come that the Son of man might be glorified.* 24 *Amen, amen, I say to*

---

93. Gr. οὐκ ὠφελεῖτε οὐδέν.
94. Gr. τί γὰρ ὠφεληθήσεται.
95. For another such example, see 11:50, where we saw that the proposal of Caiaphas, "it is to your advantage that one man die for the people, and the whole nation not be lost," echoed the form, if not the substance, of Jesus' pronouncement in other Gospels that "it is to your advantage that one of your members be lost, and your whole body not thrown into Gehenna."
96. Gr. ὁ κόσμος.

you, unless the grain of wheat dies by falling to the earth, it remains alone by itself; but if it dies, it bears a great crop. 25 *The person who loves his life loses it, and the person who hates his life in this world will keep it to eternal life.* 26 *If anyone would serve me, let him follow me, and where I am, there my servant will be. If anyone would serve me, the Father will honor him.* 27 *Now my soul is shaken, and what shall I say? 'Father, save me from this hour'? No, for this reason I came to this hour.* 28 *Father, glorify your name."*

Then a voice came from the sky, "I have both glorified, and I will glorify again." 29 *So the crowd standing by, when they heard, were saying thunder had come. Others were saying, "An angel has spoken to him."* 30 *Jesus answered and said, "This voice was not for my sake but for yours.* 31 *Now is the judgment of this world. Now the ruler of this world will be driven out.* 32 *And I, if I be lifted up from the earth, will draw them all to myself."* 33 *This he said signifying by what death he was going to die.* 34 *So the crowd answered him, "We have heard from the law that the Christ remains forever, and how can you say that the Son of man must be lifted up. Who is this Son of man?"*

35 *Jesus said to them, "Yet a short time the Light is in you. Walk while you have the Light, lest darkness overtake you — and the person who walks in that darkness does not know where he is going.* 36 *While you have the Light, believe in the Light, that you might become sons of light." These things Jesus spoke, and he went away and was hidden from them.*

As if confirming the lament of the Pharisees, "Look, the world has gone after him!" (v. 19), some "Greeks" who had come to the Passover festival approached one of Jesus' disciples, asking, "Sir, we want to see Jesus!" (v. 21). The request is passed along to Jesus, triggering his decisive announcement, "The hour has come that the Son of man might be glorified" (v. 23), and an accompanying parable introduced by the characteristic "Amen, amen" formula: "unless the grain of wheat dies by falling into the earth, it remains alone by itself; but if it dies, it bears a great crop" (v. 24). The tension of the preceding section between the prospect of Jesus' death and the hope of "glorification" or universal kingship is maintained, in the simple biological fact that life, represented here by a "great crop" or harvest, comes through death, and only through death. The parable is short and simple, barely long enough to qualify as a parable,[1] yet with its explicit application to Jesus himself (v. 32), it frames the whole of his two-part speech (vv. 24-28, 30-32) to "the

---

1. It is not widely recognized as a parable, but see Homer A. Kent Jr., *Light in the Darkness*, 157.

crowd standing by" (v. 29). This can be clearly seen by placing verses 24 and 32 side by side (with italics added):

> "Amen, amen, I say to you, *unless* the grain of wheat dies by falling *to the earth*, it remains alone by itself; but *if* it dies, it bears a great crop" (v. 24).
> "And I, *if* I be lifted up *from the earth*, will draw them all to myself" (v. 32).

If verse 32 is seen as in some sense the interpretation of verse 24, Jesus is identifying himself with "the grain of wheat" that dies, yielding a "great crop," but with a conspicuous and decisive twist: he dies *not* by "falling to the earth" like a seed, but on the contrary, by being "lifted up from the earth," a clear allusion to what he said much earlier, at the first Passover (see 3:14, "And just as Moses lifted up the snake in the desert, so the Son of man must be lifted up"). The Gospel writer spells it out for us, reminding us that Jesus was "signifying what death he was going to die" (v. 33). The "great crop" comes to expression in the notice that as a result of being "lifted up," evidently on the cross, Jesus will "draw them all" to himself. This is his real answer to the request of the Greeks that he seems to have ignored, "Sir, we want to see Jesus" (v. 21).

The material framed by the parable and its interpretation (vv. 25-31) falls into two parts. In the first, Jesus applies the principle of life through death to his followers (vv. 25-26). In the second (vv. 27-31) he applies it to himself, in light of his announcement that "the hour has come" (v. 23). He speaks to the Father, asking first if he should pray (in words recalling Gethsemane in the other Gospels), "Father, save me from this hour" (v. 27), but then praying instead, "Father, glorify your name" (v. 28). The answer is immediate, and heard by all (vv. 28-29), but Jesus is quick to tell the crowd that the audible voice "was not for my sake but for yours" (v. 30). Then he boldly announces that his "hour" will mean judgment on "this world," and on "the ruler of this world" (v. 31). And when the crowd responds with confusion over how his talk of death and of "the Son of man" fits their common expectations of "the Christ" (v. 34), he ignores that issue and warns them instead of the judgment soon to come (vv. 35-36).

20 The writer's notice that "Greeks" as well as Jews were present at the Passover festival (v. 20) serves as a reminder that the Pharisees' remark, "Look, the world has gone after him!" was not as farfetched as it appeared to be. "Greeks"[2] have been mentioned only once before in the Gospel, and that by "the Jews," clearly distinguishing "the Greeks" from

---

2. Gr. Ἕλληνες.

themselves (7:35).³ Even though they have come "that they might worship" at a Jewish festival, the distinction likely still holds. Because they have come to worship the God of Israel, J. A. T. Robinson's argument that they are in fact Jews of the diaspora has somewhat more plausibility here than in 7:35,⁴ yet the designation "Greeks" makes it clear that they are in some sense still "the other." Like the Samaritans earlier, who worshiped the same God on a different mountain, they represent "the world" (see 4:42), not in the loose rhetorical sense in which the Pharisees have just used the word (v. 19), but in clear distinction from "the Jews" who have been Jesus' interlocutors all along. Yet John's Gospel never calls them "the Gentiles,"⁵ preferring either "Greeks" or a designation referring to the elect status of those among them who believe, such as "other sheep" (10:16), or "the children of God who are scattered" (11:52). Their presence is historically realistic in that Greek-speaking Jews, as well as other Greeks and other foreigners, did attend Jewish festivals on occasion, whether out of curiosity or genuine admiration for the Jewish way of life.⁶ But more important to the narrative, their presence gives notice that the relationship of Jesus to the whole "world," Jewish and non-Jewish alike, is soon to be addressed.

21 These "Greeks" who had come to the festival (however many there were) "came to Philip," who is further identified as being "from Bethsaida of Galilee" (see 1:44, where the identification served to link him with Andrew and Peter). Whether they approached him *because of* his Galilean connections is uncertain. Most of Jesus' disciples, after all, were Galileans. Possibly the fact that he, like Andrew (v. 22), had a Greek name is significant, and the reader will assume from their identity as "Greeks" that their request to him, "Sir, we want to see Jesus"⁷ (v. 21) was uttered in Greek. Readers familiar with Luke's Gospel may also be reminded of Herod Antipas, who "when he saw Jesus was very glad, for he had been wanting to see him⁸ for a long time and was hoping to see some sign done by him" (Lk 23:8; compare 9:9). There too the one "wanting to see" Jesus was, if not a Greek, at least someone not numbered among "the Jews" in Jerusalem, and viewed by them with suspicion. Herod's motivation ("to see some sign done

---

3. The distinction between "Jew" and "Greek" is common both in the letters of Paul (Rom 1:16; 2:9, 10; 3:9; 10:12; 1 Cor 1:22, 24; 10:32; 12:13; Gal 3:28; Col 3:11) and in the book of Acts (14:1; 16:1; 18:4; 19:10, 17; 20:21).

4. See Robinson's *Twelve New Testament Studies*, 107-25.

5. Gr. τὰ ἔθνη.

6. Josephus speaks of "foreigners [ἀλλοφύλοις] present for worship" at Passover, who were not permitted to eat of the Passover sacrifice, even though "a large number of these assemble from abroad" (*War* 6.427; LCL, 3.499).

7. Gr. θέλομεν τὸν Ἰησοῦν ἰδεῖν.

8. Gr. θέλων ἰδεῖν αὐτόν.

12:20-36 THE HOUR OF GLORIFICATION

by him," Lk 23:8) raises at least the possibility that the same desire may have been at work among these "Greeks" at the Passover. If so, it is little different from that which motivated the Jewish crowds in the city (see v. 9, "that they might also see Lazarus, whom he raised from the dead"; also v. 18, "because they heard that he had done this sign"). In contrast, perhaps, to Paul (see 1 Cor 1:22), *both* Jews and Greeks are looking for signs — something they can see — not wisdom, and definitely not "the message of the cross" (1 Cor 1:18), which Jesus will soon begin to reveal (vv. 24, 32). In a quite different vein, the scene also evokes Luke's version of an account in which Jesus' mother and brothers could not reach him because of the crowds around him, and Jesus was told that they were standing outside, "wanting to see you"[9] (Lk 8:20). The parallel lies in the fact that in neither of the two instances in Luke is Jesus ever said to grant the wish, or even reply to it directly. Both are undeveloped or "vestigial" scenes, like others in John's Gospel (for example, 2:12; 11:54; 12:9).

Instead of acknowledging the Greeks, Jesus seizes the opportunity to make a point to his disciples, who have passed along the request (see vv. 23-26). "Seeing Jesus" redemptively depends not on "wanting" to do so, but on Jesus himself "wanting" to be seen (see 17:24, "Father, that which you have given me, I want them to be with me where I am, that they might see my glory which you have given me").

22 Philip and Andrew make their appearance in tandem, as in 6:5-9, where Jesus first tested Philip with a question (6:6), and Philip and Andrew both responded, raising the reader's expectations of a miracle. Their appearance together here also recalls Jesus' first encounter with John and his disciples, when Andrew was the first disciple named (even before his brother Simon Peter, 1:40-41), and Philip was the third (1:43), followed by Nathanael. That scene is an even closer parallel if Philip was in fact (as Schnackenburg has suggested) the unnamed disciple accompanying Andrew when they first heard John's testimony (1:40). Here Philip, instead of taking the Greeks' request directly to Jesus, "comes and tells Andrew, Andrew comes with Philip, and they tell Jesus" (v. 22). While it is doubtful that the biblical principle that "the testimony of two men is true" is in play here (see 8:17), the involvement of two of Jesus' disciples rather than one does lend a ceremonious quality to the occasion, so that the reader is primed to listen eagerly for Jesus' response.

23 The reader is not disappointed. It is indeed a decisive moment, even though we have heard the last of the Greeks, and their desire to "see Jesus." Instead of responding to their request by granting an interview, Jesus answers with an announcement: "The hour has come that the Son of man might be glorified" (v. 23). What this might have meant to the two disciples

---

9. Gr. ἰδεῖν θέλοντές σε.

— much less to the Greeks — is unclear, but it means a great deal to the reader. Jesus had spoken of his "hour" only once before, to his mother (2:4), where his meaning was far from clear. But the Gospel writer twice intimated that his "hour" would be a time of risk or danger. If Jesus could not be arrested "because his hour had not yet come" (7:30; 8:20), it follows that if and when his "hour" did come, he could and would be arrested and put to death, just as the Jewish authorities had intended all along. Yet the Gospel writer has also hinted at a time to come when Jesus would be "glorified" (7:39; 12:16), a notion confirmed by Jesus' own words ("so that . . . the Son of God might be glorified," 11:4; see also 8:54).

What then is the relationship between the prospect of mortal danger and the prospect of "glorification"? The only possible answer is that Jesus' "glorification" and his "hour" — the hour of his death — are one and the same. That answer is immediately confirmed by his references to a seed "dying" by falling into the earth (v. 24) and a person "losing his soul" or life (v. 25), and then by his aborted prayer, "Father, save me from this hour" (v. 27). Jesus' "hour" is now so imminent that he can speak of it as if it were already here. It is already but not yet, in that he can say "the hour has come" (v. 23) and yet in almost the same breath speak of being "saved" or rescued from it (v. 27). The bittersweet tension between death and life that was evident in the raising of Lazarus (11:40), in the council's decree "that one man die for the people" (11:50), in the anointing of Jesus by Mary "for the day of my burial" (12:7), and in Jesus' triumphal entry into the city (12:12-18) comes to a head here in Jesus' own explicit acknowledgment that the decisive "hour" has come. Somehow the contours of resurrection or ascension, or a vindication of some kind, have been imposed upon the grim reality of the death itself. Death and resurrection are no longer viewed as two successive events, the one negating or undoing the other, but mysteriously as the *same* event viewed from a human perspective as death but from God's perspective as glorification.

24 Jesus continues his reply to Andrew and Philip with an "Amen, amen" formula, for the seventeenth time in the Gospel (the most recent being in 10:7, introducing "I am the Door of the sheep"). The plural "you" in "Amen, amen, I say to you" are clearly the two disciples. This time the formula introduces an "unless"[10] clause reminiscent of "unless someone is born from above, he cannot see the kingdom of God" (3:3), or "unless you eat the flesh of the Son of man and drink his blood, you do not have life in yourselves" (6:53). In each instance, the accent is not on who Jesus is but on what it means to become Jesus' disciple and gain eternal life. And in each instance what is required is something very radical: to be reborn from above, to eat

---

10. Gr. ἐὰν μή.

flesh and drink blood, and here to fall down and die — all in order to live. But the "unless," or "if not," clause here differs from the other two examples in that it is followed by a positive "if" clause. That is, "unless the grain of wheat dies by falling to the earth, it remains alone by itself; but if[11] it dies, it bears a great crop" (v. 24). In the first instance (3:3), the positive side was unexpressed and had to be inferred: that is, if a person *is* "born from above," then he *can* "see the kingdom of God." In the second, the positive side was expressed differently, not with an "if" clause but repeatedly in a series of distinct pronouncements (6:54, 55, 56, 57, 58).

Here the single pronouncement looks at both scenarios: *either* the grain of wheat stays where it is and remains "alone by itself," *or* it "dies by falling to [or into] the earth" (that is, by being planted) and "bears a great crop." New life comes through death, and only through death. Paul makes the same point in arguing for a bodily resurrection: "You fool, what you plant does not come to life unless it dies" (1 Cor 15:36). Jesus does not speak of resurrection here (at least not explicitly), but simply of "a great crop," in keeping with the agricultural metaphor. "A great crop"[12] recalls his words to his disciples at the approach of the Samaritan villagers eight chapters earlier: "Lift up your eyes and look at the fields, that they are white for harvest. Already the harvester is receiving payment and gathering a crop for eternal life" (4:35-36). Here too the "crop" has to do with "eternal life," in contrast to the "death" of the seed in the ground, as the next verse will reveal (v. 25). This hints at resurrection, as in Paul's use of the metaphor, but the context, with the Greeks still waiting in the wings as the Samaritans were earlier, suggests that the "great crop" may also hint at a coming mission to the Gentiles.

The question remains whether "the grain of wheat" and its "death" in the ground represent simply the "glorification" of Jesus in the "hour" of his death, or whether the image has a wider application. As we have seen, the analogous "Amen, amen" pronouncements introducing "unless" clauses (3:3, 5; 6:53) had to do with disciples and discipleship, not with christology per se, and the same appears to be true here. If so, the "grain of wheat" does not represent Jesus, at least not Jesus uniquely, but *anyone* who would be his disciple. This is borne out by what immediately follows.

25 As is often the case in John's Gospel (for example, 3:5, 11; 5:19, 25; 6:26, 32, 53; 8:34; 10:1, 7), "Amen, amen" introduces a series of pronouncements, not just one. Jesus moves quickly from parable to application, from the dying "grain of wheat" to Andrew and Philip standing before him in person, representing simultaneously the rest of the disciples, the Greeks and the readers of the Gospel. "The person who loves his life loses it," Jesus tells

---

11. Gr. ἐάν.
12. Gr. πολὺν καρπόν.

them, "and the person who hates his life in this world will keep it to eternal life" (v. 25). The pronouncement has parallels in other Gospels, above all "For whoever wants to save his life will lose it, but whoever loses his life for my sake will find it" (Mt 16:25//Lk 9:24).[13] The version here differs only in framing the contrast as one between "loving" and "hating" one's own soul or life,[14] and in omitting the explicit connection with Jesus himself (that is, losing one's life "for my sake"). Both of these distinctives suggest that John's Gospel may be fairly close to the earliest form of the tradition.[15] The first, the contrast between "loving" and "hating," shows an affinity with another traditional — and likely authentic — saying of Jesus preserved by Luke: "If anyone comes to me and does not hate his own father and mother and wife and children and brothers and sisters, and even his own life,[16] he cannot be my disciple" (Lk 14:26).[17] The second, omitting "for my sake" (as in Matthew) or "for my sake and that of the gospel" (as in Mark), is also likely to be original, given the tendency of the tradition to add such words, not take them away.[18]

That said, it is also likely that John's Gospel has added two "Johannine" touches of its own, qualifying the expressions "hates his life" and "will keep [his life]" respectively. As to the first, one's "life" is defined as life "in this world,"[19] and as to the second, to "keep" or preserve one's life is understood to mean keeping it "to eternal life," or forever[20] (as in 4:14, 36; 6:27). "The world," or "this world," and "eternal life" are polar opposites, nowhere

---

13. Mark 8:35 is slightly different: "For whoever wants to save his life will lose it, and whoever will lose his life for my sake and that of the gospel will save it." Matthew and Luke agree in wording against Mark, suggesting that the pronouncement was handed down in more than one strand of the tradition. See also Matthew 10:39 ("The person who finds his life will lose it, and the person who has lost his life for my sake will find it"), and Luke 17:33 ("Whoever seeks to secure his life will lose it, but whoever loses will stay alive").

14. Gr. ὁ μισῶν τὴν ψυχὴν αὐτοῦ.

15. See the discussion in C. H. Dodd, *Historical Tradition*, 338-43. As he summarizes (343), "There is nothing against the view that the couplet, simple, rhythmical, and genuinely biblical as it is in language, was handed down by tradition substantially in the terms preserved in John xii. 25 (without the qualifying clauses)."

16. Gr. μισεῖ . . . καὶ τὴν ψυχὴν ἑαυτοῦ.

17. Matthew's gentler version is probably secondary to Luke's: "The person who loves [ὁ φιλῶν] father or mother more than me is not worthy of me, and the person who loves [ὁ φιλῶν] son or daughter more than me is not worthy of me" (Mt 10:37).

18. So Bultmann, 425, n. 1. At the same time, Dodd cautions that "The omission of the ἕνεκεν-clause we could understand; John does not use this preposition, nor does he use εὐαγγέλιον" (*Historical Tradition*, 341).

19. Gr. ἐν τῷ κόσμῳ τούτῳ.

20. Gr. εἰς ζωὴν αἰώνιον.

12:20-36 THE HOUR OF GLORIFICATION

more so than in the Gospel of John. This pronouncement stands as Jesus' answer not so much to the Greeks who wanted to see him as to the Pharisees, and their comment when he entered the city, "Look, the world has gone after him!" (v. 19). As we have seen, he cares nothing about "gaining the whole world" or even about saving his own "life in this world." Instead, he "lays down his life" for his sheep, not least his "other sheep . . . not from this courtyard" (see 10:15b-16), and the reader now knows that "the hour has come" (v. 23) for him to do exactly that.

26 While lacking the words from the synoptic tradition, "for my sake," in the pronouncement about "hating one's own life" (v. 25), John's Gospel more than makes up for it in Jesus' next pronouncement: "If anyone would serve *me*, let him follow *me*, and where *I* am, there *my* servant will be. If anyone would serve *me*, the Father will honor him" (v. 26, italics added). With or without the exact words, Jesus makes it very clear that the rejection of the world that he demands is unquestionably "for my sake." This saying too has a parallel (albeit a more remote one) in the synoptic tradition, where just before saying "whoever wants to save his life will lose it, but whoever loses his life for my sake will find it" (Mt 16:25//Lk 9:24), Jesus had said, "If anyone wants to come after me, let him deny himself and take up his cross and let him follow me" (Mt 16:24). There is a minor redundancy here, in that to "come after" Jesus and to "follow" him amount to the same thing, and the redundancy is heightened a bit in Mark: "If anyone wants to follow after me, let him . . . follow me" (Mk 8:34). What keeps it from being totally redundant is its definition of what "coming after" or "following" Jesus entails, that is, risking death by denying oneself and taking up one's cross. In John's Gospel, no trace of redundancy remains, for instead of "If anyone wants to come after me," Jesus says, "If anyone would serve me."[21] Little has been said so far in the Gospel of anyone "serving" or "ministering" to Jesus.[22] The only exceptions are the sisters Mary and Martha at the supper in Bethany, where Martha was explicitly said to have "served" Jesus and others (12:2), but where Mary's act of anointing Jesus' feet with perfume for the day of his burial seems to have been the more significant act

---

21. Gr. ἐὰν ἐμοί τις διακονῇ. The "if" clauses are different, in that in Matthew and Mark it is a condition of reality with εἰ and a verb in the present indicative, and in John's Gospel a future condition with ἐάν and a verb in the present subjunctive. But they are similar in meaning because the helping verb "wants to" (θέλει) in the synoptic texts attaches the same note of contingency to the notion of "coming" to Jesus that the subjunctive attaches here to that of "serving" him. Even in English, "If anyone wants to" and "If anyone would" amount to more or less the same thing.

22. As we have seen, "the servants" (οἱ διάκονοι) at the Cana wedding who did as they were told (2:5) functioned as surrogates or stand-ins for the disciples, but the designation "servants" is never directly applied to the disciples themselves.

of service, even though not called that in so many words. Much the same is true in the other Gospels, where those who "serve" or minister to Jesus are characteristically women (see Mt 8:15//Mk 1:31//Lk 4:39; Mt 27:55//Mk 15:41; Lk 8:3; 10:40),[23] but where Jesus himself is quite emphatic that "the Son of man did not come to be served but to serve, and to give his life a ransom for many" (Mt 20:28//Mk 10:45), or that "I am in your midst as the one who serves" (Lk 22:27; see also 12:37). Here, "serving" Jesus or "ministering" to him is defined as "following" him, to the point that "where I am, there my servant[24] will be." The unspoken implication is that "serving" Jesus involves imitating his behavior, doing what he did by serving others, or each other. This will become explicit later on, when Jesus speaks privately to all his disciples about what discipleship means (see, for example, 13:14-15, 34-35; 15:12).[25]

For now, the accent is rather on the reward of true discipleship and the logical outcome of "following" him, that is, as he says, "where I am, there my servant will be."[26] This is understood as an "honor," for as Jesus rephrases it, "If anyone would serve me, the Father will honor him." Jesus has already told the Pharisees that "where I am you cannot come" (7:34), or "Where I go you cannot come" (8:21), and even his own disciples (including Martha and Mary) that "me you do not always have" (12:8; compare 13:33). Yet now he signals that this will not be the case forever as far as his true "servants" are concerned. Wherever he is going, if they "follow" him faithfully, even, if need be, to martyrdom, their place with him is assured. Here more than anywhere else in the first twelve chapters, Jesus anticipates the themes of his farewell discourses (see 14:3; 17:24).[27]

27 Jesus' speech continues, now addressed to the Father as a prayer: "Now my soul is shaken, and what shall I say? 'Father, save me from this hour'? No, for this reason I came to this hour" (v. 27). The scene obviously

---

23. In one other instance, "angels served him" (Mt 4:11//Mk 1:13), and in an indirect reference those rejected at the last judgment ask, "Lord, when did we see you hungry or thirsty or a stranger or naked or sick or in prison, and we did not serve you?" (οὐ διηκονήσαμέν σοι, Mt 25:44, in which the verb applies to any of the stated conditions so as to involve providing food, water, lodging, clothing, or support and companionship).

24. Gr. ὁ διάκονος ὁ ἐμός.

25. The same principle is at work in the synoptic Gospels, where Jesus himself is the supreme example of the principle that "whoever wants to become great among you will be your servant" (Mt 20:26//Mk 10:43; see also Lk 22:26; Mt 23:11; Mk 9:35).

26. This was what the disciples had desired from the beginning (see 1:39, "So they came, and saw where he was staying, and they stayed with him that day").

27. Compare Lincoln, 351: "One who serves Jesus will follow him in self-giving, even if that leads to death. But just as Jesus' death will be his glory, so that pattern will be reproduced for his followers."

12:20-36 THE HOUR OF GLORIFICATION

invites comparison with the synoptic accounts of Jesus' prayer in the garden of Gethsemane (see Mt 26:39//Mk 14:35-36//Lk 22:41-42), but there are significant differences as well. Most conspicuously, Jesus' prayer is answered (v. 28), and the answer is heard publicly (v. 29), suggesting that the prayer was public as well. Also, the prayer, "Father, save me from this hour," which most closely parallels the Gethsemane accounts,[28] is not Jesus' actual prayer in John's Gospel. Rather, it is precisely what he does *not* pray. Instead he prays, "Father, glorify your name" (v. 28a). The text does not suggest any real uncertainty on Jesus' part, along the lines of what Paul describes in Romans 8:26 ("For we do not know what to pray as we ought").[29] The petition "Father, save me from this hour" is introduced only as a rhetorical question, the wrong prayer setting the stage for the right one.[30] As soon as the words are out of his mouth, Jesus adds, "No,[31] for this reason I came to this hour."[32] If John's account is at all aware of the Gethsemane tradition, it is (at the very least) shifting the emphasis dramatically from "If it is possible, let this cup pass from me," to "not what I want but what you want" (Mt 26:39// Mk 14:36).

28 Whether with the "wrong" prayer or the "right" one, Jesus addresses God as "Father" just as at the raising of Lazarus (11:41), and in his last prayer (see 17:1, 5, 11, 21, 24, 25). The "right" prayer, "Father, glorify your name"[33] (v. 28a), could easily be read as a variant of the Lukan form of the so-called "Lord's Prayer" ("Father, hallowed be your name," Lk 11:2), a prayer not oriented toward a particular decisive "hour," but one appropriate for Jesus or his followers at any time or in any place ("When you pray, say . . . ," Lk 11:2).[34] The "right" prayer, in short, seems to have been for Je-

---

28. The closest parallel is with the Markan account, which begins with the notice that Jesus "fell on the earth and was praying that if it is possible the hour [ἡ ὥρα] might pass from him" (Mk 14:35).

29. So Schnackenburg: "For the Johannine Jesus there is no real lingering in the depths of death and annihilation, and the approach to the Father which follows should therefore be understood not as a petition but as a question" (2.387). This is supported by the textual editors, who have punctuated it as a question, and by most modern translations.

30. Within the narrative, Jesus is asking himself what he should pray (see BDF, §448[4], "a question to one's self"), but the reader's impression is that the question is rhetorical, because Jesus already knows the answer.

31. Gr. ἀλλά.

32. As Bultmann paraphrases, "Is such a desire the right answer for the question of this hour? No! Flight from this hour would destroy its significance" (427).

33. Gr. πάτερ, δόξασόν σου τὸ ὄνομα.

34. Elsewhere in this Gospel, Jesus can adapt the prayer, to make it more specific to the occasion, or more centered on himself: "Glorify your Son [δόξασόν σου τὸν υἱόν], that your Son may glorify you" (17:1); "And now you, Father, glorify me [δόξασόν με] in your presence with the glory I had with you before the world was" (17:5).

sus a "normal" prayer, one that he prayed quite commonly and consistently, not a special or exceptional prayer designed for this one occasion.[35]

This is perhaps in keeping with the answer given at once, and audibly: "Then a voice came from the sky, 'I have both glorified, and I will glorify again'" (v. 28b). The voice "from the sky" (or from heaven)[36] recalls the voice at Jesus' baptism and the voice "from the cloud" at his transfiguration in the synoptic accounts, and like them has to be understood as the voice of the Father, this time in response to Jesus' prayer. Aside from God's (presumably private) words to John (1:33), it is the *only* time God speaks in the entire Gospel. On the assumption that the glorification of God's name is the same as the glorification of Jesus himself, "the Son of man" (v. 23), it appears that the promise, "I will glorify again," refers to Jesus' "hour" now at hand.[37] But what is meant by the first part of the pronouncement, "I have . . . glorified"? It is probably pointless to look for precise references within the story such as Jesus' birth or baptism, neither of which are even mentioned in this Gospel. Rather, the voice is reminding Jesus of the consistent relationship he has *always* enjoyed with the Father, not just from the beginning of his ministry but from eternity (see, for example, 8:29, "for I always do the things that please him"; 11:42, "I knew that you always hear me"). As Jesus told "the Jews" four chapters earlier, "If I glorify myself, my glory is nothing. It is my Father who glorifies me, him whom you say that 'He is our God'" (8:54). The Gospel's presupposition is that God "glorifies his name" by glorifying his Son, and in one sense that glorification goes on continually throughout the narrative (see, for example, 1:14; 2:11; 11:4, 40; 17:4), having begun presumably with the sending of the Son into the world.[38] Nevertheless, the voice does not let us forget that a final "glorification" is imminent, and will be the dominant theme from here on.

29-30 As far as we know, Jesus has been speaking to Philip and Andrew (v. 22), but now we are introduced to "the crowd standing by," of which we have heard nothing before. This crowd, like other crowds in the Gospel (for example, 7:12, 40-42), seems to have been divided, though not to the

---

35. Alternatively, even the "wrong" prayer, "Father, save me from this hour," could be viewed as an adaptation of the *last* petition of the Lord's Prayer, either "Lead us not into temptation" (Lk 11:4; see also Mt 26:41//Mk 14:38//Lk 22:46) or "Deliver us from the Evil One" (Mt 6:13). But this is probably too subtle, and therefore less likely.

36. The phrase "from the sky" (ἐκ τοῦ οὐρανοῦ) could also be translated "from heaven" (see, for example, 3:31; 6:32-33, 41) but the crowd's confusion of the voice with thunder (v. 29) suggests that the Gospel writer is using the language of appearance here (as perhaps is done in the synoptic baptism and transfiguration scenes as well).

37. See 13:31, "Now the Son of man is glorified, and God is glorified in him."

38. So Schnackenburg, 2.388; Bultmann, 429. See also 10:36, where the operative word is "consecrated," and 17:22, where this consecration for mission (17:19) is understood as glorification: "And I, the glory you have given me I have given them."

12:20-36 THE HOUR OF GLORIFICATION

point of a "split" or schism (as in 7:43). The crowd "heard" something, and what they heard sounded to them as if "thunder had come," but "others" (probably *within* the crowd, presupposing that only "some" heard thunder) were saying, "An angel has spoken to him" (v. 29). The latter suggests real communication, not just noise (see 1:51, "the sky opened, and the angels of God going up and coming down over the Son of man"), yet it is difficult to tell whether or not anyone in the crowd heard the actual words that were spoken.

Whatever they may have heard, Jesus is quick to tell them, "This voice was not for my sake but for yours" (v. 30). With this he recalls an earlier scene in which he told the Father that his prayer at the tomb of Lazarus was "for the sake of the crowd standing around, so that they might believe that you sent me" (11:42). The point there was not that the crowd knew the content of Jesus' prayer, only that they knew he was praying, showing his dependence on the Father. So here, the voice is "for the sake" of the crowd,[39] not because it tells them anything specific, but only as a signal that Jesus' prayer has prompted a response from the sky, and therefore that a decisive moment has come. This decisive moment, he hastens to explain, no longer to his disciples (as in vv. 24-26) but now to an anonymous "crowd standing by," represents in some way the whole Jewish community.

31 Jesus focuses the crowd's attention on his "hour" (without using the actual word), first as judgment (v. 31) and then as redemption (v. 32). Instead of "the hour" (v. 23) or "this hour" (v. 27), he speaks of it simply as "now," twice in quick succession: "*Now* is the judgment of this world. *Now* the ruler of this world will be driven out" (v. 31, italics added). The second sentence explains the first: the world is "now" judged, in that its ruler is "now" to be "driven out."[40] The language can easily be read as the language of exorcism, especially with "the ruler of this world" as its object.[41] This is the case even though Jesus has performed no exorcisms in this Gospel, and

---

39. Gr. δι' ὑμᾶς.
40. Gr. ἐκβληθήσεται ἔξω. The expression is strong, to the point of redundancy (the adverb ἔξω being unnecessary): literally, he will be "driven out outside." Some ancient manuscripts (including P[66] and D) get rid of the redundancy with the reading βληθήσεται ἔξω. Yet the redundancy is thoroughly characteristic of Johannine style. Other ancient manuscripts (including Θ, some of the old Latin, Sy[s], and Chrysostom) read βληθήσεται κάτω ("thrown down"), evoking an apocalyptic image of "the ruler of this world" being thrown down either from heaven to earth (see Lk 10:18; Rev 12:9), or into the pit of hell (Rev 20:2-3).
41. There are over 30 examples of ἐκβάλλειν in connection with exorcisms in the synoptic Gospels. Admittedly, it is used in other ways as well, and the full expression "to drive out outside" (ἐκβάλλειν ἔξω) is used in other ways in this Gospel (as in 9:34-35, where it refers to excommunication from the synagogue, and 6:37 and 15:6, where it implies rejection by God or Jesus without demonic implications).

even though he is not explicitly said to perform this one.[42] Instead of many exorcisms of demons, there will be just one. "The ruler[43] of this world" (see 14:30; 16:11) can only be the devil,[44] referred to in the synoptic tradition as "the ruler of the demons" or "Beelzebub" (see Mt 12:24//Mk 3:22//Lk 11:16; also Mt 9:34). There, when Jesus asks, "How can Satan drive out Satan?" (Mk 3:23; see also Mt 12:26), the implication is that he himself has done exactly that, in "binding the strong man" (see Mt 12:29//Mk 3:27). In another synoptic passage, he observes it happening by virtue of his disciples' exorcisms: "I saw Satan as lightning fallen from heaven" (Lk 10:18).

Here Satan, or the devil, is ruler not "of the demons" but "of this world."[45] In that sense the Pharisees are profoundly wrong in claiming that "the world has gone after" Jesus (v. 19). On the contrary, "this world" has given its allegiance to its own demonic ruler. For that reason, only those who *hate* their life "in this world" will gain "eternal life" (v. 25), and for that reason "this world" now faces judgment. Instead of the exorcism of demons, this Gospel contemplates a kind of exorcism of "the world" itself, by virtue of the "throwing out" of its ruler.[46] The thought recalls John's pronouncement near the beginning of the Gospel, in which Jesus himself, as the "Lamb of God," purifies the world by "taking away" its sin (1:29). In spite of the repeated "now," the verb "will be driven out" is future, allowing for the presence of "the devil" or "Satan" in the chapters to follow (see 13:2, 27; also 14:30).[47] Clearly, there is an "already-but-not-yet" to Jesus' solemn pronouncement, for at this point in the narrative the world is still very much "the world," not yet judged and not yet purified from sin.

---

42. The passive ἐκβληθήσεται ("will be thrown out") is an impersonal passive, introduced perhaps to avoid the use of the divine name (see BDF, §130[1]). That "the ruler of this world will be thrown out" may imply "*God* will throw him out." Presumably it is all part of what is involved in God "glorifying his name" (v. 28).

43. Gr. ὁ ἄρχων.

44. For roughly equivalent expressions in Paul's letters, see 1 Corinthians 2:6 ("the rulers of this age"), Ephesians 2:2 ("the ruler of the power of the air"), and 2 Corinthians 4:4 ("the god of this age").

45. Gr. τοῦ κόσμου τούτου. Some manuscripts, including the first hand of P[66], D, W, Sy[s], some old Latin versions, and the Vulgate have simply "the ruler of the world" (as in 14:30), but "this" (τούτου) has stronger attestation, and should probably be retained, as in v. 25 and 16:11.

46. The Christian reader cannot help but remember Martin Luther's lines, "And though this world with devils filled should threaten to undo us, we will not fear, for God hath willed His truth to triumph through us."

47. Only in 16:11 is "the ruler of this world" said to be finally "judged" (κέκριται), and there it is entirely possible that this is spoken within the framework of the future ministry of "the Advocate" or "Spirit of truth" who comes only after Jesus has gone away (see 16:5-7).

32-33 In the two pronouncements, "Now is the judgment of this world" and "Now the ruler of this world will be driven out" (v. 31), Jesus said nothing explicitly of his own role in bringing those things about, even though his role will doubtless be crucial. But now he abruptly puts himself back at the center (v. 32). The pronouncement comes as a kind of postscript to the parable of verse 24, so that it too is now centered on Jesus himself. Instead of the "if" clause with which verse 24 ended ("if it dies, it bears a great crop"), he adds a new "if" clause identifying *himself* with the "grain of wheat" that "dies by falling to the earth" (v. 24): "And I, if I be lifted up from the earth, will draw them all to myself."[48] The contrast between "to [or into] the earth"[49] and "from [or out of] the earth"[50] is striking. Jesus' parables of growth in the synoptic tradition are well known, and in keeping with the agricultural metaphor, he seems to be identifying himself here with the plant that grows to full stature from a seed planted in the ground, perhaps in reference to his resurrection from the grave (see 1 Cor 15:36-38, where Paul adopts such a metaphor). This is consistent with what follows, in that being "lifted up from the earth" Jesus promises to "draw them all to myself" — that is, to bring about the general resurrection of "all who are in the tombs" (see 5:28-29).

This interpretation would be a viable one even without the narrative aside that immediately follows: "This he said signifying by what death[51] he was going to die" (v. 33). That is, the phrase "lifted up from the earth" refers to Jesus' *death,* not just his resurrection. While the text is building on the parable of "the grain of wheat" (v. 24), its application to Jesus himself is qualified in one important respect: Jesus will die *not* like a seed, by "falling to the earth" (v. 24), but rather by being "lifted up from the earth" (v. 32).[52] Without that qualification, the image of "the grain of wheat," applicable to Jesus' disciples (see vv. 25-26), is not directly applicable to Jesus himself. The terminology introduced here revisits two earlier pronouncements. In the first, Je-

---

48. As is often noticed, even though "if" (ἐάν) introduces a conditional clause, its fulfillment is not in doubt. "If" has virtually the force of "when," for Jesus will in fact be "lifted up" (see v. 34, where δεῖ ὑψωθῆναι confirms that it "must" happen; also 3:14). So also Bultmann, 432, n. 2, citing 14:3 as a parallel. The matter is clear in 14:3, because the "if" clause is preceded by a flat statement that "I am going away to prepare a place for you" (14:2). Here too we have the flat statement, "And I . . . will draw them all to myself," with the "if" clause simply a parenthesis. Possibly recognizing this, some ancient witnesses (including 1241 and some old Latin versions) read "when" (ὅταν) in place of "if" (others, with B, shorten ἐάν to ἄν).

49. Gr. εἰς τὴν γῆν.

50. Gr. ἐκ τῆς γῆς.

51. Gr. ποίῳ θανάτῳ.

52. He does, however, "fall to the earth" (ἔπιπτεν ἐπὶ τῆς γῆς, with a different preposition) in the garden of Gethsemane (Mk 14:35), as he prays for the "cup" of death to pass from him.

sus told Nicodemus and those he represented that "just as Moses lifted up the snake in the desert, so the Son of man must be lifted up, so that everyone who believes might have eternal life in him" (3:14-15). In the second, he told the Pharisees, "When you lift up the Son of man, then you will know that I am" (8:28). In both instances he refers to himself as "the Son of man," but in neither does he explain what it means to be "lifted up," except to imply that something good will come of it. The perceptive Christian reader has suspected all along that he was referring to his death by crucifixion, and now that interpretation is explicitly confirmed.

Here too something good comes of Jesus' being "lifted up," as he promises, "I will draw them all[53] to myself" (v. 32b). The apparently universal scope of "all" is striking. Because nothing else in the Gospel even hints at universal salvation, and a number of texts speak against it (for example, 3:36; 5:29; 8:21, 24), interpreters have proposed a variety of alternatives. For instance, some important ancient texts (including P^{66}, the first hand of א, and all the Latin versions) read the neuter plural "all things"[54] in place of the masculine plural ("them all," or "all people"), suggesting a kind of cosmic redemption of the universe. If so, it might include human beings corporately rather than individually.[55] Either way, the reference would not necessarily require the salvation of every individual person. But the neuter reading is slightly less strongly attested than the masculine, and may well have come into being precisely to alleviate a theological difficulty.[56] Another recourse is to understand "all" (whether read as masculine or neuter) in relation to ethnic groups rather than individuals. That is, both Jews and Greeks.[57] This could be supported by an appeal to Paul (especially in Romans), for whom "all" frequently comes to mean "Jew and Greek" (or "Jew and Gentile") alike (see,

---

53. Gr. πάντας ἑλκύσω.

54. Gr. πάντα, with P^{66}, the first hand of א, and the Latin versions.

55. In certain other Johannine texts a neuter *singular* is used in that way; for example, 6:39 ("that of all he has given me I might not lose *anything,* but raise *it* up at the last day"), and 10:29 ("*That which* my Father has given me is greater than all things, and no one can seize [it] out of my Father's hand"). But this usage is not attested for a neuter plural (see Schnackenburg, 2.528, n. 98).

56. Augustine's discussion is instructive: "But He did not say, All men, but 'all things'; for all men have not faith. And, therefore, he did not allude to the totality of men, but to the creature in its personal integrity, that is, to spirit, and soul, and body; or all that which makes us the intelligent, living, visible, and palpable beings we are." As a kind of fallback position, he argued, "Or if by 'all things' it is men that are to be understood, we can speak of all things that are foreordained to salvation; of all which He declared, when previously speaking of His sheep, that not one of them would be lost" (*Homilies on the Gospel of St. John* 52.11; NPNF, 1st ser., 7.390).

57. So Chrysostom, on "all men": "That is, 'even those of the Gentiles'" (*Homilies on John* 67.3; NPNF, 1st ser., 14.250).

for example, Rom 1:18; 2:9, 10; 3:9, 23; 10:12; 11:32).[58] It can also appeal, obviously, to the actual presence of "Greeks" in the narrative context (vv. 20-22). This option has much in its favor, and many modern interpreters have adopted it.[59] Less likely is the supposition that "all" really does mean every individual, but that Jesus is promising to draw "all" or "everyone" to himself for judgment, not salvation. This view can appeal to the strong accent on judgment in the immediate context (v. 31), viewing this verse simply as the explication of the preceding one.[60] It can also appeal to Jesus' earlier statements that the Father "has given all judgment to the Son," or given him "authority to do judgment because he is the Son of man" (see 5:22, 27). But while final judgment of the wicked was emphasized both in early Judaism and early Christianity (see, for example, 5:29), nowhere are those judged said to be "drawn" to God or to Jesus for that purpose. The difficulty lies with the verb "I will draw,"[61] used earlier in the Gospel to refer unambiguously to being "drawn" to Jesus redemptively (6:44), as a synonym for being "given" to him by the Father (6:37), or being "given" the privilege of coming to him for salvation (6:65).

The verb "I will draw" is in fact the likely key to the meaning of the verse. Those "drawn" are a specific group, those who actually "come" to Jesus in faith, for salvation. The repeated expression, "to come to me" (6:37, 44, and 65),[62] corresponds to the promise here that Jesus will draw these people "to myself,"[63] suggesting that the same specific group is in mind here.[64] If so, then "all" is qualified by the previous references to those "drawn" or "given" to Jesus by the Father, that is, believers (hence the trans-

---

58. The neuter reading πάντα might even be understood as a kind of abbreviation for πάντα τὰ ἔθνη ("all the nations" or "all the Gentiles"), a term which never occurs in John's Gospel.

59. See, for example, Barrett, 427; Keener, 2.881; Lindars, 434; Carson, 444; Moloney, 355; Morris, 531-32.

60. See Kent, *Light in the Darkness,* 157-58: "Others explain this as the drawing of all men to the crucified Christ in judgment. Judgment is clearly the subject of the immediate context (12:31). Every man must stand before the crucified Christ, either as a penitent sinner to receive judicial pardon, or else to face him as the judge to hear his doom pronounced."

61. Gr. ἑλκύσω.

62. See also, for example, 3:2, 26, 5:40, 6:5, 7:37, and 10:41, where the term consistently denotes allegiance (or potential allegiance) to Jesus.

63. Gr. πρὸς ἐμαυτόν. See also 14:3, "I will receive you to myself" (πρὸς ἐμαυτόν).

64. As Morris puts it (531), "all those who come to Christ are there because they have been drawn. Jesus is not affirming that the whole world will be saved; he is affirming that all who are saved are saved in this way." (Morris combines this, not altogether consistently, with the notion that "all" refers to Jew and Gentile alike.)

lation, "them all").⁶⁵ The point is not that every human being is "drawn," but that all those drawn by the Father are drawn by the Son. Instead of the Father drawing believers to Jesus, he himself, now "lifted up from the earth," draws "them all" to himself. As he put it in the earlier setting, "I will raise him up at the last day" (6:44). Jesus will "draw" believers first to the cross on which he is "lifted up" (see v. 33), but beyond that to wherever he is going (see v. 26, "where I am, there my servant will be").⁶⁶ The place is unknown to Jesus' enemies (7:34; 8:21), and even to his own disciples (see 13:36; 14:5), but the reader of the Gospel knows at least that he is going back to where he came from (see 6:62, "[what] if you see the Son of man going up where he was at first?" 7:33, "I go to the One who sent me"), and he now repeats in different words the thought that "where I am, there my servant will be" (v. 26). Just as in verses 24-26, however, the only way to get there is by way of the cross. To be "drawn" to Jesus "lifted up" on the cross is to be drawn into the pattern of discipleship set forth in those verses — and earlier, in 6:53-58, under the metaphor of "eating Jesus' flesh and drinking his blood." Thus the way of discipleship, not the worldwide mission to the Gentiles, is the likely *primary* meaning of Jesus' "drawing them all" to himself. He has indeed promised a "great crop" (v. 24), pointing to eternal life for his followers (v. 25), and hinting at a missionary harvest like that in Samaria (see 4:36-38), yet the hint remains only a hint, for the "Greeks" are not heard from again.

Perhaps surprisingly, the Gospel writer's narrative aside (v. 33) seems to ignore Jesus' main assertion — that he "will draw them all to myself" — in favor of something he said only in a subordinate clause ("if I be

65. Chrysostom asks, "How then said He that the Father draweth? Because when the Son draweth, the Father draweth also." Then he links the reference with the preceding verse about judgment on the world and its ruler: "He saith, 'I will draw them,' as though they were detained by a tyrant, and unable of themselves alone to approach Him, and to escape the hands of him who keepeth hold of them. In another place He calleth this 'spoiling'; no man can spoil a strong man's goods except he first bind the strong man, and then spoil his goods (Matt. xii. 29). This He said to prove His strength, and what there he calleth 'spoiling,' He hath here called 'drawing'" (*Homilies on John* 67.3; NPNF, 1st ser., 14.250).

66. Bultmann too notices this parallel (432): "it is self-evident that he certainly offers this possibility to all men, but that this is realised only in those who belong to him, who as his servants will be with him (v. 26; 14.3; 17.24)." So also Schnackenburg: "For John the cross is so much the place of glorification and the beginning of Jesus' saving rule . . . that Jesus does not just draw people to him on the cross, but in the heavenly realm. The one who is 'lifted up' is the Son of man, who has gone up again to where he was before (cf. 3:13; 6:62). This goal, which Jesus also describes in 12:26; 14:3; 17:24 as the place 'where I am,' and to which he wants to take his own (14:3: πρὸς ἐμαυτόν!), is envisaged in the 'drawing'" (2.393).

lifted up from the earth"). The effect is to focus attention solely on the *manner* of his death: "This he said signifying[67] by what death he was going to die" — that is, simply that his death would involve being "lifted up." This is clearly the case when the pronouncement is mentioned again later in retrospect (18:32), as it becomes apparent that Jesus will die at the hands of the Romans by crucifixion. It is also the case here if Jesus was "signifying," or signaling something to the immediate bystanders, "the crowd standing by" (v. 29), for they seem to hear nothing of Jesus' "drawing" anyone to himself. Their response, given immediately (v. 34), focuses instead on the verb "lifted up," and only on that. This is perhaps why the Gospel writer pauses to highlight the manner (rather than the redemptive purpose) of Jesus' death.[68] The strange fact is that Jesus will die not in the normal way, by "falling to the earth" like a seed (v. 24), but by being "lifted up from the earth" like — what? Like a full-grown plant or tree? Or more like a snake upon a pole (see 3:14)?

34 As if taking their cue from the Gospel writer's narrative aside (v. 33), the crowd responds to Jesus' speech. Ignoring Jesus' words about the voice they had heard (v. 30), about "this world" being judged and its ruler "driven out" (v. 31), and about Jesus "drawing them all" to himself (v. 32), they too fasten solely on one verb in one subordinate clause, "if I be lifted up . . ." (v. 32). "We have heard from the law," they claim, "that the Christ remains forever, and how can you say that the Son of man must be lifted up.[69] Who is this Son of man?" (v. 34). "From the law" can only mean "from the Scripture" (see 10:34, where the quotation is from Psalms), not from a legal code or the five books of Moses in particular. While nothing is said in the Hebrew Scriptures in so many words about a personal Messiah "remaining forever," the thought may come from Psalm 110:4 ("You are a priest forever"), or Isaiah 9:6-7, or from any number of passages about an eternal, messianic, Davidic line (see, for example, 2 Sam 7:13; Ps 132:12), including the closest parallel of all to the present passage, the promise to David that his line "will continue forever" (Ps 89:36 LXX).[70]

---

67. Gr. σημαίνων.

68. Yet if Jesus is understood as also "signifying" something to the *readers of the Gospel* as well as the crowd, it would certainly include not only the manner but the redemptive *purpose* of his death — that is, that by dying on the cross he would "draw them all" to himself. Such a possibility is supported by the similar notice at the end of the Gospel, after the risen Jesus has described Peter's future: "This he said signifying [σημαίνων] by what death [ποίῳ θανάτῳ] he [that is, Peter] will glorify God" (21:19). There, Jesus' comment is meant as a sign *both* to Peter and to the readers of the Gospel, and the same is probably true here.

69. Gr. δεῖ ὑψωθῆναι.

70. Gr. εἰς τὸ αἰῶνα μενεῖ.

If taken out of context, the crowd's comment could be interpreted in either of two ways. If they understand "lifting up" as exaltation to heaven or to a divine status with God (see, for example, Acts 2:33; 5:31), they could be saying, "Scripture tells us that the Messiah is to be the Exalted One who remain forever and rules over Israel, but you are telling us that it is instead this mysterious 'Son of man.' Who is this 'Son of man,' anyway?" On this reading, their problem is with the title "Son of man," and they are unsure whether or not Jesus is using it to mean the Messiah. But if they understand "lifting up" to refer to death by crucifixion, then they are saying, "Scripture tells us that the Messiah will remain forever, but you are telling us that the Son of man — by which we assume you mean the Messiah — will *not* remain forever, but die by crucifixion." On this reading, their problem is not with the title "Son of man," but with the notion of a dying Messiah.

If the crowd's question is read in context, the second reading is the only one possible, for the Gospel writer has just now settled the interpretation of "lifted up." In using that word, he tells us, Jesus was "signifying by what death he was going to die" (v. 33, my italics).[71] This is in keeping with the two previous occurrences of the term, where "lifting up" was compared to a snake being fastened to a pole (3:14), and was said to be something Jesus' enemies would do to him (8:28). Moreover, the crowd's paraphrase sounds more like what he said nine chapters earlier (3:14) than what he has said to them just now. Here he has used the emphatic "I" followed by a conditional clause, "if I be lifted up"; there he used the self-designation "Son of man" and the expression "must be lifted up," accenting necessity. In both respects, the crowd offers only a loose paraphrase of what he has just said in their presence, but an almost exact quotation of what he said to Nicodemus and his friends much earlier, during his first visit to Jerusalem.

Various explanations of this have been given, most commonly the suggestion that the crowd's remark originally followed 3:14 (or perhaps 8:28),[72] and that in the final redaction of the Gospel two distinct scenes have become confused with one another.[73] But if we take the text as it stands, the

---

71. Even though the crowd was obviously not privy to the Gospel writer's narrative aside (v. 33), the verb "signifying" (σήμαινων) implies that Jesus communicated something not just to the readers of the Gospel but to the actual bystanders. What he communicated to them, as we have just seen, was not the redemptive purpose of his death, but simply the fact of death by crucifixion.

72. Bultmann's rearrangement (354, n. 6) places it after 8:28 (possibly because of its polemical context) rather than 3:14, but it is just as awkward there as here, for Jesus has not said there that the Son of man "must" be lifted up. If any rearranging were to be done, it would have to be with 3:14 and not 8:28.

73. Brown (1.478) takes seriously a proposal offered years ago by J.-G. Gour-

better explanation is that Jesus' interlocutors, whether identified as "the Jews" or "the Pharisees" or "the crowd" (even disciples, as in 6:60), are in some sense always the same, a stereotyped audience raising the same sorts of objections chapter after chapter to his self-revelation. Here it is as if "the crowd" (like the readers of the Gospel!) remembers what Jesus said earlier to Nicodemus, and hears it echoed in his words about being "lifted up from the earth." He has, since then, repeatedly called himself (as recently as v. 23) "the Son of man," and (in spite of the "if" clause)[74] left no doubt that he will in fact be "lifted up." The crowd takes it for granted that Jesus is using "Son of man" to refer to himself, and their comment is, if not an exact quotation, at least an acceptable paraphrase of what he actually said.

In a way, it gathers up the whole of his self-revelation, from the dialogue with Nicodemus to the present moment, and voices the classic Jewish objection to it. Jesus does not qualify as "the Christ," or Messiah, of Jewish expectation because the Messiah "remains forever," while he claims that he must be "lifted up," signaling thereby that he must die by crucifixion. This is in keeping with similar objections: he cannot be the Christ because "we know where this man is from, but the Christ, when he comes, no one knows where he is from" (7:27), or (contradicting themselves) because "the Christ comes from the seed of David and from Bethlehem" (7:41-42). In each instance, as we have seen, the reader knows better, for the Jewish leaders do not in fact know where Jesus is from (see 8:14; 9:29).[75] The same is true here. They are wrong again, in that both things are true: he must be "lifted up," and yet he "remains forever." He has said as much parabolically, and applied it to himself: "But the slave does not remain in the household forever; the son remains forever.[76] So if the Son sets you free, you will really be free" (8:35-36). The crowd cannot grasp this. To them, death has a finality that makes it incompatible with "remaining forever." When they conclude with the question, "Who is this Son of man?" they are really asking Jesus, "Who are you?"[77] How can you claim to be the Christ if you admit you are going to be crucified?"

35 Again the question goes unanswered. Instead of identifying him-

---

billon ("La Parabole du Serpent d'Airain," *RB* 51 [1942], 213-26), that at one stage of the tradition 3:14-21 in its entirety stood between 12:31 and 32. But even if this very speculative suggestion were true, it would merely tell us something about the Johannine tradition, not about any Gospel that actually exists.

74. See above, n. 48.

75. That is, they do not know that he comes from God, or that he was in fact born in Bethlehem, as "the Scripture" (7:42), which "cannot be abolished" (see 10:35), requires.

76. Gr. ὁ υἱὸς μένει εἰς τὸν αἰῶνα.

77. For that question, compare 8:25, "Who are you?" and 8:53, "Who do you make yourself to be?" (see also 10:24, "If you are the Christ, tell us plainly").

self outright as "the Son of man" or claiming explicitly to be "the Christ," Jesus revisits the Gospel's opening verses, speaking of himself in the third person as "the Light" (as in 1:4-5, 8-9). "Yet a short time the Light is in you," he begins (v. 35a).[78] Other pronouncements during the course of Jesus' ministry come into play as well. Just after the early notice at the first Passover that "the Son of man must be lifted up" (3:14), he referred to himself repeatedly as "the Light" (3:19, 20, 21) on the basis of which all people are judged, and later made the identification explicit at the Tent festival: "I am the Light of the world. Whoever follows me will not walk in darkness, but will have the light of life" (8:12).

That there was a time limit to his manifestation as "the Light" became evident in the next chapter when Jesus told his disciples, "We must work the works of the One who sent me as long as it is day. Night is coming when no one can work" (9:4), and "When I am in the world, I am the Light of the world" (v. 5). In 11:9 we learned that there was still time ("Are there not twelve hours of the day?"), but now time is running out. "Yet a short time[79] the Light is in you," Jesus tells the crowd, just as he told the Pharisees at the Tent festival, "Yet a short time I am with you, and I go to the One who sent me" (7:33; see also 8:21-22). Here it comes as Jesus' final appeal to unbelievers who are nevertheless potential disciples. "Walk while you have the Light,"[80] he continues, "lest darkness overtake you — and the person who walks in that darkness does not know where he is going" (v. 35b). Echoing the invitation and promise of 8:12 ("Whoever follows me will not walk in darkness, but will have the light of life"), he gives the crowd at the Passover one last opportunity to "walk" with him. In this respect, the pronouncement also recalls Jesus' reminder to his own disciples after Mary anointed his feet, "For the poor you always have with you, but me you do not always have" (12:8). Like his disciples, these bystanders "have" Jesus the Light, if only for "a short time." The door is still open, but closing fast. With the invitation comes a warning: "lest darkness overtake you." The reader knows that darkness did not "overtake" the light that dawned with the coming of Jesus (1:5), but it is evident here that it will "overtake" those who do not "walk in the light" (see 1 Jn 1:6-7). Jesus adds

---

78. "In you" (ἐν ὑμῖν) is to be preferred to the variant reading "with you" (μεθ' ὑμῶν, as in A, Γ, Δ, 700, 1424, sy^s, and certain Coptic versions), and (in contrast to Mt 6:23 and Lk 11:36) must be understood here as "among you," for Jesus is referring to the crowd, not to individuals in the crowd.

79. Gr. ἔτι μικρὸν χρόνον.

80. Gr. ὡς τὸ φῶς ἔχετε. The variant reading ἕως (as in 9:4, "as long as," with P^{66}, ℵ, Θ, some old Latin versions, the Vulgate, and the majority of later witnesses) brings out even more clearly the notion of a limited time, but ὡς is probably to be preferred on the basis of manuscript evidence (including B, D, A, K, L, W, Ψ, 1, and 565).

a further warning, "the person who walks in that darkness[81] does not know where he is going." Then, without explaining all that this entails,[82] he goes on to renew the invitation positively (v. 36).

36 Having used the clause, "while you have the Light," in the framework of a metaphor about "walking in the light" as opposed to "walking in darkness" (v. 35), Jesus now repeats the same clause in a straightforward nonmetaphorical invitation to believe: "While you have the Light, believe in the Light, that you might become sons of light." More and more, the metaphor of "the Light" has become interchangeable with Jesus himself. To "believe in the Light,"[83] an expression found nowhere else in the Gospel, means simply "believe in me," just as "coming to the Light" (3:20-21) was understood earlier to be synonymous with "coming to Jesus" (see 3:26; 6:35, 37). Yet at the end, "light" retains its metaphorical quality, in that the purpose of believing is to become "sons of light,"[84] a phrase that obviously does not mean "sons of Jesus," but rather (in keeping with Hebrew idiom), "people of the light," that is, people who belong to God (see 1 Thess 5:5, "For you are all sons of light and sons of day; we are not of night nor of darkness").[85] So Jesus ends his appeal not with a threat (as in v. 35), but on a note of promise.

Jesus' speech — and with it his whole public ministry — comes to an end abruptly with a brief notice: "These things Jesus spoke, and he went away and was hidden from them" (v. 36b). As we have seen, expressions such as "these things he spoke" have been the Gospel writer's way of terminating scenes and making transitions again and again. Here he uses it to terminate not just one brief encounter with a crowd of bystanders, but all that Jesus has had to say to "the world" from the beginning of his ministry. "Hidden from them" means hidden from all his interlocutors, whether "the crowd" (as here), or "the Jews," or "the Pharisees." He has nothing more to say to any of them, and what he says from now on will be directed either to no audience in particular (as in vv. 44-50), or to his own disciples (as in chap-

---

81. "In that darkness," because the definite article (ἐν τῇ σκοτίᾳ) refers back to the darkness referred to in the preceding clause (see BDF, §252[1]).

82. But see 11:10 ("he stumbles"), and 1 John 2:11 ("the darkness has blinded his eyes").

83. Gr. πιστεύετε εἰς τὸ φῶς.

84. Gr. υἱοὶ φωτός.

85. See also Luke 16:8: "For the sons of this age are wiser than the sons of light [ὑπὲρ τοὺς υἱοὺς τοῦ φωτός] in their own generation"; Ephesians 5:8: "For you were once darkness, but now light in the Lord. Walk as children of light" (ὡς τέκνα φωτός); 1 Peter 2:9, "You, however, are a chosen race, the King's priesthood, a holy nation, a people destined for vindication — all to sound the praises of him who called you out of darkness into his marvelous light."

ters 13–17 and 20–21), or to the Roman authorities (as in chapters 18–19).[86] Instead of saying anything more, Jesus "went away" — we are not told where — and was "hidden"[87] — we are not told how, whether naturally or supernaturally — just as he "was hidden, and went out of the temple" at the end of the Tent festival (8:59b). In contrast to the earlier passage, there is no threat of a stoning here. Jesus simply brings the encounter to an end, without waiting for a response to his invitation to believe. The "short time" (v. 35) is all but over. Jesus is on his way out of the world; "the Light of the world" is receding (see 9:5).

T. THE VERDICT ON THE WORLD (12:37-50)

> 37 *Even after he had done so many signs before them, they would not believe in him,* 38 *so that the word of Isaiah the prophet might be fulfilled, which he said, "Lord, who believed the message we have heard, and to whom was the arm of the Lord revealed?"* 39 *Therefore they were unable to believe, because, again, Isaiah said,* 40 *"He has blinded their eyes, and hardened their heart, lest they see with the eyes and understand with the heart, and turn, and I will heal them."* 41 *These things Isaiah said because he saw his glory, and he spoke about him.*
>
> 42 *Nevertheless many, even some of the rulers, did believe in him, but because of the Pharisees would not confess, lest they be put out of synagogue.* 43 *For they loved the glory of humans rather than the glory of God.*
>
> 44 *But Jesus cried out and said, "The person who believes in me believes not in me but in the One who sent me,* 45 *and the person who sees me sees the One who sent me.* 46 *I have come [as] light into the world, so that everyone who believes in me might not remain in the darkness.* 47 *And if anyone hears my words and does not keep them, I do not judge him, for I did not come to judge the world but to save the world.* 48 *The person who rejects me and does not receive my words has that which judges him. The word which I spoke, that will judge him in the last day,* 49 *for I did not speak on my own, but the Father who sent me, he has given me a command what I should say and what*

---

86. The only exceptions are Jesus' repeated self-identifications (with "I am") at his arrest (see 18:2-11), his reply to the High Priest (18:20-21), the substance of which was that he had already said all he had to say, and a defiant challenge to an officer standing by (18:24).

87. Gr. ἐκρύβη.

12:37-50 THE VERDICT ON THE WORLD

I should speak. 50 And I know that his command is eternal life; so then the things I speak, just as the Father has told me, thus I speak."

Jesus has invited crowd to "believe in the Light" (v. 36), and we quickly learn their response not from their own lips but from the Gospel writer, who tells us that "they would not believe in him" (v. 37). "They could not believe," he hastens to add (v. 39), because Isaiah had prophesied in Scripture that they would not (vv. 38-41). Even while acknowledging that "many," including some of the religious leaders, did "believe in him" (v. 42), he insists that their faith was not genuine because they were afraid to confess him publicly (v. 43). Then he invokes the now "hidden" Jesus (see v. 36b) to explain that believing in him means believing in the One who sent him, the Father, and that he has still not finished saying all that the Father has given him to say (vv. 44-50). Just as the Gospel's opening verses (1:1-5) and the farewell speech of John (3:31-36) framed the first three chapters of the Gospel, so those same opening verses and this transitional speech of Jesus with no narrative context of its own frame the Gospel's first twelve chapters, preparing the reader for more to come.

37 The notion that when Jesus was "hidden from them" (v. 36), he was hidden not just from this crowd but from *all* his interlocutors throughout his public ministry — crowds, Pharisees, and "Jews" alike — is confirmed by the Gospel writer's verdict that "Even after he had done so many signs before them,[1] they would not believe in him" (v. 37). "Them" apparently refers to the same group in both instances — a group by no means limited to the crowd of bystanders who had just insisted that "the Christ remains forever" (v. 34). The reference to "so many signs"[2] done "before them" looks back at all of Jesus' "signs" — with the possible exception of the two numbered as "first" and "second" (2:11 and 4:54).[3] In some sense it looks back as well at everything Jesus has said or done up to now.[4] But even if attention is focused on the mira-

---

1. Gr. ἔμπροσθεν αὐτῶν.
2. Gr. τοσαῦτα . . . σημεῖα.
3. The first two signs (set apart by being numbered) seem to belong in a different category, in that they were known and witnessed only within a family circle (see 2:11-12; 4:53-54). They were not "before them" (ἔμπροσθεν αὐτῶν) in the sense of being done in the presence of the crowds or the Pharisees, and, more important, they were *not* met with unbelief.
4. As we have seen, there is a sense in which Jesus' "signs" (σημεῖα) actually include all his words and actions. There is therefore some truth in Bultmann's contention (452) that in this Gospel "the concepts σημεῖα and ῥήματα (λόγοι) flow together: the σημεῖα are deeds that speak, and their meaning is developed in the discourses; moreover, the ῥήματα are not human words but words of revelation, full of divine and miraculous power — they are indeed miraculous works. Hence the Evangelist also, when looking back, could characterise the work of Jesus as a σημεῖα ποιεῖν."

cles in particular, these miraculous signs are not limited to seven, as some have suggested, nor to the unnumbered five described in chapters 5, 6, 9, and 11, but are presumed to include many others as well (see 2:23; 3:2; 6:2; 7:31; 11:47), all done publicly in Jerusalem or Galilee and all the subject of controversy between Jesus and either the crowds or the Jewish leaders or both.[5] Those who "would not believe in him" (v. 37) are therefore not just one crowd at one Passover (vv. 29, 34), but *all* the crowds and *all* the Jewish leaders from the first Passover until now. While Jesus has repeatedly charged one or another group of his hearers with unbelief (see 3:12; 5:38, 44; 6:36, 64; 8:45-46; 10:25),[6] this is the first time the Gospel writer has made such a sweeping generalization about them, confirming from the preceding narrative the principle stated at the outset that "his own did not receive him" (1:11).

38 That the people "would not believe in him" requires an explanation, and the Gospel writer is quick to supply one. The reason they did not believe was "so that the word of Isaiah the prophet might be fulfilled, which he said, 'Lord, who believed the message we have heard, and to whom was the arm of the Lord revealed?'" The quotation (from Isa 53:1, LXX) is linked to the context in John's Gospel by the rhetorical question, "Who believed?" — implying "No one believed" and thus picking up from the preceding verse the stark verdict, "they would not believe in him." It is for the sake of those words, evidently, that the quotation is introduced. Still, it is worth asking if perhaps the "we" of the quotation (that is, "the message *we* have heard," or "*our* message") has an implied antecedent in the Christian community — either the Gospel writer himself, or the writer and his implied readers. They at least have "heard" the message of Jesus and have the opportunity to believe it, and to them at least "the arm of the Lord" has been revealed in the signs Jesus has done (see 20:30-31).[7] This would be in keeping with the context in

---

5. Brown (1.485) cites as a parallel Deuteronomy 29:2-4: "Moses summoned all the Israelites and said to them: Your eyes have seen all that the LORD did in Egypt to Pharaoh, to all his officials and to all his land. With your own eyes you saw those great trials, those miraculous signs and great wonders. But to this day the LORD has not given you a mind that understands or eyes that see or ears that hear" (NIV). While the parallel is not the one the Gospel writer chooses to highlight explicitly, it is part of a series of intriguing similarities between Jesus in John's Gospel and Moses in Deuteronomy, based perhaps on the notion of Jesus as the Prophet like Moses mentioned in Deuteronomy 18:15-18.

6. In one additional instance the Gospel writer took note of Jewish unbelief, in relation not to Jesus but to the man born blind, to the effect that they "did not believe [οὐκ ἐπίστευσαν οὖν οἱ Ἰουδαῖοι] . . . that he was blind and could see, until they summoned the parents of the one himself who could see" (9:18).

7. Alternatively, Richard Bauckham identifies the "we" as Jesus himself — the "we," as he put it, of authoritative testimony (*Jesus and the Eyewitnesses*, 382). This is less likely, for it is difficult to argue that the speaker in Isaiah 53:1 is himself the suffering Servant.

Isaiah itself, where the question "Who believed the message we have heard?" does *not* necessarily expect only a negative answer. There the immediately preceding words suggest that some would in fact believe, but not those who were expected to: "So shall many nations marvel at him, and kings shall shut their mouths. Those to whom no announcement about him was made, will see, and those who have not heard will understand" (Isa 52:15, LXX).[8] Backing up still further, it is likely that the Gospel writer was fully aware of Isaiah's context, for his accent on the "lifting up" and "glorification" of Jesus has all along echoed Isaiah's introductory words, "Look, my servant will understand, and he will be lifted up and glorified exceedingly"[9] (Isa 52:13, LXX). None of this, however, changes the fact that in the present context the accent is on unbelief, and on that alone. If there is any intimation of belief on the part of the readers of the Gospel, or of the salvation of Gentiles ("many nations," Isa 52:15) through the "lifting up" or "glorification" of Jesus (see 12:32), it remains only a subtle hint, nothing even approaching an explicit promise or prophecy.

39-40 The writer goes a step beyond "they would not believe," adding, "Therefore[10] they were unable to believe" (v. 39) on the basis of another text in Isaiah: "because, again,[11] Isaiah said, 'He has blinded their eyes, and hardened their heart, lest they see with the eyes and understand with the heart, and turn, and I will heal them'" (v. 40, from Isa 6:10, LXX). This was a quotation used elsewhere by early Christians to explain the unbelief they faced, especially from the Jewish people (see Mt 13:15; Acts 28:27). The first part of the quotation here (in contrast to the other two examples) is very free, allowing the Gospel writer to assign the blinding of eyes and hardening of hearts to the direct action of God, even though this creates an abrupt change from third to first person, as God himself intervenes to forestall any possibility that "I will heal them." This is clearly sufficient to explain why

---

8. Moreover, the clause that follows, "and to whom was the arm of the Lord revealed?" suggests that "the arm of the Lord" was revealed to *someone,* not that the display of God's power was altogether in vain.

9. Gr. ὑψωθήσεται καὶ δοξασθήσεται σφόδρα.

10. "Therefore" (διὰ τοῦτο) looks forward rather than back; the reason "they were *unable* to believe" was "because" (ὅτι) Isaiah "said" what he said in the quotation to follow. As Brown recognizes (1.483), "the basic thought is not that the unbelief resulted in the fulfillment of the prophecy, but that the prophecy brought about the unbelief." Even though the writer is not citing Isaiah explicitly as "Scripture," the principle that "the Scripture cannot be abolished" (10:35) is understood to apply as well to Isaiah's spoken prophecy.

11. The placement of "again" (πάλιν) in our translation implies not that the second quotation actually comes second in Isaiah (which of course it does not), only that it comes second in the Gospel writer's argument. The variant reading in D (καὶ γάρ) might perhaps be traced to a scribe who failed to take account of this.

"they were unable to believe" (v. 39; compare 5:44; 8:43). Jesus had said elsewhere that "No one can come to me unless the Father who sent me draw him" (6:44), or "unless it is given him from the Father" (6:65), and Isaiah's ancient words now put the judgment in even starker terms. Not only has God not "drawn" these people or "given" them faith, but he has "blinded their eyes and hardened their hearts" to make sure they would *not* repent and be healed!

41 The two citations from Isaiah are of great importance to the writer, for they help explain what is otherwise difficult to understand: why the world, even though it "came into being" through Jesus the Word, "did not know him," and why even "his own did not receive him" (1:10-11). Perhaps surprisingly, he cites Isaiah not as "Scripture," or "what is written," invoking the principle that "the Scripture cannot be abolished" (10:35), but instead simply as spoken prophecy. Now for the third time he mentions Isaiah by name. Having appealed to "the word of Isaiah the prophet . . . which he said" (v. 38; also v. 39, "again, Isaiah said"), he concludes, "These things Isaiah said because he saw his glory, and he spoke about him."[12] The reference is to Isaiah's vision in the temple, the setting of the second quotation (in vv. 39-40). There "I saw the Lord," he claimed, "seated on a throne, high and lofty, and the house was full of his glory" (Isa 6:1, LXX), and he heard the seraphs crying out to one another, "Holy, holy, holy is the Lord of hosts; all the earth is full of his glory"[13] (6:3, LXX). The Gospel writer's startling claim is that "the Lord," or "Lord of hosts," in Isaiah's vision was none other than Jesus, that the "glory" filling both "the house" (or temple) and "all the earth" was Jesus' glory, and consequently that when Isaiah spoke he was speaking of Jesus. If this is so, then in some sense he who "has blinded their eyes, and hardened their heart, lest they see with the eyes and understand with the heart, and turn, and I will heal them" (v. 40) is Jesus himself, or God acting through him.[14] This is not as far-fetched as it sounds, given that Jesus earlier claimed for himself a role in this hardening process after the healing of the man born blind: "For judgment I came into this world, so that those who do not see might see, and so that those who see might go blind" (9:39).

On the face of it, the comment that Isaiah saw Jesus' glory and spoke about him might seem to refer *only* to the second of the two Isaiah quotations, for that was the one growing immediately out of the prophet's inaugu-

---

12. So Brodie: "The actual name 'Isaiah' is mentioned three times, and the triple reference forms a crescendo effect" (419).

13. Gr. πλήρης . . . τῆς δόξης αὐτοῦ, in both instances.

14. Without being quite so explicit, Bultmann admits that "in v. 40 the subject of ἰάσομαι ["I will heal"] is Jesus" (453). He does not explore the implication that if Jesus is seen as the speaker he is quite pointedly *refusing* to heal, a refusal that Jesus himself subsequently explains (see vv. 47-48).

12:37-50 THE VERDICT ON THE WORLD

ral vision (see Isa 6:1-10).[15] Yet the plural, "These things Isaiah said," implies that the first quotation (v. 38) is in view as well. Isaiah is, of course, being read as one book, in which 53:1 ("Lord, who believed the message we have heard, and to whom was the arm of the Lord revealed?") grows out of the prophet's call and reflects the prophet's experience just as surely as 6:10, with its talk of blindness and hardness of heart. How then does the comment that Isaiah was speaking of Jesus affect the interpretation of 53:1? A possible answer is that just as "the Lord" is described as "high and lofty" in the inaugural vision, and the temple filled with "his glory" (Isa 6:1, LXX), so (as we have seen) the Lord's "servant" is described in the context of 53:1 as destined to be "lifted up and glorified exceedingly" (52:13, LXX). From the Gospel writer's perspective, the "glory" of the Lord (Isa 6:1, 3) and the "glory" of his servant (Isa 52:13) seem to have merged into one, yielding a certain ambiguity (possibly intentional) in the notice that Isaiah "saw *his* glory, and he spoke about *him*" (v. 41, italics added). While Jesus is without question the intended antecedent of "his" and "him," Jesus has not been mentioned by name since verse 36, and the Gospel writer leaves it to the reader to infer that the "glory" of the God that Isaiah saw was in fact the glory of Jesus, now revealed in his signs and in his words (see 1:14; 2:11). It is not a difficult inference, given Jesus' own claims earlier that Abraham "rejoiced that he would see my day, and he saw and was glad" (8:56), and that "before Abraham came to be, I am" (8:58). As in that passage, the point is not simply that Isaiah saw the glory of Jesus by seeing into the future, but that Isaiah saw the glory of the preexistent Jesus, the Word who was "in the beginning" (1:1-2), already in his own time.

42 The writer goes on to acknowledge something that at this point in the Gospel can hardly be denied: "Nevertheless many, even some of the rulers, did believe in him" (v. 42a).[16] One has only to remember the "many" who "believed in his name" at the first Passover (2:23), with Nicodemus, "a

---

15. This would clearly be the case if the variant reading ὅτε ("when") were adopted in place of ὅτι ("because"), yielding the translation, "These things Isaiah said *when* he saw his glory" (for a similar variation, see 12:17). But the manuscript support (limited to D, family 13, the Syriac versions, and the majority of later witnesses) is far weaker than the support for ὅτι (with P⁶⁶, P⁷⁵, ℵ, A, B, L, Θ, and others), and it is also an "easier" reading in that it is quite literally true that the temple vision was in fact the occasion for the second quotation (vv. 39-40). See Metzger, *Textual Commentary,* 238.

16. The mention of "rulers" (καὶ ἐκ τῶν ἀρχόντων) exposes the ignorance behind the Pharisees' disdainful question, "Has any of the rulers believed in him?" (7:48). The point is that because they did not go public with their faith, the Pharisees knew nothing about it (see Brown, 1.487). The inclusion of "rulers" in these "many," however, should not be exaggerated. The text is saying not that "many rulers" believed, but that "many" believed, including "some" rulers (for the partitive construction with ἐκ, see BDF, §164).

ruler of the Jews" (3:1) as the prime example, or the "many" from the crowd who "believed in him" at the Tent festival because of his miracles (7:31), or the "many" Jews at the same festival who "believed in him" in response to his words (8:30), or the "many" who "believed in him" when he raised Lazarus from the dead (11:45), or the "many" (possibly the same group) who "were going off and believing in Jesus" on account of Lazarus (12:11).[17] Such obvious exceptions to the rule that "they would not believe in him" (v. 37) require some explanation. Two of these have already been discredited in the course of the narrative (see 2:24-25; 8:31-59), and the Gospel writer now adds a further consideration that fits them and all the rest: the "many" (all of the groups mentioned above) who were said to have "believed" were in fact disqualified. This is consistent with the fact that nothing is said to have come of the "belief" of the crowds at the Tent festival (7:31) or of those who witnessed the raising of Lazarus (11:45; 12:11), even though the latter may well have "testified" to what they saw (12:17). "Because of the Pharisees," he explains, they "would not confess" (that is, publicly acknowledge) their faith in Jesus,[18] "lest they be put out of synagogue"[19] (v. 42b).

With this, he revisits an earlier notice that "the Jews had already reached an agreement that anyone who confessed that he was Christ would be put out of synagogue" (9:22). If that notice was an anachronism, referring only to what happened decades later, this one is as well, but more likely the reference is (as we have seen) not to formal excommunication but to some kind of temporary expulsion from the synagogue. This may indeed be the writer's point — that those who were said to have "believed in Jesus" allowed themselves to be intimidated not by actual threats, but by imagined ones. Jesus himself was clearly in danger, and Lazarus as well (see 12:10), but there is no clear evidence that the authorities were ready to invoke drastic measures against the "many" who (in their view) were being led astray by Jesus and his followers. What they were actually facing seems to have been, at worst, synagogue discipline of some kind and consequent loss of prestige.

43 This is borne out by the Gospel writer's verdict on their behavior, a verdict just as grim as the verdict on those who "would not believe in him" (see vv. 37-41): "For they loved the glory of humans rather than the glory of

17. The expression is virtually the same every time: always "many" (πολλοί), who either "believed in his name" (ἐπίστευσαν εἰς τὸ ὄνομα αὐτοῦ, 2:23), "believed in him" (ἐπίστευσαν εἰς αὐτόν, 8:30; 11:45), or "were believing in Jesus" (καὶ ἐπίστευον εἰς τὸν Ἰησοῦν, 12:11).

18. The verb "confess" (ὡμολόγουν) has no direct object in the Greek text. The object could be "him" (as in 9:22), referring to Jesus, or "it," referring to their faith. There is no substantial difference in meaning.

19. Gr. ἵνα μὴ ἀποσυνάγωγοι γένωνται.

God" (v. 43). His verdict echoes that of Jesus himself on those who "loved the dark rather than the Light, because their works were evil" (3:19), and those who "receive glory from each other, but do not seek the glory that comes from the Only God" (5:44). Here, as in 3:19, the verb "loved"[20] means "chose" or "preferred." Just as humans (3:19) consciously chose darkness over the Light, these so-called "believers" consciously chose human glory (precisely the glory of those who preferred darkness, 3:19) over "the glory of God." As in 5:41 and 44, "glory" is used here in the sense of praise or approval, whether "from humans" in general (5:41), or "from each other" (5:44), or from God. At the same time, the vocabulary of "glory" does double duty, evoking once more Isaiah's vision of the glory of Jesus (see v. 41), now explicitly identified as "the glory of God." In opting for human approval over God's approval, these "believers" have shown themselves blind to "the glory of God" revealed in the "glorification" of the Son (see 11:4, 40; 12:23, 28) — just as blind as any of those who would not and could not believe (see vv. 37-40). Their "belief" cannot save them, and to that extent the principle that "whoever believes has eternal life" (6:47) has its exceptions.

That said, even though it is too late for those within the narrative who "loved the glory of humans rather than the glory of God," it is *not* too late for those reading the Gospel. The fate of those who "would not believe" (v. 37) and those who "did believe in him" but out of fear "would not confess" their faith (v. 42) stands as a cautionary tale for certain readers, or potential readers. As has often been suggested,[21] the Gospel writer perhaps knows of Jewish believers still in the synagogue who have become convinced that Jesus is the Messiah, yet are unwilling to sacrifice their standing by acknowledging their belief openly. His implied warning to them is, "Don't let this happen to you! While it is true that 'whoever believes has eternal life,' there is no genuine belief without public confession — and perhaps by implication, Christian baptism." Near the end of the Gospel, he finally makes an explicit appeal, if not to Jewish believers in particular at least to an audience broad enough to include them: "These things are written," he will say, "that you might believe that Jesus is the Christ, the Son of God, and that believing you might have life in his name" (20:31).

44-45 Jesus, presumably "hidden" somewhere (v. 36), abruptly

---

20. Gr. ἠγάπησαν.
21. As Bultmann concludes, "Obviously such secret disciples still have the possibility of their faith becoming genuine," adding "How then will the man who surveys this result decide? The conclusion makes it plain to him that the issue at stake is to put the δόξα τοῦ θεοῦ before the δόξα τῶν ἀνθρώπων. Will he summon up courage to dare it?" (454). See also Brown (1.487), and Schnackenburg (2.418), but with less emphasis on the note of appeal, and more on the steadfast opposition of the synagogue at the time the Gospel was written.

comes out of hiding to speak at some length: "But Jesus cried out and said, 'The person who believes in me believes not in me but in the One who sent me, and the person who sees me sees the One who sent me.'" He has "cried out"[22] twice before (7:28, 37), at a carefully designated time and place,[23] but in this instance we are not told where or under what circumstances he made the speech. In that respect, his "outcry" is more like that of John, for we were never told when or where "John testifies about him and has cried out, saying . . ." (1:15). As we have seen, "cried out" implies a solemn announcement or formal proclamation of some kind, but here (as in 1:15) the proclamation has no narrative context at all.[24] Jesus is preaching to no one but the reader. The purpose of the speech is to confirm and explain, from Jesus' own lips, the Gospel writer's summary of his ministry so far (vv. 37-43), and at the same time to serve as a transition to what Jesus has to say from now on, mainly to his own disciples (chapters 13–17).

Above all, its purpose is to explain what it means to "believe in him," and what it means to disbelieve (see vv. 37, 42). There is little or nothing here that he has not said before. That someone who "believes in me believes not in me but in the One who sent me" (v. 44) simply brings out the obvious implication of his recurring theme that (for example) "My teaching is not mine, but belongs to the One who sent me" (7:16). In both places, he is fond of putting things paradoxically ("The person who believes in me believes not in me," and "My teaching is not mine"), but the point is clear enough. If what Jesus speaks is only what the Father has given him to speak, then to "believe in him" is to believe in the Father who sent him. The principle that what is done to, or for, a person's agent or emissary is actually done to, or for, the person who sent him appears frequently in the Gospel tradition (see, for example, Mt 10:40; Mk 9:37; Lk 9:48; 10:16), but just once so far (negatively) in John's Gospel ("Whoever does not honor the Son does not honor the Father who sent him," 5:23). Here Jesus states it for the first time positively, adding for good measure, "the person who sees me sees the One who sent me" (v. 45). In the following chapters, he will make this principle of agency explicit to his disciples, telling them that "the person who receives me receives the One who sent me" (13:20), "the person who has seen me has seen the Father" (14:9), and (again negatively) "the person who hates me also hates my Father" (15:23).

---

22. Gr. ἔκραξεν.

23. That is, "teaching in the temple" (7:28), and "on the last day, the great day of the festival" (7:37).

24. Bultmann's rearrangement (313) arbitrarily gives it a context, right after 8:12. But even if this was its "original context," he admits that it is now "divorced" from that context, for the Gospel writer has placed it where it now stands.

The reference to "the person who sees me"[25] (v. 45), like the reference to "the person who believes in me" (v. 44), draws on what was said in the Gospel writer's summary ("lest they see with the eyes," v. 40; Isaiah "saw his glory," v. 41). In that sense, "seeing is believing," or perhaps "believing is seeing" (compare 6:40, "For this is the will of my Father, that every person who sees the Son and believes in him might have eternal life"). The principle of agency applies to seeing no less than to believing: to see the Son is to see the Father. Moreover, if it is literally true that "No one has seen God, ever" (1:18), then seeing the Son is the *only* way to see the Father (so 14:9). On this assumption, when Isaiah "saw the Lord seated on a throne, high and lofty, and the house was full of his glory" (Isa 6:1), he must necessarily have seen Jesus (or the "glory" of Jesus, v. 41), and only in that way the Lord God of Israel.

46 The metaphor of "seeing" (v. 45) brings Jesus back to the metaphor of "light" (as in vv. 35-36). "I have come [as] light into the world," he continues, "so that everyone who believes in me might not remain in the darkness" (v. 46). With this he revisits the language of the Gospel's opening verses (1:4-9), and of several of his own earlier pronouncements (3:19-21, 8:12, 9:5, and 12:35-36). As in two of these (8:12 and 9:5), he makes his self-identification as "light" (or "the Light") explicit.[26] In contrast to 3:19, he accents salvation rather than judgment as the result of his coming as the Light. He has come into the world "so that everyone who believes in me might not remain in the darkness" — this in keeping with 8:12b, "Whoever follows me will not walk in the darkness, but will have the light of life."[27]

47-48 At the same time, it is all too apparent to the reader that the *actual* result of Jesus' coming, at least so far, has been unbelief (see vv. 37-43). Therefore he turns now to the central question, "What of those who do *not* believe?"[28] In response to this question, he keeps his focus resolutely on

---

25. Gr. ὁ θεωρῶν ἐμέ.

26. The identification of Jesus as "light" is unmistakable. Following the Greek word order, the first clause is literally "I, light [ἐγὼ φῶς], into the world have come." Φῶς ("light") is not exactly in apposition to ἐγω ("I"), however, as Abbott supposes (*Johannine Grammar,* 40), but is a predicate nominative with the verb "have come" instead of the verb "to be." The addition of "as" (to make better sense in English) simply turns the metaphor into a simile.

27. Schnackenburg (2.422) distinguishes between 12:35, where darkness is viewed as "a threatening force which attacks human beings," and the present passage, where it is "a sphere within which they continually exist," but the distinction is overly subtle. Those who "remain" (as here) or "walk" (8:12) in darkness are in fact those who are ever in danger of being "overtaken" or "overcome" (see 1:5) by the darkness of eternal death (see 1 Jn 2:11).

28. Bultmann recognizes this, but goes a step too far in commenting that "the sentence here [that is, v. 46] is used only as a foil for the decisive thought of the following verses" (345). This is to overlook the importance of v. 46 in its own right, as a follow-up to Jesus' closing words in vv. 35-36.

salvation rather than judgment: "And if anyone hears my words and does not keep them, *I* do not judge him, for I did not come to judge the world but to save the world" (v. 47, my italics). The emphatic "I" implies that even though Jesus himself does not judge them, they are nevertheless judged, and this becomes explicit in the following verse: "The person who rejects me and does not receive my words has that which judges him. The word which I spoke, that will judge him in the last day" (v. 48). In this way, he resolves (or at least relieves) the tension between what he has said here and such earlier pronouncements as 3:19 ("This then is the judgment, that the Light has come into the world"), 5:22 ("For the Father judges no one, but has given all the judgment to the Son"), 5:27 ("he gave him authority to do judgment, because he is the Son of man"), and especially 9:39 ("For judgment I came into this world, so that those who do not see might see, and so that those who see might go blind").

At the same time, the accent on salvation over judgment is consistent with Jesus' earlier claims that "God sent his Son into the world not to judge the world, but so that the world might be saved through him" (3:17), and that "'I' judge no one" (8:15). Each time Jesus says something of the kind, he signals — as he does here — that nevertheless judgment does take place. After 3:17, he immediately added, "Whoever believes in him is not judged; whoever does not believe is already judged, because he has not believed" (3:18), and after 8:15 he continued, "And yet if I judge, my judgment is true, because I am not alone, but I and the Father who sent me" (8:16). Here too, as we have seen, he goes on to explain that "The person who rejects me and does not receive my words has that which judges him. The word which I spoke, that will judge him in the last day" (v. 48). The reader's first impression is that Jesus is standing on a mere technicality. Not he but his word will carry out the judgment — a distinction without a real difference, it seems. But this is not the case. The point is rather that Jesus does not judge anyone "by himself," or "on his own" (as in 7:18). The Son does not carry out judgment apart from the Father (3:17; 8:15), nor the Father apart from the Son (5:22, 27). It is never "I," but always "I and the Father who sent me" (8:16).

In short, the answer to the riddle lies in the notion of agency with which Jesus began this final speech of his ministry so far (see vv. 44-45), and to which he will shortly return (vv. 49-50). He evokes it even now with his reference to "the person who rejects me[29] and does not receive my words," recalling the traditional saying in another Gospel that "the person who rejects me rejects the One who sent me" (Lk 10:16b), and at the same time anticipating its positive equivalent a chapter later, when he will tell his disciples that "the

---

29. Gr. ὁ ἀθετῶν ἐμέ.

person who receives me receives the One who sent me" (13:20).³⁰ If so, then Jesus' "words" are supremely important, for "the word that I spoke" is the very word of the Father.³¹ To say that "the word" is what carries out the judgment "in the last day" is to acknowledge the role of Father and Son alike in the final judgment. "In the last day" makes it clear that judgment in the present (see 3:18-19, 5:30, 8:16, 9:39, 12:31, and 16:11) does not preclude a final judgment at the end of the age (see 5:29), even as "eternal life" in the present does not preclude a literal resurrection at the end (see 6:39-40, 44, 54).

49-50 In conclusion, Jesus makes his dependence on the words of the Father explicit: "for I did not speak on my own,³² but the Father who sent me, he has given me a command³³ what I should say and what I should speak: (v. 49). The only such "command" mentioned before was the "authority" he was given to "lay down his life" and "receive it back" ("This command I received from my Father," 10:18). Here the "command" has to do not with the action of laying down his life and receiving it back again, but with his speech: "what I should say and what I should speak."³⁴ Yet in the end it is all the same "command," for Jesus' speech so far has made his death inevitable, and his speech in the next five chapters will have as its central theme his death and resurrection, or departure and return. The Father's "command" from the start pointed Jesus first toward death ("I lay down my life"), but then toward life ("that I might receive it back again," 10:17).

Now he reinforces this by adding, "And I know that his command is eternal life; so then the things I speak, just as the Father has told me, thus I speak"³⁵ (v. 50). This final verse of the chapter serves as a transition to the latter half of the Gospel. When Jesus said "I did not speak on my own" (v. 49), he was looking back at his ministry so far, and when he claimed that the Father "has given me a command what I should say and what I should speak," he was referring to *all* that he had said or ever would say.³⁶ But now

---

30. The use of λαμβάνειν for "receive" rather than δέχεσθαι (as in Mt 10:40; Mk 9:37; Lk 9:48) in connection with agency appears to be a distinctly Johannine feature (4:45 is an exception).

31. "Word" (λόγος) and "the words" (or "utterances," τὰ ῥήματα) are used interchangeably, as in 6:60, 63.

32. Gr. ἐξ ἐμαυτοῦ.

33. Gr. ἐντολήν.

34. Gr. τί εἴπω and τί λαλήσω, respectively. For the redundant use of "say" and "speak," compare 8:43, where "word" and "speech" are similarly interchangeable.

35. Gr. οὕτως λαλῶ.

36. The perfect "has given" (δέδωκεν, with P⁶⁶, ℵ, A, B, W, Ψ, 33, and others), which is to be preferred over the aorist "gave" (ἔδωκεν, with D, L, Θ, and the majority of later witnesses), emphasizes that the Father's "command" is by no means a thing of the past but is still very much in effect.

he turns his attention toward the immediate future: "the things I speak" (that is, from now on), and "thus I speak" (that is, in the chapters to follow). In short, Jesus has a great deal more to say. Later, when he is well into that last series of speeches, he will anticipate the future once again, and in a similar way, looking directly at the impending passion: "and just as the Father commanded me, thus I do"[37] (14:31). As is often noticed,[38] Jesus' language evokes the prophecy given to Moses that "I will raise up for them a prophet like you from among their brothers; I will put my words in his mouth, and he will speak to them whatever I command him"[39] (Deut 18:18; for this "prophet," see Jn 1:21; 7:40, 52).[40] The most conspicuous feature of God's "command,"[41] whether in Deuteronomy or in John's Gospel, is that it means "life" or "eternal life" for those who obey it.[42] First of all it means life for Jesus himself (see 10:18, both "authority to lay it down," and "authority to receive it back"), and then on that basis eternal life for those who follow him (see 10:10, 28). Even Jesus' words about death (in 6:51-58, for example) turn out finally to be "words of eternal life" (see 6:63, 68). The Gospel began with the notice that "In him was life" (1:4), and its first major section ended with John's testimony that "Whoever believes in the Son has eternal life, but whoever disobeys the Son will never see life" (3:36). Now its second major section ends with Jesus' own claim, "I know that his command is eternal life" (v. 50), and when the Gospel writer finally comes to state what he wants for his readers, it is "that believing you might have life in his name" (20:31). "Life" is the Gospel's overarching theme, and even though Jesus will rarely mention it explicitly in the next five chapters, all that he says from now on will serve to define what it means for his disciples and for the reader of the Gospel (see especially 17:2-3).

---

37. Gr. οὕτως ποιῶ.

38. See, for example, Hoskyns, 431; Brown, 1.491-92; Schnackenburg, 2.424; Lincoln, 361; Moloney, 369; Beasley-Murray, 218; Whitacre, 326.

39. Gr. ἐντείλωμαι αὐτῷ.

40. Brown (1.491-92) calls attention as well to the words that follow in Deuteronomy: "And whoever does not hear the words which the prophet will speak in my name, I shall take vengeance on him" (Deut 18:19; see vv. 47-48 in our text).

41. Gr. ἐντολή.

42. In Deuteronomy, see, for example, 32:47, "They are not just idle words for you — they are your life. By them you will live long in the land you are crossing the Jordan to possess" (also Deut 8:3, "man does not live on bread alone but on every word that comes from the mouth of the LORD").

III. JESUS' SELF-REVELATION TO THE DISCIPLES (13:1–17:26)

In the next five chapters Jesus speaks again, this time to his disciples after a last meal in Jerusalem, preparing them for his departure from the world. His discourse in two parts (13:36–14:31 and 15:1–16:33) overcomes the scandal of his departure with promises of his return and of the coming of the Advocate, or Spirit of truth, bringing joy, peace, and answered prayer. This time the transition to the next major section (comparable to the earlier transitions at 3:31-36 and 12:44-50) is longer, taking the form of Jesus' prayer to the Father (17:1-26), spoken as if in private, with the disciples no longer present. In this way the stage is set for the chain of events leading to Jesus' crucifixion and resurrection (chapters 18–21).

A. JESUS AT SUPPER (13:1-20)

> 1 *Now before the festival of the Passover, Jesus, knowing that his hour had come that he should be taken out of this world to the Father, having loved his own who were in the world, he loved them to the end. 2 And while supper was going on, the devil having already put it into the heart so that Judas Iscariot of Simon might hand him over, 3 knowing that the Father had given him all things into his hands, and that he had come from God and was going to God, 4 he rises from the supper and lays his garments down, and, taking a towel, girded himself. 5 Then he pours water into the basin, and he began to wash the feet of the disciples and wipe with the towel with which he was girded. 6 So he comes to Simon Peter, [who] says to him, "You, Lord, are washing my feet?" 7 Jesus answered and said to him, "What I am doing you do not understand now, but afterward you will understand." 8 Peter says to him, "You shall never ever wash my feet!" Jesus answered him, "Unless I wash you, you have no part with me." 9 Simon Peter says to him, "Lord, not my feet only, but also the hands and the head!" 10 Jesus says to him, "The person who has bathed does not have need to wash, except for the feet, but is clean all over, and you men are clean — but not all of you." 11 For he knew the one who was handing him over. That is why he said that "You are not all clean."*
>
> *12 So, when he had washed their feet, he took his garments and reclined again. He said to them, "Do you understand what I have done for you? 13 You call me 'Teacher' and 'Lord,' and you say well, for I am. 14 So now that I, the Teacher and the Lord, washed your feet, you too ought to wash each other's feet. 15 For I have given you an exam-*

ple, so that just as I did for you, you too might do. 16 *Amen, amen, I say to you, a slave is not greater than his lord, nor is a messenger greater than the person who sent him.* 17 *Now that you understand these things, blessed are you if you do them.* 18 *I am not speaking about all of you. I know which ones I chose. But the Scripture must be fulfilled, 'The one who eats my bread lifted up his heel against me.'* 19 *From now on I tell you before it happens, so that when it happens you might believe that I am.* 20 *Amen, amen, I say to you, the person who receives whomever I send receives me, and the person who receives me receives the One who sent me."*

A new major section of the Gospel of John begins with two breathless sentences (v. 1 and vv. 2-4), gathering up a number of themes both from what has preceded and what follows, in order to set the stage for a dramatic action on Jesus' part. These themes involve Jesus "knowing"[1] certain things in advance: first, "that his hour had come that he should be taken out of this world to the Father" (v. 1), and second, "that the Father had given him all things into his hands, and that he had come from God and was going to God" (v. 3). These were things already evident to the reader (see 3:35; 7:29, 33; 8:42), as was the thought that Judas would "hand him over" (v. 2) and that Jesus knew that as well (see 6:64, 71; 12:4).[2] But what the reader has not heard before is the explicit statement that he "loved"[3] his own who were "in the world" (v. 1b). It is his love which he now demonstrates by a specific loving act. He rises from supper, takes off his garment, girds himself with a towel, and washes the disciples' feet (vv. 4-5). In response to Simon Peter's protest, he explains why he must wash their feet, and only their feet (not the whole body), in the same breath hinting at what Judas will do by reminding them, "You are not all clean" (vv. 6-11). Then he puts his garment back on, takes his place again at the table (v. 12b), explaining his action as an example to his disciples (vv. 12-17), that they ought to "wash each other's feet" (v. 14). After this he cites a biblical text warning of possible betrayal or treachery (vv. 18-19). Finally, he articulates again the notion of agency (see 12:44-45), applying it both to the disciples as his agents (in that they follow his example), and to himself as agent of the Father who sent him (v. 20).

1 The first verse serves as a kind of heading to the whole chapter, if

---

1. Gr. εἰδώς.
2. Each of these becomes, if anything, even more conspicuous in the chapters to follow: above all, that Jesus would depart from the world (see 13:33; 13:36–14:31; 16:5-33), but also that "the Father had given him all things" (see 17:2), "that he had come from God and was going to God" (see 16:28), and of course that Judas Iscariot would "hand him over" (see 13:21-30).
3. Gr. ἀγαπήσας.

not to the whole of chapters 13–17. The two participles, "knowing" and "having loved," set the stage for the main verb of the sentence, "he loved," calling attention to what he will do next (see vv. 4-5). The notice that this was "before the festival of the Passover" implies "just before" the Passover was to start, updating earlier notices that "the Passover of the Jews was near" (11:55), that it was "six days before the Passover" (12:1), and then "the next day" (12:12). Jesus has by now gone into hiding (12:36, 44-50), and we are still not told where he is, only that he "knew" what was coming and that he "loved" his disciples. That he knew "his hour had come" is evident because he has said so (12:23, 27). His knowledge that this would mean being "taken out of this world to the Father" is almost as explicit, for he told the Pharisees, "Yet a short time I am with you, and I go to the One who sent me" (7:33), reminded his disciples that "the poor you always have with you, but me you do not always have" (12:8), and at the end told the crowd, "Yet a short time the Light is in you" (12:35).

What he has *not* said before, and what the Gospel writer has never quite told us explicitly, is that he "loved" his disciples, or that viewed them as "his own."[4] We have heard that God "loved" the world (3:16), that the Father "loves" the Son (3:35; 5:20), that the disciples were the Father's gift to the Son (6:37, 39), that Jesus "chose" them (6:70) and valued them as "greater than all things" (10:29), even that he "loved" certain individuals (Martha, Mary, and Lazarus, 11:5), but never in so many words that he "loved" his disciples as a group. Perhaps most important was the notice that he "chose" them (6:70), for, as we have seen, "love" in the Gospel of John is often a matter of choice or preference (see, for example, 3:19; 12:43). Jesus' love for his disciples ("the Twelve" in particular) has been expressed in the first half of the Gospel in his choice of them as "his own," signaled metaphorically by the image of "the shepherd of the sheep" summoning "his own sheep" by name and leading them out of the courtyard (10:3). The expressions "his own sheep" and "all his own" (10:4) in that passage, and "his own" in the present one, stand in apparent contrast to the principle stated in the beginning that Jesus "came to what was his own, and his own[5] did not receive him" (1:11). Yet that negative verdict, as we have seen, was immediately qualified by the notice that some of "his own" *did* in fact "receive him" (1:12), evidently because it was "given" to them to do so (see 3:27; 6:65). It is "his own" in this sense who now claim Jesus' attention — and his love.[6]

The text makes two things clear: first, that Jesus had "loved his own" all

---

4. Gr. τοὺς ἰδίους.
5. Gr. οἱ ἴδιοι.
6. Barrett comments (438) that "the meaning is perhaps best brought out by 15.19; Jesus loves his own, and the world similarly loves its own (τὸ ἴδιον)." But this is no help to the reader who has not had the benefit of reading 15:19.

along, and, second, that he (now) "loved them to the end." "To the end"[7] can be either temporal (as the translation implies) or qualitative ("to the utmost," or to the greatest extent possible). Both nuances fit the context, and both may well be intended.[8] Yet the obvious contrast between Jesus being about to be taken "out of this world" and his disciples being still "in the world" suggests that a separation is imminent. This, together with the explicit statement that "his hour had come," suggests that the temporal meaning, "to the end," or "to the very last, is primary.[9] Jesus would love his disciples right up to the moment he was to be taken from them — as he will shortly demonstrate.

2 The second sentence is much longer (vv. 2-4), and begins the narrative proper in that it concludes by describing a specific action of Jesus (v. 4).[10] Having set the time "before the festival of the Passover" (v. 1), the writer now sets the occasion (although very vaguely) as "while supper was going on" (v. 2).[11] What supper? Where? We are not told. Obviously if this is "before the festival of the Passover," it is not the Passover meal. In contrast to the supper at Bethany (12:2), no circumstances are given. It is relegated to a subordinate clause.

The next subordinate clause does give "circumstances" of sorts, but they are not the kind that would have been visible to an observer at the scene: "the devil having already put it into the heart so that Judas Iscariot of Simon[12]

---

7. Gr. εἰς τέλος.
8. See BDAG, 998.
9. Compare Jesus' last cry from the cross, "It is done" (τετέλεσται, 19:30).
10. The structure of the sentence resembles that of the preceding one in that a series of participles (in this case three, "going on," "having already put," and "knowing") sets the stage for a series of finite main verbs, in which Jesus "rises" (ἐγείρεται), "lays [τίθησιν] his garments down," and "girded" (διέζωσεν) himself with a towel (v. 4).
11. Gr. δείπνου γινομένου. Some ancient witnesses (including P[66], a corrector of ℵ, A, D, Θ, and the majority of later manuscripts) have the aorist participle δείπνου γενομένου ("when supper was over"). But the present ("while supper was going on") has stronger manuscript support (including ℵ, B, L, W, Ψ, and others), and is probably to be preferred (Jesus "reclined again" in v. 12, and supper seems to be still going on as late as v. 26!). Possibly the aorist was introduced by scribes who wanted to harmonize John's Gospel with the other Gospels by implying that all this took place *after* the traditional institution of the Eucharist as described in the other three. Alternatively, Metzger (*Textual Commentary*, 239) suggests that the aorist might have been original, but intended "as an ingressive aorist, 'supper having been served'" (that is, "when supper was on the table").
12. In contrast to 6:71 and 13:26, "Iscariot" (Ἰσκαριώτης, according to P[66], ℵ, and B) modifies "Judas" here, not "Simon," the father of Judas (compare 12:4, "Judas the Iscariot"). Other witnesses (including L, Ψ, 1241, and others) have Ἰσκαριώτου, modifying "Simon" (so Metzger, *Textual Commentary*, 239), but this reading is not as well attested and appears to be an attempt to conform the name to the two other passages that mention Judas's father (6:71 and 13:26).

might hand him over." This is something only an omniscient narrator could know, building on Jesus' remark long before in Galilee that "one of you is 'the devil'" (6:70). As the text stands,[13] it is unclear into whose heart the devil put the idea[14] that Judas would "hand over" Jesus — into Judas's heart, or into his own (that is, that the devil "made up his mind" that Judas would hand Jesus over). While the notion of putting something into one's heart (in the sense of deciding or making up one's mind) is attested in Hebrew and in biblical Greek,[15] it seems odd that the writer would explore the thought processes of the devil!

Whichever is meant, the point is the same: Judas will fulfill the devil's purpose. The notice here anticipates the comment later in the chapter ("after the morsel") that "then Satan entered into him" (v. 27). Far from contradicting the latter,[16] "already" underscores the inevitability of what Judas will shortly do. "Already" does not mean "just now," but takes us back to a time well *before* the supper even began. This may be a tacit acknowledgment that Judas's plans with the Jewish authorities were already in place, as we are explicitly told in the other Gospels (see Mk 14:10-11//Mt 26:14-16//Lk 22:3-6).[17] Within John's Gospel itself, the notice takes us back to when Jesus first identified Judas as "the devil" (6:70), calling him "the devil" because he would be the devil's agent and fulfill the devil's purpose. Here the writer con-

---

13. As Metzger points out (*Textual Commentary,* 239-40), certain manuscripts (including A, D, K, Δ, Θ, family 1, and others) have an "easier" reading, with the genitive Ἰούδα, yielding the translation, "the devil having already put it into the heart *of* Judas of Simon, the Iscariot, that he [Judas] might hand him over." The better-attested nominative, Ἰούδας (with P⁶⁶, ℵ, B, L, and others), yields the translation as we have it. This is a more ambiguous and therefore more difficult reading, in that it leaves open the question of whose "heart" (εἰς τὴν καρδίαν) is in view here, and is therefore almost certainly the correct reading.

14. The construction "the devil having already put" (τοῦ διαβόλου ἤδη βεβληκότος), like the preceding one (δείπνου γενομένου), is a genitive absolute. "Having put" (βεβληκότος) is literally "having thrown" (for the weakened sense of the verb βάλλειν, "to throw," see BDAG, 163).

15. See, for example, Luke 21:14, and other texts adduced by Barrett (439).

16. Schnackenburg, for example (3.17), speaks of an apparent contradiction, yet concludes with the suggestion that "this statement in v. 2 is the work of an editor who was already familiar with the sentence in v. 27 and wanted to anticipate the attack of the devil (note the word ἤδη in v. 2), but had to express himself more cautiously in order to avoid an open contradiction with 13:27." But why an editor? Why not the author? And if the notice is truly an "anticipation" of v. 27, why speak of a contradiction at all? According to Bultmann (464, n. 2), the reading we have adopted (see above, n. 11) represents "a correction made in the attempt to avoid the contradiction with v. 27." It is difficult to see how this is the case (Schnackenburg finds it puzzling as well: 399, n. 37).

17. This, according to Luke, was the moment when "Satan entered into Judas" (Lk 22:3), something which does not occur in John's Gospel until 13:27.

firms that the devil's purpose was indeed that Judas would "hand over" Jesus to the authorities, and, finally (v. 27), we will see him beginning to do exactly that. As we have seen, "hand over"[18] is, in itself, a neutral term (see 6:64, 71; 12:4), but now it is identified explicitly as the devil's own purpose, to that extent justifying the more common translation as "betray," and the common designation of Judas as "the betrayer" or "traitor."

3 Again, building up to a simple and straightforward description of Jesus' actions at this supper (vv. 4-5), the Gospel writer reminds us of the full extent of what Jesus "knew." The participle "knowing"[19] echoes the same word in the chapter heading (v. 1), so as to frame the chapter's first three verses. In the chapter heading, Jesus knew "that his hour had come that he should be taken out of this world to the Father" (v. 1); here he knew "that the Father had given him all things into his hands, and that he had come from God and was going to God" (v. 3). The second "knowing" confirms the first, while expanding its horizons to look at Jesus' world-encompassing authority (see 3:35; 17:2), and at his origin from God no less than his destiny with God (see 16:28). The effect is to put the act of girding himself with a towel and washing the disciples' feet (vv. 4-5) into a cosmic perspective by reminding us who it is who undertakes this simple act of service. It is not simply a host showing kindness to his guests, nor even an authority figure known as "Teacher" and "Lord" (v. 13), but it is One to whom "all things" have been given, One who is "from God," and on his way back "to God."[20] And while there is no verifiable link between this passage (or the event it narrates) and Philippians 2:5-11, it is not difficult to see why interpreters have often viewed Jesus' action here as a paradigm for "being in the form of God," yet "taking the form of a slave" (2:6-7), only to be exalted again to Lordship over all things.

4 With the stage so elaborately set, what follows next becomes a kind of acted parable of what the Christian gospel — this Gospel in particular — is all about: "the Word" coming in human flesh (1:14), or "the good Shepherd" laying down his life and receiving it back again (10:17-18). The Gospel writer moves on, now with great economy of language, as the main verbs of a long sentence (vv. 2-4) finally make their appearance. Jesus "rises from the supper[21] and lays his garments down, and, taking a towel, girded himself" (v. 4). When his work is done, he will reverse those actions: "So, when he had

---

18. Gr. ἵνα παραδοῖ.
19. Gr. εἰδώς.
20. The phrase "was going to God" (πρὸς τὸν θεόν ὑπάγει) evokes 1:1, "was with God" (ἦν πρὸς τὸν θεόν). While the similarity is probably coincidental, the point is that Jesus will shortly resume the relationship with God that was his from the beginning (see 17:5).
21. Gr. ἐγείρεται ἐκ τοῦ δείπνου.

washed their feet, he took his garments and reclined again" (v. 12). Placed side by side, the two notices recall, even verbally, the "Shepherd" discourse, where Jesus said, "I lay down my life, that I might receive it back again" (10:17).[22] In this way, all that comes between — the footwashing itself — hints at Jesus' death for "his own" (v. 1), and his departure "to the Father" (v. 1) or "to God" (v. 3). In this way, the Gospel of John accomplishes with a narrative what Mark and Matthew accomplish with a pronouncement: "For even the Son of man did not come to be served but to serve, and to give his life a ransom for many" (Mk 10:45). Yet the writer is content to let the death of Jesus remain implicit here, just as it remained implicit in the account of Mary anointing Jesus' feet at the earlier "supper" in Bethany (see 12:3-8). The narrative here bears comparison to the Bethany anointing in other ways as well, not least in its abruptness.[23] Why does Jesus interrupt the meal (v. 2), instead of performing his act of service when the guests arrived (as a host might normally do), or at the beginning of the meal?[24] In contrast to the anointing story, where no explanation was given of why Mary did what she did, the answer has been given here — somewhat mysteriously — in the first three verses. All the participles about what Jesus "knew," how much he "loved," and what the devil was up to combine to make the point that the moment for action came in the middle of the meal. There is a note of urgency here, as there is in much that will follow; for example, "What you do, do quickly" (v. 27); "Yet a short time I am with you" (v. 33); "Rise, let's get out of here!" (14:31).

As for Jesus' act of service itself, it is (as we have seen) as remarkable for its role reversal as Mary's was for its extravagance. That it is by no means "normal" becomes evident both in Jesus' comment to Peter ("What I am doing you do not know now," v. 7) and in Peter's instinctive reaction (v. 8). For a comparable role reversal, we must look to a Lukan parable, where Jesus exclaims, "Blessed are those slaves whom the lord will find watching when he

---

22. The parallel centers on the verbs τίθησιν ("he *lays* his garments down"), λαβών ("*taking* a towel" instead), and finally ἔλαβεν ("he *took* his garments"), and on the adverb πάλιν ("and reclined *again*").

23. J. Christopher Thomas (*Footwashing,* 57) goes so far as to characterize Mary's action (as well as that of the anonymous woman in Lk 7:36-50) as footwashing, but this is doubtful, given that water was not involved, and that Jesus was the only recipient of the action.

24. Thomas describes two occasions when footwashing commonly took place: either "as a sign of welcome," or "where the washing precedes a meal or banquet" (*Footwashing,* 46-47). Here Thomas comments, "Clearly, the Evangelist is underscoring the importance of the footwashing by its unusual placement, with Jesus interrupting the meal to perform it" (83-84). So too B. J. Malina and R. L. Rohrbaugh, *Social Science Commentary,* 223: "Since the foot washing in the scene depicted here is not upon arrival, something else is going on."

comes. Amen, I say to you that he will gird himself and have them recline, and will come along and serve them" (Lk 12:37), or perhaps to Luke's account of the last supper, where Jesus asks (*without* reference to his death), "Who is greater, the one who reclines or the one who serves? Is it not the one who reclines? But I am in your midst as the one who serves" (Lk 22:27). Any reader of Luke familiar with John's Gospel might easily visualize Jesus in that passage washing the disciples' feet. John's Gospel instead uses the verb "to serve" only in connection with Jesus *being* "served" (see 12:2, 26), and describes Jesus' own action not as generalized "serving," but instead very concretely and ceremoniously, as "rising" from the table, "laying" aside his garments, "taking" a towel, and "girding" himself (as in Lk 12:37). Yet the effect is much the same. We are not explicitly told *that* Jesus "served," but we are allowed to see him serving.

5 The sentence (vv. 2-4) has gone on long enough. Pausing for breath, the narrator continues, as we quickly learn what the towel was for: "Then he pours water into the basin, and he began to wash the feet of the disciples and wipe with the towel with which he was girded" (v. 5). In itself, the procedure was unremarkable. Footwashing by a host (if he was poor), or by the host's slaves, was a gesture of hospitality. Slaves washed their masters' feet after a journey, wives the feet of their husbands, disciples the feet of their teachers.[25] If Jesus was in any sense the host of this "supper," his action may not have been quite so extraordinary (despite Peter's misgivings) as it is commonly represented. What was extraordinary, as we have seen, was the timing, and presumably the fact that Jesus had never done anything like this before.

6 Nothing is said of the washing of any of the disciples' feet except Simon Peter's. Whether Jesus came to him first, second, or last, in some sense Peter speaks for all the disciples (vv. 6-11), just as he did earlier when he said, "Lord, to whom shall we turn? You have words of life eternal, and we believe and we know that you are the Holy One of God" (6:68-69). He has not been heard from since, and all we are told now is that Jesus "comes to Simon Peter," who "says to him, 'You, Lord, are washing my feet?'" The placement of the personal pronouns accents each one, highlighting Peter's incredulity; literally, "Lord, *you?* Of *me?*[26] Washing the feet?"[27] Clearly, Peter is scandalized. To him it is inappropriate that "the Holy One of God" should lower himself to perform such menial service for one so unworthy.

---

25. For a concise survey of footwashing in "The Jewish and Graeco-Roman Environment," see Thomas, *Footwashing,* 26-60.

26. Gr. κύριε, σύ μου.

27. In a quite different setting in another Gospel, John the Baptist hesitates to baptize Jesus, because "I [ἐγώ] have need to be baptized by you [ὑπὸ σοῦ], and you [σύ] are coming to me?" (πρός με, Mt 3:14).

13:1-20 JESUS AT SUPPER

7 Jesus' reply to Peter deserves close attention because it is his first utterance in this setting, the first since he promised that he had more to say ("so then the things I speak, just as the Father has told me, thus I speak," 12:50). He takes no offense at Peter's skepticism, but cautions him, "What *I* am doing *you* do not understand now, but afterward you will understand" (v. 7, my italics). Both "I" and "you" are emphatic, echoing (and perhaps gently mocking) Peter's emphatic personal pronouns in addressing Jesus.[28] "You" is singular, for Jesus is speaking to Peter alone even though his words apply just as well to all the disciples. Yet the comment is puzzling. What exactly does Peter "not understand now," and how long "afterward," or "after these things" will it be until he finally "understands"?[29] The reader may recall the narrative aside at the triumphal entry, "These things his disciples did not understand at first, but when Jesus was glorified, then they remembered that these things were written about him and these things they did for him" (12:16; see also 2:22, "So, when he was raised from the dead, his disciples remembered that this was what he meant"). If these are the proper parallels,[30] then what Peter does not understand is that Jesus is soon to be "taken out of this world to the Father," and that when he has gone the meaning of what he has done will become clear — that is, that "having loved his own who were in the world, he loved them to the end" (see v. 1). On such a reading, Peter seems to have less insight than the silent Mary of Bethany, whom Jesus credited with having kept her perfume "for the day of my burial," because "me you do not always have" (12:7). Yet if Jesus had washed or anointed Mary's feet instead of allowing her to anoint his, one has to wonder if her reaction might not have been the same as Peter's. There is no way to know, but as the text stands, her silence is far more eloquent than Peter's indignant question.

Another possibility is that "afterward" refers not solely to Jesus' departure (or glorification as in 12:16, or resurrection as in 2:22), but to things closer at hand as well. A few verses later he will ask his disciples, "Do you understand what I have done for you?" (v. 12), and without waiting for an answer will explain to them their obligation to do for each other what he has

---

28. Compare Jesus' answers to Nicodemus (3:3), and to the Samaritan woman (4:10).

29. The phrase μετὰ ταῦτα ("after these things") can be simply a way of carrying forward the narrative (see, for example, 3:22; 5:1, 14; 6:1; 7:1), or it can refer (as here) in a general way to "the future" (as in Rev 1:19, or 4:1, where it is used both ways in the same verse).

30. So, for example, Bultmann, for whom "μετὰ ταῦτα refers to the decisive turning-point that is now imminent, to the death and resurrection of Jesus" (467); also Schnackenburg: "It can only be the time after Jesus' death and resurrection" (3.19), as well as Brown (2.552), Barrett (440), and most others.

just done for them (vv. 14-15), ending with a beatitude, "Now that you understand these things,[31] blessed are you if you do them" (v. 17). Two chapters later, he will tell them, "I no longer say that you are slaves, because the slave does not know what his lord is doing, but I have said that you are friends, because everything I heard from my Father I made known to you" (15:15). Such texts suggest that "understanding" what Jesus has done — and will do — is a process, not something that comes in a magic moment of remembrance. There is more than one aspect to Jesus' act of washing their feet, and they will not grasp it all at once. As we will see, in this Gospel the future, or "afterward," has a way of imposing itself on the present (see 4:23; 5:25; 16:32), all the more now that Jesus' final "hour" (v. 1) is under way.

8 Unwilling to wait for further illumination, Peter insists, "You shall never ever wash my feet!" (v. 8a). As in several other places, the combination of an emphatic negative[32] with an expression meaning "forever"[33] strengthens the assertion (in this case the denial) to the point of redundancy. All the other examples were on the lips of Jesus, promising eternal life,[34] but on Peter's lips they amount (though unintentionally) to a denial of life. Peter's redundant "never ever" stands squarely against both the writer's affirmation of Jesus' love for his own "to the end" (v. 1), and Jesus' promise of understanding "afterward" (v. 7). Jesus' reply to Peter is equally blunt: "Unless I wash you, you have no part with me" (v. 8b). The "unless" clause recalls other such clauses in John's Gospel (3:3, 5; 6:53; 8:24; 12:24) in which failure to accept what Jesus offers means failure to attain life or salvation. The expression "to have a part" or "a share"[35] with someone is used negatively in Matthew and Luke, of "one's part" being with either "the hypocrites" (Mt 24:51) or "the unfaithful" (Lk 12:46). In the book of Revelation, it is used both positively and negatively, as some have "a part in the first resurrection" (20:6), and others "in the lake that burns with fire and brimstone, which is the second death" (21:8; compare 22:19).[36] Quite simply, Jesus is telling Peter that refusing the love about to be displayed in the washing of his feet would sim-

---

31. Gr. εἰ ταῦτα οἴδατε, a first-class conditional clause, implying that they do know.

32. Gr. οὐ μὴ νίψῃς.

33. Gr. εἰς τὸν αἰῶνα.

34. See 4:14, 8:51-52, 10:28, and 11:26, with εἰς τὸν αἰῶνα (also 6:35, with the equally redundant πώποτε, "ever").

35. Gr. ἔχειν μέρος.

36. See also Ignatius, *To Polycarp* 6.1, "May it be mine to have my part with them [μετ' αὐτῶν μοι τὸ μέρος] in God"; *Martyrdom of Polycarp* 14.2, "that I may receive a part [μέρος] among the number of the martyrs." In Acts 8:21, Peter himself (using slightly different vocabulary) tells Simon Magus, "You do not have a part or a share [μερὶς οὐδὲ κλῆρος] in this matter, for your heart is not right before God."

ply prove that he was not one of Jesus' "own who were in the world" (v. 1), but belonged instead to "the world" itself.[37]

9 Peter's reply seems to take a comic turn, as he says, "Lord, not my feet only, but also the hands and the head!" (v. 9). If washing his feet will give him "a part" or "share" with Jesus in eternal life, how much more the cleansing of his whole body?[38] On the face of it, it is difficult to tell whether Peter is being serious here, or ironic. Is he expressing his devotion to Jesus, or simply reducing the whole thing to an absurdity? We are reminded of Nicodemus, who replied to another of Jesus' "unless" pronouncements by asking, "How can a person be born when he is old? Can he enter his mother's womb a second time and be born?" (3:4). Or we might think of Peter himself in other Gospels who "did not know what he was saying" when at the transfiguration he proposed, "let us make three tents, one for you and one for Moses and one for Elijah" (Mk 9:5//Mt 16:4//Lk 9:33). The second is the more likely parallel. Throughout the Gospel tradition, Peter is known more for his naiveté than for irony. Mindless as it may be, his comment is probably sincere, and, more important, it gives Jesus the opportunity to make a point to all the disciples, and to the reader.

10 Jesus' answer is still "to him," that is, to Peter alone, but he then states a general principle ("The person who has bathed does not have need to wash, except for the feet, but is clean all over"), which he goes on to apply to "his own" who were present at the supper ("and you men[39] are clean, but not all of you"). The meaning of the pronouncement hinges on a textual variant. A few ancient witnesses[40] omit the entire phrase "except for the feet,"[41] yielding a somewhat different thought: "The person who has bathed does not have need to wash, but is entirely clean."[42] Despite its weak attestation, this

---

37. See 15:19, "If you were of the world, the world would love its own" (τὸ ἴδιον). In 14:30, when Jesus tells his disciples, "the ruler of the world is coming, and he has nothing in me" (καὶ ἐν ἐμοὶ οὐκ ἔχει οὐδέν), the meaning is not the same as what he says to Peter here, yet it does strike the same chord of dissociation.

38. Thomas (*Footwashing,* 95-97) offers a number of plausible reasons for mentioning the hands and the head in particular, but at the same time admits that "along with the feet, they are the only parts of the body normally left exposed" (95). Jesus' answer (v. 10) seems to imply that Peter is asking to have his whole body washed.

39. Gr. ὑμεῖς. The translation "you men" brings out the abrupt shift from the singular "you" (σύ and σε) with which Jesus addressed Peter in verses 7 and 8, to the plural ὑμεῖς. "You all" would have been unsatisfactory because of the way the pronouncement ends, but "you men" brings out the meaning — at least on the widely shared assumption that only men were present.

40. Codex Sinaiticus (ℵ) above all, but also the Vulgate and one or two old Latin versions, plus Tertullian and Origen.

41. Gr. εἰ μὴ τοὺς πόδας.

42. While this is the only variant that substantially affects meaning, there are

shorter reading has gained an impressive array of adherents.[43] Their preference for it is based on two assumptions. First, it is assumed that the verbs for "bathed"[44] and "wash"[45] are synonymous, and not to be contrasted in any way.[46] As Lindars puts it, "'He who has washed does not need to wash, but is clean all over.' In other words, there is no need to wash twice."[47] The phrase "except for the feet" only clouds the issue by implying that the person is *not* in fact "clean all over."[48] The second assumption is that Jesus' act of washing the disciples' feet is a decisive redemptive act (see v. 8, "Unless I wash you, you have no part with me"), and therefore (in Barrett's words) "not a secondary 'washing' subordinate to an initial 'bath.'"[49] By pointing to the same reality to which baptism points, redemption through the death of Jesus, footwashing becomes the Gospel of John's equivalent of Christian baptism, for some perhaps solving the riddle of when and under what circumstances Jesus' first disciples were baptized. From this, a kind of ambivalence toward the act of footwashing emerges. On the one hand, it is seen as primary and not secondary, essential to salvation, or so it would seem. But on the other, the outward act itself is dissolved into symbolism, turned into something other than what it is on the surface, the simple washing of feet.

How valid are these assumptions, and these conclusions drawn from the shorter reading? Are they sufficient to overturn the weight of manuscript evidence in favor of the longer reading?[50] The difficulty with the notion that

---

other small variations in the text, affecting mostly word order (see Thomas, *Footwashing*, 19; Metzger, *Textual Commentary*, 240).

43. For example, Hoskyns, 438-39; Bultmann, 469, n. 2; Barrett, 441-42; Brown, 2.567-68; Schnackenburg, 3.20-22; Lindars, 451; Beasley-Murray, 229; Moloney, 378-79, and others.

44. Gr. ὁ λελουμένος.

45. Gr. νίψασθαι.

46. Appeal is made to a fondness for synonyms in the Gospel of John (see, for example, 21:15-17), and especially to the narrative in Papyrus Oxyrhynchus 840, a fourth-century account of a controversy between Jesus and "a Pharisee, a chief priest [*sic*], Levi by name," over ritual purity" (see Thomas, *Footwashing*, 97-98).

47. Lindars, 451.

48. Gr. καθαρὸς ὅλος.

49. Barrett, 441.

50. While there are a number of minor variants (see above, n. 27), the support for the inclusion of the phrase "except for the feet" (εἰ μὴ τοὺς πόδας) is overwhelming (with B, C, D, L, Θ, W, Ψ, Syriac, Coptic, most old Latin versions, and P[66], which even accents the phrase by the addition of μόνον ("alone"), echoing Peter's request, "not my feet alone" (v. 9). The only other reading worthy of note is that of Codex D: "does not have need to wash the head, except for the feet alone" (again responding more directly to Peter's confused remark). Interpreters favoring the longer reading include Thomas, *Footwashing*, 19-25; Sanders and Mastin, 308; Morris, 618; Haenchen, 2.108; Carson, 464-66; Lincoln, 369-70, and others.

Jesus is pronouncing his disciples "clean" simply on the basis of the footwashing itself is the fact that as he speaks those words the footwashing is not yet complete! Peter has still not permitted Jesus to wash his feet, and we are not told how many of the other disciples (if any) have had their feet washed. Not until the notice is given, "So, when he had washed their feet, he took his garments and reclined again" (v. 12) do we learn that the footwashing is over. This suggests that Jesus' disciples were "clean"[51] *not* by virtue of the footwashing, but already before it began — in short, that a distinction *is* intended between "bathing" or taking a bath and "washing."[52] The former refers to bathing one's whole body, and the latter to a partial washing, whether of the head, hands, or feet.[53] Consequently, the phrase "except for the feet" is not only supported by stronger manuscript evidence, but is necessary to the logic of the pronouncement and the flow of the narrative. That Jesus is directly responding to Peter's odd plea for a thorough washing of feet, hands and head (v. 9) is clear from the words "Jesus says to him" (v. 10), an expression little different from those used to introduce what he said to Peter before (vv. 7, 8b), and what Peter said to him (vv. 6, 8a). He simply continues the conversation, even while turning it toward the wider audience. Jesus replies to Peter not with a parable or proverb, but with an illustration from everyday life: "The person who has bathed" — whether at home or at a public bath — and then walked somewhere "does not have need to wash, except for the feet [which have picked up dust from the streets], but is clean all over."[54] Then he makes the application, not just to Peter but to all the disciples: "and you men are clean[55] — but not all of you." They were "clean" even before the footwashing began, and consequently needed only to have their feet washed.

Was there a literal "bath" prior to the footwashing that made them

51. Gr. καθαροί.
52. That is, between ὁ λελουμένος and νίψασθαι.
53. See, for example, *Testament of Levi* 9.11: "Before you enter the sanctuary, bathe [λούου]; while you are sacrificing, wash [νίπτου]; and again when the sacrifice is concluded, wash" [νίπτου]" (*OTP*, 1.792); see also Tobit 7.9: "And when they had bathed [ἐλούσαντο], and washed their hands [ἐνίψαντο], and laid them down to dine . . ." (*APOT*, 1.221). The distinction is rather widely acknowledged (see, for example, BDAG, 603; LSJ, 1176; F. Hauck, *TDNT*, 4.947), Papyrus Oxyrhynchus 840 (see above, n. 29) being a rather late and far from conclusive exception (see Thomas, *Footwashing*, 99).
54. Seneca (a contemporary of Jesus) wrote of "the old-time ways of Rome," that "the Romans washed [*abluebant*] only their arms and legs daily — because those were the members that gathered dirt in their daily toil — and bathed [*lavabantur*] all over [*toti*] only once a week. Here someone will retort, 'Yes; pretty dirty fellows they evidently were! How they must have smelled!' But they smelled of the camp, the farm, and heroism. Now that spick-and-span bathing establishments have been devised, men are really fouler than of yore" (*Epistulae Morales* 86.12; LCL, 2.317-19).
55. Gr. καὶ ὑμεῖς καθαροί ἐστε.

"clean," even "clean all over"? Baptism again comes to mind, because baptism seems to have been "about purification,"[56] and because Jesus was said to have baptized quite successfully in Judea (3:22, 26), even "making and baptizing more disciples than John" (4:1). Yet Jesus says nothing of baptism here, nor does he even explicitly claim that his disciples have "bathed" — that belongs to the illustration, not the application. All he says is that they are "clean," needing only the washing of their feet. What made them clean? The most plausible answer is found in the scene at Capernaum (6:60-71), where he had been "teaching in synagogue" (6:59). There he told his disciples, "The words I have spoken to you are spirit, and they are life" (6:63), yet "many" of them (6:60, 66) were offended and turned away. When he "said to the Twelve, 'Do you want to go away too?'" Simon Peter spoke on their behalf, just as he does here: "Lord, to whom shall we turn? You have words of life eternal" (6:68), and declared their faith in him (v. 69). To this, Jesus replied, "Did I not choose you as the Twelve? And one of you is 'the devil'" (6:70). Aside from the water and the basin, the scene matches the present one. The cast of characters was the same: Jesus, his disciples, Peter in particular, and in the background Judas, who "was going to hand him over" (6:71). As we have seen, the notice that Jesus "chose" his disciples (6:70) to be "the Twelve" was the clearest intimation up to now that he "loved his own who were in the world." All that remained was to show that "he loved them to the end" (v. 1), and now he does just that by washing their feet. While nothing was said of water or of cleansing in the earlier passage, the "words" of Jesus as "spirit" and "life" (6:63), or as "life eternal" (6:68), surely hinted at the same realities to which the metaphor of water in this Gospel commonly points (see 3:5; 4:14; 7:39; 9:7). In any event, the link is confirmed two chapters later when Jesus will remind his disciples that "You are already clean,"[57] not because of baptism nor even because of the footwashing, but "because of the word I have spoken to you" (15:3). While this "cleansing by the word" is doubtless viewed as an ongoing process in John's Gospel, it seems to have had its beginning in the winnowing out of the doubtful and the consolidation of "the Twelve" at the synagogue in Capernaum. On that basis, Jesus is willing to pronounce his disciples "clean — but not all of you."[58]

The last phrase, "but not all of you,"[59] brings us up short. Exception is piled upon exception: first, "clean all over," *yet* "except for the feet"; now

---

56. Gr. περὶ καθαρισμοῦ (3:25).
57. Gr. ἤδη ὑμεῖς καθαροί ἐστε.
58. The rendering in the *Good News Bible,* "All of you are clean — all except one," is both inaccurate and too specific, for Jesus says nothing about only "one" being unclean. That point is made only in the narrative aside that follows (v. 11).
59. Gr. ἀλλ' οὐχὶ πάντες.

"you men are clean," *yet* "not all of you." In keeping with what has just preceded, we might have expected "clean," yet not "clean all over," making allowance again for the need of footwashing. Instead, Jesus introduces a different word for "all,"[60] moving the thought in a different direction by considering the disciples individually, and not just as a group. When this is done, the *degree* of cleanliness or purity is no longer the only issue. Now they must look at themselves — and each other — as individuals, with the question of individual purity in mind. The notion that a corporate unit (labeled earlier as "the Twelve") is "clean" or "clean all over" is a mere abstraction unless the same is true of each person in its number. Jesus already warned of this (even more pointedly) when, in the same breath that he pronounced them "chosen," and "the Twelve," he immediately added, "and one of you is 'the devil'" (6:70). They paid no attention then, and they are paying no attention now.

11 Again (just as in 6:71), a narrative aside alerts us that what Jesus has just said may have been intended as much for the reader as for the silent disciples: "For he knew[61] the one who was handing him over. That is why he said that 'You are not all clean.'" The comment itself echoes not so much 6:71, however ("He meant Judas of Simon Iscariot") as 6:64: "For Jesus knew[62] from the beginning who they are who do not believe, and who it is who will hand him over." Once again, readers are reminded of Jesus' knowledge of "what was in the person" (2:25), and in particular this special knowledge, shared with them repeatedly (in addition to 6:64 and 6:71, see 12:4, 6; 13:2) but still withheld from his disciples, about who would "hand him over."

The narrative aside focuses attention on just the one exception to the notion that the disciples are "clean" (that is, on "Judas of Simon Iscariot," v. 2), but in theory there could be more (again, see 6:64, where Jesus knew *both* those "who do not believe" *and* the one person "who will hand him over"). If the principle that "you men are clean — but not all of you" is applied beyond the immediacy of the supper at which Jesus washed the disciples' feet — that is, to Christian communities familiar to the Gospel writer in his own time, then the exception, "but not all of you," could have a wider application as well. Within the story of Jesus, there is only one Judas, but in the Christian communities as constituted in the Graeco-Roman world there could — and would — be others. This will be confirmed later on, when Jesus speaks of "every branch in me that does not bear fruit" being "taken away" (15:2), or "thrown out like the branch and withered" (15:6).

---

60. That is, πάντες instead of ὅλος.
61. Gr. ᾔδει γὰρ.
62. Gr. ᾔδει γὰρ.

The Gospel of John

12 The narrative assumes that Peter, satisfied with Jesus' answer (v. 10), allowed his feet to be washed, and that the other disciples did the same. "So, when he had washed their feet," it continues, "he took his garments and reclined again" (v. 12a). He simply reverses his previous actions, taking up the garments he had laid down, and returning to his place at the table.[63] Then he asks the disciples, "Do you understand what I have done for you?" (v. 12b). He already knows the answer. They do *not* understand, any more than Peter did (see v. 7, "What I am doing you do not understand now, but afterward you will understand"). Therefore he will not wait for their reply, but will instead go on to explain, in the simplest terms possible, just "what I have done for you."[64] That at least will be a beginning.

13 Jesus continues, "You call me 'Teacher' and 'Lord,' and you say well,[65] for I am" (v. 13). The nouns are literally "the Teacher" and "the Lord,"[66] but the clause cannot be translated "You call me the Teacher and the Lord" (indirect discourse), for this would require accusatives. Rather, the nouns are in the nominative case, which must therefore be understood as the nominative with the definite article used in place of a vocative for direct address.[67] Yet it is a ceremonious, almost confessional, vocative,[68] perhaps something closer to Thomas's famous words of confession, "My Lord and my God!"[69] (20:28). Almost from the Gospel's beginning, Jesus' disciples have in fact addressed him as "'Rabbi' — which means teacher" (1:38),[70] and as "Lord."[71] They also, on occasion, refer to him in the third person as "the Teacher" (11:28), and as "my Lord" (20:13) or "the Lord" (20:2, 13;

---

63. The reversal is signaled (in part) by the notice that he reclined at table "again" (πάλιν; see above, n. 22). This assumes that "again" goes with the preceding verb, "reclined" (ἀνέπεσεν), as most English versions read it (for example, "returned to his place," NIV; "returned to the table," NRSV; "sat down again," REB). If πάλιν goes with what follows (that is, "again he said to them," as in Westcott and Hort's punctuation, and Richmond Lattimore's translation), then Jesus is resuming his speech to Peter (v. 10), ending with a few words to them all ("You men are clean," v. 10b). See Abbott, *Johannine Grammar*, 490. Even without πάλιν, however, the reversal is clear.

64. Gr. τί πεποίηκα ὑμῖν.

65. On "say well" (καλῶς λέγετε) in the sense of saying what is true, see 4:17-18; 8:48.

66. That is, ὁ διδάσκαλος and ὁ κύριος, respectively.

67. See Barrett, 443; also BDF, §147[3]).

68. Thus implying perhaps more than the actual vocatives, διδάσκαλε and κύριε.

69. Gr. ὁ κύριός μου and ὁ θεός μου.

70. See also 1:49; 4:31; 9:2; 11:8; 20:16. He is also addressed as "Rabbi" or "Teacher" by those who do not necessarily believe (see 3:2; 6:25; 8:4).

71. See 6:68; 9:38; 11:3, 12, 21, 27, 32, 34, 39; 13:6, 9, 25, 36, 37; 14:5, 8, 22; 21:15, 16, 17, 20, 21. As we have seen, this designation on the lips of strangers can also simply mean "Sir" (as in 4:11, 15, 19, 49; 5:7; 6:34; 9:36; 12:21; 20:15).

21:7, 12), to the point that even the Gospel writer within the narrative sometimes follows their example (see 6:23; 11:2).

14-15 From these titles, which Jesus accepts,[72] he draws a conclusion: "So now that I, the Teacher and the Lord, washed your feet, you too ought to wash each other's feet" (v. 14), adding by way of explanation, "For I have given you an example, so that just as I did for you, you too might do" (v. 15). The noun "example"[73] and the repetition of "you too" make it clear that Jesus is calling on his disciples to do for each other exactly what he has done for them. The repetition of the verb "to do" — "just as I did" and "that you might do" — confirms that he is urging them to imitate not just his humble attitude, but the literal action of washing feet. Moreover, the present subjunctive, "might do,"[74] in contrast to the aorist, "just as I did," implies that he is urging them to continue to do repeatedly what he has done for them once and for all.

The language suggests either that footwashing was already the practice of Christian communities known to the writer of the Gospel, or that the writer is advocating the adoption of such a practice. The latter is perhaps more likely, given the Gospel's omission of the institution of the Lord's Supper, which would almost certainly have been practiced in the Johannine communities (see 6:52-58). Quite possibly the Gospel writer is urging the practice of footwashing, not as an independent third sacrament alongside baptism and the Lord's Supper, but simply as an aspect of the eucharistic meal.[75] It is difficult to be certain, given the Gospel writer's reticence about sacraments generally.[76] Nor should it be forgotten that the Gospel writer views Jesus as an example to his disciples on a rather wide front, not just with reference to the washing of feet. This is the case not only in connection with the "new command" to "love each other, just as I loved you" (v. 34; see also 15:12, 17), but in several passages in 1 John, with the same verb "ought" that is used

---

72. See v. 13, "for I am" (εἰμὶ γάρ).
73. Gr. ὑπόδειγμα.
74. Gr. ἵνα . . . ποιῆτε.
75. Even Richard Bauckham, who argues forcefully against footwashing as a ritual practice, admits (in connection with 1 Tim 5:10) that "another possible context for the widows' footwashing . . . is the agape meal, at which the feet of all who arrived for the meal would have to be washed in some way" (*Testimony of the Beloved Disciple*, 203). If the agape, why not the Eucharist?
76. For a detailed defense of this view, see Thomas, *Footwashing*, 126-89. With rare candor, the editors of the 1582 Rheims New Testament admitted in a note on verse 14: "Our Maister neuer spake plainer, nor seemed to command more precisely, either of Baptisme or the Eucharist or any other Sacrament: and yet by the Churches judgement directed by the Holy Ghost, we know this to be no Sacrament nor necessarie ceremonie, and the other to be."

here.⁷⁷ For example, "The person who claims to remain in him ought himself to walk just as he walked" (1 Jn 2:6); "In this we know love, because he laid down his life for us, and we too ought to lay down our lives for the brothers" (1 Jn 3:16); "Beloved, if God so loved us, we too ought to love each other" (1 Jn 4:11). To imitate Jesus in a concrete, visible way by washing each other's feet seems to have served as a sign of a broader commitment to imitate him in every area of life. What remains uncertain is whether or not the washing of feet was also intended to represent within the Christian community the mutual forgiveness of sins committed by believers after baptism. If so, it is never made explicit.⁷⁸

16 Jesus continues with an "Amen, amen" formula, the eighteenth so far in the Gospel (the most recent being in 12:24). This time the formula seems to introduce not a series of pronouncements (as, for example, in 3:5, 11; 5:19, 25; 6:26, 32, 53; 8:34; 10:1, 7; 12:24), but a single unified pronouncement: "Amen, amen, I say to you, a slave is not greater than his lord, nor is a messenger⁷⁹ greater than the person who sent him" (v. 16). The pronouncement, moreover (aside from the double "Amen, amen"), is not distinctly "Johannine" in character, but is quite similar to one found in Matthew. "A disciple is not above the teacher, nor a slave above his lord. It is enough for the disciple that he be as his teacher, and the slave as his lord" (Mt 10:24-25a).⁸⁰ Ironically, Matthew's version of the saying admirably fits the context in John's Gospel, given Jesus' preceding reference to himself as both "the Teacher" and "the Lord" (vv. 13-14). But Matthew's first clause ("A disciple

---

77. Gr. ὀφείλετε (v. 14)

78. Thomas addresses the question at considerable length (*Footwashing*, 155-72), making an impressive case from 1 John and from church fathers that this was in fact the case. But John's Gospel, with the exception of 20:23, is silent on the subject of the forgiveness of sins. Thomas argues that the pronouncement in 20:23 about "forgiving" or "retaining" sins refers to "not only conversion, but forgiveness of those within the community" (155). Interestingly, Jesus in this Gospel sometimes "retains" sin (see 9:41; 15.22) but never explicitly "forgives." As I once put it, in John's Gospel "The accent is on salvation positively as the impartation of life, not negatively as cleansing or forgiveness" (Michaels, "By Water and Blood," 151). Thomas makes his case largely by reading the perspective of 1 John back into the Gospel, a method which legitimately sheds light on practices in "Johannine" communities even though it cannot be allowed to settle the interpretation of John 13.

79. Or "apostle" (Gr. ἀπόστολος).

80. The saying in Matthew is not directly introduced by "Amen, I say to you," but the preceding verse (10:23) does contain that formula, and it is possible that in Matthew (as in John) the formula can be regarded as governing a whole series of distinct pronouncements. The parallel in Luke, "A disciple is not above the teacher, but everyone when he is instructed will be as his teacher" (Lk 6:40), lacks altogether that which Matthew's and John's Gospels have in common.

is not above [or greater than] his teacher") is nowhere to be found in our passage. Instead, we have an almost exact parallel to Matthew's *second* clause ("a slave is not greater than his lord"), followed by another clause unparalleled in any other Gospel: "nor is a messenger greater than the person who sent him."

What is Jesus' point? In Matthew, it is quite clear: if Jesus encountered opposition and persecution, his disciples can expect to fare no better (see Mt 10:25b, "If they called the master of the house Beelzebul, how much more those of the household?"). John's Gospel makes exactly the same point two chapters later, where Jesus recalls the first part of the present saying ("a slave is not greater than his lord"), and draws from it the conclusion, "If they persecuted me, they will persecute you" (15:20). But here the application is different, simply reinforcing the argument from the greater to the lesser two verses earlier: "now that I, the Teacher and the Lord, washed your feet, you too ought to wash each other's feet" (v. 14). That is, if the one greater is not ashamed to be a servant (even a "slave") to his subordinates, why should they be ashamed to be servants to each other? Surely, Jesus insists, "a slave is not greater than his lord." But instead of making the same point again, redundantly, by adding Matthew's principle that "a disciple is not above the teacher" (Mt 10:24), he introduces a new thought: "nor is a messenger greater than the person who sent him."

Surprisingly, this added clause, despite the more "Johannine" flavor of the phrase "the person who sent him," does not appear to fit the context of the footwashing very well. Nothing has been said of a mission, or of the disciples being "sent" (at least not since 4:38, where it may have referred to their baptizing activity in Judea). While those gathered for supper have come to be traditionally known as "the apostles" (as in Lk 22:14), they are never called that in John's Gospel. If anyone is "a messenger" or "apostle," it is Jesus. One need only recall his many references to "the One who sent me," or "the Father who sent me."[81] That Jesus is not "greater" than the Father who sent him will become explicit later on (see 14:28). Still, it is doubtful that "messenger" (or "apostle") here is anything more than a generic term for *anyone* "sent" as an agent or representative of someone else. As such it is applicable either to Jesus or his disciples. So far, Jesus is the "messenger" or "sent one" par excellence (1:6 and 4:38 being the only exceptions), but the parallel with the preceding clause, "a slave is not greater than his lord," offers a hint that the disciples too are (or soon will be) "messengers," with Jesus as "the person who sent them" (see v. 20; also 17:18; 20:21). In retrospect, this

---

81. "For the One who sent me" (ὁ πέμψας με), see 4:34; 5:24, 30; 6:38, 39; 7:16, 18, 28, 33; 8:26, 29; 9:4; 12:44, 45; for "the Father who sent me" (ὁ πέμψας με πατήρ), see 5:23, 37; 6:44; 8:16, 18; 12:49. For Jesus as ἀπόστολος, see Hebrews 3:1; also Justin Martyr, *First Apology* 12.9; 63.10, 14.

is perhaps inevitable in view of the introductory notice that while Jesus "knew that his hour had come that he should be taken out of this world," those whom he called "his own" were still emphatically "in the world" (v. 1), with responsibilities to "the world" as well as to each other (this too becomes explicit later on; see 17:11, 15).

17 Ignoring for a moment the last clause, Jesus draws a conclusion from the "example" he has just given, and from the accompanying command to "do just as I did for you" (v. 15). "*Now that* you understand these things," he tells his disciples, "blessed are you *if* you do them" (v. 17, italics added). There are two conditional clauses in this sentence, one a first-class condition presupposing reality ("Now that [literally "if"] you understand these things,"[82] like "now that I . . . washed your feet," in v. 15), and the other a future condition expressing what he presumes will happen ("if you do them").[83] The repetition of "do" (vv. 15, 17) makes it clear that Jesus is still insisting on the disciples' obligation to "wash each other's feet" (v. 14), just as in another Gospel he insists, "This do in remembrance of me" (Lk 22:19; compare 1 Cor 11:24-25). Here again (as in v. 15), the present subjunctive suggests that the disciples are to do repeatedly what Jesus has done for them once for all. To this, he attaches a beatitude, "blessed are you,"[84] one of only two in the Gospel of John (one for "believing," 20:29, and this one for "doing"). Matthew, by contrast, has thirteen beatitudes in all, and Luke fifteen (Mark has none). Of these, the closest parallel to the Gospel of John's "Blessed are you if you do them" is one found almost word for word the same in Matthew and Luke: "Blessed is that slave whom his lord will find doing so when he comes" (Mt 24:46//Lk12:43). The contrast between "that slave" and "his lord" evokes again the principle that "a slave is not greater than his lord" (see v. 16), and while the contexts in Luke and Matthew are different both from each other and from the present one, all three passages have in common the prospect of Jesus' absence,[85] and the need to prepare the disciples accordingly. While he is absent, they are "blessed" on one condition: in John's Gospel "if they do" (v. 17) what Jesus has just commanded, that is, "wash each other's feet" (v. 14), but more vaguely in Matthew

---

82. Gr. εἰ ταῦτα οἴδατε (see n. 31).

83. Gr. ἐὰν ποιῆτε αὐτά. In this instance the "if" clause (with ἐάν) comes close to presupposing reality (see BDF, §372[1a]), as if to say, "Blessed are you when you do them" (or, "in doing them"; see Jas 1:25, "blessed [μακάριος] in the doing of it").

84. Gr. μακάριοί ἐστε.

85. This is explicit in John's Gospel (see vv. 1, 3), but implicit in Matthew and Luke. There the preparation for Jesus' departure is couched in the form of parables about the lord of a household going away and leaving his slaves in charge (see, for example, Mt 24:42, 45; Lk 12:35, 42). In each case, the application ("You too must be ready, for the Son of man is coming at an hour when you do not expect him," Mt 24:44//Lk12:40) makes it clear that to these Gospel writers as well the absent lord is indeed Jesus.

13:1-20 JESUS AT SUPPER

and Luke, if a slave is found "doing so."[86] But "doing" what? Providing for the needs of his fellow slaves, not by the washing of feet to be sure, but by the daily provision of food (see Mt 24:45; Lk 12:42).[87] Moreover, Luke's version of the parable concludes, "That slave who knew his lord's will, and did not get ready or do what was wanted will be beaten with many blows, but the one who did not know and did things that deserved a beating will be beaten with few blows. From everyone to whom much is given, much will be required of him, and from one to whom much has been entrusted, much will be demanded" (Lk 12:47-48). Such parallels give special force to Jesus' words here in the Gospel of John, "Now that you understand these things, blessed are you if you do them."

18 Jesus immediately qualifies the beatitude he has just pronounced: "I am not speaking about all of you. I know which ones[88] I chose." (v. 18a).[89] At first glance he seems to contradict what he said earlier in Capernaum, "Did I not choose you as the Twelve?" (6:70), heightening the irony of the revelation that "one of you is 'the devil'" (6:70). But it is simply another way of saying the same thing: the disciples are "chosen" corporately as "the Twelve," but not all are individually chosen. Jesus is simply repeating in different words what he said a few verses earlier, "and you men are clean, but not all of you" (v. 10). Moreover, in saying, "I know[90] which ones I chose," he seems to confirm the Gospel writer's narrative aside ("he knew the one who was handing him over," v. 11). This time, however, there is no narrative aside, and Jesus does not mention Judas Iscariot either by name or as "the one who was handing him over." Instead, he refers to a verse from the Psalms: "But the Scripture must be fulfilled [or, more literally, "that the Scripture might be fulfilled"],[91]

---

86. The word order varies (between οὕτως ποιοῦντα and ποιοῦντα οὕτως) between Matthew and Luke according to modern textual editors, but also within the manuscript tradition of each Gospel.

87. Also possibly relevant is the preceding parable in Luke, where Jesus urges his disciples, "Let your loins be girded and your lamps burning. You then are like men awaiting their lord when he returns from the wedding, so that when he comes and knocks they might open to him. Blessed [μακάριοι] are those slaves whom the lord will find awake when he comes. Amen, I say to you, he will gird himself and have them recline, and will come along and serve them" (Lk 12:35-37). There too the girding of the loins (whether by the slaves or by their lord) implies a servant's role, and possibly even footwashing in particular.

88. Instead of "which ones" (τίνας), some important ancient witnesses (including P[66], A, D, W, Θ, Ψ, and the majority of later manuscripts) have "the ones" (οὕς), but the support for τίνας is even stronger (with ℵ, B, L, C, 33, and others), and the variants are in any case interchangeable in meaning.

89. The emphatic "I" may help to mark a subtle transition from v. 17, "Now that you understand [οἴδατε] these things," to what Jesus himself (ἐγὼ οἶδα) "knows" or "understands."

90. Gr. οἶδα.

91. This is the first instance in John's Gospel of the formula, "that it might be ful-

'The one who eats my bread[92] lifted up his heel against me'" (v. 18b, from Ps 41:9 [40:10, LXX]).[93] The quotation speaks of rebellion and open disdain on the part of a trusted friend or family member, exactly the opposite action and attitude from that represented in the washing of one another's feet. The question for the reader is whether the narrative aside of verse 11 is somehow still in effect, so that Jesus must be understood as referring to Judas and Judas alone, or whether the fulfillment of the psalm should be understood in a wider framework. Such a framework is provided by the preceding "Amen, amen" pronouncement (v. 16), hinting (as we have seen) at an ongoing mission, and by another such pronouncement to follow (v. 20), confirming just such a mission.

Most readers have assumed that the focus is solely on Judas, for two main reasons. First, Judas is undeniably the center of attention in the preceding narrative aside (v. 11) and in the drama that plays out in the section to follow (vv. 21-30). Second, the psalm quotation, "The one who eats my bread lifted up his heel against me," is singular, not plural, and it is natural to take the singular as referring specifically to Judas. The quotation is widely believed to find at least a faint echo in Mark 14:18, where Jesus very explicitly predicts that "one of you will hand me over, the one eating with me."[94] The difficulty with the second of these arguments is that the Markan reference is

---

filled" (ἵνα . . . πληρωθῇ), more commonly associated with Matthew but used in John in relation both to biblical texts (see 15:25; 17:12; 19:24, 36) and to sayings of Jesus (18:9, 32). For the translation, "must be fulfilled," compare 15:25.

92. Gr. ὁ τρώγων μου τὸν ἄρτον. Some important ancient witnesses (including P[66], א, A, D, and the majority of later manuscripts) have "the one who eats bread with me" (ὁ τρώγων μετ' ἐμοῦ τὸν ἄρτον), but this reading looks suspiciously like an assimilation either to Mark 14:18 or to Mark 14:20, Matthew 26:23, and Luke 22:21 (see n. 95 below). The shorter reading (ὁ τρώγων μου τὸν ἄρτον, with B, C, L, and others) is in closer agreement with both the Hebrew and the LXX, and has the support of most textual editors (see Metzger, *Textual Commentary*, 240) and most English versions (see NIV, TNIV, RSV, NRSV, and NAB; NEB and REB are exceptions).

93. The quotation agrees more closely with the Hebrew (אוכל לחמי הגדיל עלי עקב, literally 'the one who ate my bread made the heel great against me') than with the LXX (ὁ ἐσθίων ἄρτους μου ἐμεγάλυνεν ἐπ' ἐμὲ πτερνισμόν, literally "the one who eats my loaves made treachery great against me"). The lifting up of the heel seems to have been an obscene gesture (regarded as such by Arabs to this day), implying a "malicious kick" (BDAG, 895), a desire to dominate or trample under foot the person to whom the gesture is directed, or perhaps to shake the dust of his city from the feet (see E. F. F. Bishop, *Expository Times* 70 [1958-59], 331-32).

94. Gr. ὁ ἐσθίων μετ' ἐμοῦ. See Brown, 2.571, who claims that the psalm is "cited implicitly in Mark xiv 18," adding "(That Mark was aware of a scriptural background for what was happening can be deduced from xiv 21: 'The Son of man goes his way *as it is written of him*')"; also Dodd, *Historical Tradition*, 36. It is likely that the two expressions for "the one who eats" (ὁ τρώγων in Jn 13:18 and ὁ ἐσθίων in Mk 14:18 and in the LXX) are interchangeable in meaning.

so brief that nothing substantial can be made of it.[95] The singular "one who eats my bread" may indeed refer to Judas, but as in the psalm itself the singular reference to one person may well invite generalization. More important, the notion that Jesus is referring solely and unequivocally to one of the disciples seated right there at the table makes it hard to explain why there is no immediate reaction from the disciples, as there is shortly afterward (v. 22), when he says explicitly, "Amen, amen, I say to you that one of you will hand me over" (v. 21). Why the apparent duplication? Why does Jesus find it necessary to predict Judas's treachery twice?[96] And how would the disciples have understood the psalmist's words, "The one who eats my bread lifted up his heel against me"?

19 More specifically, how would those dire words be "fulfilled"? Jesus gives no direct answer, but claims that their fulfillment, when it comes, will only vindicate his authority: "From now on I tell you before it happens,[97] so that when it happens you might believe that I am" (v. 19). His language suggests that the "fulfillment" he has in mind will come not (or at least not *only*) in a few seconds right there at the table (vv. 21-30), but in a rather more distant future. His pronouncement seems to belong with several others in the chapters to follow, warning the disciples of certain things ahead of time so that when they take place the disciples will "believe" (14:29) or at least "not be scandalized" (16:1), or simply "remember" what he told them (16:4) and "have peace" (16:32-33). The parallel with 14:29 is especially close (with verbal agreements in italics):

> "From now on I tell you before it happens,[98] *so that when it happens you might believe* that I am" (13:19).
> "And now I have told you before it happens,[99] *so that when it happens you might believe*" (14:29).

---

95. It is doubtful that anyone would have even seen a connection between Mark's phrase, "the one eating with me," and Psalm 41:9 were it not for the fuller quotation here. The only parallel would have been "the one eating" (ὁ ἐσθίων), for the words "with me" (μετ' ἐμοῦ) in Mark simply anticipate the reference two verses later to "the one who dips with me [μετ' ἐμοῦ] in the dish" (14:20) with its parallels in Matthew and Luke. As for the reference to what "is written" (14:21), nothing suggests that it refers to one specific passage. It can as easily be simply a general reference to Scripture (as in the parallel, Mt 26:24; see also Mk 14:49).

96. Ernst Haenchen notices this (2.109), commenting that the Scripture quotation "awkwardly presupposes what is said in verses 21ff., and thereby destroys the tension with which the text is obviously concerned."

97. Gr. πρὸ τοῦ γενέσθαι.
98. Gr. πρὸ τοῦ γενέσθαι.
99. Gr. πρὶν γενέσθαι.

At the same time, the pronouncement evokes certain sayings of Jesus in the other Gospels in which he predicts what will happen after his departure in the course of the Christian mission. After a series of predictions about persecution and false prophets, he warns his disciples, "Watch out! I have told you everything ahead of time" (Mk 13:23; see also Mt 24:25). Conspicuous among the dangers to come are dissension within the believing community and hatred from without: "And brother will hand brother over to death," Jesus warns, "and father hand over child, and children will rise against parents and will put them to death. And you will be hated by all for my name's sake" (Mt 10:21-22//Mk 13:12-13). In the same chapter in Matthew (the chapter in which he says, "A disciple is not above his teacher, nor a slave above his lord," 10:24), Jesus issues other warnings about division within households: "For I have come to split up a man against his father, and a daughter against her mother, and a bride [or daughter-in-law] against her mother-in-law — and a man's enemies will be those of his household" (Mt 10:35-36; see also Lk 12:52-53).[100] In John's Gospel he addresses the same two issues: here, dissension and betrayal within the Christian community, and two chapters later the grim prospect being "hated" by the world (15:18-25). Each time, Jesus draws on the language of a psalm: there, "They hated me [ἐμίσησάν με] without cause" (15:25, from either Ps 35:19 or 69:4), where "they" refers to "the world" (see 15:18-19); here Psalm 41:9, where "the one who eats my bread" (v. 18) refers first to any anonymous member of a household, and only as an afterthought to Judas Iscariot (see v. 21). While it is impossible to know how the disciples would have heard these words of Jesus, it is more likely that they heard them in this way than as an explicit prediction of a betrayal by one of their number right then and there.

What sets Jesus' pronouncement here apart from those in the synoptic Gospels is his claim that the fulfillment of his grim prophecy will actually vindicate his authority. The phrase "from now on"[101] seems to imply that he is predicting a future event or situation well "before it happens,"[102] with the intent that "when it happens[103] you might believe that I am" (v. 19). His lan-

---

100. While these words of Jesus are drawn largely from Scripture (see Mic 7:6), they are not explicitly identified as such, or said to be in any way a "fulfillment."

101. Gr. ἀπ' ἄρτι.

102. There is wide agreement among commentators that "from now on" (ἀπ' ἄρτι, 13:19) means simply "now" (like καὶ νῦν, 14:29) (see Brown, 2.554; Bultmann, 478, n. 4; Schnackenburg, 3.403, n. 77; Barrett, 445; also BDAG, 97). Still, the more literal translation, "from now on," has something to be said for it, suggesting "from this time on," or "already, this long before the event actually takes place." The language is, if anything, more applicable to events after Jesus' death and resurrection than to an incident at the table only minutes later (that is, to vv. 21-30).

103. Gr. ὅταν γένηται.

guage is at least as applicable, possibly more so, to events after his death and resurrection as to an incident at the table only minutes later (that is, to vv. 21-30).[104] The fulfillment of his prediction will serve as testimony to his disciples "that I am."[105] In the immediate context, "I am" could simply mean, "I am the one who speaks in this psalm" (like the "me" and the "I" and the "my" in the psalm citations in 2:17, 15:25, and 19:24 and 28). But more likely, the expression has a wider, more explicitly christological application, as it does elsewhere in the Gospel (see 4:26; 8:24, 28; and, above all, 8:58). The mention of a particular future moment of verification recalls 8:28 in particular, where Jesus told the Jewish authorities, "When you lift up the Son of man, then you will know that I am, and [that] on my own I do nothing, but just as the Father taught me, these things I speak." To "the Jews" in that passage, Jesus would be vindicated as God's agent by his death on the cross, and to his disciples here he will be vindicated, he says, precisely in his betrayal and in their own trials and dissension, simply by virtue of the fact that he was not taken by surprise, but predicted it all in advance.[106] According to Deuteronomy, one of the tests of a true prophet was that his prophecies came to pass: "If what a prophet proclaims in the name of the LORD," said Moses, "does not take place or prove true, that is a message the LORD has not spoken. That prophet has spoken presumptuously" (Deut 18:22, NIV). Even God's own authority is vindicated in the same way, for God can summon the nations, asking, "Which of them foretold this and proclaimed to us the former things? Let them bring their witnesses to prove they were right, so that others may hear and say, 'It is true.' You are my witnesses, declares the LORD, and my servant whom I have chosen, so that you may know and believe me and understand that I am he" (Isa 43:9-10a, NIV), and can claim, "I make known the end from the beginning, from ancient times what is still to come" (Isa 46:9-10a, NIV). Jesus presses in much the same way his own claim to know

---

104. So Bultmann, who comments that the Gospel writer "does not refer to Jesus' prior knowledge in order to overcome the difficulty caused by a single fact, which is what Judas's betrayal is. On the contrary, just as the allusion to the betrayer is intended to shake the disciple's assurance and to draw attention to a possibility he always has to face, so too the difficulty that the Evangelist is concerned with is the ever present one, that there are disloyal disciples. It is this, fundamentally, that Jesus knows beforehand. . . . We are not of course told here as clearly as we are later (16.1, 4, 32f.; 14:29) that Jesus' foreknowledge is of this kind" (478; see also Michaels, "Betrayal and the Betrayer," especially 467-72).

105. Gr. ὅτι ἐγώ εἰμι.

106. As far as the betrayal by Judas is concerned, it is natural to cite as the moment of vindication the moment in which Jesus says "I am" (ἐγώ εἰμι) at his arrest (18:5, 6, 8; see Schnackenburg, 3.224), yet at that moment none of Jesus' disciples responded explicitly in faith, as Jesus would have intended that they should. While this may have been a provisional fulfillment of Jesus' prophecy within the narrative, it is clearly not the final fulfillment of 13:19.

the future, and readers who remember him saying "before Abraham came to be, I am" (8:58) can scarcely mistake the import of his words. Like the God of Israel, he not only knows, but reveals himself, in things yet to come no less than in things past and present.

20 Jesus concludes his brief discourse with yet another "Amen, amen" pronouncement, the nineteenth in the Gospel: "Amen, amen, I say to you, the person who receives whomever I send receives me, and the person who receives me receives the One who sent me" (v. 20). The two clauses are not distinct, but are closely linked, with the second building immediately on the first. That is, the person who "receives" (or welcomes) the disciples and accepts their message actually "receives" (in faith) Jesus himself, and therefore God the Father, because Jesus represents the Father. Here the earlier hint that the notion of agency applies to the disciples no less than to Jesus (v. 16) becomes an explicit claim. The disciples, like Jesus, will be "sent,"[107] and Jesus, like the Father, will take on the role of Sender. The notion that his disciples will act as his agents or messengers implies his absence — something the reader has known about at least from the beginning of the chapter (see vv. 1, 3), yet something of which the disciples have been — and continue to be — only dimly aware. The effect of the pronouncement is to place all of verses 18-20, and to some extent the whole of verses 12-20, in the framework of the disciples' mission "in the world" (v. 1) and to the world after Jesus' impending departure. Within that framework they have a responsibility both to "each other" (vv. 14-15) and those to whom they are "sent" (vv. 16, 20). Here (as in v. 16) the "Amen, amen" formula introduces a pronouncement found elsewhere in the Gospel tradition (see Mt 10:40; Lk 10:16), and it is tempting to many interpreters to view both sayings as parenthetical at best, or at worst as interpolations in John's Gospel.[108] Yet the vocabulary is thoroughly Johannine, and quite different from that of Matthew and Luke.[109] One need

---

107. And in that sense "apostles" (see ἀπόστολος as "messenger," v. 16),

108. Brown, for example, calls v. 20 "strangely out of place" (2.571). According to Haenchen: "Verse 20 does not belong to this context at all; it is loosely connected with verse 16 by means of the catchword 'send'" (2.110). Schnackenburg (3.25) attributes both vv. 16 and 20 to an editor, even while admitting that v. 20 at least is characteristically Johannine in style. Godet is closer to the truth in arguing that if anything is parenthetical, verses 18-19 are: "Vv. 18, 19 are a simple digression occasioned by the contrast between the fate of Judas and the happiness of the faithful disciples (ver. 17). Ver. 20 is immediately connected with the idea of this happiness declared in vv. 16, 17" (2.253).

109. Matthew, by contrast, has δέχεσθαι instead of λαμβάνειν for "receive," and ἀποστέλλειν instead of πέμπειν for "send": "The person who receives you [ὁ δεχόμενος ὑμᾶς] receives me, and the person who receives me receives the One who sent me" (τὸν ἀποστείλαντά με, Mt 10:40). Luke has, "The person who hears you hears me, and the person who rejects you rejects me, but the person who rejects me rejects the One who sent me" (τὸν ἀποστείλαντά με, Lk 10:16).

only remember 12:44-45, "The person who believes in me believes not in me but in the One who sent me, and the person who sees me sees the One who sent me."

If the two "Amen, amen" pronouncements are "interpolations," they are the Gospel writer's own interpolations, by no means parenthetical, but on the contrary crucial to the writer's flow of thought. In the text as it stands, Jesus' disciples are to be imitators of him in two ways: first, by doing for one another what Jesus has done for them (see vv. 14, 17), and second, by representing him as his agents in the world after his departure, so that what is done to them or for them is done to or for him, just as Jesus has represented the Father as the Father's agent in the world. John's Gospel has taken the notion of agency, intimated in Matthew and Luke, and made it the very foundation of both christology and ecclesiology. As we have seen, however, the response to Jesus as the Father's agent can be negative as well as positive (see 5:23; 12:47-48), and the same will be true of the world's response to the disciples as Jesus' agents. Jesus gives no hint of a negative response here, only of the possibility of betrayal and treachery among the disciples themselves (vv. 18-19). But that other shoe will drop two chapters later (see 15:18-25).

B. THE DEPARTURE OF JUDAS (13:21-35)

>21 *Having said these things, Jesus was shaken in the spirit, and he testified and said, "Amen, amen, I say to you that one of you will hand me over."* 22 *The disciples kept looking at each other, perplexed as to which one he meant.* 23 *One of his disciples was reclining at Jesus' side, one whom Jesus loved.* 24 *So Simon Peter nods to this one to inquire who it might be that he meant.* 25 *So, having leaned on Jesus' breast like this, that one says to him, "Lord, who is it?"* 26 *Jesus answers, "That one it is to whom I will dip the morsel and give to him." Then, having dipped the morsel, he takes and gives to Judas of Simon Iscariot.* 27 *And after the morsel, then Satan entered into that one. So Jesus says to him, "What you are doing, do quickly!"* 28 *But none of those reclining found out for what reason he said this to him.* 29 *For some thought, since Judas had the money box, that Jesus was saying to him, "Buy the things we have need of for the festival," or that he should give something to the poor.* 30 *So that one, having taken the morsel, went out immediately, and it was night.*
>
>31 *So when he had gone out, Jesus says, "Now the Son of man is glorified, and God is glorified in him,* 32 *and God will glorify him in him, and he will glorify him immediately.* 33 *Children, yet a short time I am with you. You will seek me, and just as I said to the Jews that*

The Gospel of John

> '*Where I am going, you cannot come,*' *so I say to you now.* 34 *A new command I give you, that you love each other, just as I loved you, that you too love each other.* 35 *By this they all will know that you are my disciples, if you have love for each other.*"

With his brief discourse (vv. 12-20) at an end, Jesus invokes the "Amen, amen" formula yet again (see vv. 16, 20), this time with deep emotion, as testimony to his disciples: "one of you will hand me over" (v. 21). This time his words provoke a strong reaction among them as they wonder to whom he can be referring (v. 22), and we are introduced to an anonymous disciple we have not met before — at least not as designated here — "one whom Jesus loved," seated right beside Jesus (v. 23). Peter motions to him to find out from Jesus which one is meant, and he does so (vv. 24-26), but we are not told that he passed the information on to Peter, or anyone else. On the contrary, when Jesus tells Judas, "What you are doing, do quickly?" (v. 27), they do not understand that Judas has been singled out as the one who will "hand over" Jesus — to death as it turns out (vv. 28-29). Consequently when Judas goes out into the night (v. 30), only Jesus himself, the "one whom Jesus loved," and the reader know the significance of what has just happened. The other disciples, no less than Judas, are in the dark.

Virtually the whole of verses 21-30 is seen and told through the eyes of this disciple "whom Jesus loved." Novelist Reynolds Price has argued that much of John's Gospel is in fact told in this way: "Hovering just at the edge of each event," he writes, "or caught in its center, is the powerful sense of a pair of human eyes, so fixed in a lover's rapt attention as to vanish nearly from our reading minds and leave us face-to-face with the act itself and the moving bodies."[1] His test is whether or not a third-person narrative can be easily changed to first person by a mere switching of certain pronouns. He tries to illustrate this with some brief examples drawn from 21:3-14, and implies (without much concrete evidence) that it works almost everywhere in the Gospel.[2] This is extremely doubtful, yet 13:21-30 is one place where it does work rather well (better, perhaps, than in Price's examples from chapter 21). So transformed (and somewhat shortened), our passage would read like this:

> Jesus said, "Amen, amen, I say to you that one of you will hand me over." We kept looking at each other, perplexed as to which one he meant. I was reclining at Jesus' side. Simon Peter nods to me to inquire who it might be. So, having leaned on Jesus' breast like this, I say to him, "Lord, who is it?" Jesus answers, "That one it is to whom I will dip

---

1. Price, *Three Gospels,* 176.
2. Price, *Three Gospels,* 175-76.

13:21-35 THE DEPARTURE OF JUDAS

the morsel and give to him." Then, having dipped the morsel, he takes and gives to Judas. And after the morsel, then Satan entered into that one. So Jesus says to him, "What you are doing, do quickly!" But none of them found out for what reason he said this to him. Some thought, since Judas had the money box, that Jesus was saying to him, "Buy the things we have need of for the festival," or that he should give something to the poor. So that one, having taken the morsel, went out immediately, and it was night.

As soon as Judas is gone, Jesus goes on to speak to the disciples openly of three things: his glorification (vv. 31-32), his imminent departure from the world (v. 33; compare vv. 1, 3), and mutual love (vv. 34-35; see vv. 1, 14). Nothing more is heard of the disciple "whom Jesus loved," but these three programmatic themes will reappear in the next four chapters: first, and at considerable length, his departure (13:36–14:31); then all three in reverse order — mutual love (15:1-17) with its corollary of being hated by the world (15:18–16:4a), the departure again (16:4b-33), and, finally, Jesus' glorification (17:1-26). Whether or not they are the dominant themes, or the key to the structure of those chapters (as I once argued)[3] is another question altogether.

21 "Having said these things"[4] terminates the preceding discourse (vv. 12-20), just as the same phrase terminates the much longer series of discourses that will shortly follow (see 18:1). It is as if Jesus pauses for breath before stating something even more immediate and portentous. It an emotional pause, for he is "shaken in the spirit," just as he was at the tomb of Lazarus (see 11:33, 38). Nothing is said of anger here, yet the situation is similar to the extent that someone is present who should not be present. Jesus' intent here is that that person must leave so that he can say what he has to say to his disciples in private, and in due course he does leave (v. 30). At the raising of Lazarus, as we have seen, Jesus seems to have been angry because he was forced to perform the miracle in public, and here too the issue may well be privacy. But instead of being angry, Jesus simply "testified and said, 'Amen, amen I say to you that one of you will hand me over'" (v. 21).

For the twentieth time in the Gospel, and for the third time in fairly quick succession, Jesus invokes his characteristic formula, now with even greater immediacy and solemnity than it had a moment before (vv. 16, 20). The verb "testified" gives it greater solemnity, for Jesus' "testimony" (as if in a court of law) is everywhere else in the Gospel directed toward "the world," or "the Jews" or "the Pharisees" or "the crowd," not toward his own disciples. He has been on trial, and has "testified" on his own behalf as part of that trial.

---

3. Michaels, *John*, 253-54.
4. Gr. ταῦτα εἰπών.

The Gospel of John

It is not altogether clear, in fact, whether Jesus is here "testifying" to, or against, his disciples, for his words, "one of you[5] will hand me over" (exactly as in Mk 14:18 and Mt 26:21), have an accusatory tone that we have heard only once before, when he told them, "one of you is 'the devil'" (6:70). With such pointed words here, Jesus brings much closer to home the scriptural principle that "The one who eats my bread lifted up his heel against me" (v. 18). Not only is it true that "brother will hand brother over[6] to death" in the course of the Christian mission (as in Mt 10:21 and Mk 13:12), but more specifically, "*one of you* will hand *me* over"[7] (v. 21) right here and now (italics added). The notion that Jesus will be "handed over" by one of his disciples is old news to the reader, who has been reminded of it again and again (6:64, 71; 12:4; 13:2, 11), but here for the first time it comes on the lips of Jesus himself, and it draws an immediate reaction.

22 In sharp contrast to 6:70, where we were not told how the disciples responded to the revelation that "one of you is 'the devil,'" here we learn that "The disciples kept looking at each other, perplexed[8] as to which one he meant"[9] (v. 22). But instead of asking him each in turn, "Is it I, Lord?" (see Mt 26:22; Mk 14:19), they remained silent,[10] communicating at first only with their eyes.

23 At this tense moment, we are introduced for the first time to a character who will make four more cameo appearances in the Gospel (19:26; 20:2-8; 21:7, 20-23), and who will finally be identified as "the one who testifies about these things and who wrote these things" (20:24). "One of his disciples," we are told, "was reclining at Jesus' side, one whom Jesus loved"[11] (v. 23). The phrase "one of his disciples,"[12] coming right on the heels of Jesus' prediction that "one of you [εἷς ἐξ ὑμῶν] will hand me over" (v. 21), could give the impression that this is none other than the disciple who will "hand over" Jesus to the authorities who were seeking his life. Such a thought would not be inconsistent with the notice that "Jesus loved" this man, and that he was "re-

---

5. Gr. εἷς ἐξ ὑμῶν.
6. Gr. παραδώσει.
7. Gr. παραδώσει με.
8. Gr. ἀπορούμενοι.
9. Gr. περὶ τίνος λέγει. Here, as elsewhere, λέγειν περί, literally, "to speak about," is legitimately translated as "meant" (see 2:21; 7:39, and compare 6:71)

10. In Luke, although no actual words are given, the disciples carry on a discussion among themselves [πρὸς ἑαυτούς] about "which one of them it might be" (τίς ἄρα εἴη ἐξ αὐτῶν, Lk 22:23).

11. Gr. ὃν ἠγάπα ὁ Ἰησοῦς.

12. Gr. εἷς ἐκ τῶν μαθητῶν αὐτοῦ. Once again, compare the expressions, "one of you [ἐξ ὑμῶν εἷς] is 'the devil'" (6:70), and "Judas of Simon Iscariot . . . one of the Twelve" (εἷς ἐκ τῶν δώδεκα, 6:71).

13:21-35 THE DEPARTURE OF JUDAS

clining at Jesus' side," for the implication of the text Jesus had just cited (v. 18) was that the betrayer would indeed be a trusted member of the household. A first-time reader could be momentarily teased (perhaps deliberately, to build suspense) into thinking this was the case, but any such impression will be quickly corrected. The "one whom Jesus loved" is not the man who will hand him over, but the one to whom Jesus reveals the identity of the one who will hand him over. His own identity, however, remains a secret. If he is himself the author (as 21:24 claims), the choice to remain anonymous is his own choice. Whoever he may be, this disciple's defining moment is the present moment of discovery (see 21:20, where he is identified in relation to this very incident). And if he is the author, the inordinate authorial interest in Judas Iscariot (as evidenced in the narrative asides in 6:64, 71, 12:6, and 13:11, and in the narrative introduction in 13:2) is plausibly explained.

Still, the question persists: Who *was* this disciple? The question is not answerable from the passage here. Surely, the notice that he was "one whom Jesus loved" does not distinguish him from any of the others, for we have been told regarding them all that "having loved his own who were in the world," Jesus "loved them to the end" (v. 1).[13] Nor does the detail that he was "reclining at Jesus' side" help very much. "At the side,"[14] recalling Jesus' own close relationship to the Father (see 1:18, "right beside the Father"),[15] seems to express a relationship to Jesus which all his true disciples, not just one, would have enjoyed, at least in a spiritual sense.[16]

As to the actual seating arrangements at a meal around the table, little is known, only that "James and John, the sons of Zebedee" (or their mother) wanted the seats immediately on either side of Jesus "in your glory" (or "in your kingdom"), presumably at the end of the age (Mk 10:35-37; also Mt 20:20-21). Whether or not they wanted this because it was *already* the cus-

---

13. As we have seen, the only disciples Jesus was said to have "loved" individually were Lazarus, Mary, and Martha (see 11:3, 5, 36). From this, some have inferred that the disciple mentioned here is Lazarus. One might just as easily propose Martha or Mary, but the difficulty with all such conjectures is that no satisfactory explanation has ever been given of why someone mentioned repeatedly by name would suddenly become anonymous. As for the anonymous rich man in Mark, whom Jesus is said to have "loved" (Mk 10:21), he is far too removed from the present context to be anything but an extremely speculative option.

14. Gr. ἐν τῷ κόλπῳ, literally, "in the bosom."

15. This interpretation is as old as Origen: "John . . . was reclining in the bosom of the Word, analogous also to the Word being in the bosom of the Father" (*Commentary on John* 32.264; FC, 89.391).

16. That Jesus' relationship to the Father becomes the model for Jesus' own relationship to all his disciples, or to Christian believers generally, has been hinted at already (see 6:57), and will soon become apparent in a variety of ways, for example, with respect to indwelling (14:20), love (15:9), being sent (17:18; 20:22), and glorification (17:22).

tomary seating arrangement at shared meals is uncertain. Nor is it certain whether the future "glory" or "kingdom" was visualized as a banquet scene (as in Mk 14:25//Mt 26:29//Lk 22:18), or a throne room (as in Mt 19:28//Lk 22:30), or both. The traditional inference from the other Gospels has been that Peter, James, and John were viewed as a kind of inner circle of three among the twelve apostles (see, for example, Mk 9:2; 14:33), that this "beloved" disciple is distinguished from Peter (v. 24), and must therefore be either James or John, that he cannot be James because James was martyred early (Acts 12:2), and that he must therefore have been John the son of Zebedee.[17] Such considerations, while intriguing and deserving of respect, are far from conclusive. This disciple whom Jesus is said to have "loved," like a number of other significant characters in the Gospel,[18] remains anonymous, and the reader has no choice but to respect his anonymity.

24 In three of the other four instances in which the disciple "whom Jesus loved" makes an appearance, he is seen with Simon Peter (20:2-8, 21:7, and 21:20-23), and the same is true here: "So Simon Peter nods to this one to inquire who it might be that he meant." The silence (v. 22) is not broken.[19] The expression "who it might be that he meant"[20] (v. 24) echoes the implied but unspoken question "as to which one he meant" (v. 22).[21] Peter signals with a mere nod of the head[22] to his fellow disciple to ask the question that

---

17. The classic argument is that of Westcott (ix-lix, especially xlv-xlvi).

18. These include two major exemplars of faith, the Samaritan woman (chapter 4) and the man born blind (chapter 9), as well as two slightly less significant figures, the royal official whose son was sick (chapter 4) and the sick man at the pool (chapter 5). Quite possibly these characters are anonymous because the writer did not know their names, but in the case of this disciple the anonymity is evidently deliberate.

19. This is not the case with a variant reading in which Peter not only "nods" but "says to him, 'Tell who it is'" (εἰπὲ τίς ἐστιν, with B, C, L, X, Origen, and others), omitting the entire clause, "to inquire who it might be that he meant" (ℵ combines the two: "to inquire who it might be that he meant, and he says to him, 'Tell who it is'"). While the simpler reading has support among commentators (including Barrett, 447; Bultmann, 481, n. 6), the text as it stands is strongly and widely attested (with P⁶⁶, A, D, K, W, Δ, and the majority of later witnesses), and is probably to be preferred (see Metzger, *Textual Commentary,* 240-41; Brown 2.574-75). While the longer reading of ℵ makes good sense, it appears to be a conflation. As for the shorter reading, it is odd that Peter would have been represented as just saying, "Tell who it is," as if he thought the other disciple would know (Bultmann's assertion that his words mean "ask Jesus who is intended" is unwarranted). More likely, "Tell who it is" was a scribe's way of explaining further what Peter's silent gesture implied.

20. Gr. τίς ἂν εἴη περὶ οὗ λέγει.

21. See above, n. 9. The purposeful, almost singsong repetition offers additional confirmation of the preferred textual reading (see n. 19).

22. On νεύειν, to "nod to someone as a signal, perh. by inclination of the head," see BDAG, 670 (compare ἐκνεύειν in 5:13).

13:21-35 THE DEPARTURE OF JUDAS

was on everyone's mind.[23] The silent gesture implies a rather close relationship between the two. Words were unnecessary. It also implies that Peter was probably *not* seated "at Jesus' side" — that is, at his other side, across from the disciple "Jesus loved" — but further away, with that disciple (and perhaps others) between him and Jesus. In sharp contrast to what happens a few moments later (see vv. 36-37), Peter does not feel free to question Jesus directly, but quietly prompts the disciple "Jesus loved" to ask the question for him — and for all the disciples.

25 The question is finally asked, as the anonymous disciple "having leaned on Jesus' breast like this, . . . says to him, 'Lord, who is it?'" (v. 25). The reference to "leaning on Jesus' breast" sounds strangely redundant after being told that he was already "reclining at Jesus' side" (v. 23).[24] The effect of the redundancy is to heighten the impression of intimacy between this disciple and Jesus, and therefore of the privacy and confidentiality of this particular exchange. The disciple "leans" on Jesus as if to whisper in his ear, and the expectation is that the answer will similarly be for his ears alone. The Gospel writer — identified finally as this very disciple (21:24) — adds to the intimacy by confiding to the reader that it went "like this," as if performing or acting out (in this case) his own body language.[25] "Lord, who is it?" the disciple asks — his only spoken lines in the entire Gospel until after Jesus' resurrection, when he tells Peter by the lakeshore, "It is the Lord" (21:7).

26 Jesus "answers" immediately:[26] "That one[27] it is to whom I will dip the morsel and give to him," and then without hesitation, "having dipped

---

23. The disciples show a similar disinclination to ask questions in 16:5-6 and 21:12, though not necessarily for similar reasons.

24. That the verbs for "reclining" and "leaning over" (BDAG, 65, 70), and the nouns for "breast" and "side" (BDAG, 556-57, 944), are nearly synonymous in meaning is in keeping with this Gospel's fondness for synonyms (the classic example being 21:15-17). The reading ἐπιπεσών ("pressing close to," as in the first hand of ℵ, D, A, Θ, W, a corrector of P⁶⁶, and the majority of later witnesses) for ἀναπεσών "leaning on") may have come into being as an attempt to lessen the redundancy.

25. Gr. οὕτως. For οὕτως used similarly, see 4:6, where Jesus was sitting *like this* at the spring," and the textual gloss appended to 8:59, "and having come through the midst of them, he was going on, and passing by *like this*" (οὕτως).

26. This is one of only three instances where Jesus "answers" someone in the present tense (ἀποκρίνεται). Elsewhere he uses uses the aorist (overwhelmingly ἀπεκρίθη, though in two cases, 5:17 and 19, the aorist middle ἀπεκρίνατο). In each instance of the present ἀποκρίνεται (the others being 12:23 and 13:38), Jesus is speaking privately to either one or two disciples.

27. The pronouns are somewhat confusing because the disciple "whom Jesus loved" is spoken of first as "this one" (τούτῳ, v. 24) and then as "that one" (ἐκεῖνος, v. 25), just before Judas is called "that one" (ἐκεῖνος), not once but three times (vv. 26, 27, 30). The awkwardness is reflected, deliberately, in the translation.

the morsel, he takes and gives[28] to Judas of Simon Iscariot" (v. 26). Once again (as in vv. 22 and 24), verbal repetition carries the narrative forward, making the identification of Judas unmistakable. "The morsel"[29] is a small piece of bread which Jesus dips in a sauce and offers to Judas, fulfilling the role of host and acting out in a specific setting the generalized prophecy he has just quoted, that "The one who eats *my* bread lifted up his heel against me" (v. 18, italics added).[30] Offering "the morsel" was an act of hospitality that could hardly be refused. In this way Jesus maintains the initiative, in contrast to the Synoptics, where Judas's own action of "dipping with me in the dish" is what triggers the identification (see Mk 14:20//Mt 26:23).[31] All this is seen through the eyes of the disciple "whom Jesus loved" (v. 23). While Jesus' action in giving the morsel to Judas may have been visible to all the disciples, the impression given is that they were not privy to the words that immediately preceded it, and therefore would not have seen it as the answer to their unspoken question about "which one he meant" (v. 22).

27 What happened next was not visible to anyone: "And after the morsel, then Satan entered into that one" (v. 27a). Who could have seen such a thing? How did the writer know? Only by resuming his role as omniscient narrator, the role he has adopted all along in his narrative asides and in his extraordinary introduction to the chapter (vv. 1-3), the same role Luke adopted in alerting his readers to what Judas was up to (see Lk 22:3, "Satan entered into Judas").[32] But here, as we have seen, the narrator is

---

28. There are a number of textual variants in this verse, and the evidence is complex. The main question is whether Jesus "takes and gives" (λαμβάνει καὶ δίδωσιν) the morsel to Judas (with B, the first corrector of ℵ, C, L, 33, Origen, and others), or merely "gives" it (δίδωσιν) to him (with the first hand of ℵ, P⁶⁶, D, and others). Metzger (*Textual Commentary*, 241) sees it as a question of "whether λαμβάνει καί was added by copyists to recall Jesus' deliberate action at the Last Supper in *taking* bread (Mt 26.26; Mk 14.22; Lk 22.19; 1 Cor 11.23), or whether the words were omitted as irrelevant and unnecessary." Perhaps more likely, λαμβάνει καί was original, but was omitted by scribes to avoid confusion with the final notice just before Judas "went out," that he had "taken" (λαβών) the morsel Jesus offered him.

29. Gr. τὸ ψωμίον.

30. So Schnackenburg, 3.30.

31. Luke's wording (22:21) is slightly different: "But see, the hand of him who is handing me over is with me [μετ' ἐμοῦ] on the table." Keener (2.919) notices that "Jesus does not identify the betrayer by the betrayer's choice but by his own. In the Synoptics, Judas stretches out his own hand 'with' Jesus," although Keener's further observation that this may indicate "a deliberate violation of rank, hence rebellion," is less than convincing. According to Schnackenburg, "This is a clear expression of Jesus' initiative, taken to remove the traitor, and is as such completely in accordance with the rest of the image of the Johannine Jesus" (3.30).

32. The parallel is striking. According to Luke, "Satan entered into Judas"

13:21-35 THE DEPARTURE OF JUDAS

also an eyewitness, the one through whose eyes the story is told (see 21:20, 24). In which capacity (eyewitness or omniscient narrator) does he tell us that "after the morsel, then Satan entered into that one"? If he did not literally see Satan entering Judas's body, what did he see? The answer comes only belatedly, and in a subordinate clause, "having taken the morsel," just as Judas leaves the scene (v. 30). What he saw, evidently, was Judas receiving "the morsel" from Jesus' hand, the completion of the transaction. "The morsel" becomes for him not a mere piece of bread, but a moment in time, an event of decisive import, prompting the odd expression "after the morsel,"[33] which can only mean "after the passing of the morsel."[34] His conclusion that "Satan entered into that one" at just that moment is probably intended not as something immediately apparent to him on witnessing the transaction, but as something evident in retrospect, long after the fact, something for which the reader is by now more than amply prepared (see 6:70-71; 13:2).

Jesus then speaks again, no longer confidentially to the disciple he loved, but now to Judas, apparently within earshot of all: "What you are doing, do quickly!" (v. 27b). The urgency of those words is a corollary of the fact that Jesus' "hour had come that he should be taken out of this world to the Father" (v. 1) and at the same time an anticipation of his warning to the disciples that "yet a short time I am with you" (v. 33). As far as Jesus is concerned, time is running out (see 9:4; 11:9-10; 12:35-36), and is not to be wasted (see 14:30-31; also Mk 14:41-42). Once "the hour has come," events must (and will) move rapidly toward their inevitable conclusion. What Judas was "doing" was the very antithesis of what a disciple of Jesus should have been "doing" (vv. 15, 17), and the implication of Jesus' words is that Judas is being dismissed. He must leave at once.

28-29 That everyone at the table heard what Jesus had said is clear from the notice that "none of those reclining found out for what reason he said this to him" (v. 28). The statement is, of course, not literally true. Jesus knew. Judas presumably knew. And the disciple "whom Jesus loved" must

---

(εἰσῆλθεν δὲ σατανᾶς εἰς Ἰούδαν, 22:3), and here, "then Satan entered into that one" (τότε εἰσῆλθεν εἰς ἐκεῖνον ὁ σατανᾶς). The possibility of influence from a Lukan tradition of some kind is heightened by the fact that only here in John's Gospel is "Satan" used as a designation for "the devil" (6:71; 8:44; 13:2), or "the ruler of this world" (see 12:31; 14:30; 16:11).

33. Gr. μετὰ τὸ ψωμίον.

34. The phrase μετὰ τὸ ψωμίον is also somewhat redundant alongside "then" (τότε), which is omitted (possibly for that reason) by a number of witnesses, including ℵ, D (which omits "after the morsel" as well), L, Sy^s, and certain old Latin and Coptic versions. The redundancy, however, adds to the solemnity of the notice, and is in all likelihood original.

have known, by virtue of "the morsel," that Jesus was referring to his imminent betrayal. So in saying "none of those reclining found out," he is speaking as an eyewitness observer of all the *other* disciples gathered around the table.[35] Obviously, he did not report back to Peter and the other disciples what he learned from Jesus. For whatever reason, he held his peace, and he will continue to do so through most of the rest of the Gospel. His silence remains a mystery at this point. In ascribing to the other disciples the erroneous theories that "since Judas had the money box, . . . Jesus was saying to him, 'Buy the things we have need of for the festival,' or that he should give something to the poor" (v. 29),[36] it is unclear whether he is looking into their minds (as omniscient narrator) or simply passing along conjectures which they later put into words.

Their theories were reasonable enough (though wrong) in light of the earlier notice that Judas indeed "had the money box" (12:6). The first, moreover, about needs "for the festival," stands as important evidence that the meal described here was *not* itself part of "the festival of the Passover" (v. 1). The second revisits Judas's question (which any of them might have asked), "Why was this perfume not sold for three hundred denarii and given to the poor?" (12:5).[37] Their conjectures are not inherently absurd (like Peter's request for a full bath, v. 9), but simply the consequence of not having heard what Jesus had said privately to "the disciple whom he loved." While it is odd (as interpreters have pointed out) that Judas would leave for either of those reasons so abruptly, and at night (v. 30),[38] it is just as odd that he would leave

---

35. This is more likely than that the disciple's privileged knowledge simply contradicts verse 28, where that knowledge is suddenly ignored. Lincoln argues that "the account would proceed smoothly" if one were to move directly from verse 22 to verse 26b, where Jesus "dipped the morsel" and gave it to Judas (see Lincoln, 378-79). But as we have seen, v. 26b is so closely tied (verbally) to Jesus' answer (v. 26a) to the beloved disciple (with the words, "dipped," "morsel," and "give") that the two can scarcely be separated. Alan Culpepper asks whether or not the disciple whom Jesus loved understood Jesus' gesture, and comments that if he did understand, "then one faces the question of why he did not tell the others or do anything to stop Judas. Naturally one could conjecture that the Beloved Disciple is presented as a disciple so close to Jesus that when Jesus shared with him the knowledge of his coming death and its significance, the Beloved Disciple guarded Jesus' divine knowledge" (*John the Son of Zebedee*, 60-61).

36. The abrupt shift from direct to indirect discourse is not without parallel in John's Gospel (see 20:18).

37. In view of the earlier narrative aside that Judas "was a thief," and "was stealing from what was being put in" the money box (12:6), the conjecture here carries more than a touch of irony.

38. There is considerable discussion over whether or not the shops would have been open at night, particularly in connection with the question of just how near the Passover festival was (see, for example, Brown, 2.576; Barrett, 448; Keener, 2.919-20;

in that way and at that time for any reason, including the real one. He does so, apparently, only because Jesus told him to.[39] He has been dismissed — this in contrast to the other three Gospels, where he is never said to have exited by himself, separating himself from the other disciples only after the meal (see Mk 14:26//Mt 26:30) but before their arrival at Gethsemane (see Mk 14:43// Mt 26:47//Lk 22:47).

30 The impression of haste is confirmed when Judas, "having taken the morsel, went out immediately,[40] and it was night" (v. 30). Both the adverb "immediately" and the mention of "night" imply a quick and abrupt departure. Earlier, Jesus warned his disciples that "Night is coming when no one can work" (9:4), yet assured them that at least a short time of daylight remained (see 11:9-10). Now, however, time is of the essence. "Night" is upon him and the other disciples, no less than upon Judas.[41] The expression, "having taken the morsel," belatedly confirms (as we have seen) what the "disciple whom Jesus loved" witnessed with his own eyes (v. 27). Here at the end of the account, it simply heightens the finality of Judas's action, and his consequent departure. Yet despite the finality, there is much more to tell. Judas "went out" here, but it will be more than four chapters later before we read that "Jesus went out with his disciples" (18:1). And despite the press of time, Judas's departure makes it possible for Jesus to speak to those other disciples at far greater length and with far greater openness than ever before.

31-32 Having shifted from discourse (vv. 12-20) to the narrative of Judas's departure (vv. 21-30), the text now shifts back again to discourse. The transition is accomplished by the simple repetition of a verb: Judas "went out immediately" (v. 30), and "when he had gone out" (v. 31), Jesus began speaking again in the presence of the disciples but in an oracular vein, as if to no one in particular. "Now the Son of man is glorified,[42] and God is glorified in him, and God will glorify himself in him,[43] and he will immedi-

---

Schnackenburg, 3.31). But Lincoln is surely correct that the point is "simply to illustrate graphically the gap between Jesus' awareness and his followers' incomprehension of what is taking place" (380).

39. So Barrett: "Judas was now simply and entirely a servant of Satan. Even so, and though he no longer holds his place with the Eleven, he is instantly obedient to the word of Jesus and goes out as he is bidden" (448).

40. Gr. εὐθύς.

41. It is unlikely that there is any real connection between the mention of "night" here and the detail that Nicodemus first came to Jesus "by night" (3:2).

42. Gr. ἐδοξάσθη.

43. That God will "glorify him in him" (δοξάσει αὐτὸν ἐν αὐτῷ) is as odd in Greek as it sounds in English. Consequently, a number of ancient manuscripts (including a corrector of ℵ, A, D, L, W, Θ, Ψ, and the majority of later witnesses) have "in himself"

ately glorify him" (v. 32).[44] The pronouncement echoes several others that Jesus made to his disciples in the first half of the Gospel: first, his claim that "If I glorify myself, my glory is nothing. It is my Father who glorifies me" (8:54); second, his comment on learning of the sickness of Lazarus, that "This sickness is not toward death, but for the glory of God, so that through it the Son of God might be glorified" (11:4); finally his speech to Andrew and Philip on learning of the desire of certain Greeks to see him, beginning with "The hour has come that the Son of man might be glorified" (12:23) and ending with "Father, glorify your name" (12:28).

Two things emerge from these comparisons. First, "Son of God" (11:4) and "Son of man" (12:23) are used interchangeably, suggesting that the same is true here.[45] More important, God is glorified precisely in and through the glorification of "the Son" (or "Son of man"), and this mutual glorification is the point that Jesus "now" drives home repeatedly. "Now" (v. 31) is pretty much equivalent to "the hour has come" (see 12:23, 27, 31; 13:1), but in the present context, "now" is the specific moment brought about by the departure of Judas (v. 30). "Now" Judas is gone, and Jesus announces to the gathered disciples his glorification, which is at the same time the glorification of God "in him." It is a moment both present — by virtue of Judas's departure, making Jesus' death on the cross a certainty — and future, anticipating the literal event itself. To paraphrase: "the Son of man is glorified" — *in*

(ἐν ἑαυτῷ). But the more difficult reading (with P⁶⁶, B, and the first hand of ℵ) is to be preferred (see Metzger, *Textual Commentary*, 242). Some interpreters resolve the problem by assuming a rough breathing (ἐν αὐτῷ), translated the same as ἐν ἑαυτῷ ("in himself"), or by an appeal to Hellenistic usage in which either form could be used reflexively as "in himself" (see Metzger, 615-16).

44. Most texts and versions follow a longer reading: "Now the Son of man is glorified, and God is glorified in him. If God is glorified in him [εἰ ὁ θεὸς ἐδοξάσθη ἐν αὐτῷ], God will also glorify him in himself, and he will glorify him immediately." The added words have modest support (with A, correctors of ℵ and C, K, Δ, Θ, Ψ, and the majority of later witnesses), but the external evidence for the shorter reading is overwhelming (with P⁶⁶, B, the first hand of ℵ and C, D, L, W, and others). It is commonly assumed that a whole clause was omitted accidentally by a scribe's eye dropping down to the next line (homoeoteleuton), but it is just as likely that ὁ θεὸς ἐδοξάσθη ἐν αὐτῷ was written once too often when a scribe's eye slipped back to the preceding line (haplography). Quite possibly a scribe, trying to make sense of the reduplication, added "if" (εἰ), creating a conditional sentence. By contrast, the shorter text preserves a straightforward series of coordinate clauses linked by "and" (καί): "*and* God [καὶ ὁ θεός] is glorified in him, *and* God will glorify [καὶ ὁ θεὸς δοξάσει] him in himself, *and* he will immediately glorify him" (καὶ εὐθὺς δοξάσει). Yet it should be acknowledged on all sides that the variant makes relatively little difference in meaning.

45. As we have seen, this is the case generally in John's Gospel (see, for example, 3:13-17; 5:25-27).

13:21-35 The Departure of Judas

his death; "and God is glorified in him" — that is, *in his death;* "and God will glorify him in him" — again, *in his death;*[46] and he will immediately glorify him" — in that *his death* is imminent).

Death, in short, is what Jesus' "glorification" is all about, and for his disciples his death means his departure from them and from the world. The writer intimated this at the very beginning of the chapter when he wrote that Jesus knew "his hour had come" (v. 1), an expression that seemed to imply the "hour" of his glorification (see 12:23, 27-28). Yet instead of his "hour to be glorified," the writer calls it "his hour . . . that he should be taken out of this world to the Father" (v. 1), adding that "he had come from God and was going to God" (v. 3). The implication is that Jesus' "glorification" (with its accompanying glorification of the Father) and his departure from the world take place at the same time and amount to the same thing. This will be confirmed in the next verse. The metaphor changes, but the reality to which it refers — death on the cross — is the same.

33 Jesus continues, now addressing his disciples very directly and personally: "Children, yet a short time I am with you. You will seek me, and just as I said to the Jews that 'Where I am going, you cannot come,' so I say to you now" (v. 33). Only here in the entire Gospel does he address them as "Children,"[47] that is, as actual small children, not simply offspring. This is perhaps a corollary of their characterization earlier as "his own" (v. 2), whom he loved. The affectionate address softens the bad news, that "yet a short time I am with you," that "You will seek me," and that "Where I am going you cannot come."

As Jesus reminds them, he said the very same thing "to the Jews," and in fact his words are virtually identical to what he told the delegation from "the chief priests and Pharisees" at the Tent festival: "Yet a short time I am with you, and I am going to the One who sent me. You will seek me and you will not find, and where I am you cannot come" (7:33-34), words that puzzled them (7:35-36) and prompted them to report back, "No man ever spoke

---

46. This interpretation provides an alternative to the reflexive understanding of ἐν αὐτῷ as "in himself." The parallel between ἐν αὐτῷ in v. 31 (referring to "the Son of man") and ἐν αὐτῷ here suggests that the antecedent is the same (Jesus), despite the awkwardness in translation. The awkwardness is reduced (though perhaps not removed) by reading "in him" (in both instances) as referring to Jesus' death on the cross: that is, God "glorifies" the Son by means of his death (while not exact equivalents, Eph 2:15, 16 and Col 2:15 are at least comparable, in that Jesus accomplishes certain things "in him" in the sense of "by his death").

47. Gr. τεκνία, the diminutive of τέκνα (see 1:12-13; 11:52). The author of 1 John commonly uses this designation (see 1 Jn 2:1, 12, 28; 3:7, 18; 4:4; 5:21; also παιδία in Jn 21:5 and in 1 Jn 2:14, 18). Jesus' use of the term here suggests that it does not necessarily imply a great difference in age between the speaker and those addressed.

like that" (7:46).[48] The only differences in wording are that here Jesus says nothing about "going to the One who sent me," and that instead of "where I am you cannot come," he says "Where I am going you cannot come."[49] He seems to be saying to his disciples that they are no better off than those Jewish authorities in that earlier scene, but hidden beneath that surface comparison lies a far deeper and more significant contrast. At the Tent festival, the authorities were "seeking" Jesus in order to arrest and kill him (see 5:18; 7:1, 19, 25, 30), but their threat against his life will be thwarted, for no one takes his life from him; as he says, "I lay it down on my own" (10:18). As far as they are concerned, Jesus' departure will vindicate him against them, for he will go "to the One who sent him," while they will "die in their sins" (see 8:21, 24). Here, by contrast, his disciples "will seek" him simply to be with him again, overcoming the pain of his absence. His imminent departure will not brand them as enemies, but only make them "orphans," and that temporarily (see 14:18). All this will come out in a series of questions and answers (13:36–14:31), but for the moment the prospect is grim. What kind of "glory" is it that produces only sorrow? Even "the Jews" were told where Jesus was going — "to the One who sent me" (7:33) — even though they did not understand (see 7:35-36; 8:22).[50] Here, by contrast, he does *not* tell his disciples where he is going, because, as far as they are concerned, there is far more to it than simply, "I am going to the One who sent me." The reader knows where Jesus is going, but the disciples do not. The question, "Where are you going?" will be asked — and answered — more than once, with ever deepening implications.

34 The most important question raised by Jesus' "glorification," understood as his departure from the world, is that of the disciples' responsibility in his absence. This he now states, in the simplest possible terms: "A new command[51] I give you, that you love each other, just as I loved you, that you too love each other" (v. 34). This "new command" could be viewed as the Johannine equivalent of "the new covenant" instituted similarly at a last meal according to Luke and Paul (Lk 22:20; 1 Cor 11:25). All our literary witnesses, in fact (see Mk 14:24; Mt 26:28), agree that something decisive occurred at Jesus' last meal with his disciples, something that determined how they would live, but the other sources connect that something to the church's observance of the Lord's Supper, while John's Gospel connects it instead

---

48. While this delegation of "officers" is not initially identified as "the Jews," they are so identified when their reaction is given (7:35).

49. "Where I an going" (ὅπου ἐγὼ ὑπάγω) agrees instead with 8:21, a similar pronouncement addressed later to "the Jews" at the same Tent festival.

50. The reason they did not understand was that they did not know "the One who sent him" (7:28-29).

51. Gr. ἐντολὴν καινήν.

with the everyday life of Jesus' disciples during his absence, particularly with their obligation to love and serve one another.

What makes the command "new"? Is it a new command *replacing* one or more older commands? Or a new command *in addition to* commands already familiar? Surely the latter. As we have seen, Jesus' references earlier to "doing the truth" (3:21), "doing good things" (5:29), or "doing his will" (7:17; see also 9:31; 1 Jn 2:17), imply an understanding of right conduct based on the Hebrew Scriptures and commandments handed down from Moses. Jesus' assumption all along has been that "if you believed Moses, you would believe me" (5:46). The acceptance of Jesus as God's unique messenger and agent has been the evidence of faithfulness to the "will of God" revealed in those ancient commandments (see especially 7:17, where those who "choose to do his will" are the ones who "will know about the teaching, whether it is from God, or whether I speak on my own"). Moreover, Jesus from here on will speak of his "commands" (plural) three times (14:15, 21; 15:10), and of the love "command" (singular) only once (15:12).[52] So we may not assume that the love command is the only command to be obeyed, much less that it is meant to replace (for example) the two great commands in the other three Gospels, love of God and love of neighbor (see Mk 12:28-34// Mt 22:34-40//Lk 10:25-28). If John's Gospel knows of that tradition (as 14:15, 21, 23, and 31 may well suggest), this "new" love command is an additional one placed alongside the "great, and first" command and the "second, like it" (Mt 22:38-39), "new" in two ways. First, it focuses attention not on the "neighbor" (defined in the Synoptics so broadly as to include the enemy), but rather on the fellow believer or disciple, thus accenting love's mutuality.[53] Second, and perhaps more important, it bases the command very explicitly on Jesus' love for "his own" disciples (v. 1), based in turn on the Father's love for his Son (see 3:35; 5:20; 15:9).

The form of this "new" command — "*just as* I loved you, that *you too* love each other" — matches the form of Jesus' stated "example" of footwashing — "so that *just as* I did for you, *you too* might do" (v. 15, italics added).[54] While Jesus did not speak of the latter as a "command," only as an

---

52. See also 15:14, "You are my friends if you do the things [plural] I command you" (ἃ ἐγὼ ἐντέλλομαι ὑμῖν), and 15:17, "These things [plural] I command you [ταῦτα ἐντέλλομαι ὑμῖν], that you love each other." For the plural "commands," see also 1 John 2:3, 4; 3:22, 24; 5:2; 3 (twice); 2 John 6 (eight times in all, as opposed to ten occurrences of the singular "command" in 1 and 2 John).

53. Yet while this emphasis may have been "new" on the lips of the historical Jesus, it was not exactly new at the time the Gospel was written, for it is common in early Christian traditions quite distinct from John's Gospel (see, for example, 1 Thess 4:9; Rom 12:10; Eph 5:2; Heb 13:1; 1 Pet 1:22; 2:17; 4:8).

54. Gr. καθὼς . . . καὶ ὑμεῖς in both instances.

obligation, something the disciples "ought" to do (v. 14), and are "blessed" for doing (v. 17), the similarity of structure is evident. Both pronouncements combine a "vertical," one-way relationship (that is, from a Lord or King to subordinates) with a "horizontal," two-way relationship (that is, a mutual relationship among peers). Jesus takes the initiative to love (and show his love for) his disciples. Nothing is said of their loving him first, or even in return, and they are not allowed to reciprocate by washing his feet. Instead, they extend his love to "each other," whether specifically by washing each other's feet (vv. 14-15), or more generally in the daily conduct of their lives (vv. 34-35). Such a structure, with its "vertical" and "horizontal" axis, can be seen not only here but in several other New Testament passages, whether the subject matter is mutual love (see 15:12; 1 Jn 3:16; 4:11; Eph 5:2), forgiveness (Eph 4:32; Col 3:13), or acceptance (Rom 15:7).

The parallel between the love command and the footwashing offers a possible answer to the question raised earlier, as to whether or not footwashing represented within the Christian communities the mutual forgiveness of sins committed after baptism, in the sense that believers actually "cleansed" each other as Jesus by his death had cleansed them once and for all. "Wash each other's feet" could easily enough be heard as "Forgive each other, as I have forgiven you" (see Eph 4:32; Col 3:13; and compare Mt 6:14-15; 18:21-35; Mk 11:25;). But as we have seen, any such theory must remain only implicit, not explicit, as far as John's Gospel is concerned. As I have stated elsewhere, "Just as John's Gospel views Christian conversion and baptism positively as the giving of life rather than negatively as repentance from sin, so it views footwashing among believers positively as mutual love rather than negatively as mutual forgiveness of sins."[55] While the principle common in the ancient church that "love covers many sins" (see 1 Pet 4:8; Jas 5:20; *1 Clement* 49.5; *2 Clement* 16.4) may well have been a tacit presupposition of the Gospel writer, it never quite comes to the surface. Because John's Gospel — in contrast to 1 John[56] — says little about the sins of believers, it says nothing explicitly about how such sins are forgiven, only about the responsibility of believers to "love each other."

35 Jesus next reinforces the "new command" of mutual love with a promise: "By this they all will know that you are my disciples, if you have love for each other"[57] (v. 35), drawing together their responsibility to one another (see vv. 14-15) and their responsibility to the whole world as Jesus' messengers (see vv. 16, 20). "They all" are all those who have the opportunity to observe the conduct of Jesus' disciples in his absence, potentially at least everyone in

---

55. Michaels, "By Water and Blood," 153.
56. See, for example, 1 Jn 1:7, 9; 2:1-2; 4:10; 5:16-17.
57. Gr. ἐν ἀλλήλοις (literally, "among each other").

the world. Jesus will spell out the point more eloquently later in his final prayer to the Father "that they might be perfected into one, so that the world might know that you sent me and loved them just as you loved me" (17:23).

Here, however, it should not be assumed that their status as Jesus' "disciples" was an assured fixed relationship that they could afford to take for granted, and that only needed to be "made known" to the rest of the world. He has said elsewhere to another group, "If you remain in my word, you are truly my disciples" (8:31), and he will say again to this group, "In this my Father is glorified, that you bear much fruit and become my disciples" (15:8). Therefore, the likely meaning here is something like, "By this you will become my disciples — or prove to be my disciples — and everyone will know it." With this, Jesus drives home the "new command" of love in the same way he drove home the command to wash each other's feet, with a concluding conditional clause, "*if* you have love for each other" (italics added; compare v. 17, "Now that you understand these things, blessed are you *if* you do them"). The rest is up to those who call themselves "disciples." Interestingly, Jesus' disciples on the scene never respond directly either to the footwashing or the love command. John's Gospel leaves that to the reader.

C. FOUR QUESTIONS (13:36–14:31)

13:36 *Simon Peter says to him, "Lord, where are you going?" Jesus answered him, "Where I am going you cannot follow now, but you will follow later."*

37 *Peter says to him, "Why can I not follow you now? I will lay down my life for you!"*

38 *Jesus answers, "You will lay down your life for me? Amen, amen, I say to you, never will a rooster crow until you have denied me three times.*

14:1 *Let no one's heart be shaken! Believe in God, and believe in me!* 2 *In my Father's household are many dwellings. If not, I would have told you that I am going off to prepare a place for you.* 3 *And if I go off and prepare a place for you, I am coming back and I will take you to myself, so that where I am you too might be.* 4 *And where I am going, you know the way."*

5 *Thomas says to him, "Lord, we do not know where you are going. How can we know the way?"*

6 *Jesus says to him, "I am the Way, and the Truth, and the Life. No one comes to the Father except through me.* 7 *If you all have known me, you will know my Father too, and from now on you know him, and you have seen him."*

8 *Philip says to him, "Lord, show us the Father, and it's enough for us."*

9 *Jesus says to him, "Such a long time I am with you all, and you, Philip, have not known me? The person who has seen me has seen the Father. How can you say, 'Show us the Father'?* 10 *Do you not believe that I am in the Father, and the Father in me?*

"The words that I am saying to you all I am not speaking on my own, but the Father, dwelling in me, is doing his works. 11 Believe me, that I am in the Father, and the Father in me, but if not, believe because of those very works. 12 Amen, amen, I say to you all, the person who believes in me, the works I am doing that person will also do, and greater than these he will do because I am going to the Father. 13 And whatever you ask in my name, this I will do, so that the Father might be glorified in the Son. 14 *If you ask me anything in my name, I will do.*

15 *If you love me, you will keep my commands.* 16 *And I will ask the Father, and he will give you another advocate, that he might be with you forever,* 17 *the Spirit of truth, which the world cannot receive, because it neither sees it nor knows it. You do know it, because it dwells beside you, and is in you.* 18 *I will not leave you orphaned. I am coming to you.* 19 *Yet a short time, and the world no longer sees me, but you see me, because I live — and you too will live.* 20 *In that day, you will come to know that I am in my Father, and you in me, and I in you.* 21 *The person having my commands and keeping them, that person it is who loves me, and the person who loves me will be loved by my Father, and I will love him, and I will reveal myself to him."*

22 *Judas, not the Iscariot, says to him, "Lord, and how come you are going to reveal yourself to us and not to the world?"*

23 *Jesus answered and said to him, "If anyone loves me, he will keep my word, and my Father will love him, and we will come to him, and we will make a dwelling right beside him.* 24 *The person who does not love me does not keep my words, and the word which you all hear is not mine but the Father's who sent me.*

25 "These things I have spoken to you while dwelling beside you. 26 But the Advocate, the Holy Spirit, whom the Father will send in my name, he will teach you all things and remind you of all things that I said to you. 27 Peace I leave with you, my peace I give you. Not as the world gives do I give to you. Let no one's heart be shaken, nor let it be fearful! 28 You heard that I said to you, 'I am going away, and I am coming to you.' If you loved me, you would rejoice that I am going off to the Father, because the Father is greater than I. 29 And now I have told before it happens, so that when it happens you might believe. 30 I will no longer speak with you very much, for the ruler of the world is

13:36–14:31 FOUR QUESTIONS

coming, and in me he has nothing. 31 But that the world might come to know that I love the Father, and just as the Father commanded me, thus I do. Rise, let's get out of here!"

Ignoring for the moment Jesus' pronouncements about glorification (13:31-32) and the "new command" to love each other (vv. 34-35), his disciples fasten their attention solely on his words, "Children, yet a short time I am with you. You will seek me, and just as I said to the Jews that 'Where I go, you cannot come,' so I say to you now" (v. 33). Four disciples in turn question him on that issue: Peter (13:36-37), Thomas (14:5), Philip (14:8), and Judas (another Judas; not the Iscariot, who has left the scene, 14:22). Jesus answers each in turn, speaking first to the individual and then to the whole group, explaining where he is going, what the benefits of his departure will be, and how he will return to them. The answer to Philip (vv. 9-21, 28 lines of Greek text) is markedly longer than the answer to the first two, and the answer to Judas (vv. 23-31) is not much shorter (21 lines of Greek text). As the chapter goes on, the question-and-answer exchanges give way to an almost unbroken discourse of Jesus, ending with a sort of rallying cry, "Rise, let's get out of here!" (v. 31). And even that cry will not bring the discourse to an end, for Jesus will continue an uninterrupted monologue (on a variety of issues, not limited to his departure) from 14:23 all the way to 16:16, his longest continuous speech in the entire Gospel.

This observation is based on the canonical Gospel as it has been handed down through the centuries. Much recent scholarship, however, has centered on the abrupt break at 14:31, which seems to terminate the discourse, leading us to expect something immediately that actually turns out to be deferred for three whole chapters: "Having said these things, Jesus went out with his disciples" (18:1) — just as Judas "went out" after taking the morsel (13:30). On this basis, two distinct "farewell discourses" of Jesus have been posited:[1] 13:36–14:31,[2] centering on the single theme of Jesus' impending departure, and 15:1–17:26, a much longer discourse embracing several themes,

---

1. Most famously in the commentaries of Brown (as part of his well-known five-stage theory of composition, 1.xxxiv-xxxix; also 2.581-604), and Schnackenburg (for example, 3.89-93).

2. Or more commonly 13:31–14:31 (with both Brown and Schnackenburg), on the obvious ground that 13:36 is Peter's response to a pronouncement made already in v. 33. Yet vv. 31-35 introduce issues which are not addressed in 13:36–14:31, only in chapters 15–17, suggesting that those verses may be linked as closely to the latter as to the former, or even had an existence of their own independent of (and perhaps prior to) *both* of the proposed "farewell discourses." It is not impossible that the text at one stage of the tradition might have moved directly from 13:35 to 18:1 ("Having said these things") and on into the passion narrative.

including mutual indwelling and the love command (15:1-17), persecution and hatred by the world (15:18–16:4a), Jesus' departure (16:4b-33), and a long prayer of Jesus (17:1-26) picking up the themes of glorification, the unity of believers, and their mission to the world. Beyond the obvious difference in scope, a number of other small but significant differences in emphasis and terminology have also been noticed between the two discourses, and these will be discussed as they come up. If one is looking for chiasm, it is possible (as we have seen) to structure chapters 15–17 in relation to 13:31-35 in reverse order: first — if one is willing to subordinate the theme of indwelling in Jesus to that of mutual love — the love command (15:1-17, corresponding to 13:34-35), with the world's hatred as the price of love (15:18–16:4a); second, a slightly different treatment of the departure theme (16:4b-33, corresponding to 13:33); finally, Jesus's glorification (as in 13:31-32, if one is willing to see that as the major theme of Jesus' last prayer in chapter 17).

While such a construct is attractive, it is also speculative, and should not be allowed to override the particulars of the text when we come to them. Nor should anything that has been said, or can be said, about two farewell discourses be allowed to override the canonical text as it stands. No textual evidence exists suggesting that either discourse was added later, whether by the same author or someone else. Whatever the *history* of its composition, the Gospel of John now contains a very extensive farewell discourse of Jesus, punctuated at some points by questions from his disciples, and at other points an unbroken monologue. While it can be fairly divided into two parts, 13:36–14:31 and 15:1–17:26, no reader is given a right to change their order, choose between them, or in any way privilege one over the other. The task of interpreting the Gospel is formidable enough without undertaking to rewrite it.

36 Undaunted by his failure to learn the betrayer's identity, Simon Peter pursues another question, "Lord, where are you going?" (v. 36a), fastening on Jesus' words, "Where I am going, you cannot come" (v. 33). The reader already knows where Jesus is going — to "the One who sent him" (see 7:33) — and expects Peter to know as well, but he does not. Quite possibly Peter is thinking of death, and not so much asking information about Jesus' destination as uttering a plaintive cry, "Lord, *why* are you going? Why must you leave us?" Jesus answers him accordingly, not giving a destination but instead assuring him, "Where I am going you cannot follow now, but you will follow later."[3] If Jesus' departure is his death, Peter will indeed "follow later" in due course. Peter's death, like Jesus' own, will even "glorify God" (see 21:18-19).

37 Peter seems to understand that "following" Jesus means death, at

---

3. The form of the answer recalls Jesus' earlier response to Peter, "What I am doing [ὃ ἐγὼ ποιῶ] you do not understand now [ἄρτι], but afterward [μετὰ ταῦτα] you will understand" (v. 7).

13:36–14:31 FOUR QUESTIONS

least potentially. "Lord,"[4] he exclaims, "why can I not follow you now? I will lay down my life for you!" (v. 37). Not "later" (v. 36), but "now." Readers familiar with other Gospels will remember Peter's rash promises,[5] but here one senses an added note of absurdity. The promise, "I will lay down my life for you!"[6] echoes almost verbally Jesus' own claim as "the good Shepherd" that "I lay down my life for the sheep" (10:15), with "authority to lay it down," and "authority to receive it back" (10:18). Whether Peter means "I will risk my life for you" (as any good shepherd does for his sheep, 10:11), or "I will give my life for you" (as Jesus does for his disciples, 10:15, 18), his words come through as an absurd parody of Jesus' own,[7] putting him in control of his own "soul," or life, as if to say (with Jesus), "No one took it away from me, but I lay it down on my own" (see 10:18). Eventually, Jesus will make it clear to him that "later," when he does "follow," exactly the opposite will be true (see 21:18). He is not in control, now or later.

38 Jesus' skeptical reply, "You will lay down your life for me?" (v. 38a), echoing Peter's own words, exposes the emptiness of his rash promise on different grounds from those just mentioned — grounds the reader knows nothing about. "Amen, amen, I say to you," he continues, "never will a rooster crow until you have denied me three times." This is the twenty-first "Amen, amen" saying in the Gospel, but Jesus has not used it in addressing a single individual[8] since chapter 3 (Nicodemus in 3:3, 5, and 11). While he addressed Nicodemus there as representative of a group (see 3:11-12), here he speaks to Peter individually about his personal history. The pronouncement has to do with Peter and no one else (see also 21:18). It is little different

---

4. Some important ancient witnesses (including the first hand of א, 33, 565, the Vulgate, and Sy^s) omit "Lord" (κύριε), as in v. 8, where Peter's emphatic disclaimer, "You shall never ever wash my feet!" similarly lacked an accompanying address to Jesus as "Lord." The omission is plausible because Peter is just as emphatic and excited here as he was there. All the other questions Jesus is asked in this sequence (by Peter, v. 36; Thomas, 14:5; Philip, 14:8; and Judas, 14:22) begin with "Lord," and it is possible that the address was added for the sake of consistency. Still, the textual evidence for retaining "Lord" (with P^{66}, B, a corrector of א, A, C, D, L, W, Δ, Θ, Ψ, and the majority of later witnesses) is somewhere between strong and overwhelming. The longer reading deserves the benefit of the doubt (see Metzger, *Textual Commentary,* 242).

5. These include a willingness to die (see Lk 22:33, "ready to go with you to prison and to death"; also Mk 14:31//Mt 26:35).

6. Gr. τὴν ψυχήν μου ὑπὲρ σοῦ θήσω.

7. As Barrett puts it, "John makes Peter assume language which is peculiarly applicable to Jesus. But this is absurd; to lay down one's life in the sense in which Jesus lays down his means complete obedience to the Father and perfect love for men, neither of which does Peter possess. . . . In fact, the truth is the reverse of what Peter thinks" (453).

8. That is, Ἀμὴν ἀμὴν λέγω σοι ("you" singular) rather than Ἀμὴν ἀμὴν λέγω ὑμῖν ("you" plural).

from what Jesus tells Peter at the end of the meal in the other three Gospels,[9] and it is fulfilled just as literally (see 18:17, 25, 27). In contrast to Matthew (26:35) and Mark (14:31), Peter says nothing in response.[10]

14:1 With this, Jesus abruptly stops speaking to Peter alone, and begins to address the whole group: "Let no one's heart be shaken! Believe in God, and believe in me!" (v. 1). The twin imperatives for "believe" are plural,[11] signaling the change of audience from Peter to all the disciples gathered at the table (vv. 1-4). In contrast to the grim warning to Peter (v. 38), the words addressed to the group are words of comfort. Jesus encourages them to "believe" or "keep on believing" in God and in him not in a generalized or merely confessional sense, but specifically in relation to his departure and their hope for the future. That is, "trust God, and trust me; there is no need to be troubled or fearful." This is in keeping with his consistent claim that he is sent from God, and that to believe in him and to believe in "the One who sent him" amount to exactly the same thing (see 12:44). It is also in keeping with the principle in the Mosaic law that "the testimony of two men is true," in the sense that "I am the one who testifies about myself, and the Father who sent me testifies about me" (see 8:17-18).

"Let no one's heart be shaken!" is literally, "Let not your heart be shaken!"[12] (with "heart" singular but "your" a plural pronoun). One might have expected "your hearts" (plural), but "heart" is always singular in this Gospel, even when it is the heart of many.[13] With Judas gone, Jesus' disciples share a common "heart," with common concerns and similar kinds of questions. Let it not be "shaken,"[14] he tells them, even though he himself has

---

9. See Matthew 26:34//Mark 14:30//Luke 22:34. The differences are minor: Matthew and Mark use the "Amen, I say to you" formula, while Luke has simply, "I say to you." Matthew mentions "this night," while Luke speaks of "today," and Mark (somewhat redundantly) mentions both. Mark alone allows one crowing of the rooster, insisting only that it will not happen "twice" before Peter's triple denial.

10. See, however, Luke 22:34, where Peter is similarly silent. On balance, the account of Peter in John's Gospel is more like Luke's than the others, for Luke also hints at Peter's restoration (see Lk 22:32).

11. Gr. πιστεύετε, which can be read as either indicative ("you believe") or imperative ("believe"). While some English versions have translated the first as the one and the second as the other (see the KJV, "Ye believe in God, believe also in me"), there is no reason to translate them differently. The preceding imperative "Let no one's heart be shaken" strongly supports that reading. An indicative is unlikely to have been sandwiched between two imperatives.

12. Gr. ὑμῶν ἡ καρδία.

13. See 14:27; 16:6, 22 (all with the expression ὑμῶν ἡ καρδία). Even those who do not believe in Jesus share a common "heart," albeit a hardened and uncomprehending one (see 12:40).

14. Gr. μὴ ταρασσέσθω.

been "shaken" or troubled in spirit more than once (see 11:33; 12:27), even at this very meal (v. 21). But all that is over, as he now offers them peace and reassurance.

2 "In my Father's household are many dwellings," he continues. "In my Father's household"[15] does not mean in the Jerusalem temple, as in 2:16 ("Stop making my Father's house[16] a house of trade!"), nor in the heavenly temple (which is not mentioned at all in John's Gospel), but in heaven itself, understood as a household, in keeping with the household imagery of certain passages in the Gospel. Above all, the "household" of God recalls 8:35-36, where Jesus told some "Jews who had believed" that "the slave does not remain in the household[17] forever; the son remains forever. So if the Son sets you free, you will really be free." Jesus offered them freedom, and with it the opportunity to "remain" or dwell in God's household. They refused, but here Jesus reiterates to his disciples that there are indeed "many dwellings,"[18] that is, plenty of room in that household for those whom the Son sets free.[19] While the verb "remain" or "dwell" is very common in John's Gospel, the noun "dwelling" or dwelling place occurs only twice (here and in v. 23, the only occurrences in the entire New Testament). The traditional "many mansions" (KJV) is based on the Latin Vulgate's *mansiones multae,* "many stations" or "stopping places," from an ancient interpretation of the saying as referring to places of rest along the way on the soul's journey to heaven — a view that has few adherents today.[20] More commonly, parallels from Jewish apocalyptic literature are duly noted about "dwelling places of the holy ones" in heaven.[21] Yet the emphasis here is not on separate or individual rooms or

---

15. Gr. ἐν τῇ οἰκίᾳ τοῦ πατρός μου.
16. Gr. τὸν οἶκον.
17. Gr. ἐν τῇ οἰκίᾳ.
18. Gr. μοναὶ πολλαί.
19. The "household" (οἰκία) in both passages evokes the world of Jesus' parables. It is a patriarchal and (to us) curiously incomplete household, with a father but no mother, a son (or sons) but no daughter, and slaves, presumably male (see 5:20 and 15:15 for further glimpses of that parabolic "household," though without using the actual word). For the "household" as the sphere of God's authority in the other Gospels (especially in parables), see, for example, Matthew 10:25; 13:27; 24:45-51; Mark 13:34, 35; Luke 12:35-38; 13:25; 14:21; 15:11-32.

20. See, however, Westcott, 2.167. Brown (2.618-19) adds the comment that although the Latin had this meaning, the word "mansion" in Old English had no such meaning, nor did it mean a palatial estate. It meant simply "dwelling place."

21. See *1 Enoch* 39.4-5 (*OTP,* 1.30-31); also, for example, *2 Enoch* 61.2, "Many shelters have been prepared for people, good ones for the good, but bad ones for the bad, without number" (*OTP,* 1.186), or *4 Ezra* 7.95, where the righteous are "gathered into their chambers and guarded by angels in profound quiet" (*OTP,* 1.540). Even in the New Testament itself, see Luke 16:9, "make friends for yourselves from the unrighteous

compartments, but simply on the fact that there are "many" such dwellings in heaven, more than enough for the disciples around the table, and all of the "many" who were said to have "believed" in Jesus in the course of the narrative (4:39, 41; 10:42; 11:45) — even those who will never go there (see 2:23; 8:30; 12:42) — and for all future believers (see 17:20, 24).

Jesus goes on to provide added assurance that this is in fact the case: "If not, I would have told you that I am going off to prepare a place for you." The translation is based on one of three (at least) possible ways of reading the text. The traditional strategy has been to divide the pronouncement into two sentences: "If not, I would have told you. For I am going off to prepare a place for you" (see KJV, NIV, NEB, REB). The implication is that Jesus' disciples already knew (by default, as it were) that in the Father's household were "many dwellings," so that there would be plenty of room for them. They would only need to be notified if that were *not* the case. Consequently, the accent falls on Jesus' solemn promise right here and now, "I am going away to prepare a place for you." With "many dwellings" available, he is able to go on ahead and make room in heaven for all "his own who are in the world" (see 13:1). The difficulty with this is that dividing the pronouncement is very unnatural.[22] A new sentence begins with a conjunction[23] which has to be translated "For" or "Because." It is far more natural, however, to translate it as "that," particularly when it immediately follows "I would have told you."[24] The latter prompts the question "Told them what?" Merely that there was no room in the Father's household? Not likely. The more likely answer by far is that he told them "that I am going away to prepare a place for you."

The second way of reading the text acknowledges this point, but turns the declarative sentence into a question: "If not, would I have told you that I am going off[25] to prepare a place for you?" (see RSV, NRSV, TNIV,

---

wealth, so that when it runs out they may receive you into the eternal dwellings (σκηναῖς, literally "tents"). On the entire Jewish, Hellenistic, and gnostic background of the expression, see G. Fischer, *Die himmlischen Wohnungen: Untersuchungen zu Joh. 14.2f.* (Bern/Frankfurt: Lang, 1975).

22. Barrett avoids dividing it into two sentences, but his strategy of creating a parenthesis has the same effect, and is open to the same objection: "There will be many abiding-places (and if it had not been so I would have told you), for I am going to prepare a place for you" (457; so too Morris, 568 and others).

23. Gr. ὅτι.

24. Gr. εἶπον ἂν ὑμῖν. A number of ancient witnesses (including the first hand of P[66], Δ, Θ, 28, 700, and the majority of later manuscripts) omit the ὅτι altogether, but this reading is highly suspect as an attempt to relieve a very real difficulty (Metzger, *Textual Commentary*, 243, agrees, but on the simpler ground that ὅτι introducing a direct or indirect quote is "often omitted as superfluous").

25. Gr. πορεύομαι.

NAB, NLT). The point is that Jesus did tell them just that, and would not done so unless there were plenty of room for them in the Father's household. This sets the stage perfectly for the next verse: "And if I go off and prepare a place for you, I am coming back and I will take you to myself, so that where I am you too might be" (v. 3).[26] The difficulty, however, is that Jesus is never represented as saying such a thing anywhere else in the Gospel. He could be referring to a text known from the tradition but not actually found in the Gospel, or (more likely) he could be drawing on something that was implicit rather than explicit in his words.[27] Once again, 8:35-36 comes to mind, where Jesus offers his hearers a permanent place in the "household" of God, a place that would otherwise not be theirs. Yet nothing was said there about "going away" in order to make such a thing possible. Other texts might conceivably come into play, such as "I, if I be lifted up from the earth, will draw them all to myself" (12:32), especially when the latter is coupled with the preceding promise that "where I am, there my servant will be" (12:26). Yet these shed more light on the next verse (14:3) than on the present one. The absence of any explicit precedent for the saying remains a problem.

The most straightforward reading of the text is like the preceding one, except as a declarative statement rather than as a question: "If not, I would have told you that I am going off to prepare a place for you." The point seems to be that if there were *not* "many dwellings" in his Father's household, Jesus would have had to go away in order to provide them, and in that case he would have told the disciples so. But in fact he has not told them that, because there was adequate room already. This obviously agrees with the fact that no such explicit statement to that effect can be found in earlier chapters of the Gospel. The difficulty comes in the next verse ("And if I go off and prepare a place for you . . ."), which implies the contrary — that Jesus *is* in fact going off for that very purpose.[28] Consequently this way of reading the text has few advocates among modern interpreters or translators of the Gospel.[29]

---

26. If there is a difference between "going away" (ὑπάγειν, 13:33, 36; 14:4) and "going off" (πορεύεσθαι, 14:2, 3), it is that the former emphasizes departure or absence, while the latter means simply to embark on a journey. Abbott (*Johannine Grammar*, 109-10) makes a great deal, too much in fact, out of this distinction.

27. In at least one other instance Jesus mentions something he said previously which is difficult to verify in the actual text of the Gospel (see 6:36, which quite possibly refers back to 5:37-38).

28. While "if I go" (ἐὰν πορευθῶ) is a future condition, not a first-class condition implying reality, the clause functions here (as in 12:32) to imply future reality, as if to say "when I go" (see also 16:7).

29. One exception among modern translators is Richmond Lattimore: "Were there not, I would have said to you that I was going to make ready a place for you." Among an-

Is there a way out of the dilemma? Perhaps the answer lies with the expression, "if not," or "otherwise."[30] It is commonly assumed that it refers to the immediately preceding words, "In my Father's household are many dwellings" — that is, "if it were not so" (as in the KJV), meaning if in fact there were *not* "many dwellings" in the household.[31] But then Jesus should have said, "I would have gone off to prepare a place for you," rather than "I would have *told you* that I am going off to prepare a place for you." It appears to have been a question not of whether there was actually room enough in the Father's household for the disciples, but of whether or not they believed, or understood, that there was room enough. Edwin Abbott calls attention to this, pointing out that "if not" characteristically follows "an expressed or implied imperative."[32] He cites a conspicuous example within this same chapter: "Believe me, that I am in the Father and the Father in me, but if not, believe because of those very works" (v. 11). Here too, Abbott reminds us, are preceding imperatives, "Believe in God, and believe in me!" (v. 1), suggesting that "if not," or "otherwise," is introduced in relation to these, not in relation to the adequacy "the Father's household." The passage might then be paraphrased roughly as follows: "Trust me, that there is enough room in my Father's household. If I thought you did not believe or understand that, then instead of saying 'Where I am going, you cannot come' (13:33), I would have told you, in order to reassure you, 'I am going off to prepare a place for you.'"[33] Jesus has in fact moved halfway in that direction already by confiding to Peter, "Where I am going you cannot follow now, but you will follow later" (13:36). The fact that Peter would follow later implied already that Jesus' departure would have the positive purpose of making a way or "prepar-

---

cient interpreters, it seems to have been Chrysostom's reading of the text (see *Homilies on St. John* 73.2; ANF, 1st ser., 14.268), and Augustine's as well (*Tractates on John* 68.1), the latter of whom struggled at length with its difficulties: "How is it that He goes and prepares a place, if there are many mansions already? If there were not such, He would have said, 'I go to prepare.' Or if the place has still to be prepared, would He not then also properly have said, 'I go to prepare'?" (NPNF, 1st ser., 7.322).

30. Gr. εἰ δὲ μή.

31. "If it were not so" would be a literal translation of εἰ δὲ μὴ οὕτως ἦν, not εἰ δὲ μή, "if not" or "otherwise" (see Abbott, *Johannine Grammar*, 110).

32. *Johannine Grammar*, 109, citing evidence from the LXX and the New Testament.

33. This appears to be Abbott's view (*Johannine Grammar*, 109-11), although he weakens his case somewhat by drawing an overly sharp distinction between "going away" (ὑπάγειν) and "going off" (πορεύεσθαι). His contention that ὑπάγειν necessarily means to "go back" or "go home" is unsubstantiated. While the two verbs are not exact synonyms (see above, n. 26), they do overlap considerably in meaning (see, for example, v. 28; also 16:7, where πορεύεσθαι is used interchangeably with ἀπέρχεσθαι, another word meaning "to go away").

ing a place," not just for Peter but for all the disciples.[34] That is their hope and consolation.

3 Building on that reassurance, Jesus draws a conclusion. Verbal repetition carries the thought forward. He could have said merely, "And if go off, I am coming back," but instead he repeats the whole clause from the preceding verse. "And if I go off and prepare a place for you, I am coming back,"[35] adding that "I will take you to myself, so that where I am you too might be" (v. 3). This is the only instance in the entire New Testament in which Jesus speaks of "coming back" or "coming again,"[36] and thus the only explicit evidence in the Gospels of a "second" coming of Jesus (see, however, Heb 9:28). Evidence for a "second coming" in the other Gospels rests on a number of passages where Jesus speaks in the third person of the Son of man "coming."[37] These can be set over against just one passage (in a context corresponding roughly to the present one) in which the Son of man "goes away" (Mt 26:24; Mk 14:21) or "goes off" (Lk 22:22) — apparently as a result of being "handed over" to death. A striking feature of the synoptic tradition is that it speaks repeatedly of the Son of man's impending death and repeatedly of his future "coming," but never of both in the same pronouncement.[38] Consequently, some interpreters (Rudolf Bultmann most famously) have concluded that Jesus meant someone other than himself when he spoke of the Son of man "coming." John's Gospel, by contrast, draws together the "going" (in death) and the "coming," so that the "coming" is explicitly defined as "coming back" or "coming again," at the same time substituting "I" for "the Son of man."[39] This step is not altogether un-

---

34. As Chrysostom paraphrased it, "The same place which receiveth Peter shall receive you" (*Homilies on St. John* 73.2; ANF, 1st ser., 14.268).

35. Gr. πάλιν ἔρχομαι.

36. He does say, two chapters later, "A short time and you no longer see me, and again [πάλιν] a short time and you will see me" (see 16:16, 17, 19), and "I will see you again" (πάλιν δὲ ὄψομαι, 16:22).

37. In still other passages the Son of man is represented as having already "come" (ἦλθεν or ἐλήλυθεν), just as Jesus can claim, "I have come" (ἦλθον or ἐλήλυθα).

38. The nearest thing to an exception is Luke 17:24-25 (albeit without the use of the words "come" or "coming"): "For as the lightning flashes and lights the sky from one end to the other, so the Son of man will be in his day. *But first* [πρῶτον δέ] he must suffer many things and be rejected by this generation" (italics added).

39. Andrew Lincoln also notices this: "John creatively brings together the two issues of Jesus' going and coming, draws traditional material from Jesus' apocalyptic discourse into a farewell speech, and in the process reinterprets what is meant by the coming, so that it is no longer simply an event at the end of history but one which is already being experienced by Jesus' followers in the present" (384). This is the case in the chapter as a whole, but these opening verses, as we will see, are still dealing with "an event at the end of history."

precedented even in the Synoptics, where (without mentioning "the Son of man") Jesus can speak in a parable of "a man on a journey leaving his household, and giving authority to his slaves," commanding his disciples, "Keep watch, then, for you do not know when the lord of the household is coming" (Mk 13:34-37). In John's Gospel "the lord of the household" — or at least the Son in the Father's "household" (see v. 2 and 8:35-36) — speaks for himself in the first person: "If I go off, . . . I am coming back" (v. 3a).

Then Jesus continues, explaining to his disciples what his "coming back" or "coming again" will mean to them: "and I will take you[40] to myself, so that where I am you too might be" (v. 3b). This is consistent with the future "coming" of the Son of man in the other three Gospels, where Jesus promises that the Son of man will "send his angels and will gather his elect from the four winds, from the ends of the earth to the ends of the sky" (Mk 13:27; also Mt 24:31), and with Paul's vision of that same event (see 1 Thess 4:16-17).[41] It is also consistent with certain passages in John's Gospel itself that contemplate a time when "all who are in the tombs will hear his voice, and those who have done good things will go out to a resurrection of life" (5:28-29), or when, as Jesus said, "I will raise him up at the last day" (see 6:39, 40, 44, 54). Moreover, it helps to clarify two other passages, one in which Jesus spoke of "other sheep" that he "must bring," so that all will become "one flock, one Shepherd" (10:16), and another where Caiaphas prophesied that Jesus would die "in order that the children of God who are scattered might also be gathered into one" (11:52). Now we learn that in "bringing" or "gathering into one" those who belong to him, Jesus is taking them, as he says, "to myself" (as in 12:32, 'And I, if I be lifted up from the earth, will draw them all to myself'). He promises his disciples, "I will take you to myself,[42] so that where I am[43] you too might be," drawing together 12:32 with 12:26, "If anyone would serve me, let him follow me, and where I am, there my servant will be." In doing so, he combines two competing images, that of "following" Jesus of one's own volition (12:26; also 13:36), and that of being "taken" (as here) or "drawn" to him almost forcibly (12:32), and solely at his sovereign initiative (see also 6:44). The tension between those two images is never fully resolved in

40. Gr. καὶ παραλήμψομαι ὑμᾶς.
41. The expression, "I will take you [παραλήμψομαι ὑμᾶς] to myself," evokes another synoptic saying of Jesus about two individuals, of whom "the one shall be taken [παραλημφήσεται] and the other left" (Lk 17:34-35; see also Mt 24:40-41), even though commentators are divided as to whether being "taken" in those passages implies salvation or judgment.
42. Gr. πρὸς ἐμαυτόν.
43. Gr. ὅπου εἰμὶ ἐγώ.

the course of the chapter, nor for that matter in the entire Gospel or the entire New Testament.

4 "And where I am going," Jesus concludes, "you know the way" (v. 4). He does not claim in so many words that they know *where* he is going, though he has implied, almost unmistakably, that he is going to "my Father's household" (v. 2), that is, to the Father himself in heaven. Instead, he claims only that they know "the way."[44] His point is that if they truly know "the way," they do not even need to know the destination, for their arrival at the right destination is guaranteed. There is an ambiguity to "the way"[45] that the reader must be aware of, even though the disciples are not. "The way" is not a literal road or path, nor a mere set of directions, but metaphorically a "way" of life, a commitment to "follow" Jesus, as stated earlier (again, see 12:26, "If anyone would serve me, let him follow me, and where I am, there my servant will be").

The best commentary on "the way" as it is used in the Gospel of John comes not from the professional commentators, but from John Bunyan's classic, *The Pilgrim's Progress,* where Christian, the pilgrim, encounters Formalist and Hypocrisy climbing over a wall to join him on the "way" to the Celestial City. When he challenges them (citing Jn 10:1), they reply, "so be we get into the way, what's matter which way we get in; if we are in, we are in: thou art but in the way, who, as we perceive, came in at the Gate; and we are also in the way that came tumbling over the wall: wherein now is thy condition better than ours?" His answer is, "I walk by the rule of my master, you walk by the rude working of your fancies. You are counted thieves already by the Lord of the way,[46] therefore I doubt that you will not be found true men at the end of the way." The result was that they joined him anyway, "so that they went on every man in his way, without much conference one with another."[47] As Stanley Fish points out, "for them the 'way' is any way which finds them in an external conformity with the directions they have

---

44. This is obviously *not* the case in a number of ancient witnesses that preserve a longer reading: "And where I am going you know, and the way you know" (ὅπου ἐγὼ ὑπάγω οἴδατε καὶ τὴν ὁδὸν οἴδατε; see P⁶⁶, A, D, Θ, Ψ, families 1 and 13, the old Latin and Syriac versions, and the majority of later manuscripts). But the stronger manuscript evidence (including ℵ, B, C, L, Q, W, and 33) favors the shorter reading, οἴδατε τὴν ὁδόν (see Metzger, *Textual Commentary,* 243). It appears that the longer reading may have come into being as a result of conforming Jesus' pronouncement to Thomas's answer, "Lord, we do not know where you are going. How can we know the way?" (v. 5).

45. Gr. ἡ ὁδός.

46. "Thieves" because of John 10:1, as Bunyan quotes it, "He that cometh not in by the door, but climbeth up some other way, the same is a thief and a robber."

47. See Bunyan, *The Pilgrim's Progress* (ed. Roger Sharrock; London: Penguin, 1987), 83-84.

been given. We are, they say to Christian, in the same *place* as you; are we not therefore in the same way? Christian answers by internalizing the metaphor," so that "for him the 'way' refers to an inner commitment of the spirit, . . . a commitment to the rule of his master, and as long as he walks by *that*, any road he walks in is the way. Being in the way is paradoxically independent of the way you happen to be in, for you will be in the way only if the way is in you."[48] He goes on to make the point that "This rule[49] is nowhere given, but the several scriptural allusions in the passage point us unmistakably to it: I am the way, the truth and the life; no man cometh to the Father, but by me (John 14:6)."[50]

5 At this point, of course, Jesus has not yet said, "I am the Way." All he has said is that his disciples "know the way" (v. 4), even though it quickly becomes evident that they do not know that they know it. Thomas says as much: "Lord, we do not know where you are going. How can we know the way?" (v. 5). With this, he takes up Peter's question once more, "Lord, where are you going?" (13:36), as if Jesus had not answered it. Even if Thomas heard Jesus mention "my Father's household" (v. 2), he does not presume to know where that is, and if we do not know the destination, he reasons, "How can we know the way?" Thomas is still thinking of "the way" as a road or at least a road map, not as an "inner commitment," or way of life, and in his own literalistic terms he is right. It is useless to ask directions if one does not know where one is going. Unlike Peter (see 13:37), Thomas speaks not just for himself but for all the disciples ("*we* do not know where you are going? How can *we* know the way?").[51] His question affords Jesus the opportunity to set all the disciples straight — and instruct the reader as well.

6 Although Thomas speaks for all the disciples, Jesus replies at first "to him" alone: "I am the Way, and the Truth, and the Life. No one comes to

---

48. "Progress in *The Pilgrim's Progress*," in *Self-Consuming Artifacts* (Berkeley: University of California Press, 1974), 227-28. This is borne out again and again in *The Pilgrim's Progress,* not least near the end, when Christian asks the Shepherds in the Delectable Mountains, "Is this the way to the Celestial City?" and they answer him, "You are just in your way." When he continues, "How far is it thither?" they reply, "Too far for any but those that shall get thither indeed," and when he asks, "Is the way safe or dangerous?" the answer is "Safe for those for whom it is to be safe, *but transgressors shall fall therein*" (Bunyan, 170). Their three nonanswers deconstruct the questions, eloquently confirming Stanley Fish's interpretation.

49. That is, "the rule of his master."

50. Fish, 228-29.

51. In contrast to his other appearances in the Gospel (see 11:16; 20:24; 21:1), Thomas is not introduced as "the one called Didymos." It is unlikely that any conclusions can or should be drawn about Thomas's character or personal history from this passage, as from 20:24-28 and possibly 11:16. Here (as in 21:2) he is simply one of the group. His question does not differentiate him from the others.

the Father except through me" (v. 6). This is the first "I am" pronouncement since "I am the Resurrection and the Life" (11:25), which it resembles in two ways: first, in that Jesus says it only once, and second, in having more than one predicate (one of which is "the Life"). The dominant predicate here is "the Way." Jesus could have just said, "I am the Way. No one comes to the Father except through me," and the dynamic of the exchange would have been the same. "The Truth" and "the Life" simply spell out for his disciples the benefits of the salvation to which "the Way" leads. Jesus has already told Martha explicitly that he was "the Life" (11:25), and he implicitly claimed to be "the Truth" by telling a group of "believing" Jews at the Tent festival that "the truth will set you free" (8:32), and "if *the Son* sets you free, you will really be free" (8:36, italics added).

The central pronouncement, "I am the Way," is profoundly significant within the chapter as a whole, for it states in so many words what Bunyan knew, that "the way" is not what Thomas thought it was, a literal route or pathway, but a Person, Jesus himself. The destination, accordingly, is not a place (not even precisely "my Father's house"), but also a Person, the Father himself: "No one comes *to the Father* except through me" (italics added). The terms of the whole discussion now begin to change, from talk of a departure, a journey, a "way," and a destination, to talk of Jesus and the Father. There is profound mutuality in their relationship, for the claim that "No one comes to the Father except through me" stands as a kind of sequel to the principle stated much earlier that "No one can come to me unless the Father who sent me draw him" (6:44), or "unless it is given him from the Father" (6:65). That is, only the Father can bring anyone to Jesus, and only Jesus can bring anyone to the Father.[52] Those who are quite willing to press the exclusivity of the latter principle — that is, that salvation is possible only through Jesus Christ — are sometimes less willing to acknowledge the exclusivity of the former — that is, that no one comes to Christ without being "drawn" or "given" by the Father to the Son. But both things are true, and therein lies the characteristic exclusivism, even dualism, of the Gospel of John.[53] At the same time, the invitation is universal, for the last phrase, "through me,"[54] recalls an earlier pronouncement that accented its positive side: "I am the Door. Through me, if anyone goes in he will be saved, and will go in and go out and find pasture" (10:9). Such is the dialectic of salvation throughout this Gospel.

52. Or, as Jesus puts it in other Gospels, "No one [οὐδείς] knows the Son except the Father, nor the Father except the Son and anyone to whom the Son chooses to reveal him" (Mt 11:27; see also Lk 10:22).

53. This is the case elsewhere in the New Testament as well (for example, Acts 4:12). On the exclusivism of this verse, see Carson, 491-93 (especially telling is his line, "Your way to God is not my way but me").

54. Gr. δι' ἐμοῦ.

7 Jesus now turns from Thomas alone to the whole group, though the transition (in contrast to the transition from Peter to the group, v. 1) is barely noticeable: "If you all[55] have known me, you will know my Father too, and from now on you know him, and you have seen him" (v. 7). If this is the correct reading, Jesus is assuming that they do in fact know him,[56] but some ancient manuscripts have it instead as a contrary-to-fact condition, "If you all had known me, you would have known my Father too."[57] This reading implies that they have not known either Jesus or his Father, but that "from now on" they will.

While the contrary-to-fact condition is not without parallel in this very chapter (see v. 28), the simple conditional sentence implying that they *do* know Jesus has wider textual support, and is virtually demanded by the logic of his argument.[58] He has just told them, after all, that "you know the way" (v. 4), and then explained, "I am the Way" (v. 6). And two verses later he will express great surprise that Philip still does *not* know him (v. 9). If they truly did not know him, they would be no better off than the Pharisees at the Tent festival to whom he said, "You know neither me nor my Father; if you knew me, you would know my Father" (8:19). The disciples, by contrast, are those Jesus has identified as his "sheep," who know their Shepherd and their Shepherd's voice (see 10:4, 14), just as surely, he said, "as the Father knows me, and I know the Father" (10:15). His promise here is not simply that "you will know my Father" sooner or later,[59] but that "from now on[60] you know him, and you have seen him." The last clause, "and you have seen him,"[61] is particularly striking when we remember Jesus' earlier statement of a sweeping principle, "Not that anyone has seen the Father except he who is from God, he has seen the Father" (6:46; also 1:18, 5:37).

---

55. The translation "you all" signals that the verbs are plural, referring to the whole group, not just Thomas.

56. This (with only minor variations) is the reading of P⁶⁶, ℵ, D, W, and a few others (among English versions, see the NAB, TEV, NRSV, and TNIV).

57. For this reading (with ἂν ᾔδειτε), see B, C, L, Q, Ψ, 1, 33 and (with ἐγνώκειτε ἄν) A, Θ, family 13, the Vulgate, and the majority of later witnesses (it is also presupposed by most English versions, including the KJV, NASV, RSV, NIV, NEB, REB, and NLT).

58. So Metzger (*Textual Commentary*, 243), who comments that the contrary-to-fact condition may have arisen "because Philip's question (ver. 8) and Jesus' reply (ver. 9) suggested to them that the disciples knew neither Jesus nor the Father." His other alternative — that "copyists recalled Jesus' reproach against unbelieving Jews in 8:19" — is less likely.

59. That is, conditioned on something they must do (as, for example, in 7:17; 8:28, 32).

60. Gr. ἀπ' ἄρτι.

61. Gr. καὶ ἑωράκατε αὐτόν.

8 The third questioner is Philip, picking up on the last clause, "and you have seen him" (v. 7b). Philip, like Thomas, ventures to speak for the whole group: "Lord, show *us* the Father, and it's enough for *us*" (v. 8, my italics). At one level, he is asking in another way the same question Peter and Thomas asked, "Where are you going?" (13:36; 14:5), given that Jesus' destination has now been defined as "the Father" (v. 6). Yet it is difficult to say just what Philip has in mind. How exactly does he expect Jesus to "show us the Father?" Is he asking for a sign, like Jesus' other signs? Or a literal vision of God, something Jesus has explicitly ruled out (see 6:46)? Superficially, his question echoes that of the Pharisees at the Tent festival who asked Jesus, "Where is your father?" (8:19), but the circumstances are very different. As we have seen, those Pharisees did not even understand that Jesus was speaking of his heavenly Father, and were simply challenging him to call his second witness (see 8:18). Philip, by contrast, is expected to know both Jesus and the Father (v. 7). His confusion seems to come as a surprise to Jesus (v. 9), yet given the repeated misunderstandings of Jesus' pronouncements in this Gospel (for example, 2:20; 3:4; 4:11-12; 7:35-36; 8:22), it is perhaps less surprising to the reader, for even the disciples are not immune (see 13:9). The importance of Philip's remark lies not so much in what he may have meant by it as in the opportunity it gives Jesus to reveal more and more of the truth.

9 Jesus responds to Philip and to the whole group of disciples simultaneously, interweaving plurals and singulars: "Such a long time I am with you all,[62] and you, Philip, have not known me? The person who has seen me has seen the Father. How can you [singular] say, 'Show us the Father?'" (v. 9). The gentle rebuke is addressed to Philip alone; the words of reminder and instruction are for all the disciples. "Such a long time" that Jesus has been with them stands in contrast to the "short time" left before his departure (13:33). His reply, "The person who has seen me has seen the Father," is simply a corollary of the principle of agency that he has already presented, first to the reader (12:44-45) and then to the disciples at the meal (13:20). The reader at least has even been told explicitly, "the person who sees me sees the One who sent me" (12:45), and now Philip and his companions are given that information as well. In a larger sense, the reply to Philip is also a corollary of everything Jesus has said in the first half of the Gospel about his dependence on the Father, speaking only what the Father had given him to say and doing only what the Father commissioned him to do. And from the beginning, the bad news that "No one has seen God, ever," has been balanced against the good news that "It was God the One and Only, the One who is right beside the Father, who told about him" (1:18). To say, "The person who has seen me has seen the Father," is simply to say that the Son reveals the Father.

---

62. Gr. μεθ' ὑμῶν.

10-11 Continuing in the same vein, Jesus asks Philip, "Do you not believe that I am in the Father, and the Father in me?" Then he reminds the whole group, "The words that I am saying to you all I am not speaking on my own, but the Father, dwelling in me, is doing his works" (v. 10). The hint of mutuality that came to expression in "No one comes to the Father except through me" (see v. 6), now becomes the dominant theme of the discourse, replacing the themes of Jesus' departure and his destination. Jesus has spoken before of mutual glorification (13:31-32), but here he defines mutuality as mutual indwelling.[63] He is "in the Father," he claims, and the Father "in me."[64] None of this is new. He has said it all before, not to the disciples but to "the Jews" at the Rededication festival in Jerusalem: "If I do not do the works of my Father, don't believe me. But if I do them, even if you don't believe me, believe the works, so that you might learn and know that the Father is in me and I in the Father" (10:37-38). The parallel is striking, not just because of the reference to mutual indwelling but because of the accent on Jesus' "works" as "the works of my Father" (10:37). The equivalent here is that "the Father, dwelling in me, is doing his works" (v. 10). All of this was wasted on Jesus' audience at the Rededication, who instead of listening merely "sought to arrest him again" (10:39). Jesus seems to have said it only for the benefit of the reader, who was left to ponder how the Father could be "in" Jesus and Jesus "in" the Father all at the same time. Beyond a vague sense that he was trying to explain in what way "I and the Father are one" (10:30), the reader has had little to go on.

Now Jesus makes a similar claim to Philip and the other disciples at supper. "Do you not believe?" he asks Philip, who says nothing, but then he drives the question home to the rest of the disciples by underlining the great authority with which he speaks (vv. 10b-11). In referring to "The words that I am saying to you all," he means the specific words he has just said to Philip about the mutual indwelling of the Father and the Son. These words, he reminds them, are not spoken "on my own, but the Father, dwelling in me, is doing his works" (v. 10b). He has said as much before, about other claims he has made (see, for example, 5:30; 7:16-18; 8:28), but the thought of the Father "dwelling in me" gives this claim added credibility. He then confirms the claim by repeating it verbatim before the group: "Believe me, that I am in the Father and the Father in me, but if not, believe because of those very works" (v. 11).

It is quite noticeable that Jesus speaks of his "words" and his "works" interchangeably.[65] Where we might have expected, "I am not speaking on my

---

63. Again, compare Stanley Fish's comment on *The Pilgrim's Progress:* "for you will be in the way only if the way is in you" (Fish, in *Self-Consuming Artifacts,* 228).

64. Gr. ἐν τῷ πατρί and ἐν ἐμοί, respectively.

65. So Bultmann, 609: "In the light of v. 10, these ἔργα can only be Jesus' revela-

own, but the Father is speaking through me," he says instead, "the Father, dwelling in me, is doing his works," and he commands them to believe on the basis of "those very works." He told them earlier that "The words I have spoken to you are spirit, and they are life" (6:63), and they acknowledged that "You have words of life eternal" (6:68), yet he also made clear to his opponents that words are cheap. Even if he calls himself "God" or "the Son of God," it means little or nothing (see 10:34-36). What really counts are the "works" the Father has given him to do: "If I do not do the works of my Father, don't believe me. But if I do them, even if you don't believe me, believe the works, so that you might learn and know that the Father is in me and I in the Father" (10:37-38). Now, in the presence of his disciples, he expects them to recognize those same words about mutual indwelling as words bringing to realization the Father's "works" of giving life and executing judgment (see 5:20-22). "Believe me" (that is, believe what I say), he tells them, or else "believe because of those very works." It amounts to the same thing.

12 It is unclear precisely where Jesus' answer to Philip ends. A case could be made for extending it all the way to verse 22, where "Judas, not the Iscariot" asks a fourth question. Yet here an "Amen, amen" formula (the twenty-second in the Gospel) marks a definite break. While he has had the group as a whole in view as well as Philip in particular as far back as verse 9, Philip is now forgotten and Jesus turns his full attention to them all without distinction: "Amen, amen, I say to you all,"[66] in contrast to "Jesus says to him" (v. 9). As for the pronouncement itself, it has occasioned much discussion among interpreters: "the person who believes in me, the works I am doing that person will also do, and greater than these he will do because I am going to the Father." The reference to "believing" and to "the works I am doing" signal that the subject matter has not changed, but the added promise is startling. Those who "believe" (as the disciples are now being invited to do) will do the same "works" Jesus has done, and even "greater than these,"[67] he promises, all because "I am going to the Father." Much earlier, he distinguished between the works of the Father "until now" (5:17) which the Father has shown him, and the "greater works than these" (5:20) of raising the dead and executing judgment, both now and at the last day (see 5:21-29). But in what sense are the works of believers after his departure "greater" than Jesus' works? It is generally agreed that they will not perform "greater" or more

---

tory works in the word he speaks" (see also his *Theology of the New Testament,* 2.60: "But 14:11 is the continuation of 14:10, and together they indicate that the 'works' of v. 11 are neither more nor less than the 'words' of v. 10"). For another instance of this interchangeability, see 8:28, "on my own I *do* nothing, but just as the Father taught me, these things I *speak*" (italics added).

66. Gr. λέγω ὑμῖν.
67. Gr. μείζονα τούτων.

spectacular miracles than he did (as is hinted, for example, in the longer ending of Mark, 16:16-18). Possibly their works are "greater" in that more people (Gentiles as well as Jews) will benefit from Jesus' death than from the works he did while on earth (see, for example, 10:16; 11:52; 12:24, 32). We have known all along that he had a limited time to complete his works (9:4; 11:9-10), and that certain things could not take place and other things could not be understood until after he was "glorified" (see 7:39; 12:16). Here he looks more closely at the impending time of his absence, assuring his disciples that his works will nonetheless continue and, yes, be even "greater" than when he was present. Still, the question persists: In what sense "greater"?

It is important to recognize that Jesus is not settling for second place. The disciples' works are, first of all, the same as "the works *I* am doing," and only "greater than these" because "*I* am going to the Father" (italics added). The emphatic "I" is quite noticeable. The "greater" works are no less the works of Jesus than of his disciples, for it is he who makes them possible. Just as the distinction in 5:20 was not between Jesus' works and those of the Father but between the Father's works "until now" (5:17) and those yet to come, so the distinction here is not between what Jesus does and what the disciples do, but between what Jesus has done so far and what he will do (through them) by "going to the Father."

Most conspicuous among the "works" of Jesus promised but not yet accomplished are those of "taking away the sin of the world" (1:29), and "baptizing in Holy Spirit" (1:33) — two expressions, it may be, for the same act of purification. Jesus has turned water to wine, healed the sick, multiplied loaves, given sight to the blind, raised the dead, but he has not — at least not explicitly[68] — forgiven or taken away anyone's sin.[69] Those who have come to him have come not as sinners but as "true Israelites" (1:47), who "do the truth" and whose works have been "wrought in God" (see 3:21). Those who opposed him have been told that their sin "remains" (9:41), and left to "die in their sins" (8:21, 24; see also 15:22). Clearly, something is missing — something that will not be explicitly supplied until Jesus' resurrection, when he will breathe on his disciples and say to them, "Receive Holy Spirit. Whosoever's sins you forgive, they are forgiven them; whosoever's you retain, they are retained" (20:22-23). If there is a prime candidate for one of these "greater"

---

68. "Not explicitly," because of the references to Jesus baptizing in water (3:22, 26; 4:1). If this baptism was "for the forgiveness of sins" (as John's baptism was said to be in the Synoptics, though not in this Gospel), then we have here an exception. Although there is mention of "purification" (3:25), nothing is said of the forgiveness of sins, and in any case the Gospel writer makes every effort to downplay Jesus's personal involvement in a ministry of baptism (4:2).

69. See my articles "By Water and Blood," 149-51, and "Atonement in John's Gospel and Epistles," 109-12.

works, it is the forgiveness of sins, possibly because it could only come by virtue of the actual shedding of Jesus' blood on the cross, just as the gift of the Spirit could only come by virtue of Jesus' glorification (see 7:39).[70]

13-14 The forgiveness of sins is not explicitly mentioned here as one of the "greater" works. Instead, Jesus singles out the assurance of answered prayer, quite possibly with prayer for the forgiveness of sins particularly in mind. "And whatever you ask in my name," he promises, "this I will do, so that the Father might be glorified in the Son" (v. 13). Then, for emphasis, he says it again: "If you ask me anything in my name, *I* will do"[71] (v. 14). The emphatic "I" is evident once more, signaling again that Jesus is not simply backing off, leaving the authority to do "greater" works in the hands of his disciples. We might have expected, "And whatever you ask in my name, *the Father* will do, so that the Father might be glorified in the Son," and "If you ask *the Father* anything in my name, *he* will do." We have come to expect Christian prayer to be directed *to* the Father *through* the Son, and this is in fact what we find in this Gospel's other passages on prayer (see 15:16, "so that whatever you ask *the Father* in my name, *he* might give you"; 16:23, "whatever you ask *the Father* in my name, *he* will give you").[72] Here, by contrast, even though the prayer is offered in Jesus' name, it is Jesus himself (now "gone to the Father," v. 12) who "will do" what is asked.[73] In a sense, the promise that "I will do" (v. 14) echoes and reaffirms his previous reference to the works that "I am doing"[74] (v. 12). He who carries out the Father's works in his ministry on earth will continue to perform "greater" works from heaven in response to the prayers of the disciples he left behind.

---

70. In contrast to John's Gospel, much is said about the forgiveness of sins in 1 John (see 1:7, "But if we walk in the light as he is in the light, we have fellowship with one another, and the blood of Jesus his Son cleanses us from all sin"; 1:9, "If we confess our sins he is faithful and righteous, so as to forgive us the sins and cleanse us from all unrighteousness"). See also Luke 24:46, "And he said to them that thus it is written that the Christ is to suffer and be raised the third day, and that repentance for the forgiveness of sins is to be proclaimed to all the Gentiles."

71. Gr. ἐγὼ ποιήσω.

72. Italics added. See also 15:7, "you will ask whatever you want, and *it will be done* for you" (γενήσεται ὑμῖν, the future passive signaling the work of God the Father); also Mt 18:19, "If two of you agree on earth about any matter whatever they ask, *it will be done* for them [γενήσεται αὐτοῖς] by my Father in heaven."

73. Particularly odd is the wording the second time around, "If you ask *me* [με] anything in my name, *I* [ἐγώ] will do" (italics added). It is difficult to picture the disciples asking Jesus for something in his own name (rather than asking the Father "in his name"). For this reason, certain manuscripts (including A, D, L, K, Q, and Ψ) have omitted "me." But the more difficult longer reading should be retained, with the effect of heightening even more the emphasis on "I" (ἐγω).

74. Gr. ἐγὼ ποιῶ.

What is the reader to make of such promises of answered prayer? They should be looked at one at a time, for a single interpretation does not necessarily fit them all. The promise here is notable for what it does *not* say. Jesus does not invite them to ask "whatever you want" (as he will in 15:7!), but to ask "in my name,"[75] a phrase that seems to mean "Ask as if I were asking," or "Ask what I would ask."[76] This would suggest that the prayer is directed ultimately to the Father after all, yet Jesus the Son promises to answer it, "so that the Father might be glorified in the Son" (v. 13, echoing 13:31, "Now the Son of man is glorified, and God is glorified in him"). The disciple is invited to come to the Father "in the name of" Jesus, with the promise of enjoying the same access to God that Jesus enjoys (see 9:31, and especially 11:41-42). It is not a matter of an individual's personal whims or desires, but of bringing to realization all that Jesus wants to accomplish in the world.

15 Jesus continues to address his disciples, with another "If" clause: "If you love me, you will keep my commands" (v. 15).[77] Perhaps surprisingly, he does not pick up on the "new command" he has just given them (13:34) by speaking of his love for them or their responsibility to "love one another." Instead, he speaks of love in a very traditional way, and of a plurality of "my commands," not of a single "new command." His language evokes the covenantal language of the Hebrew Bible, in which the people of Israel are repeatedly characterized as those who "love God" and "keep his commands."[78] It also evokes his words in the other three Gospels about the two great commands to "love the Lord your God" and "love your neighbor as

---

75. Gr. ἐν τῷ ὀνόματί μου.

76. This is supported by several other uses of "the name" (τὸ ὄνομα) in this Gospel. For example, to believe in Jesus' "name" (1:12; 2:23; 3:18) is simply to believe in Jesus, and for Jesus to come in the Father's "name" (5:43), or to perform works in the Father's "name" (10:25), is to act on the Father's behalf as the Father's agent. In the same way, to suffer for Jesus' "name" is to suffer for his sake (15:21), and to have life in his "name" (20:31) is to have life in him.

77. Instead of "you will keep" (τηρήσετε), some ancient manuscripts (including A, D, W, Θ, and the majority of later witnesses) have the imperative, "keep" (τηρήσατε). While this reading lacks the support to be considered original, it reminds us that the future indicative "you will keep" could have a mildly imperatival force, as if to say, "you should keep" (see BDF, §362). While this is possible, the analogy with verse 23 ("If anyone loves me, he will keep my word") suggests otherwise.

78. See, for example, Exodus 20:6 (NIV), where the God of Israel describes himself as "showing love to a thousand generations of those who love me and keep my commandments" (see also Deut 5:10; 7:9; 11:1). The classic statement, perhaps, is the daily prayer known as the Shema: "Hear, O Israel: The LORD our God, the LORD is one. Love the LORD your God with all your heart and with all your soul and with all your strength. These commandments that I give you today are to be upon your hearts" (Deut 6:4-6, NIV).

yourself" (see Mt 22:37-39//Mk 12:29-31; also Lk 10:26-27). It resonates with these more than with anything we have encountered up to now in the Gospel of John itself. But there is one enormous difference: the command is not simply to love the God of Israel, but quite specifically to "love me," and keep "my commands,"[79] presumably including — though not limited to — the "new command" to love one another.[80] In short, Jesus stands before his disciples at this last meal in the place of God, and representing God.

16-17 Closely linked to the promise of "greater" things (v. 12), answered prayer in particular (vv. 13-14), is the promise of the Spirit. On the basis of the disciples' love for him and the keeping of his commands, Jesus continues, "And I will ask[81] the Father, and he will give you another advocate, that he might be with you forever" (v. 16). The phrase "another advocate"[82] implies that Jesus himself is an "advocate" for his disciples, presumably by virtue of "going off to prepare a place" for them with the Father (vv. 2-3; see 1 Jn 2:1, "we have an advocate with the Father, Jesus Christ the righteous").[83] This

---

79. Gr. τὰς ἐντολὰς τὰς ἐμάς.

80. As we have seen, the "new command" was not intended to replace a plurality of "old" commands, but to be added to them, for the old biblical "commands" were understood to be Jesus' commands as well. In the synoptic Gospels, by contrast, the "commands" remain the commands of God, not Jesus, with the single exception of Matthew 28:20, where the *risen* Jesus at the very end tells his disciples to teach the Gentiles to obey "everything I commanded you" (πάντα ὅσα ἐνετειλάμην ὑμῖν).

81. Jesus uses a different word for his own prayer to the Father (ἐρωτᾶν, as in 16:26; 17:9, 15, 20) from the word used for the disciples' prayers (αἰτεῖν, as in vv. 13-14; 15:7; 16:23-24, 26). When this word is used of the disciples, it means to ask a question rather than to pray (see 16:5, 19, 23, 30, and even 1 Jn 5:16). The distinction was noticed over a century ago by Ezra Abbot, "The Distinction between *aiteō* and *erōtaō*," in *The Authority of the Fourth Gospel* (Boston: Ellis, 1888), 113-36.

82. Gr. ἄλλον παράκλητον. There is no agreement among English versions as to how παράκλητος should be translated, whether as "Paraclete" (with the Douay, giving up the effort from the start), or as "Comforter" (Tyndale, KJV), "Counselor" (RSV, NIV), "Helper" (TEV), or "Advocate." A growing trend favors the latter (see NRSV, NEB, REB, NAB, TNIV, NLT), possibly because of the legal connotations of the term, and because of its appropriateness in 1 John 2:1. The term implies someone "called in" or "called alongside" to help or intercede, often in legal matters. Translations such as "Comforter" or "Counselor" seem to have arisen out of efforts to accent the Spirit's active role of exhortation or encouragement (παράκλησις, from the active verb παρακαλεῖν, "to make an appeal").

83. For this reason, the alternative of reading "advocate" in a kind of predicate relationship to "another" — that is, "he will give you another [ἄλλον], as an advocate [παράκλητον]," without implying that Jesus was himself an "advocate" (see, for example, NEB, REB) — is very unlikely. Jesus' earlier reference to "another" (ἄλλος), who "testifies about me" (5:32), quite clearly referred to the Father, while his warning about "another" (ἄλλος) who "comes in his own name" (5:43) is obviously a different matter altogether.

other "advocate," he promises, will be "with you forever" (v. 16), in contrast to Jesus himself, who said he would be "with you" only "a short time" (13:33). He then further identifies the "advocate" as "the Spirit of truth"[84] which the world cannot receive, because it neither sees nor knows it," adding "You know it, because it dwells beside you, and is in you" (v. 17).[85]

The neuter pronouns in the English translation ("which" and "it") reflect neuter pronouns in Greek,[86] with the neuter noun "Spirit" as antecedent. This is somewhat misleading, for the noun "advocate" is masculine,[87] and in subsequent passages the personality of "the Spirit of truth" (or "Holy Spirit," v. 26) will emerge more clearly than anywhere else in the New Testament (see v. 26; 15:26; 16:7-15). For now, nothing is said of how this other "advocate" will carry out its advocacy for the disciples,[88] only that it is given specifically to them, not to "the world," to dwell "beside" them, or "in" them. That "the world cannot receive" and "neither sees nor knows" this advocate comes as no surprise, given that the world "did not know" Jesus the Word either (1:10). Nor does Jesus promise that his disciples will literally "see" it, for it is "Spirit" and not flesh. But "You do know it," he promises them, "because it dwells beside you,[89] and is in you."[90] It is important to understand that even though all the verbs are in the present tense,[91] they all have a future meaning (no less than the verbs "I am going" and "I am coming" in vv. 2-3).

---

84. Gr. τὸ πνεῦμα τῆς ἀληθείας.

85. Here for the first time "the Spirit" (τὸ πνεῦμα), elsewhere further identified as "Holy Spirit" (1:33), is called "the Spirit of truth," yet as we have seen, the expression "in Spirit and truth" (4:23, 24) conveys much the same idea.

86. Gr. ὅ and αὐτό.

87. Gr. ὁ παράκλητος.

88. As we will see, the "advocate" is an advocate *for* the disciples, just as Jesus was, to strengthen them before God in their prayers (see vv. 13-14), and defend them against the world (see 16:8-11), not primarily an advocate on *God's* behalf to touch their conscience or convict them of sin (rather, he will "convict *the world* of sin," 16:8).

89. Gr. παρ' ὑμῖν μένει. "Beside you" (παρ' ὑμῖν, v. 17) is scarcely distinguishable from "with you" (μεθ' ὑμῶν, v. 16) in meaning, even though we have distinguished them in the English translation.

90. Gr. ἐν ὑμῖν ἐστιν.

91. There is one exception according to some important textual witnesses (including P[75], ℵ, A, Θ, family 13, and the majority of later manuscripts) that read, "it dwells beside you and *will be* in you" (ἔσται instead of ἔστιν). But the present tense (ἔστιν) has the support of P[66], B, D, W, 1, 565, and the old Latin). While the future may be correct, it may have been occasioned by the desire of scribes to distinguish between the Spirit's presence "beside" (παρά), or with, the disciples now, and "in" them (ἐν ὑμῖν) later, when the Spirit actually "comes." No such distinction is evident in the text. If the future is adopted as the original reading, it should be read simply as confirming the future reference of *all* the verbs used in verse 17.

Jesus' point is that the world *will not* recognize the advocate when it comes, *will not* see or know it, but that the disciples *will* know it (presumably because Jesus has told them in advance), and that it *will* "dwell beside you" and *will* "be in you." This is quite clearly the case because of what has preceded. Jesus has said, "I *will* ask the Father, and he *will* give you another advocate, that he might be with you forever" (v. 16, italics added). The "other advocate" will not come until the first "advocate" has gone to the Father (this becomes explicit in 16:7). And when the advocate comes, it will "dwell beside" the disciples, or be "in" them. No distinction is intended (see n. 91).

18 What Jesus says next is startling: "I will not leave you orphaned. I am coming to you" (v. 18). Without an advocate, the disciples would be "orphaned,"[92] destitute and alone in the world, but as it is they will not be alone. But how can he say, "I am coming"? What has *his* "coming" to do with that of the "other advocate"? This time he does not say, "I am coming back," nor does he promise to "take you to myself, so that where I am you too might be" (v. 3). Nor is the "I" emphatic, as if to say, "I" in addition to that "other" advocate. He simply says, "I am coming to you," and at this point the reader can only conclude that he is promising to come to them in the person of the "advocate . . . the Spirit of truth," of whom he has just spoken. If so, this is not the same "coming" promised earlier, after a period of absence and the preparation of "a place for you" (v. 2), but a different "coming" altogether.

19 Further explanation is required, and Jesus quickly supplies it: "Yet a short time, and the world no longer sees me, but you see me, because I live — and you too will live" (v. 19). The phrase, "Yet a short time,"[93] recalls the pronouncement with which the whole sequence began, "Children, yet a short time I am with you" (13:33), but with a crucial difference. Now, instead of accenting his physical absence from the disciples ("Where I am going you cannot come," 13:33), he brings good news.[94] He will be truly absent only as far as "the world" is concerned.[95] Even though "the world no longer sees me," he promises them, "you see me, because I live — and you too will live." Here again (as in v. 17) the present verbs have a future meaning, as if to say that after Jesus' departure from the world, "the world *will* no longer see me, but you *will* see me, because I *will* live — and you too *will* live" (italics added; only the last of these verbs is actually future).

It is the same with Jesus as with the "other advocate." Just as the

---

92. Gr. ὀρφανούς.
93. Gr. ἔτι μικρόν.
94. He has already mitigated the prospect of his absence somewhat in his answer to Peter, "Where I am going you cannot follow now, but you will follow later" (13:36).
95. This is in keeping with what he said earlier to "the Jews," that "Where I am going you cannot come" (8:21), just before reminding them that "You are from this world [ἐκ τούτου τοῦ κόσμου], I am not from this world" (8:23).

world "neither sees it nor knows it," but "You do know it" (v. 17), so here, Jesus says, "the world no longer sees me, but you see me."[96] The disciples and the world perceive things differently. They will "know" and "see" what the world cannot. The only difference is that Jesus is a human being who can literally be "seen" (as in v. 9) while the "other advocate," being "Spirit," can be "known" but not actually "seen," even by the disciples. This raises the question, *When* will the disciples "see" Jesus after his departure from the world? The next clause provides a clue: "because I live[97] — and you too will live." The reference to Jesus' "living," or coming to life, in a setting dark with the prospect of his impending death suggests that he has in view here his resurrection. This is supported by the close link in this Gospel between "resurrection" and "life" (see, for example, 5:21; 6:40; 11:25-26). Only twice before has he hinted at his own resurrection, once at the first Passover when he said, "Destroy this sanctuary, and in three days I will raise it up" (2:19; see 2:21), and once at the Rededication when he said, "I lay down my life, that I might receive it back again. . . . I have authority to lay it down, and I have authority to receive it back" (10:17-18).[98] Here he speaks of it in similarly guarded language, but the reference is almost unmistakable. Then, and then only, was Jesus literally "seen" by his disciples after his death on the cross (for example, 20:18, 20, 25, 29), and it was then too that he "breathed" on his disciples and said, "Receive Holy Spirit" (20:22), so that he "came" (20:19, 24, 26) bringing with him, as it were, the "other advocate." None of this is clear to the disciples here at the meal (and much is still unclear to the reader), but the one thing that is clear is that they will not only "know" but "see" with their own eyes what "the world" cannot know — that Jesus is theirs, and they are his.

20 "In that day," Jesus continues, "you will come to know that I am in my Father and you in me, and I in you" (v. 20). "In that day"[99] places the events of the preceding verse (that is, "seeing" Jesus because he "lives") on a specific "day," not "the last day," to be sure (as in 6:39, 40, 44, and 54), yet an eschatological "day" full of hope and expectancy.[100] "That day" is under-

---

96. Gr. ὑμεῖς δὲ θεωρεῖτέ με.

97. Gr. ὅτι ἐγὼ ζῶ.

98. Other passages, of course, have to do with Jesus' "glorification," or "lifting up" (with the cross in view no less than the resurrection), or "going up to heaven" or to "where he was before" (see 3:13; 6:62), but not with resurrection from death per se.

99. Gr. ἐν ἐκείνῃ τῇ ἡμέρᾳ.

100. The Old Testament instances of "that day" or "in that day" with reference to the "day of the LORD" or a decisive day of judgment or vindication are too numerous to list (in the New Testament see, for example, Mt 24:26; 26:29; Mk 13:32; 14:23). Yet the phrase can also be used in a noneschatological sense in simple narrative (as in Mt 13:1; 22:23; Mk 4:35; Jn 5:9).

stood here on the one hand as the literal day on which Jesus rose from the dead ("that first day of the week," 20:19) and on the other as the whole age in which the Johannine community now lives, the age of the risen Lord (see 16:23, 26).[101] In connection with "that day," Jesus again speaks of mutual indwelling, but with a decisive addition. Instead of "I am in the Father, and the Father in me" (vv. 10 and 11; also 10:38), it is now "I am in my Father, and you in me, and I in you." Jesus has said nothing quite like this before. The closest he came was "The person who eats my flesh and drinks my blood dwells in me, and I in him" (6:56), with the added claim that "Just as the living Father sent me and I live because of the Father, so the person who eats me, even that person will live because of me" (6:57, italics added). That was a scandal and an offense to those who heard it at the time (see 6:60), but now Jesus tells his disciples that "in that day" they will "come to know"[102] the mutual indwelling of Father and Son — to the point that they are themselves drawn into it! To them belongs the unrealized promise to "the Jews who had believed" at the Tent festival: "If you remain in my word, you are truly my disciples, and you will know the truth, and the truth will set you free" (8:32). To know "the truth," we now learn, is to know "the Spirit of truth" (v. 17), and so be united with the Father and the Son (v. 20).

21 Returning to the thought of verse 15, "If you love me, you will keep my commands," Jesus now translates the mystical notion of mutual indwelling into more traditional language: "The person having my commands and keeping them, that person it is who loves me, and the person who loves me will be loved by my Father, and I will love him, and I will reveal myself to him" (v. 21). He could have merely said, "the person who loves me I will love," but because of what he has just said about mutual indwelling (v. 20), he brings the Father into the picture first — that person "will be loved by my Father" — adding (almost as an afterthought) "and I will love him." Finally, repeating in different words his promises that "I am coming to you" (v. 18)," and "the world no longer sees me, but you see me" (v. 19), he concludes, "and I will reveal myself to him."[103] The "coming" promised here (unlike the "coming back" mentioned in v. 3) is defined not as a return from heaven or "the Father's house," but as a revelation or self-disclosure prompted by the Father's (and Jesus') love for those who "love him and keep his commands."

22 After the long response, direct and indirect, to Philip's request to "Show us the Father" (vv. 9-21), the fourth and last question is asked, as "Ju-

---

101. The closest New Testament parallel outside the Gospel of John is perhaps Mark 2:20, "But days will come when the bridegroom will be taken from them, and then they will fast in that day" (ἐν ἐκείνῃ τῇ ἡμέρᾳ).
102. Gr. γνώσεσθε.
103. Gr. καὶ ἐμφανίσω αὐτῷ ἐμαυτόν.

das, not the Iscariot, says to him, 'Lord, and how come[104] you are going to reveal yourself to us and not to the world?'" (v. 22). This "Judas" is otherwise unidentified. The only "Judas" mentioned in the lists of the apostles other than "the Iscariot" is "Judas of James," who appears only in Luke (6:16) and Acts (1:13).[105] Unlike the first three, Judas's question is not one that betrays a lack of understanding or failure to pay attention.[106] On the contrary, it is a legitimate question that might well have been on the minds of many of the Gospel's readers. "To reveal yourself"[107] echoes Jesus' promise, "I will reveal myself to him" (v. 21), but the notion that this revelation is "not to the world" shows the speaker's awareness of Jesus' previous words as well, that "the world cannot receive, because it neither sees . . . nor knows" the Spirit (v. 17), and that "the world no longer sees me, but you see me" (v. 19). It may even look back to the still earlier promise that "if I go off and prepare a place for you, I am coming back and I will take you to myself" (v. 3), which did not mention the world but held out for the disciples a very personal relationship with Jesus in a "place" prepared just for them.

The question is a natural one against the background of certain primitive Christian expectations that when the Son of man comes, "every eye will see him," and "all the tribes of the earth will mourn over him" (Rev 1:7), or "then will appear the sign of the Son of man in the sky, and then all the tribes of the earth will mourn, and they will see the Son of man coming on the clouds with power and much glory" (Mt 24:30; see also Mk 13:26; Lk 21:27),[108] or even the very last words of the second-century *Didache:* "Then

---

104. The colloquial "how come" is an almost literal translation of τί γέγονεν (even more literally, "Lord, and how has it come about that . . .").

105. Perhaps significantly, this Judas's name appears next-to-last in Luke's list (6:16), just before that of "Judas Iscariot," and last in the book of Acts. Certain insignificant variant readings substitute the name "Judas the Cananaean" (probably on the basis of a harmonization of Lk 6:16 with "Simon the Cananaean" in Mk 3:18 and Mt 10:4), or the name "Thomas" (probably on the basis of later identifications of Thomas as "Didymus Judas Thomas," for example, in the *Gospel of Thomas*).

106. Brown, by contrast, calls the question "disturbingly like" the request of Jesus' unbelieving brothers to "reveal yourself to the world" (φανέρωσον σεαυτὸν τῷ κόσμῳ, 7:4), commenting that "We might have expected that by this time Judas would have had more faith in Jesus than the disbelieving brothers" (2.647). The parallel between the two passages, however, is superficial at best. Jesus' brothers were urging him to "go" from Galilee to Judea to perform miracles, while here it is a matter of Jesus "coming" or "coming back" from heaven or "my Father's house." Moreover, there is no imperative here. Judas is not saying "reveal yourself to the world," but simply asking why Jesus has chosen not to.

107. Gr. ἐμφανίζειν σεαυτόν.

108. Matthew's wider context finds its parallel elsewhere in Luke, suggesting that this expectation was common both to the Markan tradition and the so-called early "Q"

the world will see the Lord coming upon the clouds of the sky" (*Didache* 16.7). This expectation did not necessarily imply redemption for "the world"; on the contrary, the rhyming "they will see" and "they will mourn"[109] suggests the opposite. Still, Judas is puzzled. What happened to this expectation of a public visible "coming," he wonders, and possibly readers of the Gospel are wondering the same thing.[110] Whether he (or they) were expecting universal salvation on the one hand, or the public vindication of Jesus and his disciples before the entire world on the other is not altogether clear, but in any event Judas's question is the best anyone has asked yet. It deserves an answer, but the answer is complex. It will not come all at once, but the reader will do well to keep the question in mind.

23 For the time being Jesus contents himself with a kind of nonanswer: "If anyone loves me, he will keep my word, and my Father will love him, and we will come to him, and we will make a dwelling right beside him" (v. 23). For the most part, he merely repeats the very thing he said that provoked the question in the first place (see v. 21),[111] adding only that when he "comes" (v. 18) and "reveals himself" (v. 21), he will not come alone, but the Father will come with him. "We will come," he promises, and "we will make a dwelling right beside him."[112] The imagery of "many dwellings" in a "place" prepared for the disciples "in the Father's house" (v. 2) is here reversed, as the Father himself comes with Jesus to make his own "dwelling" alongside the believer. Startling as the addition sounds, it does not speak to Judas's question. It has no bearing on why the revelation is only to the disciples and not to the world. It is simply a corollary of what Jesus has said already: that "I am in the Father, and the Father in me" (v. 11), and "I am in my Father, and you in me, and I in you" (v. 20). If there is such a thing as in-

---

source: "For as the lightning comes forth from the east and shines to the west, so will be the coming of the Son of man" (Mt 24:27; see Lk 17:24). Here too the event is pictured as public and visible in nature.

109. Gr. ὄψονται . . . κόψονται.

110. Alternatively, it is possible that his question is related to the thought Peter expresses in Acts 10:40-41, that God gave Jesus "to be revealed [ἐμφανῆ γενέσθαι] not to all the people, but to witnesses handpicked by God — to us, who ate and drank with him after he rose from the dead." This view is attractive because of the likelihood that the resurrection is what Jesus is actually referring to here. But from a literary standpoint, the notion of Judas formulating such a question with the resurrection explicitly in view lacks credibility. It is far more likely that he is represented as envisioning a public eschatological coming at the end of the age.

111. That is, changing only a participle to a conditional clause, "my commands" (v. 21) to "my word" (τὸν λόγον μου, v. 23), and "he will be loved by my Father" (v. 21) to "my Father will love him" (v. 23).

112. Gr. μονὴν παρ' αὐτῷ.

dwelling, then when Jesus comes the Father comes, and if Jesus is "in" the disciples or "beside" them, so too is the Father.[113]

24 If there is a real answer here to Judas's question, it comes not in the added promise (v. 23), but in the negative saying that follows: "The person who does not love me does not keep my words" (v. 24a). The reference to "the person who does not love me"[114] is Jesus' way of defining "the world." Jesus will not reveal himself to those who do not love him or keep his "words" or "commands" (v. 21),[115] therefore not to "the world" (later he will be even more emphatic: "If the world hate you, you know that it has hated me first," 15:18). But even this briefest of answers is overshadowed by what he immediately adds, returning to his overarching theme, his relationship to the Father: "and the word which you all hear is not mine but the Father's who sent me" (v. 24b). Instead of responding in detail to Judas's question, the pronouncement concludes and frames the whole of verses 10-24, beginning with Jesus' answer to Philip, "The words that I am saying to you all I am not speaking on my own, but the Father, dwelling in me, is doing his works" (v. 10). Jesus' "word" — or "words," or "commands" — are not his own, he insists, but those of "the Father who sent him," who dwells in him and in whom he dwells. This is, of course, true not only of the foregoing speech, but of everything Jesus says, always and everywhere. Therein lies his authority.

25-26 "These things I have spoken to you while dwelling beside you," Jesus continues, as if signaling an end to his speech, and an imminent departure (v. 25). He speaks as if the end is approaching, yet it is not quite here, for the expression "these things I have spoken to you"[116] is one that he is quite capable of repeating again and again (see 15:11; 16:1, 4, 6, 25), before finally using it to conclude the entire discourse (16:33). He introduces it here to set the stage for a second glimpse of the "other advocate" he has promised (vv. 16-17). His reference to himself as "dwelling beside you"[117] recalls that promise, particularly the words "it dwells beside you and is in

---

113. For the interchangeability of "in" (ἐν) and "beside" (παρά), not to mention "with" (μετά), in relation to the "other advocate," see verses 16-17.

114. Gr. ὁ μὴ ἀγαπῶν με.

115. Compare perhaps Paul's pronouncement, "The eye has not seen, the ear has not heard, nor has there come up in the human heart the things which God has prepared for those who love him" (1 Cor 2:9). Also, James 1:12, "the crown of life which he has promised to those who love him"; James 2:5, "heirs of the kingdom which he has promised to those who love him"; 2 Timothy 4:8, "the crown of righteousness reserved . . . not only for me but for all who love his appearing" (πᾶσι τοῖς ἠγαπηκόσι τὴν ἐπιφάνειαν αὐτοῦ).

116. Gr. ταῦτα λελάληκα ὑμῖν.

117. Gr. παρ' ὑμῖν μένων. See also verse 23, with its promise that Jesus and the Father "will make a dwelling right beside him."

you" (v. 17). What Jesus does for them now, "another advocate" will continue to do after his departure, for in spite of all he has said about mutual indwelling, the departure is real. With this, the "other advocate" takes on a definite identity, and with it a title, along with a job description (hence the capitalization): "But the Advocate,[118] the Holy Spirit,[119] whom the Father will send in my name, he will teach you all things, and remind you of all things that I said to you" (v. 26).[120] Like Jesus himself, the Spirit is "sent"[121] from the Father, but "in my name," Jesus says, that is, in response to his intercession (see v. 16). The "he" and the "I" are both emphatic, framing the last clause.[122] That is, *"He* [the Advocate] will teach you all things and remind you of all things that *I* [Jesus] said to you." The effect of the "he"[123] is to highlight the personality of "the Advocate," corresponding to the personal "I" who speaks. The Advocate, moreover, will do things only a person can do, the very things Jesus has done from the start. He will "teach," and his teaching will be a continuation of Jesus' own, in that it will include "reminding"[124] the disciples of what Jesus has already taught them. In contrast to Je-

---

118. Gr. ὁ δὲ παράκλητος.

119. Only here is the Advocate called "the Holy Spirit" (τὸ πνεῦμα τὸ ἅγιον) rather than "the Spirit of truth" (as in v. 16; 15:26; and 16:13). The importance of the designation here is that it links the promise of the Advocate both with John' prediction that Jesus would "baptize in Holy Spirit" (1:33), and with the risen Jesus' word to his disciples as he "breathed on them" and said, "Receive Holy Spirit" (20:22).

120. Nowhere outside of John's Gospel is the "Holy Spirit" (or "Spirit of truth") ever given the title of "the Advocate" (ὁ παράκλητος). There is no conceptual background in either Jewish or Hellenistic literature, for Jesus and Jesus alone is the model for who the Advocate is and what he does. A better paradigm, perhaps, is the notion of two successive prophetic or redemptive figures, in which either the first anticipates the second, or the second completes the work of the first: for example, Moses and Joshua, Elijah and Elisha, or John and Jesus. As Jesus followed John, so the Advocate follows Jesus. But in sharp contrast to John, Jesus never says, "The One coming after me has gotten ahead of me" (1:15). On the contrary, his own role remains primary and the Advocate's role derivative — more like Joshua's role in relation to Moses, or Elisha's in relation to Elijah.

121. Gr. ὃ πέμψει (the relative pronoun is again neuter because τὸ πνεῦμα is neuter.

122. That is, the clause begins with "he" (ἐκεῖνος), and the emphatic "I" (ἐγώ) comes at the very end, not before εἶπον ("said"), where we might have expected it. At the same time it must be noted that the emphatic ἐγώ is omitted in some important manuscripts (including ℵ, A, D, Θ, Ψ, family 1 and 13, and the majority of later manuscripts). But it is present in B, L, and some important later minuscules. Internal evidence favors its retention, for if it was added by a later scribe, it is difficult to see why it was placed where it is, at the end of the sentence. If on the other hand it was original, it is not difficult to see how a scribe might have ignored or omitted it as redundant because of its odd placement.

123. Gr. ἐκεῖνος, masculine, in agreement with ὁ παράκλητος.

124. Gr. ὑπομνήσει.

sus, the Advocate will not be under time constraint, for he will teach them "all things," and remind them of "all things"[125] that Jesus ever said. While there is no evidence that the disciples themselves grasped the full significance of this promise, it helps the reader understand why, after Jesus was "glorified" or "raised from the dead," his disciples "remembered" not just the words that he spoke, but what his words and his actions meant (see 2:22; 12:16). In this way, it gives authority to the text of the Gospel, implying that with the help of the Advocate the disciples — and by implication the Gospel writer — finally "got it straight," whatever their limitations might have been during the course of Jesus' ministry. The accent on "all things that I said to you" could even suggest that they came to know far more than they ever put into writing (see 20:30; 21:25).[126]

27 The impression that Jesus' speech is drawing to a close (v. 25) is heightened by his next words, "Peace I leave with you, my peace[127] I give you. Not as the world gives do I give to you" (v. 27a). This first mention of "peace" in the entire Gospel stands as the positive sequel to the words with which he began, "Let no one's heart be shaken!" (v. 1), and to those very words he now returns, framing the entire discourse: "Let no one's heart be shaken, nor let it be fearful!" The added words, "nor let it be fearful"[128] (v. 27b), are significant. Jesus himself, as we have seen, had been "shaken," or troubled (11:33; 12:27; 13:21), but never "fearful," a term implying cowardice or lack of courage.[129] With these words (right on the heels of the promise of the Advocate!), he implies that his disciples are still badly in need of his "peace," with some distance yet to go before truly "believing" in him" (vv. 1, 10, 11) or "loving" him (vv. 15, 21, 23) as they should. In the same breath, he takes another opportunity (as in vv. 17 and 19) to distance himself and the disciples from "the world" and the way the world sees things. In saying, "Not as the world gives do I give you," his point is that the "peace" he leaves with his disciples is not necessarily what the world calls peace — that is, the absence of conflict. Without quite saying so, he hints that persecution may await them, and that this would *not* be incompatible with the "peace" he is offering them, for the peace he offers is in their "heart,"[130] not in their outward circumstances. He

---

125. Gr. πάντα.
126. A later promise, even more sweeping, is that "he will lead you in all the truth" (ἐν τῇ ἀληθείᾳ πάσῃ, 16:13), this in contrast to Jesus, who says, "I have much yet to say to you, but you are unable to bear it now" (16:12).
127. Gr. εἰρήνην τὴν ἐμήν.
128. Gr. μηδὲ δειλιάτω.
129. BDAG, 215. See Jesus' words to his disciples, "Why are you fearful?" (τί δειλοί ἐστε, Mt 8:26; Mk 4:40), implying their lack of faith; also Rev 21:8, where the lake of fire is τοῖς δειλοῖς καὶ ἀπίστοις, "for the cowardly and unbelieving").
130. Gr. ὑμῶν ἡ καρδία (see above, n. 13).

will make this explicit later on when he finally bids them farewell: "These things I have spoken to you that in me you might have peace. In the world you have distress, but take courage, I have overcome the world!" (16:33).

28 Summing up the whole discourse, Jesus continues, "You heard that I said to you, 'I am going away, and I am coming to you'" (v. 28a). The summary draws on a number of pronouncements all the way back to 13:33, when he first told them that "where I am going you cannot come" (for "going away," see 13:36, 14:4; for "going" or "going off," 14:2, 3, 12; and for "coming," 14:3, 18). Only once has he spoken of "going" and "coming," in one breath, "And if I go off and prepare a place for you, I am coming back" (v. 3),[131] and only once has he used the exact words, "I am coming to you" (v. 18). It is not altogether clear, therefore, whether the "coming" to which he now refers is his "coming back," presumably at "the last day" (v. 3), or "coming to you" in the person of the Advocate (v. 18). Nor is it all that important, for the accent here is on the "going," not the "coming."[132]

Jesus quickly makes this explicit: "If you loved me, you would rejoice[133] that[134] I am going off to the Father, because the Father is greater than I" (v. 28b). What is striking is that "If you loved me, you would rejoice," is a contrary-to-fact condition, suggesting that the disciples do *not* in fact love Jesus as they should.[135] That he loves them is beyond question (13:1, 34), and it is easy to assume that they love him as well. Clearly they do, in the sense that they do not belong to "the world" (see vv. 23-24). Yet their love is less than perfect. The contrary-to-fact condition is not as surprising as it sounds, given the implication that they are still "fearful," or lacking in courage (see v. 27).[136]

---

131. This on the assumption that ὑπάγω and πορεύομαι are being used interchangeably, as they seem to be here.

132. So too Bultmann: "Whether the ἔρχομαι is that of v. 3, which finally frees the disciple from life within the bounds of the κόσμος, or whether it is that of v. 18, which is realized in the experiences of earthly life within history, what is significant is that the saying does not end in the comforting tones of the promise, but in a warning which takes up again the thought contained in 16.7" (628; this in keeping with Bultmann's rearrangement in which 16:7 actually *precedes* 14:28!).

133. Gr. ἐχάρητε ἄν.

134. "That" (ὅτι) could also be translated "because," but the difference in meaning would be slight. "That" is preferable, given that the next ὅτι can only be rendered as "because" ("because I am going off to the Father").

135. As we have seen, a variant reading in verse 7 calls for a contrary-to-fact condition as well ("If you had known me, you would have known my Father"), but without conclusive evidence either in the manuscripts or in the context.

136. See 1 John 4:17-18, where love is deemed inconsistent even with the more common word for "fear" (φόβος): "There is no fear in love, but perfect love casts fear out; for fear has to do with punishment, and the person who fears has not been perfected in love."

Their four questions have given evidence of their emotional dependence on Jesus, but love is another matter. Three times he has set forth obedience to his "commands" (vv. 15, 21) or his "word" (v. 23) as the undeniable evidence that a person "loves" him, but neither he nor the disciples have ever said in so many words that they do. As late as the very last chapter of the Gospel, he can still ask Peter (not once but three times!), "Do you love me?" (21:15, 16, 17). This time the test of love is not simply keeping Jesus' commands, but something more difficult: rejoicing and not grieving that he is "going off to the Father, because the Father is greater than I."

Theologians have long debated in what sense the Father is "greater"[137] than the Son, and how this assertion relates to Jesus' earlier claim that "I and the Father are one" (10:30). But in the immediate context Jesus is doing little more than reinforcing his earlier pronouncement that the true disciple will do "the works I am doing . . . and greater than these he will do *because I am going to the Father*" (v. 12, italics added). Now we learn that the works will be "greater" because the Father is "greater." The Advocate will come only because Jesus "will ask the Father" (v. 16), probably in the Father's presence when he has "gone away" (see 16:7). Despite the accent on mutuality (as in vv. 10, 11, 20), there are certain respects in which it has been clear all along that the Father is "greater." Certain statements about the Father and the Son are not reversible. That is, the Father sent the Son, not the other way around. The Son does what he sees the Father doing, does the works of the Father, says what the Father gives him to say (see, for example, v. 24, "and the word which you all hear is not mine but the Father's who sent me"). None of these pronouncements makes sense when turned around: the Father does not imitate the Son; the Father does not do the works of the Son, nor speak the Son's words. In that sense the Father's priority is undeniable. If Jesus is "the Way," he is the way "to the Father" (v. 6), who sent him in the first place, not an end in himself. His disciples should rejoice in his "going," because only by "going to the Father" can he "come" to them and be able to say, "I am in my Father, and you in me, and I in you" (v. 20). The promise of mutual indwelling is Jesus' answer to their fear of his departure, while at the same time their acceptance of that departure is the key to their experience of mutual indwelling. Thus when Jesus "comes back" at last to take them to himself in the Father's spacious household (v. 3), it is simply the natural and inevitable consummation of an already existing vital relationship in the present world.

29 "And now I have told before it happens," Jesus concludes, "so that when it happens you might believe" (v. 29). When what happens? The parallel with his words just after the footwashing in connection with the cita-

---

137. Gr. μείζων.

tion of Psalm 41 is striking, as we have seen: "From now on I tell you before it happens, so that when it happens you might believe that I am" (13:19). There he was speaking of the prospect of dissension and betrayal within the community of disciples after his departure. Here too he has hinted at impending trouble (v. 27), but what he has said explicitly is far more positive — a reason to "rejoice," in fact: "I am going away, and I am coming to you," and "I am going off to the Father" (v. 28). His intent is that when this happens, "you might believe." The reader is left to wonder, When *did* it happen, and did the disciples in fact "believe"? As we have just seen, there is an ambiguity about the "coming." It could be the traditional "second coming" at the last day (v. 3), or it could be the coming of Jesus to his disciples after his resurrection (see vv. 18-20, 23). But the coming at the last day is hardly an appropriate occasion for the disciples to "believe." It is rather too late for that. More likely, the "coming" he has in mind is the day of his resurrection, when Jesus "came" (20:19, 26), and his disciples "saw" (20:20, 25, 29), "rejoiced" (20:20), and finally, in the person of Thomas, explicitly "believed" (20:29). The stronger accent here, however, has been on the "going away," or "going off to the Father" (v. 28). That seems much less ambiguous. Jesus seems to be referring simply to his impending death. But why will his death become the occasion for his disciples to "believe"? By itself it cannot, even if it confirms to them that in fact he correctly predicted it. Only the "coming" can validate the "going away." Only the resurrection can prove that in dying Jesus actually did "go to the Father," and "prepare a place" in the Father's household. Or so it would seem. Yet as the narrative plays out, one of them, significantly, will "believe," even *before* the decisive "coming" (see 20:8, "and he saw and believed"). Jesus wants his disciples to believe that "I am going off to the Father" no less than that "I am coming to you," for as he has just told them, "the Father is greater than I" (v. 28). Only by coming to terms with his absence can they fully experience his presence.[138]

30 Finally, after repeated signals that his discourse may be drawing to a close ("These things I have spoken to you," v. 25; "Peace I leave with you," v. 27; "now I have told before it happens," v. 29), Jesus finally sounds ready to wrap things up: "I will no longer speak with you very much, for the ruler of the world is coming, and in me he has nothing" (v. 30). Still, the adverb "very much"[139] leaves the door open a crack for a little more to come.[140]

---

138. Bultmann puts it just as concisely: "Only the man who has grasped the meaning of Jesus' departure will experience his coming" (628-29).

139. Gr. πολλά.

140. This is a telling enough point that Brown (2.649) puts "much" in brackets on the basis of negligible manuscript evidence (Sinaitic Syriac alone), on the theory that "a scribe, thinking the statement 'I shall no longer speak with you' strange when three chap-

Whether the crack is wide enough to accommodate all of the next two (or three) chapters is another question. Probably Jesus is saying no more than that he will be around for only "a short time," which he has already stated twice (13:33; 14:19), so who knows how much more he will have to say?

Again we hear of "the ruler of the world."[141] Earlier, Jesus said, "Now is the judgment of this world. Now the ruler of this world will be driven out" (12:31).[142] There we observed a certain tension between "now" and the future verb, "will be driven out." As we saw, the world's "ruler" can only be "the devil," or "Satan," and here we learn that he is still very much in the picture (see already 13:2, 27). He is "coming,"[143] Jesus says, no less surely than Jesus himself is "coming" (vv. 3, 18, 28), and presumably sooner. The reader is left to wonder: If the devil, or Satan, "entered into" Judas (13:27), and went out when Judas "went out" (13:30), in what way is this world "ruler" now "coming"? In the person of Judas still, or in other ways? Jesus has just one more thing to say about him, "And in me he has nothing," distancing himself once again both from "the world" and from its "ruler."[144] Just as "the world" cannot receive, see, or know "the Spirit of truth" (v. 17), and "no longer sees" Jesus when he goes away (v. 19), and just as he is not "from this world" (8:23), and gives peace "Not as the world gives" (v. 27), so here, he and the world's "ruler" have nothing in common.

31 No sooner has Jesus finished distancing himself from "the world" and all it represents than he offers a ray of hope that this dissociation will not last forever. "But"[145] signals the contrast: "But that the world might come to know that I love the Father, and just as the Father commanded me,

---

ters of discourse were yet to follow, may have inserted the word" (2.651; also Bultmann, 630, n. 4, "certainly an early interpolation"). Thus the compositional theory of two farewell discourses is allowed to trump the clear textual evidence.

141. Gr. ὁ τοῦ κόσμου ἄρχων.

142. The precise term, "the ruler of the world," occurs only here; in 12:31 and 16:11 he is called "the ruler of this world," but the difference is insignificant. Each time the phrase occurs, it is with an accompanying reference of some kind either to "the world" (as here and in 16:9) or "this world" (see 12:31).

143. Gr. ἔρχεται.

144. "And in me he has nothing" (καὶ ἐν ἐμοὶ οὐκ ἔχει οὐδέν) recalls certain passages in John's Gospel which speak of believers "having" (ἔχειν) something "in" Jesus or "in" his name, such as "life" (3:15; 20:31) or "peace" (16:33). By contrast, the world has "nothing" in him, at least as long as "the ruler of the world" continues to be its ruler (see also 13:8, where Jesus warns Peter, "Unless I wash you, you have no part [οὐκ ἔχεις μέρος] with me"). Appeal to an underlying Hebrew idiom yields the related notion that this "ruler" has no claim on Jesus, and certain minor variant readings, such as "he will find nothing in me" (K) and "he has nothing to find in me" (D), suggest that he has no charges that he can legitimately bring against Jesus. But the basic idea is simple dissociation.

145. Gr. ἀλλά.

thus I do. Rise, let's get out of here!" (v. 31). We have heard already that Jesus is both "Savior of the world" (4:42) and "Light of the world" (8:12), and that his very flesh is given "for the life of the world" (6:51), and we will hear more later of the hope that "the world" might "believe" (17:21) and "know" (17:23) certain things of which it is now ignorant.[146] Therefore, his intent "that the world might come to know that I love the Father" is by no means out of place here, even after all he has said of the world's blindness and hostility to his claims.[147] Nowhere in the entire Gospel of John (or the entire New Testament for that matter) does Jesus himself ever say either "I love God" or "I love the Father"[148] except here, but the measure of his love is a familiar one: "just as the Father commanded me, thus I do." Jesus "loves" the Father in that he keeps the Father's commands (see 15:10), just as the measure of his disciples' love for him is that they keep his commands (see vv. 15, 21, 23). Without using the actual word "love," he has said that the Father "has given me a command what I should say and what I should speak" (12:49), adding that "I know that his command is life eternal; so then the things I speak, just as the Father has told me, thus I speak" (12:50). Earlier, he said, "This command I received from my Father," referring to his intention of "laying down" his life and "receiving it back" (10:18). Here too it is a matter not of things he is about to "speak" (12:50), but of something he is about to "do"[149] (v. 31), that is, "lay down his life" and "receive it back." It is hard to avoid the conclusion that Jesus' words here place him right on the threshold of the arrest, and the events that will quickly unfold in chapters 18–21. For this reason there has been a growing consensus that at some point in the composition history of the Gospel, this verse was followed immediately by 18:1, "Having said these things, Jesus went out with his disciples across the valley of the Kidron, where there was a garden into which he entered, he and his disciples." The reader might have been able to infer all this even without the final exclamation, "Rise, let's get out of here!"[150] but the added words seem to put the matter beyond doubt.

The whole scene bears a striking resemblance to the synoptic ac-

---

146. These references from Jesus' farewell prayer of chapter 17 are comparable to the present reference in that they follow such statements as "I pray not for the world" (17:9) and "They are not from the world even as I am not from the world" (17:16), distancing Jesus and his disciples from all that the world represents.

147. Compare Jesus' words to "the Jews" at the Tent festival, even as he points to their role in his own death: "When you lift up the Son of man, then you will come to know [τότε γνώσεσθε] that I am, and [that] on my own I do nothing, but just as the Father taught me, these things I speak" (8:28).

148. Gr. ἀγαπῶ τὸν πατέρα.
149. Gr. οὕτως ποιῶ.
150. Gr. ἐγείρεσθε ἄγωμεν ἐντεῦθεν.

The Gospel of John

counts of Jesus and his sleeping disciples in Gethsemane, when Jesus said to them, "Look, the Son of man is handed over into the hands of the sinners. Rise, let us go![151] Look, the one handing me over has come near!" (Mk 14:41-42//Mt 26:45-46). As in John's Gospel, the "one handing over" Jesus is clearly Judas, who immediately makes his appearance (Mk 14:43//Mt 26:47; also Lk 22:47). Jesus is summoning the disciples to wake up and face the approaching enemy. That parallel has largely shaped the interpretation of our text here, where the one "coming" is not explicitly Judas but "the ruler of the world" (v. 30). Here too, most commentators have assumed that Jesus is calling the disciples to confront him head-on, not escape him.

Yet there are differences that give us pause. Chronologically, Jesus' summons here is parallel not to anything that happened in Gethsemane (which has no place in John's Gospel), but to the notice at the end of the last supper in Mark and Matthew that "when they had sung a hymn they went out to the Mount of Olives" (Mk 14:26//Mt 26:30). Jesus and the disciples are together at a last meal, not already in the garden, and the disciples are being summoned to get up from the table, not awakened from sleep. The change of location is evident in the wording: not "Rise, let us go!" but "Rise, let's get out *of here!*"[152] accenting flight fully as much as confrontation.[153] If in fact "the ruler of the world is coming, and in me he has nothing" (v. 30), is that a reason to go out to meet him, or a reason to escape, as Jesus repeatedly escaped before (see 8:59; 10:39; 12:36)? It is difficult to say, because we are not told what the approach of "the ruler of the world" might have meant concretely. "The Jews" and "the Pharisees" who had tried to arrest him before are for the moment out of the picture, so that if Jesus and the disciples are fleeing, it is unclear just what they are fleeing from. Moreover, the intervening words "just as the Father commanded me, thus I do" (v. 31a), evoking the words "not what I want but what you want" (Mk 14:36//Mt 26:39; Lk 22:42), point forward toward the arrest and the passion, just as in the Synoptics, giving the scene a certain finality.

At the end of the day it is doubtful that either the aspect of escape or the aspect of imminent confrontation can be excluded. If there is an aspect of escape, then Jesus may be buying time (as in 8:59, for example), and in the canonical text as it stands, there clearly is still time for considerable instruction on mutual indwelling, love, and impending persecution (15:1–16:33), even for a long prayer (17:1-26), all of it cut off somewhat from its narrative

---

151. Gr. ἐγείρεσθε ἄγωμεν.
152. Gr. ἐντεῦθεν.
153. Contrast 11:8, "Let us go [ἄγωμεν] back to Judea," and 11:15, "Let us go [ἄγωμεν] to him" (that is, to Lazarus), where the accent is on the destination, not the point of departure.

15:1-17 INDWELLING AND THE LOVE COMMAND

setting. Not until Jesus finally goes out "with his disciples across the valley of the Kidron" (18:1) are we reminded again of the setting in which these chapters have taken place.

D. INDWELLING AND THE LOVE COMMAND (15:1-17)

> 1 *"I am the true Vine, and my Father is the Vinekeeper. 2 Every branch in me that does not bear fruit he takes it away, and every branch bearing fruit he trims it clean, to bear more fruit. 3 Already you are clean, because of the word which I have spoken to you. 4 Make your dwelling in me, and I in you. Just as the branch cannot bear fruit on its own unless it dwells in the vine, so you cannot unless you dwell in me. 5 I am the Vine, you are the branches. The person who dwells in me and I in him, he bears much fruit, so that apart from me you cannot do anything. 6 Unless someone dwells in me, he is thrown out like the branch, and withered, and they gather them and throw them into the fire, and they are burned up. 7 If you make your dwelling in me, and my words come to dwell in you, ask whatever you want, and it will be done for you. 8 In this my Father is glorified, that you bear much fruit and become my disciples. 9 Just as the Father loved me, so I loved you. Make your dwelling in my love. 10 If you keep my commands, you will dwell in my love, just as I have kept the commands of my Father and dwell in his love.*
>
> 11 *"These things I have spoken to you so that my joy might be in you, and that your joy might be fulfilled. 12 This is my command, that you love each other just as I loved you. 13 No greater love has anyone than this, that he lay down his life for his friends. 14 You are my friends, if you are doing the things I command you. 15 I no longer say that you are slaves, because the slave does not know what his lord is doing. But I have said that you are friends, because everything I heard from my Father I made known to you. 16 You did not choose me, but I chose you, and appointed you that you might go and bear fruit, and that your fruit might last — that whatever you ask of the Father in my name he might give you. 17 These things I command you, that you love each other."*

Almost without stopping for breath Jesus continues, "I am the true Vine, and my Father is the Vinekeeper" (15:1), without the slightest narrative introduction, such as "So again Jesus spoke to them, saying" (as in 8:12), or "So again he said to them" (as in 8:21), or "But Jesus cried out and said" (as in 12:44). The closest analogy is with John's farewell speech, where, after seeming to conclude with "He must grow, but I must diminish" (13:30), John instead

799

plunged ahead with "The One coming from above is above all" (v. 31), and further testimony to Jesus (vv. 31-36). The question confronting the reader here is, What are these words of Jesus meant to follow? Are we to presuppose all that has been said in the preceding chapter, as the canon would dictate, or are we back to square one, building on the narrative of the footwashing and the exit of Judas, as modern theories of the Gospel's composition have suggested? Surely the notices that "Every branch in me that does not bear fruit he takes it away" (v. 2) and "Unless someone dwells in me, he is thrown outside like the branch" (v. 6) come appropriately after the apostasy of Judas.[1] Yet just as surely, Jesus' abrupt self-identification as "the true Vine" cannot be read as following immediately upon 13:30, for in that case it would have been introduced with "Jesus said," or something to that effect. It could, however, be read as following 13:35, expanding on the themes of 13:31-35, and in particular the "new command" of mutual love (vv. 34-35). This is plausible because Jesus does get around fairly soon to reiterating that the disciples must love each other as he has loved them (see 15:12-17). Yet that is not the starting point. The starting point is rather the theme of indwelling, introduced only in the intervening discourse, specifically in answer to Philip's question (14:10-11, 20) and the question of Judas (v. 23). Jesus now speaks as if the relationship to be revealed "in that day" that "I am in my Father, and you in me, and I in you" (14:20) has already gone into effect, as indeed it has, the Gospel writer believes, for the readers of the Gospel. For this reason, the traditional "canonical" reading of the text as it stands is preferable. Jesus uses the metaphor of the Vine to explain further what the "indwelling" of which he has just spoken will mean concretely in the disciples' experience.

The Vine metaphor, however, has its limitations, for it does not explain the love Jesus has for the disciples or the love they must have for one another. While Jesus has spoken of loving him as one would love God and keeping his commands in connection with indwelling (see 14:15, 21), he has not yet revisited the "new command" of love given earlier, with its accent on love's mutuality (13:34-35). The true measure of dwelling in the Vine (vv. 1-8), he now reminds them, is dwelling in his love and "keeping his commands" (vv. 9-10), just as before (14:15, 21), but the one "command" now highlighted above all others is the "new" command grounded in Jesus' initiative: "love each other just as I loved you" (see vv. 12, 17). On this basis, Jesus envisions the disciples "bearing fruit" (vv. 2, 3, 4, 5, 8, 16), fruit left undefined, but apparently understood as a "crop," or harvest, of eternal life, both for themselves and others (see 4:36; 12:24-25), the equivalent, perhaps, of Jesus' own "works." Bearing "fruit" is what makes them his "disciples"

---

1. If 13:31–14:31 comprise the first farewell discourse, as Brown proposes (2.545, 586), then 15:1 would indeed come directly after 13:30.

15:1-17 INDWELLING AND THE LOVE COMMAND

(v. 8), that is, not just his "slaves" but his "friends," who "know what he is doing" and for whom he "lays down his life" (vv. 13-15).

1 "I am the true Vine" (v. 1), like "I am the Bread of life" (6:35, 48), "I am the Light of the world" (8:12; 9:5), "I am the Door" (10:7, 9), and "I am the good Shepherd" (10:11, 14), is the first of two parallel "I am" pronouncements. First Jesus says, "I am the true Vine, and my Father is the Vinekeeper" (v. 1), and five verses later, "I am the Vine, you are the branches" (v. 6). He is "the Vine" both in relation to his Father and in relation to his disciples, corresponding to the claim that "I am in my Father, and you in me, and I in you" (14:20). The notion of the Father as "Vinekeeper" is not surprising, given the parables in the Gospel tradition about vineyards (see Mt 20:1-16; 21:28-32; Lk 13:6-9; Mk 12:1-12//Mt 21:33-46//Lk 20:9-19), going back to biblical imagery about Israel as God's vineyard (for example, Ps 80:8-18; Isa 5:1-7; Ezek 15:1-8; 17:5-8; 19:10-14).

More surprising is Jesus' self-identification as "the Vine,"[2] for his only possible self-reference in the synoptic parables is as the vineyard owner's "beloved son" and "heir" (Mk 12:6-7), not as "the vine" or vineyard itself.[3] Still, his earlier self-identification as a "grain of wheat" that "bears a great crop" by becoming a full-grown plant "lifted up from the earth" (see 12:24, 32) has already opened the door to a similarly bold deployment of vineyard imagery here. Jesus is the "true"[4] Vine in the same sense in which he is "the true bread from heaven" (6:32), or "the good Shepherd" (10:11, 14). The point is not to differentiate him from other "vines" (Israel, for example), but simply to claim him as the very embodiment of what every vine should be — above all, the source of life to its branches.[5] Later, it is sufficient to call himself simply "the Vine" (v. 5). Yet as always, the "I am" does not represent a claim to independence or self-sufficiency. Even "the Vine" depends on the love and care of "the Vinekeeper." Just as "my Father" is the one who "gives you the true bread from heaven" (6:32), and just as "the good Shepherd" concludes by acknowledging that "I and the Father are one" (10:30), so here "my Father is the Vinekeeper," on whom everything that follows depends.

---

2. Gr. ἡ ἄμπελος.

3. See, however, the table prayer in the *Didache,* which at least approaches such an identification: "We thank you, Father, for the holy vine of David your servant, which you made known to us through Jesus your servant. To you be the glory forever!" (*Didache* 9.2). Here "the holy vine" still seems to represent Israel, the people of God, rather than Jesus personally, yet even in John 15, Jesus as "the true Vine" encompasses its "branches" as well, the new people of God.

4. Gr. ἡ ἀληθινή.

5. In much the same way, "bread" is seen as the source of life, to the point that Jesus calls himself "the Bread of life" (6:35, 48; see also vv. 50, 51, 58), and so too (in an even more active way) is the "shepherd" (10:10, 28).

2 Still focusing on the Father as Vinekeeper, Jesus makes the Father the subject of the next sentence: "Every branch in me that does not bear fruit he takes it away, and every branch bearing fruit he trims it clean so that it bears more fruit" (v. 2). Several of the preceding "I am" pronouncements in the Gospel have been followed by an invitation or promise of some kind (see 6:35; 8:12; 10:9; 11:25-26; also 14:6, where the invitation was stated negatively). This one, by contrast, focuses on those who have *already* responded to Jesus' invitation, urging them to maintain their commitment so as to "bear fruit." The accent on "fruit," or "a crop," is simply part of the metaphor of the "vine," and is consequently left (for the moment) unexplained, but the reader can at least infer that the absence of "fruit" implies the absence of life, that is, of a life-giving relationship to the vine. As he did in introducing the metaphors of "the Door" and "the good Shepherd" (10:1),[6] Jesus begins here with the negative: "Every branch in me that does *not* bear fruit[7] he takes it away" (italics added), before coming to the positive: "and every branch bearing fruit he trims it clean, to bear more fruit."

Two things are noticeable here. First, Jesus speaks of "Every branch in me," even though he has not yet explicitly identified the "branches" of the vine as the disciples (see v. 5), or urged them to "Make your dwelling in me" (v. 4). Second, he plays on the rhyme of the two verbs, "takes away" and "trims clean,"[8] to describe the Father's work as Vinekeeper. The grim work of "taking away" the dead and fruitless branches he will spell out shortly (v. 6). Judas Iscariot is still fresh in memory as the classic example. "Trimming clean" is what applies to the rest of the disciples, and, as we will see, Jesus' goal for them is "more fruit," or "much fruit" (see vv. 5, 8).

3 Jesus immediately adds that the Father's work of "trimming clean" is now complete: "Already you are clean, because of the word which I have spoken to you" (v. 3). The emphatic "you" makes it clear that the disciples themselves are the branches in the vine. "Clean"[9] involves a certain play on words. Jesus introduced the verb "trims clean"[10] as a agricultural term, in keeping with the metaphor of the vine,[11] while the adjective "clean" comes rather from the world of ritual or moral purity (as if from the verb "to cleanse" or "purify").[12] The reminder, "Already you are clean," recalls the

---

6. There he began, "the one who does *not* enter through the door . . . is the thief and robber" (v. 1, italics added), before continuing, "But the one who enters through the door is the shepherd of the sheep" (v. 2).
7. Gr. μὴ φέρον καρπόν.
8. Gr. αἴρει and καθαίρει.
9. Gr. καθαροί.
10. Gr. καθαίρει.
11. See BDAG, 488; "to remove superfluous growth from a plant."
12. Gr. καθαρίζειν. This verb does not occur in John's Gospel, but see 1 John 1:7,

footwashing, yet even back then, as we have seen, Jesus pronounced the disciples (except for Judas) *already* "clean" (see 13:10-11). Confirming what he said then, he now makes it clear that they are clean not because of the footwashing itself, nor because of baptism, but "because of the word[13] which I have spoken to you." Jesus' "word," or spoken "words,"[14] are the means by which the Father has "given" or "drawn" the disciples to Jesus (see 6:37, 44, 65), trimming them "clean" to be his messengers. The implication is that now they are ready to bear "more fruit."

4 How are they to do this? "Make your dwelling in me, and I in you," Jesus tells them. "Just as the branch cannot bear fruit on its own unless it dwells in the vine, so you cannot unless you dwell in me" (v. 4). "Make your dwelling in me, and I in you"[15] (v. 4a) is an extraordinary command. Extraordinary for two reasons. First, the verb "to dwell," or "stay," or "remain" somewhere,[16] ordinarily implies a continuing relationship, one in which a person is already involved, and this is supported by the present context ("Already you are clean"). In the imperative it should mean "stay where you are," or "maintain the relationship which now exists" (that is, do nothing; don't change a thing); therefore, one would expect the present imperative.[17] But the imperative here is aorist,[18] suggesting an act of the will, a conscious decision to "dwell," or make a home, in one's present relationship to Jesus. Hence the translation, "Make your dwelling in me," evoking the promise in the preceding chapter that Jesus and the Father will come and "make a dwelling"[19] with those who love him (14:23).[20] But how exactly does one go about "making one's dwelling" not just "with" or "right beside" Jesus, but "in"

9; for the noun "purification" (καθαρισμός), see 2:6 (with reference to Jewish rules of purity) and 3:25 (probably with reference to baptism).

13. Gr. διὰ τὸν λόγον.

14. Gr. τὰ ῥήματα, as in 6:63, 68.

15. Gr. μείνατε ἐν ἐμοί, κἀγὼ ἐν ὑμῖν.

16. Gr. μένειν.

17. As Abbott notices (*Johannine Grammar*, 318-19), the imperative is aorist (μείνατε) both times it occurs on Jesus' lips in John's Gospel (here and in v. 9), but present (μένετε) in 1 John (2:28).

18. Gr. μείνατε.

19. Gr. μονήν . . . ποιησόμεθα.

20. This is consistent with the few other occurrences of the aorist imperative (μείνατε) in the New Testament (see Mt 10:11, where the meaning is "stay there," that is, make that city your home until it is time to leave; also, Mt 26:38//Mk 14:34, where Jesus is telling the disciples, "stop here," while he goes on further, and Lk 24:29, where the disciples urge the risen Jesus to "stay with us," that is, sit down and join us at table). In John's Gospel (without an imperative), see 1:39, "and they stayed [ἔμειναν] with him that day," meaning they "made their dwelling" with him.

him? What does such a command mean concretely? What steps must a person take? At this point, the answer is far from clear.

The second extraordinary thing is the corollary, "and I in you."[21] Is this the equivalent of a conditional sentence, an elliptical promise of a reward, as if to say, "*If* you dwell in me, I will dwell in you"? Or is it part and parcel of the imperative itself, as if to say, "Making your dwelling in Jesus is equivalent to Jesus' making his dwelling in you"? Probably the latter, provided that this mutual indwelling is not viewed as something the disciple simply wills into being.[22] Mutual indwelling is God's doing, not theirs, the work of the Father through the Son. Once more, 14:20 provides the key: "In that day, you will come to know that I am in my Father, and you in me, and I in you." Nothing said here, in fact, makes much sense apart from that immediate background, thus confirming the text's canonical order. The command, "Make your dwelling in me, and I in you," simply means to accept and embrace that relationship, probably not at that very moment in narrative time, between the meal and the garden, but "in that day" (14:20), the day of resurrection when Jesus "comes" (14:18) and, with the Father, makes his "dwelling" with those who love him (14.23). Consequently it is intended as much (or more) for the readers of the Gospel as for the eleven disciples still trying to cope with Jesus' impending departure.

Jesus next ties the command back to the metaphor of the vine: "Just as the branch cannot bear fruit on its own *unless* it dwells in the vine, so you cannot *unless* you dwell in me" (v. 4b, italics added).[23] Several previous "unless" clauses, by now familiar to the reader of the Gospel, had to do with salvation or eternal life (see 3:3, 5, 27; 6:44, 53, 65), and one was drawn, like this one, from the world of agriculture: "Unless the grain of wheat dies by falling to the earth, it remains alone by itself; but if it dies, it bears a great crop" (12:24). The similarities are striking. Both statements are truisms: a seed amounts to nothing "unless" it is planted, and a branch amounts to nothing "unless" it is part of the vine. A "grain of wheat," planted, eventually "bears a great crop," and a branch on a vine "bears fruit" — the vocabulary is the same. The English translations differ only in that one expects a "crop" from wheat and "fruit" from a grapevine! In the very next verse, matching the earlier terminology exactly, Jesus will speak

---

21. Gr. κἀγὼ ἐν ὑμῖν.

22. This is close to the view of Abbott, who does not altogether avoid putting the disciples in control. He paraphrases, "Your abiding in me shall be mine in you.... Cause yourselves to abide in me and [thereby] me also to abide in you," adding that "The two 'abidings' are regarded as inseparable" (*Johannine Grammar,* 174).

23. The phrase "on its own" (ἀφ' ἑαυτοῦ) corresponds to what Jesus has frequently said about himself. He too never acts "on his own," but always in dependence on the Father (see, for example, 5:19, 30; 7:17-18).

of "bearing much fruit"[24] (v. 5). In both instances, the agricultural facts serve as metaphors for the disciples' experience: like the "grain of wheat," they too must "die" in order to live (12:25), and like the branches they must continually "dwell" in Jesus, and he in them.[25] The one superficial difference is in the use of the verb "dwell": unlike the fruitless branches, the useless seed that is not planted does "remain" or "dwell" somewhere, but "alone by itself" (12:24), in the end no different from fruitless branches cut off from the vine.

5 Jesus now repeats the "I am" (see v. 1), stating explicitly what he has been assuming from the start: "I am the Vine, you are the branches" (v. 5a), the emphatic "you" pointedly echoing the direct address of verses 3 and 4. This pronouncement serves as a heading to a sequence that follows (vv. 5-8), setting before the disciples two stark alternatives. These can be usefully set forth in a chiastic *(a-b-b-a)* pattern (not because the writer intended it but simply as a help to the reader):

a. The person who dwells in me, and I in him, he bears much fruit,
b. so that[26] apart from me you cannot do anything (v. 5).
b'. Unless someone dwells in me, he is thrown outside like the branch, and withered, and they gather them and throw them into the fire, and they are burned up (v. 6).
a'. If you make your dwelling in me, and my words dwell in you, ask whatever you want and it will be done for you. In this is my Father glorified, that you bear much fruit and become my disciples (vv. 7-8).

The point of the sequence is simple. When branches "dwell" or remain in the vine *(a* and *a')*, they bear fruit (even "much fruit"); when they do not *(b* and *b')*, they die, and the same is true of Jesus' disciples in relation to him. In the first half of the sequence (or chiasm, if we may call it that), Jesus

---

24. Gr. φέρει καρπὸν πολύν (compare 12:24).
25. Two textual variants must be noted. In both clauses, instead of "unless it dwells [μένῃ] in the vine," and "unless you dwell [μένητε] in me," in which the verb "dwell" is in the present subjunctive, some manuscripts (including D, Ψ, families 1 and 13, the majority of later witnesses, and for the former variant A as well) have the aorist subjunctive (which might be rendered as "make a dwelling") — this in agreement with the aorist imperative μείνατε, "Make your dwelling," at the beginning of the verse. But this is likely a scribal error prompted by the preceding aorist. The present subjunctive has the support of ℵ, B, L, and (in the second variant) A.
26. "So that" (ὅτι) carries no causal significance here ("because" or "for"), but merely signals a loose connection to what precedes (see BDAG, 732). If it is true that "dwelling in me [ἐν ἐμοί], and I in him" is a condition for "bearing much fruit," then it follows that "apart from me" [χωρὶς ἐμοῦ] no fruit is possible.

states the alternatives briefly *(a* and *b),* in the second half, he repeats them at greater length and in reverse order *(b'* and *a').* Throughout the sequence, he interweaves generalizations about a "person" (any person, or "someone") with words directed explicitly to the disciples (that is, to "you"). First he issues a generalized promise that "The person who dwells in me, and I in him, he bears much fruit," and then a very plainly worded warning to the disciples, "so that apart from me you cannot do anything" (v. 5b). If they were confused over what it meant to "dwell" in him and he in them, or to "bear fruit," there is no room for confusion here. For the moment at least, the metaphor and the mystery disappear, and there is no mistaking what he means. It is a matter of total dependence upon him. Later, we will see a dramatic illustration of this pronouncement, as the disciples after the resurrection fished all night and "caught nothing" (21:3) until the risen Jesus told them where to cast their net.[27]

6 The rest of the sequence, or chiasm (vv. 6-7), looks first at what happens, "*Unless* someone dwells in me" (v. 6), and then at what happens, "*If* you make your dwelling in me, and my words dwell in you" (v. 7, italics added).[28] The first clause introduces a cautionary tale: "Unless someone dwells in me, he is thrown out like the branch, and withered, and they gather them and throw them into the fire, and they are burned up" (v. 6). The subject of the tale is an indefinite "someone,"[29] but the warning is a very real one, whether directed to the disciples on the scene or (more likely) to the readers of the Gospel. "Thrown out" evokes memories of "the ruler of this world" being "driven out" (12:31), or of the Jewish authorities "driving out" the former blind man from the synagogue (9:34), or of that which Jesus explicitly promised *not* to do to "the person who comes to me" (6:37).[30] Here it spells out in what way the Father "takes away" every fruitless "branch" (v. 2). The phrase "like the branch," in fact, revisits that statement quite explicitly, replacing the metaphor with a simile. Jesus then adds that the anonymous "someone" is "withered," again like a branch,[31] and goes on to explain (in unnerving detail)

---

27. A number of commentators (including Bultmann, 537; Brown, 2.661) have also detected in these words an echo of the Gospel's sweeping claim at the beginning that "apart from him [χωρὶς αὐτοῦ] not one thing [οὐδὲ ἕν] that has come to be was made" (1:3). Intriguing but probably unintended.

28. Again, 12:24 offers a useful point of comparison: "unless [ἐὰν μή] the grain of wheat dies by falling to the earth, it remains alone by itself; but if [ἐὰν δέ] it dies, it bears a great crop."

29. Gr. τις.

30. All of these are similar in vocabulary, but with the compound verb (ἐκβάλλειν ἔξω).

31. This is the predominant usage of the verb "withered" (ἐξηράνθη), although it can also be used of the human body (see Mk 3:1; 9:18).

what happens to "withered" branches: "and they gather them and throw them into the fire, and they are burned up." He is obviously speaking of literal branches, not people, yet his point is unmistakable: those who do not "dwell" or remain in him so as to "bear fruit" are in mortal danger.[32] The verb "dwells" is present, not aorist (as in v. 4, "Make your dwelling in me"), implying that those to whom he refers are in some sense already "in" the vine (see v. 2, "Every branch in me"). For this reason, the verse has played a significant role in theological debates over the question of apostasy, or whether individuals can lose their salvation.

Clearly, Judas is still very much in mind, and the question is whether or not Jesus is raising the possibility of other Judases among the disciples or among the readers of the Gospel. In the case of Judas, the Gospel writer went out of his way to make it clear that "from the beginning" Jesus knew who would "hand him over" (6:64), and Jesus himself identified Judas as one of the "chosen" group, yet in the same breath as "the devil" (6:70). He also hinted at others (not "chosen") who in the course of the disciples' mission would "lift up the heel" in treachery against them (13:18), and reminded the disciples pointedly that "From now on I tell you before it happens" (13:19). But on the other hand, he stated clearly that his own "sheep" will "never ever be lost, and no one will seize them out of my hand" (10:28). And in the present context nothing is said about the fruitless branches being "cut off," only of being "taken away" (v. 2), or "thrown out" (v. 6). That they do not "bear fruit" (v. 2), and do not "dwell" or remain in the vine (v. 6), signal that they are *already* dead, not put to death by the Vinekeeper. Whether they were once alive and truly united to the Vine is left unexplored, but the very term "life eternal," so characteristic of this Gospel, renders it doubtful.[33] They are evidently viewed as having separated themselves from the believing community, and it is quite possible that the Gospel writer's view is the same as that expressed in 1 John: "Children, it is the last hour, and just as you have heard that antichrist is coming, so now many antichrists have come. They went out from us, but they were not of us, for if they were of us, they would have remained [or

---

32. Such imagery is not uncommon in the New Testament. See, for example, John the Baptist: "Already the axe is laid to the root of the tree. So every tree that does not bear good fruit is cut down and thrown into the fire" (Mt 3:10//Lk 3:9); and from Jesus the same: "Every tree that does not bear good fruit is cut down and thrown into the fire" (Mt 7:19); and Hebrews: "But if [the ground] brings forth thorns and thistles, it is worthless, and nearly cursed; its end is for burning" (Heb 6:8).

33. See 10:28, where the promise quoted above that they will "never ever be lost" is preceded by the words, "And I give them life eternal" (see also 6:39-40, where the Father's will is that Jesus not "lose anything" of those the Father has given him, and that they "might have life eternal").

"dwelt"]³⁴ with us, but [they did it] in order to make it known that they were not of us" (1 Jn 2:18-19).

7 Jesus now completes the sequence on a positive note: "If you make your dwelling in me, and my words come to dwell in you, ask whatever you want, and it will be done for you" (v. 7). With this, he begins to clarify one or two points that have so far been obscure. First, he offers a definition, or at least an illustration, of what "I in you" (v. 4) or "I in him" (v. 5), which by itself sounds very mystical, means concretely. One thing it can mean is that Jesus' spoken "words"³⁵ take root, or "come to dwell," in the disciples' minds and hearts so as to govern their attitudes and actions. Long before, in a futile attempt to win over some "Jews who had believed him" (8:30), he had said, "If you dwell on³⁶ my word, you are truly my disciples, and you will know the truth, and the truth will set you free" (8:31-32). They took offense, and nothing came of it (8:33), and now he holds out much the same hope to those who have all along been designated his "disciples" already.³⁷ Second, Jesus provides a specific illustration of what "bearing fruit" might mean. Just as he introduced answered prayer a chapter earlier as an example of "greater" works the disciples would do after his departure (see 14.12-14), so he tells them here, "ask whatever you want, and it will be done for you."³⁸ The phrase "whatever you want"³⁹ could imply a more sweeping promise than before,⁴⁰ but the promise is in effect only on the stated condition that "you make your dwelling in me, and my words come to dwell in you." If answered prayer is not itself the "fruit" of which Jesus speaks, it is at least the means — perhaps the only means — by which the expectation of "much fruit" is to be fulfilled.

8 Jesus confirms this by immediately adding, "In this my Father is glorified, that you bear much fruit and become my disciples" (v. 8).⁴¹ "In

---

34. Gr. μεμενήκεισαν.
35. Gr. τὰ ῥήματά μου.
36. Gr. ἐὰν ὑμεῖς μείνητε ἐν. The translation "dwell on" in that verse was an attempt to make this point.
37. His acknowledgment of his own role as their "Teacher" and "Lord" (13:13) further confirmed this.
38. The expression "it will be done for you" (γενήσεται ὑμῖν) implies the activity of God the Father. It is comparable to such expressions as "Ask, and *it will be given you*" (δοθήσεται ὑμῖν), or "Knock, and *it will be opened to you*" (καὶ ἀνοιγήσεται ὑμῖν; see Mt 7:7//Lk 11:9).
39. Gr. ὃ ἐὰν θέλητε.
40. Jesus himself speaks boldly in prayer of what "I want" (θέλω, 17:24), yet even he in one classic instance pointedly avoided doing so (see Mk 14:36; Mt 26:39).
41. The accent on the Father being "glorified" in connection with the promise of answered prayer also corresponds to what Jesus said in the preceding chapter, that "whatever you ask in my name, this I will do, so that the Father might be glorified in the Son" (14:13).

15:1-17 Indwelling and the Love Command

this" looks simultaneously forward and back, in effect linking the promise of answered prayer (v. 7) to the bearing of "much fruit," which in turn means that the disciples "become my disciples"[42] (v. 8b). This kind of statement made sense in 8:31, where Jesus told the "believing" Jewish authorities, "If you dwell on my word, you are truly[43] my disciples," because the genuineness of their commitment (as "the Jews"!) was inevitably suspect. Here it seems to make less sense because we have grown accustomed to a definite group of "disciples," so designated, and even "chosen" out of a larger group (see 6:66-70) as in some way "genuine" disciples, a gift from the Father "greater than all" (see 10:29). It comes as something of a shock that at this late date they have yet to "become my disciples" (without even an adverb such as "truly" to cushion the blow!).[44] No ground for complacency here, yet no trace of a rebuke either. One is reminded of Ignatius of Antioch, facing the prospect of martyrdom in Rome: "Then I will truly be a disciple of Jesus Christ" (*To the Romans* 4.2; LCL, 1.275), "But I am becoming more of a disciple" (5.1), and "Now I am beginning to be a disciple" (5.3; LCL, 1.277).[45] "Discipleship," it seems, means different things at different stages of a person's spiritual growth. Jesus' so-called "disciples" still have a ways to go.

9 Jesus continues to adapt the Vine metaphor to his audience, to make it less abstract or mystical, more practical and concrete. To do so, he explains mutual indwelling as mutual love (vv. 9-17, especially vv. 12 and 17). Nothing in the Vine metaphor per se would have required this. The relation of branches to a vine is a life-giving relationship, not a love relationship. Branches do not "love" the vine, much less each other! Jesus therefore looks elsewhere, at least for the moment, drawing on the "new command" of mutual love (13:34-35). "Just as the Father loved me," he begins, "so I loved you. Make your dwelling in my love" (v. 9). Only the imperative "Make your dwelling" links the pronouncement to the metaphor of the Vine (see v. 4,

---

42. Gr. καὶ γένησθε ἐμοὶ μαθηταί.
43. Gr. ἀληθῶς.
44. This is no less the case if the variant reading, "you will become" (γενήσεσθε), is adopted (with ℵ, A, Ψ, and the majority of later manuscripts) instead of "that you become" (ἵνα ... γένησθε, with P⁶⁶, B, D, L, Θ, and others); see Metzger, *Textual Commentary*, 246.
45. This in fact is the predominant usage of μαθητής in Ignatius; see also *To the Ephesians* 1.2, "I was hoping, through your prayer, to be allowed to fight the beasts in Rome, that by doing so I might be able to be a disciple" (LCL, 1.221); *To the Trallians* 5.2, "For not even I am a disciple already. ... For many things are still lacking to us, that we may not be lacking God" (LCL, 1.261); *To the Magnesians* 9.1, "Through this mystery we came to believe, and for this reason we endure, that we may be found to be disciples of Jesus Christ, our only teacher" (LCL, 1.251).

"Make your dwelling in me"). Otherwise the metaphor is dropped until verse 16, where he finally speaks again of "bearing fruit."

Jesus does not immediately repeat the "new command" verbatim ("that you love each other, just as I loved you," 13:34), but instead starts further back, with the Father's love for him (see 3:35; 5:20; 10:17; 17:24): "Just as the Father loved me, so I loved you" (v. 9a). The Father's love for the Son is the basis of the Son's love for the disciples, which in turn is the basis of their love for each other. But instead of coming immediately to the "new command" of mutual love (see vv. 12, 17), Jesus simply tells them, "Make your dwelling[46] in my love" (v. 9b), that is, make my love for you your very identity. Who are you? Those whom Jesus loved. If the consistent designation of a certain disciple as "one whom Jesus loved" (see 13:23) is, as many believe, a self-designation of the author (or implied author) of the Gospel, then this is how he identifies himself (even to the exclusion of his actual name!). If the Son is "the beloved Son" (in the other Gospels), or "the One and Only" (in this Gospel), by virtue of being loved and chosen by the Father, so the disciples will find their identity as "his own" (13:1) or as "friends" of the Son (see vv. 14-15) by virtue of the Son's (and consequently the Father's) love for them (see 16:27; 17:23, 26).

10 The disciples display their identity as those whom Jesus loves by keeping his commands (as in 14:15 and 21), and this too is rooted in his own relationship to the Father. "If you keep my commands," Jesus continues, "you will dwell in my love, just as I have kept the commands of my Father and dwell in his love" (v. 10). Jesus' obedience to the Father (4:34; 5:30; 6:38; 8:29), and more explicitly the Father's "command,"[47] has been evident all along (see 10:18, 12:49-50, 14:31).[48] Here he makes it the model for the disciples' obedience to his "commands," above all (as we will quickly see) the one command to "love each other" (v. 12). This will define their identity (see 13:35, "By this they all will come to know that you are my disciples, if you have love for each other"). The only difference between Jesus' teaching here and in the preceding chapter is that there "keeping the commands" was the measure of the disciples' love for Jesus (14:15, 21) and of Jesus' love for the Father (14:31), whereas here it is the measure of the Father's love for Jesus and Jesus' love for the disciples (see v. 9).

11 Jesus pauses momentarily, again using the expression "These

---

46. Gr. (once again) μείνατε.
47. Gr. ἐντολή, singular.
48. Only here does Jesus speak explicitly of "commands" (τὰς ἐντολάς, plural) that he has received from the Father, for the accent has been on the single "command" of laying down his life (10:18 and presumably 14:31). Yet see 8:29, "the things that please him" (τὰ ἀρεστὰ αὐτῷ). He has also, of course, spoken freely of the plural "works" (τὰ ἔργα) that the Father has given him to do.

15:1-17 Indwelling and the Love Command

things I have spoken to you" (as in 14:25) to state the implications of what he has just said. His intent is "that my joy[49] might be in you, and that your joy might be fulfilled" (v. 11). He wants the disciples, in being the object of his love, to experience joy as well. Up to now, he has mentioned "joy" only to notice its absence ("If you loved me, you would rejoice," 14:28), but now he envisions his own "joy" dwelling "in" them, just as he himself (vv. 4, 5), or his "words" (v. 7) will dwell "in" them. We have heard little of Jesus' own joy, but it is clearly presupposed here (and later in 17:13), evidently on the basis of his relationship to the Father and the completion of the Father's work.[50] As for the disciples' joy being "fulfilled,"[51] we have glimpsed that in the person of John (in a very real sense Jesus' first disciple), who spoke of "the friend of the bridegroom who . . . rejoices with joy at the bridegroom's voice," and who made that joy his own by adding, "So this, my joy, is fulfilled" (3:29). But the joy of these disciples, as of the readers of the Gospel, is a shared joy. It is shared with Jesus, for it is his joy to begin with, and by implication with each other, but its ultimate "fulfillment" is yet to come. "Grief" will come first (16:6, 20), but grief will give way to joy when they see Jesus again (16:20-22; compare 20:20). Joy's "fulfillment" is never quite an accomplished fact as it was in the end for John (3:29), but always an object of hope and of prayer, whether their own prayers (16:24) or the prayer of Jesus (17:13).[52]

12 Finally, having laid the groundwork, Jesus repeats verbatim the "new command" (without calling it "new"): "This is my command, that you love each other just as I loved you" (v. 12, as in 13:34). By this they "make their dwelling" in Jesus' love (see v. 9), acting out their new identity in their relationship to one another. Oddly, Jesus does not spell out what this means in practice. He does not, for example, repeat the command to "wash each other's feet" (13:14), nor does he provide any concrete illustration of love for one another, as is done, for example, in 1 John: "But whoever has the world's livelihood and sees his brother having need and closes off his heart from him, how does the love of God dwell in him?" (1 Jn 3:17). In the verses to follow, Jesus will focus on his own love for the disciples more than on theirs for one another (vv. 13-16), returning to the explicit command to "love each other"

---

49. Gr. ἡ χαρὰ ἡ ἐμή.
50. Jesus has been said to be "glad" (χαίρω) only once, in anticipation of the raising of Lazarus and the consequent faith of the disciples (11:15), while 4:36 hints at his joy (ἵνα . . . χαίρῃ), along with others, in the completion of a "harvest" among the Samaritans.
51. Gr. πληρωθῇ.
52. The "fulfillment" of joy is expressed in a purpose clause both here (ἵνα . . . πληρωθῇ) and in its other occurrences in the Gospel (ἵνα . . . ᾖ πεπληρωμένη, 16:24; ἵνα ἔχωσιν . . . πεπληρωμένην, 17:13; see also 1 Jn 1:4; 2 Jn 12).

only at the end, still without explanation (v. 17), so as to frame the whole paragraph (vv. 12-17).

13 Speaking of his own love for them, Jesus continues, "No greater love has anyone than this, that he lay down his life for his friends" (v. 13).[53] The expression "lay down his life," or "soul," recalls what Jesus as the "good Shepherd" does for his sheep (10:11, 15). When the sheep metaphor is dropped, Jesus' "sheep" become "his friends," those whom he loves and cares about. The author of 1 John seems to know these passages (or something very like them), extending the principle to cover the disciples' responsibilities as well: "In this we know love, that he laid down his life for us, and we ought to lay down our lives for the brothers" (1 Jn 3:16).

As is often noted by commentators, love for one's "friends" (even to the point of death) was a virtue widely commended in the Graeco-Roman world,[54] but some readers of the New Testament might object that love for one's enemies is an even "greater" love (see Mt 5:43-47//Lk 6:32-35; Rom 5:6-8). It is important to remember that Jesus is not here comparing love for one's "friends" to any other kind of love — whether for parents or spouse or children, or "neighbors" (however defined), or for one's enemies — but simply making the point that there is no "greater" expression of love than giving one's life for someone.[55] Those for whom Jesus' gives his life are his "friends" for that very reason, whoever or whatever they may have been before that. His love for them — and consequently his death on their behalf — transforms them into "friends."[56]

---

53. The addition of "someone" (τις) in most manuscripts (including some important early ones) in order to provide a specific subject for the verb "lay down his life" looks suspiciously like a later grammatical correction (τις is omitted in P[66], the first hand of ℵ and of D, and in Θ and some old Latin witnesses. For the construction without τις, see BDF, §394).

54. See Keener, 2.1004-11; among the texts frequently quoted are Aristotle, *Nicomachean Ethics* 1169a ("To a noble man there applies the true saying that he does all things for the sake of his friends . . . and, if need be, he gives his life for them"), and Plato, *Symposium* 179b ("Only those who love wish to die for others").

55. So Barrett: "It does not claim that love for friends is better than love for enemies; only that there is nothing greater you can do for your friends than die for them. Life sacrificed is the supreme gift, and the mark of love" (476-77). But 1 John obviously contemplates situations short of that (once more, see 1 Jn 3:17). It is one thing to say, "I would die for you if need be," when no such contingency is on the horizon, and another to supply a specific lesser need that is actually present.

56. Such considerations may help to resolve the obvious tension between what Jesus says here and what Paul says in Romans: "For while we were still weak, at the right time, Christ died for the ungodly [ὑπὲρ ἀσεβῶν]. For scarcely will anyone die for a righteous person — for a good person, someone might possibly dare to die — but God proves his own love for us, in that while we were still sinners, Christ died for us" (ὑπὲρ ἡμῶν,

15:1-17 INDWELLING AND THE LOVE COMMAND

14 Jesus now announces the transformation: "You are my friends,[57] if you are doing the things I command you." This sounds like a conditional sentence, but if it were truly conditional we would have expected, "If you do the things I command you, you *will be* my friends," making friendship dependent on performance.[58] Instead, Jesus says, "You are my friends," right up front, as if without qualification, just as he said without qualification, "Already you are clean" (v. 2). The condition attached, "if you are doing[59] the things I command you," has a force akin to that of a first-class condition ("assuming you are doing"), or even a participle ("in doing what I command you").[60] That they are Jesus' "friends" is a given, just as it is by now a given that he has "loved" them (see vv. 9, 12; 13:1, 34).[61] It is unclear to what extent "friends" became a widespread self-designation among early Christians. Jesus calls his disciples "my friends" only once outside of John's Gospel, and that quite casually (Lk 12:4), yet 3 John concludes with a notice that "The friends[62] greet you. Greet the friends by name" (3 Jn 15), using the phrase much as other writers use "the saints," "the brothers."

15 Jesus next goes on to explain more of what the designation implies: "I no longer say that you are slaves,[63] because the slave does not know what his lord is doing. But I have said that you are friends, because everything I heard from my Father I made known to you" (v. 15). Jesus has never called his disciples "slaves" explicitly, although he acknowledged his own status as their "Lord" (13:13), and pointedly reminded them that "a slave is not greater than his lord, nor is a messenger greater than the person who sent him" (13:16).[64] Nor has he literally dropped the term, for within five verses

---

Rom 5:6-8). As we have seen, John's Gospel does not deal explicitly with the issue of sin and its remedy.

57. Gr. φιλοί μου.

58. The clause, "if you are doing the things I command you," echoes v. 10, "If you keep my commands." But what was conditional there on keeping Jesus' commands was not his love for the disciples, but their ability to "dwell," or make their home, in his love.

59. Gr. ἐὰν ποιῆτε.

60. The construction recalls 13:17, "Blessed are you [μακάριοί ἐστε] if you do them" (ἐὰν ποιῆτε, that is, 'in doing them'). As Bultmann puts it, "It is not a question of their still having to *become* his friends by fulfilling his commands; they *are* his friends already, as v. 15 states; the phrase ἐὰν κτλ. specifies the condition whereby what they already are can be fully realised in them" (543).

61. As we have seen, there is no discernible difference in this Gospel between the two verbs for "love" (φιλεῖν, from which φίλοι is derived, and ἀγαπᾶν).

62. Gr. οἱ φίλοι.

63. Gr. δούλους.

64. He has also referred to a disciple — any disciple — as his "servant" (διάκονος), without the connotation of slavery (to illustrate the distinction, see Mk 10:43-44).

he will use it again (v. 20, "A slave is not greater than his lord"). His point is rather that he does not view his disciples as his "slaves" in the proper sense of the word, but as his "friends." The distinction is not exactly what we might have guessed. It is different, for example, from 8:35, where the slave's limitation (in contrast to the son) is that he "does not remain in the household forever," but can be sold. It is not so much a question of freedom as of knowledge. A slave "does not know what his lord is doing," Jesus says, while his "friends," by contrast, presumably do know because "everything I heard from my Father I made known to you."[65]

With these words, Jesus revisits three earlier pronouncements, two addressed to "the Jews" in Jerusalem, and one to the disciples themselves just after the footwashing. In the first instance, he said, "For the Father loves the Son and shows him everything that he himself is doing" (5:20). The principle is the same as here: love in the sense of friendship involves "full disclosure." The Father and the Son are "friends"[66] with no secrets between them. And knowledge implies imitation: what the Father "is doing" the Son does as well (5:19). In the second instance, Jesus addressed "the Jews who had believed him" at the Tent festival: "If you dwell on my word, you are truly my disciples, and you will know the truth, and the truth will set you free" (8:31-32). While nothing was said there about friendship (rather, he said, "you are truly my disciples," as in 15:8), Jesus did make the point — as he does here — that freedom comes through knowledge. There knowledge of "the truth" was refused, on the ground that "We are Abraham's seed, and have never been in slavery to anyone" (8:33), but here, by contrast, Jesus credits his disciples with knowledge of what he is doing, "because everything I heard from the Father I made known to you." The prospect that "if the Son sets you free, you will really be free" (8:36) belongs to them, not "the Jews," and what "sets them free" is nothing other than "the truth" made known to them by the Son, truth that they must "do" as well as "believe." In the third instance, Jesus told Peter when he washed his feet, "What I am doing you do not understand now, but afterward you will understand" (13:7). Yet when the footwashing was over, he asked the disciples, "Do you understand what I have done for you?" (13:12), and after explaining what he had done, he told them, "Now that you know these things, blessed are you if you do them" (13:17). Again, knowing requires doing. The disciples for their part gave no signal that they did in fact

---

65. Whether Jesus "heard" (ἤκουσα) from God or "my Father" in some preexistent state or during the course of his ministry is not further explained here or elsewhere (see 3:32; 5:30; 8:26, 40). The expression can on occasion be used of others as well (see 6:45; 8:38, 47; 14:24).

66. The friendship in 5:20 is expressed with the verb φιλεῖ instead of the noun φίλοι.

understand, nor do their questions in the ensuing discourse (13:36–14:31) show any great measure of understanding, but Jesus now gives them the benefit of the doubt. His assurance to them is carefully worded, however. He does not claim explicitly that they, in contrast to a slave, *do* know "what he is doing,"[67] but only that "everything I heard from my Father I made known to you."[68] The implication is that they ought to know if they do not.

16 "*You* did not choose me, but *I* chose you,"[69] Jesus goes on (v. 16a), in keeping with the priority of his love for them over their love for one another (see vv. 9, 12; also 13:1, 14, 34). Love, as we have seen, is understood as choice, or preference. The disciples are Jesus' "friends" because he has chosen them as his friends. What he says here is said just as emphatically in 1 John: "In this is love, not that *we* have loved God, but that *he* loved us" (1 Jn 4:10), and "*We* love, because *he first* loved us" (1 Jn 4:19, italics added). He has twice spoken of his love as choice or election: "Did I not choose you as the Twelve? And one of you is 'the devil'" (6:70), and "I am not speaking about all of you. I know which ones I chose" (13:18). Now that Judas is gone, he can say without qualification, "I chose you."[70] His choice of these disciples is not so much divine "election" in the classic theological sense of the term as simply the selection of "Twelve" (now eleven) out of all who followed him, to accompany him in his ministry and carry on his work after his departure.

This he now makes explicit: "and appointed you that you might go and bear fruit, and that your fruit might last — that whatever you ask the Father in my name he might give you" (v. 16b). So far he has only hinted at a mission of some kind (see 13:16 and 20), without telling the disciples explicitly that it is their mission, or that he is actually "sending" them into the world as the Father sent him (see 13:20). Without using the actual word "send" (as he will in due course; see 17:18; 20:21), he reveals that his purpose for the disciples he has chosen is that they "go" and "bear fruit,"[71] and that their fruit "last,"[72] that is, "dwell" in the Vine, just as they dwell in the Vine. "Go and bear fruit" are closely linked, almost to the point that "go"[73] functions as a helping verb (as in "I'm going fishing," 21:3).[74] The accent is

---

67. Gr. τὶ ποιεῖ.
68. Despite the use of πάντα ("everything"), we will learn later that this "making known" is an ongoing process (see 16:12; 17:26).
69. Italics added because both pronouns, ὑμεῖς and ἐγώ, are emphatic.
70. Gr. ἐγὼ ἐξελεξάμην ὑμᾶς.
71. Gr. (again) καρπὸν φέρητε.
72. Gr. μένῃ.
73. Gr. ὑπάγητε.
74. Compare Matthew 28:20, "Go and make disciples of all the Gentiles," where the emphasis is on "making disciples," and the verb for "go" (πορευθέντες) functions similarly as a helping verb.

not on "going away" as Jesus will "go away" (13:33; 14:28), but on "bearing fruit" in the sense of making disciples or winning new converts (see 17:20, "those who believe in me through their word").[75] Then Jesus adds, in words that sound curiously anticlimactic, "that whatever you ask of the Father in my name he might give you." This should not be read as an additional goal *beyond* "bearing fruit," as if answered prayer depends on success in evangelism. Rather, the reverse is true. The two purpose clauses are both saying the same thing, reminding the disciples that whatever success they may have in "bearing fruit" in the course of their mission to the world is gained through answered prayer, and only through answered prayer.[76] At times we were reminded that this was true even of Jesus himself (see 9:31; 11:22, 41-42), and he has made it clear in the present discourse that prayer was indeed the key both to the disciples' "greater works" (14:13-14) and to the bearing of "much fruit" (vv. 7-8).[77]

17 These things I command you," Jesus adds, "that you love each other" (v. 17), reiterating what he has already said twice (v. 12 and 13:34), but still not spelling out what it means in actual practice, beyond washing one another's feet (13:14). All we can infer beyond that is that they must remain "friends" to one another (see 3 Jn 15), willing to lay down their lives for each other, in imitation of what Jesus has done for them (see 1 Jn 3:16). This, as we will see, they may well be called upon to do.

---

75. Chrysostom makes the point somewhat differently by drawing the image of "going" into the metaphor of the vine: "'that you should go,' (He still useth the metaphor of the vine,) that is, 'that ye should extend yourselves,'" which he then explains as "extending your branches through all the world" (*Homilies on St. John* 77.1; NPNF, 1st. ser., 14.282).

76. As Abbott puts it, "According to this view, the meaning is, "*That* ye may save souls — *that [I say]* your prayers for the souls of men may ever be heard" (*Johannine Grammar*, 128). Possibly Jesus is making a similar point in Matthew: "The harvest is great, but the workers are few. Therefore pray [δεήθητε] the Lord of the harvest, that he send out workers to his harvest" (Mt 9:37-38).

77. In 14:13-14, as we have seen, Jesus promised that he himself would answer prayers in his name (whether addressed to him or to the Father), while here (as implicitly in v. 7) prayer in Jesus' name is both addressed to the Father and answered by the Father (see also 16:23). While this could signal a distinction between the prayer terminology in the so-called "first" discourse (13:36–14:31) from that in the "second" (15:1–16:33), it can also be explained by the immediate context of 14:13-14, in which Jesus wants to accent his own authority at work in the "greater" things that the disciples will accomplish after his departure.

E. THE WORLD AND THE ADVOCATE (15:18–16:16)

18 *"If the world hates you, you know that it has hated me before you.* 19 *If you were from the world, the world would love its own, but because you are not from the world, but I chose you out of the world, for this reason the world hates you.* 20 *Remember the word that I said to you, 'A slave is not greater than his lord.' If they persecuted me, they will also persecute you. If they kept my word, they will also keep yours.* 21 *No, all these things they will do to you for my name's sake, because they do not know the One who sent me.* 22 *If I had not come and spoken to them, they would not have sin, but now they have no excuse for their sin.* 23 *The person who hates me hates my Father too.* 24 *If I had not done the works among them that no one else did, they would not have sin, but now they have both seen and hated both me and my Father.* 25 *But the word that is written in their law must be fulfilled, that 'They hated me without cause.'* 26 *When the Advocate comes, whom I will send to you from the Father, the Spirit of truth that goes forth from the Father, he will testify about me,* 27 *and you too must testify because you are with me from the beginning.*

16:1 *"These things I have spoken to you so that you will not be made to stumble.* 2 *They will put you out of synagogue. And yes, an hour is coming when everyone who kills you might think he is offering worship to God.* 3 *And they will do these things because they did not know the Father or me.* 4 *But these things I have spoken to you so that when their hour comes you might remember them, that I told you. And these things I did not tell you from the beginning, because I was with you.* 5 *But now I am going to the One who sent me, and none of you asks me, 'Where are you going?'* 6 *But because I have spoken these things to you, grief has filled your heart.* 7 *I, however, am telling you the truth: it is to your advantage that I am going away, for unless I go away, the Advocate will not come to you. But if I go, I will send him to you.* 8 *And he, when he comes, will convict the world of sin, and of justice, and of judgment.* 9 *Of sin because they do not believe in me,* 10 *and of justice because I am going to the Father and you no longer see me,* 11 *and of judgment because the ruler of this world has been judged.* 12 *I have still much more to say to you, but you are unable to bear it now.* 13 *But when that one comes, the Spirit of truth, he will lead you in all the truth. For he will not speak on his own, but whatever he hears he will speak, and he will announce to you the things to come.* 14 *That one will glorify me, because he will take from what is mine and announce it to you.* 15 *All things that the Father has are mine; that is why I said that he takes from what is mine and will an-*

nounce it to you. ₁₆ *A short time, and you no longer see me, and again a short time, and you will see me."*

Jesus' lengthy monologue (14:23–16:16) continues, and finally draws to a close. The command that the disciples "love each other" (15:17) gives way to a solemn warning that "the world," by contrast, will "hate" them just as it hated Jesus, and that the world's hatred will come to expression in active persecution as they go about fulfilling their mission to the world (15:18-25). Against this background, Jesus promises once again (as in 14:16-17, 26) that the "Advocate," or "Spirit of truth," will come and testify to the world about him even as they themselves bear testimony to what he has said and done (vv. 26-27). All this will happen, he warns them, in the setting of excommunication from the synagogue and even martyrdom, but they must not be discouraged, knowing that he has warned them of what is coming well in advance (16:1-4).

Jesus then returns to the immediate issue of his departure from the world (16:5-7), explaining more fully the nature of the Advocate's ministry. The Advocate will prove "the world" wrong, he promises (vv. 8-11), and teach the disciples all that they need to know in his absence (vv. 12-15). Finally he brings the discourse to an end with a riddle, designed to elicit from them (at last) a response: "A short time, and you no longer see me, and again a short time, and you will see me" (v. 16).

18-19 The dualism of John's Gospel could imply that the corollary of loving "each other" (rather than the "neighbor," or the "enemy") might be "hating" everyone else — that is, "the world." This was in fact the case in some branches of sectarian Judaism, notably the *Community Rule* at Qumran (". . . that they may love all the sons of light, each according to his lot in God's design, and hate all the sons of darkness, each according to his guilt in God's vengeance").[1] At the very least, the Gospel's characteristic understanding of love as choice or preference could lead us to expect a "hatred" of the world analogous to the "hatred" of parents, wife, children, and siblings of which Jesus speaks in Luke's Gospel (Lk 14:26). But such is not the case. The closest Jesus comes to urging hatred of the world is his promise that "the person who hates his life in this world will keep it to life eternal" (12:25).[2]

What we find instead is the expectation of being hated by the world. "If the world hates[3] you," Jesus tells his disciples, "you know that it has hated me

---

1. See 1QS 1.9-11 (Vermes, 99).
2. This in agreement with the last few words of Luke 14:26, "or even his own life" (ἔτι τε καὶ τὴν ψυχὴν ἑαυτοῦ). In 1 John, readers are told, "Love not the world, nor the things in the world. If anyone love the world, the love of the Father is not in him" (2:15) — but never in so many words, "hate the world."
3. Gr. μισεῖ.

before you" (v. 18).⁴ The pronouncement invites comparison with something he said to his unbelieving brothers just before the Tent festival: "The world cannot hate you, but it hates me because I testify about it that its works are evil" (7:7). His disciples, in contrast to his brothers, will be hated, and just as Jesus' love for them is prior to their love for one another (see v. 12), so the world's hatred of him is prior to its hatred of them. Jesus continues, as if revisiting in his mind that earlier scene with his brothers, "If you were from the world, the world would love its own,⁵ but because you are not from the world, but I chose you out of the world, for this reason the world hates you" (v. 19). The reminder that "I chose you"⁶ echoes verbatim the preceding "You did not choose me but I chose you" (16), making clear that their relationship to the world has been severed on Jesus' initiative, not their own.⁷ He, and he alone, is the reason the world hates them. If he had not chosen them, they would be no different from Jesus' unbelieving brothers, whom the world "cannot hate" (7:7). That the world can also "love" may come as something of a surprise after all the talk of Jesus' "love" for those whom he made his "friends," and it may be tempting, especially to modern interpreters, to contrast the world's narrow-minded love for "its own" with Jesus' universal love for everyone, not least his enemies. This is a valid point when all four Gospels are taken into consideration, but not in the Gospel of John, where Jesus too loves not his "neighbors" (much less his "enemies"), but precisely "his own⁸ who were in the world" (13:1). Jesus and "the world" have this much in common — that they each love their "own," and the two loves are mutually exclusive. On this point, John's Gospel is at one with the very different Epistle of James: "Do you not know that friendship with the world is enmity with God? So whoever wants to be a friend of the world becomes an enemy of God" (Jas 4:4). The principle here is the same, but the conclusion drawn is the opposite: those who become Jesus' "friends" will quickly discover that "the world" is their enemy.⁹

---

4. Compare 1 John 3:13, "And do not be surprised [μὴ θαυμάζετε], brothers, if the world hates you."

5. Gr. τὸ ἴδιον ἐφίλει. "Its own" (τὸ ἴδιον) is neuter, "that which is its own," referring corporately to those who belong to the world (just as Jesus uses neuter singular pronouns in 6:37, 39 and 10:28 to refer to those who corporately belong to him). P⁶⁶ and 1241 change the neuter to masculine (τὸν ἴδιον), as if referring to an individual person, but this reading is clearly secondary.

6. Gr. ἐγὼ ἐξελεξάμην ὑμᾶς.

7. The verb "chose" (ἐξελεξάμην) alters the meaning of the preposition ἐκ (and consequently of the phrase ἐκ τοῦ κόσμου). The disciples are no longer "from" or "of" the world (ἐκ τοῦ κόσμου) in the sense of belonging to it, but are chosen "out of" the world (ἐκ τοῦ κόσμου), and thus separated from it.

8. Gr. τοὺς ἰδίους.

9. This helps explain a number of passages in 1 John, in which hatred of the

20 From being Jesus' "friends," the disciples are temporarily demoted (for illustrative purposes only) back to being "slaves." "Remember the word that I said to you," Jesus continues, citing 13:16: "A slave[10] is not greater than his lord." There the pronouncement was linked to footwashing: if he, the "Lord" (13:13), washed the disciples' feet, they should not be too proud to wash each other's feet (see 13:14-15). Here he applies it quite differently: "If they persecuted me, they will also persecute you.[11] If they kept my word, they will also keep yours" (v. 20).[12] He seems to be drawing as much on what is *not* explicitly quoted from 13:16 ("nor is a messenger greater than the person who sent him") as from what *is* quoted, for the "persecution" in question surely comes as a result of being "sent" as Jesus' "messengers" (see v. 16, "that you might go and bear fruit"). As such, the disciples can expect no better treatment from the world than what Jesus himself received.

"If they persecuted me,[13] they will also persecute you" is a first-class conditional sentence, built on the assumption that Jesus has been consistently "persecuted," or "pursued" by "the world," more specifically by the Jewish authorities. The beginning of that persecution was explicitly noted, shortly after he healed the sick man at the pool: "And for this the Jews began pursuing [that is, "persecuting"] Jesus, because he did such things on the Sabbath" (5:16). More broadly, we have known from the start that "the world did not know him" (1:10), "hated" him, in fact (7:7), and that "Even after he had done so many signs before them, they would not believe in him" (12:37). More surprising is the next sentence: "If they kept my word, they will also keep yours." This too is a first-class conditional sentence which, if read in the same way, could imply that "the world" did in some way "keep Jesus' word," and might keep theirs as well. But the reader knows that this was not the case, for the verdict on Jesus' public ministry to the world is already in (see 1:10-11; 12:37-43). Therefore, the conditional sentence is ironic — a contrary-to fact condition masquerading as a simple condition: "If they kept my word — which they did not! — they will also keep yours — which they will not!"[14] It

---

"brother" (that is, the fellow believer) places one "in the darkness" (1 Jn 2:9, 11), or makes one a "murderer," like Cain (3:15), or a "liar" (4:20). To hate "the brother" is to be no longer a "brother," but to align oneself rather with "the world."

10. Gr. δοῦλος.

11. See Matthew 5:11-12, where "the prophets" are cited as the precedent; also Luke 21:12.

12. John's Gospel has precedent in other Gospels for such an application (see Mt 10:25b, "If they called the master of the house Beelzebul, how much more those of the household?").

13. Gr. εἰ ἐμὲ ἐδίωξαν.

14. As Brown paraphrases it (2.687), "they will keep your word to the extent they have kept mine (and they have not kept mine)."

is of course true that some "kept Jesus' word" during the course of his ministry — the disciples themselves are living proof of that — and some will keep theirs as well (see 17:20), but Jesus is not looking here at "some" in contrast to "others."[15] He is looking rather at "the world" as a unified entity arrayed in opposition to him and his Father, and to the disciples.

21 Jesus signals his use of irony, moving beyond it to dead seriousness, with an emphatic "But no,[16] all these things they will do to you for my name's sake, because they do not know the One who sent me" (v. 21). "All these things" are presumed to be bad things — persecution, and worse (see 16:2) — not the supposedly positive response of some who might "keep your word" (compare 16:3).[17] "For my name's sake"[18] recalls a similar tradition common to the other three Gospels, "and you will be hated by all for my name's sake" (Mk 13:13//Mt 10:22//Lk21:17; also Mt 24:9, "by all the Gentiles"). Jesus' disciples will suffer persecution simply because they belong to him, and represent him. But John's Gospel gives us the deeper reason: because "they do not know the One who sent me" — in short, they do not know God, a charge Jesus has leveled at them before (see 7:28-29; 8:19, 55). With these words, he gives the disciples not only a necessary warning but a message of consolation: when they suffer persecution they can be assured that they are doing so for Jesus' sake and following in his footsteps, and (as Chrysostom put it) that "the Father also is insulted together with them."[19]

22-23 "If I had not come and spoken to them," Jesus continues, "they would not have sin,[20] but now they have no excuse for their sin" (v. 22), adding "The person who hates me hates my Father too" (v. 23). The contrary-to-fact conditional clause reinforces a remarkable feature of this Gospel's understanding of "sin." Even though Jesus was introduced as "the Lamb of God who takes away the sin of the world" (1:29), the world's "sin" comes to expression only in its rejection of him, and consequently of God the Father. Although sin was obviously present long before Jesus came into the world (the devil, after all, was a murderer and a liar "from the beginning," 8:44),[21] it was

---

15. This is a common view among interpreters (see, for example, Schnackenburg, 3.115: "The Johannine community took both possibilities into account: rejection and persecution on the one hand, and acceptance in faith of their proclamation on the other hand"; also Barrett, 480: "John means, If there are some who persecute you, there will also be others who will keep your word").
16. Gr. ἀλλά.
17. As Brown notes (2.687), "Those who think that the last clause in 20 has a positive tone find difficulty with this verse," to the point that some see it as an interpolation!
18. Gr. διὰ τὸ ὄνομά μου.
19. *Homilies on St. John* 77.2; NPNF, 1st ser., 14.283.
20. Gr. ἁμαρτίαν οὐκ εἴχοσαν.
21. See also 1 John 3:8, "for the devil sins [ἁμαρτάνει] from the beginning."

somehow not counted as sin until the coming of Jesus brought it "to light," as it were (see 3:19). In short, there was plenty of sin before Jesus came, but no formal attribution of guilt.[22] In contrast to Paul, who claimed that "sin was in the world before the law, but sin is not reckoned where there is no law" (Rom 5:12), John's Gospel has a different point of reference. Sin is identified as sin not in relation to the law of Moses, but only in relation to Jesus (see 16:9, "About sin because they do not believe in me").

The contrary-to-fact condition also recalls what Jesus said to the Pharisees after he healed the man born blind: "If you were blind, you would not have sin.[23] But now you say that 'we see.' Your sin remains" (9:41). This too he said against the background of an announcement that "I came into this world" for a dual purpose — not only "that those who do not see might see," but "so that those who see might go blind" (9:39). In this sense the "coming" of Jesus creates not only "friends," but "sinners" as well. In both passages, the phrase "but now," or "as it is,"[24] brings us back to reality, and the reality is that "Your sin remains" (9:41), or, here more specifically, "they have no excuse for their sin" (v. 22).[25] That is, they are now fully accountable. They cannot claim innocence on the basis that they have not been warned, or have not heard the word of God! They have heard it from the lips of Jesus, but have not recognized his words as words from God. In hating him and persecuting him (see vv. 18, 20) they have (unwittingly) hated as well the One they worship as God: "The person who hates me hates my Father too" (v. 23).[26]

24 For emphasis, Jesus says almost the same thing again, using the same contrary-to-fact conditional sentence structure: "If I had not done the works among them that no one else did, they would not have sin, but now they have both seen and hated both me and my Father." The differences are, first, that Jesus now speaks of his "works" rather than his words — what he has "done among them" rather than "said to them" (v. 22), and, second, that he draws the pronouncement about hating both him and his Father into the "but now" clause, defining the "sin" for which there is no "excuse" (22) — the ultimate sin, and the one with which Jesus is mostly concerned in this

---

22. This is reflected in several modern English translations: "they would not be guilty of sin" (NIV, TNIV, NEB, REB); RSV, NRSV, and NAB retain the more traditional "they would not have sin," probably on the theory that guilt is implied in any case).

23. Gr. οὐκ ἂν εἴχετε ἁμαρτίαν.

24. Gr. νῦν δε.

25. "Excuse" (πρόφασιν) means a "valid reason" for doing what they do (see BDAG, 889), anticipating the biblical citation that "They hated me without cause" (δωρεάν, v. 25).

26. See 8:54, "It is my Father who glorifies me, him whom you say that 'He is our God.' And you have not known him, but I know him."

15:18–16:16 The World and the Advocate

Gospel.[27] As for the "works," Jesus identifies them here as works "that no one else did," recalling the former blind man's observation that "It is unheard of that anyone ever opened the eyes of one born blind" (9:32; see also 10:21). But even his works, for all their uniqueness and magnitude, have not produced faith (see 5:36; 10:25, 38; 14:11) among those who hated him. While the contexts are very different, Jesus here is recognizably the same Jesus who railed against the cities of Galilee in Matthew and Luke:

> "Woe to you, Chorazin! Woe to you, Bethsaida! For if the miracles done in you had been done in Tyre and Sidon, they would have repented long ago in sackcloth and ashes. Nevertheless, I say to you, It will be easier in the day of judgment for Tyre and Sidon than for you. And you, Capernaum, will you be lifted up to heaven? You will be thrown down to Hades! For if the miracles done in you had been done in Sodom, it would have remained until today. Nevertheless, I say to you that it will be easier in the day of judgment for the land of Sodom than for you." (Mt 11:21-24; see also Lk 10:12-15)

Here, instead of threatening the world with final judgment, Jesus simply levels the charge that "they have both seen and hated both[28] me and my Father" (repeating the thought of v. 23). "Seeing" Jesus probably refers first of all to seeing his works, but the notion that the unbelieving world has also "seen" the Father is odd in light of 1:18 ("No one has seen God, ever"), 5:37 ("You have never heard his voice nor seen his form") and 6:46 ("Not that anyone has seen the Father except he who is from God"). Jesus seems to have in mind here what he said to Philip ("The person who has seen me has seen the Father," 14:9), and more broadly the principle that "the person who sees me sees the One who sent me" (12:45). But he reminds his disciples that to "see" him is not necessarily to believe in him (compare 6:36), and therefore not necessarily to believe in the Father either.[29] To "see" and to "hate" are, unfortunately, quite compatible, making it impossible to explain away the world's hatred as mere ignorance or unfamiliarity. Rather, as Jesus has said (v. 22), it is an unreasoning hatred, in defiance of all that is "seen," with no valid excuse or justification.

---

27. The only exceptions to the notion of "sin" as the rejection of Jesus are (possibly) 5:14 and 8:11. Never in the Gospel, but only in 1 John do we hear of "sin" which is "not to death" (μὴ πρὸς θάνατον, 1 Jn 5:16-17). Unless we are told otherwise, we can generally assume that "sin" is mortal (see 8:21, 24, 34, 35).

28. "Both" (καί) is omitted in P66, D, and some old Latin versions. There are four occurrences of καί in a single verse, but the repetition of "both . . . and" (καὶ . . . καί) for rhetorical effect may well be deliberate. There is no difference in meaning in any event.

29. Brown (2.688) disagrees, arguing that 14:9 "is addressed to the disciples and presupposes the acceptance of Jesus in faith," and that "The world has seen Jesus but has not had the faith to see the Father in him."

25 Jesus clinches the point with a biblical citation, and he could not have chosen a more appropriate one: "But the word that is written in their law[30] must be fulfilled,[31] that 'They hated me without cause.'"[32] The text, in slightly different form,[33] appears twice in the Greek Old Testament, Psalm 34(35):19 and 68(69):5 (LXX).[34] The adverb "without cause," or gratuitously, captures perfectly what Jesus has just said — that the world has no "excuse" (v. 22), no valid reason or provocation, for its sin of hating the Father and the Son.

The citation stands as a kind of sequel to the earlier one from Psalm 41:9 (40:10, LXX), introduced similarly: "But the Scripture must be fulfilled, 'The one who eats my bread lifted up his heel against me'" (13:18). In both instances, Jesus makes the words of the anonymous psalmist his own, speaking there of betrayal or treachery at the hands of someone who eats at the same table, and here more generally of "the world" and its unprovoked hatred. Just as there he had in view not only his own imminent betrayal by Judas Iscariot, but the prospect of further betrayals among the disciples in the course of carrying out their mission to the world, so here he looks both at the world's present hatred of him and its future hatred of the disciples. As we have seen, the two texts together echo what Jesus said in very different settings in other Gospels: "And brother will hand brother over to death, and father hand over child, and children will rise against parents and will put them to death. And you will be hated by all for my name's sake" (Mt 10:21-22//Mk 13:12-13). The psalmist's lament, "They hated me without cause," becomes the lament of the true disciple (and the faithful reader of the Gospel) no less than of Jesus himself. They too, as he has said plainly (vv. 18-19) will be "hated," and for no better reason than he was.

26-27 In the face of the world's hatred, the disciples' only recourse is "the Advocate."[35] "When the Advocate comes," Jesus promises, "whom I will send to you from the Father, the Spirit of truth that goes forth from the Father, he will testify about me" (v. 26). The term "Advocate" is introduced here with the definite article, implying that the disciples have heard it before,

---

30. "Their law" (ἐν τῷ νόμῳ αὐτῶν), like the expression "your law" (8:17; 10:34), places Jesus at a certain distance from the Jewish law, yet without denying its authority. It is still that which is "written" (ὁ . . . γεγραμμένος), and which must be "fulfilled." As in 10:34, Jesus uses the term "law" (νόμος) to refer to Jewish Scripture generally (in this case, the Psalms), not just to the Torah or to legal matters.

31. Gr. ἵνα πληρωθῇ.

32. Gr. ἐμίσησάν με δωρεάν.

33. Gr. οἱ μισοῦντές με δωρεάν.

34. See also the postbiblical *Psalms of Solomon* 7.1, "they hated us without cause" (ἐμίσησαν ἡμᾶς δωρεάν).

35. Gr. ὁ παράκλητος.

15:18–16:16 THE WORLD AND THE ADVOCATE

as indeed they have (see 14:16, 26). This is additional evidence that the material beginning at 15:1 is intended to follow chapter 14, and is not, as some have theorized, an independent discourse originally composed to follow 13:30 or 13:36.

Yet there are also small differences between the notice here and the two earlier ones. For one thing, this is the first time the Advocate is explicitly said to "come"[36] (see also 16:8, 13). In the preceding chapter, Jesus was the one who promised to "come" (14:18, 28), yet there was little doubt that he was promising to come in the person of the Advocate. Second, Jesus says, "I will send" the Advocate, in contrast to earlier pronouncements that the Father would "give" or "send" the Advocate (14:16, 26). This should not be exaggerated, however. In the first instance, the Father gives the Advocate in answer to Jesus' prayer (14:16), and sends him in Jesus' "name" (14:26), while in the present instance Jesus "sends" the Advocate explicitly "from the Father,"[37] and not content with that adds, redundantly, that this "Spirit of truth . . . goes forth from the Father" (v. 26). The most substantial difference is that in the preceding chapter the Advocate's ministry was to the disciples only, to be "with" them (14:16-17), to "teach" them, and to "remind" them of all that Jesus said. The "world," he said, could neither "receive" nor "see" nor "know" the Advocate (14:17). Here, by contrast, the Advocate "will testify[38] about me," Jesus says (v. 26), with the implication that the testimony is not to the disciples but to the hostile "world," even as Jesus' own "testimony" was directed mainly to the world.[39] This he immediately confirms by adding, "and you too must testify[40] because you are with me from the beginning" (v. 27). If their testimony is to the world, it is natural to suppose that the Advocate's testimony is as well. These twin testimonies, in fact, are not two but one, for the Advocate will testify solely in and through the lives and lips of the disciples.

This is very much in keeping with what the few references in the other Gospels to a future "Holy Spirit" might have led us to expect. In Mark and Matthew, just before warning his disciples of "betrayal" and "hatred" (again, see Mt 10:21-22//Mk 13:12-13), Jesus told them, "When they lead you to trial and hand you over, don't worry beforehand about what to say, but say whatever is given you in that hour, *for it is not you who speak but the Holy Spirit*"

36. Gr. ὅταν ἔλθῃ.
37. Gr. παρὰ τοῦ πατρός.
38. Gr. μαρτυρήσει.
39. Explicitly so in 7:7 ("it hates me because I testify about it that its works are evil") and 18:37 ("for this I came into the world, that I might testify to the truth"); implicitly almost everywhere else (see 3:11, 32; 5:31; 8:14, 18). Only twice (4:44; 13:21) does Jesus "testify" to his own disciples or to the readers of the Gospel.
40. Gr. καὶ ὑμεῖς δὲ μαρτυρεῖτε.

(Mk 13:11, italics added; see also Mt 10:19-20). And in Luke he said, "When they bring you to the synagogues, and the rulers and the authorities, don't worry about how or what to do in your own defense, or what to say, for the Holy Spirit will teach you in that very hour what you must say" (Lk 12:11). The context here is much the same, centering on the hatred and persecution they will face in the world. While Jesus emphasized in the previous chapter that the world "cannot receive," and "neither sees . . . nor knows," the Advocate in the way the disciples know him (14:17), he now insists that the Advocate can and will at least "testify" to — perhaps against! — the world (compare 16:8), and that the disciples are called to make that testimony their own.

This they must do, and this they are qualified to do because they have been with Jesus "from the beginning"[41] (v. 27), that is, from the beginning of — and throughout — his ministry (see 2:11, "This Jesus did in Cana of Galilee as a beginning of the signs, and revealed his glory, and his disciples believed in him").[42] "From the beginning" signals Jesus' ministry in its entirety, right up to his death on the cross (see also Acts 1:21-22). That is the perspective of 1 and 2 John, for example (see 1 Jn 1:1; 2:7, 13, 24; 3:11; 2 Jn 5, 6), and it is likely intended here as well.[43] It was surely on the basis of this text — or something close to it — that the author of 1 John began his tract with the words, "That which was *from the beginning,* which we have heard, which we have seen with our eyes, which we have looked at and our hands have touched concerning the word of Life — and the Life was revealed, and we have seen and *testify*" (1 Jn 1:1-2, italics added).

16:1 For the third time (as in 14:25 and 15:11), Jesus signals a momentary pause with the expression, "These things I have spoken to you." He has forewarned them of hatred and persecution, he says, "so that you will not be made to stumble" (16:1). The words "made to stumble"[44] are not unexpected, for Jesus warned in the eschatological discourse in Matthew that "you will be *hated* by all the Gentiles for my name's sake, and then many will be *made to stumble,* and will *hand over* each other and *hate* each other" (Mt 24:9-10, italics added). A natural consequence of the world's hatred and persecution is that believers themselves "stumble" and fall away, treating each other in much the same way that the hostile world treats them. And in a context similar to the present one, Jesus warns the disciples just after leaving for the Mount of Olives that "you will all be made to stumble," prompting

---

41. Gr. ἀπ' ἀρχῆς.
42. See also 6:64, "For Jesus knew from the beginning [ἐξ ἀρχῆς] who they are who do not believe, and who it is who will hand him over." If those who would *not* believe were known, surely those who would believe were known from the beginning as well.
43. So too 16:4b (Gr. ἐξ ἀρχῆς).
44. Gr. σκανδαλισθῆτε.

Peter to claim that even if the others are, he will not be (see Mk 14:17-19//Mt 26:31-33). Here, instead of predicting outright that the disciples will "stumble," Jesus simply states his own firm intention that they do not. At this point in Mark and Matthew, his prediction made it virtually certain that they would in fact fail him in the time of crisis. Here the outcome remains unclear.

2 The preceding verse, introduced by "These things I have spoken to you," leads us to expect a further reason why the disciples need not "stumble," and such a reason will be given shortly (v. 4). But Jesus interrupts himself, taking the opportunity to speak more explicitly of two dangers facing them, excommunication and martyrdom. "They will put you out of synagogue," he begins (v. 2a). To be put "out of synagogue"[45] now becomes no longer a mere threat of temporary discipline (as in 9:22 and 12:42), but a decisive break with the Jewish community. Here if anywhere the Gospel of John looks beyond the setting of Jesus' ministry to conditions which may have prevailed at the time the Gospel was written — not necessarily the so-called *Birkath ha-Minim*,[46] but rather more drastic measures of excommunication practiced sporadically and perhaps unpredictably. As we have seen, on this point John's Gospel stands in contrast to the other three, where the accent is rather on being judged and punished "in the synagogues" (Mt 10:17; also 23:34; Mk 13:9; Lk 21:12). Even more striking are Jesus' next words, "And yes,[47] an hour is coming when everyone who kills you[48] might think he is offering worship to God" (v. 2b).[49] The expression, "an hour is coming" (as in 4:21; 5:28; see also 16:25), looks beyond present circumstances to the time after Jesus' departure when the disciples will experience the world's hatred and persecution in the course of their mission.[50] In the other Gospels, Je-

---

45. Gr. ἀποσυναγώγους.

46. As we have seen (in connection with 9:22), the *Birkath* seems to have been a policy not of outright excommunication, but of forcing "heretics" to leave on their own.

47. For the use of ἀλλά to introduce something even stronger ("rhetorically ascensive") as if to say, "and not only this," see BDAG, 45.

48. Gr. πᾶς ὁ ἀποκτείνας ὑμᾶς.

49. The purpose clause (with ἵνα) is surprising because one expects merely a "when" or "in which" clause identifying the decisive hour. The purpose clause accents the divine purpose in what happens, and consequently its inevitability. For ἵνα with Jesus' "hour" (instead of "when," as in 4:21, 23; 5:25, or "in which," as in 5:28), see 12:23; 13:1; also 16:32). Abbott comments, "When once the stupendous admission is made that evil in some sense may be decreed by God, there ceases to be any difficulty in xvi. 2.... If persecution is 'decreed,' it must be decreed that some shall persecute" (*Johannine Grammar*, 115). This should not be pressed to imply, however, that the *motivation* for killing (that is, as a way of worshiping God) is also divinely decreed.

50. Thus not the very last day (as in 5:28), but a time that may well have been already present to the Gospel writer. He could as easily have said, "an hour is coming, and now is" (καὶ νῦν ἐστιν), as in 4:23; 5:25, or "and has come" (καὶ ἐλήλυθεν), as in 16:32.

sus only occasionally speaks of his disciples being "killed" in the course of their world mission, but two references in Matthew are noteworthy: one in which he tells the Pharisees, "I am sending you prophets and sages and scribes; some of them you will kill and crucify, and some of them you will flog in your synagogues" (Mt 23:34), and one in which he tells the disciples, "Then they will hand you over to tribulation and will kill you" (Mt 24:9; this in a context in which Mark had spoken of being "handed over" to councils and "beaten in synagogues").[51]

It comes as no surprise that Jews executed Christians in the first century. Not only do the martyrdoms of Stephen (Acts 7) and James (Acts 12), and the frenzied efforts of Saul of Tarsus to bring Jewish Christians to justice provide evidence of this, but the Gospel of John itself offers repeated glimpses of the efforts of Jewish leaders to kill Jesus (beginning at 5:18; see also 7:1, 19, 25; 8:37, 40, 59; 10:31; 11:50), and at least one of his disciples (Lazarus, 12:10).[52] Jesus has surely prepared his disciples for possible martyrdom metaphorically in speaking of the "dying" grain of wheat (12:24), and literally in adding that "The person who loves his life loses it, and the person who hates his life in this world will keep it to life eternal" (12:25). Also, as we have seen, the metaphor of eating his flesh and drinking his blood (6:53-56) seems to have pointed in the same direction. More surprising is the notice that "everyone who kills you will think he is offering worship[53] to God." While it is not difficult to imagine such a thought motivating Saul, with his "zeal" for the God of Israel and the "ancestral traditions" (see Gal 1:14; Phil 3:6; Acts 22:3; 26:9-11), he never quite makes it explicit.[54] If such a motivation existed among Jews, whether in reality or in rhetoric, it is likely to have gone back to traditions about Phinehas, who averted a plague against the people by killing a fellow Israelite who brought a foreign woman into the camp, gaining for himself "a covenant of a lasting priesthood because he was zealous for the honor of his God, and made atonement for the Israelites" (see

---

51. See Mark 13:9. In fairness it has to be added that Matthew immediately continues with, "and you will be hated *by all the Gentiles* for my name's sake" (24:9b, italics added). Whether the force of this is to attribute the "killing" specifically to the Gentiles or whether Jesus is attributing tribulation and murder to *both* Jews and Gentiles is uncertain.

52. According to the *Martyrdom of Polycarp* 13.1 (mid-second century), when Polycarp of Smyrna was burned, "The crowds immediately gathered wood and kindling . . . with the Jews proving especially eager to assist, as is their custom" (ὡς ἔθος αὐτοῖς; LCL, 1.384-85). In the case of the stoning of James, the brother of Jesus, however, there is no evidence of unanimity among Jewish leaders (see Josephus, *Antiquities* 20.200, and Eusebius, *Ecclesiastical History* 2.23).

53. Gr. λατρείαν προσφέρειν.

54. Rather, in referring to the earnest "worship" (λατρεῦον) of "our tweve tribes," he links it with their hope of final resurrection (Acts 26:6-8).

Num 25:13, NIV). Phinehas was remembered in connection with Mattathias, and the killing of the king's officer and a Jew about to offer pagan sacrifice on the altar in Modein, precipitating the Maccabean revolt (see 1 Maccabees 2.23-26), and in later rabbinic tradition as well.[55]

3 "And they will do these things," Jesus adds, "because they did not know the Father or me" (v. 3). With this, he repeats almost verbatim the charge that "all these things they will do to you . . . because they do not know the One who sent me" (15:21). His point is not to make allowance for their actions on the ground of ignorance (as in Lk 23:34, or Acts 3:17), for he has already stated plainly that they have no "excuse" (15:22), and that they do what they do "without cause" (15:25). Rather, he is underscoring the irony that although they claim to be "offering worship to God" (v. 2), they do not even know God, for God can be known only as Jesus' Father, or "the One who sent" Jesus (again see 7:28-29; 8:19, 55).

4 "But these things I have spoken to you," Jesus continues, resuming what he started to say about his intention that they not "stumble" (v. 1). He has spoken of "these things," he says, "so that when their hour[56] comes you might remember them that I told you" (v. 4a). The repetition of "their" and "them"[57] is confusing.[58] The antecedent of the second "them" is quite clearly "these things," that is, all the predictions of hatred, persecution, excommunication, and martyrdom (15:18–16:3). But what about the first (that is, "*their* hour")? Does it also refer to the things predicted — that is, their "hour" to be fulfilled? Or does it refer to the unidentified "they" (the people of "the world," or possibly "the Jews") who have been the object of the whole series of warnings, from "If *they* persecuted me" (15:20) right up to "And *they* will do these things because *they* did not know the Father or me" (16:3) — that is, their "hour" to carry out their evil plans? Most commentators favor the latter option, pointing to Luke 22:53, where Jesus says to those who come

---

55. Reflecting on Numbers 25:13, a later midrash (*Numbers Rabbah* 21.3) asks, "But did he offer a sacrifice, to justify the expression ATONEMENT in this connection? No, but it serves to teach you that if a man sheds the blood of the wicked it is as though he had offered a sacrifice" (*Midrash Rabbah: Numbers* [London: Soncino, 1961], 2.829-30).

56. Gr. ἡ ὥρα αὐτῶν.

57. Gr. αὐτῶν.

58. Each, in fact, is omitted in certain early manuscripts: the first in א, D, Ψ, the majority of later manuscripts, Sy^s, and some old Latin; the second in the first corrector of א, D, L, family 13, Sy^s, and others. Either or both of these omissions would yield a clearer sentence: "so that when *the* hour [that is, the "hour" mentioned in v. 2] comes, you might remember [or, remember "them"] that I told you." But both are retained, despite the awkwardness, in P^{66}, A, B, Θ, and 33. It is far more likely that a later scribe would have dropped αὐτῶν (particularly the first one) rather than adding it (see Metzger, *Textual Commentary*, 247).

to arrest him, "this is your hour,"⁵⁹ and the authority of darkness."⁶⁰ Yet it is odd that the two instances of the same word⁶¹ so close together have different antecedents. Clearly, what Jesus wants his disciples to "remember" are his words of warning (as in 13:19), not his enemies.⁶² While difficult to decide, it is marginally more likely that "their hour" also refers to Jesus' words (in 15:18–16:3) and to the time for them to be fulfilled, not to the anonymous haters and persecutors. A passage from Luke should not be determinative here. The expression, "when their hour comes," is therefore best understood simply as the equivalent of "when it happens" (as in 13:19; 14:29).⁶³

This is consistent with what comes next, as Jesus continues to focus on "these things": "And these things I did not tell you from the beginning, because I was with you" (v. 4b).⁶⁴ The implication is that he knew "these things" all along (for example, "he knew them all . . . he himself knew what was in the person," 2:23; "he knew who they are who do not believe, and who it is who will hand him over," 6:64). But there was no need to warn the disciples of persecution because he also knew that he was its primary target, not they,⁶⁵ and that in any event he would keep them safe as long as he was "with" them (see 6:39, 10:28, and especially 17:12, "when I was with them"). Yet even with this in mind, the last clause, "because I was with you,"⁶⁶ brings the reader up short. While it will be quickly explained by what follows ("But now I am going to the One who sent me," v. 5), it still sounds

---

59. Gr. ὑμῶν ἡ ὥρα.

60. See, for example, Brown, 2.692; Schnackenburg, 3.122; Morris, 616. Barrett puts it neatly: "The 'hour' of Jesus appears to mean his failure but is in fact his exaltation; that of his enemies appears to mean their victory but is in fact their defeat" (485). Lindars is an exception ("i.e. the time of these things," 498), yet he too, oddly, cites Luke 22:53. To Bultmann, "It makes no difference" (556, n. 6).

61. That is, αὐτῶν.

62. Many English versions (including NASB, RSV, TNIV, NRSV) obscure this point with some such translation as "so that when their hour comes, you might remember that I told you of them" (making αὐτῶν dependent on εἶπον rather than the object of μνημονεύητε). The effect of this is either to identify "them" as Jesus' enemies, or preserve the ambiguity while concealing the awkwardness of the language.

63. Translations that adopt this interpretation tend to ignore the two instances of αὐτῶν altogether (again concealing the awkwardness of the Greek); for example, "I have told you this, so that when the time comes, you will remember that I warned you" (NIV; see also NEB, REB, NLT).

64. There is no discernible difference in meaning between ἐξ ἀρχῆς (here and in 6:64, but nowhere else in the New Testament) and ἀπ' ἀρχῆς (as in 15:27); see Morris, 341, n. 155.

65. So Morris: "The implication is that persecution then would fall on him, not them (cf. 18:8-9). But not at the time of which he speaks. Things will be different" (616).

66. Gr. ὅτι μεθ' ὑμῶν ἤμην.

strange, for it seems to imply that he has *already* gone away. It is as if he speaks as the Risen One, looking back at his ministry on earth (as in Lk 24:44, "while I was still with you"). Both here and in 17:12, he stands so close to the "hour" of his departure (see 13:1) that he can speak as if he is with the Father already.[67]

5 Jesus immediately confirms this, while at the same time remarking on the disciples' prolonged silence: "But now I am going to the One who sent me, and none of you asks me, 'Where are you going?'" (v. 5). "But now" has temporal significance here (in contrast to 15:22 and 24): "now," as distinguished from an earlier time when "I was with you" (v. 4b). His imminent departure changes things, making it necessary to warn the disciples of what is ahead. The notice that "none of you asks me, 'Where are you going?'"[68] provides one of the pillars for the theory of two distinct farewell discourses, 13:36–14:31 and 15:1–16:33, for Jesus seems to have no recollection here of the disciples' plaintive refrain in the so-called "first" discourse: "Lord, where are you going?" (13:36), "Lord, we do not know where you are going" (14:5), and "Lord, show us the Father" (14:8).[69] If there are in fact two farewell discourses, and if the second was composed as an alternative to the first, the contrast is indeed striking, as if the one is consciously distancing itself from the other. But even if this is the case, it does not relieve us of the responsibility of making sense of the text as it stands. As we have seen, the disciples have been silent for a long time (all the way back to 14:22), and it would not be at all odd for Jesus to comment on their silence, and the reason for it. He could have said, "I am going to the One who sent me, and none of you says anything," but instead he builds on what they had been saying earlier: thus, "none of you asks me — as you repeatedly did before — 'Where are you going?'" The announcement, "Where I am going you cannot come" (13:33), had prompted a string of questions. Now the announcement that "I am going to the One who sent me" draws no response at all. The accent is not on their failure to ask a *particular* question, but on their failure to say anything at all. Why the long silence, after so many questions? What has happened in the meantime?

6 Jesus answers his own implied question: "But because I have spoken these things to you, grief has filled your heart" (v. 6).[70] Here again (as in

---

67. Compare Tobit 12.18, LXX (S), where the angel Raphael, bidding farewell to Tobit and Tobias, also speaks as if no longer present: "When I was with you [ἐγὼ ὅτε ἤμην μεθ' ὑμῶν], it was not by my favor that I was with you [ἤμην μεθ' ὑμῶν], but by the will of God." Then, in very "Johannine" language: "I am going up [ἐγὼ ἀναβαίνω] to the One who sent me" (v. 20; compare Jn 20:17!).

68. Gr. ποῦ ὑπάγεις.

69. As we have seen, those are simply different ways of asking the same question.

70. For the singular "heart" with the plural pronoun (ὑμῶν, "your"), see 14:1, 27.

vv. 1 and 4), the expression "these things I have spoken to you"[71] recalls his warnings of hatred and persecution, and more explicitly excommunication and martyrdom (15:18–16:3). No such dire predictions had accompanied his first announcement of his imminent departure (13:33), and they are the reason, he now tells the disciples, that "grief[72] has filled your heart," leaving them speechless. Ironically, the same expression, "these things I have spoken to you," a chapter earlier introduced his ultimate intention for them "that your joy might be fulfilled" (15:11), but now we learn that "grief" comes first and then "joy" (see vv. 20-22).[73]

7 Again Jesus promises the Advocate: "I, however, am telling you the truth:[74] it is to your advantage that I am going away,[75] for unless I go away, the Advocate will not come to you. But if I go, I will send him to you" (v. 7). Here, as in the preceding chapter (see 14:12, 28), Jesus accents the benefits of his departure — and beyond that, its sheer necessity. "Unless" he goes away, "the Advocate will not come," but "if" he goes, he will send the Advocate (for the sentence structure, again compare 12:24). For this reason, his departure should be a cause of rejoicing, as he has said before (14:28), not grief. It is not simply an act of resignation by which he gets out of the way so that Another can take his place. Rather, as the two uses of the emphatic "I" suggest ("I, however," and "I am going away"), it is the positive means by which he makes "greater" things possible (compare 14:12). This is the only instance in which Jesus does not further identify "the Advocate" as "the Spirit of truth" or "the Holy Spirit," probably because the identification in 15:26 is presumed to be still in the reader's mind. Just as in 15:26, Jesus (not the Father) "sends" the Advocate, who is thereby identified as One who will "come," or not come, to the disciples, depending on whether or not Jesus goes away. The disciples, however, do not have a choice: Jesus *will* "go away," the Advocate *will* "come to you," and it *will* turn out "to your advantage."[76] Jesus has already explained why (see especially 14:26), but he will

---

71. Once again, ταῦτα λελάληκα ὑμῖν.

72. Gr. ἡ λύπη.

73. Note the same verbs for "filled" or "fulfilled" (ἵνα . . . πληρωθῇ, 15:11; πεπλήρωκεν here).

74. The solemn opening clause, "I am telling you the truth" (τὴν ἀλήθειαν λέγω ὑμῖν), functions as the equivalent of the customary "Amen, amen, I say to you" formula (last heard in 14:12; see vv. 20, 23). Luke occasionally uses a similar equivalent: "Truly [ἀληθῶς] I say to you" (Lk 9:27; 12:44; 21:3).

75. Gr. ἐγὼ ἀπέλθω. Here Jesus introduces yet a third word (ἀπέρχεσθαι, alongside ὑπάγειν and πορεύεσθαι) for "going off" or "going away" (see 13:36; 14:3-4, 28), but with little difference in meaning.

76. The expression, "it is to your advantage" (σύμφερει ὑμῖν) occurs only here and in 11:50, where Caiaphas the high priest said to his fellow priests, "Don't you realize that

tell them more, particularly in relation to the dangers they face in, and from, "the world."

8-11 Confirming that the Advocate will in fact "come," Jesus continues, "And he, when he comes, will convict the world of sin, and of justice, and of judgment" (v. 8). Then he expands briefly on each of the three: "Of sin because[77] they do not believe in me" (v. 9); "and of justice[78] because I am going to the Father and you no longer see me" (v. 10); "and of judgment because the ruler of this world has been judged" (v. 11). Even though the Advocate will come *to* the disciples (v. 7),[79] his activity is directed *through* them to "the world" (v. 8), just as in 15:26-27. Interpreters have defined his role here as that of a prosecuting attorney, in contrast to a defense attorney. Using judicial language, Jesus claims that the Advocate will "convict[80] the world of[81] sin." The verb "convict" in the sense of "expose," or "bring to light" (see 3:20), is particularly appropriate with "sin," its first object here (see 8:46, "Who among you convicts me of sin?").[82] To "convict the world of sin" probably does not mean to bring the world to a conscious recognition of its sin, and consequently to repentance, but simply to expose it before God as sinful. This is what Jesus himself has done (see 9:41; 15:22). "Sin" is defined here, in characteristically Johannine fashion, not as moral failure or the transgression of law, Jewish or otherwise, but simply as rejecting Jesus and his message (see 15:22-24; also 8:24).

"Sin" and "justice" and "judgment" are carefully linked into a deliberate triad.[83] If so, all three — the latter two as much as the first — are given distinctively Johannine interpretations. The verb "convict" is obviously less appropriate with "justice" and "judgment" than with "sin," for the latter two

---

it is to your advantage [σύμφερει ὑμῖν] that one man die for the people, and the whole nation not be lost?" Just as that ironic prediction of Jesus' passion (see 11:51-52) seemed to echo a synoptic saying of Jesus (Mt 5:29-30), so in turn Jesus' choice of words here (intentionally or not) seems to revisit Caiaphas's remark, turning the high priest's irony into straightforward prophecy: Jesus must "go away" (in death) in order for the Advocate to come, protecting the scattered "children of God" (see 11:52).

77. As Abbott notices, the conjunction ὅτι in vv. 9, 10, and 11 should probably be read "because" (rather than "that"), but with the meaning, "[I say this] because" (*Johannine Grammar,* 158). The meaning would be little different, however, if it were rendered as "in that," or "in the sense that."

78. Gr. περὶ δικαιοσύνης.

79. Gr. πρὸς ὑμᾶς, not once but twice in v. 7.

80. Gr. ἐλέγξει.

81. Literally, "about" (Gr. περί).

82. There too the construction is ἐλέγχειν with the preposition περί (BDAG, 315; see also Jude 15).

83. This by means of a μὲν . . . δὲ . . . δέ construction (that is, περὶ ἁμαρτίας μέν, v. 9; . . . περὶ δικαιοσύνης δέ, v. 10; . . . περὶ δὲ κρίσεως, v. 11).

are not wrongful deeds to be "exposed," or crimes of which one can be "convicted." The point is rather that the Advocate will "reprove" the world, or prove it wrong, about both "justice" and "judgment," thereby proving Jesus right.[84] "Justice," or "righteousness," is mentioned only here (vv. 8 and 10) in John's Gospel, and its connection to the promise that "I am going to the Father and you no longer see me" (v. 10) is not immediately obvious. Its only occurrences in 1 John (2:29; 3:7) have to do simply with right behavior, which does not particularly fit the present context.[85] Rather, it seems to mean something more like justification, or vindication.[86] Jesus is proven right by going to the Father, so that the world — and, we now learn, even the disciples — no longer sees him. Earlier he said, "the world no longer sees me, but you see me" (14:19). Now he acknowledges that even his own disciples "do not see me," at least for a time. He will explain this shortly (vv. 16, 19-22). His point is not to relegate the disciples to a position no better off than the world (as he seemed to do back in 13:33), but simply to emphasize that he is literally leaving the world by "going away" to the Father, hidden from human view.[87] To put it in terms more characteristic of other New Testament writers, Jesus will be "justified," or vindicated against the world, in his resurrection and ascension (see 14:19-20).[88]

---

84. So the NRSV, "prove the world wrong" (see also TNIV). The NIV ("convict the world of guilt in regard to sin and righteousness and judgment") is rather more cumbersome, for to convict of "guilt in regard to sin" is redundant. Again, see BDAG, 315: "to express strong disapproval . . . *reprove, correct.*"

85. This is the apparent meaning in another triadic construction, in which Paul, in connection with "faith in Christ Jesus," speaks to Felix and Drusilla "about righteousness and self-control and the coming judgment" (περὶ δικαιοσύνης καὶ ἐγκρατείας καὶ τοῦ κρίματος τοῦ μέλλοντος, Acts 24:25), yet R. B. Rackham's comment (*The Acts of the Apostles: An Exposition* [London: Methuen, 1951], 449), that "The first two chapters of the Epistle to the Romans shew us how the apostle could treat the subject," could imply that Paul spoke of "justice" or "righteousness" to Felix in a more theological sense (in keeping with Acts 13:38-39 and 17:31).

86. As Bultmann puts it, "Insofar as the terminology is that of the lawsuit, dik. means 'innocence'; not, however, in the moral sense of uprightness, but in the forensic sense of being in the right, of winning one's case" (564).

87. Jesus has shifted his ground somewhat from 6:62, where he implied that if they actually saw "the Son of man going up where he was at first," it would prove him right). Here, by contrast, it is a matter of what they will *not* see. Again we may compare Ignatius's aspiration (derivative, no doubt, from what he understood to be true of Jesus): "Then I will truly be a disciple of Jesus, when the world does not see even my body" (*To the Romans* 4.2; LCL, 1.275).

88. Compare perhaps 1 Timothy 3:16 ("He who was revealed in the flesh, justified [ἐδικαιώθη] in the Spirit . . . received up in glory"), and 1 Peter 3:18-22 ("Put to death in the flesh, made alive in the Spirit . . . gone to heaven").

15:18–16:16 THE WORLD AND THE ADVOCATE

He makes much the same point with regard to "judgment"[89] (vv. 8 and 10). "Judgment," or condemnation (unlike "justice," or righteousness), has been mentioned explicitly before as something that takes place in connection with the coming of Jesus, or that which he has been given the authority to carry out (see 3:19; 5:22, 27, 30; 8:16; 12:31). Here he claims that the Advocate will prove the world wrong about "judgment" by proving that "the ruler of this world" — not Jesus — "has been judged." With this, he draws together the two affirmations of 12:31: "Now is the judgment of this world," and "Now the ruler of this world will be driven out." From Jesus' standpoint, the "exorcism" of Satan, the world's ruler, was a work in progress. Even after the departure of Judas, Satan's instrument, he still had to warn his disciples that "the ruler of the world is coming," and remind them that "in me he has nothing" (14:30). From the future perspective of the Advocate, however, Satan's defeat is an accomplished fact. "The ruler of this world," and consequently "the world" itself, is "judged," or condemned,[90] just as surely as "whoever does not believe is already judged, because he has not believed in the name of the One and Only Son of God" (3:18). "Judgment" too (like "justice") is accomplished through Jesus' departure to the Father and the coming of the Advocate. In short, the Advocate will redefine three familiar terms (familiar especially to the Jews), each one in relation to Jesus: "sin" as rejecting *Jesus,* "justice" as what God has done for *Jesus,* and "judgment" as what *Jesus* carries out by his death.

12 Pausing for a moment before continuing to describe the Advocate's ministry, Jesus tells the disciples, "I have still much more[91] to say to you, but you are unable to bear it now" (v. 12).[92] While this might appear to contradict 14:30, "I will no longer speak with you very much," in actuality it does not, for Jesus is simply explaining *why* he will not have much more to say. Not because there is nothing left to say, nor even because he is about to leave, but because the disciples are "unable to bear it now." The verb "to bear," or endure, is appropriate in view of Jesus' grim warnings of hatred and persecution (15:18–16:3).[93] He implies that he could have spoken of these at greater length and in more detail, but did not do so because the Father did not tell him to.[94] There is much that the disciples will face in the course of their

---

89. Gr. περὶ κρίσεως.
90. Gr. κέκριται.
91. Gr. Ἔτι πολλά.
92. Barrett cites v. 4b ("these things I did not tell you from the beginning"), with the comment that "There were things Jesus had not said during the course of his ministry; some, he could not say even at the end" (488).
93. See BDAG, 171: "be able to bear up under especially trying or oppressive circumstances."
94. This is probably the key to resolving another possible contradiction that some

mission for which they are not prepared, and for which it would be premature to try to prepare them. Above all, their mission will reach beyond the "world" of Judaism to that of the Gentiles. Jesus in this Gospel has confined his warnings mainly to the former,[95] with little explicit attention to the fate awaiting them in the Graeco-Roman cities, and at the hands of the Roman authorities.

13 By itself, Jesus' announcement that "I have still more to say to you" (v. 12) could imply further revelation beyond what he reveals in the Gospel — that is, that the Advocate (vv. 7-11) is "not only his interpreter, but also his 'successor,' who will continue his revelation."[96] Jesus had promised earlier that the Advocate "will teach you all things and remind you of all things that I said to you" (14:26), but now his role seems to have expanded, so that "when that one comes, the Spirit of truth, he will lead you[97] in all the truth" (v. 13a). The phrase, "in all the truth,"[98] surely the most sweeping statement of the Spirit's ministry to be found anywhere in the New Testament, must obviously be read in context. "All the truth" is *not* the scientific or philosophical truth about the natural world, not the things humans can learn on their own by rational inquiry or observation. Rather, as Jesus will quickly point out, it is *his truth, in the sense of the truth the Father has given him to* make known, the "still much more" that is left to say (v. 12). But before defining "the truth" more explicitly as "what is mine" (see vv. 14 and 15), Jesus continues to describe the Advocate's ministry, a ministry remarkably like his own: "For he will not speak on his own, but whatever he hears[99] he will

---

commentators (for example Bultmann, 573; Brown, 2.714) have noticed with the earlier pronouncement that "everything I heard [πάντα ἃ ἤκουσα] from my Father I made known to you" (15:15). Jesus has more that he could say, but he does not say it because it is not what he has "heard" from the Father (compare 8:26, "I have many things [πολλά] to say about you and to judge, but the One who sent me is True, and the things I heard [ἃ ἤκουσα] from him are the things I say to the world").

95. This in contrast to Matthew 10:18, "and you will be led before governors and kings for my sake, for a testimony to them and to the Gentiles" (see also Mk 13:9-10) and Matthew 24:9, "and you will be hated by all the Gentiles for my name's sake."

96. So Schnackenburg, 3.133; see also Brown, 2.714: "Does this imply there will be new revelations after his death? Some have thought so, and a certain mystique has been built on the basis of this statement."

97. Gr. ὁδηγήσει ὑμᾶς.

98. Gr. ἐν τῇ ἀληθείᾳ πάσῃ.

99. More literally, "whatever he will hear" (ὅσα ἀκούσει, as in B, D, W, Θ, and Ψ). A variant reading, ὅσα ἀκούσῃ, with A and the majority of later witnesses) looks like a purely grammatical correction. Another variant, ὅσα ἀκούει (literally, "whatever he hears," with ℵ, L, 33), is probably *not* "a dogmatic improvement, introduced to suggest the eternal relationship of the Holy Spirit" (as Metzger, *Textual Commentary,* 247 suggests), but simply another grammatical correction, possibly even the original reading. There is no difference in meaning.

15:18–16:16 THE WORLD AND THE ADVOCATE

speak, and he will announce to you the things to come" (v. 13b). The first two of these characteristics match perfectly Jesus' own self-revelation, for he too does not speak "on his own" (see 5:19; 7:17-18; 12:49; 14:10), and he too says only what he has "heard" (that is, from the Father; see 5:30; 8:26, 40; 15:15). The third is more distinctive. Although Jesus has shown that he can predict the future "before it happens" (13:19; 14:29; also 16:4), he has for the most part left "the things to come"[100] to the Advocate.[101] Whether that phrase refers to eschatological events (such as those described in the book of Revelation),[102] or simply to more detailed instruction about what the disciples will face in their mission to the world and how to face it, is uncertain. Possibly no distinction is intended between those two alternatives. In any event, Jesus provides here the reason why he is not saying all that he has to say or could say (v. 12). Rather, the disciples will take their directions from "that one[103] . . . the Spirit of truth."

14-15 "That one will glorify me," Jesus continues, "because he will take from what is mine and announce it to you" (v. 14). Why "from what is mine"? Has Jesus not said that the Advocate would speak "whatever he hears" (v. 13b) — presumably from the Father, not Jesus? And before that, that he would lead the disciples "in all the truth" (v. 13a)? How can he characterize "all the truth" as "mine," or claim that the Advocate will "glorify me"?[104] Even though Jesus has spoken this way before,[105] an explanation is required, and he is quick to supply it: "All things that the Father has are mine; that is why I said that he takes from what is mine and will announce it to you" (v. 15). He defines "all the truth" (v. 13) as "All things that the Father has," which he then explicitly claims in turn as "mine" (in keeping with 3:35, "The Father loves the Son and has given all things into his hand"). "All the truth" is

---

100. Gr. τὰ ἐρχόμενα.

101. In subsequent narrative, however, Jesus himself is said to know "all things coming upon him" (πάντα τὰ ἐρχόμενα ἐπ' αὐτόν) before they happen (18:4).

102. It is intriguing to ask, on the basis of a canonical reading of Scripture, if perhaps this very pronouncement may have functioned as a legitimation of Christian prophecy as contained in the Revelation.

103. Gr. ἐκεῖνος.

104. That the Advocate "will glorify me" raises a further question. Earlier we were told that the Spirit would not come until Jesus was "glorified" (7:39), while here the Spirit himself "glorifies" Jesus. This reminds us that Jesus' "glorification" is not a single act (such as his death on the cross), but a process (see 12:28; also, perhaps, 17:10, "and I am glorified in them"; quite possibly the Advocate will "glorify" Jesus first to, and then through, the disciples).

105. The Advocate's close relationship to Jesus is by now a given. He is, after all, "another advocate" (like Jesus, 14:16); he will "remind" the disciples of what Jesus said (14:26); he will, Jesus promises, testify "about me" (περὶ ἐμοῦ, 15:26), and in fact Jesus himself will "send" him (15:26; 16:7).

Jesus' truth, or the truth about Jesus — the only truth that matters in the Gospel of John. The added explanation (v. 15) functions in much the same way as the Gospel writer's classic narrative asides, and some have regarded it as such.[106] Yet the fact that it is placed on Jesus' own lips can hardly be overlooked. Whether it comes from Jesus or the Gospel writer, the writer clearly wants us to regard it not as his comment but as Jesus' own explanation of what he has just said, in much the same way that Jesus will almost immediately utter a riddle (v. 16) and then explain it (vv. 19-22).

16 If what he has just said (vv. 14-15) sounded like a riddle followed by an explanation, then what Jesus says next is another riddle, this time without explanation, well calculated to draw a response from the long silent disciples: "A short time,[107] and you no longer see me, and again a short time,[108] and you will see me" (v. 16). The disciples have heard something like this before ("Yet a short time, and the world no longer sees me, but you see me," 14:19).[109] This time, by contrast, there are *two* "short times," which can be understood in at least three possible ways:

(a) The two "short times" are consecutive, and of roughly equal length. The first is the brief interval before Jesus dies, and the second the interval between his death and his resurrection, when the disciples will see him once more (see 2:19, "in three days"). On this view, the reader's impression is that of living in the age of the resurrection, with Jesus present in the Spirit, having already gone away and returned.

(b) The two "short times" are consecutive, but not necessarily of equal length. The first is the brief interval before Jesus' death and resurrection, and the second the whole present age, after which Jesus will be

---

106. It is in fact missing in P[66] and the first hand of ℵ. According to Bultmann, "In a note (v. 15) the Evangelist comments on what has been said in v. 14 by reminding us of the unity of Father and Son" (576). In a footnote, Bultmann refers to 13:11, which similarly cites what Jesus has just said, but explicitly from the writer's standpoint (thus, "For he knew. . . . That is why he said"). This is not a true analogy. Somewhat more analogous are 6:65 (which Bultmann also mentions), and 4:44 (which he does not), where pronouncements of Jesus are invoked within narrative asides introduced by the Gospel writer. Yet they are not true parallels either. While verse 15 may reflect the thought of the Gospel writer, formally at least it is a saying of Jesus, not one of the author's narrative asides.

107. Gr. μικρόν.

108. Gr. πάλιν μικρόν.

109. It is worth noticing that (in contrast to 14:19), Jesus uses two different words for "see" (both here and in vv. 17 and 19): "you no longer see me" (θεωρεῖτέ με, as in 14:19) and "you will see me" (ὄψεσθέ με). Yet no convincing case has ever been made that the two verbs are anything but synonymous in meaning — for example, that one refers to physical sight and the other to spiritual insight. While such a distinction does exist, it rests on context, not simply on the choice of words.

seen again. On this view, the reader's impression is that Jesus has gone away and will soon return.[110]

(c) The two "short times" are *not* consecutive, but are in fact the same "short time" viewed in two different ways — first through the eyes of "the world" (14:19, "the world no longer sees me"), and then through the eyes of the disciples (14:19, "but you see me"). The adverb "again" does not imply succession, or introduce a second "short time," but simply presents a different way of looking at the "short time" already mentioned.[111] On this view, the reader's impression is that of living within this "short time," a time in which Jesus has literally gone away, yet is still accessible to the believer through faith, prayer, and the ministry of the Advocate (see 20:29, "Blessed are those who did not see, and yet believed").

The third alternative perhaps requires further explanation. As we have seen, Jesus emphasized earlier that the disciples and "the world" perceive things differently, for they will see him (as the Risen One) even when the world no longer does (see 14:19). Here, by contrast, he acknowledges that at one level the disciples' perception is no different from the world's. As he has just said (v. 10), the Advocate will convict the world "of justice because I am going to the Father and you no longer see me" (not simply that "the world" no longer sees him). In short, Jesus' absence is real, just as real to the disciples as to the world.[112] Yet absence is not the last word, for he quickly adds, "And again a short time, and you will see me." Thus, in one sense "you no longer see me," while in another "you will see me." Obviously, the disciples are confused by Jesus' riddle (see vv. 17-18). But this is not one of those instances in which the reader clearly understands while the disciples do not. Rather, the riddle remains a riddle, not only to the disciples on the scene but even to the readers of the Gospel. They, no less than the disciples, stand to benefit from the detailed explanation Jesus will give (vv. 20-24).

---

110. So Augustine: "For the whole of that space over which the present dispensation extends, is but a little while; and hence this same evangelist says in his epistle, 'It is the last hour'" (*Tractates on John* 101.6; NPNF, 1st ser., 7.388-89).

111. See BDAG, 753, where πάλιν is defined not only as a marker of repetition, or something added, but as a "marker of contrast or an alternative aspect, *on the other hand, in turn*" (see, for example, v. 28, "Again, I am leaving the world"). This could be expressed in English by saying, "*or* again, a short time and you will see me."

112. This in fact has been his presupposition from the start (see 13:33, "just as I said to the Jews that 'Where I am going, you cannot come,' so I say to you now").

F. THE DISCIPLES' RESPONSE (16:17-33)

> 17 So some of his disciples said to each other, "What is this that he is saying to us? 'A short time, and you do not see me, and again a short time, and you will see me'? And 'because I am going to the Father'?" 18 So they said, "What does this 'short time' mean? We don't know what he is talking about." 19 Jesus could tell that they wanted to ask him, and he said to them, "Are you questioning each other because I said, 'A short time, and you no longer see me, and again a short time, and you will see me'? 20 Amen, amen, I say to you that you will weep and mourn, but the world will rejoice. You will be grieved, but your grief will be turned into joy. 21 The woman, when she gives birth, has grief because her hour has come. But when the child is born, she no longer remembers the distress on account of the joy that a human being is born into the world. 22 And so you have grief now, but I will see you again, and your heart will rejoice, and no one takes your joy from you. 23 And in that day you will ask me nothing. Amen, amen, I say to you, whatever you ask of the Father in my name he will give you. 24 Up to now you have asked for nothing in my name. Ask, and you will receive, that your joy might be fulfilled.
>
> 25 These things I have spoken to you in parables. An hour is coming when I will speak to you no longer in parables, but I will report to you plainly about the Father. 26 In that day you will ask in my name, and I am not saying to you that I will ask the Father on your behalf. 27 For the Father himself loves you, because you have loved me, and have believed that I came forth from God. 28 I came forth from the Father, and I have come into the world. Again, I am leaving the world and going off to the Father."
>
> 29 His disciples said, "Look, now you are speaking plainly, and no longer telling a parable. 30 Now we know that you know all things and have no need that anyone ask you. By this we believe that you came forth from God." 31 Jesus answered them, "Now you believe! 32 Look, an hour is coming and has come that you will be scattered, each to his own home, and leave me all alone, and yet I am not alone, because the Father is with me. 33 These things I have spoken to you so that in me you might have peace. In the world you have distress, but take courage, I have overcome the world!"

Finally the disciples break their long silence. For the first time since Judas's question (14:22), they offer a reaction to what Jesus has said. Yet in contrast to 13:36–14:31, they speak not as individuals, but as a group, and quite noticeably not to Jesus directly, but only "to each other" (v. 17). They express

16:17-33 THE DISCIPLES' RESPONSE

somewhat repetitiously (vv. 17-18) their confusion about what he has just said (v. 16), while ignoring all that preceded it (14:23–16:15). Jesus takes note of the fact that they have still not questioned him directly and summarizes their confusion yet again (v. 19). Then he offers by way of explanation a parable about a woman in labor (vv. 20-21), which he promptly interprets for them (vv. 22-24). Finally, picking up some threads of his preceding long discourse, he tries to get through to them once again (vv. 25-28). At last they answer him directly, claiming that "now" they understand what he is saying (vv. 29-30). Whether they actually do or not is unclear (vv. 31-33), for his final verdict on their faith and understanding awaits the next chapter.

17-18 If Jesus' riddle (v. 16) was designed to elicit a response from the disciples, it succeeds. The Gospel writer describes their confusion over it at some length. First, "So some of his disciples said to each other, 'What is this that he is saying to us? "A short time, and you do not see me, and again a short time, and you will see me"?[1] And "because I am going to the Father"?'" (v. 17). Then, somewhat redundantly, "So they said, 'What does this "short time" mean? We don't know what he is talking about'" (v. 18). In contrast to earlier questions voiced by single individuals and directed to Jesus as "Lord" (13:36; 14:5, 8, 22), these questions are spoken "to each other" (v. 17), like the questions and murmurings of Jesus' antagonists in the first half of the Gospel (see, for example, 6:41-43, 52, 60-61; 7:35-36; see also 7:15, 25-27; 8:22; 10:19-21). Yet this hesitancy to speak directly to him is not unprecedented even for the disciples (see v. 5; also 4:27, 33; and compare 21:12). Jesus has noticed it already, and attributed it to their "grief" (vv. 5-6). The writer is less kind, accenting the disciples' bewilderment by the use of repetition and redundancy. First, they quote the riddle in full, asking "What is this that he is saying to us?" Then, drawing on something Jesus said earlier, they cite the reason *why* they would not see him: "because I am going to the Father" (v. 10; this shows that they have heard more than just the final riddle). Not content with that, they continue, "What does this 'short time' mean? We don't know what he is talking about." In just two verses they speak of "a short time," "again a short time," and "this 'short time,'" asking twice, "What is this?" and concluding "We don't know what he is talking about." Their ignorance sounds almost invincible.

19 Noticing that they still have not spoken to him directly, "Jesus could tell[2] that they wanted to ask him, and he said to them, 'Are you question-

---

1. The quotation of Jesus' words is verbatim, except for "do not [οὐ] see me" instead of "no longer [οὐκέτι] see me" (both here and in v. 16, as well as in v. 19). In each instance, certain later manuscripts have attempted to achieve word-for-word correspondence, but their harmonization is secondary.

2. Gr. ἔγνω.

ing each other[3] because I said, "A short time, and you do not see me, and again a short time, and you will see me"?'" (v. 19). The word-for-word repetition of the riddle, now for the third time (see vv. 16, 17), gently mocks the disciples, calling attention to their bewilderment. Yet at the same time Jesus gives them the benefit of the doubt, acknowledging that, far from ignoring him, they "wanted to ask him" but did not, whether out of grief (as in v. 6) or for some other reason. Therefore he will answer the questions they have asked each other, but could not bring themselves to ask him: "What is this that he is saying to us?" (v. 17), and "What does this 'short time' mean?" (v. 18).

20 The explanation begins with an "Amen, amen" saying, the twenty-third in the Gospel (and the first since 14:12): "Amen, amen, I say to you that you will weep and mourn, but the world will rejoice. You will be grieved, but your grief will be turned into joy" (v. 20).[4] The original riddle (v. 16) said nothing about "the world," nor did the disciples in questioning each other about it. But now Jesus returns to the subject of "the world," and the sharp contrast between what the "short time" (or "times") of which he has just spoken will mean to "you" and what it will mean to "the world." In that sense he revisits 14:19, where the contrast between the world's perception and that of Jesus' disciples was evident. But this time the contrast is not so much between two different *perceptions* of reality as between two different *responses* toward what is perceived. The reality is that Jesus is literally going away. He will be absent not only from the world, but also from the disciples. For a "short time" at least, they must put up with his absence, and consequently "weep and mourn."[5] What differentiates them from the world is not the experience of Jesus' "real absence" but their emotional response to it. The world will "rejoice"[6] at his absence, even as they are "grieved"[7] (v. 20a). This is not surprising in view of the earlier warning that "If the world hates you, you know that it has hated me before you" (15:18). Because he has been a thorn in the world's side, exposing its sin (see 15:22), the world will rejoice that he is gone.[8]

---

3. Gr. ζητεῖτε μετ' ἀλλήλων.

4. Notice that "you" is emphatic (ὑμεῖς), not once but twice in this verse, accenting the contrast to "the world." The first emphatic ὑμεῖς is particularly conspicuous by virtue of being placed last — and unexpectedly — in its clause (κλαύσετε καὶ θρηνήσετε ὑμεῖς).

5. The two verbs, "weep" (κλαύσετε) and "mourn" (θρηνήσετε) evoke the image of mourning the dead (for the first, see 11:31, 33 at the tomb of Lazarus, and Mary Magdalene at the tomb of Jesus in 20:11, 13, and 15; the second, perhaps implying a more formal ritual of mourning [BDAG, 458-59], occurs nowhere else in John's Gospel).

6. Gr. χαρήσεται.

7. Gr. λυπηθήσεσθε.

8. For an analogy within the so-called "Johannine" writings, see the account of

16:17-33 THE DISCIPLES' RESPONSE

That much is essentially an explanation of the first half of the riddle: "A short time, and you no longer see me." As for the second half, "and again a short time, and you will see me," Jesus addresses that with the promise, "but your grief will be turned into joy" (v. 20b). His intention for the disciples all along has been "joy" (see 15:11), but "grief" has gripped them instead, even before his departure (see v. 6). "You will be grieved" (v. 20a), he now says, but in fact they are already grieved at even the prospect of his absence, too grieved to question him directly (vv. 17-18). Yet his original intent "that my joy might be in you, and that your joy might be fulfilled" (15:11) will not be thwarted, for their grief "will be turned into joy." What will be the turning point? Clearly, it has to do with the promise that they will "see" Jesus once more.[9] Taking our cue from 14:19-20, we suspect that it is his resurrection (see also 20:20, "so the disciples rejoiced, seeing the Lord"). This is confirmed in part by what is *not* said. He does not say that the world's "joy" will turn to "grief," suggesting that this turning point is something of which the world is not even aware — quite plausibly his resurrection (see 14:19, "the world no longer sees me"; also Acts 10:41-42). Still, the riddle is not quite solved. Will the disciples' grief turn to joy after "a short time," or after two successive "short times" (see v. 16). They are still puzzled. An illustration or parable of some kind is needed, and Jesus quickly supplies one.

21 The parable centers on the two key words, "grief" and "joy," in connection with childbirth: "The woman, when she gives birth, has grief because her hour has come.[10] But when the child is born, she no longer remembers the distress, on account of the joy that a human being is born into the world" (v. 21). "The woman"[11] is generic. While childbirth was a common metaphor for eschatological "distress" or tribulation prior to "the day of the Lord" in Judaism and early Christianity, this is *any* woman giving birth (as in 1 Thess 5:3), just as "the slave" (8:35; 15:15) is any slave, or "the son" (5:19; 8:35) is any son.[12] She is not an allegorical figure representing either Israel or

---

the deaths of the two witnesses in the book of Revelation, in which their bodies lie unburied on the main street of "the Great City" for three and a half days (Rev 11:8-9), and "the dwellers on the earth are rejoicing over them [χαίρουσιν ἐπ' αὐτοῖς], and celebrating and sending gifts to one another, because these two prophets tormented the dwellers on the earth" (11:10).

9. Gr. ὄψεσθέ με (vv. 16, 17, 19).

10. "Grief" (λύπη) is not as appropriate within the parable itself as in the application (v. 22). What a woman giving birth feels is not so much "grief" as actual physical pain — something closer to "the distress" (τῆς θλίψεως) which, Jesus says, she "no longer remembers." Probably "grief" (λύπη) is retained here simply to preserve the continuity of verses 20, 21, and 22.

11. Gr. ἡ γυνή.

12. Other examples include "the bridegroom" (3:29), "the doorkeeper" (10:3),

Jerusalem or the people of God (as, for example, in Isa 26:16-19; 66:7-9; Mic 4:9-10; 5:3; or Rev 12:2). Yet the parable does involve a comparison between her experience and that of the disciples. The comparison is a simple one: there is "grief" and then "joy," but the joy far outweighs the grief.[13] Jesus' point is much the same as Paul's: "For I reckon that the sufferings of the present time are not worthy to be compared to the glory about to be revealed to us" (Rom 8:18), and "For this light temporary distress is achieving for us an immeasurable and eternal weight of glory" (2 Cor 4:17).[14] Most mothers will dispute the accuracy of the claim that "when the child is born, she no longer remembers the distress" (evidence perhaps that the Gospel writer was a man!), but the words are not intended literally. They are simply a way of making the point that the prospect of "joy" renders all the "grief" or "distress" that precedes it worthwhile (see Heb 12:2).

The parable comes as a surprise in one respect, in that the reason for the woman's overwhelming joy is "that a human being[15] is born into the world." To be born "into the world" is evidently a good thing, even in the face of all that has been said about "the world" hating the disciples (15:18-25) and rejoicing at their grief (see v. 20). The positive imagery recalls "the true [Light] that illumines every human being[16] who comes into the world" (1:9), reminding us that the dualism of this Gospel never lapses into world-denying Gnosticism. The disciples themselves, while not "of," or "from" the world, are, and will be, emphatically "in" the world (see 17:11, 16), not only by virtue of having been "born" into it but by virtue of being "sent" (17:18), even as Jesus himself was both "born" (18:37) and "sent into the world" (for example, 3:17; 10:36). Yet implicit in the imagery is also an argument from the lesser to the greater, as the very real joy at physical birth hints at a greater joy transcending even that of a new mother.[17]

"the thief" (10:10), "the wolf" (10:12), and "the grain of wheat" (12:24). See Abbott, *Johannine Grammar,* 47 (although his identification of "the woman" as "the woman [of the house], *i.e.* the wife," is not necessary to the argument).

13. Schnackenburg is right: "The childbearing woman cannot be interpreted allegorically as pointing to the disciples. The only point of comparison is the transition from sorrow to joy" (3.158).

14. See also the book of Revelation, where a brief, truncated period of distress ("1260 days," "42 months," or "a time, times and half a time") finally gives way to a thousand-year reign with Christ (Rev 20:1-10).

15. Gr. ἄνθρωπος.

16. Gr. πάντα ἄνθρωπον.

17. The contrast between physical and spiritual birth has been firmly established in the Gospel (see 1:13; 3:3-8). As we have seen, "every human being [πάντα ἄνθρωπον] who comes into the world," however "illumined" (1:9), is also mortal, born to die (see 3:6, "What is born of the flesh is flesh"), so that the joy at a child's birth is by definition temporary.

16:17-33 THE DISCIPLES' RESPONSE

Jesus immediately makes the application explicit: "And so you have grief now, but I will see you again, and your heart will rejoice, and no one takes your joy from you" (v. 22). "Now" confirms that "grief" (as in v. 6) is a *present* experience for the disciples, not something that begins only after "a short time." The "short time" has already begun, for they have already felt the pain of their Teacher's absence and expressed it, first by their questions (13:36–14:22), and then by their confused silence (vv. 5-6, 17-18). Here at least — in keeping with option (c) above (see pp. 838-39) — Jesus seems to leave room for only one "short time," the one in which they already find themselves, a brief period after which their present grief will turn to joy. His use of the adverb "again" signals that he is accenting this second way of looking at the "short time."[18] The reader expects something like "but you will see me again," in keeping with the thrice-repeated promise, "and you will see me" (vv. 16, 17, and 19). Instead, quite unexpectedly, he promises, "but I will see *you* again,"[19] pointedly reminding them that their reunion with him, and consequently their heart's joy, depends on his initiative alone, not on their moods or perceptions.[20]

The promise, "I will see you again," also recalls Jesus' terminology earlier in answering the questions of individual disciples: "I am coming back" (14:3), and "I am coming to you" (14:18, 28). The vocabulary of "not seeing" and "seeing" has now replaced that of "going away" and "coming," yet the experience described is the same, and with the same ambiguities. There Jesus' "coming" could refer either to his resurrection and the coming of the Advocate (14:18), or to his "second" coming at the close of the age (14:3), or it could be left uncertain (14:28). The same is true here. A reader who knows the end of the story will know that Jesus and the disciples saw each other again when he was raised from the dead (20:14, 18, 20, 25, 29), and that they "rejoiced" (20:20), yet it could hardly be said of them that "no one takes your joy from you." Their life from then on was *not* uninterrupted joy, nor is that of the reader. Rather, grief and joy exist alongside each other in the present age, even after Jesus' resurrection (see 21:17, "Peter was grieved"). The resurrection appearances of chapters 20 and 21 provide a glimpse of eternal joy, but only a glimpse. Turning from grief to joy is not something that happens once for all in the life of the disciple, but something that happens again and again. The "short time" in which we live as disciples of Jesus and readers of the Gospel can be a time of either grief or joy, de-

---

18. See πάλιν μικρόν (vv. 16, 17, 19).
19. Gr. πάλιν δὲ ὄψομαι ὑμᾶς.
20. It is tempting to detect here an echo of Isaiah 66:14, LXX, καὶ ὄψεσθε, καὶ χαρήσεται ὑμῶν ἡ καρδία ("and you will see, and your heart will rejoice"), particularly in view of the preceding reference in Isaiah to pain in childbirth (66:7-9). If this is the case, it is all the more telling that Jesus changes "you will see" (ὄψεσθε) to "I will see" (ὄψομαι).

pending on a variety of factors — external circumstances, our prayers, our faith, and above all the ministry of the risen Jesus in the person of the Advocate. As readers we will resonate at times with the first way of looking at it ("you do not see me"), and at other times ("again") with the second ("you will see me," or "I will see you"). Jesus is conspicuous among us, whether by his presence or his absence. Ambiguity is evident among the disciples in the rest of the chapter (see vv. 31-33), even as it doubtless was among the Gospel's first readers, and no less so today.

23-24 Jesus' explanation of the parable (v. 21) continues (vv. 23-24), confirming the conclusion that "your heart will rejoice, and no one takes your joy from you" (v. 22). "And in that day," he promises, "you will ask me nothing" (v. 23a). "In that day" recalls an earlier promise that "In that day, you will come to know that I am in my Father, and you in me, and I in you" (14:20). "Joy" rests on knowledge, and he has repeatedly promised the disciples knowledge (see also 15:15). "You will ask me nothing"[21] could mean either "you will ask me *for* nothing" — that is, in prayer,[22] or "you will ask me no questions."[23] In support of the former, the emphatic "me" suggests to some translators that Jesus is distinguishing himself from the Father. the disciples will not need to pray to him or through him, but will have direct access to the Father (see vv. 26-27).[24] Yet the verb "to ask"[25] is used only of Jesus' prayers in this Gospel (see 14:16; 16:26; 17:9, 15, 20), not of the prayers of disciples or believers (1 Jn 5:16 is a possible, though unlikely, exception). When the disciples are the subject, it normally means to ask questions (as in vv. 5 and 19; also 9:2). In the very next sentence, when the subject turns to prayer (v. 23b), a different verb for "ask" is used,[26] not once but three times.

21. Gr. ἐμὲ οὐκ ἐρωτήσετε οὐδέν.
22. See, for example, NRSV, NEB: "you will ask nothing of me"; NLT: "you won't need to ask me for anything." These are somewhat ambiguous, however, in that the uses of ἐρωτᾶν as "ask for" are not necessarily prayers (see, for example, 4:31, 40, 47; 12:21; 19:31, 38; 2 Jn 5). Abbott (*Johannine Grammar,* 468) similarly straddles the fence, commenting that "xvi. 23 is doubtful and perhaps includes both 'ask a question' and 'ask a boon'" (see also Schnackenburg, 3.159).
23. So Brown: "you will have no more questions to put to me" (2.718); so too NAB: "you will not question me about anything"; NIV, TNIV: "you will no longer ask me anything"; REB, "you will ask me nothing more."
24. The NLT makes this explicit: "I tell you the truth, you will ask the Father *directly,* and he will grant your request because you use my name" (v. 23b, italics added). But this is to state prematurely what Jesus will say in verses 26-27 in any case. Also, the use of "me" (ἐμέ) is not unexpected, given the precedent of verse 5 ("none of you asks me"), and verse 19, where the placement of "him" (αὐτόν) before ἐρωτᾶν closely matches the word order here.
25. Gr. ἐρωτᾶν.
26. Gr. αἰτεῖν.

Here the meaning is, "you will ask me no questions" — not because they are too grieved (as in v. 6) or too confused to ask (as in v. 19), but because they will have no need to ask.[27] "In that day" (here as in 14:20) they will understand what they do not understand now. Their questions will have been answered. The emphatic "me" simply identifies Jesus as the Source of truth, who will reveal all things freely without being questioned (see v. 30).[28]

Another kind of "asking" is needed, however, even commanded. While the disciples will have no more need to ask questions (v. 23a), they will always need to "ask"[29] in prayer. Without hesitation Jesus continues: "Amen, amen, I say to you, whatever you ask of the Father in my name he will give you" (v. 23b). This twenty-fourth "Amen, amen" pronouncement in the Gospel does not introduce a new topic, but adds a necessary qualification to what has already been said. "Joy" (v. 22) rests on knowledge to be sure, but the transition from grief to joy is accomplished only through prayer. The pronouncement itself is nothing new, for he has already expressed his intent (in almost the same words) "that whatever you ask of the Father in my name he might give you" — this as the means by which the disciples would "go and bear fruit" (15:16). What he stated there as an intention is stated here as a fact. Prayer "in his name" will be answered because it is the prayer of those who know him, and do not have to be told what he would want.

The promise of answered prayer is for "that day"[30] (v. 23a) when Jesus will see them again (v. 22) and make himself known to them, yet he boldly invites them to claim it even now: "Up to now you have asked for nothing in my name. Ask, and you will receive, that your joy might be fulfilled" (v. 24).[31] The reference to "your joy" brings him full circle back to the application of the parable about the woman ("but I will see you again, and your heart will rejoice, and no one takes your joy from you," v. 22), and back still further to his stated intention "that my joy might be in you, and that your joy might be fulfilled" (15:11). With this, he confirms that the transition from "grief" to "joy" is not limited to an eschatological moment, whether the res-

27. So Bultmann, 585, n. 5; Barrett, 494; Brown, 2.722-23; Lincoln, 424-25; Morris, 627; Lindars, 510.

28. See also verse 12 ("I have still more to say to you"), and v. 13 ("the Spirit of truth . . . will lead you in all the truth").

29. Gr. αἰτεῖν.

30. Gr. ἐν ἐκείνῃ τῇ ἡμέρᾳ.

31. "Ask, and you will receive" (αἰτεῖτε καὶ λήμψεσθε) looks like a simple variation on Jesus' pronouncement about prayer in Matthew and Luke: "Ask, and it will be given you" (αἰτεῖτε καὶ δοθήσεται ὑμῖν, Mt 7:7; Lk 11:9), paired with "Seek, and you will find," and "Knock, and it will be opened to you"; see also Matthew 21:22, "And whatever things you ask [αἰτήσητε] in prayer believing you will receive" (λήμψεσθε).

urrection of Jesus or his final coming, but is something that happens again and again, above all through the prayers of those who grieve.

25 Once again (as in 14:25; 15:11; 16:1, 4, 6), the expression "These things I have spoken to you"[32] marks a rhetorical pause in the discourse, drawing a distinction (as in 16:1) between the present and a future "hour" to come: "These things I have spoken to you in parables. An hour is coming when I will speak to you no longer in parables, but I will report to you plainly[33] about the Father" (v. 25). But here (in contrast to 16:2), Jesus speaks of the coming "hour" as a time not simply of persecution, but of open revelation and free access to God — all the more necessary, perhaps, because of persecution to come. The phrase "in parables"[34] is probably broad enough to refer both to the riddle that first aroused the disciples' curiosity, "A short time, and you no longer see me, and again a short time, and you will see me" (v. 16), and to the actual parable that followed, about a woman giving birth (v. 21, like 10:1-5 a "parable of normalcy" in everyday life). The former confused them (vv. 17-19); the latter was an attempt to clarify, yet nothing in the text suggests that the clarification was successful. Confusion still reigns. But when "parable" gives way to "plain" speech, then (and only then) will they understand.

"Plainly" is the same word used earlier to mean "openly" or "publicly" (7:4, 13, 26).[35] The meaning, however, is closer to what was implied by the Jews at the Rededication, "If you are the Christ, tell us plainly" (10:24, in contrast to figurative language about shepherds and sheep), or to the instance in which Jesus, after referring to Lazarus as having "fallen asleep" (11:11), finally told the disciples "plainly" that "Lazarus died" (11:14). Here, by contrast, the promise to speak "plainly" looks beyond the present scene to a coming "hour" when Jesus will continue to speak to the disciples (see v. 12, "I have still more to say to you, but you are unable to bear it now"), but only through the Advocate (see v. 13, "But when that one comes, the Spirit of truth, he will lead you in all the truth"). In this way, he promises, "I will report to you plainly about the Father." The verb "report," or "report back,"[36] occurs only here in John's Gospel,[37] but is particularly appropriate in a set-

---

32. Gr. ταῦτα . . . λελάληκα ὑμῖν.
33. Gr. παρρησίᾳ.
34. Gr. ἐν παροιμίαις.
35. Jesus in retrospect makes this his stated policy throughout his "public" ministry: "I have spoken publicly [παρρησίᾳ] to the world. I always [πάντοτε] taught in synagogue and in the temple, where all the Jews come together, and I spoke nothing in secret" (18:20). It appears that the opposite of παρρησίᾳ in the sense of "publicly" was "in secret" (ἐν κρυπτῷ), while its opposite in the sense of "plainly" was "in parables" (ἐν παροιμίαις, 16:25; also v. 29).
36. Gr. ἀπαγγέλλειν.
37. See, however, 4:51 and 5:15, where it occurs in some manuscripts as a variant

16:17-33 THE DISCIPLES' RESPONSE

ting which seems to presuppose Jesus' departure to the Father and his return in the person of the Advocate.[38] The content of his "report" is "about the Father," in keeping with what has been the content of his revelation all along (see, for example, 8:28; 14:9, 24; 15:15). From here on (vv. 26-28) his emphasis is resolutely on "the Father."

26-27 "In that day," Jesus continues, "you will ask in my name, and I am not saying to you that I will ask the Father on your behalf" (v. 26). "In that day" confirms the impression that he is speaking of a future time after his departure (as in v. 23 and 14:20), a "day" indistinguishable from that coming "hour" when he will speak "plainly" and not in parables (v. 25). It is, as we have seen, a day not for questions but for prayer (v. 23). He has invited the disciples even now to "Ask, and you will receive, that your joy might be fulfilled" (v. 24), but he implies that "in that day" their relation to the Father will be closer and more direct than it is now. "You will ask in my name," he says, just as he has said all along (vv. 23-24; also 14:13; 15:16), but he goes on to define what that means, or more precisely what it does not mean. It does *not* mean that he will intercede for them with the Father, or that he will somehow take their prayers and present them to the Father. On the contrary, he says, "I am not saying that I will ask[39] the Father on your behalf." In the following chapter, he will still be heard "asking" on the disciples' behalf (see 17:9, 15, 20), but "in that day," after he goes to the Father, he will no longer need to do so, for their own access to the Father will be immediate and direct.[40] He makes this explicit by adding, "For the Father himself loves you, because you have loved me, and have believed that I came forth from God" (v. 27). This implies that of course their prayers to the Father will be answered (as we knew already from v. 23), but there is no need to spell it out.

---

reading (though not with Jesus as the subject). Some manuscripts (including Ψ, families 1 and 13, and the majority of later witnesses) have ἀναγγελῶ, but with little difference in meaning (see BDAG, 59 and 95). The textual support for ἀπαγγελῶ (with P⁶⁶, A, B, C*, D, K, L, W, Θ, 33, and others) is quite conclusive. One important manuscript (ℵ) has the present ἀπαγγέλλω, but the parallel with the future λαλήσω in the preceding clause dictates a future meaning in any instance.

38. Schnackenburg (with the uses of ἀπαγγέλλομεν in 1 Jn 1:2, 3 in mind) finds that "a material shift of emphasis or a transposition in the perspective has taken place" here, adding that "the obvious conclusion is that this discourse originated in the circle of the evangelist's pupils, who were pursuing a special interest that was of concern to the community" (3.162). But this is unconvincing. There is no more reason to link the verb ἀπαγγέλλειν to the later community than, say, the verb μαρτυρεῖν, "to testify" (see 1 Jn 1:2; Jn 15:26-27), and no greater evidence of a later situation here than in any other part of the farewell discourse (or, for that matter, the Gospel as a whole).

39. Gr. ἐγὼ ἐρωτήσω.

40. The distinction in vocabulary between the disciples' prayers (αἰτεῖν) and the prayers of Jesus (ἐρωτᾶν, as in 14:16) is here maintained.

849

The Father's love for the disciples, of course, consists of far more than just answering their prayers.

The notion that the Father loves us because we love Jesus echoes 14:21 ("the person who loves me will be loved by my Father") and 14:23 ("If anyone loves me, . . . my Father will love him") almost verbatim.[41] The main difference is that there the proof that a person loved Jesus was keeping his "commands" (14:21), or his "word" (14:23), while the proof here, he says, is believing "that I came forth from God" (v. 27). The test is creedal here, not behavioral. Jesus' acknowledgment that the disciples have in fact believed this can be grounded in Peter's confession that "we believe and we know that you are the Holy One of God" (6:69), in light of Jesus' subsequent self-identification as he "whom the Father consecrated [that is, "made holy"] and sent into the world" (10:36).

28 Jesus next expands the brief clause, "that I came forth from God,"[42] into a full summary of his mission that could serve admirably as a summary of the whole Gospel of John: "I came forth from the Father, and I have come into the world. Again,[43] I am leaving the world[44] and going off to the Father" (v. 28).[45] The first two clauses echo what he said long before to the Jews at the Tent festival ("I came forth from God, and here I am," 8:42),

---

41. I am assuming no substantial difference between the use of the verb ἀγαπᾶν for "love" in 14:21 and 23, and the use of φιλεῖν here.

42. Gr. ἐγὼ παρὰ θεοῦ ἐξῆλθον. Some ancient manuscripts (including P⁵, ℵ*, N, Θ, 33) have the definite article (παρὰ τοῦ θεοῦ), and others (including B, C*, D, L) have "from the Father" (παρὰ τοῦ πατρός). The latter is suspect as an assimilation to the same phrase in the following verse. The former could well be original, but could also be a conflation of the two other options, so the article is bracketed in the Nestle text (see Metzger, *Textual Commentary*, 248). "From the Father" is unlikely here because in this Gospel neither the disciples nor anyone else but Jesus has ever spoken of God as "the Father" except to ask, "Where is your father?" (8:19), or "Show us the Father" (14:9). Two verses later, for example, the disciples will say, "By this we know that you have come forth from God" (ἀπὸ θεοῦ), *not* "from the Father" (v. 30).

43. "Again" (πάλιν) evokes the mysterious πάλιν of v. 16 ("A short time, and you no longer see me, and again a short time, and you will see me"), repeated in vv. 17 and 19. While the pronouncement here should not necessarily be read as the interpretation of that earlier riddle, the use of the same adverb does accent the fact that by contrast he is now speaking "plainly," and this is how the disciples hear it (v. 29).

44. Gr. ἀφίημι τόν κόσμον, introducing yet another verb for Jesus' departure.

45. Certain textual witnesses (including D, W, b, and Sy^s) drop the entire clause, "I came forth from the Father," making vv. 27 and 28a into one sentence (". . . because you have loved me, and have believed that I came forth from God, and have come into the world"). This is almost certainly an accidental omission. The text as it stands has far stronger support (with P⁵, P²², ℵ, B, A, C*, Θ, L, Ψ, 33, and the majority of later witnesses (of these, B, C*, L, Ψ, and 33 have ἐκ τοῦ πατρός instead of παρὰ τοῦ πατρός, possibly influenced by the preceding verb ἐξῆλθον). See Metzger, *Textual Commentary*, 248.

while the first and last clauses state in his own words what the reader has known from the very beginning of the present scene ("that he had come from God and was going to God," 13:3). This is the whole package, the sum of what he wants his disciples to understand and believe.

29 At long last the disciples are able to speak directly to Jesus: "His disciples said,[46] 'Look, now you are speaking plainly, and no longer telling a parable. Now we know that you know all things and have no need that anyone ask you. By this we believe that you came forth from God'" (vv. 29-30). These are the only words the disciples as a group have addressed to Jesus in the entire farewell discourse. At first, some of them had spoken to him individually, addressing him repeatedly as "Lord" (13:6, 9, 25, 36; 14:5, 8, 22), but since then they have spoken only once, and that to each other, not to Jesus (vv. 17-18). Finally, they break their long silence, but these are also their last words before the discourse comes to an end. Have they understood, or not?

Clearly, the disciples think that "now" they understand Jesus. Their repetition of "now" (vv. 29, 30) has the effect of finishing his sentence for him. He has said, "An hour is coming"[47] (v. 25), and they in effect supply the conclusion, "and now is" (in keeping with 4:23 and 5:25). He spoke of a coming "hour" in which "I will speak to you no longer in parables, but I will report to you plainly about the Father" (v. 25), and their response is that the "hour" has already begun. The question is, Are they being premature. Have they "jumped the gun" with their jubilant claim? Earlier, the expressions "the hour is coming" and "the hour is coming and now is" could either be used interchangeably (as in 4:21, 23), or differentiated (as in 5:25, 28). In the present discourse, the shorter form ("the hour is coming") seems to have been used for events that are future from the standpoint of Jesus, but present in the experience of the readers (vv. 2, 25). The question is whether or not the Gospel writer intends a sharp distinction between the experience of the readers of the Gospel and the experience of these original disciples on the scene. Probably not. The disciples' impression that Jesus is "speaking plainly, and no longer telling a parable" (v. 29) is, after all, accurate. "I came forth from the Father, and I have come into the world," and "I am leaving the world and going off to the Father," are about as "plain" as speech can be.[48]

---

46. Some manuscripts (including A, D, L, W, the majority of later manuscripts, and most Latin, Syriac, and Coptic versions) make this explicit by adding "to him" (αὐτῷ). This is probably not original, but is implied in any case.

47. Gr. ἔρχεται ὥρα.

48. Modern theologians might well object that such claims as "I came forth from the Father" and "I am going off to the Father" are anything but "plain," in that they do not signal a journey in space but a change in a relationship. Such changes, they would say, cannot be verified in the "real" world, and in that sense these pronouncements are no less "parabolic" than "now you see me, now you don't," or the images of shepherds and sheep,

30 From the disciples' recognition of "plain" speech a confession of faith emerges: "Now we know that you know all things and have no need that anyone ask you," and "By this we believe that you came forth from God" (v. 30).[49] The acknowledgment "that you know all things and have no need that anyone ask you" is somewhat anticlimactic, for it simply repeats in the disciples' own words something Jesus has said already: that "in that day you will ask me nothing" (v. 23). They seem to have understood that pronouncement correctly: "in that day" their questions will have been answered.[50] To a modern reader, the words, "you know all things and have no need that anyone ask you," sound somehow wrong, for one expects, "you know all things and have no need to ask anyone." But the notion that Jesus "knows all things" is not an abstract theological claim. It is closely linked to his role as Revealer. If he knows all things, he will reveal all things without being questioned. This he will do, he has implied, through the Advocate who "will lead you in all the truth" (see vv. 12, 13). The initiative in revelation rests with him, not with the disciples.

The use of questions to solicit divine revelation was a familiar technique in Jewish and Christian apocalyptic literature (and in later gnostic writings), and not least in this very Gospel (quite conspicuously in the four questions of Peter, Thomas, Philip, and Judas after the footwashing). But as the discourse moved toward its close, Jesus seized the initiative by answering the disciples' unspoken questions without being asked (see vv. 19-22). This, he claimed, would be the model for the coming "day" when he would see them again (v. 23), and his disciples, echoing his words, now claim that it has already gone into effect. The same principle appears to be at work in the second-century *Shepherd of Hermas,* in which the prophet is told that "no spirit given by God is consulted,[51] but having divine power it speaks all things from its own authority, because it comes from above, from the power of the divine spirit. But the spirit that, when consulted, speaks in light of human desires is earthly and insubstantial, having no power. And it does not speak at all unless

---

or a woman in labor. Yet it is doubtful that such subtleties are of much interest to the Gospel writer, who more likely views these sayings as ordinary language. If not precisely "literal," they are metaphors so fixed and so well understood in first-century Mediterranean culture that they would have been viewed as "plain" speech even by those who denied that they were true.

49. Again, compare their earlier confession, voiced by Peter: "Lord, to whom shall we turn? You have words of life eternal, and we believe [καὶ ἡμεῖς πεπιστεύκαμεν] and we know [καὶ ἐγνώκαμεν] that you are the Holy One of God" (6:68-69).

50. Their assumption that "that day" is "now" (νῦν) is also supported by Jesus' accompanying invitation, "Up to now [ἕως ἄρτι] you have asked for nothing in my name. Ask, and you will receive" (v. 24).

51. Gr. ἐπερωτᾶται.

it is consulted."⁵² Here, too, the point seems to be that Jesus does not have to be "questioned" or consulted, but takes the initiative in revelation.

The recognition that Jesus knows and reveals all things triggers the disciples' confession "that you came forth from God."⁵³ In comparison to most confessions in this Gospel, it is a modest confession indeed, for it is not attributed to a particular person, nor does it draw on any of the great christological titles, such as "the Christ" (11:27), or "Son of God" (1:34, 49; 11:27), or "Holy One of God" (6:69), or "Lord" and "God" (20:28). It shows no advance, in fact, over what Nicodemus recognized almost from the beginning, that Jesus had "come from God as a teacher" (3:2)! In the present context, moreover, it too is anticlimactic, merely confirming what Jesus already said: "you have loved me, and have believed that I came forth from God" (v. 27). It does not begin to match the full confession he seemed to want to elicit from them when he added, "Again, I am leaving the world and going off to the Father" (v. 28) — much less the joyful affirmation that "I am coming back" (14:3), or "I am coming to you" (14:18, 28), or "I will see you again" (v. 22). Unless the reader is expected to fill in the gaps to encompass the full scope of Jesus' mission to the world, their confession is not so much premature and overblown as weak, belated, and long overdue. Not much here for Jesus to build on, but build on it he will (see 17:6-8).

31 The disciples' confession of what they "know" and "believe" (v. 30) will form the basis of Jesus' long prayer in the following chapter, but first he pauses to remind them that they still have a long way to go (vv. 31-33). His ironic reply to their confession⁵⁴ can be read as either a question ("Do you now believe?"), or an exclamation, probably intended ironically ("Now you believe!"). Most English translations read it as a question,⁵⁵ yet Jesus has already stated without qualification that they do in fact believe precisely what they have just said they believe (see v. 27). It is unlikely that their confirmation of it (v. 30) would have led him to have second thoughts as to their sincerity. Their belief is real, but it is "now," that is, temporary. It will

---

52. Hermas, *Mandates* 11.5-6; LCL, 25 (2003), 287 (see D. E. Aune, *Prophecy in Early Christianity,* 226-27). "From its own authority" (ἀφ' ἑαυτοῦ) means in contrast to human authority or initiative (as in Jn 10:18, "I lay it down ἀπ' ἐμαυτοῦ," or "on my own"), not in contrast to divine authority. The same principle applies in the book of Revelation, where John the Seer never asks a question in the entire book (see, for example, Rev 5:2-5 and 7:13-14, where angels or "elders" both ask the questions and supply the answers, and 17:6, where John "marvels" but never formulates a question).
53. Gr. ὅτι ἀπὸ θεοῦ ἐξῆλθες.
54. Gr. ἄρτι πιστεύετε.
55. For example, the KJV, RSV, NRSV, TNIV, NEB, REB, NAB, and NLT (so too most commentators; see also the punctuation in the Nestle Greek text). The one major exception (NIV) reads it as an exclamation, but without irony ("You believe at last!").

not stand the test of time, and of persecution (see v. 2). In choosing a different word for "now" from the one his disciples have just used,[56] he avoids mocking them, yet his comment reminds them that their confidence is misplaced. "Now," on their lips means "already," while on Jesus' lips it means "for the time being." Hard times are coming, and they are not prepared.[57]

32 "Look," he continues, "an hour is coming and has come that you will be scattered, each to his own home, and leave me all alone, and yet I am not alone, because the Father is with me" (v. 32). For the third time in the chapter he uses the expression "an hour is coming," recalling simultaneously his dire prediction of excommunication and death (v. 2) and the glad prospect of "plain" speaking and direct access to God in prayer (v. 25). In the second instance, as we have seen, the disciples virtually finished his sentence for him, announcing that the "hour" had already come (vv. 29-30). This time he finishes his own sentence (as in 4:23 and 5:25) — "an hour is coming and has come"[58] — revisiting instead the earlier warning of persecution (v. 2).

The focus of the prophecy is not on the specifics of what the disciples will suffer at the hands of either "the world" or "the Jews" (as in v. 2), but on the effect all this will have on them. "You will be scattered,"[59] Jesus tells them, "each to his own home, and leave me all alone." Having warned them explicitly against being "made to stumble" (v. 1), he now acknowledges that they will in fact do exactly that. The prediction, "you will be scattered," corresponds to Jesus' words in Mark that "you will all be made to stumble" (Mk 14:27; also Mt 26:31). The verb "scattered," in fact, recalls the accompanying biblical quotation in Mark and Matthew (from Zech 13:7): "I will strike the shepherd, and the sheep will be scattered." In John's Gospel, as in the other two, the reference functions as an explicit prediction of the disciples' desertion and flight at Jesus' arrest (see Mk 14:50-51; Mt 26:56), even though in John's Gospel, as we will see, that event is narrated differently (see 18:8-9). This is evident from the words, "and leave me all alone," referring to Jesus' suffering and death. Yet those "scattered, each to his own home" are not just the disciples on the scene but all believers everywhere, all those in danger of being "made to stumble" at the prospect of expulsion from the synagogue, or even death (see v. 2). Their time of being "scattered" is their time of "grief" (see vv. 20, 22). Not only will Jesus' immediate disciples leave him "all alone"[60] in his passion, but they themselves, and their followers, will be

---

56. That is, νῦν (vv. 29 and 30).
57. For this reason, Bultmann's comment, "Even if the sentence is taken as a statement, the sense is no different" (591), is only a slight exaggeration.
58. Gr. ἔρχεται ὥρα καὶ ἐλήλυθεν.
59. Gr. ἵνα σκορπισθῆτε.
60. Gr. μόνον.

16:17-33 THE DISCIPLES' RESPONSE

left alone in the wake of his departure. He has said, "I will not leave you orphaned" (14:18), yet he now acknowledges times in their experience when their sense of his absence and their own isolation (temporary though it may be) will be very real and very strong.

Closing on a note of hope, Jesus adds, "and yet I am not alone, because the Father is with me." He has said as much twice before to the Pharisees at the Tent festival, first to enhance his authority to pass judgment (8:16), but then in a more sweeping way to assert a relationship that "always" exists: "And the One who sent me is with me. He has not left me alone, for I always do the things that please him" (8:29). If the Father has been with the Son throughout his ministry, there is no reason to believe that he will desert him just because the disciples do. And if the pronouncement holds out hope for Jesus in his passion, it does so for the scattered disciples as well. They have been told that "the Father himself loves you" (v. 27), and while it has not yet been made explicit, they have every reason to believe that as "children of God who are scattered" they will at last be "gathered into one" (see 11:52). Their grief will turn to joy, as we have seen, not once for all in a single moment but again and again, through prayer and through the ministry of the Advocate.

33 The expression, "These things I have spoken to you,"[61] finally does what the reader expected it to do all along. It brings the discourse to a close. Here (as in 15:11; 16:1, 4) it is followed by a purpose clause: "These things I have spoken to you so that in me you might have peace. In the world you have distress, but take courage, I have overcome the world!" (v. 33). Earlier, he stated his purpose both positively (to bring joy, 15:11), and negatively (to warn against "stumbling," 16:1, 4). This time he combines warning and assurance, with the good news that in the end assurance and hope have the last word. He visualizes the disciples after his departure living simultaneously "in me" (as in 14:20; 15:2, 4-7), where they will have "peace," and "in the world," where "distress"[62] awaits them. His final word to them is "Take courage, I have overcome[63] the world." If chapters 15 and 16 are indeed a "second" farewell discourse, as many have proposed, then the second discourse ends on a note reminiscent of Jesus' words near the close of the first, "Peace I leave with you, my peace I give you. Not as the world gives do I give to you. Let no one's heart be shaken, nor let it be fearful!" (14:27). The dualism is evident in both places. Jesus and his disciples are at war with "the world," and "the world" is already defeated in principle. His victory over the world is theirs as well, a victory confirmed and accomplished in the long prayer to follow (17:1-26), and explicitly claimed for Christian believers both in 1 John (see 2:13-14; 4:4;

---

61. Gr. ταῦτα λελάληκα ὑμῖν (as in 14:25; 15:11; 16:1, 4, 25).
62. Gr. θλῖψιν.
63. Gr. ἐγὼ νενίκηκα τὸν κόσμον.

5:4-5) and in the book of Revelation (see 3:21; 5:5; 12:11; 15:2; 17:14; 21:7). But as for the disciples on the scene, they are not heard from again.

G. THE PRAYER FOR THE DISCIPLES (17:1-26)

1 *These things Jesus spoke, and when he had lifted his eyes to heaven he said, "Father, the hour has come. Glorify your Son, so that the Son might glorify you,* 2 *just as you gave him authority over all flesh, so that all that you have given him he might give them life eternal.* 3 *And this is the eternal life, that they might know you, the only true God, and him whom you sent, Jesus Christ.* 4 *I glorified you on the earth, having completed the work you have given me that I should do.* 5 *And now you, Father, glorify me in your own presence, with the glory I had in your presence before the world was.*

6 *I revealed your name to the men you gave me out of the world. Yours they were, and you gave them to me, and they have kept your word.* 7 *Now they have known that all things you have given me are from you,* 8 *because the words that you gave me I have given to them, and they received, and they came to know truly that I came forth from you, and they believed that you sent me.*

9 *I ask on their behalf. I do not ask on behalf of the world, but on behalf of those you have given me, because they are yours,* 10 *and all mine are yours and yours mine, and I am glorified in them.* 11 *And I am no longer in the world, and they are in the world, and I am coming to you. Holy Father, keep them in your name which you have given me, so that they may be one just as we are.* 12 *When I was with them, I kept them in your name which you have given me, and I guarded them, and none of them is lost except the son of destruction, that the Scripture might be fulfilled.* 13 *But now I am coming to you, and these things I am speaking in the world so that they might have my joy fulfilled in themselves.* 14 *I have given them your word, and the world hated them, because they are not from the world, just as I am not from the world.* 15 *I am asking not that you take them out of the world but that you keep them from the Evil One.* 16 *They are not from the world, just as I am not from the world.* 17 *Consecrate them in the truth. Your word is the truth.* 18 *Just as you sent me into the world, I also sent them into the world,* 19 *and on their behalf I consecrate myself, so that they too might be consecrated in truth.*

20 *And not for these alone do I ask, but also for those who believe in me through their word,* 21 *so that all might be one, just as you, Father, are in me and I in you, that these too might be in us, so that the*

17:1-26 THE PRAYER FOR THE DISCIPLES

> *world might believe that you sent me. 22 And I, the glory that you have given me I have given to them, so that they might be one just as we are one — 23 I in them and you in me — so that they might be perfected into one, so that the world might know that you sent me and loved them just as you loved me. 24 Father, that which you have given me, I want them to be with me where I am, so that they might see my glory, which you have given me because you loved me before the foundation of the world. 25 Righteous Father, and yet the world did not know you, but I knew you, and these men knew that you sent me. 26 And I made known to them your name, and I will make known, so that the love with which you loved me might be in them, and I in them.*

Discourse now gives way to prayer, a long prayer addressed to God as "Father" (vv. 1, 5, 11, 21, 24, 25), revisiting most of the themes of the preceding discourse. In particular, the prayer builds positively on the disciples' rather modest confession that "By this we believe that you came forth from God" (16:30). Their confession means that they "have kept your word," he reports to the Father (v. 6), in that "they have known that all things you have given me are from you" (v. 7), and have come to "know truly that I came forth from you, and . . . believed that you sent me" (v. 8; also v. 25). At the same time the prayer builds negatively on Jesus' warning that they "will be scattered, each to his own home, and leave me all alone" (16:32). The repeated petitions "that they may be one just as we are" (see vv. 11, 21-23) are best understood against the background of that prediction. Those "scattered" in the world are those who stand in need of prayer for protection and unity (compare 11:52, "that the children of God who are scattered might also be gathered into one"). In that sense the prayer, traditionally known as Jesus' "high-priestly" prayer (on the basis of vv. 17 and 19), could equally be viewed as the Shepherd's prayer (see 10:16), for its concerns are both pastoral and priestly.

Structurally, the prayer can be divided into six parts: first, Jesus prays to the Father for his own glorification on the basis of what he has accomplished in the world (vv. 1-5); second, he points to his disciples as trophies of his ministry in the world (vv. 6-8); third, he prays for their safety in the world, their unity, and their mission to the world (vv. 9-19); fourth, he prays for those who are not yet disciples, but "believe in me through their word," and for the unity of them all in the Father and the Son, so that even the world might believe and know what the Father has done (vv. 20-23); fifth, he states what he "wants" finally for his disciples (v. 24); sixth and last, he summarizes once again both the results of his ministry and his intent for those who believe (vv. 25-26).

1-2 Echoing Jesus' own concluding words ("These things I have spoken to you," 16:33), the Gospel writer continues the narrative: "These things Jesus spoke,[1] and when he had lifted his eyes to heaven he said, 'Father, the hour has come. Glorify your Son, so that the Son might glorify you, just as you gave him authority over all flesh, so that all that you have given him he might give them life eternal'" (vv. 1-2). In "lifting his eyes to heaven" he turns his attention away from the disciples and toward God. They are presumably still present, because when he makes his exit they leave with him (18:1), but they are silent throughout, and there is no evidence that they can even hear what he is saying. To all intents and purposes, he is alone with the Father, just as he was at Gethsemane in the other Gospels when the disciples were asleep. Jesus has "lifted his eyes" upward in prayer once before, at the tomb of Lazarus (11:41),[2] where instead of offering a petition he simply thanked the Father that he had *already* been heard (11:42). In both places, he addresses God as "Father," as he does consistently in the Gospel tradition, but the petition, "Glorify your Son," recalls rather 12:28, where he corrected "Father, save me from this hour" (12:27) to "Father, glorify your name." The parallel is heightened by a common reference to the "hour," echoing 12:23, "The hour has come that the Son of man might be glorified" (see also 13:1). Here the coming "hour" does double duty, alluding both to Jesus' own impending death and to the consequent scattering of the disciples in an "hour" that is both "coming" and "has come" (16:32).

The prayer, "Glorify your Son, so that the Son might glorify you" (v. 1) evokes at the same time Jesus' first words after the departure of Judas Iscariot, "Now the Son of man is glorified, and God is glorified in him" (13:31).[3] The "glorification" of which he speaks is mutual. The prayer here suggests that the Father first glorifies the Son, and the Son consequently glorifies the Father, but it can just as easily be the other way around (as in vv. 4 and 5). When the Son is glorified the Father is glorified, and vice versa (see also 11:4). But what does "glorified" mean concretely, whether for the Father or for the Son? Its meaning has to be determined from the context. As far as the Son is concerned, it is an oversimplification to say that Jesus is simply praying that he might die on the cross. Throughout the farewell discourse he has spoken of his death as a departure to the Father, and it appears likely here that he wants to be "glorified" in the sense of being reunited with the Father (he will make this explicit in v. 5). And what does it mean for the Son to "glorify" the Father? He explains this in the next clause, "just as you gave him au-

---

1. Gr. ταῦτα ἐλάλησεν Ἰησοῦς.
2. The expression does not always refer to prayer. In two other instances (4:35 and 6:5) he "lifted his eyes" (or told his disciples to do so) not in prayer, but in order to see an approaching crowd ripe for mission or ministry.
3. As we have seen, "the Son" and "the Son of man" are used interchangeably in this Gospel (see, for example, 3:13-18; 5:25-27; 6:27).

17:1-26 THE PRAYER FOR THE DISCIPLES

thority over all flesh, so that all that you have given him he might give them life eternal" (v. 2). This second purpose clause clarifies the first: the Son will "glorify" the Father, he says, by giving "life eternal" to "all that you have given him" — that is, to the disciples (see 6:37, 39).[4] Most immediately, the disciples are those whose feet Jesus washed and who have just now confessed, "By this we believe that you came forth from God" (16:30). Yet they represent a wider group of all who have believed in Jesus so far, including the Samaritans, the royal official and his household in chapter 4, the man born blind, and women disciples such as Martha and Mary. While "authority over all flesh"[5] hints at even broader horizons,[6] the accent is specifically on believers, as the rest of the prayer will demonstrate (see, for example, v. 9, "I do not ask on behalf of the world"). His words to the Father here echo his words to "the Jews" at the Rededication festival, where he referred to his disciples as his "sheep," adding, "And I give them life eternal, and they will never ever be lost" (10:28).[7] For the moment at least, "authority over all flesh" matters less than the authority to confer eternal life on those who believe.[8]

3 So crucial is this "eternal life" that the Gospel writer, blending his words with the words of Jesus, inserts a definition: "And this is the eternal life,[9] that they might know you, the only true God, and him whom you sent, Jesus Christ" (v. 3). The definition functions much like the Gospel writer's characteristic narrative asides, yet it is not a narrative aside, for the writer clearly wants to put it on the lips of Jesus. Its closest kinship is with certain passages where Jesus is abruptly represented as speaking of himself in the third person and from the Gospel writer's postresurrection viewpoint (see, for example, 3:13, 16-21; 6:27, 33). Its uniqueness lies in its being part of a prayer and in its use of the actual name, "Jesus Christ" — one of only two occurrences of the full name in the entire Gospel (the other being 1:17). Obvi-

---

4. "All" (πᾶν) is neuter singular, referring to the disciples corporately (as in 6:37 and 39).

5. Gr. ἐξουσίαν πάσης σαρκός.

6. Compare John's testimony: "The Father loves the Son and has given all things [πάντα δέδωκεν] into his hand" (3:35); also, of course, Matthew 28:18: "All authority was given to me [ἐδόθη μοι πᾶσα ἐξουσία] in heaven and on earth."

7. We have already noticed there the juxtaposition of the neuter plurals αὐτοῖς and αὐτά (10:28), referring to πρόβατα, "sheep") with the neuter singular (ὃ δέδωκέν μοι, "*that which* he has given me"), referring to "the disciples" corporately.

8. Again, compare John's testimony: "Whoever believes in the Son has eternal life, but whoever disobeys the Son will never see life, but the wrath of God remains on him" (3:36; also 1 Jn 5:11-12).

9. The definition reverses the order of "life eternal" (ζωὴν αἰώνιον, the normal word order in John's Gospel, v. 2) to "the eternal life" or "that eternal life" (ἡ αἰώνιος ζωή, v. 3), creating a kind of chiasm ("life eternal . . . the eternal life"), with the definite article noting the previous reference (BDF, §252).

ously, the use of the name undercuts to some degree the writer's intention of attributing the words to Jesus himself, yet it is little more than an extension of the practice of representing Jesus as speaking of himself in the third person as "the Son of man" (a title he almost certainly did use), and "the Son" (a title he may well have used).

Like the narrative asides, the definition of eternal life is for the reader's benefit, despite being addressed to God, as is the designation of the Father as "the only true God." God the Father knows who he is, and does not need to have "eternal life" defined for him! But for the reader of John's Gospel it is crucial that "eternal life" be defined as knowledge revealed through Jesus the Word. The phrase "the only true God," though firmly rooted in Jewish monotheism, nevertheless echoes some of Jesus' rebukes to "the Jews" themselves in earlier settings. Despite their monotheism, they did not "seek the glory that comes from the Only God" (5:44), nor did they understand that "the One who sent me is True, whom you do not know" (7:28). In this Gospel, "you, the only true God," and "him whom you sent, Jesus Christ," are inextricably linked. Neither can be known apart from the other. The ending of 1 John draws the same conclusion: "We know that the Son of God has come, and has given us understanding, that we might know the True One, and we are in the True One, in his Son Jesus Christ. This is the true God, and life eternal" (1 Jn 5:20). In much the same way, the definition of eternal life here upholds Jewish monotheism as the writer understands it, while at the same time reinforcing for the reader the Gospel's opening line, that "In the beginning was the Word, and the Word was with God, and the Word was God" (1:1).

4-5 Jesus now reverses the order of his opening petition ("Glorify your Son, so that the Son might glorify you," v. 1) in such a way that the Son's glorification of the Father comes first: "*I* glorified *you* on the earth.[10] . . . And now *you*, Father, glorify *me* in your own presence, with the glory I had in your presence before the world was" (vv. 4-5, italics added).[11] More specifically, he has glorified the Father on earth by "having completed the work[12] you have given me that I should do" (v. 4). Long before, and in a very different setting, he has said, "My food is that I might do the will of the One who sent me and complete his work" (4:34). The nature of that "work" he will spell out shortly (vv. 6-8), but for the moment he mentions it only

---

10. In this instance, "on the earth" (ἐπὶ τῆς γῆς) is pretty much equivalent to "in the world" (ἐν τῷ κόσμῳ, as in v. 13). The choice of words may be dictated by a desire to accent the contrast (as in 3:31) between "earth" below and "heaven" above (see v. 1, "lifted up his eyes to heaven").

11. The placement of the pronouns side by side creates the emphasis: literally, "I you [ἐγώ σε] glorified on the earth. . . . And now glorify me you" (με σύ).

12. Gr. τὸ ἔργον τελειώσας.

17:1-26 THE PRAYER FOR THE DISCIPLES

briefly, as the basis for the twin petitions, "Glorify your Son" (v. 1) and "glorify me in your own presence" (v. 5). The result is a kind of chiasm:

a "Glorify your Son" (v. 1a)
b "So that the Son might glorify you" (v. 1b)
b' "I have glorified you" (v. 4)
a' "And now glorify me" (v. 5)

Jesus is asking the Father for "glorification" (*a* and *a'*) on the basis of having glorified the Father already on earth *(b')*, and with the promise of continuing to do so *(b)*. This continuing glorification of the Father by the Son is probably best understood as the continuing gift of eternal life to all those whom the Father has given him (see v. 2), with life understood as knowledge of "the only True God" (v. 3).[13] This will take place through the testimony of the Advocate among those who are disciples already, and in the end through the written Gospel itself (see 20:31).

The "glory" for which Jesus is asking is here defined as "the glory that I had in your presence[14] before the world was" (v. 5). This is consistent with the notion that this "glory" is understood as the Son's reunion with the Father, but more specifically it revisits the Gospel's opening affirmation that "the Word was with God,[15] and the Word was God" (1:1). While the allusion to the Gospel's beginning is indirect rather than direct,[16] the reader is expected to know that Jesus was "with God in the beginning" (1:2), and that he shared in the Father's glory (see 1:14b). He alluded occasionally to his preexistence in such expressions as "I came down from heaven" (6:38), or "[what] if you see the Son of man going up where he was at first?" (6:62), or "The things I have seen in the Father's presence I speak" (8:38), or "before Abraham came to be, I am" (8:58). But more often he spoke ambiguously of having "come into the world," or being "sent" from the Father, expressions consistent with preexistence while not quite demanding it (see 1:6, where John too is a man "sent from God"). Jesus' language here in prayer to the Fa-

---

13. See verse 26, near the very end of the prayer: "And I made known to them your name, *and I will make known*" (italics added).
14. Gr. παρὰ σοί.
15. Gr. πρὸς τὸν θεόν.
16. For one thing, Jesus uses the preposition παρά here (παρὰ σεαυτῷ, "in your own presence"; παρὰ σοί, "in your presence"; compare 8:38), while in 1:1-2 the expression was "with God" (πρὸς τὸν θεόν). For another, the phrase "before the world was" (πρὸ τοῦ τὸν κόσμον εἶναι) places the emphasis simply on the world's existence, not on its creation or on Jesus as its creator. The variant reading in D (πρὸ τοῦ γενέσθαι τὸν κόσμον, "before the world came to be") comes closer to the language of 1:10 (καὶ ὁ κόσμος δι' αὐτοῦ ἐγένετο, "and the world came into being through him").

ther, accenting where he came from and where he is going, recalls his "plain" revelation to the disciples just a few verses earlier, "I came forth from the Father, and I have come into the world. Again, I am leaving the world and going off to the Father" (16:28). Turning his face now toward the Father, he asks that his journey back to the Father might begin. At the same time, the disciples are very much on his mind (see vv. 2-3), and the future glorification for which Jesus prays is, as we will see (v. 24), as much for their sakes as for his.

6 Jesus now interrupts the petition proper in order to report to the Father more explicitly in just what way "I glorified you on the earth, having completed the work you have given me that I should do" (v. 4). What exactly was "the work" he was given to do, and has he in fact "completed" it? At this point in the narrative, it cannot be the work of dying on the cross (see 19:30, "It is finished!"). Rather, it is the work of revealing the Father's "name" (that is, the Father himself) in the world. From the start, Jesus made it clear that "I have come in my Father's name," but his experience with the Jewish leaders was that "you do not accept me" (5:43). All his works were done "in my Father's name," he said, but were met with unbelief, except by those whom he called his "sheep" (see 10:25-26). They alone accepted him, and in doing so accepted his Father as well. In learning to know Jesus as Son of God, they have come to know God in a new way, as Father of Jesus — and so, though still only implicitly, as their own Father (see 20:17). Accordingly, he can report to the Father that "I revealed your name[17] to the men[18] you gave me out of the world. Yours they were, and you gave them to me, and they have kept your word" (v. 6). He speaks of his gathered disciples as if they were not in the same room. They are, he claims, the Father's gift to him, the living trophies of his mission (see v. 2; also 6:37, 39; 10:29).

In all this, he is giving them the benefit of the doubt, just as he did earlier when he said, "you are friends, because everything I heard from my Father I made known to you" (15:14). He also said, "If anyone loves me, he will keep my word" (14:23), and "The person who does not love me does not keep my words, and the word which you all hear is not mine but the Father's who sent me" (14:24), with the implicit invitation to do exactly that — love him and thereby "keep his word," which he claimed was the very word of the Father. Now we learn that they have in fact done so, for Jesus explicitly tells the Fa-

---

17. Gr. ἐφανέρωσά σου τὸ ὄνομα.

18. "The men" (τοῖς ἀνθρώποις) here may or may not be generic, but there is no evidence that any women were among those who uttered the confession on which this part of the prayer is built (16:30). While Jesus clearly had female disciples (notably Martha and Mary at Bethany), no women are represented in John's Gospel as belonging to the "Twelve" (6:70), or even (as, for example, in Lk 8:1-3) as having traveled with Jesus. Moreover, those present here are said to have later been "scattered" (16:32), while several of the women who believed evidently were not (see 19:25).

17:1-26 THE PRAYER FOR THE DISCIPLES

ther, "they have kept your word" (v. 6). This is by no means obvious to the reader, for, as we have seen, after an initial set of questions the disciples have been silent through most of Jesus' farewell discourse. The conclusion that they have "kept the Father's word" appears to be based on their sole declarative statement at the end, "Now we know that you know all things.... By this we believe that you came forth from God" (16:30).[19] To be sure, a stronger case can be made in their favor by going further back, to when Peter, speaking for them all, said, "Lord, to whom shall we turn? You have words of eternal life, and we believe and we know that you are the Holy One of God" (6:68-69). Implicit in the title "the Holy One of God" was, as we have seen, the notion that Jesus was the One "whom the Father consecrated and sent into the world" (10:36). It was on that basis, presumably, that Jesus said, "My sheep hear my voice, and I know them, and they follow me" (10:27), and yet they seem to have made little if any progress since then. They have been slow learners at best throughout the farewell discourse. Jesus himself practically articulated their confession for them when he said, "I came forth from the Father, and I have come into the world. Again, I am leaving the world and going off to the Father" (16:28), and all they did was echo the first half of what he said ("By this we believe that you came forth from God," v. 30).[20] The reader's impression is that seldom has so much been built on so little.[21] It appears that this final prayer of Jesus is itself an operation of divine grace, transforming the shaky faith of the disciples into something firm and lasting.[22]

---

19. Bultmann (497-99) is unable to admit this because of his rearrangement, placing chapter 17 well *before* the farewell discourse, between 13:30 and 31.

20. Notice that in partially echoing Jesus' words, they still avoided calling God "Father."

21. Schnackenburg, sensing this, comments that "Jesus' words about the disciples who belong to God are spoken so unconditionally and in such a fundamental way that they must apply not only to the disciples who were with Jesus, with their very defective understanding (see 14:9-12; 16:18f., 29-32), but also to all those who accept Jesus' revelation and show that they belong to God" (3.175). Barrett goes even further: "This can hardly refer to the period of the ministry (especially in view of 16.31f. and similar passages). John is looking back (perhaps from the end of the first century) upon the work of the apostles" (505). This view is widely held among commentators (see also Brown, 2.743; Lindars, 522). Yet it ignores the very explicit transition from the one group to the other, a transition not yet made in the text (see v. 20). Quite clearly, Jesus is referring at this point to his disciples gathered with him in the same room, and only to them.

22. So (correctly) Carson (559): "At the fundamental level, Jesus' assessment of his closest followers is entirely realistic, and in no way a contradiction of 16:31-32. After all, despite the generous assessment in 17:6, Jesus goes on to ask the Father to keep them safe (17:11). That they have kept the revelatory 'word' that Jesus has mediated to them from the Father does not mean that they have already become 'Christians'.... It simply means that, as compared with the world, they have been drawn out of it (v. 6), and constitute

7-8 As Jesus, continues, the reference to 16:30 becomes more and more unmistakable: "Now they have known that all things you have given me are from you, because the words that you gave me I have given to them, and they received, and they came to know truly that I came forth from you, and they believed that you sent me" (vv. 7-8). "Now they have known"[23] echoes almost verbally the disciples' own claim, "Now we know"[24] (16:30a). What they "knew," as we have seen, was that Jesus knew all things and revealed all things freely from God without being asked (see 16:30a). This, they believed, was because he "came forth from God" (16:30b). Putting their confession into his own words, Jesus tells the Father, "they came to know truly that I came forth from you, and they believed that you sent me" (v. 8b). At the same time, in claiming that "the words[25] that you gave me I have given to them, and they received" (v. 8a), he still seems to have in mind Peter's earlier acknowledgment that "You have words of life eternal, and we believe and we know that you are the Holy One of God" (6:68), and even prior to that the principle that "to as many as did receive him he gave authority to become children of God, to those who believe in his name" (1:12). Just as in verse 6, Jesus builds immediately on 16:30, but at the same time more broadly on all that has gone before.

In this report to the Father, Jesus focuses attention on the Father, not himself. The repetition of the emphatic "you," "your," and "yours" is striking: "*your* name" (v. 6), "*Yours* they were" (v. 6), "*your* word" (v. 6), "all things you have given me are *from you*" (v. 7),[26] "I came forth *from you*" (v. 8), "that *you* sent *me*" (v. 8; italics added throughout). Jesus commends his disciples to the Father not so much because they have recognized something about him as because they have recognized the Father — even though they are still unable to speak of "the Father" explicitly. Convinced as ever that "the Father himself loves" the disciples because they have "loved me, and have believed that I came forth from God" (16:27), he will now present them to the Father in prayer.

9-10 Jesus now begins intercessory prayer: "I ask[27] on their behalf. I

---

the nucleus of what will become the expanding messianic community, the church. Only this interpretation makes sense of the verses that follow." So too Morris (641): "The disciples still had misconceptions and their faith was still weak. But Jesus recognizes that their attitude to him is right. They know that he has come from God (cf. 16:30)."

23. Gr. νῦν ἔγνωκαν.
24. Gr. νῦν οἴδαμεν.
25. Gr. τὰ ῥήματα.
26. While the first "you" in this clause is not emphatic, the striking redundancy ("all things you have given me are from you," where we might have expected "all things that I have are from you") centers all the attention on the Father.
27. Gr. ἐρωτῶ.

17:1-26 THE PRAYER FOR THE DISCIPLES

do not ask on behalf of the world, but on behalf of those you have given me, because they are yours, and all mine are yours and yours mine, and I am glorified in them" (vv. 9-10). The verb "to pray"[28] is never used in this Gospel, only the verbs for "ask."[29] In keeping with the dualism of this Gospel, Jesus does not "ask," or pray, "on behalf of the world," but solely on behalf of the disciples, whom he continues to refer to as "those you have given me" (as in vv. 2, 6), for all the reasons he has just set forth (vv. 6-8). This does not mean that he is unconcerned about the world, only that his concern for the world is indirect rather than direct. His plans for the world, whatever they may be, are channeled through the disciples, and them alone (see vv. 21, 23). His mission to the world is over, even as theirs is about to begin (see v. 18).

Even though the Father has given the disciples to Jesus, he has not given them *away*. They still belong to the Father, and for this reason Jesus prays to the Father on their behalf. "They are yours," he tells the Father, adding that "all mine are yours[30] and yours mine," and "I am glorified in them." The abrupt neuter plurals[31] are striking. The apparent antecedents are masculine plurals: "the men you gave me out of the world" (v. 6), and who "received" and "came to know" and "believed" the truth (v. 8). Why does he switch to the neuter? It is tempting to think of the clause as wholly parenthetical, a virtual narrative aside placed on the lips of Jesus, as if he were generalizing, reflecting on the universality of what he and the Father had in common — that is, "*all things* mine are yours and *things* of yours are mine" (see 16:15, "All things that the Father has are mine"; also 3:35).[32] This is possible, yet there is no denying that the focus is strongly on persons, the disciples in particular, not on things. More likely, therefore, Jesus is tacitly (and abruptly) reintroducing the metaphor of himself as Shepherd and the disciples as sheep, so that the unspoken antecedent of the neuter plurals, "all mine" and "yours" *(ta sa),* is the neuter plural "sheep,"[33] as if to say, "and all my sheep are yours and yours are mine." There is a kind of precedent for this in 10:14-

---

28. Gr. προσεύχεσθαι.
29. That is, either αἰτεῖν for the prayers of the disciples (as in 14:13-14; 15:7, 16; 16:23-24), or ἐρωτᾶν for the prayers of Jesus (as in 14:16 and 16:26, and consistently in this chapter with περί, "concerning," or "on behalf of").
30. Gr. τὰ ἐμὰ πάντα σά ἐστιν.
31. Gr. τὰ ἐμά and σά.
32. This could also be supported by an appeal to verse 2, "just as you gave him authority over all flesh" (ἐξουσίαν πάσης σαρκός). This seems to be the view of most commentators. Brown (2.758) calls it a "parenthetical sentence . . . similar to xvi.15." Barrett speaks of a "complete mutuality of interest and possession between the Father and the Son" (507), and Lindars of a "complete community of possessions between the Father and Jesus" (523).
33. Gr. τὰ πρόβατα.

15, where Jesus said, "I am the good Shepherd, and I know mine[34] and mine know me, just as the Father knows me and I know the Father." There, to be sure, the sheep metaphor was explicit, yet, as we have seen, "the Father" was not part of that metaphorical world, and the thought expressed was quite independent of the world of shepherds and sheep. Quite possibly here, the generalization involved in the expression "all mine are yours and yours are mine" has to do with persons only, not things, embracing both the disciples on the scene and Jesus' "other sheep" (see 10:16), thus anticipating the later reference to "those who believe in me through their word" (v. 20). If so, although the words in question have a mildly parenthetical quality, they in no way interrupt the prayer's consistent focus on the disciples.[35] In a very real sense, this chapter can be understood as the Good Shepherd's prayer for his soon-to-be-scattered sheep (see 16:32).

Jesus draws the conclusion, "and I am glorified in them" (v. 10b), evidently in much the same sense in which God is "glorified" in him (see 13:31). To put it in more contemporary terms, the disciples (whatever their shortcomings) are his pride and joy, just as he is the Father's pride and joy. They are his "glory" in that they are the living proof that he has indeed "completed the work" the Father gave him to do (see v. 4), making possible his return to the Father to resume the glory that was his "before the world was" (v. 5). They are his "sheep," for whom he has already risked his life and for whom he will lay down his life. And just as the glorification of the Father and the Son has been mutual (see 13:31-32), so the glorification of Jesus and the disciples will turn out to be mutual. Just as he is "glorified in them," so they will be in him as they continue his work in the world (see v. 22, "And I, the glory that you have given me I have given to them").

11 True to the principle that his "glorification" is nothing other than his departure to the Father, Jesus finishes the thought of the preceding verse: "And I am no longer in the world, and they are in the world, and I am coming to you" (v. 11a), With this, he simply reiterates the recurring themes of the farewell discourse, except that he is now voicing them to the Father instead of to the disciples. The two clauses, "And I am no longer in the world," and "I am coming to you," echo such pronouncements as "A short time, and you no longer see me" (16:16), and "I go to the Father" (16:10, 17), respectively, and

---

34. Gr. τὰ ἐμά (neuter).

35. Schnackenburg puts it well, carefully avoiding the word "parenthesis": "Ornamental additions should cause no surprise in a prayer of praise. The logical progress of the ideas is undoubtedly impeded by the phrase 'all mine are thine and all thine are mine,' but these words follow the last words in the previous verse quite naturally. In the more restricted context, they can only refer to the disciples." Then, without quite speaking of "sheep" as the antecedent, he goes on to cite the shepherd and sheep imagery of chapter 10, concluding that "The same theme is present in 17:10" (3.178-79).

17:1-26 THE PRAYER FOR THE DISCIPLES

now frame the assertion that will govern most of the rest of the prayer: "and they[36] are in the world." Jesus is poised between "the world" and heaven, neither "in the world" in the same way as before, nor quite in the Father's presence either. When he says, "I am coming to you," he speaks of what he is *about to do,* not what he has already done, and two verses later, when he says the same thing again, he immediately adds, "these things I am speaking in the world" (v. 13). So there is a sense in which he is still "in the world," and a sense in which he is not.[37] What is clear in any event is a growing distance between Jesus and the disciples. They are fully "in the world" even as he leaves it, and for that reason they stand in need of prayer.

The intercession proper begins with the words, "Holy Father, keep them in your name which you have given me, so that they may be one just as we are" (v. 11b). This is where the verse division should have come. Jesus has said that he is "asking" on the disciples' behalf (v. 9), but here for the first time he "asks" for something specific. He marks the specificity with the direct address "Holy Father,"[38] echoing the address, "Father," in verses 1 and 5. Like the prayer for his own glorification (vv. 1, 5), the prayer is a simple imperative, "keep[39] them in your name," corresponding perhaps to the claim just made, that "they have kept your word" (v. 6).[40] The mention of the Father's "name" takes us back to verse 6, where Jesus said, "I have revealed your name," probably in the sense of revealing the Father himself. But here the identification of the Father's name as a name "which you have given me" is puzzling.[41] What "name" has the Father given to the Son? It is unlikely that

---

36. Gr. καὶ αὐτοί. Here he reverts to the masculine plural pronoun, as in verses 6 (αὐτούς) and 8 (καὶ αὐτοί). Whether "in them" (ἐν αὐτοῖς) in v. 10 is neuter or masculine is impossible to tell. Clearly the masculine and neuter are interchangeable.

37. This must have been so evident to certain scribes that they made it explicit in the text. After the words, "and I am coming to you," D and one or two old Latin versions have, "and I am no longer in the world, and in the world I am" (καὶ ἐν τῷ κόσμῳ εἰμί). See F. H. Scrivener, *Bezae Codex Cantabrigiensis* (Cambridge: Deighton, Bell, 1864), 151.

38. Gr. πάτερ ἅγιε.

39. Gr. τήρησον.

40. Again, after the words, "keep them in your name," D has another longer reading, "and when I was with them, I kept them in your name" (anticipating v. 12).

41. "Which" is ᾧ, referring to the name as that which the Father has given him. Because it is puzzling, some ancient witnesses (including a corrector of D, one or two minuscules, the Vulgate, and certain other ancient versions) changed ᾧ to οὕς, yielding the translation, "keep in your name those you have given me" (that is, the disciples; see the KJV, Douay, NEB). Others (including D, X, and a few minuscules) changed it to ὅ, yielding the translation, "keep in your name that which you have given me" (that is, the disciples corporately, as in 6:39 and 10:29). But the reading ᾧ, with "the name" as antecedent, has overwhelming manuscript support (with P[60], P[66], ℵ, A, B, C, K, Θ, Ψ, family 13, and the majority of later witnesses). See Metzger, *Textual Commentary,* 249-50.

the name is "Lord," the common LXX translation of the divine name, because "Lord" in this Gospel is consistently either a mere term of respect ("Sir") or at most a divine title (as in 20:28), not a name. Raymond Brown (already in v. 6) suggested that the "name" in question is "I Am," in keeping with certain LXX passages in which it seems to function in that way. In revealing himself as "I Am" (above all in 8:58), Jesus reveals himself by a name the Father has given him, and thereby reveals the Father.[42] While the specificity of such an interpretation is appealing, it is doubtful that most readers would have understood such a subtle allusion. More likely, perhaps, the Father has given Jesus his own "name" simply in the sense of delegating to him the authority to act on the Father's behalf, thereby revealing who the Father is (see, for example, v. 2, "authority over all flesh"; also, 13:20, "the person who receives me receives the One who sent me"; 16:15, "All things that the Father has are mine"). In this sense the petitions "Glorify your name" (12:28) and "Glorify your Son" (17:1) amount to the same thing.[43]

All this, Jesus says, is "so that they may be one[44] just as we are" (v. 11b),[45] the first of four notices of such an intention in the prayer (see vv. 21, 22, 23). Again, the Shepherd discourse is in play, where he had said, "they will become one flock, one Shepherd" (10:16), and "I and the Father are one" (10:30). The Shepherd's prayer for the sheep is what accomplishes his intention. And even apart from the Shepherd and sheep imagery, we have been told that Jesus himself would die "in order that the children of God who are scattered might also be gathered into one" (11:52). The analogy here between the unity of the disciples and the unity of the Father and the Son is striking, yet not without precedent. Jesus has, after all, said first, that "the Father is in me and I in the Father" (10:38), and later, to the disciples, that "I am in my Father, and you in me, and I in you" (14:20). As we have seen, there is little that is new in the prayer. Most of what is said has been said before, ex-

---

42. Brown, 2.755-56.

43. Perhaps in part under the influence of John's Gospel, the notion that the Father has given his name to the Son reappears in certain early Gnostic texts, as, for example, *Gospel of Truth* 38.6-11 ("Now the name of the father is the son. It is he who in the beginning named what emanated from him.... And he begot him as a son and gave him his name"), and *Gospel of Philip* 54.5-7 ("Only one name is not uttered in the world, the name that the father bestowed on the son; it is above every other — that is, the name of the father"). See B. Layton, *The Gnostic Scriptures: A New Translation* (New York: Doubleday, 1995), 262, 330.

44. Gr. ἵνα ὦσιν ἕν.

45. The whole clause, "so that they may be one just as we are," is omitted in the first hand of P[66] and in a number of old Latin versions, either accidentally or because it seemed premature (see vv. 21-23), interrupting the flow from "keep them in your name which you have given me" (v. 11) to "When I was with them, I kept them in your name which you have given me" (v. 12).

17:1-26 The Prayer for the Disciples

cept that now it is spoken to the Father in prayer rather than to the disciples in discourse.

12 "When I was with them," Jesus explains, "I kept them in your name" (v. 12a). "When I was with them" recalls 16:4, "And these things I did not tell you from the beginning, because I was with you." Here again, Jesus looks back on his ministry in the world as if it were already in the past, in keeping with what he has just said ("I am no longer in the world," v. 11). The notice affords him the opportunity to add a postscript to what he has already reported to the Father about the "work" he accomplished on earth (see vv. 4, 6-8). What he has just asked the Father to do (that is, "keep them in your name," v. 11) is what he himself has done up to now: "I kept them in your name which you have given me, and I guarded them." The shared responsibility of the Father and the Son to "keep" or "guard"[46] the disciples "so that they may be one just as we are" (v. 11) corresponds to their own responsibility to "dwell" or "remain" in the Father and the Son (see 14:20; 15:4, 7). Jesus concludes that he has done so successfully because "none of them is lost except the son of destruction, that the Scripture might be fulfilled." In short, he announces that the intention stated in 3:16, 6:39, and 10:28 has been realized. That is, none of those who believe in Jesus — his "sheep," according to 10:27-28 — are "lost." As we have seen, there is a grim finality in this Gospel to being "lost" which is not present in other Gospels or the letters of Paul.

Jesus' words here, particularly his reference to the one exception, are more for the reader's benefit than a real part of a prayer to the Father. He is not by any means offering an excuse to the Father for the one exception — the "son of destruction," who is in fact "lost" — but simply informing the reader that this is the case. The "son of destruction" (that is, the one destined to be lost) can only be Judas Iscariot,[47] and the God who assigned Judas his fate hardly needs to be reminded of it! Like the definition of eternal life near the beginning of the prayer (v. 3), the notice that this happened in order "that the Scripture might be fulfilled"[48] is intended solely for the reader, who

---

46. "Keep" is τηρεῖν; "guard," φυλάσσειν.

47. For the exact phrase, "the son of destruction" (ὁ υἱὸς τῆς ἀπωλείας), see 2 Thessalonians 2:3, with reference to an Antichrist figure ("the man of sin"), who will appear before Christ is finally revealed in glory. Judas too is an Antichrist figure, probably in much the same sense as the heretics in 1 and 2 John (see 1 Jn 2:18, 22; 4:3; 2 Jn 7). In view of the finality of "destruction" (τῆς ἀπωλείας, a cognate of ἀπώλετο, "lost") in John's Gospel (see preceding note), its application to Judas is telling. In form, "the son of destruction" is a Semitic expression, like "sons of light" (see 12:36), meaning one whose destiny it is to be irrevocably "lost." In later traditions, the phrase is applied even to Satan himself (see the Greek of the fifth-century *Acts of Pilate* IV [20.3]: 'Ο inheritor of darkness, son of perdition [υἱὲ τῆς ἀπωλείας], devil'; see M. R. James, *Apocryphal New Testament,* 131).

48. Gr. ἵνα ἡ γραφὴ πληρωθῇ.

might have been wondering now for several chapters how one of twelve "chosen" disciples could also have been "the devil" (see 6:70). But what "Scripture" had to be fulfilled? The one nearest at hand is Psalm 41:9 (40:10, LXX), introduced in exactly the same way as here in 13:18: "The one who eats my bread lifted up his heel against me." Yet as we have seen, that text seems not to have referred to Judas exclusively, and even to the extent that it did refer to him, it was in relation to his betrayal of Jesus at the table, not in relation to the inevitability that he would be "lost," or to the "destruction" awaiting him (Ps 68[68]:26 and 109[108]:8, as cited in Acts 1:20, are better suited to that purpose). Of the four instances in John's Gospel of the expression "that the Scripture might be fulfilled" (the others being 13:18 and 19:24, 36), this is the only one in which a specific text is not cited. In that respect it is closer to 19:28, "that the Scripture might be completed," where (as we will see) no one biblical text is in view. Quite possibly, readers of John's Gospel were expected to be familiar in a general way with the notion that Judas's betrayal and his subsequent fate were prophesied in Scripture (see not only 13:18 and Acts 1:20, but also Matt 27:9). If this was the case, and "the Scripture cannot be abolished" (10:35), then Judas's grim fate was inevitable — even in the face of the principle that "none of them is lost." He has in any case hinted at Judas's "destruction" in connection with the metaphor of the vine and the branches (see 15:6, "thrown out like the branch, and withered, and they gather them and throw them into the fire, and they are burned up").

13 "But now I am coming to you," Jesus continues, in sharp contrast to "When I was with them" (v. 12). With this, he picks up the thought of verse 11, giving it an added note of immediacy. Even so, he tacitly acknowledges that he is still "in the world" (despite his words to the contrary in v. 11): "And these things I am speaking in the world so that they might have my joy fulfilled in themselves" (v. 13). Again the prayer simply replicates in words directed to the Father what Jesus has already told the disciples about his joy and theirs being fulfilled (see 15:11; 16:24). It is not altogether clear whether "these things I am speaking in the world" refers to what he said earlier to the disciples or to what he is saying to the Father right now. Probably the ambiguity is deliberate, for the discourse and the prayer both have the same intention. Jesus wants "joy," his own joy, for the disciples, even in their time of "grief" in the world (see 16:22). Their joy will be "fulfilled in themselves,"[49] by virtue of their relationship to him, not in the external circumstances they face, which may well be dire and difficult (see 15:18–16:3). Of these circumstances he now speaks.

14 "I have given them your word," he continues, "and the world hated them, because they are not from the world, just as I am not from the

---

49. Gr. πεπληρωμένην ἐν ἑαυτοῖς.

17:1-26 THE PRAYER FOR THE DISCIPLES

world" (v. 14). The first clause is repetitious (see v. 8a, "the words that you gave me I have given to them"), but serves here to heighten the force of what follows: "and the world hated them,"[50] once again echoing to the Father what he has already said to the disciples (15:18, "If the world hates you, you know that it has hated me before you"). He also reiterates the reason for the world's hatred: "because they are not from the world just as I am not from the world" (compare 15:19). Because the world hates the disciples, they are in danger of persecution (see 15:20–16:3), and in need of protection, just as sheep need protection from predators (see 10:10, 12). Jesus himself has already "guarded" them (v. 12) in the course of his ministry, and he will do so once more before his departure (see 18:8-9), but now he entrusts them to the Father's care.

15-16 As we have seen, Jesus' words to the Father in verses 12-14 were not so much petitionary or intercessory prayer as simply a continuation of his rehearsal of his ministry on earth.[51] But now he resumes the intercession that broke off when he prayed "that they may be one, just as we are" (v. 11b). The verb "ask" (as in v. 9) signals the next petition: "I am asking not that you take them out of the world, but that you keep them from the Evil One." The disciples, although *chosen* "out of the world" (15:19), are not to be *taken* "out of the world." To "take them out of the world"[52] should not be understood as equivalent either to "I will take you to myself" redemptively (14:3), or to "taking away" in judgment the branches of the vine that do not bear fruit (15:2). Rather, it is purely hypothetical, like Paul's comment that in telling the Corinthians not to mingle with immoral people he did not mean the immoral "of this world," for then they would have to "go out of the world" (1 Cor 5:10). It is not something that either this writer or the Apostle Paul envisions as actually happening. The accent falls instead on the last clause, the real object of the petition: "that you keep them from the Evil One," corresponding to the earlier petition, "keep them in your name" (v. 11).

---

50. The aorist "hated" (ἐμίσησεν) is surprising, because up to now Jesus has spoken primarily of the world's hatred of the disciples in the near future, after his departure (see 15:18-19). He speaks of the world's hatred here as a given, an accomplished fact, which of course it is for the earliest readers of the Gospel. Schnackenburg (3.183) offers a comparison to the aorist, "I sent" (ἀπέστειλα, v. 18), referring to a sending that had not yet taken place (see 20:21). Even so, the tense also presupposes that the world hated the disciples right from the beginning, for Jesus has "guarded" them all along, lest they be "lost" (see v. 12).

51. The closest he comes to explicit intercession within those three verses is his stated intent "that they might have my joy fulfilled in themselves" (v. 13b), but as we saw, that was not so much the content of a petition as simply the intent of all that Jesus has said or will say in chapters 13–17.

52. Gr. ἵνα ἄρῃς ἐκ τοῦ κόσμου.

Like "Father" (v. 1; 11:41; 12:27, 28), "Holy Father" (v. 11), and the references to God's "name" in prayer (vv. 11, 12; 12:28), "keep them from the Evil One" evokes the Lord's Prayer, which (according to Matthew and the *Didache*) ends with the petition, "deliver us from the Evil One" (Mt 6:13), traditionally rendered as "deliver us from evil." The reference to the devil is unmistakable, for he has already been identified as "the ruler of the world" (14:30), or of "this world" (12:31), and near the end of 1 John the reader is reminded that "the whole world lies in the Evil One."[53] Thus, to "keep them from the Evil One" is to keep them safe in the hostile "world." Jesus then adds, "They are not from the world, just as I am not from the world" (v. 16), repeating verse 14b verbatim. The redundancy reinforces even more the dualism governing both the prayer and the preceding discourse (again, see 15:18-19).

17 Jesus next adds to the imperatives "glorify" (vv. 1, 5) and "keep" (v. 11) a third imperative: "Consecrate[54] them in the truth. Your word is the truth" (v. 17).[55] Appropriately, the One addressed as "Holy Father" (v. 11) is the One who "consecrates" or "makes holy" Jesus' disciples, for it was he who first "consecrated" Jesus and sent him into the world (10:36), as "the Holy One of God" (6:69). This is the first hint within the prayer of the traditional notion of it as a "high-priestly" prayer, for a prayer of "consecration" is the appropriate work of a priest. Jesus prays that the Father might consecrate or sanctify the disciples "in the truth," which he then immediately defines (not for the Father's benefit but for the reader's, just as in v. 3!) as "your word." By "your word" he does not mean the written Scriptures (as in 10:35), but the "word" or message from the Father which he has given the disciples and which they have "received" and "kept" (see vv. 6, 8). That word is "the truth" that has set them free (see 8:32), so as to become no longer "slaves" but "friends" (see 15:15). The identification of "your word" and "the truth" is thoroughly in keeping with Jesus' identification of himself as "the Truth" (14:6), the coming Advocate, as "the Spirit of truth" (14:17; 15:26; 16:13), and the Father as "the only true God" (v. 3).

18 The connection between "consecration" and "sending" evident in 10:36 is maintained here as well. "Just as you sent me into the world," Jesus goes on, "I also sent them[56] into the world" (v. 18). He speaks of the disciples' mission to the world in the past tense, as if it has already started, or

---

53. 1 John 5:19; see also Matthew 5:37 and 2 Thessalonians 3:3.
54. Gr. ἁγίασον.
55. Once again, Colwell's rule ("definite predicate nouns which precede the verb usually lack the article") suggests the translation "is the truth" rather than simply "is truth" for ἀλήθειά ἐστιν.
56. Gr. κἀγὼ ἀπέστειλα αὐτούς.

17:1-26 THE PRAYER FOR THE DISCIPLES

even been completed,[57] and yet it will not "officially" begin until he tells them after the resurrection, "just as the Father has sent me, so I am sending you" (20:22). It is commonly suggested that the pronouncement is worded in this way for the benefit of the readers of the Gospel, who would hear it in relation to their own ongoing mission in the world, and this is undoubtedly the case. And yet he had said long before in a Samaritan village, "I have sent you[58] to harvest that on which you have not labored" (4:38). Quite possibly there are echoes both there and here of certain synoptic (or synoptic-like) traditions in which Jesus sent the disciples on certain missionary journeys already during the course of his ministry (see Mk 6:6-13; Mt 10:5-16; Lk 9:1-6; 10:1-12). The difference here comes in the phrase "into the world," which occurs in none of those passages, and which looks beyond those early preaching tours toward a worldwide mission that would begin with Jesus' resurrection.[59] In principle, Jesus has just now sent his disciples "into the world" by praying to the Father, "Consecrate them" (v. 17), that is, "Set them apart for mission, just as you set me apart."

19 Still, there is a sense in which the "consecration" of the disciples is not yet accomplished, for Jesus continues, "and on their behalf I consecrate myself,[60] so that they too might be consecrated in truth" (v. 19). The priestly language of the two preceding verses continues. What does it mean for Jesus to "consecrate" himself, given that the Father, in sending him into the world, has already "consecrated" him (10:36)? And in what sense does his self-consecration "consecrate" the disciples? Having been "consecrated" by being sent into the world, Jesus as priest now "consecrates himself" to fulfill a priestly role — evidently to offer himself as a sacrifice. According to the book of Hebrews (5:3; 9:7), Jewish priests repeatedly offered sacrifices both for their own sins and for the sins of the people, while Jesus, being "holy, blameless, pure, set apart from sinners, exalted above the heavens," had no need to do this, but instead "sacrificed for their sins once and for all when he offered himself" (Heb 7:26-27, NIV). The accent, both in Hebrews and here, is not only on Jesus' priestly role but on his initiative in carrying it out. Here he can say that "on their behalf[61] I consecrate myself," just as he said earlier in the voice of the Good Shepherd, "I lay down my life for [or "on behalf of"] the sheep" (10:15) and "No one took it away from me, but I lay it

---

57. See above, n. 50.
58. Gr. ἐγὼ ἀπέστειλα ὑμᾶς.
59. It is not surprising — it is even appropriate in a way — that just as the synoptic accounts of mission tours within Jesus' ministry on earth contain intimations of a worldwide mission to come (see, for example, Mt 10:17-18, 23), so the worldwide mission is announced here as if it had already begun.
60. Gr. ἐγὼ ἁγιάζω ἐμαυτόν.
61. Gr. ὑπὲρ αὐτῶν.

down on my own" (10:18). The "Lamb of God" of John's prophecy (1:29, 36) has become both Shepherd[62] and High Priest, offering himself to the Father so that his disciples "might be consecrated in truth" (v. 19)![63] It is unclear how far the priestly imagery should be pressed. Are the disciples "consecrated" as a priesthood (see, for example, 1 Pet 2:5, 9), or perhaps as sacrificial victims facing the prospect of eventual martyrdom? Or are they simply set apart for a mission, without specific reflection on what that mission will entail? Probably the latter, although the precedent of 6:53-58 and 16:2 suggests that martyrdom remains a very real threat. Jesus' awareness of such a possibility has been evident already in his prayer "not that you take them out of the world but that you keep them from the Evil One" (v. 15). Yet the emphasis is not so much on a priestly role for the disciples or on the prospect of martyrdom as it is on "truth," that is, the word of God with which they are entrusted (see v. 17).

20-21 Jesus now looks beyond the small group of disciples whose feet he had washed after the meal to a larger group: "And not for these alone do I ask, but also for those who believe[64] in me through their word, so that all might be one, just as you, Father, are in me and I in you, that these too might be in us,[65] so that the world might believe that you sent me" (vv. 20-21). This broader awareness corresponds to his words much earlier about the "other sheep I have, which are not from this courtyard. Those too I must bring, and they will hear my voice, and they will become one flock, one Shepherd" (10:16). Even the form of the pronouncement ("not for these alone . . . but also") corresponds to the principle that Jesus dies "not for the nation alone, but also in order that the children of God who are scattered might be gathered into one" (11:52). Jesus' prayer now reveals just how these "other sheep," or "children of God," will be brought in. It will be "through their word," that is, through the message proclaimed by Jesus' disciples, the very "word" of the Father (v. 17) by which they have been consecrated in answer to Jesus' prayer. Here, as in the other two passages, the accent is not on futurity — that

---

62. Interestingly, in the book of Revelation as well, "the Lamb" (τὸ ἀρνίον) takes on the role of "shepherding" the people of God (Rev 7:17).

63. Gr. ἡγιασμένοι ἐν ἀληθείᾳ. The thought is not unlike that of Hebrews 2:11, "For the one who consecrates [ὁ ἁγιάζων] and those who are consecrated [οἱ ἁγιαζόμενοι] are all of one family" (ἐξ ἑνός).

64. Gr. περὶ τῶν πιστευόντων.

65. Instead of "might be in us" (ἵνα . . . ἐν ἡμῖν ὦσιν) some ancient witnesses (including ℵ, A, L, Θ, and the majority of later manuscripts) have "might be one in us" (ἵνα . . . ἐν ἡμῖν ἓν ὦσιν), but the better-attested reading (with P[66], B, C, W, and the old Latin, Syriac, and Coptic versions) lacks the redundant repetition of ἕν, or "one," and is to be preferred (see Metzger, *Textual Commentary*, 250). The accent is not merely on unity or oneness, but also on dwelling "in us," that is, in the Father and the Son.

is, that these "others" necessarily belong to a later generation — but simply on the fact that the "word" reaches them not directly from Jesus, but indirectly through his disciples. Just as in 10:16 he could say, "other sheep I have," as if they were already his, and in 11:52 they were already called "children of God," so here they are "those who believe," whenever and wherever that might be, not "those who will believe" at some unstated time in the future.[66] As in the two earlier passages, the end and goal of the process is unity. Just as he had said, "they will become one flock, one Shepherd" (10:16), and just as his death would be "in order that the children of God who are scattered might also be gathered into one" (11:52), so here his prayer is that "all might be one, just as you, Father, are in me and I in you, that these too might be in us" (v. 21a; compare v. 11). Because the accent is not on futurity, the point of the prayer for unity is not that later generations of believers should bond with earlier generations by holding fast to the apostolic tradition, but simply that all believers everywhere should be united with each other in their commitment to Jesus and to the Father.

Jesus goes beyond the earlier passages (10:16 and 11:52) in two ways. The first is that he grounds the unity of all believers in the unity of the Father and the Son, as the preceding discourse might have led us to expect (see 14:20, "In that day, you will come to know that I am in my Father, and you in me, and I in you"). Here his use of direct address, almost redundantly ("just as you, Father, are in me, and I in you") accents the intimacy between Father and Son. The second is that he adds an additional object and purpose to his prayer — perhaps its ultimate purpose: "so that the world might believe[67] that you sent me" (v. 21b). This abrupt enlargement of the scope of the prayer (going beyond v. 11 as well) qualifies the earlier disclaimer that "I do not ask on behalf of the world, but on behalf of those you have given me" (v. 9). Even though Jesus' prayer is not for the world, the whole world is within his horizons. He views the unity of the disciples and their mission to the world as inseparable. His vision is that their unity with one another will send a message to the world that will bring people to faith in him and in the Father. He builds here on 13:35 ("By this they all will come to know that you are my disciples,

---

66. The participle "those who believe" is present (τῶν πιστευόντων), according to the earliest and best manuscripts, even though some witnesses (including a corrector of D and some Latin and Coptic versions) have changed the participle to the future (τῶν πιστευσόντων).

67. Gr. ἵνα ὁ κόσμος πιστεύῃ. Once again there is variation in the manuscript tradition between the present and the aorist subjunctive (that is, between πιστεύῃ, "to be convinced," with P[66], ℵ, B, C, W, and others, and πιστεύσῃ, 'to come to faith,' with P[60], A, D, L, and correctors of ℵ and C). The weight of manuscript evidence favors the former, suggesting that the emphasis is not on the world coming to faith, but simply on it being convinced of what is true.

if you have love for each other"), implying that the unity of which he speaks must be something visible to the outside world, visible, for example, in love shown to each other. Going even beyond 13:35, his intent is that many who now belong to "the world" will recognize not only that the disciples belong to Jesus but that Jesus belongs to the Father and comes from the Father. In this way he reveals at last the implication of his announcements early on that "God so loved the world" (3:16), or that he himself came to "save" the world (3:17; 12:47). God's plan for the world will come to realization not through Jesus during his limited time on earth, but through the band of disciples he has gathered around him. Moreover, the promise held out to the world is very carefully worded here (as it is in 3:16). The negative verdict that "the world did not know him" (1:10) and "his own did not receive him" (1:11) is not rescinded. Jesus does not say that the whole world will believe *in* him (that is, that everyone will become his disciple), or even that he intends this. His intent is only that the world might believe, or recognize, *that* he was sent from God, whom he calls Father.[68] This could mean either than the world will come to faith, as the disciples have done (16:30), and in that sense cease to be "the world," or that Jesus and his mission from the Father will be vindicated before the world, and the world consequently proven wrong (see 16:8-11). In that event, the world becomes simply a theater for the vindication of Jesus' followers as those chosen and beloved of God.

Jesus' petition thus holds out hope for the world, but nothing approaching certainty. It is not a prophecy of what must happen, but simply a generalized expression of divine intent comparable to 3:17 ("For God sent his Son into the world not to judge the world, but so that the world might be saved through him") or 12:47 ("I did not come to judge the world but to save the world"). Readers of the Gospel in every generation have known that the outcome of the disciples' mission to the world remains undecided. In any event, the focus is not on the question of whether or not "the world" will be saved, but on the disciples themselves, and on the nature of their unity in the Father and the Son. The point is that it must be a visible unity, a "sign" to the world, testifying not only to their relationships with each other but to their relationship with Jesus and to the Father. Implicit in the notion of unity — in itself a very abstract concept — is the concrete imperative of loving one another (as in 13:34-35; 15:12, 17), and obeying Jesus' commands (as in 14:15 and 15:10). Those are things even "the world" can see, and those things, he implies, are the heart and soul of the disciples' mission to the world — consequently the world's only hope

22-23 "And I, the glory that you have given me I have given to

---

68. The word order, ὅτι σύ με ἀπέστειλας, tends to bear this out, accenting both the second- and first-person pronouns: "that *you* sent *me*."

17:1-26 THE PRAYER FOR THE DISCIPLES

them," Jesus continues (v. 22a). What is this "glory" that the Father has given him? What does it mean for him to give it to his disciples? And when did he confer on them this glory? Was it during the course of his ministry when, as he said, "I revealed your name to the men you gave me out of the world" (v. 6), and passed on to them "the words that you gave me" (v. 8)? Or was it just now, in the course of the prayer itself, when he asked the Father, "Consecrate them in the truth" (v. 17), and consecrated himself on their behalf (v. 19)?[69] It is tempting to place it during the ministry because of the structural parallel between "the words that you gave me I have given to them" (v. 8), and "the glory that you have given me I have given to them" (v. 22). But this is unlikely because during Jesus' ministry, as described in this Gospel, the "glory" seems to have been his and his alone, something the disciples can see (1:14; 2:11; 11:4, 40), but in which they do not share. Even though he can say "I am glorified in them" (v. 10), the glory is still his and not yet theirs. His "glorification," moreover, is repeatedly linked to his impending death (see 7:39; 11:4; 12:23; 13:31-32; 17:1, 5).[70] It is therefore more plausible that he has conferred his "glory" on the disciples at this very moment, in the act of "consecrating" himself as a sacrifice "so that they too might be consecrated in truth" (v. 19).[71] The "glory" he gives them is the mission on which he has just now "sent them" (v. 18), continuing his own revelatory mission as those "consecrated" to that task.

The purpose of consecrating the disciples, or giving them glory, is indistinguishable from the purpose of the prayer itself: "so that they might be one just as we are one — I in them and you in me — so that they might be perfected into one, so that the world might know that you sent me and loved them just as you loved me" (vv. 22b-23). Here he repeats almost verbatim, with three slight elaborations, verse 21 ("so that all might be one, just as you,

---

69. Many commentators do not clearly distinguish between these two alternatives (see, for example, Bultmann, 515-16; Schnackenburg, 3.192).

70. So Barrett: "The glory is the glory of Christ, and the glory of Christ is acquired through, and is most completely expressed in, the crucifixion. The church received glory on precisely the same terms, by unity in faith with the death and resurrection of Jesus, and expresses it in obedience, and pre-eminently in humiliation, poverty, and suffering" (513). Brown cites v. 1, "Glorify your Son, that the Son might glorify you," suggesting "that glory will be given after the exaltation of Jesus, since the Son glorifies the Father through the disciples. Consequently the tenses in 22 seem to be from the standpoint of the time in which the Johannine writer is living" (2.771). While this may be true, the event is seen as already accomplished in principle by Jesus' prayer, which effectively confers on the disciples the "glory" of which it speaks.

71. As we have seen, Jesus' prayer, "Father, glorify your name" (δόξασόν σου τὸ ὄνομα, 12:28) can be read as the equivalent of the beginning of the Lukan version of the Lord's Prayer, "Father, hallowed [or consecrated] be your name" (ἁγιασθήτω τὸ ὄνομά σου, Lk 11:2).

Father, are in me and I in you, that these too might be in us, so that the world might believe that you sent me"). The first elaboration is that becoming "one" (v. 21a) is defined as being "perfected into one"[72] (v. 23), recalling the "gathering into one" of the "children of God" (11:52). The second is that the world's "believing" (v. 21b) is defined as "knowing" or recognizing[73] (v. 23). The third is that what the world is intended to "know" is not just "that you sent me" (v. 21), but "that you sent me and loved them as you loved me" (v. 23). Jesus has not spoken of the love of God so far in the prayer itself, but the Father's love is by now a major theme of the Gospel, whether for the Son (3:35; 5:20; 10:17; 15:9) or for the disciples (14:21, 23; 16:27).

The modest changes are interrelated. The notion of being "perfected" is less characteristic of John's Gospel than of the "priestly" Epistle to the Hebrews, where "by one offering" Jesus is said to have "perfected forever those who are being consecrated" (Heb 10:14; also Heb 2:10-11). But more in keeping with the theology of John's Gospel is the notion that the "perfecting into one" of Jesus' disciples means first of all having the love of God "perfected" or brought to realization in their love for one another.[74] This was evident in the preceding discourse, where "dwelling" in Jesus (15:4) was defined as dwelling in his love (15:9-10) by extending his love to one another (15:12, 17). In 1 John, this relationship is explicitly characterized as having the love of God "perfected"[75] in us (1 Jn 4:12; also 2:5; 4:17-18), and this is likely implied here by the phrase "perfected into one."

With these subtle changes, the implicit link to 13:35 ("By this they all will know that you are my disciples, if you have love for each other") becomes almost explicit. The world cannot see, or "know," a merely "spiritual" unity or indwelling of the disciples in each other, or in the Father and the Son, but it can recognize the love believers have for each other as a sign of God's love for them. On that recognition, and on that alone, rests the possibility "that the world might believe" (v. 21). Perhaps surprisingly, nothing is said here of the world recognizing the Father's love for the world itself (see 3:16). Possibly this is because Jesus has been addressing God as "Father" (vv. 1, 5, 11), and will immediately do so again (vv. 24, 25). While God in-

72. Gr. τετελειωμένοι εἰς ἕν.
73. Gr. ἵνα γινώσκῃ.
74. The verb τελειοῦν, to "perfect" or "complete," is used differently here from its previous occurrences in the Gospel, where it had to do with Jesus "completing" or simply finishing the work he was given to do (see 4:34; 5:36; 17:4). Here, as in 1 John, it comes closer to "make perfect" (see BDAG, 996), not in the sense of an abstract perfectionism, but in the sense of a relationship of love or unity becoming all that it can be. Closer in meaning, perhaps, is 19:28, where all Scripture "comes true" or comes to a realization of its purpose in Jesus' death on the cross.
75. Gr. τετελειωμένη.

17:1-26 THE PRAYER FOR THE DISCIPLES

deed "loves" the world (3:16), he does not love it in the same way that he loves Jesus and the disciples — that is, as a father loves a child.

24 The prayer so far has been punctuated with the address, "Father" (vv. 1, 5), framing Jesus' petitions for his own glorification, "Holy Father" (v. 11), beginning a series of petitions for his disciples, and "Father" again (v. 21), highlighting the last and arguably most important of his petitions. Now he uses it again: "Father, that which you have given me, I want them to be with me where I am" (v. 24a). This time it introduces something more than a petition, a forthright declaration to the Father of what "I want."[76] The contrast with his prayer in the garden of Gethsemane in other Gospels is striking, for there he is represented as praying, "Not what I want,[77] but what you want" (Mk 14:36; also Mt 26:39 and Lk 22:42). He is more assertive here, in keeping with his invitation to the disciples to ask "whatever you want,[78] and it will be done for you" (15:7). There, as we saw, the sweeping promise was given on the condition that "you make your dwelling in me and my words come to dwell in you," and if the promise was valid for the disciples, it is all the more so for Jesus himself.[79]

Obviously, what he "wants" is far different here from what it was at Gethsemane in the synoptic accounts. What he wanted there was to be spared the "cup" of suffering and death, something to which he has already consecrated himself here (see v. 19). What he wants rather is for his disciples "to be with me where I am," something he has already promised them (14:3 and 12:26), and he is not afraid to make his wants known boldly.[80] In characteristic fashion (as in 6:37, 39; 10:29; 17:2) he speaks of his disciples corporately as "that which you have given me." The phrase focuses on the disciples ("Twelve" according to 6:70) who accompanied Jesus during his ministry, but implicitly at least it refers as well to others who believed during his ministry (such as the Samaritans at Sychar, the man born blind, and Martha), and be-

---

76. Gr. θέλω. Ernst Käsemann notices this (5), although his comment that the "majestic 'I desire' dominates the whole chapter" is an exaggeration. He adds that "This is not a supplication, but a proclamation directed to the Father in such manner that his disciples can hear it also. The speaker is not a needy petitioner, but the divine revealer and therefore the prayer moves over into being an address, admonition, consolation and prophecy. Its content shows that this chapter, just like the rest of the farewell discourse, is part of the instruction of the disciples." If not instruction of the disciples, one can agree that it is at least instruction of the reader.

77. Gr. οὐ τί ἐγὼ θέλω.

78. Gr. ὃ ἐὰν θέλητε.

79. As Barrett puts it, "He expresses his will, but his will is identical with the Father's" (514).

80. See 5:21, where he claims to give life to "those he wants" (οὓς θέλει), and 21:22, where he "wants" (θέλω) to decide whether or not the disciple whom he loves shall "remain until I come."

yond that to those who would "believe in me through their word" (v. 20). Jesus has just envisioned them all as "one," after all (vv. 21, 23), and the presumption all along has been that even those who do not yet believe nevertheless belong to him in some sense already.[81] But what does it mean for them to be, as he says, "with me where I am"? The phrase "where I am"[82] echoes 12:26 and 14:3 verbatim. Clearly, he is not referring to the present moment but to the disciples' presence with him in the Father's presence *after* he has gone away and come back, and taken them to himself (as in 14:3). The promise is further explained in light of the prayer's opening paragraph, in particular his petition to the Father to "glorify me in your own presence, with the glory I had in your presence before the world was" (v. 5). That petition, we now learn, was more than just a private transaction between the Father and the Son that had nothing to do with the disciples. Already in those opening lines, Jesus was in some sense praying on their behalf as much as for himself, for he now adds, "so that they might see my glory, which you have given me because you loved me before the foundation of the world" (v. 24b). His future glorification with the Father, resuming the glory he had "before the world was" (v. 5), or "before the foundation of the world"[83] (v. 24), is for their benefit no less than his own.

In what way will Jesus' disciples "see" the glory that will be his on his return to the Father, and in what way will that vision of future glory go beyond what they have "seen" already in the course of his ministry (1:14; 2:11)? At one level, it is impossible to say. How does one quantify "glory"? The best answer, perhaps, is that the glory Jesus had "before the world was" (v. 5), and will have again on his return to the Father, is the measure of the Father's love for him. The Son's glory is that "which you have given me because you loved me before the foundation of the world." What he wants the disciples to "see" is the full extent of that love. The measure of Jesus' love for his disciples is clear: he gives his life for them. But the measure of the Father's love for the Son is more difficult to comprehend. It has come to expression in certain pronouncements earlier in the Gospel — for example, John's testimony that because the Father loves the Son he has "given all things in his hand" (3:35), and Jesus' testimony to the Jews that the Father loves the Son and "shows him everything that he himself is doing" (5:20). Yet it is not something the disciples will fully comprehend short of that future day when they will stand with Jesus in the Father's presence, and see for themselves the "glory" of the Father's love for Jesus, and consequently for them, the same love they in turn have displayed to the world by their love for one another (see vv. 21, 23).

25-26 Again Jesus punctuates the prayer with an address, this time

---

81. See 10:16, "other sheep *I have*," and 11:52, "children of God."
82. Gr. ὅπου εἰμὶ ἐγώ.
83. Gr. πρὸ καταβολῆς κόσμου.

17:1-26 THE PRAYER FOR THE DISCIPLES

"Righteous Father,"[84] setting the last two verses off as a distinct unit summarizing the prayer in its entirety: "Righteous Father, and yet the world did not know you, but I knew you, and these men knew that you sent me. And I made known to them your name, and I will make known, so that the love with which you loved me might be in them, and I in them" (vv. 25-26). While "Righteous Father" has much the same rhetorical effect as "Holy Father" (v. 11), the vocabulary of "righteous" and "righteousness" has been used very sparingly in this Gospel. Jesus has attributed "righteousness" or "justice" to God by telling the Jewish leaders that "my judgment is right, because I am not seeking my will but the will of the One who sent me" (5:30), and by telling his disciples that the Advocate will convict the world "of justice, because I am going to the Father" (16:10). Here his point is simply that those who know the Father (Jesus and his disciples) are "right" and those in "the world" who do not are wrong.

The "and" which immediately follows the direct address is puzzling, but should probably be assigned an adversative force: "and yet."[85] That is, despite what Jesus has just said about the world's potential belief and knowledge (vv. 21 and 23), and about the disciples' future vision of Jesus' "glory" (v. 24), he can still say to the Father, "the world did not know you." The verdict stated from the beginning that "the world did not know him" (1:10) still stands, repeated now almost verbatim. Jesus, in contrast to the world, has known the Father (see 10:15; Mt 11:27), and so too, he adds, have his disciples, for he adds, "these men knew that you sent me" (v. 25b).[86] As in verse 6-8, he is referring here primarily to those who had said, "By this we believe that you came forth

---

84. Gr. πάτερ δίκαιε. Some witnesses (including A, B, and N) have instead πατὴρ δίκαιε, combining a nominative with a vocative (a nominative used as a vocative normally has the defintite article). While it could be argued that this ungrammatical construction is a more "difficult" reading and therefore possibly original, similar constructions are attested in certain early papyri (see BDAG, 786). It could therefore just as easily be the correction of a scribe. The better-attested vocative πατέρ should be retained.

85. See BDF, §442(1). Abbott (*Johannine Grammar*, 148) offers an alternate view, in which καί is coordinate with a second καί in the next line (see BDF, §444). Thus, on the one hand, the world did not know the Father (καὶ ὁ κόσμος σε οὐκ ἔγνω, v. 25a), but on the other the disciples did know (καὶ οὗτοι ἔγνωσαν, v. 25b). On this reading, the intervening clause, "but I knew you" (ἐγὼ δέ σε ἔγνων), is taken as parenthetical (so also Barrett, 515). But such a reading is oversubtle and difficult to sustain because "the world did not know you, but I knew you" creates a symmetrical contrast, with the same object, "you" (σε), while Abbott's proposed contrast between not knowing "you" (σε) and knowing "that [ὅτι] you sent me" is awkward and asymmetrical.

86. The translation "these men" (for οὗτοι; compare τοῖς ἀνθρώποις, "the men," v. 6) is intended not to call attention to gender *per se* but to help distinguish between the (presumably male) group already identified as "what the Father has given" to Jesus, and the much larger group (obviously not all male) of those who would, he said, eventually "believe in me through their word" (v. 20).

from God" (16:30). He has said of them once, "they came to know truly that I came forth from you, and they believed that you sent me" (v. 8), and now he commends their knowledge once again. They already know what he wants "the world" to know (see v. 23, "that you sent me"). How do they know? Because he has revealed to them the Father's "name" (v. 6), that is, who God is in relation to Jesus — "'the Father' who sent him."

Now he speaks again of what he has revealed to them, not for the Father's benefit, but for the reader's: "And I made known to them your name, and I will make known, so that the love with which you loved me might be in them, and I in them" (v. 26). "I made known[87] to them your name" (v. 26a) recalls what he told them two chapters earlier, that "everything I heard from my Father I made known to you" (15:15), and at the same time his report to the Father that "I revealed your name to the men you gave me out of the world" (v. 6), both referring to his now-completed ministry on earth. "I will make known,"[88] by contrast, looks to the future. For the first time in the prayer, we learn that the revelation Jesus brought will continue after his departure. Nothing has been said in the prayer of the ministry of the Advocate, but here it is clearly presupposed. What he "will make known" will be known through the Advocate, for the benefit both of those whom the Father has already given him and those others "who believe in me through their word" (v. 20). He has said, "I have still much more to say to you" (16:12), and implied that he will say it in the person of the Advocate (16:13-15). Now, in the presence of the Father, he confirms that the revelation will continue. More important, he confirms that the content of the revelation is, above all, the Father's "name," that is, the Father' identity as "Father," in relation to Jesus as Son, and by extension to all those whom the Father has given to the Son (see 20:17, "my Father and your Father"). Finally, this relationship is again defined in very characteristically Johannine terms as a relationship of love: "so that the love with which you loved me might be in them, and I in them."

Jesus' final pastoral and priestly prayer thus ends with a triple affirmation of the love with which all other love begins (vv. 23, 24, 26), the love with which, he tells the Father, "you loved me"[89] (v. 26b; see also v. 23, "just as you loved me," and v. 24, "because you loved me"). From the Father's love for the Son (15:9) comes the Son's love for the disciples (13:34; 15:12) and their love for one another (13:34-35; 15:12, 17) . His prayer is that the Father's love for him might be "in them" as well, and in that sense, consequently, he can add "and I in them," for (as we have seen throughout the farewell discourse) the concrete expression of "indwelling" (14:20; 15:1-8) is love.

87. Gr. ἐγνώρισα.
88. Gr. γνωρίσω.
89. Gr. ἡ ἀγάπη ἣν ἠγάπησάς με.

18:1-27   THE ARREST AND HEARING

IV. VERIFICATION OF JESUS' SELF-REVELATION IN HIS PASSION AND RESURRECTION (18:1–21:25)

Jesus is abruptly with his disciples once more, as discourse ends and narrative begins again with Jesus' arrest in a garden across the Kidron valley. Conspicuous in the Gospel's passion narrative (chapters 18–21) are a series of verifications or confirmations of promises made earlier in the course of Jesus' self-revelation: that his scattered disciples would not be lost (18:8-9), that he himself would be "glorified" (19:13) and "lifted up" (19:17-18), and that he would return again to the disciples, bringing with him the Holy Spirit, and the joy and peace he had promised (20:19-29). The Gospel ends with a new beginning reminiscent of other Gospels, as Jesus, having revealed himself, now reveals some of the implications of being his disciples (chapter 21).

A. THE ARREST AND HEARING (18:1-27)

1 Having said these things, Jesus went out with his disciples across the valley of the Kidron, where there was a garden, into which he entered, he and his disciples. 2 Now Judas too, who was handing him over, knew the place, because Jesus had often gathered there with his disciples. 3 So Judas, taking along the band of soldiers and officers both from the chief priests and from the Pharisees, comes there with lanterns and torches and weapons. 4 Then Jesus, knowing everything that was happening to him, came out, and says to them, "Whom are you seeking?" 5 They answered him, "Jesus the Nazorean." He says to them, "I am he." And Judas, who was handing him over, was standing there with them. 6 Then, as he said to them "I am he," they drew back and fell to the ground. 7 So again he asked them, "Whom are you seeking?" They said, "Jesus the Nazorean." 8 Jesus answered, "I told you that I am he. So if you are seeking me, let these go," 9 so that the word that he said, that "I have lost none of those whom you have given me," might be fulfilled. 10 Then Simon Peter, having a sword, drew it and struck the servant of the Chief Priest and cut off his right ear. And the servant's name was Malchus. 11 So Jesus said to Peter, "Put the sword in the sheath. The cup the Father has given me, shall I not drink it?"

12 So the band of soldiers and the captain and the officers of the Jews arrested Jesus and bound him, and led him first to Annas. 13 For he was the father-in-law of Caiaphas, who was Chief Priest of that year. 14 And Caiaphas it was who counseled the Jews that it was advantageous for one man to die for the people. 15 Now Simon Peter was following Jesus, with another disciple, and that disciple was known to the Chief Priest and went in with Jesus into the courtyard of the Chief Priest. 16 So Peter was standing at the door outside. Then the other disciple who was known to the Chief Priest came out, and spoke to the doorkeeper, and led Peter in. 17 So the servant girl who was the doorkeeper says to Peter, "Are you also one of this man's disciples?" He says, "I am not." 18 Now the servants and the officers were standing there, having made a charcoal fire because it was cold, and warming themselves. And Peter too was with them, standing there and warming himself.

19 So the Chief Priest asked Jesus about his disciples and about his teaching. 20 Jesus answered him, "I have spoken publicly to the world. I always taught in synagogue and in the temple, where all the Jews come together, and I spoke nothing in secret. 21 Why do you ask me? Ask those who heard what I spoke to them. Look, they know what I said." 22 When he had said these things, one of the officers standing by said, "Is that how you answer the Chief Priest?" and gave Jesus a slap in the face. 23 Jesus answered him, "If I have spoken badly, testify to what is bad, but if well, why do you strike me?" 24 So Annas sent him bound to Caiaphas the Chief Priest.

25 And Simon Peter was standing there and warming himself. So they said to him "Are you also one of his disciples?" He denied, and said, "I am not." 26 One of the servants of the Chief Priest, being a relative of him whose ear Peter cut off, says, "Did I not see you in the garden with him?" 27 So again Peter denied, and immediately a rooster crowed.

Now that the long prayer (17:1-26) is over, we are reminded that despite the privacy of his conversation with the Father, Jesus is still, after all, "with his disciples" (v. 1), as he now "went out" with them "across the valley of the Kidron." Their destination is a "garden," evidently a walled garden into which Jesus "entered" (v. 1) and from which he shortly "came out" (v. 4).[1] "Jesus often gathered there with his disciples," we are told (v. 2), making this enclosed space an equivalent in real life to the "courtyard" in his discourse about sheep and the Shepherd (10:1, 16), where the sheep, he had said, would "go in and go out and find pasture" (10:9). This is the first we have heard of this customary gathering place, nor do we know at what hour Jesus and the disciples arrived there or how long it was before Judas and his contingent of soldiers, priests, and Pharisees came to arrest him. It was already "night" when Judas had made his departure (13:30), and the reference to "lanterns and torches" (v. 3) makes it fair to assume that it is now either very late at

---

1. To Barrett as well (517) the verbs suggest "a walled enclosure."

18:1-27 THE ARREST AND HEARING

night or very early morning, well before dawn. Once again (as in 13:1, 3) we are reminded that Jesus was not taken by surprise, but already knew "everything that was happening to him" (v. 4). Fully in control of the situation, he asks, "Whom are you seeking?" and identifies himself as the object of their search: "I am he" (v. 5). At those majestic and now familiar words of self-revelation (see 6:20; 8:58), "they drew back and fell to the ground" (v. 6), and that might have been the end of it. It is not. Again he asks them, and again he identifies himself, this time simply to make sure that they arrest only him, and let his disciples go (v. 8). In this way the good Shepherd "lays down his life for the sheep" (see 10:11), so as to fulfill the text, "I have lost none of those whom you have given me" (v. 9; see 17:12).

Woven into the narrative from here on is an account of how one disciple in particular, Simon Peter, is spared and kept safe. In a manner reminiscent of Mark (14:53-72) and Matthew (26:57-75), the narrative moves back and forth between Peter's story (vv. 10-11, 15-18, and 25-27) and the story of Jesus' arrest and interrogation (vv. 12-14 and 19-24). Peter, admitted to the Chief Priest's courtyard by the intercession of an anonymous second disciple (v. 16), tries to protect himself by lying three times (vv. 17, 25, 27), just as Jesus said he would (13:38), but in the end it is not his lies but Jesus himself who (once again) protects him and all the disciples, refusing to divulge their identity, or the nature of their allegiance to him (vv. 19-21). As for Peter's story, it is left unfinished, but only for a time (see 21:15-23).

1 "Having said these things"[2] (v. 1) marks a transition from prayer to narrative, just as "These things Jesus spoke" (17:1) marked a transition from discourse to prayer. His disciples, about whom he has said much in the prayer, but who have not been heard from since 16:30, are back in the picture. They are, apparently, still in the room where they had dined and where he had washed their feet. Jesus now "went out" as Judas had done much earlier (13:30), not alone like Judas but "with his disciples," putting into action at last his almost-forgotten words three chapters earlier, "Rise, let's get out of here!" (14:31). Their destination is out of the city, "across the valley of the Kidron,"[3] to a "garden, into which he entered, he and his disciples." The singular verbs, "went out" and "entered," place Jesus at the center of the action, but the phrases "with his disciples" and "he and his disciples" make it clear

2. Gr. ταῦτα εἰπών, as in 12:20.
3. The "valley" (χειμάρρου) is literally "the winter torrent," or wadi (BDAG, 1082), referring to a ravine filled with water in winter but dry the rest of the year (see also Josephus, *Antiquities* 8.17). The Kidron ravine, while not mentioned in the other Gospels, divides Jerusalem from the Mount of Olives, in keeping with their accounts of the arrest in Gethsemane. In itself, the use of the term here gives no clue as to the actual time of year, but we know it is Passover season (see 13:1; 18:28), when there would likely have been some water in the ravine.

from the outset that the story is about them as well. The "garden"[4] is consistent with the synoptic accounts, in which Jesus and the disciples go out to the Mount of Olives (Lk 22:39-40), or to a "field by the name of Gethsemane" (Mk 14:32; also Mt 26:36). Here the location is just as specific, even without being named, for like the "courtyard" in Jesus' parable (10:1) it seems enclosed, with a definite entrance and exit.[5] While it cannot be identified with the "garden" where Jesus' body was later buried (19:41) and where he appeared to Mary Magdalene (20:11-18), the two "gardens" effectively frame the story of Jesus' passion.

2 Judas Iscariot has not been heard from since his abrupt departure after the footwashing (13:30), except for the notice (without naming him) that as "son of destruction" he is "lost" (17:12). Although "lost" spiritually, he is very much alive, and fully committed to "handing over" Jesus to the religious authorities. He was identified first as the one who "was going to hand him over" (6:71; also 12:4), and then, after the devil "put it into his heart" (13:2), as the one who "was handing him over" (13:11). Here the "handing over" goes into effect, as Judas is identified in the same way: "Now Judas too, who was handing him over, knew the place, because Jesus had often gathered[6] there with his disciples" (v. 2). "The place,"[7] like certain other "places" in the Gospel narrative (for example, 4:20; 10:40-42; 11:6, 48; 19:13, 17, 41) is evidently of significance to the Gospel writer.

Nothing has been said in John's Gospel of these frequent gatherings of Jesus with his disciples in Jerusalem. The analogy in the Gospel itself is not with times spent together outside Jerusalem, whether in Capernaum (2:12), Bethany "across the Jordan" (1:39; 10:40–11:6), or Ephraim "near the desert" (11:54), for those were extended retreats, not temporary meetings for teaching or prayer. The closer parallel is with Luke's notice that during his last week in Jerusalem, Jesus spent his nights on the Mount of Olives (Lk 21:37), presumably with his disciples.[8] The major difference is that in Luke this goes on for only a week, while in John's Gospel, given Jesus' far more extensive Jerusalem ministry (see chapters 2, 5, 7-10, 12-17), it emerges (belatedly, to be sure) as a major aspect of his ministry as a whole. Judas "knew" the place because he would have been present at those gatherings just as he was at the last meal, and in fact the best analogy within the Gospel of John itself is with that last meal and those farewell discourses just concluded. In

---

4. Gr. κῆπος.
5. This is evident in the verbs εἰσῆλθεν (v. 1) and ἐξῆλθεν (v. 4).
6. Gr. πολλάκις συνήχθη.
7. Gr. τὸν τόπον.
8. Luke too speaks of it as "the place" (ἐπὶ τοῦ τόπου, 22:40), and signals the presence of the disciples by a subsequent notice that on the night of the arrest, when Jesus, "as was his custom," went to the Mount of Olives, "the disciples followed him" (22:39).

18:1-27 THE ARREST AND HEARING

fact, what we have just witnessed is simply a transition from one private place and private gathering to another. The implication is that Jesus spent more time in private with his disciples than what is recorded in chapters 13–17, and perhaps told them more than what is found written in the Gospel (see 20:30; 21:25). As we will see, all this stands somewhat in tension with his later disclaimer to the Chief Priest that "I always taught in synagogue and in the temple, where all the Jews come together, and I spoke nothing in secret" (v. 20). We have just been treated to five chapters of private (though not exactly "secret") instruction and prayer, and we learn here that there had been even more.

3 Judas's prior knowledge sets the stage for an account of his action: "So Judas, taking along the band of soldiers, and officers both from the chief priests and from the Pharisees, comes there with lanterns and torches and weapons" (v. 3). "The band of soldiers"[9] is literally "the cohort," that is, one-tenth of a Roman legion — about six hundred men,[10] obviously an enormous number for such an undertaking. The extraordinary size of the contingent — particularly in light of what would follow, when they all "drew back and fell to the ground" (v. 6) — recalls other instances in which things that Jesus does, or things that happen to him, are seen as far larger than life: turning more than a hundred gallons of water into wine (chapter 2), or feeding five thousand men with twelve baskets left over (chapter 6), or having a whole pint of perfume poured on his feet (chapter 12), or being embalmed with seventy-five pounds of spices (chapter 19), or bringing in 153 large fish (chapter 21). The definite article suggests that "the cohort" is already known to the readers, perhaps from some previous account, written or oral.

Initially, Judas is the main figure in the arrest. He, single-handedly, is "taking along" this small army, and with them "officers both from the chief priests and from the Pharisees." These Jewish "officers"[11] have been in the picture before, at the Tent festival when "the chief priests and the Pharisees sent officers to arrest him" (7:32), and these "officers" returned to "the chief priests and Pharisees" empty-handed (7:45). On the face of it, the two groups — one priestly and linked to the temple, the other made up of laity and linked to the synagogue — do not appear to be natural allies, but the Gospel has quite consistently shown them acting in unison (see 1:19, 24; 7:32, 45; 11:47), and that is the case here. Together, they seem to be synonymous with "the Jews," and the "officers" (both here and in chapter 7) represent their common interest in bringing Jesus to justice. From here on, however, "the Pharisees" disappear from the story, as the trial and execution is left to "the chief priests" and their

9. Gr. τὴν σπεῖραν.
10. See BDAG, 936.
11. Gr. ὑπηρέτας.

"officers" (see 19:6, 15, 21), in addition, of course, to the Roman soldiers. The centrality of Judas is underscored as well by the singular verb: he it is who "comes there with lanterns and torches and weapons," possibly echoing Jesus' earlier warning that "the ruler of the world is coming, and in me he has nothing" (14:30).[12] Obviously the "lanterns and torches" — implying that it is still "night" (see 13:30) — and the "weapons" — as if expecting armed resistance — are the baggage of the whole party, not Judas alone, and probably not Judas at all. Others will do the heavy lifting. Later we will learn that the "band of soldiers" at least has a "captain" (v. 12), as a cohort should. Judas is only a guide, showing them where Jesus can be found, yet for the moment his role in the arrest is placed front and center.

4 Judas's knowledge was limited by his past experiences with Jesus and the disciples, but Jesus' knowledge, we are now reminded, was unlimited: "Then Jesus, knowing[13] everything that was happening to him, came out, and says to them, 'Whom are you seeking?'" (v. 4). The notice comes as no surprise, because what Jesus "knew" has been spelled out already, even before his last meal with the disciples: "knowing that his hour had come" (13:1) and "that the Father had given him all things into his hands, and that he had come from God and was going to God" (13:3). And long before that, he "knew from the beginning who they are who do not believe, and who it is who will hand him over" (6:64). Now comes the "handing over," the first step in the process by which he is "going to God." That he knew "everything that was happening to him"[14] means more than that he understands each step in the process as it unfolds. It means that he knows (ahead of time) everything that will happen to him from this point on (see 16:13, "things to come"). Nothing will take him by surprise. Fully in control of the situation, he then "came out" of the walled garden into which he and his disciples had "entered" a short time before (v. 1).

Speaking to the whole contingent, not Judas in particular, Jesus asks, "Whom are you seeking?"[15] The question recalls his very first words to his own disciples, "What are you seeking?" (1:38), but the situation, and consequently the implication of the question, is totally different. In the intervening chapters we have heard repeatedly of those who were "seeking" Jesus out of questionable motives (6:24, 26), or even "seeking" to arrest or kill him (see 5:18; 7:1, 11, 19, 20, 25, 30, 34, 35; 8:21, 37, 40; 10:39; 11:8, 56), and it is these latter efforts which are now coming to a head. The question is one to

---

12. This depends, of course, on the identification of "the ruler of the world" with Judas, which, as we have seen, is not altogether certain.
13. Gr. εἰδώς.
14. Gr. πάντα τὰ ἐρχόμενα ἐπ' αὐτόν.
15. Gr. τίνα ζητεῖτε.

18:1-27 THE ARREST AND HEARING

which he already knows the answer: they are "seeking" him, and more specifically to arrest him and take his life, for that has been the intention of the "chief priests and Pharisees" all along (see 7:32-36, 45-46; 11:47-50). He might have said, as he does in Luke, "Have you come out as if for a bandit, with swords and clubs? When I was with you every day in the temple, you did not lay your hands on me" (Lk 22:52-53). But he does not, because he knows they have tried again and again, and failed. His "hour" had not yet come (see 7:30; 8:20, 59; 10:39), but now it is at hand (compare Lk 22:53, "this is your hour, and the power of darkness").

5 The dramatic scene unfolds step by step: "They answered him, 'Jesus the Nazorean.' He says to them, 'I am he'" (v. 5a). After all the encounters and skirmishes of the Gospel's first twelve chapters, the reader would not expect Jesus to have to identify himself, especially given the presence of his nemeses, "the chief priests and the Pharisees." The identification is evidently for the benefit of "the band of soldiers," Romans who may not have recognized him. This is the only Gospel that even mentions the presence of Roman soldiers at the arrest, but it is noteworthy that in the three other Gospels as well Jesus has to be identified (by the kiss of Judas; see Mk 14:45; Mt 26:49; Lk 22:47).[16] As Raymond Brown puts it, "The Synoptics have Judas do it with a kiss; John has Jesus identify himself."[17] In typical Johannine fashion, Jesus takes the initiative.

The need for identification suggests that even though the synoptic Gospels do not mention the Roman cohort (contenting themselves with references to a "crowd," or a "great crowd"), the presence of Roman troops is being tacitly acknowledged (giving John's narrative some historical credibility). In the other Gospels and the book of Acts, "Jesus the Nazorean" is used mostly by Jews, or in a Jewish setting (Mt 2:23; Lk 18:37), and often either by Jesus' enemies (Mt 26:71) or in speeches directed to his enemies (Acts 2:22; 3:6; 4:10; 6:14; 22:8; 26:9). But that Romans as well as Jews might have used it is evident from its only other occurrence in the Gospel of John, the inscription Pilate placed over the cross at the crucifixion: "Jesus the Nazorean, king of the Jews" (19:19).[18] Whether the Roman soldiers, or Pilate, connected the term with Jesus' origins in the town of Nazareth, or whether they merely picked it up from the Jewish authorities, possibly as a

---

16. That the kiss was for this purpose is explicitly stated in Mark and Matthew, where it is said to have been a "signal" (Mk 14:44) or "sign" (Mt 26:48). In Luke it is implied by Jesus' reply that the kiss is what accomplishes the betrayal (Lk 22:48).

17. *Death*, 1.252. Brown even takes note of the correspondence between Mark and Matthew's "he it is" (αὐτός ἐστιν) and John's "I am he" (ἐγώ εἰμι).

18. See also Acts 24:5, where Tertullus (possibly a Roman), in making the case against Paul, accuses him of "fomenting rebellion among all the Jews throughout the world, and a ringleader of the sect of the Nazoreans."

term of reproach, is unclear. In any event, Jesus embraces the designation with the affirmation, "I am he," or "It is I."[19] On the face of it, his words are no more profound than the words of the man formerly blind who, when people wondered out loud if he was the beggar they had seen every day, said simply, "It is I" (9:9). Like that pronouncement, and like two earlier sayings of Jesus himself (4:26; 6:20), it is merely a self-identification here, not a mysterious or profound self-revelation, whether future (8:24, 28; 13:19)[20] or present (8:58). Or so it would seem. Yet as we will see, the response to it (v. 6) says otherwise, reminding us that the distinction between mere self-identification ("Jesus the Nazorean") and decisive self-revelation ("the God of Abraham, Isaac and Jacob," see 8:58) is by no means a hard-and-fast one.

Sandwiched between the terse "I am" and the arresting party's response to it (v. 6) is a brief vignette of Judas Iscariot: "And Judas, who was handing him over, was standing with them" (v. 5b). Nothing further is said of Judas's role in the arrest of Jesus. Having led the party to Jesus, he is simply there "with them." The notice appears to be another of this Gospel's undeveloped "vestigial scenes," in which a stage is set but nothing happens (see above, on 2:12; 11:54; 12:9, 20-21). Here, of course, something does happen, but Judas has no explicit role in it, and it remains unclear why he is mentioned at just this point. All that the notice does is to show him "standing there with them,"[21] that is, with Jesus' enemies, just as Peter will shortly be seen in the Chief Priest's courtyard, "standing there with them[22] and warming himself" (v. 18). The crucial difference is that this is our last, and definitive, glimpse of Judas, while for Peter there will be more to come, an opportunity for redemption (see 20:6-7; 21:7, 15-19). Judas is last seen standing on one side of the confrontation and all the rest of the disciples on the other.

6 Even though an earlier "I am" pronouncement on Jesus' lips drew a strong, instant response once before, when his hearers "took up stones that they might throw on him" (8:59), nothing quite prepares the reader for what happens here at the garden: "Then, as he said to them, 'I am he,' they drew back and fell to the ground" (v. 6). The subject of the plural expressions "drew back" and "fell to the ground"[23] can only be the whole arresting party, six hundred strong and more, "the band of soldiers and officers both from the chief

---

19. Gr. ἐγώ εἰμι.
20. Schnackenburg (3.224) finds in it a fulfillment of 13:19, "the disciples are to believe, when it happens, that Jesus rightly says: ἐγώ εἰμι." But this is unlikely because there is no evidence here that *the disciples* saw anything significant in his words. The readers, perhaps, but not the disciples. The overwhelming effect of the pronouncement (v. 6) is not on the disciples but on the Roman cohort, the chief priests, and the Pharisees.
21. Gr. εἱστήκει . . . μετ' αὐτῶν.
22. Gr. μετ' αὐτῶν ἑστώς.
23. Gr. ἀπῆλθον εἰς τὰ ὀπίσω καὶ ἔπεσαν χαμαί.

priests and from the Pharisees" (v. 3). It is tempting to emend the text by making the plurals singular, so that only the guilty Judas (v. 5b) "draws back and falls to the ground," but there is not a shred of evidence for such an expedient. Clearly, the Gospel writer intends us to visualize an extraordinary scene in which more than six hundred men are literally "bowled over" by two simple words *(esō eimi)*. Just to make sure we perceive the connection, he repeats the two words: "Then, as he said to them, 'I am he,' they drew back and fell to the ground."

In itself the notice that they "drew back" is manageable enough. The same expression was used of Jesus' own disciples who "turned back and would no longer walk with him" (6:66). It does not have to mean any more than that they lost their nerve and failed (momentarily at least) to carry out their mission.[24] The reader of the Gospel is aware that this has happened more than once before (see 7:30, 32, 45-46; 8:20, 59; 10:39). What is more shocking is that the whole company "fell to the ground" as if vanquished by a greater army. Nothing in the Gospel of John — not the quantity of wine at Cana, not the five thousand fed with twelve baskets left over, not the pint of perfume at Bethany, not the load of spices at Jesus' burial, not the net heavy with fish — quite matches the present scene. For that we have to go to Mark's Gospel, where Jesus sent a "legion" of demons into a herd of "about two thousand" pigs (Mk 5:13), roughly one-third of a Roman legion — even more than the cohort or "band of soldiers" here in John's Gospel (see v. 3). While there is no discernible link between the two passages, the enormity of the scene is comparable. The effect within John's Gospel is to put a very large exclamation point after Jesus' words spoken eight chapters earlier, "I lay down my life, that I might receive it back again. No one took it away from me, but I lay it down on my own" (10:17-18a). "No one!!"[25] — not even six hundred Roman soldiers, plus "officers both from the chief priests and from the Pharisees" — can take Jesus' life from him. The "authority to lay it down," like the "authority to receive it back" (10:18b), is his and his alone. This he will do, freely and voluntarily, "for the sheep" (10:15), as he will quickly demonstrate (v. 8).

7-9 There is more than a touch of comedy here. As if nothing has happened, Jesus asks the Roman soldiers and Jewish officers lying on the

---

24. Parallels from the Psalms are often cited: for example, Psalm 27:2, "When my enemies and my foes attack me, they will stumble and *fall*"; 35:4, "May those who seek my life be disgraced and put to shame; may those who plot my ruin be turned *back* in dismay"; 56:10, "Then my enemies will turn *back* when I call for help. By this I will know that God is for me" (NIV, with italics indicating verbal similarities). But it is doubtful that such texts are in the writer's mind. This is, after all, only a temporary setback for Jesus' enemies, for the arrest will take its course.

25. Gr. οὐδείς.

ground the same question he asked before: "So again he asked them, 'Whom are you seeking?'" Evidently picking themselves up and regaining their composure, they give the same answer, "Jesus the Nazorean" (v. 7).[26] Like a patient instructor explaining things to slow-witted pupils, he says again, "I told you that I am he. So if you are seeking me, let these go" (v. 8). This third occurrence of the characteristic "I am" formula within four verses (see vv. 5, 6) is as much for the reader's benefit as for theirs. The reader has heard the formula again and again (6:20; 8:24, 28, 58; 13:19), and finds here a confirmation that Jesus is who he said he was all along.[27] As for the arresting party, Jesus takes advantage of the fact that they have twice said that they were seeking him, and presumably him alone. For them, the formula (whatever its mysterious power may have been in v. 6) now simply distinguishes Jesus from the disciples gathered around him, as the sole object of the search. Therefore he commands them, "let these go." Nothing is said of how the Roman soldiers and the Jewish officers reacted. They evidently do not fall to the ground a second time, yet they seem to have obeyed Jesus' command to let the disciples go, to the point of ignoring even Simon Peter's provocative attack on "the servant of the Chief Priest" (v. 10). In short, the Shepherd willingly gives up his life to the "wolves" (see 10:11-12, 15), and the sheep go free.

Instead of recording immediately what the arresting party said or did, the Gospel writer pauses to tell the reader that Jesus said this "so that the word that he said, that 'I have lost none of those whom you have given me,' might be fulfilled" (v. 9). The temporary safety of the disciples stands as a sign of what has come to be called their "eternal security," that is, their assurance of eternal life. This is in sharp contrast to Mark and Matthew, where the disciples flee and are scattered at the time of Jesus' arrest (Mk 14:50//Mt 26:56), just as Jesus had predicted (see Mk 14:27//Mt 26:31). In John's Gospel as well Jesus has predicted that they will be "scattered" (16:32), but the Shepherd's prayer for the sheep (chapter 17) has intervened, so that their unity and security in the Father's hand is now restored. That they are not taken into custody along with Jesus is a sign not of their unfaithfulness, as in Matthew and Mark, but of Jesus' sovereign choice and initiative. The formula, "so that [something] might be fulfilled,"[28] has been used repeatedly in Matthew, and four times so far in John's Gospel, for the fulfillment of "Scripture" (13:18, 17:12),[29] or of what is "written in their law" (15:25), or of "the

---

26. For a similarly comic touch, see 7:45-46.

27. This is perhaps the element of truth in Schnackenburg's proposal (above, n. 20) that this is in some sense a fulfillment of 13:19.

28. Gr. ἵνα . . . πληρωθῇ.

29. It will be used twice more of Scripture fulfillments (19:24, 36), making six occurrences in all in John's Gospel (see also ἵνα τελειωθῇ, 19:28).

word" of a biblical prophet (12:38). Here, by contrast (and again in v. 32), it is used of "the word" of Jesus, something he has said in this very Gospel: "I have lost none of those whom you have given me." The citation does not agree verbatim with any one saying of Jesus recorded in the Gospel, but 6:39 ("that . . . I might not lose anything"), 10:28 ("they will never ever be lost"), and 17:12 ("none of them is lost") are reasonably close. The third of these is quite clearly the one in mind here, for it alone speaks of the disciples' security as an accomplished fact, not simply a hope or intention. The only difference is that the notice here substitutes "I have lost none" (drawing on the language of 6:39), for "none of them is lost" (17:12). The "word" of Jesus that is now fulfilled was a word uttered in prayer. There, conspicuously, Jesus mentioned one exception, "the son of destruction," Judas, who is very much in evidence here as well. Interestingly, Jesus invoked there "the Scripture" and its fulfillment to account for Judas's defection (17:12b), but now that Judas stands irrevocably on the other side (v. 5), his defection a *fait accompli,* there is no further need to mention it.

The appearance of a formula normally used of the fulfillment of Scripture in connection with a saying of Jesus is striking. The text is not so much equating "the Scripture" with the spoken "word" of Jesus, as it is equating Jesus' spoken "word" with "the word" of Isaiah (see 12:38) or any other biblical prophet. J. A. Bengel's concise comment was that this showed that Jesus "was a Prophet,"[30] and this is true as far as it goes. Even Matthew, who repeatedly cites fulfillments of Scripture, cites them not *as* written "Scripture" but as "what was spoken"[31] either "by the Lord through the prophet" (Mt 1:22; 2:15), or simply "through the prophets" (2:23), or "through" a particular prophet (2:17; 4:14; 8:17; 13:35; 21:4; 27:9). Only once does Matthew explicitly identify them all as in fact fulfillments of "the Scriptures of the prophets" (Mt 26:56). But the text here implies more than that Jesus was a prophet like Isaiah or Jeremiah. In John's Gospel, as early as chapter 2, "the scripture" and "the word Jesus spoke" stood together as common objects of the disciples' faith (see 2:22). "The word" encompasses *both* the message given to Israel long ago and embodied in the Scripture that "cannot be abolished" (see 10:35), *and* the message the Father has now given to the Son, the word that is "the truth" (17:17; see also 14:24; 17:6, 8).[32] Behind all of it stands the mystery that this message — identified at the outset as "the Word" — *is* Jesus (see 1:1, 14).

30. *Gnomon,* 2.468.
31. Gr. τὸ ῥηθέν.
32. The principle that "the Scripture cannot be abolished" (Jn 10:35), with its equivalent in Matthew 5:18, has its parallel in the words of Jesus in Matthew 24:35: "The heaven and the earth will pass away, but my words [οἱ δὲ λόγοι μου] will never pass away."

10-11 The reaction of the arresting party to Jesus' bold words (v. 8) is still not given. Instead, one of the disciples who has just been set free by Jesus' words steps in to aggravate the situation: "Then Simon Peter, having a sword, drew it and struck the servant of the Chief Priest and cut off his right ear. And the servant's name was Malchus. So Jesus said to Peter, 'Put the sword in the sheath. The cup the Father has given me, shall I not drink it?'" (vv. 10-11). There is agreement among the four Gospels that such an incident happened, but considerable variation in the details. Only here, for example, is the assailant identified as Simon Peter. In Mark (14:47) it is "one of the bystanders," who may or may not have been one of Jesus' disciples; in Matthew (26:51) it is "one of those with Jesus," evidently a disciple; in Luke (22:49-50) it is one of "those around him," similarly a disciple, but unidentified. In much the same way that it identified Judas by name as the disciple who asked about the poor at the dinner in Bethany (12:4-5),[33] John's Gospel identifies Peter as the disciple who cut off the ear of the Chief Priest's servant. Thus the incident becomes part of Peter's personal history. His impetuous act appears to be the acting out of his rash resolve (found only in this Gospel) that "I will lay down my life for you!" (13:37) — as if he were the Shepherd, and Jesus one of his sheep! For this Jesus rebuked him ("You will lay down your life for me?"), and prophesied his triple denial (13:38), a prophecy that will shortly come to pass (see vv. 17, 25-27). No explanation is given as to why Peter (or any of the disciples) was carrying a sword in the first place. Only Luke (22:35-38) addresses that question. In John's Gospel it is perhaps simply part of Peter's misguided resolve to "lay down his life," if need be, as Jesus' protector and defender.

In contrast to the other Gospels, "the servant of the Chief Priest" is also named. In each of the Gospels, he is *"the* servant,"[34] implying either that there was only one, or that he was in some way a known figure, but this Gospel goes a step further is assigning him a name, "Malchus." It is hardly the case that there was only one "servant," for we read later of "one of *the servants* of the Chief Priest" (my italics), who was in fact "a relative of him whose ear Peter cut off" (v. 26). Possibly the definite article, *"the* servant of the Chief Priest," simply reflects the fact that the story — and perhaps other stories about this servant — had been told often enough that he would have been a familiar figure to Christian readers.[35] That John's Gospel is able to

---

33. There, as we have seen, the pattern was similar: Mark (14:4) said "some" objected; Matthew (26:8) said "the disciples"; John's Gospel supplied a name. Interestingly, John's Gospel alone also gives the name of the woman (Mary) who poured the perfume on Jesus' feet, just as here it also names the Chief Priest's servant.

34. Gr. τὸν δοῦλον.

35. In an apocryphal account of the resurrection of Jesus in the *Gospel According to the Hebrews* preserved by Jerome (*Of Illustrious Men* 2), we read, "Now the Lord,

18:1-27   THE ARREST AND HEARING

supply a name could be attributable to the fact that one of Jesus' disciples who was present on the scene was "known to the Chief Priest" (vv. 15-16), and therefore might have known the names and relationships of some of the Chief Priest's servants. Both Luke (22:50) and John specify that the servant lost his "right ear," which would not have been expected if the assailant was righthanded and facing him, but this may be nothing more than a signal that real harm was done (like a person's "right eye" or "right hand," Mt 5:29-30). Luke adds (22:51) that Jesus "touched the ear and healed him," but John's Gospel (like Mark and Matthew) knows nothing of this. The provocation remains, yet Peter is not arrested.

In all this, there is (again) a comic touch. Jesus has floored the whole company with a word (v. 6), and poor Peter thinks his sword is necessary to save the day! But Jesus' answer is serious. His words found in Matthew would have been appropriate: "Or do you think I cannot call on my Father, and he will even now furnish me with over twelve legions of angels?" (Mt 26:53). Or he could have told Peter what he later tells Pilate: "If my kingdom were from this world, my officers would fight, so that I would not be handed over to the Jews. But now my kingdom is not from there" (see v. 36b). Instead, he tells Peter, "Put the sword in the sheath.[36] The cup the Father has given me, shall I not drink it?" (v. 11). This is the first we have heard of the metaphor of "the cup,"[37] so conspicuous in the synoptic accounts of Jesus in Gethsemane. The closest we have come to it was a pronouncement about food rather than drink, "My food is that I might do the will of the One who sent me and complete his work" (4:34). In this Gospel we do not hear Jesus praying that the cup might "pass from him" (as in Mk 14:36//Mt 26:39//Lk 22:42), for here he acknowledges "the cup" without question as one of the many things he says "the Father has given me" — the last thing, in fact, after "authority over all flesh" (17:3), the disciples themselves (17:6) and the "words" to teach them (17:8), God's own name (17:11-12), and God's own glory (17:22, 24). It is implicit in all of these, the epitome of them all, for it is his mission.

In place of the Gethsemane prayer, the Gospel of John has given us

---

when he had given the shroud [*sindonem*] to the servant of the priest [*servo sacerdotis*], went to James and appeared to him" (*Apocrypha*, II: *Evangelien* [ed. E. Klostermann; 3d ed., Berlin: de Gruyter, 1929], 10). It may be of interest that in Mark (14:51-52) the arresting party (including "the servant of the Chief Priest," v. 47) are left holding the "shroud" (τὴν σινδόνα) of the mysterious "certain young man" (νεανίσκος τις) who fled naked on the occasion of Jesus' arrest.

36. Compare Matthew 26:52, where the command is the same but the vocabulary is different: "Return your sword to its place," with the added words, "For all who take the sword will perish by the sword."

37. Gr. τὸ ποτήριον.

two other prayers, one in which Jesus rejects the petition, "Father, save me from this hour," in favor of "Father, glorify your name" (12:27-28), and the other in which he brings all that "the Father has given" to bear on his mission of "consecrating" himself as Shepherd and High Priest on behalf of his disciples (chapter 17). In John's Gospel, no less than in the other three, "the cup" is the equivalent of "the hour," the looming prospect of suffering and death.[38] In Jesus' own words, it is nothing other than the "command I received from my Father," to "lay down my life, that I might receive it back again" (10:17-18). From this moment on, he will begin to "drink the cup."

12-14 Ignoring the attack on "the servant of the Chief Priest" (v. 10), the arresting party carries out its mission of seizing Jesus, and him alone. The power of Jesus' word is still in evidence, for the only apparent reason Peter is not arrested is that Jesus has commanded, "let these go" (v. 8). Accordingly, "the band of soldiers and the captain and the officers of the Jews arrested Jesus and bound him, and led him first to Annas," identifying "Annas" as "the father-in-law of Caiaphas, who was Chief Priest of that year" (vv. 12-13). "The captain"[39] is here simply the officer in charge of the Roman cohort.[40] He was not mentioned before (v. 3), only because Judas was pictured as the one who led the party to the garden because he "knew the place" (v. 2), but the mere mention of a "band of soldiers" (or cohort) clearly presupposed such a "captain" or "chiliarch." With Judas's work now done, the "captain" appears as leader of the Roman troops, while the "officers both from the chief priests and from the Pharisees" (v. 3) are now simply "the officers of the Jews."

Jesus is bound and taken "first[41] to Annas," identified not as Chief Priest but as "the father-in-law of Caiaphas, who was Chief Priest of that year" (v. 13). Caiaphas is known to the readers of the Gospel precisely as "Chief Priest of that year" (11:49, 51), and just to make sure they do not miss it, the Gospel writer now reminds them that "Caiaphas it was who counseled the Jews that it was advantageous for one man to die for the people" (v. 14; see 11:51b). According to Luke, Annas and Caiaphas seem to have shared the high priesthood (Lk 3:2), and Annas bears the title by himself in the book of Acts (4:6).[42] Yet in John's Gospel only Caiaphas is identified (now for the

---

38. Brown (*Death*, 1.278) puts it well: "Mark has two prayers in Gethsemane, for the passing of the hour [14:35] and for the taking away of the cup [14:36]. John has two rhetorical questions, one earlier in the ministry and one in the garden across the Kidron: the first indicating that Jesus does not want to be saved from the hour; the second, that he must not be prevented from drinking the cup" (references added in brackets).

39. Gr. ὁ χιλίαρχος, literally "leader of a thousand."

40. See BDAG, 1084.

41. Gr. πρῶτον.

42. See also Josephus, *Antiquities* 18.34, where the name is given as "Ananus."

18:1-27 THE ARREST AND HEARING

third time!) as "Chief Priest of that year." For this reason it appears likely that the "Chief Priest" who will shortly interrogate Jesus (vv. 19-23) will be Caiaphas and not Annas. The notice that Jesus was led "first" to Annas (v. 13) implies that this may not have been his actual destination, but for the moment nothing is said of where he was taken after that. Only *after* the interrogation by "the Chief Priest" will we learn that "Annas sent him bound to Caiaphas the Chief Priest" (v. 24). Consequently, the identity of "the Chief Priest" who questioned Jesus "about his disciples and about his teaching" (vv. 19-23) remains an open question. If it is Annas, why go to such lengths to identify Caiaphas as "Chief Priest of that year," but if it is Caiaphas, why introduce Annas, the father-in-law, at all? Either way, we have another of this Gospel's characteristic "vestigial scenes," in which a stage is set but nothing happens (see, for example, v. 5).[43] The question is whether it comes here, where Jesus is taken to Annas and nothing happens, or at verse 24, where he is sent to Caiaphas and nothing happens. Each time we expect something to happen we are told instead what is going on with Peter (see vv. 15-18, 25-27). For the moment, the word "first" (v. 13) simply leaves us to wonder where Jesus will be taken "second" or "next," and where he will finally end up. We will cross that bridge when we come to it (that is, at vv. 19 and 24).

15 In agreement with Matthew and Mark, but not Luke,[44] the narrative in John's Gospel alternates back and forth between the arrest and interrogation of Jesus (vv. 12-14, 19-23) and the three denials of Simon Peter (vv. 15-18, 25-27). Having brought Jesus "first to Annas" (v. 13), the writer abruptly turns his attention to Peter, who was last seen holding a sword (v. 11): "Now Simon Peter was following Jesus, with another disciple, and that disciple was known to the Chief Priest, and went in with Jesus into the courtyard of the Chief Priest" (v. 15). The glimpse of Peter still "following," even though he and the other disciples have been freed by Jesus' word (v. 8), is surprising, but perhaps less so than in the other Gospels, where they have all fled (Mk 14:50//Mt 26:56) and he alone follows "from afar" (Mk 14:54// Mt 26:58//Lk 22:54). Only here does Peter have as his companion "another disciple,"[45] who makes possible his entry into the Chief Priest's courtyard (see v. 16). It is common in some quarters to identify this anonymous "other

---

43. See also 2:12; 11:54; 12:9, 20-21.
44. Matthew moves from the presentation of Jesus to the Chief Priest (26:57), to Peter in the courtyard (v. 58), to the interrogation (vv. 59-68), and back to Peter and his denials (vv. 69-75). Mark moves similarly from the presentation of Jesus to the Chief Priest (14:53), to Peter in the courtyard (v. 54), to the interrogation (vv. 55-65), and back to Peter and his denials (vv. 66-72). Luke, by contrast, recounts Peter's denials in a continuous account, moving from the presentation of Jesus to the Chief Priest (22:54a), to Peter and his three denials (vv. 54b-62), and thence to the interrogation (vv. 63-71).
45. Gr. ἄλλος μαθητής.

disciple" with the "one whom Jesus loved" and who reclined at his side at the last meal (13:23),[46] but there is no evidence here to support such a claim. At most, the case could be argued from a subsequent passage where Mary Magdalene ran "to Simon Peter and to the other disciple, whom Jesus loved" to tell them of the empty tomb (20:2; see also vv. 3, 4, 8, where he is called simply "the other disciple"). But this would be a very belated and very indirect identification of this anonymous disciple who was "known to the Chief Priest" with the disciple "whom Jesus loved" (13:23). This identification, however, has at times been made the basis for certain conclusions about the disciple "whom Jesus loved" — either that he was not a Galilean but a Judean, familiar with Jerusalem and the temple, or, if he was a Galilean (John the son of Zebedee, for example), that he had in the past sold fish to the priestly aristocracy in Jerusalem.[47]

There is no real basis for any of this. Even if the narrative in chapter 20 were intended to identify the "other disciple" here, it is not something the reader can possibly know at this point, or is meant to know. Peter's companion here is anonymous, probably intentionally so.[48] His presence in the story accomplishes two things: first, it explains how Peter gained entrance to the Chief Priest's courtyard (something left unexplained in the other three Gospels); second, it provides an eyewitness (other than Peter himself) to the events in the courtyard, specifically Peter's three denials (vv. 15-18, 25-27), and possibly — though by no means certainly — to Jesus' interrogation by the Chief Priest (vv. 19-24). That function at least — of being able to testify to what he has seen — he does have in common with "the disciple whom Jesus loved" (see 21:24). Why then is he not named (given that even a character as minor as Malchus *is* named)? That remains a mystery, but no more so than why the beloved disciple is not named — or, for that matter, the anonymous witness to the spear thrust and the blood and water from Jesus' side a chapter later (19:35). The truth of John's Gospel rests on the testimony not of just one, but of two or more (see 8:17), and in fact of many witnesses, some named and some unnamed, from John (1:7, 15, 19, 34) and Jesus (repeat-

---

46. Brown goes so far as to claim that "the main point of the description is the contrast between that other (beloved) disciple and Peter. . . . By denying [Peter] fails, while the other disciple will go on to stand at the foot of the cross" (*Death*, 1.598).

47. This text may have been the basis of the notice attributed to Polycrates of Ephesus at the end of the second century about "John, who leaned on the Lord's breast, who was a priest wearing the mitre, and martyr and teacher, and he sleeps at Ephesus" (Eusebius, *Ecclesiastical History* 3.31.3; LCL, 1.271).

48. Schnackenburg makes a strong case that this "other disciple" is not the beloved disciple (3.235), but is less convincing in attributing the reference to a source, implying that the Gospel writer himself did not know the disciple's identity. This is no more likely to be true of the "other disciple" here than of "the disciple whom Jesus loved."

18:1-27 THE ARREST AND HEARING

edly), to the disciples as a group and the Advocate who will instruct them (15:26-27). All we need to know about this particular disciple is that he was "known to the Chief Priest,"[49] and therefore "went in with Jesus into the courtyard of the Chief Priest." We have last seen Jesus' disciples gathered in a "garden" (v. 1), an enclosed space into which they "entered" with Jesus, and from which Jesus "came out" (v. 4). Now we see one of them entering with Jesus into another enclosed space, the Chief Priest's "courtyard,"[50] coincidentally (or perhaps not!) the same term Jesus used for an enclosure in which a shepherd keeps his sheep (10:1, 16). That it is in fact coincidental is likely, for the Chief Priest's "courtyard" is conspicuous in the other Gospels as well (see Mk 14:54; Mt 26:3, 58; Lk 22:55; also of Pilate's praetorium, Mk 15:16). But if so, it is a happy coincidence for the Gospel writer, for there are hints of a deliberate contrast between the Shepherd's "courtyard" (chapter 10) and that of the Chief Priest. The former is specifically for Jesus' disciples, while the latter is closed to them unless, like Peter's companion here, they are "known to the Chief Priest." In the former, Jesus the Shepherd is in charge. In the latter, the Chief Priest is in charge, or so it would seem, yet the events that will happen here (vv. 15-18, 25-27) are exactly what Jesus said would happen (see 13:38).

At this point, Jesus and the "other disciple" have entered the courtyard, but whether or not this will also be the scene of Jesus' interrogation by the Chief Priest (vv. 19-23) is not altogether clear. In Matthew the "courtyard" is "outside" (Mt 26:69), and in Mark "below" (Mk 14:66) the room where Jesus is being questioned.[51] In Luke, by contrast, Jesus seems to be with Peter in the courtyard, for he has only to "turn and look at him" (Lk 22:61), but Jesus is not interrogated until the next morning, when Peter is not present. In John's Gospel there are no clear signals as to where the interrogation takes place, only changes of scene as the writer turns his attention from the "other disciple" and Peter (vv. 15-18), to Jesus and the Chief Priest (vv. 19-24), and then back again to Peter and his denials (vv. 25-27). The reader has no way of knowing whether these contrasting scenes are both within the courtyard, within earshot of one another, or whether Jesus has been taken to a different venue for questioning. For the time being, at least, the notice that the unnamed disciple "went in with Jesus" seems to place Jesus in the courtyard as well.

49. Gr. γνωστός. The phrase "known to the Chief Priest" does not, of course, mean that he was known to be a disciple of Jesus (according to v. 19, the Chief Priest has to ask Jesus about his disciples), but simply that he was (for whatever reason) an acquaintance of the Chief Priest (see BDAG, 204).

50. Gr. εἰς τὴν αὐλήν.

51. In Mark there is also a "forecourt" (προαύλιον), still further "outside" (ἔξω), where Peter goes after the first denial and hears the first crowing of a rooster (Mk 14:68).

16 There are further reminders that the courtyard was an enclosed space, as "Peter was standing at the door outside."[52] Then the other disciple who was known to the Chief Priest came out, and spoke to the doorkeeper, and led Peter in" (v. 16). This courtyard, like the Shepherd's, has a definite "outside" and "inside,"[53] with a "doorkeeper" to check on the legitimacy of anyone seeking entrance. In this case the doorkeeper is not a man as in chapter 10 (see 10:3) but a woman.[54] Peter, who would have "laid down his life" like a shepherd (13:37), now has to yield the shepherd role to "another disciple," to whom "the doorkeeper opens" (see 10:3).[55] This disciple, "known to the Chief Priest," is apparently known to the doorkeeper as well. Having been admitted without question, but realizing that Peter has not been allowed to enter with him, he comes out again, and has only to speak a word to her to have Peter admitted. She does not have to check with the Chief Priest, or anyone else. This is consistent with the notion that the disciple was familiar enough with the circle of the Chief Priest's servants to have known such things as Malchus's name (v. 10) and the identity of one of his relatives (v. 26). As for Peter, aside from the fact that he had been "following Jesus" (v. 15), it is unclear why he even wants to enter the courtyard, given that he will repeatedly deny any allegiance to his Lord.[56]

17 The doorkeeper, now fully identified as "the servant girl who was the doorkeeper," questions Peter, apparently not as a test for allowing him to enter (for he is already in), but simply for information. "Are you also one of this man's disciples?" she asks, and Peter answers, "I am not" (v. 17). The "also" does not necessarily imply that she knows that Peter's companion is a disciple, for a similar construction is used in Matthew (26:69), in Mark (14:67), and in Luke (22:56), where no other disciple is in the picture. The question merely reflects a general awareness that Jesus had disciples, and that

---

52. Gr. ἔξω.
53. See Mark 14:54, "He followed him inside [ἔσω] into the courtyard"; Matthew 26:58, "he went inside [ἔσω] and sat with the officers."
54. Gr. τῇ θυρωρῷ (in contrast to the masculine ὁ θυρωρός, 10:3; see also v. 17, "the servant girl [ἡ παιδίσκη] who was the doorkeeper"). In the other Gospels too there is a "servant girl" (παιδίσκη) who questions Peter (Lk 22:56; twice in Mk 14:66, 69), and in Mt 26:69 one "servant girl," followed by "another" in v. 71), but only in John's Gospel is she identified as the "doorkeeper." For another incident involving Peter and a "servant girl" (παιδίσκη) who served as a doorkeeper (without the word being used, and without actually admitting him), see Acts 12:13-15.
55. The subject of "led Peter in" (εἰσήγαγεν) has to be the "other disciple" and not the doorkeeper, not only because he is the subject of the two preceding verbs as well, but because the doorkeeper has to be reintroduced at the beginning of the next verse.
56. Matthew tells us that he simply wanted "to see the ending" (Mt 26:58). John's Gospel, like Mark and Luke, mentions only the warm fire (vv. 18, 25), explaining why he stayed but not why he came in the first place.

Peter, being unknown to her, just might be one of them.[57] The form of her question[58] should probably not be overtranslated (as most English versions have done) with a construction such as "You are not also one of this man's disciples, are you?"[59] All the writer wants to do is make clear that this is not an accusation, as if to say, "Are you not also one of his disciples?"[60] but a simple question. In the other Gospels, by contrast, it is not even a question but an outright accusation (see Mt 26:69//Mk 14:66//Lk 22:56). Here in John's Gospel the word of Jesus has already set the disciples free (v. 8), so that if Peter had answered "Yes," he still would have been safe. But Peter does not trust the word of Jesus, any more than he did when he drew his sword and cut off the ear of the Chief Priest's servant, so he answers, "I am not,"[61] the first of three such denials (see vv. 25, 27), in stark contrast to Jesus' thrice-repeated "I am" (vv. 5, 6, 8).[62] His self-serving denials are not only unfaithful but redundant, for his safety and salvation are already assured (see v. 9).

18 The narrative is about to take leave of Peter as it shifts to the interrogation of Jesus by the Chief Priest (vv. 19-24), but before doing so it sketches a memorable scene: "Now the servants and the officers were standing there, having made a charcoal fire because it was cold, and warming themselves. And Peter too was with them, standing there and warming himself" (v. 18). Again a scene is set, but nothing happens immediately. The reader is expected to remember it, for the narrative will resume seven verses later, with Peter *still* "standing there and warming himself" (v. 25).[63] That it might have been "cold" *(psychos)* at Passover season, with the Kidron "valley" (v. 1) still flooded (see n. 3), is not surprising, and whatever Peter's reasons for coming may have been, the warm fire gives him reason to stay.

The point of the scene is that Peter, having just denied his relationship with Jesus (v. 17), now stands "with them,"[64] that is, on the other side, with Jesus' enemies, just as surely as Judas Iscariot stood "with them" at Jesus' arrest (v. 5). The unanswered (and unasked) question is, Where is the "other disciple" standing, the one who brought Peter into the courtyard? If he was "known to the Chief Priest," and to the doorkeeper, is he too standing with Peter and all

---

57. See Bultmann, 645; Brown, *Death,* 1.597-98.

58. Gr. μὴ καὶ σύ (with μή expecting a negative answer; see BDF, §427[2], 440).

59. See, for example, the NRSV, NIV, TNIV, NLT, ESV, NAB. The NEB and REB are better: "Are you another of this man's disciples?"

60. That is, with οὐ instead of μή. Oddly, the RSV ("Are not you also one of this man's disciples?") and CEV ("Aren't you one of that man's followers?") translate the verse in just that way, as a veiled accusation.

61. Gr. οὐκ εἰμί.

62. See Brown, *Death,* 1.599.

63. Gr. ἑστὼς καὶ θερμαινόμενος, in both places (vv. 18 and 25).

64. Gr. μετ' αὐτῶν.

"the servants and the officers"? If he is a witness to Peter's unfaithfulness, is he at the same time a witness to his own? Could the incriminating phrase "with them" be replaced with an even more incriminating "with us," as if he too belonged to that number? Or, having gone "in with Jesus into the courtyard of the Chief Priest" (v. 15), is the unnamed disciple now with Jesus at the interrogation? We will never know, for the story is not about him but about Peter. Peter's unfaithfulness is comparable to that of Judas, but with two decisive differences: first, Peter has been set free by Jesus' word ("let these go," v. 8, and "I have lost none of those whom you have given me," v. 9), and Judas has not; second, Judas's story is over, and Peter's is not. In the end, Peter will be warmed (and fed) at another "charcoal fire"[65] (21:9).

19 Abruptly the scene changes: "So the Chief Priest asked Jesus about his disciples and about his teaching" (v. 19). Two issues present themselves. First, who is "the Chief Priest" who is questioning Jesus? Is it Annas, "the father-in-law of Caiaphas, who was Chief Priest of that year," to whom Jesus was taken "first" (v. 13)? This is supported by the fact that nothing has been said of Jesus being taken anywhere else, and especially by the notice a few verses later, "So Annas sent him bound to Caiaphas the Chief Priest" (v. 24). Consequently, this is the view of virtually all modern commentators.[66]

On the other hand, it can be argued that the "Chief Priest" is Caiaphas, on the grounds that only he is ever referred to as "Chief Priest" anywhere else in John's Gospel, three times conspicuously as "Chief Priest of that year" (v. 13 and 11:49, 51)?[67] As we have seen, the identification of Annas as Chief Priest depends on Luke (3:2; Acts 4:6) and on Josephus, not on anything in the Gospel of John itself. The difficulty with this view, and the reason few have adopted it, is that it requires either reading verse 24 retrospectively, "Now Annas *had* sent him bound," as in the KJV (italics added),[68] or rearranging the text (as was done in certain ancient manuscripts and versions).[69]

---

65. Gr. ἀνθρακιάν.

66. See, for example, Brown (2.820-21; *Death,* 1.404-11), Bultmann (642), Schnackenburg (3.236), Lindars (549), Carson (583), Morris (668). Others posit that Caiaphas was already present with Annas and carried out the interrogation (see Barrett, 524-25), but this seems to contradict the subsequent notice that Annas "sent him" to Caiaphas the "Chief Priest" (v. 24).

67. Among commentators, Bengel (*Gnomon,* 2.472), John Wesley (*Explanatory Notes,* 278), and Westcott (2.274-75) can be cited in favor of this identification.

68. See also the Ronald Knox translation: "Annas, you must know, had sent him on, still bound."

69. For example, certain late Greek manuscripts, plus the Harclean Syriac version and Cyril of Alexandria, interpolated verse 24 either within or just after verse 13 (as well as in its present position!), so as to make it clear that Jesus was sent from Annas to Caiaphas *before* the questioning began. Even more ambitiously, the Sinaitic Syriac re-

18:1-27 THE ARREST AND HEARING

A decision is difficult, but on balance it is probably better to maintain the consistency of the designation, "the Chief Priest," instead of allowing it to refer to Caiaphas in verse 13 (where the two are clearly distinguished) and probably in verse 15 as well,[70] and then abruptly shifting it to Annas, the father-in-law, in verses 19-23. The reader, after all, does not yet have the "benefit" of verse 24 to give the impression that Jesus is still with Annas. The text claims that "the Chief Priest" was questioning Jesus, and there is no reason to assume a different "Chief Priest" from the one named as "Chief Priest of that year" (v. 13), the one who had "the courtyard," and to whom the "other disciple" was "known" (v. 15) — surely Caiaphas and not Annas. By default as it were, Caiaphas must (for now at least) be understood as the interrogator. If so, then it must be assumed that Jesus, having been taken to Annas "first" (v. 12b), has moved on from there.

The second issue, still unresolved, has to do with the location of the scene. Are Jesus and the Chief Priest in the "courtyard," within sight and hearing of Peter and those gathered around the fire (as in Luke), or are they somewhere else in the building (as in Matthew and Mark)? John's Gospel gives no clear answer. The last we heard of Jesus, the disciple "known to the Chief Priest," was entering the courtyard with him (v. 15), and we can only assume — again by default — that the Chief Priest's courtyard is where they both still are. As it happens, however, the location makes little difference, for the contrasting scenes — Peter at the charcoal fire and Jesus being questioned by the Chief Priest — are kept separate. Neither seems aware of the other, even though the possibility exists that the "other disciple," Peter's mysterious companion, may have been witness to both.

What the two contrasting scenes have in common is an interest in the question, "What about Jesus' disciples?" Jesus must die (see v. 14), but what about them? Peter has been asked explicitly, "Are you also one of this man's disciples?" (v. 16), and now the Chief Priest asks Jesus just as explicitly "about his disciples"[71] and "about his teaching"[72] (v. 19). Those are not two

---

arranged the whole of verses 13-27, yielding the following order: verses 13, 24, 14-15, 19-23, 16-18, 25-27 (see Metzger, *Textual Commentary,* 251-52, who notices that Luther rearranged the text similarly).

70. Lindars, for example (549), who identifies the interrogator as Annas, nevertheless admits that "in verse 15 the reference was certainly to Caiaphas in John's source (cf. Mk 14.54)." Similarly, Schnackenburg struggles with the fact that "The source spoke only of *one* high priest," while (he thinks) John's Gospel knows of two, but simply takes the phrase "the high priest" (in v. 15, for example) from the source (2.234). But as we have seen, John's Gospel, no less than its "source" (if it has one), also knows of only one "Chief Priest."

71. Gr. περὶ τῶν μαθητῶν αὐτοῦ.
72. Gr. περὶ τῆς διδαχῆς αὐτοῦ.

questions, but one.⁷³ As for his "teaching," Jesus could have said what he said once before, "If anyone chooses to do his will, he will know about the teaching, whether it is from God, or whether I speak on my own" (7:17), but he does not, for the Chief Priest neither knows the teaching nor does the Father's will. What he wants to know is whether or not Jesus' disciples will keep his teaching alive after he is executed. Are they a unified group, and consequently a danger, or not? In response to the fear expressed earlier that "If we let [Jesus] go on like this, they will all believe in him, and the Romans will come and take away both our place and our nation" (11:48), he had counseled that getting rid of "one man" would take care of matters (11:50). But Lazarus also had been a wanted man (see 12:10-11), and now Caiaphas wonders about all the disciples. What are their names? Should they not at the very least be rounded up and questioned? Or even hunted down and executed, even as the council had resolved to kill Lazarus? Jesus already addressed that issue in the presence of the company that came to arrest him (v. 8, "So if you are seeking me, let these go"), and his words had the power to carry out his intention. But the Chief Priest was not present then, and now Jesus must protect his disciples once again. Simon Peter thinks he is protecting himself in the Chief Priest's courtyard, but in reality it is Jesus who protects him, now for the second time.

20-21 Jesus answers the question "about his disciples and about his teaching" with a rather unexpected redefinition of discipleship. Instead of something like, "My disciples are those whom the Father has given me" (see 6:37, 39; 17:6-8, etc.), he seems to change the subject: "I have spoken publicly⁷⁴ to the world. I always taught in synagogue and in the temple, where all the Jews come together, and I spoke nothing in secret.⁷⁵ Why do you ask me? Ask those who heard what I spoke to them. Look, they know what I said" (vv. 20-21). But he is not avoiding the question. Rather, he is blurring, if not eradicating, any distinction between potential and actual discipleship, by implying that *all* who heard his message, whether "in synagogue" or "in the temple," are at least potential disciples, and therefore qualified to testify to what he said. In other words, there is no need to question an inner circle of his adherents, for his "teaching" (v. 19) is a matter of public record.

The references to teaching "in synagogue" and "in the temple" recall

---

73. So Bultmann (646, n. 2): "If Jesus is questioned concerning his disciples and concerning his teaching, it is difficult to think that two different points are stated. The answer of Jesus ignores the question about the disciples; it is included in that concerning his teaching." I would say the opposite: he ignores the question about the teaching, for it is included in the question about the disciples.

74. Gr. παρρησίᾳ.

75. Gr. ἐν κρυπτῷ ἐλάλησα οὐδέν.

18:1-27 THE ARREST AND HEARING

the summary statements in 6:59 ("These things he said *teaching in synagogue* in Capernaum") and in 8:20 ("These words he spoke in the treasury, *teaching in the temple*"), respectively (italics added), taking us back to the major discourses of his public ministry, where his real "trial" had already taken place.[76] In particular, the first of those settings (6:59) was when "many of his disciples" complained, "This word is hard. Who can hear it?" (6:60), and finally "turned back and would no longer walk with him" (6:66). Their unfaithfulness proved that while all of Jesus' hearers were potential disciples, only a few (twelve in particular, 6:70) turned out to be actual disciples who continued to "walk with him" in Galilee and Judea. Here Jesus seems to have in mind that same distinction, teasing the Chief Priest by invoking the broader definition of "disciple" to encompass the general public, all who had heard Jesus' message "in synagogue and in the temple, where all the Jews come together." They are the ones to interrogate, he urges, not the pitiful band of followers who used to gather from time to time in the "garden" across the Kidron valley (see v. 2).

There are even stronger echoes here of the Tent festival, when Jesus' brothers urged him to "go to Judea, so that your disciples may see your works that you do" (7:3), and in this way "reveal yourself to the world" (7:4). There too, as we have seen, a broader definition of "disciple" may have been in evidence. Now, in the presence of the Chief Priest, he claims to have done just what his brothers asked — "I have spoken publicly to the world" — with "the world" defined as the Jewish world, "where all the Jews come together" (v. 20).[77] While the Chief Priest does not need to be reminded that the Jerusalem temple is "where all the Jews come together" (a notice intended as much for the reader as for him), it does underscore even for him the truly "public" character of Jesus' teaching. This Jesus reinforces with the claim that "I spoke nothing in secret," and in fact, as we have seen, Jesus' ministry at the Tent festival followed a trajectory from initial "secrecy" (7:4, 10) to a very "public" self-disclosure midway through the festival (see 7:26), and back finally into "secrecy" when his life was threatened (8:59). Technically, perhaps, the claim that he "always"[78] taught in the public square and said "noth-

---

76. See also Mark 14:49, "I was with you every day in the temple teaching [ἐν τῷ ἱερῷ διδάσκων], and you did not arrest me" (compare Mt 26:55; Lk 22:53). While that pronouncement is made at the arrest rather than the hearing, and looks not at the whole of Jesus' ministry but only at the final week in Jerusalem, it does have in common with the pronouncement here before the Chief Priest an emphasis on the very public character of Jesus' teaching.

77. See the Pharisees' lament on Jesus' entry into Jerusalem (12:19, "Look, the world has gone after him!"), in the wake of the concern that "many of *the Jews* were going off and believing in Jesus" (12:11, italics added).

78. Gr. πάντοτε.

ing" privately or "in secret" could be viewed as an overstatement,[79] given his lengthy discourses to his disciples after the footwashing (13:36–16:33) and his intimate prayer to the Father (17:1-26), yet the point is clear enough.[80] He made no claims to his disciples in private that he did not also make publicly.[81] While he did not say exactly the same things to the crowds and "the Jews" in the first half of the Gospel that he said to the inner circle in the latter half (the circumstances being different), his teaching has been consistent and coherent throughout. For this reason, there is no need to question his so-called "disciples," for his message was the same everywhere. All "those who heard"[82] (v. 21) are in effect his "disciples," for they are just as qualified to testify to his claims as the "twelve," or however many they may have been, who traveled with him and gave him their allegiance. In this way, Jesus answers the Chief Priest's question in such a way as to protect his actual disciples (including Peter) from interrogation — even while Peter is being asked, "Are you also one of this man's disciples?" (v. 17; also vv. 25, 26).

22-23 The reaction is swift, though not from the Chief Priest himself, who says nothing. In contrast to the synoptic Gospels, Jesus has not been asked such questions as "Are you the Christ, the Son of the Blessed?" (Mk 14:61; see also Mt 26:63; Lk 22:67), only about his disciples and his teaching. Consequently he has said nothing so provocative as "I am" (see 8:58; Mk 14:62), or "I and the Father are one" (10:30), and there is nothing so drastic as an attempted stoning (8:59; 10:31), or even a rending of garments and cry of blasphemy from the Chief Priest (as in Mk 14:63-64; Mt 26:65).

Instead, "When he had said these things, one of the officers standing by said, 'Is that how you answer the Chief Priest?' and gave Jesus a slap in the face. Jesus answered him, 'If I have spoken badly, testify to what is bad, but if well, why do you strike me?'" (vv. 22-23). If this interrogation is in any way the Gospel of John's equivalent to the so-called "trial" in the Synoptics before the Chief Priest (Mt 26:57-68//Mk 14:53-65; see also Lk 22:66-71), the slap in the face stands as the equivalent to the conclusion of that scene, when "they spat in his face and beat him, and some slapped him, saying, 'Prophesy to us,

---

79. As perhaps in Mark 4:34, "He did not speak to them except in parables."

80. Beyond this, there were unquestionably times when Jesus withdrew from the public eye, and "would no longer walk openly [παρρησίᾳ] among the Jews" (11:54; see also 7:1) because of the danger to his life from the religious authorities. That very notice, in fact, implies that "walking openly [or publicly] among the Jews" was his normal practice.

81. As we have seen, when the Jewish authorities demanded, "If you are the Christ, tell us plainly" (παρρησίᾳ, 10:24), they betrayed their ignorance of what he had already said and done in the public square (see 7:26).

82. Gr. τοὺς ἀκηκοότας.

18:1-27 THE ARREST AND HEARING

Christ! Who is it that struck you?'" (Mt 26:67-68).[83] Yet the two scenes have little in common, for the similarities serve only to highlight the differences. The far closer parallel is Paul's appearance before a later Chief Priest, Ananias, who without provocation "ordered those standing by to strike him in the mouth," to which Paul replied, "God will strike you, you whitewashed wall! You sit there judging me according to the law, and yet in violation of the law you command that I be struck?" (Acts 23:2-3). The same "bystanders" then said to Paul, "How dare you insult God's Chief Priest?" and Paul backed down: "I did not know, brothers, that he was Chief Priest, for it is written that 'You shall not speak badly[84] of a leader of your people'" (Acts 23:4-5). There is no way to assess the literary relationship between the two passages. Does John's Gospel know the book of Acts, or the other way around? Is Paul being pictured as more compliant than Jesus, or Jesus as more defiant than Paul? Or is it sheer coincidence?[85] Instead of attempting a judgment on literary dependence, it is best to start with what the two texts have in common: an awareness of the command in Exodus 22:28, "You shall not revile God, or curse a leader of your people" (NRSV). To "curse" is literally to "speak badly,"[86] as in the book of Acts. Paul quotes the text almost verbatim, and it seems to be the text the officer of the Chief Priest has in mind when he slaps Jesus in the face. Jesus' answer reflects this: "If I have spoken badly,[87] testify to what is bad, but if well, why do you strike me?" (v. 23).

In the other Gospels, Jesus is convicted on the grounds of "blasphemy" (Mt 26:65; Mk 14:64; implicitly in Lk 22:71), and the text in Exodus equates blasphemy against God with speaking ill of "a leader of your people." Jesus in the Gospel of John (even more than in the Synoptics) has made extraordinary claims for himself (5:17; 8:58; 10:30), and, as we have seen, has had to defend himself already against charges of "blasphemy" (see 10:33, 36). Here he does so again, this time by redefining what it means to speak ill or "badly" of someone, whether of God or a human leader. He contrasts speaking "badly" with speaking "well,"[88] a term used consistently in this Gospel for speaking the truth (see 4:17; 8:48; 13:13). The issue is not whether something he has said is insulting or blasphemous, but whether or

---

83. Mark has it slightly differently: "And some began to spit on him and to cover his face and beat him and say to him, 'Prophesy!' And the officers took and slapped him" (14:55). In Luke (22:63-65) a rather similar scene takes place shortly after the arrest and *before* the trial the next morning.
84. Gr. οὐκ ἐρεῖς κακῶς.
85. Lake and Cadbury (*Beginnings*, 4.287) ask, "What is the relation between the two episodes?" without venturing an answer.
86. Gr. κακῶς ἐρεῖς (Exod 22:28, LXX).
87. Gr. εἰ κακῶς ἐλάλησα.
88. Gr. καλῶς. The rhyme with κακῶς is noticeable.

907

not it is true. If it is true, it is not blasphemy, and if it is false, it should be labeled as such, and testimony brought to the contrary. The reader cannot help but notice that Jesus has said nothing even remotely insulting to the Chief Priest, nor does the Chief Priest act as if he had. The slap in the face is an egregious overreaction. Moreover, what he has said to the Chief Priest (vv. 20-21) *is* the truth, in that it points back to and reinforces the truth that he has repeatedly spoken "in synagogue and in the temple" throughout his public ministry in Jerusalem and Galilee.

The words of Jesus here, "If I have spoken badly, testify to what is bad, but if well, why do you strike me?" are his last words to the Jewish community or the Jewish hierarchy in the Gospel of John. At the end of the day, they refer not simply to verses 20 and 21, but to all that he has said publicly, from "Destroy this sanctuary, and in three days I will raise it up" (2:19) right up to the present. As such they stand as a lasting challenge to that religious establishment, echoing and reinforcing his words near the end of the Tent festival, "Who among you convicts me of sin? If I speak truth, why do you not believe me?" (8:46). In contrast to the synoptic accounts (Mt 26:68//Mk 14:65; Lk 22:71), Jesus has the last word. Neither the officer who slapped him nor the Chief Priest has anything to say.

24 Curiously, as we have seen, the hearing in the presence of someone called "the Chief Priest" (vv. 19, 22) ends with the notice, "So Annas sent him bound to Caiaphas the Chief Priest" (v. 24). If, as we have been assuming, the reader understands "the Chief Priest" to be Caiaphas (in keeping with vv. 13-15 and 11:49-51), the notice brings him up short, leaving him with two alternatives. It is either (1) a *correction,* to the effect that the so-called "Chief Priest" in verse 19-23 was Annas all along, not Caiaphas; or (2) a belated *clarification,* to the effect that of course Annas, to whom Jesus had "first" been taken (v. 12b), had by this time sent the prisoner along to the real Chief Priest, his son-in-law Caiaphas. Of the two, the first is the more awkward, for it necessitates going back and rereading verse 19-23 with Annas now in mind as the interrogator.

Despite the near consensus against it among commentators, the second option (as in the KJV and the Knox translation) is the more attractive one. Moreover, the reading of the aorist ("So Annas sent[89] him") as if it were a pluperfect ("So Annas had sent him") is quite legitimate. The difficulty is that the connective "so"[90] normally carries the narrative forward (in the sense of "therefore," or "then"), rather than looking back at something that has already happened.[91] Yet if the notice is taken as parenthetical, that is, as one of

---

89. Gr. ἀπέστειλεν.
90. Gr. οὖν.
91. The οὖν is missing in A and the majority of later textual witnesses, and δέ is

18:1-27 THE ARREST AND HEARING

this Gospel's characteristic "narrative asides,"[92] a retrospective reference is not out of the question. As we have seen, the writer has a way of introducing some of his narrative asides belatedly. Among his belated clarifying notices are 1:24 ("And they were sent from the Pharisees"), 1:28 ("These things came about in Bethany, across the Jordan"), 3:24 ("For John was not yet put in prison"); 4:2 ("although Jesus himself was not baptizing, his disciples were"), 4:8 ("For his disciples had gone into the town to buy provisions"),[93] 4:39 ("Now many of the Samaritans from that town had believed in him because of the woman's word"), 5:9 ("But it was the Sabbath that day"); 9:14 ("Now it was Sabbath on the day Jesus made the mud and opened his eyes"), 11:30 ("Now Jesus had not yet come into the village, but was still in the place where Martha met him"), and especially 12:10 ("And the chief priests resolved that they would also kill Lazarus"), where the aorist verb quite clearly has the force of a pluperfect. If verse 24 is read as a belated notice that Jesus, having been sent "first" to Annas (v. 12b), has by now been sent on to Caiaphas, it may simply be an example of that same tendency.[94]

Alternatively, if the "Chief Priest" here is Annas (as most commentators believe), then when Jesus is finally sent on to Caiaphas (v. 24), it must be acknowledged that nothing happens there. The scene is left undeveloped, the mother of all "vestigial" scenes.[95] If Caiaphas had any questions of his own, we are not privy to them. Instead, we are privy to Peter's second and third denials (vv. 25-27), and Jesus is sent on "from Caiaphas" (v. 28) to the praetorium and Pontius Pilate. Why would a hearing before Caiaphas be hinted at, only to be suppressed? One possible reason is that John's Gospel knows of an extended narrative about a hearing before Caiaphas (possibly

---

substituted in א but is supported by the preponderance of textual evidence, including P[60], B, C*, L, N, W, Θ, 33, 565, 700, and others. The variation actually makes little difference, for the alternatives no less than οὖν seem to imply (at least on the face of it) that Jesus is sent to Caiaphas *after* the interrogation rather than before.

92. John Wesley, in his *Explanatory Notes* (278), translated the text as in the KJV, but in parenthesis, with the comment, "as is implied ver. 15." That is, he seems to have felt that consistency in the use of the designation "Chief Priest" required that Caiaphas be understood as the questioner in verses 19-23.

93. Abbott (*Johannine Grammar,* 470) points out a rearrangement by the Sinaitic Syriac in John 4:6-9 rather similar to what that version has done here in 18:13-27.

94. So Bengel (*Gnomon,* 2.472): "Sometimes in a narrative there is put something out of the regular order of time, which is connected with those circumstances that receive light from it," citing 5:9, 9:14, and 11:30 (see also Westcott, 2.274-75).

95. On the other hand, of course, if Caiaphas is the interrogator in verses 19-23, then the notice that Jesus was sent "first to Annas" (v. 12) is the "vestigial" scene, the one left hanging, as it were, with only the adverb "first" (πρῶτον) hinting that the real hearing will come later. Quite possibly, Jesus' encounter with Annas has no significance for the Gospel writer beyond the simple recollection that such an encounter took place.

with the whole Sanhedrin present), and has deliberately chosen to leave it out. Just such a hearing, the so-called "trial" of Jesus before Caiaphas and the Sanhedrin, is found in both Mark (14:53-65) and Matthew (26:57-68).[96] John's Gospel has no need for such a trial because, as we have seen, the whole public ministry of Jesus has been his "trial," and the verdict is already in (see 11:47-53). If the "Chief Priest" now questioning Jesus is Annas, then the silence about what went on with Caiaphas (vv. 24 and 28) could be a tacit acknowledgment of another narrative that the Gospel writer knows about but deliberately omits. On the other hand, if the "Chief Priest" now questioning Jesus is the one identified as such everywhere else in the Gospel — that is, Caiaphas, "a certain one among them" (11:49) — then the Gospel writer is boldly substituting his account for that of Matthew and Mark, on the ground that whatever else may have happened that night, Jesus' fate was settled long before, throughout his public ministry and finally by Caiaphas himself at a private meeting with "the chief priests and the Pharisees" ("So from that day,"11:53). But either way, there is no formal trial of Jesus before the Sanhedrin in John's Gospel, and he is not legally convicted of anything.

25 Without so much as a "Meanwhile," the narrative shifts back to Simon Peter, right where we left him (see v. 18), "standing there and warming himself"[97] (v. 25). He is asked the same question as before, "Are you also one of his disciples?" (compare v. 17), except that it is asked by an indefinite "they" rather than the doorkeeper, implying perhaps some general skepticism about his previous answer. But the answer is the same, this time explicitly labeled a denial: "He denied,[98] and said, 'I am not.'"[99]

26-27 The third and last question follows immediately: "One of the servants of the Chief Priest, being a relative of him whose ear Peter cut off, says, 'Did I not see you in the garden with him?'" (v. 26). On the surface, the question seems to raise only the issue of Peter's presence in the garden. But the phrase "with him" gives it away — not "with them" around the fire (v. 18), not "with them" who arrested Jesus in the garden (v. 5), but "with him," implying allegiance to Jesus.[100] Moreover, the form of the question[101] is confrontational. In contrast to the first two questions, this one expects a

---

96. Luke differs, in that all that occurs in the Chief Priest's house that night is a time of mocking and beating (Lk 22:63-65); the "trial" (if it is that) before the Sanhedrin takes place the next morning (22:66-71), without explicit mention of any "Chief Priest."

97. Gr. ἑστὼς καὶ θερμαινόμενος.

98. Gr. ἠρνήσατο.

99. Gr. οὐκ εἰμί, as in verse 17. Stylistically, compare (and contrast) the testimony of John: "And he confessed, and did not deny [καὶ οὐκ ἠρνήσατο]; he confessed that 'I am not [οὐκ εἰμί] the Christ'" (1:20).

100. See, for example, 6:66; also Mark 3:14; 5:18, 40.

101. That is, introduced by οὐκ rather than μή.

18:1-27 THE ARREST AND HEARING

positive answer, and the juxtaposition of "I" and "you"[102] gives to both personal pronouns extra emphasis, as if to say, "*I* — did not *I* see *you* — yes, *you* — in the garden with him?"[103] Even more to the point is the identification of the third questioner as "a relative[104] of him whose ear Peter cut off." Evidently the same source that knows Malchus's name (quite possibly Peter's companion who was "known to the Chief Priest") knows the kinsman as well, and therefore knows how incriminating the question is. Clearly the kinsman knows more about Peter than what he is asking about. In fact, he knows what Peter has done, and his question is nothing less than an accusation. Peter, for his part, seems to have no idea of the relationship between Malchus and the questioner, and consequently no awareness that the question is loaded: "So again Peter denied, and immediately a rooster crowed" (v. 27). This time he does not say "I am not," because the question was not cast in the form, "Are you also one of his disciples?" (vv. 17 and 25). Consequently he denies not only his allegiance to Jesus, but his very presence at the scene of the arrest. The notice that "immediately a rooster crowed" has no particular significance if the story told in this chapter is the whole story. It acquires significance only in the light of Jesus' solemn pronouncement five chapters earlier, "Amen, amen, I say to you, never will a rooster crow until you have denied me three times" (13:38). Here again the Gospel writer could have added (as in v. 9), "so that the word that he said, that 'never will a rooster crow until you have denied me three times' might be fulfilled," but there is no need to labor the point. The fulfillment of Jesus' word is crystal clear. Even readers with a shorter attention span than five chapters are expected to grasp it, simply because they are likely to have heard the story told again and again, as in all the Gospels.

In contrast to all the other Gospels, Peter's reaction is not given. We are not even told that he heard the crowing of the rooster. He is not said to have "remembered" Jesus' prediction,[105] nor to have "wept" at what he had done. The notice that "a rooster crowed" is in fact more for the reader's benefit than Peter's, reminding us again that Jesus' prophecies always come true. No attempt is made to get inside Peter's head or record his feelings, and we will not meet him again until Mary Magdalene summons him, with "the other disciple whom Jesus loved," to Jesus' empty tomb (20:2). From this we know that he was not arrested. His denials were at some level "successful,"

---

102. Gr. οὐκ ἐγώ σε εἶδον.
103. Compare 13:6, "Lord, *you?* Of *me?* Washing the feet?"
104. Gr. συγγενής.
105. According to Luke (22:61), Peter "remembered the word of the Lord" only because Jesus "turned and looked" at him. In Matthew (Mt 26:75) and Mark (14:72), the crowing of the rooster itself was enough to jog his memory.

not by virtue of his own repeated lies (vv. 17, 25, 27), but by virtue of the Shepherd's willingness to "lay down his life" for him, not once but twice — first at the arrest (vv. 8-9), and then in the presence of the Chief Priest (vv. 20-21). As for Peter's feelings, and his love (or lack of love) for Jesus, that issue is deferred to the very end of the Gospel (see 21:15-17, 18-23).

B. JESUS, PILATE, AND THE JEWS (18:28–19:15)

28 *So they are leading Jesus from Caiaphas into the praetorium — it was early morning — and they themselves did not go into the praetorium, so that they might not be defiled but might eat the Passover.*

29 *Therefore Pilate came outside to them, and said, "What charge do you bring against this man?"* 30 *They answered and said to him, "If he were not doing what is bad, we would not have handed him over to you."* 31 *Then Pilate said to them, "You take him, and judge him according to your law." The Jews said to him, "It is not lawful for us to kill anyone,"* 32 *so that the word of Jesus that he said signifying by what death he was going to die might be fulfilled.*

33 *Then Pilate went in again into the praetorium and summoned Jesus and said to him, "You are the King of the Jews?"* 34 *Jesus answered, "Are you saying this on your own, or did others tell you about me?"* 35 *Pilate answered, "Am I a Jew? Your nation and the chief priests handed you over to me. What have you done?"* 36 *Jesus answered, "My kingship is not from this world. If my kingship were from this world, my officers would fight so that I would not be handed over to the Jews. But now my kingship is not from here."* 37 *So Pilate said to him, "So you are a king!" Jesus answered, "You say that I am a king; I was born for this, and for this I have come into the world, that I might testify to the truth. Everyone who is from the truth hears my voice."* 38 *Pilate said to him, "What is truth?"*

And having said this, he went outside again to the Jews, and he says to them, "I find in him no probable cause, 39 *and there is a custom you have that I release to you one at the Passover. So shall I release to you the King of the Jews?"* 40 *Then they cried out again, saying, "Not this one but Barabbas." And Barabbas was a terrorist.*

19:1 *So then Pilate took Jesus and had him flogged.* 2 *And the soldiers wove a crown of thorns and put it on his head and wrapped a purple robe around him,* 3 *and they kept coming at him and saying, "Hail, King of the Jews," and giving him slaps in the face.*

4 *And Pilate again went outside, and says to them, "Look, I am leading him outside to you, so that you might know that I find in him*

18:28–19:15 JESUS, PILATE, AND THE JEWS

no probable cause." 5 Then Jesus came outside, wearing the thorny crown and the purple robe. And he said to them, "Look, the man!" 6 So when the chief priests and the officers saw him, they cried out, saying, "Crucify, crucify!" Pilate said to them, "You take him, and crucify, for I find in him no probable cause." 7 The Jews answered him, "We have a law, and according to the law he ought to die, because he made himself the Son of God."

8 Then, when Pilate heard this word, he was all the more afraid, 9 and he went into the praetorium again, and he says to Jesus, "Where are you from?" But Jesus gave him no answer. 10 So Pilate says to him, "Are you not speaking to me? Do you not know that I have authority to release you, and I have authority to crucify you?" 11 Jesus answered him, "You would have no authority against me at all if it were not given to you from above. For this reason the one who handed me over to you has greater sin." 12 From this time, Pilate kept seeking to release him, but the Jews cried out, saying, "If you release this one, you are not a friend of Caesar. Everyone who makes himself king opposes Caesar. 13 Then Pilate, when he heard these words, led Jesus outside and sat down on the judge's bench at a place called Stone Pavement, and in Hebrew Gabbatha. 14 Now it was the preparation of the Passover; it was about the sixth hour. And he says to the Jews, "Look, your king!" 15 They then cried out, "Take, take! Crucify him!" Pilate says to them, "Shall I crucify your king?" The chief priests answered, "We have no king except Caesar!"

When Jesus is transferred from the Chief Priest's courtyard to the praetorium, the headquarters of Pontius Pilate, the Roman governor (18:28), a series of scenes follow, alternating back and forth between the "outside" (18:29, 38; 19:4, 5, 13) and inside of the praetorium. The alternation is necessary because the Jewish leaders who led Jesus to Pilate "did not go into the praetorium, so that they might not be defiled, but might eat the Passover" (18:28). Again the narrative features an enclosed space, not the Chief Priest's courtyard this time but the residence of a Gentile, a place of uncleanness for the devout Jew. The notice that they stayed outside the praetorium (v. 28) governs the seven scenes that follow, as Pilate accommodates himself to their religious scruples:

1. Pilate "went outside" and addressed the Jews (18:29-32).
2. Pilate "went in again into the praetorium" and questioned Jesus (18:33-38a).
3. Pilate "went outside again" and told the Jews they had no case against Jesus (18:38b-40).

913

4. Pilate had Jesus flogged and mocked, evidently within the praetorium (19:1-3).
5. Pilate "again went outside," brought Jesus out, and said, "Look, the man!" (19:4-7).
6. Pilate "went into the praetorium again," and again questioned Jesus (19:8-11)
7. Pilate "led Jesus out," and said, "Look, your king!" (19:12-15).

In the end, Pilate will accommodate himself as well to the desires of the chief priests to have Jesus executed (see 19:16), but not before exploring thoroughly the issue of whether or not Jesus is claiming to be a king. His questioning of Jesus convinces him that whatever kind of a king Jesus might be, he is no threat to the Roman emperor. Three times he tells the Jews, "I find in him no probable cause" (18:38; 19:4, 7). And yet, fascinated with the phrase, "the King of the Jews" (see 18:33; 19:3), he repeatedly uses it to mock them: "Shall I release to you the King of the Jews?" (18:39); "Look, your king!" (19:13); "Shall I crucify your king?" (19:15). Ironically, those who at the beginning of the narrative refused even to enter the Roman praetorium for fear of ritual defilement, in the end cry out, "We have no king except Caesar!" (v. 15b).

28 The narrative shifts back again from Peter (vv. 25-27) to Jesus the following morning: "So they are leading Jesus from Caiaphas into the praetorium — it was early morning — and they themselves did not go into the praetorium, so that they might not be defiled but might eat the Passover" (v. 28). Jesus is "led" from the Chief Priest's courtyard, just as he was "led" to it in the first place (v. 13), but this time it is not specified who "they" are who are doing the leading. Before, it was "the band of soldiers and the captain and the officers of the Jews" (v. 12),[1] but here the comment that "they themselves"[2] stayed outside the praetorium to avoid ritual defilement makes it clear that "they" no longer include "the band of soldiers" (that is, the Roman cohort) with its "captain." They will in fact be identified in due course as "the Jews" (vv. 31, 38; 19:7, 12), or, more specifically, "the chief priests and the officers" (19:6). Once Jesus had been handed over to the Jewish Chief Priest, the Roman cohort and its captain seem to have made their exit. Now the process is reversed, as the Jewish priests and officers hand him back again to the Roman authority.

---

1. It is difficult to say whether any distinction is intended between Jesus being "led" to the Chief Priest's courtyard and then to the praetorium (vv. 13, 28), and being "sent" (ἀπέστειλεν) by Annas to Caiaphas (v. 24), evidently within the courtyard. That he is still "bound" (v. 24) suggests that there is little if any distinction.

2. Gr. καὶ αὐτοί.

The "praetorium" was the headquarters and residence in Jerusalem of the Roman governor, Pontius Pilate (see Mt 27:27//Mk 15:16). There was another praetorium at Caesarea on the coast (known as "Herod's praetorium," Acts 23:35), where a later governor, Felix, had his headquarters, and which Pilate may have used as well. Roman governors seem to have commandeered preexisting Herodian structures, and it is debated whether Pilate's praetorium was the Antonia fortress north of the temple area which went back to Maccabean times (see Josephus, *War* 1.75; *Antiquities* 15.403), and which Herod had converted into a palace, or Herod's more elaborate palace on the western height of the city near the present Jaffa gate (see Josephus, *War* 5.176-83).[3] What matters in the narrative is not the precise location of the praetorium, but the simple fact that it is now a Roman, and thus a Gentile, residence. As we have seen, participation in the Passover festival required ritual purification (11:55),[4] and to enter the residence — even the temporary residence — of a Gentile, even the governor, would have compromised ritual purity, particularly since it was now "early morning"[5] of the day before they were to "eat the Passover."[6] The notice makes it clear that the Passover meal has not yet taken place, confirming what the reader already knows, that Jesus' last meal with his disciples was *not* the Passover meal (see 13:1, "Now *before* the festival of the Passover").

The scene is heavy with irony. Those bringing Jesus to Pilate are so scrupulous about the laws of purity that they will not even enter the praetorium, yet their scruples do not extend to murder. Their intent all along has been to kill Jesus (see 5:18; 7:1, 19; 8:37, 40), and now the opportunity has come. The irony was recognized already by Origen, who (in commenting on 11:55) wrote that those who "purified themselves" for the Passover did so for an act of worship that was "not a work of God's feast, but a polluted work that they performed when they killed Jesus" at the Passover. They thought their Passover worship "offered service to God" (see Jn 16:2, which Origen also cited explicitly), but in fact it only made them "more polluted than they were before they purified themselves."[7]

---

3. Tradition favors the former, inasmuch as the Antonia became the starting point of the traditional Via Dolorosa, while modern scholarship rather consistently favors the latter (see Brown, *Death*, 1.706-10).

4. The relevant biblical texts were Numbers 9:6-12 and 2 Chronicles 30:17-18.

5. Gr. πρωί.

6. See, for example, in the Mishnah, *'Oholoth* 18.7, "The dwelling-places of Gentiles are unclean" (Danby, 675). Within the New Testament itself, see Acts 10:28; also, perhaps, Matthew 8:8; Luke 7:6-7.

7. See Origen, *Commentary on John* 28.230-32 (FC 89.339). By "polluted" Origen meant "guilty of bloodshed" (ἐναγές and ἐναγέστεροι). His comments on 18:28 in its proper sequence are not extant.

29-30 Because they would not enter the praetorium, the Roman governor came out to meet them: "Therefore Pilate came outside[8] to them, and said, 'What charge[9] do you bring against this man?'" (v. 29). While the phrase "this man" could imply that Jesus is with him, this is unlikely, for Jesus plays no role in the interchange, and later, when Pilate does bring him out (19:4-5), it is made explicit. Just as in Mark (15:1), Pilate himself is introduced abruptly, without being identified as governor (as in Mt 27:2 and Lk 3:1), perhaps because it was already widely known that, as the earliest creeds declared, Jesus was crucified "under Pontius Pilate" (see, for example, 1 Tim 6:13; Ignatius, *To the Trallians* 9.1; *To the Smyrnaeans* 1.2). Pilate's first words to them, "What charge do you bring against this man?" echo Jesus' parting words, "If I have spoken badly, testify to what is bad, but if well, why do you strike me?" (v. 23). They had no answer for Jesus, and they have no real answer for Pilate: "They answered and said to him, 'If he were not doing what is bad, we would not have handed him over to you'" (v. 30). Still unwilling to "testify to what is bad" (v. 23), they nevertheless expect Pilate to take their word for it that Jesus is "doing what is bad,"[10] that is, that he is an "evildoer" or criminal, in the sight of the Romans and the empire no less than in theirs.[11] In sharp contrast to Luke (23:2), where they list three specific charges ("We found this man leading our nation astray, and hindering the paying of taxes to Caesar, and saying that he himself is Christ the king"), they refuse to say what Jesus has done wrong.[12]

31 With no charges filed, Pilate refuses to consider the matter: "Then Pilate said to them, 'You take him,[13] and judge him according to your law'" (v. 31a). There is every evidence within the Gospel that they could have done so. A few verses later they will tell Pilate, "We have a law, and according to the law he ought to die, because he made himself Son of God" (19:7), and on that ground (5:18; 10:33) they have repeatedly tried to kill Jesus, culminating in two attempts at a stoning (8:59; 10:31).[14] But if they are

---

8. Gr. ἔξω.
9. Gr. τίνα κατηγορίαν.
10. Gr. κακὸν ποιῶν.
11. That this was how the expression κακὸν ποιῶν was widely read can be seen from the variant readings κακοποιῶν (C*, Ψ, 33, and others), and κακοποιός (A, Θ, old Latin versions, and the majority of later witnesses). See BDAG, 501 on κακοποιεῖν and κακοποιός respectively.
12. Mark (15:1) and Matthew (27:13) speak of "many" charges (πολλά in Mark; πόσα in Matthew), but without listing them.
13. Gr. λάβετε αὐτὸν ὑμεῖς.
14. This is not to mention the account of the woman taken in adultery (7:53–8:11), in which the apparent intention of "the scribes and Pharisees" was to stone her to death on the ground that "in the law Moses commanded us to stone such women" (8:5). Nor does it

free to "take him and judge him according to your law," and if stoning is still their intention, why have they brought Jesus to Pilate at all? Their answer is puzzling. Instead of confirming (as in 19:7) that their law condemns Jesus to death, they seem to imply the opposite: "The Jews said to him, 'It is not lawful for us to kill anyone'" (v. 31b).

The words, "It is not lawful,"[15] are commonly interpreted to mean that Roman law did not permit the Jews to impose the death penalty, so that consequently Jesus would die not by stoning but by crucifixion, a Roman and not Jewish method of execution (hence v. 32, citing Jesus' pronouncements about being "lifted up," as on a cross). Yet it is odd that the Jews would have to remind Pilate of what Roman law did or did not permit. It is just as odd that Pilate seems to have just given them permission to do what they are now saying was forbidden ("You take him," v. 31a), and odder still that he will give them permission again, in the same three words, later on: "You take him, and crucify him" (19:6). Moreover, such expressions as "It is lawful"[16] or "It is not lawful" are more often used of what is allowed or forbidden by the law of Moses than by Roman law.[17] Viewed in this way, "It is not lawful for us to kill anyone" sounds more like a simple allusion to the Decalogue: "You shall not murder" (Exod 20:13; Deut 5:17, NIV, NRSV). To be sure, the vocabulary does not exactly match in Greek any more than in English.[18] Yet "kill"[19]

---

take account of the stoning of Stephen in the book of Acts a few years later (see Acts 7:54-60), or the stoning of James the Just, the brother of Jesus, around A.D. 62 (see Josephus, *Antiquities* 20.200 [LCL, 9.497]; also Clement of Alexandria, *Hypotyposes,* in Eusebius, *Ecclesiastical History* 2.3-5 [LCL, 1.105], and Hegesippus, in Eusebius 2.23.4-18 [LCL, 1.171-75]). All these sources assume that the Jews had the authority to impose the death penalty, with or without a formal trial.

15. Gr. οὐκ ἔξεστιν.
16. Gr. ἔξεστιν.
17. See Josephus, who at the very end of his *Antiquities* proposes to write further "concerning the laws, that is, why according to them we are permitted [ἔξεστιν ἡμῖν] to do some things while we are forbidden to do others" (*Antiquities* 20.268; LCL, 9.533). Aside from the present verse, 20 of the 21 uses of ἔξεστιν and ἐξόν in the Gospels have to do with what is permitted or forbidden in Jewish law, whether with regard to the Sabbath (Mt 12:2//Mk 2:24//Lk 6:2; Mk 3:4; Lk 14:3; Jn 5:10), divorce (Mt 19:3//Mk 10:2; Mt 14:4//Mk 6:18), Corban (Mt 27:6), or the payment of taxes to Caesar (Mt 22:17//Mk 12:14//Lk 20:22). The only exception is Matthew 20:15, where it refers more generally to what is right or proper (see also 1 Cor 6:12; 10:23; 2 Cor 12:4). Only in the book of Acts are such expressions used in connection with Roman law as it applied to Roman citizens (see Acts 16:21, 22:25; and in a more general rhetorical sense, 21:37). See my "John 18.31 and the 'Trial' of Jesus," *NTS* 36 (1990), 475.
18. "You shall not murder" is οὐ φονεύσεις (Exod 20:13; Deut 5:17, LXX; compare Mt 19:18, Mk 10:19, and Lk 18:20).
19. Gr. ἀποκτεῖναι.

is also not quite what we would expect in speaking of a formal execution, for which the more judicial verb "put to death"[20] would have been more appropriate.[21] What the vocabulary does match perfectly is what this Gospel has been saying of the Jewish authorities all along, that they were seeking "to kill" Jesus (5:18; 7:1, 19, 20, 25; 8:37, 40). This terminology extends even to the judicial decision of the council chaired by Caiaphas the Chief Priest "that they would kill"[22] Jesus (11:53), and Lazarus as well (12:10).

The consistency of language was not lost on Origen, who once again savored the irony, citing first verse 31b ("It is not lawful for us to kill anyone"), and then in quick succession verses 35 and 40 and 19:7, 12, and 15 to demonstrate that in effect they did exactly what it was "not lawful" for them to do. Then he cites 16:2 ("The hour is coming when everyone who kills you will think he offers service to God") with the comment that this prophecy of Jesus was "fulfilled, beginning with himself." Finally he repeats verbatim Jesus' last charge against them, "But now you seek to kill me, a man who has spoken the truth to you, which I have heard from God" (8:40).[23] The point is that now, in saying "It is not lawful for us to kill anyone," the Jewish chief priests have condemned themselves, validating at last Jesus' judgments on them long before at the Tent festival: "Has Moses not given you the law? And none of you does the law? Why are you seeking to kill me?" (7:19), and "If you are Abraham's children, you would be doing the works of Abraham. But now you are seeking to kill me" (8:39-40a). It is indeed "not lawful . . . to kill anyone," but they have plotted from the beginning to kill not just "anyone," but even worse, "a man who has spoken to you the truth which I heard from God. This Abraham did not do" (8:40b). Their lawlessness is now condemned again, this time from their own lips.[24]

This is all very well within the framework of the Gospel, and the Gospel writer's intention, but what is going on in the minds of the Jews themselves? What are they thinking? They are saying it to Pilate after all, not just to the reader.[25] What is he to conclude from their disclaimer, "It is not lawful

---

20. Gr. θανατοῦν or θανατῶσαι.

21. So Mt 26:59, 27:1 and Mk 14:55 in connection with the trial of Jesus (in other judicial connections, see Mt 10:21, Mk 13:12 and Lk 21:16). "Put to death" (θανατοῦν) is also the dominant terminology in Old Testament passages regarding the death penalty for Sabbath breaking, blasphemy, and the worship of other gods (see, for example, Exod 31:14; Lev 24:16-17; Deut. 13:6, 11, LXX), even though the terminology of "killing" (ἀποκτεῖναι) is not unknown (see Lev 20:15, 16; Deut 13:10; 22:22, 25, LXX).

22. Gr. ἵνα ἀποκτείνωσιν.

23. See Origen, *Commentary on John* 28.232-38 (FC 89.339-40).

24. So Paul Duke, *Irony,* 136: "'The Jews' have confessed that their law forbids them to kill, but the law is forsaken along with their faith." See also Schnackenburg, 245.

25. Brown comments that "The dialogue, however, is obviously for the informa-

for us to kill anyone"? As we have seen, it is not plausible to assume that they would be lecturing Pilate on the fine points of Roman law. Possibly they are tacitly acknowledging that they have not held a formal trial and consequently do not have a conviction. While the other Gospels seem to imply a trial of some sort before the Jewish Sanhedrin or ruling council (see Mt 26:55-66// Mk 14:55-64; Lk 22:66-71), it is true that in John's Gospel itself there has been no formal trial and no conviction. Therefore if they were to execute Jesus without a formal conviction, it would be murder, or a lynching, in violation of the ancient command, "You shall not murder." These points I argued some years ago.[26] Yet it must be acknowledged that such rules did not stop the Jews from attempting to stone Jesus without a trial on two previous occasions (8:59 and 10:31).[27]

Evidently something else is going on here. For some reason, it is important to the Jewish authorities that the Romans carry out the execution of Jesus. Quite possibly they may have feared that they did not have broad enough popular support, and that if they were to stone Jesus to death there would be repercussions among "the crowds," who have all along been ambivalent about Jesus (see 7:49, "this crowd that does not know the law"; also 12:19, "Look, the world has gone after him!"; also Mt 26:5, "Not during the festival, so as not to cause an uproar among 'the people'"). The stated fear of the chief priests was that if Jesus were allowed to continue to perform signs, "they will all believe in him, and the Romans will come and take away both our place and our nation" (11:48), and Caiaphas had proposed that the wrath of Rome be visited on one man so that the whole nation might be spared (11:50). To this end, it was not enough that Jesus be arrested, tried, and put to death by the Jewish authorities. That would gain them no particular favor with the Romans, and might cause them to lose favor with the people. It would be far better if the Roman governor himself came to perceive Jesus as a threat, and if possible be persuaded to carry out the execution on his authority, in the process giving them due credit for their loyalty to Rome. Jesus has implied that they are liars (see 8:44, 55), and their claim that "It is not lawful for us to kill anyone" is, if not an outright lie, at least an attempt to deceive Pilate by leading him to believe that their law prevents them from putting Jesus to death. Pilate, with only a cursory knowledge of Jewish teaching, might well have known that there was some-

---

tion of the readers, not of Pilate" (*Death*, 1.747). But clearly, this is not an either/or matter. Whatever its literary function, the dialogue must have credibility as genuine dialogue.

26. See Michaels, "John 18:31," 478-79.

27. As Brown notes in critiquing my article, "the various OT *commands* to execute a blasphemer or seducer do not specify a trial or what the investigation would consist of" (*Death*, 1.748, n. 40).

thing in their law about not committing murder, and been willing to take them at their word.[28]

32 In any event, the Gospel writer's comment that this exchange took place "so that the word of Jesus that he said signifying by what death he was going to die might be fulfilled" (v. 32) sounds a bit premature. Its point is that since the Jews will not execute Jesus, he will die not by stoning (as he would have in 8:59 and 10:31) but by crucifixion, the Roman method of execution. That is, he will be "lifted up" on a cross just as he said he would (3:14; 12:32, 34; see also 8:28). This is by no means a foregone conclusion. Pilate has not yet agreed to crucify Jesus. Three times he will tell them, "I find in him no probable cause" (v. 38; 19:4, 6), before he finally yields to their demands (19:16). Yet the writer's comment signals already what is coming: Pilate *will* capitulate. Jesus *will* be crucified. His word "signifying by what death he was going to die" *will* be fulfilled. Here for a second time (as in v. 9) the formula "that it might be fulfilled"[29] occurs with a saying of Jesus rather than a citation of Scripture. In contrast to verse 9 the actual saying of Jesus (this time about being "lifted up," 3:14; 12:32) is not quoted or paraphrased. Instead the writer simply identifies it as the pronouncement by which Jesus "signified" the manner of his death (see 12:33). Yet the earlier citation, "I have lost none of those whom you have given me" (v. 9) did have the same premature-sounding quality seen here, for at the moment of Jesus' arrest it was by no means a foregone conclusion that the lives of his disciples would be spared.[30] The "fulfillment" of what he had said before was at the same time a prophecy of what was to come, and the same is true here. Jesus' fate is sealed, his destiny assured, for "just as Moses lifted up the snake in the desert, so the Son of man *must* be lifted up" (3:14, italics added).

33 The scene changes, as "Pilate went in again[31] into the praetorium and summoned Jesus and said to him, 'You are the King of the Jews?'" (v. 33). That he "summoned" Jesus after reentering the praetorium confirms that Jesus was still inside, presumably under guard. Pilate's question, "You are the King of the Jews?"[32] is exactly the same question, word for word, that he asks in all four Gospels (compare Mt 27:11//Mk 15:2//Lk 23:3), leaving us to wonder where the title came from, and where Pilate got the idea that

---

28. The apocryphal *Acts of Pilate* 3.1 (fourth century or later) adds a final question by Pilate, implying that he knows they are referring to their own law: "Has God forbidden you to slay [μὴ ἀποκτεῖναι], but allowed me?" (Hennecke-Schneemelcher, 1.454).

29. Gr. ἵνα . . . πληρωθῇ.

30. As we have seen, Peter tried to save his own life in denying Jesus three times, and Jesus had to protect the lives of the disciples once again in the answer he gave to the Chief Priest (vv. 20-21).

31. Gr. εἰσῆλθεν οὖν πάλιν.

32. Gr. σὺ εἶ ὁ βασιλεὺς τῶν Ἰουδαίων.

this was what Jesus might be claiming. The answer (to the second question at least) is found only in Luke, where the Jewish authorities who bring Jesus to Pilate level certain explicit charges, the last of which is that of claiming to be "Christ, a king," or, perhaps, "an anointed king"[33] (as in Lk 23:2b). In Matthew and Mark, Pilate's question is not fully explained, for we are told merely that they "handed him over" to Pilate (Mt 27:2//Mk 15:1). No charges are mentioned. Here in John's Gospel it is even more puzzling in that Pilate has asked them, "What charge do you bring against this man?" (v. 29), and they have refused (v. 30). How then does Pilate know that the charge is that of claiming to be "King of the Jews"? It is as if Luke 23:2 is needed in order to make sense of the Gospel of John (not to mention Matthew and Mark!).[34]

While the phrase "the King of the Jews" makes an abrupt first appearance here, the reader of John's Gospel has known almost from the beginning that Jesus is indeed both "the Son of God" and "the King of Israel" (1:49). And even though he himself thwarted those who tried "to seize him to make him king" (6:15), the crowds welcomed him publicly into Jerusalem as "the One coming in the name of the Lord, even the King of Israel" (12:13), in the face of which the Pharisees lamented, "Look, the world has gone after him!" (12:19). This may have been enough to prompt Pilate's question, "You are the King of the Jews?" Pilate's terminology as a Gentile, and as governor of Judea only, would have been "the Jews" and not "Israel," but he might well have known of the public clamor (even without an enumeration of the charges mentioned in Luke), and framed the question for himself.

34 The whole of verses 34-37 appears to be an expansion of the cryptic "You say so,"[35] which is what we find in the other three Gospels (Mt 27:11//Mk 15:2//Lk 23:3), followed by resolute silence (see Mt 27:12//Mk

33. Gr. χριστὸν βασιλέα.

34. Warren Carter *(Pontius Pilate: Portraits of a Roman Governor)* appeals to the fact that the Roman troops involved in the arrest of Jesus (v. 3) "could not have been deployed without Pilate's command. It seems, then, that at a previous meeting or meetings Pilate heard the Jerusalem elite's concern over Jesus as a major threat to the society over which he as governor and they as the Jerusalem elite rule (cf. 11:45-48). The presence of Roman troops at Jesus' arrest expresses Pilate's consent to remove Jesus." This is why "His inquiry about a charge after the arrest seems out of place and surprises them" (141). On this ground Carter justifies their refusal to name any charges (v. 30), and goes on to build a far-reaching case that all Pilate's efforts to release Jesus are merely a pretense designed to subjugate and humiliate the Jewish leaders. But surely if the Gospel writer intended us to believe that Pilate was complicit in the Jewish plot against Jesus (that is, in 11:47-53), he would have given us clues to that effect. Instead, all the clues point in the opposite direction. The presence of Roman troops at the arrest need not signal Pilate's complicity, but only an effort to make sure that the arrest did not eventuate in an uprising that would upset the social order.

35. Gr. σὺ λέγεις.

15:4-5; compare Lk 23:9). Here in John's Gospel, by contrast, he speaks freely, turning the words, "You say so," into a question, "Are you saying this[36] on your own, or did others tell you about me?" — the same question, in fact, that is in the mind of the reader.[37] That is, where does the phrase "King of the Jews" come from? Have "the Jews" themselves made some charge to that effect (as they do explicitly in Lk 23:2), or is Pilate's question strictly his own?

35 Pilate's reply is unambiguous: "Am I a Jew? Your nation and the chief priests handed you over to me. What have you done?" (v. 35). The question "Am I a Jew?" is rhetorical, emphatically dissociating Pilate from "the Jews," just as emphatically as when he told the chief priests a moment before, "You take him, and judge him according to your law" (v. 31). In the same breath he dissociates himself from Jesus, identifying Jesus' accusers as "Your nation." There is ironic truth in this, for as Caiaphas prophesied, the "nation" is Jesus' own nation, destined to be redeemed by his death (see 11:51[38]). Pilate views Jesus and "the Jews" in much the same way. He wants nothing to do with either, and he asks Jesus the same question he asked them. Of them he had asked, "What charge do you bring against this man?" (v. 29), and of Jesus, "What have you done?" that is, "What are they charging you with?" But as he has already revealed (v. 33), kingship is on his mind.

36 Jesus knows this, and responds accordingly: "My kingship[39] is not from this world. If my kingship were from this world, my officers would fight so that I would not be handed over to the Jews. But now my kingship is not from here"[40] (v. 36). He tacitly acknowledges that he is a king, just as Nathanael and the crowds in Jerusalem confessed him to be, but he is careful to explain what kind of king he is *not,* leaving the reader to infer the kind of king he is. In contrast to 3:3 and 5, it is not a question of a "kingdom," a realm that human beings can "see" (3:3) and "enter" (3:5), but rather "kingship," something belonging to Jesus alone, his royal authority as Son of God (see 1:49, "Son of God" and "King of Israel").

It is important here to avoid a common misunderstanding. That Jesus' kingship is not "from this world"[41] does not mean that it is merely "spiritual" in the sense of being inward or subjective. It is not simply Christ reigning in the hearts of individuals. The phrase does not so much define the nature of

---

36. Gr. σὺ τοῦτο λέγεις.

37. In the end, he will echo the synoptic saying again: "You say [σὺ λέγεις] that I am a king" (v. 37). Barrett (536) assumes that our Gospel is expanding on Mark in particular, but this is not necessarily the case.

38. Gr. ὑπὲρ τοῦ ἔθνους.

39. Gr. ἡ βασιλεία ἡ ἐμή.

40. Gr. ἐντεῦθεν.

41. Gr. ἐκ τοῦ κόσμου τούτου.

Jesus' kingship as locate its origin. It is not "from" this present world, just as Jesus himself is not "from this world" (8:23b). Rather, he is "from above" (8:23a), or "from heaven" (3:13; 6:33, 41, 50, 51, 58), and he now wants the reader to know that the same is true of his "kingship." He says it twice: "My kingship is not from this world," and "But now my kingship is not from here." In the same way that "not from this world" implies "from heaven," or "from above," the notice that Jesus' kingship is not "from here" implies that it is "from above"[42] (3:31). In short, it comes not from Jerusalem or Rome, but from heaven, from the very presence of God, and therefore belongs to God. Divine origin implies divine ownership. "Not from this world" implies no allegiance to this world, but allegiance only to God. Jesus' kingship is not merely "spiritual" but eschatological, rather like the Holy City in Revelation, always coming down "out of heaven from God" (Rev 3:12; 21:2, 10). It is nothing less than Jesus' all-encompassing "authority over all flesh" (17:2; also Mt 28:18), and in the end it will supersede all human authority.[43] Pilate in the end will pronounce it politically harmless (see v. 38b), but it is more dangerous than he imagines.

The two assertions that Jesus' kingship, or royal authority, is not "from this world" (or "from here") frame a contrary-to-fact condition. The second one, "But now my kingdom is not from here," brings matters back to reality, but the conditional clause itself addresses the question, "What if Jesus' kingship were from this world? What difference would it make?" The difference, he says, is that "my officers would fight so that I would not be handed over to the Jews." To begin with, he would have "officers"[44] under him, like the "officers" of the chief priests who came to arrest him (18:3, 12, 18, 22; also 7:32, 45), not just "disciples." These "officers" would fight back, and he would not have been taken. Admittedly, the logic is not airtight. First, one of Jesus' disciples, evidently fancying himself an "officer," had in fact drawn a sword and cut off Malchus's ear (v. 10). Second, even a king whose kingship was "not from this world" might (according to a different tradition) have called on "twelve legions of angels" for reinforcements (see Mt 26:53).

---

42. Gr. ἄνωθεν.
43. Bultmann (654, n. 3) accents the eschatological nature ("in a Johannine sense") of Jesus' kingship, comparing the answer given (according to Hegesippus) by the grandsons of Jude the brother of Jesus to Domitian when he asked them about "the Christ and his kingship." They said it was "not worldly nor earthly [οὐ κοσμικὴ μὲν οὐδ' ἐπίγειος], but would turn out to be heavenly [ἐπουράνιος] and angelic, coming at the close of the age when, having come in glory, he will judge the living and the dead, each according to his works." Despite the eschatological claims, Domitian "did not condemn them, but despised them as simple folk, set them free, and by decree ceased the persecution against the church" (Eusebius, *Ecclesiastical History* 3.20.4).
44. Gr. οἱ ὑπηρέται.

But the first was irrelevant because Jesus renounced Peter's misguided attempt to help (v. 11), and was in fact arrested despite the token resistance. The second scenario — even if known to the writer of John's Gospel — would have made no sense at all to a Roman governor. The contrary-to-fact condition is ambiguous as far as tense is concerned. It could be translated either "my officers *would fight* so that I would not be handed over to the Jews" (as we have done), or "my officers *would have fought* so that I would not be handed over to the Jews" (italics added).[45] We might have expected "so that I would not be handed over *to you,*" for Pilate has just said, "Your nation and the chief priests handed you over to me" (v. 35). The present tense, "my officers would fight," is marginally more appropriate because the reference to being "handed over to the Jews" anticipates not the present moment but rather the end of the whole sequence of events when, as we will learn, Pilate finally "handed him over *to them* [that is, to "the Jews"] to be crucified" (19:16, italics added). Already here, Jesus drops a hint that he will die at the hands of "the Jews" after all.

37 The subtlety of the contrary-to-fact condition is wasted on Pilate, who seems to have heard only the phrase, "My kingship," implying that Jesus is a king of some sort. Pilate, therefore, "said to him, 'So, you are a king!'" (v. 37a).[46] Jesus replies, "You say[47] that I am a king. I was born for this, and for this I came into the world, that I might testify to the truth.[48] Everyone who is from the truth hears my voice" (v. 37b).

With this, the "Johannine" expansion of the simple "You say so" in all three synoptic Gospels (Mt 27:11//Mk 15:2//Lk 23:3) is complete. Jesus does not deny his kingship, for it is evident in this Gospel no less than in the others (1:49, 12:13), but he prefers to speak of something else — his calling to "testify to the truth," just as John had done before him (5:33). "For this," he tells Pilate, "I was born, and for this I have come into the world."[49] The solemn

---

45. See BDF, §360(3): "the imperfect is temporally ambiguous," rendering ἠγωνίζοντο ἄν as "'would have fought and continued to fight' (the outcome and result being uncertain)."

46. Gr. οὐκοῦν βασιλεὺς εἶ σύ. The force of οὐκοῦν (found only here in the New Testament) is to draw a conclusion in the form of a rhetorical question expecting a positive answer (see BDAG, 736. In effect, the rhetorical question, "So are you not a king?" amounts to a declarative statement, "So, you are a king!" (see Abbott, *Johannine Grammar,* 193: *"Well then . . . thou art a king"*).

47. Gr. σὺ λέγεις.

48. Gr. ἵνα μαρτυρήσω τῇ ἀληθείᾳ.

49. The parallel between "I was born" (γεγέννημαι) and "I have come into the world" makes it clear that Jesus' language about having "come down from heaven" (for example, 3:13; 6:38) was metaphorical. Despite the absence of a birth narrative in John's Gospel, Jesus is understood to have "come into the world" like every other human being (see 1:9), by being born.

18:28–19:15 JESUS, PILATE, AND THE JEWS

repetition of "for this"⁵⁰ makes this the simplest and most emphatic statement of Jesus' mission to be found anywhere in the Gospel.⁵¹ Throughout his public ministry, he has spoken "the truth which I heard from God" (see 8:40, 45). Even those who mistakenly wanted to "come and seize him to make him king" (6:15) did so because they believed he was "truly the Prophet who is coming into the world" (6:14). His role as king cannot be separated from his role as the revealer of God, for his authority to "testify to the truth" rests on his kingship, the royal authority the Father has given him over "all flesh" (17:2) to make known "the truth" — that is, "the only true God," and himself as God's messenger (17:3).

His final words to Pilate here add a cautionary note, "Everyone who is from the truth⁵² hears my voice." The implication is that those who are not "from the truth," that is, do not belong to the truth or stand on the side of truth, do not hear Jesus' voice. In effect he is asking Pilate, "Do *you* belong to the truth? Are *you* hearing my voice?" Earlier, after telling "the Jews who had believed him" at the Tent festival, "If you dwell on my word, you are truly my disciples, and you will know the truth, and the truth will set you free" (8:31-32), he found that this did not happen, and he had to say to them in the end, "Whoever is from God hears the words of God. This is why you do not hear, because you are not from God" (8:47). Again at the Rededication he told them: "But as for you, you do not believe, because you do not belong to my sheep [literally, "you are not from my sheep"]. My sheep hear my voice, and I know them, and they follow me" (10:26-27). That was his verdict on the Jewish authorities: they were not "from God" in that they did not belong to God; they were not "from" his sheep in that they were not numbered among his sheep; by implication, they were not "from the truth," for they refused to believe the One who told them the truth (8:45-46) and repeatedly tried to kill him.

38a Pilate is no better. Jesus does not state the negative, but Pilate states it for him: "What is truth?"⁵³ (v. 38). The question poses no challenge to the reader. We are not intended to ponder these "profound" words, or say to ourselves, "Good question. What *is* truth, anyway?" On the contrary, it tells us that Pilate has no clue what truth is, consequently that he is *not* "from the truth" (v. 37) any more than the Jewish leaders were, and has by no means

---

50. Gr. εἰς τοῦτο.
51. So Lincoln, 463. Among his other declarations of his mission are 6:38 ("not to do my will but the will of the One who sent me"), 9:39 ("so that those who do not see might see, and so that those who see might go blind"), 10:10 ("that they might have life, and have [it] in abundance"), 12:46 ("so that everyone who believes in me might not remain in the darkness"), 12:47 ("to save the world").
52. Gr. ἐκ τῆς ἀληθείας.
53. Gr. τί ἐστιν ἀλήθεια.

"heard Jesus' voice." Readers of the Gospel, by contrast, know what "the truth" is, for Jesus has acknowledged to the Father, "Your word is the truth" (17:17), and has even told the disciples, "I am the Way, and the Truth, and the Life" (14:6). Pilate's question, moreover, is dismissive. He does not want an answer, only an end to the conversation, and as far as the reader is concerned, the answer has already been given.[54]

With this, Jesus' brief encounter with the Gentile world in the person of one Roman governor is over, and the result is the same as that of his far longer series of encounters with the Jewish people and their leaders. If it is true that "He came to what was his own, and his own [that is, the Jews] did not receive him" (1:11), it is just as true that "He was in the world, . . . and the world [that is, the whole world — Jew and Gentile alike] did not know him" (1:10). But who was privy to this brief encounter? In contrast to Peter's denials — and possibly Jesus' interrogation by the Chief Priest — this appears to have been a very private conversation between Jesus and Pilate, with no anonymous disciple "known to the Chief Priest" (v. 15) to pass along what might have been said. On what basis was the Gospel writer able to expand the cryptic, "You say so," of earlier traditions (Mk 15:1 and par.), not to mention the conspicuous silence that followed (Mk 15:5 and parallel), into the significant dialogue that we find in this Gospel? It is an intriguing question for which there is no sure answer. The account looks like the Gospel writer's own composition. Possibly the writer claimed as his source another who, like Jesus, would "testify to the truth" — that is, the Advocate or "Spirit of truth," who, Jesus promised, would "testify about me" (15:26; see also 14:26). Who better to play the role — or give the Gospel writer the right to play the role — of omniscient narrator?

38b-39 Nothing Jesus has said about his kingship has convinced Pilate to regard him as a criminal or in any way a threat to the empire. Once more the scene changes: "And having said this, he went out again to the Jews, and he says to them, 'I find in him no probable cause'" (v. 38b).[55] The verse division is such that the change of scene comes in the middle of a verse, confirming the impression that Pilate expected no answer to the question, "What

---

54. Later traditions were unable to leave it at that. According to the apocryphal *Acts of Pilate* 3.2, "Jesus answered him, 'Truth is from heaven' [Ἀλήθεια ἐξ οὐρανοῦ]. Pilate said, 'Is there not truth upon earth?' [ἐπὶ γῆς]. Jesus said to Pilate: 'You see how those who speak the truth are judged by those who have authority [τὴν ἐξουσίαν] on earth'" (Hennecke-Schneemelcher, 1.455). To a surprising degree, the fertile imaginations of those who composed that account seem to have stayed within the limitations of what might be inferred from the Gospel of John itself. Yet the Gospel's silence is far more eloquent.

55. Gr. οὐδεμίαν . . . αἰτίαν. Αἰτίαν is literally "cause," and when used as a legal term, "probable cause" in the legal sense, or grounds on which to build a case (see BDAG, 31). Οὐδεμίαν is emphatic: no cause whatsoever (see also 19:4).

is truth?" (v. 38a). As quickly as he "said this,"[56] he went back outside the praetorium to speak to the Jewish priests, resuming the conversation that had broken off when they said, "It is not lawful for us to kill anyone" (v. 31b). His declaration, "I find in him no probable cause," is emphatic, as if to say, "*I* find none, but perhaps *you* might." This would amount simply to a reiteration of his earlier words, "You take him, and judge him according to your law" (v. 31a). Pilate and "the Jews" were at a stalemate, and he now looks for a way out by appealing to a "custom you have[57] that I release to you one at the Passover," and asking, "So shall I release to you the King of the Jews?" (v. 39). The repetition of "you" is conspicuous, suggesting that in "releasing" Jesus he would not be granting him unconditional freedom (certainly not guaranteeing him any sort of protection), but simply returning him to the jurisdiction of the Jewish leaders. As far as Pilate is concerned, they could still "take him, and judge him" according to Jewish law (v. 31a), or even, if they wished, "take him, and crucify him" (19:6).

This is rather different from what appears to be the case in the other three Gospels, where Pilate had made no previous attempt to return Jesus to the jurisdiction of the Jewish authorities. There Pilate proposed to "release" Jesus (see Mk 15:9//Mt 27:17; Lk 23:16), not to them for judgment but to the crowds — and presumably to freedom. The crowds, under pressure from the chief priests (so Mt 27:20//Mk 15:11), cried out for Barabbas to be released instead. Here, by contrast, "the Jews" have a second opportunity (as in v. 31) to do with Jesus what they will, as Pilate asks them, "So shall I release to you the King of the Jews?" For the first time, he throws in their face the title "the King of the Jews," and it does not make them happy.

40 While Pilate's proposal to "release" may have a slightly different meaning in John's Gospel than in the other three, the response is just the same: "Then they cried out again, saying, 'Not this one but Barabbas' [compare Mt 27:21; Mk 15:11; Lk 23:18]. And Barabbas was a terrorist" (v. 40). "Again"[58] sounds odd because they have not "cried out"[59] before, but the probable meaning is that they shouted "back," in response to what he had just said.[60] They are

---

56. Gr. τοῦτο εἰπών.
57. Gr. συνήθεια ὑμῖν.
58. Gr. πάλιν.
59. Gr. ἐκραύγασαν.
60. See BDAG, 752; Brown, *Death,* 1.808. This is in keeping with the repeated use of πάλιν in the context to refer to Pilate's "back"-and-forth movements between the inside and the outside of the praetorium (see vv. 33, 38b; 19:4, 9). To Bultmann, by contrast, πάλιν implies that "an account must have been given earlier of the κραυγάζειν of the Jews" because "a suppressed piece of the source's text has obviously been replaced by 18.33-37" (649). Oddly, πάλιν is *not* used the second, third, and fourth times that the Jewish leaders "cried out" (ἐκραύγασαν) against Pilate (see 19:6, 12, 15).

in no mood to negotiate. "Barabbas" is introduced very abruptly, more so than in the other three Gospels (all of which mention and name him), and he is identified in just one word, as a "terrorist,"[61] a term quite compatible with the more detailed information given in Mark (15:7), Matthew (27:16), and Luke (23:19).[62] John's Gospel shows less interest in Barabbas than the other Gospels, and unlike the others (see Mt 27:26; Mk 15:15; Lk 23:25), never states explicitly that he was in fact ever released. The characteristically Johannine narrative aside, "And Barabbas was a terrorist," calls attention to the same irony that is so evident in the other Gospels (not to mention Acts 3:14), but here it is merely one small irony among many. More important, perhaps, Pilate's offer to turn Jesus back to the Jewish authorities is once again refused. "The Jews" are relentless in their determination that Rome and not Jerusalem will put Jesus to death.

19:1 While we are not told explicitly that Pilate "went back inside" (as in 18:33), this is implied by the notice that "then Pilate took Jesus and had him flogged" (19:1).[63] In Matthew and in Mark, this happens just as Pilate "handed him over to be crucified" (Mt 27:26//Mk 15:15). In Luke, by contrast, it is not actually carried out. Rather, as a strategy or conciliatory gesture, Pilate twice offers to "have him flogged and release him" (Lk 23:16, 22), but the strategy proves futile. Here in John's Gospel, it is evident that Pilate has not yet given in. He still has no intention of bending to the wishes of the chief priests (see vv. 4, 6, 12). Yet it is doubtful that he does this simply to conciliate "the Jews," for his action is closely linked to what immediately follows (vv. 2-3), an elaborate mockery of "the Jews."

2-3 That the "flogging" was carried out by Pilate's soldiers is confirmed by the accompanying notice, "And the soldiers wove a crown of thorns and put it on his head and wrapped a purple robe around him, and they kept coming at him[64] and saying, 'Hail, King of the Jews,' and giving him slaps in the face" (vv. 2-3). In Matthew and Mark, this takes place only after

---

61. Gr. λῃστής.

62. Λῃστής can refer either to a common robber or bandit (see 10:8), or to a revolutionary or insurrectionist of some kind (see BDAG, 594). Both Mark and Luke are explicit in claiming that Barabbas had not only taken part in an insurrection, but had committed murder (see also Acts 3:14).

63. "Flogging" or beating (μαστιγῶσαι) is mentioned in the synoptic passion predictions as something that will happen to Jesus at the hands of the Gentiles (see Mt 20:17// Mk 10:34//Lk 18:33). The translation "had him flogged" is based on the assumption that Pilate did not "take" and "flog" Jesus with his own hands, but commanded his soldiers to do so (compare vv. 4, 13, where Pilate probably did not personally bring Jesus outside, and especially vv. 19 and 22, where it is fair to assume that he did not personally "write" the inscription over the cross).

64. Gr. ἤρχοντο πρὸς αὐτόν.

18:28–19:15   JESUS, PILATE, AND THE JEWS

Jesus has been handed over to be crucified, and in the presence of "the whole cohort" (Mt 27:27//Mk 15:16), six hundred troops in all.[65] The "horseplay" described here is more private, and reminiscent of what was recorded a chapter earlier in the other Gospels, in connection with the trial before Caiaphas and the Jewish council — but with one important exception. There Jesus was mocked by Jews for his reputation as a prophet (Mt 27:68; Mk 14:65; Lk 22:64). Here the mockery is the work of the Romans, aimed as much at "the Jews" themselves as at Jesus. The soldiers — apparently at Pilate's instigation — are acting out the governor's obsession with the title "King of the Jews" (see 18:33, 39). The idea of this pitiful subject people having their own "king" is an absurdity to Pilate, and he allows his soldiers the sport of dressing up this pitiful, beaten figure as a ridiculous "King of the Jews."[66] The "purple robe" proclaims his kingship, while the "crown of thorns," the flogging, and the slaps in the face expose him as a "king" thoroughly humiliated and powerless, a fitting potentate for a despised and subjugated people.[67]

4-5 The elaborate mockery of Jesus by Pilate and the Roman soldiers is not simply a matter of private amusement, but turns out to be for the benefit of the Jewish leaders as well: "And Pilate again went outside, and says to them, 'Look, I am leading him outside to you, so that you might know that I find in him no probable cause'" (v. 4). For the second time, he pronounces his verdict: "no probable cause" (as in 18:38), at least as far as the death penalty is concerned. "Look, I am leading him outside" probably means that Pilate has ordered his soldiers to bring Jesus out, not that he went back in and escorted Jesus out personally. Immediately, "Jesus came outside,[68] wearing the thorny crown and the purple robe. And he said to them, 'Look, the man!'"[69] (v. 5). Given the

---

65. In Luke there is no flogging at this point, but something of the kind takes place earlier, when Pilate sent Jesus to Herod (an event reported only in Luke) at the hands of Herod and his soldiers. Herod, we are told, "insulted him and mocked him and clothed him in an elegant robe" before sending him back to Pilate (see Lk 23:11).

66. On Pontius Pilate's often anti-Semitic track record in relation to the Jews, see Philo, *Embassy to Gaius* 299-305 (LCL, 10.151-53); Josephus, *Antiquities* 18.55-62 (LCL, 9.43-47), 18.85-89 (LCL, 9.61-65); *War* 2.169-77 (LCL, 2.389-93); also Luke 13:1 (for a convenient chart, see Carter, *Pontius Pilate,* 14).

67. Despite centuries of tradition, it is not self-evident that the crown of thorns was intended as torture. Brown comments (*Death,* 1.866), "In the Gospels, however, there is no stress on torture; and the crown is part of the royal mockery, like the robe and [in Matthew] the scepter," adding the consideration that "stiff thorns cannot be woven (even if the branches can be entangled)." The notice that they kept "giving him slaps in the face" (ἐδίδοσαν αὐτῷ ῥαπίσματα, v. 3) recalls the Jewish officer who "gave Jesus a slap in the face" (ἔδωκεν ῥάπισμα τῷ Ἰησοῦ) for how he had answered the Chief Priest (18:22), but this too is closer to mockery or humiliation than to torture.

68. Gr. ἔξω, now for the third time in two verses.

69. Gr. ἰδοὺ ὁ ἄνθρωπος.

way Jesus is clothed, we might have expected, "Look, your king!" (as in v. 14). Pilate is not ready to say that, and when he does say it he will make it far more of a production, formally installing Jesus (albeit ironically) as "the King of the Jews" (see v. 13). "Look" *(idou)* does not have the same performative quality that "Look" *(ide)* has, at least in some places (as, for example, in v. 14). Pilate is not, by his words, appointing Jesus to be "the man," but simply calling attention to him so that "the Jews" can draw their own conclusions about him. "Look, the man!" recalls the repeated references to Jesus as "this man"[70] throughout the Gospel, usually by the Jewish authorities, and often with disdainful connotations (see 5:12; 9:16, 24; 11:47; 18:17, 29).[71] It is as if Pilate is now saying to them, "Look, here is 'the man' you were looking for, and arrested and brought to me. Now what are you going to do with him?"

To the reader, the pronouncement evokes something quite different, Jesus' characteristic self-identification as "the Son of man." As we have seen, he himself has used "Son of man" conspicuously in connection with his impending death, whether by being "glorified" (12:23; 13:31) or "lifted up" (3:14, 8:28; 12:34), and now the moment of death is drawing near.[72] But the title "the Son of man" (literally, "the son of the man")[73] would make no sense to a Roman Gentile. "The man" is about as close to the idiomatic Jewish expression "the Son of man" as Pontius Pilate could be expected to come. It is commonly agreed, in fact, that "a man," or "the man," is precisely what "the Son of man" means when translated back into Hebrew or Aramaic.[74] To the reader, therefore, Pilate — like Caiaphas before him (11:51-52) — is speaking more wisely than he knows, designating Jesus in much the same way Jesus designated himself, as "the Son of man,"[75] in Caiaphas's words the "one man"[76] destined to "die for the people" (11:50).

70. Gr. οὗτος ὁ ἄνθρωπος.

71. Sometimes the pronoun "this one" (οὗτος) is used by itself, with similarly negative connotations (see, for example, 6:52; 7:15, 27, 35; 9:29; 18:30, 40). In a more neutral vein, the once blind beggar speaks of "the man [ὁ ἄνθρωπος] called Jesus" (9:11).

72. See also 6:53, where the terminology of "eating the flesh" and "drinking the blood" of the Son of man also presupposes his violent death. "Son of man" is linked just as closely to Jesus' death in the other Gospels as well (see, for example, Mk 8:31; 9:31; 10:33, 45; 14:21, 41 and par.).

73. Gr. ὁ υἱὸς τοῦ ἀνθρώπου.

74. Aramaic בר נשא *("bar nasha")*. This can be seen most clearly in John's Gospel in connection with Jesus' question to the man born blind, "Do you believe in the Son of man?" (that is, in "that man," the one who had healed him).

75. The closest parallel anywhere in the Gospel tradition to Pilate's "Look, the man!" (ἰδοὺ ὁ ἄνθρωπος) is perhaps Mark 14:41, where Jesus tells his sleeping disciples in Gethsemane, "Look, the Son of man is handed over [ἰδοὺ παραδίδοται ὁ υἱὸς τοῦ ἀνθρώπου] into the hands of the sinners" (compare Mt 26:45).

76. Gr. εἷς ἄνθρωπος.

18:28–19:15 JESUS, PILATE, AND THE JEWS

So much for christological hints and allusions.[77] The more immediate question is, What response does Pilate expect from the Jewish leaders by showing them "the man," crowned with thorns, beaten, and wearing a purple robe? According to Raymond Brown, all this is "arranged by Pilate as a ploy to win the sympathy of 'the Jews' for a Jesus thus pitiably disfigured."[78] This is perhaps consistent with the fact that "Look, the man!" is framed by Pilate's second and third announcements that "I find in him no probable clause" (vv. 4, 6), but it is hardly consistent with the cruel mockery that has just gone on inside the praetorium. Pilate is not trying to elicit compassion from the Jewish leaders, but only to dramatize his impression that Jesus is a pathetic and therefore harmless figure as far as the Roman government is concerned. The sight of him is calculated to evoke not so much pity as ridicule, and they can hardly be unaware that the ridicule is aimed as much at them as at Jesus. Ordinarily the kind of treatment to which Jesus has been subjected is preliminary to execution,[79] and the presentation of "the man" to the Jewish chief priests appears to be yet another invitation to them (as in 18:31) to "take him, and judge him according to your law." Once more Pilate is offering to "release to you the King of the Jews" (18:39), that they might finish the job he has started for them and put the wretched prisoner to death.[80] In short, the battle of wills goes on. Jesus must die, but at whose hands, the Romans or the Jews?

6 It appears that the Jewish "chief priests and officers" themselves

---

77. Schnackenburg (3.256-57) finds such allusions unlikely. Bultmann, without committing himself on "Son of man," makes a different point: "The declaration ὁ λόγος σὰρξ ἐγένετο has become visible in its extremest consequence" (659), that is, "It is in this sphere [flesh] that the Logos appears, i.e. the Revealer is nothing but a man. And the men who meet him take him for a man, as is seen most clearly in the ἰδοὺ ὁ ἄνθρωπος (19.5)."

78. *Death,* 1.865.

79. See Mark 15:15-20//Matthew 27:26-31, where the flogging and mockery take place after Jesus' fate has been decided, and just prior to his crucifixion (also, for example, Josephus, *War* 5.449: "They were accordingly scourged [μαστιγούμενοι] and subjected to torture of every description before being killed, and then crucified [ἀνεσταυοῦντο] opposite the walls" (LCL, 3.341). While this does not appear to be the case in Luke 23:16 ("Having disciplined him, I will release him"), the verb "disciplined" (παιδεύσας) is a much weaker verb, and may not imply the same degree of brutality.

80. Schnackenburg virtually grants this, interpreting Pilate's third pronouncement of no probable cause (v. 6) to mean "*You* do with the prisoner what you will, *I* want nothing to do with him" (3.258). This, however, comes in the context of Schnackenburg's own (and widely held) view that the Jews were not allowed (by the Romans) to execute Jesus (see 18:31b). Consequently, Pilate's only purpose, according to Schnackenburg, is to "provoke and humiliate them." But, on the other hand, if (as we have argued), they *were* allowed to impose the death penalty, then Pilate is in effect sentencing Jesus to death, only at the hands of the Jews and not the Romans.

view the flogging and mockery as preliminary to execution, for at the sight of "the man" they "cried out,[81] saying, 'Crucify, crucify!' "[82] Then "Pilate said to them, 'You take him, and crucify, for I find in him no probable cause'" (v. 6). The scene is a virtual reenactment of 18:30-31, when they first brought Jesus to Pilate without naming a specific charge, and he told them, "You take him, and judge him according to your law" (18:31). This time he is more explicit: "You take him, and crucify," that is, "you" rather than "I." The conventional wisdom among modern commentators is that "Pilate is not serious," but is simply "refusing to have anything to do with crucifying Jesus by telling them to do what both parties knew was impossible."[83] But at this point conventional wisdom is sorely tested, for Pilate's reply here (as in 18:31) implies just the opposite, that "the Jews" were perfectly free to put Jesus to death if they so chose. They had, after all, attempted to do just that, not once but twice (8:59; 10:31). On the other hand, Pilate probably does know that if "the Jews" were to put Jesus to death, it would not be by crucifixion.[84] He simply wants to throw their own words ("Crucify, crucify!") back in their faces. All he is saying is, "*You* take him. I don't care what you do with him! As for me, *I* find in him no probable cause" (this now for the third time).

7 The Jewish chief priests respond to Pilate's emphatic pronouns[85] with an emphatic pronoun of their own: "We[86] have a law, and according to the law he ought to die, because he made himself the Son of God" (v. 7).[87] That is, "Even if your law does not condemn him, ours does." And with this they reveal their real reason for wanting Jesus dead — not that he made himself "King of the Jews," posing a threat to the Romans (as in Lk 23:2, for example), but that he "made himself the Son of God."[88] This, of course, has been their charge against Jesus ever since that unnamed festival when they

---

81. Gr. ἐκραύγασαν, as in 18:40.
82. Gr. σταύρωσον σταύρωσον.
83. Brown, 2.877, who adds that they "understood that he was not serious, for they did not hasten to seize Jesus and execute him themselves. Rather they continued to press Pilate to order the execution because that was the only way it could be effected" (so also Schnackenburg 3.258; see the preceding note).
84. So Brown, 2.877: "(Moreover, John could scarcely mean that Pilate thought the Jewish leaders would carry out a *crucifixion,* for this form of punishment was not acceptable among the Jews . . .).")
85. That is, ὑμεῖς and ἐγώ.
86. Gr. ἡμεῖς.
87. The text in mind is presumably Leviticus 24:16 ("anyone who blasphemes the name of the LORD must be put to death. The entire assembly must stone him. Whether an alien or native-born, when he blasphemes the Name, he must be put to death," NIV).
88. Gr. υἱὸν θεοῦ ἑαυτὸν ἐποίησεν. Here as elsewhere it is quite plausible that υἱὸν θεοῦ (without the article) be translated "the Son of God" on the basis of Colwell's rule (see above, on 1:1), for the predicate noun precedes the verb.

began by asking, "Who is *the man?*" (5:12), and ended by "seeking all the more to kill him, because he was . . . claiming God as his own Father, making himself equal to God" (5:18), and later at the Rededication when they tried to stone Jesus to death for "blasphemy, and because you, *being a man,* are making yourself God" (10:33, italics added). Here again, Pilate's "Look, the man!" (v. 5) prompts them to forget their strategy with the governor, and recall again what this "man" has been "making himself" to be — nothing less than the Son of God! On the face of it, the notion that "according to the law he ought to die, because he made himself the Son of God" contradicts their earlier excuse that "It is not lawful for us to kill anyone" (18:31b). Once again the Gospel writer wants to expose their hypocrisy. They have told Pilate on the one hand that their law forbids the taking of life, and on the other that their law requires it in cases of blasphemy.[89] Why then do they not act on what their law requires? They have attempted to do so before (8:59 and 10:31), but now, whether because they do not have a formal conviction, or (more likely) because they lack support among the people, they are determined that Pilate will do it for them, even though he does not perceive Jesus as a political threat. In the heat of the moment they have inadvertently revealed their true reason for wanting Jesus dead, not that he claimed to be king, or posed a threat to the Romans or to the social order, but (just as before) that "he made himself the Son of God."

8-9 The effect on Pilate is unexpected, as the scene changes again: "Then, when Pilate heard this word, he was all the more afraid,[90] and he went into the praetorium again, and he says to Jesus, 'Where are you from?' But Jesus gave him no answer" (vv. 8-9). "All the more" (v. 8) sounds strange because Pilate has shown no sign of fear thus far.[91] For this reason, some have proposed that the meaning is simply that he became "very afraid."[92] More likely, "all the more" is used precisely because fear has *not* been mentioned before. That is, it is used to mean "rather," introducing an alternative. The point is that Pilate's demeanor was not what it had been before; *rather,* he became fearful.[93] Still the question remains, What was Pilate afraid of? His fear

---

89. So Chrysostom: "How then when the judge said, 'Take ye him, and judge him according to your law,' did ye reply, 'It is not lawful for us to put any man to death,' while here ye fly to the law"? (NPNF, 1st ser., 14.314).

90. Gr. μᾶλλον ἐφοβήθη.

91. Some (for example, Schnackenburg 3.260) find a hint of fear in Pilate's question "What is truth?" (18:38), but this is highly speculative.

92. That is, with μᾶλλον (the comparative of μάλα, "very," or "exceedingly") simply intensifying that idea (see Barrett, 542; Brown, 2.877). No examples are listed in BDAG, 613-14.

93. On μᾶλλον as "rather," introducing alternatives, see BDAG, 614. This is in keeping with two other uses of μᾶλλον in the Gospel: "the dark *rather than* the Light"

is said to be triggered by "this word" (v. 8), apparently the chief priests' claim that Jesus "made himself the Son of God" (v. 7). He promptly breaks off the conversation and goes back again into the praetorium, evidently taking Jesus with him. The questioning that had broken off with Pilate's dismissive "What is truth?" (18:38) now resumes. "Where are you from?"[94] (v. 9), he asks Jesus, a question that could be simply routine,[95] but more likely arises out of Pilate's fear. If Jesus "made himself the Son of God," what sort of being is he claiming to be? For the first time, Pilate seems to sense that he may be dealing with more than he bargained for. Has he scourged a god of some sort?[96]

The question of where Jesus is from[97] is not a new one.[98] The Jerusalemites at the Tent festival thought they knew (7:27), and Jesus agreed that, at least in a geographical sense, they did know, but quickly added, "I have not come on my own, but the One who sent me is true, whom you do not know" (7:28; see also 8:14, "I know where I came from and where I am going. But you do not know where I come from or where I am going"). Later, after the healing of the man born blind, they admitted that "as for this man, we don't know where he is from"[99] (9:29), just as the wedding guests did not know where the good wine was from (2:9), and the Samaritan woman did not know where the living water came from (4:11; see also 3:8). Yet no one up to

---

(3:19), and "the glory of humans *rather than* the glory of God" (12:43). More problematic is 5:18, "the Jews kept seeking *all the more* to kill him," where "all the more" (μᾶλλον) implies "more than" merely pursuing or persecuting him (5:16), and yet where the intent to kill is present already in the intent to persecute. Here, by contrast, there is nothing to prepare for or anticipate the abrupt reference to Pilate's fear.

94. Gr. πόθεν εἶ σύ.

95. That is, he could merely be asking where Jesus was from geographically. See, for example, Luke 23:6, where Pilate, before sending Jesus to Herod, asked "if the man was a Galilean." Also Josephus, *War* 6.305, where a later Roman governor, Albinus, asks "one Jesus, son of Ananias" (6.301), "who [τίς] and whence [πόθεν] he was," and the latter (like Jesus in this situation) "answered him never a word" (LCL, 3.465). The questions "who" (τίς) and "whence" (πόθεν) seem to have been standard in routine interrogations (see Abbott, *Johannine Grammar,* 568-69; see also Rev 7:13). Pilate has already asked "who" Jesus is (18:33: "king of the Jews?"), but the "whence" now takes the interrogation to another level.

96. See Philostratus, *Life of Apollonius of Tyana* 1.21, where Apollonius is asked, "'Whence [πόθεν] do you come to us, . . . and who sent you?' as if he were asking questions of a spirit" (LCL, 1.59).

97. That is, πόθεν, literally "whence."

98. It is hard to know what to make of Bultmann's comment (661, n. 6) that "It is on the lips of Gentiles that the theme of the πόθεν occurs," particularly when he goes on to cite all the right passages where it came up already in Jesus' interactions with "the Jews."

99. Gr. πόθεν ἐστίν.

now has asked him in so many words, "Where are you from?"[100] It is the perfect opportunity for Jesus to say something like "You are from below, I am from above. You are from this world, I am not from this world" (8:23), or words to that effect. Instead he says nothing at all, confirming the tradition found in other Gospels that at some point Jesus was silent in the presence of Pontius Pilate, in the face of charges leveled by the Jewish chief priests (see Mt 27:12-14//Mk 15:3-5). But here, by contrast, only Pilate is present, and the reader knows why Jesus is silent. He already answered Pilate's question when he said, "My kingship is not from this world," and "my kingship is not from here" (18:36). If it is "not from this world," it is, as we have seen, "from heaven," and if it is not "from here," it is "from above." And if Jesus' kingship is "from heaven" or "from above," he himself is from there as well (as John told us, 3:31). Jesus does not answer because he has already done so — if Pilate would only listen.

10 In contrast to Matthew and Mark, where Jesus is unresponsive to the accusations of the Jewish priests, Pilate knows that the silence is directed at him, and him alone. "Are you not speaking to me?" he persists. "To me" is placed first in the sentence for emphasis (literally, "*To me* are you not speaking?"). And "Do you not know," he adds "that I have authority[101] to release you, and I have authority to crucify you?" (v. 10). The sentence bears a striking resemblance to Jesus' claim nine chapters earlier that "I lay down my life, that I might receive it back again. . . . I have authority[102] to lay it down, and I have authority to receive it back" (10:17-18). The redundant repetition of "I have authority" in both passages links them unmistakably together, as if on a collision course. Where *does* the "authority" to settle Jesus' fate lie? With Jesus himself, as he has repeatedly claimed, or with the Roman governor? Without question, Pilate does have the legal right to have Jesus crucified, but as to his first claim, that "I have authority to release you," it is conspicuously evident that he has so far been unable to do so. Even from the standpoint of raw political power, his claim is on shaky ground.

11 Jesus could have responded by throwing in Pilate's face the earlier pronouncement, which Pilate of course has not heard: "No, you are wrong. *I* have authority to lay down my life, and *I* have authority to receive it back" (see 10:17-18). But he does not. Instead, avoiding the collision course, "Jesus answered him, 'You would have no authority against me at all[103] if it

---

100. The emphatic "you" (σύ) has drawn the attention of some interpreters (for example, Abbott, *Johannine Grammar*, 569-70, who views it as "superfluous"), but it appears to be merely part of the standard vocabulary by which Pilate and Jesus address each other (see 18:33, 34, 35, 37; 19:10).
101. Gr. ἐξουσίαν ἔχω.
102. Gr. ἐξουσίαν ἔχω.
103. Gr. οὐκ εἶχες ἐξουσίαν κατ' ἐμοῦ οὐδεμίαν.

were not given to you from above.¹⁰⁴ For this reason the one who handed me over to you has greater sin'" (v. 11). It is a very gentle response, for it applies to Pilate the same principle that applied to John, to Jesus himself, or indeed to anyone: "A person cannot receive anything unless it is given him from heaven" (3:27).¹⁰⁵ It is a response intended more for the reader of the Gospel than for Pilate, who would not have understood it. To him, "from above" would likely have meant from higher up in the imperial chain of command, ultimately from the emperor himself. But the reader is expected to understand that "from above"¹⁰⁶ means "from heaven," the place where Jesus himself is from (see 3:31). Jesus had said, "I have authority to lay down my life, and I have authority to receive it back," yet he was quick to add, "This command I received from my Father" (10:18b). Even Jesus' "authority" over his own life and death is not self-contained, but is contingent on his Father's "command." The same is true many times over of Pilate's self-proclaimed "authority" in the political and legal sphere, for Pilate is but an unknowing instrument in God's hands, while Jesus is, as he claimed, the very "Son of God," the Father's obedient messenger "from above."

The more difficult pronouncement is the corollary, "For this reason the one who handed me over to you has greater sin." Superficially, the pronouncement recalls the scene in Matthew where Pilate washes his hands and declares himself innocent of Jesus' blood, and "all the people" reply, "His blood is on us and on our children" (Mt 27:24-25). But here "the one who handed over" Jesus is singular,¹⁰⁷ obviously not "all the people."¹⁰⁸ Most immediately, the Jewish chief priests handed him over (see 18:30, 35), but the singular calls attention to Caiaphas in particular (see 18:28,

---

104. It is important to make a subtle distinction. Strictly speaking, what is "given" is not "authority" (ἐξουσίαν), for that word is feminine, while the participle "given" (δεδομένον) is neuter. Rather, what is "given" from God is the entire series of events by which Jesus has been handed over to Pilate, and Pilate now has the "authority" to exercise judgment. As Carson comments (601), "although it is true that all civil authority is mediated authority from God himself (cf. Pr. 8:15; Rom 13), that is not the point here" (so too Hoskyns, 524). Jesus is appealing rather to God's sovereignty over *all things*. For a similar use of the participle, see 6:64, "no one can come to me unless it is given [δεδομένον] him from the Father" (that is, it is "given" to a person to carry out the will of God).

105. See also 6:37, 44, 65. Also 1 Corinthians 4:7 ("What do you have that you did not receive"?) and James 1:17 ("Every good gift and every perfect gift is from above [ἄνωθεν], coming down from the Father of lights . . .").

106. Gr. ἄνωθεν.

107. Gr. ὁ παραδούς με.

108. In spite of this, Bultmann (662, n. 6) and Lindars (569) interpret it as a reference to the Jewish people as a whole, very much in keeping with Matthew 27:25. More often the onus is placed on the chief priests (Lincoln, 468; Schnackenburg, 3.262; Keener, 2.1127), again ignoring the singular (ὁ παραδούς).

"from Caiaphas").[109] Here again Pilate's understanding and that of the reader part company. Pilate could only have understood the reference to be to Caiaphas, for Caiaphas had in fact done the "handing over." Yet the words, "You would have no authority against me at all if it were not given to you from above," could just as easily have been said to Caiaphas as to Pilate. As "Chief Priest of that year," and as someone able to "prophesy" (11:51), Caiaphas surely stood as much (or more) under the sovereignty of God as Pilate. Therefore, the reader will inevitably think of Judas as "the one who handed over" Jesus to the authorities, Jewish and then Roman, thus betraying him death.[110] This is in keeping with the way Judas has been designated quite consistently in the Gospel (see 6:64, 71; 12:4; 13:2, 11, 21). And yet even Judas's act of betrayal was "so that the Scripture might be fulfilled" (13:18; 17:12), implying that it too was in some way decreed or given "from above."

Quite possibly the reader is meant to go even a step further back, remembering that before the last meal and the footwashing, "the devil ... put it into the heart so that Judas Iscariot of Simon might hand him over" (13:2). While Judas himself is called "the devil" for doing the devil's work (6:70), and the Jewish leaders have been told, "You are from the father [who is] the devil, and you choose to do the desires of your father" (8:44), the one with "greater sin"[111] is perhaps best identified as the original devil of the Genesis story, "homicidal from the beginning," both "the liar and the father of it" (8:44).[112] As we have seen, while Jesus never explicitly forgives sin in this Gospel, he does retain or convict of sin repeatedly (see 8:21, 24; 9:41; 15:22, 24), and now he does so again. "Greater sin" implies that Pilate too is guilty of sin (and Caiaphas and Judas all the more), but he places the ultimate guilt right where it belongs (see 1 Jn 3:8, "the devil sins from the beginning; for this the Son of God is revealed, that he might destroy the works of the devil"). At this point, the stark dualism of the Gospel is evident, for Jesus is

---

109. So Morris (705); Carson (601); Moloney (500); Beasley-Murray (340); also Brown (2.879), but specifically "as representative of the Jews."

110. So, for example, Barrett, 543. It is difficult to say whether or not Pilate would have known anything about Judas. The only possible evidence that he might have is Judas's role in leading Roman troops as well as Jewish priests and Pharisees to the place where Jesus was arrested (see 18:2-3).

111. Gr. μείζονα ἁμαρτίαν.

112. Still, it is arguable that there is no point in distinguishing between the devil and his human instrument (see above, on 6:70). Hoskyns (524) summarizes, "the greater sin attaches to the Jews who delivered Jesus into Pilate's hands, and especially to the apostate disciple who betrayed Him (xiii. 2, 11, 21, xviii. 2, 5). This murderous activity, however, has its ultimate source in the homicidal energy of the Devil, who is the prince of the world (viii. 44, xii. 31, xiii. 2, 27)."

unwilling to say of the devil what he says of Pilate, that is, that anything about him is "from above" (see 14:30, "in me he has nothing").

12 The conversation is over. We may assume that at this point Pilate went out again (alone) to address the Jewish chief priests, for we are told, "From this time, Pilate kept seeking to release him, but the Jews cried out,[113] saying, 'If you release this one, you are not a friend of Caesar. Everyone who makes himself king opposes Caesar'" (v. 12). "From this"[114] could mean either "From this moment on," or "As a result of this," but in this case (as in 6:66) it is clearly the latter. Pilate has, after all, been trying to have Jesus released ever since he first questioned him (see 18:38, 39; 19:4, 6). The tense of the verb ("was seeking," or "kept seeking")[115] suggests that he simply continued what he was trying to do all along, either by saying yet again, "I find in him no probable cause," or in other ways. But what is it that happened "as a result of this"? Not that he tried to have Jesus released, for he had done that already. Rather, that "the Jews" responded in the way they did, going over Pilate's head as it were to invoke the power of the emperor: "If you release this one, you are not a friend of Caesar."[116] Unfortunately for Pilate, the words of Jesus, "You would have no authority against me at all if it were not given to you from above" (v. 11) are still ringing in his ears, words which, as we have seen, he would have heard as a reference to Caesar and the Roman imperial authority. The Jewish priests, abruptly changing their tactics, are now invoking that very authority "from above" as a veiled threat against him.[117] Surely

---

113. Gr. ἐκραύγασαν, now for the third time (see 18:40; 19:6).

114. Gr. ἐκ τούτου.

115. Perhaps coincidentally, the notion of "seeking" (ἐζήτει) to release Jesus stands in sharp contrast to the now familiar language about the Jewish authorities "seeking" (ἐζήτουν) to arrest and kill him (see 5:18; 7:1, 11, 19, 25, 30, 34; 8:37, 40; 10:39; 11:8).

116. It is debated whether or not the phrase "friend of Caesar" (φίλος τοῦ Καίσαρι) refers to a specific honorific title *(amicus Caesaris)* bestowed on certain senators and other officials for service to the empire (for the argument that it does, see E. Bammel, *"Philos tou Kaisaros," Theologische Literaturzeitung* 77 [1952], 205-10). This is often made the basis of a supposition that Philo's patron had been Sejanus, prefect of the praetorian guard, who was deposed and put to death right around this time. According to Tacitus (*Annals* 6.8), "Whoever was close to Sejanus had a claim on the friendship of Caesar" *(ad Caesaris amicitiam)*. Philo characterizes Sejanus as notoriously anti-Semitic (*Against Flaccus* 1; *Embassy to Gaius* 160), but if this was the case (and it is not verified by other sources), it is the only link between Sejanus and Pilate, and even Philo draws no direct connection between the two. If "friend of Caesar" was a technical term, it is unclear whether Pilate already enjoyed this status and was fearful of losing it, or whether he merely aspired to it.

117. The threat invites comparison with a threat (to send an embassy to Caesar) leveled against him by Jewish authorities in response to his having brought Roman shields

a coincidence, it seems, for "the Jews" were not privy to the conversation between Pilate and Jesus (vv. 8-11). And yet, we are told, their appeal to the higher authority arises "from this," or "as a result of this." Where is the connection? Possibly in the redemptive plan of God, although the Gospel writer does not press the point. But whether that is the case or not, the connection in Pilate's mind is very real. That is, the threat that if he releases Jesus, he will lose favor with the emperor (v. 12) serves to reinforce his misunderstanding of Jesus' warning that the only authority he has is "from above" (v. 11). Its inevitable effect will be to heighten his fears (see v. 8), and bring him finally to the point of handing Jesus over to death (see v. 16).

Yet why should the release of one fugitive cause Pilate to lose favor with the emperor? The Jewish priests explain themselves further, shifting their ground once more: "Everyone who makes himself king opposes Caesar" (v. 12b). Previously, the charge had been that Jesus "made himself the Son of God" (v. 7), a religious charge which, as we have seen, was their real reason for wanting to kill Jesus (see 5:18; 10:33). Now they have changed it back to the political charge that was implied in bringing Jesus to Pilate in the first place (see 18:30; also Lk 23:2), the charge that Jesus "makes himself king."[118] This means that he "opposes Caesar,"[119] and by implication that Pilate himself is "opposing Caesar" in refusing to prosecute such a person. The identification of "Son of God" and "King" is something the reader understands, for Nathanael paired the two titles right from the start (1:49), and the reader knows full well that Jesus *is* both "Son of God" and "King of Israel" (see also 10:36; 12:13). What is not true is that he has "made himself" either of those things. He is, on the contrary, One "whom the Father consecrated and sent into the world" (10:36), and "the One coming in the name of the Lord" (12:13), who speaks and acts *not* "on his own" (*aph' heautou;* see, for example, 5:18; 7:18), but always at the Father's command. The accusation by the chief priests that he "makes himself king" simply ignores Pilate's thrice-repeated verdict that "I find in him no probable cause" (18:38; 19:4, 6), made on the basis of a conversation with Jesus specifically about kingship (18:33-37). There is nothing new here, but circumstances

---

into Herod's palace, in violation of Jewish law (see Philo, *Embassy to Gaius* 302, where we are told, "he feared that if they actually sent an embassy they would also expose the rest of his conduct as governor by stating in full the briberies, the insults, the robberies, the outrages and wanton injuries, the executions without trial constantly repeated, the ceaseless and supremely grievous cruelty" (LCL, 10.153). While Philo claims that these shields "had no image work traced on them" (299), Josephus (*War* 2.169) speaks of "effigies of Caesar," which would explain the uproar.

118. Gr. βασιλέα ἑαυτὸν ποιῶν.

119. Gr. αντιλέγει τῷ Καίσαρι. Ἀντιλέγει is literally "to speak against" or "contradict," but also "to oppose" or "reject" (see BDAG, 89).

have changed. Pilate now fears for his political future, and he takes immediate action.

13-14 Pilate's action here is triggered (just as in v. 8) by a pronouncement of "the Jews." In verse 8 they spoke of Jesus "making himself the Son of God," and "when Pilate heard this word" he was afraid and went in to speak with Jesus. Here they have just spoken of Jesus "making himself king," and "Pilate, when he heard these words,[120] led Jesus outside and sat down on the judge's bench at a place called Stone Pavement, and in Hebrew *Gabbatha*. Now it was the preparation of the Passover; it was about the sixth hour. And he says to the Jews, 'Look, your king!'" (vv. 13-14). That he "led Jesus outside" probably does not mean that he went back into the praetorium but (as in v. 4) that he ordered guards to bring Jesus out. He then "sat down on the judge's bench"[121] as if to issue a definitive verdict, just as he did (according to Josephus) when he was challenged by the Jews over the issue of bringing effigies of Caesar into Jerusalem.[122] Some have argued that the verb is transitive (as it sometimes can be),[123] so as to yield the translation, "Pilate seated [Jesus] on the judge's bench."[124] This is in fact the case in certain second-century traditions in which Jesus is seated and mockingly commanded, "Judge us" (Justin, *First Apology* 35),[125] or "Judge righteously, O King of Israel" (*Gospel of Peter* 3.7).[126] But this is no mocking scene. The mockery is over (see vv. 2-5), and (as Brown notices)[127] Jesus is no longer said to be wearing the purple robe and the crown of thorns. It is a solemn and decisive moment, and the Gospel writer underscores the solemnity by taking careful notice of the exact place and time. Pilate takes his seat in order to an-

---

120. Gr. ἀκούσας τῶν λόγων τούτων. The distinction between ἀκούειν ("to hear") with the accusative (v. 8) and with the genitive (v. 13), in which the former means simply to hear and the latter to take heed and obey, should not be pressed (as Edwin Abbott does; see *Johannine Vocabulary,* 116; *Johannine Grammar,* 435). Pilate is in no sense "obeying" the Jewish chief priests at this point.

121. Gr. ἐκάθισεν ἐπὶ βήματος.

122. See Josephus, *War* 2.172, καθίσας ἐπὶ βήματος.

123. See BDAG, 491-92.

124. In particular, see I. de la Potterie, "Jésus, Roi at Juge d'Après Jn 19, 13: *ekathisen epi bēmatos*," *Biblica* 41 (1960), 217-47.

125. Here, however, the verb is plural, "*they* seated him on the judge's bench" (ἐκάθισαν ἐπὶ βήματος), "they" being "the Jews," not Pilate.

126. Here too the verb is plural, "*they* seated him on the seat of judgement" (ἐκάθισαν αὐτὸν ἐπὶ καθέδραν κρίσεως), and again the perpetrators are "the Jews" or "the people," not Pilate. Both here and in Justin Martyr, the procedure is more akin to what goes on in the synoptic Gospels after the trial before Caiaphas and before Jesus is sent to Pilate, when he is mockingly commanded to "Prophesy!" (see Mt 27:67-68//Mk 14:65// Lk 22:63-65).

127. *Death,* 1.848.

nounce his decision "at a place called Stone Pavement,[128] and in Hebrew Gabbatha."

This location is now unknown. Tourists today are shown a very ancient pavement (over two thousand square yards in area!) at the site of the Fortress Antonia, but this is unlikely. Not only is the Antonia no longer believed to be the site of Pilate's praetorium,[129] but the text seems to require a more specific location than the pavement shown today, which has the same general appearance that any large public square would have had, and in any event probably dates from no earlier than the second century. More likely, the "Stone Pavement" was a platform of some kind (possibly marked by a mosaic) on which the "judge's bench"[130] stood. Moreover, "Gabbatha" is not the Hebrew translation of the Greek word for "Stone Pavement," but rather an Aramaic word of uncertain meaning, possibly referring to a height or ridge of some kind (whether natural or man-made).[131] It seems to have been simply the name given by the Jews to the specific "place" known to Pilate and the Romans as "Stone Pavement." It is doubtful that the Gospel writer actually expected his readers to know and visualize the location, any more than he expected them to know the location of the pool of Bethsaida (5:2), or Siloam (9:7), or the "portico of Solomon" (10:23), or for that matter "Golgotha" (19:17). The notice simply lends concreteness to the narrative, telling the reader that these were real events that happened at a particular time and place, not forgotten but known and remembered by the author and other witnesses.

To the same end the Gospel writer adds a narrative aside, "Now it was the preparation of the Passover;[132] it was about the sixth hour," and, resuming the narrative, goes on to tell us that Pilate then "says to the Jews, 'Look, your king!'"[133] (v. 14). The two designations of time ("preparation of the Passover," and "the sixth hour"), closely linked to the presentation of Jesus as king, seem to carry more weight than the two designations of place ("Stone Pavement" and "*Gabbatha*"). The "preparation" normally meant Friday, the day before Sabbath (see Mk 15:42), but in connection with "the Passover" it refers to the day before Passover, when lambs were slaughtered in "preparation" for the Passover meal. Although the Gospel writer does not labor the point, Jesus, "the Lamb of God" (1:29), will die on that very day. That it was

128. Gr. Λιθόστρωτον.
129. See above, n. 3.
130. Gr. βῆμα.
131. See BDAG, 185-86, which cites a reference in Josephus (*War* 5.51) to Gibeah, Saul's birthplace north of Jerusalem as Γαβὰθ Σαούλ, which he translates as λόφον Σαούλου ("Saul's ridge").
132. Gr. παρασκευὴ τοῦ πάσχα.
133. Gr. ἴδε ὁ βασιλεὺς ὑμῶν.

indeed the "preparation" in that sense was clear from the moment Jesus was brought to Pilate, when those who brought him "did not go into the praetorium, so that they might not be defiled but might eat the Passover" (18:28). Later, however, we will learn that it was the "preparation" in *both* senses, for it seems to have been a year in which the Passover also fell on a Sabbath (see below, vv. 31, 42).[134]

As for the notice that "it was about the sixth hour,"[135] any reader familiar with other Gospels will notice a conflict with the tradition that "It was the third hour when they crucified him" (Mk 15:25). It is commonly agreed that in the Gospels (as in the Mediterranean world generally) daytime was reckoned from 6:00 a.m. on,[136] so that "the third hour" would be 9:00 a.m. and "the sixth hour" noon.[137] A surprising number of commentators have theorized that "the sixth hour" is a Johannine invention designed to make the point that Jesus was crucified at the precise time the Passover lambs were being slaughtered in the temple.[138] But the evidence for this is late and obscure (according to Exod 12:6, the lambs were to be slaughtered "at twilight"), and one would expect the Gospel writer to call attention to such a remarkable correspondence. It is better to content ourself with the recognition that while the text "does link Jesus' death with the slaughter of the Passover lambs in the temple," the link is "of the day rather than the hour."[139] This means that "the sixth hour" as the approximate time of the presentation and crucifixion of Jesus is not merely a theological construction, but is to be taken seriously as a tradition independent of Mark. It should also be noted that all three synoptic Gospels testify to "the sixth

---

134. For another instance in which a Jewish festival overlaps with the Sabbath, see 5:1 ("there was a festival of the Jews") in connection with 5:9 ("But it was the Sabbath that day"). Some have argued that this was the case also in 9:14 ("Now it was Sabbath on the day Jesus made the mud and opened his eye"), but this is unlikely.

135. Gr. ὥρα ἦν ὡς ἕκτη.

136. See above, on 1:39.

137. Instead of "sixth" (ἕκτη), some ancient witnesses (including a corrector of ℵ, an addition to D, plus L, Ψ, and a few others) have "third" (τρίτη), as Metzger puts it, "an obvious attempt to harmonize 'the chronology with that of Mk 15.25'" (*Textual Commentary*, 252). This is reflected also in John Wesley's 1755 translation (*Explanatory Notes*, 280, "about the third hour").

138. See, for example, Brown, 2.883, 895; Schnackenburg, 3.265; Bultmann, 664, 677. The arguments for moving from "twilight," or "between two evenings" (Exod 12:6), to midday (see Brown, *Death*, 1.847, n. 47) are too complex and cumbersome to be convincing.

139. Keener, 2.1131, who also comments helpfully, "Even if our information concerning the time of the paschal sacrifice is correct, however, it was not widely known to John's audience; even those who had gone as pilgrims had undoubtedly simply gotten their own lambs slaughtered when they could" (2.1130).

hour" as the time when darkness began to "cover the whole earth" (Mt 27:45//Mk 15:33//Lk 23:44).[140]

In the interest of harmonization, some have proposed that in this instance, the new day began at midnight (as in Roman law),[141] so that "the sixth hour" would be 6:00 a.m., but besides being inconsistent with other time references in the Gospel of John (1:39; 4:6, 52), this expedient creates more problems than it solves. Too much has happened since "early morning" (18:28) for "the sixth hour" to be only 6:00 a.m. Moreover, if we are to have the crucifixion at 9:00 a.m. (as in Mark), the three hours that must still elapse between verse 14 and verse 17 (when Jesus is crucified) are left unaccounted for. And why would the Gospel writer fix the time of Jesus' presentation as king so precisely and the time of his crucifixion not at all? It appears rather that the Gospel writer wants to call attention to *two* decisive events, close together in time — the presentation as king (vv. 13-14), and the crucifixion (vv. 17-18) — each linked to a specific place identified with both a Greek and a Semitic name (vv. 13, 17), with an approximate time designation in between, sufficient to locate both ("it was *about* the sixth hour"). If — as is generally agreed — the crucifixion is Jesus' "lifting up" (as in 3:14; 8:28; 12:32), it is just as plausible to think of the presentation, "Look, your king!" as his "glorification" (as in 7:39; 11:4; 12:16, 23, 28; 13:31-32; 17:1, 5), for the one is no less ironic than the other. As far as the Gospel writer is concerned, whatever the shame of crucifixion, Jesus *was* in fact "lifted up" to the Father, and whatever Pilate's motivation, "glorified" here as "Son of God" and "King" (see vv. 7, 12).

And what was Pilate's motivation? It appears that "Look,[142] your king!" has a performative quality that "Look,[143] the man!" (v. 5) does not have. Jesus is obviously a man, but not so obviously a king, and, rhetorically at least, Pilate is making him a king. Clearly, the pronouncement is a direct response to the threat of "the Jews" that "If you release this one, you are not a friend of Caesar," because "Everyone who makes himself king opposes Caesar" (v. 12). The accent, therefore, in the words, "Look, your king!" falls on "your."[144] Pilate is saying, in effect, "How dare you threaten me! He is *your* king after all!" The reader cannot help but recall his earlier words, whether to them ("*You* take him, and judge him according to *your* law,"

---

140. Strictly speaking, it is only Mark that places the crucifixion at "the third hour" (Mk 15:25); Matthew and Luke set no time for the actual crucifixion, but simply take note of the onset of darkness at noon and of Jesus' death at "the ninth hour."

141. See Westcott, 2.324-26, who is nevertheless willing to admit that "this mode of reckoning was unusual in ancient times" (2.326).

142. Gr. ἴδε.

143. Gr. ἰδού.

144. Gr. ὑμῶν.

18:31, and "*You* take him, and crucify," 19:6), or to Jesus ("Am *I* a Jew? *Your* nation and the chief priests handed you over to me," 18:35). All along he has tried to dissociate himself from them and their grievances. Now that they have threatened to accuse him of disloyalty to Caesar, he throws the word "king" back in their faces. If Jesus is in any sense "King of the Jews" (18:33, 39; 19:3), then it is they, not he, who are disloyal to Caesar.

15 The drama continues: "They then cried out, 'Take, take! Crucify him!' Pilate says to them, 'Shall I crucify your king?' The chief priests answered, 'We have no king except Caesar!'" (v. 15). Dodging for a moment the issue of their own loyalty, they once again "cried out,"[145] now for the fourth time (see 18:40; 19:6, 12), as the redoubled "Take, take! Crucify him!" picks up the redoubled "Crucify, crucify!" of verse 6. Again Pilate throws their own word back in their faces, this time (as in v. 6), the word "Crucify." "Shall I crucify your king?" he asks, reminding them once again that the issue is not his loyalty to Caesar but rather, "Who is *your* king?"

On the positive side, Pilate's question, "Shall I crucify your king?"[146] juxtaposes for the reader crucifixion and kingship, allowing two seemingly incompatible notions to illumine and interpret each other. Jesus will indeed reign as king in this Gospel — of the Jews, and of all people — not from a throne but from a cross, for his violent and shameful death will reveal once and forever his eternal kingship. But on the negative side, deliberately or not, Pilate's question forces from the Jewish priests a pledge of allegiance to Rome: "We have no king except Caesar!" (v. 15b). It is the final irony. Not content with rejecting Jesus, "the Jews" reject their own Jewishness. Any discussion of the so-called anti-Semitism or anti-Judaism of the Gospel of John must take account of the fact that in the eyes of the Gospel writer those who crucify Jesus are no longer "Jews" in any meaningful way, but loyal subjects of Rome who acknowledge "no king except Caesar" — in that sense Romans! Their bold words, "We are Abraham's seed, and have never been in slavery to anyone" (8:33), now ring more hollow than ever. In denying Jesus they have denied as well any hope of a messianic king, and beyond that even the kingship of their God, the God of Israel. While not as hurtful or anti-Semitic in its long-range effects, "no king except Caesar" in John's Gospel is in its way no less disturbing than Matthew's "His blood be on us and on our children" (Mt 27:25), for it presents a Judaism that — momentarily at least — denies its very existence.[147]

---

145. Gr. ἐκραύγασαν.
146. Gr. τὸν βασιλέα ὑμῶν σταυρώσω.
147. See Brown's discussion in *Death*, 1.848-49.

C. THE CRUCIFIXION AND BURIAL (19:16-42)

16 *So then he handed him over to them that he might be crucified. Then they received Jesus,* 17 *and bearing the cross for himself, he went out to what is called Skull Place, which is called in Hebrew Golgotha,* 18 *where they crucified him, and with him two others on either side, Jesus in the middle.* 19 *And Pilate wrote a title and placed it on the cross. And it was written, "Jesus the Nazorean, the King of the Jews."* 20 *Now many of the Jews read this title, because the place where Jesus was crucified was near the city, and it was written in Hebrew, Latin, and Greek.* 21 *So the chief priests of the Jews said to Pilate, "Do not write 'the King of the Jews,'" but that he said, "I am the King of the Jews."* 22 *Pilate answered, "What I have written I have written."*

23 *Then the soldiers, when they crucified Jesus, took his garments and made four parts, a part for each soldier, and the tunic. But the tunic was seamless, woven throughout from the top.* 24 *So they said to one another, "Let us not tear it, but let us gamble for it, whose it will be," that the scripture might be fulfilled that says, "They divided my garments to themselves, and for my garment they cast lots." So the soldiers did these things.*

25 *Now standing by the cross of Jesus were his mother and the sister of his mother, Mary of Clopas, and Mary Magdalene.* 26 *So Jesus, seeing the mother, and the disciple whom he loved standing by, says to the mother, "Woman, look, your son!"* 27 *Then he says to the disciple, "Look, your mother!" And from that hour the disciple took her to his own home.*

28 *After this, Jesus, knowing that all things are already finished, so that the scripture might be completed, says, "I am thirsty."* 29 *A vessel full of sour wine was set there, so they put a sponge full of sour wine on a stalk of hyssop and brought it to this mouth.* 30 *Then when he received the sour wine, Jesus said, "It is finished," and he bowed the head and handed over the Spirit.*

31 *Now the Jews, because it was the preparation, so that the bodies would not remain on the cross on the Sabbath — for great was the day of that Sabbath — asked Pilate that their legs be broken and that they be taken away.* 32 *So the soldiers came, and broke the legs of the first, and of the other who was crucified with him.* 33 *But when they came to Jesus, as they saw he was already dead, they did not break his legs,* 34 *but one of the soldiers punctured his side with a spear, and at once blood and water came out.* 35 *And he who has seen has testified, and his testimony is true, and that one knows that he tells the truth, so that you too might believe.* 36 *For these things happened so that the*

scripture might be fulfilled, "No bone of him shall be broken," 37 *and again, another scripture says, "They will see him whom they pierced."*
38 *Now after these things, Joseph from Arimathea, being a disciple of Jesus secretly for fear of the Jews, asked Pilate that he might take away the body of Jesus, and Pilate gave permission. So he came, and took away his body.* 39 *And Nicodemus also came — he who at the first came to him at night — bringing a mixture of myrrh and aloes, about a hundred pounds.* 40 *So they took the body of Jesus and bound it in linen cloths with the spices, as is the custom of the Jews to bury.* 41 *And there was in the place where he was crucified a garden, and in the garden a new tomb in which no one had yet been laid.* 42 *So there, on account of the preparation of the Jews, because the tomb was nearby, they laid Jesus.*

Taking the Jewish chief priests at their word that they are loyal Romans, with "no king but Caesar" (v. 15), Pilate finally hands Jesus over *to them* to be crucified (v. 16). The implication is that even though crucifixion was a distinctly Roman method of execution, in the end "the Jews" crucified Jesus, as surely as if they drove the nails with their own hands. The crucifixion takes place almost immediately (vv. 16-18). Jesus carries his own cross to the place of execution, and four Roman soldiers quickly carry out the will of the Jewish chief priests. At the same time, the ironic title over the cross gives the lie to their insistence that Caesar is their only king (vv. 19-22). Then, in a series of brief vignettes, Jesus is stripped of his clothing (vv. 23-24), and gives up his closest human relationships (vv. 25-27) and finally life itself (vv. 28-30), the first and last of these in explicit fulfillment of scripture (vv. 24, 28).

The theme of fulfillment continues after his death, as the legs of two other prisoners are broken to hasten death (before the beginning of Sabbath), but his are not because he is already dead (vv. 31-33). Instead a spear is thrust into his side, blood and water come out (v. 34), and an anonymous witness is introduced, solemnly testifying to what has happened (v. 35). All this, we are told, was to fulfill two specific passages of scripture (vv. 36-37). The burial is carried out by Joseph of Arimathea, a disciple "secretly for fear of the Jews," with the help of Nicodemus, "who first came to him at night" (see 3:2) and who brings now an enormous quantity of spices for embalming the body. Because the Passover festival is about to begin, Jesus is quickly buried in a new tomb, in a garden right near the place where he was crucified. The account of his arrest and execution ends, as it began (18:1), in a garden.

16-18 The account of the crucifixion begins with a startling reversal: "So then he [Pilate] handed him over to them[1] that he might be crucified"

1. Gr. παρέδωκεν αὐτόν αὐτοῖς.

19:16-42 THE CRUCIFIXION AND BURIAL

(v. 16a). Pilate's involvement had begun when they first "handed over" Jesus to him (see 18:30) for crucifixion, and now, it seems, he returns the favor! "To them" can only refer to "the Jews" (v. 14,) or "the chief priests" (v. 15). In spite of the clear implication that crucifixion was a Roman and not a Jewish method of execution (see 18:32), we now learn that "the Jews" will crucify Jesus after all![2] This is not totally unexpected, for Jesus told them long before at the Tent festival that they would one day "lift up the Son of man" (8:28), nor is it inconsistent with other early Christian narratives of Jesus' death.[3] Here, moreover, it is qualified by the new reality that they are no longer "Jews" at all, but true Romans with allegiance to no one but Caesar (v. 15).

In any event, they are quick to carry out their assigned task: "Then they received Jesus, and bearing the cross for himself he went out to what is called Skull Place, which is called in Hebrew Golgotha, where they crucified him, and with him two others on either side, Jesus in the middle" (vv. 16b-18). "The Jews" are clearly the subject of the verb "received"[4] and probably of the verb "crucified" as well. Alternatively, it is possible that the third person plural, "crucified,"[5] is impersonal, with an indefinite subject: that is, "they crucified him" — as in the old spiritual, "Were you there when they crucified my Lord?" — meaning simply that Jesus "was crucified" by someone.[6] Later, as we will see, Roman soldiers will be said to have "crucified" him (v. 23). But the more likely meaning here is that the Jewish chief priests "crucified" Jesus

---

2. This is deliberate, and by no means the result of "careless narrative style" (so Brown, *Death,* 1.855). Brown's comments that "Johannine Christians knew perfectly well that Roman soldiers did the crucifying," and that "One should not press grammatical antecedents as if the readers knew nothing of 'the passion' before the Gospel was written" (1.856) are quite true, but also quite irrelevant.

3. See, for example, Luke 23:25 ("he handed Jesus over to their will"); also Acts 2:36 ("this Jesus whom you crucified") and 4:10 ("whom you crucified"). In a more eloquent vein, see Melito, *On the Passover* 75-77: "it was necessary for him to be crucified, but not by you, nor by your right hand. . . . You ought to have cried aloud to God with this voice, . . . 'Let him be crucified by the tyrannical right hand, but not by mine.' But you, O Israel, did not cry out to God with this voice, nor did you absolve yourself of guilt before the Lord, nor were you persuaded by his works" (G. F. Hawthorne, "A New English Translation of Melito's Paschal Homily," in *Current Issues in Biblical and Patristic Interpretation* [Grand Rapids: Eerdmans, 1975], 167).

4. Gr. παρέλαβον. There is irony — unintended, to be sure — in the verb "received" (παρέλαβον) in light of 1:11, "and his own did not receive him" (οὐ παρέλαβον). Here, just as in the vocabulary of "handing down" tradition (see 1 Cor 15:3), the verb "received" is simply the corollary to "handed over" (παρέδωκεν, v. 16a). As such, it probably has a relatively passive meaning here ("received" rather than "took"), in contrast to "crucified," and in contrast to their own earlier outcry, "Take, take [ἆρον ἆρον]! Crucify him!" (v. 15).

5. Gr. ἐσταύρωσαν.

6. See BDF, §130[2]; Abbott, *Johannine Grammar,* 310-11.

in the sense of having him crucified,[7] even though the Roman soldiers would finally drive the nails. There is no way to tell how much time elapses between the moment "they received Jesus" from Pilate, presumably "about the sixth hour" (v. 14), and the time of his actual crucifixion. However long it may have been in real time, it is very short in narrative time, and there is little doubt that "about the sixth hour" was intended to fix the approximate time of both.

There is no Simon of Cyrene to carry (or help carry) Jesus' cross, as in the other Gospels (see Mt 27:32//Mk 15:21//Lk 23:26), and no *Via Dolorosa* as in Luke (23:27-31). Rather, "bearing the cross for himself, he went out to what is called Skull Place, which is called in Hebrew *Golgotha*" (v. 17). "For himself"[8] keeps alive his firm commitment that no one takes his life from him (even to the extent of helping him on his way to the cross), but that "I lay it down on my own" (10:18). That he "went out" no longer refers to coming out of the praetorium (as in 18:29, 38; 19:4, 5,13), but now presumably to going out of the city (see also Mt 27:32; Mk 15:20; Lk 23:26) to a definite "place"[9] both public and "near the city" (see v. 20), and carefully identified with both Greek and Hebrew names, like Pilate's "Stone Pavement" (v. 14). Unlike the latter, this place is so identified in two other Gospels as well (see Mt 27:33//Mk 15:22), as "Skull Place,"[10] or *"Golgotha,"*[11] names attested nowhere outside the New Testament. In later tradition, "Skull Place" was understood as a hill or promontory, probably because of the comparison to a rounded skull,[12] and this assumption may well have guided the fourth-century placement of the site at what became the traditional location within the Church of the Holy Sepulchre, now inside the walls of Jerusalem but in the time of Jesus outside the walls. Certainly it helped guide modern theorists to the so-called "Gordon's Calvary" next to the Garden Tomb. While the latter is by no means the authentic site, it does capture something of the very

---

7. This in the same sense in which Pilate "took Jesus and had him flogged" (v. 1), and "led" him outside" (vv. 4, 13), and later "wrote a title and placed it on the cross" (v. 19).

8. Gr. ἑαυτῷ.

9. Gr. τόπον.

10. Gr. Κρανίου Τόπον.

11. In Luke 23:33 it is called simply "Skull" (Κρανίον; in Latin *calvaria* and in KJV, "Calvary"). John's Gospel differs from Matthew and Mark only in putting the Greek name first, as he has done also in verse 13 ("Stone Pavement [Λιθόστρωτον], and in Hebrew *Gabbatha*"), and this contrary to his usual practice (see 1:38, 41, 42, where the Hebrew comes first and then the Greek translation). The apparent reason for this is there the Gospel writer was interpreting Hebrew words used by participants in his story, while here, choosing his own words, he names the places first in the language his readers will understand before providing the esoteric-sounding Semitic equivalent.

12. *Golgotha,* like *Gabbatha,* is Aramaic rather than biblical Hebrew. As we have seen, the name *Gabbatha* (v. 14) is actually more evocative of a height or a hill than the name *Golgotha.*

19:16-42 THE CRUCIFIXION AND BURIAL

public nature of Jesus' crucifixion, for it stands visible to all, right over a bus station and just outside the Damascus Gate.

The crucifixion itself is told simply, with an economy of words: "they crucified him, and with him two others on either side, Jesus in the middle" (v. 18). The "two others," identified more explicitly in Matthew (27:38) and in Mark (15:27) as "terrorists"[13] and in Luke (23:33) as "criminals," are introduced abruptly, with no explanation as to why they are being crucified, or whether they too were "handed over" from Pilate to the Jews for execution. Presumably they were among those on "death row" from whom Barabbas had been chosen as the "one at the Passover" to be spared (see 18:39). Just as in the other three Gospels, the writer is careful to describe the scene so that readers can visualize it: Jesus in the center, with "two others on either side,"[14] each on his own cross. But in contrast to the synoptic Gospels (notably Lk 23:39-43, but see also Mt 27:44//Mk 15:32), we will hear nothing more of them until after Jesus has died. They are introduced here simply to set up the contrast between what is eventually done to them and what is done to Jesus (see vv. 31-33).

19 The reader's attention is focused on the middle cross: "And Pilate wrote a title and placed it on the cross. And it was written, 'Jesus the Nazorean, the King of the Jews'" (v. 19). The "title"[15] or notice over Jesus' cross is mentioned in all the Gospels,[16] but only here is Jesus called "Jesus the Nazorean," drawing together the whole narrative from the moment the Jewish priests and Roman soldiers first announced that they were seeking "Jesus the Nazorean" (18:5, 7) up to the present. And only here is it Pilate himself who "wrote" it (that is, had it written) and had it fastened to the cross. Only here, consequently, does it become an issue between Pilate and "the Jews," who are not satisfied with the wording.[17]

20 The issue arises because the site was so public, and the notice so plain for all to see: "Now many of the Jews read this title, because the place where Jesus was crucified was near the city, and it was written in Hebrew,[18]

---

13. Gr. λῃσταί.
14. Gr. ἐντεῦθεν καὶ ἐντεῦθεν. John's Gospel is obviously not influenced by the *precise language* of the other Gospels, all of whom say "one on the right and one on the left" (Mt 27:38//Mk 15:27//Lk 23:33), rather than "on either side" (ἐντεῦθεν καὶ ἐντεῦθεν, literally "from here and from here").
15. Gr. τίτλον, from the Latin *titulus*.
16. The wording varies from "This is Jesus, the King of the Jews" (Mt 27:37), to simply "The King of the Jews" (Mk 15:26), or "This is the King of the Jews" (Lk 23:38).
17. In Matthew and Mark it is not called a "title," or "inscription" (ἐπιγραφή), as in Luke, but rather the "charge" (αἰτία) or "probable cause" against Jesus (something Pilate does not even recognize in John's Gospel; see 18:38; 19:4, 6).
18. As in the case of *Golgotha* (v. 17) and *Gabbatha* (v. 13), Aramaic is probably meant.

Latin, and Greek" (v. 20). That it was "near the city" confirms the impression that it was outside the city wall (see v. 17), in keeping both with Jewish customs regarding executions (see Lev 24:14; Num 15:35; 1 Kgs 21:3; Acts 7:58),[19] and with other ancient traditions about Jesus' death (see, for example, Heb 13:12; Mt 21:39//Mk 12:8//Lk 20:15). As for the notice itself, its implication that the Jews are a people whose miserable "king" hangs on a cross, offends them, and is made all the worse by being publicly accessible as well to Gentiles passing by who read only Greek or Latin. Pilate is rubbing salt in old wounds, the wounds that were opened when he repeatedly called Jesus "the King of the Jews" (see 18:33, 39; 19:3, 5), and finally presented him as "your king" (see vv. 14, 15).

21-22 Knowing that they cannot persuade Pilate to remove the notice altogether, "the chief priests of the Jews" urge him, "Do not write 'the King of the Jews,' but that he said, 'I am the King of the Jews'" (v. 21). In fact, Jesus had carefully avoided saying any such thing (see 18:34-37), even though the reader knows it is true (see 1:49; 12:13, 15), and the reader is vindicated by Pilate's abrupt and dismissive answer, "What I have written I have written"[20] (v. 22). The repeated accent on "writing," and what "was written" (vv. 19, 20), gives the notice an authoritative quality, almost comparable to the authority of Scripture (see 2:17; 6:31, 45; 8:17; 10:34; 12:14, 16; 15:25), or the Gospel of John itself (20:30, 31). What is "written" is fixed and not subject to change: Jesus is truly "the King of the Jews"! Regardless of Pilate's intentions, the "title" over the cross takes its place alongside the other "titles" (in a rather different sense) given to Jesus in the classic confessions of faith found throughout the Gospel (such as 1:29, 49; 4:42; 6:69; 11:27). While this does not make Pilate what he becomes in later traditions (that is, a confessing Christian),[21] it does highlight the irony that the Jews recognize "no king except Caesar" (v. 15), and yet Pilate the Roman governor now publicly assigns them a king other than Caesar.[22]

23-24 The next sequence, looking back momentarily at the actual

---

19. The story found in 7:53–8:11 is an exception (for it takes place in the temple), raising a question as to whether the intent was actually to stone the woman to death right then and there.

20. Gr. ὃ γέγραφα, γέγραφα.

21. See Carter, *Pontius Pilate,* 6-11. The earliest example of this is probably Tertullian, who wrote, "The whole story of Christ was reported to Caesar (at that time it was Tiberius) by Pilate, himself in his secret heart [*et ipse iam pro sua conscientia*] already a Christian" (*Apologeticus* 21.24; LCL, 113), but it becomes a major theme in later traditions, above all the apocryphal *Acts of Pilate* (no earlier than the fourth century; see M. R. James, *The Apocryphal New Testament,* 94-146).

22. Brown compares Pilate's "present role to that of Caiaphas in John 11:49-52," who was "brought by God unknowingly to speak the truth about Jesus" (*Death,* 2.966).

moment of crucifixion (v. 18), belatedly introduces the Roman soldiers (last heard from in v. 2), as those who *literally* crucified Jesus in the sense of nailing him to the cross: "Then the soldiers, when they crucified[23] Jesus, took his garments and made four parts, a part for each soldier, and the tunic. But the tunic was seamless, woven throughout from the top. So they said to one another, 'Let us not tear it, but let us gamble for it, whose it will be,' that the scripture might be fulfilled that says, 'They divided my garments to themselves, and for my garment they cast lots.' So the soldiers did these things" (vv. 23-24).[24] Because Jesus was crucified naked, his clothing was available for the taking, but by whom? All the Gospels mention that "they" (implicitly the soldiers) divided his garments among themselves by lot (see Mt 27:35// Mk 15:24//Lk 23:34), but only here is the procedure described in detail, and only here is it said to be the fulfillment of a biblical text (specifically Ps 21[22]:19, LXX). The text from the Psalms, like those Jesus himself quoted at 13:18 and 15:25, has to do with a righteous sufferer who speaks in the first person, but in contrast to the two earlier ones,[25] the application here is to Jesus and to him alone, not to his disciples as well.

Clearly, the synoptic writers are also aware of the text. In fact they reproduce its actual vocabulary more closely than John's Gospel does![26] But here the Gospel writer goes to the trouble of actually quoting it in full: "They divided my garments[27] to themselves, and for my garment[28] they cast lots" (v. 24).[29] The text is a Hebrew parallelism, in which the two clauses are two

---

23. Gr. ἐσταύρωσαν.

24. For the formula, "that the scripture might be fulfilled" (ἵνα ἡ γραφὴ πληρωθῇ), see 13:18 and 19:36 (with a particular verse of scripture in mind, as here; compare 12:38; 15:25), and 17:12 (referring to scripture more generally; compare 19:28).

25. That is, it was true of both Jesus and the disciples after his death that they would be betrayed (13:18) and hated (15:25). Here, however, the dividing of garments has a one-time application to Jesus in his passion, and only to that.

26. See Brown, *Death,* 2.953-54. In particular, Matthew's διεμερίσαντο ("divided") reproduces verbatim the διεμερίσαντο of the psalm (Mark has διαμερίζονται, and Luke διαμεριζόμενοι), and the ἔβαλον κλῆρον ("cast lots") of the psalm shows up in Matthew and Mark as βάλλοντες κλῆρον, and in Luke as ἔβαλον κλήρους. John's Gospel, like the others, speaks of "his garments" (τὰ ἱμάτια αὐτοῦ, v. 23), but refers only to the "parts" (μέρη) of Jesus' clothing, and uses a different word, "gamble" (λάχωμεν, v. 24), for the casting of lots.

27. Gr. τὰ ἱματιά μου.

28. Gr. ἐπὶ τὸν ἱματισμόν μου.

29. Not surprisingly, certain manuscripts and versions of Matthew 27:35 (including Δ, Θ, families 1 and 13, 1424, and others) quote the same text from Psalm 22:19, introducing it in more typically Matthean fashion with the formula, "that what was spoken through the prophet might be fulfilled." It is by no means certain that this variant is a harmonization to the Gospel of John. Just as plausibly Matthew's language may have seemed

different ways of saying the same thing. But the Gospel writer, ignoring the parallelism, anticipates the first clause ("They divided my garments to themselves") by first describing how the soldiers "took his garments and made four parts, a part for each soldier." This is done not by "lot" or chance, but simply by attempting to divide the four pieces of clothing (which are not specifically named) as equally as possible among the four soldiers (this is the first we learn that they are four in number). The "tunic," however (evidently the grand prize),[30] poses a problem. Whoever gets the tunic gets more than his share, and it cannot be divided up without destroying it, for it is "seamless, woven throughout from the top" (v. 24). It is solely for the tunic, therefore, that the soldiers say, "let us gamble for it,[31] whose it will be," anticipating the second clause in the psalm quotation. The tunic is the single "garment" in the psalm for which "they cast lots."[32] This, we are told, is what the soldiers then did (v. 24b), though we are not told which of them acquired it. Ignoring Hebrew parallelism in order to draw added meaning from a biblical text handed down in Greek is far from unique in the New Testament. Matthew has done it in his account of Jesus' triumphal entry into Jerusalem (Mt 21:2-5, in relation to Zech 9:9), Luke has done it in his record of the prayer of early Christian believers in Jerusalem after warnings had been issued against Peter and John (Acts 4:25-27, in relation to Ps 2:1-2), and the Gospel of John has done it here. In none of these instances is it likely that the writer is ignorant of biblical poetry. More likely, each has seized an opportunity to draw an exact correspondence between the literal wording of a biblical text and events which he believes actually happened in the way he describes them (that is, in Matthew two animals at the triumphal entry, in Acts the involvement of both Jews and Gentiles in the death of Jesus, and here two distinct procedures in disposing of Jesus' garments). Much has been written about the possible symbolic significance of the "seamless" tunic[33] (v. 23), whether representing the unity of those who belong to Jesus, or Jesus' role as High Priest,[34] or both of these at once (see 17:17-19, 20-23). The reader may won-

---

to some ancient scribes to require the actual quotation of the text to which he was implicitly referring.

30. Gr. ὁ χιτών. According to BDAG, the tunic was "a garment worn next to the skin, and by both sexes" (1085); thus it would have been the garment stripped last from Jesus' body (so NIV and TNIV, "undergarment"). The corresponding word in the biblical psalm (τὸν ἱματισμόν), like the preceding τὰ ἱμάτιά μου, refers more generally to any article of clothing.

31. Gr. λάχωμεν περὶ αὐτοῦ.

32. Gr. ἔβαλον κλῆρον.

33. Gr. ὁ χιτὼν ἄρραφος.

34. See Josephus, *Antiquities* 3.161, referring to the "tunic" (χιτών) worn by the Jewish High Priest: "But this tunic is not composed of two pieces, to be stitched at the

der if there is any connection between the untorn tunic and Jesus' unbroken bones (see vv. 33, 36), or perhaps the unbroken net when Jesus' disciples after the resurrection hauled in 153 large fish (see 21:11). But it is far too speculative. All such theories stumble on the simple fact that the tunic thought to be so rich in symbolism no longer belongs to Jesus, but is taken from him.[35]

If there is any significance here at all beyond the very literal fulfillment of a biblical text, it is that Jesus is now stripped of his material possessions, the last of these being his clothing. This begins the process of dying, as he gives up first his clothing (vv. 23-24), then his closest human relationships (vv. 25-27), and finally life itself (vv. 28-30). In that sense his passion corresponds to what he requires of his disciples — more conspicuously in synoptic traditions than in the Gospel of John itself. Consider, for example, such pronouncements as "from anyone who takes away your garment, do not withhold even your tunic" (Lk 6:29),[36] or "go sell your possessions, and give to the poor, and you will have treasure in heaven" (Mt 19:21), or "everyone who has left households or brothers or sisters or father or mother or children or fields for my name's sake will receive hundredfold, and will inherit eternal life" (Mt 10:29), or "whoever wants to save his life will lose it, but whoever will lose his life for my sake and the gospel will save it" (Mk 8:35; see also Jn 12:25). Jesus in this Gospel exemplifies all these things. Now naked and poor, he is ready to sever old relationships (see vv. 25-27) and lay down his life, that he might receive it back again (see vv. 28-30).

25 The narrative continues, hinting at some of Jesus' human relationships that must now end: "Now standing by the cross[37] of Jesus were his mother and the sister of his mother, Mary of Clopas, and Mary Magdalene" (v. 25). As every commentator notices, it is unclear how many women are in the picture here, two, three, or four. If the two named women, Mary of Clopas[38] and Mary Magdalene, are read in apposition to the two that are un-

---

shoulders and at the sides: it is one long woven cloth, with a slit for the neck, parted not crosswise but lengthwise from the breast to a point in the middle of the neck." This, however, was an outer tunic, contrasted with an undergarment already described (3.153), and except for the word "tunic" the vocabulary does not correspond to the vocabulary in John's Gospel (on the whole issue of symbolism, see Brown, *Death,* 2.955-58).

35. So Brown, who notices that both the unity interpretation and the priestly interpretation are "forced to deal with the symbolic import of having this undivided tunic *taken away* from Jesus" (*Death,* 2.958).

36. Oddly, Matthew (5:40) has it the other way around, in that the χιτών (supposedly the inner garment) is taken first and then the ἱμάτιον, but this may be because it is taken in a judgment by a court of law.

37. Gr. Εἰστήκεισαν δὲ παρὰ τῷ σταυρῷ τοῦ Ἰησοῦ.

38. This is probably "Mary the *wife* of Clopas," but it could also be the mother, daughter, or sister of Clopas. It is impossible to be certain (see Schnackenburg, 3.277).

named (that is, Jesus' mother and his mother's sister), then there are only two: Mary the mother of Jesus (with the understanding that Clopas is her second husband, Joseph having died) and Mary Magdalene. This is highly implausible, not only because it identifies Mary Magdalene as Jesus' aunt (!), but because it requires that two sisters were both named Mary, which would have been very unlikely. It can be safely ruled out. If "Mary of Clopas" is understood to stand in apposition to "the sister of his mother," then there are three women, Jesus' mother, her sister Mary of Clopas, and Mary Magdalene, who is not further identified. This is almost as difficult, for it leaves us with the same problem of imagining two sisters with the same name. Only if we theorize that so far as John's Gospel is concerned Jesus' mother was not named Mary (she is, after all, nowhere named in this Gospel) does it make any kind of sense, and the unanimous testimony of the other three Gospels that Mary was in fact her name tells mightily against it. It too has to be set aside. Consequently, we are to picture four women "standing by the cross of Jesus," two of whom (his mother's sister and Mary of Clopas) are mentioned nowhere else in the Gospel.[39] Mary Magdalene is also a new face, but we will hear much more of her in the following chapter (see 20:1-2, 11-18). The only one who actually plays a part in the present scene is "his mother," whom we have encountered just once before, at the Cana wedding and shortly thereafter at Capernaum (see 2:3-5, 12; see also 6:42).

John's is the only Gospel in which the mother of Jesus is explicitly said to have been present at the crucifixion. The key word here is "explicitly," for a case can be made that she is *implicitly* present (or at least nearby) in two other Gospels as well. In the other Gospels, the women are not "standing by the cross," but either "standing" (Luke) or "watching" (Matthew and Mark) "from a distance."[40] Matthew and Mark agree that Mary Magdalene was one of them, but she is accompanied in Mark by "Mary, the mother of James the little and Joses," and by "Salome" (Mk 15:40), and in Matthew by "Mary, the mother of James and Joseph" (later called "the other Mary," Mt 27:61; 28:1), and by "the mother of the sons of Zebedee" (see Mt 27:56). In both Gospels, the three women are identified as those who had "followed him and ministered to him in Galilee" (Mk 15:41; Mt 27:55). In Luke, the women are anonymous, but described in much the same way (Lk 23:49). The enigma is the woman so elaborately named in Mark, "Mary, the mother of James the little and of Joses" (Mk 15:40), who shows up a little later as "Mary, the [mother] of Joses" (15:47) and as "Mary, the [mother] of James" (16:1).[41] Much ear-

---

39. This is the verdict of Brown as well (*Death*, 2.1014-15), and of Barrett (551), Schnackenburg (3.277), Bultmann (672), and most commentators.
40. Gr. ἀπὸ μακρόθεν.
41. That is, as Μαρία ἡ Ἰωσῆτος, and Μαρία ἡ τοῦ Ἰακώβου, respectively.

19:16-42 THE CRUCIFIXION AND BURIAL

lier in Mark, both "James" and "Joses" are named (along with "Simon" and "Judas") as brothers of Jesus, in the same breath in which Jesus is called "the son of Mary" (Mk 6:3). The parallel passage in Matthew (13:55) substitutes "Joseph" for "Joses," just as Matthew does in the scene near the cross.

It is hard not to conclude from this that "Mary the mother of James and Joses [or Joseph]" is in fact "Mary the mother of Jesus"![42] But if Mark meant that, why did he not say so? Possibly because of Mark 3:31-35, when Jesus' mother and brothers stood at the door, and he asked, "Who is my mother and my brothers?" and, pointing to the disciples seated around him, said, "Look, my mother and my brothers!" adding, "For whoever does the will of God, this is my brother and sister and mother" (see also Mt 12:46-50). If Mark took this literally, it is not so surprising that when Jesus' mother appears at the end of the story she is not acknowledged as his mother, but simply as "Mary, the mother of James the little and of Joses" (Mk 15:40).[43] She is important in the story not because of a blood relationship but because she had "followed him and ministered to him in Galilee" (15:41) — that is, she had "done the will of God."[44] Whether Matthew does the same thing for the same reason, or whether he simply follows Mark by default, without reflecting on who "the other Mary" might have been, is uncertain.[45] In short, there

---

42. Brown (*Death*, 2.1017, n. 84) considers this a "dubious interpretation" of Mark because "it has to suppose the three other evangelists went in the opposite direction because they gave Mary a favored role in Christian memory." While his point is well taken with respect to Luke, it is less so with respect to Matthew. As for John's Gospel, this interpretation actually draws Mark and John together in placing the mother of Jesus at the cross.

43. More commonly, this Mary is identified with "Mary of Clopas" in John's Gospel, on the theory that she was the sister of Jesus' mother, and that the two named sons were Jesus' cousins (for a refutation, see J. Painter, *Just James* [Columbia, SC: University of South Carolina Press, 2004], 18-19). But in defense of the view that she is Jesus' own mother, see R. H. Gundry (*Mark*, 977), albeit without reference to Mark 3:31-35. Gundry also suggests that "Mark describes James as 'the little' in reference to 6:3, i.e. as younger than his brother Jesus." But his further suggestion that Mark avoids calling Mary Jesus' mother "because the centurion has just identified Jesus as God's Son and Mark does not want Mary's being the mother of Jesus to lessen the emphasis in this passage on his divine sonship," is less than convincing.

44. As Gundry points out (977), "An inclusion of Mary the mother of Jesus' brothers among those women who were following him in Galilee and waiting on him there disfavors that Mark polemicizes against Jesus' family" (the latter is the view of J. D. Crossan, "Mark and the Relatives of Jesus," *Novum Testamentum* 15 [1973], 81-113, who in some other respects agrees with Gundry).

45. Gundry (*Matthew*, 579) argues that "In both Mark and Matthew, but especially in Matthew because of the identical revisions [that is, "Joses" to "Joseph" in Mt 13:55 and 27:56], the parallel between the two passages favors a reference to Mary the mother of Jesus."

is a tendency in all the Gospels except Luke to distance Jesus in certain respects from his birth family, and in particular from his mother.[46] There were hints of this at the Cana wedding, when Jesus addressed his mother as "Woman," and made it clear to her that the agenda for what would happen was his, not hers (see 2:4). Here she makes her reappearance, being introduced again as "his mother," but in a moment she will be identified rather as *someone else's* mother, just as she appears to be in Mark and Matthew.

26-27 "So Jesus," the narrative continues, "seeing the mother, and the disciple whom he loved standing by, says to the mother, 'Woman, look, your son!' Then he says to the disciple, 'Look, your mother!' And from that hour the disciple took her to his own home" (vv. 26-27). Conspicuously, he calls his mother "Woman," just as at the Cana wedding (2:4), and she is not called "his mother" (as in v. 25), but simply "the mother." As for "the disciple whom he loved," he appears as it were out of nowhere. We have just been told who was "standing by the cross" (v. 25): four women, corresponding perhaps to the four soldiers who had just divided up his garments, but no male disciples at all. Where then did "the disciple whom he loved" come from? He has not been heard from since that moment around the table when Jesus announced that someone would hand him over (see 13:21-25). Perhaps the best explanation of why he was not included in the snapshot of those present at the cross (v. 25) is that he was the one taking the picture. That is, the four women mentioned in the preceding verse are seen through his eyes, in much the same way that the departure of Judas (13:21-30) was seen through his eyes. By adopting again the strategy of changing a third-person narrative to the first-person,[47] it is possible to reconstruct (paraphrastically) how this disciple might have first handed down the story:

> Now standing by the cross of Jesus were his mother and the sister of his mother, Mary of Clopas, and Mary Magdalene. So Jesus, seeing his mother standing there, says to her, "Woman, look, your son!" Then he says to me, "Look, your mother!" And from that hour I took her to my own home.

---

46. Even in Luke, when a woman says, "Blessed is the womb that bore you and the breasts that nourished you," Jesus replies, "Blessed rather are those hearing and keeping the word of God" (Lk 11:27-28). But Luke has already resolved the issue with Jesus' pronouncement, "These, my mother and my brothers, are those who hear and do the word of God" (Lk 8:21, in contrast to Mk 3:34-35; so J. A. Fitzmyer, *Luke,* 1.723, 725).

47. See Reynolds Price, *Three Gospels,* 175-76. See also 13:28, where the notice that "none of those reclining found out" what Jesus meant obviously does not include the beloved disciple, but is written from his point of view as an eyewitness observing all the *other* disciples gathered around the table.

19:16-42 THE CRUCIFIXION AND BURIAL

The presence of "the disciple whom he loved" at the cross obviously stands as an exception to Jesus' grim prediction earlier that "you will be scattered, each to his own home, and leave me all alone" (16:32). He goes "to his own home" indeed[48] (v. 27), but this is a good thing, for he takes the mother of Jesus with him, in obedience to Jesus' implied command. This comes as no great surprise, for the prediction that the disciples would be scattered has already been qualified, first by Jesus' long prayer for their unity and security (chapter 17) and then by his charge to the soldiers who came to arrest him, "if you are seeking me, let these go" (18:8), setting the disciples free. The unfaithfulness of the disciples after Jesus' arrest — in any case more evident in the other Gospels than here — should not be exaggerated. Even Peter, after all (despite his subsequent denials), and at least one other, kept "following" Jesus after his arrest (18:15).[49] Therefore the presence of one male disciple at the cross is not as remarkable as it might seem. And if there is one, it is hardly surprising that it is he who reclined closest to Jesus at the table (13:23).

Does the scene tell us anything further about the identity of "the disciple whom he loved"? The analogy with Mark and Matthew, where a woman at the cross seems to have been identified as the mother of Jesus' two brothers, James and Joses (or Joseph), could suggest that "the disciple whom he loved" is one of those brothers, allowed to remain anonymous just as Mary herself is anonymous in this Gospel. In this case, the pronouncements, "Woman, look, your son!" and "Look, your mother!" would be literally true![50] Jesus would be committing his mother into the care of one whom we might logically expect to be her caregiver, one of her own sons. This is consistent with the book of Acts, where "Mary the mother of Jesus" is seen along with "his brothers" after the ascension, joining with eleven disciples and some women in constant prayer together (Acts 1:14).

It is an intriguing possibility, and one that has not received adequate attention, but difficulties remain. Most conspicuously, we were told just before Jesus went to the Tent festival in Jerusalem that "his brothers did not believe in him" (7:5). Even in Markan tradition, the notion that Jesus distanced himself from his mother is part of the larger tradition of distancing himself

---

48. Gr. εἰς τὰ ἴδια.

49. Each of the other Gospels is careful to report that Peter (and Peter alone) was following "from a distance" (ἀπὸ μακρόθεν, Mt 26:58//Mk 14:54//Lk 22:54), in much the same way that they later place the women at a "distance" (ἀπὸ μακρόθεν) from the cross.

50. This is not necessarily inconsistent with the fact that "look" (ἴδε) in both instances somehow *constitutes* or *appoints* Jesus' mother as the disciple's mother, and he as her son (see above, in connection with 1:29). Even if they are already literally mother and son, the pronouncement places on each of them new responsibilities, as evidenced by the disciple immediately taking the mother "to his own home."

from his brothers and sisters as well (see Mk 3:31-35, and especially 6:4, "a prophet is not without honor except in his hometown, and among his kin, and in his own household"). Is it possible that by the time he came to Jerusalem for the last Passover one of his unbelieving brothers had become not only his disciple, but his closest disciple, "reclining at Jesus' side" at their last meal together (13:23)? Yes, it is possible, but it presupposes a considerable gap in the narrative, with much that the reader is not told. Certainly if one of his brothers did become a disciple (belatedly), it would not be surprising if he thought of himself as "one whom Jesus loved" as a brother, nor would it be surprising for Jesus to have assigned him a place of honor in the seating arrangement at the table.

Still, the identification remains speculative. For a short time, Jesus, his mother, his brothers, and his disciples were together at Capernaum (see 2:12), but since then he and his disciples have taken center stage. In the following chapter he will send Mary Magdalene to "my brothers," with the news that "I am going up to my Father and your Father, even my God and your God," and she goes straight to "the disciples," not to his natural brothers (see 20:17-18). It appears that he has two kinds of brothers, those who have the same mother as he, and those who have the same (heavenly) Father, and it would be easy to conclude that the latter — his disciples, as in Mark 3:34-35 — have displaced the former. Yet matters are not that simple. If his mother was a disciple — as her presence at the cross implies — then it is not impossible that one or more of his brothers were as well, perhaps even before his resurrection, and if so, the possibility that one of them was "the disciple whom he loved" cannot be ruled out (see Introduction). The other side of the coin is that if the disciple "whom Jesus loved" was *not* one of his brothers, then assigning his mother into the care of that disciple would have been an apparent affront to them, distancing him from his natural (and presumably unbelieving) brothers even more than before.

Whether "the disciple whom he loved" was one of Jesus' brothers or not, the question remains as to the theological significance of the scene. Much has been written about its possible symbolic import. Specifically, if the beloved disciple is in some way a typical disciple or an example of what is true of every believer — such as being the object of Jesus' love, or reclining "at Jesus' side," even as Jesus was "right beside the Father" (1:18) — then what does the scene imply about the believer's relationship to Mary the mother of Jesus? Is she the spiritual mother of all believers? Is she whom Jesus twice addressed as "Woman" in some way the "the woman" in Jesus' parable who, "when she gives birth, has grief because her hour has come. But when the child is born, she no longer remembers the distress, on account of the joy that a human being is born into the world" (16:21)? Is "that hour" (v. 27) in which the beloved disciple takes her home her "hour" of giving birth to a new community of faith? Is she even perhaps the "woman" in the book of Revelation, "clothed with the sun, and the moon under her feet, and on her head a crown of twelve stars," who is pregnant and brings to birth a male child who will "shepherd all the nations with a rod of iron" (see Rev 12:1-6)?[51]

The answer is No, no, no, and no! None of those things are even hinted at in the text. First, Jesus addresses at least two and possibly three other women as "Woman" in this Gospel (see 4:21; 20:15; also 8:10, the only exceptions being Martha and Mary at Bethany; see also Mt 15:28 and Lk 13:12). Nothing more should be read into the designation than the same distancing tendency that is evident in 2:4. Second, it is the beloved disciple (whoever he may be) — not Peter or any other disciple, and not all believers generally — who takes Jesus' mother to his home. He is present at the scene in all of his particularity and individuality, not as a representative of anyone else. Rather, the significance of the scene is to be found within the Gospel of John itself. As in the farewell discourses, Jesus is making preparation for his departure from the world. Implicit in the words, "Look, your son!" and "Look, your mother!" is a command, and the command is simply a particular instance of the "new command I give you, that you love each other, just as I loved you, that you too love each other" (13:34), a command that came right on the heels of the announcement that "Where I am going, you cannot come" (13:33). In short, he is saying to two of his disciples (for his mother too is a disciple), or, possibly, two of his family members, "Take care of each other, for I am going away!" Yes, perhaps even "Wash each other's feet!" (see 13:14). The moment of departure now looms even nearer than before, and Jesus, divested of his clothing (vv. 23-24), takes the initiative to divest himself of family and loved ones (at least those within earshot), giving them into each other's care. This is the second step in his — perhaps anyone's — process of dying.[52]

---

51. See the extensive discussions in Brown (2.924-27, and in *Death,* 2.1019-26). He appears to be more skeptical about symbolic interpretations in the later work than in the earlier. Symbolic interpretations are by no means limited to Roman Catholics, nor to precritical eras in the history of interpretation. Bultmann, for example, comments, "The mother of Jesus, who tarries by the cross, represents Jewish Christianity that overcomes the offence of the cross. The beloved disciple represents Gentile Christianity, which is charged to honour the former as its mother from whom it has come, even as Jewish Christianity is charged to recognise itself as 'at home' within Gentile Christianity, i.e. included in the membership of the one great fellowship of the Church" (673)! Surprisingly, modern interpreters show far more imagination here than, say, Chrysostom, who commented simply, "But He on the Cross, committeth His mother to the disciple, teaching us even to our last breath to show every care for our parents" (NPNF, 1st ser., 14.318; so too Augustine, NPNF, 1st ser., 7.432-33).

52. As I once wrote, even though he is in control throughout his passion, "Jesus' sovereign control is as appropriate to a mortal man as to the Son of God. His calm acceptance of physical death corresponds to the acceptance psychologists tell us we should all

Without hesitation, "the disciple whom he loved" obeys the implicit command: "And from that hour the disciple took her to his own home" (v. 27b). "That hour," presumably still "about the sixth hour" (v. 14), is surely not the "hour" for the mother to give birth to a new community, but simply the "hour" Jesus told her about from the beginning (2:4), the hour of his crucifixion (see 7:30; 8:20; 12:23, 27; 13:1; 17:1). The prediction that "you will be scattered, each to his own home" (16:32) is fulfilled, not as we might have anticipated by the disobedience of the disciples, but precisely by one's obedience as he took Jesus' mother "to his own home," wherever that might have been. It cannot have been far away, for the beloved disciple remains in the vicinity, and will be heard from again (see 20:2-10; 21:7, 20-24).

28-29 Whether the disciple and the mother left the scene immediately or whether they stayed at the cross until Jesus had died remains an open question. In any event, the third and last step in the process of dying comes after an unspecified interval, possibly bringing the time of Jesus' actual death somewhat closer to what is stated in the other Gospels.[53] "After this,"[54] the narrative continues, "Jesus, knowing that all things are already finished, so that the scripture might be completed, says, 'I am thirsty'" (v. 28). Yet again we are reminded of his knowledge of everything that was happening or would happen to him. "Knowing"[55] echoes 13:1 ("knowing that his hour had come that he should be taken out of this world to the Father"), 13:3 ("knowing that the Father had given him all things into his hands, and that he had come from God and was going to God"), and 18:4 ("knowing everything that was happening to him"). What he "knows" now is that "all things are already finished."[56] The journey from the world back to the Father must now begin. It is time to go. In providing for the needs of his mother and his closest disciple (vv. 25-27), he has discharged his final responsibilities, or, as we have been told, "having loved his own who were in the world, he loved them to the end" (13:1). Now at last he thinks of his own needs, but what are they? "I am thirsty," he says, and we are told that this was "so that the scripture might be completed."[57] The formula resembles the more common "so that the scrip-

---

reach at some point in the process of our dying. Jesus lets go first of personal possessions . . . then of personal relationships . . . finally, after an open acknowledgement of his helplessness and immediate needs ('I am thirsty'), he lets go of life itself (19:28-30). The death of Jesus in the Gospel of John is a fully human death, not the painless or bloodless return of a Heavenly Messenger to the Divine Realm from which he came" ("John 12:1-11," in *Interpretation* 43.3 [1989], 291).

53. That is, "the ninth hour," or 3:00 p.m. (see Mt 27:45//Mk 15:33//Lk 23:44).
54. Gr. μετὰ τοῦτο.
55. Gr. εἰδώς.
56. Gr. ἤδη πάντα τετέλεσται.
57. Gr. ἵνα τελειωθῇ ἡ γραφή.

ture might be fulfilled" (as in v. 24). "Completed" is perhaps occasioned by the preceding (and following) uses of "finished," in the sense of "completed" (vv. 28, 30).[58]

The words "I am thirsty" recall an earlier scene (also "about the sixth hour," 4:6) when Jesus was thirsty (although the word was not used), and said to a Samaritan woman, "Give me to drink" (4:7, 10). There we never learned whether or not he ever got his drink, but we did learn from him that "whoever drinks of the water that I will give him will never ever thirst" (4:14). Here he is not only thirsty again, and with a far more desperate thirst, but he puts it into words. The irony is evident. He who quenches all thirst cries out, "I am thirsty."[59] But what is he thirsty for? Clearly, the thirst that he promises to quench forever is not a thirst for water (believers get just as thirsty as unbelievers!), but thirst for God, and for eternal life. The pronouncement here takes us again into the world of the Psalms, and of the righteous sufferer who speaks in the first person in many of those psalms (as in v. 24; see also 13:18; 15:25), yet it is not a precise quotation of any known biblical text. Several texts in the Psalms come close, most notably "As the deer longs for springs of water, so my soul longs for you, O God. My soul was thirsty[60] for the living God! When shall I come and see the face of God?" (Ps 42:1-2 [41:2-3, LXX]), and "My God, my God, I seek you early. My soul was thirsty for you! How often my flesh has longed for you in a barren and trackless land without water!" (Ps 63:1 [62:2, LXX]). In both of these passages, thirst is not so much a literal reality as a metaphor. The suffering psalmist is thirsty for God, as one thirsts for water in an arid desert.[61] The same is true here. "I am thirsty" can be regarded as this Gospel's equivalent of "My God, my God, why have you forsaken me?" (Mk 15:34//Mt 27:46). Jesus may well have been literally thirsty, but, like the psalmist, he was really thirsty for God. The pronouncement is addressed, therefore, not to the Roman soldiers, but to God, signaling his intense longing to rejoin the Father by "drinking the cup" the Father has given him (see 18:11). As such, it brings to "completion" not a particular passage of scripture about "thirst," but Scripture as a whole, for it triggers that to which all Scripture points, the death and resurrection of the Messiah. The accent is on the whole biblical testimony that (as Luke puts it),

---

58. Some important witnesses (including ℵ, Θ, and families 1 and 13) substitute πληρωθῇ for τελειωθῇ, but this appears to be simply an accommodation to the Gospel's more common usage.

59. Gr. διψῶ.

60. Gr. ἐδίψησεν.

61. For literal thirst we must look rather to Psalm 22:15, where the actual verb for thirst does not appear: "My strength is dried up like a potsherd, and my tongue sticks to the roof of my mouth, you lay me in the dust of death" (NIV). Brown suggests this is "the scripture" referred to here (*Death*, 2.1073-74).

"The Christ will suffer and rise from the dead the third day" (Lk 24:46; in John's Gospel see 2:17, 22; 12:16; 20:9).

A less likely interpretation is that the specific "scripture" triggered by the pronouncement is Psalm 69:22, "And they gave gall for my food, and for my thirst they made me drink sour wine"[62] (Ps 69:22).[63] In that case, the actual citation comes in the following verse, "A vessel full of sour wine was set there, so they put a sponge full of sour wine[64] on a hyssop and brought it to this mouth" (v. 29). But this is by no means a quotation of Psalm 69:22, for that text mentions no "vessel," no "sponge," no "hyssop,"[65] and John's Gospel mentions no "gall."[66] The only word in common is the word for "sour wine" or vinegar.[67] Moreover, in the psalm the "gall" and the "sour wine" are

62. Gr. ἐπότισάν με ὄξος.
63. So, for example, Barrett, 553; Schnackenburg, 3.283.
64. Gr. τοῦ ὄξους.
65. The "sponge" (σπόγγον) is mentioned in Matthew and Mark as well, but only John's Gospel refers to the "vessel" (σκεῦος) that was "set there" (ἔκειτο), presumably for quenching the soldiers' thirst. The same is true of "hyssop" (ὑσσώπῳ), a strange word in this connection. The hyssop plant was a small bush with blue flowers used in the purification of sacrifices by sprinkling, but with no stalk capable of bearing the weight of a wet sponge. Matthew and Mark speak rather of a "reed" (καλάμῳ), which makes sense. For this reason, some have looked for symbolic significance in "hyssop" on the basis of Exodus 12:22, where it was that by which the blood of the Passover lambs was sprinkled on the doorposts. More generally, it was considered a means of purification (see, for example, Lev 14:4; Num 19:6, 18; Ps 51:7; Heb 9:19). Yet a symbolic meaning is doubtful here. In view of the strong accent on Jesus' initiative in this Gospel, would bystanders be agents of his purification? Others have emended ὑσσώπῳ to ὑσσῷ, "javelin" (a variant actually found in a few late manuscripts and versions). Metzger (*Textual Commentary*, 253-54) discounts the variant as haplography, but an accidental variation could as easily have gone in the other direction (that is, repeating a syllable), either because of the symbolic connotations of hyssop or simply because "hyssop" was a far more common word in biblical vocabulary than "javelin" (see BDAG, 1043). The emendation would allow us a glimpse of another weapon (besides a "spear," v. 34) in the soldiers' arsenal. Yet "hyssop" should be allowed to stand, not only because of overwhelming manuscript evidence but as the more difficult reading.
66. "Gall" (χολή) does, however, make an appearance in certain later manuscripts at this point (including Θ and some late minuscules; μετὰ χολῆς καὶ ὑσσώπου, "with gall and hyssop"), possibly signaling the scribes' awareness of either Psalm 69 or Matthew 27:34 (see Metzger, *Textual Commentary*, 254).
67. Matthew (27:48) and Mark (15:36) have in common the same word (as does Lk 23:36), plus one other parallel, the phrase "made him drink" (ἐπότιζεν αὐτόν, corresponding to ἐπότισάν με in the psalm). Yet not even Matthew cites it as fulfillment of scripture. At an earlier moment when Jesus is first crucified, Matthew (27:34) and Mark (15:23) record a similar incident but with different vocabulary: "wine" (οἶνος) instead of "sour wine" (ὄξος), in Mark treated with "myrrh" and in Matthew mixed with "gall" (χολή).

part of the psalmist's torment,[68] not (as the sour wine appears to be here)[69] a small act of mercy intended to lessen thirst and pain.[70] It is unlikely, therefore, that this text is in play.[71] The words "I am thirsty," while addressed to God, are heard and (in characteristically Johannine fashion) misunderstood — that is, taken literally — by someone, an anonymous "they" (whether soldiers or women),[72] as Jesus is offered "sour wine" from a vessel that is handy (that is, "set there"). If "their" action is wrong, it is not because of hostility or mockery, but simply because it rests on a misunderstanding of what (or rather, Whom) Jesus is thirsty for. It is not so much wrong as beside the point. Jesus' fate is in his own hands, not theirs and not Pilate's. But whatever its motivation, the act of bringing to his mouth the sponge soaked in sour wine accomplishes one thing. It dramatizes the metaphor he had used earlier in telling Peter to put down his sword: "The cup the Father has given me, shall I not drink it?" (18:11).

30 Consequently, Jesus accepts the drink: "Then when he received[73] the sour wine, Jesus said, 'It is finished,' and he bowed the head and handed over the Spirit" (v. 30). His acceptance of "the cup" prompts him to say, "It is finished,"[74] putting into words what he knew in advance to be true (see v. 28, "that all things are already finished"). He stated almost from the beginning his intention to "do the will of the One who sent me and complete his work" (4:34), and reported to the Father that he had "finished the work you have given me that I should do" (17:4). Now the pronouncement, "It is finished,"

---

68. This is evident both from the preceding words, "I looked for sympathy, but there was none, for comforters, but I found none," and the words that follow, "May the table set before them become a snare; may it become retribution and a trap" (Ps 69:20, 22, NIV).

69. Brown sees elements of mockery in the other Gospel accounts (on the basis of Lk 23:36, plus the references to calling for Elijah in Matthew and Mark), but he finds John's Gospel "alone in portraying no clear mockery" (*Death,* 2.1059). "Nothing in 19:29," he concludes, "suggests mockery; rather the soldiers seem to be responding spontaneously to Jesus' request for a drink" (2.1075).

70. On "sour wine" (ὄξος) as a desirable drink and thirst-quenching agent, see Brown, *Death,* 2.1063, and the texts cited there, including Numbers 6:3; Ruth 2:14.

71. So persistent is the assumption that Psalm 69:22 is in play that it is allowed to override what John's Gospel actually says, to the point of assuming that "John apparently expects his audience to presuppose the hostility of those providing the drink, for they fulfill the role of the persecutors in the psalm to which John here alludes" (Keener, 2.1146).

72. Only in Luke (23:36) is it definitely the soldiers who did this. In Matthew (27:48) and in Mark (15:36) it is one unidentified person.

73. This in contrast to an earlier scene in two other Gospels (Mt 27:34//Mk 15:23), where he refused to drink. According to Mark, "he did not receive" (οὐκ ἔλαβεν) what was offered, while in Matthew he "tasted but chose not to drink."

74. Gr. τετέλεσται.

encompasses all that and more, embracing as well "everything that was happening to him" (18:4) from the moment of the arrest in the garden up to the present.

Having said this, Jesus "bowed the head and handed over the Spirit."[75] To "bow the head"[76] does not occur in any other Gospel account of the crucifixion, nor is it, as we might have expected, a customary expression for dying. It can evoke any number of associations, including physical weakness, submission or humility,[77] prayer, affirmation, or approval,[78] or simply pointing in a certain direction.[79] But what is it here? Its only other occurrence in the Bible is in the well-known saying of Jesus, "Foxes have holes, and the birds of the sky have nests, but the Son of man does not have anywhere to bow the head"[80] (Mt 8:20//Lk 9:58). There, "bow the head" (or "lay his head," as it is normally translated) meant simply to sleep, or have a place to sleep — that is, a home. It is as if the Gospel writer here remembers just such a saying, and is reminding us that at last the Son of man, constantly on the move in all the Gospels, is home, and free to take his rest.[81] As for the expression, "handed over the

---

75. Referring to the order of the clauses, Chrysostom wrote, "For He did not, when He had expired, bow His head, as happens with us, but when He had bent His head, then He expired. By all which things the Evangelist hath shown, that He was Lord of all" (*Homilies on John* 85.3; NPNF, 1st ser., 14.319). Even though there is in the writer's mind probably "no thought of a temporal relation" between the two clauses (see Bultmann, 675, n. 1), the point that Chrysostom makes about Jesus' initiative is well taken.

76. Gr. κλίνας τὴν κεφαλήν.

77. This is conspicuous in the hymnal of the anabaptist Old German Baptist Brethren (*Hymns and Sacred Songs;* Dayton: Lithoprint, 1999), where the gesture is linked not only to Jesus' death but to his baptism, and consequently to the baptism of believers (performed in that tradition by having the candidate bow forward into the water). See, for example, #149 ("See where he bows his sacred head! He bows his head and dies!"), #271 ("Down to the sacred wave The Lord of Life was led; and he who came our souls to save In Jordan bowed his head"), #273 ("O Thou who in Jordan did'st bow thy meek head, O'erwhelmed in our sorrow did'st sink to the dead. . . . Thy footsteps we follow to bow in the tide, And buried with thee in the death thou has died"), and #274 ("Choose ye his cross to bear, Who bowed beneath the wave? Clad in his armor, will ye share, In faith, a watery grave?")

78. See Keener, 2.1148.

79. According to Brown (*Death,* 2.1080), "The participial 'bowing his head' modifies the main action of giving over the spirit. Might it not indicate the direction of the giving, namely, down to those who stood near the cross?" (so too Hoskyns, 532). Lindars, by contrast (582), sees it simply as a clue that when Jesus said "It is finished," he said it "with an upward, heavenly look" (as perhaps in 6:5, 11:41 and 17:1, none of which Lindars mentions), and that he then looked down.

80. Gr. τὴν κεφαλὴν κλίνῃ.

81. So Morris (721, n. 79): "That resting place for his head that he did not have on earth he found on the cross."

Spirit,"[82] it is fairly close to what we find in the other Gospels,[83] but its interpretation in this Gospel is powerfully shaped by what has preceded it. The verb "handed over" comes as the last in a chain of occurrences of this verb. The devil, through Judas Iscariot (13:2), "handed over" Jesus to Caiaphas and the Jewish authorities (18:2), who "handed him over" to Pilate (18:30), who "handed him over" again to the Jews again for crucifixion (19:16).

Now, Jesus himself "hands over" himself — that is, his "Spirit" — to someone, but to whom? To the Father (as in Lk 23:46, and implicitly in Mt 27:50)? Or, as some have suggested, to the beloved disciple and the women gathered around the cross?[84] The latter will not work, for Jesus gives the Spirit to his disciples a chapter later, after his resurrection (see 20:22), and it is unlikely that there would be a special bestowal in advance on four women and one man simply because they were present at the crucifixion. As we have seen (v. 27), it is not even certain that his mother and the disciple whom he loved were still present. If they were not, why would the Spirit be given to Mary Magdalene and Mary of Clopas and no one else? And if the gift is somehow implicitly for the whole believing community, what is its relationship to the later "breathing" of the Spirit on the gathered disciples (20:22)? Quite clearly, Jesus "handed over the Spirit" to the Father, just as in the other Gospels. But why capitalize "Spirit" here and not in the other Gospels?[85] The answer lies back near the beginning of the story, when John testified, "I have watched the Spirit coming down as a dove out of the sky, and it remained on him" (1:32), confirming that the person "on whom you see the Spirit coming down and remaining on him, this is he who baptizes in Holy Spirit" (1:33). How long did "the Spirit," evidently the "Holy Spirit" (v. 33), "remain" on Jesus? We are not told, but two chapters later John can still say, "the one God sent speaks the words of God, for he gives the Spirit without measure" (3:34), and we are never told that the Spirit left Jesus — until now! That he "handed over the Spirit" means just what it does in the other three Gospels — that he stopped breathing — but his "breath" or "spirit" is the Holy Spirit, the very Spirit of God that was his "without measure," not from birth but from the day John witnessed it "coming down as a dove out of the sky" (1:32), presumably at his baptism. Jesus dies willingly, not by his own hand yet clearly on his own initiative and at the moment he chooses. As he has said (10:18), no one takes his

---

82. Gr. παρέδωκεν τὸ πνεῦμα.

83. Matthew is the closest, with "he dismissed the spirit" (ἀφῆκεν τὸ πνεῦμα, Mt 27:50); Mark (15:37) has simply "expired" (ἐξέπνευσεν, literally "breathed out," the verb being a cognate of "spirit"); Luke has the same, but immediately preceding it is the prayer, "Father, into your hands I commit my spirit" (παρατίθεμαι τὸ πνεῦμά μου, Lk 23:46).

84. So Hoskyns, 532; Brown, *Death,* 2.1080 (see above, n. 79).

85. See above, n. 83, where (with most translations) I have left "spirit" uncapitalized.

life from him, but he lays it down on his own, and the reader knows that if he has the authority to lay it down, he has the authority to receive it back.

31 The purpose of the next three verses is to verify that Jesus is in fact dead. Death by crucifixion would normally have been a long, slow process, and it appears that neither "the Jews," wherever they might be, nor the Roman soldiers on the scene are aware that Jesus has just died. They seem not to have heard him say, "It is finished," or seen him bow his head, nor could they know when he "handed over the Spirit." Death by crucifixion was a long, slow process, and they did not have time for it: "Now the Jews, because it was the preparation, so that the bodies would not remain on the cross on the Sabbath — for great was the day of that Sabbath — asked Pilate that their legs be broken, and that they be taken away" (v. 31). According to biblical law, "If anyone guilty of a capital offense is put to death and their body is exposed on a pole, you must not leave the body hanging on a pole overnight. Be sure to bury it that same day, because anyone who is hung on a pole is under God's curse" (Deut 21:22-23, TNIV). The only way to insure that the law was kept was to break the legs of the three who were crucified, hastening death so that the bodies could be removed.

Obviously "the Jews," as a people subject to Roman authority, were in no position to enforce biblical law. It was the Roman custom to leave bodies hanging on crosses for extended periods of time as a warning to potential criminals, and a grim public reminder of imperial authority. But the circumstances here are exceptional. It is not just a matter of "overnight," but of the "preparation" for the Sabbath, and not just any Sabbath but a "great," or special, Sabbath,[86] probably in the sense that it would fall on the fifteenth day of Nisan, the first day of the Passover festival (see v. 14, "the preparation of the Passover").[87] Even so, Pilate was under no obligation to accede to the request, yet certain concessions were customary at festival times (see 18:39).[88] Pilate evidently grants their request, for it is promptly carried out.

---

86. While this terminology is not attested in early Jewish sources, a "great Sabbath" is mentioned (possibly in dependence on John's Gospel) in connection with the death of Polycarp (*Martyrdom of Polycarp* 8.1, σαββάτου μεγάλου; 21.1, σαββάτῳ μεγάλῳ). For the adjective "great" (μεγάλη) in connection with a particular day of a Jewish festival, see 7:37, referring to the last day of the Tent festival.

87. When "preparation" was mentioned previously, it was as "preparation" for the Passover festival (v. 14, παρασκευὴ τοῦ πάσχα), while here it is used in the sense of "preparation" for the Sabbath (that is, Friday; see also v. 42).

88. Philo quotes himself pleading his case before the Roman governor Flaccus in Egypt: "I have known cases when on the eve of a holiday of this kind [not a Jewish festival, to be sure, but an emperor's birthday], people who have been crucified have been taken down and their bodies delivered to their kinfolk, because it was thought well to give them burial and allow them the ordinary rites" (*Against Flaccus* 83; LCL, 9.347-49).

32-33 The request of the Jewish authorities "that they might break" the legs of the three condemned men could imply that they were asking permission to do it themselves, but this is of course not the case. Rather, just as the crucifixion itself was carried out by Romans soldiers, so is this final act of hastening death: "So the soldiers came, and broke the legs of the first, and of the other who was crucified with him. But when they came to Jesus, as they saw he was already dead, they did not break his legs" (vv. 32-33). This is the point: Jesus was "already dead,"[89] and the attempt to break his legs to hasten death verified it. There is no particular reason why the soldiers would have come to him last. One would have expected them to go either from left to right or right to left, and so come to him second (see v. 18, "two others on either side, Jesus in the middle"), but he is mentioned last either for dramatic effect,[90] or perhaps because he was the last of the three to be given up for crucifixion. As we have seen, the other two are not identified in any way as "terrorists" or "criminals," as in the synoptic Gospels, only as "two others." Neither of them mocks him (as in the other three Gospels), and neither of them comes to faith (as in Lk 23:40-43). They are in the story only to have their legs broken and die, in contrast to Jesus, who dies on his own initiative and whose legs are not broken.

34 Instead of breaking his legs, "one of the soldiers punctured his side with a spear, and at once blood and water came out" (v. 34). The action appears redundant if Jesus is in fact dead and his death verified, perhaps a gratuitous act of sheer meanness. Raymond Brown attributes it to "the illogic of ordinary life: Like the other soldiers he has seen that Jesus is dead, yet to make sure he probes the body for a telltale reaction by stabbing Jesus' side." Others, as he notes, view it as "a coup de grace aimed to pierce the heart" but this is less likely because the verb is "punctured,"[91] not "pierced" (as in v. 37).[92]

In another tradition, a variant reading in Matthew 27:49, the "puncturing" takes place *before* Jesus dies. According to this variant, two things happen just before he "dismisses the spirit" (Mt 27:50). First, "one of them, running and taking a sponge full of sour wine, put it on a reed and made him drink" (27:48). Then "another, taking[93] a spear, punctured his side, and water and blood came out" (27:49a). The added words are almost universally judged by editors, translators, and textual critics to be a harmonization to

---

89. Gr. ἤδη αὐτὸν τεθνηκότα (compare Mk 15:44, ἤδη τέθνηκεν).
90. See Bultmann, 676, n. 7; Brown, *Death,* 2.1176.
91. Gr. ἔνυξεν.
92. See Brown, *Death,* 2.1177. This is "ordinarily not a violent or deep piercing" (BDAG, 682). Some Latin and Syriac versions have "opened," probably based on a misreading of the unexpected ἔνυξεν as ἠνοίξεν, "opened."
93. Gr. ἄλλος δὲ λαβών.

John's Gospel, and for that reason discounted.[94] Yet a number of features favor their retention as part of Matthew's text, or if not that at least an independent tradition, possibly known to the writer of John's Gospel.[95] First, the manuscript evidence in favor of the longer reading in Matthew is strong.[96] Second, the variant is well integrated into the Matthean passion narrative, and in certain ways different from its parallel in the Gospel of John. For example, the one wielding the spear is not explicitly said to be a Roman soldier, but simply "another" bystander, in addition to "one of them" who offered Jesus the sponge full of sour wine on a reed. Also, what comes out of Jesus' side is "water and blood," the word order accenting "blood," in contrast to John's Gospel, which, as we will see, emphasizes "water."[97] This is in keeping with a strong emphasis in Matthew's passion narrative on the shedding of Jesus' blood, whether for the forgiveness of sins (Mt 26:28), or as a sign of Jewish guilt (Mt 23:35; 27:4, 6, 8, 24, 25). And only in the variant reading do we see the literal shedding of Jesus' blood in Matthew. Third, and most important, it comes before rather than after the death of Jesus, making it at least open to the interpretation that it is a mortal wound, the actual cause of Jesus' death. This, of course, stands in sharp contrast to John's Gospel, where every attempt to "kill" Jesus fails. No one takes his life, for he gives it freely, and on his own initiative. Matthew, to be sure, acknowledges this to the extent that Jesus then, "having cried out again with a great voice, dismissed the spirit" (Mt 27:50), yet in the variant reading the death cry is arguably the result of the spear thrust. If the author of John's Gospel is aware of such a tradition, whether in Matthew or as an independent tradition, it is quite plausible that he might have wanted to correct it by placing the spear thrust *after* Jesus' death so as to make it redundant.[98] This might in fact have been one reason

---

94. See Metzger, *Textual Commentary*, 71.

95. For a defense of this tradition, if not as an original part of Matthew at least as an independent tradition, see S. Pennells, "The Spear Thrust (Mt. 27:49b, v. l./Jn. 19:34)," *JSNT* 19 (1983), 99-115.

96. The long addition has the support of both א and B, as well as C, L, a few other witnesses, and some manuscripts of the Vulgate.

97. That the Johannine community knows of the other word order is evident from 1 John 5:6, where the accent on blood is explicit: "This is he who came through water and blood, Jesus Christ, not in the water alone but in the water and in the blood."

98. See Pennells, "The Spear Thrust," 109-10, who regards the order of events in Matthew 27:49b as more plausible because of the obvious problem that normally a dead body does not bleed (because the heart is no longer pumping blood). This was an issue raised already by Celsus against Origen, who in response cited John 19:35, candidly claiming a miracle: "Now, in other dead bodies the blood congeals, and pure water does not flow forth; but the miraculous feature in the case of the dead body of Jesus was, that around the dead body blood and water flowed forth from the side" (*Against Celsus* 2.36; ANF, 4.446).

— though probably not the only reason — for introducing an eyewitness (v. 35) to verify exactly what happened, and in what order.

What happens next is that "at once blood and water came out" (v. 34b). "Blood," mentioned first, is what we expect; "water" is not, and consequently "water" is what seizes our attention. Yet the statement is remarkably simple and matter-of-fact, with no interest either in medical explanations on the one hand, or in asserting a miracle on the other.[99] Miracle or not, the event is fraught with "significance" — that is, it qualifies as a "sign" in the full Johannine sense of the word, no less than the "lifting up" in crucifixion (see 3:14; 12:33). "Water" from inside the body of Jesus evokes a number of thoughts First, it confirms that when Jesus said "I thirst" (v. 28), his real thirst was for God, not water, for he is the very Source of water. It confirms as well his two promises that "whoever drinks of the water that I will give him will never ever thirst," but "the water I will give him will become in him a spring of water rushing to eternal life" (4:14), and that "Whoever believes in me, . . . from his insides will flow streams of living water" (7:38). What is true of those who drink of the Fountain of life is first of all true of him who is that Fountain. Last, and perhaps most important, "water" in this scene does not stand alone, but rather in close connection with "blood." Jesus has spoken in very shocking language of drinking his blood as if it were water, and thereby gaining eternal life (6:53-56). Now the blood and the water appear together, as a graphic reminder that life (represented by water) emerges from death, the shedding of blood. As we have seen, "eat my flesh and drink my blood," whatever else it means, presupposes first of all Jesus' violent death, and now the "blood and water" from his side invites us again, "If anyone thirst, let him come to me and drink" (7:37), an invitation never truly heard at the Tent festival, but now at last in effect because Jesus has been "glorified" (see 7:39).[100] As for the more "institutional" interpretation of the "blood and water" — that is, symbolizing the Eucharist and Baptism respectively — there is no more reason to look in that direction here than anywhere else in John's Gospel. Nothing here corresponds to the eucharistic bread, and if there is a symbolic dimension to the water, it is the symbolism not of sprinkling or washing but of "drinking," that is, simply "coming" to Jesus and believing in him (see 7:37-38), an act which might or might not have resulted in water baptism.

99. Brown, after an extensive summary and discussion of "The Physiological Cause of the Death of Jesus" (*Death,* 2.1088-92), rightly concludes, "Clearly none of that discussion dedicated to discovering the natural cause of the blood-and-water phenomenon is germane to John's purpose in recording it" (2.1179).

100. To be sure, "water" is there defined more specifically as "the Spirit, which those who had believed in him were later to receive" (7:39), and that will in fact come a bit later (see 20:22).

35 At this point an anonymous testimony is introduced, apparently the testimony of an eyewitness to what has just happened: "And he who has seen has testified,[101] and his testimony is true, and that one knows that he tells the truth, so that you too might believe" (v. 35). The notice strikingly echoes the words of John at the beginning of Jesus' ministry, when he saw the dove coming down and remaining on Jesus: "And I have seen, and have testified[102] that this is the Son of God" (1:34). The two eyewitness testimonies stand like bookends framing the ministry of Jesus.[103] We know who John was, but who is this eyewitness to Jesus' death on the cross? A near consensus identifies him as "the disciple whom he loved" (see v. 26), partly because he is the only male disciple said to be present at the scene (the participle and the pronouns being masculine), and partly because of the analogy with a notice at the end of the Gospel, "This is the disciple who testifies about these things and who wrote them, and we know that his testimony is true" (21:24). That final notice refers to the disciple whom Jesus loved (see 21:20-23), identifying him as the witness *par excellence,* whose "testimony is true," and on whose authority the whole Gospel was written. In short, the author of the Gospel is pausing at a crucial point in the story to verify the details of Jesus' death, assuring us that he writes what he himself has seen.

The argument is plausible, but far from conclusive. If the eyewitness is the beloved disciple, it is strange that he is not so identified, as he was in verse 26, and in 13:23 (and as he will be in 20:2 and in 21:7 and 20).[104] Moreover, we were told a few verses earlier, when Jesus committed his mother into that disciple's care, that "from that hour[105] the disciple took her to his own home" (v. 27). If this was literally the case, then the disciple whom Jesus loved is no longer present to witness personally the death of Jesus, the spear thrust, and the flow of blood and water.[106] Jesus' word to the disciple and his mother is, after all, separated from the account of his death by an unspecified

---

101. Gr. καὶ ὁ ἑωρακὼς μεμαρτύρηκεν.

102. Gr. κἀγὼ ἑώρακα καὶ μεμαρτύρηκα.

103. Again, compare 1 John 5:6, where "the water and the blood" form a pair, framing the whole ministry of Jesus from his baptism in water to the shedding of his blood on the cross. The writer assumes that the ultimate Witness to both events is the Spirit, for "the Spirit is the truth," and "there are three that testify, the Spirit and the water and the blood, and the three are as one" (5:8).

104. As we have seen, in two other instances (1:40 and 18:15) there have been some who proposed that the disciple whom Jesus loved is present without being so identified, but on even shakier grounds than here.

105. Gr. ἀπ' ἐκείνης τῆς ὥρας.

106. See Dodd, *Historical Tradition,* 133, n. 1. Dodd concludes that "someone, not the author, had, to the author's knowledge, witnessed the occurrence, and that it is here recorded on the testimony of that witness, whoever he may have been" (133-34).

period of time indicated by the phrase "after this" (v. 28). Quite possibly, therefore, the purpose of the reference is just the opposite of what is commonly assumed. That is, the writer of the Gospel (the beloved disciple himself, according to 21:24) wants to assure the reader that *even though he himself had left the scene,* nevertheless there was someone present who could — and did — verify what happened. C. H. Dodd, one of the few who does not identify the witness with the beloved disciple, concludes "that someone, not the author, had, to the author's knowledge, witnessed the occurrence, and that it is here recorded on the testimony of that witness, whoever he may have been."[107] If we do not join the prevailing consensus, must we leave it at that, or are there other clues to this person's identity?

Two alternatives present themselves. One is that the eyewitness verification does not take place right here on the scene, but a chapter later, after the resurrection, when Jesus appeared to his disciples in a locked room and "showed them the hands and the side" (20:20), and finally said to Thomas, "Bring your finger here and see my hands, and bring your hand and put it in my side, and do not be faithless but faithful" (20:27). Thomas then said, "My Lord and my God!" and Jesus replied, "Because you have seen me,[108] you have believed. Blessed are they who did not see, and believed" (20:28-29). Is it possible that the writer, with the later passage already in mind, is thinking of Thomas as "he who has seen"[109] and "testified" to the wound in Jesus' side? It is not as far-fetched as it sounds, for the notice here concludes with the intention "that *you too* might believe" (v. 35b, italics added), implying that the eyewitness himself "believed," just as Thomas is said to have done (20:29). Yet there are major difficulties, even apart from the obvious one that the writer is bringing Thomas into the narrative prematurely. What the anonymous witness is said to have "seen" (v. 35) surely includes more than just the wound in Jesus' side and the spear thrust that made it. It must include also the blood and water (of which Thomas shows no knowledge), possibly the *order* of events (that is, that the spear thrust and the blood and water came after Jesus had died and not before, as in another tradition), and beyond that perhaps *all* that transpired on the cross at least from 19:28 on: the thirst, the sour wine, the handing over of the Spirit, and the unbroken bones. All Thomas has "seen" is the wound verifying that the risen Jesus is indeed the crucified one, and it must be acknowledged that the other disciples saw that as well (20:20). This alternative, therefore, can be safely eliminated.[110]

---

107. *Historical Tradition,* 133-34.
108. Gr. ἑωρακάς με.
109. Gr. ὁ ἑωρακώς.
110. The only interpreter (that I know of) to identify Thomas as the anonymous eyewitness is James Charlesworth (*The Beloved Disciple,* 226-33), but his scenario is

The second alternative is more promising. If we press the parallel between this testimony near the end of the story and John's testimony near the beginning, what stands out is that the actual content of John's testimony was that "this is the Son of God" (1:34). The title "Son of God," moreover, is conspicuous in the apparent echo in 1 John of these two passages. There the writer asks, "Who is it who overcomes the world except the person who believes that Jesus is the Son of God? This is he who came through water and blood, Jesus Christ, not in the water alone but in the water and in the blood" (1 Jn 5:5-6), and finally concludes that "this is the testimony of God that he has testified concerning his Son. The person who believes in the Son of God has the testimony in himself" (5:9-10), and "the person who has the Son has life; the person who does not have the Son of God does not have life" (5:12). Here, however, the title "Son of God" does not appear in the testimony of our anonymous eyewitness. No actual content is given, only that he "has testified, and his testimony is true, and that one knows that he tells the truth, so that you too might believe." Yet, as we have noticed, the words "so that you too might believe"[111] not only invite the reader to believe, but presuppose some kind of prior belief on the part of the anonymous witness — belief that presumably has content. The analogy with 20:31 suggests (once again) that the implied content of this belief is that Jesus is the Son of God, for there the writer concludes, "But these things are written that you might believe that Jesus is the Christ, the Son of God, and that believing you might have life in his name."[112] These are the only two passages in the Gospel where the reader is explicitly invited to "believe," and it is natural to conclude that what is to be believed is the same in both instances — that Jesus is

---

quite different from the preceding in that he also identifies Thomas as "the disciple whom Jesus loved." From the fact that Thomas seems to know of the wound in Jesus' side without being told (20:25), Charlesworth assumes that Thomas was actually present on the scene in the person of the anonymous witness, and since he also presupposes without question that the beloved disciple is that witness, he concludes that Thomas and the beloved disciple are the same person. This theory is not credible because Jesus also showed the wound to the other disciples as verification (20:20), implying that they too knew by this time that such a wound existed. Moreover, as in the case of certain other identifications (Lazarus, for example), Charlesworth's theory is open to the objection that the beloved disciple is unlikely to have been named in some instances and anonymous in others.

111. Gr. ἵνα καὶ ὑμεῖς πιστεύ[σ]ητε.

112. The analogy between the two passages is evident even in the textual tradition, where the form πιστεύ[σ]ητε signals the same divergence in the manuscript tradition between the present subjunctive πιστεύητε, that "you might believe" in the sense of be convinced or assured, and the aorist subjunctive πιστεύσητε, that "you might come to believe," as if for the first time. While the texual evidence is not exactly the same in both instances, B and the first hand of ℵ support the former in both passages, while A, D, L, W, families 1 and 13, and the majority of later witnesses support the latter. In short, scribes tended to conform the two to one another as if aware of the parallel.

the Son of God. If this is so, then it is also that which the anonymous eyewitness believed, and to which he testified.

Just such a testimony is found in Mark, where a Roman centurion present at the crucifixion, "when he saw that Jesus died thus, said, 'Truly this man was the Son of God'" (Mk 15:39; see also Mt 27:54).[113] For this reason it is possible that "he who has seen" and "testified" is none other than one of the four Roman soldiers, possibly the one who punctured Jesus' side with a spear.[114] Traces of such an identification linger in later traditions,[115] but the strongest argument for it comes two verses later, when the writer cites Zechariah 12:10, "They will see him whom they pierced" (v. 37). If attention is given to the verb "see" as well as to the verb "pierced," the effect of the quotation is to draw together verses 34 and 35 in such a way that those who "see" and those who "pierce" are the same.[116] While the plural verbs for "see" and "pierce" might caution us against pinning down the identification to the one soldier who actually threw the spear, this is surely the strongest argument in favor of identifying the anonymous eyewitness at least with one of the four who were present on the scene. It should be noted that the centurion in Mark acknowledges Jesus as "Son of God" simply by observing how Jesus died (Mk 15:39), not on the basis of any visible miracle or accompanying event (unless blood from the body of a corpse qualifies as such), and the same is true here.[117]

---

113. Despite the absence of the article, Colwell's rule again justifies the translation "the Son of God," rather than "a son of God." The issue here is not what may or may not have been in the centurion's mind, but rather the significance that Mark saw in the confession (as a sequel perhaps to Mk 1:1 and 11).

114. See my article, "The Centurion's Confession and the Spear Thrust," *CBQ* 29.1 (1967), 102-9; also Paul S. Minear, *John: The Martyr's Gospel* (New York: Pilgrim Press, 1984), 71-72.

115. This is most notably the case in the fourth-century *Acts of Pilate,* where the same name ("Longinus," apparently related to λόγχη, the word for "spear") is given to the soldier who threw the spear in John's Gospel (*Acts of Pilate* 16.7, recension A) and to Mark's confessing centurion (11.1, recension B). The hybrid figure Longinus then came to be widely celebrated in medieval art and legend (see Michaels, "Centurion's Confession," 102).

116. This is the argument of Minear as well (71), who does not even bring Mark 15:39 into the equation.

117. This is not the case in Matthew, where the centurion (and others as well who were guarding Jesus) made the confession on the basis of the rending of the temple veil and an earthquake opening the tombs of sleeping saints (see Mt 27:51-54). While Mark also mentions the rending of the veil (15:38), he states clearly that the centurion's confession is based on Jesus' death (15:37), and on that alone. It is even possible that the rending of the temple veil in Mark is itself meant as a symbolic reference to Jesus' death (see Jn 2:21; Heb 10:19; see Michaels, "Centurion's Confession," 107-9; also J. E. Yates, *The Spirit and the Kingdom* [London, 1963], 234).

The Gospel of John

If we must have an alternative to simply leaving the anonymous witness anonymous (like Peter's anonymous companion in 18:15-17), this is the most plausible option, more plausible on balance than attributing the testimony to the beloved disciple. While it could be open to the charge of harmonization in that it seems to import something from Mark to explain what we find in John's Gospel,[118] it does not necessarily presuppose John's dependence on Mark. All it presupposes is a tradition (written or oral, and possibly pre-Markan) that one of the Roman soldiers at the cross publicly acknowledged Jesus as "Son of God" (whatever he might have meant by that), and it calls attention to the truth of that confession.

To this end, the Gospel writer adds, "and his testimony is true, and that one knows that he tells the truth, so that you too might believe" (v. 35b). Who is "that one"[119] who "knows" and vouches for the truth of the eyewitness testimony? While it is possible to make an argument that the pronoun refers to the disciple whom Jesus loved (v. 26), in that he is the witness underlying everything that is recorded in the Gospel (21:24), or even that it refers to God, or the living Christ, or the Holy Spirit (as if to say, "God knows he is telling the truth"), it is virtually certain that it refers to the anonymous eyewitness himself.[120] Grammatically, "he who has seen" is the nearest antecedent. Although it would tempting to introduce a second witness on the ground that "it is written that the testimony of two men is true" (see 8:17), it is presupposed in any event that the beloved disciple, not to mention the community to which he belongs (21:24), has already added his own testimony to that of the witness on the scene, quite explicitly in the words, "and his testimony is true." The point of the added words, "and that one knows that he tells the truth," is, as C. H. Dodd puts it, "that the witness himself spoke with full knowledge of the facts and was conscious of speaking the truth. His identity therefore must have been known to the evangelist, who had complete confidence in his credibility (as one who knew the facts) and his good faith."[121] Such an interpretation might also seem to presuppose that the witness is still alive and presumably part of a

---

118. One cannot help but wonder if the hymn writer William Cowper envisioned yet another possibility, based on a harmonization with Luke: "The dying thief rejoiced to see that fountain in his day, and there may I, though vile as he, wash all my sins away."

119. Gr. ἐκεῖνος.

120. See the detailed survey of the uses of ἐκεῖνος in the Gospel of John, in Dodd, *Historical Tradition* (134, n. 1). This stands in sharp contrast to Bultmann's dictum that "It cannot be the eyewitness himself, but must be another who is in a position to guarantee the truth of the testimony" (678). He ends up wanting to emend the text to read, "and we know that one, that he tells the truth," thus conforming it to 21:24 (679).

121. Dodd, *Historical Tradition,* 134, n. 1. He drives the point home with the masterful sentence, "To brush aside this cumulative asseveration is temerarious in any critic."

19:16-42 THE CRUCIFIXION AND BURIAL

Christian community known to the Gospel writer,[122] yet this is not absolutely certain. The precedent of John, who "testifies about him and has cried out," even long after he has died (see 1:15-18), leaves open the possibility that the eyewitness (say, a Roman soldier at the cross) is, like John, by now long dead yet alive with God and aware of the truth of his memorable words, "This is the Son of God" — words to be echoed and reechoed in the Christian community, "so that you too might believe" (compare 20:31). The same possibility exists even if we do not identify the eyewitness with a Roman soldier, but leave him anonymous (as the Gospel writer has done). Nor should we forget that the beloved disciple himself still "testifies" (21:24) as if he were alive, even though he too may well have been dead by the time the Gospel's concluding words were written (21:20-25).

36-37 The account of the crucifixion and death of Jesus concludes with two citations of scripture: "For these things happened so that the scripture might be fulfilled, 'No bone of him shall be broken,' and again, another scripture says, 'They will see him whom they pierced'" (vv. 36-37). The first citation relates to verses 31-33, and the second to verse 34 and perhaps (as we have seen) verse 35. The words, "No bone of him will be broken,"[123] do not match exactly the vocabulary of the preceding narrative in which the "legs" (vv. 31, 32, 33) of the other two victims are "broken"[124] and Jesus' "legs" are not. Yet the reference to what has just happened is unmistakable, just as the Scripture citation about gambling for Jesus' clothing (v. 24) unmistakably mirrored the procedure that had just been described (v. 23) despite differences in terminology.[125] But what biblical text is in mind? Is it Exodus 12:10, 46, LXX, referring to the Passover lamb, "You shall not break a bone of it"?[126] Or is it Psalm 33(34):21, LXX, referring to the suffering righteous collectively, "The Lord guards all their bones; not one of them shall be broken"?[127] It is difficult to decide. The singular "bone" corresponds to the texts in Exodus and Numbers, while the future passive, "shall not be broken," matches the terminology of the psalm. Those who accent the theme of Jesus

---

122. This would be comparable to the reference in Mark to Simon of Cyrene as "the father of Alexander and Rufus," possibly referring to individuals known to the Gospel writer's audience (Mk 15:21). Yet the notion that a Roman soldier present at the crucifixion was still alive and active when the Gospel of John was written might stretch credulity a bit more.

123. ὀστοῦν οὐ συντριβήσεται αὐτοῦ.

124. Gr. κατεαγῶσιν, v. 31; κατέαξαν, vv. 32, 33.

125. See above, n. 26.

126. Gr. καὶ οστοῦν οὐ συντρίψετε ἀπ' αὐτοῦ (see also Num 9:12)

127. Gr. κύριος φυλάσσει πάντα τὰ ὀστᾶ αὐτῶν, ἓν ἐξ αὐτῶν οὐ συντριβήσεται (see also Ps 22:18, "I counted all my bones [πάντα τὰ ὀστᾶ μου], and they observed and looked at me" — this immediately after "they pierced my hands and feet," v. 17).

975

as the Passover lamb in the Gospel of John naturally look to Exodus, pointing to John 1:29, and to the timing of the crucifixion on the day (and for some even the hour) of the slaughter of the Passover lambs. Yet as we have seen, "the Lamb of God who takes away the sin of the world" (1:29) has little in common with the Passover lamb, and the Gospel writer gives no hint that his chronology of the passion is in any way intended to synchronize Jesus' death with that of the sacrificial animals. Moreover, most other biblical quotations in connection with Jesus' suffering and death in this Gospel are drawn from the Psalms, not from biblical narratives (see, for example, 2:17; 13:18; 15:25; 19:24, 28), and it is at least marginally more likely that this is the case here as well.

As for the second quotation, "They will see him whom they pierced"[128] (v. 37), its vocabulary is slightly closer to that of the preceding narrative, in that "They will see" corresponds grammatically (more or less) to "he who has seen" (v. 35). Yet "pierced" implies a more violent action than merely "punctured" (v. 34). Again the Gospel writer is more interested in quoting accurately the biblical text as he knows it than in conforming it to his own vocabulary in telling the story — or for that matter conforming his own vocabulary to the language of the biblical text.[129] This time the quotation is from Zechariah 12:10, and the form of the text is much closer to the Hebrew ("and they shall look at me whom they pierced")[130] than to the Greek ("and they shall look toward me because they mockingly danced").[131] The quotation seems to be based on someone's (not necessarily the Gospel writer's) fairly literal translation of the Hebrew.[132] The tendency of some commentators has been to assign significance only to the verb "pierced" with reference to the spear thrust (v. 34), not to the verb "will see" in relation to him who "has seen" and "testified" (v. 35).[133] Those who have already made up their minds that the anony-

128. Gr. ὄψονται εἰς ὃν ἐξεκέντησαν.

129. Brown (rightly) cites this as evidence that the citation "did not give rise to the episode but has been added to bring out the theological depth of an existing account" (*Death,* 2.1187).

130. Heb. והביטו אלי את אשר־דקרו.

131. Gr. (LXX): καὶ ἐπιβλέψονται πρός με ἀνθ' ὧν κατωρχήσαντο.

132. For example, the Greek translations of Aquila and Theodotion are much closer than the LXX to the Hebrew text. While the discrepancy between "*him* whom they pierced" and "*me* whom they pierced" (italics added) is a variation already present in the textual tradition of Zechariah 12:10, it is also true that the third-person singular here (εἰς ὅν) matches the third-person singular (αὐτοῦ) in the companion quotation from the psalm (v. 36). It may in fact be more than coincidental that Scripture citations about Jesus in this Gospel tend to be couched in the first-person singular while he is alive (see 2:17; 13:18; 15:25; 19:24, 28), but in the third person as soon as he dies (vv. 36, 37). Since this is the last such quotation in the Gospel, it is difficult to say whether or not this is deliberate.

133. See, for example, Barrett ("It is not the look but the piercing that fulfills

mous eyewitness is "the disciple whom Jesus loved" are naturally puzzled by the apparent identification of those who "see" with those who "pierce" the side of Jesus.[134] Yet the Scripture fulfillments in John's Gospel tend to be both simple and literal, referring to something mentioned in the immediate context, with few wasted words (this is evident in v. 36, but the best example is v. 24, where the two parts of a parallelism are assigned distinct meanings in relation to what has just happened). Even Raymond Brown, who identifies the anonymous eyewitness as "the disciple whom Jesus loved," candidly admits that "the only 'seeing' that takes place after the stabbing of Jesus' side occurs in v. 35 in reference to the beloved disciple [sic] who has borne witness to the flow of blood and water."[135] Thus the Zechariah quotation (v. 37) draws together verses 34 and 35 in much the same way that the psalm quotation (v. 36) draws together verses 31 to 33.

It is tempting to read more into the Zechariah quotation than is actually there. It says nothing, for example, about the flow of blood and water from Jesus' side (v. 34), and some, therefore, have proposed linking it in some way with the words just preceding the Zechariah text ("And I will pour out on the house of David and the inhabitants of Jerusalem a spirit of grace and supplication," Zech 12:10a), and the beginning of the following chapter ("On that day a fountain will be opened to the house of David and the inhabitants of Jerusalem, to cleanse them from sin and impurity," 13:1, NIV). Here on the cross, it appears, just such a fountain has been "opened" from the side of Jesus.[136] But if so, the Gospel writer shows no interest in the parallel, and the interpreter will be well advised to exercise comparable restraint. As we

---

prophecy that interests him," 559); so too Bultmann ("only the fact of the piercing is of importance," 677, n. 3).

134. Others address the issue differently. According to Schnackenburg, "Who the people are looking on the one who has been pierced, remains indefinite. They do not need to be the same as those who have pierced him; the plural can, indeed, be understood impersonally.... Is one to regard the Jews as the subject of ὄψονται (v. 31)? That is not to be ruled out with the evangelist's thinking; he makes them answerable for the fact that Jesus was 'lifted up,' that is, crucified (cf. 8:28). But also in general, the thought can be of those guilty of Jesus' death, or of all those whose glance is now fixed on the crucified one" (3.293). Similarly Lindars: "As the subject is unspecified (it can hardly be simply the soldiers), it can be people in general, including those who did the act of crucifixion, but not confined to them" (591).

135. *Death*, 2.1187-88. Brown ignores the difficulty that the beloved disciple was not among those who literally "pierced" Jesus.

136. Among those making such a connection are Lincoln (482), Lindars (591), and Malina and Rohrbaugh (*Social Science Commentary*, 275). Hoskyns (536) goes so far as to appeal even to the variant reading "opened" (ἠνοίξεν) for "punctured" (ἔνυξεν) in v. 34 (see above, n. 92), apparently as a reference to the fountain being "opened" (διανοιγόμενος) according to Zechariah 13:1.

The Gospel of John

have suggested, what the anonymous eyewitness saw and testified to was not simply the flow of blood and water from Jesus' side, but all that preceded it from the moment of his death, and perhaps even before. Somewhat more plausible is the notion that John's Gospel shares with Zechariah an interest in the "mourning" of the people of Israel, with its implication of repentance and cleansing (see Zech 12:10-12). It is tempting to read such overtones into the Zechariah quotation here, in part because of Jesus' prediction to "the Jews" at the Tent festival that "When you lift up the Son of man, then you will come to know that I am" (8:28), in part because of certain other citations of the same text in Zechariah (for example, Rev 1:7, "Look, he comes with the clouds, and every eye will see him, and those who pierced him, and all the tribes of the earth will mourn over him"),[137] and in part because of the faithfulness of two Jewish leaders, Joseph and Nicodemus, in the section that immediately follows (vv. 38-42). Yet if such hopes are implicit here, they are just that — implicit, not explicit — and the commentator's wisest course is to leave them at that. What is certain in any event is that the point of the two Scripture citations (vv. 36-37) is simply to confirm the testimony of the anonymous eyewitness to the reality of Jesus' death, and its meaning — that is, that he is the Son of God, and that the circumstances of his death, being foretold in Scripture, are in the plan of God — all for the reader's sake, "so that you too might believe" (v. 35).

38 With this, Joseph of Arimathea,[138] known to all four Gospel writers, makes his appearance: "Now after these things, Joseph from Arimathea, being a disciple of Jesus secretly for fear of the Jews, asked Pilate that he might take away the body of Jesus, and Pilate gave permission. So he came, and took away his body" (v. 38). Joseph is introduced in Mark (15:43) as "a

---

137. See also Justin, *Apology* 1.52.12, where the prophecy is applied even more specifically to the Jewish people: "Tribe by tribe they shall mourn [κόψονται], and then they shall look [ὄψονται] on Him whom they have pierced; and they shall say, Why, O Lord, hast Thou made us to err from Thy way? The glory which our fathers blessed, has for us been turned into shame" (ANF, 1.180; also Justin's *Dialogue with Trypho* 14.8; 32.2). These texts speak of Jewish repentance only in relation to Christ's second coming, not to anything that happens at the time of his crucifixion, but in the *Gospel of Peter* 25 there is mention of immediate mourning and repentance: "Then the Jews and the elders and the priests, when they perceived how great evil they had done themselves, began to lament [κόπτεσθαι] and to say: Woe unto our sins: the judgment and the end of Jerusalem is drawn nigh" (James, *Apocryphal New Testament*, 92).

138. The Gospels are unanimous in linking Joseph to this place in northwest Judea, probably to be identified with "Ramathaim," the city of Elkanah and Samuel (see 1 Sam 1:1; Eusebius, *Onomasticon* 33-34), making him a Judean and not a Galilean disciple. John's Gospel seems to presuppose that its readers are already familiar with this person, either from other Gospels or from traditions of the passion story (see Keener, 2.1158).

19:16-42 THE CRUCIFIXION AND BURIAL

prominent member of the Council, who was himself waiting for the kingdom of God," in Matthew (27:57) as a "rich man" who had "become a disciple of Jesus," and in Luke (23:50-51) as "a member of the Council, a good and upright man, who had not consented to their decision and action," and who was "waiting for the kingdom of God" (NIV). Here he is described quite briefly, and in terms familiar to the reader of this Gospel, as "a disciple of Jesus secretly for fear of the Jews." The phrase "for fear of the Jews"[139] recalls 7:13, where the very same words are used of the crowds at the Tent festival, and 9:22, where the former blind man's parents are said to have "feared the Jews." It also recalls the notice in 12:42 that "many, even some of the rulers" believed in Jesus, "but because of the Pharisees would not confess, lest they be put out of synagogue." Of these it was said, "For they loved the glory of humans rather than the glory of God" (12:43). It is unclear whether that negative verdict was meant to apply to Joseph of Arimathea or not. Unlike Nicodemus (3:1), he is not explicitly identified as a "ruler" in this Gospel, although it can certainly be inferred from what is said about him in Mark and Luke ("member of the Council"). And in fairness to him it must be noted that in the following chapter we find a whole group of Jesus' disciples gathered behind locked doors "for fear of the Jews"[140] (20:19, as presumably again in v. 26). If Joseph has been less than faithful, he is not the only one. And if he is a disciple "secretly,"[141] he is a disciple nonetheless. We have only to remember several instances in which even Jesus resorted to secrecy for his own protection until his appointed "hour" (see 7:10; 8:59; 12:36).

Now Joseph's time has come. He makes almost the same request of Pilate that "the Jews" made earlier, when, in order to ensure that "the bodies would not remain on the cross on the Sabbath," they "asked Pilate that their legs be broken and that they be taken away" (v. 31). The legs were broken (vv. 32-33), and even though no mention is made of the bodies being "taken away," we would have presumed, given the concerns expressed by "the Jews," that this was done, and that Jesus' unbroken, though pierced, body was taken away as well. But this was apparently *not* the case as far as Jesus is concerned, for Joseph now weighs in with this own version of the same request. Quite possibly, Jesus and the two others are still on the cross because the breaking of the legs only hastened death. It did not bring it on immediately. In any event, we are told not only that Joseph "asked Pilate that he might take away[142] the body of Jesus," but that "Pilate gave permission," something we were not told explicitly in connection with the earlier request by "the Jews."

---

139. Gr. διὰ τὸν φόβον τῶν Ἰουδαίων.
140. Gr. διὰ τὸν φόβον τῶν Ἰουδαίων.
141. Gr. κεκρυμμένος.
142. Gr. ἵνα ἄρῃ.

One suspects that the two accounts (vv. 31-33 and v. 38) may, at some stage of the tradition, have been two versions of the same event, the latter (v. 38) common to all the Gospels, and the former (vv. 31-33) preserved only in the Gospel of John. This is supported, perhaps, by the fact that in Mark the issue of whether or not Jesus is "already dead" is raised in connection with Joseph's request for the body (Mk 15:44), while in John's Gospel, as we have seen, it comes up at the time the legs of the other two victims are broken (v. 33). John's Gospel, instead of substituting the one for the other, has combined the two, resulting in a sharp contrast. "The Jews" (in vv. 31-33) are interested only in "the bodies"[143] (v. 31) as corpses to be disposed of before sundown, without particular concern for "the body of Jesus"[144] (v. 38), while Joseph's attention is focused on Jesus' body, and on that alone.[145] Consequently, with Pilate's permission, Joseph "came, and took away his body" (v. 38b).[146] It was to the cross that Joseph came, presumably, not to "the Jews" or to soldiers who had already commandeered the body, for in that case he would have had to ask their permission as well.[147] For whatever reason, the body of Jesus seems to have remained on the cross until Joseph took it away.

39 Only John's Gospel tells us that Joseph of Arimathea had a companion, someone we have met before: "And Nicodemus also came — he who first came to him at night — bringing a mixture of myrrh and aloes, about a hundred pounds" (v. 39). That Nicodemus "came" echoes what was just said of Joseph, and in case we have forgotten, he is further identified as "he who at the first came to him at night," repeating almost verbatim the words used when Nicodemus was first introduced: "He came to him at night" (3:2). He who came "at the first" now comes again, also at night, presumably (see

---

143. Gr. τὰ σώματα.

144. Gr. τὸ σῶμα τοῦ Ἰησοῦ.

145. See Brodie, 558: "In other words, the two pictures of a request to Pilate are not the result of a confused history or poor editing, but come rather from a deliberate effort to depict two contrasting attitudes and two contrasting groups." He is on less firm ground in comparing it to "the Pauline distinction between those who do, and do not, discern the body of the Lord (1 Cor 11:27-29)."

146. Instead of ἦλθεν ("he came") and ἦρεν ("he took away"), certain manuscripts (including the first hand of ℵ, N, W, and some old Latin versions) have plurals ἦλθον ("they came") and ἦραν ("they took away"), a reading that either reflects a different (possibly earlier) tradition in which "the Jews" (or the Roman soldiers) are removing the body, or (more likely) anticipates the following verse in which Nicodemus joins Joseph in the project (see the verbs ἔλαβον, "they took," and ἔδησαν, "bound," in v. 40). The singular verbs, however, should be retained on the basis of much stronger and more diverse manuscript evidence.

147. This in contrast to the *Gospel of Peter* 23: "And the Jews rejoiced, and gave the body unto Joseph to bury it" (James, *Apocryphal New Testament*, 91).

19:16-42 THE CRUCIFIXION AND BURIAL

v. 42), but under very different circumstances. That early encounter, as we saw, was inconclusive, and Nicodemus surfaced only once since then, when he asked his fellow Pharisees at the Tent festival, "Does our law judge the man unless it hear from him first and learn what he is doing?" (7:51), and for his trouble was called a Galilean sympathizer (v. 52).[148] Now at last, with Joseph of Arimathea, Nicodemus makes his move, a move the two of them must have planned together. We can probably learn a little about each from the other. The designations of Nicodemus as "a ruler[149] of the Jews" (3:1) and as "one of them" (7:50) are consistent with the information in Mark (15:43) and Luke (23:50) that Joseph of Arimathea was "a member of the Council," although we are not told whether or not Joseph, like Nicodemus, was a Pharisee. Conversely, the notice here that Joseph was "a disciple of Jesus secretly for fear of the Jews" (v. 38) is also consistent with what little we know of Nicodemus. In short, they were both "Jews" in the distinctly Johannine sense of being religious leaders, yet they also seem to have feared "the Jews" because of their secret allegiance to Jesus.

Nicodemus brings with him, evidently by prearrangement, "a mixture[150] of myrrh and aloes, about a hundred pounds" (v. 39), evidently to help Joseph prepare the body for burial. The notice is remarkable in several ways. First, this is the only Gospel account in which Jesus' body is embalmed or anointed prior to burial. In the other Gospels, Joseph simply takes the body and wraps it in a shroud before laying it in the tomb (see Mt 27:59-60//Mk 15:46//Lk 23:53). Second, it is the only account in which men carry out this preparation. According to Mark (16:1) and Luke (23:56), it was women who anointed Jesus' body with spices, and they did so only *after* the body was in the tomb. Third, and far more remarkable, is the sheer quantity of the spices that Nicodemus brings, "about a hundred pounds,"[151] more like seventy-five by today's measurement,[152] but still an enormous amount, "a burial fit for a

---

148. There too Nicodemus was identified in almost the same way as "he who came to him previously" (ὁ ἐλθὼν πρὸς αὐτὸν [τὸ] πρότερον, 7:50). Perhaps πρότερον, "previously," was used there because one earlier incident was in view, and τὸ πρῶτον, "at the first," in 19:39 because two earlier appearances of Nicodemus are presupposed.

149. Gr. ἄρχων.

150. Instead of "mixture" (μίγμα), some very important manuscripts (including B, W, and the first hand of ℵ) have ἑλιγμα, "roll" or "wrapping" (from the verb ἑλίσσειν, "to roll up," possibly anticipating the wrapping of the body in linen cloths, v. 40). But μίγμα enjoys more diversified support and makes more sense because it was indeed the "mixture" of the two spices that made them useful for embalming (see Metzger, *Textual Commentary*, 254). A decision is difficult, but the difference is small in any case. On the use of these two spices for embalming, see BDAG, 28 and 933, and Brown, *Death*, 2.1261-64.

151. Gr. ὡς λίτρας ἑκατόν.

152. The Roman "pound" (λίτρα) was twelve ounces, not sixteen (327.45 grams according to BDAG, 597).

king," as Brown puts it, "that would correspond well to the solemn proclamation that on the cross he was truly 'the King of the Jews.'"[153] That Joseph and Nicodemus are intentionally planning a royal burial is also consistent with the characterization of Joseph in Mark and Luke as one "waiting for the kingdom of God" (Mk 15:43//Lk 23:51), and perhaps with Nicodemus's recollection of certain words of Jesus about "seeing" or "entering" that kingdom (3:3, 5). Whether or not their action is misguided, either in light of Jesus' unwillingness to be made into a king (6:15), or because such an elaborate burial implies that the dead king is going to stay dead, is a question often asked, but one for which there is no clear answer. The Gospel writer passes no judgment on their action. It is what it is. The two men act according to their understanding, limited though it may be, and as the story unfolds it will become clear that not even Jesus' closest disciples were expecting him to rise from the dead (see 20:9). Moreover, the huge quantity — and presumed cost — of the spices is hardly unexpected in John's Gospel, given the hundred gallons (and more) of water turned into wine at Cana (2:6), the twelve baskets of fragments left over after the feeding of five thousand (6:13), or the 153 large fish that the disciples will catch in Galilee two chapters later (21:11).

Finally, there is an apparent redundancy in this narrative, in view of Jesus' pronouncement seven chapters earlier, when Mary of Bethany "took a pound of expensive perfume of genuine nard, anointed the feet of Jesus, and dried his feet with her hair" (12:3), and he justified her action as something done "for the day of my burial" (12:7). As we saw in that passage, Mary's "pound" was in its way just as extraordinary and extravagant as Nicodemus's "hundred pounds," given Mary's circumstances and the cost of the "expensive perfume of genuine nard," the fragrance of which filled the whole house.[154] The same question Judas asked about that extravagance (12:4-5) could have been asked of Nicodemus as well, and the answer (12:8) would surely have been the same. Mary's action "six days before the Passover" (12:1) and the action of Nicodemus and Joseph on the very day of "preparation" (see v. 42) represent not so much redundancy as a deliberately matched pair, one before the fact and one after, each an overwhelming response of disciples to the overwhelming fact of the death of God's Son, yet each the product of limited understanding. Like the unidentified woman who anointed Je-

---

153. Brown, *Death*, 2.1261. For example, Josephus's description of the funeral of Herod the Great concludes with the mention of "five hundred of Herod's servants and freedmen carrying spices [ἀρωματοφόροι]. The body was thus conveyed for a distance of two hundred furlongs to Herodion, where, in accordance with the directions of the deceased, it was interred" (*War* 1.673; LCL, 2.321; also *Antiquities* 17.199).

154. Keener's estimate (2.1163-64) that "if her gift had been worth 300 denarii, Nicodemus's was perhaps worth 30,000, a gift befitting 'a ruler of the Jews' (3:1)," is a bit too confident. Not all spices cost the same.

19:16-42 THE CRUCIFIXION AND BURIAL

sus in Mark, Joseph and Nicodemus, no less than Mary, "did what they could" (see Mk 14:8). Even though "the Son of man came not to be served but to serve" (Mk 10:45), he too is "served" in the hour of his death, and the promise that "If anyone would serve me, the Father will honor him" (12:26) is presumed to be still in effect. As we have seen, those who "serve" Jesus are characteristically women (Martha and Mary above all), and Nicodemus and Joseph are rare exceptions.

40 Once Joseph has been properly introduced, and Nicodemus reintroduced, the actual embalming procedure is described quickly and concisely. Now that Joseph has "taken away" (v. 38) the body from Golgotha, he and Nicodemus together "took the body of Jesus and bound it in linen cloths with the spices, as is the custom of the Jews to bury" (v. 40). The reader will remember Lazarus emerging from his tomb "bound with bandages on his feet and hands, and his face wrapped in a cloth" (11:44), except that here "linen cloths"[155] take the place of "bandages." The "linen cloths" will be seen again (20:6-7), and only then will we learn that Jesus' face, like that of Lazarus, was wrapped in a "cloth"[156] (20:7). The body is bound in the linen cloths "with the spices," that is, the hundred-pound "mixture of myrrh and aloes" that Nicodemus has brought. The writer reminds his (presumably Gentile) audience that the procedure was in keeping with "the custom of the Jews to bury,"[157] yet the enormous load of spices would have made it a formidable task, and certainly no ordinary burial.

41-42 None of what has just been described would have happened if Joseph had not already known of a burial place: "And there was in the place where he was crucified a garden,[158] and in the garden a new tomb[159] in which no one had yet been laid. So there, on account of the preparation of the Jews, because the tomb was nearby, they laid Jesus" (vv. 41-42). Only Matthew supplies the information that Joseph actually owned the tomb (27:59),[160] but in all the Gospels it is immediately available, and in three of them "new," as if waiting for the body of Jesus. The redundancy here ("a new tomb, in which

---

155. Gr. ὀθονίοις.
156. Gr. τὸ σουδάριον.
157. The comment belongs to a class of comments in which the Gospel writer makes reference to "the Jews" in a rather neutral explanatory way: for example, "the purification rituals of the Jews" (2:6), or this or that "festival of the Jews" (2:13; 5:1; 7:2; 11:55), or (in the present context) "the preparation of the Jews" (v. 42).
158. Gr. κῆπος.
159. Gr. μνημεῖον καινόν.
160. See, however, *Gospel of Peter* 24: "And he took the Lord and washed him and wrapped him in linen and brought him unto his own sepulchre [εἰς ἴδιον τάφον], which is called the Garden of Joseph" (Κῆπον Ἰωσήφ; see James, *Apocryphal New Testament*, 92).

no one had yet been laid") combines Matthew's "new" with Luke's "where no one had yet been laid" (see Mt 27:59; Lk 23:53). One cannot help but remember Mark and Luke's colt at the triumphal entry, "on which no one has ever yet sat" (Mk 11:2//Lk 19:30). It appears that the tomb here, like the colt there, was meant for Jesus, and for him alone.

John's Gospel is the sole source of the long-standing tradition that the site of the crucifixion and the site of the tomb of Jesus were almost side by side, and the sole canonical source of the tradition that the tomb stood within an enclosed "garden." The "place where he was crucified" can only be "Skull Place," or Golgotha (v. 17), suitable precisely because it was "nearby." Haste was in order for the same reason the bones of the two victims were broken to hasten death (v. 31), "on account of the preparation of the Jews" (v. 42).[161] The "garden" is significant because it recalls that other "garden" (18:1) where "Jesus had often gathered" with his disciples (18:2), and where the account of his passion began. The two enclosed "gardens" frame the entire Johannine passion narrative, recalling the Shepherd's enclosed "courtyard" (10:1, 16) and his care for the sheep. In the first, at his arrest, he protected them and kept them safe (18:8-9). In the second, in due course, he will meet one of them again, and call her by name (see 20:16). There Joseph and Nicodemus laid the body of Jesus. In contrast to the other three Gospels, nothing is said of the tomb being hewn from the rock or sealed with a stone.

D. THE EMPTY TOMB AND THE FIRST APPEARANCE: JESUS AND MARY (20:1-18)

1 On the first day of the week, Mary Magdalene comes early, while it was dark, to the tomb, and sees the stone taken away from the tomb. 2 So she runs, and comes to Simon Peter and to the other disciple, whom Jesus loved, and says to them, "They have taken away the Lord out of the tomb, and we do not know where they have laid him." 3 So Peter went out, and the other disciple, and they were coming to the tomb. 4 The two were running together, but the other disciple ran faster than Peter and came first to the tomb. 5 And he stooped down and sees the linen cloths lying, yet did not go in. 6 Then comes Simon

---

161. Gr. διὰ τὴν παρασκευὴν τῶν Ἰουδαίων. The explanation that "the preparation" was "of the Jews" (τῶν Ἰουδαίων) seems unnecessary here as an accommodation to Gentile readers (as, for example, in v. 40). The writer has, after all, spoken before of "the preparation of the Passover" (v. 14), and simply "preparation" (v. 31) without such explanation. More likely, the words "of the Jews" are added simply to recall the explicit concern of "the Jews" (Οἱ οὖν Ἰουδαῖοι) that the bodies should not be left overnight because the next day was both Sabbath and Passover (ἐπεὶ παρασκευὴ ἦν, v. 31).

20:1-18 THE EMPTY TOMB AND THE FIRST APPEARANCE

Peter also following him, and entered into the tomb, and he looks at the linen cloths lying, 7 and the cloth which was at his head, not with the linen cloths but rolled up separately in one place. 8 So then the other disciple who came first to the tomb went in, and he saw and believed. 9 For they did not yet know the Scripture, that he must rise from the dead. 10 Then the disciples went away again to themselves.

11 Now Mary was standing at the tomb outside, crying. Then as she was crying, she stooped down into the tomb, 12 and she looks at two angels in white, seated one at the head and one at the feet, where the body of Jesus had lain. 13 And they say to her, "Woman, why are you crying?" She says to them that "They have taken away my Lord, and I do not know where they have laid him." 14 And having said these things, she turned around and looks at Jesus standing there, and she did not know that it was Jesus. 15 Jesus says to her, "Woman, why are you crying? Whom are you seeking?" She, thinking that he is the gardener, says to him, "Sir, if you have carried him off, tell me where you have laid him, and I will take him away." 16 Jesus says to her, "Mary!" Turning, she says to him in Hebrew, "Rabbouni" (which means "Teacher!"). 17 Jesus says to her, "Don't take hold of me, for I have not yet gone up to my Father. But go to my brothers and say to them, 'I am going up to my Father and your Father, and my God and your God.'" 18 Mary Magdalene comes, announcing to the disciples that "I have seen the Lord," and [that] he said these things to her.

The time is fast forwarded to "the first day of the week" (v. 1). John's Gospel, like Matthew and Mark, tells nothing of what happened on the great "day of that Sabbath" (19:31; only Luke tells us that "they rested on the Sabbath according to the commandment," 23:56). The discovery on Easter morning that Jesus is risen unfolds in stages involving three individuals: Mary Magdalene, Peter, and "the other disciple, whom Jesus loved." The account of their discoveries (whether intentionally or not) forms what is commonly called a "chiasm," or *a-b-b-a* pattern:

a) *Mary Magdalene* came first to the tomb and saw that the stone had been removed (v. 1).
b) She ran to *Peter* and *the other disciple, whom Jesus loved,* told them what she had seen, and the two ran together to the tomb (vv. 2-4a).
c) The *other disciple* outran Peter, bent down to look in the tomb, saw linen cloths, but did not go in (vv. 4b-5).
d) *Peter* arrived, entered the tomb, saw the linen cloths "and the cloth that was at his head, not with the linen cloths but rolled up separately in one place" (vv. 6-7).

c') *The other disciple* finally entered the tomb, "and he saw and believed" (v. 8).

b') *The two disciples* "went back to their quarters" (v. 10).

a') *Mary Magdalene,* still weeping outside the tomb, stooped down to look in the tomb, and saw "two angels in white, seated one at the head and one at the feet, where the body of Jesus had been." Then she turned and saw Jesus, and when he revealed himself to her, she went and told the disciples, "I have seen the Lord" (vv. 11-18).

Thus Peter is at the center *(d),* the other disciple at *(c)* and *(c'),* the two together at *(b)* and *(b'),* Mary at *(a)* and *(a').* The story is Mary's, in that it begins and ends with her. She is the first to see the risen Lord and carry the good news of his resurrection. Yet it is also Peter's story, and the other disciple's, for at the center of the chiasm is the unmistakable evidence, seen first through Peter's eyes, that the tomb is empty, and the consequent faith of the "disciple whom Jesus loved." This is the only Gospel in which the fact of the empty tomb is verified by two male witnesses, in keeping with Jewish law (see 8:17).[1] The narrative invites reflection not only on the nature of Jesus' resurrection, but on gender roles and the relation between faith and sight — the faith of a man (v. 8) and the prophetic vision of a woman (v. 12).

1 The woman known as "Mary Magdalene" (identified consistently by her place of origin, Magdala on the lake of Galilee) has made only one cameo appearance in the Gospel so far (see 19:25). Just as in the other Gospels, she is the first named person to come to the tomb of Jesus, but here (in contrast to the other Gospels)[2] she comes alone: "On the first day of the week, Mary Magdalene comes early, while it was dark, to the tomb, and sees the stone taken away from the tomb" (v. 1). We are not told why she came. In Mark (16:1) and Luke (24:1) it was to anoint the body with spices, but in our Gospel that has already been done (19:40); in Matthew (28:1) it was merely to "see the grave," and that seems to be the case here as well. What she sees is "the stone taken away from the tomb." The definite article, "*the* stone,"[3] like "*the* tomb," implies that a "stone" has been mentioned before[4] (as it is in Matthew and Mark),[5] but as we have seen (19:42), this is not the case. The

---

1. So, for example, Lincoln, 490.
2. In Mark (16:1) she comes with "Mary the [mother] of James, and Salome"; in Matthew (28:1) with "the other Mary"; in Luke (24:10) with "Joanna, and Mary the [mother] of James, and the rest with them," but she is consistently named first.
3. Gr. τὸν λίθον.
4. "The tomb" (τὸ μνημεῖον), by contrast, has been mentioned before (19:41-42).
5. In Mark (15:46), the tomb is "carved out of rock, and a stone [λιθόν] rolled at the door of the tomb"; in Matthew (27:60) the tomb is "carved in the rock, and a great stone [λιθὸν μέγαν] rolled at the door of the tomb." Luke merely refers to the tomb as

notice implies some familiarity, therefore, with other accounts of the burial, whether oral or written. In much the same way, the reader is likely expected to have more knowledge of who Mary was than the meager information supplied in the Gospel itself — at least that she had accompanied Jesus and the disciples in their travels and contributed to their support, and possibly that she had been healed of demon possession (see Lk 8:2; Mk 16:9).

2 For whatever reason (perhaps because she is alone), Mary does not enter the tomb (as in Mark and Luke), nor does she encounter anyone to tell her that Jesus is risen (as in Matthew, Mark, and Luke). Instead, she simply assumes that the body has been stolen: "So she runs, and comes to Simon Peter and to the other disciple, whom Jesus loved, and says to them, 'They have taken away the Lord out of the tomb, and we do not know where they have laid him'" (v. 2). If the stone is "taken away from the tomb" (v. 1), she reasons, the body must have been "taken away out of the tomb" as well! It is unclear whether she thinks someone has stolen the body (see Mt 27:62-66; 28:11-15), or whether she imagines a reburial of some kind (the words, "where they have laid him,"[6] echoing the account of the burial in 19:42, could imply the latter). To Mary, the dead body is not just "the body of Jesus" (as in 19:38, 40), but "the Lord,"[7] confirming (along with her presence at the cross) a level of discipleship stronger than death. The unexpected "we"[8] is not, as is sometimes suggested, a relic of an earlier account (as in the Synoptics) in which Mary is one of several women coming to the tomb. Even in the Synoptics, the women say no such thing. Rather, the plural "we" simply reflects a consciousness of belonging to a larger community — in this case a community of disciples, embracing Peter and the other disciple as well as herself — an indefinite "we," over against the indefinite "they" whom she suspects of stealing the body.[9]

Mary ran from the tomb, and came "to Simon Peter and to the other disciple, whom Jesus loved." The repetition of the pronoun "to" could imply that the two did not live together, and this is consistent with the reader's impression that the disciple "whom Jesus loved" had "his own home, where he

---

"hewn" (23:53), yet like John's Gospel, he later refers to "the stone [τὸν λιθόν] rolled away from the tomb" (24:2).

6. Gr. ποῦ ἔθηκαν αὐτόν.

7. Gr. τὸν κύριον. See 13:13; also 11:28, where Martha speaks similarly in the third person of "the Teacher" (ὁ διδάσκαλος).

8. Gr. οὐκ οἴδαμεν ("we do not know where they have laid him").

9. We may compare Nicodemus, speaking for his community: "we know [οἴδαμεν] you have come from God" (3:2). Also, perhaps, Jesus himself in 3:11, and the former blind man in 9:31. This is in keeping with the expression "the Lord," yet stands in contrast with v. 13, where she says "my Lord," and "I do not know where they have laid him."

had taken Jesus' mother" (19:27).[10] Mary seems to have gone first "to Simon Peter" and from there (possibly with Peter) "to the other disciple," and said the same thing to each. They could not have been far away, either from Mary or each other. Simon Peter has been out of the picture ever since we heard him denying Jesus for the third time in the Chief Priest's courtyard as the rooster crowed (18:27). He was there with the help of "another disciple . . . known to the Chief Priest" (18:15). Now he is again in the company of "the other disciple,"[11] and it is tempting to assume because of the definite article (as if to say "the aforementioned other disciple") that it is the same person. But the assumption is precarious at best. The "other disciple" there was explicitly identified, both times he was mentioned, as someone "known to the Chief Priest" (18:15, 16), while "the other disciple" here is identified as one "whom Jesus loved,"[12] recalling rather the "one whom Jesus loved"[13] at the last meal together (13:23), and the disciple at the cross "whom he loved" and into whose care he entrusted his mother.[14] If the Gospel writer's intention is to identify the "other disciple" in the Chief Priest's courtyard with "the disciple whom Jesus loved," he is going about it in an extremely subtle way, demanding great ingenuity from the reader. More likely, the one "whom Jesus loved" is remembered here as "the other" (although the word was not used) in the drama that unfolded when Jesus predicted that one of them would hand him over, and Peter nodded to him "to inquire who it might be that he meant" (13:24; this is the point of reference in 21:20 as well, when we last see the two together).[15]

3-4 Just as Mary seems to come to the two disciples one at a time at their respective dwellings (v. 2), so the two of them seem to respond one at a time, running together for awhile, but then arriving at the tomb separately: "So Peter went out, and the other disciple, and they were coming to the tomb.

---

10. See Abbott, *Johannine Grammar*, 276. This is also consistent with 16:32, "each to his own home" (ἕκαστος εἰς τὰ ἴδια).

11. Gr. τὸν ἄλλον μαθητήν.

12. Gr. ὃν ἐφίλει ὁ Ἰησοῦς.

13. Gr. ὃν ἠγάπα ὁ Ἰησοῦς.

14. No sharp distinction should be made between "loved" (ἐφίλει) and "loved" (ἠγάπα), certainly not to the point of positing two different individuals. Note the interchangeability of the two verbs in relation to Jesus' love for Lazarus and his sisters (11:3, 5, 36), and the Father's love for the Son (see 3:35 and 5:20).

15. The placement of the commas in English translation can be significant. If we punctuate the sentence as I have done ("to Simon Peter and to the other disciple, whom Jesus loved"), it supports the interpretation proposed here. But if we drop the comma ('to Simon Peter and to the other disciple whom Jesus loved'), the implication is that *both* Peter and the other disciple were "disciples whom Jesus loved." This is of course true, yet nowhere else is Peter singled out individually as the object of Jesus' love (the issue rather is his love for Jesus, 21:15-17). It makes more sense, therefore, to leave the comma in and read the clause, "whom Jesus loved," as nonrestrictive.

20:1-18 THE EMPTY TOMB AND THE FIRST APPEARANCE

The two were running together,[16] but the other disciple ran faster than Peter and came first to the tomb" (vv. 3-4). The implication is that Peter started out first, perhaps because Mary reached him first, but that "the other disciple" soon accompanied him and then overtook him en route to the tomb. The footrace has no obvious significance beyond the fact that it is something that someone — evidently the beloved disciple himself — was apt to have remembered. Inferences that this disciple must have been younger than Peter because he was fleeter afoot, or that he was more eager to see the tomb are beside the point. If there is any significance at all in the order of their arrival, it lies in what comes next.

5 What comes next is that the disciple "whom Jesus loved," having reached the tomb first, seems to defer to Peter: "And he stooped down and sees the linen cloths lying, yet did not go in" (v. 5). "The linen cloths"[17] were part of the burial (19:40), and the sight of them lying in the tomb with no sign of a body must, at the very least, have aroused his curiosity. If someone stole the body, as Mary has assumed (v. 2), they have left something behind. The effect on the reader is to begin a process of revealing in three stages (vv. 5, 6-7, and 12) what is, and, more important, what is not, in the tomb. Instead of satisfying his curiosity at once, the beloved disciple holds back and waits for the arrival of Peter, so that Peter might enter first. Peter's threefold denial of Jesus, if it is known, seems not to have damaged his standing among the disciples.

6-7 Peter's arrival at the tomb affords the Gospel writer the opportunity to give a fuller description of what is inside: "Then comes Simon Peter also following him, and entered into the tomb, and he looks at the linen cloths lying, and the cloth which was at his head, not with the linen cloths but rolled up separately in one place" (vv. 6-7). The detailed description sounds like an actual eyewitness report. Because "the disciple whom Jesus loved" is eventually identified as the witness behind much, or all, of what is found in this Gospel (21:24), we would have expected that the contents of the tomb would have been described as viewed through his eyes (see vv. 5 and 8), but it is presented first of all as what *Peter* saw. This is surprising, yet consistent with Luke 24:12, where it was Peter who "got up and ran to the tomb, and stooped down and sees the linen cloths alone, and went home, amazed at what had happened." This notice, lacking in some important manuscripts of Luke,[18] is the only instance outside of the Gospel of John in which any of Je-

---

16. Gr. ὁμοῦ.
17. Gr. τὰ ὀθόνια.
18. The text is one of Westcott and Hort's so-called "non-Western interpolations," omitted in Codex D and in some of the old Latin versions, textual witnesses more often known for their longer and more expansive readings (see Metzger, *Textual Commentary*, 184).

sus' male disciples actually visit the tomb of Jesus. If the author of John's Gospel knows of such a tradition (whether as part of Luke's Gospel or not), he may well have deferred to that tradition, just as "the disciple whom Jesus loved" in the narrative deferred to Peter by allowing him to be the first to enter the tomb. But if, as the Gospel claims (21:24), the author is *himself* that disciple, then he in fact may be the very source of the tradition preserved in Luke as well.[19]

In any event, the description here is far more detailed. In Luke, Peter sees little more than what the other disciple saw in John's Gospel (v. 5). Like that other disciple, he does not even enter the tomb but merely "stoops down"[20] and "sees the linen cloths alone." In our Gospel, he sees also "the cloth which was at his head, not with the linen cloths but rolled up separately in one place" (v. 7). "The cloth" with the definite article[21] (as if to say "the aforementioned cloth") is odd because, in contrast to "the linen cloths," no head cloth was mentioned in connection with the preparation of Jesus' body for burial — just as no "stone" was mentioned in connection with the burial itself. The only such "cloth" we know of was wrapped around the face of Lazarus nine chapters earlier,[22] as he emerged from his tomb. Possibly the intent here is precisely to contrast this tomb with the tomb of Lazarus, and these empty graveclothes and head cloth with the very much present and still bound Lazarus hopping from his tomb! The whole scene — the empty "linen cloths," with the head cloth "rolled up separately in one place" — speaks eloquently against Mary's hasty conclusion that "They have taken away the Lord out of the tomb, and we do not know where they have laid him" (v. 2). "The Lord" is indeed missing, but who would carefully unwrap a body, separate the head cloth, rolling the latter up by itself, and then make off with the naked and mutilated body? It makes no sense, and yet we are not told what conclusion Peter drew from what he saw. His silence here is quite consistent with Luke's description of him as "amazed"[23] at what had happened" (Lk 24:12). The conclusion is left to Peter's companion.

8 Having stepped aside to make room for Peter, the beloved disciple now takes his turn: "So then the other disciple who came first to the tomb went in, and he saw and believed"[24] (v. 8). If this disciple is indeed the author

---

19. The notion that the beloved disciple accompanied Peter to the tomb is consistent with the information supplied in retrospect on the road to Emmaus that "*Some of those* who were with us went to the tomb and found it just as the women had said, but him they did not see" (Lk 24:24, italics added).

20. Gr. παρακύψας, as here in v. 5.

21. Gr. τὸ σουδάριον.

22. Gr. σουδαρίῳ (11:44).

23. Gr. θαυμάζων.

24. Gr. καὶ εἶδεν καὶ ἐπίστευσεν.

of the Gospel, this verse stands as a kind of personal testimony, as if to say, "I went in, and I saw, and I believed." What he does not tell us explicitly is what he saw, and what he believed. The first is not normally discussed in commentaries because the answer seems obvious: he has already told us what he saw, only he told it as if seen through Peter's eyes rather than his own. That is, presumably he saw exactly what Peter saw a moment before: "the linen cloths lying, and the cloth which was at his head, not with the linen cloths but rolled up separately in one place" (v. 7). From this, drawing the conclusion that Peter did not draw (at least not explicitly), he "believed." The aorist tense implies not that he came to faith, having been previously an unbeliever, but that he became convinced or persuaded of something on the basis of what he had just seen.

The brief notice raises two other questions. First, does this disciple's stated "belief" imply Peter's unbelief,[25] or is he in some sense testifying on behalf of both Peter and himself?[26] While his belief contrasts sharply with Peter's "amazement" according to Luke 24:12, it should not be too quickly assumed that Peter is intended to suffer by comparison. The author is, after all, telling Peter's story as an external observer and the beloved disciple's story, presumably, as his own. Quite possibly the reason he does not give Peter's reaction is simply that he is not in a position to do so. He ventures to speak only for himself. In the end, he and Peter are on the same page as far as their faith is concerned (see vv. 9-10), even as the so-called "doubting" Thomas and the other ten disciples (as we will see) end up on the same page, with Thomas finally (and belatedly) speaking for them all (20:28). The second question is, what exactly did this disciple "believe"? Did he believe in the resurrection of Jesus on the basis of the empty tomb and that alone, not having yet seen Jesus alive?[27] There is no other example of such belief in any of the Gospel accounts of the resurrection. He cannot say, as Mary will say later (v. 18), or as the disciples will say to Thomas (v. 25), that he has "seen the Lord." Did he then merely believe Mary's report that "They have taken

---

25. According to Barrett, "It is implied that Peter had not been convinced of the resurrection by the sight of the empty tomb and the grave-clothes" (563); so too Carson (639, appealing to Lk 24:12), Hoskyns (who speaks of the "pre-eminence of the faith of the Beloved Disciple," 540), and Lincoln (491).

26. So Bultmann (684): "Clearly, it is presupposed that Peter before him was likewise brought to faith through the sight of the empty grave; for if the writer had meant otherwise, and if the two disciples were set over against each other with respect to their πιστεῦσαι, it would have had to be expressly stated that Peter did not believe" (see also Morris, 737).

27. This is by far the majority view (see Bultmann, 684; Schnackenburg, 3.312; Lincoln, 490-91; Lindars, 602; Carson, 638; Beasley-Murray, 373; Hoskyns, 540; Keener, 2.1184).

away the Lord out of the tomb, and we do not know where they have laid him" (v. 2).[28] That would be a strange kind of "belief," actually more like unbelief, in a Gospel in which "believing" is of such supreme importance. It would be a case not so much of false or inadequate faith in Jesus (as, for example, in 2:23, or 8:30-31, or 12:42), as of sincerely or genuinely believing something that was not true — that is, that the body of Jesus had been stolen. Moreover, as we have seen, the presence and position of the linen cloth and the head cloth in the tomb have sent just the opposite message: the body cannot have been stolen. What then *did* the disciple "believe"? Is there a third alternative, a middle way between full-fledged resurrection faith on the one hand and Mary's confusion and near despair on the other?

A number of commentators, while acknowledging that in some sense the disciple did believe in the resurrection, nevertheless argue (particularly in light of v. 9) that his understanding of it was still limited.[29] The best answer, perhaps, is to be found in Jesus' farewell discourse: "If you loved me, you would rejoice *that I am going off to the Father,* because the Father is greater than I" (14:28), adding, "And now I have told before it happens, so that when it happens *you might believe*"[30] (14:29, italics added). The disciple "whom Jesus loved," when he entered the tomb and saw what Peter saw, had only to remember those words in order to "believe" that Jesus had in truth gone to the Father, just as he said he would.[31] While his belief is exactly what Jesus intended (14:29), it is not full-fledged resurrection faith, at least not in the Johannine sense, for the latter (as we have seen) involves not only Jesus' departure to the Father but also his return to the disciples (for example, "I will not leave you orphaned. I am coming to you," 14:18, and "You heard that I said to you, 'I am going away and I am coming to you,'" 14:28a).[32] It is by definition an experience of faith, in response to actually seeing Jesus again ("the world no longer sees me, but you see me," 14:19; "again a short time

---

28. So Augustine (on the basis of v. 9): "What then did he see? what was it that he believed? What but this, that he saw the sepulchre empty, and believed what the woman had said, that He had been taken away from the tomb" (*Tractates on John,* 120.9; NPNF, 1st ser., 7.436). Morris allows this as at least a possibility, urging that in any case the notice that he himself "saw and believed" shows not his pride but his humility, in that he "did not attain to the blessing promised to those who believed without seeing" (see v. 29).

29. Typical of these is Whitacre (474): "He has faith in that he recognizes God's fingerprints at the scene. But he still does not understand the full meaning of what he sees."

30. Gr. ἵνα ὅταν γένηται πιστεύσητε.

31. So Charlesworth, *The Beloved Disciple,* 80-81.

32. Andrew Lincoln, questioning this distinction, asks, "What is a bodily glorification and return to the Father if not a resurrection of some sort?" (490-91). "Of some sort," to be sure, but not in the sense that Jesus has described it to his disciples in chapters 14–16.

and you will see me," 16:16; "I will see you again," 16:22). It is not a response to seeing what is *not* there ("but him they did not see," Lk 24:24). True resurrection faith comes to expression in this chapter not when the beloved disciple "saw and believed," but only when Mary is able to say, "I have seen the Lord" (v. 18), and later when the gathered disciples "rejoiced at seeing the Lord" (v. 20; also v. 25). The faith of "the disciple whom Jesus loved," while no less genuine, is to that extent a limited faith.

9 The limitation of the beloved disciple's faith is made explicit in one of his characteristic narrative asides: "For they did not yet know the Scripture, that he must rise from the dead" (v. 9). The plural "they did not know"[33] confirms the notion that the Gospel writer is not setting Peter and the disciple "whom Jesus loved" sharply against one another. They both shared the same limitations, limitations inevitable in the very nature of the case, and for which they are not necessarily being blamed. Twice before we have heard that only *after* Jesus had been "glorified" (12:16) or "raised from the dead" (2:17, 22) did the disciples "remember" and come to understand the scriptures that pointed to him. Even more explicitly in Luke, it is only when the disciples have met the risen Jesus that he "interpreted to them in all the scriptures the things about himself" (Lk 24:27), and "opened their mind to understand the scriptures," telling them that "Thus it is written that the Christ is to suffer and rise from the dead the third day" (24:45-46).[34] This has not yet happened in John's Gospel, for the risen Jesus has not yet made an appearance, and it never happens explicitly, as it does in Luke. At most it can be inferred, possibly from verse 22, when Jesus breathes on the disciples and tells them, "Receive Holy Spirit," and certainly from the earlier promises that the Advocate, or Holy Spirit, "will teach you all things and remind you of all things that I said to you" (14:26), and "lead you in all the truth" (16:13).[35] The disciple "whom Jesus loved," and perhaps Peter as well, "believed" purely on the basis of what they "saw" in the tomb, not on the basis of what Scripture led them to expect.

10 The two disciples, having each entered the tomb, now abruptly depart (just as they came) together, not to appear again individually until

---

33. Gr. οὐδέπω γὰρ ᾔδεισαν.

34. It is likely that in John's Gospel, as in Luke, it is not a matter of one particular passage of Scripture (for example, Ps 16:10, as in Acts 2:31), but of Scripture as a whole (as in Lk 24:44, "everything written in the law of Moses and the prophets and the psalms about me").

35. The NEB and the REB offer a different interpretation: "until then they had not understood the scriptures, which showed that he must rise from the dead," implying that the sight of the graveclothes was what opened their eyes to the true meaning of Scripture. The translation of οὐδέπω as "until then" (instead of "not yet") is unwarranted (see BDAG, 735-36).

chapter 21: "Then the disciples went away again to themselves," or more literally, "to them,"[36] that is, to their respective living quarters. Not a word is spoken. If the beloved disciple alone believed, he is not said to have shared his faith with Peter or with Mary, and if both disciples believed, they seem to have said nothing to Mary, who is left crying at the tomb alone (v. 11). The other disciple's reticence is consistent with his silence in chapter 13 after he found out who it was who was going to hand Jesus over to the Jewish authorities (see 13:25-30). Whatever faith he or Peter may have had, it does not seem to have moved them to immediate action. They merely went home, the beloved disciple presumably to care for the mother of Jesus (see 19:27), and Peter just as he did in Luke's Gospel, where, after looking into the tomb, he "went home,"[37] amazed at what had happened" (Lk 24:12).

11-12 Mary has not been heard from since she summoned the two disciples (v. 2). She had no part in the footrace, and we have not even been told that she returned to the tomb. But with the departure of the men, her story resumes: "Now Mary was standing at the tomb outside, crying. Then as she was crying, she stooped down into the tomb" (v. 11). What she saw was strikingly different from what Peter had seen on entering the tomb. She saw *not* "the linen cloths lying, and the cloth which was at his head . . . rolled up separately in one place" (vv. 6-7), but "two angels in white, seated one at the head and one at the feet, where the body of Jesus had lain" (v. 12).[38] Her "vision of angels" (see Lk 24:23) is to some extent reminiscent of what the women see in the other three Gospels, Luke in particular (Lk 24:4-7, but also Mk 16:5-7 and Mt 28:5-7), but in this Gospel it comes belatedly, only *after* two male disciples have looked into the tomb. Because they have said nothing to her, Mary is unaware of the stark contrast between what she sees and what Peter saw, but the reader cannot help but notice it. The two descriptions of the contents of the tomb are only moments apart, at least in narrative time, but one is forced to wonder: What are we supposed to conclude was actually in that tomb, a few scattered grave clothes, or two angels in white? Why does Peter see one thing, and Mary Magadalene another? And Mary's vision

---

36. Gr. πρὸς αὐτούς. This is the better-supported reading (with ℵ*, B, L, and others), as against πρὸς ἑαυτούς (with a corrector of ℵ, A, D, W, Θ, Ψ, and the majority of later manuscripts), which unmistakably means "to themselves." Πρὸς αὐτούς can mean either "to themselves" in the sense of to their quarters, or "to them," meaning to the apostles as a group, wherever they might be. The latter is unlikely because of πάλιν, "again" or "back," that is, back to where they came from in the first place (v. 2), wherever they were previously staying.

37. Gr. πρὸς ἑαυτόν.

38. That the two angels are "in white" (ἐν λευκοῖς) agrees with every other resurrection account, whether of "a young man" (Mk 16:5), "an angel of the Lord" (Mt 28:3), or "two men" ("in dazzling clothes," Lk 24:4; "dressed in white," Acts 1:10).

20:1-18 THE EMPTY TOMB AND THE FIRST APPEARANCE

prompts us to revisit another question that we thought was already answered: What did the beloved disciple "see" that led him to "believe" (v. 8)? Did he see what Peter saw a moment before, or what Mary saw a short time after? Why is he so reticent about what he himself saw, contenting himself with describing two different scenes through the eyes of two different people? The questions multiply, and there are no obvious answers.

Most commentators ignore such questions, solving the problem instead by the use of source or tradition criticism, and in the process sacrificing the coherence and integrity of the narrative. We do not have to ask why the male disciples and Mary viewed contrasting scenes within the tomb, they reason, because their differing visions originally belonged to two different stories. Raymond Brown is a good example. Brown isolates three distinct traditions behind the Johannine narrative:[39]

(a) A story about women disciples coming to the tomb, finding it empty, and seeing a vision of some kind (Jn 20:1 and 11-13; this is comparable to the opening verses of Mark 16, Matthew 28, and Luke 24).
(b) A story about male disciples visiting the empty tomb and going away puzzled (20:2-10; this is comparable to Lk 24:12, 24).
(c) A story about a resurrection appearance to Mary Magdalene (20:14-18; this is comparable to Mt 28:9-10, and to the Markan appendix, 16:9).

Mark's Gospel has only the first of these; the appendix to Mark adds the third; Matthew has the first and the third; Luke has the first and the second; only the Gospel of John includes all three. John's Gospel also differs from the others in postponing Mary's vision of angels in the tomb until after Peter and the other disciple have entered the tomb and seen the graveclothes, thus creating the odd discrepancy between what they saw and what Mary sees. In all three synoptic Gospels, by contrast, Mary's vision comes first, and a considerable body of scholarly opinion assumes that this was originally the case in the Johannine tradition as well — as if to say that verse 11 was originally intended to follow verse 1.[40] At that stage of the tradition, Mary

---

39. See Brown, 2.998-1004.
40. Lindars, for example, commenting on verse 11, says, "it seems to have been forgotten that Mary has left the tomb, though it is possible to get round the difficulty by imagining that she followed the two disciples back to the tomb. But it is really due to imperfect interweaving of two separate traditions. John is now back at the situation of verse 1, and what follows is the material which was omitted from the story of the women" (603). So too Bultmann: "It is remarkable, for example, that in v. 11 Mary is standing at the grave, whereas according to v. 2 she had departed from it and no account is given of her return to it. Since, nevertheless, her return has to be presupposed, it is remarkable in

saw that the stone had been taken away from the tomb (v. 1), and instead of running to tell Peter and the other disciple (v. 2), she stood "at the tomb outside, crying," and then "stooped down into the tomb" and saw what she saw (vv. 11-12). Because nothing precedes it, her vision stands on its own. There is no need to compare or contrast it with anything that someone else saw.

Such constructions make for fascinating reading, and something of the kind may even have happened. But a commentator's job is not to interpret a text by describing how it came to be, but by describing it as it actually is, in its present form. When all is said and done, if the Gospel of John has made the kind of adaptations and rearrangements that are proposed, what is the effect of its artistry? What are we left with? Are we absolved of all responsibility to understand Mary's vision in relation to what has preceded it? No. The way to interpret a text is to interpret the text, not its sources or what preceded it.[41] When Mary's "vision of angels" is read seriously in its present context, certain parallels are evident between her experience and that of the male disciples, even though what she saw was quite different. Like the beloved disciple at first (v. 5), she did not enter the tomb but "stooped down,"[42] and like Peter (who did enter the tomb, v. 6), she "looked" in.[43] The two angels, positioned as they were "one at the head and one at the feet, where the body of Jesus had lain" (v. 12), sent the same message that the empty linen cloths and the head cloth had sent. They did not need to say, like the young man in Mark (for example), "He is risen; he is not here. See the place where they laid him" (Mk 16:6; compare Mt 28:6; Lk 24:5-6). Their body language said it all, more eloquently (if not more plainly) than the scattered grave clothes a few verses earlier. Jesus' body was gone, and the presence of angels implied that God had something to do with it.

And yet Mary's remarkable vision did not lead her to "see and believe," as the beloved disciple had done just moments before. Instead she kept on "crying."[44] It becomes evident that the disciple "whom Jesus loved" had not alleviated her tears by sharing with her his newfound faith that Jesus had gone to the Father (v. 8). Instead, he had simply gone home with Peter (v. 10). He showed the same reticence toward Mary that he showed toward

---

the extreme that the experience of the two disciples, whom she must have met at least on their return from the grave, holds no significance for her. In vv. 11ff. she stands at the grave, as if the events recounted in vv. 3-10 had not happened" (681).

41. In short, and in somewhat more technical vocabulary, I am privileging a *synchronic* over a *diachronic* reading (as I have tried to do throughout).

42. Gr. παρέκυψεν.

43. Gr. θεωρεῖ.

44. The present and imperfect tenses, "crying" (κλαίουσα, v. 11), "as she was crying" (ὡς οὖν ἔκλαιεν, v. 11), and "Why are you crying?" (τί κλαίεις, vv. 13, 15), bear this out.

the reader in not revealing exactly what he himself "saw" in the tomb that led him to "believe," and the same reticence he showed toward all the disciples at the last meal, when he learned who would hand Jesus over, yet did not share with them that information (see 13:25-30). Whatever we may say of his silence here, it is in keeping with what little we know of this disciple's character and behavior. If he is, as the Gospel claims, the author of the Gospel (21:24), he has left us with two cameo glimpses of what was in the tomb of Jesus: one through a man's eyes (v. 6) and one through a woman's (v. 12), one consisting of so-called hard evidence, the other a "vision of angels" (see Lk 24:23). The first is a stereotypical "male" vision, the second just as stereotypically "female."[45] The question of which vision the beloved disciple himself saw, or (to put it another way) what was "really" in the tomb, is left to the reader to decide. More important by far is what was *not* there: the body of Jesus ("but him they did not see," Lk 24:24). Ambiguities remain, but ambiguities are part of the reading experience. They should not be made to disappear by source or tradition criticism.[46]

13 Instead of stating the obvious ("He is not here. See the place where they laid him"), the two angels ask Mary a question,[47] "Woman, why are you crying?" (v. 13a), addressing her in the same way Jesus customarily addresses women (2:4; 4:21; 8:10; 19:26; see v. 15). The question is simply a corollary of "He is not here." His absence from the tomb is a reason for joy, not tears. Why then the tears? Mary's reply is surprisingly (and depressingly) familiar: "They have taken away my Lord, and I do not know where they have laid him" (v. 13b), simply echoing verse 2, in slightly more personal language: "*my* Lord," and "*I* do not know" (italics added). In sharp contrast

---

45. The gender stereotypes are more evident in Luke, where the women "told all these things to the eleven and to the rest," but their testimony seemed to the men "like an idle tale [ὡσεὶ λῆρος], and they did not believe them" (Lk 24:11), after which Peter ran to the tomb and saw only graveclothes (v. 12).

46. A possible analogy presents itself in British author John Fowles's imaginative novel *A Maggot* (Boston: Little, Brown, 1985), about the origins of Mother Ann Lee and the Shakers. There we find two conflicting testimonies about what was seen in a mysterious cave in the west of England not far from Stonehenge. One witness claimed to have seen a dark Satanic ritual centering on an evil, black-haired woman dressed all in silver, while another testified of a woman similar in demeanor but pure and holy in her intentions who led the heroine to a place "All green, as high summer. And the sun shone on all, like to June eternal" (p. 369), a place of joy and beauty, a vision of heaven itself, though not explicitly Christian. The vision transforms Rebecca Lee into a prophetess and the mother of a prophetess, and — in Fowles's imagination — the Shakers are born. At the end of the day the reader is left to decide what was really in the cave — and perhaps what the word "really" really means! The alternatives are not nearly so stark here in John's Gospel because the two scenes send the same message: Jesus has gone to the Father.

47. As in Luke (24:5-7) and Acts (1:11), the two speak as one.

to the disciple who "saw and believed" (v. 8), Mary sees but does *not* believe. Her vision of two angels in white trumps Peter's vision of scattered graveclothes (v. 6) and possibly the beloved disciple's vision as well, yet it produces no faith. It does not enter her mind that Jesus has gone to the Father. Instead she clings to her misguided assumption that someone (an indefinite "they") has taken away the body for reburial. And yet she, not Peter and not even "the disciple whom Jesus loved," will be the first to experience and articulate true resurrection faith.

14 How does this happen? Only at the initiative of Jesus, who stands behind Mary, waiting for her to "turn around": "And having said these things she turned around and looks at Jesus standing there, and she did not know that it was Jesus" (v. 14). Because she has not actually entered the tomb, Mary has only to "turn around"[48] in order to see him. Having "looked" into the tomb (v. 13), she now "looks" in the opposite direction and sees him, yet "she did not know that it was Jesus." The transition from seeing one or more angels to seeing Jesus is found also in Matthew, where an angel tells the two women (Mary Magdalene and "the other Mary") not to fear because Jesus is risen, and sends them to the disciples, and as soon as they start on their way, Jesus himself meets them and tells them much the same thing (Mt 28:5-10). Here, however, instead of recognizing him and falling down to worship him (Mt 28:9), Mary "did not know that it was Jesus," confirming her own admission that "I do not know where they have laid him" (v. 13). Her failure to recognize him, while not paralleled in Matthew, is consistent with certain other resurrection appearances in which the risen Jesus' identity is similarly concealed, at least temporarily, from his disciples (see 21:4; Lk 24:16).

15 Just as in Matthew (28:10), the risen Jesus says to Mary just what the angels said, "Woman, why are you crying?" (v. 15a, as in v. 13). But he adds, "Whom are you seeking?"[49] not "What are you seeking?" as he once said to his first potential disciples (1:38), but "Whom," as he said to those who came to arrest him in another garden (18:4, 6). His words recall those of the young man at the tomb in Mark (16:6) and the angel in Matthew (28:5), "You are seeking Jesus, the Crucified One," and even more the question of the two men at the tomb in Luke: "Why do you seek the living with the dead?" (Lk 24:5). Whether she knows it or not, Mary is looking for a living person, not a dead body, as she has already intimated in speaking of "the Lord" (v. 2) and "my Lord" (v. 13).

---

48. Gr. ἐστράφη εἰς τὰ ὀπίσω. For the expression ἀπῆλθον εἰς τὰ ὀπίσω in a negative sense, see 6:66 ("turned back"), and 18:6 ("drew back"). Here a different verb (ἐστράφη) gives it a different meaning: Mary simply "turned around" to face away from the tomb and into the garden.

49. Gr. τίνα ζητεῖς.

20:1-18 THE EMPTY TOMB AND THE FIRST APPEARANCE

Mary's answer confirms this: "She,[50] thinking that he is the gardener, says to him, 'Sir, if you have carried *him* off, tell me where you have laid *him*, and I will take *him* away'" (v. 15b, italics added). Always "him"[51] and not "it."[52] Like the man born blind after he was healed (see 9:36), Mary is talking *to* Jesus *about* Jesus, without realizing to whom she is speaking. Nothing that she has seen — not the stone rolled away from the tomb, not the sight of two angels in the tomb guarding an empty space, not even the sight of Jesus himself — has shaken her stubborn conclusion that he has been taken away and reburied. In contrast to the beloved disciple, Mary has seen but has not believed. She is seeking and not finding, but at least she has named the Object of her search correctly — "my Lord" (v. 13). Ironically, she addresses the Stranger she believes to be "the gardener" as "Sir," the same word she might have used had she known who he was.[53]

16 What sight could not do, hearing finally accomplishes. Only one word is necessary: "Jesus says to her, 'Mary!' Turning, she says to him in Hebrew, 'Rabbouni,' which means 'Teacher!'" (v. 16). Once again (as in 11:43), Jesus puts into practice the principle that the Good Shepherd "summons his own sheep by name" (10:3).[54] This time he is not calling someone out of a tomb (as he did Lazarus), but away from an empty tomb and toward himself. The sound of her own name awakens Mary as if out of sleep — the sleep of despair. Again she is described as "turning,"[55] a term that sounds redundant after she has already "turned around" from the vision in the tomb to face Jesus. This time, perhaps, it refers to her state of mind no less than to her body language,[56] yet, as we will see (v. 17), she may have turned her body toward Jesus as well.[57]

As one who "knows his voice" (see 10:4-5), she responds to his one word, "Mary!" with a one-word answer of her own. "Rabbouni," literally "my Teacher," is often regarded as a more personal and affectionate title than

---

50. Gr. ἐκείνη. In both of her answers to Jesus (in contrast to her answer to the two angels, v. 13), Mary is identified with an emphatic pronoun (ἐκείνη), accenting her back-and-forth dialogue with Jesus (ἐκείνη δοκοῦσα here, and στραφεῖσα ἐκείνη in v. 16).

51. Gr. αὐτόν.

52. That is, as if referring to τὸ σῶμα ("the body").

53. Gr. κύριε, translated as "sir" when addressed to a stranger, but elsewhere, "Lord." Again, compare the words of the man born blind in speaking to Jesus (see 9:36 and 38).

54. This is widely recognized among commentators (see Bultmann, 686; Barrett, 564; Schnackenburg, 3.317).

55. Gr. στραφεῖσα.

56. See BDAG, 948: "to turn," but also "to experience an inward change" (see 12:40; Mt 18:3).

57. Compare Revelation 1:12, "And I turned [ἐπέστρεψα] to see the voice that was speaking with me."

"Rabbi," yet the difference should not be pressed. The Gospel writer translates the "Hebrew" (actually Aramaic)[58] title for his Greek-speaking readers simply as "Teacher," exactly as he translated "Rabbi" on the lips of those who would become his first disciples (1:38). Jesus later told his male disciples, "You call me 'Teacher' and 'Lord,' and you say well, for I am" (13:13), and there is every evidence that his female disciples spoke of him in the same way. At Bethany, Martha "summoned Mary her sister, and told her privately, 'The Teacher is here, and is summoning you'" (11:28). Mary Magdalene, like Mary of Bethany, and like the sheep in 10:3, has also been "summoned" (although the word is not used),[59] and she responds accordingly.[60]

17 Jesus immediately cautions Mary, "Don't take hold of me, for I have not yet gone up[61] to my Father. But go to my brothers and say to them, 'I am going up to my Father and your Father, and my God and your God'" (v. 17). He seems to have interpreted her "turning" toward him (vv. 14, 16) as an attempt to embrace him, or perhaps to "clasp his feet" in an act of worship (see Mt 28:9).[62] "Don't take hold of me"[63] could mean either "Let go of me," implying that she had already taken hold of him, or (more likely), "Do not attempt to hold on to me." The reason he gives recalls his repeated statements to the male disciples earlier that "Where I am going, you cannot come" (13:33), or "Where I am going you cannot follow now, but you will follow later" (13:36), except that instead of "going," or "going off" (14:2, 3), he speaks here of "going up" to the Father (as in 3:13 and 6:62). Mary must not "hold on" to him. Like the male disciples, she must prepare for her Lord and Teacher's absence. She has already wept because "They have taken away my

---

58. On "Hebrew" as Aramaic, see 19:13, 17; in 5:2 and 19:20 it could be either.

59. The use of Mary's name takes the place of the verb "summon" (φωνεῖ). It is the sound of her name, plus the sound of Jesus' "voice" (φωνή), that triggers the moment of recognition (in addition to 10:4-5, see 11:43, where it is Jesus' "voice" calling Lazarus's name that brings him from the tomb; also 5:25 and 28, where the "voice" of the Son of God summons all the dead).

60. It is noteworthy that the only other occurrence of "Rabbouni" in the New Testament is on the lips of blind Bartimaeus in Jericho, who is also repeatedly said to have been "summoned": "Jesus stopped, and said, 'Summon him' [φωνήσατε αὐτόν], and they summon [φωνοῦσιν] the blind man, saying to him, 'Take heart, arise! He summons you!'" (φωνεῖ σε). When Jesus asked him, "What do you want me to do for you?" the blind beggar said, "Rabbouni, that I might receive my sight" (Mk 10:51).

61. Gr. οὔπω γὰρ ἀναβέβηκα.

62. Some ancient witnesses, including the first corrector of ℵ, Θ, Ψ, and some manuscripts of the Vulgate, add the words, "and she ran toward him to take hold of him" (καὶ προσέδραμεν ἀψάσθαι αὐτοῦ) at the end of verse 16 as a transition to the present verse, and an explanation of why he said what he did. This reading would surely not have been omitted had it been original.

63. Gr. μή μου ἅπτου.

20:1-18 THE EMPTY TOMB AND THE FIRST APPEARANCE

Lord, and I do not know where they have laid him" (v. 13), and now she must learn that her reunion with him is a momentary reunion, one that cannot last.

The reader who reads on will be tempted to contrast this warning to Mary with Jesus' bold invitation to Thomas a few verses later to "Bring your finger here and see my hands, and bring your hand and put it in my side" (v. 27). Why is Mary forbidden to take hold of him and Thomas explicitly invited to do so? Is it because she is a woman and Thomas is a man? Or does the contrast mean that somehow by the time Jesus appears to Thomas, he has already gone up to the Father and come back again, so that they are now free to touch him? One must be careful about such assumptions, for the two situations are not comparable. Mary wants to take hold of Jesus (at least if the analogy with Mt 28:9 is in play) as an act of devotion or worship, while Thomas wants to do so (as we will see) for verification (v. 25). While worship is appropriate — even *before* Jesus' resurrection (see 9:38) — the time is not right. Jesus has other plans for Mary. The point is not that she is in danger of preventing Jesus from ascending — how could she do so even if she tried? — but that the longer she stayed with Jesus, the later she would be in delivering the message Jesus gave her. The command, "Don't take hold of me," is strictly preliminary to the main thing Jesus wants to say to Mary, "But go to my brothers[64] and tell them, 'I am going up to my Father and your Father, and my God and your God'" (v. 17b). He has "not yet gone up to the Father," but now he is "going up[65] to my Father." It is unclear whether the present tense actually refers to something in the near or immediate future, like "going" or "going off" in the farewell discourse, or whether the process of "going up" has in some sense already begun.

Whichever it is, it involves a change in his relationship to the Father, a change involving the disciples as well. Up to now, Jesus' "brothers" and his "disciples" have been clearly distinguished from one another (see 2:12). His disciples "believed in him" (2:11), while his brothers did not (7:5). Yet now, abruptly, the term "brothers" refers to the disciples, for it is to them that Mary will deliver the message (v. 18). Once again, the statement recalls the risen Jesus' command to Mary Magdalene and "the other Mary" in Matthew, "Don't be afraid. Go tell my brothers[66] that they should go away into Galilee, and there they will see me" (Mt 28:10), yet with significant differences. Here, instead of "Don't be afraid," which is more or less expected (after 28:5), we have "Don't take hold of me," which is quite unexpected. Also, instead of promising a visit to Galilee, where the disciples will see him, he merely confirms that he is going away — more specifically, "going up" to the Father — and makes no promise about seeing him again. Yet the two stories

---

64. Gr. πορεύου δὲ πρὸς τοὺς ἀδελφούς μου.
65. Gr. ἀναβαίνω.
66. Gr. τοῖς ἀδελφοῖς μου.

have in common the sending of the woman (or women) to the disciples with a message, and — more remarkably — Jesus' reference to his male disciples as "my brothers." Matthew offers no explanation for the abrupt change in terminology, for the angel at the tomb had referred previously to "his disciples" (v. 7). At most, the shift could be inferred (if the reader had a good memory) from Mt 12:49, where Jesus "pointed his hand at his disciples and said, 'Look, my mother and my brothers!'" John's Gospel, however, provides a definition of "brothers" in the immediate context, for Mary is to "say to them, 'I am going up to my Father and your Father,[67] and my God and your God'" (v. 17b). Jesus' disciples are his "brothers" in that they have the same "Father" in heaven, the God of Israel whom they worship. One of them, as we have seen (19:27), even has the same mother! This is a milestone in the Gospel, for it is the first and only instance (out of 120 in all!) in which God is explicitly identified as "Father" of anyone except Jesus himself. Once or twice Jesus has come close to such an identification, as when he told the Samaritan woman of a day "when the true worshipers will worship the Father in Spirit and truth" (4:23), or when he called the disciples his "friends" (15:14-15), and reminded them that "the Father himself loves you,[68] because you have loved me" (16:27; also 14:21, 23). Still, it has always been either "the Father" or "my Father," never until now "your Father" — this despite the designation of believers as "children of God" (1:13; 11:52). It is almost the exact opposite of the other Gospels, notably Matthew and most notably the Sermon on the Mount, where Jesus begins by referring to God over and over again (beginning in Mt 5:16) as "Your Father," or "Your Father in heaven," and only near the end discloses that the key to it all is "doing the will of *my* Father who is in heaven" (Mt 7:21; see also Mt 11:27). In John's Gospel, by contrast, "the Father" is Jesus' Father first of all, and only by virtue of his resurrection the Father of those who believe.[69]

The question remains, Is the message Mary is to deliver a message for her as well? Is she included among those to whom Jesus says, "I am going up to my Father and your Father, and my God and your God"? If the male disciples are his "brothers," is she numbered among his "sisters"?[70] What does the

---

67. Gr. πρὸς τὸν πατέρα μου καὶ πατέρα ὑμῶν.

68. Gr. φιλεῖ ὑμᾶς (just as he "loves the Son," 5:20).

69. In 1-2 John, where Jesus is the risen One, God is Father both to the Son and to those who believe in the Son, (see, for example, 1 Jn 3:1, 5:1), even though they never explicitly lay claim to being Jesus' "brothers" (for that, see Heb 2:11-12).

70. For obvious reasons, even English translations firmly committed to inclusive language (NRSV, TNIV) translate τοὺς ἀδελφούς μου as "my brothers," not "my brothers and sisters." Yet see *The New Testament and Psalms: An Inclusive Version* (New York: Oxford, 1995): "But go to my sisters and brothers and say to them, 'I am ascending to my Father-Mother and your Father-Mother, to my God and your God'"(!).

message mean for the messenger? Perhaps the answer depends in part on whether Jesus is using direct or indirect discourse. It is a matter of definition. Strictly speaking, he is using direct discourse, in that "I am going up to my Father and your Father, and my God and your God," is exactly what he wants to tell his disciples. Yet it is indirect, in that Mary will not use just those words, and those alone. She will not presume to speak for Jesus in the first person, like a prophet speaking for God. Rather, she will speak for herself, referring to him in the third person as she repeats what he told her to say: either "Jesus is going up to his Father and your Father," and so on, or (more likely) "Jesus said to me, 'I am going up to my Father and your Father. . . .'"[71] The words are spoken, after all, first to Mary, representing all who believe or would believe, male or female — not least the presumably male and female readers of the Gospel! It is Mary's job to pass the message along in her own words to the male disciples, wherever they might be, thereby making them the first of Jesus' honorary "brothers." If the pronouncement elevates humankind to the point of being able to address God directly as "Father," even as Jesus has done, it confirms at the same time Jesus' humanity, to the point of worshiping "my God and your God" as any human being might do, even though he has been introduced from the very beginning of the Gospel as himself "God" (see 1:1, 18).[72]

18 We are not told how the encounter between Jesus and Mary Magdalene ended. Having said, "I am going up to my Father," did he take his leave and visibly ascend in her presence, as the angel Raphael did in the book of Tobit?[73] Or did she obey him and immediately take her leave, with Jesus still standing in the garden? As far as we know, it was the latter, for we see her next delivering her message to the disciples. That she does not simply repeat Jesus' words verbatim is confirmed by what follows: "Mary Magdalene comes, announcing to the disciples that 'I have seen the Lord,' and [that] he said these things to her" (v. 18). Her first words are, "I [Mary] have seen the Lord," not "I [the Lord] am going up to my Father and your Father," and when she goes on to convey the Lord's message, she does so by switching abruptly to indirect discourse — so abruptly as to attract attention, whether in Greek or in English. She delivers the message, but *in her own words,* making

---

71. See BDF, §470[1]: "Also Jn 20:17 εἰπὲ αὐτοῖς (my Master says to tell you,) ἀναβαίνω." The author classifies this as direct discourse, but it could just as easily be viewed as indirect.

72. See 17:3, where Jesus himself is represented as praying "that they might know you, the only true God, and him whom you sent, Jesus Christ."

73. Raphael's words in Tobit signal an actual departure: "And now give thanks to God, for I am ascending to him who sent me [ἀναβαίνω πρὸς τὸν ἀποστείλαντά με]. Write in a book everything that has happened. Then they stood up; but they saw him no more" (Tobit 12:20-21, RSV).

it unmistakably clear that Jesus "said these things to her"[74] first. Clearly, she implies, the words "my Father and your Father" were meant for her no less than for the male disciples.

Who were "the disciples" to whom Mary came, and whom Jesus has called his "brothers" (v. 17)? The last we knew, "the disciples" were just two in number, Peter and the one "whom Jesus loved," returning to their quarters after visiting the tomb (v. 10). Mary knew where to find them before (v. 2), and it is natural to suppose that she would know where to find them again. If the present narrative were all we had, we would assume that they were "the disciples" to whom she came. As it is, the scenes that follows (vv. 19-23 and 24-29) virtually require that Mary brought the message to a larger group, perhaps as many as ten or eleven. In any event, we learn nothing of how "the disciples," however many they may have been, reacted to her message, nor what the message may have led them to expect. All we know is that they will echo Mary's words — her own words, not the ones she was given to deliver — making them their words as well: "We have seen the Lord" (v. 25).

E. THE SECOND APPEARANCE: THE DISCIPLES AND THOMAS (20:19-31)

> 19 *Then when it was late on that first day of the week, and the doors being locked where the disciples were for fear of the Jews, Jesus came and stood in the midst and says to them, "Peace to you." 20 And having said this, he showed them the hands and the side. Then the disciples rejoiced, seeing the Lord. 21 Then Jesus said to them again, "Peace to you. Just as the Father has sent me, so I am sending you." 22 And having said this, he breathed, and he says to them, "Receive Holy Spirit. 23 Whosoever's sins you forgive, they are forgiven to them; whosoever's you retain, they are retained."*
>
> *24 Now Thomas, one of the Twelve, the one called Didymos, was not with them when Jesus came. 25 So the other disciples were saying to him, "We have seen the Lord." And he said to them, "Unless I see in his hands the print of the nails, and put my finger into the print of the nails, and put my hand into his side, I will never believe." 26 And after eight days the disciples were again inside, and Thomas with them. Jesus comes, the doors being locked, and stood in the midst, and said, "Peace to you." 27 Then he says to Thomas, "Bring your finger here and see my hands, and bring your hand and put it into my side, and be no longer faithless but faithful." 28 Thomas answered and said to him, "My Lord*

---

74. Gr. ταῦτα εἶπεν αὐτῇ.

20:19-31 THE SECOND APPEARANCE: THE DISCIPLES AND THOMAS

and my God!" 29 Jesus says to him that "Because you have seen me, you have believed. Blessed are those who did not see, and believed."

30 Now Jesus did many, and other, signs in the presence of his disciples which are not written in this book. 31 But these are written so that you might believe that Jesus is the Christ, the Son of God, and that believing you might have life in his name.

In this Gospel, in contrast to Matthew, Jesus has given Mary no promise that the disciples will see him again, whether in "Galilee" (Mt 28:10) or anywhere else. She herself has "seen the Lord" (v. 18), but the message she delivers is that he is on his way to the Father (v. 17), not that he will appear to them. Nothing that she tells them, but only what they might have remembered of Jesus' own words (for example, 14:3, 18-19, 21, 23, 28; 16:16-23), gives them hope of seeing him once more, and they seem not to have been expecting him. Yet he does appear to them, and quickly verifies first that he is their crucified Lord (v. 20) and second that he is nonetheless alive (v. 22), at the same time empowering them by the Holy Spirit to carry on his mission (vv. 21-23). Like Mary (v. 18), they are able to say "We have seen the Lord," passing the testimony along to their absent companion, Thomas (vv. 24-25). Thomas demands the verification they themselves have been given, and more (v. 25), and when Jesus comes back again eight days later, he offers Thomas the verification, just as before (v. 20), without being asked (v. 27). Thomas can only say, "My Lord and my God!" (v. 28).

The two appearances are best viewed as a single appearance in two parts. In the other Gospel traditions the disciples reacted with unbelief to the report of the women (see Lk 24:11; Mk 16:11), and even when Jesus appeared to them, "on seeing him they worshiped, but some doubted" (Mt 28:17; also Lk 24:41; Mk 16:13, 14). In this Gospel, the doubt is shifted to Thomas alone, yet he is in no way differentiated from the other disciples. Their "joy" at seeing Jesus, and their experience of having "seen the Lord," is incomplete without Thomas's participation in it, and in the end his decisive confession, "My Lord and my God!" (v. 28), is theirs as well. Who would want to argue that they but not he are "sent" (v. 21), that they but not Thomas "receive Holy Spirit" (v. 22), or that the power to forgive or retain sins belongs to all of them but Thomas (v. 23)? No, what is said to the rest of the disciples in verses 19-23 is, in effect, said to Thomas as well, and what is said to him in verses 26-29 is said to them all. Jesus' concluding words, "Because you have seen me, you have believed" (v. 29), are just as true of them as of Thomas. Clearly, he functions as their representative and spokesman *both* in his skepticism and in his faith. It is hard not to wonder if there is just a touch of skepticism in the disciples' joy on "seeing the Lord" (v. 20), just as in Luke, when he "showed them his hands and feet" (see Lk 24:40-41).

In contrast both to Thomas and the rest of the disciples, Jesus reserves a beatitude for those who believe *without* the need of such verification (v. 29), and finally, echoing this beatitude, the Gospel writer tells the reader that he has given only a sampling of Jesus' many "signs in the presence of his disciples." He could have provided many more, he implies, but "these are written so that you might believe that Jesus is the Christ, the Son of God, and that believing you might have life in his name" (v. 31). It has become almost a commonplace in the interpretation of John's Gospel that these words at some stage of the tradition concluded the Gospel. They sound so much like an ending that something close to a consensus has developed that chapter 21 was added later to the Gospel, either by the author of the first twenty chapters or by someone else. This is quite possibly the case, but going even further such interpreters frequently treat these verses as if they were *even now* the Gospel's last words — as if chapter 21 did not exist. The trouble is that there is no evidence in any existing manuscript of the Gospel of John that it ever circulated without chapter 21. If 20:30-31 were at some point prior to the Gospel's circulation intended to be its conclusion, they are no longer. The job of a commentary is not to interpret what the Gospel might have been "at some point," but what it was by the time it was released into the world.

Consequently, the last two verses of this chapter are not quite so momentous as some modern interpreters have made them out to be. The Gospel writer is not so much summarizing his overall purpose in writing the Gospel as simply turning to his readers to explain to them that Jesus' beatitude on "those who did not see and believed" (v. 29) applies to them, for they have seen none of these things firsthand. They are asked instead to believe what is "written." The question of whether the Gospel was written to convert unbelievers or to strengthen the faith of those who — like Thomas and the others — have already "believed" should not be settled on the basis of these verses, and these alone. As for the "signs in the presence of the disciples" (v. 30), another near consensus among scholars identifies them as the series of "signs" or miracles that Jesus performed in the first half of the Gospel, beginning with the wedding at Cana (2:1-11, the "first sign") and the healing of the nobleman's son (4:43-54, the "second sign"), and continuing with the healing of the sick man at Bethsaida (chapter 5), the feeding of the five thousand and walking on the water (chapter 6), the healing of the blind man (chapter 9), and the raising of Lazarus from the dead (chapter 11). This too, as we will see, is open to question.

19 The scene shifts from one enclosed space — the garden, with the enclosed tomb inside it — to another, a locked room: "Then when it was late on that first day of the week, and the doors being locked where the disciples were for fear of the Jews, Jesus came and stood in the midst and says to them,

20:19-31   THE SECOND APPEARANCE: THE DISCIPLES AND THOMAS

'Peace to you'" (v. 19). The expression "late[1] on that first day of the week" establishes continuity with the opening lines of the preceding section: "On the first day of the week, Mary Magdalene comes early, while it was dark" (v. 1). "That first day" is unmistakably the same day, now drawing to a close. Yet there is also a disconnect. Mary has delivered the message Jesus gave her to deliver (v. 18), but we have no information as to how, or even if, the disciples received it. Has she been to this locked room "where the disciples were for fear of the Jews"? Odd as it is, the disconnect is to some degree common to all the Gospels. In Mark (16:8) the women "said nothing to anyone, for they were afraid"; in the longer ending to Mark and in Luke they delivered the message, but the male disciples did not believe them (see Mk 16:11; Lk 24:11); in Matthew they ran to deliver the message (28:8,10), and the disciples went accordingly to a mountain in Galilee (28:16), but nothing was said as to when or how the message was received, or whether it included any mention of a mountain. Similarly here, we do not find the disciples rejoicing in Mary's good news that she has "seen the Lord" (v. 18). Instead, they are hiding out behind locked doors.[2] For the moment at least they are reduced to being, like Joseph of Arimathea, disciples "secretly for fear of the Jews" (see 19:38) — this even though Jesus has taken every precaution to ensure their safety (see 18:8-9, 19-21).

Still, their reception of the message is likely presupposed even though not explicit. Assuming that they had heard the words, "I am going up to my Father and your Father, and my God and your God" (v. 17), and that Mary had seen the risen Lord, this would not have led them to expect that *they* would see Jesus. On the contrary, if he was on his way to the Father, as he had told them again and again before, and as the beloved disciple already believed (v. 8), they would *not* have expected to see him immediately. At least "a short time" (16:16) would have to pass, a time of mourning and weeping, before they would see him again (see 16:16-22). His coming, therefore, is unexpected, and possibly miraculous, although nothing is made of its miraculous character.[3] Did he just appear suddenly behind the locked doors, or did he knock and gain admission (like Peter in Acts 12:13)? Miraculous it may well be, but if it is a miracle, the miracle is

---

1. Gr. ὀψίας.
2. Some ancient manuscripts (including a corrector of ℵ, Θ, L, Δ, Ψ, 33, families 1 and 13, and the majority of later manuscripts, as well as some ancient versions) add that they were "gathered" (συνηγμένοι), evoking the imagery of Shepherd and sheep and possibly also weekly Christian worship as readers of the Gospel might have practiced it. But the overwhelming manuscript evidence (including ℵ, B, A, D, W, and most Latin and Syriac versions) is against it.
3. It is unclear whether the "locked doors" (τῶν θυρῶν κεκλεισμένων) are literally locked or simply closed (see BDAG, 546-47).

not the point.⁴ The accent is not on *how* he came but on the simple fact *that* "Jesus came⁵ and stood in the midst and says to them, 'Peace to you.' "⁶ The language echoes the farewell discourses: "I will not leave you orphaned. I am coming to you" (14:18); "Peace I leave with you, my peace I give you" (14:27); "I am going away, and I am coming to you" (14:18); "These things I have spoken to you so that in me you might have peace" (16:33). What he promised in departing comes to realization anew in what might otherwise have seemed a routine greeting, "Peace to you" (see Lk 10:5-6), one that we will hear twice more (vv. 21, 26).

20 With the greeting goes an action: "And having said this,⁷ he showed them the hands and the side. Then the disciples rejoiced, seeing the Lord" (v. 20). The apparent purpose of showing the disciples "the hands and the side"⁸ is to verify that he is indeed Jesus, who was crucified. Yet it is a strange kind of verification, for the piercing of Jesus' hands was not even mentioned in the account of his crucifixion, and the puncturing of his side (19:34) was witnessed by only one of them (at most), the disciple whom he loved — if indeed that disciple was still on the scene (see 19:25-27), and if he is present here.⁹ Obviously, the account presupposes that the circumstances of the crucifixion had somehow become generally known among the disciples, and the now absent Thomas will shortly confirm that this was the case (v. 25).

The disciples' only reaction to anything Jesus does in the entire scene is stated immediately and concisely. They "rejoiced,¹⁰ seeing the Lord." The

---

4. Bultmann argues precisely to the contrary: "The stated reason for this circumstance is their fear of the Jews, but essentially it is because by this means the coming of Jesus is shown to be a miracle, and thus from the first his form is characterized as divine" (690-91).

5. Gr. ἦλθεν ὁ Ἰησοῦς.

6. Gr. εἰρήνη ὑμῖν. Compare Luke 24:36, "While they were saying these things, he stood in their midst and says to them, 'Peace to you'" (καὶ λέγει αὐτοῖς· εἰρήνη ὑμῖν). The last words, "and says to them, 'Peace to you,'" are missing in Codex D and some of the old Latin versions, another example (as in Lk 24:12) of so-called "non-Western interpolations."

7. Gr. τοῦτο εἰπών. For this transitional expression, see, for example, 7:9; 9:6; 11:43; 13:21; 18:1.

8. The definite articles ("*the* hands and *the* side") are ways of saying "*his* hands" and "*his* side" (see Robertson, *Grammar,* 684), but at the same time also give the impression that Jesus' hands and side have been mentioned before. Some manuscripts, including the majority of later ones, actually supply the missing possessive pronoun αὐτοῦ (for αὐτοῖς, placing the latter up front just after the verb "showed").

9. Again, John's Gospel is not unique in this respect. In Luke as well Jesus says to the disciples, "See my hands and my feet, that I am he" (Lk 24:39; also v. 40), even though no piercing of the hands or feet has been mentioned in Luke's account of the crucifixion.

10. Gr. ἐχάρησαν.

echo of 16:16 and 22 could hardly be more explicit: "A short time, and you no longer see me, and again a short time, and you will see me" (16:16), and "I will see you again, and your heart will rejoice, and no one takes your joy from you" (16:22). The promise of the farewell discourse is fulfilled both in Jesus' "coming" (v. 19) and in the disciples' "seeing"[11] (v. 20). Joy is the only emotion attributed to the disciples here — not fear and not surprise — and in contrast to Luke (24:41), their joy is not mixed with unbelief, at least not explicitly (that will come later, v. 25). The expression "seeing the Lord" is a rare instance in which the Gospel writer himself uses "the Lord" as his designation for Jesus.[12] We would have expected either "Jesus" or simply "him." The most likely explanation is that the writer is deliberately echoing in his own words Mary's announcement, "I have seen the Lord" (v. 18), in order to anticipate the disciples' announcement in turn to the absent Thomas that "We have seen the Lord" (v. 25). In a subtle way, the vocabulary confirms that the disciples have indeed received Mary's message, even though their explicit reaction to it is never stated. We are reminded of the Samaritan villagers who, on verifying the report of the woman who had met Jesus at the well, said to her, "We no longer believe because of your speech, for we ourselves have heard, and we know that this is truly the Savior of the world" (4:42).

21 Jesus repeats the greeting of peace: "Then Jesus[13] said to them again, 'Peace to you. Just as the Father has sent me, so I am sending you.'" The added words are something he has not said to them explicitly before, yet they come as no surprise to the reader, who has heard him acknowledge to the Father in prayer, "Just as you sent me into the world, I also sent them into the world" (17:18).[14] Nor can the disciples themselves be surprised, for their mission was everywhere presupposed in Jesus' last discourses. For example, "a slave is not greater than his lord, nor is a messenger greater than the person who sent him" (13:16), and "the person who receives whomever I send receives me, and the person who receives me receives the One who sent me"

---

11. Gr. ἰδόντες.
12. See 4:1 (where "the Lord" is the preferred reading), 6:23, and 11:2.
13. Some important witnesses (including ℵ, D, L, W, Ψ, and some ancient versions) omit the name "Jesus" at this point (that is, simply "he said to them again"). Others, just as important (including B, A, Θ, families 1 and 13, and the majority of later witnesses) retain the name. There is obviously no difference in meaning, but a deliberate sequel to verse 19 ("*Jesus* came and stood in the midst and said . . .") may be intended, as he now says the same thing again, and this would favor retaining the proper name.
14. In contrast to 17:18, where the same word for "send" is used in both clauses (ἀπέστειλας . . . ἀπέστειλα), two different words are used here: "Just as the Father has sent me [ἀπέσταλκέν με], so I am sending [πέμπω] you." Yet the structure of the sentence (as a comparison introduced by καθώς) requires that the two verbs for "send" are used interchangeably.

(13:20, both prefaced by "Amen, amen, I say to you"); also "You did not choose me, but I chose you, and appointed you that you might go and bear fruit, and that your fruit might last" (15:16), and the section that follows on how they will be treated in the world (15:18-25).[15] The salutation, "Peace to you," is all the more necessary in the face of what they will encounter in the course of their mission (see 16:33, "These things I have spoken to you so that in me you might have peace").

22 Just as before (v. 20), words are followed by action — and this time by more words, interpreting the action: "And having said this, he breathed, and he says to them, 'Receive Holy Spirit'" (vv. 22-23). "Having said this" echoes verse 20,[16] where it introduces Jesus' act of showing the disciples his hands and side to verify who he is and the reality of his death. Here it introduces a second act of verification: "he breathed"[17] (v. 22a). What does breathing verify? That he is alive. It is the triumphant sequel to the notice that on the cross, just after he received the sour wine, Jesus "handed over the Spirit" (19:30). As we saw there, the "Spirit" he handed over was the Holy Spirit that came down on him and "remained" (1:32-33), and was his "without measure" (3:34). When the Spirit left him, he stopped breathing and died, but now he "breathed" again, and again we are reminded of a text from the farewell discourse, "you see me, because I live — and you too will live" (14:19). The Spirit, who once rested on Jesus alone, is back, not for him now but for the disciples. Accordingly, having "breathed," Jesus added, "Receive Holy Spirit"[18] (v. 22b), and for this reason it is customary to translate the text, "he breathed *on them,*" presumably conferring on them the Spirit with his very breath, much as God in the beginning, having "formed the man from the earth, breathed[19] in his face the breath of life, and the man became a living soul" (Gen 2:7, LXX).[20] While it is doubtful that this biblical text is explicitly in view, Jesus has laid down the principle that "The Spirit is that which makes alive" (6:63), that is, that the Spirit brings about resurrection.[21] Here the Spirit is both the evidence of resurrection —

---

15. As we have seen (4:38), Jesus seems to have sent his disciples on one or more missions even *within* the course of his public ministry.

16. Gr. τοῦτο εἰπών (see above, n. 7).

17. Gr. ἐνεφύσησεν.

18. Gr. λάβετε πνεῦμα ἅγιον.

19. Gr. ἐνεφύσησεν.

20. According to Philo (*On the Creation of the World* 135; LCL, 1.107), "that which He breathed in [ἐνεφύσησεν] was nothing else than a Divine breath" (πνεῦμα θεῖον); see also *Wisdom of Solomon* 15.11: "for he did not know the one who formed him and inspired him with an active soul and breathed [ἐμφυσήσαντα] into him a living spirit."

21. This is the case also in Ezekiel: "Thus says the Lord, 'Come from the four winds and breathe [ἐμφύσησον] into these dead, and they will live'" (Ezek 37:9, LXX).

that is, that Jesus is alive — and the empowerment of the disciples to do what he has just sent them to do.

The tantalizingly brief notice of the Spirit's coming raises two difficulties, one having to do with the internal consistency of the Gospel of John itself, and the other having to do with its relationship to other New Testament witnesses, Luke-Acts in particular. First, the notion of the Spirit as an empowerment, as that which can be "breathed" on the disciples from Jesus' mouth, seems inconsistent with that of the Spirit as Advocate (or "another Advocate"), a divine Person who will teach the disciples after Jesus' departure, leading them into all the truth (see 14:16-17, 26; 15:26; 16:7, 13). The masculine "Advocate,"[22] implying personality, is repeatedly linked to the neuter "Spirit,"[23] either "the Holy Spirit" (14:26) or "the Spirit of truth" (14:16; 15:26; 16:13). Here, as in the first half of the Gospel (1:32-33; 3:5, 6, 8, 34; 4:23-24; 6:63; 7:39),[24] only the neuter "Spirit" is used (without even the definite article!), leaving little room for the Spirit's personality. Marianne M. Thompson addresses this issue helpfully and at considerable length.[25] She understands the Spirit theologically (as the Spirit of God), not christologically (as Jesus' "replacement"), and concludes with an analogy between the coming of the Word of God into the world as a Person, Jesus the Son, and the coming of the Spirit of God into the world as a Person, the Advocate.[26] In the Gospel itself, a variety of expressions have been used for the Advocate's coming: "I will ask the Father, and he will give you . . ." (14:16); "the Father will send in my name" (14:26); "whom I will send to you from the Father" (15:26); "if I go, I will send him to you" (16:7). None of these quite match the present scene in which "Holy Spirit"[27] comes on the disciples as breath from Jesus' mouth. The description here is better attuned to the promise John received that Jesus would baptize "in Holy Spirit" — as here without the definite article (1:33) — or to the experience of being "born of water and Spirit" as the qualification for entering the kingdom of God (see 3:5-6).[28] In short, the accent is on "Life," even as Jesus is alive (14:19), not on a new personal Companion to be with them forever and lead them into all the truth. And yet, this is the only "Spirit" that comes on the disciples within the pages of this Gospel. Perhaps the best answer to the riddle is to acknowledge that this "Life," this empowerment, be-

22. Gr. ὁ παράκλητος.
23. Gr. τὸ πνεῦμα.
24. To these may be added 11:33 and 13:21, where "the Spirit" is so linked to Jesus (on the basis of 1:32-33) as to be designated simply his "spirit."
25. Thompson, *The God of the Gospel of John*, 145-88.
26. Thompson, *The God of the Gospel of John*, 185-86.
27. Gr. πνεῦμα ἅγιον.
28. Here "Spirit" without the article (3:5) and with the article (3:6) seem to be used interchangeably.

comes "the Advocate" in a personal sense only later, in the course of their mission and its accompanying persecutions, when, as we learn in this Gospel (15:26-27) and in others as well, "the Holy Spirit will teach you in this hour what you must say" (Lk 12:11; see also Mk 13:11, "for you are not the ones speaking, but the Holy Spirit").

The second difficulty is that another, better-known, tradition places the coming of the Holy Spirit on the disciples fifty days later, on the day of Pentecost (Acts 2:1-4). In the other three Gospels, the baptism "in Holy Spirit" (Mk 1:8), or "in Holy Spirit and fire" (Mt 3:10//Lk 3:16), promised by John the Baptist remains unfulfilled as the Gospel story ends. According to Luke, the risen Jesus tells the disciples to wait in Jerusalem "until you are clothed with power from on high" (Lk 24:49) because "John indeed baptized in water, but you will be baptized in Holy Spirit after not many days" (Acts 1:5). "You will receive power," he adds, "when the Holy Spirit has come upon you, and you will be my witnesses" (Acts 1:8). And so they wait. In John's Gospel, by contrast, they are not waiting for anything. The Holy Spirit comes here and now, right from Jesus' mouth. Nothing remains unfulfilled. And obviously, the coming of the Spirit at Pentecost in the book of Acts cannot be made to correspond to the emergence of "the Advocate" in the course of the disciples' mission to the world. In both passages the role of the Spirit is to equip the disciples for mission; the difference between them is not that the Spirit is personal in Acts 2 and not in John 20. It is rather that the Spirit is represented in Acts 2 as "Power" and in John 20 as "Life." That (aside from the phenomenon of speaking in tongues) is the only real difference between them. Thus when Jesus breathes on the disciples and says, "Receive Holy Spirit," it is not an anticipation of Pentecost, but "Pentecost" itself — the only coming of the Spirit of which this Gospel knows.

The same cannot be said of the book of Acts, for there, at the very beginning, the writer speaks of "all that Jesus began to do and teach until the day he was taken up, having commanded *through the Holy Spirit*[29] the apostles whom he had chosen" (Acts 1:1-2, italics added). Although John's Gospel seems to know nothing of Luke's Pentecost, Luke here shows just a trace of knowledge of John's. Nothing in Luke 24 (for example, 24:31-32) explains this notice in Acts 1 quite as well as what we find in John 20:22. In John's Gospel, the coming of the Spirit — the baptism in the Spirit, if you like — is within the story, not beyond the story, in the same way that Jesus' own coming, and the experience of seeing him again and realizing the peace and joy that he brings (vv. 19-20), are within the story. It has to be that way because, unlike Luke, he has no second volume, and unlike Mark, he is not content to leave the story unfinished.

29. Gr. διὰ πνεύματος ἁγίου.

23 Jesus has told the disciples much already about what their mission entails, and what the Spirit will do for them and through them in the course of their mission to the world (see, for example, 14:12-14; 15:18–16:13). There is little to add, and what little there is he adds here: "Whosoever's sins you forgive, they are forgiven to them; whosoever's you retain, they are retained" (v. 23). As we have seen, this may well be what Jesus had in mind when he promised that they would do works "greater" than his own (see 14:12). Elsewhere in the Gospel tradition, Jesus claims for himself "authority on earth to forgive sins" (Mt 9:6//Mk 2:10//Lk 5:24), yet in this Gospel he never exercises that authority, at least not explicitly. He has come close once (5:14), and in material added to the Gospel (8:11) even closer, and he has hinted at the disciples' own need for forgiveness and responsibility to forgive in the washing of their feet (13:14), but when he has spoken of "sin" explicitly, it has been to retain and not forgive sin (see 8:21, 24, "you will die in your sin[s]"; 9:41, "Your sin remains"; 15:22, "they have no excuse for their sin"). The Gospel writer has consistently characterized Jesus' redemptive ministry positively as the giving of life, rather than negatively as the forgiveness of sin. The promise still stands that the Lamb of God "takes away the sin of the world" (1:29), but as we have seen, that promise only comes to realization when Jesus "baptizes in Holy Spirit" — that is, from now on. The Gospel remains true to its apparent assumption that sin is not truly "taken away" (whether in forgiveness or in judgment) until Jesus dies on the cross. That work is now "finished" (19:30). He that was dead is alive again (20:22), and now the risen Jesus commissions his disciples to carry out the "greater" works of forgiving sin and preparing for judgment.

The pronouncement, "Whosoever's sins you forgive, they are forgiven[30] to them; whosoever's you retain, they are retained,"[31] is generally acknowledged to be linked in some way to the pronouncement in Matthew, "Whatever you bind on the earth will be bound in heaven, and whatever you loose on the earth will be loosed in heaven" (Mt 18:18).[32] The similarities are substantial. Both passages have to do with the forgiveness of sins (see Mt 18:15-17, 21-35).[33] In both, conditional relative clauses[34] are followed by main clauses with verbs in the perfect or future perfect, signaling that something definite has been

---

30. Gr. ἀφέωνται.

31. Gr. κεκράτηνται.

32. See, for example (among many others), Dodd, *Historical Tradition,* 347-48; Brown, 2.1039.

33. This is not the case in Matthew 16:19, which is structurally parallel to 18:18. The context there has nothing in particular to do with the forgiveness of sins, but more broadly with what is to be forbidden and allowed in the "congregation" or community (ἐκκλησία) of which Jesus speaks (16:18).

34. Both with ἄν or ὅσα ἐάν and verbs in the aorist subjunctive.

accomplished. Also, in each instance a signal is given (without explicitly mentioning God) that this accomplishment is in fact the work of God — either by the use of the passive voice ("are forgiven," and "are retained"),[35] or (even more explicitly in Matthew) by the passive voice combined with a reference to "heaven" (a circumlocution for God: "bound in heaven," and "loosed in heaven"). Moreover, the verbs "forgive" and "retain" are widely regarded as at least rough equivalents of "bind" and "loose" on the basis of presumed Aramaic or Hebrew originals.[36] Yet Matthew's context is very different from the present one: preresurrection not postresurrection, and focused not on a mission to the world but on relationships *within* the Christian community, more analogous to the footwashing and the responsibility to love one another in the Gospel of John than to the present passage. Moreover, it is unlikely that John's Gospel is simply editing Matthew (or a text that uses Matthean vocabulary), and substituting his own terminology for Matthew's. While "bind" and "loose" are not John's vocabulary, neither are "forgive" and "retain." As we have seen, nowhere else does this Gospel mention the "forgiveness of sins,"[37] and the verb translated "retain," that is, to hold or seize,[38] is nowhere else used in just that sense in the New Testament. It is likely, therefore, that John's Gospel is drawing independently on a source, oral or written, other than Matthew, a source in fact that Matthew himself may have used.[39]

What exactly, then, is Jesus promising his disciples? It appears to be a corollary of 13:20, "the person who receives whomever I send receives me, and the person who receives me receives the One who sent me," while taking into account as well the negative equivalent now preserved in Luke 10:16: "The person who hears you hears me, and the person who rejects you rejects me, but the person who rejects me rejects the One who sent me." In short, the disciples are being given authority to act as Jesus' agents in the course of their mission, and consequently as agents of God himself. Through them the

---

35. For the use of the passive voice to avoid speaking of God in so many words, see BDF, §130(1).

36. This is fairly certain with respect to "forgive" as "loose," but rather less so with respect to "retain" as "bind" (see Dodd, *Historical Tradition,* 348; Brown, 2.1039-40).

37. This in sharp contrast to the other three Gospels (see, for example, Mt 6:14-15; 9:6; 18:35; 26:28; Mk 1:4; 2:10; 3:28; 11:25; Lk 1:77; 23:34; 24:47).

38. Gr. κρατεῖν.

39. Dodd speaks of it as "a special form of the common oral traditon" (*Historical Tradition,* 349). It is quite possible that Matthew also knew this source and substituted his own "bind and loose" for the source's "forgive and retain" — perhaps in order to link Matthew 18:18 more closely to 16:19. Tobias Hägerland finds (both here and in Matthew) a possible allusion to Balak's words to Balaam in Numbers 22:6, LXX, where the operative verbs are "bless" and "curse" ("The Power of Prophecy: A Septuagintal Echo in John 20:19-23," *CBQ* 71.1 [2009], 84-103), but the latter looks more like a parody of Genesis 12:3 than an anticipation of these New Testament passages.

20:19-31 THE SECOND APPEARANCE: THE DISCIPLES AND THOMAS

Holy Spirit, or Advocate, will both "convict the world of sin" (16:8) and forgive sin. The sins they will forgive are not sins against them personally (as, for example, in Mt 6:14-15; 18:21-35; Mk 11:25; Lk 17:3-4), but the sins of the world generally (see Lk 24:47), unbelief in particular (see 16:9) but sins of every kind. Those whom they forgive (because their message is accepted), God will forgive; those whose sins they "retain," as Jesus sometimes did (because the message was rejected), God will not forgive. In short, God will ratify and validate their mission because God is their Father (see v. 17). He has given them "authority to become children of God" (1:12), and consequently to act on his behalf.

24 Nothing is said of how the disciples reacted to any of this. No explicit confession of faith in Jesus. No report of how he made his departure from the locked room.[40] Instead, we learn (belatedly) that one of "the disciples" (v. 19) was *not* present: "Now Thomas, one of the Twelve, the one called Didymos, was not with them when Jesus came" (v. 24). We have met Thomas twice before, in 11:16, where he was identified similarly as "the one called Didymos," and 14:5, where (with three other disciples) he questioned Jesus about his departure. Here, for the first time, he is identified further as "one of the Twelve," the only disciple other than Judas Iscariot (6:71) to be so identified. Why just these two, when we have reason to believe that Simon Peter, Philip, Andrew, Nathanael, and the other Judas (and perhaps "the disciple whom Jesus loved") also belonged to "the Twelve"? As for Judas Iscariot, it is clear that he is so identified because *even though* he was "one of the Twelve," he handed Jesus over to the Jewish authorities. Similarly, in the case of Thomas it appears that he is so identified because *even though* he was "one of the Twelve," he was not present with the others in the locked room when Jesus appeared to them. This suggests that those who were gathered there in the five preceding verses were precisely "the Twelve," still bearing that identity even after the departure of Judas (in Mt 28:16 and Mk 16:14 they are called "the Eleven").

25 The ten other disciples bring their testimony to Thomas in the same words Mary used (v. 18) in bringing her testimony to them: "So the other disciples were saying to him, 'We have seen the Lord.'[41] And he said to them, 'Unless I see in his hands the print of the nails, and put my finger into the print of the nails, and put my hand into his side, I will never believe'" (v. 25). The form of the pronouncement echoes — one might even say mimics — certain classic sayings of Jesus himself about salvation, with "unless"[42] and a strong negative: for example, "*unless* someone is born from above, he *cannot* see the

---

40. See Bultmann, 693.
41. Gr. ἑωράκαμεν τὸν κύριον.
42. Gr. ἐὰν μή.

kingdom of God" (3:3, italics added); "*unless* you eat the flesh of the Son of man and drink his blood, you do *not* have life" (6:53).[43] It is unclear whether or not Thomas has heard the same testimony ("I have seen the Lord") from Mary's lips (v. 18) that he now hears from his fellow disciple, and just as unclear how he knew about "the print of the nails" and the wound in Jesus' side. James Charlesworth argues from Thomas's knowledge that Thomas himself is the anonymous witness who testified to the spear thrust and the blood and water from Jesus' side (19:35),[44] but this is surely to argue too much from too little. As we have seen (v. 20), Jesus showed his hands and side to the other disciples for verification, even though they did not ask for it, implying that the nature of his wounds had by that time become common knowledge — whether through the testimony of a Roman soldier, the beloved disciple, the women at the cross, or Joseph of Arimathea and Nicodemus. Thomas is by no means alone in knowing about the wounds even though he alone demands verification. Whether the other disciples would have demanded the same verification had Jesus not given it freely remains an unanswered question. Any reader familiar with the other Gospels (see Mt 28:17, "but some doubted"; also Mk 16:13-14; Lk 24:41) may well suspect that there is something unfinished about the revelation that has just taken place (vv. 19-23), that there is still a little matter of unbelief to be dealt with. If sin is defined chiefly as unbelief (as in 16:9), then the unbelief of the disciples themselves must be addressed before they can deal with the sins of those to whom they are sent.[45] While the issue is addressed in the person of just one of them, the unbelief of one is in some sense the unbelief of all, just as the final confession of faith attributed to just one (see v. 28) belongs finally to them all.[46]

26 For this reason, the drama enacted in verses 19-23 is repeated. What was left unfinished is now finished: "And after eight days the disciples were again inside, and Thomas with them. Jesus comes, the doors being locked, and stood in the midst, and said, 'Peace to you'" (v. 26). The account repeats verse 19 almost verbatim. The doors are still locked, and although the

---

43. Other examples include 3:5; 6:44, 65; 8:24; 12:24; 13:8; 15:4, and (on the lips of John) 3:27.

44. See Charlesworth, *The Beloved Disciple,* 226-33.

45. Oddly, however, this is not the case in the longer ending of Mark, where the disciples are repeatedly rebuked for their unbelief (Mk 16:11, 13, 14), yet in the end are sent out to proclaim the gospel "to the whole creation; the one who believes [ὁ πιστεύσας] and is baptized will be saved, but the one who does not believe [ὁ ἀπιστήσας] will be condemned" (16:16).

46. There is reason to agree with Brown that "Thomas has become here the personification of an attitude" (2.1031), but it should be added that Thomas dramatizes not only "apostolic doubt" (2.1032), but in the end apostolic faith as well. At this point in the story at least, Thomas is the representative disciple.

reason is not repeated ("for fear of the Jews," v. 19), the reason is unquestionably the same. They are still afraid of the Jewish authorities. Nothing has really changed, and a repeat performance is necessary.[47] "After eight days" probably means a week later, thus again on the *next* "first day of the week" (see vv. 1, 19),[48] the exchange between Thomas and the other disciples having taken place in the meantime. Jesus comes and stands among them, and says "Peace to you," now for the third and last time (see vv. 19, 21).

27 Jesus speaks to Thomas as if he has heard exactly what Thomas said to the other disciples two verses earlier. Responding to Thomas's demand to both see and touch "the print of the nails," and put his hand into Jesus' side (v. 25), he says, "Bring your finger here and see[49] my hands, and bring your hand and put it into my side"; then, responding to Thomas's emphatic "I will never believe" (v. 25), he adds, "and be no longer[50] faithless but faithful"[51] (v. 27). The invitation to believe (as, for example, in 14:1, "Believe in God, and believe in me!") is explicit. A popular interpretation of Mark 9:24 ("I believe; help my unbelief") implies that belief and unbelief can somehow rest side by side in the same heart, but that is no more the case there than it is here.[52] Thomas must choose between being "faithless" and "faithful." To believe is to renounce unbelief. There is no middle ground. Nor is Jesus asking Thomas to believe without verification. On the contrary, he is asking for faith based on seeing what the other disciples saw, and beyond that on physically touching Jesus' wounds.[53] He is offering Thomas exactly what Thomas demanded.

---

47. So Lincoln: "It is as if the earlier scene has been restaged for Thomas's benefit" (502). For Thomas's benefit, yes, but for the other disciples' benefit as well.

48. The Sinaitic Syriac version makes this explicit: "And after eight days, on the next first [day] of the week" (Lewis, 204). Quite possibly the repeated references to "the first day," or Sunday, are intended to evoke in the reader the awareness that this is indeed "the Lord's day," on which Christian believers are now accustomed to gather for worship (see *Barnabas* 15.9, "Therefore also we celebrate the eighth day with gladness, for on it Jesus arose from the dead, and appeared, and ascended into heaven" (LCL, 2.71).

49. There is quite possibly a touch of gentle humor here, as if Thomas needs to put his finger into the print of the nails in order truly to "see" Jesus' wounds — as he would if he were blind!

50. The use of μή with a present imperative (γίνου) implies the cessation of Thomas's unbelief (see BDF, §336[3]).

51. Gr. καὶ μὴ γίνου ἄπιστος ἀλλὰ πιστός.

52. The fact that Jesus drives out the unclean spirit (Mk 9:25-26) shows that the man indeed believes. In saying "I believe; help my unbelief," he is in effect renouncing the latter.

53. For a fascinating account of the practice of adoration of the wounds of Jesus, especially the side wound as a kind of portal to eternal life, among the early Moravians, see Craig D. Atwood, *Community of the Cross: Moravian Piety in Colonial Bethlehem* (University Park: Pennsylvania State University Press, 2004), 203-21.

28 Instead of taking advantage of the offer, Thomas responds immediately and emphatically to the invitation to "be no longer faithless but faithful." In reply he "answered and said to him, 'My Lord and my God!'"[54] (v. 28). The disciples have routinely called Jesus "Lord" (see 13:13), and Mary Magdalene has spoken of him as "my Lord" even in death (v. 13), but this is the first time anyone (aside from the Gospel writer) has called him "God," or "my God." Finally the introduction of Jesus to the reader as "God" (1:1), or "God the One and Only" (1:18), is confirmed from within the narrative. He has not "made himself God" (10:33), or "equal to God" (5:18), as his opponents charged, yet he is God, and now at last his disciples know it. The confession is all the more striking because the message Jesus sent to the disciples through Mary Magdalene was "I am going up to my Father and your Father, and my God and your God" (v. 17). Even Jesus recognized the Father as "my God," and he invited his disciples to do the same. Yet Thomas does not hesitate to address Jesus himself in exactly the same way. He realizes that at the end of the day, "Believe in God, and believe in me!" (14:1) amount to the same thing. Those commands were addressed to all the disciples, not just one, and Thomas's confession too (like Peter's in 6:69) is best understood as representing the conviction of all the disciples gathered behind locked doors on those two successive first days of the week.

Admittedly, the identifications of Jesus as God (1:1 and 20:28) form an admirable pair of bookends framing the whole Gospel and contributing to the commonly held notion that the Gospel at some stage ended with chapter 20. But caution is necessary because the story is not only about Jesus but about the disciples whom he has just sent out into the world. How will they carry out their mission to "forgive" or "retain" sin? How are they themselves forgiven? What are their responsibilities to one another? Who will their leaders be? These questions have not been fully answered, and whether the answers finally given (chapter 21) were an afterthought or planned from the beginning is not obvious at this point. That can be determined only by looking carefully at the verses that follow, and at chapter 21 itself.

29 As a rule, Jesus does not respond with enthusiasm to confessions of faith in him in any of the Gospels. The exception is Peter's confession in Matthew, to which Jesus replies with a beatitude, "Blessed are you, Simon Barjona, because flesh and blood has not revealed it to you, but my Father in the heavens" (Mt 16:17). Here too is a beatitude, but not for Thomas: "Jesus says to him that 'Because you have seen me, you have believed. Blessed[55] are those who did not see, and believed'" (v. 29). Yet it should not be read as a

---

54. Gr. ὁ κύριός μου καὶ ὁ θεός μου.
55. Gr. μακάριοι.

20:19-31 THE SECOND APPEARANCE: THE DISCIPLES AND THOMAS

rebuke to Thomas either.[56] He believed because he saw, just as John did (1:34), just as the anonymous witness to the spear thrust did (19:35), just as the beloved disciple did (v. 8), just as Mary Magdalene did (v. 18), and just as the other disciples did (v. 20). The only real exception within the narrative is the royal official who "believed" simply on the basis of Jesus' word that his son would live (4:50), and even he had his faith eventually verified by sight (4:53). As we have seen, his faith stands as the paradigm for the faith Jesus commends here, on the part of those who "did not see, and believed."

To whom is Jesus referring? Quite clearly to the readers of the Gospel, and others of their generation, whether Jews or Gentiles, who now believe in Jesus without having lived through the events of his ministry. Yet the aorist participles are surprising: "Blessed are those who *did not* see, and *believed*."[57] We might have expected, "Blessed are those who *will* believe — or even just 'believe,' as in 17:20 — without having seen." How seriously are we to take the past tenses? The only past example of such faith is, as we have noted, the royal official at Cana (4:50). It is as if Jesus is speaking here not in narrative time — a week after his resurrection — but in the reader's time, looking back on his ministry from the reader's perspective long after the fact. The reader knows of "those who did not see, and believed," because the reader is, almost by definition, one of them. The beatitude is for the reader's benefit. In that sense, the pronouncement parallels Revelation 1:3: "Blessed is he who reads [aloud], and those who hear the words of the prophecy, and keep the things written in it, for the time is near." And yet, the aorists also have a certain credibility within the narrative as well, for Jesus has said, "other sheep I have, which are not from this courtyard" (10:16), and the Gospel writer has spoken of "the children of God who are scattered," and yet to be "gathered into one" (11:52). Here Jesus speaks of these "other sheep" or "children of God" as if they have *already* believed, knowing that when they do believe, it will in fact be without seeing, at least in the way Thomas and his fellow disciples have seen. The beatitude is one of just two in the Gospel of John, the first for those who "do" (see 13:17), the second for those who "believe."

---

56. A certain measure of rebuke is implied when Jesus' pronouncement is punctuated as a question, as in the Nestle and Bible Society Greek texts: "Because you have seen me, have you believed?" (see also RSV, NRSV, NASB, TEV, NAB, ESV). Other English versions (including Douay-Rheims, KJV, ERV, ASV, NIV, TNIV, NEB, REB, NJB, NLT), read it as a declarative statement. The issue is analogous to that surrounding 16:31, and the case for reading it as a statement is, if anything, even stronger here than it was there. The genuineness of Thomas's faith is not in question, nor is there any disgrace attached to believing on the basis of what he has seen. Jesus' words to Thomas here also recall his words to Nathanael (1:50), where he does not rebuke Nathanael for believing on the basis of what he has heard, but simply promises something "greater."

57. Gr. οἱ μὴ ἰδόντες καὶ πιστεύσαντες.

30-31 The reader of the Gospel, implicitly in the picture in the preceding verse, is addressed quite explicitly in the two verses that follow: "Now Jesus did many, and other, signs in the presence of his disciples which are not written in this book. But these are written so that you might believe that Jesus is the Christ, the Son of God, and that believing you might have life in his name" (vv. 30-31). As in the book of Revelation (22:18-19), the self-reference to what is "written" and to "this book" (v. 30) hints that the "book" is now drawing to a close.[58] A corollary of this conclusion could be that the "many, and other, signs in the presence of his disciples" are the signs or miracles that Jesus performed throughout the course of his ministry, and that those "written" are the series of seven miracles (several of them explicitly identified as "signs") that comprise much of the first half of the Gospel. It is clear from certain summary statements throughout the first half of the Gospel that Jesus indeed performed "many, and other, signs" beyond those seven (2:23; 3:2; 6:2; 7:31; 9:16; 11:47).[59] Yet the last of the seven to be explicitly "written" occurred nine chapters earlier (with the raising of Lazarus in chapter 11). The series has been formally terminated and the verdict on it pronounced. "Even after he had done so many signs before them, they would not believe in him" (12:37). Those signs, moreover, were done not (at least not solely or primarily) "in the presence of the disciples," but "before them" (12:37) — that is, in the presence of either "the crowds" or "the Jews" — for the most part those who did *not* believe. One time-honored theory is that the summary here in chapter 20 originally terminated a pre-Johannine "Signs Source" consisting of those miracle stories and little else. Whoever created the "Signs Source," so the theory goes, believed that signs produced faith, so that simply enumerating Jesus' impressive signs, one after the other, would bring people to believe that Jesus was "the Christ, the Son of God." The Gospel writer knew better, and relegated the signs to the first half of the Gospel

---

58. See, for example, Rev 22:18, "the words of the prophecy of this book" (τοῦ βιβλίου τούτου), and "the plagues that are written in this book" (τὰς γεγραμμένας ἐν τῷ βιβλίῳ τούτῳ); 22:19, "the words of the book [τοῦ βιβλίου] of this prophecy," and "the things written in this book" (τῶν γεγραμμένων ἐν τῷ βιβλίῳ τούτῳ).

59. The phrase "many, and other, signs" (πολλὰ μὲν οὖν καὶ ἄλλα σημεῖα) sounds redundant, but the likely meaning is that Jesus performed different kinds of miracles beyond those that are "written" (as if the writer had used ἕτερα instead of ἄλλα; see BDAG, 47, and compare Lk 3:18, "So with many, and other [πολλὰ μέν οὖν καὶ ἕτερα], exhortations, he [John] evangelized the people"). If the reference is to signs performed in the course of Jesus' ministry, it could include such things as cleansing lepers, healing the deaf, or driving out demons. If it refers to resurrection signs, it could include such things as making himself known in the breaking of bread (Lk 24:30-31), eating a piece of broiled fish (Lk 24:42-43), ascending visibly to heaven (Acts 1:9-10), and, yes, bringing in an enormous catch of fish at the lake of Tiberias (Jn 21:1-14)!

20:19-31 THE SECOND APPEARANCE: THE DISCIPLES AND THOMAS

with a negative verdict attached, accenting the blindness of the world (perhaps of "the Jews" in particular). The Gospel writer then took over the more positive summary as a formal conclusion to chapters 1–20 as a whole, which at that stage of composition was the whole of the Gospel of John.[60] The difficulty is that "signs" by itself is not a particularly apt term for the content of John's Gospel as a whole. Jesus' miracles have long since yielded center stage, first to his words (chapters 14–17) and then to his passion and resurrection (chapters 18–20).

It is wise, therefore, to look at another possibility — that the "many, and other, signs in the presence of his disciples" (v. 30) are resurrection signs verifying that the Crucified One is alive, and that the Risen One is indeed Jesus who was crucified. He has rolled away the stone, made himself known to Mary in the garden, appeared suddenly within a locked room (twice), showed the disciples his hands and side, breathed on them proving that he is alive, and invited them to touch him. What more is needed? This, the writer insists, is only a sampling of all that Jesus actually did, yet it is — or should be — more than enough to engender faith among those who have not seen any of it, but who now read what is "written in this book." In short, the "many, and other, signs"[61] in the Gospel of John correspond to the "many convincing proofs" mentioned at the beginning of the book of Acts (1:3).[62] If so, the notice to the reader (vv. 30-31) is intended to conclude and summarize a series of resurrection appearances of Jesus, not necessarily the Gospel as a whole.[63] The Gospel

---

60. The theory of the Signs Source obviously has many variations and nuances. It is still most evident in the work of Rudolf Bultmann, but for a detailed treatment, see R. T. Fortna, *The Fourth Gospel and Its Predecessor: From Narrative Source to Present Gospel* (Philadelphia: Fortress, 1988).

61. Gr. πολλὰ μὲν οὖν καὶ ἄλλα σημεῖα.

62. Gr. ἐν πολλοῖς τεκμηρίοις. For the classic distinction between σημεῖον ("sign") and τεκμήριον ("index," a more conclusive demonstration), see Aristotle, *Prior Analytics* 70b (LCL, 1.526). It is fair to assume, however, that they are more or less interchangeable in John's Gospel and the book of Acts.

63. This is a distinctly minority opinion, yet see Hoskyns, 549: "The Evangelist is, however, aware, that there were in existence many other traditions of Resurrection appearances of the Lord, which were of great significance for the revelation of the nature of the Christian religion. He has but made a selection, sufficient for his readers to believe sincerely that Jesus is in very truth the Christ, the Son of God, in order that, secure in this belief, they may possess life everlasting (i.12, vi.47, xix.35)." Even Schnackenburg, while holding on to the Signs Source theory, seems nevertheless to feel the impact of this argument, commenting that "the fact that he makes the statement *in this place,* after the appearances of the risen one, indeed, in the event that it was originally the concluding remark of the σημεῖα-source, that he *transfers* it to this place, certainly requires a more far-reaching explanation. Has he not here included Jesus' appearances among the σημεῖα? (3.337). So too W. Nicol: "In c. 20 John reports two appearances of Jesus before the disci-

writer first claims that these appearances to Mary and the male disciples are enough (out of all he could have told) to verify Jesus' resurrection — yet for good measure he adds one more (see 21:1-14)! Whether the "one more" is an afterthought or planned from the start has yet to be determined.

To the reader, the Gospel writer promises that "these are written so that you might believe that Jesus is the Christ, the Son of God, and that believing you might have life in his name" (v. 31). As in 19:35, there is a textual problem as to whether the verb, "so that you might believe" is present or aorist subjunctive, but the evidence for the present is stronger.[64] The consequent debate over whether the Gospel of John is written primarily to convert unbelievers to faith in Jesus as "the Christ, the Son of God," or to confirm and strengthen the faith of Christian believers is largely beside the point. The aorist is supposed to support the former and the present the latter. But both here and in 19:35 (the only other instance in the Gospel in which the readers are addressed directly), the point is rather to encourage readers — whoever they may be — to emulate the faith of those mentioned in the narrative, the anonymous witness at the cross in the first instance, Thomas and his fellow disciples in the locked room in the second. In this way, readers are invited to claim the mantle of honor as "those who did not see, and believed" (v. 29). This is not necessarily to emulate the terminology of the narrative. In the case of the witness to the spear thrust there was no terminology; he simply "testified" (19:35), even if one wishes to infer that he may have confessed Jesus as "Son of God." In Thomas's case the terminology was "my Lord and my God" (v. 28), but the conclusion here is not "so that you might believe that Jesus is both Lord and God." Rather, the more familiar titles, "the Christ, the Son of God"[65] are retained, probably because they were the titles best known to readers of the Gospel, whether in connection with Christian initiation or Christian worship.

That Jesus is "the Son of God" or God's "One and Only" has been part and parcel of this Gospel's witness from the start (see 1:14, 18, 34, 49), and has been the predominant way in which Jesus has spoken of himself, whether as "the Son," or "the Son of man," or simply by continually referring to the God of Israel as his "Father." As for "the Christ," this title was mentioned first as that which John was not (1:20), and then as the translation of

---

ples. Immediately following them he writes in v. 30: 'There were many other signs that Jesus performed in the presence of his disciples.' The concept *sēmeion* is widened to include the appearances" (*The Sēmeia in the Fourth Gospel,* 115).

64. The present tense (ἵνα πιστεύητε) is supported by P⁶⁶ (probably), by the first hand of ℵ, B, and Θ. The aorist is supported by a corrector of ℵ, A, C, D, L, W, Ψ, families 1 and 13, and the majority of later manuscripts.

65. Gr. ὁ χριστὸς ὁ υἱὸς τοῦ θεοῦ.

"the Messiah" (1:41), that is, Israel's coming Anointed One, he "of whom Moses wrote in the law, and of whom the prophets wrote" (1:45). This is who Jesus' first disciples took him to be, because of John's introduction of him to them as "the Lamb of God" (1:36; see also 1:49, "the King of Israel"), yet he himself explicitly embraces the designation only once, in the presence of the Samaritan woman at Sychar (4:26). Among "the Jews," the debate goes on and on as to whether or not he has the qualifications or meets the expectations; the prevailing suspicion is that he does not (see 7:26-27, 31, 41-42; 9:22; 12:34). Jesus himself, when challenged to "tell us plainly" that he is "the Christ," refuses to do so in so many words, appealing instead to "The works that I do in my Father's name" (see 10:24-25) and pressing his claim to be "Son of God" (10:36). At the end of the day, the title "Son of God" decisively interprets "the Christ," rather than the other way around. It is Martha finally, at Bethany, who puts into words the full confession that the Gospel writer wants to elicit from his readers: "Yes, Lord, I have believed that you are the Christ, the Son of God, who is coming into the world" (11:27). Thomas's confession may be more profound and climactic, but Martha's is the explicit paradigm for faith among Johannine Christians.

The last clause, "and that believing you might have life[66] in his name" (v. 31b), goes to the very heart of this Gospel's theology (for example, "so that everyone who believes might have eternal life in him," 3:15; "so that everyone who believes in him might not be lost but have eternal life," 3:16; "whoever believes has eternal life," 6:47) — not to mention that of 1 John ("These things I wrote to you so that you might know that you have life eternal, you who believe in the name of the Son of God" (1 Jn 5:13).

If this interpretation is correct, then the things specifically "written so that you might believe" are the resurrection appearances of Jesus, not the Gospel as a whole and not the seven signs performed in the first half of the Gospel. Of course, it must be admitted in the same breath that the same thing is nevertheless true of the Gospel as a whole. It too is "written so that you might believe," and so for that matter are the Gospels of Matthew, Mark, and Luke. This Gospel is no more entitled than any of the others to be called the "Gospel of Belief." But are "these," that is, "these signs," to be identified only as the resurrection appearances recounted so far, or do they have a forward reference as well, so as to include to Jesus' appearance at the lake of Tiberias and the extraordinary catch of fish in the following chapter (21:1-14)? As we will see (in 21:1 and 14), chapter 21 is aware of chapter 20, but is chapter 20 aware of chapter 21? Is chapter 21 an afterthought, or something already in mind as chapter 20 concludes. It depends on what is meant by an afterthought. The transition from chapter 20 to chapter 21 is not so different

66. Gr. ζωὴν ἔχητε.

from two earlier transitions within the Gospel: the writer concluded the narratives of each of Jesus' first two signs in Galilee with summary formulas introduced by the pronoun "this":

"This Jesus did in Cana of Galilee as a beginning of the signs" (2:11).
"And this Jesus did again as a second sign when he came from Judea to Galilee" (4:54).

In each instance the pronoun "this" refers back to what has just preceded, yet in each instance the narrative continues, with the expression "after this" (2:12) or "after these things" (5:1). If the present passage is in any way analogous, "these" does refer back to the appearances described in chapter 20, not forward to chapter 21, and yet a continuation of the narrative is by no means unexpected. Similarly in Jesus' discourses, a summary introduced by "these things" or "these words" does not necessarily terminate anything; see, for example, "These words he spoke in the treasury, teaching in the temple" (8:20), followed by, "So again he said to them" (8:21); "As he was speaking these things, many believed in him" (8:30), followed by "So Jesus said to the Jews who had believed him" (8:31). In short, the transition between John 20 and 21 is not inconsistent with other narrative transitions in the Gospel. If it is a less-than-smooth transition — particularly given the shift from Jerusalem to the lake of Tiberias in Galilee — it is no more difficult than the transition from chapter 5 to chapter 6 (from Jerusalem to the same lake in Galilee!).

This, together with the fact that no manuscript evidence exists for separating chapter 21 from the rest of the Gospel as an appendix (much less assigning it to a different author or a redactor), suggests that John's Gospel be read canonically, with no thought that 20:30-31 is intended as a conclusion or definitive statement of purpose for the Gospel as a whole.[67] Afterthought or not, chapter 21 continues the narrative of chapter 20 in much the same way as chapter 5 continues that of chapter 4, chapter 6 that of chapter 5, and chapter 7 that of chapter 6 — all with exactly the same phrase, "After these things."[68]

---

67. For an attempt at just such a canonical approach, see Fernando Segovia, "The Final Farewell of Jesus: A Reading of John 20:30–21:25," *Semeia* 53 (1991), 167-90. Segovia regards verses 30-31 as transitional, linked as closely to chapter 21 as to chapter 20. With them, he maintains, "the narrator proceeds to introduce one more 'sign,' the final sign, of Jesus in the presence of the disciples."

68. Gr. μετὰ ταῦτα (see 5:1; 6:1; 7:1; 21:1).

F. THE THIRD APPEARANCE AND SIMON PETER'S COMMISSION (21:1-25)

1 *After these things, Jesus revealed himself again to the disciples, at the lake of Tiberias. And he revealed like this:* 2 *there were together Simon Peter, and Thomas, the one called Didymos, and Nathanael, the one from Cana of Galilee, and the sons of Zebedee, and two others of the disciples.* 3 *Simon Peter says to them, "I'm going fishing." They say to him, "We too are coming with you." They went out and got into the boat, and in that night they caught nothing.* 4 *But as soon as early morning had come, Jesus stood on the shore, yet the disciples did not know that it was Jesus.* 5 *Then Jesus says to them, "Lads, do you have any catch?" They answered him, "No,"* 6 *and he said to them, "Throw the net to the right side of the boat, and you will find." So they threw, and they were no longer strong enough to draw it in because of the great number of fish.* 7 *Then that disciple whom Jesus loved said to Peter, "It is the Lord." Then Simon Peter, hearing that "It is the Lord," secured the outer garment (for he was naked), and threw himself into the lake,* 8 *and the other disciples came in the boat (for they were not far from the land, about two hundred cubits), dragging the net of fish.* 9 *Then when they got out onto the land, they see a charcoal fire laid, and fish laid on, and bread.* 10 *Jesus says to them, "Bring some of the fish you caught just now."* 11 *So Simon Peter went up and drew the net onto the land, full of 153 great fish, and even with so many the net was not torn.* 12 *Jesus says to them, "Come, have breakfast." And none of the disciples dared inquire of him, "Who are you?" — knowing that "It is the Lord."* 13 *Jesus comes and takes the bread and gives to them, and the fish likewise.* 14 *This third time now Jesus was revealed to his disciples after being raised from the dead.*

15 *Then, when they had had breakfast, Jesus says to Simon Peter, "Simon of John, do you love me more than these?" He says to him, "Yes, Lord, you know that I love you." He says to him, "Tend my lambs."* 16 *He says to him again a second time, "Simon of John, do you love me?" He says to him, "Yes, Lord, you know that I love you." He says to him, "Shepherd my sheep."* 17 *He says to him the third time, "Simon of John, do you love me?" Peter was grieved because he said to him the third time, "Do you love me?" and he says to him, "Lord, you know all things; you know that I love you." Jesus says to him, "Tend my sheep.* 18 *Amen, amen, I say to you, when you were young, you used to gird yourself and walk wherever you chose, but when you are old, you will stretch out your hands, and another will gird you and bring you where you do not choose."* 19 *This he said signifying by what*

death he will glorify God, and having said this, he says to him, "Follow me."

20 Turning, Peter sees the disciple whom Jesus loved following, he who also leaned on his breast at the supper and said, "Lord, who is the one handing you over?" 21 Then, seeing this man, Peter says to Jesus, "Lord, what about this man?" 22 Jesus says to him, "If I want him to remain until I come, what [is that] to you? You, follow me!" 23 So this word went out to the brothers that that disciple would not die, but Jesus did not say to him that he would not die, but "If I want him to remain until I come, what [is that] to you?" 24 This is the disciple who testifies about these things and who wrote these things, and we know that his testimony is true. 25 There are also many other things that Jesus did which, if they were written every one, I suppose the world itself would not hold the books being written.

This chapter confirms that there were indeed "many, and other, signs" that Jesus did after his resurrection, signs that the reader should not expect to find "written in this book" (20:30). But one at least is now added. As the story line continues, Jesus is abruptly "at the lake of Tiberias" in Galilee (as in 6:1). Nothing is said of how he got there, only that he "revealed himself" there, and specifically "to the disciples" (vv. 1, 14), just as his previous appearances were "in the presence of his disciples" (20:30). If locked doors are no barrier to the risen Lord (20:19, 26), neither is distance. To a considerable degree, the chapter tells Simon Peter's story. His is the first name mentioned (v. 2); he takes the initiative to go fishing on the lake (v. 3); and he it is who hears the words, "It is the Lord" (v. 7), and drags the net full of fish onto the shore (v. 11). After the meal, Jesus questions him three times, appoints him shepherd over the flock (vv. 15-17), prophesies his death, and commands him, "Follow me" (vv. 18-19). When Peter sees "the disciple whom Jesus loved" already following and asks about him, Jesus ignores the question and repeats the command to "follow me" (vv. 20-22).

While the brief concluding notices about "the disciple whom Jesus loved" have an obvious bearing on that disciple's identity and on the authorship of the Gospel (see vv. 23-25), they do not change the fact that this final chapter is mainly about Simon Peter. There are unmistakable echoes here of Jesus' promise to the disciples in the Gospel of Mark that "after I am raised, I will go before you into Galilee" (Mk 14:28), followed by the prediction of Peter's threefold denial (14:29-30), and eventually confirmed by the young man's command to the women at the tomb to "go and tell my disciples, *and Peter*, that 'he goes before you into Galilee. There you will see him, just as he

21:1-25 THE THIRD APPEARANCE AND SIMON PETER'S COMMISSION

told you'" (Mk 16:7, italics added). Mark's Gospel[1] leads us to expect just such an appearance of Jesus in Galilee as we find here in the Gospel of John.[2] It is as if Mary Magdalene had delivered to the male disciples the message given her in Mark and Matthew along with the message given her in John's Gospel itself (see 20:17).

Other elements in the chapter as well point to a knowledge of traditions outside the Gospel of John as well as traditions within it. The reader recalls that Jesus has been at "the lake of Galilee, or Tiberias" before (6:1), that he performed a miracle there involving bread — and, secondarily, fish (see 6:5-11) — and that he revealed himself to his disciples (although the word "revealed" was not used) as they sat in a boat (see 6:16-21).[3] Here he "revealed himself"[4] (v. 1) by performing a miracle involving fish (v. 11) — and, secondarily, bread (vv. 9, 13). If we did not know better, we might have assumed that 6:1-21 was the postresurrection account and 21:1-14 a record of something within Jesus' earthly ministry. Just such an event, in fact, does occur within the earthly ministry, according to Luke (5:1-11), and there too Simon Peter is the central figure. We have here a kind of reenactment of the call of the disciples, not as told in John's Gospel but as told in the other three, Luke in particular. Nothing in this Gospel so far has connected any of the disciples with fishing, yet here we find them fishing in Galilee, just as when they first met Jesus in those other accounts. Here they meet him again under similar circumstances, even though nothing is the same. The narrative is realistic — they are literally fishing — but also metaphorical, for in doing what

---

1. Matthew's Gospel less so. Matthew parallels the promise that Jesus will go before the disciples into Galilee (26:32), but the later confirmation, whether by an angel (Mt 28:7) or by the risen Jesus himself (28:10), does not single out Peter. Matthew, moreover, does actually record an appearance in Galilee, not at the lake but "on a mountain where Jesus had directed them" (28:16), and Peter has no explicit part in that final scene (28:16-20).

2. The *Gospel of Peter* seems to know of such a tradition as well, for at the end of the fragment we possess, after each of the disciples "departed unto his own house," the narrative continues, "But I, Simon Peter, and Andrew my brother, took our nets and went unto the sea: and there was with us Levi the son of Alphaeus, whom the Lord . . ." (*Gospel of Peter* 59–60; James, *Apocryphal New Testament,* 94). There is, however, no mention of Galilee, and the apostles named do not match the names in John's Gospel.

3. The similarities to the accounts of the feeding of the five thousand and walking on the lake in Matthew and Mark are equally close (Luke does not have Jesus walking on the lake), but the use of the name Tiberias (rather than Galilee) for the lake suggests that the account in John 6 is the one primarily in view. This is perhaps confirmed by a possible parallel between the gathering of pieces of bread into twelve baskets "so that nothing is lost" (6:12, a detail found only in John's Gospel) and the net that "was not torn" (21:11), implying that none of the 153 fish were lost either.

4. Gr. ἐφανέρωσεν ἑαυτόν.

many of them have always done, the disciples now dramatize what they have been "sent" to do, that is, "fish for people" (see Mk 1:17//Mt 4:19//Lk 5:11), or, as this Gospel puts it, forgive or retain sins (see 20:22-23).

If the fishing incident dramatizes the disciples' evangelistic mission, the breakfast by the lake after the extraordinary catch (vv. 12-13) dramatizes Christian worship, centering on common meals, possibly (as in 6:11) the Eucharist in particular. And in much the same way, Jesus' subsequent encounter with Simon Peter one-on-one (vv. 15-19) evokes the need for pastoral ministry among them by reintroducing the familiar image of the shepherd and the sheep. In this exchange, Peter is reinstated — rehabilitated, if you will — and appointed shepherd of the flock in Jesus' absence. In keeping with a text quoted in two other Gospels (Mk 14:27//Mt 26:31) — "I will strike the shepherd, and the sheep will be scattered" (Zech 13:7) — this shepherd too will die (vv. 18-19), and yet the reader knows it will not matter. Whatever happens, the promise stands: the sheep will be kept safe until Jesus comes again (see 10:28-29; 17:12; 18:8). Peter wonders about the fate of "the disciple whom Jesus loved," but that too, Jesus reminds him, is irrelevant. All that matters is that Peter — and all the disciples — "follow" him, as they have been called to do (vv. 20-23).

1 The phrase "after these things," following close on "these things" (20:31), signals that there is at least one more resurrection appearance to come: "After these things, Jesus revealed himself again to the disciples, at the lake of Tiberias. And he revealed like this" (v. 1). That he revealed himself "again"[5] implies that this is what he has done before (although the same words were not used) in Jerusalem, first in a garden (20:16) and then twice in a locked room (20:19-20, 26-27). The vocabulary of "revealing"[6] is thoroughly characteristic of this Gospel. John's intent from the start was that Jesus be "revealed to Israel" (1:31); at Cana he "revealed his glory" (2:11); his brothers urged him to "reveal yourself to the world" (7:4); in the course of time he did just that, and in the end he was able to tell the Father, "I revealed your name to the men you gave me out of the world" (17:6). But these "revelations" are different. Now that Jesus is risen, "revealing himself" means establishing his identity as the Crucified One, the Jesus his disciples have known all along. He did this for Mary Magdalene by speaking her name (20:16), for the gathered male disciples by showing them his hands and his side (20:20), and for Thomas by inviting his touch (20:27). Now we learn that he did it one more time in a very different venue, "at the lake of Tiberias" (identified earlier with the lake of Galilee; see 6:1).

2 The story of how Jesus "revealed himself" is now told: "And he

---

5. Gr. πάλιν.
6. Gr. φανεροῦν.

revealed like this:[7] there were together Simon Peter, and Thomas, the one called Didymos, and Nathanael, the one from Cana of Galilee, and the sons of Zebedee, and two others of the disciples" (vv. 1b-2). These disciples are "together"[8] at the lake just mentioned. In contrast to 20:19-29, they are not the Twelve, nor the Eleven, nor even the Ten. Three are named, two others identified as "sons of Zebedee," and two others mentioned without being named — a total of seven, or so it would seem. Simon Peter is mentioned first, and will speak first (v. 3). Thomas, who has just been heard from (20:28), is still in the picture, but Nathanael, who has not been heard from since chapter 1, is a bit of a surprise. We now learn belatedly that he is from Cana, the place to which Jesus was on his way when he found Nathanael (see 1:43) and to which he seems to have accompanied Jesus (2:2). "The sons of Zebedee," named in the other Gospels as James and John, are mentioned here for the first (and only) time in this Gospel. Simon Peter's brother Andrew and his companion Philip (seen together in 6:7-9 and 12:21-22) are conspicuous by their absence, unless they are the two who are unnamed. It is unclear why they would not be named if they were present.

Somewhere in the picture is "the disciple whom Jesus loved" (see v. 7), but the presence of two unnamed disciples makes it impossible to identify him. It is normally assumed that he is one of the two unnamed disciples, but if he is indeed the one writing the account (see v. 24), he has quite possibly left himself out of the stage setting because the scene is viewed through his eyes.[9] This seems to have been the case in 13:28, where he stated that "none of those reclining" understood why Jesus told Judas to do quickly what he was going to do — obviously he himself understood — and in 19:25, where he listed four who were present at Jesus' crucifixion, but conspicuously excluded himself (only to appear abruptly in the next two verses).[10] If it is the case here, then the number of disciples on the scene is eight, not seven, and he is distinguishing himself not only from Simon Peter, Thomas, and Nathanael, but from "the sons of Zebedee" as well — thus eliminating the traditional identification of this disciple as John, son of Zebedee. Such a possibility is intriguing, and must be taken into account in any effort to identify this disciple. In any event, we have at least seven disciples "together" here at the lake of Tiberias. The "disciple whom Jesus loved," whoever he may be, is

---

7. Gr. οὕτως, the language of storytelling, this time not calling attention to a gesture (as in 4:6 and 13:25) but introducing a narrative.

8. Gr. ὁμοῦ, as in 20:4.

9. This would answer Bultmann's question (702) in connection with his assumption that the beloved disciple's appearance in verse 7 is "an editorial addition": "(why was he not named in v. 2?!)," Bultmann asks. This would explain why.

10. See the reconstructions above (at 13:28 and 19:26), based on Reynolds Price's suggestions about transforming a third-person into a first-person account.

still hidden. He will "reveal himself" only in the act of revealing Jesus ("It is the Lord," v. 7).

3 The story begins as a fishing trip: "Simon Peter says to them, 'I'm going fishing.' They say to him, 'We too are coming with you.' They went out and got into the boat,[11] and in that night they caught nothing" (v. 3). Moralistic observations to the effect that the disciples are somehow disobedient because they have returned (some of them at least) to their former occupation instead of fulfilling their mission of forgiving and retaining sin (20:23) are beside the point. It is of course possible to read this as the first of Jesus' appearances, with the disciples going back to fishing because they know nothing of any resurrection.[12] This could be the case in a source that the Gospel writer might have been using, but in the Gospel as it stands it is ruled out by the simple adverb "again" (v. 1), and by the concluding notice insisting that it is *not* the first but actually the "third" of Jesus' appearances "after being raised from the dead" (v. 14).[13]

In fact, nothing is said of Peter's motivation. The accent is not on why he and the other disciples went fishing, but simply on the fact that they did so, and in particular on the concluding statement that "in that night they caught nothing"[14] — dramatizing Jesus' caution to them six chapters earlier that "apart from me you cannot do anything" (15:5). The phrase "in that night"[15] is the first indication of time, and for those familiar with other Gospel traditions it cannot help but evoke Simon Peter's protest one morning early in the ministry when Jesus urged him to put out from shore and lower his nets: "Master, we have labored all night and have taken nothing" (Lk 5:5). If there is no catch at night, when fishing is at its best, how can there be a great catch in the morning? Symbolic echoes of 9:4 ("We must work the works of the One who sent me as long as it is day. Night is coming when no one can work") are possible here, but not likely. The symbolism would be rather too subtle, because day follows night here (as in Rom 13:12-13) rather than night following day.

4 In any event, Jesus comes in the morning, just as Mary came to the tomb in the morning (20:1): "But as soon as early morning[16] had come,[17] Je-

---

11. "The boat" (τὸ πλοῖον, with the definite article) sounds like the retelling of a familiar story about a familiar group of fishermen.

12. See, for example, Schnackenburg, 3.353; Bultmann, 705; Brown, 2.1078.

13. It could be argued that John's Gospel presupposes something rather like Luke's forty days of resurrection appearances (see Acts 1:3), not only in Jerusalem, however (as in the book of Acts), but in Galilee as well.

14. Gr. ἐπίασαν οὐδέν.

15. Gr. ἐν ἐκείνῃ τῇ νυκτί.

16. Gr. πρωίας.

17. Instead of the aorist "had come" (γενομένης, with ℵ, D, W, Θ, Ψ, and the ma-

21:1-25 THE THIRD APPEARANCE AND SIMON PETER'S COMMISSION

sus stood on the shore, yet the disciples did not know that it was Jesus"[18] (v. 4). The echoes of chapter 20 are striking, suggesting continuity and common authorship. First, Jesus "stood[19] on the shore," just as he "stood in the midst" (twice) in the presence of the disciples behind locked doors in the preceding chapter (20:19, 26).[20] Second, the echo of Mary Magdalene in the garden is even more conspicuous, for she too "did not know that it was Jesus"[21] (20:14). Once again, the stage is set for his self-revelation.

5-6 Jesus appears first as a stranger, in much the same way he appeared to Mary as the gardener (20:15), or in Luke to the two disciples on the way to Emmaus (Lk 24:15-16): "Then Jesus says to them, 'Lads,[22] do you have any catch?'[23] They answered him, 'No,' and he said to them, 'Throw the net to the right side of the boat, and you will find.' So they threw, and they were no longer strong enough to draw it in because of the great number of fish" (vv. 5-6). With these few words, the core of the story is told, and a good share of what follows (vv. 7, 8, 11) simply accents the enormous size of their catch and the difficulty of getting it to shore. Jesus in the guise of the inquisitive stranger does not ask the question because he is hungry — he already has a hearty meal on the fire (v. 9) — but to elicit from the disciples a negative

---

jority of later manuscripts), some important witnesses (including A, B, C, and L) have the present, "was coming" (γινομένης). A choice is difficult, but the use of ἤδη (literally, "already") plus the breadth of textual support slightly favors the aorist.

18. Gr. οὐ μέντοι ᾔδεισαν . . . ὅτι Ἰησοῦς ἐστιν.

19. Gr. ἔστη.

20. "On the shore" (εἰς τὸν αἰγιαλόν) corresponds to "in the midst" (εἰς τὸ μέσον) in the two earlier instances. According to Metzger (*Textual Commentary*, 256), the variant reading (ἐπὶ τὸν αἰγιαλόν, supported by ℵ, A, D, L, Θ, Ψ, 33, and others) is more correct grammatically, but εἰς (with B, C, E, G, H, K, P, S, W, G, D, L, family 1 and 13, and the majority of later manuscripts) is to be preferred as the more difficult reading. In his words, "the latter preposition with ἔστη in accounts of appearances of the risen Christ occurs elsewhere in the Fourth Gospel (20:19 and 26)."

21. Gr. οὐκ ᾔδει ὅτι Ἰησοῦς ἐστιν. The only real difference in terminology, the use of μέντοι in chapter 21, is, as Barrett notices (579), thoroughly characteristic of Johannine style (he cites 4:27, 7:13, 12:42, and 20:5) and occurs only three other times in the New Testament. This strongly favors viewing chapter 21 as an original part of the Gospel.

22. "Lads" (παιδία) is literally "children," but it does not necessarily have here the tender affectionate connotation that it has, for example, in 1 John (2:14, 18, though more commonly τέκνια, as in Jn 13:33). The disciples would more likely have heard it as a colloquialism — a pleasantry of sorts from the lips of a stranger: hence, "Lads" (see Bernard, 2.696; Brown, 2.1070).

23. "Catch" (προσφάγιον) is literally something to be eaten with bread, in this case obviously fish (BDAG, 886). The assumption is that of course they have brought with them bread to eat, as one would customarily do when traveling by boat (see Mk 8:14!). Bread in fact appears as a matter of course later in the story (see v. 13).

answer.[24] Their answer is a simple "No," appropriate to a stranger, nothing like "Master, we have labored all night and have taken nothing" (Lk 5:5).

Jesus' rejoinder, however, "Throw the net to the right side of the boat, and you will find"[25] begins to reveal who he is, for it evokes Jesus' speech as handed down in other Gospel traditions; for example, "Ask, and it will be given you; seek, and you will find;[26] knock, and it will be opened to you" (Mt 7:7//Lk 11:9).[27] Within John's Gospel itself, it evokes (if negatively) Jesus' words to the Pharisees at the Tent festival, "You will seek me, and you will not find" (7:34; see also 13:33). The difference here, because it is a fishing scene, is "throw,[28] . . . and you will find" instead of "seek, and you will find." Just such language occurs in Matthew, where Jesus tells Peter, "Go to the lake; throw a hook, and take the first fish that comes up, and open its mouth, and you will find a coin" (Mt 17:27), and in the *Gospel of Thomas:*

> The Man is like a wise fisherman who *threw* his net into the sea; he drew it up from the sea full of small fish; among them he *found* a large good fish. That wise fisherman, he *threw* all the small fish down into the sea, and chose the large fish without regret. (*Thomas* 8, italics added)[29]

Whether it is the familiarity of Jesus' language or simply the magnitude of the ensuing catch that triggers the moment of recognition (v. 7) is unclear. In any event, Jesus told them to throw their net "to the right side," and they did so, solely on the word of a stranger. The "right" side (whether in Greek or in English) implies the proper, or favorable, side,[30] but the point of the command is simply to urge the disciples to move the net from its present position.[31] The re-

---

24. The question (with μή τι) expects a negative answer, perhaps not so strongly as to merit the rendering, "You don't have any catch, do you?" — that is, "an ironical hint that Jesus knew the helplessness of the disciples when left on their own" (Brown, 2.1071) — yet it has much the same effect. It is a simple inquiry, yet it does in fact uncover their helplessness.

25. Gr. καὶ εὑρήσετε.

26. Gr. ζητεῖτε καὶ εὑρήσετε.

27. See also the Coptic *Gospel of Thomas* 2 ("Let him who seeks not cease seeking until he finds"), 92 ("Seek, and you will find") and 94 ("Whoever seeks will find"). See Guillaumont, Puech, Quispel, etc., *The Gospel According to Thomas* (Leiden: Brill, 1959), 3, 49.

28. Gr. βάλετε.

29. Adapted from the translation of Guillaumont et al., 5, 7. The Coptic word for "threw" then becomes a catchword linking the saying to the next two (*Thomas* 9, where the sower "threw," and 10, where Jesus says, "I have thrown fire upon the world"; see also *Thomas* 16 and 93).

30. See W. Grundmann, *TDNT*, 2.38.

31. This in contrast to Luke 5:4, where he tells the disciples to "lower your nets," as if for the first time.

21:1-25 The Third Appearance and Simon Peter's Commission

sult is immediate and startling, as "they were no longer strong enough to draw it in because of the great number[32] of fish." The next few verses will document their struggles in getting "the great number of fish" to shore.

7 At this point the beloved disciple abruptly reveals himself to the reader, even as he reveals Jesus to the other disciples: "Then that disciple whom Jesus loved said to Peter, 'It is the Lord.'[33] Then Simon Peter, hearing that 'It is the Lord,' secured the outer garment (for he was naked), and threw himself into the lake" (v. 7).[34] "It is the Lord" is only the second (and last) pronouncement of this disciple in the entire Gospel of John, and it is eerily, yet superficially, similar to the first, at the table when Jesus predicted that one of them would hand him over: "Lord, who is it?"[35] (13:25). He has said nothing since then, either to identify Judas to the other disciples as the betrayer (see 13:28-29), or to share with Peter or Mary Magdalene exactly what he "believed" when he looked into the empty tomb (20:8). And when Jesus gave his mother into the disciple's care, he "took her to his own home" without a word (19:27). Now at last he breaks his silence. He is the first to recognize Jesus, and at last he shares that recognition. His testimony to Peter, "It is the Lord," echoes both the words of Mary to the disciples ("I have seen the Lord," 20:18) and their words to the absent Thomas ("We have seen the Lord," 20:25). Presumably all the other disciples heard it (see v. 12), but Simon Peter is the first to act. The next sentence could be legitimately translated as indirect discourse ("Then Simon Peter, hearing that it was the Lord . . ."), but it is worthwhile noticing the repetition of the exact words, "It is the Lord," and the translation has shown this by preserving direct discourse. What Peter hears is exactly what "that disciple whom Jesus loved" has said, and before it is over, those very words will reecho yet a third time in the minds of all the disciples (v. 12).

On hearing the testimony, Simon Peter immediately "secured the outer garment (for he was naked), and threw himself into the lake" (v. 7b). It

---

32. Gr. ἀπὸ τοῦ πλήθους.

33. Gr. ὁ κύριός ἐστιν.

34. This is the crucial verse that we miss in Reynolds Price's attempted transformation of the present passage from a third-person to a first-person account: "Simon Peter said to us, 'I'm going fishing.' We said, 'We're coming with you.' So we went out and got into the boat and all that night caught nothing. . . . We others came on in the little boat dragging the net of fish since we were only about a hundred yards from land. When we got out on land we saw a charcoal fire laid, a fish lying on it and bread. . . . Jesus came, took the bread and gave it to us, also the fish. This was the third time Jesus was shown to us raised from the dead" (*Three Gospels,* 175). He would have made his point more effectively by transforming verse 7 as well: "Then I said to Peter, 'It is the Lord' " — or words to that effect.

35. Gr. κύριε, τίς ἐστιν.

is important to recognize that he does this not in order to bring the catch ashore, but to get to shore first to greet "the Lord."[36] The other disciples will drag the loaded net to shore in the boat (v. 8), and Peter will come back and help them finish the job (v. 11). It is odd that he is described as "naked," and at the same time clothed in "the outer garment." While the word we have translated "secured"[37] can also mean "put on,"[38] it hardly makes sense that if Peter was naked to begin with, he would then clothe himself in order to jump into the water! More likely, the verb means to "tie around" or "secure" a garment one is already wearing.[39] The garment in question[40] was normally worn loosely over another garment,[41] but in this instance, we are being told, it was the only garment Peter was wearing. He was "naked" underneath it. Consequently, instead of taking it off he merely tied or "secured" it so as have freedom in the water, yet without coming ashore to meet "the Lord" naked. Perhaps in this avoidance of shame there is an impulse akin to the actual shame Peter expresses in the preresurrection narrative in Luke, "Get away from me, for I am a sinful man, Lord!" (Lk 5:8).

8 Only Simon Peter left the boat. His companions heard the same words he did, "It is the Lord" (v. 7a), but they had the responsibility of getting the enormous catch to shore: "and the other disciples came in the boat[42] (for they were not far from the land, about two hundred cubits),[43] dragging the net of fish" (v. 8). Instead of trying to take on board a catch that would have sunk the boat, they haul it with difficulty toward shore. Hoskyns assumes (without discussion) that they reached shore before Peter did,[44] but that is most unlikely. He is presumably ashore already, greeting the Lord, but the "pair of human eyes" of which Reynolds Price speaks, "hovering just at the edge of each event, or caught in its center"[45] (that is, the eyes of the "disciple whom Jesus loved") are not looking in Peter's direction. For the mo-

36. See Schnackenburg, 3.355.
37. Gr. διεζώσατο.
38. See BDAG, 228: "*tie around* oneself (i.e. *put on*) *an outer garment*." Some such translation is presupposed by most English versions.
39. So, for example, Brown, 2.1072, who paraphrases it (2.1066) as "tucked in his outer garment (for he was otherwise naked)."
40. Gr. τὴν ἐπενδύτην.
41. See BDAG, 361.
42. Literally, "the little boat." The word for "boat" here is a diminutive (τῷ πλοιαρίῳ, instead of τὸ πλοῖον, v. 3), but the words are used interchangeably (as in 6:17, 19, 23).
43. That is, about a hundred yards.
44. Hoskyns, 553.
45. *Three Gospels,* 176. Price suggests (175) that this applies, "though less directly" (whatever that means), to all the miracle stories in the Gospel — a generalization harder to defend.

ment, they are focused rather on "the other disciples" and their experience, at least until Peter comes back to help them (v. 11).

9 Next we are told what the disciples saw on disembarking: "Then when they got out onto the land, they see a charcoal fire laid, and a fish laid on, and bread" (v. 9). Presumably they saw Jesus and Simon Peter as well, but the accent here is on something unexpected — both to them and to the reader: a fire already lighted and a meal already prepared. The "charcoal fire"[46] recalls the "charcoal fire" at which Peter warmed himself when he denied the Lord (18:18, 25), thus preparing the reader (though not necessarily the disciples) for Peter's reinstatement (vv. 15-17). The fire is not for warmth this time, but for cooking. "Fish" has been laid on it, "fish" as food,[47] not "fish" as a sea creature.[48] "Fish," like "bread," both without the article) is probably generic — that is, not "*a* fish" and "*a* loaf of bread," as if there were just one of each, but an unspecified amount of food.[49] The accent is not on the amount of food, but on its careful preparation; the fire has been "laid,"[50] and fish carefully "laid on." Who has prepared it? Who else but "the Lord" (v. 7)?

10 The Lord speaks again: "Jesus says to them, 'Bring some of the fish you caught just now'" (v. 10). The expression, "Bring some of the fish," is a partitive expression, literally, "bring from the fish."[51] Here again (as in v. 9), "fish" is fish to be eaten, not fish swimming in the lake (vv. 8 and 11). Is Jesus then asking for more fish to be added to those already roasting on the fire? That might seem to be the case, yet no hint is given that any of the fish in the net were ever actually cleaned and eaten. Moreover, if, as we have suggested, there is a symbolic dimension to this narrative in which fishing some-

---

46. Gr. ἀνθρακιάν.
47. Gr. ὀψάριον, like προσφάγιον (v. 5).
48. That is, like τῶν ἰχθύων (v. 8); see BDAG, 746.
49. So Bultmann, 708, n. 8. Contrast 6:9, where the amount is carefully specified: "five barley loaves [πέντε ἄρτους κριθίνους] and two pieces of fish" (δύο ὀψάρια). Schnackenburg comments (3.356), "The singular without the article possibly originally had a generic meaning (as also ἄρτον). Probably, when adding v. 10, the editor understood it numerically: *one* fish, so that several more fish from the present haul of fish are required for the meal (there are, after all, seven men)." Yet there is no evidence that the disciples actually brought any of their catch to Jesus to be cleaned and added to the menu. Jesus alone provides the meal, and as host invites the disciples to partake (v. 12).
50. Some of the old Latin versions have misread κειμένην as καιομένην; hence *incensos,* "lighted," or "burning."
51. Gr. ἐνέγκατε ἀπὸ τῶν ὀψαρίων. Such expressions can occur with either ἀπό or ἐκ, but as Barrett (581) points out, "In John 1–20 it is ἐκ, not ἀπό, which is commonly used partitively." According to Brown (2.1073), "The partitive use of *apo* is found only here in John, as contrasted with fifty-one uses of partitive *ek*" (see also Abbott, *Johannine Grammar,* 89-90). Schnackenburg draws from this the extraordinary conclusion that "the evangelist is indeed to be ruled out as the author" (3.357).

how represents the disciples' assigned task of "fishing" for human beings, the thought of eating even a part of their enormous catch is incongruous, stretching the metaphor to the breaking point. But if not this, what *is* Jesus asking?

His odd terminology — "bring from the fish" (see n. 51) — evokes the language of sacrifice, in particular the first example of sacrifice in the Greek Bible, when "Cain brought an offering from[52] the fruits of the earth, and Abel, he too brought from the firstborn of his sheep and from their fat" (Gen 4:3-4, LXX).[53] That this story was familiar to early Christians is clear from *1 Clement* 4.1, where it is quoted verbatim. While nothing quite like it appears in John's Gospel, Jesus has spoken to the disciples repeatedly about the need to "bear [that is, "bring"] fruit" (see 15:2, 4, 5, 8, 16). The word translated "bear" in that expression[54] is the same word used here as an aorist imperative, and translated "Bring." As we have seen, the notice that "in that night they caught nothing" (v. 3) has already evoked for the reader the imagery of the vine, with its warning that "apart from me you cannot do anything" (15:5). It is fitting, therefore, that what they have now accomplished with Jesus' help should be viewed precisely as the "fruit" which they have to offer him — "much fruit," in fact (see v. 6, "the great number").[55] He asks for their offering, and they will bring it, not to the table but simply to "the Lord," in fulfillment of their mission. What happens to it after that is not part of the story.

11 Peter, ashore before the others, takes the initiative to respond to Jesus' words: "So Simon Peter went up and drew the net onto the land, full of 153 great fish, and even with so many the net was not torn" (v. 11). "Went up"[56] could mean that he got back into the boat, but more likely he came up to the boat in order to bring the loaded net, still lying in shallow water, onto the land. "Drew" is the same word used of the Father "drawing" people to Jesus (6:44), or Jesus "drawing" them to himself (12:32), and some have theorized that it is chosen here for that reason, in keeping with the symbolic import of "fishing" for human beings.[57] But this is unlikely because the writer uses the verb almost interchangeably with another verb for "drawing" or "dragging" (*thyrontes;* v. 8), a word with no such associations.

Once the net is on land, we learn that it is "full of 153 great fish," a number which ordinary readers take at face value — the disciples must have

---

52. Gr. ἤνεγκεν . . . ἀπό.

53. This may account for the most unusual aorist imperative (ἐνέγκατε) instead of the present (φέρετε; see BDF, §336[3]), evoking the aorist verbs in Genesis 4.

54. Gr. φέρειν.

55. See 15:2, "more fruit" (καρπὸν πλείονα), and 15:5, 8, "much fruit" (καρπὸν πολύν).

56. Gr. ἀνέβη; see BDAG, 58 (that is, the reverse of ἀπέβησαν, "got out," in v. 9).

57. So, for example, Lincoln, 512-13.

21:1-25 THE THIRD APPEARANCE AND SIMON PETER'S COMMISSION

counted their catch![58] — yet one which continues to baffle and fascinate scholars. The number is remarkable both because it is very large (in keeping with similar extravagances in 2:6, 6:13, 12:3, and 19:39), and because it is so specific without being a round number (like one hundred) or an obviously symbolic one (like twelve). It is not an approximation ("*about* five thousand," 6:10; "*about* a hundred pounds," 19:39), nor an estimate ("each holding *two or three* measures," 2:6), but an exact figure, like the "thirty-eight years" the man at the pool had been sick (5:5). It is quite possible that the figure of 153 (with or without symbolic significance) was part and parcel of the story from the time it began to be told orally, just as the "thirty-eight years" seems to have been part and parcel of the story of the man at the pool. It hints unmistakably at the presence of an eyewitness, something the text already claims for itself (see v. 7, where "that disciple whom Jesus loved" has already made his appearance).

Needless to say, such simple explanations have not satisfied commentators. It is pointless to reinvent the wheel by cataloguing all the valiant efforts to extract symbolic meaning from this number.[59] Already in the fourth century, Augustine recognized it as a triangular number, the sum of every integer from one through seventeen — "triangular" because if one dot is printed and above that two dots and above that three, and so on up to seventeen, the result is a triangle made up of dots. Triangular numbers, like squares and square roots, were of great interest to the ancients. In that sense, 153 reduces to 17 (just as 144, for example, reduces to 12, its square root), and from there one can draw any number of conclusions. Augustine, for example, saw 17 as the sum of 10 and 7, and opined, "Accordingly, when to the number of ten, representing the law, we add the Holy Spirit as represented by seven, we have seventeen; and when this number is used for the adding together of every several number it contains, from 1 up to itself, the sum amounts to one hundred and fifty-three."[60] Somewhat more promising is the statement of Jerome (in his commentary on Ezekiel), that certain Greek zoologists (Oppian of Cilicia in particular) listed 153 varieties of fish known to exist.[61] Superficially, this might correspond to the parable of the net in Mat-

---

58. If the disciples as good commercial fishermen simply counted the fish in the net, they obviously did so in real time, probably after the fact, not in narrative time, for in the narrative they proceed at once to the meal (vv. 12-13).

59. See, for example, Brown, 2.1074-76, Beasley-Murray, 401-4, and most recently Bauckham, *Testimony*, 271-84. I once heard Raymond Brown, in an entertaining lecture long after he had written his commentary, speak of a dream he had had in which a voice from heaven spoke to him, saying, "You fool, 'the reason I said there were 153 fish in John 21 was that there WERE 153 fish!' " (that at least is how I remember it).

60. *On the Gospel of John* 72.8; NPNF, 1st ser., 7.442.

61. *Commentary on Ezekiel* 47.6-12 (*PL*, 25.474C). Jerome's text in particular

thew, in which the net gathered fish "of every kind" (Mt 13:47), except that in the parable the phrase seems to mean not every species of fish, but simply the good and the bad (13:48). Moreover, Jerome's testimony cannot be verified from any of the Greek zoologists,[62] and even if it could, it is something of a reach to suppose that the writer of John's Gospel would have known about them. Quite possibly Jerome is reading into them what he thinks he has already discovered in the Gospel of John! It is unlikely, therefore, that 153 signals the ethnic diversity of the people of God (as, for example, in the vision of "a great multitude which no one can number, out of every nation and tribe and people and tongue," Rev 7:9).

As far as the symbolism is concerned, we are back where we started. While the writer (or his source) may well have known that 153 was a triangular number, the point may be simply that it is a very large number of fish to be caught at one time in a net, and that it is not a mere approximation — that is, every single one counts, as if counted one by one (compare Mt 10:29-31//Lk 12:6-7). In any case (in contrast to the parable of the net in Matthew), there is no need to separate good from bad among the fish that are caught in the net. The catch consists of 153 "great fish,"[63] "great" implying not only "large" but "good" (as perhaps in *Gospel of Thomas* 8). None will be "thrown out" (Mt 13:48),[64] nor will any be lost, for "even with so many[65] the net was not torn." Here is where the emphasis lies, not on the characteristics of the number 153. In striking contrast to the fishing scene in Luke, where "their nets were breaking" (Lk 5:6), the net is unbroken despite the enormous weight. The point is much the same as when Jesus, after the feeding of the multitude, told the disciples to "Gather the leftover broken pieces, so that nothing is

---

was Ezekiel 47:10, "People will stand fishing beside the sea from En-gedi to En-eglaim; it will be a place for the spreading of nets; its fish will be of a great many kinds, like the fish of the great sea" (NRSV). Other solutions have centered on the names "En-gedi" and "En-eglaim," noticing that by the practice of *gematria* (that is, assigning numerical values to letters of the alphabet), the consonants in those two names (in Hebrew) add up to 17 and 153, respectively (so J. A. Emerton, *JTS* 9 [1958], 86-89). That the present scene is the lake of Galilee, where fish are abundant, not (as in Ezek 47) the Dead Sea, where no fish swim, seems not to bother those bent on finding such profound symbolism. The examples given here do not even scratch the surface of the wonders proposed.

62. Brown (citing R. M. Grant, *HTR* 42 [1949], 273-75) comments: "Oppian states that there are countless types of fish and actually lists 157," while "Pliny (*Natural History* ix. 43) knew of 104 varieties of fish and crustaceans" (2.1074).

63. Gr. ἰχθύων μεγάλων.

64. This in keeping with 6:37, but in contrast to 15:6, where those who bear no fruit are, in fact, "thrown out [ἐβλήθη ἔξω] like the branch." The present narrative looks at the disciples' world mission, not on potential issues of apostasy or church discipline that might arise later.

65. Gr. τοσούτων ὄντων.

21:1-25 THE THIRD APPEARANCE AND SIMON PETER'S COMMISSION

lost," and "they gathered, and filled up twelve baskets with pieces left over" (6:12-13).[66] Here the conservation of fish, like the conservation of fragments there, hints at Jesus' repeated promise that he will keep his disciples safe, and that none of those whom the Father has given him will ever be lost (see 3:16; also 6:39; 10:28; 17:12; 18:9). And what is true of them is true as well of "those who believe . . . through their word" (17:20). As "fishers" in the world, they will "go and bear fruit," and their fruit will last (15:16).

12 The meal is ready: "Jesus says to them, 'Come, have breakfast,'"[67] and instead of giving the disciples' response, the Gospel writer offers a rare glimpse of what was going on in their minds — not what they said but what they did *not* say: "And none of the disciples dared inquire of him, 'Who are you?' — knowing that 'It is the Lord'" (v. 12). Like Mary Magdalene (20:14), they had not recognized him at first (see v. 4), but unlike Mary, who as soon as she recognized him said, "'Rabbouni' (which means 'Teacher!')," they hesitate. They have heard from the disciple whom Jesus loved that "It is the Lord!" (v. 7a), and the words echoed in Peter's ears as he threw himself into the lake (v. 7b). Now we hear the same words yet again. Again, strictly speaking, the last clause should be translated as indirect discourse — "knowing that it was the Lord" — but again I have rendered it as direct discourse to emphasize that we are now hearing the same recognition formula for yet a third time. "It is the Lord"[68] has echoed verbatim from the disciple whom Jesus loved, to Simon Peter, and now finally to the rest of the disciples.

Why then the hesitation? Why the unwillingness to speak to "the Lord" directly? Why not Mary's "Rabbouni," or "Teacher!" (as in 20:16)? Why not Thomas's "My Lord and my God!" (as in 20:28)? Nothing of the kind is even contemplated. Perhaps it would be anticlimactic after 20:28! Their confession, "It is the Lord," remains unspoken. What is contemplated instead is a question, "Who are you?" as if addressing the supposed stranger who asked them, "Lads, do you have any catch?" (v. 5). But to ask it now, after hearing that "It is the Lord" (v. 7), would be to ask for verification,[69] something Thomas had already embarrassed himself by demanding, and something Jesus had given twice before without being asked (20:20, 27).

---

66. Just as broken fragments can come to represent the people of God (as in *Didache* 9.4), so on occasion can fish. Tertullian wrote (though not in relation to the present passage) that "we, being little fishes, as Jesus Christ is our great Fish, begin our life in the water"; *Homily on Baptism* 1.3 (ed. E. Evans, 1964), p. 1039.

67. Gr. δεῦτε ἀριστήσατε.

68. Gr. ὁ κύριός ἐστιν.

69. See 1:19, where the question "Who are you?" was a hostile question directed to John, and 8:25, where "the Jews" at the Tent festival asked it of Jesus, also in a setting of mounting hostility.

Therefore "none of the disciples dared inquire of him," and they remain silent, recalling their silence during Jesus' farewell discourse when they questioned what he was saying but were unwilling to ask him (see 16:5, 16-19). Here, however, their embarrassed silence fulfills Jesus' promise that "in that day you will ask me nothing" (16:23). Now that he has "revealed himself" (v. 1), no questions are asked because no further verification is needed.[70]

13 Jesus has just said, "Come, have breakfast" (v. 12), yet it is he who makes the first move: "Jesus comes and takes the bread and gives to them, and the fish likewise" (v. 13). He "comes," just as he "came" to the disciples twice before (20:19, 26). What he does next confirms the connection between the present scene and the feeding of the five thousand, in particular the connection between the 153 fish in the unbroken net and the twelve baskets of leftover fragments with nothing lost. Reenacting the earlier scene in which he

> "took the loaves, and when he had given thanks he gave them out to those who were seated, and of the fish, as much as they wanted" (6:11),

Jesus now

> "takes the bread and gives to them, and the fish likewise."[71]

Even though the story has to do with fish and not bread, the bread comes first, just as at the earlier meal, and then the fish "likewise."[72] The narrative is simplified in comparison to the earlier one, notably by the omission of any reference to the giving of thanks.[73] The omission is probably not of great significance. The reader is evidently expected to fill in the gaps by assuming that Jesus either "blessed" or "gave thanks" for the meal, in keeping with all other such Gospel accounts.[74] Yet given the absence of wine, there is

---

70. See also 16:30, "Now we know that you know all things and have no need that anyone ask you." Here, however, the vocabulary of "asking" is different: not ἐρωτᾶν, "ask," as in 16:5, 19, 23, and 30, but ἐξετάσαι, "inquire," used nowhere else in the Gospel.

71. The definite articles, "*the* bread" (τὸν ἄρτον) and "*the* fish" (τὸ ὀψάριον) look back to verse 9, when the disciples first saw "fish" (ὀψάριον) and "bread" (ἄρτον) laid on the fire. The definite articles tell us that this is "the aforementioned bread," and, more importantly, "the aforementioned supply of fish" — therefore *not* fish caught by the disciples in the boat (see BDF, §252).

72. Gr. ὁμοίως. The fish, after all, is προσφάγιον, something to eat with bread (v. 5).

73. The lack is supplied in a few textual witnesses, notably Codex D, which has (in place of δίδωσιν) the words εὐχαριστήσας ἔδωκεν. But this is clearly a harmonization.

74. That is, either εὐχαριστεῖν (Mt 15:36//Mk 8:6; Lk 22:19//1 Cor 11:24) or εὐλογεῖν (Mt 14:19//Mk 6:41//Lk 9:16, Mt 26:26//Mk 14:22, and Lk 24:30).

21:1-25 THE THIRD APPEARANCE AND SIMON PETER'S COMMISSION

no need to view the scene as "Eucharistic" in any proper sense of the word, despite the liturgical-sounding language — less so even than at the feeding of the five thousand, where the imagery of drinking (and drinking blood in particular) is at least introduced in the appended discourse (see 6:35, 53-56). More likely, the narrative intends to evoke simply the fellowship meals that Jesus shared with his disciples (see 12:2; 13:1-5), with Jesus as host and the disciples his guests.

14 Did Jesus himself eat any of the bread or fish? We are not told. Instead, the writer summarizes and concludes the incident: "This third time now Jesus was revealed to his disciples after being raised from the dead" (v. 14). The notice recalls many other such summary notices in the Gospel beginning with "this" or "these": for example, "This Jesus did . . . as a beginning of the signs" (2:11); "And this Jesus did again as a second sign" (4:54); "These things he said teaching in synagogue" (6:59); "These words he spoke in the treasury, teaching in the temple" (8:20). The question here is "third"[75] in relation to what? If this was the "third" time Jesus revealed himself, what were the first two?[76] Clearly, chapter 20 is presupposed, just as it was in verse 1 ("After these things, Jesus revealed himself again to the disciples"). But how much of chapter 20 is presupposed, only the two-stage appearance to the male disciples in a locked room (20:19-31), or the appearance to Mary in the garden as well (20:11-18)? Most commentators assume the former without even bothering to raise the issue. The repetition of "again" (*palin*, v. 1), after the *palin* separating the two appearances to the male disciples (20:26) points in that direction, and so does the repetition of "Jesus came" (or "comes") in 20:19, 26 and now 21:13.[77] Moreover, the appearances in 20:19-23 and 26-29 and in chapter 21 are appearances to a group, not an individual, and specifically to a group called "the disciples" (20:19, 26; 21:1, 14), a term reserved in this Gospel for male followers of Jesus.

Yet it is not quite an open-and-shut case. As we have seen, there is a sense in which the two appearances a week apart in 20:19-23 and 26-29 respectively are actually one, with a certain solidarity between Thomas and the other disciples. If the two incidents are counted as one, then the appearance in the garden to Mary Magdalene is the first "revelation" of the risen Lord, the appearance to the male disciples in the locked room the second, and the appearance at the lake of Tiberias the third. Mary testifies, "I have seen the

---

75. Gr. τρίτον.
76. Robert Fortna theorized that in the pre-Johannine Signs Source, this event was "third" precisely in relation to the first two "signs" identified in 2:11 and 4:54 (*The Fourth Gospel and Its Predecessor*, 65-66). But whatever its merits as source criticism, this hypothesis is of no help in interpreting the text as it stands, where it is excluded by the words, "after being raised from the dead."
77. Gr. ἔρχεται Ἰησοῦς.

Lord" (20:18), the disciples echo her words, "We have seen the Lord" (20:25), and "the disciple whom Jesus loved" testifies, "It is the Lord" (21:7) — a cry that echoes not once but three times through the narrative (vv. 7a, 7b, 12). Moreover, the group designated as "the disciples" in chapter 21 is not exactly the same group so designated (with or without Thomas) in chapter 20. They are only seven in number, or at most eight,[78] and it is by no means certain that the two anonymous disciples (v. 2) were even present in the preceding chapter. The possibility, therefore, that the first "revelation" to which verse 14 refers was to just one "disciple" — and a woman at that! — cannot be summarily dismissed.[79] Whatever resurrection appearances may be in view, the accent on the "third time" is noteworthy — as though the sheer repetition attests the reality of the events.

15 At this point, all of the disciples except Simon Peter (and later, "the disciple whom Jesus loved," vv. 20-24) disappear from the story and are not heard from again. It is as if Jesus and Peter are alone: "Then, when they had had breakfast, Jesus says to Simon Peter, 'Simon of John, do you love me more than these?' He says to him, 'Yes, Lord, you know that I love you.' He says to him, 'Tend my lambs'" (v. 15). The address, "Simon of John," takes us back to Jesus' first encounter with this disciple when he looked at him and said, "You are Simon, the son of John," and predicted that his name would be "Cephas," or Peter (1:42). It is no clearer here than it was there whether Jesus is alluding to Simon's father in order to distinguish him from some other Simon, or whether he is simply reminding him that he was John's disciple before he met Jesus.

The question "Do you love me?"[80] revisits the farewell discourse, when Jesus said to all the disciples, "If you love me, you will keep my commands" (14:15; see also vv. 21, 23). When Peter says "Yes," Jesus will give him a command. And yet the question has in it a possible trap, for it is not just "Do you love me?" but "Do you love me *more than these?*" (italics added). Jesus is quite capable of "testing" his disciples (as he did Philip; see 6:6), and here he seems to be doing just that. Grammatically, "more than these"[81] could mean "more than you love these other disciples," but this makes no sense because he has repeatedly urged them to "love one another" (13:34-35; 15:12, 17). Or it could mean "more than you love your boat and your nets, the instru-

---

78. That is, if "the disciple whom Jesus loved" is not counting himself as one of the seven.

79. While most interpreters do not even entertain this possibility, Fortna at least mentions it: "Strictly speaking there are in fact three appearances in chap. 20, not two, but one of them — the first — is to a lone woman, Mary Magdalene, and for that reason perhaps was not included in the enumeration" (*Predecessor,* 66, n. 145).

80. Gr. ἀγαπᾷς με.

81. Gr. πλέον τούτων.

ments of your livelihood" (see Mk 1:18//Mt 4:20, "and immediately leaving the nets they followed him"), but no such "love" for material things has played any part in the story. The meaning we are left with — the only possible meaning — is "more than these other disciples — who are present right here on the scene — love me." Here, as elsewhere in the chapter (and occasionally in the Gospel as a whole), Jesus builds on an incident or pronouncement found in other Gospels — in this case Peter's confident claim, in the face of Jesus' prediction that the disciples would abandon him, "Even if they all are offended, yet not I" (Mk 14:29; also Mt 26:33). John's Gospel has nothing quite so explicit, although Peter did say, "I will lay down my life for you!" (13:37), a rash promise that no other disciple was willing to make.

Peter does not fall into the trap. He could have said, "Yes, I do love you more than these" — sticking to all his rash promises. Or he could have said, "No, I do not love you more than these," which would have been technically true, but would have given the impression that he did not love Jesus at all. Instead, he says simply, "Yes, Lord, you know that I love you," wisely forswearing any comparison between his love for Jesus and anyone else's. If it is a test, he has passed, at least to this point. Much has been written as to whether his use of a different word for love[82] in any way limits or qualifies his answer.[83] But the two words, whatever their different nuances,[84] are used interchangeably in this Gospel for the Father's love for the Son (for example, 3:35; 5:20), the disciples' love for Jesus (see 14:15; 16:27), Jesus' love for Lazarus (see 11:3, 5), and Jesus' love for "the disciple whom he loved" (see 13:23; 20:2). Other synonyms or near synonyms, moreover, are used interchangeably both in the immediate context — "lambs" (v. 15) and "sheep" (vv. 16, 17), "tend" (vv. 15, 17), and "shepherd" (v. 16) — and in the wider context: "drawing" (vv. 6, 11) and "dragging" (v. 8), live "fish" (vv. 6, 8, 11) and "fish" as food (vv. 9, 13; also v. 5), "boat" (vv. 3, 6) and little "boat" (v. 8). The accent in Peter's reply, therefore, is not on the choice of verbs but on the omission of the phrase "more than these." Whatever he may have said before, Peter will now make no such claim. And in the same breath he ac-

---

82. That is, φιλεῖν instead of ἀγαπᾶν, the verb Jesus had used.

83. As Brown points out (2.1102), most ancient commentators saw the two verbs as interchangeable, early modern scholarship (for example, Westcott, 367-68, and Abbott, *Johannine Vocabulary,* 240-42) argued for various kinds of subtle distinctions, and most contemporary interpreters have reverted to the notion that the differences are purely for the sake of stylistic variation.

84. The distinction most commonly made is that ἀγαπᾶν implies conscious choice or preference, while φιλεῖν implies something more like simple affection or friendship. See, however, James 4:4, where "friendship" or φιλία, with the world is similarly viewed as a choice, being defined as "enmity with God, for whoever wants to be a friend [φίλος] of the world is counted as an enemy of God."

knowledges that Jesus knows what is in his heart: "Yes, Lord, you know[85] that I love you." From the beginning, the Gospel writer has assured us that Jesus "knew them all" (2:24), or "knew what was in the person" (2:25), so for Peter there can be no dissimulation or deception.

Taking Peter at his word, Jesus gives the command, "Tend my lambs." As Good Shepherd (10:11, 14), he commissions Peter to act as shepherd in his absence, in view of his imminent departure. Neither the verb "tend" nor the noun "lambs" have been used up to now in John's Gospel,[86] but it is clear that the same "flock" is in view as in chapter 10, for the "lambs" are Jesus' "lambs."[87] He, and not Peter, is still the "one Shepherd," acting on the Father's behalf (10:16). Peter's voice in a New Testament letter attributed to him bears this out: "And when the Chief Shepherd is revealed, you will receive the unfading crown of glory" (1 Pet 5:4). Peter will act as shepherd in Jesus' place, yet the "lambs" belong not to him but to Jesus. Peter does not immediately accept the commission, and instead of waiting for an answer Jesus questions him again.

16 The question is virtually the same: "He says to him again a second time, 'Simon of John, do you love me?' He says to him, 'Yes, Lord, you know that I love you.' He says to him, 'Shepherd my sheep'" (v. 16). The phrase "again a second time"[88] is as redundant as it sounds in English, suggesting that the repetition is unexpected, at least to Peter. The only difference in the question is that Jesus, taking his cue from Peter, has dropped the phrase "more than these." Without reference to anyone else's love, he is asking simply, "Do you love me [as you say you do]?" The answer is exactly the same as before, and the commission too is the same, but in different words, "Shepherd my sheep,"[89] words more familiar to the reader than "Tend my lambs" (v. 15).[90] That "shep-

---

85. Gr. σὺ οἶδας.

86. "Tend" (βόσκε) can also mean "feed" (see BDAG, 181), but the broader meaning is probably in view. "Lambs" (τὰ ἀρνία) is, grammatically speaking, a diminutive, but is probably used here synonymously with "sheep" (τὰ πρόβατα, vv. 16 and 17;3 see BDAG, 13).

87. Gr. τὰ ἀρνία μου.

88. Gr. πάλιν δεύτερον.

89. In place of πρόβατα, some important ancient manuscripts (including B, C, and 565) have προβάτια, a diminutive form, both here and in verse 17 (A also has the variant in v. 17). But πρόβατα has much wider support (with ℵ, D, W, Θ, Ψ, family 13, and the majority of later manuscripts). Possibly the diminutive was introduced by later scribes to correspond with the diminutive ἀρνία (v. 15). Or, alternatively, the diminutive could have been original, and changed to πρόβατα in conformity with the vocabulary of the Shepherd discourse in chapter 10. There is no difference in meaning in any case (see BDAG, 865).

90. For the words "my sheep" (τὰ πρόβατα τὰ ἐμά) on Jesus' lips, see 10:26; also "mine" (τὰ ἐμά, 10:14, and, as we have seen, probably 17:10 as well). While the verb

21:1-25 THE THIRD APPEARANCE AND SIMON PETER'S COMMISSION

herding"[91] became a dominant metaphor for pastoral care is evident already within the New Testament (see Acts 20:28; 1 Pet 5:2), but in John's Gospel the "sheep" are Jesus' disciples. Peter's commission, therefore, is not simply to be a pastor to new converts but in some way a pastor right away to his fellow disciples[92] — this, instead of boasting of a love for Jesus surpassing theirs! Once again, Jesus does not wait for Peter to accept the commission.

17 Taking his cue from Peter once again, Jesus repeats the question, this time using the same word for "love" that Peter himself had used twice: "He says to him the third time,[93] 'Simon of John, do you love me?'[94] Peter was grieved because he said to him the third time, 'Do you love me?' and he says to him, 'Lord, you know all things; you know that I love you.' Jesus says to him, 'Tend my sheep'" (v. 17). Peter is "grieved"[95] not because Jesus uses a different word for "love" the third time, but simply because there is a "third time." The use of "the third time," not once but twice (especially in the wake of the redundant "again a second time," v. 16), makes this abundantly clear. Moreover, "the third time" echoes the phrase "This third time" in verse 14. The risen Lord, revealed to his disciples for a "third time," as if to prove beyond doubt the reality of his resurrection, now questions Peter's love for yet a "third time" as if to elicit proof beyond doubt of the reality of that love.

What is less clear is whether Peter is "grieved" simply because he feels that Jesus does not believe him, or because he remembers his three denials in the courtyard of the Chief Priest (see 18:17, 25, 27). While the denials are not enumerated as first, second, and third, they are predicted (in all four Gospels) as precisely "three" in number (see 13:38; also Mt 26:34//Mk 14:30//Lk 22:34). There can be little doubt that the three questions, with Peter's three positive answers, are intended by the Gospel writer as a record of Peter's reinstatement, signaled in advance to the reader by a "charcoal fire" (v. 9) recalling the setting of those three denials (see 18:18, 25).[96] Whether

---

ποιμαίνειν has not occurred before, it does evoke the image of the Shepherd (ὁ ποιμήν, 10:2, 11, 14).

91. Gr. ποιμαίνειν.

92. See Luke 22:31, where Jesus tells Peter, "and you, when you have turned around, strengthen your brothers."

93. Gr. τὸ τρίτον.

94. Gr. φιλεῖς με.

95. Gr. ἐλυπήθη.

96. This is acknowledged by most interpreters, but Bultmann (712) is an exception. While he admits that the Gospel writer (in distinction from his source) may have understood it in this way "since he attached it to the Gospel which relates the threefold denial of Peter," he still argues that even "so far as he too is concerned, the real point cannot lie there; he looks on vv. 15-17 as a foil for vv. 18-23, and in any case if the section is taken by itself, it provides no hint of a relation to the account of the denial" (!) . He cites

the fire prompts Peter himself to remember the denials, as the crowing of the rooster did in the other Gospels (see Mt 26:75//Mk 14:72//Lk 22:61-62), is uncertain. In any event, Peter answers, even more emphatically than before: "Lord, you know all things; you know that I love you."[97] Oddly, the absence of "Yes" (*nai,* as in vv. 15 and 16) makes the answer even stronger. It is unnecessary to say "Yes" for a third time because Peter acknowledges not only Jesus' knowledge of his heart, but his knowledge of "all things,"[98] just as the disciples had done at the end of his farewell discourse: "Now we know that you know all things" (16:30). If he knows "all things," he knows the answer is "Yes" without Peter having to say it again. Consequently, the command is the same, now for the third time: "Tend my sheep."[99] Clearly, Jesus is commissioning Peter as shepherd to the flock in his absence, and just as clearly the principle that "The good shepherd lays down his life for the sheep" (10:11) is still in effect. Peter's rash words to Jesus, "I will lay down my life for you!" (13:37), will find a fulfillment of sorts after all. He conspicuously failed to "lay down his life" for Jesus (13:38), but what he failed to do for Jesus he will one day do for his sheep — as Jesus will promptly explain.

18 If the shepherd's task is to lay down his life for his sheep, then the corollary of Peter's commissioning as shepherd is martyrdom. Jesus could have repeated what he said earlier to all the disciples, "Remember the word that I said to you, 'A slave is not greater than his lord.' If they persecuted me, they will also persecute you" (15:2). Instead, focusing on Peter and him alone, he continues with the twenty-fifth and last "Amen, amen" pro-

---

with approval Goguel, who argued that "the early Christian tradition evidently did not feel that a rehabilitation of Peter was necessary; in any case nothing has been related about it" (712, n. 6). This is contradicted explicitly in Luke 22:31, and implicitly in Mark 16:7 ("Go tell his disciples *and Peter,* that he goes before you into Galilee").

97. The two words for "know" (οἶδας and γινώσκεις) are interchangeable here (as, for example, in 13:7; see also 13:12 and 17). Abbott's effort (see above, n. 83) to establish a difference ("Lord, thou knowest all things, thou *feelest* . . . that I *love* thee *still*") is as unconvincing as his notion that Peter's use of φιλεῖν "implies a humble protest on the part of the Apostle that he still retains a lower kind of love for his Master" (see *Johannine Vocabulary,* 1-2, 122).

98. Gr. πάντα σὺ οἶδας.

99. The same variation in the manuscripts between πρόβατα and προβάτια exists here as in verse 16 (see above, n. 89). Brown theorizes that the diminutive προβάτια might have been original here (with the additional support of A). "We have followed Alexandrinus," Brown writes, "and suggest that the readings in Vaticanus and in Sinaiticus are scribal attempts to bring conformity into the two verses" (2.1105). This would mean that three different words were used for sheep in verses 15, 16, and 17, presumably by design. Yet there would be little point in this, for only two verbs, βόσκε and ποίμαινε, are used for tending or shepherding the sheep. We have assumed πρόβατα to be original in both verses, accenting the link to the Good Shepherd discourse.

nouncement in the Gospel (the first since 16:23):[100] "Amen, amen, I say to you, when you were young, you used to gird yourself[101] and walk wherever you chose, but when you get old, you will stretch out your hands and another will gird you[102] and bring you where you do not choose" (v. 18). The description of a youthful Peter, girding himself and going where he chooses, fits the present scene in which, a few moments before, he impulsively "secured [literally, "girded up"] the outer garment . . . and threw himself into the lake" to meet Jesus (v. 7) and then labored mightily to bring the net ashore (v. 11), as well as another vivid scene much later in the book of Acts, when an angel appeared to him in prison and told him, "Gird yourself and put on your sandals," and he did so, after which the angel said, "Wrap your garment around you and follow me" (Acts 12:8). Here Jesus reminds him that it will not always be so.

As to form, the pronouncement appears to be based on a proverb contrasting youth and old age. When a man is "young,"[103] he controls his own life, but when he "gets old,"[104] he is at the mercy of others. The contrast is threefold:

when you were young	when you get old
you used to gird yourself	another will gird you
and walk wherever you chose	bring you where you do not choose

In short, freedom diminishes with advancing age, and it will be no different with Peter. Nothing about violent death or martyrdom is intrinsic to the proverb. Yet if it is *only* a proverb about aging, one clause is unaccounted for, "you will stretch out your hands."[105] This clause has prompted interpreters for centuries to conclude that Jesus is predicting Peter's eventual crucifixion — upside down according to some traditions.[106] Already in the second century, Barnabas argued that Moses made a "type of the cross" when he "began stretching out his hands" and Israel gained the victory over the Amalekites

---

100. The only other singular "Amen amen" pronouncement (that is, with λέγω σοι rather than λέγω ὑμῖν) that has to do with one man's personal history is 13:38, and there too it is addressed to Peter. Three other such sayings, also singular, are addressed to Nicodemus (3:3, 5, 11), but their application is general, not linked to Nicodemus in particular.
101. Gr. ἐζώννυες σεαυτόν.
102. Gr. ἄλλος ζώσει σε.
103. Gr. νεώτερος.
104. Gr. ὅταν δὲ γηράσῃς.
105. Gr. ἐκτενεῖς τὰς χεῖράς σου.
106. This for various symbolic reasons; see *Acts of Peter* 37–38 (Hennecke-Schneemelcher, 2.319-20).

(*Barnabas* 12.2; see Exod 17:11),[107] as did Isaiah when he said, "All day long I stretched out my hands to a disobedient people" (12.4; see Isa 65:2).[108] In similar fashion, Justin Martyr referred to Moses' gesture as "the sign of the cross" (*Dialogue with Trypho* 90.5), and interpreted Isaiah's words as a prophecy of the crucifixion of Christ, who "stretched forth his hands, being crucified by the Jews" (*Apology* 1.35.6). Yet neither Moses nor Isaiah was literally crucified, and there is no reason to suppose that Jesus is predicting literal crucifixion in Peter's case either. If he were, we would have expected a different word order: "when you get old, another will gird you and bring you where you do not choose, and you will stretch out your hands." More likely, the stretching out of the hands is simply a gesture of helplessness preliminary to arrest and execution — not Peter's death on a cross, but at most (in Justin's words) a "sign of the cross."

In short, Jesus seems to be predicting Peter's martyrdom (see v. 19, "by what death"), but not necessarily his crucifixion.[109] The verbs "crucify" and "lift up" (3:14; 8:28; 12:32) are conspicuous by their absence. Yet the ancient tradition in which Peter is crucified upside down does capture an important point in the Gospel's narrative, for the accent is on the contrast between Peter's death and that of Jesus, not on the similarities. Jesus has said, "I lay down my life, that I might receive it back again. No one took it away from me, but I lay it down on my own. I have authority to lay it down, and I have authority to receive it back" (10:17-18), and on the cross he "handed over the Spirit" in his own time and on his own initiative. Peter's death, by contrast, will *not* be "on his own," but at the will and command of others, like the death of any other martyr. Peter has rashly adopted Jesus' own language, "I will lay down my life for you!" (13:37), but the reality will be quite different.

19 At this point the writer adds a narrative aside, "This he said signifying by what death[110] he will glorify God," a comment corresponding almost exactly to 12:33, "This he said signifying by what death[111] he was going to die" — the latter in reference to Jesus' repeated claim that he would be "lifted up" on the cross (3:14; 12:23; see also 18:32). Having "signified" or made known the nature of his own death, Jesus now "signifies" to Peter the

---

107. The text in *Barnabas* is of interest because Barnabas goes on to cite another "type of Jesus" (τύπον τοῦ Ἰησοῦ) in which Moses "made a bronze serpent and displayed it prominently" (12.6; compare Jn 3:14).

108. Paul, by contrast, makes no such allusion in citing Isaiah 65:2 (see Rom 10:21).

109. Compare 16:2; also Jesus' words to James and John in Mark: "The cup that I drink you will drink, and the baptism I am baptized with you will be baptized with" (Mk 10:39).

110. Gr. σημαίνων ποίῳ θανάτῳ.

111. Gr. σημαίνων ποίῳ θανάτῳ.

nature of his death, and the two are not the same. Jesus was "lifted up" and Peter will not be; Jesus gave his life at his own initiative and Peter will not.[112] Nevertheless, Peter's death will "glorify God,"[113] a phrase evoking Jesus' language about his own death (see 12:28; 13:31; 17:1). Martyrdom does not have to be sought, or self-initiated; Jesus seems in fact to have taught the contrary (see Mt 10:23, "When they pursue you in this city, flee to the other").

After the narrative aside, the writer adds one more command of Jesus in addition to "Tend my lambs" (v. 15), "Shepherd my sheep" (v. 16), and "Tend my sheep" (v. 17): "and having said this,[114] he says to him, 'Follow me' "[115] (v. 19). This command not only echoes his initial command to Peter and Andrew according to Matthew (4:19) and Mark (1:17), but it also expresses exactly what Peter told Jesus he wanted above all else to do ("Why can I not follow you now? I will lay down my life for you!" 13:37). This he will do, but on Jesus' terms, not his own (see 12:26, "If anyone would serve me, let him follow me, and where I am, there my servant will be"). "Follow me" is of course the imperative for every disciple, but Peter is called to follow Jesus specifically as shepherd of the flock, with all that that entails.

20-21 What happens next is difficult to visualize: "Turning, Peter sees the disciple whom Jesus loved following, he who also leaned on his breast at the supper and said, 'Lord, who is the one handing you over?' Then, seeing this man, Peter says to Jesus, 'Lord, what about this man?'" (vv. 20-21). "Turning" implies that Peter had to turn around to see "the disciple whom Jesus loved," and "following"[116] seems to imply that Jesus and Peter had already started off, as if on a journey somewhere. Peter is literally "following" Jesus, just as he was told (v. 19), and the beloved disciple is "following" behind, bringing up the rear. At the same time, "turning" may also mark a "turn" in Peter's state of mind, as in the case of Mary Magdalene in the garden. But unlike Mary's "turning" (20:16), it is not necessarily a turn for the better.[117] To begin with, if Peter is literally "following" Jesus, it is not a good thing to "turn" around or look

---

112. While it is generally assumed that Peter had already died at the time the Gospel was written, it is not absolutely certain. The notice in 12:33 speaks of the death Jesus "was going to die" (ἤμελλεν ἀποθνῄσκειν), but the notice here speaks of the death by which Peter "will glorify God" (a simple future), which could imply — although it would not have to — that Peter's death is yet to come.

113. Gr. δοξάσει τὸν θεόν.

114. Gr. καὶ τοῦτο εἰπών, by now a familiar feature of Johannine style, sometimes marking a transition from discourse to narrative, but here (right on the heels of τοῦτο δὲ εἶπεν) simply leading from one pronouncement to another.

115. Gr. ἀκολούθει μοι.

116. Gr. ἀκολουθοῦντα.

117. Contrast Luke 22:31, where Jesus says to Peter, "and you, when you have turned around [ἐπιστρέψας], strengthen your brothers."

back (see Lk 9:57-62; 17:31-32).[118] And, more to the point, Peter's problem from the start has been comparing himself with other disciples — "Do you love me more than these?" (v. 15) — something he now begins doing again.

"The disciple whom Jesus loved" is reintroduced more elaborately than anywhere else in the Gospel (contrast 19:26; 20:2; 21:7), in relation to the scene at the table where he made his first appearance, as "he who also leaned on his breast at the supper and said, 'Lord, who is the one handing you over?'" (v. 20; compare 13:23-25).[119] This is evidently in anticipation of this disciple's identification at last as "the disciple who testifies about these things and who wrote these things" (v. 24). It is important that the reader understand just who he is within the narrative, even though his name is never given. Peter obviously knows who he is, for it was in response to Peter's unspoken request to find out the identity of the betrayer (see 13:24) that the disciple asked Jesus the question repeated here. He and Peter, moreover, ran together to the tomb of Jesus at the behest of Mary Magdalene, looked into the tomb, and returned together to their respective homes (20:3-10). And in the present scene, it was this disciple's recognition, "It is the Lord" (v. 7), that impelled Peter to swim to shore to meet his Lord (v. 7). Now, however, Peter has nothing to say *to* him, but instead asks Jesus *about* him (rather impolitely) in his very presence: "Lord, what about this man?"[120] What exactly is he asking? If we assume that Peter understood Jesus to be in some way predicting Peter's death, then he is asking the same question about "the disciple whom Jesus loved." How will *his* life end? Will *he* meet a similar fate? Characteristically, the beloved disciple himself holds his peace.

22 The reader knows that the fate of "the disciple whom Jesus loved" is none of Peter's business, but Jesus does not content himself with just saying so. Instead, he says to Peter, "If I want him to remain until I come, what [is that] to you? You, follow me!" (v. 22). To "remain" is simply to stay alive as opposed to dying, whether by martyrdom or natural death, yet the word inevitably implies as well remaining faithful or "dwelling" in Jesus as described in the farewell discourses (see 15:1-8). "I want"[121] has an almost imperious sound to it. Who is this person who presumes to decide how long

---

118. The scene is *not* to be compared to 1:38, where it was Jesus who "turned" (στραφείς, as here) and noticed John's disciples "following" him (ἀκολουθοῦντας), for Jesus was not turning around from following someone else. Rather, he was himself the one being followed, and he turned only to ask them, "What are you seeking?"

119. In the earlier scene the disciple merely asked, "Lord, who is it?" (κύριε, τίς ἐστιν;). The present citation adds the words ὁ παραδιδούς σε, "the one handing you over," in order to give the reader a sense of the context of the disciple's question (see 13:21, "one of you will hand me over").

120. Gr. οὗτος δὲ τί.
121. Gr. θέλω.

21:1-25 THE THIRD APPEARANCE AND SIMON PETER'S COMMISSION

his disciples will live, or how they will die? It recalls his bold prayer on their behalf, "I want them to be with me where I am" (17:24), except that instead of coming within a prayer (in which he is free to ask the Father "whatever he wants," as in 15:7), it expresses the sovereign will of one who knows that he has "authority over all flesh" (17:2) because the Father has already given it to him. Jesus is careful not to say that it *is* in fact his will that the disciple "remain," only that *if* this is the case (or if it is not!), the matter is not Peter's concern. "What [is that] to you?"[122] counters and gently dismisses Peter's "What about this man?"

The other noteworthy expression is "until I come." The "coming" of which he speaks is not the "coming" of 14:18 ("I am coming to you") or 14:28 ("I am going away, and I am coming to you"), for these seem to have already taken place (see 20:19, 26; 21:13). It is rather the "coming" promised in 14:3, apparently the same future "coming of the Son of man" that is generally presupposed in the synoptic tradition.[123] In contrast to the farewell discourses, however, and in agreement with the synoptic tradition, there is no mention of "going" (as in 13:33, 36; 14:2-4, 28), only of "coming." It is as if Jesus has already "gone away," and the two disciples (like the reader of the Gospel) are already awaiting his future "coming." The synoptic texts that "until I come"[124] brings most readily to mind are those that speak of the "coming" of the Son of man as a terminal point or time limit: "You will not complete the cities of Israel *until* the Son of man has come" (Mt 10:23), and (even more pointedly) "There are some of those standing here who will never taste death *until* they see the Son of man coming in his kingdom" (Mt 16:28, my italics).[125] Here too, as we have seen, "remaining" seems to imply staying alive in contrast to dying, whether by martyrdom or otherwise.

Jesus concludes by refusing to allow Peter to change the subject: "You, follow me!" He repeats what he said three verses earlier (v. 19), adding

---

122. Gr. τί πρὸς σέ.
123. So Bultmann (715), who calls it "the coming of Jesus in the sense of early Christian apocalyptic; only so is the 'misunderstanding,' and its correction in v. 23 to be explained." Oddly, however, he distinguishes it from the coming in 14:3 because in that case Jesus would have to have said, "ἕως ἔρχομαι καὶ παραλήμψομαι αὐτόν" (that is, "until I come *and take him*"). Why this is so is not explained here, but Bultmann's efforts earlier to distinguish John 14:3 from "the parousia of Jewish-Christian eschatology," assigning it rather to "the individualistic eschatology of the Gnostic myth" (Bultmann, 602, n. 1), are unconvincing.
124. Gr. ἕως ἔρχομαι.
125. Slightly different forms of this saying are found in Mark (9:1) and Luke (9:27). That John's Gospel also knows some form of it is likely in view of Jesus' pronouncement that "if anyone keeps my word, he will never ever see [or taste] death" (see 8:51-52).

only the emphatic "you" (that is, "not him, you!"), and changing the word order[126] so as to focus Peter's attention on the Lord and nowhere else. These are Jesus' last words in the Gospel of John, recalling that first scene long ago at Bethany when the first two disciples "followed Jesus," and he asked them, "What are you seeking?" (1:37-38). Only now will Peter learn what it means to "follow," and with him, perhaps, the reader of the Gospel (see 12:26).

23 A narrative aside is added for clarification: "So this word went out to the brothers that that disciple would not die, but Jesus did not say to him that he would not die, but 'If I want him to remain until I come, what [is that] to you?'"(v. 23). The expression, "this word went out[127] to the brothers," is solid evidence that Jesus' sayings circulated orally well before they were put into writing. The "brothers," a term first applied to Jesus' natural brothers (2:12; 7:3-5), and after that to his disciples (20:17-18), now seems to refer (as in 1 John) to the entire Christian community. If certain pronouncements in the Gospels (such as Mt 16:28 and par.)[128] were taken literally, early Christians would naturally have kept track of the deaths of those who were known to have been disciples of Jesus, and as their numbers dwindled, more and more attention would have focused on the few who were left. And if other, unwritten, pronouncements made such claims about particular individuals (in this case, "the disciple whom Jesus loved"), they would have drawn particular attention to those individuals as they grew older.[129]

Here someone (apparently the Gospel writer) takes pains to parse Jesus' pronouncement carefully, to warn against jumping to conclusions: "Jesus did not say to him[130] that he would not die, but 'If I want him to remain until I come, what [is that] to you?'" (v. 23b).[131] But who is doing the pars-

---

126. Gr. σύ μοι ἀκολούθει (literally, "you, me, follow").
127. Gr. ἐξῆλθεν.
128. Mark 13:30 (with its parallels in Mt 24:34 and Lk 21:32) would also have been in play: "this generation will never pass away until [ἕως ἄν] all these things happen."
129. Those who identify "the disciple whom Jesus loved" as Lazarus have argued that such rumors would naturally have clustered around him because he had already died and been raised to life.
130. There is potential for confusion in the pronouns. A casual reader might assume that "to him" (αὐτῷ) refers to "him" (αὐτόν) who is not expected to die, but this is not the case, for the words were obviously spoken to Peter (v. 22), not to "the disciple whom Jesus loved."
131. It is possible to imagine a similar parsing of Jesus' pronouncement about Peter's death (v. 18): "So this word went out to the brothers that Peter would be crucified, but Jesus did not say to him that he would be crucified, only that 'when you are old, you will stretch out your hands, and another will gird you and bring you where you do not choose.'" No such clarification was needed in that instance because it did not really matter whether or not Peter was crucified, only that his death, like Jesus' death, would "glorify God," and yet, unlike Jesus, he would not lay down his life of his own volition.

21:1-25 THE THIRD APPEARANCE AND SIMON PETER'S COMMISSION

ing? We have assumed all along that the narrative asides in the Gospel were the work of the Gospel writer, and we will be told in the very next verse that the Gospel writer is none other than "the disciple whom Jesus loved." If this is so, then the common assumption that the beloved disciple had died by the time these words were written[132] is obviously mistaken. Rather, he himself, still very much alive, is attempting to correct an anticipation on the part of some that he will go on living until his Lord returns.[133] Knowing that his own death, when it comes, might very well call into question the veracity of Jesus' pronouncement, he explains that the timing of everything — whether Jesus' coming or his own eventual death — is in Jesus' hands. It is a matter not of something Jesus said on earth long ago which may or may not turn out to be true, but rather of what the risen Jesus now "wants" (vv. 22, 23).[134] The present and future are in his hands.[135]

Alternatively, it is possible that someone else — presumably those who added "we know that his testimony is true" (v. 24b) — also added a comment after the fact to assure readers that even though "the disciple whom Jesus loved" has died, this does *not* mean that Jesus was mistaken. While certainty is impossible, the burden of proof is on those who assume that someone other than the beloved disciple himself is responsible for this disclaimer.

---

132. Typical is Bultmann's comment: "It is clear that this is a subsequent correction which became necessary when the beloved disciple had died" (715; see also Schnackenburg, 3.371; Brown, 2.1118-19; Barrett, 587). But there are dissenters; see, for example, Hoskyns, who argues that "there is no reason to suppose that this is the intention of the author, since the next verse states that the Beloved Disciple wrote the words. This passage must not therefore be used as a starting point from which to argue that the Beloved disciple cannot have written the Gospel because he was dead" (559; see also Morris, 775; Carson, 682).

133. As in three other instances (13:21-30; 19:25-27; 21:2-7), it is possible to transform the third-person narrative into the first person: "Turning, Peter sees me following and says to Jesus, 'Lord, what about this man?' Jesus says to him, 'If I want him to remain until I come, what [is that] to you? You, follow me!' So this word went out to the brothers that I would not die, but Jesus did not say to him that I would not die, but 'If I want him to remain until I come, what [is that] to you?'" This might even help explain the confusion over the antecedents of the pronouns αὐτῷ and αὐτόν (above, n. 130).

134. Lincoln (522) puts it this way: "In the form that that tradition took in attaching itself to the Beloved Disciple, any potential damage could be contained by emphasizing its first clause, which gave the prediction a conditional element, making it dependent on Jesus' will."

135. Nowhere, however, does this Gospel address the relationship between this accent on the risen Jesus' sovereign will and such pronouncements as Mark 13:32//Matthew 24:36, "But concerning that day or hour no one knows, not the angels in heaven, nor the Son, except the Father" (see also Acts 1:7; Mk 10:40). Such questions can only be answered in very general terms in light of the mutual love and mutual indwelling of the Father and the Son in John's Gospel.

That assumption could of course be right, but the verse that follows seems to be claiming just the opposite.

24 Finally "the disciple whom Jesus loved" is explicitly identified as the Gospel writer: "This is the disciple who testifies about these things[136] and who wrote these things,[137] and we know that his testimony is true" (v. 24). "These things" cannot be limited to the immediately preceding scene involving Jesus, Peter, and this disciple, nor to chapter 21 alone.[138] Rather, the notice pertains to the entire Gospel, the "testimony" on which it rests, its authorship, and consequently its authority. Many have "testified" in the course of the narrative, from John (1:34; 5:33), to Jesus himself and his works (5:31, 36; 8:14, 18), to the Father (5:37; 8:18), to the Jewish Scriptures (5:39), to an unnamed witness of Jesus' crucifixion (19:35), and finally to the Advocate, or "Spirit of truth," who will continue the testimony through the lips of Jesus' disciples after his departure (15:26-27). And yet all of it, we now learn, is somehow also the testimony of this "disciple whom Jesus loved" — as if he has taken the testimonies of all the others and added them to his own.

The notice is remarkable because, as we have seen, this disciple has been anything but forthcoming throughout the narrative. He did not even make an appearance until 13:23, and if he is indeed the author, he has given himself only two lines, one a question, "Lord, who is it?" (13:25) and the other a testimony of sorts, "It is the Lord" (21:7), his only testimony anywhere in the Gospel to anyone except the reader. Otherwise he has been silent throughout. Yet now, belatedly, we learn that he has been "testifying" all along, both to what he has seen with his own eyes and to that which others have seen and passed along to him, beginning (presumably) with the testimony of John (see 1:7-8, 15, 19, 34). Possibly for this reason, he himself has been persistently identified in the tradition as "John," whether the Apostle John, son of Zebedee, or John "the Presbyter."

The notice claims not only that "the disciple whom Jesus loved" provided the testimony underlying the Gospel, but also that he "wrote" it. Commentators have found this claim the more difficult one to accept, particularly those who find it hard to believe that any of the Gospels could have come from the pen of an eyewitness. That this Gospel in particular, with its pre-

---

136. Gr. ὁ μαρτυρῶν περὶ τούτων.

137. Gr. ὁ γράψας ταῦτα.

138. So C. H. Dodd, "Note on John 21,24," *JTS* n.s. 4 (1953), 212-13. While the Gospel does contain summary statements introduced by "these things" or "these words," referring to preceding discourses (for example, 6:59; 8:20; 18:1), the placement of the present notice refers unmistakably to a written book (see v. 25, with its reference to "books" that are "written"). This is widely acknowledged (for example, Bultmann, 717, n. 4; Lincoln, 522-23; Carson, 683).

sumed late date, its extraordinarily high christology, and its extensive deviations from earlier Gospel traditions, could be the work of an eyewitness, the closest of all the disciples to Jesus, strains credulity in the eyes of some.[139] Admittedly, it is possible to understand "wrote" as "caused to be written," just as Pilate "wrote" a title and "placed" it over the cross — but not with his own hands.[140] Yet "wrote" can also be used in another, almost trivial sense of a scribe who puts in writing the ideas of someone else, like the scribe who introduces himself at the end of Paul's letter to the Romans as "I, Tertius, who wrote the epistle" (Rom 16:22). The latter is clearly not the case here, for the Gospel is the disciple's own "testimony." The former might be, as long as it is acknowledged that "wrote" must mean something beyond merely "testifies." Two things are being asserted, not just one. The Gospel of John is claiming to be more than the product of this disciple's testimony; it is claiming him as its actual author, not necessarily in the sense that he "wrote" it with his own hand (any more than Pilate wrote the title, or Paul the letter to the Romans with their own hands), but in the sense that he composed it and takes full responsibility for its content. The claim might or might not be true, but there can be little doubt as to what the claim is.

The further claim is that the disciple's testimony — and by implication the written Gospel — is *true:* "and we know[141] that his testimony is true" (v. 24b). This is illuminating, for it tells us (rather belatedly) that the Gospel's author and its narrative voice are not exactly the same.[142] While it is remotely possible that all of this comes directly from "the disciple whom Jesus loved" himself (with "we know" understood rhetorically as "it is self-evident," or "it is common knowledge"),[143] the far likelier supposition is that

---

139. See, for example, Brown (2.1123), who does not want to "weaken unduly" the claim, yet argues that "it would be difficult to press the formula to imply more than an assertion of spiritual responsibility for what is contained in the book," attributing "only the first of five stages to the Beloved disciple, namely that he was the source of the historical tradition that has come into the Gospel." But this is to collapse the two assertions into one, for it is difficult to see how "wrote" (ὁ γράψας) in this watered-down sense goes beyond "testifies" (ὁ μαρτυρῶν).

140. Pilate's "authorship" of the title is reinforced by his words, "What I have written I have written" (19:22).

141. Gr. οἴδαμεν.

142. This is what distinguishes our text from 19:35, where the one who "has testified," and whose "testimony is true," is (apparently) the same one who "knows [ἐκεῖνος οἶδεν] that he tells the truth." A closer parallel is 5:32, where Jesus, referring to the Father, says, "There is another who testifies about me, and I know [οἶδα] that the testimony he testifies about me is true."

143. See BDAG, 693. Richard Bauckham argues that the "we" is a rhetorical device (the "we" of authoritative testimony, as he calls it), and hence the voice of the beloved disciple himself (*Jesus and the Eyewitnesses,* 370-83). He appeals to 19:35 (but see

1055

a voice other than his is speaking. This is presumably the same voice that has consistently referred to him in the third person as "the disciple whom Jesus loved." This appears to be the same "we" who said, "we looked at his glory — glory as of a father's One and Only" (1:14), and joined their voice with John's to add, "of his fullness we have all received, and grace upon grace" (1:16).[144] It appears to be an inclusive "we" (as in 1:14 and 16), as if inviting the readers to join the narrators in acknowledging the truth of all that has gone before. From time to time there have been hints of a possible transformation of a first-person narrative into the third person,[145] and the "we" who valued that first-person testimony enough to transform it and make it their own show their hand — if only for a brief moment.

The distinction introduced at the last minute, as it were, between the Gospel writer and the narrator or narrative voice, complicates the literary reading of the Gospel at least to some degree. All along I have been using the term "Gospel writer" (and occasionally "narrator") as if author and narrator were necessarily the same. Readers of modern literature are accustomed to authors creating for themselves narrative voices — sometimes more than one — to tell their stories for them, but here we have a narrative voice, introduced abruptly at the end, telling us at last who the true author is. So who is the true author? Whose voice are we hearing throughout? This final narrative voice, or the person this voice explicitly identifies as the author of the Gospel? It is not an easy question, nor does it in the end make an enormous difference. Most concretely, perhaps, it raises the question, To whom should we attribute the many "narrative asides" that we have noticed in the course of our reading? Do they represent the "we" of 21:24 providing "helps for the reader" in following and understanding the beloved disciple's narrative? Or are they his own side comments? Quite possibly some are the one and some the other, but their recurring interest in Judas Iscariot (see 6:64, 71; 12:4; 13:2, 11) suggests that a number of them do in fact go back to the beloved disciple himself, the first to identify Judas as the one who would hand Jesus over (see 13:25-26).[146]

25 If there was confusion between Gospel writer and narrator in the

---

above, n. 142), and to 3:11, where Jesus uses "we" to mean "I" (377-79). But as we have seen, the latter has a different explanation. Nor is his appeal to 12:38 persuasive (382), for Jesus' words there are obviously governed by the language of Isaiah.

144. Alternatively, of course, it is possible that the "we" of 1:14 and 18 is simply the beloved disciple himself speaking as part of the larger community to which he belongs, presumably the community identifying itself here in 21:14. The difference is minimal.

145. See above, 13:21-30; 19:25-27; 20:8; 21:2-7, 20-23.

146. Only rarely do they even come close to contradicting what is said in the narrative proper, and even when they do (for example, 4:2), it is by no means certain that they come from a different hand.

preceding verse, it is not resolved in this last verse of the Gospel: "There are also many other things[147] that Jesus did which, if they were written every one, I suppose the world itself would not hold the books being written" (v. 25). Yet another voice now makes itself heard, a first-person singular, "I suppose."[148] Despite the very real possibility that a first-person narrative underlies the third-person narrative which comprises the Gospel of John in its present form, this is the only actual first-person voice in the entire Gospel. Is this "the disciple whom Jesus loved" finally asserting himself as "I," or is it simply one anonymous member (perhaps a scribe) of the community that vouches for his reliability, assuring us that "we know that his testimony is true" (v. 24)?

The notice appears to be built on the similar acknowledgment a chapter earlier that "Jesus did many, and other,[149] signs in the presence of his disciples which are not written in this book" (20:30). Both passages acknowledge incompleteness: there is more to the story than what has been told. Yet there are differences too. The notice in chapter 20 has to do with "signs," probably limited to resurrection signs by which the risen Jesus made himself known to his disciples, while here it is a matter of "things that Jesus did," enough "things," we are told, to fill all the books the whole world could ever hold. There the writer could not resist adding just one more "sign" (see 21:1-14). Here nothing is added. We are truly at the end of the Gospel. There it was a matter of what was written in "this book"[150] (20:30). Here no one "book" is mentioned. The notice could come at the end of a single book, or just as easily after a whole series of books. That in fact is where it does come in our Bibles, at the end of Matthew, Mark, Luke, and John, the fourfold Gospel, and it is hard not to notice how appropriate it is as a colophon reminding us that even when we have finished reading all four, there are *still* "many other things that Jesus did." We have barely scratched the surface.

The matter is complicated by the absence of the entire verse in the first draft of Codex Sinaiticus (ℵ), whose scribe seems to have ended verse 24 with a flourish and a subscript, but later washed the vellum clean and added verse 25, followed by the same flourish and subscript.[151] The issue of whether or not this final verse is "original" is a matter of definition. If it was part of the

147. Gr. καὶ ἄλλα πολλά.
148. Gr. οἶμαι.
149. Gr. πολλὰ μέν οὖν καὶ ἄλλα.
150. Gr. ἐν τῷ βιβλίῳ τούτῳ.
151. See Brown, 2.1125. Brown asks, "Was the omission in the first instance an act of carelessness or was the scribe copying from a ms. that did not have vs. 25 (which he subsequently got from another ms.)? Even if the latter is the case, the textual evidence for treating vs. 25 as a scribal gloss is very slim."

The Gospel of John

Gospel when it came from the pen(s) of those who vouched for the truth of what the beloved disciple wrote (v. 24), it would have provided a good reason for placing the Gospel of John as the last of the four, thus separating the Gospel of Luke from its companion, the book of Acts.[152] On the other hand, whoever compiled the fourfold Gospel, placing this Gospel last (for whatever reason), might well have added the notice to remind readers that even these four did not come close to exhausting all that might have been told about the life and ministry of Jesus. In the first instance it is an "original" part of the Gospel of John, and therefore of the New Testament; in the second instance it is an "original" part of the fourfold Gospel, and therefore of the New Testament. In that case the "I" who says "I suppose" is neither "the disciple whom Jesus loved" nor one of the "we" who "know that his testimony is true" (v. 24), but rather an unknown individual who played a role in the compilation of the fourfold Gospel.[153] It is not easy to decide between these alternatives, nor is it altogether necessary. Either way this final verse is "original" (authentic if you will), and either way it is a kind of a disclaimer, an acknowledgment of limitations. It leaves the door open for other narratives, one of which (Jn 7:53–8:11) was in fact added in certain manuscripts, for other Gospels (which did in fact appear, even if none of them was judged canonical), and for harmonization (which took place freely as time went on). At the end we are reminded that the Gospel of John is "true"[154] (v. 24), and yet that it is not the only truth (v. 25). It is more than adequate "that you might believe that Jesus is the Christ, the Son of God, and that believing you might have life in his name" (20:31), even though it is far from complete.

---

152. In much the same way, it is easy to see how the warnings at the end of the book of Revelation (22:18-19) might have dictated the placement of that book at the end of the New Testament, warning the reader of the inviolability of that collection, or even of the whole biblical canon.

153. Aside from Luke 1:3, this is the only instance in the Gospel tradition in which a narrative voice speaks in the first person. A curious feature of the New Testament canon is that any reader of the books in their canonical order is apt to notice on the next page, as the book of Acts begins, someone still speaking as "I," and still about things that Jesus "did" (ποιεῖν, Acts 1:1; compare ἃ ἐποίησεν, Jn 21:25). Could it be the same voice?

154. Gr. ἀληθής.

INDEX OF SUBJECTS

Abraham, 1, 202-3, 505-6, 508, 511-15, 526-33, 535
Advocate, 26-30, 37, 719, 783-86, 790-92, 818, 824-26, 832-34, 836-37, 882, 1011-12
Aenon, near Salim, 214
Agent, Jesus as the Father's, 1, 39, 313, 605, 714, 716, 737, 744-45, 1014
Amen, amen, 134-35, 179-80, 182, 190-93, 249, 307, 314, 316-17, 362, 388, 394, 396, 506, 525, 533, 577, 582, 684-85, 688-89, 736, 740, 744-45, 746-47, 765, 779, 842, 847, 1046-47
Andrew, 12-13, 18, 118, 121-23, 134, 345-47, 686-87
Angels, 136-39, 290, 994-99
Anger of Jesus, 636-40, 747
Annas, 9, 896-97, 902-3, 908-10
Anonymous witnesses, 17-18, 121, 126, 897-902, 970, 974
Apostles, 11
Authority, 39, 68-70, 318, 421-22, 591, 859, 935-36, 938

Baptism, 32, 89, 95, 102-7, 111-17, 182-85, 213, 216, 231-34, 246, 266-68, 282-83, 569-70, 610, 730, 735
Baptism of Jesus, 113-15
Barabbas, 927-28
Beatitudes, 738, 1006
Believing, 40-41, 60, 68, 70-71, 154-55, 169-70, 173-74, 199-200, 203-4, 207, 231, 249, 268, 280-83, 315, 322, 330, 334, 337, 367, 375, 388-89, 396, 409-10, 426, 463, 463, 487-88, 502-5, 515, 517, 520, 565-68, 598-600, 606, 611-12, 632, 645, 647, 707-9, 711-15, 741, 766, 778, 794-95, 853, 857, 864, 874-75, 972, 990-93, 995, 1005-6, 1017-19, 1022-23
Beloved Disciple, 3, 6-7, 12-24, 38, 746, 748-49, 751, 753-54, 956-60, 970-71, 985-98, 1026, 1029, 1033, 1049-56
Bethany, 105-7, 126, 607, 612-13, 615, 617, 627-29, 660, 663
Bethesda, 288-89
Bethlehem, 469, 471
Bethsaida, 126
Bethsaida pool, 288-90, 293
Betrayal, 742, 745
Birth, 71-74, 181-84, 193-94, 540-41, 564, 843-44
Blind, the man born, 539-43, 545-50, 552-53, 556-70
Blindness, 572-75, 592, 709-10
Blood, 110-11, 392, 394-97, 399, 400, 402, 406, 967-69, 972
Bread of life, Jesus as, 371, 373, 378, 385, 389-92
Breath, 546, 1010-11
Bridegroom, 101, 151-52, 218-20, 231, 244-46
Brothers of Jesus, 20-24, 142, 155-56,

1059

Index of Subjects

420, 424-25, 427, 429, 957-58, 1001-3, 1052
Burial of Jesus, 669-70, 979-83

Caiaphas, 9, 627, 649-53, 896-97, 902-3, 908-10, 936-37
Cana, 125, 129, 139-41, 155-56, 271, 275-76, 279, 281, 284, 1029
Capernaum, 155-56, 271, 276, 279, 281, 283, 354, 358, 361, 384, 403-4, 415, 420
Chief Priest, 894, 896-97, 899-903, 905-6, 908-10
Chief priests, 36, 453-55, 661-63, 887, 936
Children of God, 68-71, 88, 653-55
Chosen One, Jesus as, 116
Christ, or Messiah, 40, 96-97, 103, 121, 123, 127, 165-66, 254-59, 450-52, 454, 469-71, 476, 554, 557, 564, 566, 595-97, 633, 701-3, 1022-23
Circumcision, 444-46
Cleansing, 720, 729-33, 802-3
Coming One, the, 104, 105, 112, 222, 633, 676
Commands, 591-92, 717-18, 758-60, 782-83, 787, 796-97, 800, 810-12, 815-16
Confessing Christ, 96, 98, 712-13
Courtyard, 577, 579, 584, 899
Covenant, 79-80, 438
Creation, 51-54, 65
Crowds, 294, 341-44, 346-53, 358, 360-64, 366-68, 370, 372-76, 381-82, 389, 405, 431, 442-44, 447, 449, 471, 473, 672-81, 694-95
Crucifixion, 199-200, 491, 702, 920, 932, 943-44, 946-49, 966, 1047

Darkness, 56-57, 178, 206, 478-79, 704-5
David, 97, 165, 451, 469, 471
Death, 299, 315-16, 486-87, 490, 505, 507-8, 520, 525-28, 628, 632, 637, 685, 688-89, 697, 764-65, 1048
Death of Jesus, 683, 701, 757
Death penalty, 496, 917-19
Demons, 443, 522-23, 526-27, 592

Departure of Jesus, 672, 719, 725, 727, 747, 757-58, 763-64, 768, 785, 793, 795, 818, 831-32, 866-67, 882, 959
Devil, or Satan, 4, 416-19, 509, 517-19, 521, 523, 637, 696, 722-24, 752-53, 796, 835, 871-72, 937
Disciples of Jesus, 141-42, 147-48, 151-52, 154-56, 161-63, 168-69, 212, 232-34, 257, 266-67, 342, 350, 354-59, 362-63, 405-7, 411, 424, 539-40, 618, 621-23, 658, 678-79, 839-43, 847, 850-57, 862-70, 872-77, 879-80, 884-85, 902-6, 957, 979, 1001, 1003-4, 1006-10, 1013, 1015-18, 1020, 1026-28, 1035, 1042-43
Discipleship, 504-5, 692, 761, 809, 1049
Dispersion, 457
Door, Jesus as, 578, 582-83
Doorkeeper, 578, 900
Dwellings, 767

Earth, the, 222, 487
Egypt, 37
Election, 14, 175, 739, 815
Elijah, 97-98
Elisha, 349, 351
Enclosed space, 884, 886, 900, 913, 1006
Ephesus, 6-11, 37
Ephraim, 656-58, 661
Eschatology, 321
Eucharist, 348, 391-92, 395-97, 408, 735, 1041

Father, 1, 22, 35-36, 40-42, 48-49, 80-82, 92, 160-61, 168, 226-27, 250, 254, 301-3, 307-14, 318-19, 323-25, 329-31, 334-36, 338, 365-66, 370, 376-77, 381, 385-88, 401-2, 411, 448, 458, 480-84, 489-90, 492-93, 509-11, 514, 516-17, 523-24, 529, 587-92, 599-600, 605, 607, 644, 685, 692-93, 717, 720, 767, 773, 775-81, 786-87, 789-90, 794, 796-97, 801-2, 814, 825, 829, 834, 849-50, 855, 857-65, 867-69, 875, 878-81, 965, 1000-1003, 1007
Festivals, 287

1060

Index of Subjects

Fire, charcoal, 901-2, 1035, 1045
Fishing, 1027, 1030-31, 1035, 1040
Flesh, 76-78, 184-86, 391-97, 399, 400, 402-3, 406-9
Food, 260, 343, 363-64, 397, 402
Footwashing, 726, 728, 730-31, 735, 737-38, 760
Forgiveness, 248, 576, 736, 760, 780-81, 1013-15
Freedom, 503-5, 508
Friends, 219-20, 812-16, 819
Fruit bearing, 14, 800, 802, 804-6, 808, 815
Fullness, 88

Gabbatha, 940-41
Galilee, 33, 139, 140-41, 230, 234-35, 271-72, 274-75, 284, 286, 339-40, 420, 422, 475-76, 1007, 1026-27
Garden, 884-86, 946, 983-84
Gentiles, 39-40, 589
Gerizim, Mount, 248-49
Gethsemane, 693, 798, 858, 879
Glory and glorification, 35, 76-77, 80-83, 181, 198, 332-35, 439-40, 468, 524, 529, 558, 613, 615-16, 642, 678-79, 687-88, 693-94, 710-13, 747, 755-58, 764, 808, 858-62, 865-66, 876-77, 880, 943, 1048-49
God, Jesus as, 47-48, 92-93, 303-4, 534-35, 594, 597, 601-2, 1005, 1018, 1022
Golgotha, 947-48, 984
Good Shepherd, Jesus as, 585-89, 999
Grace, 81-83, 89-91
Graveclothes, 646-47, 990, 994, 998
Greeks, 457, 684-86
Grief, 831-32, 842-45, 1045

Handing over of Jesus, 410, 418-19, 668, 724, 733, 748, 936
Harvest, 261-68, 343
Hatred, 426-28, 690, 742, 818-19, 822-24, 826, 871
Heaven, 194-97, 217, 222, 368-71, 378, 384, 386, 390, 407, 767, 867, 935-36
Hireling, 586-87
Holy One of God, 415-16

Honor, 314-15, 523-24, 691-92
"Hour," 35, 145-46, 146-47, 153, 249-50, 316, 320-21, 427, 453, 458, 485, 619-20, 685, 687-88, 692-92, 695, 753, 827, 829-30, 848

"I Am," or "It is I," 1, 30, 357, 488, 490, 533-35, 548, 567, 889-892
Indwelling, 400, 505, 606-7, 778, 786-87, 789-90, 794. 800. 803-6, 808-10, 868, 878-89, 882
Isaac, 202, 237-38
Isaiah, 710-11
Israel, 113, 129, 131-32, 154, 189-90, 603, 653

Jacob, 129, 136, 236-37, 242
Jacob's spring or well, 236, 241-43
James, brother of Jesus, 21, 23, 955
James, son of Zebedee, 7
Jerusalem, 33, 96-97, 157-58, 163, 172, 248, 286-87, 340, 428, 432, 660
Jesus' mother's sister, 953-54
Jewish Christians, 515
Jews, 2, 95-96, 99-101, 158, 164-68, 170, 173, 176-77, 239, 251-52, 287, 295-96, 299-301, 303-4, 312, 314, 316, 324-25, 334, 360, 368, 375-76, 382-85, 387, 390, 393-94, 396, 404-5, 420, 422-23, 430-31, 434-36, 442-43, 447, 457, 486, 491, 502-4, 552, 554, 563, 589, 595, 619, 627, 629, 634-37, 640, 644, 887, 914, 917, 920, 928-31, 966-67
John, son of Zebedee, 5-16, 24
John the Baptizer, 2, 16-18, 27-29, 31-33, 36, 45, 50, 57-61, 83-90, 93-119, 124, 211-28, 230-33, 325-28, 338. 609-12
John the Presbyter, 9-11
Joses (or Joseph), brother of Jesus, 21, 23, 955
Joseph of Arimathea, 946, 978-81, 983
Joseph, son of Jacob, 236
Joy, 219-20, 530-32, 811, 842-45, 847, 870, 1008-9
Judas Iscariot, 13, 417-18, 668-69, 671-

Index of Subjects

72, 722-24, 733, 739-41, 746-47, 752-53, 755, 800, 807, 869-70, 884, 886-90, 937
Judas, not Iscariot, 13, 763, 788-89
Jude, brother of Jesus, 21, 23
Judea, 211-13, 272, 422, 428, 430, 618
Judgment, 35, 204-5, 307, 312-15, 318-23, 447, 449, 480-81, 567, 572-73, 685, 695, 699, 716-17, 833, 835
Justice, or righteousness, 833, 881

Kingdom and kingship, 132-33, 179-81, 185, 352-54, 476, 675-78, 683, 914, 920-24, 926, 929-33, 935, 938-41, 943-44, 949-50, 982
Knowledge, Jesus', 175, 247-48, 409-10, 720-21, 724, 852, 885, 888, 960
Knowledge of God, 251-52, 452, 484, 490-92, 504, 516-17, 529, 813-14, 821, 824, 859-60, 864, 881

Lake Galilee or Tiberias, 340-41, 1026-28
Lamb of God, 107-11, 116, 118, 123
Last Supper, 722, 724
Law, 90, 324, 441, 473-74, 482-83, 496, 498, 824, 916, 932
Lazarus, 2, 15, 20, 612-18, 620-24, 627-30, 641, 645-46, 663-64, 672-74, 680-82
Life, Eternal, 3, 51-55, 185-86, 199-200, 203, 227-28, 243-45, 270, 285, 307, 311-13, 315-22, 338, 364-65, 372-74, 380, 388, 390-94, 396-403, 409, 414, 464, 467, 477-79, 487, 503, 508, 525-27, 532, 585, 598, 602, 631-32, 647, 685, 689-91, 717-18, 775, 785-86, 807, 859-60, 1010-11, 1022-23
"Lifted up," 197-98, 697-98, 701-2, 943
Light, 40-41, 46, 51, 54-69, 73, 76, 205-6, 208-10, 228, 322, 327, 424, 477-80, 487, 542, 545, 569, 572-73, 704-6, 715
Lord, Jesus as, 231-32, 241, 279, 568, 734-36, 987, 976, 1000, 1003-4, 1005, 1008-9, 1015, 1018, 1022, 1026, 1033, 1039, 1042

Lost, 203, 349-50, 364, 379-80, 598, 869, 892-93, 1039
Love, 201-2, 333-34, 516, 747, 749, 758-61, 764, 782-83, 787, 789, 793-94, 796-97, 800, 809-12. 815-16, 818-19, 849-50, 878, 882, 959, 1042-46
Lying, 518-21, 523

Malchus, 894
Manna, 363, 368-69, 389-90, 403
Martha, 14, 613-14, 616-18, 625, 627, 629-35, 638, 642, 663-64
Martyrdom, 397, 402, 409, 692, 829, 874, 1048
Mary of Bethany, 14, 613-14, 616-18, 629, 634-37, 664-66
Mary of Clopas, 953-54
Mary Magdalene, 14, 19, 953-54, 985-91, 993-1004, 1007, 1009, 1041
Mission, 737, 764, 857, 872-73, 876, 1009, 1014
Moses, 2, 79, 83, 90-91, 127, 197-99, 237, 256, 334, 336-38, 343, 363, 370, 383, 441-42, 444-46, 496, 506, 535, 559, 917-18
Mother of Jesus, 20-22, 24, 141-47, 149, 152, 156, 427, 953-56
Mount of Olives, 494
Murder, 518-19

Name of God, 693, 862, 867-69, 882
Narrative asides, 119, 126, 195, 233-34, 294, 371-72, 409, 418, 426, 497, 635, 668, 678, 700, 733, 752, 838, 859-60, 1048, 1052-53, 1056
Nathanael, 13, 122, 127-34, 137-39, 210, 1029
Nazareth, 128-29, 131, 272, 384
Nicodemus, 40, 171-72, 176-82, 184-85, 187-92, 210, 254, 472-73, 475-76, 946, 980-81, 983
Night, 177-78, 542, 544, 619-20, 755, 1030

One and Only, Jesus as the, 51, 71, 74, 80-82, 92, 201-2, 335

1062

Index of Subjects

Papias, 9-11
Parables, 577, 579-81, 620, 684-85, 697, 843-46, 848, 851
Paralytic, 293-94, 298
Passover, 156, 158, 170-74, 274-75, 287, 342-43, 660, 674, 721, 754, 913, 941-42
Paul, the Apostle, 907
Peace, 792, 855, 1007-10
Pentecost, 1012
Pharisees, 101-2, 176-77, 231-32, 453-55, 472-76, 479, 482-86, 495, 497-98, 539, 550-52, 568, 571, 573-76, 580-81, 647-48, 661-63, 682, 887
Philip, 18, 118, 122-23, 125-31, 134, 343, 345-47, 686-87, 763, 776-79, 787
Pilate, 496, 913-22, 924-40, 943-44, 946, 949-50, 966
Poor, the, 668-69, 671-72, 754
Portico of Solomon, 595
Praetorium, 915-16, 920
Prayer, 36, 561-62, 642-45, 693, 764, 781-82, 808, 816, 846-47, 849, 857-58, 864-65, 874, 879
Presbyters, 10-11
Priest, Jesus as, 111, 605-6, 872-74
Priests, Jewish, 95, 101-2, 104
Privacy, 637-39, 887
Prologue, 31-32, 37, 45
Prophecy, 651-53, 710
Prophet, Jesus as, 98-99, 248, 256, 273-74, 351-53, 469-70, 475-76, 552, 893
Purification, 110-11, 148, 150, 214-16, 915

Questions, 257-58, 763-77, 787-90, 831, 841-42, 846-47, 852, 1039-40

Rebekah, 237-38
Rebirth, 40-41, 72-73, 179-82, 184, 186, 188, 190, 193, 254, 515-17, 539-40, 547, 569-70
Rededication festival, 539, 594-95
Resurrection, 311-12, 316, 321-22, 379-81, 386, 397-98, 402, 407, 409, 528, 530-32, 535, 631-32, 646, 688
Resurrection of Jesus, 163, 167-69, 772, 786, 795, 992, 1010-11, 1021, 1023, 1026, 1028, 1041, 1057
Return of Jesus, 771-72, 785, 789, 793, 845, 1007-8, 1050-51
Revealer, Jesus as, 30, 78, 256-57
Riddles, 164, 302, 457, 572-73, 838-39, 841
Romans, the, 496, 648-49, 651
Royal official, 276-83

Sabbath, 294-96, 300-305, 307, 312, 444-46, 448, 496, 550-51, 985
Salvation, 251-52, 326, 716
Samaria and Samaritans, 231, 234-35, 238-39, 247, 249-51, 255, 268-69, 271-72, 522
Samaritan woman, 236-58, 268-69
Sanhedrin, 177, 627, 648, 655, 910, 919
Scriptures, 161-62, 169-70, 331-32, 336-37, 434-35, 438, 464, 466-67, 470, 602-3, 739, 870, 893, 951-52, 960, 962, 975-78
Second Coming, 771
Secrecy, 430-31, 436, 448, 536
Seeing, 572, 575, 686-87, 714-15, 776-77, 823, 990-91, 994-97, 1003-5, 1007-9, 1015-16, 1018-19
Serving, 691-92, 724, 726
Shechem, 236
Sheep, 576-90, 598-600, 865-66, 868, 1044, 1046
Shepherd, 36, 576-81, 590, 865-66, 868, 885, 1044, 1046, 1049
Sick man, 290-99
Signs, 31, 33, 153-54, 163-64, 172-74, 179, 271, 277-78, 280, 283-85, 300, 339, 341, 363, 367-69, 610-11, 682, 687, 707-8, 1006, 1020-21, 1024, 1026, 1057
Siloam pool, 546-48
Simon, brother of Jesus, 21, 23
Simon Peter, 12-15, 18-20, 118, 121-25, 134, 345-46, 405, 414-16, 725-29, 731, 733, 746, 750-51, 754, 763-66, 770, 774, 885, 894-95, 897-903, 910-12, 957, 985-91, 993-96, 998, 1026-30, 1033-36, 1039, 1042-51

1063

Index of Subjects

Sin, 108, 110, 297-99, 486-87, 490, 498, 505-7, 520-21, 540-41, 561-62, 575-76, 780, 821-22, 833, 1013-15
Slave, 503, 506-8, 813-14, 820
Soldiers, Roman, 951, 967, 973
Son, Jesus as the, 48-49, 51, 80, 108-10, 113, 115-16, 123, 132-33, 226-28, 250, 254-55, 285, 302-3, 307-14, 316-19, 323, 331, 334-35, 365, 371, 381, 507-8, 587, 591-92, 597, 604, 777, 794, 814, 858, 861, 868-69, 875, 932-34, 972, 975, 978, 1022-23
Son of man, Jesus as, 136-39, 194-201, 318-20, 365-66, 394, 397-98, 406, 408, 491, 504, 565-66, 687, 701-3, 755-56, 771, 788, 930
Sons of Zebedee, 7, 12-15, 1029
Spear thrust, 967-68, 973, 1016
Spirit, 82, 89-91, 102-3, 111, 113-16, 182-88, 190, 193, 225-26, 241, 244, 246, 252-55, 268, 407-9, 464-65, 467-69, 492, 780-81, 783-84, 786, 791, 825, 832, 837, 964-65, 1005, 1010-13, 1015
Stoning, 496, 498-500, 536, 594, 601, 608, 619
Storm, stilling of, 356
Sychar, 235, 259, 268
Synagogue, 37, 403, 415, 557, 904
Synagogue, expulsion from, 554-57, 564, 569-70, 712, 827

Teacher, Jesus as, 119-20, 734-35, 999-1000
Teaching of Jesus, 434, 437, 494-95, 791, 902, 904
Tent festival, 423-24, 428-29, 433, 436, 448-49, 461, 466, 500, 502, 538-39
Temple, 34, 157-62, 164-67, 432-33, 466, 484, 500, 537, 904
Temple treasury, 484-85
Thanksgiving, 348-49, 361, 643
Thief, 582-84, 668-69
Thirst, 237-38, 243-44, 462-64, 960-63
Thomas, 3, 623-24, 763, 774-76, 971, 1005-6, 1015-18, 1022, 1029, 1041
Tiberias, 361
Titles of the Gospels, 5-6

Tomb of Jesus, 946, 983-84, 986-90, 993-96
Trial of Jesus, 34-35, 324, 919
Triumphal entry, 34, 629, 674-79
Truth, 5, 24-27, 40, 82-83, 90, 207-10, 252-54, 504, 519-21, 775, 836-37, 872, 924-27, 974, 1055, 1058
Twelve, the, 12-15, 351, 405, 412-14, 416-19

Unity, 764, 857, 868, 875-78
Universalism, 698

Vine, 799-802, 804-5, 809
Virgin Birth, 73-74, 384
Voice, 100-101, 220, 317, 330, 694-95

Water, 148-52, 182-85, 213, 241-46, 290, 374, 424, 462-67, 726, 967-69, 972
Way, the, 773-75
Will of God, 261, 323, 378, 381, 437-38
Wind, 187, 193
Wine, 143-45, 148, 150-52, 154
Wisdom, 66-67
Woman, adulterous, 494-96, 498-500
Word, Jesus as the, 1, 32, 45-51, 59, 61, 63-67, 75-78, 92-93, 477, 893
Word of God, 330, 529, 603-4, 863, 872
Words of Jesus, 170, 269, 279-80, 315, 338, 414, 529, 732, 778, 789, 803, 820
Works, good, 41, 207, 322, 511-13
Works of God, 366-67, 541-43, 594, 597-98, 600-601, 605-6
Works of Jesus, 40-41, 205-10, 261, 302-5, 307, 310-11, 329, 778-80, 822-23, 862
World, 4, 62-64, 108, 201-3, 231, 252, 270, 425-26, 428-29, 477-78, 487, 521, 682-83, 686, 690-91, 696, 788, 790, 792, 795-98, 818-21, 823-26, 834-35, 839, 842, 855, 867, 870-71, 875-76, 922-23
Worship, 249-55, 568, 829
Wrath, 227-28

Zipporah, 237

INDEX OF AUTHORS

This index is not exhaustive, for I have largely ignored names which were merely part of a long list. While these are mostly modern authors, I have made exceptions in the case of early commentators on John, including Origen, Chrysostom, Augustine, Calvin, Bengel, and Wesley. I have included English translations only when linked to individual translators.

Abbot, E., 783
Abbott, E. A., 63, 68, 82, 126, 133, 162, 163, 169, 173, 190, 191, 244, 251, 277, 278, 300, 303, 317, 374, 375, 377, 379, 401, 402, 411, 414, 415, 425, 430, 482, 489, 510, 526, 575, 588, 643, 662, 666, 715, 770, 804, 816, 827, 833, 846, 909, 924, 988, 1043
Aland, K., 52
Alter, R., 237
Anderson, P., 357, 366, 391, 397, 399
Atwood, C. D., 1017
Augustine, 136, 165, 196, 216, 221, 240, 243, 289, 291, 307, 437, 438, 503, 541, 544, 545, 622, 698, 770, 839, 959, 992, 1037
Aune, D. E., 652

Bammel, E., 610, 937
Barrett, C. K., x, xi, 48, 57, 64, 67, 68, 83, 84, 88, 90, 91, 122, 128, 129, 131, 142, 148, 149, 162, 164, 181, 187, 191, 194, 195, 213, 221, 222, 223, 225, 228, 254, 258, 264, 265, 280, 296, 316, 320, 331, 334, 357, 422, 451, 453, 461, 482, 495, 496, 503, 504, 539, 548, 555, 581, 582, 590, 614, 622, 623, 624, 634, 637, 638, 641, 647, 658, 660, 665, 667, 678, 721, 730, 755, 765, 768, 812, 821, 830, 835, 863, 865, 902, 922, 937, 954, 962, 976, 991, 1031, 1035
Bauckham, R., 4, 9, 15, 24, 27, 570, 708, 735, 1037, 1055
Beasley-Murray, G. R., x, 65, 77, 109, 131, 195, 556, 595, 637, 937, 1037
Bengel, J. A., 400, 893, 902, 909
Bernard, J. H., 103, 136, 161, 191, 258, 286, 338, 356, 399, 407, 434, 443, 637, 1031
Bishop, E. F. F., 740
Black, M., 221
Boismard, M.-É., 73, 87, 93, 134
Borgen, P., 313, 375, 389, 403, 418
Bornkamm, G., 408
Brodie, T., 710, 980
Brown, R. E., x, xi, 48, 56, 64, 65, 77, 83, 84, 91, 98, 100, 102, 104, 105, 109, 131, 134, 137, 142, 144, 148, 149, 159, 160, 163, 164, 165, 174, 181, 191, 196, 201, 217, 218, 250,

Index of Authors

258, 261, 266, 280, 288, 300, 309, 318, 342, 343, 345, 354, 389, 391, 399, 404, 408, 410, 429, 438, 453, 470, 482, 488, 496, 499, 503, 504, 506, 510, 519, 520, 530, 539, 548, 568, 570, 578, 582, 587, 595, 609, 611, 613, 637, 641, 656, 658, 665, 673, 678, 680, 702, 708, 709, 713, 718, 740, 744, 763, 767, 788, 795, 800, 806, 820, 821, 823, 836, 846, 865, 868, 896, 898, 901, 918, 919, 927, 929, 931, 932, 937, 940, 944, 947, 950, 951, 953, 954, 955, 959, 961, 963, 964, 967, 969, 976, 981, 982, 995, 1014, 1016, 1030, 1032, 1034, 1035, 1037, 1038, 1043, 1046, 1055, 1057
Brownlee, W. H., 106
Bultmann, R., x, xi, 30, 41, 61, 62, 65, 66, 67, 68, 71, 72, 73, 77, 81, 89, 90, 92, 103, 121, 126, 134, 140, 141, 142, 153, 157, 160, 162, 163, 165, 174, 183, 188-90, 192, 207, 213, 219, 221, 222, 238, 246, 251, 262, 264, 269, 271, 272, 273, 274, 275, 280, 286, 318, 321, 329, 338, 349, 355, 367, 376, 391, 397, 399, 407, 408, 412, 416, 434, 439, 440, 443, 445, 462, 464, 471, 472, 473, 474, 476, 483, 489, 517, 519, 539, 541, 543, 546, 547, 548, 586, 588, 595, 605, 622, 624, 627, 637, 643, 650, 660, 665, 667, 673, 678, 680, 690, 693, 694, 700, 702, 707, 710, 713, 714, 715, 723, 727, 743, 750, 771, 778, 793, 795, 806, 813, 830, 834, 836, 837, 854, 863, 901, 904, 923, 927, 931, 934, 936, 954, 959, 964, 974, 977, 991, 995, 1008, 1015, 1021, 1029, 1030, 1035, 1045, 1051, 1053
Bunyan, John, 377, 773, 774, 775
Burney, C. F., 68
Burridge, R. A., 27

Cadbury, H. J., 72, 907
Calvin, J., 197, 269
Carson, D. A., x, 4, 12, 140, 148, 157, 170, 185, 258, 266, 438, 462, 465, 491, 556, 581, 601, 775, 863, 936, 991
Carter, W., 921, 929, 950
Charlesworth, J., 20, 971, 972, 992, 1016
Chrysostom, 67, 90, 131, 136, 152, 154, 155, 163, 166, 191, 196, 215, 216, 236, 237, 239, 246, 258, 260, 263, 275, 307, 308, 312, 320, 324, 325, 328, 338, 362, 372, 421, 425, 430, 438, 445, 446, 474, 489, 493, 520, 628, 630, 639, 698, 700, 770, 771, 816, 821, 933, 959, 964
Cohee, P., 53
Colwell, E. C., 48, 319, 320, 520, 552, 578
Cowper, William, 974
Crossan, J. D., 955
Cullmann, O., 266
Culpepper, A., 119, 754

Dalman, G., 141, 214, 656
Daube, D., 239, 240
Delling, G., 165
Dibelius, M., 439
Dickinson, Emily 1, 42
Dodd, C. H., x, 56, 59, 60, 61, 83, 84, 95, 102, 105, 109, 140, 148, 153, 160, 162, 165, 169, 209, 302, 304, 305, 307, 309, 320, 331, 470, 477, 482, 488, 506, 543, 561, 652, 690, 740, 970, 971, 974, 1014, 1054
Duke, P., 237, 918

Edwards, M. J., 533
Edwards, R. B., 89, 90
Emerton, J. A., 1038

Fee, G. D., 467
Fenton, F., 119
Field, F., 296
Fischer, G., 768
Fish, S., 773, 774, 778
Fitzer, G., 224
Fitzmyer, J. A., 956

Index of Authors

Fortna, R., 142, 153, 284, 1021, 1041, 1042
Fowles, John, 997
France, R. T., 233, 267

Garvie, A. E., 119
Giblin, C. H., 144
Ginzberg, L., 513
Godet, F., 744
Greeven, H., 254
Grundmann, W., 585
Gundry, R. H., 4, 93, 166, 168, 604, 955

Haenchen, E., x, 74, 76, 81, 150, 159, 170, 195, 207, 251, 446, 597, 740, 744
Hägerland, T., 1014
Harner, P., 48, 488
Hedrick, C. W., xiii, 119, 657
Heracleon, 90, 276, 524
Hirsch, E., 273
Horbury, W., 556
Hort, F. J. A., 85
Hoskyns, E., x, 67, 72, 191, 239, 429, 444, 462, 483, 523, 539, 596, 637, 937, 965, 977, 991, 1021, 1034, 1053
Howard, W. F., 247
Hunn, D., 503

Jeremias, J., 159

Käsemann, E., 3, 77, 78
Keener, C., x, xi, xiii, 433, 445, 452, 472, 477, 478, 482, 488, 496, 539, 545, 563, 621, 629, 637, 648, 668, 752, 812, 936, 942, 963, 964, 978, 982
Kent, H. A., xiii, 684, 699
Kimelman, R., 556
Koester, C. R., 131
Kopp, C., 214

Lake, K., 907
Lattimore, R., 144, 509, 769
Law, R., 515
Levenson, J., 202
Lewis, C. S., 312

Lightfoot, J. B., 493
Lightfoot, R. H., x, 81, 465
Lincoln, A. T., x, 644, 653, 666, 678, 692, 754, 755, 771, 925, 936, 986, 991, 992, 1017, 1036, 1053
Lindars, B., x, 126, 139, 142, 149, 157, 170, 183, 227, 239, 240, 247, 250, 251, 264, 265, 292, 300, 329, 355, 361, 422, 429, 442, 448, 503, 510, 546, 581, 594, 611, 624, 637, 666, 730, 830, 865, 903, 936, 964, 977, 995
Longenecker, B., 348

Mackowski, R. M., 288, 289
Martyn, L., 555, 556, 569
Mastin, J. A., x, 170, 276, 539, 637
Meier, J., 233, 234
Metzger, B., 52, 103, 231, 288, 290, 384, 385, 461, 481, 565, 568, 635, 671, 680, 722, 752, 776, 942, 989, 1031
Michaelis, W., 576
Michaels, J. R., x, 52, 84, 85, 86, 87, 88, 131, 173, 207, 265, 273, 365, 372, 380, 433, 442, 444, 448, 465, 476, 489, 496, 618, 736, 743, 747, 760, 791, 917, 960, 973
Miller, E., 52
Minear, P., 397, 973
Möller, M., 566
Moloney, F., x, 93, 123, 125, 127, 128, 129, 133, 134, 140, 149, 153, 159, 161, 164, 170, 178, 183, 197, 213, 223, 233, 241, 252, 256, 258, 261, 266, 275, 326, 369, 407, 425, 443, 503, 511, 539, 624, 638, 937
Moore, G. F., 305
Moore, S. D., 242
Morris, L., x, xi, 11, 16, 62, 64, 66, 67, 78, 89, 120, 127, 128, 130, 133, 149, 157, 159, 161, 170, 174, 178, 181, 183, 246, 247, 258, 262, 275, 319, 397, 421, 443, 462, 496, 545, 555, 556, 582, 624, 643, 667, 699, 830, 864, 937, 964, 991, 992
Moule, C. F. D., 131

Index of Authors

Neyrey, J. H., 221

Nicol, W., 1021
Niklas, T., 131

O'Connor, Flannery, 417
Odeberg, H., 136, 137, 183, 184, 195, 251, 303, 305, 330, 387, 407
Origen, 52, 83, 84, 85, 86, 87, 88, 90, 100, 101, 102, 106, 122, 158, 166, 173, 246, 269, 272, 274, 275, 276, 289, 409, 486, 511, 514, 518, 524, 532, 643, 650, 652, 667, 749, 915, 918, 968

Painter, J., 955
Parker, P., 106
Pennells, S., 968
Peterson, E., 629
Potterie, I. de la, 93, 940
Price, Reynolds, 144, 509, 746, 956, 1029, 1033

Rackham, R. B., 834
Reinhartz, A., 3, 4
Rengstorf, K., 418, 498
Richter, G., 76
Riesner, R., 107
Robert, R., 93
Robertson, A. T., 416
Robinson, E., 141
Robinson, J. A. T., 98, 157, 266, 288, 289, 458, 556, 578, 686
Rohrbaugh, R. L., 977

Sanders, J. N., x, 170, 276, 539, 637
Sasse, H., 194
Sayers, D., 238
Schlatter, A., 226
Schnackenburg, R., x, xi, 61, 62, 66, 72, 73, 74, 77, 79, 80, 83, 84, 108, 121, 126, 127, 133, 137, 144, 148, 149, 159, 162, 165, 166, 167, 174, 176, 178, 181, 182, 191, 195, 213, 222, 223, 244, 247, 261, 262, 264, 266, 269, 275, 286, 295, 303, 328, 329, 338, 345, 366, 378, 387, 391, 404, 408, 421, 422, 429, 434, 454, 458, 464, 466, 470, 471, 482, 491, 492, 499, 506, 510, 514, 544, 547, 548, 567, 578, 579, 582, 601, 613, 632, 637, 641, 660, 667, 675, 693, 694, 700, 713, 715, 723, 727, 743, 744, 752, 763, 821, 836, 837, 844, 849, 863, 866, 871, 890, 898, 903, 931, 933, 954, 977, 1021, 1030, 1034, 1035
Schneiders, S., 237, 244, 247
Scholer, D. M., xiii
Schrage, W., 555
Segovia, F., 1024
Smith, G. A., 289, 485
Staley, J., 118, 120, 121, 192, 292
Stauffer, E., 202

Tabor, J., 23
Tenney, M. C., xiii, 119
Thatcher, T., 249, 302, 457, 572, 573, 574
Thomas, J. C., 725, 729, 730, 735, 736
Thompson, M. M., 1, 1011

Updike, John 244

Van Belle, G., 119

Wakefield, G., 174
Wesley, J., 258, 402, 902, 909, 942
Westcott, B. F., x, xiii, 13, 16, 85, 150, 159, 170, 224, 272, 399, 443, 465, 483, 637, 750, 767, 902, 943, 1043
Whitacre, R., xiii, 199, 354, 436, 484, 496, 624, 637, 992
Wilcox, M., 644
Wilkinson, J., 289
Witherington, B., xiii, 24

Yates, J. E., 973

Zerwick, M., 90
Zimmerman, M. and R., 220

INDEX OF SCRIPTURE REFERENCES

This index does not include cross references within the Gospel of John itself. There are too many of these to make indexing feasible.

OLD TESTAMENT		17:10-13	445	34:25-29	236
		17:15-17	531	38:24	514
Genesis		17:17	532	41:55	147
1:1	49	17:23-27	445	47:29	207, 208
1:2	47	17:23	445	48:22	236, 242
1:3	50, 51, 63	18:1-15	513	49:10	128, 547
1:5	51	19:1-5	513		
1:6	50	21:1-7	531	**Exodus**	
1:8	51	21:4	445	2:15-21	237
1:9	50, 51	22:1-14	532	2:15	237
1:11	50, 51	22:8	109	2:21	246
1:13	51	22:12	110	3:6	528, 535
1:14	50	22:16	110	3:14	92, 535
1:15	51	24:1-27	237, 239	4:22	56
1:19	51	24:12-14	238	7:1	606
1:20	50, 51	24:17	238	7:3	278
1:23	51	24:18	238, 239	12:5	110
1:24	50, 51	24:23	246	12:6	942
1:26	50	25:9-10	641	12:10	975
1:29	50	25:22	541	12:22	962
1:30	51	27:35-36	130	12:46	975
2:2-3	301	28:12	136	13:15	506
2:7	91, 407, 408, 546, 1010	28:18	136	16:1-12	383
		29:1-12	237, 239	16:3	363
3:15	128	29:7	237	16:4	368
4:3-4	1036	29:12	246	16:15	368
8:21	564	32:10	207, 208	17:3	383
12:3	1014	32:28	129	17:6	466
13:15	530	33:19	236	17:8	506

Index of Scripture References

17:11	1048	9:12	975	18:15	98, 351
19:11	140	11:13	343	18:18-19	99
19:15	140	14:27	383	18:18	718
19:16	140, 330	14:29	383	18:19	718
19:19	330	15:35	950	18:22	743
20:2	336	16:41	383	19:15	324, 479, 482, 495
20:5	540	17:5	383		
20:6	782	18:16	159	19:16-17	473
20:13	442, 917	19:6	962	19:16-18	498
20:18-19	330	19:18	962	20:6	265
21:6	602	20:7-11	466	21:22-23	966
22:7-9	602	21:8-9	197, 198	22:22-24	496
22:28	202, 907	21:9	199	22:22	918
31:14	554, 918	22:6	1014	22:25	918
32:32	337	24:17	128	24:18	506
33:18	83	29:12-35	461	24:22	506
33:20	83, 91			27:4-8	249
33:23	91	**Deuteronomy**		27:4	249
34:6	83, 90	1:16-17	473	28:30	265
40:35	79	2:14	291	29:2-4	708
		5:9	540	30:12	195
Leviticus		5:10	782	32:39	336, 488, 534, 535
5:7	159	5:15	506		
11:33	148	5:17	917	32:47	718
12:3	445	6:4-5	334, 336		
14:4	962	6:4-6	782	**Joshua**	
17:10-16	395	7:9	782	7:19	558
20:10	496	8:3	261, 718	15:9	656
20:15	918	11:1	782	19:28	140
20:16	918	11:29	249		
23:33-36	423	13:6	918	**Judges**	
23:33	461	13:10	918	11:12	143
23:35-36	424	13:11	918	14:6	244
23:36	461	14:1	56	14:19	244
23:39	461	15:11	672	15:14	244
23:39-43	423	15:15	506		
23:42-43	423	16:12	506	**Ruth**	
24:14	950	16:13-17	423	2:14	963
24:16	932	16:13	461		
24:16-17	918	16:15	461	**1 Samuel**	
25:8-12	533	16:16	423	[= 1 Kingdoms LXX]	
26:11-12	79	16:18	447	1:1	978
		17:6	324, 479, 482, 495	10:6	244
Numbers				10:10	244
5:22	135	17:7	498	11:6	244
6:3	963	18:15-18	99, 128, 256, 337, 363, 708	16:7	448
9:6-12	661			16:11-13	448

1070

Index of Scripture References

16:13	244	**Nehemiah**		49[48]:5	595
		3:1	288	51:5	541, 564
2 Samuel		3:15	547	51:7	962
[= 2 Kingdoms LXX]		3:32	288	56:10	891
7:12	470	8:6	135	58:3	541
7:13-14	165	9:33	207	58:4	564
7:13	701	12:39	288	63:1[62:2]	961
7:14	304	13:28	249	66:18-19	561
16:8	72			69:4	742
16:10	143	**Job**		69[68]:5	163, 824
19:22-23	143	3:1-19	541	69[68]:10	162
22:17	386	10:9	546	69:22	962, 963
		31:8	265	69[68]:26	870
1 Kings [= 3 Kingdoms LXX]				72:19	135
		Psalms		77:16-19	358
17:18	143			78:16	465, 466
17:23	646	*The numbers in brackets are those of the LXX.*		78:17-20	466
19:10	456			78[77]:24	368, 369
19:14	456	2:1-2	952	80:8-18	801
21:3	950	2:6-7	132	82[81]:6	56, 602, 603
		7:10	175	82:7	603, 604
2 Kings [= 4 Kingdoms LXX]		8:4	319	86[85]:4	596
		8:5	602	86[85]:10	335
2:17	456	8:6	54	88[87]:17	595
3:13	143	8:7	319	89:4	470
4:36	646	16:10	170	89:29	470
5:10	547	22:15	961	89:26-27	132, 304
17:24-41	523	22[21]:16	595	89[88]:36	470, 701
17:24	247	22:17	975	89[88]:49	527
17:29-32	247	22:18	975	89:53	135
18:4	197	22[21]:19	163, 951	105[104]:40	369
19:15	335	23	589	106[105]:25	383
19:19	335	25[24]:1	596	107:23-30	358
4:38	347	27:2	891	109[108]:3	595
4:41	347	28:3	214	108[109]:8	870
4:42-44	347	32[31]:7	595	110:4	701
4:44	349	32:2	130	113–118	676
14:25	475	33:6	50	114:8	465
		34:15-16	561	118[117]:10	595
2 Chronicles		34[33]:21	975	118[117]:11	595
30:17-18	661	35:4	891	118[117]:12	595
35:21	143	35[34]:19	742, 824	118:21	644
		41:10[40:9]	740, 741, 824, 870	118:25	676
Ezra				118:26	676
10:8	554	41:10	163	126:5-6	265
5:16	165	41:14	135	132:12	701
		41:2-3[42:1-2]	961	132[131]:16-17	327

1071

Index of Scripture References

143[142]:8	596	52:13	198, 709, 711	**Daniel**	
		52:14–53:12	199	7:13-14	319
Proverbs		52:15	709	12:2	317, 322
24:12	175	53:1	708		
30:4	195	53:7	109	**Hosea**	
		53:9	130	1:1	603
Ecclesiastes		54:13	386, 436	1:2	514
6:2	265	55:1	465	1:10	56
		56:7	160	2:6	514
		58:9	643	9:10	131
Isaiah		58:11	465	14:8	143
1:13-14	482	64:1	279		
5:1-7	801	65:2	1048	**Joel**	
6:1-10	711	66:7-9	844, 845	2:13	255
6:1	710, 711, 715	66:14	845	3:18	466
6:3	710, 711				
6:10	709, 711	**Jeremiah**		**Amos**	
8:6-7	547	1:2	603	2:2	419
8:9-10	165	1:4	603	4:4	165
8:17	482	1:11	603	9:13	265
9:2	265	7:11	160		
11.1-2	470	7:21	165	**Micah**	
11:3	447	17:10	175	4:9-10	844
26:10	208	17:13	497	5:2	470, 476
26:16-19	844	23:5	470	5:3	844
28:16	136	28:6	135	6:15	265
29:18	572	31[38]:3	386		
35:5	572			**Zechariah**	
37:20	335	**Ezekiel**		1:5	528
40:3	101	6:1	603	2:10-11	79
41:4	488, 534	9:6	499	3:8	131
42:7	572	15:1-8	801	3:10	131
42:18	572	17:5-8	801	6:12-13	165
43:9-10	743	18	41	7:9	447
43:10-11	534	19:10-14	801	9:9	132, 676, 952
43:10	257, 488	34	589	12:10-12	978
43:20	465	36:25-27	102, 185	12:10	973, 976
43:25	488, 534, 535	37:4	317	13:1	102
44:3	465	37:5	408	13:7	580, 587, 854, 1028
45:18	257, 488, 534	37:9	1010		
45:19	488, 534, 535	37:27	79	14:1	466
46:9-10a	743	39:17-18	396	14:4	466
48:12	488, 534	45:25	461	14:6	466
49:26	396	47:1-12	465	14:8	465, 466
51:12	257, 488, 534, 535	47:10	1038	14:9	466
52:6	257, 488	48:24	419	14:13	466
52:13–53:12	109	48:41	419	14:20	466

Index of Scripture References

14:21	158, 160, 466	4:13	156	8:5-13	276
		4:14	893	8:5	276
Malachi		4:17	215	8:6	281
2:10	515	4:18-20	122	8:7	277
3:1	98	4:18	121	8:8	280, 281
4:5	98	4:19	1028, 1049	8:9	280
		4:20	1043	8:10	280
		4:21	7	8:11	568
NEW TESTAMENT		4:23	314	8:13	279, 281, 282
		4:34	34	8:15	282, 692
Matthew		5:1	413	8:17	893
1:1	46	5:2	342	8:19	496
1:16	256, 384	5:3-12	572	8:20	273, 964
1:21	653	5:11-12	820	8:21	413
1:22	893	5:16	1002	8:23-27	356
2:2	568	5:17	336, 438, 572, 603	8:23	413
2:4-6	470			8:26	792
2:7	256	5:18	893	8:27	310
2:11	255	5:19	303, 438	8:29	143, 416
2:12	353	5:20	182, 438	9:1	540
2:13-14	137	5:21-48	262, 535	9:6	290, 1013, 1014
2:13	353	5:25	455	9:8	319
2:14	353	5:29-30	653, 895	9:9	539
2:15	893	5:29	446, 651	9:10	413
2:17	256, 893	5:30	446, 651	9:11	413
2:22	256, 353	5:37	872	9:13	40, 475
2:23	156, 889, 893	5:40	953	9:14	413
3:1	100, 102	5:43-47	812	9:15	219
3:3	100, 112	6:6-13	873	9:18	568
3:6	106	6:10	562	9:19	413
3:7-11	205	6:13	694, 872	9:22	282
3:7	228	6:14-15	760, 1014, 1015	9:27	540
3:9	506	6:22-23	446	9:33	310, 472
3:10-12	326	6:23	704	9:34	696
3:10	807, 1012	7:7-8	456	9:36	263, 652
3:11	95, 103, 105, 110, 111	7:7	122, 362, 808, 847, 1032	9:37	263, 413
				9:38	580
3:14	726	7:14	185	10:1-4	416
3:15	543	7:16-20	185	10:1	351, 413
3:16	114, 138	7:19	326, 310	10:2-4	413
3:17	80, 107, 115, 116, 366	7:21	182, 438	10:2	7, 121, 122, 123, 256
		7:22-23	173		
4:4	261, 345, 364	7:22	334	10:3	125
4:6	137	7:24	438	10:4	788
4:9	255, 314	7:25-27	187	10:5-16	266, 873
4:11	137, 692	7:29	438	10:5	235, 380, 652
4:12	33, 215, 232, 353	8:2	568	10:6	202, 263

Index of Scripture References

10:11	803	12:26	696	15:2-3	240
10:17-18	873	12:27	124	15:3	524
10:17	557, 648, 827	12:28	535	15:14	576
10:19-20	826	12:29	696	15:17	364
10:21-22	742, 824, 825	12:33-35	185	15:19	255
10:21	748, 918	12:38	164, 278, 454, 496	15:21-28	276
10:22	821			15:21	353
10:23	736, 873, 1049, 1051	12:39-40	164, 369	15:24	202, 380, 652
		12:40	167, 198, 370	15:25	568
10:24-25	736	12:45	299	15:26	251, 277
10:24	737, 742	12:46-50	955	15:28	145, 280, 281, 282, 500
10:25	737, 767, 820	12:49	1002		
10:29-31	1038	12:50	438	15:30	342
10:29	953	13:1	786	15:31	310
10:32-33	97	13:11	69	15:32	143, 144, 355
10:34-35	572	13:14-15	573	15:33	343
10:34	336	13:15	709	15:34	346
10:35-37	749	13:24-30	581	15:36	348, 1040
10:35-36	742	13:35	893	15:37	149, 349, 363
10:38-39	397	13:36-43	581	15:39	355
10:39	586, 690	13:41-42	205	15:40	23, 955
10:40	1, 313, 714, 717, 744	13:41	137	15:41	955
		13:44-46	127, 131	15:47	23
11:2-5	454	13:47	1038	16:1	164, 278, 369, 497
11:2	215	13:48	1038		
11:3	104	13:49-50	205	16:4	164, 369, 729
11:5	576	13:54	272	16:9-10	149, 349
11:7	100	13:55	21, 23, 384, 955	16:13	567
11:11	223	13:57	66, 272	16:15	415
11:12	353	14:3-12	215	16:16-18	780
11:14	96, 98	14:4	917	16:16	402
11:18	326, 443	14:9	276	16:17-19	415
11:21-24	823	14:13	353	16:17	124, 1018
11:25	643	14:15	355	16:18-19	646
11:27	29, 226, 587, 775, 881, 1002	14:18	346	16:18	124, 1013
		14:19	347, 348, 1040	16:19	1013
12:2	917	14:20	149, 349, 363, 413	16:20	415
12:4	195			16:21	140, 167
12:5	445	14:21	348	16:22	406
12:8	302	14:22	355	16:23	406, 418
12:11-12	446	14:23	354, 355	16:24-25	397
12:11	577	14:24-33	355	16:24	86, 104, 682, 691
12:12	602	14:24	355	16:25	586, 690, 691
12:15	353	14:26	357	16:26	683
12:18-23	247	14:27	357	16:27	365
12:18	80	14:32	356	16:28	20, 527, 1051, 1052
12:24	696	14:33	568		

17:1	7, 140, 663	21:2-5	952	24:3	634
17:5	80, 115	21:4	677, 893	24:9-10	826
17:12	96, 326	21:5	677, 678	24:9	831
17:12-13	98	21:8	675	24:15	649
17:18	282	21:9	104, 675, 676, 677	24:21	50
17:23	140, 167			24:25	742
17:27	1032	21:12	157, 159	24:26	786
18:3	180, 182, 999	21:13	160	24:27	634, 789
18:6-9	651	21:20	310	24:28	586
18:8-9	227, 651	21:22	847	24:30-31	137
18:8	185	21:23–24:1	433	24:30	369, 788
18:9	185	21:25	326	24:31	772
18:12-14	127	21:28-32	801	24:34	278, 1052
18:12	254	21:32	158	24:35	893
18:13	565	21:33-46	801	24:36	1053
18:14	651	21:38	479	24:37	634
18:15-17	555, 1013	21:39	950	24:40-41	772
18:16	482	22:1-14	219	24:41	530
18:19	781	22:4	585	24:42	738
18:21-35	760, 1013, 1015	22:14	503	24:43-44	584
18:26	255, 568	22:16	496	24:44	738
18:33	186	22:17	917	24:45-51	767
18:35	1014	22:18	497	24:45	738, 739
19:3	497, 917	22:21	506	24:46	738
19:4	50	22:22	310	24:51	728
19:8	50	22:23	786	25:1-13	219, 220
19:16	185	22:24	496	25:21	266
19:17	185, 227	22:32	528	25:23	266
19:18	917	22:34-40	759	25:24	265
19:21	953	22:35-36	497	25:31-46	205, 672
19:23-24	182	22:36	496	25:31	137, 320
19:28	180, 320, 413, 653, 750	22:37-39	783	25:44	692
		22:38-39	759	26:2	655, 663
19:29	185	22:46	499	26:3-4	655
20:1-16	264, 801	23:11	692	26:3	29, 899
20:15	431, 917	23:12	572	26:5	655, 674, 919
20:16	265	23:16	576	26:6-13	614
20:17	928	23:17	576	26:6	664
20:19	167	23:19	576	26:7	614, 664, 665
20:20-21	749	23:23	186	26:8	667, 894
20:20	568	23:26	576	26:10	671
20:26	692	23:31	515	26:11	671, 672
20:28	692	23:32	165	26:13	614, 667, 670
20:30	540	23:34	515, 557, 827	26:14-16	668, 723
20:34	540	23:35	968	26:14	419
21:1-9	675	23:37	515	26:18	24
21:1-7	677	23:39	653	26:21	758

Index of Scripture References

26:22	419, 748	26:67-68	907, 940	27:68	929
26:23	740, 753	26:68	908	28	995
26:24	741, 771	26:69-75	897	28:1	670, 954, 986
26:26	348, 395, 752, 1040	26:69	899, 900, 901	28:3	994
		26:75	911, 1046	28:5-10	998
26:27-28	395	27:2	916, 921	28:5-7	994
26:27	348	27:4	968	28:5	998, 1001
26:28	758, 968, 1014	27:6	917, 968	28:6	996
26:29	750, 786	27:8	968	28:7	1027
26:30	755, 798	27:9	870, 893	28:8	1007
26:31-33	827	27:11	920, 921, 923	28:9	255, 568, 1000, 1001
26:31	587, 854, 892, 1028	27:12-14	935		
		27:12	921	28:10	29, 998, 1001, 1005, 1007, 1027
26:32	1027	27:16	928		
26:33	1043	27:17	927	28:11-15	987
26:34	766, 1045	27:20	927	28:16-20	1027
26:35	765, 766	27:21	927	28:16	342, 1007, 1015
26:36	886	27:24-25	935	28:17	68, 568, 1005, 1016
26:37	7	27:24	683, 968		
26:38	803	27:25	515, 968	28:18	226, 923
26:39	378, 693, 798, 808, 879, 895	27:26-31	931	28:19-20	232
		27:26	928	28:19	233
26:41	694	27:27	915, 929	28:20	783, 815
26:42	283	27:32	948		
26:45-46	798	27:33	948	**Mark**	
26:45	930	27:34	446, 962, 963	1:1	46
26:47	755, 798	27:35	951	1:2	98
26:48	889	27:37	949	1:3	100
26:49	889	27:38	949	1:4	100, 102, 110, 214, 1014
26:51	894	27:40	164, 165, 168		
26:52	895	27:44	949	1:5	106
26:53	137, 895, 923	27:45	944, 954, 960	1:6	95,
26:55-66	919	27:46	493, 961	1:7	105, 111
26:55	905	27:48	962, 963, 967	1:8	103, 1012
26:56	854, 892, 893, 897	27:49	29, 967, 968	1:9-11	49
		27:50	965, 967, 968	1:10	114
26:57-75	885	27:51-54	973	1:11	80, 226, 325
26:57-68	906, 910	27:54	973	1:12	580
26:57	897	27:55	692, 954	1:13	137, 692
26:58	897, 899, 900, 957	27:56	23, 954	1:14	33, 215
		27:57	979	1:15	429
26:59-68	897	27:59-60	981	1:16-20	36
26:59	648, 918	27:59	983, 984	1:16-18	122
26:61	165, 168	27:60	986	1:16	121, 539, 540
26:63	597, 906	27:61	954	1:17	86, 126, 1028, 1049
26:64	138	27:62-66	987		
26:65	906, 907	27:64	140, 167	1:18	1043

Index of Scripture References

Ref	Pages	Ref	Pages	Ref	Pages
1:19	7	3:1	806	5:21-43	628
1:20	386	3:2	295	5:24	639
1:21-28	403	3:4	296, 303, 312, 602, 917	5:25	291
1:21	403			5:30	406
1:23-26	403	3:9	639	5:31	639
1:24	143, 415	3:11	416	5:35-43	639
1:27	152	3:13-19	416	5:37	7, 639
1:29	126	3:14	216, 351, 413, 910	5:38	639
1:31	282, 692			5:39	317, 621, 639
1:34	174	3:16-19	413	5:40	216, 621, 639, 910
1:35	354, 639	3:16	122		
1:38	618	3:17	7	5:41-43	639
1:40	292	3:18	125, 788	5:42-43	646
1:41	292	3:20	639	5:43	177
1:43-44	638	3:21	592	6:1	272
1:44	442	3:22	443, 592, 696	6:2	435
1:45	638	3:23-30	523	6:3	21, 23, 141, 156, 384, 623, 955
2:1-12	151	3:23	593, 696		
2:3-4	293	3:27	696	6:4	66, 272, 426, 958
2:4	294	3:28	1014	6:6-13	266
2:5	294, 298, 299, 541	3:30	443, 592	6:9	347
		3:31-35	21, 955, 958	6:14	102, 276
2:6-8	479	3:31-33	156	6:17-29	215
2:8	406	3:34-35	956, 958	6:18	917
2:9-12	298	3:34	629	6:23	620
2:9-10	299	4:1-9	581	6:24	102
2:9	294, 541	4:1	639	6:25	102
2:10-11	290	4:2	434	6:29	215
2:10	319, 1013, 1014	4:3	586	6:32	340
2:11	294, 295	4:10-12	377	6:34	652
2:12	294, 472	4:10	629	6:35	344
2:13	540	4:11	194	6:36	344, 355
2:14-17	151	4:12	573	6:37	344, 345, 669
2:14	125, 539	4:13-20	581	6:41	348, 1040
2:17	40, 130, 572, 577	4:21	133	6:42	363
2:18-20	577	4:26-29	262	6:43	149, 349, 413
2:18	215	4:27-28	589	6:44	347
2:19-20	152, 219	4:34	639, 906	6:45-46	355
2:29	586	4:35-41	356	6:45	355
2:20	530, 787	4:35-36	639	6:46	354
2:22	152, 577	4:35	786	6:47	354, 356
2:23-28	151, 296	4:36	361	6:48	355, 358
2:23	295	4:41	152, 356, 479	6:49	355, 357
2:24	295, 917	5:7	143, 416	6:50	357
2:26	296	5:13	891	6:51	356
2:28	302, 319, 551	5:18	216, 910	7:6	522
3:1-5	151	5:20	310	7:9	522

1077

Index of Scripture References

7:10	442	9:7	80, 107, 115, 325	11:15	157, 159
7:14-15	581	9:8	294	11:17	160
7:17	639	9:13	98, 326	11:25	164, 760, 1014, 1015
7:24-30	276	9:18	806		
7:24	639	9:24	1017	11:27–13:1	433
7:27	251, 277	9:25-26	1017	11:27-28	595
7:28	278	9:29	562	11:30	217, 223
7:29	279, 281	9:30	638	11:31	479
7:33	545, 639	9:31	140, 167, 638, 930	12:1-12	801
7:34	562			12:6-7	801
8:2	144, 145, 165	9:33-37	180	12:6	80
8:3	355	9:35	692	12:8	950
8:4	343	9:37	313, 714, 717	12:14	450, 917
8:5	346	9:38	7	12:17	506
8:6	348, 1040	9:40	7	12:18-27	532
8:7	346	9:42-48	651	12:27	528, 535
8:8	149, 349, 363	9:43	185, 227	12:28-34	759
8:9	355	9:45	185, 227	12:29-31	783
8:11	164, 278, 369, 454, 497	9:47	182, 185	12:34	499
		10:2	497, 917	12:38	434
8:12	164	10:3-4	442	12:41-44	485
8:14	1031	10:6	50	12:41	485
8:16-17	479	10:13-16	180	12:43	485
8:18	573	10:17-18	431	13	34
8:19-21	149	10:19	917	13:3	7
8:19-20	349	10:21	749	13:6	334
8:22-26	563	10:23-27	181	13:9	557, 648, 827
8:23	545, 639	10:23-25	182	13:11	826, 1012
8:24-25	545	10:26	479	13:12-13	742, 824, 825
8:26	639	10:33	930	13:12	748, 918
8:29	415	10:34	140, 167, 928	13:13	821
8:30	415	10:37	7, 13	13:14	186
8:31	138, 167, 198, 930	10:39	1048	13:19	50
		10:40	1053	13:22	278, 334, 454, 554
8:32-33	406	10:43-44	572, 813		
8:33	418	10:43	692	13:23	742
8:34-35	397	10:45	586, 666, 692, 725, 930	13:26-27	137
8:34	86, 682, 691			13:26	788
8:35	572, 586, 690, 953	10:46-52	563	13:27	772
		10:46	540, 548	13:30	1052
8:36	682	10:51	292, 1000	13:31-35	426
8:38	137, 138, 365, 557	11:1-10	675	13:32	786, 1053
		11:1-6	675, 677	13:34-37	772
9:1	20, 527, 1051	11:2	984	13:34	578, 767
9:2	7, 140, 294, 663, 750	11:8	675	13:35	767
		11:9	104, 675, 676	14:1-2	674
9:5	294, 346, 729	11:10	676	14:1	655, 656, 663

1078

Index of Scripture References

Ref	Pages	Ref	Pages	Ref	Pages
14:2	655	14:49	741, 905	15:29	164, 165, 168
14:3-9	614, 665	14:50-51	854	15:32	368, 949
14:3	29, 614, 664, 665	14:50	892, 897	15:33	943, 960
14:4	479, 667, 894	14:51-52	895	15:34	493, 961
14:5	664, 667	14:53-72	885	15:36	962, 963
14:6	669, 671	14:53-65	906, 910	15:37	965, 973
14:7	671	14:53	897	15:38	973
14:8	669, 670, 983	14:54	455, 897, 899, 900, 903, 957	15:39	973
14:9	614			15:40	141, 954
14:10-11	668	14:55-65	897	15:41	692, 954
14:10	419, 723	14:55-64	919	15:42	941
14:14	24	14:55	648, 907, 918	15:43	978, 981, 982
14:17-19	827	14:58	140, 164, 165, 168	15:44	967, 980
14:18	740, 748			15:46	981, 986
14:19	419, 748	14:61	906	15:47	141, 954
14:20	740, 741, 752	14:62	138, 319, 535, 536, 597, 906	16	995
14:21	741, 771, 930			16:1	141, 670, 954, 981, 986
14:22	348, 395, 752, 1040	14:63-64	906		
		14:64	907	16:3	644
14:23	348, 786	14:65	455, 908, 929, 940	16:5-7	994
14:24	758			16:5	994
14:25	750	14:66-72	897	16:6	996, 998
14:26	755, 798	14:66	899, 900, 901	16:7	580, 589, 1027, 1046
14:27-28	580	14:67	900		
14:27	587, 854, 892, 1028	14:68	899	16:8	1007
		14:69	900	16:9	987
14:28	1026	14:70	436	16:11	1005, 1007, 1016
14:29-30	1026	14:72	911, 1046	16:13	1005, 1016
14:29	1043	15:1	648, 916, 921, 926	16:14	1005, 1015, 1016
14:30	766, 1045			16:16	203
14:31	765, 766	15:2	920, 921, 923		
14:32	886	15:3-5	935	**Luke**	
14:33	7, 750	15:4-5	922	1:2	26, 46, 50, 410
14:34	803	15:5	926	1:3	6, 24, 1058
14:35-36	693	15:9	927	1:13	16
14:35	697, 896	15:11	927	1:16	495
14:36	378, 643, 798, 808, 879, 895, 896	15:15-20	931	1:17	98
		15:16	899, 915, 929	1:35	82, 185
		15:20	948	1:60	16
14:38	694	15:21	948, 975	1:63	16
14:41-42	753, 798	15:22	948	1:77	1014
14:41	930	15:23	962, 963	1:80	100, 221
14:42	618	15:24	951	2:9	137
14:43	755, 798	15:25	942, 943	2:16	495
14:44	889	15:26	949	2:19	24
14:45	889	15:27	949	2:21	445
14:47	894	15:28	959	2:22	442

Index of Scripture References

2:26	526, 527	5:1-11	36, 122, 1027	7:19	104
2:31	495	5:1	341	7:20	102
2:35	42	5:4	1032	7:21	611
2:40	221	5:5	1030, 1032	7:22	576
2:42-51	142	5:6	1038	7:24	100
2:46-47	435	5:8	130	7:28	223
2:46	165	5:10	7, 386	7:29	495
2:49	145, 160	5:11	1028	7:33	102, 443
2:51	24	5:12	82	7:36-50	248, 614, 664, 667, 725
3:1	165, 916	5:18	294		
3:2	100, 650, 896, 902	5:19	294	7:36-38	665
		5:21	495	7:37-38	614
3:3	110	5:23	294	7:37	614, 664
3:7-14	95	5:24	294, 1013	7:38	637, 666
3:7	228	5:25	294	7:39	248, 479
3:8	506	5:26	152	7:49	479
3:9	807	5:30	495	8:1-3	862
3:15	96, 328	5:32	40	8:2-3	669
3:15-16	95	5:33	124, 215	8:3	692
3:16	103, 105, 111, 301, 1012	5:34-35	219	8:8	314
		5:39	152	8:15	21
3:17	110	6:2	917	8:16	133
3:18	1020	6:5	302	8:20	687
3:19-20	215	6:7	495	8:21	21, 956
3:21	138, 495	6:9	602	8:25	310
3:22	114	6:12-16	416	8:28	143, 416
3:23	384, 532	6:13	13, 351, 413	8:47	495
4:1	82, 83, 106	6:14-16	413	8:48	500
4:14	82	6:14	7, 121, 122, 125	8:51	7
4:16-30	403	6:16	788	9:1-6	266, 873
4:16	403	6:17	495	9:9	686
4:18	576	6:20-26	572	9:13	495
4:22-23	403	6:22	557	9:14	347
4:22	310, 403, 435	6:29	953	9:16	348, 1040
4:24	66, 272, 273	6:32-35	812	9:17	149, 349, 363, 413
4:26	818	6:39	576		
4:27	195	6:40	736	9:20	415
4:28-29	403	7:1-10	276	9:21	415
4:30	296, 537	7:1	276	9:22	140, 167, 198, 495
4:31-37	403	7:2	277		
4:31	403	7:6	277, 281	9:23-24	397
4:34	143, 415	7:7	280, 281	9:23	104, 682
4:36	479	7:8	280	9:24	586, 690, 691
4:39	282	7:9	280	9:25	683
4:41	416	7:11-17	628	9:26	137, 365
4:43	274	7:15	646	9:27	20, 181, 400, 527, 1051
4:44	128	7:18-22	454		

1080

Index of Scripture References

Ref	Pages	Ref	Pages	Ref	Pages
9:28	7	11:35	620	14:35	314
9:32	76, 81, 181	11:36	704	15	546
9:33	729	11:38	310	15:2	495
9:35	80, 115, 116	11:53	495	15:4-6	565
9:43	310	12:4	813	15:4	577
9:48	313, 714, 717	12:6-7	1038	15:6	202, 380
9:49	7	12:8-9	97, 137	15:8	254
9:51	429	12:8	557	15:11-32	767
9:52	235	12:11	557, 826, 1012	15:23	585
9:53	275	12:12	186	15:24	380
9:54	7	12:14	324	15:27	585
9:57-62	1050	12:29	586	15:30	585
9:58	273, 964	12:32	589	15:32	127, 186
10:1-12	266, 873	12:35-38	767	16:8	704
10:1	235	12:35-37	739	16:9	767
10:5-6	1008	12:35	738	16:11	173
10:7	264	12:37	692, 726	16:20	613
10:12-15	823	12:39-40	584	16:22	528
10:16	1, 313, 452, 714, 716, 744, 1014	12:40	738	16:31	127, 613
		12:42	739	17:3-4	1015
10:18	695, 696	12:43	738	17:6	512
10:22	29, 226, 587, 775	12:44	400	17:11-19	235
10:25-28	759	12:45	738	17:22	530
10:25	496, 497	12:46	728	17:24-25	198, 771
10:26-27	783	12:47-48	739	17:24	530, 789
10:29	497	12:48	254	17:30	530
10:30-33	235	12:49	572	17:31-32	1050
10:37	523	12:52-53	742	17:33	397, 586, 690
10:38-42	614, 630	13:1-5	541	17:34-35	772
10:38-39	613	13:1	929	18:1	186
10:39	636, 666	13:6-9	801	18:13	562
10:40	664, 692	13:6-7	254	18:18-19	431
10:42	630	13:10	295	18:18	177, 181, 496
11:1	215	13:11	291	18:20	917
11:2	693, 877	13:12	145, 500, 959	18:25	182
11:4	694	13:14	186	18:33	140, 167, 928
11:9-10	456	13:15-16	446, 602	18:37	889
11:9	122, 362, 808, 847, 1032	13:16	186, 291, 303	18:43	495
		13:25	767	19:5	186
11:14	310	13:31-33	144	19:10	254, 380
11:16	278, 369, 497	13:32-33	544	19:21-22	265
11:19	124	13:32	140	19:28-40	675
11:26	299	14:3	295, 303, 917	19:29-35	677
11:27-28	956	14:5	602	19:30	984
11:29-30	164, 369	14:21	767	19:36	675
11:30	198	14:26	690	19:37	675, 678
11:34	446	14:27	104, 397	19:38	104, 676

Index of Scripture References

Ref	Pages	Ref	Pages	Ref	Pages
19:39	678	22:33	765	23:22	29, 928
19:45	157, 159	22:34	766, 1045	23:25	928, 947
19:46	160	22:35-38	894	23:26	948
19:47	494, 495	22:39-40	886	23:27-31	948
19:48	495	22:39	494	23:33	948, 949
20:1–21:4	433	22:41-42	693	23:34	643, 951, 1014
20:1	495	22:42	378, 643, 798, 879, 895	23:35	116
20:6	495			23:36	962
20:9-19	801	22:43	137	23:38	949
20:15	950	22:46	694	23:39-43	949
20:19	495	22:47	755, 798, 889	23:40-43	967
20:22	917	22:49-50	894	23:44	943, 960
20:25	506	22:50	895	23:46	643, 965
20:26	310	22:51	895	23:49	954
20:38	528	22:52-53	889	23:50-51	979
20:40	499	22:53	454, 905	23:50	177, 981
20:45	495	22:54-62	897	23:51	982
21:1-4	485	22:54	897, 957	23:53	981, 984
21:1	485	22:55	899	23:56	981, 985
21:3	400	22:56	900, 901	24	995
21:12	827	22:57	145	24:4-7	994
21:14	723	22:59	436	24:4	994
21:16	918	22:61-62	1046	24:5-7	997
21:17	821	22:61	899, 911	24:5-6	996
21:27	788	22:63-71	897	24:5	998
21:32	1052	22:63-65	907, 912, 940	24:7	140, 167, 198
21:37-38	433, 494, 495	22:64	929	24:10	986
21:37	886	22:66	495, 648	24:11	1005, 1007
21:38	461, 494, 495	22:66-71	906, 910, 919	24:12	19, 310, 991, 994, 995, 1008
22:1	24	22:67	906		
22:2	495, 655, 674	22:69	565	24:15-29	565
22:3-6	723	22:71	907, 908	24:15-16	1031
22:3	419, 723, 752, 753	23:2	916, 921, 922, 932, 939	24:16	998
				24:19	495
22:8	7	23:3	920, 921, 924	24:20	177
22:14	737	23:4	29	24:21	140, 167
22:19	348, 395, 738, 1040	23:5	431	24:23	994, 997
		23:6	934	24:24	990, 993, 995, 997
22:20	758	23:8	687		
22:21	740	23:9	922	24:25-27	332
22:22	771	23:10	495	24:27	128, 993
22:23	748	23:11	929	24:29	82, 803
22:26	692	23:13	177	24:30-31	1020
22:27	692, 726	23:14	29, 431	24:30	1040
22:30	653, 750	23:16	927, 928, 931	24:31-32	1012
22:31	1045, 1046, 1049	23:18	927	24:35	93
22:32	766	23:19	928	24:36	1008

24:39	1008	3:14	928	10:15	283
24:40-41	1005	3:17-26	508	10:25	255, 568
24:40	1008	3:19-21	653	10:26	569
24:41	310, 1005, 1008, 1016	3:22	99	10:31	562
		3:26	99	10:37-41	34
24:42-43	1020	4:5	177, 435	10:38	82
24:44-47	332	4:6	9, 896, 902	10:40-41	789
24:44	442	4:8-12	7	10:40	167
24:45-46	993	4:8	177	10:41-42	843
24:46	140, 781	4:9-20	7	10:45	241
24:47	1014, 1015	4:10	889, 947	10:48	234
24:49	1012	4:12	775	11:14	246, 282, 283
		4:13	435, 436	11:15	50
Acts		4:25-27	952	11:17	241
1:1-2	1012	4:30	278	11:24	82, 83
1:1	1058	5:12	278, 595	12:2	13, 750
1:3	13, 1021, 1030	5:22	455	12:6	583
1:5	155, 1012	5:26	455	12:8	1047
1:6-7	653	5:31	197, 702	12:13	1007
1:7	1053	6:3	82, 83	12:14	583
1:8	82, 213, 1012	6:5	9, 82, 83, 125	12:17	22
1:9-10	1020	6:7	221	12:24	221
1:11	997	6:8	82, 83, 278	13:10	82, 418
1:13	122, 125, 788	6:13	649	13:13	629
1:14	957	6:14	164, 165, 649, 889	13:25	95, 105
1:20	870			13:35	170
1:21-22	826	7:37	99	13:36	621
2:1-4	1012	7:48-49	253	13:43	561
2:6	187	7:54-60	917	13:50	561
2:7	436	7:55	82, 83	14:1	458, 686
2:16	112	7:56	138, 565	14:3	278
2:22	889	7:58	950	14:8	540
2:23	515	7:60	621	14:10	244
2:24	647	8	125	14:13	583
2:31	170, 993	8:13	266	14:15	250, 251, 569
2:33	197, 702	8:14-25	13, 266	14:22	182
2:36	508, 554, 947	8:16	234	15:5	502
2:38	234, 241	8:20-23	7	15:12	93, 278
2:43	278	8:20	241	15:14	93
3:1–4:22	13	8:21	728	15:20	395
3:2	540	8:32-35	109	15:29	395
3:4-6	7	8:37	568	16:1	458, 686
3:6	889	9:33	291	16:14	561
3:8	244	9:36	82	16:15	246, 282, 283
3:11	595	10:2	562	16:21	917
3:12-26	7	10:4	562	16:31-33	246, 282, 283
3:13-15	508	10:8	93	16:34	503

Index of Scripture References

Reference	Pages	Reference	Pages	Reference	Pages
17:4	561	2:10	458, 686, 699	15:4	162
17:17	561	2:19-20	576	15:7	760
17:22	248	3:2	173	15:19	278
17:23	251	3:9	458, 686, 699	16:22	1055
17:24	250, 253	3:10	458	16:27	335
17:28	250	3:12	458		
17:29	253	3:19	450	**1 Corinthians**	
18:4	458, 686	3:23	699	1:12	124
18:8	246, 282, 283	4:17	531, 532	1:13	234
18:10	115	5:6-8	812, 813	1:15	234
19:10	458, 686	5:12	507, 822	1:16	234, 246
19:17	458, 686	5:13	507	1:17	267
19:20	221	6:14	507	1:18	380, 687
19:28	82	6:16-18	506	1:22	277, 458, 686, 687
20:21	458, 686	6:16	507		
20:28-29	589	6:23	507	1:24	458, 686, 687
20:28	1045	7:7-11	507	1:32	687
20:32	392	7:10	331	2:6	696
20:34	167	7:14	450	2:9	790
21:8	125	7:18	392	3:6-7	267
21:19	93	8:7	185	3:6	304
21:20	502	8:10-11	408	3:8	264, 265
21:25	395	8:14-15	70	3:10	267
21:28	649	8:16-17	70	3:13-15	205
22:8	889	8:18	844	3:22	124
22:25	917	8:19	70	4:4	696
22:30	648	8:21	70, 507	4:5	205
23:2-3	907	8:22	450	4:7	217, 936
23:4-5	907	8:23	70	4:12	254
23:6	380	8:26	693	5:3-5	555
23:35	915	8:28	450	5:10	871
24:5	129	8:32	110	6:12	917
24:15	311, 322, 380	9:4	70	7:16	145
26:8	311	9:7	511	7:39	621
26:9	889	9:8	70, 512	8:6	91, 515
27:40	187	9:33	466	9:5	124
28:27	709	10:12	686, 699	9:17	174
		10:21	1048	9:20-22	523
Romans		11:3	456, 515	10:1-5	389
1:16	458, 686	11:11-32	653	10:4	466
1:18	699	11:32	699	10:5	466
1:21-23	261	12:10	759	10:10	383
1:22	253	13:12-13	1030	10:23	917
1:25	519	13:12	544	10:32	458, 686
2:2	450	13:14	72	11:23	752
2:6-11	205	14:17	399	11:24-25	738
2:9	458, 686, 699	15:3	162	11:24	348, 395, 1040

Index of Scripture References

11:25	395, 758	6:18	80	5:24	73
11:27-29	980	8:23	112	5:13	206
11:30	621	12:4	917	5:25	73, 392
12:13	246, 458, 686	12:8	112		
12:17	446	12:9	115	**Philippians**	
12:27	226	12:12	278	1:7	112
13:9	226			2:5-11	725
13:10	226	**Galatians**		2:6	304
13:12	226	1:4	392	2:9	197
14:7	187	1:18	124	4:10	112
14:8	187	1:19	426		
14:10	187	2:7-8	124	**Colossians**	
14:13	187	2:7	174	1:18	50
14:25	255	2:9	124	1:22	393
15:4	140, 167	2:11	124	2:15	757
15:5	124	2:14	124	2:16	399
15:6	621	2:20	392	3:11	458, 686
15:7	21, 426	3:16	530	3:13	760
15:18	621	3:21	331	3:18-19	73
15:20	621	3:28	458, 686	4:11	256
15:23	634	4:1-7	70, 507		
15:27	54	4:1	308	**1 Thessalonians**	
15:36-38	697	4:5-7	507	1:9-10	402
15:36	689	4:5	70	1:9	251
15:45	408	4:21-26	507	2:4	174
15:47	223	4:26	180	2:15	515
15:50	186	4:28-29	180	2:19	634
15:51	262, 317, 621	4:29	185, 515	3:13	634
15:52	392	5:16	72	4:9	174, 759
15:53	392	5:17	185	4:13-15	621
15:53-54	167	6:7-8	185	4:13	174, 317
16:15	246			4:15	634
		Ephesians		4:16-17	772
2 Corinthians		1:13	224	4:16	634
1:22	224	2:2	696	4:17	629
2:15-16	380	2:3	72	5:1-11	544
3:6	408	2:13-14	393	5:2	530, 584
3:18	76	2:15	757	5:3	843
4:3-4	380	2:16	757	5:4	584
4:6	55	3:14	317	5:5	70, 705
4:17	844	4:16	515		
5:1	167, 450	4:9-10	196	**2 Thessalonians**	
5:2	167, 392	4:30	224	2:1	112, 634
5:4	167, 392	4:32	760	2:3	869
5:10	205	5:2	392, 759, 760	2:8	634
5:17	72	5:8	705	2:9	278
6:16	79	5:22	73	3:3	872

1085

3:8	364	10:19	393, 973	2:22	110, 130
3:10	364	11:8-19	513	3:12	561
5:21	585	11:17	344	3:18	408
		11:19	531, 532	4:8	759, 760
1 Timothy		11:21	255	4:17	499
1:8	450	12:2	844	5:1	499
1:11	174	12:19	330	5:2-3	589
1:17	335	12:22	249	5:2	1045
1:20	555	12:25	330	5:4	1044
2:6	392	12:26	330	5:13	124
2:11	563	13:1	759		
3:11	417, 518	13:12	950	**2 Peter**	
5:10	735	13:20	580	1:12	208
5:18	264			1:16	634
6:13	916	**James**		1:17-18	81
		1:1	21, 22	2:20	299
2 Timothy		1:12	790	3:4	50, 621, 634
3:3	417, 518	1:15	507		
4:8	324, 790	1:17	936	**1 John**	
		1:25	738	1:1-4	75
Titus		2:5	790	1:1-3	223
1:3	174	2:18	207	1:1-2	190, 192, 826
2:3	417, 518	2:21	513	1:1	50, 75, 81, 410,
2:14	392	3:3	446		826
3:5	180	3:6	446	1:2	92, 849
		3:12	185	1:3	75, 91, 849
Hebrews		4:4	819, 1043	1:4	811
1:1-2	51, 99, 226	4:12	324	1:5–2:2	130
1:1	330	5:4	264	1:5	48, 75, 206, 317
1:3	111	5:7-8	262	1:6-7	209, 620, 704
2:4	278	5:7	634	1:6	208
2:5-9	319	5:8	634	1:7	72, 111, 760,
2:10-11	878	5:9	324, 583		781, 802
2:11-12	1002	5:15	299	1:8	576
2:15	507	5:20	760	1:9	440, 562, 760,
3:1	737				781
3:17-19	389	**1 Peter**		2:1-2	760
5:3	873	1:3	180	2:1	91, 757, 783
5:7	561	1:19	109, 110, 544	2:2	111, 336, 652,
6:8	807	1:22	759		654
7:26-27	873	1:23	70, 180	2:5	878
9:7	873	2:1	130	2:6	736
9:19	962	2:5	874	2:7	50, 410, 826
9:25-26	111	2:6	136	2:8	56, 206, 316, 317
10:5	393	2:8	466	2:9	206, 302, 820
10:10	393	2:9	705, 874	2:11	188, 206, 620,
10:14	878	2:17	759		705, 715, 820

Index of Scripture References

Reference	Pages	Reference	Pages	Reference	Pages
2:12	757	4:6	188, 253	12	811
2:13-14	855	4:7	48, 71, 515		
2:13	50, 826	4:8	48	**3 John**	
2:14	50, 1031	4:9	92, 265, 333	3	208
2:15-16	72	4:10	111, 265, 760	4	208
2:15	333, 818	4:11	735, 760	15	813, 816
2:17	56, 365, 437	4:12	81, 330, 878		
2:18-22	869	4:13	210, 265	**Jude**	
2:18-19	808	4:14	81, 113, 190, 270	1	21, 22
2:18	1031	4:15	97, 210	25	335
2:22-23	97	4:16	48, 632		
2:22	520, 529	4:17-18	793, 878	**Revelation**	
2:24	50, 210, 826	4:17	265	1:2	46
2:27	174, 440	4:19	815	1:3	1019
2:28	634, 757, 803	4:20	516, 820	1:4	7, 92
2:29	71, 515	5:1	71, 333, 515, 516, 1002	1:7	492, 788, 978
3:1	70, 654, 1002			1:8	92
3:2	70, 654	5:2	70, 265, 654	1:12	999
3:2-3	110	5:4-5	856	1:13	320
3:5	108, 110, 113, 440	5:4	71, 515	1:14	263
		5:5-6	972	1:15	214
3:7	757	5:6	72, 91, 111, 407, 968, 970	1:17-18	320
3:8	50, 108, 418, 519, 821, 936			1:19	727
		5:8	111	2:1	7
3:9	70, 71, 73, 189, 515	5:9-10	972	2:2	175
		5:9	325	2:7	315
3:10	70, 265, 418, 654	5:10	225, 325	2:9-10	518
3:11	50, 410, 826	5:11-12	245, 859	2:9	175
3:12-13	186	5:11	199	2:11	315
3:12	519	5:12	228, 285, 972	2:13	175, 315
3:13	819	5:13	1023	2:19	175
3:14	315	5:14	437, 562	2:22	315
3:15	519, 820	5:16-17	130, 760, 823	2:23	175
3:16	265, 735, 760, 812, 816	5:16	616, 783, 846	3:1	175
		5:17	440	3:3	584
3:17	811, 812	5:18	71, 73, 189, 515	3:8	175
3:18	757	5:19	188	3:9	255
3:19	265	5:20-21	399	3:10	486
3:22	493, 644	5:20	91, 285, 452, 860	3:12	196
3:23	91	5:21	757	3:14	50
3:24	210, 265			3:15	175
4:1-6	522	**2 John**		3:21	856
4:2	91, 265	3	83, 91	4:1	138, 727
4:2-3	97, 516	4	208	4:8	92
4:3	252, 264, 869	5	50, 826, 845	5:2-5	853
4:4	188, 757, 855	6	50, 826	5:5	109, 856
4:5-6	522	7	91, 869	5:6	109

5:14	255	12:12	78	19:13	46
6:9	46	13:6	78, 486	19:17-18	396
6:10	486	13:9	315	20:1-10	844
7:1	187	13:12	486	20:2-3	695
7:1-8	263	13:14	486	20:4-6	322
7:9	263, 675, 1038	14:1-5	263	20:4	46
7:10	676	14:4	263	20:6	728
7:11	255	14:14-15	263	20:11-15	322
7:13-14	853	14:14	320	20:12-13	205
7:13	934	14:15	262	21:2	196, 923
7:15	78	15:2	856	21:3	78, 79
7:16	78	16:5	92	21:4	78
8:13	486	16:6	396	21:7	80, 856
11:8-9	843	16:15	584	21:8	728, 792
11:10	486, 843	17:1	214	21:10	196, 249, 923
11:12	634	17:2	486	21:27	195
11:16	255	17:6	853	22:8	255, 568
11:17	92	17:8	486	22:9	568
12:1-6	959	17:14	856	22:12	205
12:2	844	17:15	214	22:15	208
12:9-10	518	19:6	214	22:18-19	1058
12:9	695	19:9	46	22:18	377, 1020
12:11	856	19:10	255, 568, 569	22:19	728, 1020

INDEX OF EARLY EXTRABIBLICAL LITERATURE

JEWISH LITERATURE

Apocrypha

Tobit
3.3-5	540
4.6-7	208
7.9	731
8.8	135
11.12-13	563
12.20-21	1003
13.6	208

Wisdom of Solomon
8.19-20	541
9.16	193
10.10	180
15.11	1010
16.5-7	197
16.10-11	197
16.26	261

Sirach
9.1-9	239
24.3-11	66
24.31	465
26.29	160
27.2	160
32.1-2	150
43.31	93
48.1	326
48.10	98
49.13	164

Baruch
3.35–4.2	66
3.29	195

Epistle of Jeremiah
60	187

1 Maccabees
2.23-26	829
4.26	99
4.59	594
7.19	289
9.27	99
9.39	219
13.51	675
14.41	99

2 Maccabees
1.9	595
3.24	485
3.28	485
5.17-18	507
7.32-33	507
10.6	461, 595
10.7	675

4 Maccabees
7.19	528
16.25	528

1 Esdras
5.44	164
9.47	135
48.6	451

Pseudepigrapha

2 Baruch
29.5	149

1 Enoch
10.19	149
39.4-5	767
42.1	67
46.3-4	320
62.5	320
69.27	320

2 Enoch
61.2	767

3 Enoch
6.2	183

4 Ezra
3.320-27	507
4.21	193
6.56-59	507
7.10-11	507
7.95	767

Index of Early Extrabiblical Literature

12.32	103, 451	1QS 2.10	135	*Shabbat*	
13.52	103, 451	1QS 2.18	135	7.2	295, 550
		1QS 5.3	207	10.5	295
Jubilees		1QS 6.24–7.25	554	18.3	445
15.17	532	1QS 8.2	207	19.2	445
16.19	532	1QS 9.11	99	24.3	550
		3Q15	289		
Letter of Aristeas		4Q*Florilegium*	166	*Sheqalim*	
270	174	4Q*Testimonia*	99	6.5	485
139	335				
252	498	**Rabbinic Literature**		*Sukkah*	
				4.1	462
Lives of the Prophets		MISHNAH		4.8	461
1.2	547	*Abot*		4.9	462
		1.5	239	5.2-3	477, 485
Psalms of Solomon		2.6	472		
7.1	824	2.7	331	*Ta'anit*	
17.21	470	3.1	183	3.8	555
		3.2	79		
Sibylline Oracles				*Yebamot*	
12.104	340	*Baba Batra*		16.3	628
		6.8	641		
Testament of Abraham				BABYLONIAN TALMUD	
2.2	513	*Baba Qamma*		*'Abodah Zarah*	
13.2-3	319	8.6	506	5a	603
Testament of the Twelve Patriarchs		*Bekhorot*		*Berakot*	
		5.5	418	4b	282
T. Issachar		8.7	159	6b	561
7.8	641			28b	555
		Ketubbot			
T. Joseph		2.9	479	*'Erubin*	
19.11	109			53b	239
		Middot			
T. Levi		2.2	555	*Gittin*	
9.11	731			56a	176
18.1	531	*Mo'ed Qatan*			
18.14	531	3.1-2	555	*Ketubbot*	
				6b–67a	176
T. Reuben		*Nedarim*			
7.2	641	3.11	445	*Sanhedrin*	
				39a	193
Dead Sea Scrolls		*Rosh ha-Shanah*		43a	176
1QH 5.21	183	3.8	197		
1QH 9.21	183			*Shabbat*	
1QH 11.24	183	*Sanhedrin*		132a	446
1QS 1.5	207	3.5	219	108b	550
1QS 1.9-11	818				
1QS 1.20	135				

1090

Index of Early Extrabiblical Literature

Sukkah
27b	475
48b	462

Ta'anit
2a	184, 311
19b–20a	176

Yoma
85b	446

Midrashim

Mekilta Exodus
2.272	603
20.2	305

Mekilta de R. Ishmael
2.210	140
2.231-32	305

Pesiqta de Rab Kahana
28	461

Genesis Rabbah
11.12	301
60.13	561
63.6	541
68.12	136

Exodus Rabbah
22.3	561
30.9	301
32.1	603
32.7	603

Leviticus Rabbah
4.1	603
11.3	603
18.1	628
31.6	62

Numbers Rabbah
7.4	603
16.24	603
21.3	829

Deuteronomy Rabbah
7.12	603

Ruth Rabbah
1	603

Ecclesiastes Rabbah
3.16.1	603

Songs Rabbah
1.2.5	603

Sifre Deuteronomy
§329	305

Philo

Agriculture
95–96	197

Allegory of the Laws
1.5	301
1.48-49	304
2.79-81	197
3.227	265

Embassy to Gaius
160	938
299–305	929
302	939

Flaccus
1	938
83	966

Life of Moses
2.3-4	352

Migration of Abraham
107	513

On the Creation
135	1010

On Dreams
1.171	134
1.229-30	47

On Flight and Finding
71	335

On the Change of Names
50–51	499
154	532
161	531

On the Cherubim
87	304

On Rewards and Punishments
54	352

Posterity of Cain
145	89

Josephus

Life
269	235
400	276

Antiquities
1.196	513
1.244-48	239
2.257	237
3.153	953
3.161	952
3.245	423
4.219	483
8.17	885
9.288	247
11.302	249
11.321-24	249
11.341	242
12.235	595
12.396	174
13.255-56	249
13.282	652
13.299-300	652
13.380	491
13.391	140
15.112	140
15.289	276
15.380	165
15.391	164

15.395-402	289	**Samaritan Writings**		17.5	492
15.398-401	595	*Memar Markah*			
15.403	915	4.12	256	**Clement of Alexandria**	
17.266	276			*Paedagogus*	
17.270	276			2.8	667
17.281	276	**EARLY CHRISTIAN**			
18.34	650, 896	**LITERATURE**		*Stromateis*	
18.35	650			6.5	255
18.55-62	929	*Acts of Peter*			
18.85-89	929	2.3	514	**Didache**	
18.85	256	37–38	1046	7.1-2	241
18.95	650			9.2	801
18.116	326	*Acts of Philip*		9.4	350, 1039
18.117	328	110	518	10.6	676
18.119	326	119	518	11.4-5	273
20.118	235			11.8	274
20.219	165	*Acts of Pilate*		16.6	369
20.200	828, 917	3.1	920	16.7	789
20.220	595	3.2	926		
20.221	595	15.1	456	**Diognetus**	
20.228	164	16.7	973	1	255
20.268	917	20.3	869		
				Egerton Papyrus	
		Acts of Thomas		2	331, 336
Jewish War		31	623	2.2-3	337
1.68-69	652	32	517		
1.75	915	76	76	**Epiphanius**	
1.229	661	147	263	*Panarion*	
1.673	982			3.33	8
2.169-77	929	*Barnabas*		33.4.1-2	441
2.169	939	12.2	1048	33.6.5	208
2.172	940	12.4	1048		
3.57	341	12.5-7	197	*Epistle of the Apostles*	
4.456	341	12.6	1048	5	142, 156
5.149-51	289	12.7	199		
5.176-83	915	15.9	1017	**Eusebius**	
5.184-85	595			*Ecclesiastical History*	
5.190-92	289	*1 Clement*		2.3-5	917
5.200	485	4.1	1036	2.23	828
5.306	356	16.1	589	2.23.4-18	917
5.449	931	44.3	589	3.3-4	10
6.282	485	49.5	760	3.20.4	923
6.290	661	54.2	589	3.24.7-8	28
6.301	934	57.2	589	3.31.3	9, 898
6.305	934			3.39.5-7	10
6.427	686	*2 Clement*		3.39.15	9
		16.4	760	5.14	37

Index of Early Extrabiblical Literature

5.20.5-6	8
5.24.3	9
6.14.7	28
7.25.7	12
Onomasticon	106, 656, 978

Gospel According to the Hebrews — 894

Gospel of Peter
1.1-2	276
3.7	940
23	980
24	983
25	978

Gospel of Philip
48	600
54.5-7	868

Gospel of Thomas
1	623
2	1032
3	386
8	1032, 1038
9	1032
10	1032
16	1032
18	527
19	527
31	66, 273
47	152
64	160
77	641
92	1032
93	1032
94	1032
111	527

Gospel of Truth
38.6-11	868

Hermas
Mandates
11.5-6	853

Similitudes
9.16.4	224

Visions
1.1.7	145
1.2.2	263
2.4.1	263
3.10.2-5	263

Ignatius
To the Ephesians
1.2	809

To the Magnesians
7.1	38
8.2	493
9.1	809

To the Philadelphians
7.1	38, 188

To Polycarp
6.1	728

To the Romans
4.2	809, 834
5.1	809
7.2-3	397
7.3	38

To the Smyrneans
1.2	916

To the Trallians
5.2	809
9.1	916

Irenaeus
Against Heresies
1.8.5	8, 53
1.30.5-6	518
1.30.6	519
1.30.8	518
2.22.6	533
3.1.1	6
3.3.4	8
3.11.1	8
5.15.2	546
5.15.12	91
5.33.3	149

Jerome
Commentary on Ezekiel
47.6-12	1037

Justin Martyr
Apology
1.12.9	737
1.26	523, 527
1.35	940
1.35.6	1048
1.52.12	978
1.60	197, 199
1.61.4	180
1.63.10	737
1.63.14	737

Dialogue with Trypho
8.4	98, 103, 451
14.8	978
16.4	555
47.4	555
56	513
90.5	1048
91	197, 199
94	197
96.2	555
110.1	451
112	197
114.4	463
135.3	466
137.2	555
137.4	559

Martyrdom of Polycarp
8.1	966
13.1	828
14.2	728

Melito
Eclogues
5–6	110

On the Passover
12   110
75–77   947

Odes of Solomon
7.12   38, 66
8.20-21   38
10.5   38
11.23   38
18.6   38

Oxyrhynchus Papyri
1.5   641
1.6   273

Pseudo-Clementine
Homilies
6.11   489

Recognitions
1.54   60

Ptolemy
Letter to Flora   8

Tertullian
Against Marcion
3.18.7   197

Apology
21.24   950

On the Flesh of Christ
19   73

Theophilus of Antioch
To Autolycos
2.22   6

GRECO-ROMAN LITERATURE

Aristotle
Nicomachean Ethics
1169a   812

Prior Analytics
70b   1021

Corpus Hermeticum
1.28   69
11.21   143
13   69, 180
13.1-2   182

Dio Chrysostom
Discourses   272

Diodorus Siculus
24.1-2   187

Epictetus
Discourses
1.1.16   143

1.22.15   143
1.27.13   143
2.19.16   143
3.16.11   272

Lysias
Orations   448

Philostratus
Epistles
44   272, 305

Life of Apollonius
1.21   934

Plato
Symposium
179b   812

Pliny
Epistles
10.96   49

Seneca
Epistulae Morales
86.12   731

Tacitus
Annals
6.8   938